HUDSONs

Historic Houses
& Gardens
Castles and Heritage Sites

2006

Published by: NORMAN HUDSON & COMPANY

High Wardington House, Upper Wardington, Banbury, Oxfordshire OX17 1SP, United Kingdom
Tel: +44 (0) 1295 750750 • Fax: +44 (0) 1295 750800 • e-mail: enquiries@hudsonsguide.co.uk

www.hudsonsguide.co.uk

THE GLOBE PEQUOT PRESS
246 Goose Lane, Guilford, Connecticut 06437, USA

foreword

by Lord Marshall of Knightsbridge

Chairman, VisitBritain

In so many ways, Britain's historic houses, castles, gardens and other heritage sites are the jewels in the crown of our burgeoning tourism industry.

For visitors from home and overseas, they each, in their own unique way, help to define Britain, to tell the story of this country and its people from centuries past to the present day. Not only does our historic, built environment provide this rich cultural heritage, it also now offers an extraordinarily wide range of high-quality visitor attractions, facilities and experiences.

Heritage sites – whether buildings or landscapes – have done so much historically to influence the areas in which they are located. The way in which they are now presented and cared for, to be enjoyed by today's generations, means that whole communities continue to be influenced in the way of welcoming visitors.

It is my firm belief that growth in the value of tourism, for both those involved in it and the visitors they welcome, will only come about by ensuring that this is a truly customer-driven industry. It means presenting our products in ways which are attractive, informative and easily accessible, so that lasting relationships can be built with both markets as a whole and customers, as individuals.

For 20 years, *Hudson's* has fulfilled that objective for the important historic houses, castles and gardens sector of British tourism. The very existence of such an authoritative and respected annual directory has done much to encourage innovation, to raise standards and add value to the visitor experience.

Hudson's makes an outstanding contribution to British tourism and I welcome wholeheartedly this 2006 edition.

HUDSONs

Borde Hill Garden, Sussex.

from the editor
Norman Hudson

The properties featured in this book are magnets that attract hundreds of thousands of people of all ages and from all over the world. They range both in size and opulence from magnificent palaces and houses with works of art and collections that surpass in quality those in museums worldwide, to modest manor houses and ruins that in their own way can be no less exciting, charming or interesting.

Gardens in the setting of these properties may exemplify both historic and new innovative design. They brim with appeal for those seeking passive enjoyment of their design, scents, colour and ambience as well as for the avid and knowledgable garden visitor. Furthermore gardens change throughout the year and may merit repeat visits. Many have plants for sale and this is mentioned in the entries.

Just because you have visited somewhere before, do not assume you have 'done it'. Many places have changing exhibitions, displays and a series of special events throughout the year, making a return visit really worthwhile. Go out and enjoy seeing ever more places. This sector of our heritage is exceptional by world standards and all of us have a need to capture something of the past and benefit from a tangible glimpse of the art forms and way of life that has influenced what we do and enjoy today.

Happy visiting.

Norman Hudson

Norman Hudson OBE

Hudson's Historic Houses & Gardens

Publisher and Editor-in-Chief .... Norman Hudson

Production Co-ordinator & Advertising .... Sue Wintersgill

Administration .... Jennie Carwithen

Graphic Design/Page Layout .... Karen Cooper, Victoria Lavery

Maps .... Taurus Graphics

Scanning & Pre-press .... Spot-On Design & Print

Sales .... Fiona Rolt

Printed by .... Körner Rotationsdruck

UK & European Distribution .... Portfolio - tel: 020 8997 9000

USA Distribution .... The Globe Pequot Press - tel: 001 203 458 4505

Published by:
Norman Hudson & Company
High Wardington House,
Upper Wardington, Banbury,
Oxfordshire OX17 1SP, UK
Tel: 01295 750750
Fax: 01295 750800
enquiries@hudsonsguide.co.uk
www.hudsonsguide.co.uk
ISBN: 1 904387 03 9

Co-published in the USA by:
The Globe Pequot Press
246 Goose Lane, Guilford,
Connecticut 06437, USA

**Library of Congress
Cataloging-in-Publication
data is available.**

ISBN: 1-904387-05-5

UK Cover: 18 Folgate Street, London- Dennis Severs House. ©James Brittain.
US Cover: The Tower of London ©HRP 2006
Frontispiece: Lake Sculpture, Burghley House, Lincolnshire ©Burghley House

CONTENTS

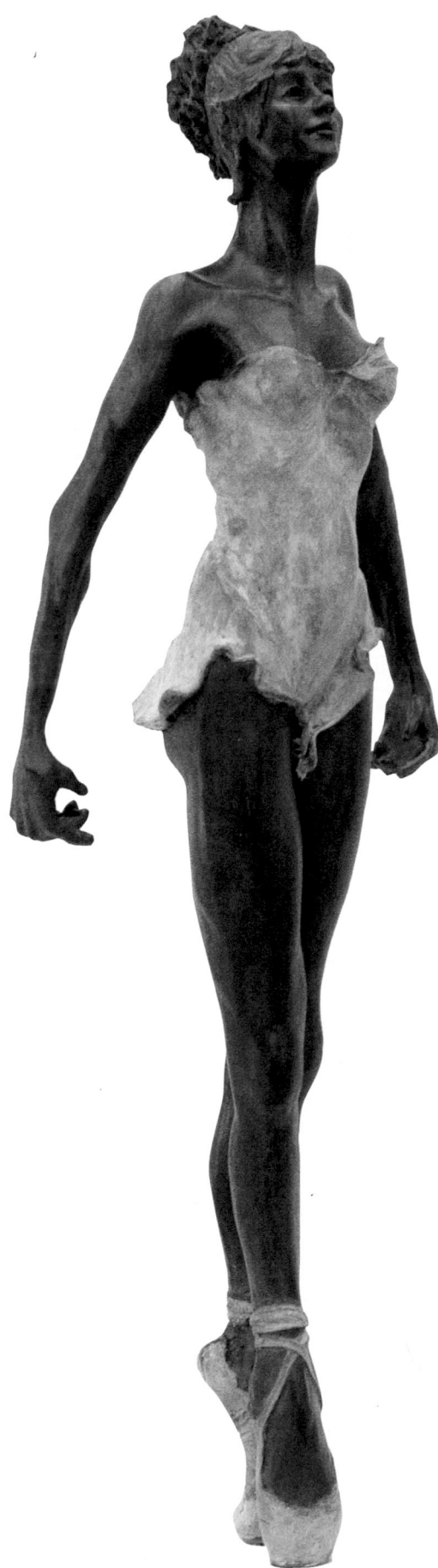

© Sue Wiley 'Points'

Burghley House – *Pride & Prejudice.*

The backdrop business
– historic houses as film locations

Burghley House.

Filming on location gives an authenticity that cannot be created in the studio and this last year has been a busy time for some historic houses, discovers **Lucy Denton.**

The treasure houses of Britain have long been used as dramatic stages in cinematography, with commercial filmmakers attracted to their sumptuous, lavish decoration for the provision of distinctive and atmospheric period backdrops. It might not necessarily be the richness in country house interiors that will catch the eye of a director, but the bleak austerity of a ruined castle in cruel remoteness that may be used to evoke dreariness and enhance a feeling of despair. Filming on location provides an authenticity, a sense of truth that cannot be recreated on a set.

Despite the disruption often caused by a film crew, the financial incentives are strong, especially as the majority of the houses used in films are in the private sector and many need supplementary income to

Basildon Park, Berkshire featured as 'Netherfield' in the recent film *Pride & Prejudice*. In 2006 an exhibition at the house will show much of the work involved in connection with the film. See page 104.

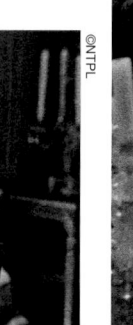

Filming in the Heaven Room at Burghley House.

ensure their maintenance and conservation. The outcomes of filming are usually encouraging for the house, especially if it is open to the public, as it provides a substantial and otherwise unachievable degree of publicity. Other rewards include the opportunities for restoration, especially if the film company requires the redecoration of a room for the purposes of the film - the two necessities may be beneficially combined.

The use of the country house as a film set is a burgeoning business – and with good reason. The authoritative retelling of a story through film depends on the character interpretation on the part of the cast. Perhaps it is easier to fall into rôle when a genuine environment sets the scene, whether this is the shadowy hall of a medieval mansion, or a sweeping Capability Brown landscape – the atmosphere is absorbing and spellbinding. It is often the theatrical, imaginative association of a place which can also be used to suspend reality – think of the brooding towers of the medieval **Alnwick Castle** in Northumberland, which became the magical 'Hogwarts School' in the *Harry Potter* films and the numerous architectural styles at enchanting **Lacock Abbey**, with the cloisters, vaulted rooms and soaring twisted stacks which were transformed into classrooms for the same adaptations of J K Rowling's famous books.

Real settings can be adapted to different purposes. The magnificent Alnwick also became the backdrop for scenes from the 16th century life of *Elizabeth* with Cate Blanchett as the indomitable and determined monarch. Often it is not necessary to faithfully reconstruct a known scene or place, but rather to create an ambience, an atmospheric evocation of the time. The beer and wine cellars at **Warkworth Castle**, near Alnwick, Northumberland, were thus turned into dungeons for the same film, made in 1998.

2005's costume drama hit, *Pride & Prejudice*, starring Keira Knightley, was filmed at several locations, among them **Basildon Park** in Berkshire and splendid **Chatsworth**, remodelled at the end of the 17th century, which became 'Pemberley', the home of Mr Darcy. **Haddon Hall** in Bakewell, a fortified manor house with fragments of stone-work from the 12th century, provided the setting for the 'Lambton Inn' and the Dining Room was transformed into Elizabeth Bennett's bedroom. The Bow Room at **Burghley House**, Lincolnshire, with its lavish painted scenes by Laguerre, also features in the film, while the Great Hall appears in *Golden Bowl* (2000) starring Kate Beckinsale. It was in this house that filming for the eagerly anticipated *Da Vinci Code*, featuring Oscar-winning actor Tom Hanks, took place in the autumn of 2005.

Another new film, this time from the well-established company, Merchant Ivory, called *The White Countess*, was filmed at the beautiful, early 18th century Thames-side villa, **Marble Hill House**. In the care of English Heritage, this property is the setting for summer concerts as well as film-making, both activities supplementing the income for the significant overheads required for the maintenance of the house.

Many houses used in films are in close proximity to London. The Entrance Hall at **Eltham Palace** in south-east London, restored in the early 1930s, has appeared in films providing diverse backdrops from a bedroom to a restaurant. It features in Guy Ritchie's newly released film, *Revolver*, a gangster movie starring Jason Statham and Ray Liotta. This opulently gilded Hall was also used in *I Capture the Castle* released in 2003 and *Bright Young Things*, Stephen Fry's witty adaptation of Evelyn Waugh's *Vile Bodies*, starring Emily Mortimer and released in 2003. **Knebworth** has been used for films such as *Wilde* (1997) starring Jude Law, and **Kingston Lacy** provided

the backdrop for several scenes in *Wimbledon* (2003).

Often the preservation of the fabric of the building necessitates extra measures on the part of the film company. To preserve the banqueting hall at **Eilean Donan Castle** in the West Highlands of Scotland, it was reconstructed in a film studio at Pinewood for the scene in the 1999 James Bond film, *The World is Not Enough* in which John Cleese demonstrates a car coming up through what appear to be the castle floorboards. Sometimes a house will not entirely fulfil the needs of film production, but adaptation of an existing structure is possible. When Zeffirelli's *Jane Eyre* (1996) was shot

Hartland Abbey, Devon used for *The Shell Seekers* by Rosamund Pilcher. For this it was not so much the Abbey that was used but its coastal location and a cottage at the estate.

Dame Judi Dench as 'Lady Catherine De Burgh in *Pride & Prejudice*.

Kirby Hall, Northamptonshire.

Ingatestone Hall, Essex – featured as 'Chesney Wold' in the recent BBC production of *Bleak House*.

Alnwick Castle, Northumberland – features as 'Hogwarts School' in the *Harry Potter* films.

Broughton Castle, featured in many productions including *'Shakespeare in Love'*.

at **Haddon**, the film crew built a false story on top of the house to make it appear larger.

Adaptability is important: the Oak Room and Great Hall at **Broughton Castle**, Oxfordshire, featured in the sumptuous 1998 production of *Shakespeare in Love* with Joseph Fiennes and Gwyneth Paltrow. The Oak Room was again used for *To Kill a King* (2003) and the Dining Room was turned into the King's bedroom at one end and Queen Charlotte's bedroom at the other for *The Madness of King George* (1994).

The Great Hall at the magnificent Elizabethan **Kirby Hall**, in Corby, Northamptonshire, was used for the ballroom scene in *Mansfield Park* (1999), appropriately so – this architecturally exuberant house was built for entertaining. It also features in a forthcoming film, *Tristram Shandy*, starring Steve Coogan, Jeremy Northam and Gillian

Anderson. For the ambience of an age, the producers of *Piccadilly Jim* (2004), used the splendid rococo decoration at **Claydon House** in Buckinghamshire as an extravagant backdrop to a film set in the 1930s.

The **Hartland Abbey** estate, in a beautiful situation on the North Devon coast, has been used for a diverse selection of productions. This last autumn part of *The Shell Seekers* by Rosamund Pilcher was filmed at Hartland, with Vanessa Redgrave playing the main role of 'Penelope Keeling'. For this it was not so much the Abbey that was used but a cottage at Blackpool Mill, a 15th century cottage by the rocky Atlantic cove familiar to visitors to the Abbey, who enjoy the walk to the beach. Despite the full force of the Atlantic gales which allow nothing to grow, let alone up the walls, the cottage was decorated with climbing roses and was surrounded by a pretty garden. An artist's studio was built

temporarily in a position overlooking the sea.

Not every house owner welcomes filming. The disruption and potential damage can be substantial and the location fee can be insufficient to make it attractive and worthwhile. To gain some idea of what is involved I put some questions to Mark Simmons, House and Visitor Services Manager for The National Trust at Basildon Park, recently featured as 'Netherfield' in the making of *Pride & Prejudice*.

Describe Basildon Park and why it was chosen to become 'Netherfield'

Basildon Park was built between 1776 and 1783 by John Carr for Francis Sykes, a Yorkshireman of great wealth who was looking for a country residence within easy reach of London. The Palladian architecture and stunning interiors made it perfect for 'Netherfield' – more of a

showpiece than a lived-in home, which was perfect for the rented house it was meant to portray.

How much effort went into the preparation of the house for filming?

This was the largest and most complex film project The National Trust has ever undertaken. The house was closed for seven weeks while staff and volunteers moved the historic contents, including curtains and carpets, into store and Working Title furnished the house with their own props. The carpet in the Octagon Drawing Room provided the greatest challenge – at 32 feet in diameter it covered the largest floor area in the house. It took fifteen staff to roll it up, an exercise lasting three hours due to the required delicacy of the operation.

Was any work required on the fabric of Basildon Park?

Many houses have evidence of building work carried out over several different generations and Basildon Park is no exception, with elements from the 18th century through to the 1950s. For the filming of *Pride & Prejudice*, a pure early 19th century look was required and the finished result had to be free from all post-Georgian interiors. Radiators were covered up with mock panelling and modern fixtures like alarm sensors and light switches were removed. The modern carpet in the Staircase Hall was also removed and replaced with an imitation marble floor. The red-coloured walls in the Octagon Room would have stood out in contrast to the muted tones of the other 19th century rooms, but as we would not allow redecoration, the film crew installed a false 'room within a room' with real doors and windows. Creating the Octagon Room was the largest

construction job on the film project and was a huge task involving much planning.

For how long did filming take place at Basildon Park?

Location filming lasted for two weeks with a working day typically lasting for twelve hours. The first four days involved shooting the large ballroom sequence with over 250 extras and all the principal actors. Other scenes took place outside, including various carriage shots; and the grand entrance to the ball, one of the most spectacular scenes of the entire film.

Filming itself is divided into two parts: the preparation and the shooting itself, after the director says, "action"! There were many moments when actors simply stood waiting for the next take. The extras had even longer days, arriving at 6am to attend costume and make-up, often for hours, prior to shooting the ball scene.

Was The National Trust comfortable allowing a film crew into Basildon Park?

It costs The National Trust over £350,000 a year to run and maintain Basildon Park. Visitor income over the summer months is insufficient to cover our costs. Even though we hold a number of events at the property ranging from weddings to open-air concerts, the Trust also has to balance conservation and access and has to consider ways in which the costs might be more easily covered. The filming of *Pride & Prejudice* will enable the Trust to continue its programme of vital conservation work and the profile of the property will be boosted – publicity the Trust could not afford. Therefore, the benefits outweigh the temporary intrusion of the film crew.

By Appointment

Columbine Hall, Stowupland, Suffolk.

Only a small proportion of the historic houses in Britain are regularly open to the public. The majority are retained and used exclusively for the purpose for which they were built – as family homes. But some of these too are opened occasionally – although only 'by appointment'.

For larger houses, those with a series of State Rooms – the true stately home – opening is much easier. The family can stay resident in the rooms which perhaps always have been used as the family quarters on a daily basis, while the principal State or reception rooms can be opened. In smaller houses, where the main rooms to be seen are those occupied on a daily basis, the management of opening is much more difficult if family occupation is to continue with any degree of normality.

In some cases, regular opening could have the effect of rendering a house virtually uninhabitable. The majority of properties featured in Hudson's are open regularly but there are many others which are open only 'by appointment'.

Towards the back of the book you will find properties which have received repair grants from English Heritage and, as a condition, are open to the public. Some of these are open by appointment only, possibly because they are small family homes or workplaces. In many respects this arrangement gives the visitor greater flexibility, possibly being able to arrange a time that suits both parties rather than being tied to a number of set dates.

In East Anglia, predominantly in Suffolk, is a scheme "Invitation to View" which is unique in Britain. The area is rich in old houses and inspiring gardens, but only a few are open to the public. This scheme gives visitors a chance to visit houses which are either closed or rarely open. Each visitor is treated as a special guest: you will be part of a small tour which is often shown around by the house owner or at least a guide with personal knowledge of the place. Being able to join a small tour can make it much easier for the visitor, who might otherwise be hesitant and shy about making an individual appointment.

Most of us love visiting other people's houses and a personal tour by an owner is a very different experience from the sometimes impersonal guides at larger properties.

The criterion for being in the scheme is that the house and garden should be capable of providing an interesting tour lasting at least an hour. Owners offer cups of tea or coffee, home-made cakes, and even lunch. While all the houses are historic they are, nevertheless, ordinary homes and there is nothing sanitised or precious about the rooms. Parties may walk through unreconstructed teenagers'

Saxham Hall, Nr Bury St Edmunds, Suffolk.

bedrooms, learn about pruning fruit trees, or hear how the rooms were brought back from dereliction.

At the beginning of each year a full calendar of opening dates is publicised on the website **(www.invitationtoview.co.uk)** and visitors are able to book in advance. The dates are so structured that anyone wishing to combine several house and garden tours may decide to make them the focus of a short break, with accommodation ranging from farmhouse B&B and country house hotels, to cosy self-catering cottages.

High Hall, Nettlestead, Suffolk.

North Cove Hall, Beccles, Suffolk.

Buxlow Manor, Saxmundham, Suffolk.

Bringing history to life

With over 400 historic sites plus Europe's biggest historical events programme, you can look forward to many wonderful days out when you become a member of English Heritage.

From music, drama, outdoor cinema, and historical tours, to battle spectaculars and tournaments, English Heritage brings you top quality entertainment in magnificent historic settings.

The highlight of the English Heritage events programme is the **Festival of History** on 12th & 13th August 2006 at Kelmarsh Hall, Northamptonshire. Celebrating over 2,000 years of history from the Romans to the Swinging Sixties, the festival offers something for all the family to enjoy. Marvel at spectacular WWI aerial displays and dramatic battle re-enactments. Wander through the colourful living history encampments, barter in the traditional street market and enjoy music, dance and an unrivalled celebrity lecture programme.

Now in its second year, **The Knights' Tournament** brings back the days of chivalry, romance and royal sporting entertainment. Follow your team's progress over the summer, as they are put through their paces in jousting, archery, sword-fighting and mounted skill-at-arms. Sixteen rounds of real battle action take place at a selection of England's best historic sites.

For those who want to get their hands on history, an **English Heritage Experience Day** provides the ideal opportunity to explore an authentic pastime or learn a new skill, such as bodice making, sword fighting or falconry – once the sport of kings.

Fans of historical action have the chance to witness famous battles first hand, as major recreations are played out at sites across the country, including the most famous of all – the **Battle of Hastings**. This year's event on the 14-15 October promises to be the biggest spectacle so far, to commemorate the battle's 940th anniversary.

For history-lovers who enjoy walking, there is a superb series of guided **Battlefield Hikes** to the sites of some of England's most significant battles. For those who

prefer a more leisurely encounter with the past, our fully-guided **Tours Through Time** are ideal. These exclusive tours include expert commentary, luxury coach travel, and on overnight trips, bed and breakfast with dinner included. **Tours Through Time** is run in conjunction with Brookland Travel (tel: 0845 121 2863).

All English Heritage events are suitable for families. Events specially designed for children, including fun days, craft workshops and trails, are held during the school holidays at most English Heritage properties.

See page 570 for some key events in 2006.

Why not join today?

By joining English Heritage, you can enjoy all these events for free or at a reduced price as well as free entry to all our properties featured in this guide.

And the benefits of membership don't end there; you will receive our award-winning quarterly magazine, *Heritage Today* and the English Heritage members' and visitors' handbook. What's more, up to six accompanying children are allowed free entry with each member.

Every penny from your membership makes a difference to our work in conserving England's historic environment. In return, we hope you'll gain a great deal of enjoyment from your membership.

Call 0870 333 1181 quoting HUDS1 to join today or visit www.english-heritage.org.uk to find out more about membership and our events.

festival of history

DON'T MISS THE GREATEST WEEKEND IN HISTORY

Saturday 12 & Sunday 13 August 2006
Kelmarsh Hall, Northamptonshire

Experience over 2,000 years of living history from the Roman Empire to the Swinging Sixties. Marvel at WW1 aerial displays, barter in the traditional street market, enjoy music, dance and an unrivalled celebrity lecture programme, all in a magnificent historical setting.

BUY TICKETS NOW AND BEAT THE QUEUES

PHONE 0870 333 1183

www.english-heritage.org.uk/festivalofhistory

ENGLISH HERITAGE

Heraldry

"Heraldry will be found in nearly all historic country houses in Britain" says **David White, Somerset Herald**. Externally you may see it carved on gatehouses and in pediments, inside houses it appears in stained glass, in plaster work and on innumerable objects such as tapestries, portraits, plate, china, bookplates and furniture. It is placed there to mark ownership and to proclaim pride in family, ancestry and social status.

Heraldry first came into being in early 12th century England and France, when knights began to bear bold and bright designs on their shields so that they might be identified. These designs became hereditary and were passed on to their sons. By the 13th century a second element had been introduced: the crest. This was an object worn by a man in armour, as its name implies, on top of his helm (fig 2).

A modern mistake is to use the word 'crest' to refer to any heraldic device, whereas in fact it is only that three-dimensional object that sits on top of the helm. Under nearly all crests you will see a strip of cord; this is known as the wreath, and was a circlet of twisted silk rope that masked the join between the crest and the helm, and helped hold the mantling on. When a crest includes a coronet at its base a wreath is often omitted. The crest is very commonly used on its own to mark smaller objects, such as cutlery.

The mantling was the small cloak which hung down beneath the crest to keep the sun off the helm so that its wearer did not become too hot. It became fashionable to show mantling as ripped and torn, as if its wearer had

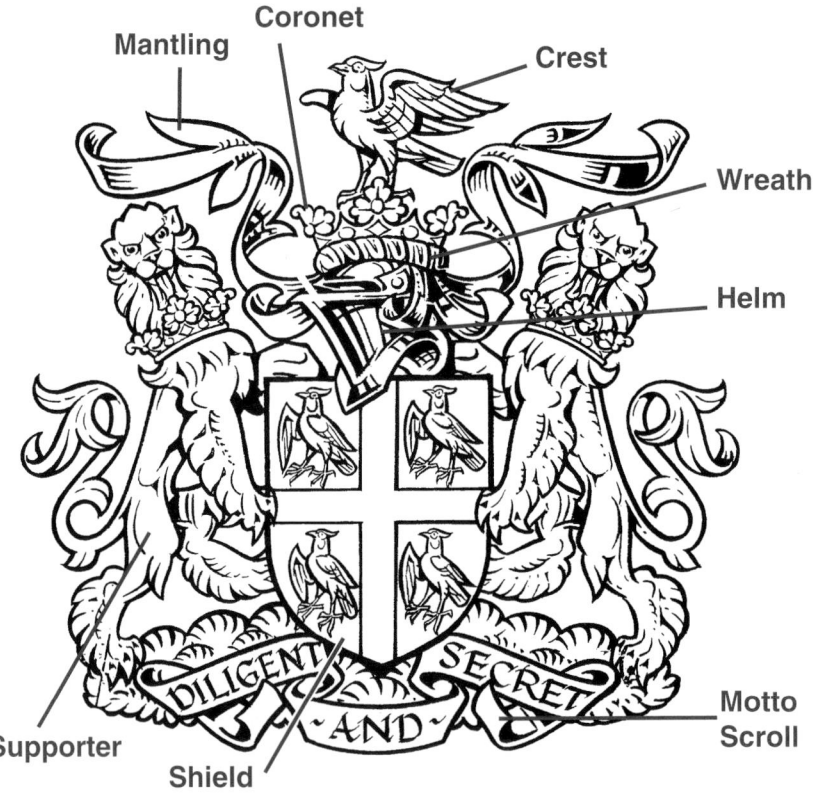

Fig 1. A coat of arms usually includes a shield, crest and a helmet of rank. A coronet can indicate rank as does the presence of supporters.

Mantling — Coronet — Crest — Wreath — Helm — Supporter — Shield — Motto Scroll

been in a particularly hard-fought battle. Over time heraldic artists have taken liberties with mantling, making it so elaborate and overblown that it is often mistaken by the uninitiated for foliage or feathers. Mantling is normally one of the standard heraldic colours on the outside, and lined with a 'metal' (ie gold or silver) on the inside, and

once one realises this it is easier to see the more exaggerated mantling as the cloak it is intended to be (fig 3).

Even if you do not know the name of the family whose heraldry you are looking at there are usually indicators in the way in which it is displayed which will tell you something of the sex, marital status and rank of its owner.

For example, while gentlemen and esquires show their helm above the shield with the vizor down, knights and baronets always show it with the vizor up so that one is looking into the empty helm (fig 4). Baronets will have on their shield a 'baronets badge' which is a much smaller white shield charged with a red hand. Holders of Scottish baronetcies created before 1707 have a different badge on their shield, involving the Scottish lion rampant surmounting a St Andrew's cross.

Around the shield there may be the ribband and motto of an order of chivalry such as TRIA JUNCTO IN UNO ('Three joined in one') for the Order of the Bath, or NEMO ME IMPECUNE LACESSIT ('No one provokes me with impunity') for the Order of the Thistle. The most famous order of chivalry is the Order of the Garter and holders of this will have a blue garter round their shield with the motto HONI SOIT QUI MAL Y PENSE ('Dishonoured be he who thinks ill of it') in gold on it (figs 4 and 5).

fig 2: The crest of a family named Bacon: on a white and red wreath, A Boar statant Ermine. Here carved in wood and painted.

fig 3: Letters patent granting arms and crest to Thomas Edmunds, of Worsbrough, Yorkshire, Gentleman, 1647. The mantling has been painted in a particularly elaborate manner.

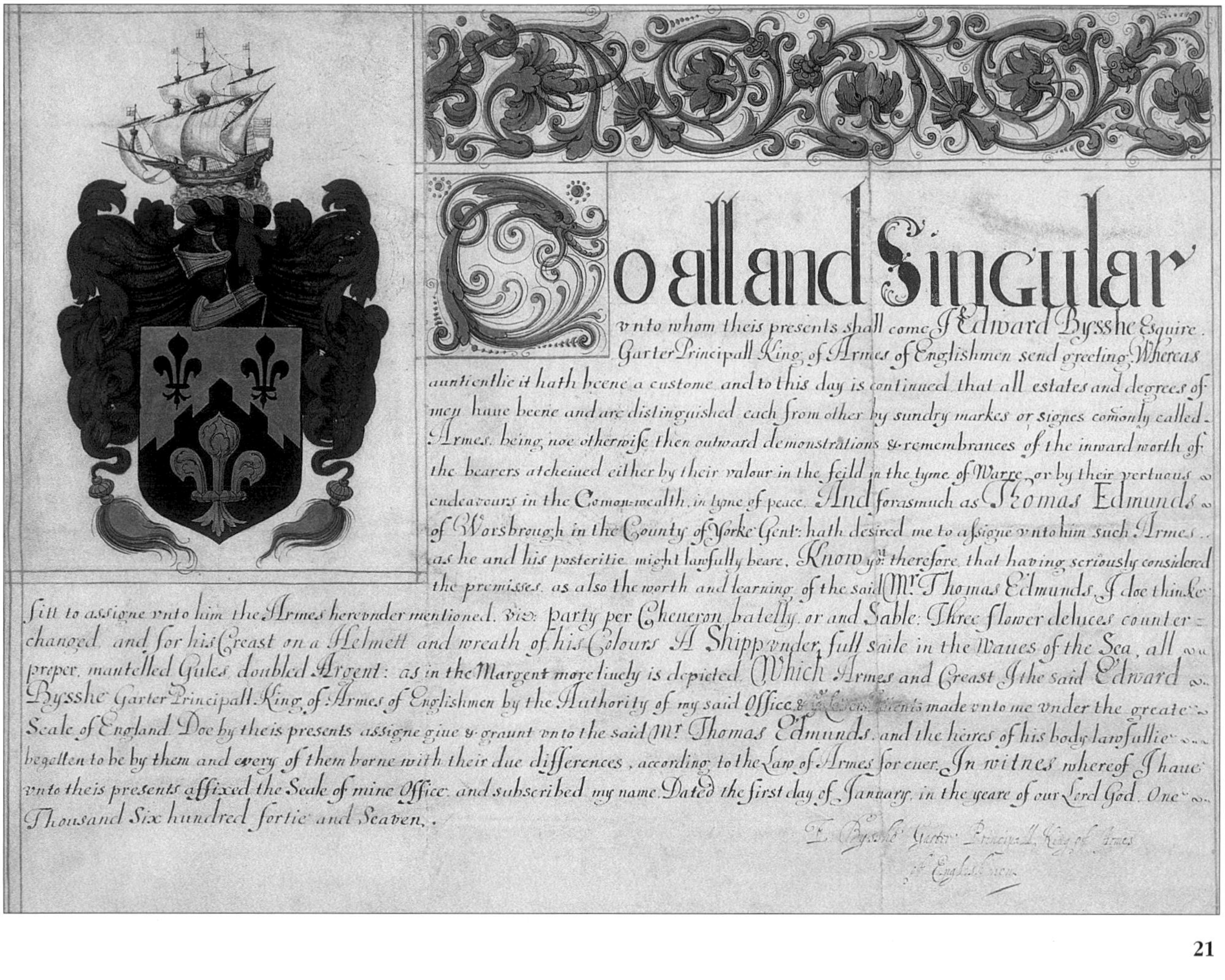

Family mottoes will often appear on a scroll beneath the shield, or if it is a Scottish coat of arms, on a scroll above the crest. While no two families may have the same coat of arms, there is no rule against them having the same motto.

The five ranks of the peerage, duke, marquess, earl, viscount and baron, each have their own distinctive coronet, and in the case of the arms of a peer this will usually be shown above the shield in place of, or in addition to, the crest. A duke's coronet is made up of five gold stylised strawberry leaves set on a gold rim; a marquess shows three strawberry leaves with two silver balls in between them; an earl's coronet has five silver balls raised on gold stalks (fig 7); a viscount's coronet has nine or more silver balls set directly on to the top of the rim (figs 5 and 6); and a baron's has four silver balls set on the rim.

Another indicator of rank are supporters. These are animals, monsters, or human figures which stand on either side of a shield 'supporting' it. The best know pair of supporters are the lion and unicorn of the Royal arms. All five ranks of peer are entitled to supporters as are clan chiefs, Knights of the Garter and of the Thistle, together with Knights Grand Cross of other orders of chivalry. The arms of many corporations, such as public companies and boroughs, also have supporters.

That a man is married is most commonly indicated in heraldry by the shield being divided in two down the middle, with the husband's arms being squeezed on to the left side as seen by the viewer, and wife's family arms being put on the right half.

If a wife has no brothers she is regarded as an heiress to her father's arms. In this case you will see her arms appearing on a small shield at

fig 4: Arms, crest and supporters of General Sir John Moore, painted 1805. The shield is encircled by the ribband of the Order of the Bath, inscribed TRIA JUNCTA IN UNO. As Sir John was a knight the vizor of the helm is shown raised.

fig 8 (facing page): Arms and crests, mostly of Tudor origin, in an early 16th century manuscript. Here the helm is omitted in each coat of arms and the crest, with its wreath, rests directly on the shield, with a small piece of mantling on either side.

fig 5: The arms, crest and supporters of Robert Sidney, Viscount Lisle, in an early 17th century manuscript. The shield is surrounded by the Garter, with the motto HONI SOIT QUI MAL Y PENSE, indicating that he was a member of the Order of the Garter. Between the shield and the helm is a viscount's coronet. On the shield only the 'quarter' in the top left bears the Sidney arms of a gold field with a blue spearhead; the other 'quarters' represent descent from various heraldic heiresses.

Thomas powle
oud of the xij parte
of the Shuudeuy

Rychard hewlett
of Aylysham in com
Kent

Antony butler
of Rottes in
com Lyncolne

Jane Collyns
wiffe to edward
west

Olenyng

Robert Morley
de com norff

John patenson
de London

Thomas Wood
Woodeut de
Barkshire

John oly▢ of sporgrave
de com Kent

Olyuer
Cawberuy

William
Tusser

Andreu reglas
west

©College of Arms, L9.28

23

the centre of her husband's (often obscuring much of the design of his arms). When she dies her children may 'quarter' her arms, the shield being divided into four and her arms placed in the second and third quarters. Over time many 'quarterings' may be acquired by a family through marriages with heiresses, and although a shield may be divided up into dozens of sections to accommodate the arms of the heiresses, each section is still referred to as a 'quarter' (fig 5).

If you see a coat of arms on a diamond shape (known technically as a lozenge) this indicates that they were borne either by a spinster (in which case there is often a ribbon tied in a bow above them) or a widow. Usually a widow's arms on a lozenge show her husband's on the viewer's left and her own family arms on the viewer's right.

Many people are confused by the fact that people of the same surname have quite different coats of arms. It is important to realise that coats of arms do not belong to surnames but to individuals. In England, Wales and Northern

fig 6: Arms and supporters of Frances, Dowager Viscountess Conway, painted 1671. As she was a widow her arms are shown on a diamond shape known as a lozenge. The coronet of a viscountess appears above.

Ireland arms and crests are granted by letters patent of the Queen's three senior heralds, known as Kings of Arms. For any person to have a lawful right to arms they must either have a grant of arms to themself or be able to prove a legitimate male line descent from somebody to whom arms were granted or confirmed in the past. The College of Arms in London makes about 140 grants of arms by

letters patent each year. Some recent examples of these and details of the process involved in petitioning a grant of arms can be found at **www.college-of-arms.gov.uk.**

Scotland has its own system of heraldry and granting arms. The heraldic authority north of the border is The Court of the Lord Lyon, HM New Register House, Edinburgh EH1.

fig 7: Arms, crest and supporters of Augustus John Hervey, Earl of Bristol, painted c1775. An Earl's coronet, with five balls raised on stalks, appears immediately above the shield.

The Landmark Trust: 40 years of rescuing historic buildings

Rescuing remarkable buildings that would otherwise have slipped through the conservation net has been the Landmark Trust's purpose since it was founded 40 years ago. Since then, the charity has saved over 180 buildings and tens of thousands of people have been able to enjoy the rare experience of living for a while in a building of historic interest.

The Ruin, polite elevation, North Yorkshire.

Fort Clonque, Alderney, Channel Islands.

Saddell Castle, Scotland.

Clavell Tower, on the Dorset coast, currently in danger of falling into the sea and needing to be rescued.

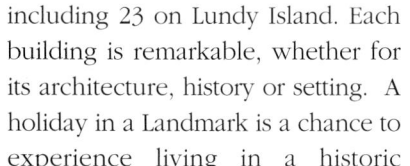

Freston Tower, Suffolk.

A unique experience

There are 183 Landmarks in the UK, including 23 on Lundy Island. Each building is remarkable, whether for its architecture, history or setting. A holiday in a Landmark is a chance to experience living in a historic building as if it were your own. It can be studied at leisure, seen in all lights and weather and an understanding of why and how it was built can be developed.

Landmark's portfolio offers the opportunity for a weekend in a folly or a family celebration in a Tudor manor house. You can watch the sunset over the ramparts of Saddell Castle on the Mull of Kintyre, or filtering through leaded windows at Tixall Gatehouse, where Mary, Queen of Scots was once held. Witness the sea crashing on the rocks around Fort Clonque on

Alderney, or sit by the tranquil stream running through the hamlet of Coombe in Cornwall. Whether you enjoy medieval or modern architecture the Landmark Trust has a building to beguile you.

Rescuing buildings: a continuing need

Whilst the letting income pays for the buildings' future upkeep, funds for new restoration projects must be raised entirely through donations. The charity receives on average three approaches a week about potential Landmarks – many are buildings at risk and in need of urgent help. However due to a lack of resources Landmark can only take on three to five new projects each year.

At the time of writing the

Landmark Trust is raising money to restore an early nineteenth century cottage orné on an estate in Dumfries, a folly on the Dorset coast in danger of collapsing into the sea below and an unusual summerhouse with four circular towers in Bedfordshire. However, there are other buildings in Landmark's sights that are in need of funds to secure their rescue and restoration. With Landmark's experience they can be given a new and secure future.

Restoration

When conserving a building, Landmark seeks to keep as much as possible of its original fabric and will endeavour to repair rather than renew. By using traditional building materials and crafts, and by following our predecessors' example in attention to detail, the aim is to retain the building's texture and personality. However, consideration is given to reversing past change; perhaps inferior work obscures a finer original, or decay has progressed so far that reinstatement would be conjectural or financially unjustifiable.

Some buildings were never designed to be lived in. By preserving them in the form in which they were built, adapting them for modern use only in minor ways, the living arrangements can be unusual. Rather than commit to unseemly alteration, Landmark trusts to its visitors' sense of adventure and asks them to adapt to the building rather than the reverse. At Swarkestone Pavilion guests have to cross the open roof to reach the bathroom and at Tangy Mill you live amongst the old mill machinery.

Architects are commissioned according to region and their familiarity with the needs of old buildings and the fragility of their patina. Often the architects have worked with the Landmark Trust before, but their ingenuity will always be tested, especially in buildings which were never intended for habitation, and where kitchens and bathrooms must be inserted where, until now, there was no water or electricity.

Likewise, local contractors and craftsmen are taken on wherever possible, helping to ensure the survival of distinctive regional techniques. There is good reason to keep faith with these traditional materials and skills. They ensure honest repair and allow an old

Gothic Temple, Stowe, Buckinghamshire. Built in 1741 and one of the last additions to the great garden at Stowe formed for Lord Cobham by Charles Bridgeman and his successor William Kent. That same year "Capability" Brown arrived as gardener to begin his own transformation of the landscape.

Gothic Temple, Stowe, Buckinghamshire.

Wilmington Priory, East Sussex.
This was a cell of the Benedictine
Abbey at Grestain in Normandy.

building quite literally to breathe and remain in healthy equilibrium with its environment. Even a specialist contractor is unlikely to carry all the crafts needed to restore a building. Conservators of paint or *papier mâché*, plasterers skilled in replacing cornices and mouldings, joiners who can transform planks into panelling may all be called upon during the long restoration process.

Living with history

Once a building is restored anyone can stay in it, enriching their lives by living for a time in an historic building, while knowing that every holiday helps ensure that building's survival.

Each building has modern bathrooms and heating, sheets and towels, open fires wherever possible and a well-equipped kitchen. There will also be good furniture and interesting pictures, specially chosen books and a history album telling the secrets of that building's past and its former inhabitants.

Visiting during Open Days

Each year the Landmark Trust opens some of its buildings for Open Days. These events allow people the chance to learn more about their local historic buildings and gives Landmark the opportunity to find out new information from people who may have known the building many years before. Details of forthcoming Open Days can be found on Landmark's website and a selection are contained in this book.

Full details of all 183 Landmark Trust buildings are available in the 40th anniversary edition of the Landmark Trust Handbook, price £11.00 including post and packing, refundable against the first booking. Telephone 01628-825925 or online at www.landmarktrust.org.uk.

Goddards, Surrey. Built by Edwin Lutyens in 1898 - 1900 it is considered one of his most important early houses. The garden was laid out in collaboration with Gertrude Jekyll.

Gothic Temple Gallery, Buckinghamshire.

Duart Castle, West Highlands & Islands

The HHA Friends scheme
provides amazing value for the interested house and gardens visitor

Athelhampton, Dorset

The HHA is a group of highly individualistic and diverse properties most of which are still lived-in family houses. They range from the great palaces to small manor houses.

Many HHA member properties are open to the public and offer free admission to Friends of the HHA.

Eastnor Castle, Herefordshire

Castle Howard, Yorkshire

Parham, Sussex

Longleat, Wiltshire.

The Peto Garden at Iford Manor, Wiltshire.

Knebworth, Hertfordshire

HISTORIC HOUSES ASSOCIATION

Become a Friend of the HHA and visit nearly 300 privately owned houses and gardens for FREE.

KINGSTON BAGPUIZE HOUSE, OXFORDSHIRE

HISTORIC HOUSES ASSOCIATION

**join on line
www.hha.org.uk**

Other benefits:

- Receive the quarterly magazine of the HHA which gives news and features about the Association, its members and our heritage

- Take advantage of organised tours in the UK and overseas

- Join the specially arranged visits to houses, some of which are not usually open to the public

LEVENS HALL GARDENS, CUMBRIA

It is not generally realised that two-thirds of Britain's built heritage remains in private ownership. There are more privately-owned houses, castles and gardens open to the public than are opened by the National Trust, English Heritage and their equivalents in Scotland and Wales put together.

Successive Governments have recognised the private owner as the most economic and effective guardian of this heritage. But the cost of maintaining these properties is colossal, and the task is daunting. The owners work enormously hard and take a pride in preserving and presenting this element of Britain's heritage.

The HHA helps them do this by:

- *representing their interests in Government*
- *providing an advisory service for houses – taxation, conservation, security, regulations, etc.*
- *running charities assisting disabled visitors, conserving works of art and helping promote educational facilities*

There is a fascinating diversity of properties to visit free with a Friends of the HHA card – from the great treasure houses such as Blenheim and Castle Howard through to small manor houses. What makes these places so special is their individuality and the fact that they are generally still lived in – often by the same family that has owned them through centuries of British history. As well as the stunning gardens which surround the houses, there are over 60 additional wonderful gardens to visit.

The subscription rate remains outstanding value for money. Individual Friend: £34. Double Friends living at the same address: £54 (each additional Friend living at same address, £16.50 – only available to holders of a Double Membership). If you wish to become a Friend of the HHA then you can join, using your credit/debit card by calling 01462 896688 or simply fill in the form below.

HOLKHAM HALL, NORFOLK

Membership: Single £34, Double £54, £16.50 additional Friend at same address. Members of NADFAS, CLA and NACF are offered special rates of £30 Individual and £49 Double (at same address).

FRIENDS APPLICATION FORM   HHHG/06

PLEASE USE BLOCK CAPITALS   *DELETE AS APPROPRIATE

MR/MRS/MS or MR & MRS* INITIALS _____

SURNAME _____

ADDRESS _____

_____

_____ POST CODE _____

ADDITIONAL FRIENDS AT SAME ADDRESS

_____

I/We* are members of NADFAS/NACF/CLA (please circle name of organisation to which you belong) our membership number is: _____

☐ I/We* enclose remittance of £ _____ payable to the Historic Houses Association.

☐ I/We* have completed the direct debit adjacent.

Please return to: Historic Houses Association, Friends Membership Department, Heritage House, PO Box 21, Baldock, Hertfordshire SG7 5SH. Tel: (01462) 896688

PHOTOCOPIES OF THIS FORM ARE ACCEPTABLE

INSTRUCTION TO YOUR BANK TO PAY DIRECT DEBITS

Please complete Parts 1 to 5 to instruct your Bank to make payments directly from your account. Then return the form to: Historic Houses Association, Membership Department, Heritage House, PO Box 21, Baldock, Herts, SG7 5SH.

1. Name and full postal address of your Bank

_____

_____

_____

Your Bank may decline to accept instructions to pay Direct Debits from some types of accounts.

2. Account holder name _____

3. Account number ☐☐☐☐☐☐☐☐

4. Bank sort code ☐☐ ☐☐ ☐☐

Originator's identification No. 9 3 0 5 8 7

Originator's reference (office use only) ☐☐☐☐☐☐☐

5. Your instructions to the Bank and signature.

- I instruct you to pay Direct Debits for my annual subscription from my account at the request of the Historic Houses Association.
- The amounts are variable and may be debited on various dates.
- I understand that the Historic Houses Association may change the amounts and dates only after giving me prior notice of not less than 21 days.
- Please cancel all previous Standing Order and Direct Debiting instructions in favour of the Historic Houses Association.
- I will inform the Bank in writing if I wish to cancel this instruction.
- I understand that if any Direct Debit is paid which breaks the terms of the instruction, the Bank will make a refund.

Signature(s) _____

_____

Date _____

DIRECT Debit Completion of the form above ensures that your subscription will be paid automatically on the date that it is due. You may cancel the order at any time. The Association guarantees that it will only use this authority to deduct annually from your account an amount equal to the annual subscription then current for your class of membership.

IF COMPLETING THE DIRECT DEBIT FORM, YOU MUST ALSO COMPLETE THE APPLICATION FORM.

RHS Partner Gardens

PROPERTY	OPENING TIMES AND DATES	FREE ACCESS DATES
Abbotsbury Sub-Tropical Gardens	All year, daily, 10am - 6pm (dusk in winter). Closed over Christmas and New Year	Oct - Feb
Aberglasney Gardens	Summer, daily, 10am - 6pm (last entry 5pm); winter, daily, 10.30am - 4pm	Jan - Mar
Arley Hall & Gardens	1 Apr - 1 Oct: Tue - Sun & BHs, 11am - 5pm. Oct: w/ends only	When open, (gardens only and not special event days)
Bedgebury National Pinetum	All year, daily, 10am - 5pm	When open
Belvoir Castle	Apr - Sept: Tue - Thur, w/e & BH Mons, 11am - 5pm	Apr - Jul, daily except Mon & Fri
Benington Lordship Gardens	4 Feb - 19Feb, 12 - 4pm and 26 Jun - 2 Jul, daily, 2 - 5pm	When open
Bicton Park Botanical Gardens	All year, daily, 10am - 6pm (5pm winter). Closed 25 & 26 Dec	Jan - Feb & Nov (excl train rides)
Blenheim Palace Park & Gardens	12 Feb - 11 Dec: daily 9am - 4.45pm (last admission) Closed Mon & Tues Nov - Dec	11 Feb - 27 May (excl. Easter) & 11 Sept - 10 Dec. Gardens only
Bodnant Garden	11 Mar - 5 Nov: daily, 10am - 5pm (last admission 4.30pm)	When open
Branklyn Gardens	Good Friday - 30 Oct, daily, 10 - 5pm	When open
Burton Agnes Hall	1 Apr - 31 Oct: daily, 11am - 5pm	When open
Cae Hir Gardens	Apr - Oct, daily, 1 - 6pm	When open
Caerhays Castle & Garden	13 Feb - 31 May: daily, 10am - 5.30pm (gardens only) last entry 4.30pm.	13 Feb - 12 Mar
Cambo Gardens	All year, daily, 10am - dusk	When open
Cawdor Castle & Gardens	1 May - 8 Oct: daily, 10am - 5.30pm	May - Jun & Sept - Oct (gardens only)
Cholmondeley Castle Garden	Apr - Sept: Wed, Thurs, Sun & BHs, 11.30am - 5pm	June
Corsham Court Gardens	20 Mar - 30 Sept: Tues - Thurs, Sat & Sun, 2 - 5pm. 1 Oct - 19 Mar: w/e only, 2 - 4pm. Closed Dec	When open (gardens only)
Cottesbrooke Hall & Gardens	May - end June: Wed, Thurs, 2 - 5.30pm. Jul - Sept: Thur & BH Mon, 2 - 5.30pm	When open (gardens only) excl special event days.
Coughton Court	Please see website: www.coughtoncourt.co.uk	When open (gardens only)
Dalemain	26 Mar - 29 Oct: Sun - Thurs, 10.30am - 5pm	5 Apr - 3 May (gardens only)
Docton Mill & Garden	Mar - Oct: daily, 10am - 6pm	Sats 1 Mar - 31 Oct inclusive
Doddington Hall	Gardens: Sun, 19 Feb - Sept & Easter Mon, 12 - 5pm. With house: May - Sept, Wed, Sun, BHs, 12 - 5pm	When open
The Dorothy Clive Garden	11 Mar - 31 Oct: daily, 10am - 5.30pm	Jul - Aug
Drummond Castle	Easter Weekend and May - Oct, daily, 1 - 6pm	May, Sept and Oct
Duncombe Park	30 Apr - 29 Oct: Sun - Thurs (please telephone for opening times)	When open
Dunrobin Castle Gardens	1 Apr - 15 Oct, daily, Apr, May and Oct 10.30am - 4.30pm, (5.30pm, Jun - Sept)	When open
Dyffryn Gardens	Easter - Sept, daily, 10am - 6pm; Oct, daily, 10am - 5pm; Nov - Easter, daily, 10am - 4pm	1 Apr - 31 Oct (not special event days)
East Bergholt Place Garden	1 Mar - 30 Sept, daily, 10am - 5pm. Closed Easter Sunday	Mar - Jun (except charity Sundays)
Elton Hall	28 - 29 May, Weds in Jun, Wed, Thurs and Sun, Jul - Aug, 28 Aug, 2 - 5pm	May - Jul
Exbury Gardens	26 Feb - 6 Nov: daily, 10am - 5.30pm. Please call for winter opening dates	Mar
Fairhaven Woodland & Water Garden	All year: daily, 10am - 5pm. May - Aug: Wed & Thurs, 10am - 9pm. Closed 25 Dec	Feb - Apr & Oct

Properties in *Hudson's* that offer free garden access at specified times to RHS Members.

Royal Horticultural Society
200 YEARS

PROPERTY	OPENING TIMES AND DATES	FREE ACCESS DATES
Floors Castle Gardens	Apr - Oct: daily, 11am - 5pm	When open (gardens only)
Forde Abbey & Gardens	Gardens open daily: 10am - 4.30pm. Abbey open Apr - Oct, Tues - Fri, Sun & BH: 12 noon - 4pm	Oct - Feb (gardens only)
Furzey Gardens	All year: daily, 10am - 5pm (dusk in winter) excl Christmas and Boxing Day	Mar - Oct
Glen Chantry	7 Apr - 2 Sept, Fri - Sat, 10am - 4pm	When open
Glenwhan Garden	1 Apr - 30 Sept, daily, 10am - 5pm	Aug - Sept and 1 - 30 Oct by appointment
Goodnestone Park Gardens	31 Mar - 26 Sept: Wed - Fri, 11am - 5pm. Sat - Sun, 12 noon - 5pm	Apr - May & Sept (gardens only, not special event days)
Harewood House	26 Mar - 29 Oct: daily, 10am - 6pm	26 Mar - 30 Jun (gardens only, not w/e, BHs & special event days)
Harmony Garden	Good Friday - 30 Sept, Mon - Sat, 10am - 5pm, Sun, 1 - 5pm	When open
Hatfield House & Gardens	Easter Sat - 30 Sept: daily, 11am - 5.30pm	When open, except Thurs (& major event days)
Hergest Croft	Mar, Sat - Sun, 12.30 - 5pm, 1 Apr - 29 Oct, daily, 12.30 - 5.30pm, May - Jun, 12 noon - 6pm	1 Mar - 30 Apr and 1 Jul - 29 Oct
Hill of Tarvit Mansionhouse & Garden	All year: daily, 9.30am - sunset	When open (gardens only)
Holker Hall Garden	26 Mar - 29 Oct: Sun - Fri, 10.30am - 5.30pm. Hall & Gardens closed Sat	Apr - Oct (gardens only excl special event days)
Houghton Hall	Easter Sun - 28 Sept: Wed - Thurs, Sun & BH Mons, 11am - 5.30pm	June (gardens only)
Kellie Castle & Garden	All year, daily, 9.30am - 5.30pm	When open
Kingston Maurward Garden	4 Jan - 21 Dec: daily, 10am - 5.30pm	When open
Leith Hall and Garden	All year, daily, 9.30am - sunset	When open
Loseley Park	May - Sept: Tues - Sun, 11am - 5pm	May & Sept (garden only) except NGS days, 7 May & 3 Sept
Mannington Gardens	May - Sept, Sun, 12 noon - 5pm; Jun - Aug, Wed - Fri, 11am - 5pm	When open (gardens only)
Mapperton Gardens	Mar - Oct: daily except Sat, 11 - 5pm	When open
Muncaster Castle Garden	Feb - Dec, daily, 10.30am - 5pm (closed Jan)	1 Jul - 5 Nov
National Botanic Garden of Wales, The	31 Oct - 26 Mar, daily, 10am - 4.30pm; 27 Mar - 30 Oct, daily, 10am - 6pm. Closed Christmas Day.	Jan - Mar & Oct - Dec
Newby Hall & Gardens	1 Apr - 1 Oct: Tues - Sun & BHs Mon, 11am - 5.30pm (daily in Jul - Aug)	Apr, May & Sept (not special event days)
Nymans Garden	15 Feb - 29 Oct: Wed - Sun & BH Mon, 11am - 6pm. Nov - Feb 2007, w/e only, 11am - 4pm (or dusk)	When open
Parcevall Hall Gardens	Good Friday - 31 Oct: daily, 10am - 6pm	May - Aug
Penshurst Place & Gardens	4 - 25 Mar: w/e, 10.30am - 6pm. 25 Mar - 29 Oct: daily, 10.30am - 6pm	Apr & Sept - Oct (gardens only)
Picton Castle	Apr - Oct: Tues - Sun & BHs, 10.30am - 5pm	Apr - Sept (not event days), gardens only
Plas Brondanw Gardens	All year, daily, 9.30am - 5pm (or dusk if earlier)	1 Oct - 31 Apr

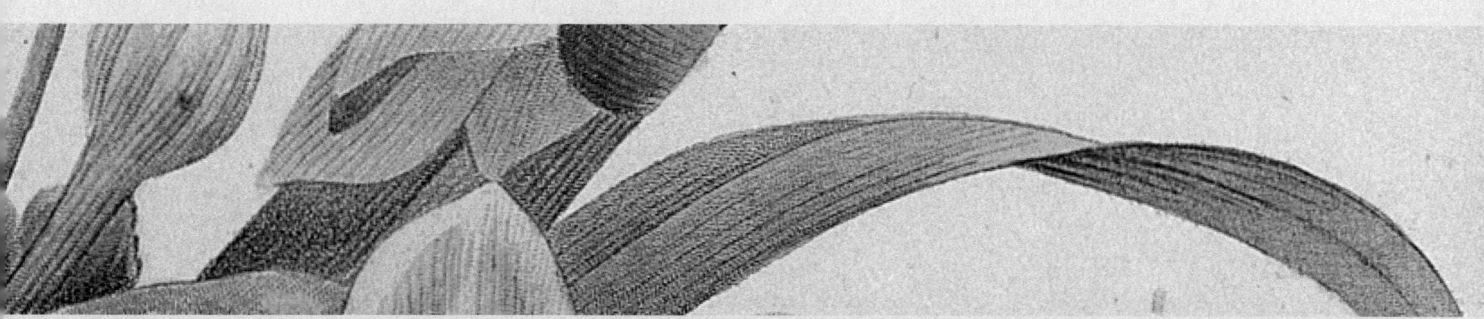

RHS Partner Gardens

PROPERTY	OPENING TIMES AND DATES	FREE ACCESS DATES
Portmeirion	All year, daily except Christmas Day, 9.30am - 5.30pm	1 Oct - 31 Apr
Raby Castle	May - Sept, Sun - Fri, 11am - 5.30pm, 5pm in Sept, Sat on BHs	When open (not special event days)
Ragley Hall	25 Mar - 1 Oct, 10am - 6pm	May - Sept, Thurs /Fri, Jul - Aug, Thurs - Sun
Renishaw Hall	Easter - end Sept, Thurs - Sun and BHs, 10.30am - 4.30pm	When open
Ripley Castle	All year, daily, 9am - 5pm (4.30pm during winter)	When open
Rode Hall	4 - 26 Feb: daily except Mon, 12 noon - 4pm 1 Apr - 30 Sept: Tues - Thur & BHs, 2 - 5pm	When open
Ryton Organic Gardens	All year: daily, 9am - 5pm. Closed Christmas week.	When open
Sandringham	15 Apr - mid Jul & early Aug - 29 Oct: daily, 10.30am - 5pm (4pm, Oct)	When open (gardens only)
Sausmarez Manor	All year, daily, 10am - 5pm. Closed 24 Dec - 6 Jan 07	First week of every month when open
Scone Palace & Grounds	Apr - Oct: daily, 9.30am - 5.45pm	When open
Seaforde Gardens	All year: Mon - Sat, 10am - 5pm, Sun, 1 - 6pm (Nov - Feb, closed Sat & Sun). Closed 24 Dec - 2 Jan	Apr - Jun (gardens only)
Sheffield Park Garden	Opening times vary throughout the year. Please contact the garden for details.	When open
Syon Park	Apr - Oct, 10.30am - 5.30pm, Nov - Mar 2007 (except Christmas and Boxing Day), 10.30am - 4pm	When open (gardens only)
Tapeley Park	26 Mar - 31 Oct: Sun - Fri, 10am - 5pm	8 Jun - 8 Jul
Tatton Park	25 Mar - 1 Oct: Tues - Sun, 10am - 6pm. 3 Oct - 23 Mar 2007: Tues - Sun, 11am - 4pm	When open (gardens only)
Thorp Perrow Arboretum	Mar - mid-Nov: daily, dawn - dusk	Mon - Fri (not BHs) when open
Threave Garden & Estate	All year: daily, 9.30am - 5pm	Apr - May & Sept - Oct
Torosay Castle & Gardens	All year: daily, 9am - sunset	When open
Trebah Garden	All year, daily, 10.30am - 5pm	Jan - Mar and Nov - end Jan 07
Trewithen Gardens	Feb - Sept: daily, 10am - 4.30pm. Closed Sun, Jun - Sept.	Jul - Sept
Waddesdon Manor	29 Mar - 23 Dec: Wed - Sun & BH Mon plus 18 & 19 Dec, 10am - 5pm. 7 Jan - 26 Mar: w/e 10am - 5pm	Mar & Sept - Oct
Wartnaby Gardens Jun)	4 Apr - 25 Jul: Tues, 9.30am - 12.30pm	When open (excl 27 Feb, 24 Apr & 19
Wentworth Castle Gardens	Mar - Oct, Sat - Sun, 2 - 5pm, guided tour available at 2.30pm - contact garden directly)	When open
West Dean	Nov - Feb, Wed - Sun, 11am - 4.30pm, Mar, Apr and Oct, daily, 11am - 5pm, May - Sept, daily, 10.30am - 5pm	Jan - Mar (except special event days)
Westonbirt Arboretum Oct	All year, daily, 10am - 8pm (or dusk if earlier)	When open except 21 - 31 Aug & 1 - 31
Wilton House	13 Apr - 30 Sept, daily, 10.30am - 5.30pm, last admission 4.30pm	When open
Wollerton Old Hall Garden	Good Fri - Sep: Fri, Sun & BHs, 12 noon - 5pm	Apr - May & Sept
Yalding Organic Gardens	Apr - Oct, Wed - Sun, 10am - 5pm, and BHs, 10am - 5pm	When open
York Gate Garden	Apr - 30 Sept, Thurs, Suns and BHs, 2 - 5pm and Thurs 22, 29 Jun and 6 Jul, 6.30pm - 9pm	Apr - May and Sept

Unlock **2000** years of Britain's heritage!

The Great British Heritage Pass is a great way of discovering Britain's unique and magical heritage, as it opens the doors of nearly 600 of our finest historic buildings, stately homes, castles, gardens, and monuments. All for one great value price!

Saving you money

Walking in the footsteps of kings and queens of the past, your Great British Heritage Pass can cover its cost in just a few visits!

Saving you time

The Great British Heritage Pass not only saves you money, it may also save you time because you won't have to stand in line to buy a ticket!

Choose from 4 durations – 4 day, 7 day, 15 day and 30 day*

*From just £2.50 per day. Offers subject to change. For up-to-date information about prices and attractions, please visit www.gbheritagepass.com

Buy your pass in advance!

Go online to
www.gbheritagepass.com

or

Contact our call centre on
+44 (0) 1664 485 020

Monday – Friday 9am – 8pm GMT
Saturday 10am – 4pm GMT

Historic Scotland
looking after Scotland's heritage

HRH The Duke of Rothesay visits Linlithgow Palace.

Historic Scotland cares for 345 historic attractions across Scotland, spanning more than 5,000 years of Scotland's history, heritage and culture. Including ancient tombs, majestic castles and soaring abbey ruins, the extent of the collection creates a colourful step into Scotland's past.

From the Highlands and islands to the Borders, Historic Scotland offers days out at Scotland's most visited, famous and enchanting attractions, and welcomes around 2.9 million visitors every year. The portfolio includes the globally famous icon of Edinburgh Castle – home to the country's 'crown jewels', Stirling Castle, and Urquhart Castle, in a dramatic location overlooking the waters of Loch Ness.

Other picturesque properties include the great Border Abbeys – magnificent ruins among some of the Borders' most beautiful countryside, and places such as Edzell Castle near Brechin and Dirleton Castle near North Berwick, which are surrounded by inspiring gardens.

Historic Scotland's collection extends to the islands including Shetland, Orkney and the Western Isles. Famous Orkney attractions include Skara Brae, a prehistoric village older than the pyramids, which is recognised as a World

Linlithgow Palace – the restored King's Fountain.

Craigmillar Castle.

Heritage Site and one of the most significant ancient monuments in the world.

Many properties have visitor centres, exhibitions and audio tours in addition to expert on-site guides and staff. Moreover some have a programme of battle re-enactments, drama and music.

As well as encouraging access to its buildings, sites and monuments Historic Scotland's rôle is to maintain and conserve them for future generations, for which it has a team of highly skilled conservators, architects and technicians. This includes experts from the Historic Scotland Conservation Centre, based in Edinburgh, who carry out specialist work including the restoration of some of the fine ornamental stone details on the interior and exterior of the properties.

In the past five years the team at the Conservation Centre has been instrumental in restoring the King's Fountain at Linlithgow Palace to its former glory. The ornate five metre stone fountain gracing the courtyard of the Palace has been closely associated with royalty since its creation in the 16th century. This link was renewed in 2003 when HRH

Sculpture restoration.

Edzell Castle - parterre.

Dallas Dhu distillery.

Prince Charles, Duke of Rothesay, visited Linlithgow Palace and admired the progress being made on the long and delicate programme of restoration on the fountain.

Once one of the glories of the Scottish Court, the elaborate King's Fountain was commissioned by James V in 1537, possibly to welcome his new French queen. Subsequently it was a centrepiece for special occasions, as in 1633 when it ran to celebrate a visit by Charles I. When Bonnie Prince Charlie visited the Palace in 1745 it is said to have flowed with wine. But for around the last 100 years the ruinous state of the fountain has prevented any water from flowing through it.

It was following an assessment of the cultural significance and condition of the fountain that in 2000, Historic Scotland embarked on the ambitious project to rectify centuries of damage and decay. An essential part of the repair work involved the removal of 1930s' concrete and iron armature repairs. Each of the 158 carved or moulded stones from the fountain was surveyed, photographed and their condition assessed. As much as

possible of the original material was retained and reinstated during the conservation work.

Many of the new stones for the fountain were carved by Historic Scotland stonemasons at a stone carving facility based at Blackness Castle. Others were produced by the Cliveden Conservation Workshop in Bath.

Every detail has been authentically restored so that the fountain now looks as impressive as in the days of James V when it was first built. Octagonal, with three basins arranged like a wedding cake, the overall appearance of the fountain is of an elaborate crown.

One of the greatest accomplishments of the project has been to restore the fountain's internal workings. It is now in full working order, although its future operation will be limited in order to minimise erosion of the stone.

This marvellous achievement further enhances Linlithgow Palace, the birthplace of Mary, Queen of Scots, as one of Historic Scotland's most popular properties and once a favoured residence of the Stewart Kings, overlooking Linlithgow Loch.

Find out more

Details on Historic Scotland attractions are available at www.historic-scotland.gov.uk.

A programme of battle re-enactments, drama, music and interpretation events can be found at many properties.

To request a programme call 0131 668 8830 or visit www.historic-scotland.gov.uk/events.

A wide range of castles, palaces and abbeys in the care of Historic Scotland are available for hire for unique corporate events or weddings.

Each offers its own distinct atmosphere, from the ruinous splendour of Dryburgh Abbey and Elgin Cathedral, to the imposing grandeur of Edinburgh, Edzell and Urquhart Castles. For further information tel: 0131 668 8958.

Email:hsfunctions@scotland.gov.uk, or go to web address: www.historic-scotland.gov.uk/weddings, or www.historic-scotland.gov.uk/corpevents.

Getting around

An Explorer Pass is a money saving pass which provides access to all Historic Scotland attractions. It is valid for three to ten day periods. For details ask at any site, visit www.historic.scotland.gov.uk/explorer/ or call +44 (0) 131 668 8797

For free entry to attractions all-year-round become a member of Historic Scotland. Annual or life membership benefits include free entry to hundreds of events, 20% discount in Historic Scotland shops and a quarterly magazine. For further information ask at any site or contact 0131 668 8999 or email; hsfriends@scotland.gov.uk for an information pack.

Facing page: A miscellany of Historic Scotland properties.

Historic Royal Palaces

Historic Royal Palaces is the independent charity that cares, conserves and presents to the public some of the greatest palaces ever built: The Tower of London, Hampton Court Palace, Kensington Palace, The Banqueting House, Whitehall and Kew Palace. Because it receives no public funding, income from visitors is crucial for the charity to continue to conserve these unique palaces for future generations.

Hampton Court Palace.

Above: Hampton Court and some of the historical re-enactments that take place there.

The Royal Ceremonial Dress Collection at Kensington Palace.

For 2006, Historic Royal Palaces will be exploring the theme of 'History Where It Happened'. This translates into fascinating stories at each of the palaces, including: the domestic life of George III and his family at Kew Palace; the rôle of the Medieval Palace at The Tower of London under Edward I and Henry III; the efficient production line that was the vast Tudor Kitchens at Hampton Court Palace; and the stunning new exhibition of world-renowned photographer Mario Testino's portraits of Diana, Princess of Wales at Kensington Palace, her former home.

So these are new events for 2006, but what is the individual history of these unique palaces, and what else is there to see and do there?

The family country home of George III and Queen Charlotte, enchanting **Kew Palace** is the sole survivor of a group of buildings that comprised the extensive royal residence in the Royal Botanic Gardens at Kew. It is where King George III was often confined, under the watchful eyes of his many doctors, during his well-documented bouts of illness, presumed as madness but now known to have been porphyria. Since the closure of the palace in 1996 for urgent conservation work, extensive and painstaking research of the physical building fabric and historical records has revealed a fascinating insight into this modest, domestic royal palace as well as the lives of the family who lived and the people who worked there.

Kew Palace has been undergoing a comprehensive conservation and representation project and will open to the public again in May 2006, featuring the fashionable Georgian décor and furnishings with which George III and his family created their tranquil retreat.

Her Majesty's Royal Palace and Fortress **The Tower of London**, founded by William the Conqueror in 1066-7, and enlarged and modified by successive sovereigns, is one of the world's most famous and spectacular fortresses. Enriched by its many living traditions, the Crown Jewels, the Royal Armouries' displays and other recent improvements, the Tower is a World Heritage Site and the most visited historic site in Britain.

The Banqueting House, Whitehall.

The Chapel Royal at Hampton Court Palace.

Visitors can also enjoy free Beefeater Tours, explore the legend of the mysterious Tower Ravens, and take part in interactive costumed events. And for this year's 400th anniversary of the Gunpowder Plot, the special exhibition 'Gunpowder Treason' presents dramatic film and audio footage of the Tower's rôle in the Gunpowder Plot story.

Hampton Court Palace became a royal palace in the 1520s, on its acquisition by Henry VIII from Cardinal Wolsey. Its Tudor buildings are among the most important in existence, and include the vast Tudor Kitchens, the finest and most complete surviving royal kitchens in the world, which had the mammoth task of feeding 600 people twice a day. William III and Mary II's improvements are an outstanding example of the English baroque. The interiors are enriched by a magnificent collection of pictures and tapestries from the Royal Collection.

The buildings are surrounded by 60 acres of garden and 750 acres of royal parkland which visitors can also enjoy, including the formal Privy Garden, East Front Garden, the historic Longwater and the world-famous Maze.

Kensington Palace became a royal residence in 1689 with the purchase of an existing house by William III and Mary II, anxious for a retreat from the unhealthy air of Whitehall. Immediately enlarged for them by Christopher Wren, and subsequently altered under George I, the State Apartments contain important interiors by William Kent, many major works of art from the Royal Collection and the Royal Ceremonial Dress Collection. A very intimate and feminine palace, it was home to a series of Royal women including Queen Victoria (who was born in the palace and declared Queen here in 1837), Princess Margaret and, most recently, the late Diana, Princess of Wales.

Tower of London White Tower (top), and by the Traitor's Gate.

The King's Staircase at Hampton Court Palace painted by Antonio Verrio.

Queen Anne's Orangery is an elegant Hawksmoor building, where after exploring the palace, visitors can relax over a very English afternoon tea.

Finally, **The Banqueting House** is the only remaining building of Whitehall Palace, the sovereign's principal residence from 1530 until 1698, when it was destroyed by fire. Designed by Inigo Jones for James I (1603 - 25), The Banqueting House was originally built for occasions of State, plays and masques. Today visitors can still gaze at the original ceiling paintings in the Main Hall by Sir Peter Paul Rubens, which were commissioned by Charles I, to celebrate his father James I's life and wise government. There are nine canvasses altogether, mounted on a carved and compartmented ceiling.

However, the Banqueting House is probably most famous for the single most significant event which took place here – the execution of King Charles I. In 1649, after years of struggle between the authority of Parliament and the power of the King, which culminated in the Civil War (1642 - 9), Charles I was found guilty of treason and sentenced to death. The carpenters set up the scaffold just south of the Whitehall Gate against the walls of the northern annexe of the Banqueting House. Although the King was hidden from the majority of the crowd by black drapery, neighbouring rooftops were thronged with spectators who gave eyewitness accounts of the King's beheading.

So between them these great palaces represent 1,000 years of stories to be explored and discovered. Visit the Historic Royal Palaces in 2006 and you can be amongst the first people to see Kew Palace restored after eight years, plus the new look Medieval Palace at the Tower and re-presented Tudor Kitchens at Hampton Court Palace. Find out more about visiting these magnificent palaces and book tickets in advance at **www. hrp.org.uk**.

What does "listing" mean?

All the buildings in Hudson's are 'listed', most of them in the highest categories of listing. But what does 'listing' mean? It varies depending on whether the building is in England, or Wales where the statutory body is CADW; or in Scotland where it is Historic Scotland and the Grades I, II* and II are replaced by the arguably more logical Grades A, B and C. **Gemma Abercrombie** of English Heritage explains the situation in England and current changes to the system.

Holkham Hall, Norfolk.

© English Heritage Photo Library.

Listing allows us to identify and protect the most interesting and important parts of our architectural heritage. The term refers to the legal process by which properties are added to the lists of buildings of special architectural and historic interest that are compiled by the government, specifically the Secretary of State for Culture, Media and Sport, acting on advice from English Heritage. The process derives from the Planning (Listed Buildings and Conservation Areas) Act 1990. The lists include the huge diversity of building types and styles that make up our architectural heritage, ranging from stately homes, cathedrals and castles, to swimming pools, steelworks, telephone boxes, bandstands and modern tower blocks. A review of this system is underway, to try to simplify and clarify what is perceived as a complex, somewhat mystifying process.

The biggest misconception surrounding the listing system is that its purpose is to fossilise buildings, preserving them in aspic. This is absolutely not the case – listing does give protection to historic buildings, but the aim is to allow their special character to be taken into account when changes are made rather than preventing change itself. It has long been acknowledged that the long-term interests of historic buildings are best served by keeping them in use, ideally that which they were designed for, but if not then a new use may have to be found. Listing ensures that those qualities and characteristics that make a building special are fully considered before changes are made.

The majority of people who own listed buildings are keen to preserve and repair them, and indeed 97% of applications to change listed buildings are approved. In many cases, having a listed house can add to its value, reflecting people's growing awareness of and engagement with our shared heritage – often listed buildings and structures are powerful expressions of our long history.

Buildings are selected for listing with great care. The older and rarer a building is, the more likely it is to be listed. Buildings built before 1700 that survive in anything like their original condition are listed, as are most built between 1700 and 1840. After that date, the criteria become tighter with time, because of the increased number of buildings erected and the much larger numbers that have survived, so that post-1945 buildings have to be exceptionally important to be listed. Buildings less than 30 years old are only rarely listed, if they are of outstanding quality and under threat.

The other main principles for selection are:

• Architectural interest: all buildings that are nationally important for the interest of their architectural design, decoration and craftsmanship; also, important examples of particular building types and techniques, as well as significant plan forms.

• Historic interest: this includes buildings that illustrate important aspects of the nation's social, economic, cultural or military history. Close historical association with nationally important figures and events.

• Group value – especially where buildings comprise an important architectural or historic unity, or are a fine example of planning (such as squares, terraces and model villages).

More detailed principles of selection, providing further guidance about the way particular building types are considered, have been the subject of public consultation over the summer. There are currently about 370,000 entries on the lists, which are graded I, II* or II. Grade II buildings make up the vast majority of the

Stone Bridge in North Cornwall

45

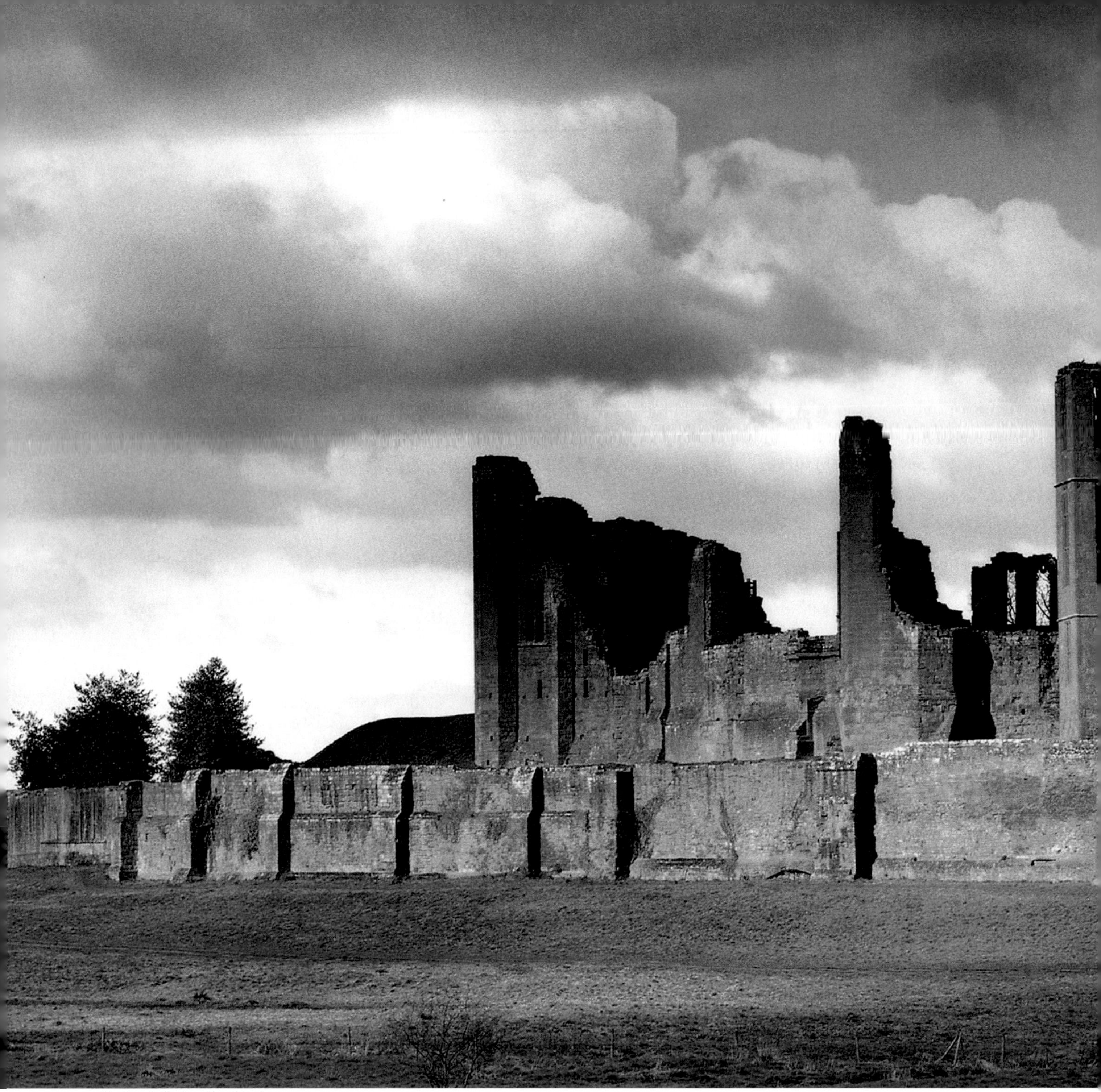

Kenilworth Castle, Warwickshire.

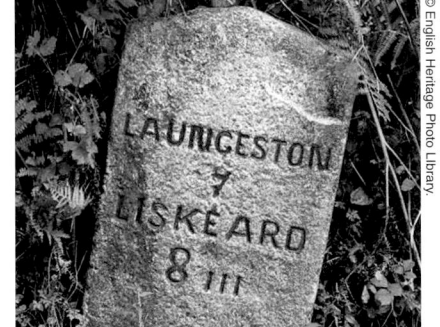

lists, at about 92% of the total, and are of special interest, warranting every effort to preserve them, whilst Grade II* are particularly important, of more than special interest, and Grade I buildings make up the elite of exceptional interest and importance.

English Heritage is the statutory adviser to government for listing, recommending buildings for listing to the Secretary of State, who makes the final decision. In April 2005, the administration of this system was transferred entirely to English Heritage, eliminating much of the bureaucracy and double-handling; now anyone applying for a property to be listed comes directly to

Milestone

© English Heritage Photo Library.

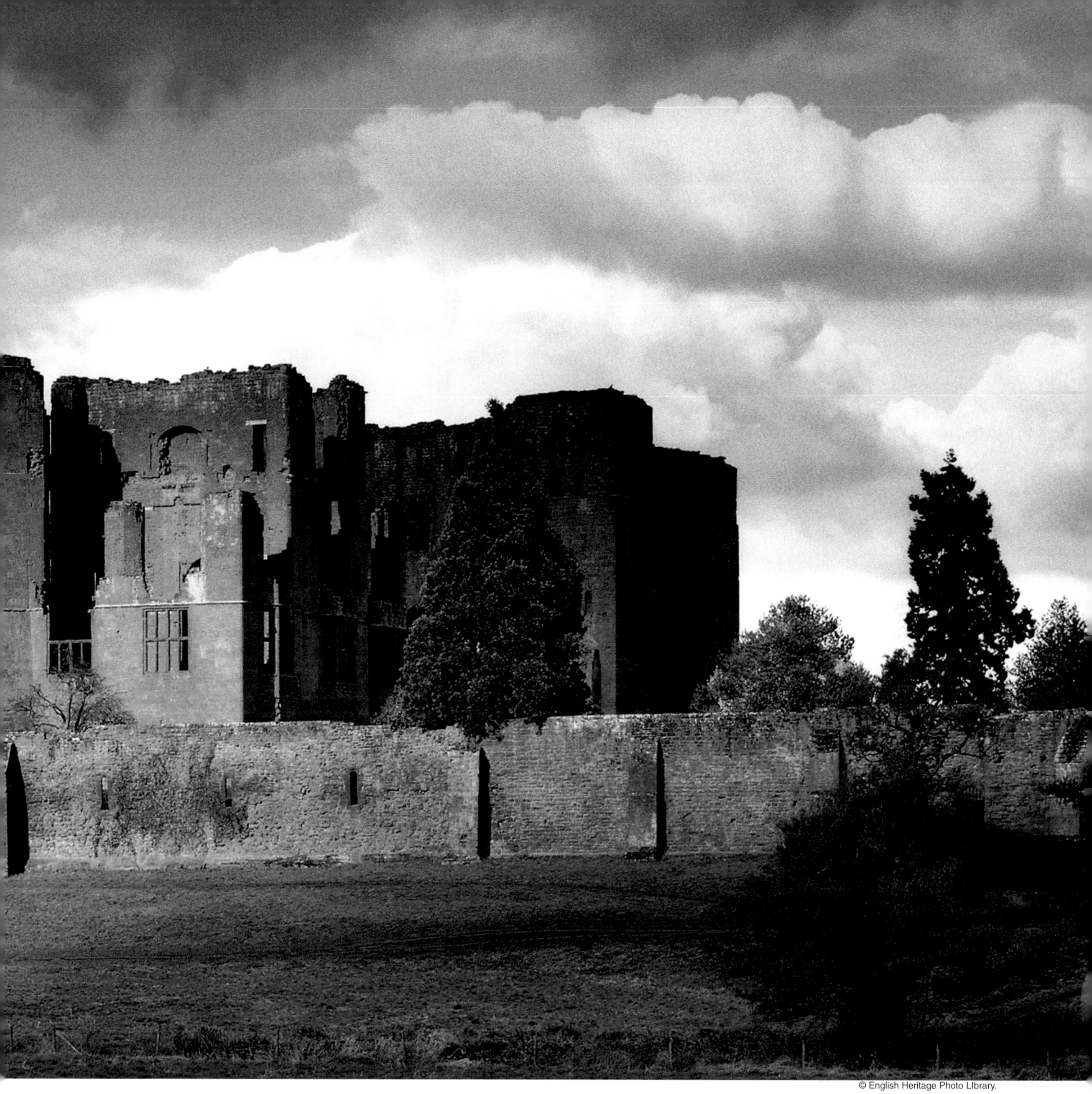

© English Heritage Photo Library.

University of East Anglia student accommodation designed by Denys Lasdun.

© English Heritage Photo Library.

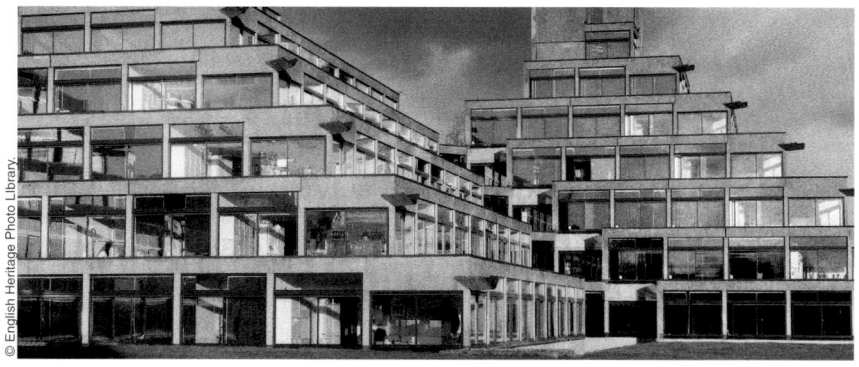

English Heritage, who then make an assessment and submit a recommendation to the Secretary of State.

Other changes to the system are also being put in place. English Heritage now notifies owners when an application for listing is made – previously, it was possible that the owners of a property could be totally unaware that their house was being considered for listing as a result of a third party application. The opportunity to open up the process further, allowing owners and local authorities a formal chance to make their comment on recommendations, will also be introduced in 2006, making the process much more open and accessible.

Helping owners and managers to understand their building and the consequences of listing is one of the main aims of this reform to the system, and another of the improvements to be implemented in 2006 is the introduction of information packs for owners of newly listed buildings, giving clear information about the listed building and its importance, and guidance on how to seek expert advice.

The government's current review of the whole heritage protection system aims to modernise and streamline the management of the historic environment, which goes beyond the listing process to encompass wider heritage management. Following public consultation in 2003 – Protecting our Past, making the system work better – widespread support for reform has led to the above short term changes. Further reform is planned – however, to fundamentally change the system primary legislation is required: this will allow the power to designate to be transferred in its entirety to English Heritage; the creation of a new Register of Historic Buildings and Sites for England, in which listed buildings are included alongside scheduled sites and parks and gardens and battlefields; a streamlined consent process for those who wish to make changes to designated items; and the introduction of statutory manage-ment agreements for large or complex sites. These agreements, provisionally termed Heritage Partnership Agreements, will allow owners and managers of such sites to enter into partnerships with local authorities and English Heritage to provide a framework for long-term strategic management of the historic assets involved. And within that framework prior consent will be given for certain defined works. Such agreements should help to shift the management of the historic environment towards a more positive, pro-active culture based on partnership rather than confrontation.

For more information on listing and the heritage protection reform visit www.english-heritage.org.uk.

Arnos Vale Cemetery, Bristol.

GARDEN OF REST

Clumber Park, Nottinghamshire – the longest avenue of lime trees in Europe.

The National Trust – providing
"a great day out"

As Europe's largest conservation charity, the National Trust looks after over 300 houses and gardens, 700 miles of coastline and 245,000 hectares of countryside across England, Wales and Northern Ireland. It is from these special and remarkable places that visitors can experience enjoyment, enrichment and quite simply, a great day out.

Many of the houses and gardens are open to visitors throughout the year. Enjoy beautiful spring bulbs and summer blooms, fêtes and outdoor theatre; autumn trees and frosted winter landscapes, carol concerts and festive feasts, as each season brings its own unique highlights. Each year brings different things to discover too, with newly renovated properties and gardens, exquisite collections and a whole host of special events.

At home with great stories and fascinating history

From grand, palatial country estates to industrial workers' cottages; opulent state bedrooms and exquisite libraries to servants' quarters and working kitchen gardens, you can observe the passing of the centuries and the changing habits, fashions and notions of the people who lived through them. Listed below are just a few examples of the many houses worth visiting during the year.

At Castle Drogo, near Exeter in Devon, you can explore the "last castle to be built in England", a grand and imposing medieval style castle built between 1910 and 1930, with all the modern interior comforts of the 20th century and jaw-dropping views over Dartmoor. On a less imposing scale, but equally interesting, Lanhydrock in Cornwall presents a perfect picture of how the Victorians lived, with fifty complete rooms dressed with original family props and accessories to create a true 'at home' atmosphere.

Experience life above and below stairs at Petworth in West Sussex, a magnificent late 17th-century mansion set in a Capability Brown landscape. The house contains the National Trust's largest collection of paintings, including works by Turner, Van Dyck and Blake, but also has marvellous servants' quarters and an authentic Victorian kitchen.

The 18th-century Wimpole Estate at Royston provides a complete day out in its own right. Start off in the mansion house with its unrivalled collection of historical books and manuscripts, before enjoying some fresh air out in the landscaped park and Home Farm, with its rare breed cattle, pigs and sheep. For a more 'spiritual' experience, visit Blickling Hall, a beautiful and reputedly haunted Jacobean mansion, near Norwich. As well as the chance of spotting the ghostly apparition of Anne Boleyn walking the corridors, you will have the opportunity to visit the impressive library containing more than 12,000 books.

Built between 1759 and 1765 for the wealthy aristocratic Curzon family, Kedleston Hall in Derby features the most complete sequence of Robert Adam interiors in England and is in stark contrast to the grim work yards, dormitories and cellars of the 19th-century paupers' Workhouse in nearby Nottinghamshire.

Powis Castle, Wales.

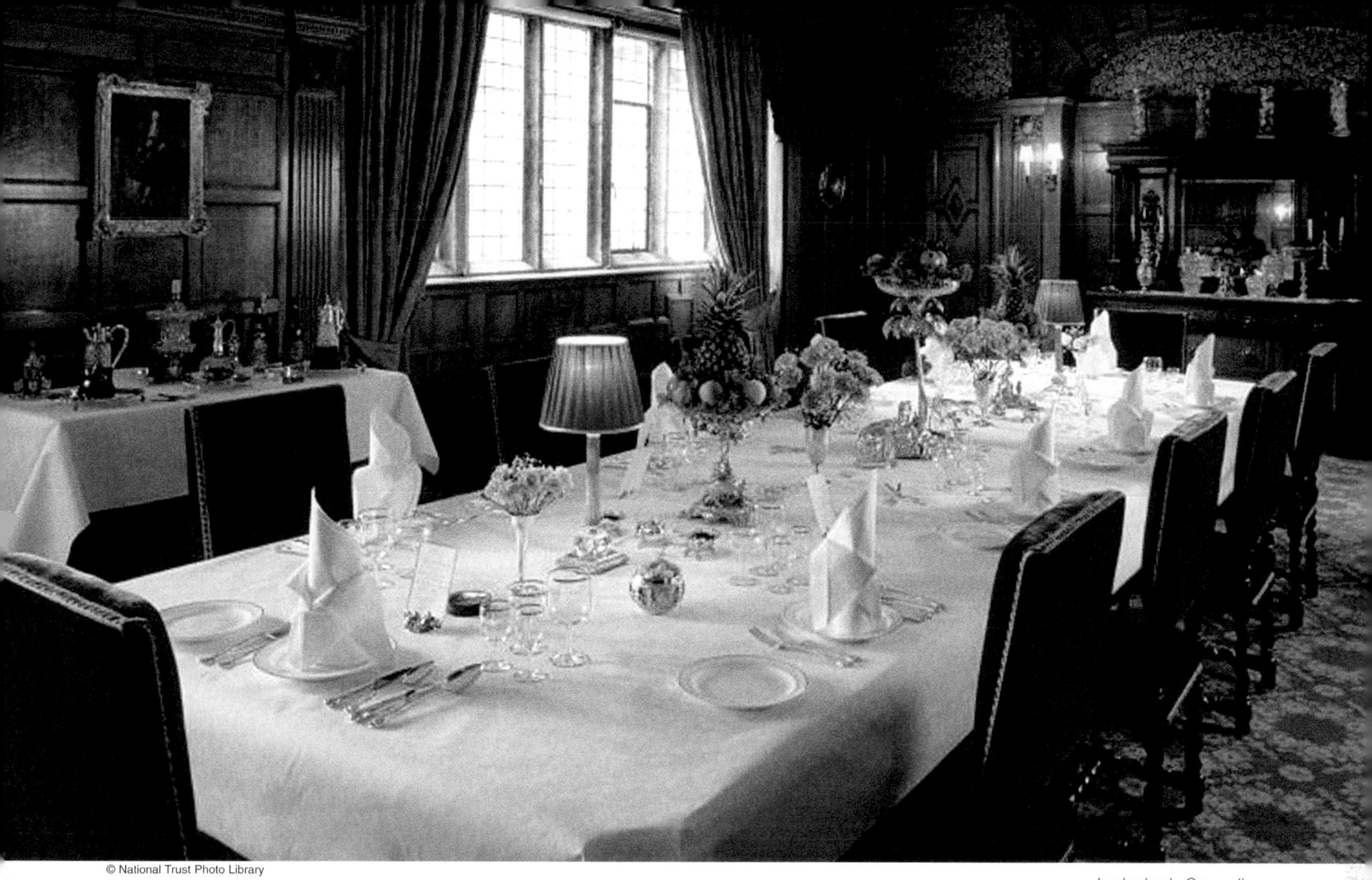

© National Trust Photo Library

Lanhydrock, Cornwall.

Over in the West Midlands, Upton House near Banbury dates back to 1695 and is home to a priceless collection of paintings, porcelain and tapestries amassed in 1927 by avid collector Lord Bearsted.

Take a whistle-stop journey through time at Speke Hall in Liverpool with an interior spanning many centuries. Tudor priest holes, William Morris décor and a fine Victorian kitchen all feature in this famous half-timbered house.

Chippendale furniture is the main attraction at Nostell Priory, near Wakefield. Even the doll's house on display there has miniature Chippendale-style furniture and fittings of its own.

Glorious gardens, breathtaking landscapes

The majority of the Trust's historic houses are just as impressive on the outside, with beautiful gardens and landscaped grounds to enjoy at various times of the year.

At Mottisfont Abbey, set amidst glorious countryside along the River Test in Hampshire, visitors can walk amongst magnificent trees, walled gardens and a National Collection of fragrant Old-fashioned roses, at their best in June and July.

You can make the most of spectacular garden displays in Spring, Summer and Autumn at picturesque Scotney Castle in Kent. Rhododendrons, azaleas and kalmia take centre stage in May and June; Wisteria and rambling roses in July and August and rich red and gold leaved trees in October.

Another garden of note is the newly restored Japanese garden at Kingston Lacy in Dorset. It features a formal Japanese Tea Garden and

© National Trust Photo Library

Nunnington Hall, Yorkshire.

Petworth, Sussex.

© National Trust Photo Library

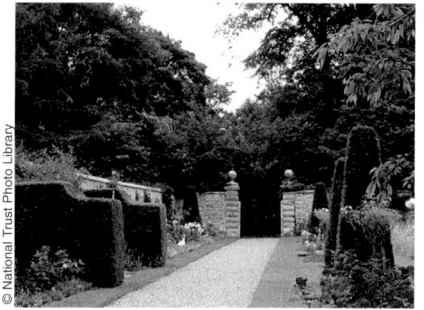

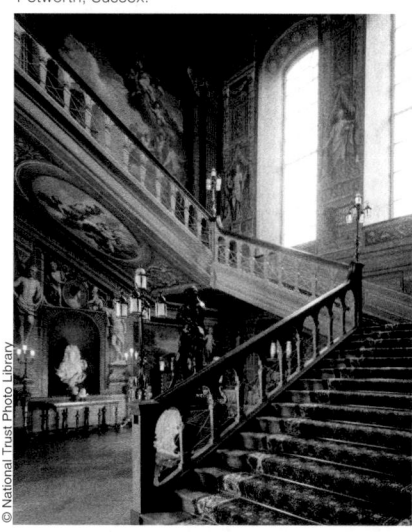

Acer Glade and is the biggest of its kind in the UK.

For sheer breathtaking beauty, it's hard to beat the amazing abbey ruins and awesome vistas of Fountains Abbey & Studley Royal Water Garden in North Yorkshire. Visit during the Autumn months and you can see the Cistercian ruins floodlit to dramatic effect against the landscape.

Romantic Powis Castle in Wales has a world-famous garden containing many rare plants, an aviary, orangery, superb rhododendrons and some exquisite lead statues. Equally celebrated Mount Stewart in Northern Ireland has an unusual series of outdoor 'rooms' and vibrant parterres containing rare plants that thrive in the mild climate of the Ards.

Exciting Events, inspiring collections

Every year sees new collections displayed and a variety of enjoyable and interesting exhibitions and events to capture the imagination. 2006 is no exception, with a packed programme of events planned throughout the year, from spring snowdrop days, countryside walks, garden tours and fairs to summer concerts and outdoor theatre to suit every taste.

At Montacute House in Somerset, lovers of art and textiles can enjoy an exhibition of 17th-century samplers, and Elizabethan artwork on loan from the National Portrait Gallery.

Basildon Park, near Reading, is hosting an exhibition of 'The Making of Pride & Prejudice', featuring props and signed memorabilia from the 2005 film starring Kiera Knightley. Between April and June 2006, visitors can also see the costumes from the film on display.

Following a huge restoration project at Snowshill Manor in the Cotswolds, the eclectic and extensive collections of craftsmanship and curios can now been seen in their best light.

In 2006 touring theatre productions will include the Shakespearian delights of Romeo & Juliet, Twelfth Night, The Merry Wives of Windsor and A Midsummer Night's Dream. Other productions will include Oscar Wilde's comedy, The Importance of Being Earnest and Edith Nesbit's beloved tale, The Railway Children.

Behind the scenes tours and 'putting the house to bed days' provide an insight into the past and modern residents of our properties, whilst Christmas festivities, ranging from lecture lunches and carol concerts to gift fairs, craft workshops and belly-busting walks, round off the year.

Tempting tea-rooms, gorgeous gifts

No visit to a National Trust property would be complete without enjoying a tasty treat in the tea-room or restaurant, or enjoying a look around the shop for gifts, quality cards and handcrafted souvenirs.

The National Trust serves a staggering 3.5 million cups of tea each year and one in five visitors treat themselves to a cream tea. The top ten most popular tea-rooms are Chartwell (Kent), family home of Sir Winston Churchill; Mottisfont Abbey (Hampshire), an atmospheric estate set in stunning countryside; Fountains Abbey (North Yorkshire), world famous Cistercian abbey with deer park and water gardens; Dunham Massey (Cheshire), where the scandal and romance of life below and above stairs is still told; Polesden Lacey (Surrey) the spectacular Edwardian honeymoon location of George VI and Queen Elizabeth; Stourhead (Wiltshire), celebrated 18th-century landscape garden; Wimpole Hall (Cambridgeshire), 18th-century house and farm with rare breed sheep, pigs, cattle and horses; Sissinghurst (Kent), celebrated

Blickling Hall, Norfolk.

Stourhead, Wiltshire.

© National Trust Photo Library

Scotney Castle, Kent.

© National Trust Photo Library

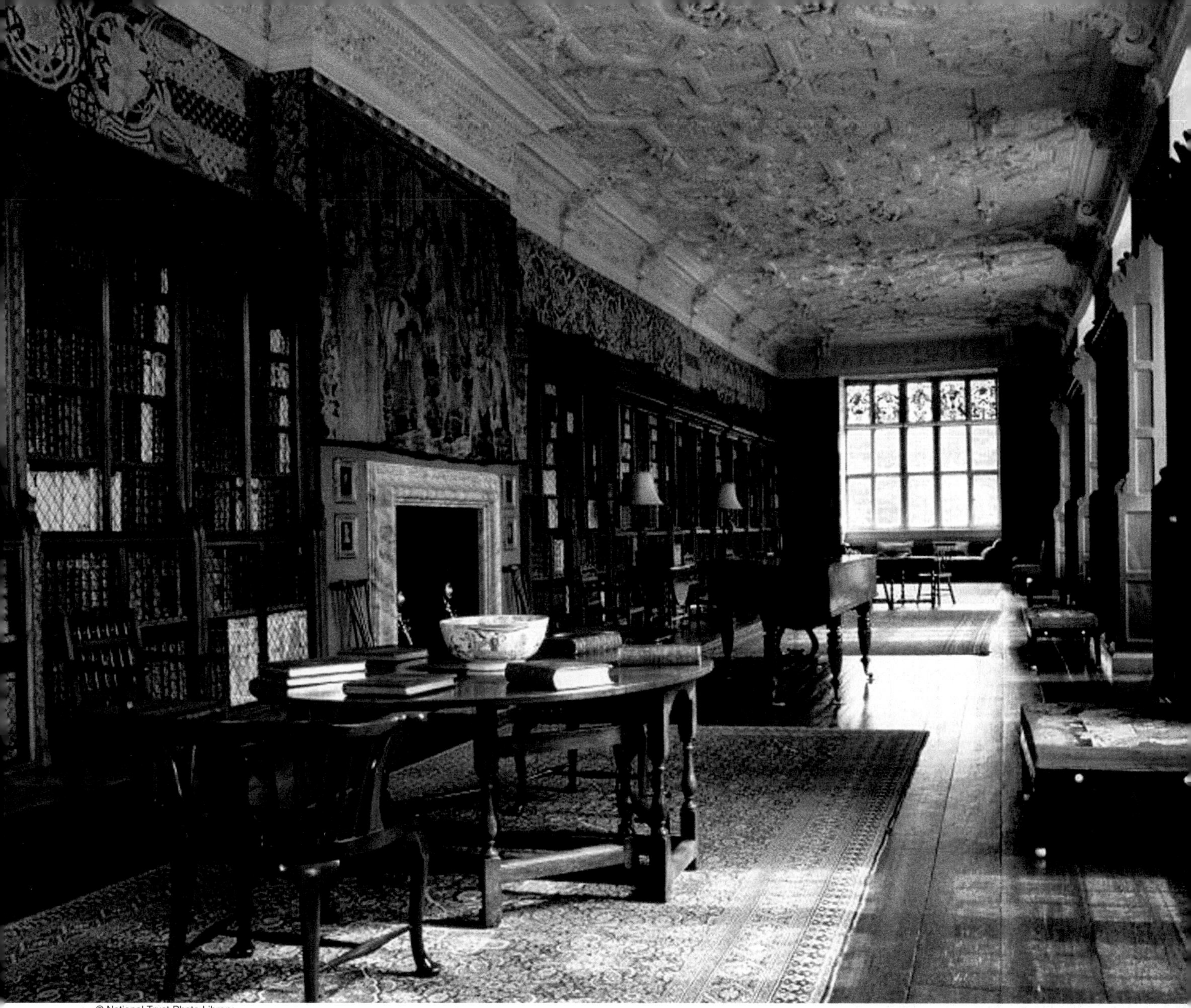

© National Trust Photo Library

Blickling Hall, Norfolk.

garden created by Vita Sackville-West; Clumber Park (Nottinghamshire), featuring the longest avenue of lime trees in Europe and Ightham Mote (Kent), a romantic Tudor moated manor.

For tea with a view, taste the good life at Nunnington Hall in North Yorkshire where cream teas are served in the family dining room of a 17th-century manor house and on sunny days, along the banks of the River Rye in the Privy Garden. For an authentic West Country experience, visit Trelissick Garden in Cornwall where the tea-room is located in a 19th-century converted barn overlooking the tranquil courtyard. Or, for a real taste of history, enjoy afternoon tea as Lady Penrhyn would have experienced it at Penrhyn Castle in Wales.

For all National Trust property opening times, entry prices and travel directions, visit www.nationaltrust.org.uk or call 0870 458 4000.

Fountains Abbey, Yorkshire.

© National Trust Photo Library

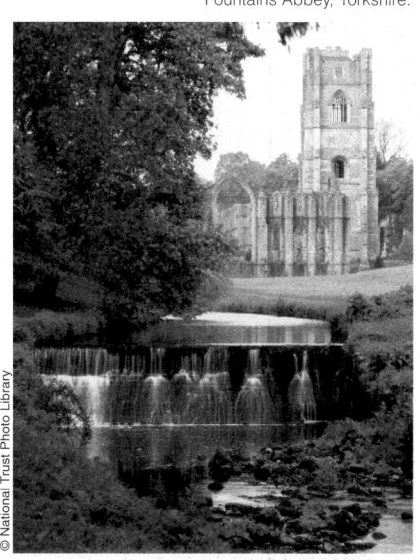

Wallington
a Northumbrian gem

'In going over the Northumberland moors near Lady Trevelyan's if you stop and listen you will hear nothing but the wind whistling – a rattling brook perhaps among some stones, now and then the cry of a curlew, now and then the bleat of a lamb; all plaintive and melancholy' – **John Ruskin** on visiting Wallington in 1852.

Wallington is near the village of Cambo in Northumberland, 20 miles north-west of Newcastle-upon-Tyne and only 20 miles from Hadrian's Wall. This huge 13,000 acre estate, with its house and contents, was given by Sir Charles Philips Trevelyan to the National Trust in 1941.

Many country houses are hidden from view by high walls, long drives or screens of trees. The visitor must wait, anticipate and then gasp at a house's exterior aspect – this is not the case with Wallington, which comes immediately into sight as one climbs the hill after crossing James Paine's Palladian bridge. The exterior of Wallington is plain, solid and dignified, built of local sandstone – only the four griffins' heads sitting on the front lawn seem to grin at you. Begun in 1688 by Sir William Blackett, a successful Newcastle businessman, the house is designed around a courtyard plan. In the 18th century, Sir William's grandson, Sir Walter Calverley Blackett, made further improvements to both the house and grounds. He laid out the garden and the park, and for the house commissioned Daniel Garrett, a member of Lord

Burlington's circle, to create a new suite of state rooms on the south front. The Francini brothers were employed to decorate the rooms with rococo plasterwork. Their work creates the exuberant yet delicate feel to the interiors.

Wallington passed to the

Trevelyan family on Sir Walter's death in 1771. When Sir Walter Trevelyan inherited the estate in 1846, he and his wife Pauline, Lady Trevelyan, made Wallington a meeting place for writers, scientists, and particularly painters and sculptors of the Pre-Raphaelite circle. The central courtyard, roofed over in 1853-54, is decorated with murals on Northumbrian history by William Bell Scott. The mural

entitled *'The Northumbrian shows the world what can be done with Iron & Coal'*, is renowned for its depiction of an image from the Industrial Revolution. The stone columns were painted with flowers by Pauline, Lady Trevelyan and Ruskin. Later generations of the family used the Hall as a central sitting room.

The Trevelyans are a family of distinguished intellectuals, politicians, historians and civil servants. Sir Charles Trevelyan, who gave Wallington to the National Trust, was a leading Socialist, and Labour MP. As early as 1929 he opened parts of the house to the public. Gifting Wallington to the Trust gave him immense satisfaction – that everyone could enjoy this beautiful place.

The garden and grounds are worth a visit just for themselves. The Walled Garden, half a mile from the

house, has a Victorian peach house, a terrace lined with 18th century statues, and an Edwardian conservatory. There are a number of helpful leaflets describing walks on the estate.

The House re-opened in 2004 after a year of extensive works – the sparkling interiors are the perfect backdrop to consider for a corporate function, or even as a wedding venue – a peaceful tranquil world which you should take time to enjoy.

For further details about Wallington see page 439.

Woodcarving, 1872, by Thomas Kendall of Warwick.

The Historic Chapels Trust – Preserving places of worship in England

Established to take into ownership redundant chapels and other places of worship in England which are of outstanding architectural and historic interest. Securing for public benefit their preservation, repair and regeneration.

Coanwood Friends Meeting House, Northumberland.

Cote Baptist Chapel, Oxfordshire.

Below are 14 of the chapels the in the care of H.C.T. which you can visit on application to the keyholder.

Biddlestone RC Chapel, Northumberland	01665 574420
	01669 630270
	01669 620230
Coanwood Friends Meeting House, Northumberland	01434 320256
Cote Baptist Chapel, Oxfordshire	01993 850421
Farfield Friends Meeting House, West Yorkshire	01756 710587
The Dissenters' Chapel, Kensal Green Cemetery, London	020 7402 2749
Penrose Methodist Chapel, St Ervan, Cornwall	01841 540737
Salem Chapel, East Budleigh, Devon	01395 445236
Shrine of Our Lady of Lourdes, Blackpool, Lancashire	01253 300100
St Benet's Chapel, Netherton, Merseyside	0151 520 2600
St George's German Lutheran Church, Tower Hamlets, London	020 7481 0533
Todmorden Unitarian Church, West Yorkshire	01706 815648
Wainsgate Baptist Church, West Yorkshire	01422 845445
Wallasey Unitarian Church, Merseyside	0151 639 9707
Walpole Old Chapel, Suffolk	01986 798308

For further information please visit our website: www.hct.org.uk or telephone: 020 7481 0533

Walpole Old Chapel, Suffolk.

St George's German Lutheran Church.

Penrose Methodist Chapel, Cornwall.

The City of London's Gardens ...

Trees and gardens are rare in the City of London but some of those that exist have their feet firmly in the past says **David Jones** – former Superintendent and Director of London's Parks and Gardens.

The City – the densely developed heart of London - has around 200 areas of open space, albeit it some of them very small. These provide visitors and the City's community with much-needed oases of calm. A maze-like array of secret gardens, churchyards, plazas and highway plantings in turn support 1,400 trees and an annual influx of 200,000 bedding plants. They are an integral part of the area's unique history, from the tiniest leafiest churchyard to the City's largest open space. All have a tale to tell.

It is not until the formation of the Livery Companies in the 14th and 15th centuries that we have any real evidence of plants being cultivated for their decorative, culinary or medicinal properties or that gardens were created just for pleasure. The tradition of green spaces in the City can be traced back to these Livery Company gardens, some of which can still be visited today. The Worshipful Company of Girdlers had a garden adjacent to their Livery Hall in 1431 and Thomas Cromwell kept an enormous garden after 1534 in Throgmorton Street, part of which remains to this day, as does part of his house (now the Hall of the Worshipful Company of Drapers).

Many wonderful gardens must have existed in the City of London throughout time. Ager's Map of 1560 and Morgan's Map of 1682 show some of them. By Chaucer's time London, even within the walls, was a scattered town ('spotted' as Walter Thornby says: 'as thick with gardens as a common meadow is with daisies'.)

The majority of the gardens seen in the City today came into being as the result of two key historical events that changed the geography of the City forever: the Great Fire of London in 1666 and the Blitz in 1940. The devastation caused by both events created small pockets of derelict land - including the ruins of former Wren churches - which were then turned into secluded havens for the City's community to enjoy. After the Burial Act of 1855 many churchyards within the City were also made available for public use as gardens.

The Worshipful Company of Barbers tended a garden at their Hall near London Wall in 1555. It was this garden that, by forming a fire-break, saved their Hall from destruction in the Great Fire. It was one of few buildings to survive. The fire consumed a staggering 13,200 houses and 87 churches, among

The Minotaur by Michael Ayrton, an English Sculpture, one of just three in the world, is a magnificent work and can be found on the Barbican High Wall near to Moorgate Station.

them the beloved St Paul's Cathedral. The destructive fury of this conflagration is thought never to have been exceeded in the world by an accidental fire. Within the walls it destroyed almost 5/6ths of the whole City.

Today the Barbers' Hall has a new garden created in the 1980s. This contains plants which have given us some of the best drugs ever known – digitalis for heart conditions and other Solanaceous plants, as heart stimulants and pain-killers, but best of all the Meadow Sweet (Spiraea ulmaria), the first plant to give us the active ingredient now called 'aspirin', later to be taken from the Willow (Salix sp.) and now, of course, synthesised. The word 'drug' is derived from the Anglo Saxon 'drigan' ('to dry') as healing herbs were always dried for preservation. Here too can be found another wonderful painkilling species of herb, the Mandrake (Mandragora officin-arum). Some say that it was the juice of this plant which was applied via vinegar-soaked sponges to the lips of those unfortunates being crucified (the ultimate sedative).

It was William Turner (who died in 1668 and is buried in St. Olave's Churchyard, Hart Street), who created the first recorded herbal, his English 'New Herball' in 1551, with more than 90 species of herbs mentioned.

Many of the City street names, you would think, give us a clue as to what trees or plants grew in the City naturally, or were cultivated there - for example, Beech Street, Wood Street, Lime Street, Elder Street and Aldersgate. But most of them were in fact derived from other sources: Wood Street is where wood was sold for burning or making charcoal; Lime Street was where lime was burned for mortar; Beech Street (according to Stowe) alludes to Nicholas de la Beech, Lieutenant of the Tower of London in the time of Edward III. Herbal and Saffron Hill in Holborn must have been the location where John Gerard made his collection of 1,030 species of plants before 1600. However, Wormwood Street does derive from the wormwood plants (Artemisia absinthium) which, until quite recent times, grew in the area; but Garlick Hill and the Church of St James Garlickhythe are both so

called after the garlic markets which traded there during the Middle Ages.

The first 'Green Belt' was created by Queen Elizabeth I by prohibiting building within 3,000 paces of the gates of London – but with disastrous results. Urban sprawl began and much more intensive building took place within the confines of the City.

How different the City of London would have looked today if Sir Christopher Wren's plans had been implemented after the Great Fire. His original plans involved rebuilding the City in brick and stone to a grid plan with Continental piazzas and avenues, but because many buildings had survived to basement level, legal disputes over ownership of land ended the grid plan idea. It was eventually rebuilt following the existing street pattern with buildings of brick and stone which included Wren's magnificent churches. There is a certain irony in that some of the most attractive gardens in the City today have been created in the ruins of some of Wren's churches destroyed in the Blitz.

But probably the best garden is around his masterpiece, St Paul's Cathedral. Here in the garden are many fine examples of trees including Ginkgo biloba, planted near the Cross of St Paul; if you look at it from a distance you will see that it spreads its high branches to form a cross. Nearby is a fine example of Abies grandis, a Grand Fir and an unusual tree to see in the centre of the City, planted in 1974 by the Oberburgermeister of Baden-Baden in Germany. Some good shrubs too can be seen here, for example Paliurus spina-christi, said to be the plant that formed the Crown of Thorns at the Crucifixion.

By the end of the 19th century the gardens in the City had been largely lost to the ravages of industry and building and the only

The Herb Garden is in the space near the Museum of London, and is situated inside bastion 13 of the Roman City Wall, next to some fine Inigo Jones brickwork, once the wall of an operating theatre.

trees of any significance that remained were the London Planes (Platyanus hispanica). Some of them are now more than 250 years old. Philip Miller (the compiler of the Gardeners' Dictionary), records the plantings of this species in 1731. The trees are tolerant of smoke pollution, and the wood is excellent for woodturning and was used to make buttons (hence the common name 'the button wood'). Today, the most magnificent Plane trees stand in St Paul's Cathedral near the Cross of St Paul, growing in soil laced with oyster shells discarded long ago by those so poor that oyster was their staple diet. (Today 'the oyster' is an Underground ticket to and from work!).

Other wonderful specimens of London Planes stand in the garden of the Stationers' Livery Company and in the corner of Wood Street and Cheapside, and it is this very tree that was mentioned by William Wordsworth in 1800 in his poem *The Reverie of Poor Susan:*

At the corner of Wood Street, when daylight appears, Hangs a Thrush that sings loud, it has sung for three years: Poor Susan has pass'd by the spot, and has heard In the silence of morning the song of the bird.

Trees in London are an important feature of the streets, not just for themselves but for the story behind the sites they occupy. The gardens and open spaces in the City are a resource for the 7,000 residents and 330,000 workers and visitors that enter the Square Mile every day. Some may enjoy the open air summer jazz in Finsbury Circus, the oldest public park in London – Finsbury Circus Garden dating back to 1606 – others the tiny street corner spaces squeezed between developments, the transformation of bombed-out remains, trees, flower beds and water features - all make a positive contribution to the contemporary city environment but attain greater interest with some knowledge of their past.

Some Livery Companies may require an appointment for garden visits. However, the Barbers' Company Herb Garden is free to view, as is St Paul's Cathedral garden and those around the City on the sites of church ruins, for example Christ Church (Newgate Street), St Dunstan in the East (St Dunstan's Hill), St Botolph (Bishopsgate) and St Alphage (London Wall).

Guidebook **innovation**

The last 50 years have seen enormous changes in guidebooks to historic properties open to the public. Guidebooks now offered to visitors are far removed from the small, unillustrated pamphlets that were once the norm.

Belsay Hall – Quarry Garden.

No longer do they comprise rather heavy and scholarly descriptive text peppered with architectural and specialist terms that the average visitor does not understand. Today they are likely to be descriptive but easily readable, larger format and highly illustrated colour souvenir books. This transition has been gradual, with first the introduction of some black and white photographs and then full colour brochures which have improved progressively as new photographic and printing techniques have allowed.

The prime purpose of any guidebook is to explain and interpret to visitors those things which they will see. This may stand alone or

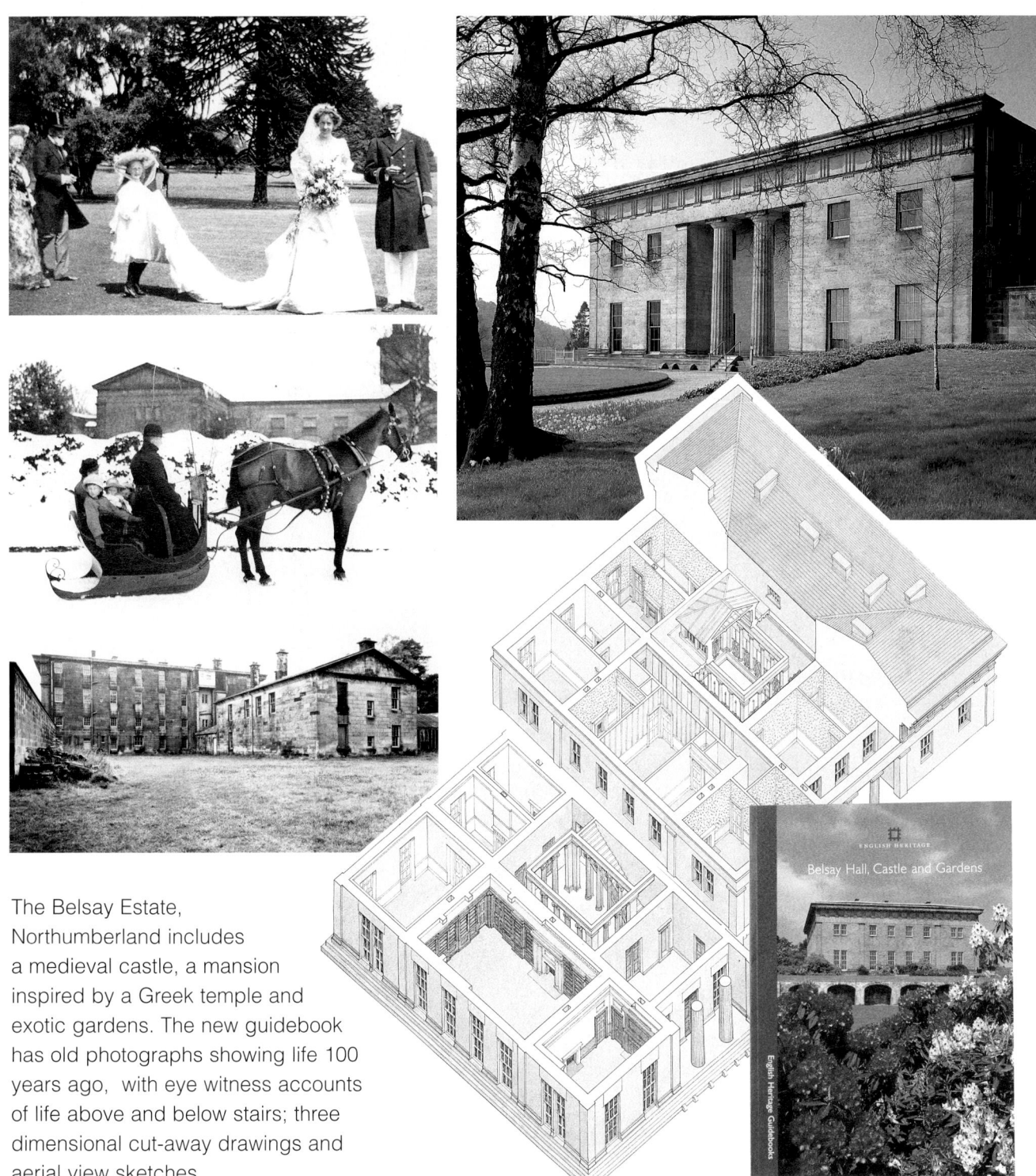

The Belsay Estate, Northumberland includes a medieval castle, a mansion inspired by a Greek temple and exotic gardens. The new guidebook has old photographs showing life 100 years ago, with eye witness accounts of life above and below stairs; three dimensional cut-away drawings and aerial view sketches.

supplement information provided on site. A secondary purpose is to provide a souvenir of the visit.

In practice it seems that most people consult a guidebook in the early part of their visit then give up, with a view to reading it later. It is then that copious illustrations are so helpful. They can provide a more full picture and help visitors'

recall of their own experience of the place – a true souvenir.

Private owners have tended to push development of the guidebook art further, each with their own individualistic form of presentation – but a new series of guidebooks just launched by English Heritage is taking things on again.

The new guidebook series, with distinctive red covers, brings the properties vividly to life. An entirely fresh approach has been taken. Both format and content have been completely revamped to make them more attractive and accessible, while at the same time providing historical information of the highest standard.

The number of photographs and

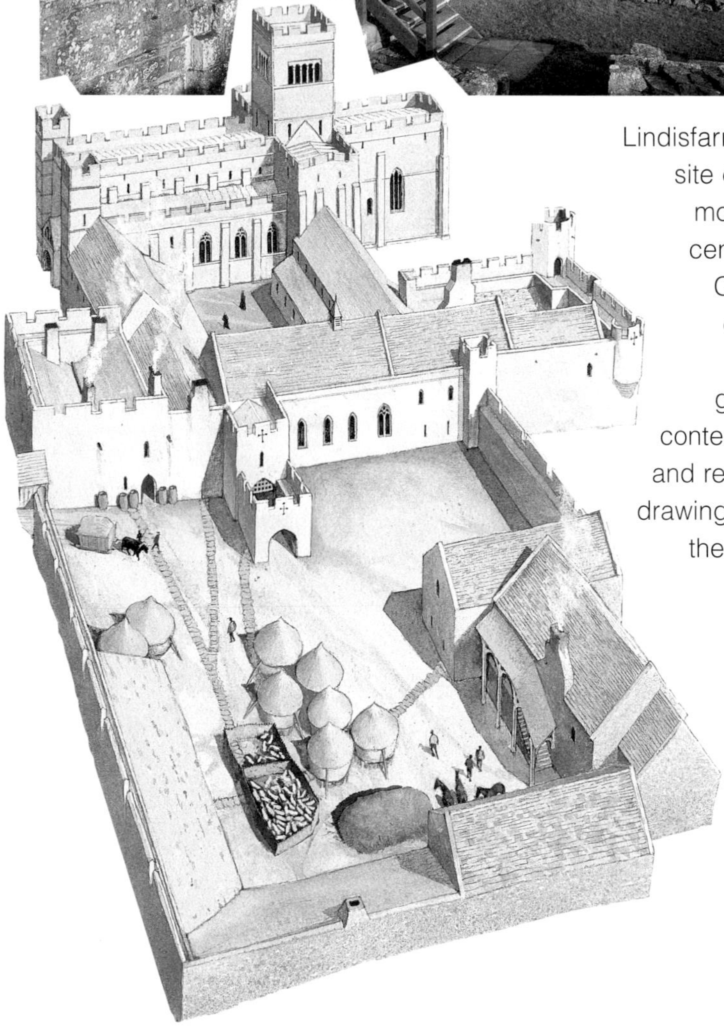

Lindisfarne Priory the site of one of the most important centres of early Christianity is described in its wider geographical context. Cut-away and reconstruction drawings help bring the ruins vividly to life.

illustrations has been dramatically increased, as well as including more maps and plans to enable people to get the most out of their visit. Also included, for the first time, are personal accounts by people who have had a connection or who have lived or worked at these historic sites. This enables visitors to have some greater feel and flavour of what life was like at the property over the last 80 years or so. Of particular note are the fold-out covers at front and back, which contain a series of specially commissioned orientation drawings of the site and elegant phase plans. Also for the first time, each property is placed in its wider geographical context and the guides show how each site and its surrounding landscape have shaped each other.

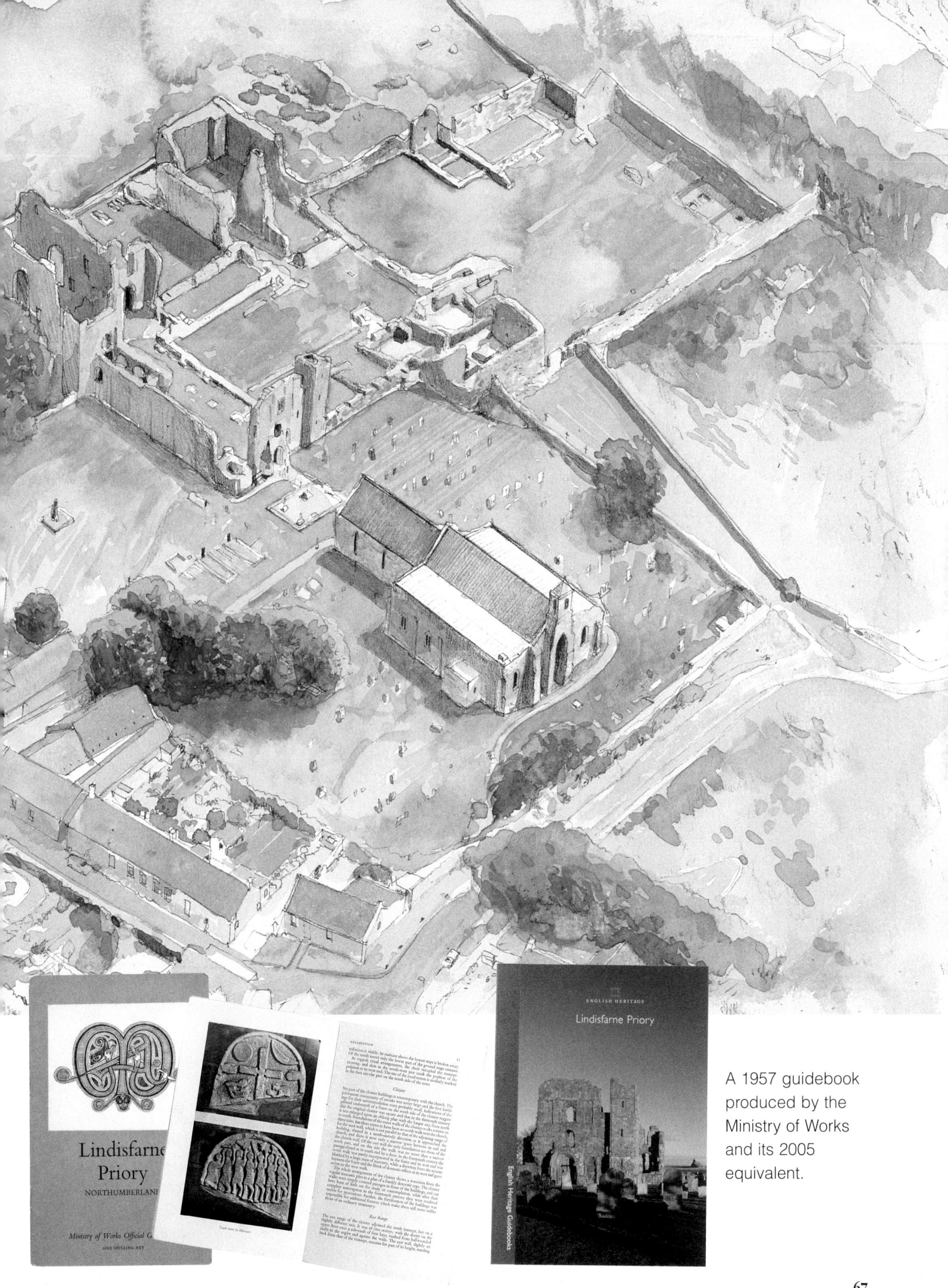

A 1957 guidebook produced by the Ministry of Works and its 2005 equivalent.

Contemporary Sculpture in the Historic House Setting

New sculpture gardens and sculpture parks in historic landscape settings are exciting a new generation of house visitors.

Works of sculpture have long been part of the historic house scene as decoration features internally and externally and collected as works of art. Many houses have sculpture galleries specifically designed or set out for the display of a sculpture collection. These may typically include pieces of antiquity collected by earlier generations when on the Grand Tour in the 18th century.

Outside pieces of sculpture have been used as punctuation marks in the garden or landscape, perhaps terminating a vista, at the centre of a pool or circus, or providing a focal point. Comparatively few new sculptures were added during the 20th century, a period disturbed by two World Wars and a dramatic change in the fortunes of country houses. But the start of the 21st century has seen a new phenomenon. The appearance of sculpture gardens: spaces designed specifically for the display of sculpture and with works of art being acquired specially to be placed and shown in particular locations. Some are purely private collections and tend to be permanent, and may not be open to the public except for occasional charity purposes; others associated with houses open to the public may also be a permanent collection to which new additions are made periodically but are more likely to be a composite of a permanent collection and a changing display of pieces that are also offered for sale.

These have provided a new dimension to the experience of visiting a house. It is one that can be enjoyed by individuals but more particularly by family groups. Together, they may enjoy the comparative freedom of walking outside at their own pace, of discovering displayed pieces in a variety of settings, often being able to touch and feel them, walk around

collections, he has advocated the use of gardens and landscapes as a gallery with changing displays and works of art for sale. For the visitor, even those who could not reasonably be expected to acquire a piece, this provides reason for repeat visits and to see new things every time.

Each year Peter de Sausmarez has something in the region of 100 artists of a dozen nationalities, exhibiting around 200 pieces. This is renewed each year so that the exhibition is fresh and up-to-date; with the largest selection in Britain it is a mammoth task of organisation and transport.

Contemporary sculpture that seems to appeal most is what has stood the test of time and has a strong figurative basis to it. This stretches back to classical times and you can usually recognise and enjoy what you are looking at. Abstract work certainly has its followers and most sculpture parks will have some on view, although you are unlikely to see too many unmade beds or half-animals (which some believe are created largely to shock and to attract an amount of media notoriety).

Half the joy of viewing and buying a sculpture in this way is that it is so easily visited. Now that people have gone beyond the sundial and birdbath stages they find it exciting to be able to choose something more adventurous.

Insurance is really not the problem some people imagine as all contemporary work is signed and numbered and sometimes dated, so that it can easily be traced and

them, and to derive their individual impressions. This often forms the subject of discussion and debate within the group, which is something less likely to be provoked by a more formal display of classical sculpture in a gallery. Already there is clear evidence of the extent to which visitors are enjoying this active engagement with sculpture parks and how they are providing a contrasting experience to that of the more customary presentation of an historic house.

An early enthusiast of sculpture parks and the inspiration for several has been Peter de Sausmarez of Sausmarez Manor in Guernsey. While some collections have been acquired as permanent private returned should anything happen. Thieves know this and on the whole avoid modern sculpture because of it. They stick to antiques or those ubiquitous lead, terracotta or stone urns.

Ragley Hall in Warwickshire, home of Lord and Lady Hertford, is the new location of the Jerwood Sculpture Park. One of the Jerwood Foundation's priorities is to develop this sculpture collection by purchase, particularly from contemporary sculptors and by commissioning new work to be placed at Ragley. Alongside sculptors of international reputation such as Frink, Chadwick, Armitage, Ayrton and Gormley, they have brought in important national sculptures and emerging young artists who have won the Jerwood Sculpture Prize.

The Sculpture Garden at Burghley in Lincolnshire originated from an initiative by the Burghley House Trustees who were conscious that only limited garden space was regularly accessible to visitors, and in 1989 Capability Brown's lost Lower Garden was designated to be cleared and planted as a natural setting in which to place contemporary sculpture.

The layout and pathways of the Sculpture Garden helped to provide a structure and focus for the development of the sculpture collection and to add to the tradition of management and innovation with in the parkland. The positioning of the sculptures, particularly those that are site specific, often accentuates and draws attention to the spaces and plantings that surround them. A symbiotic relationship has begun to develop in which neither sculpture nor horticulture dominate in an area which remains essentially natural, offering an interesting and stimulating environment in which to enjoy contemporary art or simply to wander and spend time away from the hustle and bustle of modern life. Each year there is an exhibition of sculpture in the garden from June to October together with permanent exhibits which are on display throughout the year.

In Yorkshire at Newby Hall, home of Richard and Lucinda Compton, the Sculpture Garden is now one of the most popular features – notwithstanding that the house is one of Britain's finest Adam houses, with superb contents, and one of the most renowned galleries of classical sculptures, surrounded by 25 acres of award-winning gardens.

There is a long tradition of

collecting at Newby which the Comptons, who are passionate about art, are keen to continue. Each year from January onwards, they start to select the work: always a completely new mix of pieces by artists whose work they have seen and admired – it is very much a personal choice. There is usually a combination of abstract and figurative work in a range of media from wood and glass to bronze and stone, so that there is something to suit almost all taste.

Through their selection of pieces they support young artists by providing them with a chance for

their work to be shown alongside established names.

Perhaps the reason for the Newby Sculpture Garden being one of the most popular features is not just the art but the setting. All the pieces are sited with care in a lovely area of historic woodland and adjoining orchard which lie alongside the River Ure. A varied mix of visitors seem to enjoy it, from serious art lovers to families out for the day and local schools, for which it provides a valuable educational resource.

One of the most exciting and permanent developments, however,

is at the great Palladian house of Houghton Hall in Norfolk. Over the last year some large sculptures have been constructed within the exceptional historic designed landscape surrounding the house. The 'Full Moon Circle' by Richard Long is set in the centre of the avenue providing the east view from the house. It comprises large pieces of slate set in a circular pattern but in a way in which light is reflected in a variety of ways and at some times appearing to be a formal pool of water. Even more exceptional is one of two pieces by James Turrell, the world-renowned American artist born in 1943. His

work involves explorations in light and space that speak to viewers without words, impacting the eye, body and mind with a force of a spiritual awakening. Newly constructed in the north wilderness at Houghton is his 'Skyspace' – a free-standing enclosed chamber large enough for about 15 people and designed and constructed with utmost precision to heighten one's sense of sight and perception.

Opening times of the properties mentioned can be found respectively at:

- **Sausmarez Manor, p202**
- **Ragley Hall, p359**
- **Burghley House, p321**
- **Newby Hall, p384**
- **Houghton Hall, p294**

73

Borde Hill, Sussex.

England

london

London, England's vibrant capital city, contains not just the 'must-see' attractions such as Buckingham Palace and the Tower of London, but also many smaller and no less interesting properties. Go east to Spitalfields and visit 18 Folgate Street, a time capsule of 18th century London. London's parks are the lungs of the city. From Regent's Park in the north to Battersea Park south of the river, via Hyde Park and St James's it is possible to walk for miles, hardly touching a pavement. Whether you are looking for ancient buildings, beautiful parkland, museums, classical music or world class rock concerts, London has them all. This cosmopolitan capital has something to attract everyone, the city is constantly evolving, and London's newer attractions, such as the London Eye, are every bit as popular as some of her more established landmarks.

The Wellington Arch.

©English Heritage Photo Library/Nigel Corrie.

MAP 20

APSLEY HOUSE ⊞

www.english-heritage.org.uk/visits

Apsley House (also known as No. 1 London) is the former residence of the first Duke of Wellington.

The Duke made Apsley House his London home after a dazzling military career culminating in his victory over Napoleon at Waterloo in 1815. Wellington enlarged the house (originally designed and built by Robert Adam between 1771 - 78) adding the magnificent Waterloo Gallery by Benjamin Dean Wyatt which holds many of the masterpieces from the Duke's extensive painting collection. It has been the London home of the Dukes of Wellington ever since.

The seventh Duke gave the house and contents to the Nation in 1947, with apartments retained for the family. With its collections of outstanding paintings, porcelain, silver, sculpture, furniture, medals and memorabilia largely intact and the family still in residence, Apsley House is the last great aristocratic town house in London.

Owner:
English Heritage

▶ **CONTACT**
House Manager
Apsley House
Hyde Park Corner
London W1J 7NT

Tel: 020 7499 5676
Fax: 020 7493 6576

▶ **LOCATION**
OS Ref. TQ284 799

N. side of
Hyde Park Corner

Underground:
Hyde Park Corner exit 1
Piccadilly Line.

▶ **OPENING TIMES**

1 April - 31 October
Tue - Sun & BHs
10am - 5pm.

1 November - 31 March
Tue - Sun
10am - 4pm.
Closed 24 - 26 Dec & 1 Jan.

▶ **ADMISSION**

Adult £4.95
Conc. £3.70
Children £2.50
Child (under 5yrs) ... Free

15% discount on groups of 11 or more. Free for English Heritage members and for Overseas Visitor Pass holders.

©English Heritage Photo Library/Nigel Corrie.

[i] No photography in house.

[📷]

[♿] Partial.

[👤] By arrangement.

[🎧] Free. English, French, Spanish & German.

[P] In Park Lane.

[🐕] Guide dogs only

[❄]

[⊞] Tel for details.

London - England

MAP 20

Owner:
Historic Royal Palaces

THE BANQUETING HOUSE

www.banqueting-house.org.uk

The magnificent Banqueting House is all that survives of the great Palace of Whitehall which was destroyed by fire in 1698. It was completed in 1622, commissioned by King James I, and designed by Inigo Jones, the noted classical architect. In 1635 the main hall was further enhanced with the installation of 9 magnificent ceiling paintings by Sir Peter Paul Rubens, which survive to this day. The Banqueting House was also the site of the only royal execution in England's history, with the beheading of Charles I in 1649.

The Banqueting House is open to visitors, as well as playing host to many of society's most glittering occasions.

▶ **CONTACT**

The Banqueting House
Whitehall
London SW1A 2ER

General Enquiries:
0870 751 5178
Functions:
0870 751 5185 / 5186

▶ **LOCATION**

OS Ref. TQ302 801

Underground:
Westminster,
Embankment and
Charing Cross.

Rail: Charing Cross.

▶ **OPENING TIMES**

All Year
Mon - Sat
10am - 5pm
Last admission 4.30pm.

Closed
24 December - 1 January,
Good Friday and other
public holidays.

NB. Liable to close at short notice for Government functions.

▶ **ADMISSION**

Enquiry line for
admission prices:
0870 751 5178

Concerts.
No photography inside.

Banquets.

Undercroft suitable.

Video and audio guide.

None.

Welcome.

CONFERENCE/FUNCTION		
ROOM	SIZE	MAX CAPACITY
Main Hall	110' x 55'	400
Undercroft	64' x 55'	350

The Royal Collection © 2006 HM Queen Elizabeth II.

MAP 20

BUCKINGHAM PALACE
THE STATE ROOMS
THE QUEEN'S GALLERY
THE ROYAL MEWS

www.royalcollection.org.uk

Owner:
Official Residence of
Her Majesty The Queen

▶ **CONTACT**

Ticket Sales &
Information Office
Buckingham Palace
London SW1A 1AA

Tel: 020 7766 7300
Groups (15+):
020 7766 7321
Fax: 020 7930 9625

e-mail: bookinginfo@
royalcollection.org.uk

▶ **LOCATION**
OS Ref. TQ291 796

Underground:
Green Park, Victoria,
St James's Park.

Rail: Victoria.

Sightseeing tours
A number of tour
companies include a
visit to Buckingham
Palace in their
sightseeing tours. Ask
your concierge or hotel
porter for details.

Buckingham Palace is the official London residence of Her Majesty The Queen and serves as both home and office. Its 19 State Rooms, which open for eight weeks a year, form the heart of the working palace. They are used extensively by The Queen and members of the Royal Family to receive and entertain their guests on State, ceremonial and official occasions. The State Rooms are lavishly furnished with some of the finest treasures from the Royal Collection – paintings by Rembrandt, Rubens, Van Dyck; sculpture by Canova; exquisite examples of Sèvres porcelain, and some of the most magnificent English and French furniture in the world. The garden walk offers superb views of the Garden Front of the Palace and the 19th-century lake.

Adjacent to Buckingham Palace are the Royal Mews and The Queen's Gallery. The Royal Mews is one of the finest working stables in existence and houses both the horse-drawn carriages and motor cars used for coronations, State visits, royal weddings and the State Opening of Parliament.

The Queen's Gallery hosts a programme of changing exhibitions of magnificent works of art from the Royal Collection. Exhibitions in 2006 include *Canaletto in Venice* (until 23 April); and *Watercolours and Drawings from the Collection of Queen Elizabeth The Queen Mother* (19 May - 29 October) and *Unfolding Pictures: Fans in the Royal Collection* (17 November - 11 February 2007).

All exhibitions will be shown alongside *Treasures from the Royal Collection*, which will include paintings by Duccio, Clouet, Rubens, Van Dyck, Claude and Lely, works by Fabergé, as well as furniture, sculpture and ceramics, jewellery, silver and gold.

▶ **OPENING TIMES**
As Buckingham Palace is a working royal palace, opening arrangements may change at short notice. Please check before planning a visit.

The State Rooms
August - September
Daily: 9.45am - 6pm
(last admission 3.45pm).

The Queen's Gallery
All year daily except
14 April & 25/26 Dec and
between exhibitions.
10am - 5.30pm
(last admission 4.30pm).
Entry by timed ticket.

The Royal Mews
March - October
Daily except Fridays:
11am - 4pm.
Closed 14 April and during
State Visits. Extended
opening hours during
August & September
10am - 5pm (last adm. 4.15pm)

To pre-book your tickets visit our website or contact the Ticket Sales and Information Office.

Private Evening Tours are available to Groups (15+) contact 020 7766 7322.

▶ **ADMISSION**
The State Rooms, The Queen's Gallery, The Royal Mews
For admission prices
please call the Ticket Sales
& Information Office.
Group (15+) discounts
available.

The Queen's Gallery, The Royal Collection © 2006 HM Queen Elizabeth II.

The Glass Coach © 2006 The Royal Collection/David Cripps.

🛍️ ℹ️ No photography inside.

♿ Wheelchair users are required to pre-book.

🚶 The Royal Mews.

🎧 The State Rooms and some exhibitions.

🅿️ None. ■

🦮 Guide dogs only.

London - England

© English Heritage P1 © Library

MAP 19

Owner:
English Heritage

▶ **CONTACT**

Visits:
House Manager
Chiswick House
Burlington Lane
London W4 2RP

Tel: 020 8995 0508

Venue Hire and Hospitality:
Hospitality Manager
Tel: 020 7973 3292

▶ **LOCATION**

OS Ref: TQ210 775

Burlington Lane
London W4 2RP.

Rail: ¼ mile NE of Chiswick Station.

Tube: Turnham Green, ¾ mile

Bus: 190, E3.

CHISWICK HOUSE ⊞

www.english-heritage.org.uk/visits

Chiswick House is internationally renowned as one of the first and finest English Palladian villas. Lord Burlington, who built the villa from 1725 - 1729, was inspired by the architecture and gardens of ancient Rome and this house is his masterpiece. His aim was to create a fit setting to show his friends his fine collection of art and his library. The opulent interior features gilded decoration, velvet walls and painted ceilings. In 2006, eight Old Masters paintings, including a newly discovered work by Rubens will be on display in the Red Velvet Room. The important 18th century gardens surrounding Chiswick House have, at every turn, something to surprise and delight the visitor.

Venue Hire and Hospitality

English Heritage offers exclusive use of Chiswick House in the evenings and Saturday afternoons for dinners, receptions and weddings.

© English Heritage Photo Library

▶ **OPENING TIMES***

Summer
1 April - 31 October
Wed - Sun & BHs,
10am - 5pm.
Closes at 2pm on Sats.

Winter
1 November
- 31 March 2007.
Pre-booked group
tours only.

▶ **ADMISSION***

Adult £4.00
Child (5-15yrs)....... £2.00
Conc £3.00
Family .... £ 10.00
Groups
(11+) .... 15% discount

🗄 ℹ WCs. Filming, plays, photographic shoots.

🍽 Private & corporate hospitality.

♿ Please call in advance. WC.

🏃 Personal guided tours must be booked in advance.

🎧 Free audio tours in English, French & German.

📕 Free if booked in advance. Tel: 020 7973 3485.

🐕 Guide dogs in grounds.

🔔 Civil Wedding Licence.

🅿

🛡 Tel for details.

English Heritage Photo Library/Jonathan Bailey

MAP 19

Owner:
English Heritage

▶ **CONTACT**

Eltham Palace
Court Yard
Eltham
London SE9 5QE

Visits:
Property Secretary
Tel: 020 8294 2548

**Venue Hire and
Hospitality:**
Hospitality Manager
Tel: 020 8294 2577

▶ **LOCATION**

OS Ref. TQ425 740

M25/J3, then A20
towards Eltham. The
Palace is signposted
from A20 and from
Eltham High Street.
A2 from Central
London.

Rail: 20 mins from
Victoria or London
Bridge Stations to
Eltham or Mottingham,
then 15 min walk.

CONFERENCE/FUNCTION	
ROOM	MAX CAPACITY
Great Hall	300 standing 200 dining
Entrance Hall	100 seated
Drawing Room	120 standing 80 theatre-style
Dining Room	80 standing 10 dining

ELTHAM PALACE ⊞

www.english-heritage.org.uk/visits

The epitome of 1930s chic, Eltham Palace dramatically demonstrates the glamour and allure of the period.

Bathe in the light flooding from a spectacular glazed dome in the Entrance Hall as it highlights beautiful blackbeam veneer and figurative marquetry. It is a *tour de force* only rivalled by the adjacent Dining Room – where an Art Deco aluminium-leafed ceiling is a perfect complement to the bird's-eye maple walls. Step into Virginia Courtauld's magnificent gold-leaf and onyx bathroom and throughout the house discover lacquered, 'ocean liner' style veneered walls and built-in furniture.

A Chinese sliding screen is all that separates chic '30s Art Deco from the medieval Great Hall. You will find concealed electric lighting, centralised vacuum cleaning and a loud-speaker system that allowed music to waft around the house. Authentic interiors have been recreated by the finest contemporary craftsmen. Their appearance was painstakingly researched from archive photographs, documents and interviews with friends and relatives of the Courtaulds.

Outside you will find a delightful mixture of formal and informal gardens including a rose garden, pergola and loggia, all nestled around the extensive remains of the medieval palace.

English Heritage Photo Library/Jonathan Bailey

 WCs. Filming, plays and photographic shoots.

Exclusive private and corporate hospitality.

 WC.

Guided tours on request.

Free. English, German & French.

P Coaches must book.

 Tel for details.

▶ **OPENING TIMES***

1 April - 31 October
Sun - Wed
10am - 5pm.

1 November - 20 December
Sun - Wed
10am - 4pm.

4 February - 31 March
Sun - Wed
10am - 4pm.

Closed 21 December
- 3 February.

Groups visits must be booked two weeks in advance.

**Venue Hire and
Hospitality**
English Heritage offers exclusive use of the Palace on Thu, Fri or Sat for daytime conferences, meetings and weddings and in the evenings for dinners, concerts and receptions.

▶ **ADMISSION***

House and Grounds

Adult £7.60
Child £3.80
Conc. £5.70
Family (2+3) £19.00

Grounds only

Adult £4.60
Child £2.30
Conc. £3.50

London - England

Crown Copyright: Historic Royal Palaces

Crown Copyright - Historic Royal Palaces

MAP 20

Managed by:
Historic Royal Palaces

▶ **CONTACT**
Kensington Palace
London W8 4PX

Recorded Information:
0870 751 5170

Venue Hire and Corporate Hospitality:
0870 751 5184

All Other Enquiries:
0870 751 5176

▶ **LOCATION**
OS Ref. TQ258 801

In Kensington Gardens.

Underground:
Queensway on Central Line,
High Street Kensington on Circle & District Line.

KENSINGTON PALACE

www.kensington-palace.org.uk

Kensington Palace has seen such momentous events as the death of George II and the birth of the future Queen Victoria. Visitors today enjoy the tranquillity and calm away from the hustle and bustle of this popular part of London.

The palace is home to the magnificent Royal Ceremonial Dress Collection, a display of court and ceremonial outfits dating from the 18th century. Multi-language sound guides lead visitors through the excitement of court presentation. The collection includes dresses worn on state occasions by Her Majesty The Queen as well as 14 of Diana, Princess of Wales's evening dresses.

On display during 2006 at Kensington Palace will be, *Princess Diana by Mario Testino*, an exhibition of his photographs of the Princess, taken for her last photo-shoot that appeared in *Vanity Fair* in July 1997.

Included in admission to the Palace, the exhibition will include many new images taken at the time but never previously released. The Princess was at the height of her beauty and modelled a selection of her dresses that were later auctioned in New York for charities close to her heart. The dresses will also be displayed alongside these iconic pictures.

The multi-lingual sound guides also take visitors around the magnificent State Apartments, including the lavishly decorated Cupola Room where Queen Victoria was baptised, and the beautifully restored King's Gallery.

▶ **OPENING TIMES**
March - October
Daily, 10am - 6pm
(last admission 5pm)

Nov - Feb
Daily, 10am - 5pm
(last admission 4pm)

Closed 24 - 26 Dec.

▶ **ADMISSION**
Telephone Information Line for admission prices:
0870 751 5170

Advance Ticket Sales:
0870 751 5180

Group bookings
0870 751 7070
Quote Hudson's.

Crown Copyright, HRP

FUNCTIONS

ROOM	MAX CAPACITY
Orangery	250 receptions 150 dinners
Victoria Garden Rooms	100 receptions 50 dinners
State Apartments	200 receptions 170 dinners

📷 ℹ️ No photography indoors.

🍴 🍽️ ☕ The Orangery (located nearby) serves light refreshments.

♿ Partial.

🎧

🅿️ Nearby. Cars and coaches.

🚌 Welcome, please book. 0870 751 5192.

🐕 In grounds, on leads. Guide dogs only in Palace.

❄️

©English Heritage Photo Library/Paul Highnam

MAP 20

KENWOOD ⌗

www.english-heritage.org.uk/visits

Owner:
English Heritage

▶ **CONTACT**
Kenwood House
Hampstead Lane
London NW3 7JR

Visits:
The House Manager
Tel: 020 8348 1286

▶ **LOCATION**
OS Ref. TQ271 874

M1/J2. Signed off A1,
on leaving A1 turn
right at junction with
Bishop's Ave, turn left
into Hampstead Lane.
Visitor car park on left.

Bus: London Transport
210.

Rail: Hampstead Heath.

Underground:
Archway or Golders
Green Northern Line
then bus 210.

Kenwood, one of the treasures of London, is an idyllic country retreat close to the popular villages of Hampstead and Highgate.

The house was remodelled in the 1760s by Robert Adam, the fashionable neo-classical architect. The breathtaking library or 'Great Room' is one of his finest achievements.

Kenwood is famous for the internationally important collection of paintings bequeathed to the nation by Edward Guinness, 1st Earl of Iveagh. Some of the world's finest artists are represented by works such as a Rembrandt *Self Portrait*, Vermeer's *The Guitar Player*; *Mary, Countess Howe* by Gainsborough and paintings by Turner, Reynolds and many others.

As if the house and its contents were not riches enough, Kenwood stands in 112 acres of landscaped grounds on the edge of Hampstead Heath, commanding a fine prospect towards central London. The meadow walks and ornamental lake of the park, designed by Humphry Repton, contrast with the wilder Heath below. The open air concerts held in the summer at Kenwood have become part of London life, combining the charms of music with the serenity of the lakeside setting.

▶ **OPENING TIMES**

1 April - 31 October,
Daily: 11am - 5pm.

1 November - 31 March
Daily: 11am - 4pm.

Closed 24 - 26 December
& 1 January.

Venue Hire and Hospitality
Events are available for up to 100 guests in the Service Wing. Please ring Company of Cooks on 020 8341 5384.

▶ **ADMISSION**
House & Grounds: Free.
Donations welcome.

English Heritage Photo Library

English Heritage Photo Library

🛍

ℹ WCs. Concerts, exhibitions, filming. No photography in house.

♟ Exclusive private and corporate hospitality.

♿ Ground floor access. WC.

☕ Available in the Brew House.

🕼 Available on request (in English). Please call for details.

🎧 English, French, Italian & German.

🅿 West Lodge car park on Hampstead Lane. Parking for the disabled.

▦ Free when booked in advance on 020 7973 3485.

❄

🛡 Tel for details.

© J-tonal Maritime Museum

MAP 19

ROYAL OBSERVATORY, NATIONAL MARITIME MUSEUM & QUEEN'S HOUSE

www.nmm.ac.uk

Owner: National Maritime Museum

▶ **CONTACT**

Groups: Robin Scates
Events: Jo Rough
Park Row, Greenwich
London SE10 9NF

Tel: 020 8858 4422
Fax: 020 8312 6632

Visit Bookings:
Tel: 020 8312 6608
Fax: 020 8312 6522
e-mail:
bookings@nmm.ac.uk
Functions:
Tel: 020 8312 6693
Fax: 020 8312 6572

▶ **LOCATION**
OS Ref. TQ388 773

Within Greenwich Park on the S bank of the Thames at Greenwich. Travel by river cruise or Docklands Light Railway (Cutty Sark station). M25 (S) via A2. From M25 (N) M11, A12 and Blackwall Tunnel.

The Royal Park at Greenwich provides a beautiful backdrop to the architectural landscape of Greenwich, now a World Heritage Site. The Tudor palace of Placentia, in which Henry VIII, Mary Tudor and Elizabeth I were born, is now covered by the 17th century Old Royal Naval College with its Painted Hall and Chapel.

Illustrated above is Flamsteed House (Wren 1675), built to accommodate the first Astronomer Royal. It has been restored for 2006 with new presentations of significant time-keepers, including those of John Harrison, and the story of Greenwich Mean Time. The Meridian Line, Longitude 0°, is marked in the courtyard as the base point for the calculation of the World's time zones and the 1833 timeball still drops punctually at 1 o'clock. New development is in progress for 2007 to add a new planetarium and modern astronomy displays.

The modern National Maritime Museum charts Britain's history of seafaring and empire. Nelson's uniform coat is on display and portraits and artefacts from various military and civil expeditions tell the human stories behind many great events. Contemporary themes are tackled including the ocean environment, slavery and travel at sea. Stained glass from the destroyed Baltic Exchange is in a separate memorial gallery. There are frequent events and talks for adults and children.

The Queen's House (Inigo Jones 1635) is significant as the first classical house in England. Introducing the Palladian style to England, it was called a 'House of Delights' by Henrietta Maria and was used for court entertainments and balls. The Great Hall, Orangery and 'Tulip' stairs provide an elegant setting for fine and contemporary art displays, occasional exhibitions and private functions.

▶ **OPENING TIMES**
Daily, 10am - 5pm (later opening in summer). Last admission 30 mins prior. Varies at New Year and Marathon Day (23 Apr).

Closed 24 - 26 December.

Gallery talks and drama (see notices on arrival).

Special Exhibitions
National Trust/ Magnum photography Coast Exposed until 12 Feb 2006. Life at Sea, 19 Jan - 23 Apr.

▶ **ADMISSION**

Free admission except for Planetarium shows

CONFERENCE/FUNCTION		
ROOM	SIZE	MAX CAPACITY
Queen's House	40' x 40'	Dining 120 Standing 200 Conference 120
Observatory, Octagon Rm	25' x 25'	Dining 60 Standing 150
NMM Upper Court	140' x 70'	Dining 500 Standing 1000
NMM Lecture Theatre		Conference 120

Tulip Spiral Staircase, The Queen's House © NMM

No photography.

Partial. WC.

Licensed.

Limited for coaches.

Guide dogs only.

© Newbery Smith Photography / Jarrold Publishing

MAP 20

Owner: Dean & Chapter of St Paul's Cathedral

▶ **CONTACT**

Mark McVay
The Chapter House
St Paul's Churchyard
London   EC4M 8AD

Tel: 020 7246 8348
020 7246 8346

Fax: 020 7248 3104

e-mail: chapterhouse@
stpaulscathedral.org.uk

▶ **LOCATION**

OS Ref. TQ321 812

Central London.

Underground:
St Paul's,
Mansion House,
Blackfriars, Bank.

Rail: Blackfriars,
City Thameslink.

Air: London Airports.

ST PAUL'S CATHEDRAL

www.stpauls.co.uk

A Cathedral dedicated to St Paul has stood at the heart of the City of London for 1400 years, a constant reminder of the spiritual life in this busy commercial centre.

The present St Paul's, the fourth to occupy the site, was built between 1675 - 1710. Sir Christopher Wren's masterpiece rose from the ashes of the previous Cathedral, which had been destroyed in the Great Fire of London.

Over the centuries, the Cathedral has been the setting for royal weddings, state funerals and thanksgivings. Admiral Nelson and the Duke of Wellington are buried here, Queen Victoria celebrated her gold and diamond jubilees and Charles, Prince of Wales married Lady Diana Spencer. Most recently, St Paul's hosted the thanksgiving service for the 100th birthday of HM Queen Elizabeth the Queen Mother. On 4 June 2002 the Cathedral hosted the National Service of Thanksgiving for the Golden Jubilee of HM The Queen.

Hundreds of memorials pay tribute to famous statesmen, soldiers, artists, doctors and writers and mark the valuable contributions to national life made by many ordinary men and women.

The soaring dome, one of the largest in the world, offers panoramic views across London from the exterior galleries. Inside, a whisper in the Whispering Gallery can be heard on the opposite side.

2005 will see the completion of a major programme of cleaning and repair on the interior, allowing visitors to experience the Cathedral as we imagine Sir Christopher Wren originally conceived it. Nearly 300 years of dirt has been removed returning the Portland stonework to its natural creaminess, revealing the delicacy of carvings and brilliance of the Byzantine-style mosaics. This is part of a £40m programme of work for the building's approaching tercentenary. Far more than a beautiful landmark, St Paul's Cathedral is a living symbol of the city and nation it serves.

▶ **OPENING TIMES**

Mon - Sat, 8.30am - 4.30pm, last admission 4pm.

Guided tours: daily, 11.30am, 1.30pm and 2pm.

Tours of the Triforium: Mon & Thur, 11.30am & 2.30pm.

All tours are subject to an additional charge.

Cathedral Shop & Café:
9am - 5.30pm,
Sun, 10.30am - 5pm.

Restaurant:
11am - 5.30pm.

Service Times
Mon - Sat
7.30am Mattins (Sat 8.30am)
8am Holy Communion (said)
12.30pm Holy Communion (said)
5pm Choral Evensong

Sun: 8am Holy Communion (said)
10.15am Choral Mattins & sermon
11.30am Choral Eucharist & sermon
3.15pm Choral Evensong & sermon
6pm Evening service

The Cathedral may be closed to tourists on certain days of the year. It is advisable to phone or check our website for up-to-date information.

▶ **ADMISSION**

Adult £9.00
Child £3.50
OAP/Student £8.00
Groups (10+)
Adult £8.00
Child £3.00
OAP/Student £7.00

Sampson Lloyd

constructionphotography.com

CONFERENCE/FUNCTION

ROOM	MAX CAPACITY
Conference Suite	100 (standing)

 No photography, video or mobile phones.

 Partial.

 Licensed.

None for cars, limited for coaches.   Guide dogs only.

MAP 20

SPENCER HOUSE

www.spencerhouse.co.uk

Spencer House, built 1756 - 66 for the 1st Earl Spencer, an ancestor of Diana, Princess of Wales (1961-97), is London's finest surviving 18th century town house. The magnificent private palace has regained the full splendour of its late 18th century appearance, after a painstaking ten-year restoration programme.

Designed by John Vardy and James 'Athenian' Stuart, the nine state rooms are amongst the first neo-classical interiors in Europe. Vardy's Palm Room, with its spectacular screen of gilded palm trees and arched fronds, is a unique Palladian setpiece, while the elegant mural decorations of Stuart's Painted Room reflect the 18th century

passion for classical Greece and Rome. Stuart's superb gilded furniture has been returned to its original location in the Painted Room by courtesy of the V&A and English Heritage. Visitors can also see a fine collection of 18th century paintings and furniture, specially assembled for the house, including five major Benjamin West paintings, graciously lent by Her Majesty The Queen.

The state rooms are open to the public for viewing on Sundays. They are also available on a limited number of occasions each year for private and corporate entertaining during the rest of the week.

▶ **CONTACT**

Jane Rick
Director
Spencer House
27 St James's Place
London SW1A 1NR

Tel: 020 7514 1958
Fax: 020 7409 2952

Info Line: 020 7499 8620

▶ **LOCATION**

OS Ref. TQ293 803

Central London:
off St James's Street,
overlooking
Green Park.

Underground:
Green Park.

All images are copyright of Spencer House Ltd and may not be used without the permission of Spencer House Ltd.

▶ **OPENING TIMES**

All Year
(except January & August)
Suns, 10.30am - 5.45pm.

Last tour 4.45pm.

Regular tours throughout the day. Maximum number on each tour is 20.

Mon mornings for pre-booked groups only.

Open for corporate hospitality except during January & August.

▶ **ADMISSION**

Adult £9.00
Conc.* £7.00

* Students, Friends of the V&A, Friends of the Tate, Friends of the Royal Academy and senior citizens (only on production of valid identification), children under 16. No children under 10 admitted.
Group size: min 15 - 60.

Prices include guided tour.

SPECIFIC SUNDAYS

The authentically restored garden of this 18th century London palace will be open to the public on specific Sundays during Spring and Summer.

For updated information telephone 020 7499 8620 or view www.spencerhouse.co.uk

CONFERENCE/FUNCTION

ROOM	MAX CAPACITY
Receptions	400
Lunches & Dinners	130
Board Meetings	40
Theatre Style Meetings	100

ℹ️ No photography inside House or Garden. 🍸 ♿ House only, ramps and lifts. WC.
🚶 Obligatory. Comprehensive colour guidebook £3.50. 🅿️ None.

SYON PARK

www.syonpark.co.uk

Owner: The Duke of Northumberland

▶ CONTACT

Estate Office
Syon House
Syon Park
Brentford
TW8 8JF

Tel: 020 8560 0882
Fax: 020 8568 0936

e-mail: info@ syonpark.co.uk

▶ LOCATION

OS Ref. TQ173 767

Between Brentford and Twickenham, off the A4, A310 in SW London.

Rail: Kew Bridge or Gunnersbury Underground then Bus 237 or 267.

Air: Heathrow 8m.

Described by John Betjeman as 'the Grand Architectural Walk', Syon House and its 200 acre park is the London home of the Duke of Northumberland, whose family, the Percys, have lived here for 400 years.

Originally the site of a late medieval monastery, excavated by Channel 4's *Time Team*, Syon Park has a fascinating history. The present house has Tudor origins but contains some of Robert Adam's finest interiors, which were commissioned by the 1st Duke in the 1760s. The private apartments and State bedrooms are available to view. The house is regularly used for feature films and productions.

Within the 'Capability' Brown landscaped park are 40 acres of gardens which contain the spectacular Great Conservatory designed by Charles Fowler in the 1820s. The House and Great Conservatory are available for corporate and private hire.

Syon House is an excellent venue for small meetings, lunches and dinners in the Duke's private dining room (max 22). The State Apartments make a sumptuous setting for dinners, concerts, receptions, launches and wedding ceremonies (max 120). Marquees can be erected on the lawn adjacent to the house for balls and corporate events. The Great Conservatory is available for summer parties, launches and wedding receptions (max 150).

▶ OPENING TIMES

House
22 March - 29 October
Wed, Thur, Sun & BHs
11am - 5pm
(open Good Fri & Easter Sat).

Other times by appointment for groups.

Gardens
Daily (except 25/26 Dec)
April - October
10.30am - 5.30pm
November - March
10.30am - 4pm. Last admission ¾ hr before closing.

▶ ADMISSION

House and Gardens
Adult £7.50
Child/Conc. £6.50
Family (2+2) £17.00
Groups
Adult £7.00
Child/Conc. £6.00

Gardens only
Adult £3.75
Child/Conc. £2.50
Family (2+2) £9.00
Groups (15 - 50 persons)
.................................£2.50

No photography in house. Indoor adventure playground.

Garden centre.

Partial.

By arrangement.

Guide dogs only.

Tel for details.

WEDDING/FUNCTION

ROOM	SIZE	MAX CAPACITY
Great Hall	50' x 30'	120
Great Conservatory	60' x 40'	150
Marquee		1000

THE TOWER OF LONDON

www.tower-of-london.org.uk

MAP 20

Managed by:
Historic Royal Palaces

▶ **CONTACT**

The Tower of London
London   EC3N 4AB

Recorded Information Line:
0870 756 6060

Venue Hire and Corporate Hospitality:
0870 751 5183

All Other Enquiries:
0870 751 5177

▶ **LOCATION**
OS Ref. TQ336 806

Underground:
Tower Hill on Circle/District Line.

Docklands Light Railway:
Tower Gateway Station.

Rail: Fenchurch Street Station and London Bridge Station.

Bus: 15, 25, 42, 78, 100, D1, RV1.

Riverboat: From Charing Cross, Westminster or Greenwich to Tower Pier. London Eye to Tower of London Express.

For over 900 years the Tower has served as a royal residence, a fortress, mint, armoury, menagerie, a prison and place of execution.

Start your visit with a Yeoman Warder tour. Better known as Beefeaters, the Yeoman Warders provide an introductory tour detailing the dark and sometimes deadly history of the Tower. Meanwhile, costumed interpreters bring to life the history in daily re-enactments on the south lawn.

The magnificent Crown Jewels remain one of the main attractions. See the Star of Africa, the world's largest cut diamond, mounted in the Sceptre, part of the Coronation Regalia. Also in the collection is the Imperial State Crown, still worn by The Queen

annually at the State Opening of Parliament.

Prisoners and imprisonment is a popular subject and following the recent representation in the Bloody and Beauchamp Towers, displays incorporate the latest audio and visual effects to create a very different experience. Learn more about how prisoners filled their time whilst confined in those very rooms at the Tower and contemplate the reality compared to the myth of Tower imprisonment!

Stand on the execution site, visit the White Tower housing displays of Tudor Arms and Armour and take in the Torture exhibition in the Wakefield Tower.

▶ **OPENING TIMES**

Summer
1 March - 31 October
Daily
Tues - Sat: 9am - 6pm
(last admission 5pm)
Mons & Suns: 10am - 5pm.

Winter
1 November - 28 February
Tues - Sat: 9am - 5pm
Mons & Suns: 10am - 4pm
(last admission 4pm).

Closed 24 - 26 December and 1 January.

Buildings close 30 minutes after last admission.

▶ **ADMISSION**

Telephone Information Line for admission prices:
0870 756 6060

Advance Ticket Sales:
0870 756 7070

Group bookings:
0870 751 7070
Quote Hudson's.

No photography in Jewel House.

0870 751 5183.

Partial. WC.

Yeoman Warder tours are free and leave front entrance every 1/2 hr.

None for cars. Coach parking nearby.

Welcome. To book 0870 751 5191.

Guide dogs only.

www.tower-of-london.org.uk

2 WILLOW ROAD

HAMPSTEAD, LONDON NW3 1TH

Tel: 020 7435 6166   **e-mail:** 2willowroad@nationaltrust.org.uk

Owner: The National Trust   **Contact:** The Custodian

The former home of Erno Goldfinger, designed and built by him in 1939. A three-storey brick and concrete rectangle, it is one of Britain's most important examples of modernist architecture and is filled with furniture also designed by Goldfinger. The interesting art collection includes works by Henry Moore and Max Ernst.

Location: OS Ref. TQ270 858. Hampstead, London.

Open: 4 - 25 Mar, 4 - 25 Nov: Sats, 12 noon - 5pm. 1 Apr - 28 Oct: Thurs - Sat, 12 noon - 5pm, except first Thurs each month, house opens 5 - 9pm instead. Open Good Fri. Last admission 4.30pm. Tours: 12 noon, 1 & 2 pm (5 & 6pm on first Thurs). Unguided visits 3 - 5pm & 7 - 9pm.

Admission: Adult £4.70, Child £2.35, Family £11.75. Joint ticket with Fenton House £6.70. Private groups are welcome throughout the year outside public afternoon opening times. Groups must be 5+, booking essential.

Small ground floor area accessible. Filmed tour of whole house available.

18 FOLGATE STREET

Spitalfields, East London E1 6BX

Tel: 020 7247 4013   **Fax:** 020 7377 5548   **www.**dennissevershouse.co.uk

Owner: Spitalfields Historic Buildings Trust   **Contact:** Mick Pedroli

A time capsule furnished and decorated to tell the story of the Jervis family, Huguenot silk weavers from 1724 - 1919.

Location: OS Ref. TQ335 820. 1/2 m NE of Liverpool St. Station. E of Bishopsgate (A10), just N of Spitalfields Market.

Open: "Silent Night" every Mon evening. Booking required. 1st & 3rd Sun each month: 2 - 5pm. Mons following these Suns 12 noon - 2pm.

Admission: "Silent Night" Mons £12 (pm £5), Suns £8. Christmas prices may vary.

Partial. Obligatory by private bookings. Tel for details.

ALBERT MEMORIAL

Princes Gate, Kensington Gore SW7 2AN

Tel: Bookings - 020 7495 0916. Enquiries - 020 7495 5504

An elaborate memorial by George Gilbert Scott to commemorate the Prince Consort.

Location: OS Ref. TQ266 798. Victoria Station 1 1/2 m, South Kensington Tube 1/2 m.

Open: All visits by booked guided tours; first Sun of the month Mar - Dec, 2pm & 3pm. Tours last 45 mins.

Admission: Adult £4.50, Conc £4. Booking advisable for groups of 10+.

APSLEY HOUSE

See page 79 for full page entry.

THE BANQUETING HOUSE

See page 80 for full page entry.

BLEWCOAT SCHOOL

23 Caxton Street, Westminster, London SW1H 0PY

Tel: 020 7222 2877

Owner: The National Trust   **Contact:** Janet Bowden

Built in 1709 at the expense of William Green, a local brewer, to provide an education for poor children. Used as a school until 1926, it is now the NT London Gift Shop and Information Centre.

Location: OS Ref. TQ295 794. Near the junction with Buckingham Gate.

Open: All year: Mon - Fri, 10am - 5.30pm. Easter - Christmas: Thurs, 10am - 7pm. Also Sat 18 - 23 Dec: 10am - 4pm. Closed BHs.

BOSTON MANOR HOUSE

Boston Manor Road, Brentford TW8 9JX

Tel: 0845 456 2824   **e-mail:** info@cip.org.uk

Owner: Hounslow Cultural & Community Services   **Contact:** Victoria Northwood

A fine Jacobean house built in 1623.

Location: OS Ref. TQ168 784. 10 mins walk S of Boston Manor Station (Piccadilly Line) and 250yds N of Boston Manor Road junction with A4 - Great West Road, Brentford.

Open: Apr - end Oct: Sat, Sun & BHs, 2.30 - 5pm. Due to structural works during 2005/6 please check times prior to your visit. Park open daily.

Admission: Free.

BRUCE CASTLE MUSEUM

Haringey Libraries, Archives & Museum Service,
Lordship Lane, London N17 8NU

Tel: 020 8808 8772   **Fax:** 020 8808 4118   **e-mail:** museum.services@haringey.gov.uk

Owner: London Borough of Haringey

A Tudor building. Sir Rowland Hill (inventor of the Penny Post) ran a progressive school at Bruce Castle from 1827.

Location: OS Ref. TQ335 906. Corner of Bruce Grove (A10) and Lordship Lane, 600yds NW of Bruce Grove Station.

Open: All year: Wed - Sun & Summer BHs (except Good Fri), 1 - 5pm. Organised groups by appointment.

Admission: Free.

BUCKINGHAM PALACE

See page 81 for full page entry.

BURGH HOUSE

New End Square, Hampstead, London NW3 1LT

Tel: 020 7431 0144   **Buttery:** 020 7431 2516   **Fax:** 020 7435 8817

e-mail: burghhouse@talk21.com   **www.**burghhouse.org.uk

Owner: London Borough of Camden   **Contact:** Ms Helen Wilton

A Grade I listed building of 1703 in the heart of old Hampstead with original panelled rooms, "barley sugar" staircase banisters and a music room. Home of the Hampstead Museum, permanent and changing exhibitions. Prize-winning terraced garden. Regular programme of concerts, art exhibitions, and meetings. Receptions, seminars and conferences. Rooms for hire. Special facilities for schools visits. Wedding receptions.

Location: OS Ref. TQ266 859. New End Square, E of Hampstead underground station.

Open: All year: Wed - Sun, 12 noon - 5pm. Sats by appointment only. BH Mons, 2 - 5pm. Closed Christmas fortnight, Good Fri & Easter Mon. Groups by arrangement. Buttery: Wed - Sun, 11am - 5.30pm. BHs, 1 - 5.00pm.

Admission: Free.

Ground floor & grounds. WC. Licensed buttery. By arrangement. None. By arrangement. Guide dogs only.

CAPEL MANOR GARDENS

BULLSMOOR LANE, ENFIELD EN1 4RQ

www.capel.ac.uk

Tel: 08456 122122   **Fax:** 01992 717544

Owner: Capel Manor Charitable Organisation   **Contact:** Miss Julie Ryan

These extensive, richly planted gardens are delightful throughout the year offering inspiration, information and relaxation. The gardens include various themes - historical, modern, walled, rock, water, sensory and disabled and an Italianate Maze, Japanese Garden and 'Gardening Which?' demonstration and model gardens. Capel Manor is a College of Horticulture and runs a training scheme for professional gardeners originally devised in conjunction with the Historic Houses Association.

Location: OS Ref. TQ344 997. Minutes from M25/J25. Tourist Board signs posted.

Open: Daily in summer: 10am - 5.30pm. Last ticket 4.30pm. Check for winter times.

Admission: Adult £5, Child £2, Conc. £4, Family £12. Charges alter for special show weekends and winter months.

Grounds. WC. In grounds, on leads. Tel for details.

CARLYLE'S HOUSE

24 Cheyne Row, Chelsea, London SW3 5HL

Tel: 020 7352 7087   **Fax:** 020 7352 5108   **e-mail:** carlyleshouse@nationaltrust.org.uk

Owner: The National Trust   **Contact:** The Custodian

Atmospheric home of the writer Thomas Carlyle and his wife Jane from 1834-1881. There is a small walled garden and the surrounding streets are rich in literary and artistic associations.

Location: OS Ref. TQ272 777. Off the King's Road and Oakley Street, or off Cheyne Walk between Albert Bridge and Battersea Bridge on Chelsea Embankment.

Open: 25 Mar - 29 Oct: Wed - Fri (incl. Good Fri), 2 - 5pm; Sat, Sun & BH Mons, 11am - 5pm. Last admission 4.30pm.

Admission: Adult £4.20, Child £2.10. Tel for groups visits and guided tours.

By arrangement for groups. Tel for details.

CHAPTER HOUSE ⊞

East Cloisters, Westminster Abbey, London SW1P 3PE
Tel: 020 7654 4834 **www.**westminster-abbey.org
Owner: English Heritage   **Managed by:** Dean & Chapter of Westminster
The Chapter House, built by the Royal masons c1250 and faithfully restored in the 19th century, contains some of the finest medieval sculpture to be seen and spectacular wall paintings. The building is octagonal, with a central column, and still has its original floor of glazed tiles, which have been newly conserved. Its uses have varied and in the 14th century it was used as a meeting place for the Benedictine monks of the Abbey and as well as for Members of Parliament.
Location: OS Ref. TQ301 795.
Open: All year: Daily, 10am - 4pm. Liable to be closed at short notice on State & religious occasions. Closed Good Fri, 24 - 26 Dec & 1 Jan.
Admission: Integral part of tour of Westminster Abbey.

CHELSEA PHYSIC GARDEN

66 ROYAL HOSPITAL ROAD, LONDON SW3 4HS

www.chelseaphysicgarden.co.uk

Tel: 020 7352 5646 **Fax:** 020 7376 3910
e-mail: enquiries@chelseaphysicgarden.co.uk
Owner: Chelsea Physic Garden Company
The second oldest botanic garden in Britain, founded in 1673. For many years these 4 acres of peace and quiet, with many rare and unusual plants, were known only to a few. Specialists in medicinal plants, tender species and the history of plant introductions.
Location: OS Ref. TQ277 778. Off Embankment, between Chelsea & Albert Bridges. Entrance - Swan Walk. Underground: Sloane Square/South Kensington.
Open: 2 Apr - 29 Oct: Weds, 12 noon - 5pm & Suns, 12 noon - 6pm. Special winter openings: 5 & 12 Feb: 11am - 3.30pm & 22/23, 25/26 May & 20, 22 June: 12 noon - 5pm.
Admission: Adult £6.50, Child £3.50, Carers for disabled: Free.
🅾 👻 📺 ♿ Partial. WCs. ▣ 🅺 By arrangement. ▣ 🅷 Guide dogs only. 🅥 Tel for details.

CHISWICK HOUSE ⊞   *See page 82 for full page entry.*

CHURCH FARMHOUSE MUSEUM

Greyhound Hill, London NW4 4JR
Tel: 020 8203 0130 **e-mail:** gerrard.roots@barnet.gov.uk
www.churchfarmhousemuseum.co.uk
Owner: London Borough of Barnet   **Contact:** Gerrard Roots
The building is a Grade II* 1660s farmhouse with Victorian additions, in a small public garden. There are three 19th century furnished rooms - dining room (decorated for a Victorian Christmas each December), kitchen and laundry room. Four temporary exhibitions - social history and the decorative arts - are held annually.
Location: OS Ref. TQ228 896. Greyhound Hill is a turning off the A41 (Watford Way) in Hendon. ¹/₂ m from M1/J2.
Open: All year. Mon - Thurs, 10am - 1pm & 2 - 5pm; Sat, 10am - 1pm & 2 - 5.30pm; Sun, 2 - 5.30pm. Closed: Christmas Day, Boxing Day and New Year's Day.
Admission: Free. Groups restricted to no more than 30 people.
ℹ Photography by permission. 🅾 ♿ Unsuitable. 🅺 By arrangement. 🅟 Limited. No coaches. ▣ 🅷 Guide dogs only. ✳

COLLEGE OF ARMS

Queen Victoria Street, London EC4V 4BT
Tel: 020 7248 2762 **Fax:** 020 7248 6448 **e-mail:** enquiries@college-of-arms.gov.uk
Owner: Corp. of Kings, Heralds & Pursuivants of Arms
          Contact: The Officer in Waiting
Mansion built in 1670s to house the English Officers of Arms and their records.
Location: OS Ref. TQ320 810. On N side of Queen Victoria Street, S of St Paul's Cathedral.
Open: Earl Marshal's Court only; open all year (except BHs, State and special occasions) Mon - Fri, 10am - 4pm. Group visits (up to 10) by arrangement only. Record Room: open for tours (groups of up to 20) by special arrangement in advance with the Officer in Waiting.
Admission: Free (groups by negotiation).

EASTBURY MANOR HOUSE ✄

Eastbury Square, Barking, Essex IG11 9SN
Tel: 020 8724 1000 **Fax:** 020 8724 1003 **e-mail:** eastburyhouse@lbbd.gov.uk
www.barking-dagenham.gov.uk
Owner: The National Trust   **Contact:** Julie Packham
Eastbury Manor is a unique example of a medium sized Elizabethan Manor House with attractive grounds. Leased to the London Borough of Barking and Dagenham and used for a variety of events and arts and heritage activities. In addition Eastbury can be hired for business conferences, Sunday weddings, seminars and education days.
Location: OS TQ45/ 838. In Eastbury Square off Ripple Road off A13, 10 mins S from Upney Station. Buses 287, 368 or 62.
Open: All Year: Mons & Tues and 1st & 2nd Sat of the month, 10am - 4pm.
Admission: Adult £2.50, Child 65p, Conc. £1.25, Family £5. Groups (15+) by arrangement: £2pp.
🅾 ♿ 🖥 🅺 🅟 In Eastbury Square. ▣ 🅷 In grounds only. 🅰 ✳ 🅥 Tel for details.

ELTHAM PALACE ⊞   *See page 83 for full page entry.*

The Wellington Arch

FENTON HOUSE ⚜

WINDMILL HILL, HAMPSTEAD, LONDON NW3 6RT

Tel/Fax: 020 7435 3471 **Infoline:** 01494 755563
e-mail: fentonhouse@nationaltrust.org.uk
Owner: The National Trust   **Contact:** The Custodian

A delightful late 17th century merchant's house, set among the winding streets of Old Hampstead. The charming interior contains an outstanding collection of Oriental and European porcelain, needlework and furniture. The Benton Fletcher Collection of beautiful early keyboard instruments is also housed at Fenton and the instruments are sometimes played by music scholars during opening hours. The walled garden has a formal lawn and walks, an orchard and vegetable garden and fine wrought-iron

gates. Telephone for details of demonstrations and other events.
Location: OS Ref. TQ262 860. Visitors' entrance on W side of Hampstead Grove. Hampstead Underground station 300 yds.
Open: 4 - 26 Mar: Sat & Sun, 2 - 5pm. 29 Mar - 29 Oct: Wed - Fri, 2 - 5pm; Sat, Sun & BHs, 11am - 5pm. Groups at other times by appointment.
Admission: Adult £4.90, Child £2.45, Family £12. Groups (15+) £4.10.
Joint ticket with 2 Willow Road, £6.70.
ⓘNo picnics in grounds. ♿Ground floor. Braille guide. 🎦Demonstration tours.
ⓅNone. ✉Send SAE for details.

FORTY HALL

FORTY HILL, ENFIELD, MIDDLESEX EN2 9HA

www.enfield.gov.uk/fortyhall

Tel: 020 8363 8196   **Fax:** 020 8367 9098   **e-mail:** forty.hall@enfield.gov.uk
Contact: London Borough of Enfield   **Contact:** Gavin Williams

This beautiful Grade I listed Jacobean House built in 1629 for Sir Nicholas Rainton, Lord Mayor of London, is a location for festivals, events and guided tours throughout the year. The 273-acre estate includes formal gardens, wildflower meadows and the site of Elsyng Palace, owned by Henry VIII and Elizabeth I.
Location: OS Ref. TQ336 985. 1m from M25/J25, just off A10. Tourist Board sign posted.
Open: All Year: Wed - Sun, 11am - 4pm.
Admission: Free.
ⓧ♿Partial. WCs. ▣ 🎦By arrangement. ⓅAmple for cars. Limited for coaches.
▣ ♨In grounds, on leads. ✴✉Tel for details.

THE FOUNDLING MUSEUM

40 Brunswick Square, London WC1N 1AZ

Tel: 020 7841 3600 **Fax:** 020 7841 3601
Owner: The Foundling Museum

Site of London's first home for abandoned children. Established in 1739. The museum charts the history of the Foundling Hospital and its residents until its closure in 1953.
Location: OS Ref. TQ303 822. Underground: Russell Square.
Open: Tues - Sat, 10am - 6pm; Sun, 12 noon - 6pm.
Admission: Adult £5, Child up to 16yrs Free, Conc. £4. Special rates apply for groups and schools.

FULHAM PALACE & MUSEUM

Bishop's Avenue, Fulham, London SW6 6EA

Tel: 020 7736 5821 **Fax:** 020 7736 3233
Owner: London Borough of Hammersmith & Fulham & Fulham Palace Trust

Former home of the Bishops of London (Tudor with Georgian additions and Victorian Chapel). The gardens, famous in the 17th century, now contain specimen trees and a knot garden of herbs.
Location: OS Ref. TQ240 761.
Open: Restoration in progress. Please telephone for further details.
Admission: Gardens: Free.

plant sales
see page 555

THE GEFFRYE MUSEUM

KINGSLAND ROAD, LONDON E2 8EA

www.geffrye-museum.org.uk

Tel: 020 7739 9893   **Fax:** 020 7729 5647   **e-mail:** info@geffrye-museum.org.uk

Owner: Independent Charitable Trust

The Geffrye presents the changing style of the English domestic interior from 1600 to the present day through a series of period rooms. The displays lead the visitor on a walk through time, from the 17th century with oak furniture and panelling, past the refined splendour of the Georgian period and the high style of the Victorians, to 20th century modernity. The museum's displays are complemented by a walled herb garden and a series of period gardens.

Location: OS Ref. TQ335 833. 1m N of Liverpool St. Buses: 242, 149, 243, 67 & 394. Underground: Liverpool St. or Old St.

Open: Museum: Tue - Sat, 10am - 5pm. Sun & BH Mon, 12 noon - 5pm. Closed Mon (except BHs) Good Fri, Christmas Eve, Christmas Day, Boxing Day & New Year's Day. Gardens: Apr - Oct.

Admission: Free.

🖻 🎵 ♿ 🖵 🍴 🎧 ❄ 🐕 Tel for details

GUNNERSBURY PARK & MUSEUM

Gunnersbury Park, London W3 8LQ

Tel: 020 8992 1612   **Fax:** 020 8752 0686   **e-mail:** gp-museum@cip.org.uk

Owner: Hounslow and Ealing Councils   **Contact:** Lynn Acum

Built in 1802 and refurbished by Sydney Smirke for the Rothschild family.

Location: OS Ref. TQ190 792. Acton Town Underground station. ¼ m N of the junction of A4, M4 North Circular.

Open: Apr - Oct: daily: 1 - 5pm. Nov - Mar: daily: 1 - 4pm. Victorian kitchens summer weekends only. Closed Christmas Day & Boxing Day. Park: open dawn - dusk.

Admission: Free. Donations welcome.

Tower of London.

HAM HOUSE 🌿

HAM, RICHMOND, SURREY TW10 7RS

www.nationaltrust.org.uk/hamhouse

Tel: 020 8940 1950   **Fax:** 020 8439 8241   **e-mail:** hamhouse@nationaltrust.org.uk

Owner: The National Trust   **Contact:** The Property Manager

Ham House, set on the banks of the Thames near Richmond, is perhaps the most remarkable Stuart house in the country. Formerly the home of the influential Duke and Duchess of Lauderdale, Ham was a centre for Court intrigue throughout the 17th century. In its time, the house was at the forefront of fashion and retains much of its interior decoration from that period, including outstanding collections of furniture, textiles and paintings shown in 26 rooms. The gardens are a remarkable survival of English formal gardening and have now been restored to their former glory. Replicas of the original statues of *Venus Marina* and *Mercury* have returned to the garden. The 18th century dairy, decorated with cast iron cows' legs supporting marble work surfaces and hand-painted Wedgwood tiles, is now on view as is the 17th century still house, used for distilling alcohol and essences.

Wide programme of events throughout the year, including herb week, open air theatre, ghost tours, children's activities, recitals and Christmas specific events. 2 Sept - 29 Oct "The Grand Tour" - Exhibition focusing on the effect that the "Grand Tour of Europe" had on the subsequent refurbishment and organisation of the Great Country Houses, focusing on Ham House and the 4th Earl of Dysart.

Location: OS Ref. TQ172 732. 1½ m from Richmond and 2m from Kingston. On the S bank of the River Thames, W of A307 at Petersham.

Open: House: 25 Mar - 29 Oct: Sat - Wed, 1 - 5pm. Gardens: All year, Sat - Wed, 11am - 6pm. Closed 25/26 Dec & 1 Jan. Special Christmas evening openings for house and gardens, shop and café and Christmas lunches in December.

Admission: House & Garden: Adult £8, Child £4, Family £19. Garden only: Adult £4, Child £2, Family £9. Booked groups (15+): Adult £7, Child £3.50.

🖻 🎵 🎵 ♿ Partial. WC. 🖵 🐾 🅿 🖵 🍴 Guide dogs. 🔺 🐕 Tel for details.

© Matthew Hollow

HANDEL HOUSE MUSEUM

25 BROOK STREET, LONDON W1K 4HB

www.handelhouse.org

Tel: 020 7495 1685 **Fax:** 020 7495 1759 **e-mail:** mail@handelhouse.org

Owner: The Handel House Trust Ltd **Contact:** Kate Sheerin

Handel House Museum is located at 25 Brook Street, where the great baroque composer, George Frideric Handel lived for 36 years, and where he wrote such timeless masterpieces as *Zadok the Priest*, *Messiah* and *Music for the Royal Fireworks*. The elegantly refurbished interiors create the perfect setting for 18th century furniture and fine art, evoking the spirit of Georgian London. This landmark address is also brought to life by an inspiring programme of live music, events and activities for adults and families. The Thursday evening concerts every week are particularly popular, and you are recommended to book well in advance.

Location: OS Ref. TQ286 809. Central London, between New Bond St and Grosvener Square. Bond Street Tube.

Open: Tue - Sat, 10am - 6pm (Thur until 8pm). Suns, 12 noon - 6pm. Closed Mons. Groups by arrangement.

Admission: Adult £5, Child £2, Conc. £4.50.

ℹ️No inside photography. 🎥 ♿ 🚻By arrangement. 🎧 ■ ❋

KEATS HOUSE

KEATS GROVE, HAMPSTEAD, LONDON NW3 2RR

www.cityoflondon.gov.uk/keats

Tel: 020 7435 2062 **Fax:** 020 7431 9293
e-mail: keatshouse@corpoflondon.gov.uk

Owner: Corporation of London **Contact:** The Manager

Regency home of the poet John Keats (1795 - 1821).

Location: OS Ref. TQ272 856. Hampstead, NW3. Nearest Underground: Belsize Park & Hampstead.

Open: All year: Tue - Sun & BHs, 1 - 5pm. Visits by appointment: Tue - Fri, 10am - 12 noon. Please call to confirm times prior to visit.

Admission: Adult £3.50, Under 16s Free, Conc. £1.75.

🎥 ♿ Ground floor & garden. 🅿️None. ■ 🦮 Guide dogs only. ❋

HOGARTH'S HOUSE

Hogarth Lane, Great West Road, Chiswick, London W4 2QN

Tel: 020 8994 6757 **www.**hounslow.info/hogarthshouse **email:** info@cip.org.uk

Owner: Hogarth House Foundation **Contact:** Victoria Northwood

This late 17th century house was the country home of William Hogarth, the famous painter, engraver, satirist and social reformer between 1749 and his death in 1764.

Location: OS Ref. TQ213 778. 100 yds W of Hogarth roundabout on the Great West Road - junction of Burlington Lane. Car park in named spaces in Hogarth Business Centre behind house and Chiswick House grounds.

Open: Tue - Fri, 1 - 5pm (Nov - Mar: 1 - 4pm). Sat, Sun & BH Mons, 1 - 6pm (Nov - Mar: 1 - 5pm). Closed Mon (except BHs), Good Fri, Christmas Day, Boxing Day & Jan.

Admission: Free.

🎥 🅿️ ❋

JEWEL TOWER ♯

Abingdon Street, Westminster, London SW1P 3JX

Tel: 020 7222 2219 **www.**english-heritage.org.uk/visits

Owner: English Heritage **Contact:** Visitor Operations Team

Built c1365 to house the personal treasure of Edward III. One of two surviving parts of the original Palace of Westminster. Now houses an exhibition on 'Parliament Past and Present'. The second floor now includes new illustrated panels, telling the story of this small but important building.

Location: OS Ref. TQ302 794. Opposite S end of Houses of Parliament (Victoria Tower).

Open: 1 Apr - 31 Oct: daily, 10am - 5pm, may close at short notice for functions, please call to check. 1 Nov - 31 Mar: daily, 10am - 4pm. Closed 24 - 26 Dec & 1 Jan.

Admission: Adult £2.70, Child £1.40, Conc. £2.

🎥 🚽 🦮 ❋ 🎫 Tel for details.

DR JOHNSON'S HOUSE

17 Gough Square, London EC4A 3DE

Tel: 020 7353 3745 **e-mail:** curator@drjohnsonshouse.org

Owner: The Trustees

Fine 18th century house, once home to Dr Samuel Johnson, the celebrated literary figure, famous for his English dictionary.

Location: OS Ref. TQ314 813. N of Fleet Street.

Open: Oct - Apr: Mon - Sat, 11am - 5pm. May - Sept: Mon - Sat, 11am - 5.30pm. Closed BHs.

Admission: Adult £4.50, Child £1.50 (under 10yrs Free), Conc. £3.50. Family £10. Groups: £3.50.

KENSINGTON PALACE STATE APARTMENTS

See page 84 for full page entry.

KENWOOD HOUSE ♯

See page 85 for full page entry.

LSO ST LUKE'S
THE UBS AND LSO MUSIC EDUCATION CENTRE

161 Old Street, London EC1V 9NG

Tel: 020 7490 3939 **Minicom:** 020 7490 8299 **Fax:** 020 7566 2881

e-mail: lsostlukes@lso.co.uk **www.**lso.co.uk/lsostlukes

Contact: Alison Thompson, Events Manager

Formerly St Luke's Church, a Grade I listed Hawksmoor church built in 1733. LSO St Luke's is the new home for the London Symphony Orchestra's music education and community programme, LSO Discovery. The church was derelict for 40 years, but has been rebuilt and opened in early 2003 with state-of-the-art facilities.

Location: OS Ref. TQ325 824. On corner of Old Street and Helmet Row, 5mins walk from Old Street Station (Northern Line, National Rail).

Open: By appointment only. Contact the Events Manager.

Admission: Free.

♿ 🚻By arrangement. 🅿️No cars, limited for coaches. ■ 🦮Guide dogs only.

corporate hospitality
see page 568

THE LAW SOCIETY'S HALL

113 CHANCERY LANE, LONDON WC2A 1PL

www.uniquevenue.lawsociety.org.uk

Tel: 020 7320 9555 **Fax:** 020 7320 5955 **e-mail:** m&e@lawsociety.org.uk

Owner: The Law Society **Contact:** Heidi Carlsen

This historic London venue, designed by Vulliamy in the Neo-Classical style, opened in 1832. 15 stunning air-conditioned function suites are available to accommodate meetings, conferences, or banquets. The Common Room, with its green marble pilasters and mahogany panelling, lends itself perfectly to wedding receptions.

Location: OS Ref. TQ311 812. Underground: Blackfriars, Temple, Chancery Lane. Rail: Blackfriars, Charing Cross, Waterloo.

Open: All year: daily, 9am - 11pm for pre-booked functions only.

Admission: Please contact for details.

ℹ️Not open to general public except for functions. 🕐 ♿️ 💳Licensed. 🍴Licensed. 🅿️Limited. None for coaches. 🐕Guide dogs only. 🔳✳️

LINDSEY HOUSE 🌿

100 Cheyne Walk, London SW10 0DQ

Tel: 01494 528051

Owner: The National Trust **Contact:** Area Manager

Part of Lindsey House was built in 1674 on the site of Sir Thomas More's garden, overlooking the River Thames. It has one of the finest 17th century exteriors in London. Ground floor entrance hall, main staircase and gardens only open to the public.

Location: OS Ref. TQ268 775. On Cheyne Walk, W of Battersea Bridge near junction with Milman's Street on Chelsea Embankment.

Open: 10 May & 11 Oct: daily, 11am - 4pm.

Admission: Free.

Kensington Palace

LEIGHTON HOUSE MUSEUM

12 HOLLAND PARK ROAD, KENSINGTON, LONDON W14 8LZ

www.rbkc.gov.uk/leightonhousemusem

Tel: 020 7602 3316 **Fax:** 020 7371 2467

e-mail: museums@rbkc.gov.uk

Owner: Royal Borough of Kensington & Chelsea

Contact: Curator

Leighton House was the home of Frederic, Lord Leighton 1830 - 1896, painter and President of the Royal Academy, built between 1864 - 1879. It was a palace of art designed for entertaining and to provide a magnificent working space in the studio, with great north windows and a gilded apse. The Arab Hall is the centrepiece of the house, containing Leighton's collection of Iznik tiles, a gilt mosaic frieze and a fountain. Victorian paintings by Leighton, Millais and Burne-Jones are on display.

Location: OS Ref. TQ247 793. Nearest underground: High Street Kensington (exit staircase turn left, take first right for Melbury Road after Commonwealth Institute. Leighton House is located in Holland Park Road, the first left. Bus: 9, 10, 27, 28, 33, 49, 328 (to Commonwealth Institute).

Open: Daily, except Tues, 11am - 5.30pm. Also open Spring/Summer BHs. Guided tours on Wed & Thur, 2.30pm. Closed 25/26 Dec.

Admission: Adult £3, Conc £1. Family £6. Guided tours free on Weds & Thurs. Joint group guided tour with Linley Sambourne House £10pp.

🔲 ℹ️No photography. 🕐 ♿️Unsuitable.
✈️Wed & Thurs at 2.30pm. 🔲 🅿️None. 🔳❌✳️
📋Tel for details.

LINLEY SAMBOURNE HOUSE

18 STAFFORD TERRACE, LONDON W8 7BH

www.rbkc.gov.uk/linleysambournehouse

Info: 020 7602 3316 (ext 300 Mon - Fri) **or** 07976 060160 (Sats & Suns)

Fax: 020 7371 2467 **e-mail:** museums@rbkc.gov.uk

Owner: The Royal Borough of Kensington & Chelsea **Contact:** Curatorial staff

Linley Sambourne House is the former home of the Punch cartoonist Edward Linley Sambourne and his family. Almost unchanged over the course of the last century, the house provides a unique insight into the life of an artistic middle-class family. The majority of the original decoration and furnishings remain in situ exactly as left by the Sambournes. All visits are by guided tour with special dramatic tours available and an introductory video. Larger groups can visit jointly with Leighton House Museum just 10 minutes walk away.

Location: OS Ref. TQ252 794. Parallel to Kensington High St, between Phillimore Gardens & Argyll Rd. Bus: 9, 10, 27, 28, 31, 49, 52, 70 & C1. Underground: Kensington High St. Parking on Sun in nearby streets.

Open: 18 Mar - 10 Dec: Sats & Suns; tours leaving at 10am, 11.15am, 1pm, 2.15pm and 3.30pm. Pre-booking is advised. At other times for booked groups (10+), by appointment. Larger groups (12+) will be divided for tours of the House. Access for Group tours: Mon - Fri.

Admission: Adult £6, Child (under 18yrs) £1, Conc £4. Groups (12+): Min £60.00. Joint group (10+) guided tour with Leighton House Museum £10pp.

No photography. Obligatory. None. Guide dogs only.

MARBLE HILL HOUSE ⌗

RICHMOND ROAD, TWICKENHAM TW1 2NL

www.english-heritage.org.uk/visits

Tel: 020 8892 5115

Owner: English Heritage **Contact:** Visitor Operations Team

This beautiful villa beside the Thames was built in 1724 - 29 for Henrietta Howard, mistress of George II. Here she entertained many of the poets and wits of the Augustan age including Alexander Pope and later Horace Walpole. The perfect proportions of the villa were inspired by the work of the 16th century Italian architect, Palladio. Today this beautifully presented house contains an important collection of paintings and furniture, including some pieces commissioned for the villa when it was built. A new display in 2006 recreates the Chinese wallpaper Henrietta Howard hung in the Dining Room in 1751. Summer concerts.

Location: OS Ref. TQ174 736. A305, 600yds E of Orleans House.

Open: 1 Apr - 31 Oct: Sat, 10am - 2pm. Suns & BHs, 10am - 5pm. Tours: Tues & Wed, 12 noon & 3pm. 1 Nov - 31 Mar: pre-booked group tours only.

Admission: Adult £4, Child £2, Conc. £3.

Ground floor. WC. Summer only. Tel for details.

English Heritage Photo Library

MORDEN HALL PARK ✤

Morden Hall Road, Morden SM4 5JD

Tel: 020 8545 6850 **Fax:** 020 8417 8091

e-mail: mordenhallpark@nationaltrust.org.uk

Owner: The National Trust **Contact:** The Property Manager

Former deer park centred around historic Snuff Mills and rose garden featuring an extensive network of waterways, ancient hay meadows and wetlands. Workshops now house local craftworkers.

Location: OS Ref. TQ261 684. Off A24 and A297 S of Wimbledon, N of Sutton.

Open: All year: daily. NT gift shop & Riverside Café: 10am - 5pm (closed: 25/26 Dec & 1 Jan). Car park closes 6pm.

Admission: Free.

WILLIAM MORRIS GALLERY

Lloyd Park, Forest Road, Walthamstow, London E17 4PP

Tel: 020 8527 3782 **Fax:** 020 8527 7070

Owner: London Borough of Waltham Forest **Contact:** The Keeper

Location: OS Ref. SQ372 899. 15 mins walk from Walthamstow tube (Victoria line). 5 - 10 mins from M11/A406.

Open: Tue - Sat and first Sun each month, 10am - 1pm and 2 - 5pm.

Admission: Free for all visitors but a charge is made for guided tours which must be booked in advance.

accommodation
see page 567

MYDDELTON HOUSE GARDENS
Bulls Cross, Enfield, Middlesex EN2 9HG
Tel: 01992 702200 **www**.leevalleypark.org.uk
Owner: Lee Valley Regional Park Authority
Created by the famous plantsman and Fellow of the Royal Horticultural Society. E A Bowles, the gardens contain year round interest. From the January snowdrops, through the springtime flowering daffodils to the summer roses and beyond to the autumn crocus, there is always something in the gardens to interest the visitor. The gardens are an ideal place to draw, paint, photograph or picnic. Woodland walks. Carp lake. Kitchen garden under restoration. National Collection of award-winning Bearded Iris.
Location: OS Ref. TQ342 992. ¼ m W of A10 via Turkey St. ¾ m S M25/J25.
Open: Apr - Sept: Mon - Fri, 10am - 4.30pm, Suns & BH Mons & NGS days, 12 noon - 4pm. Oct - Mar: Mon - Fri, 10am - 3pm. Last admission 30 mins before closing. Closed Christmas.
Admission: Adult £2.40, Conc. £1.80. Prices subject to change April 2006. Separate charge for guided walks.
🔲 ♿ ⬅ Some paths. 💳 📷 Please ring 01992 709849. 🅿 🐕 Guide dogs only. ✳

THE OCTAGON, ORLEANS HOUSE GALLERY
Riverside, Twickenham, Middlesex TW1 3DJ
Tel: 020 8831 6000 **Fax:** 020 8744 0501 **e-mail:** galleryinfo@richmond.gov.uk
Owner: London Borough of Richmond-upon-Thames **Contact:** The Curator
Outstanding example of baroque architecture by James Gibbs c1720. Art gallery.
Location: OS Ref. TQ168 734. On N side of Riverside, 700yds E of Twickenham town centre, 400yds S of Richmond Road. Vehicle access via Orleans Rd only.
Open: Tue - Sat, 1 - 5.30pm, Sun & BHs, 2 - 5.30pm (Oct - Mar closes 4.30pm). Closed Mons. Garden: open daily, 9am - sunset.
Admission: Free.

OSTERLEY PARK 🍂
JERSEY ROAD, ISLEWORTH, MIDDLESEX TW7 4RB

Tel: 020 8232 5050 **Fax:** 020 8232 5080 **Infoline:** 01494 755566
e-mail: osterley@nationaltrust.org.uk **www**.nationaltrust.org.uk/osterley/
Owner: The National Trust **Contact:** Visitor Services Manager
Osterley's four turrets look out across one of the last great landscaped parks in suburban London, its trees and lakes an unexpected haven of green. Originally built in 1575, the mansion was transformed in the 18th century into an elegant villa by architect Robert Adam. The classical interior, designed for entertaining on a grand scale, still impresses with its specially made tapestries, furniture and plasterwork. The magnificent 16th century stables survive largely intact.

Location: OS Ref. TQ146 780. Access via Thornbury Road on N side of A4.
Open: House: 4 - 26 Mar: Sat & Sun; 29 Mar - 29 Oct: Wed - Sun, 1 - 4.30pm. Park & Pleasure Grounds: All year: daily, 9am - 7.30pm. Open BH Mons & Good Fri. Park & Pleasure Grounds close dusk if earlier than 7.30pm. Park closes early before major events. Car park closed: 25 & 26 Dec.
Admission: Adult £5.10, Child £2.50, Family £12.80, Groups (15+) £4.20. Park & Pleasure Grounds: Free. Car Park: £3.50.

🔲 🚻 ♿ Tel for details. 💳 🅿 📷 🐕 On leads in park. 🔔 ✳ 🎥 Tel for details.

National Maritime Museum

PALACE OF WESTMINSTER
London SW1A 0AA
Tel: 020 7219 3000 **First Call:** 0870 906 3773 **Info:** 020 7219 4272
Fax: 020 7219 5839 **Contact:** Information Office
The first Palace of Westminster was erected on this site by Edward the Confessor in 1042 and the building was a royal residence until a devastating fire in 1512. After this, the palace became the two-chamber Parliament for government - the House of Lords and the elected House of Commons. Following a further fire in 1834, the palace was rebuilt by Sir Charles Barry and decorated by A W Pugin.
Location: OS Ref. TQ303 795. Central London, W bank of River Thames. 1km S of Trafalgar Square. Underground: Westminster.
Open: Aug - Oct (please ring for details). At other times by appointment. Please telephone Info line.
Admission: Adult £7, Child/Conc. £5. Free.

PITZHANGER MANOR-HOUSE
Walpole Park, Mattock Lane, Ealing W5 5EQ
Tel: 020 8567 1227   **Fax:** 020 8567 0595
e-mail: pmgallery&house@ealing.gov.uk   **www.**ealing.gov.uk/pmgalleryandhouse
Owner: London Borough of Ealing   **Contact:** Anne Ninivin
Pitzhanger Manor House is a restored Georgian villa, once owned and designed by the architect Sir John Soane (1753 - 1837). Rooms in the house have been restored using Soane's highly individual ideas in design and decoration. Exhibitions of contemporary art are programmed year-round, sited in the adjacent Gallery and often also in the House.
Location: OS Ref. TQ176 805. Ealing, London.
Open: All year: Tue - Fri, 1 - 5pm. Sat, 11am - 5pm. Summer Sunday Openings, please ring for details. Closed Christmas, Easter, New Year and BHs.
Admission: Free.

RED HOUSE
Red House Lane, Bexleyheath DA6 8JF
Tel: 01494 755588 (Booking line: Mon - Fri, 10am - 2pm)
Owner: The National Trust
Commissioned by William Morris in 1859 and designed by Philip Webb, Red House is of enormous international significance in the history of domestic architecture and garden design. The garden was designed to "clothe" the house with a series of sub-divided areas that still clearly exist today. Inside, the house retains many of the original features and fixed items of furniture designed by Morris and Webb, as well as wall paintings and stained glass by Burne-Jones.
Location: OS Ref. TQ48 1750. Off A221 Bexleyheath. Visitors will be advised on how to reach the property when booking. Nearest rail station Bexleyheath, 15 mins' walk.
Open: Mar - Dec: Wed - Sun, 11am - 4.15pm. Closed Christmas Day, Boxing Day, 1 Jan - 14 Feb. Open Easter Sun, Good Fri, BH Mons. Admission by pre-booked guided tour only.
Admission: Adult £6, Child £3, Family £15.
No WC. Ground floor only. Limited.
No Parking on site. Parking at Danson Park (15 min walk). 90p parking charge at weekends and BHs. Disabled drivers can pre-book (limited parking).

ROYAL OBSERVATORY NATIONAL MARITIME MUSEUM & QUEEN'S HOUSE
See page 86 for full page entry.

ST GEORGE'S CATHEDRAL, SOUTHWARK
Westminster Bridge Road, London SE1 7HY
Tel: 020 7928 5256   **Fax:** 020 7202 2189
e-mail: info@southwark-rc-cathedral.org.uk   **Contact:** Canon James Cronin
Neo-Gothic rebuilt Pugin Cathedral bombed during the last war and rebuilt by Romily Craze in 1958.
Location: OS Ref. TQ315 794. Near Imperial War Museum. 1/2 m SE of Waterloo Stn.
Open: 8am - 6pm, every day, except BHs.
Admission: Free.

Syon Park.

ST JOHN'S GATE
MUSEUM OF THE ORDER OF ST JOHN
ST JOHN'S GATE, LONDON EC1M 4DA
www.sja.org.uk/museum
Tel: 020 7324 4070   **Fax:** 020 7336 0587   **e-mail:** museum@nhq.sja.org.uk
Owner: The Order of St John   **Contact:** Pamela Willis
Early 16 century Gatehouse (1504 - 2004), Priory Church and Norman Crypt. The remarkable history of the Knights Hospitaller, dedicated to caring for the sick and dating back to the 11th century, is revealed in collections including furniture, paintings, armour, stained glass and other items. Notable associations with Shakespeare, Hogarth, Edward Cave, Dr Johnson, Dickens, David Garrick and many others. In Victorian times, St John Ambulance was founded here and a modern interactive gallery tells its story.
Location: OS Ref. TQ317 821. St. John's Lane, Clerkenwell. Nearest Underground: Farringdon.
Open: Mon - Fri: 10am - 5pm. Sat: 10am - 4pm. Closed BHs & Sat of BH weekend. Tours: Tue, Fri & Sat at 11am & 2.30pm. Reference Library: Open by appointment.
Admission: Museum Free. Tours of the building: £5, OAP £4 (donation).
Ground floor. WC. Guide dogs only.   Reg. Charity No. 1077265

ST PAUL'S CATHEDRAL
See page 87 for full page entry.

SIR JOHN SOANE'S MUSEUM
13 Lincoln's Inn Fields, London WC2A 3BP
Tel: 020 7405 2107   **Fax:** 020 7831 3957   **www.**soane.org
Owner: Trustees of Sir John Soane's Museum   **Contact:** Julie Brock
The celebrated architect Sir John Soane built this in 1812 as his own house. It now contains his collection of antiquities, sculpture and paintings.
Location: OS Ref. TQ308 816. E of Kingsway, S of High Holborn.
Open: Tue - Sat, 10am - 5pm. 6 - 9pm, first Tue of the month. Closed BHs & 24 Dec.
Admission: Free. Groups must book.

civil wedding venues
see page 562

SOUTHSIDE HOUSE 🏛

3 WOODHAYES ROAD, WIMBLEDON, LONDON SW19 4RJ

www.southsidehouse.com

Tel: 020 8946 7643 **e-mail:** info@southsidehouse.com

Owner: The Pennington-Mellor-Munthe Charity Trust **Contact:** The Administrator

Described by connoisseurs as an unforgettable experience, Southside House provides an enchantingly eccentric backdrop to the lives and loves of generations of the Pennington Mellor Munthe families. Maintained in traditional style, without major refurbishment, and crowded with the family possessions of centuries, Southside offers a wealth of fascinating family stories.

Behind the long façade are the old rooms, still with much of the original furniture and a superb collection of art and historical objects. John Pennington-Mellor's daughter, Hilda, married Axel Munthe, the charismatic Swedish doctor and philanthropist. The preservation of the house was left to their youngest son who led a life of extraordinary adventure during the Second World War. Malcolm Munthe's surviving children continue to care for the property.

The gardens are as fascinating as the house, with a series of sculptural "rooms" linked by water and intriguing pathways.

Location: OS Ref. TQ234 706. On S side of Wimbledon Common (B281), opposite Crooked Billet Inn.

Open: Easter Sun - 1 Oct: Weds, Sats, Suns & BH Mons. Guided tours on the hour 2, 3 & 4pm. Other times throughout the year (excluding Dec - Mar) by arrangement with the Administrator (min 15 people).

Admission: Adult £5, Child £2.50 (must be accompanied by an adult), OAP £4, Family £10.

🚫 Unsuitable. 🎫 Obligatory. 🅿 Limited. ▣ ✉

SOUTHWARK CATHEDRAL

London Bridge, London SE1 9DA

Tel: 020 7367 6700 **Fax:** 020 7367 6730 **Visitors' Officer:** 020 7367 6734
e-mail: cathedral@southwark.anglican.org **www.**southwark.anglican.org/cathedral
Owner: Church of England **Contact:** Visitors' Officer

London's oldest gothic building and a place of worship for over 1,000 years, Southwark Cathedral has connections with Chaucer, Shakespeare, Dickens and John Harvard. Included in the new riverside Millennium buildings are: the Cathedral Shop, Refectory, and Archaeological Chamber.

Location: OS Ref. TQ327 803. South side of London Bridge, near Shakespeare's Globe and Tate Modern.

Open: Daily: 8.30am - 6pm. Weekday services: 8am, 12.30pm and 5.30pm. Sat services, 9am and 4pm. Sun services: 9am, 11am, 3pm & 6.30pm. Cathedral Shop: daily, 10am - 6pm, Sun, 11am - 5pm.

Admission: Recommended donation of £4 per person. Booked groups (min 10): Adult £4, Child £2, Conc. £3.50. Trade discounts available.

ℹ Indoor photography & video recording with permit. 📷 🎫 ♿ Partial. WCs. ✉
🍴 Licensed. 🎫 By arrangement. 🔊 🅿 None. ▣ 🐕 Guide dogs only. ✱
♨ Tel for details.

SPENCER HOUSE　　　　　　　　　*See page 88 for full page entry*

STRAWBERRY HILL

ST MARY'S, STRAWBERRY HILL, WALDEGRAVE ROAD, TWICKENHAM TW1 4SX

Tel: 020 8240 4224 /Appointments: 020 8240 4044

Contact: The Conference Office

Horace Walpole converted a modest house at Strawberry Hill into his own version of a gothic fantasy. It is widely regarded as the first substantial building of the Gothic Revival and as such is internationally known and admired. A century later Lady Frances Waldegrave added a magnificent wing to Walpole's original structure. Lady Waldegrave's suite of rooms can be hired for weddings, corporate functions and conferences. Please telephone for details.

Location: OS Ref. TQ158 722. Off A310 between Twickenham & Teddington.

Open: 7 May - 24 Sept: Suns, 2 - 3.30pm. Tours commence at 2pm, 2.45pm & 3.30pm. Booking is not required. For group tours please tel: 020 8240 4044.

Admission: Adult £5.50, OAP £5. Group bookings: £5.

ℹ Conferences. 📷 ✉ 🎫 ✉

NT Photographic Library: Geoffrey Frosh

SUTTON HOUSE ✿

2 & 4 HOMERTON HIGH STREET, HACKNEY, LONDON E9 6JQ

Tel: 020 8986 2264   **e-mail:** suttonhouse@nationaltrust.org.uk

Owner: The National Trust   **Contact:** The Custodian

A rare example of a Tudor red-brick house, built in 1535 by Sir Ralph Sadleir, Principal Secretary of State for Henry VIII, with 18th century alterations and later additions. Restoration revealed many 16th century details, even in rooms of later periods. Notable features include original linenfold panelling and 17th century wall paintings.

Location: OS Ref. TQ352 851. At the corner of Isabella Road and Homerton High St.

Open: Historic rooms: 2 Feb - 22 Dec: Thur - Sun, 12.30 - 4.30pm. Café, Shop & Art Gallery: 2 Feb - 22 Dec: Thur - Sun, 12 noon - 4.30pm. Open BH Mons. Closed Good Fri.

Admission: Adult £2.50, Child 50p, Family £5.50. Group visits by prior arrangement.

▢ ⬦ Ground floor only. WC. ▣ 𝐟 🅿None. ▮ ▲ ✳ ♛ Tel for details.

© English Heritage Photo Library

WELLINGTON ARCH ⌗

HYDE PARK CORNER, LONDON W1J 7JZ

www.english-heritage.org.uk/visits

Tel: 020 7930 2726   **Venue Hire and Hospitality:** 020 973 3292

Owner: English Heritage   **Contact:** Visitor Operations Team

Set in the heart of Royal London at Hyde Park Corner, Wellington Arch is a landmark for Londoners and visitors alike. George IV originally commissioned this massive monument as a grand outer entrance to Buckingham Palace. It was completed in 1830 by architect Decimus Burton, and moved to its present site in 1882.

Take a lift to the balconies just below the spectacular bronze sculpture, which tops the imposing monument, for glorious views over London's Royal Parks and the Houses of Parliament. The statue is the largest bronze sculpture in Europe, and depicts the Angel of Peace descending on the Chariot of War. Inside the Arch, three floors of exhibits tell its fascinating history.

Location: OS Ref. TQ285 798. Hyde Park Corner Tube Station.

Open: 24 Mar - 31 Oct: Wed, Sun & BHs, 10am - 5pm, may close at short notice for functions, please call to check. 1 Nov - 31 Mar: Wed - Sun, 10am - 4pm. Closed 24 - 26 Dec & 1 Jan.

Admission: Adult £3.10, Child £1.60, Conc. £2.30. Groups (11+) 15% discount.

▢ ⊤ ⬦ 𝐟 Mondays for groups only. ✳ ♛ Tel for details.

SYON PARK 🏛   *See page 89 for full page entry.*

THE TOWER BRIDGE EXHIBITION

Tower Bridge, London SE1 2UP

Tel: 020 7940 3985   **Fax:** 020 7357 7935

Owner: Corporation of London   **Contact:** Emma Parlow

One of London's most unusual and exciting exhibitions is situated inside Tower Bridge. Enjoy spectacular views from the high level walkways.

Location: OS Ref. TQ337 804. Adjacent to Tower of London, nearest Underground: Tower Hill.

Open: 1 Apr - 30 Sep: 10am - 5.30pm (last ticket). 1 Oct - 31 Mar: 9.30am - 5pm (last ticket). Closed 25 Dec.

Admission: Adult £5.50, Child £3, Conc. £4.25. (Prices may change April 2006.)

THE TOWER OF LONDON   *See page 90 for full page entry.*

EMERY WALKER'S HOUSE

7 Hammersmith Terrace, London W6 9TS

Tel: 020 8741 4104   **e-mail:** info@emerywalker.org.uk

www.emerywalker.org.uk

Owner: The Emery Walker Trust   **Contact:** Sue Bright

Emery Walker, friend and advisor to William Morris, lived in this riverside house for 30 years and it preserves the only authentic Arts and Crafts urban interior in Britain, with furniture, wallpapers, textiles and ceramics by Morris & Co, Philip Webb, William de Morgan, etc. Small, pretty garden.

Location: OS Ref. TQ221 782. Between Chiswick Mall and South Black Lion Lane in Hammersmith, parallel with King Street (Buses 27, 190, 267, 391, H91). Underground: Stamford Brook or Ravenscourt Park (District Line, both 7 mins walk) or Hammersmith (Piccadilly Line, 15 mins walk). Very limited metered on-street parking.

Open: Apr - Jul: Guided tour. Please visit website for times, dates and booking arrangements. Admission strictly by pre-booked timed ticket.

Admission: Adult £10, Conc. £5. No children under 12yrs. Groups (max 8).

ⓘ No photography inside house. No WC. Refreshments available locally. ⬦ Limited access to ground floor, no access to garden. 𝐟 Obligatory. 🚶

THE 'WERNHER COLLECTION' AT RANGER'S HOUSE ⌗

Chesterfield Walk, Blackheath, London SE10 8QX

Tel: 020 8853 0035   **www.**english-heritage.org.uk/visits

Owner: English Heritage   **Contact:** House Manager

This attractive red-brick villa built c1700 on the edge of Greenwich Park houses the 'Wernher Collection': the life-time collection of self-made millionaire, Julius Wernher. A superb display of fine and decorative arts with objects dating from 3BC to the 19th-century, and including a stunning array of Renaissance jewellery as well as paintings, sculpture, furniture, tapestries, enamels and ivories.

Location: OS Ref. TQ388 768. N of Shooters Hill Road.

Open: 1 Apr - 30 Sept: Sun - Wed, 10am - 5pm. 1 Oct - 31 Mar: pre-booked guided tours.

Admission: Adult £5.50, Child £2.80, Conc. £4.10.

ⓘWC. ▢ ⬦ Limited, lift available. 🅿 ▮ 🐕 Guide dogs only. ♛ Tel for details.

WESTMINSTER CATHEDRAL

Victoria, London SW1P 1QW

Tel: 020 7798 9055   **Fax:** 020 7798 9090   **www.**westminstercathedral.org.uk

Owner: Diocese of Westminster   **Contact:** Revd Mgr Mark Langham

The Roman Catholic Cathedral of the Archbishop of Westminster. Spectacular building in the Byzantine style, designed by J F Bentley, opened in 1903, famous for its mosaics, marble and music. Westminster Cathedral celebrated the Centenary of its foundation in 1995.

Location: OS Ref. TQ293 791. Off Victoria Street, between Victoria Station and Westminster Abbey.

Open: All year: 7am - 7pm. Please telephone for times at Easter & Christmas.

Admission: Free. Lift charge: Adult £3. Child £1.50. Family (2+4) £7.

▢ ⬦ Ground floor. ▣ 𝐟 Booking required. 🅿None. ▮ Worksheets & tours. 🐕 Guide dogs only. ✳

Squerryes Court & Gardens, Kent

berkshire   buckinghamshire   hampshire   kent   oxfordshire

south east

Eight counties make up the this region. All are easily accessible in a day trip from London and offer a wealth of historical interest. Kent is not only 'the Garden of England', with acres of fruit orchards and hop gardens, but also houses the site of the centre of the Anglican faith at Canterbury Cathedral, founded by St Augustine, in 597AD. Following the murder of St Thomas à Becket in 1170, the Cathedral became a place of pilgrimage, which it remains today. In each of these counties you can find world-famous properties such as Windsor Castle (Berkshire), Blenheim Palace (Oxfordshire), and Leeds Castle (Kent) – but do try to visit the lesser known treasures as well. Belmont (Kent), Broughton Castle (Oxfordshire) and Great Dixter House & Gardens (Sussex) are among those that give a deeper insight into Britain's heritage and history both architectural and horticultural.

surrey   sussex   isle of wight

BASILDON PARK

www.nationaltrust.org.uk/basildonpark

This beautiful Palladian mansion stars as Netherfield in the 2005 feature film adaptation of Jane Austin's classic novel *Pride and Prejudice*, and throughout 2006 you can see a fascinating exhibition which explains the enormous amount of work which went on behind the scenes at Basildon Park.

The beauty of Basildon Park is that it is here at all. At many times during its 220-year history it has faced decay, neglect and obliteration. After the Second World War, it seemed that it would go the way of many of England's great country houses and be pulled down.

Yet today Basildon's house and grounds are a fantastic example of how a passion for architecture, interiors and landscape, a personal attachment to a fine home and, most of all, perseverance through adversity, can make grand dreams a reality.

A striking Palladian house built between 1776 and 1783 by John Carr, Basildon Park was the home of Sir Francis Sykes, a man who had made his fortune in India. In the 19th century it was sold to the Liberal MP James Morrison, who completed some of the interiors left unfurnished by Sykes when his fortunes faltered.

From the early years of the 20th century, however, it remained variously empty or utilised for the war effort, during which time most of its contents and fittings were sold, damaged, dispersed or destroyed. By the early 1950s it seemed as if demolition was inevitable.

Its saviours were Lord and Lady Iliffe, who restored and refurnished the house to a grandeur that once seemed impossible. They in turn gave the house and grounds to the National Trust, to secure their future and to enable future generations to enjoy what was very nearly lost.

The house has rich interiors with fine plasterwork, pictures and furniture, and includes an unusual Octagon Room and a decorative Shell Room.

Owner:
The National Trust

▶ CONTACT

The Property Manager
Basildon Park
Lower Basildon
Reading
Berkshire RG8 9NR

Tel: 0118 984 3040
Infoline: 01494 755558
Fax: 0118 976 7370

e-mail: basildonpark@
nationaltrust.org.uk

▶ LOCATION

OS Ref. SU611 782

2¹/₂ m NW of Pangbourne on the west side of the A329, 7m from M4/J12.

▶ OPENING TIMES

House:
22 Mar - 29 Oct: daily except Mon & Tue (open BH Mons), 12 noon - 5pm.

Property closes at 4pm 18 - 20 Aug.

Park, Garden, Woodland Walk & Restaurant:
as house, 11am - 5pm.

Shop: as house plus
1 Nov - 17 Dec:
12 noon - 4pm.

Exhibition: As house all year. Costumes from the film on display. Apr - end June.

▶ ADMISSION

House, Park & Garden:
Adult	£5.30
Child	£2.65
Family	£13.25

Park & Garden only:
Adult	£2.70
Child	£1.35
Family	£6.75

Groups (15+) by appointment £4.00

All information correct at time of going to print.

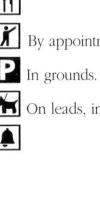 By appointment.
P In grounds.
On leads, in grounds only.

© Universal Studios

South East - England

Windsor Castle. Peter Packer/The Royal Collection © 2006 HM Queen Elizabeth II

WINDSOR CASTLE
ST GEORGE'S CHAPEL & FROGMORE HOUSE
www.royalcollection.org.uk

Owner:
Official Residence of Her Majesty The Queen

▶ **CONTACT**

Ticket Sales & Information Office
Buckingham Palace
London SW1A 1AA

Tel: 020 7766 7304
Groups (15+): 020 7766 7321
Fax: 020 7930 9625

e-mail: bookinginfo@ royalcollection.org.uk

▶ **LOCATION**
OS Ref. SU969 770

M4/J6, M3/J3. 20m from central London.

Rail: Regular service from London Waterloo and London Paddington.

Coach: Victoria Coach Station - regular service.

Sightseeing tours: Tour companies operate a daily service with collection from many London hotels. Ask your hotel concierge or porter for information.

Whichever way you approach the town of Windsor, the view is dominated by the dramatic outline of Windsor Castle, the largest inhabited castle in the world and the oldest royal residence to have remained in continuous use by the monarchs of Britain. Today, along with Buckingham Palace and the Palace of Holyroodhouse in Edinburgh, it is one of the official residences of Her Majesty The Queen.

Windsor's rich history spans more than 900 years but, as a working royal palace, the Castle plays a large part in the official work of The Queen and members of the Royal Family today. The magnificent State Rooms are furnished with some of the finest works of art from the Royal Collection, including paintings by Rembrandt and drawings by Leonardo da Vinci. Visitors should not miss the Castle Precinct Tours (which depart at regular intervals from the Admission Centre), Queen Mary's Dolls' House, a masterpiece in minature, and the last and largest suit of armour made for Henry VIII.

Within the precincts is St George's Chapel, one of the most beautiful ecclesiastical buildings in England. Ten monarchs are buried here, including Henry VIII with his favourite wife, Jane Seymour.

Frogmore House has been a favourite royal retreat for over 300 years. It is open to visitors on a limited number of days during the year. Guided pre-booked group visits are available throughout August and September. Please contact the Ticket Sales & Information Office for details.

St George's Chapel, Windsor Castle.

Frogmore House. Grand Reception Room.

 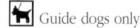 No photography. Audio Tours Windsor Castle. None. Guide dogs only.

▶ **OPENING TIMES**

March - October: Daily except 14 Apr & 19 Jun: 9.45am - 5.15pm. Last admission 4pm.

November - February: Daily except 25/26 Dec, 9.45am - 4.15pm. Last admission 3pm.

The State Rooms are closed 9 - 20 Jan & 17 - 20 Jun. (Reduced admission prices apply.)

Opening arrangements may change at short notice. 24-hr info line 01753 831118.

Private Evening Tours of the Castle for groups contact 020 7766 7322.

St George's Chapel is closed to visitors on Sundays as services are held throughout the day. Worshippers are welcome.

Frogmore House & Mausoleum
16 - 18 May and 26 - 28 Aug. For prices (Frogmore House & Mausoleum only) contact 020 7766 7305.

Private Tours of the house for pre-booked groups (15+) 1 Aug - 28 Sept. Contact 020 7766 7321.

▶ **ADMISSION**
For admission prices please contact our Ticket Sales and Information office

Groups (15+) Discounts available.

All information correct at time of going to print.

SPECIAL EVENTS

With the exception of Sundays, the Changing of the Guard takes place at 11am daily from April to the end of June and on alternate days at other times of the year.

BASILDON PARK ⚜   See page 104 for full page entry.

DONNINGTON CASTLE ⌗
Newbury, Berkshire
Tel: 01424 775705   **www**.english-heritage.org.uk/visits
Owner: English Heritage   **Contact:** 1066 Battle Abbey
Built in the late 14th century, the twin towered gatehouse of this heroic castle survives amidst some impressive earthworks.
Location: OS Ref. SU463 691. 1 mile N of Newbury off B4494.
Open: All year: Any reasonable time (exterior viewing only).
Admission: Free.
♿Steep slopes within grounds. 🅿 🚍 On leads. ✳

DORNEY COURT 🏠
WINDSOR, BERKSHIRE SL4 6QP
www.dorneycourt.co.uk
Tel: 01628 604638   **e-mail:** palmer@dorneycourt.co.uk
Owner/Contact: Mrs Peregrine Palmer
Just a few miles from the heart of bustling Windsor lies "one of the finest Tudor Manor Houses in England", *Country Life*. Grade I listed with the added accolade of being of outstanding architectural and historical importance, the visitor can get a rare insight into the lifestyle of the squirearchy through 550 years, with the Palmer family, who still live there today, owning the house for 450 of these years. The house boasts a magnificent Great Hall, family portraits, oak and lacquer furniture, needlework and panelled rooms. A private tour on a 'non-open day' takes around 1½ hours, but when open to the public this is reduced to around 40 mins. The adjacent 13th century Church of St James, with Norman font and Tudor tower can also be visited, as well as the adjoining Plant Centre in our walled garden where light lunches and full English cream teas are served in a tranquil setting throughout the day.
Location: OS Ref. SU926 791. 5 mins off M4/J7, 10mins from Windsor, 2m W of Eton.
Open: May: BH Suns & Mons; Aug: daily except Sats, 1.30 - 4pm (last admission).
Admission: Adult: £6, Child (10yrs +) £4. Groups (20+): By arrangement all year.
ℹ Film & photographic shoots. No stiletto heels. 🌱 Garden centre. 🌂
♿Garden centre. 🍴 🅵 🅿 🚍 Guide dogs only. ✳

ETON COLLEGE 🏠
Windsor, Berkshire SL4 6DW
Tel: 01753 671177   **Fax:** 01753 671029   **www**.etoncollege.com
e-mail: r.hunkin@etoncollege.org.uk
Owner: Provost & Fellows   **Contact:** Rebecca Hunkin
Eton College, founded in 1440 by Henry VI, is one of the oldest and best known schools in the country. The original and subsequent historic buildings of the Foundation are a part of the heritage of the British Isles and visitors are invited to experience and share the beauty of the ancient precinct which includes the magnificent College Chapel, a masterpiece of the perpendicular style.
Location: OS Ref. SU967 779. Off M4/J5. Access from Windsor by footbridge only. Vehicle access from Slough 2m N.
Open: Mar - early Oct: Times vary, best to check with the Visits Office.
Admission: Ordinary admissions and daily guided tours during the season at 2.15pm and 3.15pm. Groups by appointment only. Rates vary according to type of tour.
📷 🌂 ♿Ground floor. WC. 🅵 🅿 Limited. 🚍Guide dogs only.

SAVILL GARDEN
WINDSOR GREAT PARK, BERKSHIRE SL4 2HT
www.savillgarden.co.uk
Tel: 01753 847518   **Fax:** 01753 847536   **e-mail:** savillgarden@thecrownestate.co.uk
Owner: Crown Estate Commissioners   **Contact:** Jan Bartholomew
World-renowned 35 acre woodland garden, providing a wealth of beauty and interest in all seasons. Spring is heralded by hosts of daffodils, masses of rhododendrons, azaleas, camellias, magnolias and much more. Roses, herbaceous borders and countless alpines are the great features of summer, and the leaf colours and fruits of autumn rival the other seasons with a great display.
Location: OS Ref. SU977 706. Wick Lane, Englefield Green. Clearly signposted from Ascot, Bagshot, Egham and Windsor. Nearest station: Egham.
Open: Mar - Oct: 10am - 6pm. Nov - Feb: 10am - 4pm.
Admission: Mar - Oct: Adult £5.50, Child (6-16yrs) £2.75, Conc. £4.95, Family (2+2) £15 (+£2 additional child). Groups (10+) £4.40. Nov - Feb: Adult £4, Child (6-16yrs) £2, Conc. £3.60, Family (2+2) £12 (+£1.25 additional child). Groups (10+) £3.20. Child up 5yrs Free.
ℹ Film & photographic shoots. 📷 🌱Plant centre. ♿Grounds. WC. 🍴 Licensed.
🅵For groups, by appointment. 🚍 Guide dogs only. ✳

TAPLOW COURT 🏠
BERRY HILL, TAPLOW, Nr MAIDENHEAD, BERKS SL6 0ER
www.sgi-uk.org
Tel: 01628 591209   **Fax:** 01628 773055
Owner: SGI-UK   **Contact:** Michael Yeadon
Set high above the Thames, affording spectacular views. Remodelled mid-19th century by William Burn. Earlier neo-Norman Hall. 18th century home of Earls of Orkney and more recently of Lord and Lady Desborough who entertained 'The Souls' here. Tranquil gardens & grounds. Anglo-Saxon burial mound. Permanent and temporary exhibitions.
Location: OS Ref. SU907 822. M4/J7 off Bath Road towards Maidenhead. 6m off M40/J2.
Open: House & Grounds: 28 May - 30 Jul & 10 Sept: Sun & BH Mons, 2 - 5.30pm. Groups at other times by appointment.
Admission: No charge. Free parking.
📷 ♿ 🍴 🅵 🚍 🅿 🚍 Guide dogs only. 🍴 Tel for details.

WELFORD PARK

Newbury, Berkshire RG20 8HU
Tel: 01488 608203/608691
Owner/Contact: Mr J Puxley
A Queen Anne house, with attractive gardens and grounds. Riverside walks.
Location: OS Ref. SU409 731. On Lambourn Valley Road. 6m NW of Newbury.
Open: 5 Jun - 7 Jul: Mon - Sat, 11am - 5pm. Closed 17 June. Home made cream teas available for groups (10+), must book 7 days in advance.
Admission: Booked House Tour: Adult £5, Children under 16yrs free. Grounds: Free except when occasionally open in aid of charities.
Grounds. On leads, in grounds. Obligatory.

WINDSOR CASTLE, ST GEORGE'S CHAPEL & FROGMORE HOUSE

See page 105 for full page entry.

open all year
see page 557

Pride and Prejudice, Basildon Park.

MAP 7

STOWE HOUSE

www.shpt.co.uk

Owner:
Stowe House
Preservation Trust

▶ **CONTACT**

Visitor Services Manager
Stowe School
Buckingham
MK18 5EH

Tel: 01280 818229

Fax: 01280 818186
House only

e-mail:
amcevoy@stowe.co.uk

▶ **LOCATION**
OS Ref. SP666 366

From London, M1 to
Milton Keynes, 1¹/₂ hrs
or Banbury 1¹/₄ hrs,
3m NW of Buckingham.

Bus: Buckingham 3m.

Rail: Milton Keynes 15m.

Air: Heathrow 50m.

Stowe offers its pre-eminence to the vision and wealth of two great owners. From 1715 to 1749 Viscount Cobham, one of Marlborough's Generals, continuously improved his estate, calling in the leading designers of the day to lay out the Gardens and commissioning several leading architects – Vanburgh, Gibbs, Kent and Leoni – to decorate them with garden temples. From 1750 to 1779 Earl Temple, his nephew and heir, continued to expand and embellish both House and Gardens. As the House and Gardens were expanded, and political and military intrigues followed, the family eventually fell into debt, resulting in two great sales – 1848 when all the contents were sold and 1922 when the contents and the estate were sold off separately. The House is now part of a major public school, since 1923, and owned by Stowe House Preservation Trust, since 2000. Over the last four years, through the Trust, the House has under gone two phases of a six phase restoration – the North Front and Colonnades, the Central Pavilion and South Portico and the absolutely spectacular Marble Saloon, dating from the 1770s. Around the mansion is one of Britain's most magnificent and complete landscape gardens, taken over from the School by the National Trust in 1989. The Gardens have since undergone a huge, and continuing, restoration programme, and with the House restoration, Stowe is slowly being returned to its 18th century status on one of the most complete neo-classical estates in Europe.

©Jerry Hardman-Jones

ℹ️ Indoor swimming pool, sports hall, tennis court, squash courts, astroturf, parkland, cricket pitches and golf course.
No photography in house.

🔧 International conferences, private functions, weddings, and prestige exhibitions. Catering on request.

♿ Visitors may alight at entrance, tel. 01280 818229 for details. Allocated parking. WC. 'Batricars' available (from NT - tel. 01280 818825).

  Morning coffee, lunch and afternoon tea available by pre-arrangement only, for up to 80.

🚶 For parties of 15 - 60 at additional cost. Tour time: house and garden 2¹/₂ - 4¹/₂ hrs, house only 1¹/₂ hrs.

🅿️ Ample.

🚭

🐕 In grounds on leads.

⚭ Civil Wedding Licence.

❄️ Available.

▶ **OPENING TIMES**

House
Easter & Summer
School Holidays.
Wed - Sun 12noon - 5pm
(last admission 4pm),
Guided tour at 2pm & also
in term times, please check
website or telephone for
further details.

▶ **ADMISSION**

House
Adult £3.00
Child (5 - 16yrs) £2.50

House and Tour
Adult £4.00
Child (5 - 16yrs) £3.00
under 5s ....Free

Open to private groups
(15 - 60 persons), all year
round at discounted rates.
Please telephone 01280
818229 to pre-book.

Phase 3 of Restoration; will
mean restricted access,
check website
(www.shpt.org) or 24hr
telephone line (01280
818166) for details, exact
opening times and prices.

Visit both The National
Trust Gardens & the
House. For Gardens
opening times telephone
01280 822850 or visit
www.nationaltrust.org.uk
/stowegardens

▶ **SPECIAL EVENTS**
Please check website
for 2006 events:
www.stoweevents.co.uk

CONFERENCE/FUNCTION

ROOM	MAX CAPACITY
Roxburgh Hall	460
Music Room	100
Marble Hall	200
State Dining Rm	160
Garter Room	160

©NTPL, Waddesdon Manor

MAP 7

WADDESDON MANOR

www.waddesdon.org.uk

Waddesdon Manor was built (1874-89), in the style of a 16th century French château, for Baron Ferdinand de Rothschild to entertain his guests and display his vast collection of art treasures. It houses one of the finest collections of French 18th century decorative arts in the world. The furniture, Savonnerie carpets, and Sèvres porcelain rank in importance with the Metropolitan Museum in New York and the Louvre in Paris. There is also a collection of portraits by Gainsborough and Reynolds and works by Dutch and Flemish Masters of the 17th century.

Waddesdon has one of the finest Victorian gardens in Britain, renowned for its colourful parterre, seasonal displays, shady walks and views, fountains and statuary. At its heart lies the rococo-style aviary which houses a splendid collection of exotic birds and is known for breeding endangered species. Thousands of bottles of vintage Rothschild wines are found in the wine cellars.

There is a gift shop, a wine shop with a full selection of Rothschild wines, and two licensed restaurants. A full programme of events is organised throughout the year including special interest days, wine tastings and family events.

▶ CONTACT

Waddesdon
Nr Aylesbury
Buckinghamshire
HP18 0JH

Tel (24-hour recorded info):
01296 653211

Booking & Info (Mon - Fri 10am - 4pm):
01296 653226

Fax: 01296 653212
email:
waddesdonmanor@
nationaltrust.org.uk

▶ LOCATION

OS Ref. SP740 169

Between Aylesbury & Bicester, off A41.

Rail: Aylesbury 6m.

©National Trust, Waddesdon Manor

ℹ️ No photography in house.

🏬 Gift and Wine Shops.

♟ Conferences, corporate hospitality.

♿ WCs.

🍷 Licensed.

🍴 Licensed.

🚶 By arrangement. 🎧

🅿️ Ample for coaches and cars.

🐕 Assistance dogs only.

🔔 Civil Wedding Licence.

🎭 **SPECIAL EVENTS**

Wine Tasting, Special Interest Days, Family Events. Please telephone 01296 653226 for details.

NT members free. HHA Members free entry to grounds. RHS members free to grounds in Mar, Sept & Oct.

A timed ticket system to the House is in operation. Tickets can be purchased up to 24 hours in advance for a fee of £3 per transaction from the Booking Office.

Children welcomed under parental supervision in the House. Babies must be carried in a front-sling.

Reservations can be made at the Manor Restaurant. Tel: 01296 653242.

▶ OPENING TIMES

Gardens (incl. Aviary, Restaurants, and Shops)

7 Jan - 26 Mar: weekends only, 10am -5pm (Stables Restaurant open w'ends Mar).

Main Season
29 Mar - 23 Dec, Wed - Sun & BH Mons & 18/19 Dec 10am - 5pm.

House (inc Wine Cellars) Main Season
29 Mar - 29 Oct, Wed - Sun & BH Mons, 11am - 4pm (Last rec admission 2.30pm)

Bachelors' Wing
29 Mar - 29 Oct: Wed - Fri 11am - 4pm. Space is limited so entry cannot be guaranteed.

Christmas Season (East Wing decorated for the festive season)
15 Nov - 23 Dec
Wed - Sun & 18/19 Dec 12 noon - 4pm. Sat & Sun 11am - 4pm.

Timed tickets to house avail. up to 24 hrs in advance, (by Fri for w/ends). Booking fee £3 per transaction. Please call Booking Office.

▶ ADMISSION

House & Grounds

Adult	£12.00
Christmas	£9.00
Child (5-16 yrs)	£8.50
Christmas	£4.50

*Groups (15+)

Adult	£9.60
Christmas	£7.20
Child	£6.80
Christmas	£3.60

Grounds only

Adult	£5.00
Child (5-16 yrs)	£2.50

Groups

Adult	£4.00
Child	£2.00

Bachelors' Wing .. £3.00

Children under 5 free.

*No group discount w/ends.

ASCOTT ✤

Wing, Leighton Buzzard, Bucks LU7 0PS
Tel: 01296 688242 **Fax:** 01296 681904
e-mail: info@ascottestate.co.uk **www.**ascottestate.co.uk
Owner: The National Trust **Contact:** Resident Agent
Originally a half-timbered Jacobean farmhouse, Ascott was bought in 1876 by the de Rothschild family and considerably transformed and enlarged. It now houses a quite exceptional collection of fine paintings, Oriental porcelain and English and French furniture. The extensive gardens are a mixture of the formal and natural, containing specimen trees and shrubs, as well as an herbaceous walk, lily pond, Dutch garden and remarkable topiary sundial.
Location: OS Ref. SP891 230. ¹/₂ m E of Wing, 2m SW of Leighton Buzzard, on A418.
Open: House & Garden: 14 Mar - 30 Apr: daily except Mons, 2 - 6pm. 2 May - 27 Jul: Tues - Thurs, 2 - 6pm. Aug: daily except Mons, 2 - 6pm. Last admission 5pm. Closed BH Mons and Good Fri.
Admission: Adult £7, Child £3.50. Garden only: £4. Child £2. No reduction for groups which must book. NT members charged on NGS days.
♿Ground floor & grounds with assistance. 3 wheelchairs available. WCs.
🅿 220 metres. 🐾 In car park only, on leads.

BOARSTALL DUCK DECOY ✤

Boarstall, Aylesbury, Buckinghamshire HP18 9UX
Tel: 01844 237488 / 01280 822850 (Visitor Services Manager Mon - Fri)
e-mail: stowegarden@nationaltrust.org.uk
Owner: The National Trust **Contact:** Visitor Services Manager
A rare survival of a 17th century decoy in working order, set on a tree-fringed lake, with nature trail and exhibition hall.
Location: OS Ref. SP624 151. Midway between Bicester and Thame, 2m W of Brill.
Open: Apr - Aug: Sats & Suns, 10am - 4pm; 1 Apr - 31 Aug: Weds, 3.30 - 6.30pm. Displays on Sats, Suns, & BH Mons: 11am & 3pm; Weds: 3.30pm. Bird walks and woodland talks occasionally, please telephone for details. Please telephone for winter opening details.
Admission: Adult £2.40, Child £1.20. Family £6. Groups (6+) must book: £1.50.
♿Partial. 🏠 By arrangement. 🐾 In car park only, on leads.

BOARSTALL TOWER ✤

Boarstall, Aylesbury, Buckinghamshire HP18 9UX
Tel: 01844 239339 / 01280 822850 (Mon - Fri)
Owner: The National Trust **Contact:** Visitor Services Manager
The stone gatehouse of a fortified house long since demolished. It dates from the 14th century, and was altered in the 16th and 17th centuries, but retains its crossloops for bows. The gardens are surrounded by a moat on three sides.
Location: OS Ref. SP624 141. Midway between Bicester and Thame, 2m W of Brill.
Open: 5 Apr - 25 Oct: Weds, 2 - 6pm. BH Sats: 11am - 4pm & BH Mons: 2 - 6pm.
Admission: Adult £2.40, Child £1.20, Family £6.
ℹ️ No WC. ♿ Ground floor & garden (steps to entrance). 🐾 In car park only.

BUCKINGHAM CHANTRY CHAPEL ✤

Market Hill, Buckingham
Tel: 01280 822850 (Mon - Fri) **Fax:** 01280 822437
Owner: The National Trust **Contact:** Buckingham Heritage Trust
Rebuilt in 1475 and retaining a fine Norman doorway. The chapel was restored by Gilbert Scott in 1875, at which time it was used as a Latin or Grammar School.
Location: OS Ref. SP693 340. In narrow lane, NW of Market Hill.
Open: All year, Sats, 9am - 1pm. Other times by appointment with the Buckingham Heritage Trust, c/o Old Gaol Museum, Market Hill, Buckingham MK18 1JX.
Admission: Free. Donations welcome.
ℹ️ No WCs. ♿ ❄️

CHENIES MANOR HOUSE 🏛

CHENIES, BUCKINGHAMSHIRE WD3 6ER

Tel/Fax: 01494 762888
Owners: Mrs MacLeod Matthews & Mr Charles MacLeod Matthews
Contact: Sue Brock

Home of the MacLeod Matthews family, this 15th and 16th century Manor House with fortified tower, is the original home of the Earls of Bedford. Visited by Henry VIII and Elizabeth I. She was a frequent visitor, first coming as an infant in 1534 and as Queen she visited on several occasions, one being for a six week period. The Bedford Mausoleum is in the adjacent church. The House contains tapestries and furniture mainly of the 16th and 17th centuries, hiding places, a collection of antique dolls, medieval undercroft and well. In the grounds stands the newly-restored 16th century pavilion which contains various exhibitions and most unusual cellars. The house is surrounded by beautiful gardens, famed for the spring display of tulips, which have featured in many publications and on TV. Tudor sunken garden, white garden, herbaceous borders, fountain court, physic garden containing a wide selection of medicinal and culinary herbs, parterre with an ancient oak, complicated yew maze and kitchen garden in Victorian style with unusual vegetables and fruit. Attractive dried and fresh flowers arrangements throughout the house. Our renowned annual Plant Fair will be held on 16 July with stalls from some of England's best nurseries. A Nature Trail consisting of woodlands, riverside and water meadow is suitable for childrens' groups. Delicious home-made teas.

Location: OS Ref TQ016 984. N of A404, between Amersham and Rickmansworth, M25/J18 3m.
Open: 5 April - 26 Oct & BH Mons, 2 - 5pm. Last entry to house 4.15 p.m.
Admission: House & garden: Adult £5.50, Child £3. Garden only: Adult £3.50, Child £1.50. Groups (20+) by arrangement throughout the year.
🌱 Unusual plants for sale. 🍽 ♿ Grounds. ☕ 🅿 Free nearby. 🐾 ❄️
🍴 Tel for details.

open all year
see page 557
❄️

CHILTERN OPEN AIR MUSEUM

Newland Park, Gorelands Lane, Chalfont St Giles, Buckinghamshire HP8 4AB

Tel: 01494 871117   **Fax:** 01494 872774

Owner: Chiltern Open Air Museum Ltd   **Contact:** Phil Holbrook

A museum of historic buildings showing their original uses including a blacksmith's forge, stables, barns etc.

Location: OS Ref. TQ011 938. At Newland Park 1½ m E of Chalfont St Giles, 4½ m from Amersham. 3m from M25/J17.

Open: Apr - Oct: daily. Please telephone for details.

Admission: Adult £7, Child (5-16yrs) £4.50, Child under 5yrs Free, OAP £6, Family (2+2) £20.50. Groups discount available on request.

CLAYDON HOUSE ✂

MIDDLE CLAYDON, Nr BUCKINGHAM MK18 2EY

Tel: 01296 730349   **Fax:** 01296 738511   **Infoline:** 01494 755561

e-mail: claydon@nationaltrust.org.uk

Owner: The National Trust   **Contact:** The Custodian

A fine 18th century house with some of the most perfect rococo decoration in England. A series of great rooms have wood carvings in Chinese and Gothic styles, and tall windows look out over parkland and a lake. The house has relics of the exploits of the Verney family in the English Civil War and also on show is the bedroom of Florence Nightingale, a relative of the Verneys and a regular visitor to this tranquil place.

Location: OS Ref. SP720 253. In Middle Claydon, 13m NW of Aylesbury, signposted from A413 and A41. 3½ m SW of Winslow.

Open: House & Grounds: 25 Mar - 29 Oct: daily except Thur & Fri; House, 1 - 5pm, last admission 4.30pm. Restaurant (non-NT): 25 Mar - 29 Oct, daily except Thur & Fri, 12 noon - 6pm.

Admission: Adult £5.50, Child £2.70, Family £13. Groups (15+): Adult £4.50 (50p extra for guided tour). Private Gardens open this year for first time same days as House. Adult £2.50, including National Trust Members.

ℹ️ No photography. No pushchairs. No backpacks. No baby carriers. No large bags. Second-hand books, pottery & florist. Ground floor only. WC. Braille guide. Photograph album. Ramp. For groups only, by arrangement. Limited for coaches. In parkland only, on leads. Tel for details..

©National Trust Photographic Library/Derek Croucher

Cliveden.

NT Photographic Library

CLIVEDEN ✣

TAPLOW, MAIDENHEAD SL6 0JA

Tel: 01628 605069   **Infoline:** 01494 755562   **Fax:** 01628 669461

e-mail: cliveden@nationaltrust.org.uk

Owner: The National Trust   **Contact:** Property Manager

152 hectares of gardens and woodland. A water garden, 'secret' garden, herbaceous borders, topiary, a great formal parterre, and informal vistas provide endless variety. The garden statuary is one of the most important collections in the care of The National Trust and includes many Roman antiquities collected by 1st Viscount Astor. The Octagon Temple (Chapel) with its rich mosaic interior is open on certain days, as is part of the house (see below).

NT Photographic Library: Ian Shaw

Location: OS Ref. SU915 851. 3m N of Maidenhead, M4/J7 onto A4 or M40/J4 onto A404 to Marlow and follow signs. From London by train take Thames Train service from Paddington to Burnham (taxi rank and office adjacent to station).

Open: Estate & Garden: 15 Mar - 29 Oct, daily, 11am - 6pm; 30 Oct - 22 Dec, daily, 11am - 4pm. House (part)& Octagon Temple: 2 Apr - 29 Oct: Thurs & Sun, 3 - 5.30pm. Admission to house by timed ticket, obtainable from information kiosk only. Woodlands: 1 Apr - 29 Oct, daily, 11am - 5.30pm; 30 Oct - 22 Dec & 2 Jan - 31 Mar, daily, 11am - 4pm. Restaurant: 15 Mar - 29 Oct, daily, 11am - 5pm; 4 Nov - 17 Dec, Sat & Sun, 11am - 3pm. Shop: 15 Mar - 29 Oct, daily, 12 noon - 5.30pm; 30 Oct - 22 Dec, daily, 12 noon - 4pm. Some areas of formal garden may be roped off when ground conditions are bad.

Admission: Grounds: Adult £7.50 Child £3.70, Family £18.70, Groups (must book) £6.50 House: £1 extra, Child 50p extra. Note: Mooring charge on Cliveden Reach.
🖰 ⬇Partial. WC. 🍴Licensed. 🐕Specified woodlands only. ✳ 📺Tel for details.

COWPER & NEWTON MUSEUM

Home of Olney's Heritage, Orchard Side, Market Place, Olney MK46 4AJ

Tel: 01234 711516   **e-mail:** cnm@mkheritage.co.uk

www.cowperandnewtonmuseum.org.uk

Owner: Board of Trustees   **Contact:** Mrs J McKillop

Once the home of 18th century poet and letter writer William Cowper and now containing furniture, paintings and belongings of both Cowper and his ex-slave trader friend, Rev John Newton (author of "Amazing Grace"). Attractions include re-creations of a Victorian country kitchen and wash-house, two peaceful gardens and Cowper's restored summerhouse. Costume gallery, important collections of dinosaur bones and bobbin lace, and local history displays.

Location: OS Ref. SP890 512. On A509, 6m N of Newport Pagnell, M1/J14.

Open: 1 Mar - 23 Dec: Tue - Sat & BH Mons, 10am - 1pm & 2 - 5pm. Closed on Good Fri. Open on Sundays in June, July & August, 2 - 5pm.

Admission: Adult £3, Conc. £2, Child & Students (with card) £1.50, Family £7.50.
ℹNo photography. 🖰 ⬇Gardens. 𝑓By arrangement. 🖰 🐕Guide dogs only.

FORD END WATERMILL

Station Road, Ivinghoe, Buckinghamshire

Tel: 01582 600391   **Contact:** David Lindsey

The Watermill, a listed building, was recorded in 1616 but is probably much older.

Location: OS Ref. SP941 166. 600 metres from Ivinghoe Church along B488 (Station Road) to Leighton Buzzard.

Open: Easter Mon - end Sept: 2nd & 4th Suns of each month & BHs, 2.30 - 5.30pm. Milling between 3 - 5pm on BHs and the 2nd Sun in May (National Mills Day) and 4th Sun in Sept.

Admission: Adult £1.50, Child 50p (5 - 15yrs). Schools: Child 75p, Adults Free.

Chenies Manor House & Garden.

NT Photographic Library, Matthew Antrobus

HUGHENDEN MANOR ❧
HIGH WYCOMBE HP14 4LA

Tel: 01494 755573/ 755565 - Infoline   **Fax:** 01494 474284
e-mail: hughenden@nationaltrust.org.uk
Owner: The National Trust   **Contact:** The Property Manager
Home of Prime Minister Benjamin Disraeli from 1847 - 1881. The interior is a comfortable Victorian home and still holds many of Disraeli's pictures, books and furniture. The surrounding park and woodland have lovely walks, and the formal garden has been recreated in the spirit of Mary Anne Disraeli's colourful designs.
Location: OS 165 Ref. SU866 955. 1½ m N of High Wycombe on the W side of the A4128.
Open: House: 1 Mar - 5 Nov, 11am - 4.30pm (11am - 1pm by guided tour only, £1pp).

Wed - Sun & BH Mon. Open Good Fri. On BHs & busy days entry is by timed ticket. Gardens open same days as house, 11am - 5pm. Shop and Restaurant: open 11am - 5pm also 8 Nov - 23 Dec, 11am - 4pm. Park & Woodland: All year.
Admission: House & Garden: Adult £6, Child £3, Family £15. Groups: Adult £5, Child £2.50. Garden only: Adult £2.50, Child £1.80. Park & Woodland Free. No groups at weekends or BHs.

⬛ ♿ Ground floor only. WC. 🍴 🎫 For booked groups. 🎧
🐕 In grounds, on leads. Guide dogs in house & formal gardens. ❉ 🅱 Tel for details.

THE KING'S HEAD ❧
King's Head Passage, Market Square, Aylesbury, Buckinghamshire HP20 2RW
Tel: 01296 381501   **Fax:** 01296 381502   **e-mail:** kingshead@nationaltrust.org.uk
Owner: The National Trust   **Contact:** The Custodian
This enchanting inn dates back to 1455 and remains a unique place to enjoy real ale or even a glass of Rothschild wine. It has many noteworthy architectural features including a medieval stained glass window, extensive timber framing and an ancient cobbled courtyard. Once a base for Oliver Cromwell it now houses a bookshop, coffee shop and visitor centre.
Location: OS Ref. SP818 138. At NW corner of Aylesbury Market Square.
Open: All year: Mon - Sat, 10am - 3pm and normal pub hours. Guided tours on Wed, Fri & Sat at 2pm.
Admission: Adult £2 (incl tour). NT members Free.
🎫 ♿ Partial. WC. 🍴 Licensed. 🎫 Obligatory. 🅿 None. ⬛ 🐕 Guide dogs only. ❉

LONG CRENDON COURTHOUSE ❧
High St, Long Crendon, Buckinghamshire
Tel: 01280 822850 (Mon - Fri)   **e-mail:** stowegarden@nationaltrust.org.uk
www.nationaltrust.org.uk
Owner: The National Trust   **Contact:** Visitor Services Manager
A fantastic opportunity to see very clearly a 15th century building. The exposed timber beams and early oak floorboards are a rare sight.
Location: OS Ref. SP698 091. 3miles N of Thame.
Open: 1 Apr - 30 Sept: Weds: 2 - 6pm. Sats, Suns & BH Mons, 11am - 6pm.
Admission: Adult £1, Child 50p.

JOHN MILTON'S COTTAGE
21 Deanway, Chalfont St. Giles, Buckinghamshire HP8 4JH
Tel: 01494 872313   **e-mail:** info@miltonscottage.org   **www.**miltonscottage.org
Owner: Milton Cottage Trust   **Contact:** Mr E A Dawson
Grade I listed 16th century cottage where John Milton lived and completed 'Paradise Lost' and started 'Paradise Regained'. Four ground floor museum rooms contain important first editions of John Milton's 17th century poetry and prose works. Amongst many unique items on display is the portrait of John Milton by Sir Godfrey Kneller. Well stocked, attractive cottage garden, listed by English Heritage.
Location: OS Ref. SU987 933. ½ m W of A413. 3m N of M40/J2. S side of street.
Open: 1 Mar - 31 Oct: Tue - Sun, 10am - 1pm & 2 - 6pm. Closed Mons (open BH Mons). Coach parking by prior arrangement only.
Admission: Adult £3, under 15s £1.50, Groups (20+) £2.
⬛ ♿ Ground floor. 🎫 Talk followed by free tour. 🅿 🐕

NETHER WINCHENDON HOUSE 🏠
Nether Winchendon, Nr Aylesbury, Buckinghamshire HP18 0DY
Tel: 01844 290101   **Fax:** 01844 290199   **www.**netherwinchendonhouse.com
Owner/Contact: Mr Robert Spencer Bernard
Medieval and Tudor manor house. Great Hall. Dining Room with fine 16th century frieze, ceiling and linenfold panelling. Fine furniture and family portraits. Home of Sir Francis Bernard Bt (d1779), the last British Governor of Massachussetts Bay. Continuous family occupation since mid-16th century. House altered in late 18th century in the Strawberry Hill Gothick style. Interesting garden (5 acres) and specimen trees.
Location: OS Ref. SP734 121. 2m N of A418 equidistant between Thame & Aylesbury.
Open: 1 - 29 May & 28 Aug: 2.30 - 5.30pm (conducted tours only at ¼ to each hour). Groups at any time by prior written agreement (minimum charge £100, no concessions).
Admission: Adult £5, OAP £4 (no concession at weekends or BHs), Child (under 12yrs) £2. HHA members free (not on special groups).
ℹ No WC. ♿ Please tel in advance. 🍴 By arrangement. 🎫 Obligatory. ❉

PITSTONE WINDMILL ❧
Ivinghoe, Buckinghamshire
Tel: 01442 851227   Group organisers: 01296 668223   **Fax:** 01442 850000
email: ashridge@nationaltrust.org.uk
Owner: The National Trust   **Contact:** William Hawkins
One of the oldest post mills in Britain; in view from Ivinghoe Beacon.
Location: OS Ref. SP946 158. ½ m S of Ivinghoe, 3m NE of Tring. Just W of B488.
Open: 4 Jun - 27 Aug: Sun & BHs, 2.30 - 6pm.
Admission: Adult £1, Child 30p.
ℹ No WC. ♿ Difficult access. 🅿

PRINCES RISBOROUGH MANOR HOUSE ❧
Princes Risborough, Aylesbury, Buckinghamshire HP17 9AW
Tel: 01494 755573   **Fax:** 01494 463310
Owner/Contact: The National Trust
A 17th century red-brick house with Jacobean oak staircase.
Location: OS Ref. SP806 035. Opposite church, off market square.
Open: House (hall, drawing room & staircase) and front garden by written appointment only with the lessee. 2 Mar - 25 Oct: Weds, 2.30 - 4.30pm.
Admission: Adult £1.40, Child 70p, Family £3.50.

STOWE LANDSCAPE GARDENS & PARK

Nr BUCKINGHAM MK18 5EH

www.nationaltrust.org.uk/stowegardens

Tel: 01280 822850   **Infoline:** 01494 755568   **Fax:** 01280 822437
Group Visits: 01280 822850   **e-mail:** stowegarden@nationaltrust.org.uk

Owner: The National Trust   **Contact:** The Property Manager

Discover one of Europe's most influential landscape gardens. Hidden amongst spectacular views and vast open spaces there are magical secret corners, hidden meanings, and over 40 monuments and temples waiting to be discovered. Visitors can also take a tour of Stowe House or explore the 750 acres of surrounding historic parkland, including the newly restored 250 acre Deer Park. Stowe is the perfect setting for a family picnic or those seeking peace and tranquility, with walks and trails for all to enjoy. With the changing seasons, continuing restoration and a calendar of events for all the family, each visit provides something new to discover. **New for 2006:** Completion of major work to the Corinthian Arch. Views not seen for over 200 years opened up with the restoration of the original 18th century Hermitage pathway. Recently completed work to the Central Pavilion, South Portico and Marble Saloon. Part of the ongoing restoration of the House.

Location: OS Ref. SP665 366. Off A422 Buckingham - Banbury Rd. 3m NW of Buckingham.

Open: Gardens, Shop & Tearooms: 1 Mar - 29 Oct, Wed - Sun, 10.30am - 5.30pm; 4 Nov - 25 Feb, Sat & Sun, 10.30am - 4pm. Open BH Mons. Last admission 1 hr. before closing. Gardens closed 27 May, 24/25 Dec, may close in extreme weather conditions. House not NT. For house opening times 01280 818166.

Admission: Gardens: Adult £6, Child £3, Family £15. Groups (by arrangement, 15+) Adult £5. House (incl. NT members): Phone 01280 818166. House admission payable at NT reception.

Pre-booked self-drive powered chairs available. WC. By arrangement. In grounds, on leads. Tel for details.

STOWE HOUSE   *See page 108 for full page entry.*

WADDESDON MANOR   *See page 109 for full page entry.*

WOTTON HOUSE

Wotton Underwood, Aylesbury, Buckinghamshire HP18 0SB

Tel: 01844 238363   **Fax:** 01844 238380

e-mail: david.gladstone@which.net   **Owner/Contact:** David Gladstone

The Capability Brown Pleasure Grounds at Wotton, currently undergoing restoration, are related to the Stowe gardens, both belonging to the Grenville family when Brown laid out the Wotton grounds between 1750 and 1767. A series of man-made features on the 3 mile circuit include bridges, follies and statues.

Location: OS Ref. 468576, 216168. Either A41 turn off Kingswood, or M40/J7 via Thame. Rail: Haddenham & Thame 6m.

Open: 12 Apr - 13 Sep: Wed only, 2pm - 5pm. Also 15 Apr, 29 May, 1 Jul, 5 Aug, 2 Sep: 2pm - 5pm.

Admission: Adult £5, Child Free, Conc. £3. Groups (max 25).

Obligatory. Limited.

WYCOMBE MUSEUM

Priory Avenue, High Wycombe, Buckinghamshire HP13 6PX

Tel: 01494 421895   **Fax:** 01494 421897

e-mail: museum@wycombe.gov.uk

Owner: Wycombe District Council   **Contact:** John Sugg

Set in historic Castle Hill House and surrounded by peaceful and attractive gardens.

Location: OS Ref. SU867 933. Signposted off the A404 High Wycombe/Amersham road. The Museum is about 5mins walk from the town centre and railway station.

Open: Mon - Sat, 10am - 5pm. Open Suns, 2 - 5pm. Closed BHs.

Admission: Free.

WEST WYCOMBE PARK

WEST WYCOMBE, HIGH WYCOMBE, BUCKINGHAMSHIRE HP14 3AJ

Tel: 01494 513569

Owner: The National Trust   **Contact:** The Head Guide

A perfectly preserved rococo landscape garden, created in the mid-18th century by Sir Francis Dashwood, founder of the Dilettanti Society and the Hellfire Club. The house is among the most theatrical and Italianate in England, its façades formed as classical temples. The interior has Palmyrene ceilings and decoration, with pictures, furniture and sculpture dating from the time of Sir Francis.

Location: OS Ref. SU828 947. At W end of West Wycombe S of the A40.

Open: House & Grounds: 1 Jun - 31 Aug: daily except Fri & Sat, 2 - 6pm. Weekday entry by guided tour only every 20 mins (approx), last admission 5.15pm. Grounds only: 2 Apr - 31 May: daily except Fri & Sat, 2 - 6pm.

Admission: House & Grounds: Adult £5.70, Child £2.80, Family £14.50. Grounds only: Adult £3, Child £1.50. Groups by arrangement. Note: The West Wycombe Caves and adjacent café are privately owned and NT members must pay admission fees.

Grounds partly suitable. Obligatory on weekdays. In car park only, on leads.

Waddesdon Manor – East Gallery.

115

MAP J

BEAULIEU 🏛

www.beaulieu.co.uk

The Beaulieu Estate has been owned by the same family since 1538 and is still the private home of the Montagus. Thomas Wriothesley, who later became the 1st Earl of Southampton, acquired the estate at the time of the Dissolution of the Monasteries when he was Lord Chancellor to Henry Vlll.

Palace House, overlooking the Beaulieu River, was once the Great Gatehouse of Beaulieu Abbey with its monastic origins reflected in the fan vaulted ceilings of the 14th Century Dining Hall and Lower Drawing Room. The rooms are decorated with furnishings, portraits and treasures collected by past and present generations of the family. Visitors can enjoy the fine gardens or take a riverside walk around the Monks' Mill Pond.

Beaulieu Abbey was founded in 1204 when King John gave the land to the Cistercians and although most of the buildings have now been destroyed, much of the beauty and interest remains. The former Monks' Refectory is now the local parish church and the Domus, which houses an exhibition and video presentation of monastic life, is home to beautiful wall hangings.

Beaulieu also houses the world famous National Motor Museum which traces the story of motoring from 1894 to the present day. 250 vehicles are on display including legendary world record breakers plus veteran, vintage and classic cars and motorcycles.

The modern Beaulieu is very much a family destination with many free and unlimited rides on a transportation theme to be enjoyed, including a mile long, high-level monorail and replica 1912 London open-topped bus.

Owner:
Lord Montagu

▶ CONTACT

John Montagu Building
Beaulieu
Brockenhurst
Hampshire SO42 7ZN

Tel: 01590 614769/87
Fax: 01590 612624

e-mail: conference@
beaulieu.co.uk

▶ LOCATION
OS Ref. SU387 025

M27 to J2,
A326, B3054 follow
brown signs.

Bus: Local service
within the New Forest.

Rail: Stations at
Brockenhurst 7m away.

▶ OPENING TIMES

Summer
May - September
Daily, 10am - 6pm.

Winter
October - April
Daily, 10am - 5pm.

Closed Christmas Day.

▶ ADMISSION

All Year

Individual rates upon
application.

Groups (15+)
Rates upon application.

CONFERENCE/FUNCTION

ROOM	SIZE	MAX CAPACITY
Brabazon (x3)	40'x40'	85 (x3)
Domus	69'x27'	150
Theatre		200
Palace House		60
Motor Museum		250

🎭 SPECIAL EVENTS

APR 23
Boatjumble & Boatworld

MAY 20/21
Spring Motormart &
Autojumble

JUNE (TBC)
Motorcycle World

SEPT 9/10
International Autojumble

OCT 28
Fireworks Spectacular

All enquiries should be made
to our Special Events Booking
Office where advance tickets
can be purchased. The contact
telephone is 01590 612888.

BEAULIEU…

CATERING AND FUNCTIONS

Beaulieu also offers a comprehensive range of facilities for conferences, company days out, product launches, management training, corporate hospitality, promotions, film locations, exhibitions and outdoor events.

The National Motor Museum is a unique venue for drinks receptions, evening product launches and dinners or the perfect complement to a conference as a relaxing visit.

The charming 13th century Domus hall with its beautiful wooden beams, stone walls and magnificent wall hangings, is the perfect setting for weddings, conferences, dinners, buffets or themed evenings.

Palace House, the ancestral home of Lord Montagu is an exclusive setting for smaller dinners, buffets and receptions. With a welcoming log fire in the winter and the coolness of the courtyard fountain in the summer, it offers a relaxing yet truly 'stately' atmosphere to ensure a memorable experience for your guests whatever the time of year

A purpose-built theatre, with tiered seating, can accommodate 200 people whilst additional meeting rooms can accommodate from 20 to 200 delegates. Bespoke marquees can also be erected on a charming parkland setting, for any event or occasion. With the nearby Beaulieu River offering waterborne activities and the Beaulieu Estate, with its purpose built off road course, giving you the opportunity of indulging in a variety of country pursuits and outdoor management training, Beaulieu provides a unique venue for your conference and corporate hospitality needs.

ℹ Allow 3 hrs or more for visits. Last adm. 40 mins before closing. Helicopter landing point. When visiting Beaulieu arrangements can be made to view the Estate's vineyards. Visits, which can be arranged between Apr - Oct, must be pre-booked at least one week in advance with Beaulieu Estate Office.

🛍 Palace House Shop and Kitchen Shop plus Main Reception Shop.

🍴

♿ Disabled visitors may be dropped off outside Visitor Reception before parking. WC. Wheelchairs can be provided free of charge in Visitor Reception by prior booking.

🍴 The Brabazon restaurant seats 250. Prices start at £18.95. Further details and menus from the Sales Office: 01590 614769.

🚶 Attendants on duty. Guided tours by prior arrangement for groups.

🅿 1,500 cars and 30 coaches. During the season the busy period is from 11.30am to 1.30pm. Coach drivers should sign in at Information Desk. Free admission for coach drivers plus voucher which can be exchanged for food, drink and souvenirs.

📖 Professional staff available to assist in planning of visits. Services include introductory talks, films, guided tours, rôle play and extended projects. In general, educational services incur no additional charges and publications are sold at cost. Information available from Education at Beaulieu, John Montagu Building, Beaulieu, Hants SO42 7ZN.

🐕 In grounds, on leads only.

❄

Highclere Castle.

The Library

HIGHCLERE CASTLE & GARDENS

www.highclerecastle.co.uk

MAP 3

Owner:
Earl of Carnarvon

▶ **CONTACT**

The Castle Office
Highclere Castle
Newbury
Berkshire RG20 9RN

Tel: 01635 253210
Fax: 01635 255315
e-mail: theoffice@
highclerecastle.co.uk

▶ **LOCATION**

OS Ref. SU445 587

M4/J13 - A34 south,
M3/J8 - A303 - A34
north.

Air: Heathrow M4
45 mins.

Rail: Paddington -
Newbury 45 mins.

Taxi: 4^1/$_2$ m
07778 156392.

Designed by Charles Barry in the 1830s at the same time as he was building the Houses of Parliament, this soaring pinnacled mansion provided a perfect setting for the 3rd Earl of Carnarvon, one of the great hosts of Queen Victoria's reign. The extravagant interiors range from church Gothic through Moorish flamboyance and rococo revival to the solid masculinity in the long Library. Old Master paintings mix with portraits by Van Dyck and 18th century painters. Napoleon's desk and chair rescued from St. Helena sit with other 18th and 19th century furniture.

The 5th Earl of Carnarvon together with Howard Carter, discovered the Tomb of Tutankhamun and the Castle houses a unique exhibition of some of his discoveries. The 7th Earl of Carnarvon was the Queen's Racing Manager and in 1993, to celebrate his 50th year as a leading owner and breeder, the Racing Exhibition was opened offering a fascinating insight into a racing history which dates back four generations. The 8th Earl and his wife take a very personal interest in the Castle and they are often to be seen round and about their home, grounds and gardens.

GARDENS

The magnificent parkland with its massive cedars was designed by 'Capability' Brown. The walled gardens also date from an earlier house at Highclere but the dark yew walks are entirely Victorian in character. The glass Orangery and Fernery add an exotic flavour. The Secret Garden has a romance of its own with a beautiful curving lawn surrounded by densely planted herbaceous gardens. A place for poets and romantics.

The Saloon

🛍 ℹ Conferences, exhibitions, filming, fairs, and concerts (cap. 8000). No photography in the house.

🍽 Receptions, dinners, corporate hospitality.

♿ Visitors may alight at the entrance. WC.

☕ Tearooms, licensed. Lunches for 20+ can be booked.

🅿 Ample.

🏛 Egyptian Exhibition: £4+VAT per child. 1 adult free per every 10 children – includes playgroups, Brownie packs, Guides etc. Nature walks, beautiful old follies, Secret Garden.

🐕 In grounds, on leads.

🔔 Civil Wedding Licence.

🛡 Please visit website.

▶ **OPENING TIMES**

1 June - 31 August
Mon - Fri, 11am - 4pm
(Gates open 10am).
Last admission 3pm.

▶ **ADMISSION**

Adult £7.50
Child (4-15yrs)....... £4.00
Conc. £6.00
Wheelchair Pusher... FOC
Family (2+2/1+3). £18.00

Grounds & Gardens only
Free of charge during season.

Groups (20+)
Adult £5.50
Child (4-15yrs)....... £3.50
Conc. £5.00

Private guided tours at other times may be arranged subject to availability at a minimum cost for up to 40 persons of £600 plus VAT, each additional person £20 plus VAT.

School Groups (to visit Egyptian Exhibition only)
Child ... £4.00 (plus VAT) 1 adult Free for every 10 children. By prior arrangement.

CONFERENCE/FUNCTION

ROOM	SIZE	MAX CAPACITY
Library	43' x 21'	140
Saloon	42' x 29'	120
Dining Rm	37' x 18'	70
Library, Saloon, Drawing Rm, Music Rm, Smoking Rm		500

MAP 3

SOMERLEY

www.somerley.com

Owner:
The Earl of Normanton

▶ CONTACT

Danielle Rogers
Somerley
Ringwood
Hampshire   BH24 3PL

Tel: 01425 480819
Fax: 01425 478613
e-mail:
events@somerley.com

▶ LOCATION

OS Ref. SU134 080

Off the A31 to
Bournemouth 2m.
London 1³/₄ hrs via
M3, M27, A31.
2m NW of Ringwood.

Air: Bournemouth
International
Airport 5m.

Rail: Bournemouth
Station 12m.

Taxi: A car can be
arranged from the
House if applicable.

Somerley is the spectacular private stately home of The 6th Earl of Normanton, and is surrounded by 7000 acres of breathtaking Hampshire countryside. The classic Georgian house, designed by Samuel Wyatt in 1750, sits majestically above 2,000 acres of parkland rolling down to the River Avon. The private Estate offers total peace and seclusion and yet is only 1¹/₂ hours from Central London and 20 minutes from Southampton Airport.

Although four of the rooms are licensed for Civil ceremonies, the formal Dining Room provides a romantic and intimate setting for a service seating 80 guests.

The spectacular Gallery which stretches 80' is breathtaking, housing furniture and pictures collected by The 2nd Earl of Normanton. This opulent room seats up to 120 guests for a truly magnificent Wedding Breakfast or 200 guests for a conference.

The formal Drawing Room which features a spectacular gilded ceiling, and the East Library housing the original Wyatt bookcases, are available for parties of up to 120 people for dancing until midnight.

For larger weddings, the Gallery provides an unrivalled room for a Civil ceremony for 150 guests, followed by a drinks reception in the Drawing Room and East Library, after which guests enjoy their Wedding Breakfast and dancing in a bespoke marquee in the beautiful gardens adjacent to the house.

Eight guest bedrooms are available including The State Bedroom where King Edward VII and Queen Alexandra stayed during their visits to the house. Somerley is not open to the public and is available only on an exclusive use basis.

▶ OPENING TIMES
Privately booked
functions only.

▶ ADMISSION
Privately booked
functions only.

CONFERENCE/FUNCTION

ROOM	SIZE	MAX CAPACITY
Picture Gall.	80' x 30'	200
Drawing Rm	38' x 30'	50
Dining Rm	39' x 19'	50
East Library	26' x 21'	30
Old Somerley	40' x 20'	70
Old Game Larder	20' x 20'	30

ℹ️ No individual visits, ideal for all corporate events, weddings, activity days and filmwork.

🍽️ Dining Room and picture gallery available for private parties.

🅿️ Unlimited.

🛏️ 8 double rooms (7 en-suite).

❄️

JANE AUSTEN'S HOUSE

CHAWTON, ALTON, HAMPSHIRE GU34 1SD

www.janeaustenmuseum.org.uk

Tel: 01420 83262 **Fax:** 01420 80695 **e-mail:** enquiries@jahmusm.org.uk

Owner: Jane Austen Memorial Trust **Contact:** Ann Channon

17th century house where Jane Austen wrote or revised her six great novels. Contains many items associated with her and her family, documents and letters, first editions of the novels, pictures, portraits and furniture. Pleasant garden, suitable for picnics, bakehouse with brick oven and wash tub, houses Jane's donkey carriage.

Location: OS Ref. SU708 376. Just S of A31, 1m SW of Alton, signposted Chawton.

Open: Jan/Feb: Sats & Suns. Mar - 1 Jan: daily, 11am - 4.30pm (last adm. 4pm). Closed 25 - 26 Dec.

Admission: Fee charged.

🖻 Bookshop. 🔄 Ground floor & grounds. WC. 🖼 Opposite house. 🅿 Opposite house. 🐕 Guide dogs only. ❄

BASING HOUSE

Redbridge Lane, Basing, Basingstoke RG24 7HB

Tel: 01256 467294

Owner: Hampshire County Council **Contact:** Alan Turton

Ruins, covering 10 acres, of huge Tudor palace. Recent recreation of Tudor formal garden.

Location: OS Ref. SU665 526. 2m E from Basingstoke town centre. Signposted car parks are about 5 or 10 mins walk from entrance.

Open: Apr - Sept: Wed - Sun & BHs, 2 - 6pm.

Admission: Adult £2, Conc. £1.

BEAULIEU 🏛

See pages 116/117 for double page entry.

BISHOP'S WALTHAM PALACE ⌗

Bishop's Waltham, Hampshire SO32 1DH

Tel: 01489 892460 **www.**english-heritage.org.uk/visits

Owner: English Heritage **Contact:** Visitor Operations Team

This medieval seat of the Bishops of Winchester once stood in an enormous park. Wooded grounds, the remains of the Great Hall and the three storey tower can still be seen. Dower House furnished as a 19th-century farmhouse.

Location: OS Ref. SU552 173. In Bishop's Waltham, 5 miles NE from M27/J8.

Open: Grounds: 1 May - 30 Sept: Sun - Fri & BHs, 10am - 5pm. Farmhouse & Grounds: 1 May - 30 Sept: Sun & BH Mons, 10am - 5pm.

Admission: Farmhouse (when open): Adult £2.80, Child £1.40, Conc. £2.10. Gardens: Free. EH Members free.

ℹ WCs. Exhibition. 🖻 🔄 Grounds. 🅿 🐕 Grounds only, on leads. 🖼 Tel for details.

AVINGTON PARK 🏛

WINCHESTER, HAMPSHIRE SO21 1DB

www.avingtonpark.co.uk

Tel: 01962 779260 **e-mail:** enquiries@avingtonpark.co.uk

Owner/Contact: Mrs S L Bullen

Avington Park, where Charles II and George IV both stayed at various times, dates back to the 11th century. The house was enlarged in 1670 by the addition of two wings and a classical Portico surmounted by three statues. The State rooms are magnificently painted and lead onto the unique pair of conservatories flanking the South Lawn. The Georgian church, St. Mary's, is in the grounds.

Avington Park is a privately owned stately home and is a most prestigious venue in peaceful surroundings. It is perfect for any event from seminars, conferences and exhibitions to wedding ceremonies and receptions, dinner dances and private parties. The Conservatories and the Orangery make a delightful location for summer functions, whilst log fires offer a welcome during the winter. Excellent caterers provide for all types of occasion, ranging from breakfasts and light lunches to sumptuous dinners. All bookings at Avington are individually tailor-made and only exclusive use is offered. Several rooms are licensed for Civil wedding ceremonies and a delightful fully-equipped apartment is available for short stays.

Location: OS Ref. SU534 324. 4m NE of Winchester ½ m S of B3047 in Itchen Abbas.

Open: May - Sept: Suns & BH Mons plus Mons in Aug, 2.30 - 5.30pm. Last tour 5pm. Other times by arrangement, coach parties welcome by appointment all year.

Admission: Adult £4, Child £2.

ℹ Conferences. 🔲 🔄 Partial. WC. 🖼 📷 Obligatory. 🅿 🐕 In grounds, on leads. Guide dogs only in house. 🏠 🔼 ❄ 🖼 Tel for details.

BREAMORE HOUSE & MUSEUM 🏛

BREAMORE, FORDINGBRIDGE, HAMPSHIRE SP6 2DF

www.breamorehouse.com

Tel: 01725 512233   **Fax:** 01725 512858   **e-mail:** breamore@ukonline.co.uk

Owner/Contact: Sir Edward Hulse Bt

Elizabethan manor with fine collections of pictures and furniture. Countryside Museum takes visitors back to the time when a village was self-sufficient.

Location: OS Ref. SU152 191. W Off the A338, between Salisbury and Ringwood.

Open: Easter weekend; Apr: Tue & Sun; May - Sept: Tue, Wed, Thur, Sat, Sun & all Bank Holidays. House: 2 - 5.30pm. Countryside Museum: 1 - 5.30pm. Last admission 4.15pm.

Admission: Combined ticket for house and museum: Adult £7, Child £5, OAP £6, Family £17.

🔲 ♿ Ground floor & grounds. WC. 🐕 🚌 €

BROADLANDS

ROMSEY, HAMPSHIRE SO51 9ZD

www.broadlands.net

Tel: 01794 505010   **Event Enquiry Line:** 01794 505020   **Fax:** 01794 518605
e-mail: admin@broadlands.net

Owner: Lord & Lady Brabourne   **Contact:** Estate Manager

Broadlands, the home of Viscount Palmerston and The Earl Mountbatten of Burma, is open to the public by guided tour only. The Mountbatten Exhibition depicts the life and times of Lord Mountbatten. Limited tours, which include items normally available by appointment, are offered on certain days.

Location: OS Ref. SU355 204. On A3090 at Romsey.

Open/Admission: Details of opening times and admission charges can be obtained from the website, or by telephone.

📺 ♿ Ground floor. WC. 🚶 Obligatory. 🐕 Guide dogs only.

CALSHOT CASTLE ⌗

Calshot, Fawley, Hampshire SO45 1BR

Tel: 02380 892023   **www**.calshot.com

Owner: English Heritage   **Contact:** Hampshire County Council

Henry VIII built this coastal fort in an excellent position, commanding the sea passage to Southampton. The fort houses an exhibition and recreated pre-World War I barrack room.

Location: OS Ref. SU488 025. On spit 2 miles SE of Fawley off B3053.

Open: 1 Apr - 31 Oct: daily, 10am - 4pm.

Admission: Adult £2.50, Child £1.50, Conc. £1.80, Family £6.

ℹ️WCs. 🔲 🅿️ 🚌

ELING TIDE MILL

The Toll Bridge, Eling, Totton, Southampton, Hampshire SO40 9HF

Tel: 023 8086 9575   **e-mail:** info@elingtidemill.org.uk

Owner: Eling Tide Mill Trust Ltd & New Forest District Council

                    Contact: Mr David Blackwell-Eaton

Location: OS Ref. SU365 126. 4m W of Southampton. ¹/₂ m S of the A35.

Open: All year: Wed - Sun and BH Mons, 10am - 4pm. Closed 25/26 Dec. (Prices valid until April 2006.)

Admission: Adult £2.25, Child £1.25, OAP £1.75, Family £5.70. Discounts for pre-booked groups (10+)

© Lord Romsey

EXBURY GARDENS & STEAM RAILWAY 🏛

EXBURY, SOUTHAMPTON, HAMPSHIRE SO45 1AZ

www.exbury.co.uk

Tel: 023 8089 1203   **Fax:** 023 8089 9940

Owner: Edmund de Rothschild Esq   **Contact:** Estate Office

HHA/Christie's Garden of the Year 2001. A spectacular 200-acre woodland garden showcasing the world famous Rothschild collection of rhododendrons, azaleas and camellias. Daffodil meadow, Rock Garden, new Exotic Garden and herbaceous borders ensure year-round interest. The Steam Railway enchants visitors   of all ages, passing through a Summer Garden, and featuring a bridge, tunnel, viaduct and causeway. Licenced for Civil Weddings and a beautiful venue for marquee receptions and corporate events.

Location: OS Ref. SU425 005. 11m SE of Totton (A35) via A326 & B3054 & minor road. In New Forest.

Open: 1 Mar - 5 Nov: daily, 10am - 5.30pm (dusk in Nov).

Admission: High Season (20 Mar- 4 June*): Adult £7.50, Child (3-15yrs) £1.50, OAP/Group £7 (OAPs £6.50 Mon - Fri), Family (2+3) £17.50, Railway +£3, Rover Ticket not available. Low Season (all other open times): Adult £5, Child (3-15yrs) £1, OAP/Group £4.50, Family (2+3) £12, Railway +£2.50, Rover Ticket £3.50. Child under 3yrs Free. Buggies: £3.50. *High Season visitors receive a free Low Season Voucher to see Autumn colours.

🔲 🚼 📺 ♿ 🐕 🍴Licensed. 🚶By arrangement. 🔳 🅿️ 🐕In grounds, on leads. 🔺 🔻

FORT BROCKHURST ⌗
Gunner's Way, Gosport, Hampshire PO12 4DS
Tel: 02393 378291 **www.**english-heritage.org.uk/visits
Owner: English Heritage   **Contact:** Portchester Castle
This 19th-century fort was built to protect Portsmouth. Today its parade ground, moated keep and sergeants' mess are available to hire as an exciting setting for functions and events of all types. The fort is also open to visitors, when tours will explain the exciting history of the site and the legend behind the ghostly activity in cell no. 3.
Location: OS196, Ref. SU596 020. Off A32, in Gunner's Way, Elson on N side of Gosport.
Open: The Fort opens occasionally for pre-booked tours & Heritage Open days, 7 - 10 Sept. Call 01424 775705 for opening details.
Admission: Adult £2.80, Child £1.40, Conc. £2.10. EH Members free.
ⓘWCs. 🅶Grounds and ground floor only. 🐕Dogs on leads (restricted areas).

FURZEY GARDENS
Minstead, Lyndhurst, Hampshire SO43 7GL
Tel: 023 8081 2464 **Fax:** 023 8081 2297
Owner: Furzey Gardens Charitable Trust   **Contact:** Maureen Cole
Location: OS Ref. SU273 114. Minstead village ½ m N of M27/A31 junction off A337 to Lyndhurst.
Open: Please contact property for details.

education index
see page 564

GUILDHALL GALLERY
THE BROADWAY, WINCHESTER SO23 9GH
www.winchester.gov.uk

Tel: 01962 848289 (gallery) 01962 848269 (office) **Fax:** 01962 848299
e-mail: museums@winchester.gov.uk
Owner: Winchester City Council   **Contact:** Mr C Wardman Bradbury
A constantly changing programme of contemporary exhibitions including painting, sculpture, craft, photography and ceramics.
Location: OS Ref. SU485 293. Winchester - city centre. Situated above the Tourist Office in Winchester's 19th century Guildhall.
Open: Apr - Oct: Mon - Sat, 10am - 5pm; Sun, 12 noon - 5pm. Nov - Mar: Tue - Sat, 10am - 4pm; Sun, 12 noon - 4pm.
Admission: Free.
🅶 ✳

GREAT HALL &
QUEEN ELEANOR'S GARDEN
WINCHESTER CASTLE, WINCHESTER SO23 8PJ
www.hants.gov.uk/discover/places/great-hall.html

Tel: 01962 846476 **Fax:** for bookings 01962 841326
Owner: Hampshire County Council   **Contact:** Custodian
The only surviving part of Henry III's medieval castle at Winchester, this 13th century hall was the centre of court and government life. The Round Table closely associated with the legend of King Arthur has hung here for over 700 years. Queen Eleanor's garden is a faithful representation of the medieval garden visited by Kings and Queens of England.
Location: OS Ref. SU477 295. Central Winchester. SE of Westgate archway.
Open: Mar - Oct daily, 10am - 5pm. Nov - Feb: daily 10am - 4pm. Closed 25/26 Dec and for Civic events only – see website for details.
Admission: Free. Donations appreciated towards the upkeep of the Great Hall.
ⓘBy arrangement. ✳

HIGHCLERE CASTLE 🏰   *See page 118/119 for full page entry.*
& GARDENS

Beaulieu.

NT Photographic Library: Stephen Robson

HINTON AMPNER GARDEN

BRAMDEAN, ALRESFORD, HAMPSHIRE   SO24 0LA

www.nationaltrust.org.uk

Tel: 01962 771305   **Fax:** 01962 793101

e-mail: hintonampner@nationaltrust.org.uk

Owner: The National Trust   **Contact:** The Property Manager

"I have learned during the past years what above all I want from a garden: this is tranquillity". so said Ralph Dutton, 8th and last Lord Sherborne, of his garden at Hinton Ampner. He created one of the great gardens of the 20th century, a masterpiece of design based upon the bones of a Victorian garden, in which he united a formal layout with varied and informal planting in pastel shades. It is a garden of all year round interest with scented plants and magnificent vistas over the park and surrounding countryside.

The garden forms the link between the woodland and parkland planting, which he began in 1930, and the house, which he remodelled into a small neo-Georgian manor house in 1936. He made further alterations when the house was reconstructed after a fire in 1960. Today it contains his very fine collection of English furniture, Italian paintings and hard-stones. Both his collection and every aspect of the decoration at Hinton Ampner reflects Ralph Dutton's sure eye and fine aesthetic judgement.

He placed the whole within the rolling Hampshire landscape that he loved and understood so well.

Location: OS Ref. SU597 275. M3/J9 follow signs to Petersfield. On A272, 1m W of Bramdean village, 8m E of Winchester.

Open: House: 19 Mar - 11 Oct: Tues, Weds & Suns also Sats in Aug, 1.30 - 5pm. Garden: 18 Mar - 11 Oct, daily except Thur & Fri, 11am - 5pm.

Admission: House & Garden: Adult £6.50, Child (5-16yrs) £3.25, Child (under 5yrs) Free. Garden only: Adult £5.50, Child (5-16yrs) £2.75, Child (under 5yrs) Free.

Limited for coaches. Guide dogs only.

© Andy Williams

HOUGHTON LODGE

STOCKBRIDGE, HAMPSHIRE, SO20 6LQ

www.houghtonlodge.co.uk

Tel: 01264 810502   **Fax:** 01264 810063   **e-mail:** info@houghtonlodge.co.uk

Owner/Contact: Captain M W Busk

A haven of peace above the tranquil beauty of the River Test. 12 acres of Grade II* Gardens with fine trees surround 18th Century "Cottage Ornée". Grade II*.

Chalk Cob walls enclose traditional Kitchen Garden with espaliers, herbs and heated greenhouses, hydroponicum and orchid collection. Gardens both formal and informal. Popular TV/film location. New for 2006: An additional 14 acres adjoining the garden now provide an experience of the natural world with meadow walks through the peaceful and unspoiled surroundings of the River Test.

Location: OS Ref. SU344 332. 1¹/₂ m S of Stockbridge (A30) on minor road to Houghton village.

Open: All year (closed 22 Dec - 4 Jan except by appointment): daily (Weds by appointment only), 10am - 5pm. House: by appointment.

Admission: Adult £5, Child Free. Groups (35+) (booked): Adult £4.50.

By arrangement. In grounds, on leads.

HURST CASTLE

Keyhaven, Lymington, Hampshire SO41 0TP

Tel: 01590 642344   www.english-heritage.org.uk/visits

Owner: English Heritage   **Contact:** (Managed by) Hurst Castle Services

This was one of the most sophisticated fortresses built by Henry VIII, and later strengthened in the 19th and 20th centuries, to command the narrow entrance to the Solent. There is an exhibition in the castle, and two huge 38-ton guns form the fort's armaments.

Location: OS196 Ref. SZ319 898. On Pebble Spit S of Keyhaven. Best approach by ferry from Keyhaven. 4 miles SW of Lymington.

Open: 1 Apr - 31 Oct: daily, 10.30am - 5.30pm. Café: open Apr - May weekends & Jun - Sept: daily.

Admission: Adult £3, Child £1.80, Conc. £2.80. EH Members free.

WCs. Unsuitable. Dogs on leads (restricted areas).

special events see page 571

KING JOHN'S HOUSE & HERITAGE CENTRE

CHURCH STREET, ROMSEY, HAMPSHIRE SO51 8BT

www.kingjohnshouse.org.uk

Tel/Fax: 01794 512200   **e-mail:** annerhc@aol.com

Owner: King John's House & Tudor Cottage Trust Ltd   **Contact:** Anne James

Three historic buildings on one site: Medieval King John's House, containing 14th century graffiti and rare bone floor, Tudor Cottage complete with traditional tea room and Victorian Heritage Centre with recreated shop and parlour. Beautiful period gardens, special events/exhibitions and children's activities. Gift shop and Tourist Information Centre. Receptions and private/corporate functions.

Location: OS Ref. SU353 212. M27/J3. Opposite Romsey Abbey, next to Post Office.

Open: Apr - Sept: Mon - Sat, 10am - 4pm. Oct - Mar: Heritage Centre only. Limited opening on Sundays. Evenings also for pre-booked groups.

Admission: Adult £2.50, Child 50p, Conc. £2. Heritage Centre only: Adult £1.50, Child 50p, Conc. £1. Discounted group booking by appointment.

⬚ ⊤ ⬚Partial. ⬚ ⬚ By arrangement.
⬚ Off Latimer St with direct access through King John's Garden.
⬚ ⬚Guide dogs only. ✳ ⬚Tel for details.

MEDIEVAL MERCHANTS HOUSE ⌗

58 French Street, Southampton, Hampshire SO1 0AT

Tel: 02380 221503   **www.**english-heritage.org.uk

Owner: English Heritage   **Contact:** Visitor Operations Team

The life of the prosperous merchant in the Middle Ages is vividly evoked in this recreated, faithfully restored 13th-century townhouse.

Location: OS Ref. SU419 112. 58 French Street. 1/4 mile S of Bargate off Castle Way. 150yds SE of Tudor House.

Open: 1 Apr - 30 Sept: Sat, Sun & BHs, 10am - 5pm.

Admission: Adult £3.50, Child £1.80, Conc. £2.60. EH Members free.

⬚ ⬚ ⬚ ✳

Sandham Memorial Chapel.

NETLEY ABBEY ⌗

Netley, Southampton, Hampshire

Tel: 02392 378291   **www.**english-heritage.org.uk/visits

Owner: English Heritage   **Contact:** Portchester Castle

A peaceful and beautiful setting for the extensive ruins of this 13th-century Cistercian abbey converted in Tudor times for use as a house.

Location: OS Ref. SU453 089. In Netley, 4 miles SE of Southampton, facing Southampton Water.

Open: Any reasonable time.

Admission: Free.

⬚ ⬚ ⬚Dogs on leads. ✳

NORTHINGTON GRANGE ⌗

New Alresford, Hampshire

Tel: 01424 775705   **www.**english-heritage.org.uk/visits

Owner: English Heritage   **Contact:** 1066 Battle Abbey

Northington Grange and its landscaped park as you see it today, formed the core of the house as designed by William Wilkins in 1809. It is one of the earliest Greek Revival houses in Europe.

Location: OS 185, SU562 362. 4 miles N of New Alresford off B3046 along farm track - 550 metres.

Open: Grounds only: 1 Apr - May, Aug - Sept: daily, 10am - 6pm. Jun - July: daily, 10am - 3pm. Nov - Mar: daily, 10am - 4pm. Closed 24 - 26 Dec and 1 Jan.

Admission: Free.

⬚ Wheelchair access (with assistance). ⬚ ⬚Dogs on leads. ✳

PORTCHESTER CASTLE ⌗

Portsmouth, Hampshire PO16 9QW

Tel/Fax: 02392 378291   **www.**english-heritage.org.uk/visits

Owner: English Heritage   **Contact:** Visitor Operations Team

The rallying point of Henry V's expedition to Agincourt and the ruined palace of King Richard II. This grand castle has a history going back nearly 2,000 years including the most complete Roman walls in Europe. Exhibition telling the story of the castle and interactive audio tour.

Location: OS196, Ref. SU625 046. On S side of Portchester off A27, M27/J11.

Open: 1 Apr - 30 Sept: daily, 10am - 6pm. 1 Oct - 31 Mar: daily, 10am - 4pm. Closed 24 - 26 Dec & 1 Jan.

Admission: Adult £3.90, Child £2, Conc. £2.90. 15% discount for groups (11+). EH Members Free.

ℹ︎WCs. Exhibition. ⬚ ⬚Partial. ⬚ ⬚ ⬚In grounds, on leads. ✳ ⬚ Tel for details.

MOTTISFONT ABBEY & GARDEN ✿

MOTTISFONT, Nr ROMSEY, HAMPSHIRE SO51 0LP

www.nationaltrust.org.uk/mottisfontabbey

Tel: 01794 340757   **Fax:** 01794 341492   **Recorded Message:** 01794 341220

e-mail: mottisfontabbey@nationaltrust.org.uk

Owner: The National Trust   **Contact:** The Property Manager

The Abbey and Garden form the central point of an 809 ha estate including most of the village of Mottisfont, farmland and woods. A tributary of the River Test flows through the garden forming a superb and tranquil setting for a 12th century Augustinian priory which, after the Dissolution, became a house. It contains the spring or "font" from which the place name is derived. The magnificent trees, walled gardens and the National Collection of Old-fashioned Roses combine to provide interest throughout the seasons. The Abbey contains a drawing room decorated by Rex Whistler and the remains of the old Priory. In 1996 the Trust acquired Derek Hill's 20th century picture collection.

Location: OS185 Ref. SU327 270. Signposted off A3057 Romsey to Stockbridge road, 4 1/2 m N of Romsey. Also signposted off B3084 Romsey to Broughton. Station: Dunbridge (U) 3/4 m.

Open: Garden only: 4 - 26 Feb: Sat & Sun, 11am - 4pm. House & Garden: 27 Feb - 31 May: daily except Thur & Fri, 11am - 5pm. 3 - 30 Jun: daily, 11am - 5pm (Garden 8.30pm); 1 July - 3 Sept: daily except Fri, 11am - 5pm. 4 Sept - 29 Oct: daily except Thur & Fri, 11am - 5pm. Shop/Kitchen Café: same as Garden. Open Good Fri, 11am - 5pm. Car Park gates close at 6pm.

Admission: Adult £7, Child (5-18yrs) £3.50, Family £17.50. (June: Adult £8, Child (5-18yrs) £4, Family £20. Group (15+) discount available.

⬚ ⬚Partial. ⬚ ⊞Licensed. ⬚ ⬚Guide dogs only. ⬚ ⬚Tel for details.

PORTSMOUTH CATHEDRAL

Portsmouth, Hampshire PO1 2HH

Tel: 023 9282 3300 **Fax:** 023 9229 5480

e-mail: rosemary.fairfax@portsmouthcathedral.org.uk

Contact: Rosemary Fairfax

Maritime Cathedral founded in 12th century and finally completed in 1991. A member of the ship's crew of Henry VIII's flagship Mary Rose is buried in Navy Aisle.

Location: OS Ref. SZ633 994. 1½ m from end of M275. Follow signs to Historic Ship and Old Portsmouth.

Open: 7.45am - 6pm all year. Sun service: 8am, 9.30am, 11am, 6pm. Weekday: 6pm (Choral on Tues and Fris in term time).

Admission: Donation appreciated.

SANDHAM MEMORIAL CHAPEL

Burghclere, Nr Newbury, Hampshire RG20 9JT

Tel/Fax: 01635 278394 **e-mail:** sandham@nationaltrust.org.uk

www.nationaltrust.org.uk/Sandham

Owner: The National Trust **Contact:** The Custodian

This red brick chapel was built in the 1920s for the artist Stanley Spencer to fill with paintings inspired by his experiences of the First World War. Influenced by Giotto's Arena Chapel in Padua, Spencer took five years to complete what is arguably his finest achievement. The chapel is set amidst lawns and orchards with views across Watership Down. Pictures best viewed on a bright day as no artificial lighting.

Location: OS Ref. SU463 608. 4m S of Newbury, ½m E of A34, W end of Burghclere.

Open: 4 - 19 Mar & 4 - 26 Nov: Sat & Sun, 11am - 4pm. 2 - 23 Dec: Sat & Sun 11am - 3pm. 22 Mar - 29 Oct: Wed - Sun, 11am - 5pm. Open BH Mons. Other times by appointment.

Admission: Adult £3, Child £1.50. Groups by prior arrangement, no reduction.

Portable ramp for entrance. By arrangement. In grounds, on leads.

SOMERLEY

See page 120 for full page entry.

STRATFIELD SAYE HOUSE

Stratfield Saye, Basingstoke RG7 2BZ

Tel: 01256 882882 **Fax:** 01256 881466 www.stratfield-saye.co.uk

Owner: The Duke of Wellington **Contact:** The Administrator

Family home of the Dukes of Wellington since 1817.

Location: OS Ref. SU700 615. Equidistant from Reading (M4/J11) & Basingstoke (M3/J6) 1½ m W of the A33.

Open: 13 - 18 Apr (Easter weekend) & 6 Jul - 31 July: daily, 11.30am (Sats & Suns, 10.30am) - 3.30pm (last admission).

Admission: Weekends: Adult £8, Child £5, OAP/Student £7. Weekdays Adult £7, Child £4, OAP/Student £6. Groups by arrangement only.

WC. Obligatory. Guide dogs only.

TITCHFIELD ABBEY

Titchfield, Southampton, Hampshire PO15 5RA

Tel: 01329 842133 www.english-heritage.org.uk/visits

Owner: English Heritage **Contact:** The Titchfield Abbey Association

Remains of a 15th-century abbey overshadowed by the grand Tudor gatehouse. Reputedly some of Shakespeare's plays were performed here for the first time. Under local management of Titchfield Abbey Society.

Location: OS Ref. SU544 067. ½ mile N of Titchfield off A27.

Open: 1 Apr - 31 Oct: daily, 10am - 6pm (5pm in Oct). 1 Nov - 31 Mar (closed 25 Dec): daily, 10am - 4pm.

Admission: Free.

Dogs on leads.

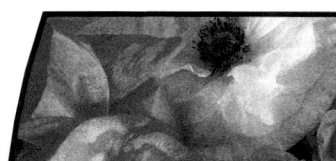 

NT Photographic Library: Andrea Jones

THE VYNE

SHERBORNE ST JOHN, BASINGSTOKE RG24 9HL

www.nationaltrust.org.uk

Tel: 01256 883858 **Infoline:** 01256 881337 **Fax:** 01256 881720

e-mail: thevyne@nationaltrust.org.uk

Owner: The National Trust **Contact:** The Property Manager

Built in the early 16th century for Lord Sandys, Henry VIII's Lord Chamberlain, the house acquired a classical portico in the mid-17th century (the first of its kind in England) and contains a fascinating Tudor chapel with Renaissance glass, a Palladian staircase and a wealth of old panelling and fine furniture. The attractive grounds feature herbaceous borders and a wild garden, with lawns, lakes and woodland walks. Weddings & Functions: Stone Gallery licensed for Civil Weddings. Receptions and private/corporate functions in Walled Garden or Brewhouse restaurant.

Location: OS Ref. SU639 576. 4m N of Basingstoke between Bramley & Sherborne St John.

Open: House: 25 Mar - 29 Oct: Sat & Sun, 11am - 5pm; 27 Mar - 25 Oct: Mon - Wed, 1 - 5pm. Grounds/Shop/Restaurant: 4 Feb - 19 Mar: Sat & Sun; 25 Mar - 29 Oct: Sat - Wed; 3 Feb - 25 Mar 2007: Sat & Sun, 11am - 5pm. Open BH Mons & Good Fri. Shop & Restaurant also 2 Nov - 23 Dec, Thur - Sun, 11am - 3pm. Group visits: 27 Mar - 25 Oct: Mon - Wed, by appointment only 11am -1pm.

Admission: House & Grounds: Adult £7.50, Child £3.75, Family £18.75. Groups £6.30. Grounds only: Adult £4.50, Child £2.25.

No photography in house. Tel for details.

GILBERT WHITE'S HOUSE & THE OATES MUSEUM

THE WAKES, HIGH STREET, SELBORNE, ALTON GU34 3JH

Tel: 01420 511275   **email:** info@gilbertwhiteshouse.org.uk

Owner: Oates Memorial Trust   **Contact:** Carey Hides

Charming refurbished 18th century house, home of Rev Gilbert White, author of *The Natural History of Selborne*. Over 25 acres of garden and parkland with many plants of the Georgian era. Tea parlour with fare based on 18th century recipes and excellent gift shop. Exhibition on Captain Oates of Antarctic fame.

Location: OS Ref. SU741 336. On W side of B3006, in village of Selborne 4m NW of the A3.

Open: 1 Jan - 24 Dec: Tues - Sun & BHs, 11am - 5pm. Groups by arrangement.

Admission: Adult £6, Child Free (accompanied by Adult), OAP £5.

ℹ️ No photography in house. ⬜ 🔳 ♿ Partial. ⬛ 🔧 By arrangement. 🅿️ 🐕 Guide dogs only. 🔳 ⬛ Tel for details.

Highclere Castle – 1st Earl of Carnarvon's children.

WINCHESTER CATHEDRAL

Winchester, Hants SO23 9LS

Tel: 01962 857200   **Fax:** 01962 857201

The Cathedral was founded in 1079.

Location: OS Ref. SU483 293. Winchester city centre.

Open: 8.30am - 6pm. East end closes 5pm. Access may be restricted during services. Weekday services:7.40am, 8am, 5.30pm. Sun services: 8am, 10am, 11.15am, 3.30pm.

Admission: Recommended donations. Adult £4, Conc. £3. Photo permits £2, Video permits £3. Library & Triforium Gallery: £1, Tower & Roof tours: £4 (age restrictions 12 - 70). Groups (10+) must book, tel: 01962 857225. Special tours available.

©National Trust Photographic Library

WINCHESTER CITY MILL ✿

BRIDGE STREET, WINCHESTER

www.nationaltrust.org.uk/winchestercitymill

Tel/Fax: 01962 870057   **e-mail:** winchestercitymill@nationaltrust.org.uk

Owner: The National Trust   **Contact:** Anne Aldridge

Spanning the River Itchen and rebuilt in 1744 on an earlier medieval site, this corn mill has a chequered history. The machinery is completely restored making this building an unusual survivor of a working town mill. It has a delightful island garden and impressive mill races roaring through the building.

Location: OS Ref. SU485 293. M3/J9 & 10. St Swithun's Bridge nr King Alfred's statue. 15 min walk from station.

Open: 4 Mar - 2 Apr: Sat & Sun; 8 - 23 Apr & 1 Jul - 23 Dec: Mon - Sun; 26 Apr - 25 Jun: Wed - Sun; 11am - 5pm. Last entry 4.30pm.

Admission: Adult £3.20, Child £1.60, Family £8. NT members Free.

⬜ ♿ Partial. 🔧 By arrangement. 🅿️ Nearby public car park. ⬛ ✖️

WOLVESEY CASTLE ⚑

College Street, Wolvesey, Winchester, Hampshire SO23 8NB

Tel: 02392 378291   **www**.english-heritage.org.uk/visits

Owner: English Heritage   **Contact:** Portchester Castle

The fortified palace of Wolvesey was the chief residence of the Bishops of Winchester and one of the greatest of all medieval buildings in England. Its extensive ruins still reflect the importance and immense wealth of the Bishops of Winchester, occupants of the richest seat in medieval England. Wolvesey was frequently visited by medieval and Tudor monarchs and was the scene of the wedding feast of Philip of Spain and Mary Tudor in 1554.

Location: OS Ref. SU484 291. ¾ mile SE of Winchester Cathedral, next to the Bishop's Palace; access from College Street.

Open: 1 Apr - 30 Sept: daily, 10am - 5pm.

Admission: Free.

⬜ ♿ Grounds. 🐕 In grounds, on leads.

BOUGHTON MONCHELSEA PLACE

www.boughtonplace.co.uk

MAP 4

Owner:
Mr & Mrs D Kendrick

▶ CONTACT

Mrs M Kendrick
Boughton
Monchelsea Place
Boughton Monchelsea
Nr Maidstone
Kent   ME17 4BU

Tel: 01622 743120
e-mail: mk@
boughtonplace.co.uk

▶ LOCATION
OS Ref. TQ772 499

On B2163, 5$^1/2$ m from
M20/J8 or 4$^1/2$ m from
Maidstone via A229.

Boughton Monchelsea Place is a battlemented manor house dating from the 16th century, set in its own country estate just outside Maidstone, within easy reach of London and the channel ports. This Grade I listed building has always been privately owned and is still lived in as a family home.

From the lawns surrounding the property there are spectacular views over unspoilt Kent countryside, with the historic deer park in the foreground. These views are shared by the 20 acre event site set back a little way from the house. A wicket gate leads from the grounds to the medieval church of St Peter, with its rose garden and ancient lych gate. At the rear of the house are to be found a pretty courtyard and walled gardens, together with an extensive range of Tudor barns and outbuildings.

Inside the house, rooms vary in character from Tudor through to Georgian Gothic; worthy of note are the fine Jacobean staircase and sundry examples of heraldic stained glass. Furnishings and paintings are mainly Victorian, with a few earlier pieces; the atmosphere is friendly and welcoming throughout.

The premises are licensed for Civil marriage ceremonies, although wedding receptions in the house may only be held on weekday afternoons. In addition we welcome conferences, group visits, location work and all types of corporate, private and public functions, but please note times of availability. Use outside these hours is sometimes possible, subject to negotiation. All clients are guaranteed exclusive use of this prestigious venue.

▶ OPENING TIMES
All year by prior arrangement only.

House & Garden
Not open to individual visitors.

Group visits/ house tours:
(15-50),
Tues - Thur, 10am - 4pm.

Private functions:
Mon - Fri, 9am - 10pm.

Outdoor Event Site
365 days a year:
8am - 11.30pm.

▶ ADMISSION
**Gardens &
Guided House Tour**
Adult £5.00

Venue Hire
Prices on application.

Day Delegate Rate
From £40.

SPECIAL EVENTS

JULY 10
Open Air Shakespeare:
'Macbeth'.
JULY 31
Open Air Theatre: 'The Importance of being Earnest'.

 Film location.

By arrangement.

By arrangement.

By arrangement.

CONFERENCE/FUNCTION

ROOM	SIZE	MAX CAPACITY
Entrance Hall	25' x 19'	50 Theatre
Dining Room	31' x 19'	50 Dining
Drawing Room	28' x 19'	40 Reception
Courtyard Room	37' x 13'	60 Theatre

South East - England

NTPL / Rupert Truman

MAP 4

Owner:
The National Trust

▶ CONTACT

The Property Manager
Chartwell
Westerham
Kent TN16 1PS

Tel: 01732 866368
01732 868381

Fax: 01732 868193

e-mail: chartwell@
nationaltrust.org.uk

▶ LOCATION
OS Ref. TQ455 515

2m S of Westerham,
forking left off B2026.

Bus: 246 from Bromley
South, 401 from
Sevenoaks, Buses4U
from Oxted
(All services Suns &
BHs only).
Please check times.

CHARTWELL ❧
www.nationaltrust.org.uk/chartwell

The family home of Sir Winston Churchill from 1924 until the end of his life. He said of Chartwell, simply *'I love the place - a day away from Chartwell is a day wasted'*. With magnificent views over the Weald of Kent it is not difficult to see why.

The rooms are left as they were in Sir Winston & Lady Churchill's lifetime with daily papers, fresh flowers grown from the garden and his famous cigars. Photographs and books evoke his career, interests and happy family life. Museum and exhibition rooms contain displays, sound recordings and superb collections of memorabilia, including gifts, uniforms and family photographs, and give a unique insight into Sir Winston's political career and personal life.

The garden studio contains Sir Winston's easel and paintbox, as well as many of his paintings. Terraced and water gardens descend to the lake, the gardens also include a golden rose walk, planted by Sir Winston and Lady Churchill's children on the occasion of their golden wedding anniversary, and the Marlborough Pavilion decorated with frescoes depicting the battle of Blenheim. Visitors can see the garden walls that Churchill built with his own hands, as well as the pond stocked with the golden orfe he loved to feed.

The Mulberry Room at the restaurant can be booked for meetings, conferences, lunches and dinners. Please telephone for details.

▶ OPENING TIMES

25 March - 2 July and
6 Sept - 29 October
Wed - Sun & BHs

4 July - 3 Sept
Tue - Sun & BHs
11am - 5pm.

Last admission 4.15pm.

▶ ADMISSION

House, Garden & Studio
Adult £10.00
Child £5.00
Family £25.00

**Pre-booked groups
(minimum 15)**
Adult £9.00
Child £4.50

Garden & Studio only
Adult £5.00
Child £2.50
Family £12.50

NTPL / Andreas von Einsiedel

NTPL / Ian Shaw

📷 ℹ️ Conference facilities.　🍷　♿ Partial. WC. Please telephone before visit.　🍴 Licensed.
👤 By arrangement.　🅿️　🐕 In grounds, on leads.　🛏️ Tel for details.

CHIDDINGSTONE CASTLE

www.chiddingstone-castle.org.uk

MAP 4

Henry Streatfeild, Squire of Chiddingstone, intoxicated by the current passion for medieval chivalry, embarked on the transformation of his ancient home into a fantasy castle in 1803, the first major commission of young William Atkinson, which a contemporary guidebook predicted would be the 'fairest house' in Kent. After five hectic years work ceased, leaving a random mixture of old and new. The Establishment was not impressed: today, we find the place enchanting. In 1955 the now decrepit castle was bought by the distinguished collector Denys Bower. He died in 1977, leaving everything to the Nation, for the enjoyment of

posterity, to be run as a living home, not a museum. The place is now administered by a registered private Charitable Trust. The restoration to the fabric of the building by the Trust has captured Denys Bower's passion for collecting in the setting of a unique country house. The fascinating array of Royal Stuart portraits and mementoes, Buddhist and Ancient Egyptian artefacts and a superb gathering of Japanese lacquer and armour celebrates 20th century collecting at its best .

The 35-acre landscaped park (listed garden of Kent) has been restored – a haven for wildlife, providing idyllic walks.

Owner:
Denys Eyre Bower Bequest Reg. Charity Trust

▶ CONTACT
Administrator
Chiddingstone Castle
Edenbridge
Kent TN8 7AD

Tel: 01892 870347

▶ LOCATION
OS Ref. TQ497 452

B2027, turn to Chiddingstone at Bough Beech, 1m further on to crossroads, then straight to castle.

10m from Tonbridge, Tunbridge Wells and Sevenoaks. 4m Edenbridge. Accessible from A21 and M25/J5.

London 35m.

Bus: Enquiries: Tunbridge Wells TIC 01892 515675.

Rail: Tonbridge, Tunbridge Wells, Edenbridge then taxi. Penshurst then 2m walk.

Air: Gatwick 15m.

CONFERENCE/FUNCTION

ROOM	SIZE	MAX CAPACITY
Assembly Rm	14' x 35'	50
Stable Block	36' x 29'	

White Rose Drawing Room.

▶ OPENING TIMES
Summer
Easter Hol, All BHs.

June - September

Thur: 2 - 5.30pm

Sun & BHs:
11.30am - 5.30pm
Last admission 5pm.

Winter
Open only for specially booked groups (20-80).
First Sun in Dec: Christmas Fair, 10.30am - 4pm – please enquire.

▶ ADMISSION
Adult	£5.00
Child*	£3.00
OAP	£5.00
Student	£5.00

Groups** (Booked 20-80)
Adult	£4.00
Child*	£3.00
OAP	£4.00
Student	£4.00

* Child under 16yrs accompanied by paying adult. Under 5 yrs Free.

** Usual hours, other times by appointment. School groups only by appointment.

▶ SPECIAL EVENTS
Chiddingstone may be closed without notice for Special Events.

ℹ️ Conferences, receptions, concerts. No photography in house; no smoking, prams/buggies, large bags or mobile phones.

🅿️ Licensed.

🅿️ Ample for cars. Limited for coaches, please book.

See facing page.

🍴 Available for special events. Wedding receptions.

In grounds, on leads.

♿ Partial (grounds unsuitable). WC.

CHIDDINGSTONE CASTLE...

Japanese Armour.

Rose Garden.

© Images by Helen Menges.

SMALL CONFERENCES
AND FUNCTIONS:

We have some facilities for small conferences and functions. They can provide a delightful alternative to traditional meeting facilities and can be viewed prior to booking. More details upon request.

CIVIL MARRIAGES:

The Great Hall is licensed by Kent County Council, and is specially attractive to those who desire the dignity of a church ceremony without the religious aspect. We offer all features of wedding celebrations, including reception of guests and refreshments.

EDUCATION:

We welcome visits from schools who wish to use the collections in connection with classroom work. No anxiety for the teacher (admitted free). Please contact our Education Officer for more details.

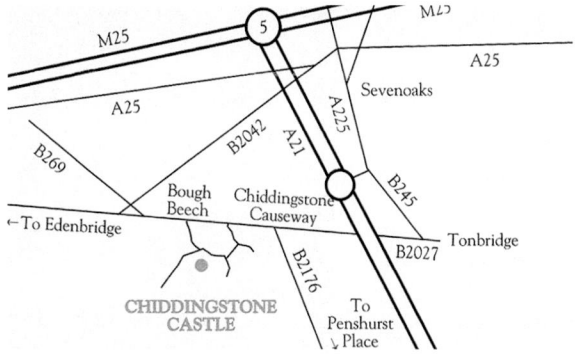

COBHAM HALL

www.cobhamhall.com

Owner:
Cobham Hall
School

▶ CONTACT

Mr N Powell
Bursar
Cobham Hall, Cobham
Kent DA12 3BL

Tel: 01474 823371
Fax: 01474 825904
e-mail:
taylorb@cobhamhall.
com

▶ LOCATION

OS Ref. TQ683 689

Situated adjacent to the
A2/M2. ¹/₂ m S of A2 4m
W of Strood. 8m E of
M25/J2 between
Gravesend & Rochester.

London 25m
Rochester 5m
Canterbury 30m

Rail: Meopham 3m
Gravesend 5m
Taxis at both stations.

Air: Gatwick 45 mins.
Heathrow 60 mins,
Stansted 50 mins.

CONFERENCE/FUNCTION

ROOM	SIZE	MAX CAPACITY
Gilt Hall	41' x 34'	180
Wyatt Dining Rm	49' x 23'	135
Clifton Dining Rm	24' x 23'	75
Activities Centre	119' x 106'	300

Cobham Hall is now a leading Girls Boarding &
Day School, and has been visited by several
English monarchs from Elizabeth I to Edward VIII.
Charles Dickens used regularly to walk through
the grounds from his house in Higham to the
Leather Bottle Public House in Cobham Village.

Cobham Hall is one of the largest, finest and
most important houses in Kent, it is an
outstanding beautiful red brick mansion in
Elizabethan, Jacobean, Carolean and 18th
century styles, it yields much interest to the
students of art, architecture & history. The
Elizabethan Wings were begun in 1584, whilst
the central section, which contains the Gilt Hall,
was wonderfully decorated by John Webb.

Further rooms were decorated by James Wyatt in
the 18th century.

In 1883 the Hon Ivo Bligh, later the 8th Earl of
Darnley, led the victorious English cricket
team against Australia bringing the Ashes home
to Cobham.

GARDENS

The Park was landscaped for the 4th Earl by
Humphry Repton, and is now gradually being
restored. The Gothic Dairy, Aviary and the Pump
House are all being restored. The gardens are
beautiful at all times of the year but especially
delightful in the spring when the spring flowers
are out in full bloom.

ℹ Conferences, business or social
functions, 150 acres of parkland for sports,
corporate events, open air concerts, sports
centre, indoor swimming pool, art studios,
music wing, tennis courts, helicopter
landing area. Filming and photography.
No smoking.

⎙ ⍋ In-house catering team for private,
corporate hospitality and wedding
receptions. (cap. 100).

♿ House tour involves 2 staircases,
ground floor access for w/chairs.

☕ Cream teas 2 - 5pm on open days.
Other meals by arrangement.

🏃 Obligatory guided tours; tour time 1¹/₂
hrs. Garden tours arranged outside standard
opening times.

🅿 Ample. Pre-booked coach groups are
welcome any time.

▦ Guide provided, Adult £4.50, Child /
OAP £3.50.

🐕 In grounds, on leads.

🛏 18 single and 18 double with
bathroom. 22 single and 22 double without
bathroom. Dormitory. Groups only.

🔔

▶ OPENING TIMES

March: 29.

April: 2, 5, 9, 12, 14, 16,
17, 19.

July:
12 - 30, Weds & Suns.

August:
2 - 30, Weds & Suns.

House & Shop:
2 - 5pm (5.30pm Shop).
Last tour at 4pm.

Garden:
Closes at 6pm.

Dates could change, please
telephone to confirm.

▶ ADMISSION

Adult	£4.50
Child (4-14yrs.)	£3.50
OAP	£3.50

Gardens & Parkland
Self-guided tour £2.50

**Historical/Conservation
tour of Grounds**
(by arrangement)

Per person £3.50

▣ SPECIAL EVENTS

APR 9
National Garden Scheme.
(+ House open 2 - 5pm).
APR 14, 16/17
Easter Opening.
(+ House open 2 - 5pm).
JUL 23
National Garden Scheme.
Summer Stroll, 7pm.
(Guidebook Tour & Glass of
Wine £5pp).
(+ House open 2 - 5pm).
AUG 13
British Red Cross.
(+ House open 2 - 5pm).

MAP 4

Owner:
Bexley Heritage Trust

▶ **CONTACT**

Miss Sarah Fosker
Danson House
Danson Park
Bexleyheath
Kent   DA6 8HL

Tel: 020 8303 6699
Fax: 020 8304 6641

e-mail: info@
dansonhouse.com

▶ **LOCATION**
OS Ref. TQ475 768

Signposted off the A2
and A221 Danson Park,
Bexley, 5 minutes
London-bound from
M25 J/2.

Rail: Welling or
Bexleyheath (10 min
walk).

Bus: B15 bus to
Danson Park.

DANSON HOUSE

www.dansonhouse.com

The most significant building at risk in London in 1995, Robert Taylor's villa has undergone extensive restoration by English Heritage over a period of ten years. Restored to its former Georgian glory and open to the public for the first time in 35 years by Bexley Heritage Trust.

The house was built by wealthy merchant Sir John Boyd, for his young bride Catherine Chapone. The design and layout of the house reflect its original purpose, to be a country house dedicated to the entertainment and enjoyment of its inhabitants. The sumptuous interior decoration including the paintings and fireplaces tell stories that reveal the passion of Sir John for his wife and the love that they shared.

The route around the principal floor takes in the austere entrance hall that would have held Boyd's collection of sculpture – trophies from the Grand Tour, followed by the Dining Room that houses a complete cycle of wall paintings by Charles Pavillon. The Salon (pictured below) houses an original painting from the house, showing it with the wings that were demolished in 1805, that has been reframed to the original designs of Sir William Chambers, who made considerable changes to the house shortly after it was completed. The impressive Library is home to a George England Organ built, for the house in 1766, that remains in working order.

The bedroom floor presents further period room displays and exhibitions relating to the history of the house and its inhabitants.

The principal floor is licensed for Civil wedding ceremonies and can accommodate up to 65 guests.

There is a programme of events and concerts throughout the year, please telephone for details.

▶ **OPENING TIMES**
2 April - 29 October.
Wed, Thur, Sun &
BH Mons, 11am - 5pm.
Last entry 4.15pm.

▶ **ADMISSION**
Adult £5.00
Child (with Adult)... Free
OAP....................... £4.50

 Two.

 WCs.

Licenced.

By prior arrangement.
Please telephone 01322 526574.

Limited for coaches.

Tel for details.

English Heritage Photo Library / Jonathan Bailey

MAP 4

THE HOME OF CHARLES DARWIN

www.english-heritage.org.uk/visits

A visit to Down House is a fascinating journey of discovery for all the family. This was the family home of Charles Darwin for over 40 years and now you can explore it to the full.

See the actual armchair in which Darwin wrote 'On the Origin of Species', which shocked and then revolutionised the way we think about the origins of mankind. His study is much the same as it was in his lifetime and is filled with belongings that give you an intimate glimpse into both his studies and everyday life.

At Down House you will discover both sides of Darwin - the great thinker and the family man.

Explore the family rooms where the furnishings have been painstakingly restored. An audio tour narrated by Sir David Attenborough will bring the house to life and increase your understanding of Darwin's revolutionary theory. Upstairs you will find state-of-the-art interpretation of the scientific significance of the house – especially designed to inspire a younger audience.

Outside, take the Sandwalk which he paced daily in search of inspiration, then stroll in lovely gardens. Complete your day by sampling the delicious selection of home-made cakes in the tea room.

Owner:
English Heritage

▶ **CONTACT**

Visitor Operations Team
Down House
Luxted Road
Downe
Kent   BR6 7JT

Tel: 01689 859119
Fax: 01689 862755

▶ **LOCATION**
OS Ref. TQ431 611

In Luxted Road, Downe, off A21 near Biggin Hill.

Rail: From London Victoria or Charing Cross.

Bus: Orpington (& Bus R8) or Bromley South (& Bus 146). Buses R8 & 146 do not run on Sundays or BHs.

▶ **OPENING TIMES**

1 Apr - 30 Sept:
Wed - Sun, 10am - 6pm.

17 July - 31 August: daily
11am - 5pm (10am House)

October: Wed - Sun
10am - 5pm.

1 November - 31 March:
Wed - Sun, 10am - 4pm.

Closed:
18 Dec 2006 - 6 Feb 2007

▶ **ADMISSION**

Adult £6.90
Child £3.50
Conc. £5.20
Family (2+3) £17.30
EH Members Free.

Groups (11+)
.... 15% discount

Tour leader and coach driver have free entry. 1 extra place for every 20 additional people.

English Heritage Photo Library / Jonathan Bailey

i   WCs.

♿

🎧 Free. English, French, German, Japanese & for visually impaired.

P   Limited for coaches.

🐕 Guide dogs only.

❄ Closed January.

Tel for details.

English Heritage PHoto Library / Jonathan Bailey

English Heritage Photo Library

MAP 4

DOVER CASTLE ⊞
AND THE SECRET WARTIME TUNNELS
www.english-heritage.org.uk/visits

Journey deep into the White Cliffs of Dover and discover the top secret World War II tunnels. Through sight, sound and smells, relive the wartime drama of the underground hospital as a wounded Battle of Britain pilot is taken to the operating theatre in a bid to save his life. Discover how life would have been during the planning days of the Dunkirk evacuation and Operation Dynamo as you are led around the network of tunnels and casements housing the communications centre.

Above ground you can explore the magnificent medieval keep and inner bailey of King Henry II. Visit the evocative Princess of Wales' Royal Regiment Museum. There is also the Roman Lighthouse and Anglo-Saxon church to see or take an audio tour of the intriguing 13th-century underground fortifications and medieval battlements. Enjoy magnificent views of the White Cliffs from Admiralty Lookout.

See the exciting '1216 Siege' exhibition, and discover, through a dramatic light and sound presentation, how it must have felt to be a garrison soldier defending Dover Castle against the French King in 1216. In the keep, see a reconstruction of the castle in preparation for a visit from Henry VIII and visit the hands-on exhibition explaining the travelling Tudor court. The land train will help you around this huge site.

Throughout the summer there are many fun events taking place, bringing the castle alive through colourful enactments and living history.

Owner:
English Heritage

▶ CONTACT
Visitor Operations Team
Dover Castle
Dover
Kent   CT16 1HU

Tel: 01304 211067
Info Line: 01304 201628

Venue Hire and Hospitality:
Hospitality Manager
Tel: 01304 209889

▶ LOCATION
OS Ref. TR326 416

Easy access from A2 and M20. Well signed from Dover centre and east side of Dover. 2 hrs from central London.

Rail: London Charing Cross or Victoria 1^1/2 hrs.

Bus: Freephone 0870 6082608.

CONFERENCE/FUNCTION

ROOM	MAX CAPACITY
The Castle Keep	standing 120 dining 90
Keep Yard Café	theatre-style 150
Secret Wartime Tunnels	standing 120 dining 80 theatre-style 80
Marquee on Palace Green	standing 400 dining 265

ℹ WCs.   📷 Two.

▼ Exclusive private and corporate hire. Tel: 01034 209889.

♿ Lift for access to tunnels. Courtyard and grounds, some very steep slopes.

🍴 3 restaurants, hot and cold food and drinks.

🚶 Tour of tunnels approx. every 20 mins, more at peak times when waits can occur.

🅿 Ample.

■ Free visits available for schools. Education centre. Pre-booking essential.

✱

🎭 Tel for details.

English Heritage Photo Library

▶ OPENING TIMES
Summer
1 April - 30 September:
Daily, 10am - 6pm
(August opens 9.30am).

October:
Daily, 10am - 5pm.

Winter
1 November - 31 January
Thur - Mon, 10am - 4pm.
(Closed 24 - 26 Dec & 1 Jan.)

NB. Keep closes at 5pm on days when events are booked.

Venue Hire and Hospitality
English Heritage offers exclusive use of the castle keep or tunnels in the evenings for receptions, dinners, product launches and themed banquets.

▶ ADMISSION
Adult	£9.50
Child	£4.80
Conc.	£7.10
Family (2+3)	£23.80

EH Members Free.

Groups: 15% discount for groups (11+). Free entry for tour leader and coach driver. One free place for every additional 20 paying.

MAP 4

GROOMBRIDGE PLACE GARDENS 🏛

www.groombridge.co.uk

Owner:
Groombridge Asset
Management

▶ **CONTACT**

The Estate Office
Groombridge Place
Groombridge
Tunbridge Wells
Kent TN3 9QG

Tel: 01892 861444

Fax: 01892 863996

e-mail: office@
groombridge.co.uk

There's magic and mystery, history and intrigue, romance and peace at this beautiful venue – which provides such an unusual combination of a traditional heritage garden with the excitement, challenge and contemporary landscaping of the ancient woodland – appealing to young and old alike.

First laid out in 1674 on a gentle, south-facing slope, the formal walled gardens are set against the romantic backdrop of a medieval moat, surrounding a classical Restoration manor house (not open to the public) and were designed as outside rooms. These award-winning gardens include magnificent herbaceous borders, the enchanting White Rose Garden with over 20 varieties of white roses, a Secret Garden with deep shade and cooling waters in a tiny hidden

corner, Paradise Walk and Oriental Garden, the Knot Garden and Nut Walk and the Drunken Garden with its crazy topiary. The gardens feature wonderful seasonal colour throughout spring, summer and autumn.

In complete contrast on a high hillside above the walled gardens and estate vineyard is the Enchanted Forest, where quirky and mysterious gardens have been developed in the ancient woodland by innovative designer, Ivan Hicks, to challenge the imagination. Children love the Dark Walk, Tree Fern Valley, Village of the Groms, the Serpent's Lair and the Mystic Pool, the Romany Camp, Double Spiral and the Giant Swings Walk. There are also Birds of Prey flying displays three times a day, a canal boat cruise to and from the Forest – plus a full programme of special events.

▶ **LOCATION**

OS Ref. TQ534 375

Groombridge Place Gardens are located on the B2110 just off the A264. 4m SW of Tunbridge Wells and 9m E of East Grinstead.

Rail: London Charing Cross to Tunbridge Wells 55mins. (Taxis).

Air: Gatwick.

▶ **OPENING TIMES**

Summer
Gardens
1 April - 4 November
Daily, 10am - 5.30pm (or dusk if earlier).

The house is not open to visitors.

▶ **ADMISSION**

Adult	£8.70
Child* (3-12yrs)	£7.20
Senior	£7.20
Family (2+2)	£29.50

Groups (20+)

Adult	£7.25
Child/School	£5.50
Senior	£5.50/£6.25
Student	£6.25
Youth	£5.50

*Child under 3yrs Free.

ℹ️ Film location.

📷

❄

🍸

♿ Partial. WCs.

☕ 🍴 Licensed.

👤 By arrangement.

🅿 Limited for coaches.

🎭

🐕 Guide dogs only.

🔔

▶ **SPECIAL EVENTS**

APR 16/17
Easter Eggstravaganza.

APR 30 & 1 MAY
Robin Hood.

JUL 16
Wings, Wheels & Steam.

AUG 6
Hot Air Balloons & Ferraris.

NOV 4
Spectacular Fireworks.

MAP 4

Owner:
Bexley Heritage Trust
Management

▶ **CONTACT**
Mrs Janet
Hearn-Gillham
Bourne Road, Bexley,
Kent DA5 1PQ

Tel: 01322 526574

Fax: 01322 522921

e-mail: jhearn-
gillham@btconnect
.com

▶ **LOCATION**
OS Ref. TQ502 743.

On the A2 less than
5m from the M25/J2
(London bound).

HALL PLACE & GARDENS

www.hallplaceandgardens.com

A fine Grade I listed country house built c1537 for Sir John Champneys, a wealthy merchant and former Lord Mayor of London, with a 17-century extension added by Sir Robert Austen.

Managed by Bexley Heritage Trust since 2000, this beautiful estate of 65 hectares stands on the banks of the River Cray at Bexley. Surrounding the house are award winning gardens with magnificent topiary, a herb garden, a secret garden, an Italianate garden, a grass maze and inspirational herbaceous borders. In the former walled gardens are a plant nursery, with plant sales, a sub-tropical plant house where you can see ripening bananas in mid-winter, and model display gardens. A recent addition is the Educational Enviromental Garden (wheelchair access), divided into Tudor Garden (looking at plants used for dyeing, medicine, beauty and cooking), meadow land, bug hunt ground and dipping pond. Beyond are recreational sports grounds and park land.

The house boasts a panelled Tudor Great Hall overlooked by a minstrel's gallery and various period rooms including a vaulted Long Gallery and splendid Drawing Room with a fine 17th-century plaster ceiling. There is a shop and numerous exhibitions, including an opportunity to purchase artists' work, throughout the year. There is also an extensive programme of events, concerts and open-air theatre, both in the house and outside, including a special Christmas programme. Several rooms are available to hire for meetings and other events, including the Great Hall and Drawing Room, which are also licensed for Civil wedding ceremonies. Its close proximity to London makes Hall Place & Gardens an ideal location for photographic, film and television use.

The Education Team offer an extensive Education & Outreach Service for schools and adult groups and organised activities for the holidays.

▶ **OPENING TIMES**

1 April - 31 October:
Mon - Sat, 10am - 5pm;
Sun & BHs, 11am - 5pm.
1 Nov - 31 Mar: Tue - Sat,
10am - 4.15pm.

▶ **ADMISSION**

Free. Charge made for
some Special Events.
Prearranged guided tours
(10+) £4.

House, lift & WC.
Licensed.
By arrangement (10+).
Guide dogs only.
Tel for details.

HEVER CASTLE & GARDENS

www.hevercastle.co.uk

Owner:
Hever Castle Ltd

▶ **CONTACT**
Anne Watt
Hever Castle
Hever, Edenbridge
Kent TN8 7NG

Infoline: 01732 865224
Fax: 01732 866796
e-mail:
mail@HeverCastle.co.uk

▶ **LOCATION**
OS Ref. TQ476 450

Exit M25/J5 & J6
M23/J10,
1¹/₂ m S of B2027 at
Bough Beech,
3m SE of Edenbridge.

Rail: Hever Station
1m (no taxis),
Edenbridge Town
3m (taxis).

Hever Castle dates back to 1270, when the gatehouse, outer walls and the inner moat were first built. 200 years later the Bullen (or Boleyn) family added the comfortable Tudor manor house constructed within the walls. This was the childhood home of Anne Boleyn, Henry VIII's second wife and mother of Elizabeth I. There are many items relating to the Tudors, including two books of hours (prayer books) signed and inscribed by Anne Boleyn. The Castle was later given to Henry VIII's fourth wife, Anne of Cleves.

In 1903, the estate was bought by the American millionaire William Waldorf Astor, who became a British subject and the first Lord Astor of Hever. He invested an immense amount of time, money and imagination in restoring the castle and grounds. Master craftsmen were employed and the castle was filled with a magnificent collection of furniture, tapestries and other works of art.

'From Castles to Country Houses' the Miniature Model Houses exhibition, a collection of 1/12 scale model houses, room views and gardens, depicts life in English Country Houses.

GARDENS

Between 1904-8 over 30 acres of formal gardens were laid out and planted, these have now matured into one of the most beautiful gardens in England. The unique Italian garden is a four acre walled garden containing a superb collection of statuary and sculpture. The award-winning gardens include the Rose garden and Tudor garden, a traditional yew maze and a 110 metre herbaceous border. A water maze has been added to the other water features in the gardens. The Sunday Walk Garden has a stream meandering through a mature woodland with borders filled with specimen plants.

▶ **OPENING TIMES**

Summer
1 March - 30 November
Daily:
Grounds: 11am - 6pm.
Castle: 12 noon - 6pm.
Last admission 5pm.

Winter
Grounds: 11am - 4pm.
Castle: 12 noon - 4pm.

▶ **ADMISSION**
Castle & Gardens
Adult £9.80
Child (5-14 yrs) £5.30
OAP £8.20
Family (2+2).......... £24.90

Groups (15+)
Availble on request.

Gardens only
Adult £7.80
Child (5-14 yrs) £5.00
OAP £6.70
Family (2+2).......... £20.60

Groups (15+)
Available on request.

Pre-booked private guided tours are available before opening, during season.

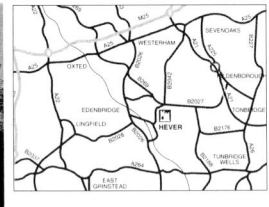

CONFERENCE/FUNCTION

ROOM	SIZE	MAX CAPACITY
Dining Hall	35' x 20'	70
Breakfast Rm	22' x 15'	12
Sitting Rm	24' x 20'	20
Pavilion	96' x 40'	250
Moat Restaurant	25 'x 60'	75

ⓘ ❀ Suitable for filming, conferences, corporate hospitality, weddings, product launches. Outdoor heated pool, tennis court and billiard room. No photography in house.

🎁 Gift, garden & book.

🍴 250 seat restaurant available for functions wedding receptions, etc.

♿ Access to gardens, ground floor only (no ramps into castle), restaurants, gift shop, book shop and water maze. Wheelchairs available. WC.

🍽 Two licensed restaurants. Supper provided during open air theatre season. Pre-booked lunches and teas for groups.

🚶 Pre-booked tours in mornings. 1 Mar - 30 Nov. Tour time 1 hr. Tours in French, German, Dutch, Italian and Spanish (min 20). Garden tours in English only (min 15).

🅿 Free admission and refreshment voucher for driver and courier. Please book, group rates for 15+.

▦ Welcome (min 15). Private guided tours available (min 25). 1:6 ratio (up to 8 year olds: 1:10 9yrs+. Free preparatory visits for teachers during opening hours. Please book.

🐕 In grounds, on leads.

❄ Tudor Village.

⬡ Call infoline: 01732 865224.

©NTPL/Andrew Butler.

MAP 4

IGHTHAM MOTE 🌿

www.nationaltrust.org.uk/ighthammote

Owner:
The National Trust

Beautiful moated manor house covering 650 years of history from medieval times to the 1960s. Discover the stories and characters associated with the house from the first owners in 1320 to Charles Henry Robinson, the American businessman who bequeathed Ightham Mote to the National Trust in 1985.

Following the completion of the largest conservation project ever undertaken by the National Trust on a house of this age and fragility, it is now possible to enjoy the most extensive visitor route to date. This includes the refurbished Great Hall and Jacobean staircase, along with the Old Chapel, Crypt, Tudor Chapel with painted ceiling, Drawing Room with Jacobean fireplace, frieze and 18th century hand-painted Chinese wallpaper and Victorian Billiards Room, plus the recently refurbished South West Quarter including the apartments of Mr Robinson. A special exhibition 'Conservation in Action' explains the project and gives insights into the techniques and skills used.

Extensive gardens with lakes and woodland walk. Surrounding 550 acre estate also provides many country walks including way-marked routes.

Free introductory talks, garden and tower tours. Varied events programme including children's events and lecture lunches through the season. Group and Educational Tours available, plus educational facility. For details please telephone: 01732 810378.

▶ CONTACT

The Property Manager
Ightham Mote
Mote Road
Ivy Hatch
Sevenoaks
Kent   TN15 0NT

Tel: 01732 810378
Info: 01732 811145
Fax: 01732 811029

e-mail: ighthammote@ nationaltrust.org.uk

▶ LOCATION

OS Ref. TQ584 535

6m E of Sevenoaks off A25. 2$^{1}/_{2}$ m S of Ightham off A227.

▶ OPENING TIMES

12 March - 29 October:
Daily except Tues & Sats.

Gardens, Shop & Restaurant:
10am - 5.30pm
(last admission 5pm).

House: 10.30am - 5.30pm
(last admission 5pm).

Restaurant & Shop, winter opening times:
please call property.

▶ ADMISSION

Adult...................... £8.50
Child...................... £4.00
Family.................. £21.00

Groups (booked)
Adult...................... £7.50
Child...................... £3.50

Charles Henry Robinson's Bedroom. © Stuart Page Architect

  Ground floor. WC.

On leads, Estate only.
Tel for details.

139

Knole ©National Trust Photographic Library

KNOLE

www.nationaltrust.org.uk/knole

MAP 4

Owner:
The National Trust

▶ **CONTACT**

Property Manager
Knole
Sevenoaks
Kent TN15 0RP

Tel: 01732 462100

Info: 01732 450608

Fax: 01732 465528

e-mail: knole@
nationaltrust.org.uk

▶ **LOCATION**
OS Ref. TQ532 543

M25/J5.
25m SE of London.
Just off A225 at S end of
High Street, Sevenoaks.

Rail: ¹/₂ hr from
London Charing Cross
to Sevenoaks.

Bus: Arriva 402
Tunbridge Wells -
Bromley North.

Knole's fascinating historic links with kings, queens and the nobility, as well as its literary links with Vita Sackville-West and Virginia Woolf, make this one of the most intriguing houses in England. Thirteen superb state-rooms are laid out much the same as they were in the 18th century, to impress visitors by the wealth and status of the Sackville family, who continue to live at Knole today. The house contains Royal Stuart furniture, paintings by Gainsborough, Van Dyck and Reynolds, as well as many 17th century tapestries, some of which came from the royal palaces of Hampton Court and Whitehall.

Learn about the history of the billiard cue and what gentlemen used to strengthen their sword arm! From the lives of the servants to the reckless behaviour of the aristocracy, every room in Knole holds its own

secrets and nearly 500 years of history.

The house inspired not only Vita Sackville-West, who was born at Knole, to write her best-selling novel *The Edwardians* but was also the setting for Virginia Woolf's famous novel *Orlando*.

Knole is set at the heart of the only remaining medieval deer park in Kent where Sika and Fallow deer still roam freely amongst ancient oak, beech and chestnut trees, as they have since the days of Henry VIII. It is the ideal spot to enjoy the picturesque surroundings, sit back and relax and watch the world go by.

Pre-booked groups can take advantage of premium guided tours of the house while it is closed to the general public. Please telephone for further information.

© National Trust Photographic Library

Knole, The Great Stairs. ©National Trust Photographic Library.

 Full range of NT goods and souvenirs of Knole.

❄

♿ Wheelchair access to Green Court, Stone Court and Great Hall. WC. Virtual reality tour of upstairs showrooms.

☕ Serving morning coffee, lunch and teas. Also ice-creams and snacks in courtyard.

🚶 Guided tours for pre-booked groups, by arrangement. Short guides to the house available in French, Dutch & German.

🅿 Ample.

👤 Welcome. Contact Education Officer.

🐕 Guide dogs only.

❄ Park open all year to pedestrians.   🎭 Tel for details.

▶ **OPENING TIMES**

House
25 March - 29 October:
Wed - Sun & BH Mons,
12 noon - 4pm.
Last admission 3.30pm.

Premium guided tours for
pre-booked groups while
house is closed to public,
Wed, Fri & Sat, 11am.
Please telephone for
further information.

Garden
Weds throughout the
season, 11am - 4pm (last
admin 3pm).

Shop & Tearoom
As House: 10.30am - 5pm.

Christmas Shop
November - December:
Wed - Sun, 11am - 4pm.

▶ **ADMISSION**
House
Adult	£7.50
Child	£3.75
Family	£18.75

Groups (booked 15+)
Adult	£6.50
Child	£3.25
Parking	£2.50

Garden
Adult	£2.00
Child	£1.00

NT members Free.

LEEDS CASTLE & GARDENS

www.leeds-castle.com

MAP 4

Owner:
Leeds Castle
Foundation

▶ CONTACT

Marketing Department
Leeds Castle
Maidstone
Kent ME17 1PL

Tel: 01622 765400
Fax: 01622 735616

▶ LOCATION

OS Ref. TQ835 533

From London to
A20/M20/J8, 40m, 1 hr.
7m E of Maidstone,
¼ m S of A20.

Rail: Combined ticket
with South Eastern
Trains available,
(train and admission).
London - Bearsted.

Coach: Nat Express
coach and admission
from Victoria.

Air: Gatwick 45m.
Heathrow 65m.

Channel Tunnel: 25m.

Channel Ports: 38m.

This "loveliest castle in the world", surrounded by 500 acres of magnificent parkland and gardens and set in the middle of a natural lake, is one of the country's finest historic properties. Leeds is also proud to be one of the Treasure Houses of England.

The site of a Saxon royal manor, a Norman fortress and a royal palace to the Kings and Queens of England, the chequered history of Leeds Castle continues well into the 20th century. The last private owner, the Honourable Olive, Lady Baillie, purchased the Castle in 1926. Her inheritance helped to restore the Castle and, prior to her death, she established the Leeds Castle Foundation, which now preserves the Castle for the nation and hosts important international conferences.

The Castle has a fine collection of paintings, tapestries and furnishings and is also home to a unique collection of antique dog collars. The Park and Grounds include the colourful and quintessentially English Culpeper Garden, the delightful Wood Garden, and the terraced Lady Baillie Garden with its views over the tranquil Great Water. The Aviary houses over 100 rare and endangered species from around the world and, next to the Vineyard can be discovered the Maze with its secret underground grotto.

A highly popular and successful programme of Special Events is arranged throughout the year, details of which can be found on the website.

▶ OPENING TIMES

Summer
1 April - 31 October
Daily, 10am- 5pm (last adm).

Winter
1 November - 31 March
Daily, 10am - 3.30pm (last adm).

Special private tours for pre-booked groups by appointment.

Castle & Grounds closed 24 Jun & 1 July prior to open air concerts and 4 Nov prior to Grand Firework Spectacular.

▶ ADMISSION

Castle, Park & Gardens

Individuals (valid 1 year)
Adult £13.50
Child (4 -15yrs) £8.00
OAP/Student £11.00

Group 15+ prices
Adult £10.00
Child (4 -15yrs) £6.50
OAP/Student £9.50

Call for rates for visitors with disabilities or visit our website.

A guidebook is published in English, French, German, Dutch, Spanish, Italian and Japanese.

CONFERENCE/FUNCTION

ROOM	SIZE	MAX CAPACITY
Fairfax Hall	19.8 x 1m	200
Gate Tower	9.8 x 5.2m	50
Culpeper	7.65 x 7.34m	40
Terrace	8.9 x 15.4m	80

Residential conferences, exhibitions, sporting days, clay shooting off site, laser shooting, falconry, field archery, golf, croquet and heli-pad. Talks can be arranged for horticultural, viticultural, historical and cultural groups. No radios.

Corporate hospitality, large scale marquee events, wedding receptions, buffets and dinners.

Land train for elderly/disabled, wheelchairs, wheelchair lift, special rates. WC.

Restaurants, group lunch menus. Refreshment kiosks.

Guides in rooms. French, Spanish, Dutch, German, Italian and Russian speaking guides.

Free parking.

Welcome, outside normal opening hours, private tours. Teacher's resource pack and worksheets.

Tel for details.

PENSHURST PLACE & GARDENS

www.penshurstplace.com

Owner:
Viscount De L'Isle

▶ CONTACT

Bonnie Vernon
Penshurst Place
Penshurst
Nr Tonbridge
Kent TN11 8DG

Tel: 01892 870307
Fax: 01892 870866

e-mail: enquiries
@penshurstplace.com

▶ LOCATION
OS Ref. TQ527 438

From London M25/J5
then A21 to
Hildenborough,
B2027 via Leigh;
from Tunbridge Wells
A26, B2176.

Visitors entrance at SE
end of village,
S of the church.

Bus: Maidstone &
District 231, 232, 233
from Tunbridge Wells.

Rail: Charing Cross/
Waterloo - Hildenborough,
Tonbridge or Tunbridge
Wells; then taxi.

Penshurst Place is one of England's greatest family-owned stately homes with a history going back six and a half centuries.

In some ways time has stood still at Penshurst; the great House is still very much a medieval building with improvements and additions made over the centuries but without any substantial rebuilding. Its highlight is undoubtedly the medieval Barons' Hall, built in 1341, with its impressive 60ft-high chestnut-beamed roof.

A marvellous mix of paintings, tapestries and furniture from the 15th, 16th and 17th centuries can be seen throughout the House, including the helm carried in the state funeral procession to St Paul's Cathedral for the Elizabethan courtier and poet, Sir Philip Sidney, in 1587. This is now the family crest.

GARDENS

The Gardens, first laid out in the 14th century, have been developed over successive years by the Sidney family who first came to Penshurst in 1552. A twenty-year restoration and re-planting programme undertaken by the 1st Viscount De L'Isle has ensured that they retain their historic splendour. He is commemorated with a new Arboretum, planted in 1991. The gardens are divided by a mile of yew hedges into "rooms", each planted to give a succession of colour as the seasons change. There is also a Venture Playground, Woodland Trail, Toy Museum and a Gift Shop.

A variety of events in the park and grounds take place throughout the season.

📷 ℹ️ Product launches, garden parties, photography, filming, fashion shows, receptions, archery, clay pigeon shooting, falconry, parkland for hire. Conference facilities. Adventure playground & parkland & riverside walks. No photography in house.

🍽 Private banqueting, wedding receptions.

♿ Limited, disabled and elderly may alight at entrance. WC.

🍴 Licensed tearoom (waitress service can be booked by groups of 20+).

🧑‍🏫 Mornings only by arrangement, lunch/dinner can be arranged. Out of season tours by appointment. Guided tours of the gardens and house.

🅿️ Ample. Double decker buses to park from village.

🎒 All year by appointment, discount rates, education room and packs.

🐕 Guide dogs only

🔔

❄️

🛡 Tel for details.

CONFERENCE/FUNCTION

ROOM	SIZE	MAX CAPACITY
Sunderland Room	45' x 18'	100
Barons' Hall	64' x 39'	250
Buttery	20' x 23'	50

▶ OPENING TIMES

Summer
4 - 24 March:
Sats & Suns only.
25 March - 29 October
Daily.

House
Daily, 12 noon - 4pm.

Grounds
Daily, 10.30am - 6pm.

Shop
Open all year.

Winter
Open to Groups by
appointment only
(see Guided Tours).

▶ ADMISSION

House & Gardens
Adult £7.50
Child* £5.00
Conc. £7.00
Family (2+2) £21.00
Groups (20+)
Adult £7.00

Garden only
Adult £6.00
Child* £4.50
Conc. £5.50
Family (2+2) £18.00

Garden Season
Ticket £35.00

House Tours (pre-booked)
Adult £7.50
Child £4.50

Garden Tours (pre-booked)
Adult £8.50
Child £5.00

House & Garden ...£11.00

* Aged 5-16yrs; under 5s Free.

SQUERRYES COURT 🏛
MANOR HOUSE & GARDENS

www.squerryes.co.uk

Squerryes Court is a beautiful 17th century manor house which has been the Warde family home since 1731. It is surrounded by 10 acres of attractive and historic gardens which include a lake, restored parterres and an 18th century dovecote. Squerryes is 22 miles from London and easily accessible from the M25. There are lovely views and peaceful surroundings. Visitors from far and wide come to enjoy the atmosphere of a house which is still lived in as a family home.

There is a fine collection of Old Master paintings from the Italian, 17th century Dutch and 18th century English schools, furniture, porcelain and tapestries all acquired or commissioned by the family in the 18th century. General Wolfe of Quebec was a friend of the family and there are items connected with him in the Wolfe Room.

GARDENS

These were laid out in the formal style but were re-landscaped in the mid 18th century. Some of the original features in the 1719 Badeslade print survive. The family have restored the formal garden using this print as a guide. The garden is lovely all year round with bulbs, wild flowers and woodland walks, azaleas, summer flowering herbaceous borders and roses.

MAP 4

Owner:
John St A Warde Esq

▶ **CONTACT**
Mrs P A White
Administrator
Squerryes Court
Westerham
Kent   TN16 1SJ

Tel: 01959 562345
Fax: 01959 565949

e-mail: squerryes.court
@squerryes.co.uk

▶ **LOCATION**
OS Ref. TQ440 535

10 min from M25/J5 or 6 off A25, ¹/₂ m W from centre of Westerham

London 1-1¹/₂ hrs.

Rail: Oxted Station 4m.
Sevenoaks 6m.

Air: Gatwick,
30 mins.

© Clive Boursnell

▶ **OPENING TIMES**
Summer
2 April - 28 September
Wed, Thu, Sun &
BH Mons.

Grounds:
11.30am - 5pm
House: 1 - 5pm
Last admission 4.30pm.

NB. Pre-booked groups welcome any day except Saturday during season.

Winter
October - 31 March
Closed.

▶ **ADMISSION**
House & Garden
Adult	£6.00
Child (under 16yrs)	£3.00
Senior	£5.50
Family (2+2)	£13.50
Groups (20+)	
Adult	£5.00
Child (under 16yrs)	£3.00

Garden only
Adult	£4.00
Child (under 16yrs)	£2.00
Senior	£3.50
Family (2+2)	£8.00
Groups (20+, booked)	
Adult	£3.50
Child (under 16yrs)	£2.00

CONFERENCE/FUNCTION

ROOM	SIZE	MAX CAPACITY
Hall	32' x 32'	60
Old Library	20' x 25' 6"	40

ℹ Suitable for conferences, product launches, filming, photography, outside events, garden parties. No photography in house. Picnics permitted in grounds.

⬠ Small.

⛺ Wedding receptions (marquee).

♿ Limited access in house and garden. WCs.

☕ Teas and light refreshments on open days. Licenced.

🚶 For pre-booked groups (max 55), small additional charge. Owner will meet groups by prior arrangement. Tour time 1 hr.

🅿 Limited for coaches.

🐕 On leads, in grounds.

TURKEY MILL
www.turkeymill.co.uk

MAP 4

Owner:
Turkey Mill
Investments Ltd

▶ **CONTACT**

Turkey Mill Events Ltd
The Events Office
Turkey Court
Turkey Mill
Ashford Road
Maidstone
Kent ME14 5PP

Tel: 01622 765511
Fax: 01622 765522

e-mail: events@
turkeymill.co.uk

▶ **LOCATION**
OS Ref. TQ773 555

Turkey Mill is located
1½ miles from M20/J7
(follow the signs).

The entrance is off
the A20 ½ mile east of
Maidstone Town Centre.

Turkey Mill has a long and distinguished history. Originally a fulling mill, it was converted to papermaking at the end of the 17th century. Under the ownership of James Whatman, father and son, it became world famous. James Whatman pioneered the development of 'wove' paper, a superior quality white paper which was in great demand and the paper of choice for artists such as Thomas Gainsborough and J M W Turner. Whatman paper was used by William Blake for four of his illuminated books and by Queen Victoria for her personal correspondance. Napoleon wrote his long and detailed Will on Whatman paper only three weeks before his death in 1821, and George Washington used it for signing many State documents. In the 1930s Soviet leaders used the paper to publish their five-year plan for the future of the USSR while the Peace Treaty with Japan was signed on Whatman paper at the close of World War II.

Today Turkey Mill is a business park and home to more than 60 companies.

Alongside the business park are nine acres of exquiste landscaped grounds and a lake through which runs the River Len. The focus of the gardens is the Orangery, completed in 2002, the perfect venue for wedding receptions, corporate functions, conferences and private parties.

The waterfall, lake, giant Wellingtonias and Blue Cedars create the perfect backdrop for filming, photography and product launches; the grounds are floodlit at dusk.

▶ **OPENING TIMES**

Available for privately booked functions only.

The Orangery and Grounds are available all year round for private and corporate events.

CONFERENCE/FUNCTION

ROOM	SIZE	MAX CAPACITY
The Orangery	82' x 30'	Dining 200 Dinner Dance 160 Theatre-style 200 (160 catered) Open block 38
The Whatman Room	23' x 19'	Theatre-style 40 (25 catered) Classroom-style 20 Open block 18

| Film location. |

| Private and Corporate events. |

| Licensed. |

 80 spaces weekdays. Unlimited weekends.

BEDGEBURY NATIONAL PINETUM
Goudhurst, Cranbrook, Kent TN17 2SL
Tel: 01580 211781 **Fax:** 01580 212423
Owner: Forestry Commission **Contact:** Mrs Elspeth Hill
Location: OS Ref. TQ714 337 (gate on B2079). 7m E of Tunbridge Wells on A21, turn N on B2079 for 1m.
Open: All year: daily, 10am - 5pm (or dusk if earlier).
Admission: Adult £4, Child £2, Conc £3.50, Family £10. Prices will alter end Mar 2006. Please telephone for details.

BOUGHTON MONCHELSEA PLACE
See page 128 for full page entry.

BELMONT 🏛
BELMONT PARK, THROWLEY, FAVERSHAM ME13 0HH
www.belmont-house.org

Tel: 01795 890202 **Fax:** 01795 890042 **e-mail:** belmontadmin@btconnect.com
Owner: Harris (Belmont) Charity **Contact:** Mr J R Farmer
Belmont is a charming late 18th century country mansion by Samuel Wyatt, set in delightful grounds, including a restored 2 acre kitchen garden and a greenhouse. The seat of the Harris family since 1801 it is beautifully furnished and contains interesting items from India and Trinidad as well as the unique clock collection formed by the 5th Lord.
Location: OS Ref. TQ986 564. 4¹/₂ m SSW of Faversham, off A251.
Open: 1 Apr - 30 Sept: Sats, Suns & BH Mons, 2 - 5pm. Last admission to house 4.15pm. Gardens: Sat - Thurs, 10am - 6pm. Groups (15+): Mon - Thurs, by appointment.
Admission: House & Garden: Adult £5.25, Child £2.50, Conc. £4.75. Groups (15+): Adult £4.75, Child £2.50. Garden: Adult £2.75, Child £1. Prices subject to change April 2006.
ⓘNo photography in house. 📷 ♿ ♿Partial. WC. ▣ 🚻Obligatory. 🅿 🐕On leads only.

THE HOME OF ⚜ CHARLES DARWIN
See page 134 for full page entry.

CHART GUNPOWDER MILLS
Chart Mills, Faversham, Kent ME13 7SE
Tel: 01795 534542 **e-mail:** faversham@btinternet.com
Owner: Swale Borough Council **Contact:** John Breeze
Oldest gunpowder mill in the world. Supplied gunpowder to Nelson for the Battle of Trafalgar, and Wellington at Waterloo.
Location: OS Ref. TQ615 015. M2/J6. W of town centre, access from Stonebridge Way or South Road.
Open: Apr - Oct: Sat, Sun & BHs, 2 - 5pm, or by arrangement.
Admission: Free.
📷 🅿

CHARTWELL ✿
See page 129 for full page entry.

CHATHAM HISTORIC DOCKYARD
Chatham, Kent ME4 4TZ
Infoline: 01634 823807 **e-mail:** info@chdt.org.uk
Owner/Contact: Chatham Historic Dockyard Trust
An 80 acre site, in which the visitor can journey through 400 years of the history of Chatham and the Royal Navy, from its origins in the reign of Henry VII to the Falklands Crisis.
Location: OS Ref. TQ759 690. Signposted from M2/J1,3&4. From M2/J1&4 follow A289 to the Medway Tunnel. From M2/J3 follow the signs to Chatham, A229 then A230 and A231 and the brown tourist signs.
Open: 11 Feb - 29 Oct: daily, 10am - 6pm (dusk if earlier). Nov: Sat & Sun only.
Admission: Adult £10, Child (5-15yrs) £6.50, Conc £7.50. Family (2+2) £26.50, Additional family child £3.25.

CHIDDINGSTONE CASTLE 🏛
See pages 130/131 for double page entry.

COBHAM HALL 🏛
See page 132 for full page entry.

DANSON HOUSE
See page 133 for full page entry.

English Heritage Photo Library: Skyscan Balloon Photography

DEAL CASTLE ⚜
VICTORIA ROAD, DEAL, KENT CT14 7BA
www.english-heritage.org.uk/visits

Tel: 01304 372762 **Venue hire and Hospitality:** 01304 209889
Owner: English Heritage **Contact:** Visitor Operations Team
Crouching low and menacing, the huge, rounded bastions of this austere fort, built by Henry VIII, once carried 119 guns. A fascinating castle to explore, with long, dark passages, battlements and a huge basement. The interactive displays and exhibition give an interesting insight into the castle's history.
Location: OS Ref. TR378 521. SE of Deal town centre.
Open: 1 Apr - 30 Sept: daily, 10am - 6pm.
Admission: Adult £3.90, Child £2, Conc. £2.90. EH Members free.
ⓘWCs. 📷 🍴Exclusive private & corporate hospitality. ♿Restricted. 🎧 🅿 Coach parking on main road. 🐕 Guide dogs only. ▣Tel for details.

DODDINGTON PLACE GARDENS 🏛
Doddington, Nr Sittingbourne, Kent ME9 0BB
Tel: 01795 886385
Owner: Mr & Mrs Richard Oldfield **Contact:** Mrs Richard Oldfield
10 acres of landscaped gardens in an area of outstanding natural beauty.
Location: OS Ref. TQ944 575. 4m N from A20 at Lenham or 5m SW from A2 at Ospringe, W of Faversham.
Open: 16 Apr - 15 Jun: Suns & BH Mons, 2 - 5pm.
Admission: Adult £4, Child £1. Groups (10+) £3.50.

South East - England

DOVER CASTLE ⌗
AND THE SECRET
WARTIME TUNNELS

See page 135 for full page entry.

DYMCHURCH MARTELLO TOWER ⌗
Dymchurch, Kent
Tel: 01304 211067   **www**.english-heritage.org.uk/visits
Owner: English Heritage   **Contact:** Dover Castle
Built as one of 74 such towers to counter the threat of invasion by Napoleon, Dymchurch is perhaps the best example in the country. Fully restored. You can climb to the roof which is dominated by an original 24-pounder gun complete with traversing carriage.
Location: OS189, Ref. TR102 294. In Dymchurch, access from High Street.
Open: Aug BH & Heritage Open Days, 7 - 10 Sept.
Admission: Adult £2.50, Child £1.30, Conc. £1.90. EH Members Free.
🅿

EASTBRIDGE HOSPITAL OF ST THOMAS
High Street, Canterbury, Kent CT1 2BD
Tel 01227 471600   **Fax** 01227 701601   **e-mail**: eastbridge@freeuk.com
www.eastbridgehospital.co.uk   **Contact:** The Warden
Medieval pilgrims' hospital with 12th century undercroft, refectory and chapel.
Location: OS189, Ref. TR148 579. S side of Canterbury High Street.
Open: All year (except Good Fri, Christmas Day & 29 Dec): Mon - Sat, 10am 4.45pm. Includes Greyfriars Franciscan Chapel, House & Garden. Easter Mon - 27 Sept: Mon - Sat, 2 - 4pm.
Admission: Adult £1, Child 50p, Conc. 75p.

Restoration House.

NTPL / Jerry Harpur

NTPL / Jerry Harpur

EMMETTS GARDEN 🌾
IDE HILL, SEVENOAKS, KENT TN14 6AY

www.nationaltrust.org.uk/emmetts

Tel: 01732 750367/868381 (Chartwell office)   **Info:** 01732 751509
e-mail: emmetts@nationaltrust.org.uk
Owner: The National Trust   **Contact:** The Property Manager
        (Chartwell & Emmetts Garden, Mapleton Road, Westerham, Kent TN16 1PS)
Influenced by William Robinson, this charming and informal garden was laid out in the late 19th century, with many exotic and rare trees and shrubs from across the world. Wonderful views across the Weald of Kent – with the highest treetop in Kent. There are glorious shows of daffodils, bluebells, azaleas and rhododendrons, then

acers and cornus in autumn, also a rose garden and rock garden.
Location: OS Ref. TQ477 524. 1¹/2 m N of Ide Hill off B2042. M25/J5, then 4m.
Open: 25 Mar - 31 May: Tue - Sun; 1 Jun - 2 Jul: Wed - Sun, 5 Jul - 29 Oct: Wed, Sat & Sun. Open BH Mons.
Admission: Adult £5 (£7.50 with guide book), (£7 with Quebec House) Child £1, Family £11, Group Adult £4.
⬚ 🅿 Steep in places. WC. Buggy from car park to garden entrance.
🐕 ⬚ In grounds, on leads. ⬚ Tel for details.

FINCHCOCKS

FINCHCOCKS, GOUDHURST, KENT TN17 1HH

www.finchcocks.co.uk

Tel: 01580 211702   **Fax:** 01580 211007   **e-mail:** katrina@finchcocks.co.uk

Owner: Mr Richard Burnett   **Contact:** Mrs Katrina Burnett

In 1970 Finchcocks was acquired by Richard Burnett, leading exponent of the early piano, and it now contains his magnificent collection of some eighty historical keyboard instruments: chamber organs, harpsichords, virginals, spinets and early pianos. About half of these are restored to full concert condition and are played whenever the house is open to the public. The house, with its high ceilings and oak panelling, provides the perfect setting for music performed on period instruments, and Finchcocks is now a music centre of international repute. Many musical events take place here.

There is a fascinating collection of pictures and prints, mainly on musical themes, and a special exhibition on the theme of the 18th century pleasure gardens, which includes costumes and tableaux.

Finchcocks is a fine Georgian baroque manor noted for its outstanding brickwork, with a dramatic front elevation attributed to Thomas Archer. The present house was built in 1725 for barrister Edward Bathurst. Despite having changed hands many times, it has undergone remarkably little alteration and retains most of its original features. The beautiful grounds, with their extensive views over parkland and hop gardens, include the newly restored walled garden, which provides a dramatic setting for special events.

Location: 1m S of A262, 2m W of Goudhurst. 5m from Cranbrook, 10m from Tunbridge Wells, 45m from London (1 1/2 hrs). Rail: Marden 6m (no taxi), Paddock Wood 8m (taxi), Tunbridge Wells 10m (taxi).

Open: 16 Apr - 23 Sept & BH Mons, plus Wed & Thurs in Aug, 2 - 6pm. Groups & indivduals: Mid Mar - Christmas, at other times by arrangement. Closed Jan - early Mar.

Admission: Adult £8, Child £4, Student £5. Garden only: Adult £2.50, Child 50p. Group (25+): Charge dependent on numbers and programme.

Music events, conferences, seminars, promotions, archery, ballooning, filming, television. Instruments for hire. No videos in house, photography by permission only. Private and corporate entertaining, weddings. Limited. WC. Suitable for visually handicapped. Licensed. Picnics permitted in grounds. Musical tours/recitals. Tour time: 2 1/2 - 4 hrs. Pre-booked groups (25 - 100) welcome from Apr - Oct. Opportunity to play instruments. Can be linked to special projects & National Curriculum syllabus. Music a speciality. Tel for details.

Squerryes Court.

GOODNESTONE PARK GARDENS

Goodnestone Park, Nr Wingham, Canterbury, Kent CT3 1PL

Tel/Fax: 01304 840107   **e-mail:** fitzwalter@btinternet.com

www.goodnestoneparkgardens.co.uk

Owner/Contact: The Lady FitzWalter

The garden is approximately 14 acres, set in 18th century parkland. A new gravel garden was planted in 2003. There are many fine trees, a woodland area and a large walled garden with a collection of old-fashioned roses, clematis and herbaceous plants. Jane Austen was a frequent visitor, her brother Edward having married a daughter of the house.

Location: OS Ref. TR254 544. 8m ESE of Canterbury, 1 1/2 m E of B2046, at S end of village. The B2046 runs from the A2 to Wingham, the gardens are signposted from this road.

Open: 19 Feb - 1 Oct: Suns, 12 noon - 5pm. 22 Mar - 1 Oct: Wed - Sat & BH Mons, 11am - 5pm.

Admission: Adult £4, Child (under 12yrs) 50p, OAP £3.50, Student £2.50, Groups (20+): Adult £3.50. Guided garden tours: £5.50.

THE GRANGE

St Augustine's Road, Ramsgate, Kent CT11 9NY

Tel: 01628 825925   **www.**landmarktrust.org.uk

Owner: The Landmark Trust

Augustus Pugin built this house in 1843-4 to live in with his family. It was at The Grange that Pugin produced the designs for the interiors of the House of Lords and the Mediaeval Court at the Great Exhibition but he reserved some of his finest and most characteristic flourishes for his own home. The Landmark Trust, a building preservation charity, have undertaken a major restoration of the building which will be available for holidays all year round.

Location: OS Ref: TR3764

Open: Available for holidays for up to 8 people throughout the year. Parts of the ground floor will be open to the general public by appointment on Wednesday afternoons and there will be regular full Open Days. Contact the Landmark Trust for full details.

Admission: Wednesday afternoons & Open Days: Free.

Accommodation for up to 8 people.

South East - England

GREAT COMP GARDEN
COMP LANE, PLATT, BOROUGH GREEN, KENT TN15 8QS
www.greatcomp.co.uk

Tel: 01732 886154

Owner: R Cameron Esq   **Contact:** Mr W Dyson

One of the finest gardens in the country, comprising ruins, terraces, tranquil woodland walks and sweeping lawns with a breathtaking collection of trees, shrubs, heathers and perennials, many rarely seen elsewhere. The truly unique atmosphere of Great Comp is further complemented by its Festival of Chamber Music held in July/September.

Location: OS Ref. TQ635 567. 2m E of Borough Green, B2016 off A20. First right at Comp crossroads. 1/2 m on left.

Open: 1 Apr - 31 Oct: daily, 11am - 5.30pm.

Admission: Adult £4, Child £1. Groups (20+) £3.50. Annual ticket: Adult £12, OAP £8.

Teas daily. Guide dogs only. Tel for details.

HOLE PARK
█████████, ████████, ████ ████ ███
www.holepark.com

Tel: 01580 241344/241386   **Fax:** 01580 241882   **e-mail:** info@holepark.com

Owner/Contact: Edward Barham

A 15 acre garden with all year round interest, set in beautiful parkland with fine views. Trees, lawns and extensive yew hedges precisely cut are a feature. Walled garden with mixed borders, pools and water garden. Natural garden with bulbs, azaleas, rhododendrons and flowering shrubs. Bluebell walk and autumn colours a speciality.

Location: OS Ref. TQ830 325. 1m W of Rolvenden on B2086 Cranbrook road.

Open: April - Oct: Wed & Thur. 1 April - 2 July Suns. BHs: 17 April, 1 & 29 May. 8, 15 & 22 Oct. All 2 - 6pm except by arrangement. Charity openings for the National Garden Scheme (NGS), telephone or visit the website.

Admission: Adult £4, Child 50p. Groups welcome by appointment. Owner guided tours a speciality.

Suns, BHs & by arrangement. Groups, Suns & BHs only. By arrangement. Car park only. Tel for details.

LESNES ABBEY
Abbey Road, Abbey Wood, London DA17 5DL

Tel: 01322 526574

Owner: Bexley Council   **Contact:** Lynda Weaver

The Abbey was founded in 1178 by Richard de Lucy as penance for his involvement in events leading to the murder of Thomas à Becket. Today only the ruins remain.

Location: OS Ref. TQ479 788. In public park on S side of Abbey Road (B213), 500yds E of Abbey Wood Station, 3/4 m N of A206 Woolwich - Erith Road.

Open: Any reasonable time.

Admission: Free.

LULLINGSTONE CASTLE
Lullingstone Castle, Eynsford, Kent DA4 0JA

Tel: 01322 862114   **Fax:** 01322 862115

Owner/Contact: Guy Hart Dyke Esq

Fine state rooms, family portraits and armour in beautiful grounds. The 15th century gatehouse was one of the first ever to be made of bricks. This is also the site for the World Garden of Plants and for Lullingstone's Parish Church of St Botolph.

Location: OS Ref. TQ530 644. 1m S Eynsford W side of A225. 600yds S of Roman Villa.

Open: Apr - Oct: Fri & Sat, 12 noon - 5pm; Suns & BHs, 2 - 6pm. Booked groups by arrangement. Closed Good Fri.

Admission: Adult £5.50, Child £2.50, OAP £5, Family £12.50 Groups (15+): £4.50 pp plus £35 for a dedicated guide.

No interior photography. Partial. Teas at visitor centre, 1km. By arrangement. Limited.

LULLINGSTONE ROMAN VILLA ⌗

LULLINGSTONE LANE, EYNSFORD, KENT DA4 0JA

www.english-heritage.org.uk/visits

Tel: 01322 863467

Owner: English Heritage   **Contact:** Visitor Operations Team

Recognised as one of the most exciting archaeological finds of the century, the villa has splendid mosaic floors and one of the earliest private Christian chapels. Take the inclusive audio tour and discover how the prosperous Romans lived, worked and entertained themselves.

Location: OS Ref. TQ529 651. ¹/₂ mile SW of Eynsford off A225, M25/J3. Follow A20 towards Brands Hatch. 600yds N of Castle.

Open: 1 Apr - 30 Sept: daily, 10am - 6pm. 1 Oct - 30 Nov & 1 Feb - 31 Mar: daily, 10am - 4pm. 1 Dec - 31 Jan: Wed - Sun, 10am - 4pm. Closed 24 - 26 Dec & 1 Jan.

Admission: Adult £3.90, Child £2, Conc. £2.90. EH Members Free.

⬜ ♿ Ground floor & grounds. WC. ⬛ ✖ ❄ ♨ Tel for details.

MAISON DIEU ⌗

Ospringe, Faversham, Kent

Tel: 01795 534542   **www.**english-heritage.org.uk/visits

Owner: English Heritage   **Contact:** The Faversham Society

This forerunner of today's hospitals remains largely as it was in the 16th century with exposed beams and an overhanging upper storey.

Location: OS Ref. TR002 608. In Ospringe on A2, ¹/₂ mile W of Faversham.

Open: 14 Apr - 29 Oct: Sats & Suns, Good Fri & BHs, 2 - 5pm. Keykeeper in Winter.

Admission: Adult £1, Child 50p, OAP 80p. EH Members Free.

ℹ️ WCs. ✖

MILTON CHANTRY ⌗

New Tavern Fort Gardens, Gravesend, Kent

Tel: 01474 321520   **www.**english-heritage.org.uk/visits

Owner: English Heritage   **Contact:** Gravesham Borough Council

A small 14th-century building which housed the chapel of the leper hospital and the chantry of the de Valence and Montechais families and later became a tavern.

Location: OS Ref. TQ652 743. In New Tavern Fort Gardens ¹/₄ mile E of Gravesend off A226.

Open: 1 Apr - 30 Sept: Wed - Sat, 12 noon - 5pm; Sun & BHs, 10am - 5pm. 1 Oct - 17 Dec & 1 - 31 Mar: Sats & Suns, 12 noon - 4pm. Closed Jan & Feb.

Admission: Adult £1.50, Child/Conc. 75p. EH Members Free.

✖

MOUNT EPHRAIM GARDENS 🏠

Hernhill, Faversham, Kent ME13 9TX

Tel: 01227 751496   **Fax:** 01227 750940

Owner: Mr & Mrs E S Dawes & Mrs M N Dawes   **Contact:** Mrs L Dawes

10 acres of superb gardens set in the heart of family run orchards. New grass maze.

Location: OS Ref. TR065 598. In Hernhill village, 1m from end of M2. Signed from A2 & A299.

Open: Easter - end Sept: Weds, Thurs, Sats, Suns & BH Mons only, 1 - 6pm. Groups Mar - end Oct, by arrangement.

Admission: Adult £4.00, Child £1. Groups: £3.50.

NURSTEAD COURT

Nurstead Church Lane, Meopham, Nr Gravesend, Kent DA13 9AD

Tel: 01474 812368 (guided tours); 01474 812121 (weddings & functions)

Fax: 01474 815133   **e-mail:** info@nursteadcourt.co.uk   **www.**nursteadcourt.co.uk

Owner/Contact: Mrs S Edmeades-Stearns

Nurstead Court is a Grade I listed manor house built in 1320 of timber-framed, crown-posted construction, set in extensive gardens and parkland. The additional front part of the house was built in 1825. Licensed weddings are now held in the house with receptions and other functions in the garden marquee.

Location: OS Ref. TQ642 685. Nurstead Church Lane is just off the A227 N of Meopham, 3m from Gravesend.

Open: Sept: Wed & Thur & 4 - 5 Oct, 2 - 5pm. All year round by arrangement.

Admission: Adult £5, Child £2.50, OAP/Student £4. Group (max 54): £4.

ℹ️ Open by arrangement for guided tours. Weddings & functions also catered for. ▼ ◼ Licensed. ♿ WCs. 🎦 By arrangement. 🅿 Limited for coaches. 🐕 On leads, in grounds. ▲ ❄

OLD SOAR MANOR ⚜

Plaxtol, Borough Green, Kent TN15 0QX

Tel: 01732 810378   **Info Line:** 01732 811145

Owner: The National Trust   **Contact:** The Property Manager

Location: OS Ref. TQ619 541.

Open: 1 Apr - 28 Sept: daily except Fri, including BHs & Good Fri, 10am - 6pm.

Admission: Free.

Hall Place.

QUEBEC HOUSE ✤
WESTERHAM, KENT TN16 1TD

Tel: 01732 868381 (Chartwell office) **Email:** chartwell@nationaltrust.org.uk

Owner: The National Trust **Contact:** Chartwell Office

This Grade I listed gabled house is situated in the centre of the beautiful village of Westerham. Many features of significant architectural and historical interest reflect its 16th century origins as well as changes made in the 18th and 20th centuries.

Quebec House was the childhood home of General James Wolfe, and rooms contain family and military memorabilia, prints and portraits. The Tudor Coach

House houses an exhibition about the battle of Quebec (1759) and the part played there by Wolfe, who led the British forces to victory over the French.

Location: OS Ref. TQ449 541. At E end of village, on N side of A25, facing junction with B2026, Edenbridge Road.

Open: 1 Apr - 29 Oct: Wed - Sun & BH Mons 1 - 4.30pm.

Admission: Adult £3.50, Child £1.50, Family (2+3) £8.50. Group Adult £3.00. Joint ticket with Emmetts Garden £7.

PENSHURST PLACE & GARDENS *See page 142 for full page entry.*

QUEX HOUSE & GARDEN & POWELL COTTON MUSEUM
Quex Park, Birchington, Kent CT7 0BH

Tel: 01843 842168 **e-mail:** powell-cotton.museum@virgin.net

www.powell-cottonmuseum.co.uk

Owner: Trustees of Powell Cotton Museum **Contact:** Julia Walton, Director

Regency/Victorian country residence, walled gardens and Victorian explorers' museum.

Location: OS Ref. TR308 683. 1/2 m from Birchington Church via Park Lane.

Open: Please contact Museum for details.

Admission: Summer: Adult £5, Child, OAP, Disabled & Carer £4, Student £3.50, Family (2+3) £14. Winter: Adult £4, Child, OAP, Disabled & Carer £3, Family (2+3) £10. (2005 prices.)

RECULVER TOWERS & ROMAN FORT ⌗
Reculver, Herne Bay, Kent

Tel: 01227 740676 **www**.english-heritage.org.uk/visits

Owner: English Heritage **Contact:** Reculver Country Park

This 12th-century landmark of twin towers has guided sailors into the Thames estuary for seven centuries. Includes walls of a Roman fort, which were erected nearly 2,000 years ago.

Location: OS Ref. TR228 694. At Reculver 3 miles E of Herne Bay by the seashore.

Open: Any reasonable time. External viewing only.

Admission: Free.

ⓘWCs. ♿Ground floor only. Long slope up from car park. 🅿 🚍Dogs on leads. ✳

accommodation
see page 567

Turkey Mill.

David Winston, Period Piano Company

RESTORATION HOUSE 🏛

17 – 19 CROW LANE, ROCHESTER, KENT ME1 1RF

www.restorationhouse.co.uk

Tel: 01634 848520 **Fax:** 01634 880058
email: robert.tucker@restorationhouse.co.uk
Owner: R Tucker & J Wilmot   **Contact:** Robert Tucker

Unique survival of an ancient city mansion deriving its name from the stay of Charles II on the eve of The Restoration. Beautiful interiors with exceptional early paintwork related to decorative scheme 'run up' for Charles' visit. The house also inspired Dickens to situate 'Miss Havisham' here.

'Interiors of rare historical resonance and poetry', *Country Life*. Fine English furniture and pictures (Mytens, Kneller, Dahl, Reynolds and several Gainsboroughs). Charming interlinked walled gardens of ingenious plan in a classic English style. A private gem. 'There is no finer pre-Civil war town house in England than this' – Simon Jenkins, *The Times*.

Location: OS Ref, TQ744 683. Historic centre of Rochester, off High Street, opposite the Vines Park.
Open: 1 Jun - 29 Sept: Thurs, Fri & Sat 3 Jun, 10am - 5pm.
Admission: Adult £5.50 (includes 24 page illustrated guidebook), Child £2.75, Conc £4.50. Booked group (8+) tours: £6.50pp.
ⓘ No stiletto heels. No photography in house. Garden by appointment. 1st Thurs in month. By arrangement. None. Guide dogs only.

RICHBOROUGH ROMAN FORT ⌗
Richborough, Sandwich, Kent CT13 9JW
Tel: 01304 612013 www.english-heritage.org.uk/visits
Owner: English Heritage   **Contact:** Visitor Operations Team
This fort and township date back to the Roman landing in AD43. The fortified walls and the massive foundations of a triumphal arch which stood 80 feet high still survive. The inclusive audio tour and the museum give an insight into life in Richborough's heyday as a busy township.
Location: OS Ref. TR324 602. 1½ miles NW of Sandwich off A257.
Open: 1 Apr - 30 Sept: daily, 10am - 6pm.
Admission: Gardens: Adult £3.90, Child £2, Conc. £2.90. EH Members Free.
ⓘ Museum. Ground floor. P Guide dogs only. Tel for details.

RIVERHILL HOUSE 🏛
Sevenoaks, Kent TN15 0RR
Tel: 01732 458802/452557 **Fax:** 01732 458802
Owner: The Rogers Family   **Contact:** Mrs Rogers
Small country house built in 1714.
Location: OS Ref. TQ541 522. 2m S of Sevenoaks on E side of A225.
Open: Garden: 2 April - 18 June: Suns & BH weekends, 11am - 5pm. House: 2 April - 18 June, open only to pre-booked groups of adults (20+)
Admission: Adult £3, Child 50p. Pre-booked groups: £4.50.

ROCHESTER CASTLE ⌗
The Lodge, Rochester-upon-Medway, Medway ME1 1SX
Tel: 01634 402276 www.english-heritage.org.uk/visits
Owner: English Heritage   **Contact:** Visitor Operations Team
(Managed by Medway Council)
Built in the 11th century. The keep is over 100 feet high and with walls 12 feet thick.
Location: OS Ref. TQ743 685. By Rochester Bridge. Follow A2 E from M2/J1 & M25/J2.
Open: 1 Apr - 30 Sept: daily, 10am - 6pm. 1 Oct - 31 Mar: daily, 10am - 4pm. Closed 24 - 26 Dec & 1 Jan.
Admission: Adult £4, Child £3, Conc £3, Family £11. EH Members Free.
ⓘ WCs.

ROCHESTER CATHEDRAL
Garth House, The Precinct, Rochester, Kent ME1 1SX
Tel: 01634 401301 **Fax:** 01634 401410 www.rochestercathedral.org
e-mail: visitsofficer@rochestercathedraluk.org
Rochester Cathedral has been a place of Christian worship since its foundation in 604AD. The present building is a blend of Norman and gothic architecture with a fine crypt and Romanesque façade. The first real fresco in an English Cathedral for 800 years is now on view to the public.
Location: OS Ref. TQ742 686. Signed from M20/J6 & A2/M2/J3. Best access from M2/J3.
Open: All year: 8.30am - 5pm. Visiting may be restricted during services.
Admission: Suggested donation. Adult £3. Guided groups: £3.50, please book on above number. Separate prices for schools.
ⓘ Photography permit £1. By arrangement. P

ROMAN PAINTED HOUSE
New Street, Dover, Kent CT17 9AJ
Tel: 01304 203279
Owner: Dover Roman Painted House Trust   **Contact:** Mr B Philp
Discovered in 1970. Built around 200AD as a hotel for official travellers. Impressive wall paintings, central heating systems and the Roman fort wall built through the house.
Location: OS Ref. TR318 414. Dover town centre. E of York St.
Open: Apr - Sept: 10am - 5pm, except Mons.
Admission: Adult £2, Child/OAP 80p.

ST AUGUSTINE'S ABBEY ⌗
Longport, Canterbury, Kent CT1 1TF
Tel: 01227 767345 www.english-heritage.org.uk/visits
Owner: English Heritage   **Contact:** Visitor Operations Team
The abbey, founded by St. Augustine in 598, is a World Heritage Site. Take the free interactive audio tour which gives a fascinating insight into the abbey's history and visit the museum displaying artifacts uncovered during archaeological excavations of the site.
Location: OS Ref. TR154 578. In Canterbury ½ mile E of Cathedral Close.
Open: 1 Apr - 30 Sept: daily, 10am - 6pm. 1 Oct - 31 Mar: Wed - Sun, 10am - 4pm. Closed 24 - 26 Dec & 1 Jan.
Admission: Adult £3.90, Child £2, Conc. £2.90. 15% discount for groups (11+). EH Members Free.
Grounds. Free. P Nearby. Guide dogs only. Tel for details.

ST JOHN'S COMMANDERY ⌗
Densole, Swingfield, Kent
Tel: 01304 211067 www.english-heritage.org.uk/visits
Owner: English Heritage   **Contact:** Dover Castle
A medieval chapel built by the Knights Hospitallers. It has a moulded plaster ceiling and a remarkable timber roof and was converted into a farmhouse in the 16th century.
Location: OS Ref. TR232 440. 2 miles NE of Densole on minor road off A260.
Open: Any reasonable time for exterior viewing. Internal viewing by appointment only. Please call 01304 211067.
Admission: Free.

South East - England

NT Photographic Library / Jenny Harpur

SCOTNEY CASTLE GARDEN & ESTATE ❧

LAMBERHURST, TUNBRIDGE WELLS, KENT TN3 8JN

www.nationaltrust.org.uk/scotneycastle

Tel: 01892 891081 **Fax:** 01892 890110 **e-mail:** scotneycastle@nationaltrust.org.uk

Owner: The National Trust   **Contact:** Property Manager

One of England's most romantic gardens designed by Edward Hussey in the picturesque style. Dramatic vistas from the terrace of the new Scotney Castle, built in the 1830s, lead down to the ruins of a 14th century moated castle. Rhododendrons, kalmia, azaleas and wisteria flower in profusion. Roses and clematis scramble over the remains of the Old Castle, which is open for the summer. In autumn the garden's glowing colours merge with the surrounding woodlands where there are many country walks to be explored all year round.

Location: OS Ref. TQ688 353. Signed off A21 1m S of Lamberhurst village.

Open: Garden & Shop: Mar: Sats & Suns 11am - 6pm. 18 Mar - 29 Oct: Wed - Sun 11am - 6pm. Last entry 5pm or at dusk if earlier. Old Castle: 29 April - 1 Oct, Wed - Sun. Shop: as Garden. Estate: open all year round for estate walks. Closed Good Friday.

Admission: Adult £5.20, Child £2.60, Family £13.00. NT members free.

⬜ ✢ ♿ Grounds (but steep parts). 🏴 🅿 🐕 Outside garden only, on leads. ✳
♿ Tel for details.

© NT Photographic Library / Eric Crichton

SISSINGHURST CASTLE GARDEN ❧

SISSINGHURST, CRANBROOK, KENT TN17 2AB

www.nationaltrust.org.uk/sissinghurst

Tel: 01580 710700 **Infoline:** 01580 710701

e-mail: sissinghurst@nationaltrust.org.uk

Owner: The National Trust   **Contact:** The Administration Assistant

One of the world's most celebrated gardens, the creation of Vita Sackville-West and her husband Sir Harold Nicolson. Developed around the surviving parts of an Elizabethan mansion with a central red-brick prospect tower, a series of small, enclosed compartments, intimate in scale and romantic in atmosphere, provide outstanding design and colour throughout the season. The study, where Vita worked, and library are also open to visitors.

Location: OS Ref. TQ807 383. 2m NE of Cranbrook, 1m E of Sissinghurst village (A262).

Open: 18 Mar - 29 Oct: Fri - Tues, including BHs & Good Fri, 11am - 6.30pm; Sat, Sun, BHs & Good Fri, 10am - 6.30pm. Last admission 1 hour before closing or dusk if earlier.

Admission: Adult £7.80, Child £3.50, Family (2+3) £20. NT members Free.

⬜ ✢ ♿ WCs. 🍴 Licensed. 🅿 Ample. Limited for coaches.
🐕 Grounds only, on leads. Guide dogs only in Garden.

© NT Photographic Library / David Sellham

SMALLHYTHE PLACE ❧

TENTERDEN, KENT TN30 7NG

www.nationaltrust.org.uk/smallhytheplace

Tel: 01580 762334 **Fax:** 01580 762334

e-mail: smallhytheplace@nationaltrust.org.uk

Owner: The National Trust   **Contact:** Assistant Property Manager

This early 16th century half-timbered house was home to Shakespearean actress Ellen Terry from 1899 to 1928. The house contains many personal and theatrical mementoes, including her lavish costumes. The grounds include the barn theatre and beautiful cottage garden. Many events take place in the grounds and the theatre.

Location: OS Ref. TQ893 300. 2m S of Tenterden on E side of the Rye road B2082.

Open: 4 - 19 Mar: Sats & Suns. 25 Mar - 29 Oct: daily except Thur & Fri (open Good Fri), 11am - 5pm, last admission 4.30pm.

Admission: Adult £4.50, Child £2.25, Family £11.25.

ℹ️ No photography in house. ✢ ♿ Ground floor only. 🅿 Limited.
🐕 On leads, in grounds. ♿ Tel for details.

SOUTH FORELAND LIGHTHOUSE

The Front, St Margaret's Bay, Nr Dover, CT15 6HP
Tel: 01304 852463 **Fax:** 01304 215484 **e-mail:** southforeland@nationaltrust.org.uk
Owner: The National Trust **Contact:** Volunteer Co-ordinator
Distinctive Historical Victorian Lighthouse on the White Cliffs of Dover.
Location: OS138 Ref. TR359 433. 2 mile walk from White Cliffs car park, 1mile walk
from St Margaret's Village, short walk from bus stop route number 113.
Open: 4 Mar - 29 Oct, Sat & Sun, 11am - 5.30pm (last entry 5pm). Open daily during local
school holidays.
Admission: Adult £3.60, Child £1.80, Family £9.

SQUERRYES COURT

See page 143 for full page entry.
MANOR HOUSE & GARDENS

STONEACRE

Otham, Maidstone, Kent ME15 8RS
Tel/Fax: 01622 862157
Owner: The National Trust **Contact:** The Tenant
A late 15th century yeoman's house, with great hall and crownpost, surrounded by
harmonious garden, orchard and meadow.
Location: OS Ref. TQ800 535. In narrow lane at N end of Otham village, 3m SE of
Maidstone, 1m S of A20.
Open: 18 Mar - 11 Oct: Weds & Sats, 2 - 6pm (last admission 5pm).
Admission: Adult £3.00, Child £1.50, Family (2+3) £7.50. Groups £2.50.

TEMPLE MANOR

Strood, Rochester, Kent
Tel: 01634 338110 **www**.english-heritage.org.uk/visits
Owner: English Heritage **Contact:** Medway
Council
The 13th-century manor house of the Knights Templar which mainly provided
accommodation for members of the order travelling between London and the
Continent.
Location: OS Ref. TQ733 686. In Strood (Rochester) off A228.
Open: 1 Apr - 30 Sept: Suns, 10am - 6pm. Oct: Suns, 10am - 4pm. For group visits,
please call 01634 843666.
Admission: Free.
Grounds only.

TONBRIDGE CASTLE

Castle Street, Tonbridge, Kent TN9 1BG
Tel: 01732 770929 **www**.tonbridgecastle.org
Owner: Tonbridge & Malling Borough Council **Contact:** The Administrator
Location: OS Ref. TQ588 466. 300 yds NW of the Medway Bridge at town centre.
Open: All year: Mon - Sat, 9am - 4pm. Suns & BHs, 10.30am - 4pm.
Admission: Gatehouse - Adult £5, Conc. £3. Family £13.50 (max 2 adults). Admission
includes audio tour. Last tour 1 hour before closing.

TURKEY MILL

See page 144 for full page entry.

UPNOR CASTLE

Upnor, Kent
Tel: 01634 718742 **www**.english-heritage.org.uk/visits
Owner: English Heritage **Contact:** Medway Council
Well preserved 16th-century gun fort built to protect Queen Elizabeth I's warships.
However in 1667 it failed to prevent the Dutch Navy which stormed up the Medway
destroying half the English fleet.
Location: OS Ref. TQ758 706. At Upnor, on unclassified road off A228. 2 miles NE
of Strood.
Open: 1 Apr - 30 Sept: daily 10am - 6pm. Oct: daily, 10am - 4pm.
Admission: Adult £4, Child £3, Conc £3, Family £11. EH Members Free.
WCs. Grounds only. On leads in restricted areas.

education index
see page 564

WALMER CASTLE AND GARDENS

WALMER, DEAL, KENT CT14 7LJ

www.english-heritage.org.uk/visits

Tel: 01304 364288 **Venue Hire and Hospitality:** 01304 209889
Owner: English Heritage **Contact:** Visitor Operations Team
A Tudor fort transformed into an elegant stately home. The residence of the Lords
Warden of the Cinque Ports, who have included HM The Queen Mother,
Sir Winston Churchill and the Duke of Wellington. Take the inclusive audio tour and
see the Duke's rooms where he died over 150 years ago. Beautiful gardens including
the Queen Mother's Garden, The Broadwalk with its famous yew tree hedge, Kitchen
Garden & Moat Garden. Lunches and cream teas available in the delightful Lord
Warden's tearooms.

Location: OS Ref. TR378 501. S of Walmer on A258, M20/J13 or M2 to Deal.
Open: 1 Mar - 30 Sept: daily, 10am - 6pm (4pm Mar & Sats). 1 - 31 Oct: Wed - Sun,
10am - 4pm. 1 - 31 Mar: daily, 10am - 4pm. Closed 7 - 9 Jul when Lord Warden in
residence.
Admission: Adult £6.20, Child £3.10, Conc. £4.70, Family £15.50. 15% discount for
groups (11+). English Heritage members free.

WCs. Private & corporate hire. Grounds. Guide dogs only.
Tel for details.

WESTENHANGER CASTLE AND BARNS

STONE STREET, WESTENHANGER, HYTHE, KENT CT21 4HX

www.westenhangercastle.co.uk

Tel: 01227 738223 **Fax:** 01227 738278 **e-mail:** graham.forge@btopenworld.com
Owner: G Forge Ltd **Contact:** Graham Forge

Part scheduled and part Grade I listed, Westenhanger Castle is one of Kent's forgotten great houses. The monument has undergone nine phases of English Heritage assisted restoration work. This once magnificent fortified 14th century manor house of major significance in Tudor times retains many features within the ruins of the curtain wall, including Tudor fireplaces and a dovecote with 420 nesting boxes. The 16th century barn, adjoining an earlier stable range, was built extravagantly with hammerbeam roof, four wagon porches and bridges over a stream. The attractive setting offers a step back in time in a peaceful and relaxed atmosphere.

Location: OS Ref. TR123 372. Next to Folkestone Racecourse. Leave M20/J11 towards Hythe.

Open: Tue - Thurs by prior arrangement.

Admission: Mon - Fri only. Owner guided tours: £12pp. Groups (15 - 40) £5.50pp. Educational groups (schools and students): £3pp.

⊤ ⅄ ⬛ Licenced. 🅵 Obligatory. 🅿 Limited for coaches. ⬛ 🐕 On leads, in grounds. ⬛ ✷ ☑ Tel for details.

WHITE CLIFFS OF DOVER ✄

Upper Road, Langdon Cliffs, Nr Dover, CT16 1HJ
Tel: 01304 202756 **Fax:** 01304 2154840 **e-mail:** whitecliffs@nationaltrust.org.uk
The Gateway to the White Cliffs is a Visitor Centre and Coffee Shop with spectacular views across the English Channel.
Location: OS138 Ref. TR336 422. Follow White Cliffs brown signs from roundabout 1m NE of Dover at J of A2/A258.
Open: All year: 1 Mar - 31 Oct, 10am - 5pm. 1 Nov - 28 Feb: 11am - 4pm.
Admission: Car Park £2.50, Motorcycles/Blue Badge Holders £1.50, Motor homes £3, Coaches £5, Season tickets £20. NT Members Free.

WILLESBOROUGH WINDMILL

Mill Lane, Willesborough, Ashford, Kent TN24 0QG
Tel: 01233 661866
130 year old smock mill. Civil Wedding Licence.
Location: OS Ref. TR031 421. Off A292 close to M20/J10. At E end of Ashford.
Open: Apr - end Sept; Sats, Suns & BH Mons, also Weds in Jul & Aug, 2 - 5pm or dusk if earlier.
Admission: Adult £3, Conc. £1.50. Groups 10% reduction by arrangement only.

YALDING ORGANIC GARDENS

Benover Road, Yalding, Maidstone, Kent ME18 6EX
Tel: 01622 814650 **Fax:** 01622 814650 **e-mail:** enquiry@hdra.org.uk
www.gardenorganic.org.uk
Owner: Garden Organic **Contact:** Tania Neumann
Five acres of stunning gardens tracing the history of gardening from medieval times to the present day. Described by the *Daily Telegraph* as 'among the most inspirational gardens anywhere, for everyone'. Kids will love the children's garden. Home cooking a speciality. Great shop. The gardens regularly appear on TV.
Location: OS Ref. TQ698 490. 6m SW of Maidstone, ½ m S of Yalding village on B2162. Rail 1½ m. Bus from Maidstone - Yalding.
Open: Apr - Oct: Wed - Sun & BH Mons. Nov & Dec: weekends, 10am - 5pm.
Admission: Adult £4, Child £1, Conc. £3. Guided tour for groups £1.
🌳 🍴 ⅄ ⬛ 🍴 🅵 By arrangement. ⬛ 🅿 🐕 Guide dogs only.

Danson House.

MAP 3

ARDINGTON HOUSE

www.ardingtonhouse.com

Owner:
The Baring Family

▶ **CONTACT**

Nigel Baring
Ardington House
Wantage
Oxfordshire OX12 8QA

Tel: 01235 821566
Fax: 01235 821151
e-mail: info@
ardingtonhouse.com

▶ **LOCATION**

OS Ref. SU432 883

12m S of Oxford, 12m
N of Newbury,
2¹/₂ m E of Wantage.

Just a few miles south of Oxford stands the hauntingly beautiful Ardington House. Surrounded by well-kept lawns, terraced gardens, peaceful paddocks, parkland and its own romantic island this Baroque house is the private home of the Barings. You will find it in the attractive village of Ardington, close to the Ridgeway on the edge of the Berkshire Downs.

Built by the Strong brothers in 1720 with typical Georgian symmetry, the House is also famous for its Imperial Staircase. Leading from the Hall, the staircase is considered by experts to be one of the finest examples in Britain.

Away from the crowds and the hustle of the workplace Ardington House provides a private and secluded setting. The calm, exclusive use environment allows for weddings, offsite board

meetings, conferences and workshops utilising the splendid gardens and grounds. There is a heated outdoor swimming pool, tennis court, croquet lawn and trout river. Close by is the ancient Ridgeway Path, a popular place for walking or mountain biking.

Ardington House is licensed to hold civil wedding ceremonies. Receptions can range from drinks and intimate dining in the house, to a full dinner and dance reception using marquees in the grounds.

Poet Laureate Sir John Betjeman wrote of the homeliness and warmth of Ardington House, and the rooms have seen many special occasions and important visitors in the past with this tradition being continued. The astonishing mixture of history, warmth and style you'll find at Ardington truly does place it in a class of its own.

▶ **OPENING TIMES**

1 - 5, 8 - 12, 15 - 19 May
31 July, 1 - 4, 7 - 11,
14 - 18 August
2.30 - 4.30pm.

Guided tours at 2.30pm.

▶ **ADMISSION**

House & Gardens

Adult £4.50

CONFERENCE/FUNCTION

ROOM	MAX CAPACITY
Imperial Hall	
Theatre Style	80
U shape	30
Cabaret	40
Oak Room	
Theatre Style	40
U shape	20
Cabaret	30
Music Room	
Theatre Style	40
U shape	20
Cabaret	30

ℹ️ Conferences, product launches, films.

🍸

☕ Lunches and teas by arrangement for groups.

🚶 By members of the family.

🅿️ Free.

♿

🐕 Guide dogs only.

📷

🔔 Tel for details.

BLENHEIM PALACE 🏛

www.blenheimpalace.com

The state rooms of Blenheim Palace hold many treasures, from world famous tapestries to furniture, paintings, porcelain, clocks and sculptures. An unusually large collection of family portraits by great masters graces the walls. These include Joshua Reynolds' painting of the 4th Duke and family, a John Singer Sargent of the 9th Duke and family including Consuelo Vanderbilt, and a huge Clostermann of John Churchill, the 1st Duke, with his family. The collection of Chippendale and Boulle furniture is 'second to none in a historic home'. 2006 sees the restoration of the historic Terracotta statues to the façade of the Palace.

The Palace, home of the 11th Duke of Marlborough and birthplace of Sir Winston Churchill, was built for John Churchill, 1st Duke of Marlborough by Sir John Vanbrugh between 1705

and 1722. The land and sum of £240,000 were given to the Duke by Queen Anne and a grateful nation in recognition of his great victory over the French at the Battle of Blenheim in 1704. It is now considered a masterpiece of English Baroque.

The original gardens were designed by Queen Anne's gardener Henry Wise, with later alterations by Lancelot "Capability" Brown which included the creation of Blenheim's most outstanding feature, the lake. In more recent times the French architect, Achille Duchêne, built the formal gardens to the east and west of the Palace. The combination of house, gardens and park was recognised as uniquely important when Blenheim was listed as a World Heritage Site.

The Pleasure Gardens area includes the Marlborough Maze, the Butterfly House, the Herb and Lavender Garden and the Adventure Play Area.

MAP 7

Owner:
The Duke of Marlborough

▶ CONTACT

Operations Director
Blenheim Palace
Woodstock OX20 1PX

Tel: 08700 602080
Fax: 01993 810570
e-mail: administrator@
blenheimpalace.com

▶ LOCATION

OS Ref. SP441 161

From London, M40, A44 (1¹/₂ hrs), 8m NW of Oxford. London 63m Birmingham 54m.

Air: Heathrow 60m. Birmingham 50m.

Coach: From London (Victoria) to Oxford.

Rail: Oxford Station.

Bus: No.20 from Oxford Station, Gloucester Green & Cornmarket.

CONFERENCE/FUNCTION

ROOM	SIZE	MAX CAPACITY
Orangery		230
Marlborough Room		80
Saloon	50' x 30'	80
Great Hall		160
with Great Hall & Library		500
Library	180' x 30'	320

Four Shops.

Filming, product launches, activity days. No photography in house.

Corporate hospitality, including dinners and receptions and team building events.

Car park for the disabled. Adapted toilets.

1 Restaurant, 2 Cafés. Group enquiries welcome (up to 150). Menus on request.

In off peak season; guides in rooms in peak season. Private and language tours may be pre-booked.

Unlimited for cars and coaches.

Sandford Award holder since 1982. Teacher pre-visits welcome.

Dogs on leads in Park. Registered assistance dogs only in house and garden.

Full programme. Tel for details.

John Singer Sargent painting of 9th Duke and his family

Gardens & Park

Main Season: 11 - 19 Feb & 1 April - 29 Oct inclusive

Adult	£9.00
Child*	£4.50
Conc	£7.00
Family	£23.00

Groups (15+)

Adult	£6.25
Child*	£3.00
Conc	£5.25

Low Season: 20 - Feb - 31 Mar, 1 Nov - 10 Dec

Adult	£7.00
Child*	£2.50
Conc	£5.00
Family	£17.00

Groups (15+)

Adult	£5.00
Child*	£1.80
Conc	£4.00

*(5 - 16yrs)

Private tours by appointment only, prices on request.

▶ OPENING TIMES

Palace, Garden & Park

11 February - 29 October Daily

1 November - 10 December: Wed - Sun

10.30am - 5.30pm Last admission 4.45pm.

Park only

11 December 2006 - mid February 2007: Daily, 9am - Dusk.

The Duke of Marlborough reserves the right to close the Palace or Park or to amend admission prices without notice.

▶ ADMISSION

Season Tickets available.

Palace, Garden & Park

Main Season 11 - 19 Feb & 1 April – 29 Oct

Adult	£14.00
Child*	£8.50
Conc	£11.50
Family (2+2)	£37.00

Groups (15+)

Adult	£10.25
Child*	£5.30
Conc	£9.00

Low Season: 20 Feb - 31 Mar, 1 Nov - 10 Dec

Adult	£12.00
Child*	£6.50
Conc	£9.50
Family (2+2)	£31.00

Groups (15+)

Adult	£9.00
Child*	£4.80
Conc	£8.00

Park only

11 December 2006 - mid February 2007

Adult	£2.50
Child*	£1.50

BROUGHTON CASTLE

www.broughtoncastle.demon.co.uk

Broughton Castle is essentially a family home lived in by Lord and Lady Saye & Sele and their family.

The original medieval Manor House, of which much remains today, was built in about 1300 by Sir John de Broughton. It stands on an island site surrounded by a 3-acre moat. The Castle was greatly enlarged between 1550 and 1600, at which time it was embellished with magnificent plaster ceilings, splendid panelling and fine fireplaces.

In the 17th century William, 8th Lord Saye & Sele, played a leading role in national affairs. He opposed Charles I's efforts to rule without Parliament and Broughton became a secret meeting place for the King's opponents.

During the Civil War William raised a regiment and he and his four sons all fought at the nearby Battle of Edgehill. After the battle the Castle was besieged and captured.

Arms and armour from the Civil War and other periods are displayed in the Great Hall. Visitors may also see the gatehouse, gardens and park together with the nearby 14th century Church of St Mary, in which there are many family tombs, memorials and hatchments.

GARDENS
The garden area consists of mixed herbaceous and shrub borders containing many old roses. In addition, there is a formal walled garden with beds of roses surrounded by box hedging and lined by more mixed borders.

Owner:
Lord Saye & Sele

▶ CONTACT
Mrs J Moorhouse
Broughton Castle
Broughton
Nr Banbury
Oxfordshire
OX15 5EB

Tel: 01295 722547

e-mail:
admin@broughton
castle.demon.co.uk

▶ LOCATION
OS Ref. SP418 382

Broughton Castle is 2¹/₂ m SW of Banbury Cross on the B4035, Shipston-on-Stour - Banbury Road. Easily accessible from Stratford-on-Avon, Warwick, Oxford, Burford and the Cotswolds. M40/J11.

Rail: From London/ Birmingham to Banbury.

▶ OPENING TIMES
Summer
Easter Sun & Mon
1 May - 15 September
Weds & Suns
2 - 5pm.

Also Thurs in July and August and all BH Suns & Mons
2 - 5pm.

Groups welcome on any day and at any time throughout the year by appointment.

▶ ADMISSION
Adult £6.00
Child (5-15yrs)....... £2.50
OAP/Student £5.00
Groups (15 -100)
Adult £5.50
Child (5-15yrs)....... £2.50
OAP/Student £5.50

 Photography allowed in house.

❄ Partial.

♿ Teas on Open Days. Groups may book morning coffee, light lunches and afternoon teas.

🚶 Available for booked groups.

P Limited.

🐕 Guide dogs only in house. On leads in grounds.

❄ Open all year for groups.

26A EAST ST HELEN STREET
Abingdon, Oxfordshire

Tel: 01865 242918 **e-mail:** info@oxfordpreservation.org.uk
www.oxfordpreservation.org.uk

Owner: Oxford Preservation Trust **Contact:** Ms Debbie Dance

One of best preserved examples of a 15th century dwelling in the area. Originally a Merchant's Hall House with later alterations, features include a remarkable domestic wall painting, an early oak ceiling, traceried windows and fireplaces.

Location: OS Ref. SU497 969. 300 yards SSW of the market place and Town Hall.

Open: By prior appointment.

Admission: Free.

ARDINGTON HOUSE 🏛
See page 155 for full page entry.

ASHDOWN HOUSE 🌿
Lambourn, Newbury RG17 8RE

Tel: 01793 762209 **e-mail:** ashdownhouse@nationaltrust.org.uk
www.nationaltrust.org.uk

Owner: The National Trust **Contact:** Coleshill Estate Office

Location: OS Ref. SU282 820. 3½ m N of Lambourn, on W side of B4000.

Open: House & Garden 1 Apr - 30 Oct: Wed & Sat, 2 - 5pm. admission by guided tour at 2.15, 3.15 & 4.15pm. Woodland: All year: daily except Fri, daylight hours.

Admission: House & garden: £2.40. Woodland: Free.

BLENHEIM PALACE 🏛
See pages 156 for full page entry.

BROOK COTTAGE
Well Lane, Alkerton, Nr Banbury OX15 6NL

Tel: 01295 670303/670590 **Fax:** 01295 730362

Owner/Contact: Mrs David Hodges

4 acre hillside garden. Roses, clematis, water gardens, colour co-ordinated borders, trees, shrubs.

Location: OS Ref. SP378 428. 6m NW of Banbury, ½m off A422 Banbury to Stratford-upon-Avon road.

Open: Easter Mon - end Oct: Mon - Fri, 9am - 6pm. Evenings, weekends and all group visits by appointment.

Admission: Adult £4, OAP £3, Child Free.

BROUGHTON CASTLE 🏛
See page 157 for full page entry.

BUSCOT OLD PARSONAGE 🌿
Buscot, Faringdon, Oxfordshire SN7 8DQ

Tel: 01793 762209 **e-mail:** buscot@nationaltrust.org.uk
www.nationaltrust.org.uk **Contact:** Coleshill Estate Office

An early 18th century house of Cotswold stone on the bank of the Thames with a small garden.

Location: OS Ref. SU231 973. 2m from Lechlade, 4m N of Faringdon on A417.

Open: 29 Mar - 25 Oct, Weds, 2 - 6pm by written appointment with tenant.

Admission: Adult £1.50, Child 70p, Family £3.70. Not suitable for groups.
ℹ No WCs. ♿ Partial.

NTPL / Thames and Chiltern

Part of the Harold Peto Water Garden

BUSCOT PARK 🌿
BUSCOT, FARINGDON, OXFORDSHIRE SN7 8BU

www.buscot-park.com

Tel: Infoline 0845 345 3387 / Office 01367 240786 **Fax:** 01367 241794

e-mail: estbuscot@aol.com

Owner: The National Trust **Contact:** The Estate Office
(Administered on their behalf by Lord Faringdon)

The 18th century Palladian house contains the Faringdon Collection of fine paintings (including works by Murillo, Reynolds, Rossetti and the famous Briar Rose series by Burne-Jones) and furniture, with important pieces by Adam, Thomas Hope and others. The House is set in parkland, offering peaceful walks through water gardens and a well-stocked walled garden. A tearoom serves delicious home-made cream teas and cakes, and there is ample free parking.

Location: OS Ref. SU239 973. Between Faringdon and Lechlade on A417.

Open: House & Grounds: 5 Apr - 29 Sep: Wed - Fri, 2 - 6pm (last entry to house 5pm). Also open BH Mons & Good Fri and weekends 8/9, 15/16 & 29/30 Apr; 13/14 & 27/28 May; 10/11 & 24/25 Jun; 8/9 & 22/23 Jul; 12/13 & 26/27 Aug; 9/10 & 23/24 Sept. Grounds only: 3 Apr - 29 Sep: Mon & Tues, 2 - 6pm. Tearoom: as House, 2.30 - 5.30pm.

Admission: House & Grounds: Adult £7.00, Child £3.50. Grounds only: Adult £5.00, Child £2.50. Groups must book in writing, or by fax or e-mail. Booking required by disabled visitors wishing to use powered mobility vehicle.

ℹ No photography in house. 🎭 Fully equipped theatre. ♿ Partial, tel for details.
🍖 BBQ lunches for groups by arrangement. 🅿 Ample for cars, 2 coach spaces.
🐕 May be exercised in overflow car park only.

CHASTLETON HOUSE ❦

Chastleton, nr Moreton-in-Marsh, Oxfordshire GL56 0SU

Tel/Fax: 01608 674355 **Infoline:** 01494 755560 **e-mail:** chastleton@nationaltrust.org.uk

Owner: The National Trust   **Contact:** The Custodian

One of England's finest and most complete Jacobean houses, dating from 1607. It is filled with a mixture of rare and everyday objects and the atmosphere of four hundred years of continuous occupation by one family. The gardens have a Jacobean layout and the rules of modern croquet were codified here.

Location: OS Ref. SP248 291. 6m ENE of Stow-on-the-Wold. 1¹/₂ miles NW of A436. Approach only from A436 between the A44 (W of Chipping Norton) and Stow.

Open: 29 Mar - 30 Sept: Wed - Sat, 1 - 5pm, last admission 4pm. 5 - 28 Oct: Wed - Sat, 1 - 4pm, last admission 3pm. Admission for all visitors (including NT members) by timed tickets booked in advance. Bookings can be made by telephone 01608 674355.

Admission: Adult £6.50, Child £3.30, Family £16.30.

🔲 Partial. **P** Coaches limited to 25 seat minibuses. 🐕 Guide dogs only.

CHRIST CHURCH CATHEDRAL

The Sacristy, The Cathedral, Oxford OX1 1DP

Tel: 01865 276154   **Contact:** Mr Jim Godfrey

12th century Norman Church, formerly an Augustinian monastery, given Cathedral status in 16th century by Henry VIII. Private tours available.

Location: OS Ref. SP515 059. Just S of city centre, off St Aldates. Entry via Meadow Gate visitors' entrance on S side of college.

Open: Mon - Sat: 9am - 5pm. Suns: 1 - 5pm (last entry 4.30pm) closed Christmas Day. Services: weekdays 7.20am, 6pm. Suns: 8am, 10am, 11.15am & 6pm. Areas of the college (especially the Great Hall & Cathedral) are closed at various times during the year. Please telephone to check before visit.

Admission: Adult £4.50, Child under 5 Free, Conc. £3.50, Family £9.00.

DEDDINGTON CASTLE ⌗

Deddington, Oxfordshire

Tel: 01424 775705 **www.**english-heritage.org.uk/visits

Owner: English Heritage   **Contact:** 1066 Battle Abbey

Extensive earthworks concealing the remains of a 12th century castle which was ruined as early as the 14th century.

Location: OS Ref. SP471 316. S of B4031 on E side of Deddington, 17 miles N of Oxford on A423. 5 miles S of Banbury.

Open: Any reasonable time.

Admission: Free.

🐕 On leads. ❈

DITCHLEY PARK

Enstone, Oxfordshire OX7 4ER

Tel: 01608 677346 **www.**ditchley.co.uk

Owner: Ditchley Foundation   **Contact:** Brigadier Christopher Galloway

The most important house by James Gibbs, with magnificent interiors by William Kent and Henry Flitcroft. For three centuries the home of the Lee family, restored in the 1930s by Ronald and Nancy (Lancaster) Tree, it was frequently used at weekends by Sir Winston Churchill during World War II.

Location: OS Ref. SP391 214. 2m NE from Charlbury. 13 miles NW of Oxford.

Open: Visits only by prior arrangement with the Bursar, weekdays preferred.

Admission: £5 per person (minimum charge £40).

🔲 **P** ❈

GREAT COXWELL BARN ❦

Great Coxwell, Faringdon, Oxfordshire

Tel: 01793 762209 **e-mail:** greatcoxwellbarn@nationaltrust.org.uk

Owner: The National Trust   **Contact:** Coleshill Estate Office

A 13th century monastic barn, stone built with stone tiled roof, which has an interesting timber construction.

Location: OS Ref. SU269 940. 2m SW of Faringdon between A420 and B4019.

Open: All year: daily at reasonable hours.

Admission: £1.

❈

GREYS COURT ❦

ROTHERFIELD GREYS, HENLEY-ON-THAMES, OXFORDSHIRE RG9 4PG

Infoline: 01494 755564 **Tel:** 01491 628529 **e-mail:** greyscourt@nationaltrust.org.uk

Owner: The National Trust   **Contact:** The Custodian

Rebuilt in the 16th century and added to in the 17th, 18th and 19th centuries, the house is set amid the remains of the courtyard walls and towers of a 14th century fortified house. A Tudor donkey wheel, well-house and an ice house are still intact, and the garden contains Archbishop's Maze, inspired by Archbishop Runcie's enthronement speech in 1980.

Location: OS Ref. SU725 834. 3m W of Henley-on-Thames, E of B481.

Open: House: 5 Apr - 29 Sept: Wed - Fri, 2 - 5pm. Garden & Tearoom: 4 Apr - 1 Aug: Tue - Sat, 2 Aug: Tue - Sat; 1 Sept - 29 Sept: Tue - Sat; 12 noon - 5.30pm. All open BH Mons but closed Good Fri.

Admission: House & Garden: Adult £5.40, Child £2.70, Family £13.60. Garden only: £3.90, Child £1.90, Family £9.60. Coach parties must book in advance.

🔲 Grounds partial. WCs. 🔲 🐕 In car park only, on leads. 🔲 Contact Custodian.

Blenheim Palace.

KINGSTON BAGPUIZE HOUSE

ABINGDON, OXFORDSHIRE OX13 5AX

www.kingstonbagpuizehouse.org.uk

Tel: 01865 820259 **Fax:** 01865 821659 **e-mail:** virginiagrant@btinternet.com

Owner/Contact: Mrs Francis Grant

A family home, this beautiful house originally built in the 1660s was remodelled in the early 1700s in red brick with stone facings. It has a cantilevered staircase and panelled rooms with some good furniture and pictures. Set in mature parkland, the gardens, including shrub border and woodland garden, contain a notable collection of trees, shrubs, perennials and bulbs including snowdrops, planted for year round interest. A raised terrace walk leads to an 18th century panelled gazebo with views of the house and gardens, including a large herbaceous border and parkland. Available for wedding receptions, special events, corporate functions, product launches and filming. Facilities for small conferences.

Location: OS Ref. SU408 981. In Kingston Bagpuize village, off A415 Abingdon to Witney road S of A415/A420 intersection. Abingdon 5m, Oxford 9m.

Open: BH Sun & Mons: Feb: 5 - 7, 26 - 28. Mar: 19 - 21. Apr: 16 - 19 & 30. May: 1 - 3, 28 - 31. Jul: 23 - 26. Aug: 27 - 30. Sept: 17 - 19; 2 - 5.30pm. Last tour of house 4pm. House: guided tours only. Last entry to garden 5pm.

Admission: House & Garden: Adult £5, Child (5-15) £2.50, (admission to house not recommended for children under 5yrs), Conc. £4.50. Gardens: £3 (child under 16yrs Free). Groups (20 - 80) by appointment throughout the year, prices on request.

No photography in house. Grounds. WC. Home-made cakes. Light meals for groups by appointment. Obligatory

---

MAPLEDURHAM HOUSE & WATERMILL

MAPLEDURHAM, READING RG4 7TR

www.mapledurham.co.uk

Tel: 01189 723350 **Fax:** 01189 724016 **e-mail:** mtrust1997@aol.com

Owner: The Mapledurham Trust **Contact:** Mrs Lola Andrews

Late 16th century Elizabethan home of the Blount family. Original plaster ceilings, great oak staircase, fine collection of paintings and a private chapel in Strawberry Hill Gothick added in 1797. Interesting literary connections with Alexander Pope, Galsworthy's *Forsyte Saga* and Kenneth Grahame's *Wind in the Willows*. 15th century watermill fully restored producing flour and bran which is sold in the giftshop.

Location: OS Ref. SU670 767. N of River Thames. 4m NW of Reading, 1¹/₂ m W of A4074.

Open: Easter - Sept: Sats, Suns & BHs, 2 - 5.30pm. Last admission 5pm. Midweek parties by arrangement only (Tue - Thur). Mapledurham Trust reserves the right to alter or amend opening times or prices without prior notification.

Admission: Please call 01189 723350 for details.

Grounds. WCs. Guide dogs only. 11 holiday cottages (all year). Tel for details.

MILTON MANOR HOUSE

Milton, Abingdon, Oxfordshire OX14 4EN

Tel: 01488 71036 **Infoline:** 01235 862321

Owner: Anthony Mockler-Barrett Esq **Contact:** Helen Hall

Dreamily beautiful mellow brick house, traditionally designed by Inigo Jones. Celebrated Gothic library and Catholic chapel. Lived in by the family; pleasant relaxed and informal atmosphere. Park with fine old trees, stables, walled garden and woodland walk. Picnickers welcome.

Location: OS Ref. SU485 924. Just off A34, village and house signposted, 9m S of Oxford, 15m N of Newbury. 3m from Abingdon and Didcot.

Open: 1 - 31 Aug: daily, 12 noon - 5pm. Easter - Aug: BH Weekends. Guided tours of house: 2pm, 3pm & 4pm. For weddings/events etc. please write to the Administrator. Groups by arrangement throughout the year.

Admission: House & Gardens: Adult £5, Child £2.50. Garden only: Adult £3, Child £1.50. Easter Egg Hunt on Easter w/end. Georgian drama all over the place, Aug BH Weekend. For group bookings only please fax or phone 01235 831287.

Grounds. Obligatory. Free. Guide dogs only. Tel for details.

MINSTER LOVELL HALL & DOVECOTE

Witney, Oxfordshire

Tel: 01424 775705 **www.**english-heritage.org.uk/visits

Owner: English Heritage **Contact:** Battle Abbey

The ruins of Lord Lovell's 15th century manor house stand in a lovely setting on the banks of the River Windrush.

Location: OS Ref. SP324 114. Adjacent to Minster Lovell Church, ¹/₂ mile NE of village. 3 miles W of Witney off A40.

Open: Any reasonable time. Dovecote – exterior only.

Admission: Free.

On leads.

PRIORY COTTAGES ✂

1 Mill Street, Steventon, Abingdon, Oxfordshire OX13 6SP

Tel: 01793 762209

Owner: The National Trust   **Contact:** Coleshill Estate Office

Former monastic buildings, converted into two houses. South Cottage contains the Great Hall of the original priory.

Location: OS Ref. SU466 914. 4m S of Abingdon, on B4017 off A34 at Abingdon West or Milton interchange on corner of The Causeway and Mill Street, entrance in Mill Street.

Open: The Great Hall in South Cottage only: 29 Mar - 27 Sept: Wed, 2 - 6pm, by written appointment with the tenant.

Admission: Adult £1.20, Child 60p, Family £3.00.

ROUSHAM HOUSE

Nr STEEPLE ASTON, BICESTER, OXFORDSHIRE OX25 4QX

www.rousham.org

Tel: 01869 347110/07860 360407

Owner/Contact: Charles Cottrell-Dormer Esq

Rousham represents the first stage of English landscape design and remains almost as William Kent (1685 - 1748) left it. One of the few gardens of this date to have escaped alteration. Includes Venus' Vale, Townesend's Building, seven-arched Praeneste, the Temple of the Mill and a sham ruin known as the 'Eyecatcher'. The house was built in 1635 by Sir Robert Dormer. Excellent location for fashion, advertising, photography etc.

Location: OS Ref. SP477 242. E of A4260, 12m N of Oxford, S of B4030, 7m W of Bicester.

Open: House: May - Sept: Suns & BH Mons 2 - 4.30pm. Garden: All year: daily, 10am - 4.30pm. Pre-booked groups, May - Sept.

Admission: House: £3. Garden: £4. No children under 15yrs.

&Partial. Obligatory. P ⊠ ✳

RYCOTE CHAPEL ⌗

Rycote, Oxfordshire

Tel: 01424 775705   **www**.english-heritage.org.uk/visits

Owner: English Heritage   **Contact:** 1066 Battle Abbey

A 15th century chapel with exquisitely carved and painted woodwork. It has many intriguing features, including two roofed pews and a musicians' gallery.

Location: OS165 Ref. SP667 046. 3 miles SW of Thame, off A329. 1½ miles NE of M40/J7.

Open: 1 Apr - 30 Sept: Fri - Sun & BHs, 2 - 6pm.

Admission: Adult £3.50, Child £1.50, Conc. £2.50. 15% discount for groups (11+).

⊡ & P ⊠

plant sales
see page 555

Broughton Castle.

STONOR 🏠

HENLEY-ON-THAMES, OXFORDSHIRE RG9 6HF

www.stonor.com

Tel: 01491 638587 **Fax:** 01491 639348 **e-mail:** jweaver@stonor.com

Owner: Lord & Lady Camoys   **Contact:** The Administrator - John Weaver

Family home of Lord and Lady Camoys and generations of their family for over 800 years. Stonor, surrounded by deer park, sits in a beautiful wooded valley. The House and Chapel date from the 12th century, with 14th and 18th century additions and changes. Internal features include rare furniture, artworks and family portraits. Mass has been celebrated continuously since medieval times in the Chapel, sited close by a pagan stone circle. St Edmund Campion sought refuge here during the Reformation. An exhibition celebrates his life and work. Hillside gardens offer outstanding views of the Park. **New for 2006 – Exhibition about Stonor's American Ancestors.**

Location: OS Ref. SU743 893. 1 hr from London, M4/J8/9. A4130 to Henley-on-Thames. On B480 NW of Henley. A4130/B480 to Stonor. Rail: Henley-on-Thames Station 5m.

Open: 2 Apr - 24 Sept: Suns & BH Mons, also Weds 5 July - 30 Aug (closed Sun 18 Jun). House & Tearoom: 2 - 5.30pm. Garden: 1 - 5.30pm. Private groups (20+) by arrangement: Apr - Sept, Tues - Thurs.

Admission: House, Garden & Chapel: Adult £6, Child (under 14yrs) Free. Garden & Chapel: Adult £3.50. Schools £2.50 pp, 1 teacher for every 10 children admitted free. Private guided tours (20+): £7pp (one group payment). School groups £4pp, 1 teacher per 10 children admitted free.

🚫 ℹ️ No photography in house. 🚻 ♿ Unsuitable for physically disabled. 🍴 Licensed. ✗ For 20-60. 🅿️ 100yds away. 🐕 In grounds on leads. 🛏️ Tel for details.

SWALCLIFFE BARN

Swalcliffe Village, Banbury, Oxfordshire

Tel: 01295 788278   **Contact:** Jeffrey Demmar

15th century half cruck barn, houses agricultural and trade vehicles. Exhibition of 2500 years of Swalcliffe history.

Location: OS Ref. SP378 378. 6m W of Banbury Cross on B4035.

Open: Easter - end Oct: Suns & BHs, 2 - 5pm.

Admission: Free.

WATERPERRY GARDENS

WATERPERRY, Nr WHEATLEY, OXFORDSHIRE OX33 1JZ

www.waterperrygardens.co.uk

Tel: 01844 389254   **Fax:** 01844 339883

e-mail: office@waterperrygardens.co.uk

Owner: School of Economic Science   **Contact:** P Maxwell

This 3.2 Ha garden, originally a ladies' horticultural school, includes one of the best herbaceous borders in the country, rose and alpine gardens, a knot garden and a riverside walk. The Saxon church, agricultural museum and art and craft gallery are additional attractions. The teashop serves homemade lunches and teas.

Location: OS Ref. SP630 063. Oxford 9m, London 52m M40/J8, Birmingham M40/J8A 42m. Well signposted locally.

Open: Apr - Oct: 9am - 5.30pm. Nov - Mar: 9am - 5pm.

Admission: Apr - Oct: Adult £4.25, Child £3 (under 10yrs Free), OAP £3.75. Nov - Mar: Apr - Oct: Adult/OAP £3. Groups by appointment. Apr - Oct £3.50; Nov - Mar £3.

🚫 ✗ ♿ Partial. Wheelchairs available. 🍴 ✗ By arrangement. 🅿️ Limited for coaches. 🍴 ✈️ ❄️

Greys Court.

The Colleges of Oxford University

All Souls' College
High Street
Tel: 01865 279379
Founder: Archbishop Henry Chichele 1438
Open: Mon - Fri, 2 - 4pm (4.30pm in summer)

Balliol College
Broad Street
Tel: 01865 277777
Founder: John de Balliol 1263
Open: Daily, 2 - 5pm

Brasenose College
Radcliffe Square
Tel: 01865 277830
Founder: William Smythe, Bishop of Lincoln 1509
Open: Daily, 10 - 11.30am (tour groups only) & 2 - 4pm (5pm in summer)

Christ Church
St. Aldates
Tel: 01865 286573
Founder: Cardinal Wolsey/Henry VIII 1546
Open: Mon - Sat, 9am - 5.30pm; Sun, 1 - 5.30pm (last adm 4.30pm)

Corpus Christi College
Merton Street
Tel: 01865 276700
Founder: Bishop Richard Fox 1517
Open: Daily, 1.30 - 4.30pm

Exeter College
Turl Street
Tel: 01865 279600
Founder: Bishop Stapleden of Exeter 1314
Open: Daily, Term time 2 - 5pm.

Green College
Woodstock Road
Tel: 01865 274770
Founder: Dr Cecil Green 1979
Open: By appointment only.

Harris Manchester College
Mansfield Road
Tel: 01865 271011
Founder: Lord Harris of Peckham 1996
Open: Chapel only: Mon - Fri, 8.30am - 5.30pm. Sat, 9am - 12 noon.

Hertford College
Catte Street
Tel: 01865 279400
Founder: TC Baring MP 1740
Open: Daily, 10am - noon & 2pm - dusk.

Jesus College
Turl Street
Tel: 01865 279700
Founder: Dr Hugh Price (Queen Elizabeth I) 1571
Open: Daily, 2 - 4.30pm

Keble College
Parks Road
Tel: 01865 272727
Founder: Public money 1870
Open: Daily, 2 - 5pm

Kellogg College
Wellington Square
Tel: 01865 270383
Founder: Kellogg Foundation 1990
Open: Mon - Fri, 9am - 5pm

Lady Margaret Hall
Norham Gardens
Tel: 01865 274300
Founder: Dame Elizabeth Wordsworth 1878
Open: Gardens: 10am - 5pm

Linacre College
St Cross Road
Tel: 01865 271650
Founder: Oxford University 1962
Open: By appointment only.

Lincoln College
Turl Street
Tel: 01865 279800
Founder: Bishop Richard Fleming of Lincoln 1427
Open: Mon - Sat, 2 - 5pm; Sun, 11am - 5pm

Magdalen College
High Street
Tel: 01865 276000
Founder: William of Waynefleete 1458
Open: Oct - June: 1- 6pm/dusk (whichever is the earlier) and July - Sept: 12 noon - 6pm

Mansfield College
Mansfield Road
Tel: 01865 270999
Founder: Free Churches 1995
Open: Mon - Fri, 9am - 5pm.

Merton College
Merton Street
Tel: 01865 276310
Founder: Walter de Merton 1264
Open: Mon - Fri, 2 - 4pm; Sat & Sun, 10am - 4pm

New College
New College Lane
Tel: 01865 279555
Founder: William of Wykeham, Bishop of Winchester 1379
Open: Daily, 11am - 5pm (summer); 2 - 4pm (winter)

Nuffield College
New Road
Tel: 01865 278500
Founder: William Morris (Lord Nuffield) 1937
Open: Daily, 9am - 5pm.

Oriel College
Oriel Square
Tel: 01865 276555
Founder: Edward II/Adam de Brome 1326
Open: Daily, 1 - 4pm (by arrangement with TIC)

Pembroke College
St Aldates
Tel: 01865 276444
Founder: James I 1624
Open: By appointment only.

The Queen's College
High Street
Tel: 01865 279120
Founder: Robert de Eglesfield 1341
Open: By prior appointment through the Tourist Information Office.

Somerville College
Graduate House, Woodstock Road
Tel: 01865 270600
Founder: Association for the Education of Women 1879
Open: 2 - 5.30pm

St. Anne's College
56 Woodstock Road
Tel: 01865 274800
Founder: Association for the Education of Women 1878
Open: 9am - 5pm

St. Antony's College
62 Woodstock Road
Tel: 01865 284700
Founder: M. Antonin Bess 1948
Open: By appointment only.

St. Catherine's College
Manor Road
Tel: 01865 271700
Founder: Oxford University 1964
Open: 9am - 5pm

St. Cross College
St. Giles
Tel: 01865 278490
Founder: Oxford University 1965
Open: Not open to the public.

St. Edmund Hall
Queens Lane
Tel: 01865 279000
Founder: St. Edmund Riche of Abingdon c.1278
Open: Daily, daylight hours.

St. Hilda's College
Cowley Place
Tel: 01865 276884
Founder: Miss Dorothea Beale 1893
Open: Daily, 2 - 5pm

St. Hugh's College
St. Margarets Road
Tel: 01865 274900
Founder: Dame Elizabeth Wordsworth 1886
Open: 10am - 4pm

St. John's College
St. Giles
Tel: 01865 277300
Founder: Sir Thomas White 1555
Open: 1 - 5pm (or dusk)

St. Peter's College
New Inn Hall Street
Tel: 01865 278900
Founder: Rev. Christopher Charvasse 1928
Open: 10am - dusk

Trinity College
Broad Street
Tel: 01865 279900
Founder: Sir Thomas Pope 1554-5
Open: Mon - Fri 10am - noon and 2 - 4pm. Sat & Sun in term, 2 - 4pm; Sat & Sun in vacation 10am - noon and 2 - 4pm.

University College
High Street
Tel: 01865 276602
Founder: Archdeacon William of Durham 1249
Open: Contact College for details.

Wadham College
Parks Road
Tel: 01865 277900
Founder: Nicholas & Dorothy Wadham 1610
Open: Term time: daily, 1 - 4.15pm. Vacation: daily, 10.30 - 11.45am & 1 - 4.15pm.

Wolfson College
Linton Road
Tel: 01865 274100
Founder: Oxford University 1966
Open: Daylight hours.

Worcester College
Worcester Street
Tel: 01865 278300
Founder: Sir Thomas Cookes 1714
Open: Daily, 2 - 5pm.

This information is intended only as a guide. Times are subject to change due to functions, examinations, conferences, holidays, etc. You are advised to check in advance opening times and admission charges which may apply at some colleges, and at certain times of the year. Visitors wishing to gain admittance to the Colleges (meaning the Courts, not to the staircases & students' rooms) are advised to contact the Tourist Information Office. It should be noted that Halls normally close for lunch (12 - 2pm) and many are not open during the afternoon. Chapels may be closed during services. Libraries are not normally open, and Gardens do not usually include the Fellows' garden. Visitors, and especially guided groups, should always call on the Porters Lodge first. Groups should always book in advance. Dogs, except guide dogs are not allowed in any colleges.

For further details contact: Oxford Information Centre, 15 - 16 Broad Street, Oxford OX1 3AS
Tel: +44 (0)1865 726871   Email: tic@oxford.gov.uk   Fax: +44 (0)1865 240261   www.visitoxford.org

National Trust Photographic Library. Hatchlands Park

National Trust Photographic Library. Clandon Park

MAP 3

CLANDON PARK & HATCHLANDS PARK

www.nationaltrust.org.uk/clandonpark

Owner:
The National Trust

▶ **CONTACT**

The Property Manager
Clandon Park &
Hatchlands Park
East Clandon
Guildford
Surrey GU4 7RT

Tel: 01483 222482
Fax: 01483 223176
e-mail: hatchlands@
nationaltrust.org.uk

▶ **LOCATION**

Clandon
OS Ref. TQ042 512
At West Clandon
on the A247,
3m E of Guildford.

Rail: Clandon BR 1m.

Hatchlands
OS Ref. TQ063 516
E of East Clandon
on the A246 Guildford -
Leatherhead road.

Rail: Clandon BR
2¹/₂ m, Horsley 3m.

Clandon Park & Hatchlands Park were built during the 18th century and are set amidst beautiful grounds. They are two of England's most outstanding country houses and are only five minutes' drive apart.

Clandon Park is a grand Palladian mansion, built c1730 by the Venetian architect, Leoni and notable for its magnificent two-storey marble hall. The house is rightly acclaimed for its remarkable collection of 18th century porcelain, textiles and furniture, which includes the Ivo Forde Meissen collection of Italian comedy figures and a series of Mortlake tapestries. The attractive gardens feature a parterre, grotto, Dutch garden and a Maori

© David Mees

meeting house with a fascinating history. Clandon is also home to the Queen's Royal Surrey Regiment Museum. The excellent restaurant is renowned for its Sunday lunches - booking is advisable.

Hatchlands Park was built in 1756 for Admiral Boscawen and is set in a beautiful 430 acre Repton park offering a variety of park and woodland walks. There is also a small garden by Gertrude Jekyll flowering from late May to early July. Hatchlands contains splendid interiors by Robert Adam, decorated in appropriately nautical style. The rooms are hung with the Cobbe Collection of old master paintings and portraits, initially formed in the 18th century. It includes works by Bernini, Guercino, Poussin, Van Dyck, Gainsborough and Zoffany.

Hatchlands also houses the Cobbe Collection of keyboard instruments, the world's largest group of early keyboard instruments owned or played by famous composers such as Purcell, J C Bach, Mozart, Chopin, Liszt, Mahler and Elgar. Notable too are Marie Antoinette's piano and the instrument on which the world's most performed opera, Bizet's Carmen, was composed.

There are frequent concerts on instruments of the collection. For information contact:
The Cobbe Collection Trust,
tel. 01483 211474 or visit
www.cobbecollection.co.uk.

▶ **OPENING TIMES**

Clandon - House
26 March - 29 October
Tue - Thur, Suns &
BH Mons, Good Fri
& Easter Sat
11am - 5pm.

Garden
As house.

Museum
26 March - 29 October
Tue - Thur & Suns,
BH Mons, Good Fri
& Easter Sat
12 noon - 5pm.

Hatchlands - House
2 April - 29 October
Tue - Thur,
Suns & BH Mon,
Fris in August only.
2 - 5.30pm.

Park Walks
1 April - 29 October: Daily
11am - 6pm.

▶ **ADMISSION**

Clandon:
House/Grounds........ £6.50
    Child £3.20
    Family £16.00
Pre-booked Groups
    Adult £5.00

Hatchlands
House/Grounds........ £6.00
    Child £3.00
    Family £15.00
    Park Walks only £3.00
    Child £1.50
Pre-booked Groups
    Adult £5.00

Combined ticket
Clandon/Hatchlands . £9.00
    Child £4.50
    Family £22.50

CONFERENCE/FUNCTION

ROOM	SIZE	MAX CAPACITY
Marble Hall Clandon Pk	40' x 40'	160 seated 200 standing

Tel: 01483 222482. No photography.

For Clandon weddings and receptions tel: 01483 222502.

WCs. Hatchlands suitable. Clandon please tel for details.

Hatchlands: 01483 211120.

Licensed. Clandon: 01483 222502.

Clandon - by arrangement.

Hatchlands only.

Children's quizzes available.

Hatchlands Parkland only.

Clandon only.   Tel: 01483 222482.

MAP 3

THE COBBE COLLECTION
AT HATCHLANDS

www.cobbecollection.co.uk

Owner:
The National Trust

▶ **CONTACT**

Cobbe Collection Trust
Hatchlands Park
East Clandon
Guildford
Surrey
GU4 7RT

Tel: 01483 211474
Fax: 01483 225922

e-mail: enquiries@
cobbecollection.co.uk

The Cobbe Collections are set in sumptuous rooms designed by Robert Adam. The house, given to the National Trust with few contents, has been let to Mr & Mrs Alec Cobbe since 1987 and is lived in as a family home. The resulting arrangement of pictures, furniture, *objéts d'art* and the celebrated collection of keyboards, spanning 400 years and formerly belonging to some of the greatest names of classical music, has been called 'one of the most beautiful musical museums in the world'. The family art collection, formed initially in the 18th century, includes pictures by Allori, Bernini, Guercino, Poussin, Van Dyck, Gainsborough, Zoffany and many others.

World headlines were occasioned by the identification in 2002, among family portraits, of the most youthful picture of Shakespeare's friend and patron, Henry Wriothesley, 3rd Earl of Southampton, formerly thought to have been of Lady Norton!

The instruments in the collection, all in playing order, are used in lunchtime recitals on Wednesdays, master classes and evening concerts and tours from April to July and in October, giving an opportunity to hear the sounds of instruments played by Purcell, JC Bach, Mozart, Beethoven, Chopin, Liszt and Mahler.

▶ **LOCATION**
OS Ref. TQ063 516

E of East Clandon, N of
A246 Guildford to
Leatherhead road.

© David Mees

▶ **OPENING TIMES**

Hatchlands - House
2 April - 29 October
Tue - Thur,
Suns & BH Mon,
Fri in August only.
2 - 5.30pm.

Park Walks
1 April - 29 October: Daily
11am - 6pm.

▶ **ADMISSION**

Hatchlands
House/Grounds £6.00
   Child £3.00
   Family £15.00
Park Walks only........ £3.00
   Child £1.50

Pre-Booked Groups
   Adult £5.00

Combined ticket
Clandon/Hatchlands . £9.00
   Child £4.50
   Family £22.50

 Suitable. WCs.

 Licensed. No booking
required, except for groups,
tel: 01483 222502

Children's quizzes.

P

 Guide dogs only. Dogs
welcome in Parkland only.

01483 222482.

©HRP 2002

©Crown Copyright: Historic Royal Palaces

MAP 3

Managed by:
Historic Royal Palaces

▶ **CONTACT**

Hampton Court Palace
Surrey
KT8 9AU

Recorded info:
0870 752 7777
All other enquiries:
0870 751 5175
**Venue Hire and
Corporate
Hospitailty**
0870 751 5182

▶ **LOCATION**

OS Ref. TQ155 686

From M25/J15 and
A312, or M25/J12 and
A308, or M25/J10 and
A307.

Rail: From London
Waterloo direct to
Hampton Court
(32 mins).

HAMPTON COURT PALACE

www.hampton-court-palace.org.uk

Henry VIII's magnificent riverside palace also proved to be the favoured home of both George II and William III. Sir Christopher Wren remodelled the south and east fronts in the beautiful baroque style, creating the 'English Versailles'.

Today there are six routes to explore. Multi-lingual sound guides and costumed guided tours help visitors get the most from a visit. Henry VIII's State Apartments include the Great Hall and Chapel Royal, whilst the King's Apartments reveal William III's ceremonial life. The vast Tudor kitchens are alive with the smell of herbs, authentic dishes from the period and the roaring fire.

The gardens are a delight all of their own, and the Garden Exhibition charts the evolution of the Palace's gardens, as well as giving inside information on conservation and plant care. Seasonal events and exhibitions will be scheduled to enhance your visit, please see our website for the latest information.

For art lovers the lower Orangery in the South Gardens holds Andrea Mantegna's *Triumphs of Caesar*, a sequence of nine paintings, part of the Royal Collection. Painted during the period c1484-1505 they are considered to be one of the most important works of the Italian Renaissance.

Summer
March - October
Daily: 10am - 6pm
(last admission 5.15pm)

Winter
November - February
Daily: 10am - 4.30pm
(last admission 3.45pm)

Closed 24 - 26 December.

▶ **ADMISSION**

Telephone Information
Line for admission prices:
0870 752 7777.

Advance Ticket Sales:
0870 753 7777.

Group Bookings
0870 7517070,
Quote *Hudson's*.

©HRP 2002

FUNCTION ROOMS

ROOM	SIZE	MAX CAPACITY
Great Hall	88'6" x 35'6"	280/400
Cartoon Gallery	22'6" x 116'	220/350
Gt Watching Chamber	66'6" x 25'	120
Painted Room	33'3" x 21'3"	50/100
King's Guard Chamber	60'3" x 36'4"	120/150
Public Dining Room	31'6" x 55'6"	50/150

ℹ️ Information Centre. No photography indoors.

♿ Motorised buggies available at main entrance. WCs.

🅿️ Ample for cars, coach parking nearby.

Rates on request 0870 7515190.

In grounds, on leads. Guide dogs only in Palace.

Seasonal events and exhibitions will be scheduled to enhance your visit, please see website for latest information.

LOSELEY PARK

www.loseley-park.com

Owner:
Mr Michael
More-Molyneux

▶ CONTACT

Events Office
Loseley Park
Guildford
Surrey GU3 1HS

Tel: 01483 304440
Tel Events: 01483
405119/120
Fax: 01483 302036

e-mail: enquiries@
loseley-park.com

▶ LOCATION

OS Ref. SU975 471

30m SW of London,
leave A3 S of Guildford
on to B3000.
Signposted.

Bus: 1¼ m
from House.

Rail: Farncombe 1½ m,
Guildford 2m,
Godalming 3m.

Air: Heathrow 30m,
Gatwick 30m.

CONFERENCE/FUNCTION

ROOM	SIZE	MAX CAPACITY
Tithe Barn	100' x 18'	200
Marquee	sites available	
Great Hall	70' x 40'	100
Drawing Rm	40' x 30'	50
Walled Gdn	Marquee	sites
Chestnut Ldg	18' x 38'	50

Loseley Park, built in 1562 by Sir William More to entertain Queen Elizabeth I, is a fine example of Elizabethan architecture – its mellow stone brought from the ruins of Waverley Abbey now over 850 years old. The house is set amid magnificent parkland grazed by the Loseley Jersey herd. Many visitors comment on the very friendly atmosphere of the house. It is a country house, the family home of descendants of the builder.

Furniture has been acquired by the family and includes an early 16th century Wrangelschrank beautifully inlaid with many different woods, a Queen Anne cabinet, Georgian armchairs and settee, a Hepplewhite four-poster bed and King George IV's coronation chair. The King's bedroom has Oudenarde tapestry and a carpet commemorating James I's visit. Also many fine paintings and portraits of family members and a beautiful and unique chimney piece carved out of a single piece of chalk to a design by Holbein.

A Christian Cancer Help Centre meets twice monthly. Loseley House is available for dinners, functions and Civil weddings.

GARDEN

A magnificent Cedar of Lebanon presides over the front lawn. Parkland adjoins the lawn and a small lake adds to the beauty of Front Park. Walled Garden: Based on a Gertrude Jekyll design, the five gardens exist each with their own theme and character, making up the whole. These include the award-winning rose garden containing over 1,000 bushes, a magnificent vine walk, colourful fruit and flower garden and the serene white garden. Other features include an organic vegetable garden and moat walk. HDRA Seed Library plants.

🏛✳ℹ️ Chapel. New lakeside walk. Business launches and promotions. 10 - 12 acre field can be hired in addition to the lawns. Fashion shows, archery, garden parties, shows (50 acre show site), rallies, filming, parkland, moat walk & terrace. Lectures can be arranged on the property, its contents, gardens & history. Picnic area, home to Jersey herd since 1916; No unaccompanied children, no photography in house, no videos on estate. All group visits must be booked in advance.

🍽 Special functions, banquets and conference catering. Additional marquees for hire. Wedding receptions.

♿ May alight at entrance to property. Access to all areas except house first floor. WCs.

☕ Courtyard Tea Room.

🍴 Lunchtime restaurant.

🚶 Obligatory. House tour: 40 mins.

🅿 150 cars, 6 coaches. Summer overflow car park.

🐕 Guide dogs only. 🔔 ❄

▶ OPENING TIMES

Summer
Garden, Shop & Tea Room
May - September
Tues - Sun & BH Mons
in May & Aug,
11am - 5pm.

Loseley House
(guided tours)
May - Aug
Tues - Thurs, Suns &
BH Mons in May & Aug,
1 - 5pm.

Lunchtime Restaurant
May - August: Tues - Sun.
September: Sats & Suns
12 noon - 2.30pm.

All Year (Private Hire)
Tithe Barn, Chestnut Lodge, House, Walled Garden and Grounds available for private/business functions, Civil weddings and receptions. Off-road 4 x 4 course.

▶ ADMISSION

House & Gardens
Adult	£7.00
Child (5-16yrs)	£3.50
Conc.	£6.50
Child (under 5yrs)	Free
Family (2 + 3)	£17.50

Booked Groups (10+)
Adult	£6.00
Child (5-16yrs)	£3.00

Garden & Grounds only
Adult	£4.00
Child (5-16yrs)	£2.00
Conc.	£3.50
Family (2 + 3)	£10.00

Booked Groups (10+)
Adult	£3.00
Child (5-16yrs)	£1.50

🛡 **SPECIAL EVENTS**
Please telephone for details.

MAP 3

Owner:
Painshill Park Trust

▶ CONTACT

Visitor Management
Painshill Park
Portsmouth Road
Cobham
Surrey
KT11 1JE
Tel: 01932 868113
Fax: 01932 868001

e-mail:
info@painshill.co.uk

▶ LOCATION
OS Ref. TQ099 605

M25/J10 to London. W
of Cobham on A245.
Entrance 200 yds E of
A245/A307 roundabout.

PAINSHILL PARK 🏛

www.painshill.co.uk

A unique award-winning restoration of England's heritage. Painshill Park is one of the most important 18th century parks in Europe. Within its 160 acres, its Hamilton Landscapes are a work of art that influenced the future of England's countryside and culture. Between 1738 and 1773 the Hon Charles Hamilton transformed barren heathland into a sequence of subtle and surprising vistas. Around the 14 acre serpentine lake, he assembled a series of carefully designed views known as the Hamilton Landscapes. The visitor moves from scene to scene; past the vineyard to an evergreen amphitheatre and on to the Gothic Temple, from the magical crystal grotto to a ruined Mausoleum, from a wild wood to the colourful flower beds that surround the site of the

Temple of Bacchus. Following years of dereliction the Landscapes have been restored to their original pre-eminence, winning the Europa Nostra Medal for exemplary restoration. Available for corporate and private hire, location filming, wedding receptions, children's parties etc.

Full Education Programme available – Lifelong Learning for ages 5 - 95. All Key Stages. Adult Higher Education and Informal Learning. Discover American Roots at Painshill Park. In spring 2006, the American Roots Exhibition will open. This is a major horticultural exhibition recreating the 18th century exchange of plants between Europe and America. Over 250 years on, retrace the journey of these seeds from American wilds to English landscapes.

▶ OPENING TIMES

March - October:
Daily, 10.30am - 6pm
(last admission 4.30pm).

November - February:
Daily (closed Christmas
Day & Boxing Day),
10.30am - 4pm. Or dusk if
earlier (last adm 3pm).

▶ ADMISSION

Adult £6.00
Child (5-16yrs) £3.50
Under 5yrs .... Free
Conc £5.25
Family (2+2) £18.00

Multiple Season £60.00
Single Season £30.00
2 Adults Season £45.00

Pre-booked
groups (10+) £5.00

 Marquee site.

 Licensed.
 By arrangement.

P

On a lead. Restrictions apply.

BOX HILL

The Old Fort, Box Hill Road, Box Hill, Tadworth KT20 7LB

Tel: 01306 885502 **Fax:** 01306 875030 **e-mail:** boxhill@nationaltrust.org.uk
www.nationaltrust.org.uk/northdowns

Owner: The National Trust   **Contact:** Head Warden

An outstanding area of woodland and chalk downland, long famous as a destination for day-trippers from London.

Location: OS Ref. TQ171 519. 1m N of Dorking, 1¹/₂m S of Leatherhead on A24.

Open: Shop, Information Centre and Servery: All year, daily (except 25/26 Dec & 1 Jan), 11 - 5pm or dusk.

Admission: Countryside: Free. Car/coach park £2, NT members Free.

CAREW MANOR DOVECOTE

Church Road, Beddington, Surrey SM6 7NH

Tel: 020 8770 4781 **Fax:** 020 8770 4777 **e-mail:** sutton.museum@ukonline.co.uk
www.sutton.gov.uk

Owner: London Borough of Sutton   **Contact:** Ms V Murphy

An early 18th century octagonal brick dovecote with around 1200 nesting boxes and the original potence (circular ladder). Opened for tours with the adjacent late medieval Grade I listed Great Hall of Carew Manor.

Location: OS Ref. TQ295 652. Just off A232 at entrance to Beddington Park.

Open: Tours: Suns only, 26 Mar, 7 May, 2 Jul & 24 Sept: 2 & 3.30pm.

Admission: Adult £3.50, Child £2.

CLANDON PARK & HATCHLANDS PARK

See page 164 for full page entry.

Hampton Court Palace.

CLAREMONT LANDSCAPE GARDEN

PORTSMOUTH ROAD, ESHER, SURREY KT10 9JG

www.nationaltrust.org.uk/claremont

Tel: 01372 467806 **Fax:** 01372 476420 **e-mail:** claremont@nationaltrust.org.uk

Owner: The National Trust   **Contact:** The Property Manager

One of the earliest surviving English landscape gardens, restored to its former glory. Begun by Sir John Vanbrugh and Charles Bridgeman before 1720, the garden was extended and naturalised by William Kent. 'Capability' Brown also made improvements. Features include a lake, island with pavilion, grotto, turf amphitheatre, viewpoints and avenues.

Location: OS Ref. TQ128 632. On S edge of Esher, on E side of A307 (no access from Esher bypass).

Open: Jan - end Mar, Nov - end Dec: daily except Mons: 10am - 5pm or sunset if earlier. Apr - end Oct: daily: Mon - Fri, 10am - 6pm, Sats, Suns & BHs, 10am - 6pm. NB: Garden closes for major events in July, please check in advance. Closed 25 Dec.

Admission: Adult £5, Child £2.50. Family (2+2) £12.50. Groups (15+), Adult £4.20, Child £2.10. Discount if using public transport. Coach groups must book; no coach groups on Suns.

Limited. WC. No dogs (Apr - Oct). Tel for details.

THE COBBE COLLECTION � AT HATCHLANDS

See page 165 for full page entry.

FARNHAM CASTLE

Farnham, Surrey GU9 0AG

Tel: 01252 721194 **Fax:** 01252 711283 **e-mail:** conf@farnhamcastle.com

Owner: The Church Commissioners **Contact:** Farnham Castle

Bishop's Palace built in Norman times by Henry of Blois. Tudor and Jacobean additions.

Location: OS Ref. SU839 474. 1/2 m N of Farnham town centre on A287.

Open: All year: Weds, 2 - 4pm except Christmas & New Year.

Admission: Adult £2.50, Child/Conc £1.50.

FARNHAM CASTLE KEEP ♯

Castle Hill, Farnham, Surrey GU6 0AG

Tel: 01252 713393 **www**.english-heritage.org.uk/visits

Owner: English Heritage **Contact:** Visitor Operations Team

Used as a fortified manor by the medieval Bishops of Winchester, this motte and bailey castle has been in continuous occupation since the 12th century. You can visit the large shell-keep enclosing a mound in which are massive foundations of a Norman tower.

Location: OS Ref. SU839 474. 1/2 mile N of Farnham town centre on A207.

Open: 1 Apr - 30 Sept: Fri - Sun & BHs: 12 noon - 5pm.

Admission: Adult £2.80, Child £1.40, Conc. £2.10. EH Members Free.

🖩 🖥Ground floor & grounds. 🎥 Free. 🅿 🐕 In grounds, on leads.

GODDARDS

Abinger Common, Dorking, Surrey RH5 6TH

Tel: 01628 825920 or 01628 825925 (bookings) **www**.landmarktrust.org.uk

Owner: The Lutyens Trust, leased to The Landmark Trust **Contact:** The Landmark Trust

Built by Sir Edwin Lutyens in 1898 - 1900 and enlarged by him in 1910. Garden by Gertrude Jekyll. Given to the Lutyens Trust in 1991 and now managed and maintained by the Landmark Trust, which let buildings for self-catering holidays. The whole house, apart from the library, is available for up to 12 people. Full details of Goddards and 183 other historic buildings available for holidays are featured in The Landmark Handbook (price £11.00 refundable against booking), from The Landmark Trust, Shottesbrooke, Maidenhead, Berkshire SL6 3SW.

Location: OS Ref. TQ120 450. 4 1/2 m SW of Dorking on the village green in Abinger Common. Signposted Abinger Common, Friday Street and Leith Hill from A25.

Open: Strictly by appointment. Must be booked in advance, including parking, which is very limited. Visits booked for Weds afternoons from the Wed after Easter until the last Wed of Oct, between 2.30 - 5pm. Only those with pre-booked tickets will be admitted.

Admission: £3. Tickets available from Mrs Baker on 01306 730871, Mon - Fri, 9am & 6pm. Visitors will have access to part of the garden and house only.

🖩

GREAT FOSTERS

Stroude Road, Egham, Surrey TW20 9UR

Tel: 01784 433822 **Fax:** 01784 472455 **e-mail:** enquiries@greatfosters.co.uk **www**.greatfosters.co.uk

Owner: The Sutcliffe family **Contact:** Amanda Dougans

Grade II* listed garden. Laid out in 1918 by W H Romaine-Walker in partnership with G H Jenkins, incorporating earlier features. The site covers 50 acres and is associated with a late 17th century country house, converted to an hotel in 1927. The main formal garden is surrounded on three sides by a moat thought to be of medieval origin and is modelled on the pattern of a Persian carpet. Garden also includes a sunken rose garden and avenue of lime trees.

Location: OS Ref. TQ015 694. M25 J/13, follow signs to Egham town centre. Under motorway bridge, left at roundabout. Left at the mini roundabout into Vicarage Rd. Right at next roundabout. Over M25. Left into Stroude Rd. 500 yds on left.

Open: All year.

Admission: Free.

🎥 🖥Partial. WC. 🎥 🍴 🅿 🐕 Guide dogs only. 🖩🔺❄

GUILDFORD HOUSE GALLERY

155 High Street, Guildford, Surrey GU1 3AJ

Tel/Fax: 01483 444742 (Guildford Borough Council) **www**.guildfordhouse.co.uk

Owner/Contact: Guildford Borough Council

A beautifully restored 17th century town house with a number of original features including a finely carved staircase, panelled rooms and decorative plaster ceilings. A varied temporary exhibition programme including paintings, photography and craft work. Exhibition and events leaflet available. Lecture and workshop programme. Details on application.

Location: OS Ref. SU996 494. Central Guildford on High Street.

Open: Tue - Sat, 10am - 4.45pm.

Admission: Free.

🖩 🎥 🍴Public car park nearby. 🅿 🐕 Guide dogs only. ❄ 🛡 Tel for details.

HAMPTON COURT PALACE

See page 166 for full page entry.

HONEYWOOD HERITAGE CENTRE

Honeywood Walk, Carshalton, Surrey SM5 3NX

Tel: 020 8770 4297 **Fax:** 020 8770 4297

e-mail: lbshoneywood@ukonline.co.uk

www.sutton.gov.uk/leisure/heritage/honeywood.htm

Owner: London Borough of Sutton **Contact:** The Curator

A 17th century listed building next to the picturesque Carshalton Ponds, containing displays on many aspects of the history of the London Borough of Sutton plus a changing programme of exhibitions and events on a wide range of subjects. Attractive garden at rear.

Location: OS Ref. TQ279 646. On A232 approximately 4m W of Croydon.

Open: Wed - Fri, 11am - 5pm. Sat, Suns & BH Mons, 10am - 5pm. Free admission to shop & tearooms.

Admission: Adult £1.25, Child 60p, under 5 Free. Groups by arrangement.

🖩 🖥Ground floor. WC. 🎥 🍴 🅿 Limited. 🖩 🐕 Guide dogs only. ❄ 🛡 Tel for details.

KEW GARDENS

Kew, Richmond, Surrey TW9 3AB

Tel: 020 8332 5655 **Fax:** 020 8332 5610 **e-mail:** info@kew.org **www**.kew.org

Contact: Visitor Information

Kew Gardens, is a World Heritage Site. It is a mixture of stunning vistas, magnificent glasshouses and beautiful landscapes beside the River Thames. This once Royal residence represents nearly 250 years of historical gardens and today its 300 acres are home to over 40,000 types of plants from rainforest to desert. There is always something to see… as the seasons change so does Kew.

Location: OS Ref. TQ188 776. A307. Junc. A307 & A205 (1m Chiswick roundabout M4).

Open: All year: daily (except 24/25 Dec) from 9.30am. Closing time varies according to the season. Please telephone for further information.

Admission: Adult £10, Child (under 17yrs) Free, Conc. £7. Discounts for groups (10+). School groups: Free. Prices subject to change Feb 2006.

🖩🎥🖥🍴 Licensed. 🅿Limited. 🖩 🐕 Guide dogs only. 🔺❄

KEW PALACE

Kew Gardens, Kew, Richmond, Surrey TW9 3AB

Tel: Group Bookings - 020 8332 5648 Individual Bookings - 020 8332 5655

e-mail: info@kew.org

www:kew.org **Contact:** Visitor Information

Kew Palace will open again after ten years on 1 May. Built in 1631, the building became the home of George III and Queen Charlotte, and is all that remains of a group of buildings that made up the royal residences of both George II and III in their gardens at Kew and Richmond. The £6.6 million conservation project aims to give visitors the opportunity to view and understand the domestic pursuits and characters of the royal family in the late 18th and early 19th centuries.

Location: OS Ref. TQ188 776.193. A307. Junc A307 & A205 (1m Chiswick roundabout M4).

Open: 1 May - 30 Sept: daily, 9.45am - 5pm.

Admission: By joint ticket purchased through Kew Gardens.

LEITH HILL �

Coldharbour, Surrey

Tel: 01306 711777 **Fax:** 01306 712153 **www**.nationaltrust.org.uk/northdowns

Owner: The National Trust **Contact:** Head Warden

The highest point in south-east England, crowned by an 18th century Gothic tower, from which there are magnificent views. The surrounding woodland contains ancient stands of hazel and oak, and there is a colourful display of rhododendrons in May - Jun.

Location: OS Ref. TQ139 432. 1m SW of Coldharbour A29/B2126.

Open: Tower: 25 Mar - 29 Oct: Fri - Sun, and Weds in Aug, 10am - 5pm. 4 Nov - end Mar 2007: Sats & Suns, 10am - 3.30pm. Open all BHs (closed 25 Dec). Wood & Estate: All year: daily.

Admission: Tower: £1, Child 50p. Rhododendron Wood: £2 per car. (2 circular nature trails with leaflet.)

ℹ️No vehicular access to summit. 🖥Partial. 🎥When Tower open. 🍴Guided walks. 🅿Parking at foot of hill, 1/2m walk from Tower. 🐕Not in picnic area or Tower. ❄

open all year
see page 557

LITTLE HOLLAND HOUSE
40 Beeches Avenue, Carshalton, Surrey SM5 3LW
Tel: 020 8770 4781   **Fax:** 020 8770 4777
e-mail: valary.murphy@sutton.gov.uk
www.sutton.gov.uk/leisure/heritage/lhh.htm
Owner: London Borough of Sutton   **Contact:** Ms V Murphy

The home of Frank Dickinson (1874 - 1961) artist, designer and craftsman, who dreamt of a house that would follow the philosophy and theories of William Morris and John Ruskin. Dickinson designed, built and furnished the house himself from 1902 onwards. The Grade II* listed interior features handmade furniture, metal work, carvings and paintings produced by Dickinson in the Arts and Crafts style.

Location: OS Ref. TQ275 634. On B278 1m S of junction with A232.
Open: First Sun of each month & BH Suns & Mons (excluding Christmas & New Year), 1.30 - 5.30pm.
Admission: Free. Groups by arrangement, £3.50pp (includes talk and guided tour).
ⓘNo photography in house. ⬛Ground floor. 🅚 By arrangement.
🦮 Guide dogs only. ✳

LOSELEY PARK 🏛   *See page 167 for full page entry.*

PAINSHILL PARK 🏛   *See page 168 for full page entry.*

civil wedding venues
see page 562 🔔

OAKHURST COTTAGE 🌿
HAMBLEDON, GODALMING, SURREY GU8 4HF
Tel: 01483 208477   **e-mail:** oakhurstcottage@nationaltrust.org.uk
Owner: The National Trust   **Contact:** Winkworth Arboretum

A small 16th century timber-framed cottage, painted by both Helen Allingham and Myles Birket Foster, containing furniture and artefacts reflecting two or more centuries of continuing occupation. There is a delightful cottage garden and a small barn containing agricultural implements.

Location: OS Ref. SU965 385. Hambledon, Surrey.
Open: 25 Mar - 29 Oct: Weds, Thurs, Sats, Suns & BH Mons. Strictly by appointment, 2 - 5pm.
Admission: Adult £4.50, Child £2.50 (incl guided tour). No reduction for groups.
⬛Unsuitable. 🅚Obligatory, by arrangement. 🅿Limited. 🦮

POLESDEN LACEY 🌿
GREAT BOOKHAM, Nr DORKING, SURREY RH5 6BD
www.nationaltrust.org.uk/polesdenlacey

Tel: 01372 452048   **Infoline:** 01372 458203   **Fax:** 01372 452023
e-mail: polesdenlacey@nationaltrust.org.uk
Owner: The National Trust   **Contact:** The Property Manager

Originally an elegant 1820s Regency villa in a magnificent landscape setting. The house was remodelled after 1906 by the Hon Mrs Ronald Greville, a well-known Edwardian hostess. Her collection of fine paintings, furniture, porcelain and silver are still displayed in the reception rooms and galleries. Extensive grounds, walled rose garden, lawns and landscaped walks.

Location: OS Ref. TQ136 522. 5m NW of Dorking, 2m S of Great Bookham, off A246.

Open: House: 12 Apr - 29 Oct: Wed - Sun, 11am - 5pm also BH Mons starting with Easter. Grounds: All year: daily, 11am - 5pm/dusk. Closed 24 Dec - 2 Jan 2007. Due to refurbishment of the visitor entrance, shop and tea room there may be short periods of closure, please telephone for details.

Admission: Gardens, grounds and landscape walks: Adult £6, Child £3, Family £15. House: Adult £3 extra, Child £1.50 extra, Family £7.50 extra. All year, booked groups £7.65 (house, garden & walks).

🖼 ✳ ⬛ 🍴Licensed. 🅿 Limited for coaches. 🦮 In grounds on leads. ✳
📺 Tel: 01372 452048 for info.

RHS GARDEN WISLEY
Nr WOKING, SURREY GU23 6QB

www.rhs.org.uk

Tel: 01483 224234 **Fax:** 01483 211750

Owner/Contact: The Royal Horticultural Society

A garden to enjoy all year round with something to see for everyone. Wisley provides the visitor with ideas and inspiration and the benefit of experience from experts. The Wisley Plant Centre with plants for sale, The Wisley Shop with books and gifts and for refreshments the Café, Restaurant and Coffee Shop.

Location: OS Ref. TQ066 583. On A3 N of Guildford nr. M25 J/10. Brown Signs.

Open: All year: daily (except Christmas Day), Mon - Fri, 10am - 6pm (4.30pm Nov - Feb). Sat & Sun, 9am - 6pm (4.30pm Nov - Feb). Last entry 1 hr before closing.

Admission: RHS Members: Free. Adult £7.50, Child (6-16yrs) £2, Child (under 6) Free. Groups (10+): Adult £5.50, Child £1.60.

🔲 ⓕ ♿ Wheelchairs available tel: 01483 211113 & special map. WC.
🖥 ⓎLicensed. ⓕBy arrangement. 🔲 🅿 🔲
🐕 Guide & Registered Support dogs only. ✳ ♿

TITSEY PLACE & GARDENS
TITSEY PLACE, OXTED, SURREY RH8 0SD

www.titsey.org

Tel: 01273 407017 **Fax:** 01273 478995

email: kate.moisson@struttandparker.co.uk

Owner: Trustees of the Titsey Foundation   **Contact:** Kate Moisson

Beautiful gardens incorporating formal lawns, rose garden, walled kitchen garden and 4 mile woodland walk and parkland. Titsey Place houses 4 stunning Canalettos and Porcelain Collection.

Location: OS Ref. TQ406 553. 1 mile N of Limpsfield.

Open: mid May - end Sept: Weds & Suns, 1 - 5pm. Additionally Summer BHs. Gardens only Easter Mon.

Admission: Adult £5, Child £2.50.

♿Partial. ⓕ Obligatory. 🅿 Limited for coaches. 🐕 Woods and park only.

RAMSTER GARDENS
Ramster, Chiddingfold, Surrey GU8 4SN

Tel: 01428 654167 **www.**ramsterevents.com

Owner/Contact: Mrs R Glaister

An idyllic, mature flowering shrub garden of 20 acres, with unusual and interesting plants. Spring colour changes from subtle daffodils and magnolias in April to the famous fiery display of rhododendrons, azaleas and bluebells in May, followed in June by the gentle pinks of climbing roses and cascades of primulas.

Location: OS Ref. SU950 333. 1 1/2 m S of Chiddingfold on A283.

Open: 8 Apr - 25 Jun: daily. 10am - 5pm.

Admission: Adult £4, Child Free. Groups by arrangement.

ⓕ ♿Partial. 🖥 🐕 On leads. ♿ Tel for details.

RUNNYMEDE 🌿
Egham, Surrey

Tel: 01784 432891 **Fax:** 01784 479007 **e-mail:** runnymede@nationaltrust.org.uk

www.nationaltrust.org.uk

Owner: The National Trust   **Contact:** The Head Warden

Runnymede is an attractive area of riverside meadows, grassland and broadleaf woodland, rich in diversity of flora and fauna, and part-designated a Site of Special Scientific Interest. It was on this site, in 1215, that King John sealed Magna Carta.

Location: OS Ref. TQ007 720. 2m W of Runnymede Bridge, on S side of A308, M25/J13.

Open: All year. Riverside Car park (grass): Apr - 30 Sept: daily, 10am - 7pm. Tearoom Car park (hard standing): daily, all year, 8.30am - 5pm (later in Summer).

Admission: Fees payable for parking (NT members Free), fishing & mooring.

🔲 ♿Partial. 🖥 ⓕ 🅿 ✳ ♿ Tel for details.

WHITEHALL
1 Malden Road, Cheam, Surrey SM3 8QD

Tel/Fax: 020 8643 1236 **e-mail:** curators@whitehallcheam.fsnet.co.uk

www.sutton.gov.uk/leisure/heritage/whitehall.htm

Owner: London Borough of Sutton   **Contact:** The Curator

A Tudor timber-framed house, c1500 with later additions, in the heart of Cheam village conservation area. Displays on the history of the house and the people who lived here, plus nearby Nonsuch Palace, Cheam School and William Gilpin (Dr Syntax). Changing exhibition programme and special event days throughout the year. Attractive rear garden features medieval well from c1400.

Location: OS Ref. TQ242 638. Approx. 2m S of A3 on A2043 just N of junction with A232.

Open: Wed - Fri, 2 - 5pm; Sat, 10am - 5pm; Sun & BH Mons, 2 - 5pm.

Admission: Adult £1.25, Child (6-16yrs) 60p, under 5yrs Free. Groups by appt.

🔲 ♿Ground floor. 🖥 ⓕ 🔲 🔲 🐕 Guide dogs only. ✳ ♿ Tel for details.

Polesden Lacey.

NTPL / D Sellman

WINKWORTH ARBORETUM ✤

HASCOMBE ROAD, GODALMING, SURREY GU8 4AD

www.nationaltrust.org.uk/winkwortharboretum

Tel: 01483 208477   **Fax:** 01483 208252

e-mail: winkwortharboretum@nationaltrust.org.uk

Owner: The National Trust   **Contact:** Head Arborist

Established in the 20th century, the hillside arboretum now contains over 1,000 different shrubs and trees, many of them rare. The most impressive displays are in spring for bluebells and azaleas, and in autumn for colour and wildlife. New wetland area with boardwalk and circular route. In the summer it is an ideal place for family visits and a picnic.

Location: OS Ref. SU990 412. Near Hascombe, 2m SE of Godalming on E side of B2130.

Open: All year round: daily during daylight hours. May be closed due to high winds. Boathouse: Apr - Nov.

Admission: Adult £4.50, Child (5-16yrs) £2, Family (2+2) £10 (additional family member £1.75). Discounts for 15 or more.

⬛ ♿ Limited. WC. ▣ 🐕In grounds, on leads. ✳

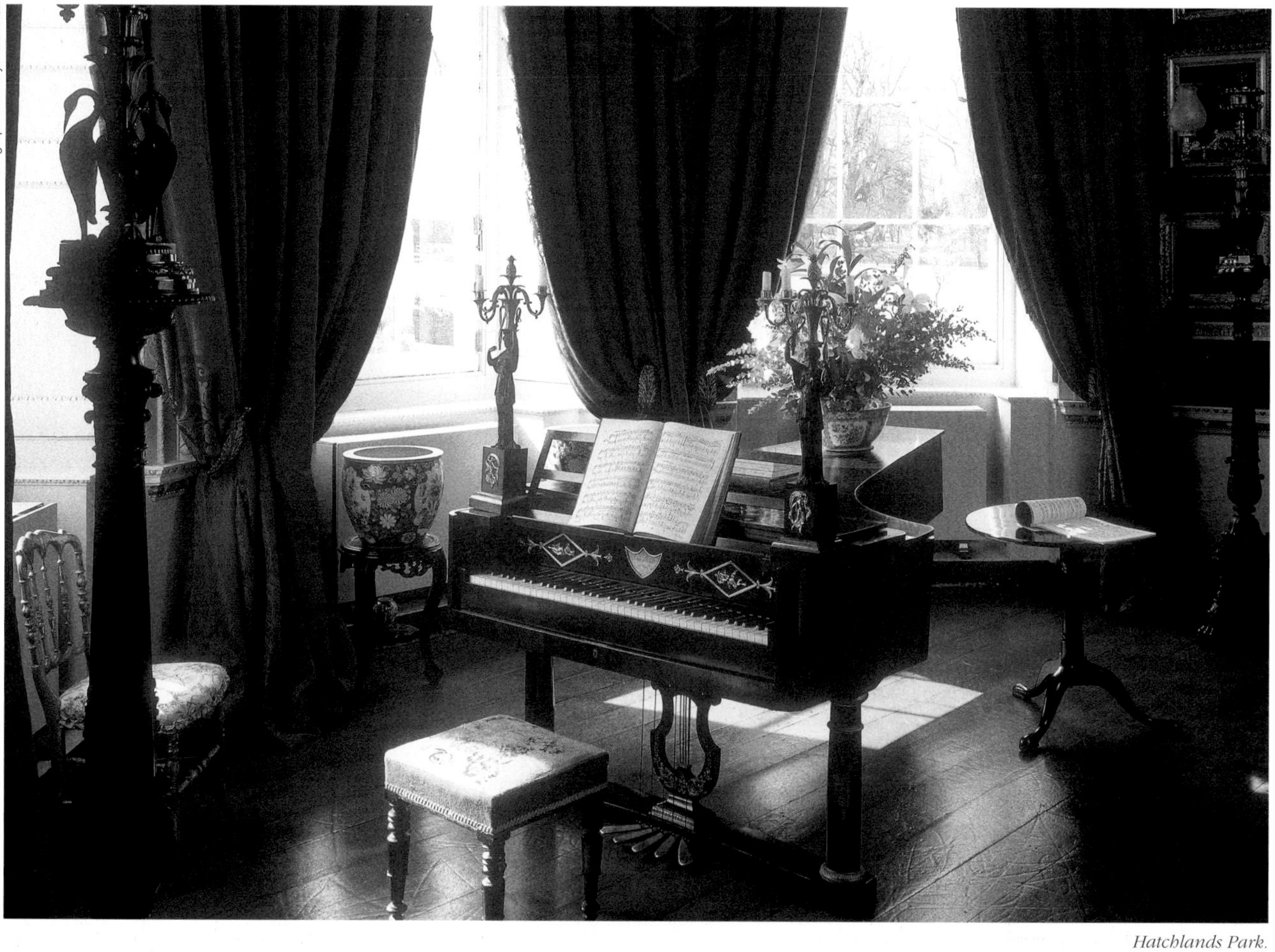

Hatchlands Park.

ARUNDEL CASTLE

www.arundelcastle.org

A thousand years of history is waiting to be discovered at Arundel Castle in West Sussex. Dating from the 11th century, the Castle is both ancient fortification and stately home of the Dukes of Norfolk and Earls of Arundel.

Set high on a hill, this magnificent castle commands stunning views across the River Arun and out to sea. Climb the Keep, explore the battlements, wander in the grounds and recently restored Victorian gardens and relax in the Fitzalan Chapel garden.

The Castle suffered extensive damage during the English Civil War and the process of structural restoration began in earnest in the 18th century and continued up until 1900. It was one of the first private residences to have electricity and central heating and has its own fire engine, which is still on view today.

Inside the Castle, 20 rooms are open to the public including the vast Baron's Hall with its fine collection of 16th century furniture, the Armoury with a unique assemblage of armour and weaponry, tapestries hang above the Grand Staircase leading to the renovated Victorian bedrooms and bathrooms, paintings by Van Dyck, Gainsborough, Canaletto and others, together with the personal possessions of Mary, Queen of Scots, including the gold and enamel rosary that she carried to her execution.

There are special events throughout the season, including jousting, medieval re-enactments and falconry.

Owner:
Arundel Castle
Trustees Ltd

▶ CONTACT

The Comptroller
Arundel Castle
Arundel
West Sussex
BN18 9AB

Tel: 01903 883136
or 01903 882173

Fax: 01903 884581

e-mail: info@
arundelcastle.org

▶ LOCATION
OS Ref. TQ018 072

Central Arundel, N of A27
Brighton 40 mins,
Worthing 15 mins,
Chichester 15 mins.
From London A3 or
A24, 1¹/₂ hrs.
M25 motorway, 30m.

Bus: Bus stop 100 yds.

Rail: Station ¹/₂ m.

Air: Gatwick 25m.

ℹ️ No photography inside the Castle. Guidebooks in French & German.

♿ Most areas accessible. Visitors may alight at the entrance, before parking in the allocated areas. WCs.

🍴 Restaurant seats 140. Special rates for booked groups. Self-service restaurant in Castle serves home-made food. Groups must book in advance for morning coffee, lunch or afternoon tea.

🚶 Pre-booked groups only. Tour time 1¹/₂ hrs. Tours available in Japanese.

🅿️ Ample. Coaches can park free in town coach park.

Items of particular interest include a Norman Motte & Keep, Armoury & Victorian bedrooms. Special rates for schoolchildren (aged 5-15) and teachers.

🛡️ Tel for details.

▶ OPENING TIMES

Summer
2 April - 27 October
Daily (except Sats)
Grounds, gardens, shop,
Fitzalan Chapel and Keep
Restaurant
11am - 5pm.

Castle Rooms
12 noon - 5pm.
Last admission 4pm.

Winter
1 November - 1 April.
Closed.

▶ ADMISSION
Summer

Adult	£12.00
Child (5-16yrs)	£7.50
Conc.	£9.50
Family (2+5 max).	£32.00

Groups (20+)

Adult	£10.00
Child (5-16yrs)	£6.00
Conc.	£8.00

Grounds only £6.50

Winter
Closed.

NTPL: Rupert Truman

BATEMAN'S

www.nationaltrust.org.uk/batemans

MAP 4

Owner:
The National Trust

▶ CONTACT

The Administrator
Bateman's
Burwash
Etchingham
East Sussex TN19 7DS

Tel: 01435 882302
Fax: 01435 882811

e-mail: batemans@
nationaltrust.org.uk

▶ LOCATION
OS Ref. TQ671 238

¹/₂ m S of Burwash
off A265.

Rail: Etchingham 3m,
then bus (twice daily).

Air: Gatwick 40m.

Built in 1634 and home to Rudyard Kipling for over 30 years, Bateman's lies in the richly wooded landscape of the Sussex Weald. Visit this Sussex sandstone manor house, built by a local ironmaster, where the famous writer lived from 1902 to 1936. See the rooms as they were in Kipling's day, including the study where the view inspired him to write some of his well-loved works including *Puck of Pook's Hill* and *Rewards and Fairies*. Find the mementoes of Kipling's time in India and illustrations from his famous *Jungle Book* tales of *Mowgli, Baloo and Shere Khan.*

Wander through the delightful Rose Garden with its pond and statues, with Mulberry and Herb gardens and discover the wild garden, through which flows the River Dudwell. Through the wild garden, you will find the Mill where you can watch corn being ground on most Saturday and Wednesday afternoons and one of the world's first water-driven turbines installed by Kipling to generate electricity for the house. In the garage, see a 1928 Rolls Royce, one of several owned by Kipling who was a keen early motorist.

Savour the peace and tranquillity of this beautiful property which Kipling described as *'A good and peaceable place'* and of which he said *'we have loved it, ever since our first sight of it…'.*

There is a picnic glade next to the car park, or you can enjoy morning coffee, a delicious lunch or afternoon tea in the licensed tearoom where there is special emphasis on using local produce. The well-stocked gift shop offers the largest collection of Kipling books in the area.

▶ OPENING TIMES

18 March - 29 October:
Sat - Wed, Good Fri &
BH Mons
11am - 5.00pm.
Last admission 4.30pm.

▶ ADMISSION

House & Garden

Adult	£6.20
Child	£3.10
Family (2+3)	£15.50
Groups	£5.20

 Ground floor & grounds.
WC. Computerised virtual tour
of upper floors.

Licensed.

Tel for details.

NTPL Geoffrey Frosh

MAP 3

GOODWOOD HOUSE

www.goodwood.co.uk

Goodwood is one of the finest sporting estates in the world. At the heart of the Estate lies Goodwood House, the ancestral home of the Dukes of Richmond, direct descendants of King Charles II. Today, it is still lived in by the Duke's son, the Earl of March and Kinrara, with his wife and young family, and is open to the public on at least 60 days a year.

The House's great flint wings with their distinctive copper-topped towers date from the Regency period: they were added to older Jacobean and Georgian wings. Set in these exquisitely decorated, gilded interiors, the art collection is at museum level, with magnificent English paintings from the 17th and 18th centuries. These include famous horse paintings by George Stubbs, and views of London by Canaletto, together with works by nearly all the great British portrait painters of the period, notably Van Dyck, Lely, Kneller, Reynolds, Ramsay, Hoppner and Raeburn. There is fine French furniture from the

18th century, as well as Gobelins tapestries and superb, personally commissioned Sèvres porcelain. Special works of art are regularly rotated and displayed. Arrangement to see the books can be made by written application to the Curator (there is a special charge for these viewings).

Goodwood is not only a beautiful house to visit on an open day, with a relaxed and friendly atmosphere, but is also renowned for its entertaining. The House enjoys a reputation for excellence as a location for exceptional weddings, parties and events. The Estate's own organic Home Farm provides premium organic meat, cream and milk for all the events. With internationally renowned horseracing and motor sport events, the finest Downland golf course in the UK, our own Aerodrome and hotel, Goodwood can offer an extraordinarily rich sporting experience.

Owner:
The Earl of March

▶ CONTACT

Curator's PA
Goodwood House
Goodwood
Chichester
West Sussex PO18 0PX

Tel: 01243 755048
01243 755042
(Weddings)
Fax: 01243 755005
Recorded info:
01243 755040
e-mail: curator
@goodwood.co.uk
or weddings@
goodwood.co.uk

▶ LOCATION
OS Ref. SU888 088

3¹/₂m NE of Chichester. A3 from London then A286 or A285. M27/A27 from Portsmouth or Brighton.

Rail: Chichester 3¹/₂m
Arundel 9m.

Air: Heathrow 1¹/₂ hrs
Gatwick ³/₄ hr.

© Goodwood Collection / Racehorses Exercising at Goodwood

CONFERENCE/FUNCTION

ROOM	SIZE	MAX CAPACITY
Ballroom	79' x 23'	200
11 other rooms also available		

 Conference facilities. No photography. Highly trained guides. Shell House optional extra on Connoisseurs' Days or by Group Appointment, or written request.

 Obligatory. **P** Ample.

In grounds, on leads. Guide dogs only in house.

Civil Wedding Licence.

▶ OPENING TIMES

Summer
26 March - 9 October:
Most Sundays & Mondays.
(Check recorded information)
August: Sunday - Thursday, 1 - 5pm.

Connoisseurs' Days
12 & 26 April, 18 May, 20 Sept, 18 Oct.
Special tours for groups: must be booked.

Closed for Special Events on 23/24 April and for 2 weekends between mid June & mid July for the Festival of Speed & for one Sunday in September for the Motor Circuit Revival Meeting. Please ring Recorded Information on 01243 755040 to check these dates & occasional extra closures.

▶ ADMISSION

House
Adult £8.00
Child (12 - 18yrs) £4.00
Child (under 12 yrs) ... Free
Senior £7.00
Student £4.00
Groups (20 - 200)
  Open Day £7.00
  Morning £9.00
  Connoisseur £9.50

SPECIAL EVENTS

Dates to be confirmed
The Festival of Speed.*
The Goodwood Revival.*

1 - 5 August
The Festival Meeting known as 'Glorious Goodwood'.

* Please visit our website for up to date information.

LEONARDSLEE
LAKES & GARDENS

www.leonardslee.com

MAP 3

Owner:
The Loder Family

▶ CONTACT

Tom Loder
Leonardslee lakes &
gardens
Lower Beeding
Horsham
West Sussex   RH13 6PP

Tel: 01403 891212
Fax: 01403 891305

e-mail: info@
leonardsleegardens
.com

▶ LOCATION

OS Ref. TQ222 260

M23 to Handcross then
B2110 (signposted
Cowfold) for 4m.
From London:
1 hr 15 mins.

Rail: Horsham
Station 4¹/₂ m.

Bus: No. 17 from
Horsham and Brighton.

Leonardslee represents one of the largest and most spectacular woodland gardens in England, in a most magnificent setting, only a few miles from the M23. The 240 acre (100 hectare) valley is world famous for its spring display of *Azalea* and *Rhododendrons* flowering throughout the valley amongst the seven lakes, providing superb views and magnificent reflections.

The gardens have evolved over 200 years and since 1889 have been maintained by the Loder family. The famous *Rhododendron loderi*, was raised by Sir Edmund Loder in 1901. The original plants can still be seen in the garden, and in May the fragrance of their huge blooms pervades the air throughout the valley. At this time the delightful Rock Garden is a kaleidoscope of colour. The many plantings of *Kalmias Cornus*

and *Hydrangeas* bring colour to the valley in the summer months.

Ducks, geese and swans swim on the lakes, and huge carp can be seen basking under the surface. Wallabies, deer and other natural wildlife roam the parks. The wallabies have lived wild within the valley for over 100 years and provide a useful environmentally-friendly mowing service.

In a secluded courtyard is a Japanese Garden with superb collection of Bonsai. Nearby, the one-twelfth scale miniature estate of 100 years ago titled "Behind the dolls house" has become a fascination to all visitors. The Loder collection of Victorian motor cars is one of the country's most impressive of this era, showing the development of the motor vehicle from 1883-1900.

Splashes of colour in the rock garden

Miniature model estate "Behind the dolls house"

▶ OPENING TIMES

Summer
1 April - 31 October
Daily 9.30am - 6pm
Last admission 4.30pm

Winter
1 November - 31 March
Closed (facilities available
for private functions)

▶ ADMISSION

April, June - October
    Adult £6.00

May (Mon - Fri)
    Adult £8.00

May (Sats & Suns)
    Adult £9.00

    Child (any time) £4.00

Coach Parties (20+)
April, June - October
    Adult £5.00

May (Mon - Fri)
    Adult £7.00

May (Sat - Sun)
    Adult £8.00

    Child (any time) £3.50

SPECIAL EVENTS

APRIL/MAY
29 Apr - 1 May
Bonsai Weekend.

MAY
Azaleas & Rhododendron
flowering season.

JULY
1/2 Vintage Engine Show.
15/16 Model Boat Regatta.

CONFERENCE/FUNCTION

ROOM	MAX CAPACITY
Clock Tower	100
Garden Room	30

Photography - landscape & fashion, film location.

Restaurant available for private and corporate functions in the evenings and out of season.

Unsuitable, due to natural valley slopes.

Restaurant/café. Morning coffee, lunches & teas.

Ample. Average length of visit 3 - 5 hours.

PASHLEY MANOR GARDENS

www.pashleymanorgardens.com

Owner:
Mr & Mrs
James A Sellick

▶ **CONTACT**

Claire Baker
Pashley Manor
Ticehurst
Wadhurst
East Sussex
TN5 7HE

Tel: 01580 200888
Fax: 01580 200102

e-mail: info@
pashleymanorgardens
.com

▶ **LOCATION**
OS Ref. TQ707 291

On B2099 between A21
and Ticehurst Village.

A winner of HHA/Christie's Garden of the Year Award. The gardens offer a sumptuous blend of romantic landscaping, imaginative plantings and fine old trees, fountains, springs and large ponds. This is a quintessential English garden of a very individual character with exceptional views to the surrounding valleyed fields. Many eras of English history are reflected here, typifying the tradition of the English Country House and its garden.

The gardens first opened in 1992 and were brought to their present splendour with the assistance of the eminent landscape architect, Anthony du Gard Pasley. A number of different gardens have been created within the 11 acres allowing the visitor to travel from blazing colour to cool creams, greens and golds.

The gardens are always evolving and never static;

it is hoped that they will be inspirational yet restful to the first-time visitor and will never disappoint those who return regularly.

Pashley prides itself on its delicious food. During warm weather, visitors can enjoy their refreshments on the terrace overlooking the moat or in the Jubilee Courtyard. Home-made soups, ploughman's lunches with pickles and patés, fresh salad from the garden (whenever possible), home-made scones and delicious cakes, filter coffee, specialist teas, fine wines are served from the Garden Room café. The gift shop caters for every taste… from postcards and local honey to traditional hand-painted ceramics and tapestry cushions. A wide selection of plants and shrubs, many of which grow at Pashley, are available for purchase.

▶ **OPENING TIMES**
8 April - 30 September:
Tues, Weds, Thurs, Sats &
all BH Mons, 11am - 5pm.
October: Mon - Fri, 10am -
4pm Garden only
(restaurant & shop closed).

▶ **ADMISSION**
Adult £6.00

Groups (20+) £5.50

Coaches must book.
Please telephone for
details.

Partial.

Licensed.

By arrangement.

P

Guide dogs only.

Telephone for details.

MAP 3

PETWORTH HOUSE & PARK

www.nationaltrust.org.uk/petworth

Owner:
The National Trust

▶ **CONTACT**

The Administration
Office
Petworth House
Petworth
West Sussex GU28 0AE

Tel: 01798 342207

Info: 01798 343929

Fax: 01798 342963

email: petworth@
nationaltrust.org.uk

▶ **LOCATION**

OS Ref. SU976 218

In the centre of
Petworth town
(approach roads
A272/A283/A285) Car
park signposted.

Rail: Pulborough
5 ¹/₄ m.

Petworth House is one of the finest houses in the care of the National Trust and is home to an art collection that rivals many London galleries. Assembled by one family over 350 years, it includes works by Turner, Dyck, Titian, Claude, Gainsborough, Bosch, Reynolds and William Blake.

The state rooms contain sculpture, furniture and porcelain of the highest quality and are complemented by the old kitchens in the Servents' Quarters. The Carved Room contains some of Grinling Gibbons' finest limewood carvings.

Petworth House is also the home of Lord and Lady Egremont and extra family rooms are open on weekdays by kind permission of the family (not Bank Holidays).

Petworth Park is a 700 acre park landscaped by 'Capability' Brown and is open to the public all year free of charge. Spring and autumn are particularly breathtaking and the summer sunsets over the lake are spectacular.

©NTPL / Rupert Truman

ⓘ 🏛 Events & Exhibitions throughout the year. Baby feeding and changing facilities, highchairs. Pushchairs admitted in house but no prams, please. No photography or mobile phones in house.

🛍 Contact Retail & Catering Manager on 01798 344975.

♿ Car park is 800 yards from house; there is a vehicle available to take less able visitors to the House.

🍴 Licensed.

🎨 By arrangement with the Administration Office on variety of subjects.

🎧 Audio House Tours.

🅿 800 yards from house. Coach parties alight at Church Lodge ebtrance, coaches then park in NT car park. Coaches must book in advance.

📖 Welcome. Must book. Teachers' pack available.

🐕 Guide dogs only in house. Dogs in park only.

❄ 🎭 Telephone for details.

▶ **OPENING TIMES**

House
1 April - 29 October. Daily except Thur & Fri, but open Good Fri, 11am - 5pm.

Last admission to House 4.30pm.

Extra rooms shown on Mons - Wed (closed BH Mons).

Pleasure Ground
18 - 29 March for spring bulbs and events, 11 am - 4pm.

1 April - 29 October. Saturday - Wednesday, 11am - 6pm.

Park
All year: Daily, 8am - sunset.

Shop & Restaurant
18 - 29 March for Mothering Sunday lunches and events, 11 am - 4pm.

1 April - 29 October. Saturday - Wednesday, 11am - 5pm.

▶ **ADMISSION**

House & Pleasure Ground
Adget £8.00
Child (5-17yrs) £4.00
Child (under 5 yrs) .... Free
Family (2+3).......... £20.00
Groups (pre-booked 15+)
Adult £7.00

Park Only ....Free

Pleasure Ground
Adult £3.00
Child (5-17yrs) £1.50

NT Members Free.

THE ROYAL PAVILION

www.royalpavilion.org.uk

Universally acclaimed as one of the most exotically beautiful buildings in the British Isles, the Royal Pavilion is the former seaside residence of King George IV.

Originally a simple farmhouse, in 1787 architect Henry Holland created a neo-classical villa on the site. It was later transformed into its current Indian style by John Nash between 1815 and 1822. With interiors decorated in the Chinese style and an astonishingly exotic exterior, this Regency Palace is quite breathtaking.

Magnificent decorations and fantastic furnishings have been re-created in the recent extensive restoration programme. From the opulence of the main state rooms to the charm of the first floor bedroom suites, the Royal Pavilion is filled with astonishing colours and superb craftsmanship.

Witness the magnificence of the Music Room with its domed ceiling of gilded scallop-shaped shells and hand-knotted carpet, and promenade through the Chinese bamboo grove of the Long Gallery.

Lavish menus were created in the Great Kitchen, with its cast iron palm trees and dazzling collection of copperware, and then served in the dramatic setting of the Banqueting Room, lit by a huge crystal chandelier held by a silvered dragon.

Set in restored Regency gardens replanted to John Nash's elegant 1820s design, the Royal Pavilion is an unforgettable experience.

Visitors can discover more about life behind the scenes at the Palace during the last 200 years with a specially commissioned interactive multimedia presentation. Public guided tours take place daily at 11.30am and 2.30pm for a small additional charge.

MAP 4

Owner:
Brighton & Hove
City Council

▶ **CONTACT**

Visitor Services
The Royal Pavilion
Brighton
East Sussex BN1 1EE

Tel: 01273 290900

Fax: 01273 292871

Email: visitor.services
@brighton-hove.gov.uk

▶ **LOCATION**

The Royal Pavilion is in the centre of Brighton easily reached by road and rail. From London M25, M23, A23 - 1 hr 30 mins.

Rail: Victoria to Brighton station 50 mins. 15 mins walk from Brighton station.

Air: Gatwick 20 mins.

CONFERENCE/FUNCTION

ROOM	MAX CAPACITY
Banqueting Room	200
Great Kitchen	90
Music Rm	180
Queen Adelaide Suite	100
Small Adelaide	40
William IV	80

ℹ️ Location filming and photography, including feature films, fashion shoots and corporate videos.

🛍️ Gift shop with souvenirs unique to the Royal Pavilion.

🍽️ Spectacular rooms available for prestigious corporate and private entertaining or wedding receptions.

♿ Access to ground floor only. Tactile and signed tours can be booked in advance with Visitor Services Tel: 01273 292820/2.

☕ Tearooms with a balcony providing sweeping views across the restored Regency gardens.

🚶 Tours in English, French and German and other languages by prior arrangement. General introduction and specialist tours provided.

🅿️ Close to NCP car parks, town centre voucher parking. Coach drop-off point in Church Street, parking in Madeira Drive. Free entry for coach drivers.

📋 Specialist tours relating to all levels of National Curriculum, must be booked in advance with Visitor Services. Special winter student rates. Slide lecture presentations by arrangement.

🔔 Civil Wedding Licence.

❄️

▶ **OPENING TIMES**

Summer
April - September
Daily: 9.30am - 5.45pm
Last admission at 5pm.

Winter
October - March
Daily: 10am - 5.15pm
Last admission at 4.30pm.

Closed 24 (from 2.30pm), 25/26 December.

▶ **ADMISSION**

Adult	£6.10
Child	£3.60
Conc.	£4.30
Groups (20+)	
Adult	£5.10

Prices subject to change in Spring 2006.

🎭 **SPECIAL EVENTS**

Autumn, Winter & Spring:
Children's Events.

Please telephone for details of other events throughout the year.

SAINT HILL MANOR

MAP 4

Owner:
Church of Scientology

▶ CONTACT

Mrs Liz Ostermann
Saint Hill Manor
Saint Hill Road
East Grinstead
West Sussex   RH19 4JY

Tel: 01342 326711
Fax: 01342 317057

e-mail:
info@hubbardfoundation.
co.uk

▶ LOCATION
OS Ref. TQ383 359

2m SW of East
Grinstead. At Felbridge,
turn off A22, down
Imberhorne Lane and
over crossroads into
Saint Hill Road,
200yds on right.

Rail: East Grinstead
station.

Air: 15 mins drive from
Gatwick airport.

Built 1792 by Gibbs Crawfurd. One of the finest Sussex sandstone buildings in existence and situated near the breathtaking Ashdown Forest. Subsequent owners included Edgar March Crookshank and the Maharajah of Jaipur. In 1959, Saint Hill Manor's final owner, acclaimed author and humanitarian L Ron Hubbard, acquired the Manor, where he lived for many years with his family. As a result of the work carried out under Mr Hubbard's direction, the Manor has been restored to its original beauty, including the uncovering of fine oak wood panelling, marble fireplaces and plasterwork ceilings. Other outstanding features of this lovely house include an impressive library of Mr Hubbard's works, elegant winter garden, and delightful Monkey Mural painted in 1945 by Winston Churchill's nephew John Spencer Churchill. This 100-foot mural depicts many famous personalities as monkeys, including Winston Churchill. Also open to the public are 59 acres of landscaped gardens, lake and woodlands. Ideal for corporate functions and also available as a film location. Annual events include open-air theatre, arts festivals, classical and jazz concerts.

▶ OPENING TIMES
All year
Daily, 2 - 5pm,
on the hour.

Groups welcome
throughout the year.

▶ ADMISSION
Free.

 Ground floor.
Teas available.
 Obligatory.
P

▣ SPECIAL EVENTS

Open-air theatre, classical and jazz concerts, exhibitions and arts festivals.

This year's open air theatre will be a production of Shakespeare's "A Midsummer Night's Dream" on Sunday 18th June. Please telephone for details.

©NTPL 2004/Lisa Barnard

SHEFFIELD PARK GARDEN

MAP 4

www.nationaltrust.org.uk/sheffieldpark

A magnificent 120 acre landscaped garden. The centrepiece of this internationally renowned, garden is the four lakes that mirror the unique planting and colour that each season brings. Displays of spring bulbs as the garden awakens, and a stunning exhibition of colour in May, of rhododendrons and the National Collection of Ghent Azaleas. Water lilies dress the lakes during the summer. Visitors to the garden during the summer months can enjoy a leisurely walk perhaps pausing to sit on a seat to enjoy the tranquil ambience. In the autumn the garden is transformed by trees planted specifically for their autumn colour including *Nyssa sylvatica*, *Amelanchier* and *Acer palmatum*. These and other fine specimen trees, particularly North American varieties, produce displays of gold, orange and crimson. *Gentiana sino-ornata* offers two borders of amazing 'Gentian Blue' colour during the autumn months. The garden is open throughout the year and has something for all, whether a quiet stroll or a family gathering, allowing the children to participate in the many activities offered. Special Events run throughout the year - please telephone for details.

Owner:
The National Trust

▶ CONTACT

Jo Hopkins
Visitor Services &
Marketing Manager
Sheffield Park
East Sussex
TN22 3QX

Tel: 01825 790231
Fax: 01825 791264

e-mail: sheffieldpark@
nationaltrust.org.uk

▶ LOCATION

OS Ref. TQ415 240

Midway between East
Grinstead and Lewes,
5m NW of Uckfield on
E side of A275.

©NTPL 2004/Lisa Barnard

▶ OPENING TIMES

14 February - 26 February,
1 November - 23
December & 13 - 25
February 2007:
Tues - Sun,
10.30am - 4pm.

28 February - 30 April,
6 June - 1 October,
Tue - Sun, 10.30am - 6pm.

1 May - 4 June &
2 - 31 October: Daily,
10.30am - 6pm.

27 - 31 December:
Wed - Sun, 10.30am - 4pm.

6 Jan - 11 Feb 2007:
Sat & Sun, 10.30am - 4pm.

Open BH Mon. Apr - Aug.

Last admission to the
garden 1 hour before
closing or dusk if earlier.

▶ ADMISSION

Adult £6.20
Child £3.10
Family £15.50
Groups (15+)
Adult £5.25
Child £2.60

Joint Ticket available with
Bluebell Railway.

NT, RHS individual &
Great British Heritage Pass
holders Free.

 Partial. WC.

(not NT).

 By arrangement.

P

Assistance dogs only.

Tel for details.

NTPL / Andrew Butler

ALFRISTON CLERGY HOUSE ✻

THE TYE, ALFRISTON, POLEGATE, EAST SUSSEX BN26 5TL

Tel: 01323 870001   **Fax:** 01323 871318   **e-mail:** alfriston@nationaltrust.org.uk

Owner: The National Trust   **Contact:** The Property Manager

Step back into the Middle Ages with a visit to this 14th century thatched Wealden 'Hall House'. Trace the history of this building which in 1896 was the first to be acquired by the National Trust. Discover what is used to make the floor in the Great Hall and visit the excellent shop with its local crafts. Explore the delightful cottage garden and savour the idyllic setting beside Alfriston's parish church, with stunning views across the meandering River Cuckmere. An intriguing variety of shops, pubs and restaurants in Alfriston village make this a wonderful day out.

Location: OS Ref. TQ521 029. 4m NE of Seaford, just E of B2108.

Open: 4 - 19 Mar: Sats & Suns, 11am - 4pm. 25 Mar - 29 Oct: daily except Tue & Fri, 10am - 5pm. 30 Oct - 17 Dec: daily except Tue & Fri, 11am - 4pm.

Admission: Adult £3.25, Child £1.60, Family (2+3) £8.10. Pre-booked groups £2.80.

ⓘ No WCs. 🅿 Parking in village car parks.

ARUNDEL CASTLE   *See page 174 for full page entry.*

ARUNDEL CATHEDRAL

Parsons Hill, Arundel, Sussex BN18 9AY

Tel: 01903 882297   **Fax:** 01903 885335

e-mail: aruncath1@aol.com   **Contact:** Rev T Madeley

French Gothic Cathedral, church of the RC Diocese of Arundel and Brighton built by Henry, 15th Duke of Norfolk and opened 1873.

Location: OS Ref. TQ015 072. Above junction of A27 and A284.

Open: Summer: 9am - 6pm. Winter: 9am - dusk. Mass at 10am, Mon - Fri (except 8.30am Thur) at Convent of Poor Clares. Sun Masses: 9.30am & 11.30am, Vigil Sat evening: 6.15pm at Convent of Poor Clares. Shop open in the summer, Mon - Fri, 10am - 4pm and after services and on special occasions and otherwise at request.

Admission: Free.

BATEMAN'S ✻   *See page 175 for full page entry.*

open all year
see page 557

ANNE OF CLEVES HOUSE

52 SOUTHOVER HIGH STREET, LEWES, SUSSEX BN7 1JA

www.sussexpast.co.uk

Tel: 01273 474610   **Fax:** 01273 486990   **e-mail:** anne@sussexpast.co.uk

Owner: Sussex Past   **Contact:** Stephen Watts

This 16th century timber-framed Wealden hall-house was given to Anne of Cleves as part of her divorce settlement from Henry VIII in 1541, and contains wide-ranging collections of Sussex interest. Furnished rooms give an impression of life in the 17th and 18th centuries. Artefacts from Lewes Priory, Sussex pottery and Wealden ironwork.

Location: OS198 Ref. TQ410 096. S of Lewes town centre, off A27/A275/A26.

Open: Open: 1 Jan - 28 Feb: Tue - Sat, 10am - 5pm. 1 Mar - 31 Oct: Tue - Sat, 10am - 5pm; Sun, Mon & BHs, 11am - 5pm. 1 Nov - 31 Dec: Tue - Sat, 10am - 5pm. Closed 24 - 26 Dec.

Admission: Adult £3.10, Child £1.55, Conc. £2.80, Family (2+2) £7.90 or (1+4) £6.30. Groups (15+): Adult £2.80, Child £1.35, Conc. £2.50. Combined ticket with Lewes Castle is also available.

🗗 🔓 By arrangement. 🅿 Limited (on road). ▦ 🐕 Guide dogs only. 🔺 ❄ 🛗 Tel for details.

West Dean Gardens.

1066 BATTLE OF HASTINGS ⊞
ABBEY AND BATTLEFIELD

BATTLE, SUSSEX TN33 0AD

www.english-heritage.org.uk/visits

Tel: 01424 773792 **Fax:** 01424 775059

Owner: English Heritage   **Contact:** Visitor Operations Team

Visit the site of the 1066 Battle of Hastings. An inclusive interactive audio tour will lead you around the battlefield and to the exact spot where Harold fell. Explore the magnificent abbey ruins and gatehouse and see fascinating displays describing the site's history. Children's themed play area.

Location: OS Ref. TQ749 157. Top of Battle High Street. Turn off A2100 to Battle.

Open: 1 Apr - 30 Sept: daily, 10am - 6pm. 1 Oct - 31 Mar: daily 10am - 4pm. Closed 24 - 26 Dec & 1 Jan. Café open from Oct 2006.

Admission: Adult £5.50, Child £2.80, Conc. £4.10, Family £13.80. 15% discount for groups (11+). English Heritage members free. From Oct 2006: Adult £6.30, Child £3.20, Conc. £4.70, Family £15.80.

🛈 WCs nearby. 📷 ♿ Ground floor & grounds. 🅿 Charge payable. 🎧 Inclusive. 🐕 In grounds, on leads. ✳ ♿ Tel for details.

BAYHAM OLD ABBEY ⊞

Lamberhurst, Sussex TN3 8DE

Tel/Fax: 01892 890381   www.english-heritage.org.uk/visits

Owner: English Heritage   **Contact:** Visitor Operations Team

These riverside ruins are of a house of 'white' canons, founded c.1208 and preserved in the 18th century, when its surroundings were landscaped to create its delightful setting. Two rooms in the Georgian dower house are also open to the public.

Location: OS Ref. TQ651 366. 1¼ miles W of Lamberhurst off B2169.

Open: 1 Apr - 30 Sept: daily, 10am - 5pm.

Admission: Adult £3.50, Child £1.80, Conc. £2.60. English Heritage members free.

📷 ♿ Grounds. WC. 🅿 🐕 In grounds, on leads.

BIGNOR ROMAN VILLA

Bignor Lane, Bignor, Nr Pulborough, West Sussex RH20 1PH

Tel/Fax: 01798 869259   **e-mail:** bignorromanvilla@care4free.net

Owner: Mr J R Tupper   **Contact:** Ging Allison – Curator

One of the largest villas to be open to the public in Great Britain, with some of the finest mosaics all *in situ* and all under cover, including Medusa, Venus & Cupid Gladiators and Ganymede. Discovered in 1811 and open to the public since 1814. See the longest mosaic on display in Great Britain at 24 metres. Walk on original floors dating back to circa 350 AD. We have a small café and picnic area available for Villa visitors only.

Location: OS Ref. SU987 146. 6m N of Arundel, 6m S of Pulborough A29. 7m S of Petworth A285.

Open: Mar & Apr: Tue - Sun & BHs, 10am - 5pm; May & Oct: daily, 10am - 5pm. Jun - Sept: daily, 10am - 6pm.

Admission: Adult £4.35, Child £1.85, OAP £2.50. Groups (10+): Adult £3.50, Child £1.50, OAP £2.50. Guided tours (max 30 per tour) £19.50. Introductory talk £10 (one room only approx. 10 mins).

📷 ♿ Partial. 🐕 ℹ By arrangement. 🅿 🐕 ✕

Petworth House.

South East - England
NT Photographic Library: D Sellman

BODIAM CASTLE ✤
BODIAM, Nr ROBERTSBRIDGE, EAST SUSSEX TN32 5UA
www.nationaltrust.org.uk/bodiamcastle

Tel: 01580 830436 **Fax:** 01580 830398 **e-mail:** bodiamcastle@nationaltrust.org.uk
Owner: The National Trust **Contact:** The Property Manager

Built in 1385 to defend the surrounding countryside and as a comfortable dwelling for a rich nobleman, Bodiam Castle is one of the finest examples of medieval architecture. The virtual completeness of its exterior makes it popular with adults, children and film crews alike. Inside, although a ruin, floors have been replaced in some of the towers and visitors can climb the spiral staircase to enjoy superb views of the Rother Valley and local steam trains from the battlements. Discover more of its intriguing past in the new Audio Visual Presentation, and wander in the peacefully romantic Castle grounds.

Location: OS Ref. TQ782 256. 3m S of Hawkhurst, 2m E of A21 Hurst Green.
Open: 7 Jan - 10 Feb: Sats & Suns, 10am - 4pm. 11 Feb - 31 Oct: daily including Good Fri, Easter Sat & Sun, 10.30am - 6pm. 4 Nov - 9 Feb 2007: Sats & Suns, 10.30am - 4pm. Last admission 1 hour before closing or dusk if earlier.
Admission: Adult £4.60, Child £2.30, Family (2+3) £11.50 Groups (15+) £3.90. Car parking £2 per car.

Ground floor & grounds. Teacher and student packs and education base. Tel for details.

BORDE HILL
GARDEN, PARK & WOODLAND 🏛
HAYWARDS HEATH, WEST SUSSEX RH16 1XP
www.bordehill.co.uk

Tel: 01444 450326 **Fax:** 01444 440427 **e-mail:** info@bordehill.co.uk
Owner: Mr & Mrs A P Stephenson Clarke **Contact:** Sarah Brook

Winner of the 2004 Historic Houses Association/Christie's "Garden of the Year" Award, this glorious garden flows into linked 'garden rooms', boasting their own distinctive character and style. Year-round colour and interest with spring flowering rhododendrens, azaleas, camellias, magnolias and the many 'champion' trees. The Rose and Italian Gardens with the herbaceous borders provide colour for summer and into autumn. Set in 200 acres of parkland with panoramic views, woodland and lakeside walks. Ideal location for filming and photographic shoots.
Location: OS Ref. TQ324 265. 1½m N of Haywards Heath on Balcombe Road, 3m from A23. 45mins from Victoria Station.
Open: Please visit our website for opening times and events listings.
Admission: Adult £6, Child £3.50, OAP £5 (excl. May & Jun). RHS members Free Jan - Feb.
Telephone for details.

BOXGROVE PRIORY ⚏
Boxgrove, Chichester, Sussex
Tel: 01424 775705 www.english-heritage.org.uk/visits
Owner: English Heritage **Contact:** 1066 Battle Abbey
Remains of the Guest House, Chapter House and Church of this 12th-century priory, which was the cell of a French abbey until Richard II confirmed its independence in 1383.
Location: OS Ref. SU909 076. N of Boxgrove, 4 miles E of Chichester on minor road N of A27.
Open: Any reasonable time.
Admission: Free.

BRAMBER CASTLE ⚏
Bramber, Sussex
Tel: 01424 775705 www.english-heritage.org.uk/visits
Owner: English Heritage **Contact:** 1066 Battle Abbey
The remains of a Norman castle gatehouse, walls and earthworks in a splendid setting overlooking the Adur valley.
Location: OS Ref. TQ187 107. On W side of Bramber village NE of A283.
Open: Any reasonable time.
Admission: Free.
Limited. On leads.

CAMBER CASTLE ⚏
Camber, Nr Rye, East Sussex TN31 7RS
Tel: 01797 223862 www.english-heritage.org.uk/visits
Owner: English Heritage **Contact:** Rye Harbour Nature Reserve
A fine example of one of many coastal fortresses built by Henry VIII to counter the threat of invasion during the 16th century. Monthly guided walks of Rye Nature Reserve including Camber Castle: telephone for details.
Location: OS189, Ref. TQ922 185. Across fields off A259, 1 mile S of Rye off harbour road.
Open: 1 Jul - 30 Sept: Sat & Sun, 2 - 5pm. Last admission 4.30pm.
Admission: Adult £2, Child/Conc. £1. Accompanied children, free. Friends of Rye Harbour Nature Reserve & EH Members Free.
Unsuitable. By arrangement. None. Guide dogs only.

185

CHARLESTON

CHARLESTON, FIRLE, NR LEWES, EAST SUSSEX BN8 6LL

www.charleston.org.uk

Tel: 01323 811265 **Fax:** 01323 811628 **e-mail:** info@charleston.org.uk

Owner: The Charleston Trust   **Contact:** Visitor Manager

When the artists Vanessa Bell and Duncan Grant moved to Charleston in 1916 they immediately began to transform the house with decorations. They painted the walls, doors, furniture and ceramics in their own unique and inspirational style and created original textiles. They also collected works of art by Renoir, Picasso, Matthew Smith, Sickert and Delacroix. Charleston became a meeting place for various members of the group of artists, writers and intellectuals known as Bloomsbury, which included the author, Virginia Woolf and the economist Maynard Keynes.

Guided tours of the house add a human touch and visitors can also explore the beautiful walled garden, with its mosaics, statues and ponds. Light refreshments are available in the Café and the Craft Council selected shop stocks a rich variety of ceramics, painted furniture, textiles, clothes and books

Location: OS Ref. TQ490 069. 7m E of Lewes on A27 between Firle & Selmeston. Rail, bus, taxi & airport.

Open: 1 Apr - 29 Oct: Wed - Sun & BH Mons. Wed & Sat, 11.30am - 6pm. Thurs & Fri, 2 - 6pm (Jul & Aug: 11.30am - 6pm), guided tours. Sun & BH Mons, 2 - 6pm, unguided. (Last entry to the house 5pm.) "A Day in the Life of Charleston" Friday tour: Fris except in July and August (1½ hr tour length), it gives a rare opportunity to see the Kitchen and Vanessa Bell's Studio.

Admission: House & Garden: Adult £6.50, Children £4.50, Disabled £4.50, Family £17.50, Conc £5.50, Wed - Thur only. Fris themed tour £7.50. Garden only: Adults £2.50, Children £1.50. Group bookings tel: 01323 811626 for rates and information.

ⓘ Filming and photography by arrangement. ▢ ⬚ ⯅
⬚ Partial. Access leaflet available. WC. ⬚ ⬚ Obligatory except Sun & BH Mons. 🅿 ▣ ⬚ Guide dogs only.

CHICHESTER CATHEDRAL

Chichester, Sussex PO19 1PX

Tel: 01243 782595 **Fax:** 01243 812499 **e-mail:** visitors@chichestercathedral.org.uk
www.chichestercathedral.org.uk   **Contact:** Ms Ruth Poyner

In the heart of the city, this fine Cathedral has been a centre of Christian worship and community life for 900 years.

Location: OS Ref. SU860 047. West Street, Chichester.

Open: Summer: 7.15am - 7pm, Winter: 7.15am - 6pm. Choral Evensong daily (except Wed) during term time.

Admission: Donation.

▢ ⬚ ⬚ ✳

CLINTON LODGE GARDEN

FLETCHING, EAST SUSSEX TN22 3ST

Tel: 01825 722952 **Fax:** 01825 723967 **e-mail:** garden@clintonlodge.com

Owner/Contact: Lady Collum

Caroline house enlarged by the Earl of Sheffield for his daughter when she married Sir Henry Clinton, one of three generals at Waterloo. The 18th century façade is set in a tree lined lawn, flanked by a newly created canal and overlooking parkland. The 6 acre garden reflects periods of English gardening history and includes a knot garden, mediaeval style herb garden with camomile paths and turf seats, potager, wild flower garden, pre-Raphaelite inspired allée, pleached lime walks; garden of old roses, double blue, white and yellow herbaceous borders; orchard planted with crinums and many yew and beech hedges.

Location: OS Ref. TQ428 238. In centre of village behind tall yew and holly hedge.

Open: 7 May, 9, 16, 18, 23 & 30 Jun, 7 & 14 Jul & 4 Aug: NGS days. 2 - 5.30pm. Other times by arrangement.

Admission: NGS Days: £4 + £2 for teas. Private groups by arrangement (minimum charge).

ⓘ WCs. ⬚⬚ Unsuitable. ⬚ ⬚ By arrangement. 🅿 Limited.
⬚ Guide dogs only. €

DENMANS GARDEN

Denmans Lane, Fontwell, West Sussex BN18 0SU

Tel: 01243 542808 **Fax:** 01243 544064 **e-mail:** denmans@denmans-garden.co.uk
www.denmans-garden.co.uk

Owner: John Brookes & Michael Neve **Contact:** Mrs Claudia Murphy
Beautiful 4 acre garden designed for year round interest - through use of form, colour and texture – the home of John Brookes MBE, renowned garden designer and writer. Beautiful plant centre and Les Routiers award winning fully licensed Garden Café (Café of the Year 2005 London & South East).

Location: OS197 Ref. SZ947 070. Off the A27 (westbound) between Chichester (6m) and Arundel (5m).

Open: Daily. Garden: 9am - 5pm (Nov - Feb, 9am - dusk). Plant centre: 9am - 5pm. Café: 10am - 5pm. Closed 24 - 26 Dec & 1 Jan.

Admission: Adult £3.95, Child (4 - 16) £2.25, OAP £3.25, Family (2+2) £11 & pre-booked groups (15+) £3.25.

▢ 👤 ♿ WC. ▣ Licensed. 🍴 Licensed. Group menus on request. 🅿
🐕 Guide dogs only. ❄

accommodation
see page 567

Jeremy Whitaker

FIRLE PLACE 📷

FIRLE, LEWES, EAST SUSSEX BN8 6LP

www.firleplace.co.uk

Tel: 01273 858307 (Enquiries) **Events:** 01273 858567
Fax: 01273 858188 **Restaurant:** 01273 858307 **e-mail:** gage@firleplace.co.uk
Owner: The Rt Hon Viscount Gage

Firle Place is the home of the Gage family and has been for over 500 years. Set at the foot of the Sussex Downs within its own parkland, this unique house originally Tudor, was built of Caen stone, possibly from a monastery dissolved by Sir John Gage, friend of Henry VIII. Remodelled in the 18th century it is similar in appearance to that of a French château. The house contains a magnificent collection of Old Master paintings, fine English and European furniture and an impressive collection of Sèvres porcelain collected mainly by the 3rd Earl Cowper from Panshanger House, Hertfordshire.

Events: The Great Tudor Hall can, on occasion, be used for private dinners, with

drinks on the Terrace or in the Billiard Room. A private tour of the house can be arranged. The paddock area is an ideal site for a marquee. The park can be used for larger events, using the house as a backdrop.

Restaurant: Enjoy the licensed restaurant and tea terrace with views over the garden for luncheon and cream teas.

Location: OS Ref. TQ473 071. 4m S of Lewes on A27 Brighton/Eastbourne Road.

Open: Easter & BH Sun/Mon. Jun - Sept: Wed, Thur, Sun & BHs, 2 - 4.30pm. Dates and times subject to change without prior notice.

Admission: Adult £6, Child £3, Conc. £5.50.

ℹ No photography in house. ▢ 📺 ♿ Ground floor & restaurant. 🍴 Licensed.
☕ Tea Terrace. 📷 Wed & Thur. 🅿 🐕 In grounds on leads. ♿ Tel for details.

Borde Hill.

FISHBOURNE ROMAN PALACE
SALTHILL ROAD, FISHBOURNE, CHICHESTER, SUSSEX PO19 3QR
www.sussexpast.co.uk

Tel: 01243 785859   **Fax:** 01243 559266   **e-mail:** adminfish@sussexpast.co.uk
Owner: Sussex Past   **Contact:** David Rudkin

A Roman site built around AD75. A modern building houses part of the extensive remains including a large number of Britain's finest *in situ* mosaics. The museum displays many objects discovered during excavations and an audio-visual programme tells Fishbourne's remarkable story. Roman gardens have been reconstructed and include a museum of Roman gardening.

Please note that owing to an exciting redevelopment programme to protect the mosaics, certain areas of the Palace may be temporarily inaccessible during early 2006. This should not affect the overall enjoyment of your visit.

Location: OS Ref. SU837 057. 1¹/₂ m W of Chichester in Fishbourne village off A27/A259.

Open: 1 Feb - 15 Dec: daily. Feb, Nov - 15 Dec: 10am - 4pm. Mar - Jul & Sept - Oct: 10am - 5pm. Aug: 10am - 6pm. 16 Dec - 31 Jan (excluding Christmas): Sats & Suns, 10am - 4pm.

Admission: Adult £6.50, Child £3.40, Conc. £5.50, Family (2+2) £16.60, Registered disabled £4.90. Groups (20+): Adult £5.40, Child £3, Conc. £4.90. (Prices from Jun 2006.)

By arrangement. Guide dogs only. Tel for details.

GLYNDE PLACE
GLYNDE, Nr LEWES, EAST SUSSEX BN8 6SX
www.glyndeplace.com

Tel/Fax: 01273 858224   **e-mail:** info@glyndeplace.com
Owners: Viscount & Viscountess Hampden   **Contact:** Sue Tester

Glynde Place is a magnificent example of Elizabethan architecture commanding exceptionally fine views of the South Downs. Amongst the collections of 400 years of family living can be seen a fine collection of 17th and 18th century portraits of the Trevors, a room dedicated to Sir Henry Brand, Speaker of the House of Commons 1872 - 1884 and furniture, embroidery and silver.

Location: OS Ref. TQ456 093. Sign posted off a A27, 4m SE of Lewes at top of village. Rail: Glynde is on the London/Eastbourne and Brighton/Eastbourne mainline railway.

Open: May - Aug: Weds, Suns & BHs, 2 - 5pm (last admission to House 4.45pm). Sculpture Garden & Tea Room: 12 noon - 5pm. Private viewings by appointment.

Admission: House & Garden: Adult £5.50, Child (under 16yrs) £2.75. Garden: Adult £2, Child (under 16yrs) £1. Child under 12yrs Free. CPRE 2 for 1. Groups (25+) by appointment.

Free. Guide dogs only. Tel for details.

GOODWOOD HOUSE

See page 176 for full page entry.

©The Landmark Trust

Wilmington Priory.

Jonathan Buckley

GREAT DIXTER HOUSE & GARDENS
NORTHIAM, RYE, EAST SUSSEX TN31 6PH
www.greatdixter.co.uk

Tel: 01797 252878   **Fax:** 01797 252879   **e-mail:** office@greatdixter.co.uk
Owner: Christopher Lloyd   **Contact:** Perry Rodriguez

Great Dixter, built c1450 is the birthplace of Christopher Lloyd, gardening author. The house boasts the largest surviving timber-framed hall in the country. The gardens feature a variety of topiary, pools, wild meadow areas and the famous Long Border and Exotic Garden.

Location: OS Ref. TQ817 251. Signposted off the A28 in Northiam.

Open: 1 April - 29 Oct: Tue - Sun, 2 - 5pm.

Admission: House & Garden: Adult £7.50, Child £3. Gardens only: Adult £6, Child £2.50. Groups (25+) by appointment.

No photography in House. Obligatory. Limited for coaches. Guide dogs only.

HAMMERWOOD PARK

EAST GRINSTEAD, SUSSEX RH19 3QE

www.hammerwoodpark.com

Tel: 01342 850594 **Fax:** 01342 850864 **e-mail:** latrobe@mistral.co.uk
Owner/Contact: David Pinnegar

Built in 1792 as an Apollo's hunting lodge by Benjamin Latrobe, architect of the Capitol and the White House, Washington DC. Owned by Led Zepplin in the 1970s, rescued from dereliction in 1982. Teas in the Organ Room; copy of the Parthenon frieze; and a derelict dining room still shocks the unwary. Guided tours (said by many to be the most interesting in Sussex) by the family.

Location: OS Ref. TQ442 390. 3¹/₂ m E of East Grinstead on A264 to Tunbridge Wells, 1m W of Holtye.

Open: 1 June - end Sept: Wed, Sat & BH Mon, 2 - 5pm. Guided tour starts 2.05pm. Private groups: Easter - Jun. Coaches strictly by appointment. Small groups any time throughout the year by appointment.

Admission: House & Park: Adult £6, Child £2. Private viewing by arrangement.
ⓘ Conferences. 🍽 💻 ✗ Obligatory. 🔲 🚻 In grounds. 🛏 B&B. ❈
🔔 Tel for details. €

HIGH BEECHES WOODLAND 🏠 & WATER GARDENS

HIGH BEECHES, HANDCROSS, SUSSEX RH17 6HQ

www.highbeeches.com

Tel: 01444 400589 **Fax:** 01444 401543 **e-mail:** gardens@highbeeches.com
Owner: High Beeches Gardens Conservation Trust (Reg. Charity)
                                                    Contact: Sarah Bray

Explore 25 acres of magically beautiful, peaceful woodland and water gardens. Daffodils, bluebells, azaleas, naturalised gentians, autumn colours. Rippling streams, enchanting vistas. Four acres of natural wildflower meadows. Rare plants. Marked trails. Recommended by Christopher Lloyd. Enjoy lunches and teas in the tearoom and tea lawn in restored Victorian farm building.

Location: OS Ref. TQ275 308. S side of B2110. 1m NE of Handcross.

Open: 17 Mar - 31 Oct: daily except Weds, 1 - 5pm (last adm. 4.30pm). Coaches/ guided tours anytime, by appointment only.

Admission: Adult £5.50, Child (under 14yrs) Free. £15. Concession for groups (30+). Guided tours for groups £10pp.

🚻 ♿ Partial. Tearoom fully accessible. 🍴 Licensed. ✗ By arrangement. 🅿 🚻
🔔 Tel for details. €

HERSTMONCEUX CASTLE GARDENS

HAILSHAM, SUSSEX BN27 1RN

www.herstmonceux-castle.com

Tel: 01323 833816 **Fax:** 01323 834499 **e-mail:** c_dennett@isc.queensu.ac.uk
Owner: Queen's University, Canada **Contact:** C Dennett

This breathtaking 15th century moated Castle is within 500 acres of parkland and gardens (including Elizabethan Garden) and is ideal for picnics and woodland walks. At Herstmonceux there is something for all the family. For information on our attractions or forthcoming events tel: 01323 834457.

Location: OS Ref. TQ646 104. 2m S of Herstmonceux village (A271) by minor road. 10m WNW of Bexhill.

Open: 15 Apr - 29 Oct (closed 25 July): daily, 10am - 6pm (last adm. 5pm). Closes 5pm from Oct.

Admission: Grounds & Gardens: Adults £4.95, Child under 15yrs & Students £3 (child under 5 Free), Conc. £3.95, Family £12.95. Group rates/bookings available.
ⓘ Visitor Centre. 📷 ♿ Limited for Castle Tour. 💻 ✗ 🅿 🚻 On leads. 🔈
🔔 Tel for details.

HIGHDOWN GARDENS

Littlehampton Road, Goring-by-Sea, Worthing, Sussex BN12 6PE
Tel: 01903 501054
Owner: Worthing Borough Council **Contact:** C Beardsley Esq
Unique gardens in disused chalk pit, begun in 1909.
Location: OS Ref. TQ098 040. 3m WNW of Worthing on N side of A259, just W of the Goring roundabout.
Open: 1 Apr - 30 Sept: Mon - Fri, 10am - 6pm. W/ends & BHs, 10am - 6pm. 1 Oct - 30 Nov: Mon - Fri, 10am - 4.30pm. 1 Dec - 31 Jan: 10am - 4pm. 1 Feb - 31 Mar: Mon - Fri, 10am - 4.30pm.
Admission: Free.

LEONARDSLEE LAKES & GARDENS

See page 177 for full page entry.

LEWES CASTLE & BARBICAN HOUSE MUSEUM

169 HIGH STREET, LEWES, SUSSEX BN7 1YE

www.sussexpast.co.uk

Tel: 01273 486290 **Fax:** 01273 486990 **e-mail:** castle@sussexpast.co.uk

Owner: Sussex Past   **Contact:** Dr Sally White

Lewes's imposing Norman castle offers magnificent views across the town and surrounding downland. Barbican House, towered over by the Barbican Gate, is home to an interesting museum of local history and archaeology. A superb scale model of Victorian Lewes provides the centrepiece of a 25 minute audio-visual presentation telling the story of the county town of Sussex.

Location: OS198 Ref. TQ412 101. Lewes town centre off A27/A26/A275.

Open: Daily (except Mons in Jan & 24 - 26 Dec). Tue - Sat: 10am - 5.30pm; Sun, Mon & BHs, 11am - 5.30pm. Castle closes at dusk in winter.

Admission: Adult £4.50, Child £2.25, Conc. £4. Family (2+2) £11.70 or (1+4) £9.20. Groups (15+): Adult £4, Child £1.85, Conc. £3.40. Combined ticket with Anne of Cleves House available.

▢ ♿ Unsuitable. 🎧 By arrangement. ▦ 🐕 Guide dogs only. ❄ 📞 Tel for details.

MARLIPINS MUSEUM

High Street, Shoreham-by-Sea, Sussex BN43 5DA

Tel: 01273 462994 or 01323 441279 **e-mail:** marlipins@sussexpast.co.uk

www.sussexpast.co.uk

Owner: Sussex Past   **Contact:** Helen Poole

Shoreham's local and especially maritime history is explored at Marlipins, an important historic building of Norman origin.

Location: OS198 Ref. TQ214 051. Shoreham town centre on A259, W of Brighton.

Open: 2 May - 31 Oct: Tue - Sat & BH Mons, 10.30am - 4.30pm.

Admission: Adult £2.50, Child £1.50, Conc. £2. Groups (15+): Adult £2, Child £1, Conc. £1.50.

Arundel Castle.

MERRIMENTS GARDENS

HAWKHURST ROAD, HURST GREEN, EAST SUSSEX TN19 7RA

www.merriments.co.uk

Tel: 01580 860666 **Fax:** 01580 860324 **e-mail:** info@merriments.co.uk

Owner: Family owned   **Contact:** Mrs Alana Sharp

Set in 4 acres of gently sloping Weald farmland, a naturalistic garden which never fails to delight. The garden is planted according to the prevailing conditions and many areas are planted only using plants suited for naturalising and colonising their environment. This natural approach to gardening harks back to the days of William Robinson and is growing in popularity, especially in Northern Europe. Most of the garden however is crammed with deep curved borders, colour themed and planted in the great tradition of English gardening. These borders use a rich mix of trees, shrubs, perennials, grasses and many unusual annuals which ensure an arresting display of colour, freshness and vitality in the garden right through to its closing in autumn.

Location: OS198, Ref. TQ737 281. Signposted off A21 London - Hastings road, at Hurst Green.

Open: Apr - Sept: Mon - Sat, 10am - 5pm, Suns, 10.30am - 5pm.

Admission: Adult £4, Child £2. Groups (15+) by arrangement £3.50pp.

▢❄ ♿ ▦ Licensed. 🍴 🎧 By arrangement. 🅿 🐕 In grounds, on leads.

South East - England

MICHELHAM PRIORY

UPPER DICKER, HAILSHAM, SUSSEX BN27 3QS

www.sussexpast.co.uk

Tel: 01323 844224   **Fax:** 01323 844030   **e-mail:** adminmich@sussexpast.co.uk

Owner: Sussex Past   **Contact:** Chris Tuckett

Set on a medieval moated island surrounded by superb gardens, the Priory was founded in 1229. The remains after the Dissolution were incorporated into a Tudor farm and country house that now contains a fascinating array of exhibits. Grounds include a 14th century gatehouse, working watermill, physic and cloister gardens and Elizabethan great barn.

Location: OS Ref. TQ557 093. 8m NW of Eastbourne off A22/A27. 2m W of Hailsham.

Open: 1 Mar - 31 Oct: Tue - Sun & BH Mons & daily in Aug. Mar & Oct: 10.30am - 4.30pm. Apr - Jul & Sept: 10.30am - 5pm. Aug: 10.30am - 5.30pm.

Admission: Adult £5.60, Child £2.90, Conc. £4.70, Family (2+2) £14.30, Registered disabled & carer £2.80 each. Groups (15+): Adult/Conc. £4.50, Child £2.60.

Licensed. By arrangement. Ample for cars & coaches Guide dogs only.

MONK'S HOUSE

Rodmell, Lewes BN7 3HF

Tel: 01323 870001 (Property Office)

Owner: The National Trust   **Contact:** Property Office

A small weather-boarded house, the home of Leonard and Virginia Woolf until Leonard's death in 1969.

Location: OS Ref. TQ421 064. 4 m E of Lewes, off former A275 in Rodmell village, near church.

Open: 1 Apr - 28 Oct: Weds & Sats, 2 - 5.30pm. Last admission 5pm. Groups by arrangement with tenant.

Admission: Adult £3, Child £1.50, Family £7.50.

PALLANT HOUSE GALLERY

9 North Pallant, Chichester, West Sussex PO19 1TJ

Tel: 01243 774557   **Fax:** 01243 536038   **Email:** info@pallant.org.uk

www. pallant.org.uk

Owner: Pallant House Gallery Trust   **Contact:** Reception

The Gallery of Modern Art in the south. A Queen Anne townhouse and a contemporary extension showcasing the best of 20th century British Art.

Location: OS Ref. SU861 047. City centre, SE of the Cross.

Open: Re-opens March 2006. Please telephone for details.

Admission: Please telephone for details.

education index see page 564

PARHAM HOUSE & GARDENS

PARHAM PARK, STORRINGTON, Nr PULBOROUGH,
WEST SUSSEX RH20 4HS

www.parhaminsussex.co.uk

Tel: 01903 742021   **Info Line:** 01903 744888   **Fax:** 01903 746557

e-mail: enquiries@parhaminsussex.co.uk

Owner: Parham Park Trust   **Contact:** Patricia Kennedy

This stunning Elizabethan house, with its award-winning Gardens, is set in the heart of a medieval deer park, below the South Downs. Parham staff are renowned for the warm welcome they give to visitors, who come to see the light panelled rooms, from Great Hall to Long Gallery, filled with early paintings, furniture and needlework.

Much admired are the large bowls of informally-arranged flowers which have been grown in the walled garden with its huge herbaceous borders, greenhouse and herbiary.

Light lunches and cream teas are served in the 16th century Big Kitchen and souvenirs and gifts can be purchased from the shop, with plants on sale from the garden shop.

Location: OS Ref. TQ060 143. Midway between Pulborough & Storrington on A283.

Open: Easter Sun - end Sept: Wed, Thur, Sun & BH Mon, 2 - 6pm (last entry 5pm), (also Tue & Fri afternoons in Aug); 8 Jul & 7 Oct. Picnic area, Big Kitchen & Gardens: 12 noon - 6pm. Guided groups by arrangement at other times.

Admission: House & Gardens: Adult £6.80, Child (5-15yrs) £3, OAP/Disabled £6, Family (2+2) £16.60. Unguided booked groups (20+) £5.50. Gardens only: Adult £5, Child £1.50, OAP/Disabled £4.50, Family (2+2) £11.00.

No photography in house. Partial. Licensed. In grounds, on leads. Special charges may apply. Annual Garden Weekend - 8/9th July; Slow Food Fair - 7/8th October. We regret that HHA passes are not valid for Special Event weekends.

SUSSEX — *South East - England*

PASHLEY MANOR GARDENS ❀   *See page 178 for full page entry.*

PETWORTH HOUSE & PARK ❀   *See page 179 for full page entry.*

PETWORTH COTTAGE MUSEUM
346 High Street, Petworth, West Sussex GU28 0AU
Tel: 01798 342100   **Email:** stevensonguk.yahoo.co.uk
Owner: Petworth Cottage Trust   **Contact:** Curator
Step into a Leconfield Estate Cottage furnished as if it were 1910. Lighting is by gas, heating by coal-fired range. The scullery has a stone sink and a copper for the weekly wash.
Open: Apr - Oct: Wed - Sun & BH Mons, 2 - 4.30pm.
Admission: Adult £2.50, Child (under 14yrs) 50p. Group visits by arrangement.

PEVENSEY CASTLE ♯
Pevensey, Sussex BN24 5LE
Tel/Fax: 01323 762604   www.english-heritage.org.uk/visits
Owner: English Heritage   **Contact:** Visitor Operations Team
Originally a 4th-century Roman fort, Pevensey was the place where William the Conqueror landed in 1066 and established his first stronghold. The Norman castle includes the remains of an unusual keep within the massive walls. An inclusive audio tour tells the story of the castle's 2,000 year history.
Location: OS Ref. TQ645 048. In Pevensey off A259.
Open: 1 Apr - 31 Oct: daily, 10am - 6pm (4pm Oct). Nov - Mar: Sats & Suns, 10am - 4pm. Closed 24 - 26 Dec & 1 Jan. EH Members Free.
Admission: Adult £3.90, Child £2, Conc. £2.90. 15% discount for groups of 11+.
ⓘWC. ⬚ ♿Grounds. ⬚ Inclusive. 🅿 In grounds, on leads. ✳ Tel for details.

THE PRIEST HOUSE
NORTH LANE, WEST HOATHLY, SUSSEX RH19 4PP
www.sussexpast.co.uk
Tel: 01342 810479   **e-mail:** priest@sussexpast.co.uk
Owner: Sussex Past   **Contact:** Antony Smith
Standing in the beautiful surroundings of a traditional cottage garden on the edge of Ashdown Forest, The Priest House is an early 15th century timber-framed hall-house. In Elizabethan times it was modernised into a substantial yeoman's dwelling. Its furnished rooms now contain 17th and 18th century furniture, kitchen equipment, needlework and household items. A formal herb garden contains over 150 different herbs.
Location: OS187 Ref. TQ362 325. In triangle formed by Crawley, East Grinstead and Haywards Heath, 4m off A22, 6m off M23.
Open: 1 Mar - 31 Oct: Tue - Sat & BHs plus Mons during Aug: 10.30am - 5.30pm; Sun, 12 noon - 5.30pm.
Admission: Adult £2.90, Child £1.45, Conc. £2.60. Groups (15+): Adult £2.60, Child £1.30, Conc £2.40.
⬚ ♿Partial. By arrangement. 🅿 Limited (on street). In grounds, on leads.

PRESTON MANOR
PRESTON DROVE, BRIGHTON, EAST SUSSEX BN1 6SD
www.prestonmanor.virtualmuseum.info
Tel: 01273 292770   **Fax:** 01273 292771   **Email:** museums@brighton-hove.gov.uk
Owner: Brighton & Hove City Council
A delightful Manor House which powerfully evokes the atmosphere of an Edwardian gentry home both 'upstairs' and 'downstairs'. Explore more than twenty rooms over four floors – from the servants' quarters, kitchens and butler's pantry in the basement to the attic bedrooms and nursery on the top floor. Plus charming walled gardens, pets' cemetery and 13th century parish church.
Location: OS Ref. TQ303 064. 2m N of Brighton on the A23 London road.
Open: Apr - Sept: Tues - Sat, 10am - 5pm. Suns, 2 - 5pm. Oct - Mar: open for pre-booked groups, school visits & special events.
Admission: Adult £3.90, Child £2.25, Conc. £3.20. Groups (20+) £3.30. Prices subject to change in 2006.
ⓘNo photography. Gift kiosk. ♿Unsuitable. By arrangement. 🅿For coaches. Spring, Summer & Autumn half-term. Easter & Summer. Children's activities all year round. Tel: 01273 292843 for details.

THE ROYAL PAVILION   *See page 180 for full page entry.*

SAINT HILL MANOR   *See page 181 for full page entry.*

SHEFFIELD PARK GARDEN ❀   *See page 182 for full page entry.*

© NTPL/Nick Meers

Sheffield Park Garden.

ST MARY'S HOUSE & GARDENS 🏛

BRAMBER, WEST SUSSEX BN44 3WE

www.stmarysbramber.co.uk

Tel/Fax: 01903 816205 **e-mail:** info@stmarysbramber.co.uk

Owner: Mr Peter Thorogood

This enchanting, medieval timber-framed house is situated in the picturesque downland village of Bramber. The fine panelled interiors, including the unique Elizabethan 'Painted Room' with its intriguing *trompe l'oeil* murals, give an air of tranquillity and timelessness. Once the home of the real Algernon and Gwendolen brilliantly portrayed in Oscar Wilde's comedy, *The Importance of Being Earnest*, St Mary's has served as a location for a number of television series including the world-famous *Dr Who*. The formal gardens with amusing animal topiary include an exceptional example of the 'Living Fossil' tree, *Gingko Biloba*, and a mysterious ivy-clad 'Monk's Walk'. In the Victorian 'Secret' Garden can still be seen the fruit-wall, potting shed (now housing the Rural Museum), circular orchard, and woodland walk. St Mary's features in Simon Jenkins' book *England's Thousand Best Houses*, was highly

commended in the Tourism ExSEllence Awards 2004, and its gardens were nominated as one of 'Britain's Fifty Best Gardens to Visit' by *The Independent*. St Mary's is a house of fascination and mystery. Many thousands of visitors have admired its picturesque charm and enjoyed its atmosphere of friendliness and welcome, qualities which make it a visit to remember.

Location: OS Ref. TQ189 105. Bramber village off A283. From London 56m via M23/A23 or A24. Bus from Shoreham to Steyning, alight St Mary's, Bramber.

Open: May - end Sept: Suns, Thurs & BH Mons, 2 - 6pm. Last entry 5pm. Groups at other times by arrangement.

Admission: House & Gardens: Adult £6, Conc. £5. Child £2.50, Groups (25+) £5.50.
ℹ️No photography in house. 🔲 🍴 ♿Partial. 📷
🎫Obligatory for groups (max 60). Visit time 2¹/₂hrs. 🅿️ 30 cars, 2 coaches.
🔲 ❌ 🔺 📺 Tel for details.

SACKVILLE COLLEGE

HIGH STREET, EAST GRINSTEAD, WEST SUSSEX RH19 3BX

www.sackville-college.co.uk

Tel: 01342 326561 **email:** sackvillecollege@yahoo.com

Owner: Board of Trustees   **Contact:** College Co-ordinator

Built in 1609 for Richard Sackville, Earl of Dorset, as an almshouse and overnight accommodation for the Sackville family. Feel the Jacobean period come alive in the enchanting quadrangle, the chapel, banqueting hall with fine hammerbeam roof and minstrel's gallery, the old common room and warden's study where "Good King Wenceslas" was composed. Chapel weddings by arrangement.

Location: A22 to East Grinstead, College in High Street (town centre).

Open: 15 Jun - 15 Sep: Wed - Sun, 2 - 5pm. Groups all year by arrangement.

Admission: Adult £3, Child £1. Groups: (10 - 60) no discount.
ℹ️Large public car park adjacent to entrance. 🔲 🍴 📺 📷 ♿Partial.
🎫Obligatory. 🅿️Limited. 🔲 🐕Guide dogs only. ❄️ By arrangement.
📺Tel for details.

NTPL/ Rupert Trueman

STANDEN 🌿

EAST GRINSTEAD, WEST SUSSEX RH19 4NE

www.nationaltrust.org.uk/standen

Tel: 01342 323029 **Fax:** 01342 316424 **e-mail:** standen@nationaltrust.org.uk

Owner: The National Trust   **Contact:** The Property Manager

Dating from the 1890s and containing original Morris & Co furnishings and decorations, Standen survives today as a remarkable testimony to the ideals of the Arts and Crafts Movement. The property was built as a family home by the influential architect Philip Webb and retains a warm, welcoming atmosphere. Details of Webb's designs can be found everywhere from the fireplaces to the original electric light fittings.

Location: OS Ref. TQ389 356. 2m S of East Grinstead, signposted from B2110.

Open: House, Garden, Shop & Restaurant: 25 Mar - 29 Oct: Wed - Sun & BHs. 11am - 5pm (last admission to house 4.30pm). Garden, Shop & Restaurant: 18 Nov - 17 Dec: Sats & Suns, 11am - 3pm.

Admission: House & Garden: £6.80, Family £17. Garden only: £4. Joint ticket with same day entry to Nymans Garden £11.50, available Wed - Fri. Groups: £5.80, Wed - Fri only if booked in advance.
🔲 🍴 📺 ♿Partial. WC. 🍽Licensed. 🅿️ 🔲
🐕In woods on leads, not in garden. 📺Tel for details.

STANSTED PARK

STANSTED PARK, ROWLANDS CASTLE, HAMPSHIRE   PO9 6DX

www.stanstedpark.co.uk

Tel: 023 9241 2265   **Fax:** 023 9241 3773   **e-mail:** enquiry@stanstedpark.co.uk

Owner: Stansted Park Foundation   **Contact:** House Administrator

'One of the South's most beautiful stately homes' set amongst 1750 acres of glorious park and woodland, Stansted House gives an insight into the social history of an English country house in its heyday. The State Rooms, containing Bessborough family furniture, portraits and a colourful collection of bird paintings, contrast with the Servants Quarters' which has a comprehensive collection of equally interesting domestic artefacts. Visit the ancient Chapel which inspired Keats, the Bessborough Arboretum, the newly restored Dutch Garden and take a ride on the Stanstead Park Light Railway. Events include the Stanstead Proms, Garden Show and Antiques Fair.

Location: OS Ref. SU761 103. Follow brown heritage signs from A3 Rowlands Castle or A27 Havant. Rail: Mainline station, Havant. Taxis: Rowlands Castle no taxis 30 minute walk.

Open: House & Chapel: Easter Sun - 25 Sept: Suns & Mons, 1 - 5pm (last entry 4pm). Jul & Aug: Sun - Wed. House closed during events. Grounds: All year, restricted access on Sats and during events. Tea Room & Garden Centre open all year.

Admission: House, Grounds, Chapel: Adult £5.50, Child (5-15yrs) £3.50, Conc. £4.50, Family (2+3) £14.50. Groups/educational visits by arrangement.

Private & corporate hire. Partial. By arrangement. Guide dogs only. Grounds. Tel for details.

Raymond Woodham

UPPARK

SOUTH HARTING, PETERSFIELD GU31 5QR

www.nationaltrust.org.uk/uppark

Tel: 01730 825415   **Fax:** 01730 825873   **e-mail:** uppark@nationaltrust.org.uk

Owner: The National Trust   **Contact:** Administrator

Marvel at the historic elegance of Uppark – with fine, late-Georgian interiors and collections of paintings, ceramics and textiles, extensive basement rooms, famous dolls house, Regency garden (stunning views to the sea), children's activities, award-winning shop and restaurant – not to mention a fascinating Exhibition – there's everything for a perfect day out.

Location: OS Ref197 SU781 181 - between Petersfield & Chichester on B2146.

Open: 2 Apr - 26 Oct: Sun - Thur; Grounds, Exhibition, Shop & Restaurant: 11.30am - 5pm; House: 12.30 - 4.30pm (Last entry 4pm). BH Suns, Mons & Good Fri 11.30am - 4.30pm. Print Room open 1st Mon of each month.

Admission: Adult £6.50, Child £3.25, Groups (15+) must book: £5.50.

By arrangement. Tel for details.

WEALD & DOWNLAND OPEN AIR MUSEUM

Singleton, Chichester, Sussex PO18 0EU

Tel: 01243 811348   **www.**wealddown.co.uk

Over 45 original historic buildings. Interiors and gardens through the ages.

Location: OS Ref. SU876 127. 6m N of Chichester on A286. S of Singleton.

Open: Apr - Oct: daily, 10.30am - 6pm. Nov - 21 Dec: daily, 10.30am - 4pm. Plus daily for 'A Sussex Christmas'. 26 Dec - 1 Jan 2007, 10.30am - 4pm. 4 Jan - 12 Feb 2006 Wed, Sat & Sun, 10.30am - 4pm. 13 Feb - 31 Mar: daily, 10.30am - 4pm.

Admission: Adult £7.95, Child/Student £4.25, OAP £6.95. Family (2+3) £21.95. Group rates on request.

Tel for details.

South East - England

Raymond Woodham

WEST DEAN GARDENS 🏛

WEST DEAN, CHICHESTER, WEST SUSSEX PO18 0QZ

www.westdean.org.uk

Tel: 01243 818210 **Fax:** 01243 811342 **e-mail:** gardens@westdean.org.uk

Owner: The Edward James Foundation **Contact:** Jim Buckland, Gardens Manager

A place of tranquility and beauty in the rolling South Downs all year round, West Dean features a restored walled kitchen garden with some of the finest Victorian glasshouses in the country. Rustic summerhouses, a 300ft Edwardian pergola, ornamental borders and a pond contrast with over 200 varieties of carefully trained fruit trees, rows of vegetables and exotic produce behind glass. For the more active, enjoy a circular walk through a 49-acre arboretum offers breathtaking views of the estate and its fine flint house and parkland setting. Do not miss the Special Events running throughout the year.

Location: OS Ref. SU863 128. SE side of A286 Midhurst Road, 6m N of Chichester.

Open: Oct, Mar - Apr: daily, 11am - 5pm. Nov - Feb: Wed - Sun, 11am - 4.30pm. May - Sept: 10.30am - 5pm.

Admission: Nov 2005 - Feb 2006: Adult £2.75, Child £1.25, Over 60s £2.50, Family £6.50. From Feb 2006: Adult £6, Child £2.50, Over 60s £5.50, Family £14.50.

ℹ️ No photography in house. 🅿️ Limited for coaches. 🎫 Licensed. 🖼 By arrangement. 🐕 Guide dogs only. 📞 Tel for details.

WILMINGTON PRIORY

Wilmington, Nr Eastbourne, East Sussex BN26 5SW

Tel: 01628 825920 or 825925 (bookings) **www**.landmarktrust.org.uk

Owner: Leased to the Landmark Trust by Sussex Archaeological Society

Contact: The Landmark Trust

Founded by the Benedictines in the 11th century, the surviving, much altered buildings date largely from the 14th century. Managed and maintained by the Landmark Trust, which lets buildings for self-catering holidays. Full details of Wilmington Priory and 183 other historic buildings available for holidays are featured in The Landmark Handbook (price £11 refundable against booking), from The Landmark Trust, Shottesbrooke, Maidenhead, Berkshire, SL6 3SW.

Location: OS Ref. TQ543 042. 600yds S of A27. 6m NW of Eastbourne.

Open: Grounds, Ruins, Porch & Crypt: on 30 days between Apr - Oct. Whole property including interiors on 8 of these days. Contact the Landmark Trust for details. Available for self-catering holidays for up to 6 people throughout the year.

Admission: Free entry on open days.

 **special events**
see page 571

High Beeches Woodland & Water Gardens.

Borde Hill Garden.

© English Heritage Photo Library

MAP 3

OSBORNE HOUSE ⌗

Osborne House was the peaceful, rural retreat of Queen Victoria, Prince Albert and their family; they spent some of their happiest times here.

Many of the apartments have a very intimate association with the Queen who died here in 1901 and have been preserved almost unaltered ever since. The nursery bedroom remains just as it was in the 1870s when Queen Victoria's first grandchildren came to stay. Children were a constant feature of life at Osborne (Victoria and Albert had nine). Don't miss the Swiss Cottage, a charming chalet in the grounds built for the Royal children to play and entertain their parents in.

Enjoy the beautiful gardens with their stunning views over the Solent and the fruit and flower Victorian Walled Garden. The Durbar Wing has been refurbished. With interactive screens it displays the exquisite Indian gifts given by the Indian people to Queen Victoria.

Owner:
English Heritage

▶ **CONTACT**

The House
Administrator
Osborne House
Royal Apartments
East Cowes
Isle of Wight
PO32 6JY

Tel: 01983 200022
Fax: 01983 297281

Venue Hire and Hospitality:
Tel: 01983 203055

▶ **LOCATION**
OS Ref. SZ516 948

1 mile SE of East Cowes.

Ferry: Isle of Wight ferry terminals.

East Cowes 1¹/₂ miles
Tel: 02380 334010.

Fishbourne 4 miles
Tel: 0870 582 7744.

CONFERENCE/FUNCTION

ROOM	MAX CAPACITY
Durbar Hall	standing 80 seated 50
Upper Terrace	standing 250
Walled Gardens	standing 100
Marquee	Large scale events possible

English Heritage Photo Library

ℹ️ WCs. Suitable for filming, concerts, drama. No photography in the House. Children's play area. WC.

📷 Private and corporate hire.

♿ Wheelchairs available, access to house via ramp, ground floor access only. WC.

☕🍴 Hot drinks, light snacks & waiter service lunches in the stunning terrace restaurant.

🚶 Open from Nov - Mar for pre-booked guided tours only. These popular tours allow visitors to see the Royal Apartments and private rooms at a quieter time of the year, and in the company of one of our expert guides.

🅿️ Ample.

📖 Visits free, please book. Education room available.

❄️

▶ **OPENING TIMES***

House
1 April - 30 September
Daily: 10am - 5pm.
Last admission 4pm.

1 - 31 October
Daily: 10am - 4pm.

1 November - 31 March
Wed - Sun: 10am - 4pm.
Guided tours only. Last tour 2.30pm. Christmas Tour Season: 11 Nov - 7 Jan, last tour 3pm. Pre-booking essential on 01983 200022.

Closed 24 - 26 December & 1 January.

May close earlier on concert days, please telephone for details.

▶ **ADMISSION***

House & Grounds
Adult £9.30
Child (5-15yrs) £4.70
Child under 5yrs ..... Free
Conc. £7.00
Family (2+3) £23.30

Grounds only
Adult £5.50
Child (5-15yrs) £2.80
Child under 5yrs ..... Free
Conc. £4.10
Family (2+3) £13.80

Groups (11+) 15% discount. Tour leader and driver have free entry. 1 extra free place for every additional 20 paying.

APPULDURCOMBE HOUSE ⌗
Wroxall, Shanklin, Isle of Wight

Tel: 01983 852484   **www**.english-heritage.org.uk/visits

Owner: English Heritage   **Contact:** Mr & Mrs Owen

The bleached shell of a fine 18th-century Baroque style house standing in grounds landscaped by 'Capability' Brown. An exhibition displays prints and photographs depicting the history of the house.

Location: OS Ref. SZ543 800. $^{1}/_{2}$ mile W of Wroxall off B3327.

Open: 1 Apr -31 Oct: daily, 10am - 4pm (5pm Jul & Aug). Last entry 1hr before closing.

Admission: House: Adult £3, Child £2, Conc. £2.75, Family £9. EH members Free.

🖼 🔊 **P** Limited. 🐾 In grounds, on leads. 📞 Tel. for details.

BEMBRIDGE WINDMILL ❧
Correspondence to: NT Office, Strawberry Lane, Mottistone,
Isle of Wight PO30 4EA

Tel: 01983 873945   **www**.nationaltrust.org.uk

Owner: The National Trust   **Contact:** The Custodian

Dating from around 1700, this is the only windmill to survive on the Island. Much of its original wooden machinery is still intact and there are spectacular views from the top.

Location: OS Ref. SZ639 874. $^{1}/_{2}$ m S of Bembridge off B3395.

Open: 26 Mar - 30 Jun & 1 - 14 Oct: daily except Sat, 1 Jul - 30 Sept: daily, 10am - 5pm. Open Easter Sat.

Admission: Adult £2.10, Child £1.05, Family £6. All school groups are conducted by a NT guide; special charge applies.

🖼 📹 🅸 By arrangement. **P** 100 yds. ♿ 🐾 Guide dogs only.

BRIGHSTONE SHOP & MUSEUM ❧
North St, Brighstone, Isle of Wight PO30 4AX

Tel: 01983 740689

Owner: The National Trust   **Contact:** The Manager

The traditional cottages contain a National Trust shop and Village Museum (run by Brighstone Museum Trust) depicting village life in the late 19th century.

Location: OS Ref. SZ428 828. North Street, Brighstone, just off B3399.

Open: 3 Jan - 1 Apr: Mon - Sat, 10am - 1pm. 3 Apr - 26 May: Mon - Sat, 10am - 4pm. 27 May - 1 Oct: daily, 10am - 5pm (Suns from 12 noon). 2 Oct - 23 Dec: Mon - Sat, 10am - 4pm. 28 - 30 Dec: 10am - 1pm.

Admission: Free.

🔊 Partial. ✳

CARISBROOKE CASTLE ⌗
NEWPORT, ISLE OF WIGHT PO30 1XY
www.english-heritage.org.uk/visits

Tel: 01983 522107   **Fax:** 01983 528632

Owner: English Heritage   **Contact:** Visitor Operations Team

The island's royal fortress and prison of King Charles I before his execution in London in 1648. See the famous Carisbrooke donkeys treading the wheel in the Well House or meet them in the donkey centre. Don't miss the castle story in the gatehouse, the museum in the great hall and the interactive coach house museum.

Location: OS196 Ref. SZ486 877. Off the B3401, 1$^{1}/_{4}$ miles SW of Newport.

Open: 1 Apr - 30 Sept: daily, 10am - 5pm. 1 Oct - 31 Mar: daily, 10am - 4pm. Closed 24 - 26 Dec & 1 Jan.

Admission: Adult £5.50, Child £2.80, Conc. £4.10, Family (2+3) £13.80. 15% discount for groups (11+). EH Members Free.

🅸 WCs. 🖼 🔊 📹 **P** 🐾 In grounds, on leads. ✳ 📞 Tel. for details.

MORTON MANOR
Brading, Isle of Wight PO36 0EP

Tel/Fax: 01983 406168   **e-mail:** mortonmanor-iow@amserver.com

Owner/Contact: Mr J A J Trzebski

Refurbished in the Georgian period. Magnificent gardens, vineyard and maize maze.

Location: OS Ref. SZ603 863 (approx.). $^{1}/_{4}$ m W of A3055 in Brading.

Open: Easter - end Oct: daily except Sats, 10am - 5.30pm. Last admission 4.30pm.

Admission: Adult £5, Child £2.50, Conc. £4.50, Group (10+) £4.

MOTTISTONE MANOR GARDEN ❧
Mottistone, Isle of Wight PO30 4ED

Tel: 01983 741302   **www**.nationaltrust.org.uk

Owner: The National Trust   **Contact:** The Gardener

A haven of peace and tranquillity with colourful herbaceous borders and a backdrop of the sea making a perfect setting for the historic Manor House. An annual open air Jazz Concert is held in the grounds in July.

Location: OS Ref. SZ406 838. 2m W of Brighstone on B3399.

Open: 26 Mar - 29 Oct: Sun - Thur, 11am - 5.30pm. House: Aug BH Mon only: 2 - 5.30pm. Guided tours for NT members on that day 10am - 12 noon.

Admission: Garden: Adult £3.10, Child £3.05, Family £7.75. Extra charges for house.

🖼 🅸 Limited ❧ ♿ 🐾

NEEDLES OLD BATTERY ❧
West High Down, Totland, Isle of Wight PO39 0JH

Tel: 01983 754772   **www**.nationaltrust.org.uk

Owner: The National Trust   **Contact:** The Fort Manager

High above the sea, the Old Battery was built in the 1860s against the threat of French invasion. Interesting exhibitions, tunnels to explore, stunning views and family activity packs

Location: OS Ref. SZ300 848. Needles Headland W of Freshwater Bay & Alum Bay (B3322).

Open: 26 Mar - 29 Jun, 1 Jul - 31 Aug, 2 Sept - 29 Oct: Sat - Thur (open Good Fri); 10.30am - 5pm. Tea Room: 14 Jan - 18 Mar 2007, Sats & Suns; 11am - 3pm. Closes in bad weather; please telephone on day of visit to check.

Admission: Adult £3.90, Child £1.95, Family £8.90. Special charge for guided tours.

🔊 Partial. 📹 🅸 By appointment. ♿ 🐾 In grounds, on leads.

NUNWELL HOUSE & GARDENS
Coach Lane, Brading, Isle of Wight PO36 0JQ

Tel: 01983 407240

Owner: Col & Mrs J A Aylmer   **Contact:** Mrs J A Aylmer

Nunwell has been a family home for five centuries and reflects much architectural and Island history. King Charles I spent his last night of freedom here. Jacobean and Georgian wings. Finely furnished rooms. Lovely setting with Channel views and five acres of tranquil gardens including walled garden. Family military collections.

Location: OS Ref. SZ595 874. 1m NW of Brading. 3m S of Ryde signed off A3055.

Open: 28/29 May & 3 Jul - 6 Sept: Mon - Wed, 1 - 5pm. House tours: 1.30, 2.30 & 3.30pm. Groups welcome by arrangement throughout the year.

Admission: Adult £4, Pair of Adults £7.50 (inc guide book), Child (under 10yrs) £1, OAP/Student £3.50. Garden only: Adult £2.50. (2005 prices.)

🖼 🅸 Obligatory. **P** 🐾 Guide dogs only. ✳

OLD TOWN HALL ❧
Newtown, Isle of Wight

Tel: 01983 531785   **www**.nationaltrust.org.uk

Owner: The National Trust   **Contact:** The Custodian

A charming 18th century building that was once the focal point of the 'rotten borough' of Newtown.

Location: OS Ref. SZ424 905. Between Newport and Yarmouth, 1m N of A3054.

Open: 26 Mar - 28 Jun, 3 Sept - 25 Oct: Mon, Wed & Sun; 2 Jul - 30 Aug: Sun - Thur, 2 - 5pm. Open Good Fri & Easter Sat.

Admission: Adult £1.80, Child 90p, Family £4.50.

P Limited. 🐾 Guide dogs only.

OSBORNE HOUSE ⌗   *See page 197 for full page entry.*

YARMOUTH CASTLE ⌗
Quay Street, Yarmouth, Isle of Wight PO41 0PB

Tel: 01983 760678   **www**.english-heritage.org.uk/visits

Owner: English Heritage   **Contact:** Visitor Operations Team

This last addition to Henry VIII's coastal defences was completed in 1547 and is, unusually for its kind, square with a fine example of an angle bastion. It was garrisoned well into the 19th century.

Location: OS Ref. SZ354 898. In Yarmouth adjacent to car ferry terminal.

Open: 1 Apr - 30 Sept: Sun - Thurs, 11am - 4pm.

Admission: Adult £2.80, Child £1.40, Conc. £2.10. EH Members Free.

🖼 🔊 Ground floor. **P** None. 🐾 In grounds, on leads.

Osborne House. © English Heritage Photo Library/Steve Cole

St Michaels Mount, Cornwall.

channel islands   cornwall   devon   dorset

south west

As you travel west from London, so the landscape changes. Neat lanes and small fields are replaced by a wilder countryside. The houses are built of stone rather than brick, villages are scarcer, and the pace of life slows. The moorlands of Devon and Cornwall are among the most dramatic in Britain, contrasting with the unspoilt beaches. Do not miss Athelhampton House & Gardens (Dorset) or Powderham Castle (Devon). For keen gardeners, The Lost Gardens of Heligan (Cornwall) contain over 200 acres of superb working Victorian gardens and pleasure grounds. The climate on the Scilly Isles means exotic and sub-tropical plants can be grown. If time permits, day trips to the islands can be made by helicopter, boat or plane from Newquay or Penzance.

somerset   wiltshire   gloucestershire

SAUSMAREZ MANOR

www.sausmarezmanor.co.uk

MAP 3

Owner:
The Seigneur de
Sausmarez

▶ **CONTACT**

Peter de Sausmarez
Sausmarez Manor
Guernsey
Channel Islands
GY4 6SG

Tel: 01481
235571/235655
Fax: 01481 235572

e-mail:
sausmarezmanor@
cwgsy.net

▶ **LOCATION**

2m S of St Peter Port,
clearly signposted.

The home of the Seigneurs de Sausmarez since c1220 with a façade built at the bequest of the first Governor of New York.

An entrancing and entertaining half day encompassing something to interest everyone. The family have been explorers, inventors, diplomats, prelates, generals, admirals, privateers, politicians and governors etc, most of whom left their mark on the house, garden or the furniture.

The sub-tropical woodland garden is crammed with such exotics as banana trees, tree ferns, ginger, 300 plus camellias, lilies, myriads of bamboos, as well as the more commonplace hydrangeas, hostas etc.

The sculpture in the art park with its 200 or so pieces by artists from a dozen countries is the most comprehensive in Britain. The dolls' house collection displays pieces from 1830 onwards and is the third largest dedicated collection in Britain. The pitch and put is a cruelly testing 500m 9 hole par 3. The Copper, Tin and Silversmith demonstrates his ancient skills in the large barn. The two lakes are a haven for ornamental wildfowl and some of the sculpture.

Sausmarez Manor is available for corporate hospitality functions and Civil weddings. It also offers guided tours, welcomes schools (has education programmes), and has a tearoom, café and gift shop.

Sea Guernsey is celebrating the *History of the Heroes of the Sea*, and much of the Activities, Pageants, and Dramas are taking place here.

▶ **OPENING TIMES**

Easter - End Oct
Daily: 10am - 5pm

Guided tours of House
Mon - Thurs:
10.30 & 11.30am.
Additional 2pm tour
during high season.

▶ **ADMISSION**

There is no overall charge
for admission.

Doll's House	3.00
Sub Tropical Garden	£4.50
Sculpture Trail	£4.50
Pitch & Putt	£4.50
Putting	£2.00
House Tour	£5.90
Ghost Tour	£10.00
Train Rides	£1.00

Discounts for Children,
Students, OAPs &
Organised Groups.

 Partial.

 Guided tours of House.

Two holiday flats
are available see
www.cottageguide.co.uk

€

National Trust/ Jon Hicks

MAP 1

Owner:
The National Trust

▶ **CONTACT**

Toby Fox
Property Manager
Cotehele
St Dominick
Saltash, Cornwall
PL12 6TA

Tel: 01579 351346
Fax: 01579 351222
e-mail:
cotehele@nationaltrust.
org.uk

▶ **LOCATION**

OS Ref. SX422 685

1m SW of Calstock by
foot. 8m S of Tavistock,
4m E of Callington,
15m from Plymouth
via the Tamar bridge
at Saltash

Trains: Limited service
from Plymouth to
Calstock (1¼ m uphill)

Boats: Limited (tidal)
service from Plymouth
to Calstock Quay
(Plymouth Boat
Cruises)
Tel: 01752 822797

River ferry: Privately
run from Calstock to
Cotehele Quay.
Tel: 01822 833331

Buses: Western
National (seasonal
variations)
Tel: 01752 222666

COTEHELE ✤

www.nationaltrust.org.uk

Cotehele, owned by the Edgcumbe family for nearly 600 years, is a fascinating and enchanting estate set on the steep wooded slopes of the River Tamar. Exploring Cotehele's many and various charms provides a full day out for the family and leaves everyone longing to return.

The steep valley garden contains exotic and tender plants which thrive in the mild climate. Remnants of an earlier age include a mediaeval stewpond and domed dovecote, a 15th-century chapel and 18th-century tower with fine views over the surrounding countryside. A series of more formal gardens, terraces, an orchard and a daffodil meadow surround Cotehele House.

One of the least altered medieval houses in the country, Cotehele is built in local granite, slate and sandstone. Inside the ancient rooms, unlit by electricity, is a fine collection of textiles, tapestries, armour and early dark oak furniture.

The chapel contains the oldest working domestic clock in England, still in its original position.

A walk through the garden and along the river leads to the quay, a busy river port in Victorian times. The National Maritime Museum worked with the National Trust to set up a museum here which explains the vital role that the Tamar played in the local economy. As a living reminder, the restored Tamar sailing barge *Shamrock* (owned jointly by the Trust and the National Maritime Museum) is moored here.

A further walk through woodland along the Morden stream leads to the old estate corn mill which has been restored to working order.

This large estate with many footpaths offers a variety of woodland and countryside walks, opening up new views and hidden places. The Danescombe Valley, with its history of mining and milling, is of particular interest.

National Trust /Tynn Lintell

ℹ️ No photography or large bags in house. *NPI National Heritage Award winners 1996 & 1999.*

🛍️ National Trust shop. ♿

🍽️ Available for up to 90 people.

♿ 2 wheelchairs at Reception. Hall & kitchen accessible. Ramps at house, restaurant and shop. Most of garden is very steep with loose gravel. Riverside walks are flatter (from Cotehele Quay) & Edgcumbe Arms is accessible. WCs near house and at Quay. Parking near house & mill by arrangement.

☕🍴 Barn restaurant daily (except Fri), 18 Mar - 31 Oct, plus light refreshments from 11 Feb. Tel for details of pre-Christmas opening. At the Quay, Edgcumbe Arms offers light meals daily, 18 Mar - 31 Oct. Both licensed.

🅿️ Near house and garden and at Cotehele Quay. No parking at mill.

🚶 Groups (15+) must book with Property Office and receive a coach route (limited to two per day). No groups Suns & BH weekends. Visitors to house limited to 80 at any one time. Please arrive early and be prepared to queue. Avoid dull days. Allow a full day to see estate.

🐕 Under control welcome only on woodland walks.

❄️

▶ **OPENING TIMES**

House & Restaurant
18 Mar - 31 Oct: Daily
except Fris (but open
Good Fri), 11am - 4.30pm
(Oct: 11am - 4pm).
Last admission 30 mins
before closing time.

Mill
18 Mar - 31 Oct: Daily
except Fris (but open
Good Fri plus Fris in July
& August) 1 - 5.30pm
(Oct: 1 - 4.30pm).

Garden
All year: Daily,
10.30am - dusk.

▶ **ADMISSION**

House, Garden & Mill
Adult £8.00
Family £20.00
1-Adult Family £12.00
Pre-booked Groups .. £7.40

Garden & Mill only
Adult £4.80
Family £12.00
1-Adult Family £7.20

*Groups must book in
advance with the
Property Office.
No groups Suns or BHs.

NT members free.
You may join here.

The National Trust / Rupert Tenison

MAP 1

LANHYDROCK

www.nationaltrust.org.uk

Lanhydrock is the grandest and most welcoming house in Cornwall, set in a glorious landscape of gardens, parkland and woods overlooking the valley of the River Fowey.

The house dates back to the 17th century but much of it had to be rebuilt after a disastrous fire in 1881 destroyed all but the entrance porch and the north wing, which includes the magnificent Long Gallery with its extraordinary plaster ceiling depicting scenes from the Old Testament. A total of 50 rooms are on show today and together they reflect the entire spectrum of life in a rich and splendid Victorian household, from the many servants' bedrooms and the fascinating complex of kitchens, sculleries and larders to the nursery suite where the Agar-Robartes children lived, learned and played, and the grandeur of the dining room with its table laid and ready.

Surrounding the house on all sides are gardens ranging from formal Victorian parterres to the wooded higher garden where magnificent displays of magnolias, rhododendrons and camellias climb the hillside to merge with the oak and beech woods all around. A famous avenue of ancient beech and sycamore trees, the original entrance drive to the house, runs from the pinnacled 17th-century gatehouse down towards the medieval bridge across the Fowey at Respryn.

Owner:
The National Trust

▶ **CONTACT**

Property Manager
Lanhydrock
Bodmin
Cornwall PL30 5AD

Tel: 01208 265950
Fax: 01208 265959

e-mail: lanhydrock@
nationaltrust.org.uk

▶ **LOCATION**

OS Ref. SX085 636

2½ m SE of Bodmin, follow signposts from either A30, A38 or B3268.

© National Trust Photo Library/Jerry Harpur

© National Trust Photo Library/Andreas Von Einsiedel

▶ **OPENING TIMES**

House:
18 Mar - 31 Oct:
Daily except Mons
(but open BH Mons)
11am - 5.30pm.
Oct: 11am - 5pm.

Last admission ½ hr before closing.

Garden:
All year: Daily.
10am - 6pm.
Charge levied from
18 Feb - 31 Oct.

Refreshments available
18 Feb - 31 Dec (except
25/26 Dec): Daily.
Jan - Mid Feb:
weekends only.

Plant Sales:
18 Feb - 17 Mar: Daily
11am - 4pm
18 Mar - 30 Sept: Daily
11am - 5.30pm.
Oct: Daily
11am - 5pm.

Shop:
Jan - 18 Feb: Sat & Sun,
11am - 4pm.
18 Feb - 17 Mar, 31 Oct -
24 Dec & 27 - 31 Dec:
Daily, 11am - 4pm.
18 Mar - 30 Sept: Daily
11am - 5.30pm.
Oct: Daily
11am - 5pm.

▶ **ADMISSION**

House, Garden & Grounds
Adult £9.00
Family £22.50
1-Adult Family £13.50
Groups.................. £7.40

Garden & Grounds only £5.00

No photography in house.

By arrangement.

Suitable. Braille guide. WC.

Licensed restaurant

In park, on leads. Guide dogs only in house.

Limited for coaches.

Please telephone for details.

©National Trust Photographic Library/Jerry Harpur

Trelissick - The Fal estuary.

National Trust/ Peter Cade

ANTONY HOUSE & GARDEN ✄
& ANTONY WOODLAND GARDEN

TORPOINT, CORNWALL   PL11 2QA

www.nationaltrust.org.uk

Antony House & Garden Tel: 01752 812191
Antony Woodland Garden Tel: 01752 814210
e-mail: antony@nationaltrust.org.uk
Antony House & Garden Owner: The National Trust
Antony Woodland Garden Owner: Carew Pole Garden Trust
Superb 18th-century house on the Lynher estuary, grounds landscaped by Repton. Formal garden with sculptures & National Collection of day lilies; woodland garden with magnolias, rhododendrons & National Collection of Camellia japonica.

Location: OS Ref. SX418 564. 5m W of Plymouth via Torpoint car ferry, 2m NW of Torpoint.

Open: House & Garden: 28 Mar - 27 Oct: Tue - Thur & BH Mons. Also Suns in June, July & Aug: 1.30pm - 5.30pm. Last adm. 4.45pm. Restaurant open from 12.30pm. Woodland Garden (not NT) 1 Mar - 30 Oct: daily except Mon & Fri (open BH Mons), 11am - 5.30pm.

Admission: House & Garden: £5.50, Family £13.75, 1-Adult Family £8.25. Groups £4.70pp. NT Garden only: £2.80. Woodland Garden: Adult £4 (Free to NT members on days when the house is open). Joint Gardens-only tickets: Adult £4.60. Groups £3.80.

◻ ⎙ ♿ Braille guide. ⑪ 🅿 ✉

BOCONNOC

ESTATE OFFICE, BOCONNOC, LOSTWITHIEL, CORNWALL PL22 0RG

www.boconnocenterprises.co.uk

Tel: 01208 872507 **Fax:** 01208 873836 **e-mail:** adgfortescue@btinternet.com

Owner/Contact: Anthony Fortescue Esq

Bought with the famous Pitt Diamond in 1717, Boconnoc remains one of Cornwall's best kept secrets. Home to three Prime Ministers, its unique combination of history, architecture, picturesque landscape and one of the great Cornish gardens created ideal film locations for *Poldark* and *The Three Musketeers*. King Charles I and the architect Sir John Soane played an influential part in Boconnoc's history. Groups visit the Boconnoc House restoration project, the gardens, church, Golden Jubilee lake walk, the Georgian Bath House and newly planted Pinetum. Ideal for private and corporate events, conferences, activities; weddings and receptions and holiday houses for long or short breaks.

Location: OS Ref. 148 605. A38 Plymouth, Liskeard or from Bodmin to Dobwalls, then A390 to Middle Taphouse.

Open: House & Garden: 23 Apr - 28 May: Suns: 2 - 5pm. Groups (15-255) by appointment all year.

Admission: House: £3, Garden £4.50. Child under 12yrs Free.

◻ ⎙ ♿Partial. 🖼 🎞By arrangement. 🅿 🖼 ✉In grounds, on leads.
🛏8 doubles, 1 single, 8 ensuite. ⬆Applied for. ❋ ☙1/2 Apr: Cornwall Garden Society Spring Flower Show. 21 - 23 Jul: Boconnoc Steam Fair.

BURNCOOSE NURSERIES & GARDEN
Gwennap, Redruth, Cornwall TR16 6BJ

Tel: 01209 860316   **Fax:** 01209 860011   **e-mail:** burncoose@eclipse.co.uk
www.burncoose.co.uk
Owner/Contact: C H Williams
The Nurseries are set in the 30 acre woodland gardens of Burncoose.
Location: OS Ref. SW742 395. 2m SE of Redruth on main A393 Redruth to Falmouth road between the villages of Lanner and Ponsanooth.
Open: Mon - Sat: 9am - 5pm, Suns, 11am - 5pm. Gardens and Tearooms open all year (except Christmas Day).
Admission: Nurseries: Free. Gardens: Adult/Conc. £2. Child Free. Group conducted tours: £2.50 by arrangement.
🔲 🚻 ♿Grounds. WCs. 🖥 🐾By arrangement. 🅿 🐕In grounds, on leads. ❊

©National Trust Photographic Library/Hugh Palmer

GLENDURGAN GARDEN ⚜
MAWNAN SMITH, FALMOUTH, CORNWALL TR11 5JZ

www.nationaltrust.org.uk

Tel: 01326 250906 (opening hours) or 01872 862090   **Fax:** 01872 865808
e-mail: trelissick@nationaltrust.org.uk
Owner: The National Trust
A valley of great beauty with fine trees, shrubs and water gardens. The laurel maze is an unusual and popular feature. The garden runs down to the tiny village of Durgan and its beach on the Helford River. Replica Victorian school room, rebuilt in 2002 in traditional thatch and cob to replace the 1876 original.
Location: OS Ref. SW772 277. 4m SW of Falmouth, $^{1}/_{2}$m SW of Mawnan Smith, on road to Helford Passage. 1m E of Trebah Garden. Accessible by ferry from Helford.
Open: 11 Feb - 28 Oct: Tue - Sat & BH Mons, 10.30am - 5.30pm. Last admission 4.30pm. Closed Good Friday.
Admission: £5, Child £2.50, Family £12.50, 1-Adult Family £7.50. Booked groups: £4.25/£2.10.
🔲 🚻 ♿Unsuitable. 🖥 🐾By arrangement. 🅿 Limited for coaches. 🐕

CAERHAYS CASTLE & GARDEN 🏛
CAERHAYS, GORRAN, ST AUSTELL, CORNWALL PL26 6LY

www.caerhays.co.uk

Tel: 01872 501310   **Fax:** 01872 501870   **e-mail:** estateoffice@caerhays.co.uk
Owner: F J Williams Esq   **Contact:** The Estate Office
One of the very few Nash built castles still left standing – situated within approximately 60 acres of informal woodland gardens created by J C Williams, who sponsored plant hunting expeditions to China at the turn of the century. Noted for its camellias, magnolias, rhododendrons and oaks. English Heritage listing - Grade I: Outstanding.
Location: OS Ref. SW972 415. S coast of Cornwall – between Mevagissey and Portloe. 9m SW of St Austell.
Open: House: 13 Mar - 31 May: Mon - Fri only (including BHs), 12.15 - 4pm, booking recommended. Gardens: 13 Feb - 31 May: daily (including BHs), 10am - 5pm (last admission 4pm).
Admission: House: £5.50. Gardens: £5.50. House & Gardens: £9.50. Guided group tours (15+) by Head Gardener, £6.50 - by arrangement.
🚻 ♿Unsuitable. 🖥 🐾By arrangement. 🐕In grounds, on leads.

GODOLPHIN 🏛
GODOLPHIN CROSS, HELSTON, CORNWALL TR13 9RE

www.godolphinhouse.com

Tel/Fax: 01736 763194   **e-mail:** info@godolphinhouse.com
Owner: Mrs L M P Schofield   **Contact:** Mrs Joanne Schofield
Unspoilt and charming Grade I mansion commenced in c1475 with early formal Side Garden (c1300 and c1500) set in beautiful, woodland surroundings. Home of Sidney, 1st Earl, Lord High Treasurer to Queen Anne. Lovely early English furnishings including a large, carved oak overmantle of c1610. Pictures by American painter Elmer Schofield and contemporary paintings in the King's Room by Robert Organ. Elizabethan stables with display of local, unrestored farm wagons, locally sourced food in the Marquee, shop, plant sales, exhibitions and events. Godolphin is a must for those who seek and appreciate beautiful, informal places. For updates, visit our website. Group tours year round by arrangement. Venue hire and weddings.
Location: OS Ref. SW602 318. Breage, Helston. On minor road from Godolphin Cross to Townshend. Follow brown signs.
Open: Easter Monday - 30 Sept, Tues - Fri and Suns: 11am - 5pm. All BH Mons: 11am - 5pm.
Admission: Adult £6, Child (5 - 15yrs) £1.50, Conc. £5. Garden: £2.
ℹ️ 🔲 🚻 ♿ 🍴 🐾By arrangement. 🅿 🐕

CHYSAUSTER ANCIENT VILLAGE ⚏
Nr Newmill, Penzance, Cornwall TR20 8XA

Tel: 07831 757934   **e-mail:** customers@english-heritage.org.uk
www.english-heritage.org.uk/chysauster
Owner: English Heritage   **Contact:** Visitor Operations Team
On a windy hillside, overlooking the wild and spectacular coast, is this deserted Romano-Cornish village with a 'street' of eight well preserved houses, each comprising a number of rooms around an open court.
Location: OS203 Ref. SW473 350. 2$^{1}/_{2}$ m NW of Gulval off B3311.
Open: 1 Apr - 30 Jun & Sept: daily, 10am - 5pm. 1 Jul - 31 Aug: daily, 10am - 6pm. 1 - 31 Oct: daily, 10am - 4pm.
Admission: Adult £2.40, Child £1.20, Conc. £1.80. 15% discount for groups (11+).
ℹ️WC. 🔲 🅿No coaches. 🐕On leads.

COTEHELE ⚜   *See page 203 for full page entry.*

THE JAPANESE GARDEN & BONSAI NURSERY
St Mawgan, Nr Newquay, Cornwall TR8 4ET

Tel: 01637 860116   **Fax:** 01637 860807   **e-mail:** rob@thebonsainursery.com

Owner/Contact: Mr & Mrs Hore
Authentic Japanese Garden set in 1½ acres.
Location: OS Ref. SW873 660. Follow road signs from A3059 & B3276.
Open: Summer: Daily, 10am - 6pm. WInter: 10am - 5.30pm. Closed Christmas Day - New Year's Day.
Admission: Adult £3.50. Child £1.50. Groups (10+): £3.

KEN CARO GARDENS
Bicton, Nr Liskeard PL14 5RF

Tel: 01579 362446

Owner/Contact: Mr and Mrs K R Willcock
4 acre plantsman's garden.
Location: OS Ref. SX313 692. 5m NE of of Liskeard. Follow brown sign off main A390 midway between Liskeard and Callington.
Open: 26 Feb - 30 Sept: daily except Sats, 10am - 6pm.
Admission: Adult £3.50, Child £1.

LANHYDROCK

See page 204 for full page entry.

LAUNCESTON CASTLE
Castle Lodge, Launceston, Cornwall PL15 7DR

Tel: 01566 772365   **Fax:** 01566 772396   **e-mail:** customers@english-heritage.org.uk
www.english-heritage.org.uk/launceston

Owner: English Heritage   **Contact:** Visitor Operations Team
Set on the motte of the original Norman castle and commanding the town and surrounding countryside. The shell keep and tower survive of this medieval castle which controlled the main route into Cornwall. An exhibition shows the early history.
Location: OS201 Ref. SX330 846. In Launceston.
Open: 1 Apr - 31 Oct: daily, 10am - 5pm (6pm in Jul & Aug & 4pm in Oct).
Admission: Adult £2.30, Child £1.20, Conc. £1.70. 15% discount for groups (11+).
☐ ⚊ Grounds. 🅿 NCP adjacent. Limited. 🐕 In grounds, on leads.
🖥 Tel for details.

LAWRENCE HOUSE
9 Castle Street, Launceston, Cornwall PL15 8BA

Tel: 01566 773277

Owner: The National Trust   **Contact:** The Property Manager
A Georgian house given to the Trust to help preserve the character of the street, and now leased to Launceston Town Council as a museum and civic centre.
Location: OS Ref. SX330 848. Launceston.
Open: 18 Apr - 29 Sept: daily, except Sat & Sun, 10.30am - 4.30pm. Other times by appointment.
Admission: Free, but contributions welcome.

St Michael's Mount.

© National Trust Photographic Library.

THE LOST GARDENS OF HELIGAN
PENTEWAN, ST AUSTELL, CORNWALL PL26 6EN

www.heligan.com

Tel: 01726 845100   **Fax:** 01726 845101
e-mail: info@heligan.com   **Contact:** Sian Batten
The award-winning restoration of Heligan's productive gardens is only one of many features which combine to create a destination with a breadth of interest around the year: Victorian pleasure grounds with spring flowering shrubs, summerhouses, pools and rockeries; a sub-tropical Jungle valley brimming with exotic foliage; woodland and farm walks through beautiful and sustainably managed Cornish countryside, and a pioneering project offering visitors a close-up view of native wildlife on site.
Location: OS Ref. SX000 465. 5m SW of St Austell. 2m NW of Mevagissey. Take the B3273 to Mevagissey – follow tourist signs.
Open: Daily except 24 & 25 Dec: 10am - 6pm (5pm Nov - Feb). Last admission 1½ hrs before closing.
Admission: Adult: £7.50. Child (5-16yrs) £4, OAP £7. Family £20. Groups by arrangement.
☐ 🎁 ⚊ 🖥 🍴 By arrangement. 🅿 ◼ 🐕 March - October ✳ 🖥 Tel for details.

MOUNT EDGCUMBE HOUSE & COUNTRY PARK
CREMYLL, TORPOINT, CORNWALL PL10 IHZ

www.mountedgcumbe.gov.uk

Tel: 01752 822236   **Fax:** 01752 822199   **e-mail:** mt.edgcumbe@plymouth.gov.uk
Owner: Cornwall County & Plymouth City Councils   **Contact:** Secretary
Former home of the Earls of Mount Edgcumbe. Miraculously the walls of the red stone Tudor House survived the bombs in 1941. Restored by the 6th Earl. Now beautifully furnished with family possessions. Set in historic 18th century gardens on the dramatic sea-girt Rame peninsula. Follies, forts; National camellia collection. Grade I listed. Exhibitions and events.
Location: OS Ref. SX452 527. 10m W of Plymouth via Torpoint.
Open: House & Earl's Garden: 2 Apr - 28 Sept: Sun - Thur, 11am - 4.30pm. Group bookings by arrangement. Country Park: All year, daily, 8am - dusk.
Admission: House & Earl's Garden: Adult £4.50, Child (5-15) £2.25, Conc. £3.50, Family (2+2 or 1+3) £10. Groups (10+): Adult £3.50, Child £2. Park: Free.
☐ 🎁 🍴 ⚊ 💺 🍴 Licensed. 🖥 By arrangement. 🅿 🐕 In grounds, on leads. ⬆
✳ 🖥 Tel for details.

PENCARROW 🏛
BODMIN, CORNWALL PL30 3AG
www.pencarrow.co.uk

Tel: 01208 841369   **Fax:** 01208 841722   **e-mail:** info@pencarrow.co.uk

Owner: Molesworth-St Aubyn family   **Contact:** J Reynolds

Still owned and lived in by the family. Georgian house and Grade II* listed gardens. Superb collection of pictures, furniture and porcelain. Marked walks through 50 acres of beautiful formal and woodland gardens, Victorian rockery, Italian garden, over 700 different varieties of rhododendrons, lake and ice house.

Location: OS Ref. SX040 711. Between Bodmin and Wadebridge. 4m NW of Bodmin off A389 & B3266 at Washaway.

Open: 2 Apr - 26 Oct: Sun - Thur, 11am - 4pm (last tour). Gardens: 1 Mar - 31 Oct: daily.

Admission: House & Garden: Adult £8, Child £4. Family £22. Garden only: Adult £4, Child £1. Groups (by arrangement): House & Garden: groups (20-30) £7, 31+ £6; Gardens only: groups (20-30) £3.50, 31+ £3. Discounts not normally available on Fri & Sat.

ℹ️ Craft centre, small children's play area, self-pick soft fruit. By arrangement. Licensed. Obligatory. 🅿️ Grounds only. Tel for details.

PINE LODGE GARDENS & NURSERY
Holmbush, St Austell, Cornwall PL25 3RQ

Tel: 01726 73500   **Fax:** 01726 77370   **e-mail:** garden@pine-lodge.co.uk
www.pine-lodge.co.uk

Owner/Contact: Mr & Mrs R H J Clemo

30 acres with over 6,000 plants all labelled. Herbaceous and shrub borders. Many water features, pinetum, arboretum, Japanese garden, wild flower meadow, lake with waterfowl and black swans. Plant hunting expeditions every year to gather seeds for our nursery which contain very unusual plants, many rare. The gardens were given a Highly Commended Award by the Cornwall Tourist Board for 2002. Plenty of seats in the gardens.

Location: OS Ref. SX044 527. Signposted on A390.

Open: Daily, 10am - 6pm, last ticket 5pm.

Admission: Adult £5.50, Child £3.

ℹ️WC. 🅿️

Godolphin.

PENDENNIS CASTLE ⌗
FALMOUTH, CORNWALL TR11 4LP
www.english-heritage.org.uk/pendennis

Tel: 01326 316594   **Fax:** 01326 319911   **e-mail:** customers@english-heritage.org.uk
Venue and Hire Hospitality: 01326 310106

Owner: English Heritage   **Contact:** Visitor Operations Team

Pendennis and its neighbour, St Mawes Castle, face each other across the mouth of the estuary of the River Fal. Built by Henry VIII in 16th century as protection against threat of attack and invasion from France. Extended and adapted over the years to meet the changing threats to national security from the French and Spanish and continued right through to World War II. It withstood five months of siege during the Civil War before becoming the penultimate Royalist Garrison to surrender on the mainland. Pendennis today stands as a landmark, with fine sea views and excellent site facilities including a hands-on discovery centre, exhibitions, a museum, guardhouse, shop and tearoom. Excellent special events venue.

Location: OS Ref. SW824 318. On Pendennis Head.

Open: 1 Apr - 30 Jun: daily, 10am - 5pm (4pm Sats). 1 Jul - 31 Aug: daily, 10am - 6pm (4pm Sats). 1 - 30 Sept: daily 10am - 5pm (4pm Sats), 1 Oct - 31 Mar: daily, 10am - 4pm. Closed 24 - 26 Dec & 1 Jan. The Keep will close for 1hr at lunch on Sats when events are booked, please telephone to check.

Admission: Adult £4.80, Child £2.40, Conc. £3.60, Family £12. 15% discount for groups (11+).

ℹ️ WC. Partial. 🅿️ In grounds only. Tel for details.

PRIDEAUX PLACE 🏛

PADSTOW, CORNWALL PL28 8RP

www.prideauxplace.co.uk

Tel: 01841 532411   **Fax:** 01841 532945   **e-mail:** office@prideauxplace.co.uk

Owner/Contact: Peter Prideaux-Brune Esq

Tucked away above the busy port of Padstow, the home of the Prideaux family for over 400 years, is surrounded by gardens and wooded grounds overlooking a deer park and the Camel estuary to the moors beyond. The house still retains its 'E' shape Elizabethan front and contains fine paintings and furniture. Now a major international film location, this family home is one of the brightest jewels in Cornwall's crown. The historic garden is undergoing major restoration work and offers some of the best views in the county. A cornucopia of Cornish history under one roof.

Location: OS Ref. SW913 756. 5m from A39 Newquay/Wadebridge link road. Signposted by Historic House signs.

Open: Easter Sun - 20 Apr, 14 May - 5 Oct. Daily except Fris & Sats. Grounds & Tearoom: 12.30 - 5pm. House Tours: 1.30 - 4pm (last tour).

Admission: House & Grounds: Adult £6.50, Child £2. Grounds only: Adult £2, Child £1. Groups (15+) discounts apply.

By arrangement. Ground floor & grounds. Obligatory. By arrangement. In grounds, on leads.

RESTORMEL CASTLE ♯

Lostwithiel, Cornwall PL22 0BD

Tel: 01208 872687   **e-mail:** customers@english-heritage.org.uk

www.english-heritage.org.uk/restormel

Owner: English Heritage   **Contact:** Visitor Operations Team

Perched on a high mound, surrounded by a deep moat, the huge circular keep of this splendid Norman castle survives in remarkably good condition. It is still possible to make out the ruins of Restormel's Keep Gate, Great Hall and even the kitchens and private rooms.

Location: OS200 Ref. SX104 614. 1½ m N of Lostwithiel off A390.

Open: 1 Apr - 31 Oct: daily, 10am - 5pm (6pm in Jul & Aug; 4pm in Oct).

Admission: Adult £2.40, Child £1.20, Conc. £1.80. 15% discount for groups (11+).

WC. Limited for coaches. In grounds, on leads. Tel for details.

ST CATHERINE'S CASTLE ♯

Fowey, Cornwall

Tel: 0121 625 6820

Owner: English Heritage   **Contact:** The South West Regional Office

A small fort built by Henry VIII to defend Fowey harbour, with fine views of the coastline and river estuary.

Location: OS200 Ref. SX118 508. 1.5 miles SW of Fowey along footpath off A3082.

Open: Any reasonable time, daylight only.

Admission: Free.

plant sales
see page 555

ST MAWES CASTLE ♯

ST MAWES, CORNWALL TR2 3AA

www.english-heritage.org.uk/stmawes

Tel/Fax: 01326 270526   **Venue Hire and Hospitality:** 01326 310106

e-mail: customers@english-heritage.org.uk

Owner: English Heritage   **Contact:** Visitor Operations Team

The pretty fishing village of St Mawes is home to this castle. On the opposite headland to Pendennis Castle, St Mawes shares the task of watching over the mouth of the River Fal as it has done since Henry VIII built it as a defence against the French. With three huge circular bastions shaped like clover leaves, St Mawes was designed to cover every possible angle of approach. It is the finest example of Tudor military architecture. The castle offers views of St Mawes' little boat-filled harbour, the passenger ferry tracking across the Fal, and the splendid coastline which featured in the *Poldark* TV series. Also the start of some delightful walks along the coastal path.

Location: OS204 Ref. SW842 328. W of St Mawes on A3078.

Open: 1 Apr - 30 June: daily, 10am - 5pm. 1 Jul - 30 Sept: Sun - Fri, 10am - 6pm (5pm in Sept). 1 - 31 Oct: daily, 10am - 4pm. (Site closed at 4pm on Sun & Fri for hospitality functions.) Closed 24 - 26 Dec & 1 Jan.

Admission: Adult £3.60, Child £1.80, Conc. £2.70. 15% discount for groups (11+).

Private & corporate hire. Grounds. WC. Limited. Grounds only. Tel for details.

ST MICHAEL'S MOUNT

MARAZION, NR PENZANCE, CORNWALL TR17 0EF

www.stmichaelsmount.co.uk   **www.nationaltrust.org.uk**

Tel: 01736 710507 (710265 tide information)   **Fax:** 01736 719930
e-mail: godolphin@manor-office.co.uk

Owner: The National Trust   **Contact:** The Manor Office

This beautiful island set in Mounts Bay has become an icon for Cornwall, and in turn there are magnificent views when you reach its summit. There the church and castle, whose origins date from the 12th century, have at various times acted as a Benedictine priory, a place of pilgrimage, a fortress, a mansion house and now a magnet for visitors from all over the world. Following the Civil War, the island was acquired by the St Aubyn family who still live in the castle today.

Location: OS Ref. SW515 300. 4m E of Penzance. At Marazion there is access on foot over causeway at low tide. In the main season, the property is reached at high tide by a short evocative boat trip.

Open: Castle: 26 Mar - 29 Oct: Sun - Fri, 10.30am - 4.45pm (last admission on the island). Nov - Mar: open when tide and weather favourable. Essential to telephone in advance. Garden (not NT): May & Jun: Weekdays only; Jul - Oct: Thur & Fri only, 10.30am - 4.45pm. Church Service: Whitsun - end Sept (also Christmas Day, Good Fri & Easter Sun): Sun, 11.15am. All visits subject to weather and tides.

Admission: Adult £6, Child (under 17) £3, Family £15, 1-Adult Family £9. Booked groups £5.50. Gardens (not NT) £3.

On mainland (not NT.) Not permitted on island.

SAUSMAREZ MANOR   *See page 202 for full page entry.*

TATE ST IVES

Porthmeor Beach, St Ives, Cornwall TR26 1TG
Tel: 01736 796266   **Fax:** 01736 794480   **e-mail:** tatestivesinfo@tate.org.uk
www.tate.org.uk

Owner: Tate Gallery   **Contact:** Arwen Fitch

Changing displays from the Tate Collection, as well as international modern and contemporary art, focusing on the modern movement that St Ives is famous for. The exhibitions are supported by an extensive range of events. Tate St Ives does close for re-hanging the new exhibitions, however the shop and café (with spectacular views over St Ives) remain open.

Tate St Ives also manages the Barbara Hepworth Museum and Sculpture Garden.

Location: OS Ref. SW515 407. Situated by Porthmeor Beach.
Open: Mar - Oct: daily, 10am - 5.30pm. Nov - Feb: Tue - Sun, 10am - 4.30pm.
Admission: Adult £5.50, Conc. £2.75, Under 18s and Over 60s Free.
Licensed. Daily. Nearby. Guide dogs only. Tel for details.

© English Heritage Photo Library

TINTAGEL CASTLE

TINTAGEL, CORNWALL PL34 0HE

www.english-heritage.org.uk/tintagel

Tel/Fax: 01840 770328   **e-mail:** customers@english-heritage.org.uk
Owner: English Heritage   **Contact:** Visitor Operations Team

The spectacular setting for the legendary castle of King Arthur on the wild and windswept Cornish coast. Clinging precariously to the edge of the cliff face are the extensive ruins of a medieval royal castle, built by Richard, Earl of Cornwall, younger brother of Henry III. Also used as a Cornish stronghold by subsequent Earls of Cornwall. Despite extensive excavations since the 1930s, Tintagel Castle remains one of the most spectacular and romantic spots in the entire British Isles. Destined to remain a place of mystery and romance, Tintagel will always jealously guard its marvellous secrets.

Location: OS200 Ref. SX048 891. On Tintagel Head, $^1/_2$ m along uneven track from Tintagel.
Open: 1 Apr - 31 Oct: daily, 10am - 6pm (5pm in Oct). 1 Nov - 31 Mar: daily, 10am - 4pm. Closed 24 - 26 Dec & 1 Jan.
Admission: Adult £4.30, Child £2.20, Conc. £3.20. 15% discount for groups (11+).
WC. No vehicles. Tel for details.

open all year
see page 557

TINTAGEL OLD POST OFFICE ✄
Tintagel, Cornwall PL34 0DB

Tel: 01840 770024 or 01208 74281

Owner: The National Trust   **Contact:** The Custodian

One of the most characterful buildings in Cornwall, and a house of great antiquity, this small 14th-century yeoman farmhouse is full of charm and interest.

Location: OS Ref. SX056 884. In the centre of Tintagel.

Open: 20 Mar - 23 July & 4 - 30 Sept: daily except Sats 11am - 5.30pm. 24 July - 3 Sept: daily 11am - 5.30pm. 1 - 29 Oct daily except Sats, 11am - 4pm. Last admission 30 mins before closing.

Admission: Adult £2.60, Child £1.30, Family £6.60, 1-Adult Family £3.90. Booked groups £2.40.

St Mawes.

© English Heritage Photo Library.

© Trebah Garden Trust

TREBAH GARDEN
MAWNAN SMITH, NR FALMOUTH, CORNWALL TR11 5JZ

www.trebah-garden.co.uk

Tel: 01326 250448   **Fax:** 01326 250781   **e-mail:** mail@trebah-garden.co.uk

Owner: Trebah Garden Trust   **Contact:** V. Woodcroft

Steeply wooded 25 acre sub-tropical ravine garden falls 200 feet from 18th century house to private beach on Helford River. Stream cascading over waterfalls through ponds full of Koi Carp and exotic water plants winds through 2 acres of blue and white hydrangeas and spills out over beach. Huge Australian tree ferns and palms mingle with shrubs of ever-changing colours and scent beneath over-arching canopy of 100 year old rhododendrons and magnolias. The striking Visitor Centre houses a garden shop, plant sales and stylish catering.

Location: OS Ref. SW768 275. 4m SW of Falmouth, 1m SW of Mawnan Smith. Follow brown and white tourism signs from Treliever Cross roundabout at A39/A394 junction through Mawnan Smith to Trebah.

Open: All year: daily, 10.30am - 5pm (last admission).

Admission: 1 Mar - 31 Oct: Adult £5.80, Child (5-15yrs)/Disabled £2, Child under 5yrs Free, OAP £5.30. 1 Nov - 28 Feb: Adult £3, Child (5-15yrs)/Disabled £1, Child under 5yrs Free, OAP £2.50. NT & RHS members: free entry 1 Nov - end Feb.

▢ ✦ ♿ Partial. ▣ ⊞ ✦ By arrangement. P ▣ ⊠ On leads. ❄

National Trust/ Tony Kent

TRELISSICK GARDEN ✄
FEOCK, TRURO, CORNWALL TR3 6QL

www.nationaltrust.org.uk

Tel: 01872 862090   **Fax:** 01872 865808   **e-mail:** trelissick@nationaltrust.org.uk

Owner: The National Trust   **Contact:** The Property Manager

A garden and estate of rare tranquil beauty with glorious maritime views over the Carrick Roads to Falmouth. The tender and exotic shrubs make this an attractive garden in all seasons. Extensive park and woodland walks beside the river. Art and Craft Gallery. Make your visit a really special day: travel to Trelissick by foot ferry from Truro, Falmouth and St Mawes by Fal River Links Partnerships Ferries, from April to September. Copeland Spode China on display in Trelissick House at 2pm on Thursdays, April to June, September and October, booking advisable 01872 864452.

Location: OS Ref. SW837 396. 4m S of Truro on B3289 above King Harry Ferry.

Open: Garden, Shop, Restaurant, Gallery and Plant Sales: 2 Jan - 9 Feb: Thur - Sun, 11am - 4pm. 11 Feb - 29 October: daily, 10.30am - 5.30pm. 30 Oct - 23 Dec: daily, 11am - 4pm. 27 Dec - 1 Jan: daily, 12 noon - 4pm. Woodland Walks: All year: daily.

Admission: Adult £5.50, Family £13.75, 1-Adult Family £8.25. Pre-arranged groups £4.60pp. Car Park £3 (refunded on admission). Garden & Copeland Spode China: £7.90 (NT members £3.60). Discounted rate for winter visits.

▢ ✦ ⊞ By arrangement. ♿ ⊞ ✦ By arrangement. P Limited for coaches. ⊠ In park on leads; only guide dogs in garden. ❄ ▣ Tel for details.

National Trust/ Giles Crawford

TRENGWAINTON GARDEN ✤
PENZANCE, CORNWALL TR20 8RZ
www.nationaltrust.org.uk

Tel: 01736 363148 **Fax:** 01736 367762

Owner: The National Trust **Contact:** David Milne - The Property Manager

Intimate and closely linked to the picturesque stream running through its valley, the garden leads up to a terrace and summer houses with splendid views across Mount's Bay to the Lizard. The walled gardens contain many rare and unusual species which are difficult to grow in the open anywhere else in the country.

Location: OS Ref. SW445 315. 2m NW of Penzance, ¹/₂ m W of Heamoor on Penzance - Morvah road (B3312), ¹/₂ m off St. Just road (A3071).

Open: 12 Feb - 29 Oct: Sun - Thur & Good Fri, 10am - 5.30pm (Feb, Mar & Oct: 10am - 5pm). Also open pre-Christmas - telephone for details.

Admission: Adult £5, Child £2.50, Family £12.50, 1-Adult Family £7.50. Booked groups: £4.10.

⬚ ⚏ ⬧Partial. ☗Tea-house. 🐾On leads.

National Trust/ Marcus Way

TRERICE ✤
KESTLE MILL, NR NEWQUAY, CORNWALL TR8 4PG
www.nationaltrust.org.uk

Tel: 01637 875404 **Fax:** 01637 879300 **e-mail:** trerice@nationaltrust.org.uk

Owner: The National Trust **Contact:** David Milne - The Property Manager

Trerice is an architectural gem and something of a rarity – a small Elizabethan manor house hidden away in a web of narrow lanes and still somehow caught in the spirit of its age. An old Arundell house, it contains much fine furniture, ceramics, glasses and a wonderful clock collection. A small barn museum traces the development of the lawn mower.

Location: OS Ref. SW841 585. 3m SE of Newquay via the A392 & A3058 (right at Kestle Mill). Or from A30 - signs at Summercourt and Mitchell.

Open: 26 Mar - 29 Oct: Daily except Sats: 11am - 5.30pm (5pm in Oct).

Admission: Adult £6, Child £3, Family £15, 1-Adult Family £9. Pre-arranged groups £5.10. Garden only: Adult £2, Child £1, Family £5, 1-Adult Family £3.

⬚ ⚏ ⬧Braille & taped guides. WC. ☗Licensed. 🐾Guide dogs only. ⬆

TREWITHEN 🏛
GRAMPOUND ROAD, TRURO, CORNWALL TR2 4DD
www.trewithengardens.co.uk

Tel: 01726 883647 **Fax:** 01726 882301
e-mail: gardens@trewithen-estate.demon.co.uk

Owner: A M J Galsworthy **Contact:** The Estate Office

Trewithen means 'house of the trees' and the name truly describes this fine early Georgian House in its splendid setting of wood and parkland. Country Life described the house as 'one of the outstanding West Country houses of the 18th century'. The gardens at Trewithen are outstanding and of international fame. It is now over 100 years since George Johnstone inherited and started developing the gardens which now contain a wide and rare collection of flowering shrubs. Some of the magnolias and rhododendron species in the garden are known throughout the world. They are one of two attractions in this county awarded three stars by Michelin. Viewing platforms and a *Camera Obscura* will be an additional interest to visitors.

Location: OS Ref. SW914 476. S of A390 between Grampound and Probus villages. 7m WSW of St Austell.

Open: Gardens: 1 Feb - 30 Sept: Mon - Sat, 10am - 4.30pm. Suns in Feb - May only. House: Apr - Jul & Aug BH Mon, Mons & Tues, 2 - 4pm.

Admission: Feb - June: Adult £5 (groups 20+ £4.50), Child (5 - 15yrs) £1, Child under 5yrs Free. July - Sept: Adult £4.50 (groups 20+ £4), Child (5 - 15yrs) £1, Child under 5yrs Free.

ℹ No photography in house. ⚏ ⬧Partial. WC. ☗ ✦By arrangement. 🅿 Limited for coaches. 🐾In grounds, on leads.

MAP 2

Owner:
Mr & Mrs S E Lister

▶ **CONTACT**

Mr Simon Lister
Bicton Park
Botanical Gardens
East Budleigh
Budleigh Salterton
Devon EX9 7BJ

Tel: 01395 568465

Fax: 01395 568374

e-mail: info@
bictongardens.co.uk

▶ **LOCATION**

OS Ref. SY074 856

2m N of Budleigh
Salterton on B3178.

Follow the brown signs
to Bicton Park from
M5/J30 at Exeter.

Rail: Exmouth 5mins,
Exeter St Davids 12m.

Air: Exeter Airport 5m.

BICTON PARK BOTANICAL GARDENS

www.bictongardens.co.uk

Spanning three centuries of horticultural history, Bicton Park Botanical Gardens are set in the picturesque Otter Valley, near the coastal town of Budleigh Salterton and 10 miles south of Exeter.

The 63-acre park's oldest ornamental area is the Italian Garden, created in the axial style of Versailles landscaper Andre le Notre, c1735. By that time formal designs were becoming unfashionable in England, which may explain why the garden was located out of view of the manor house. Today, the full grandeur of the Italian Garden can be seen from the spacious restaurant in the classically styled Orangery, built at the beginning of the 19th century.

Bicton's high-domed Palm House, one of the world's most beautiful garden buildings, was the first of many developments between 1820 and 1850. Others included an important collection of conifers in the Pinetum, now the subject of a rare species conservation project, and St Mary's Church, where Queen Victoria worshipped.

A large museum reflects changes in agriculture and rural life generally over the past 200 years. The Grade I listed gardens, which are open all year, also feature a narrow-gauge railway which meanders through the garden on its 1¹/₂ mile track. Gift shop, garden centre, children's inside and outdoor play areas.

▶ **OPENING TIMES**

Summer
10am - 6pm.

Winter
10am - 5pm.
Open all year except
Christmas Day &
Boxing Day.

▶ **ADMISSION**

Adult	£5.95
Child	£4.95
Conc	£4.95
Family (2+2)	£19.95

Groups (16-200)

Adult	£3.95
Child	£2.95
Conc.	£3.95

Children under 3yrs Free

 Children's inside & outdoor play areas.

Garden Centre.

Licensed.

By arrangement.

P

In grounds, on leads.

MAP 2

Owner:
Hon John Rous

▶ **CONTACT**

Visitor Centre
Clovelly
Nr Bideford
N Devon EX39 5TA

Tel: 01237 431781

Fax: 01237 431288

▶ **LOCATION**

OS Ref. SS248 319

On A39 10 miles W of
Bideford, 15 miles E of
Bude. Turn off at
'Clovelly Cross
Roundabout' and follow
signs to car park.

Air: Exeter & Plymouth
Airport both 50 miles.

Rail: Barnstaple
19 miles.

Bus: from Bideford.

CLOVELLY

www.clovelly.co.uk

From Elizabethan days until today, Clovelly Village has preserved its original atmosphere. The main traffic-free street, known as 'up-a-along' and 'down-a-long', tumbles its cobbled way down to the tiny harbour, which is protected by an ancient stone breakwater. It is a descent through flower-strewn cottages broken only by little passageways and winding lanes that lead off to offer the prospect of more picturesque treasures.

The New Inn, which is 400 years old, is halfway down the street, and the other, the Red Lion which is right on the quayside. Both Inns have long histories and an atmosphere rarely found in the modern world. In addition you'll find the Visitor Centre, a range of gift shops, a café and an audio-visual theatre in which visitors are treated to a history of the village. Just below is the Stable Yard with a pottery and silk workshop. There are beautiful coastal and woodland walks.

Access is restricted to pedestrians only via the Visitor Centre with a Land Rover taxi service for those unable to walk.

▶ **OPENING TIMES**

High season: 9am - 6pm.

Low season: 9am - 4.30pm.

▶ **ADMISSION**

The entrance fee covers parking and other facilities provided by Clovelly Estate, as well as admission to the audio-visual film, Fisherman's Cottage, and Kingsley Museum.

Adult £4.75
Child (7 - 16yrs) £3.25
Child (under 7yrs) ...... Free
Family (2+2) £14.00

Group Rates (20+)
Adult £4.00
Child £3.00

ℹ️ Rubber soled, low heel shoes are recommended.

🛍️ ❄️ ♿ Partial. Around the Visitor Centre.

🍷 Licensed. 🍴 Licensed. 🅿️ 🖼️ 🐕 Onleads.

🛏️ 18 double, 1 single, all en suite. ❄️

MAP 2

POWDERHAM CASTLE 🏛

www.powderham.co.uk

Owner:
The Earl of Devon

▶ CONTACT

Mrs Clare Crawshaw
General Manager
The Estate Office
Powderham Castle
Kenton, Exeter
Devon EX6 8JQ

Tel: 01626 890243
Fax: 01626 890729
e-mail: castle@
powderham.co.uk

**Functions
coordinator:**
Virginia Bowman
01626 890243
ginny@
powderham.co.uk

▶ LOCATION

OS Ref. SX965 832

6m SW of Exeter,
4m S M5/J30.
Access from A379 in
Kenton village.

Air: Exeter Airport 9m.

Rail: Starcross
Station 2m.

Bus: Devon General
No: 85, 85A, 85B to
Castle Gate.

CONFERENCE/FUNCTION

ROOM	SIZE	MAX CAPACITY
Music Room	56' x 25'	150
Dining Room	42' x 22'	90
Ante Room	22' x 18'	40
Library 1	32' x 18'	75
Library 2	31" x18'	75

Lying in a tranquil deer park with views through the ancient oaks to the Estuary of the River Exe, the castle of Powderham has long been the home of the Earl of Devon. It was built by Sir Philip Courtenay in 1390 but there may have been an earlier house defending the site in Saxon days. The Courtenays owned large parts of the West Country and it was not until the 17th century that Powderham became their principal seat. After some Civil War damage the family carried out some major embellishments and the 18th century saw the addition of the magnificent Grand Staircase and, towards the end of the century, Wyatt's fine Music Room.

The Castle remains a family home and visitors see the State Rooms by entertaining guided tours. The gardens and grounds are largely informal with walks and paths ranging from the springtime Woodland Garden to the old Victorian walled garden. The garden is also home to The Children's Secret Garden, and whilst the terraced Rose Garden has so sadly said goodbye to Timothy (the world's oldest tortoise who died in 2004 at possibly 165 years old), a youngster of some 66 years currently resides amongst the animals here. He is also a Timothy but is known as Timmy Two! The Country Store, is a great all year round destination, here you will find a Food Hall, Plant Centre, Restaurant and the House of Marbles. There is also a delightful miniature railway in the grounds, and other attractions.

Powderham has a huge events programme with everything from classic vehicles to firework displays and pop concerts. Voted Venue of the Year in 2004, some 150,000 visitors attend shows over the year (see the website for up to date details).

In addition the Castle is a popular venue for weddings, filming, private functions and corporate events, all of which help the Estate to be a diversified success in the modern world whilst retaining the charm of its past.

▶ OPENING TIMES

From 9 April - 29 Oct:
Daily* 10am - 5.30pm
Last admission 4.30pm.

*Except Sat: closed to
public, but available
for private hire.

Powderham Country Store:
Daily, 9am - 5.00pm,
(Suns, 10am - 4.00pm).

Winter
Available for hire for
conferences, receptions and
functions and private tours.

▶ ADMISSION

Group rates by arrangement
or telephone for prices.
(2005 prices.)

Adult £7.45
Child £4.10

Filming, car launches including 4WD, vehicle rallies, open air concerts, etc. Grand piano in Music Room, 3800 acre estate, cricket pitch, horse trials course. Deer park.

Conferences, dinners, corporate entertainment.

Limited facilities. Some ramps. WC.

Fully licensed restaurant and coach room access.

Fully inclusive. Tour time: 1hr.

Unlimited free parking. Commission and complimentary drinks for drivers. Advance warning of group bookings preferred but not essential.

Welcome. Fascinating tour and useful insight into the life of one of England's Great Houses over the centuries.

In part of grounds, on leads.

Civil Wedding Licence.

See website or tel for details.

NTPL / David Garner

A LA RONDE

SUMMER LANE, EXMOUTH, DEVON EX8 5BD

www.nationaltrust.org.uk

Tel: 01395 265514   **e-mail:** alaronde@nationaltrust.org.uk

Owner: The National Trust   **Contact:** John Rolfe – Custodian

A unique 16-sided house built on the instructions of two spinster cousins, Jane and Mary Parminter, on their return from a grand tour of Europe. Completed c1796, the house contains many 18th century contents and collections brought back by the Parminters. The fascinating interior decoration includes a feather frieze and shell-encrusted gallery which, due to its fragility, can only be viewed on closed circuit television.

Location: OS Ref. SY004 834. 2m N of Exmouth on A376.

Open: 20 Mar - 29 Oct: daily except Fri & Sat, 11am - 5.30pm. Last admission 1/2 hr before closing.

Admission: Adult £5, Child £2.50. No reduction for groups.

National Trust / Andreas Von Einsiedel

ARLINGTON COURT

Nr BARNSTAPLE, NORTH DEVON EX31 4LP

www.nationaltrust.org.uk

Tel: 01271 850296   **Fax:** 01271 851108   **e-mail:** arlingtoncourt@nationaltrust.org.uk

Owner: The National Trust   **Contact:** Ana Chylak - Property Manager

Nestling in the thickly wooded valley of the River Yeo, stands the 3000 acre Arlington estate. It comprises a delightful and intimate Victorian house full of treasures including collections of model ships, pewter, shells, extensive informal gardens, a formal terraced Victorian garden, a partially restored walled garden and historic parkland with breathtaking woodland and lakeside walks. The working stable yard houses the National Trust's carriage collection and offers carriage rides around the gardens.

Location: OS180 Ref. SS611 405. 7m NE of Barnstaple on A39.

Open: 26 Mar - 29 Oct: daily except Sat (open BH weekend Sats), 10.30am - 5pm. Last admission 4pm. Garden, shop, tearoom & bat-cam: 1 Jul - 31 Aug: Daily including Sats, 10.30am - 4.30pm. 1 Nov - Mar 2007: grounds open during daylight hours.

Admission: House, Garden & Carriage Collection: Adult £7, Child £3.50, Family £17.50, 1-Adult family £10.50. Group £6. Garden & Carriage Collection only: Adult £5, Child £2.50. Sats during July & Aug: Adult £2.60, Child £1.30.

Ground floor & grounds. WC. Licensed. Teachers' pack. In grounds & carriage collection, on leads. Tel for details.

ANDERTON HOUSE

Goodleigh, Devon EX32 7NR

Tel: 01628 825925   **www**.landmarktrust.org.uk

Owner: The Landmark Trust

Anderton House is a Grade II* listed building of an exceptional modern design by Peter Aldington of Aldington and Craig. It was commissioned in 1969 as a family home and is highly evocative of its time, retaining the contemporary features and materials. Anderton House is cared for by The Landmark Trust, a building preservation charity who let it for holidays. Full details of Anderton House and 183 other historic and architecturally important buildings are featured in the Landmark Trust Handbook (price £11.00 refundable against a booking).

Location: OS Ref. SS603 343. In village.

Open: Available for holidays for up to 5 people throughout the year. 2 Open Days a year. Contact Landmark Trust for details.

Admission: Free on Open Days.

BAYARD'S COVE FORT

Dartmouth, Devon

Tel: 0117 9750700

Owner: English Heritage   **Contact:** South West Regional Office

Set among the picturesque gabled houses of Dartmouth, on the waterfront at the end of the quay, this is a small artillery fort built 1509 - 10 to defend the harbour entrance.

Location: OS Ref. SX879 510. In Dartmouth, on riverfront 200 yds, S of South ferry.

Open: Any reasonable time, daylight hours.

Admission: Free.

BERRY POMEROY CASTLE

Totnes, Devon TQ9 6NJ

Tel: 01803 866618   **e-mail:** customers@english-heritage.org.uk

www.english-heritage.org.uk/berrypomeroy

Owner: The Duke of Somerset   **Contact:** Visitor Operations Team

A romantic late medieval castle, dramatically sited half-way up a wooded hillside, looking out over a deep ravine and stream. It is unusual in combining the remains of a large castle with a flamboyant courtier's mansion. Reputed to be one of the most haunted castles in the country.

Location: OS202 Ref. SX839 623. 2 1/2 m E of Totnes off A385. Entrance gate 1/2 m NE of Berry Pomeroy village, then 1/2 m drive. Narrow approach, unsuitable for coaches.

Open: 1 Apr - 31 Oct: daily, 10am - 5pm (6pm in Jul & Aug; 4pm in Oct).

Admission: Adult £3.60, Child £1.80, Conc £2.70. 15% discount for groups (11+).

Ground floor & grounds. Not EH. No access for coaches. Tel for details.

BICTON PARK BOTANICAL GARDENS

See page 213 for full page entry.

plant sales
see page 555

BRADLEY MANOR 🌿

Newton Abbot, Devon TQ12 6BN

Tel: 01626 354513   **e-mail:** greenway@nationaltrust.org.uk
www.nationaltrust.org.uk

Owner: The National Trust

A delightful small medieval manor house set in woodland and meadows. Still lived in and managed by the donor family.

Location: OS Ref. SX848 709. On Totnes road A381. 3/4 m SW of Newton Abbot.

Open: 4 Apr - 28 Sept: Tue - Thur, 2 - 5 pm. Oct weekdays by appointment only. Last admission 4.30pm.

Admission: Adult £3.50, Child £1.75, no reduction for groups.

ⓘ No WC. 🅿 From 1.30pm. Not suitable for coaches.

BRANSCOMBE MANOR MILL, THE OLD BAKERY & FORGE 🌿

Branscombe, Seaton, Devon EX12 3DB

Tel: Manor Mill - 01392 881691   Old Bakery - 01297 680333   Forge - 01297 680481
www.nationaltrust.org.uk

Owner: The National Trust   **Contact:** NT Devon Office

Manor Mill, still in working order and recently restored, is a water-powered mill which probably supplied the flour for the bakery. There are regular working demonstrations. The Old Bakery was, until 1987, the last traditional working bakery in Devon. The old baking equipment has been preserved in the baking room and the rest of the building is now a tearoom. Information display in the outbuildings. The Forge opens regularly and ironwork is on sale - please telephone to check opening times.

Location: OS Ref. SY198 887. In Branscombe 1/2 m S off A3052 by steep, narrow lane.

Open: Manor Mill: 2 Apr - 29 Oct: Suns, 2 - 5pm; also Weds in Jul & Aug. The Old Bakery: 31 Mar - 30 Oct, Wed - Sun, 11am - 5pm. The Forge Open all year round.

Admission: Adult £2.50, Child £1.30. Manor Mill only.

BUCKFAST ABBEY

Buckfastleigh, Devon TQ11 0EE

Tel: 01364 645500   **Fax:** 01364 643891   **e-mail:** education@buckfast.org.uk

Owner: Buckfast Abbey Trust   **Contact:** The Warden

Location: OS Ref. SX741 674. 1/2 m from A38 Plymouth - Exeter route.

Open: Church & Grounds: All year: 9am - 7pm.

Admission: Free.

Tiverton Castle.

BUCKLAND ABBEY 🌿

YELVERTON, DEVON PL20 6EY

www.nationaltrust.org.uk

Tel: 01822 853607   **Fax:** 01822 855448   **e-mail:** bucklandabbey@nationaltrust.org.uk

Owner: The National Trust   **Contact:** Michael Coxson - Property Manager

The spirit of Sir Francis Drake is rekindled at his home with exhibitions of his courageous adventures and achievements throughout the world. One of the Trust's most interesting historical buildings and originally a 13th century monastery, the abbey was transformed into a family residence before Sir Francis bought it in 1581. Fascinating decorated plaster ceiling in Tudor Drake Chamber. Outside there are monastic farm buildings, herb garden, craft workshops and country walks. Introductory film presentation. Beautiful new Elizabethan garden now open. Exciting new kiln gallery displays.

Location: OS201 Ref. SX487 667. 6m S of Tavistock; 11m N of Plymouth off A386. Bus: 55/56 from Yelverton (except Sun).

Open: 18 Feb - 24 Mar: Sat & Sun only, 2 - 5pm. 25 Mar - 29 Oct: daily except Thur, 10.30am - 5.30pm (last adm. 4.45pm). Nov: Sat & Sun only, 2 - 5pm. 2 - 17 Dec: Sats & Suns, 11am - 5pm.

Admission: Abbey & Grounds: Adult £7, Child £3.50, Family £17.50, 1-Adult Family £10.50. Group (15+): Adult £5.20, Child £2.60. Grounds only: Adult £3.70, Child £1.80.

ⓘ No photography in house. 🗖 🎦 🎫 ♿ Ground floor & grounds. WC.
🎦 Licensed. 🍴 Licensed. 🖊 By arrangement. 🅿 ❘ 🐕 Guide dogs only. ✳

CADHAY

OTTERY ST MARY, DEVON EX11 1QT

www.cadhay.org.uk

Tel/Fax: 01404 812999

Owner: Mr R Thistlethwayte   **Contact:** Jo Holloway

Cadhay is approached by an avenue of lime-trees, and stands in an extensive garden, with herbaceous borders and yew hedges, with excellent views over the original medieval fish ponds. The main part of the house was built about 1550 by John Haydon who had married the de Cadhay heiress. He retained the Great Hall of an earlier house, of which the fine timber roof (about 1420 - 1460) can be seen. An Elizabethan Long Gallery was added by John's successor at the end of the 16th century, thereby forming a unique courtyard with statues of Sovereigns on each side, described by Sir Simon Jenkins as one of the 'Treasures of Devon'.

Location: OS Ref. SY090 962. 1m NW of Ottery St Mary. From W take A30 and exit at Pattersons Cross, follow signs for Fairmile and then Cadhay. From E, exit at the Iron Bridge and follow signs as above.

Open: May: Fri & BH Sun/Mon. June & July: Fris; August: Fris and BH Sun & Mon: Sept: Fri, 2 - 5.30pm. Last tour 4.30pm.

Admission: Guided tours: Adult £6, Child £2. Gardens: Adults £2, Child £1.

[symbols] Ground floor & grounds. [symbols] Obligatory. [P]
[symbol] Guide dogs only. [symbols]

Arlington Court.

CASTLE DROGO

DREWSTEIGNTON, EXETER EX6 6PB

www.nationaltrust.org.uk

Tel: 01647 433306   **Fax:** 01647 433186   **e-mail:** castledrogo@nationaltrust.org.uk

Owner: The National Trust   **Contact:** Mark Agnew, Property Manager

Extraordinary granite and oak castle, designed by Sir Edwin Lutyens, which combines the comforts of the 20th century with the grandeur of a Baronial castle. Elegant dining and drawing rooms and fascinating kitchen and scullery. Terraced formal garden with colourful herbaceous borders and rose beds. Panoramic views over Dartmoor and delightful walks in the dramatic Teign Gorge.

Location: OS191 Ref. SX721 900. 5m S of A30 Exeter – Okehampton road.

Open: Castle: 4, 5, 11 & 12 Mar, 11am - 4pm. 18 Mar - 5 Nov, daily except Tues, 11am - 5pm (4pm 30 Oct - 5 Nov). Last admission ¹/₂ hr before closing. Garden, Shop & Tearoom: 4, 5, 11 & 12 Mar, 10.30am - 4.30pm. 18 Mar - 5 Nov, daily 10.30am - 5.30pm (4.30pm 30 Oct - 5 Nov) 6 Nov - 17 Dec, Fri - Sun, 11am - 4pm.

Admission: House & Garden: Adult £7, Child £3.50, Family £17.50, 1-Adult Family £10.50. Group: £5.80. Garden only: Adult £4.50, Child £2.50, Group £3.90.

[symbols] 2 rooms in castle & grounds. WCs. [symbols] By arrangement.
[symbol] Guide dogs only in certain areas. [symbol]

CHAMBERCOMBE MANOR
Ilfracombe, Devon EX34 9RJ

Tel: 01271 862624   **www** chambercombemanor.co.uk

Owner: Chambercombe Trust   **Contact:** Angela Powell

Guided tours of Norman Manor House which is mentioned in Domesday Book. Hear the legend of Chambercombe and visit Haunted Room. Set in 16 acres of woodland and landscaped gardens. Lady Jane Tea Rooms offering light lunches and cream teas.

Location: OS Ref. SS539 461. East of Ilfracombe between A399 and B3230, follow brown historic house signs. Private car park at end of Chambercombe Lane.

Open: Easter - end Oct: Mon - Fri, 10.30am - 5pm; Sun, 2 - 5pm. Last tour 4.30pm.

Admission: Adult £5, Child £3, Conc. £3, Family £14.50. Groups (max 50) conc. apply to Manor.

ⅈNo photography in house. ⒼPartial. ▣ Ⓕ Obligatory. ℗Limited for coaches.▣ ⚐On leads, in grounds.

CLOVELLY

See page 214 for full page entry.

COLETON FISHACRE HOUSE & GARDEN ❧
BROWNSTONE ROAD, KINGSWEAR, DARTMOUTH TQ6 0EQ

www.nationaltrust.org.uk

Tel: 01803 752466   **Fax:** 01803 753017   **e-mail:** coletonfishacre@nationaltrust.org.uk

Owner: The National Trust   **Contact:** David Mason, Property Manager

A 9 hectare property set in a stream-fed valley within the spectacular scenery of the South Devon coast. The Lutyensesque style house with art deco-influenced interior was built in the 1920s for Rupert and Lady Dorothy D'Oyly Carte who created the delightful garden, planted with a wide range of rare and exotic plants giving year round interest.

Location: OS202 Ref. SX910 508. 3m E of Kingswear, follow brown tourist signs.

Open: House: 29 Mar - 29 Oct: Weds - Suns & BH Mons, 11am - 4.30pm (last entry at 4pm). Garden & Tearoom: Mar: Sats & Suns only, 11am - 5pm. 29 Mar - 29 Oct: Weds - Suns & BH Mons, 10.30am - 5pm..

Admission: House & Garden: Adult £6.50, Child £3.25. Family £16.25, 1-Adult Family £9.75. Booked groups (15+): Adult £5.75, Child £2.85. Garden only: Adult £5.40, Child £2.70, Booked groups (15+) £4.75.

ⅈNo photography in house. ▣ ▣ ⒼLimited access to grounds. WC. ▣ ℗Limited. Coaches must book. ⚐Assistance dogs only in garden.

Devon Coastline near Hartland Abbey.

©National Trust Photographic Library / N Toyne

COMPTON CASTLE ✤

MARLDON, PAIGNTON TQ3 1TA

www.nationaltrust.org.uk

Tel: 01803 842382 / 01803 875740 (answerphone)

e-mail: greenway@nationaltrust.org.uk

Owner: The National Trust   **Contact:** Carol Martin

Dramatic fortified manor house built by the Gilbert family between the 14th and 16th centuries. It has been the Gilberts' home for most of the last 600 years. Sir Humphrey Gilbert (1539-1583) was coloniser of Newfoundland and half-brother to Sir Walter Raleigh. There is a lovely rose garden and knot garden to complement the interior which includes great hall, solar, spiral staircases, old kitchen and chapel.

Location: OS180 Ref. SX865 648. At Compton, 3m W of Torquay signed at Marldon. Coaches must approach from A381 Totnes Road at Ipplepen.

Open: 3 Apr - 26 Oct: Mons, Weds & Thurs, 10am - 1pm & 2 - 5pm; Last admission 1/2 hr before closing.

Admission: Adult £3.70, Child £1.85, pre-arranged groups £3.20.

🅿 🔲 WC. 🔲 (not NT) Castle Barton 01803 873314. 🔲 By arrangement. 🅿 Outside Castle or in Castle Barton Car Park. Coaches by appointment only.

CULVER HOUSE

LONGDOWN, EXETER, DEVON EX6 7BD

www.culver.biz

Tel: 01392 811885   **Fax:** 01392 811817   **e-mail:** info@culver.biz

Owner/Contact: Charles Eden Esq

Culver was built in 1836, but redesigned by the great Victorian architect, Alfred Waterhouse in a mock Tudor style. The distinctive interior of the house makes it a favoured location for functions and Culver was featured in BBC1's 'Down to Earth' series in 2001. It has also been used by German and American filmcrews.

Location: OS Ref. SX848 901. 5m W of Exeter on B3212.

Open: Not open to the public. Available for corporate hospitality.

Admission: Please telephone for booking details.

🔲

CUSTOM HOUSE

The Quay, Exeter EX2 4AN

Tel: 01392 265169   **Fax:** 01392 265165   **e-mail:** michael.carson@exeter.gov.uk

Owner: Exeter City Council   **Contact:** Michael Carson

The Custom House, located on Exeter's historic Quayside, was constructed from 1680 - 1682. It is the earliest substantial brick building in Exeter and was used by HM Customs and Excise until 1989. The building has an impressive sweeping staircase and spectacular ornamental plaster ceilings.

Location: OS Ref. SX919 921. Exeter's historic Quayside.

Open: 1 Apr - 31 Oct: Guided tour programme, telephone 01392 265203. Other times by prior arrangement with Exeter City Council.

Admission: Free.

🔲 Partial. 🔲 Obligatory. 🔲 🔲 Guide dogs only.

© English - Heritage Photo Library

DARTMOUTH CASTLE ⌗

CASTLE ROAD, DARTMOUTH, DEVON TQ6 0JH

www.english-heritage.org.uk/dartmouth

Tel: 01803 833588   **Fax:** 01803 834445

e-mail: customers@english-heritage.org.uk/visits

Owner: English Heritage   **Contact:** Visitor Operations Team

This brilliantly positioned defensive castle juts out into the narrow entrance to the Dart estuary, with the sea lapping at its foot. When begun in 1480s it was one of the most advanced fortifications in England, and was the first castle designed specifically with artillery in mind. For nearly 500 years it kept its defences up-to-date in preparation for war. Today the castle is in a remarkably good state of repair, along with excellent exhibitions, the history of the castle comes to life. A picnic spot of exceptional beauty.

Location: OS202 Ref. SX887 503. 1m SE of Dartmouth off B3205, narrow approach road.

Open: 1 Apr - 31 Oct: daily, 10am - 5pm (6pm in Jul & Aug; 4pm in Oct). 1 Nov - 31 Mar: Sat & Sun, 10am - 4pm. Closed 24 - 26 Dec & 1 Jan.

Admission: Adult £3.70, Child £1.90, Conc. £2.80. 15% discount for groups (11+).

ℹ WC. 🔲 🔲 🅿 Limited (charged, not EH). 🔲 🔲 🔲 Tel. for details.

© Hartland Abbey

Hartland Abbey.

DOCTON MILL & GARDEN

Spekes Valley, Hartland, Devon EX39 6EA

Tel/Fax: 01237 441369

Owner/Contact: John Borrett

Garden for all seasons in 8 acres of sheltered wooded valley, plus working mill.

Location: OS Ref. SS235 226. 3m Hartland Quay. 15m N of Bude. 3m W of A39, 3m S of Hartland.

Open: 1 Mar - 31 Oct: 10am - 6pm.

Admission: Adult £4, Child (under 16 yrs) Free, OAP £3.75.

DOWNES

Crediton, Devon EX17 3PL

Tel: 01392 439046 **Fax:** 01392 426183

Owner: Trustees of the Downes Estate Settlement   **Contact:** Dianne Shirazian

Downes is a Palladian Mansion dating originally from 1692. As the former home of General Sir Redvers Buller, the house contains a large number of items relating to his military campaigns. The property is now predominantly a family home with elegant rooms hung with family portraits, and a striking main staircase.

Location: OS Ref. SX852 997. Approx 1 m from Crediton town centre.

Open: 17 Apr - 11 July: Mon & Tues & Aug BH Mon & Tues, guided tours, 2.15 & 3.30pm. Open to groups (15+) between Easter & 21 June by arrangement.

Admission: Adult £4.50, Child (5-16yrs) £2, Child (under 5yrs) Free, Group (15+) £4.

THE ELIZABETHAN GARDENS

Plymouth Barbican Assoc. Ltd, New St, The Barbican, Plymouth

Tel/Fax: 01822 611027/612983   **Email:** amza36@dial.pipex.com

Owner: Plymouth Barbican Association Limited   **Contact:** Tony Golding Esq

Very small series of four enclosed gardens laid out in Elizabethan style in 1970.

Location: OS Ref. SX477 544. 3 mins walk from Dartington Glass (a landmark building) on the Barbican.

Open: Mon - Sat, 9am - 5pm. Closed Christmas.

Admission: Free.

ESCOT HISTORIC GARDENS, MAZE & FANTASY WOODLAND

ESCOT, OTTERY ST MARY, DEVON EX11 1LU

www.escot-devon.co.uk

Tel: 01404 822188 **Fax:** 01404 822903 **e-mail:** info@escot-devon.co.uk

Owner/Contact: Mr J-M Kennaway

House: an idyllic setting for weddings, conferences and product launches. Gardens: 25 acres of gardens set within 220 acres of 'Capability' Brown parkland, featuring a new 4,000 beech-tree maze, otters, wild boar, birds of prey displays in spring and summer, and including highly innovative recent garden design work by Ivan Hicks, the acclaimed gardener-artist. Estate: 1200 privately owned acres of glorious East Devon – ideal as a film location, for musical festivals and other special events.

Location: OS Ref. SY080 977 (gate). 9m E of Exeter on A30 at Fairmile.

Open: Gardens, Aquatic Centre, Restaurant & House of Marbles Gift Shop: open throughout the year as follows: Easter - 31 Oct: daily, 10am - 6pm. 1 Nov - Easter: daily, 10am - 5pm except 25, 26 Dec.

Admission: Adult £5.50, Child £4, Child (under 3yrs) Free, OAP £4, Family (2+2) £16.50. Booked groups (10+): Adult £5, Child/Conc. £3.50. Reduced rates apply in winter months.

⬚ 👶 🚆 🅃 ♿ Partial. ⬛ Licensed. 🍴 Licensed. 🎦 By arrangement. ⬛ 🅿
🐕 In grounds, on leads. ⬛ ❋ 📺 Tel for details.

EXETER CATHEDRAL

Exeter, Devon EX1 1HS

Tel: 01392 285983 (Visitors' Officer) **Fax:** 01392 285986

e-mail: visitors@exeter-cathedral.org.uk

Owner: Dean & Chapter of Exeter   **Contact:** Visitors' Officer

Fine example of decorated gothic architecture. Longest unbroken stretch of gothic vaulting in the world.

Location: OS Ref. SX921 925. Central to the City - between High Street and Southernhay. Groups may be set down in South Street.

Open: All year: Mon - Fri 9.30am - 6.30pm, Sats, 9am - 5pm, Suns, 7.30am - 6.30pm.

Admission: Donation requested of £3.50 per person. Charges apply to groups.

FINCH FOUNDRY ✂

Sticklepath, Okehampton, Devon EX20 2NW

Tel: 01837 840046

Owner: The National Trust

19th-century water-powered forge, which produced agricultural and mining hand tools, holding regular demonstrations throughout the day.

Location: OS Ref. SX641 940. 4m E of Okehampton off the A30.

Open: 25 Mar - 30 Oct: Daily except Tue, 11am - 5.30pm.

Admission: Adult £3.70, Child £1.85.

⬚ ⬛ 🅿 Not suitable for coaches. ⬛ 🐕 Except tearoom.

FURSDON HOUSE 🏠

Cadbury, Nr Thorverton, Exeter, Devon EX5 5JS

Tel: 01392 860860 **Fax:** 01392 860126 **e-mail:** enquiries@fursdon.co.uk

www.fursdon.co.uk

Owner: E D Fursdon Esq   **Contact:** Mrs C Fursdon

The Fursdons have lived here since the 13th century and the house, which was greatly modified in the 18th century, is at the heart of a small farming estate within a wooded and hilly landscape. Family memorabilia is displayed including a letter to Grace Fursdon from King Charles during the Civil War and there are fine examples of costume and textiles. The garden to the south flows naturally into the parkland beyond; to the west it slopes up to a walled and terraced area with mixed borders, roses and herbs. There are two private wings of the house for self catering holiday accommodation.

Location: OS Ref. SS922 046. 1¹/₂ m S of A3072 between Tiverton & Crediton, 9m N of Exeter turning off A396 to Thorverton. Narrow lanes!

Open: 15 - 21 Apr, 29 Apr - 6 May, 27 May - 3 June & 26 Aug - 1 Sept. Guided tours at 2.30 & 3.30pm. Groups by prior arrangement only.

Admission: Adult £4.50, Child (10-16yrs) £2 (under 10yrs Free).

ℹ Conferences. No photography or video. 🅃 ♿ Partial. 🎦 Obligatory. 🅿
🐕 Guide dogs only. ⬛ Self-catering.

THE GARDEN HOUSE

Buckland Monachorum, Yelverton, Devon PL20 7LQ

Tel: 01822 854769 **Fax:** 01822 855358 **e-mail:** office@thegardenhouse.org.uk

www.thegardenhouse.org.uk

Owner: Fortescue Garden Trust   **Contact:** Julie Beesley

'Is this the best garden in Britain?' *Sunday Express*: eight acres offer year-round colour and interest centred on an enchanting walled garden surrounding the romantic ruins of a 16th century vicarage. Modern garden planted in naturalistic style. Over 6,000 varieties feature in an idyllic valley on the edge of Dartmoor. *'You'd be mad to miss it'* – Alan Titchmarsh.

Location: OS Ref. SX490 682. Signposted W off A386 Plymouth - Tavistock Road, 10m N of Plymouth.

Open: 1 Mar - 31 Oct: daily, 10.30am - 5pm. Last admission 4.30pm.

Admission: Adult £5, Child (5-16) £1, Seniors £4.50, pre-booked groups (10+) £4. Prices subject to change.

👶 ♿ Partial. ⬛ 🎦 🅿 🐕 Guide dogs only.

©National Trust Photographic Library/Hugh Palmer

© Tony Mauley

GREENWAY ⚓

GREENWAY ROAD, GALMPTON, CHURSTON FERRERS, DEVON TQ5 0ES

www.nationaltrust.org.uk

Tel: 01803 842382 **Greenway Quay Ferry Services:** 01803 844010
Riverlink ferry: 01803 834488 **email:** greenway@nationaltrust.org.uk

Owner: The National Trust **Contact:** Carol Martin

A glorious woodland garden, held on the edge of wildness and set on the banks of the River Dart; Greenway is one of Devon's best kept secrets. Renowned for rare half-hardy trees and shrubs and underplanted with native wild flowers, this peaceful haven has magnificent views and some challenging paths. Travel by river ferry from Dartmouth or Totnes for a perfect day out.

Location: OS Ref. SX876 548.

Open: 1 Mar - 7 Oct: Wed - Sat, 10.30am - 5pm (last admission 4.30pm)

Admission: Booked groups & visitors arriving on foot or by ferry: Adult £4.25, Child £2. Others (by car): Adult £5, Child £2.50.

⬚ 🚻 🔽 ♿Partial. WC. ☕Licensed. 🍴Licensed. 🎫By arrangement.
🅿1 midi size coach only. Groups must book. Please use river travel.
🐕Tel for details.

HARTLAND ABBEY 🏛

HARTLAND, BIDEFORD, DEVON EX39 6DT

www.hartlandabbey.com

Tel: 01237 441264/234 or 01884 860225 **Fax:** 01237 441264/01884 861134

Owner: Sir Hugh Stucley Bt **Contact:** The Administrator

Founded as an Augustinian Monastery in 1157 in a beautiful valley only 1 mile's walk to a spectacular Atlantic Cove, the Abbey was given by Henry VIII in 1539 to the Sergeant of his Wine Cellar, whose descendants live here today. Remodelled in the 18th & 19th century, it contains spectacular architecture and murals. Important paintings, furniture, porcelain collected over generations. Documents from 1160. Victorian and Edwardian photographs. Museum. Dairy. Recently discovered Victorian fernery and paths by Jekyll. Extensive woodland gardens of camellias, rhododendrons etc. Bog Garden. 18th century Walled gardens of vegetables, summer borders, tender and rare plants including echium pininana. Peacocks, donkeys and Welsh Mountain sheep in the park. Monks' Pond & newly restored Gazebo overlooking sea. Film location for 'Shell Seekers' in 2005.

Location: OS Ref. SS240 249. 15m W of Bideford, 15m N of Bude off A39 between Hartland and Hartland Quay.

Open: 2 Apr - 1 Oct: Wed, Thur, Sun & BHs, plus Tues in Jul & Aug, 2 - 5.30pm. Gardens: 2 Apr - 1 Oct: daily except Sats, 2 - 5.30pm.

Admission: House, Gardens & Grounds: Adult £7.50, Child (9-15ys) £1.50, OAP £6.50. Groups (20+): Adult £6, Child £1.50. Gardens & Grounds: Adult £4, Child 50p, OAP £4.

⬚ 🚻 🔽Wedding receptions. ♿ Partial. WC. ☕ Cream teas. 🎫By arrangement.
🅿 🐕In grounds, on leads.

HALDON BELVEDERE/LAWRENCE CASTLE

Higher Ashton, Nr Dunchideock, Exeter, Devon EX6 7QY

Tel/Fax: 01392 833668 **e-mail:** turner@haldonbelvedere.co.uk
www.haldonbelvedere.co.uk

Owner: Devon Historic Building Trust **Contact:** Ian Turner

18th century Grade II* listed triangular tower with circular turrets on each corner. Built in memory of Major General Stringer Lawrence, founder of the Indian Army. Restored in 1995 to illustrate the magnificence of its fine plasterwork, gothic windows, mahogany flooring and marble fireplaces. Breathtaking views of the surrounding Devon countryside.

Location: OS Ref. SX875 861. 7m SW of Exeter. Exit A38 at Exeter racecourse for 2^1/$_2$m.

Open: Feb - Oct: Suns & BHs, 1.30 - 5.30pm.

Admission: Adult £2, Child Free.

🔽 ♿Unsuitable. 🎫By arrangement. 🅿 🚌 🐕In grounds, on leads. 📷 🏛

HEMERDON HOUSE 🏛

Sparkwell, Plympton, Plymouth, Devon PL7 5BZ

Tel: Business hours 01822 610111; other times 01752 337350 **Fax:** 01752 331477
e-mail: jim.woollcombe@btopenworld.com

Owner: J H G Woollcombe Esq **Contact:** Joseph E Hess

Late 18th century family house, rich in local history.

Location: OS Ref. SX564 575. 3m E of Plympton off A38.

Open: 1 - 17 & 25 - 29 May; 19 - 22 & 28 - 31 Aug: 2 - 5.30pm. Last admission 5pm. Provisional dates, please telephone to confirm.

Admission: £4.50.

♿ Ground floor. 🎫Obligatory. 🅿

HEMYOCK CASTLE

Hemyock, Cullompton, Devon EX15 3RJ

Tel: 01823 680745

Owner/Contact: Mrs Sheppard

Former medieval moated castle, displays show site's history as fortified manor house, castle and farm.

Location: OS Ref. ST135 134. M5/J26, Wellington then 5m S over the Blackdown Hills.

Open: BH Mons 2 - 5pm. Other times by appointment. Groups and private parties welcome.

Admission: Adult £1, Child 50p. Group rates available.

HOUND TOR DESERTED MEDIEVAL VILLAGE ⚏

Ashburton Road, Manaton, Dartmoor, Devon

Tel: 01626 832093

Owner: English Heritage **Contact:** Dartmoor National Park Authority

The remains of four bronze age to medieval dwellings.

Location: OS191 Ref. SX746 788. 1^1/$_2$ m S of Manaton off Ashburton road. 6m N of Ashburton.

Open: Any reasonable time, daylight only.

Admission: Free.

🅿 🐕 ✳

Bicton Park Botanical Gardens.

© NTPL/Chris Vile Photography

© NTPL/Chris Vile Photography

KILLERTON HOUSE & GARDEN
BROADCLYST, EXETER EX5 3LE
www.nationaltrust.org.uk

Tel: 01392 881345 **e-mail:** killerton@nationaltrust.org.uk
Owner: The National Trust **Contact:** Denise Melhuish - Assistant Property Manager
The spectacular hillside garden is beautiful throughout the year with spring flowering bulbs and shrubs, colourful herbaceous borders and fine trees. The garden is surrounded by parkland and woods offering lovely walks. The house is furnished as a family home and includes a costume collection dating from the 18th century in a series of period rooms and a Victorian laundry. New costume exhibition for 2006 'Shall we Dance?' – frothy dance dresses, glittering evening clothes and gorgeous accessories from the Killerton costume collection.

Location: OS Ref. SS977 001. Off Exeter – Cullompton Rd (B3181). M5 N'bound J30, M5 S'bound J28.

Open: House: 15 Mar - 29 Oct: daily except Tue (Oct also closed Mon); Aug: daily, 11am - 5pm. Last entry 1/2 hour before closing. Garden: All year: daily, 10.30am - dusk.

Admission: House & Garden: Adult £7, Child £3.50, Family £17.50, 1-Adult Family £10.50. Group £5.80. Garden only: Adult £5.30, Child £2.65.

⬜ 🏵 📶 💻 ♿ 🍴 🅿 🐕 Guide dogs only in house. 🎦 Tel for details.

NTPL / Chris Vile

NTPL / Stephen Robson

KNIGHTSHAYES COURT
BOLHAM, TIVERTON, DEVON EX16 7RQ
www.nationaltrust.org.uk

Tel: 01884 254665 **Fax:** 01884 243050 **e-mail:** knightshayes@nationaltrust.org.uk
Owner: The National Trust **Contact:** Penny Woollams – Property Manager
The striking Victorian gothic house is a rare survival of the work of William Burges with ornate patterns in many rooms. One of the finest gardens in Devon, mainly woodland and shrubs with something of interest throughout the seasons. Drifts of spring bulbs, summer flowering shrubs, pool garden and amusing animal topiary.
Location: OS Ref. SS960 151. 2m N of Tiverton (A396) at Bolham.

Open: House: 25 Mar - 31 Oct, daily except Fri (open Good Fri), 11am - 5pm. Last adm. 1/2 hr before closing. Garden, shop/plant centre & restaurant: 4 - 20 Mar: Sat - Mon, 11am - 4pm; 25 Mar - 31 Oct: daily, 11am - 5pm. Shop & Restaurant also open Nov & Dec, tel. for details.

Admission: House & Garden: Adult £7, Child £3.50, Family £17.50, 1-Adult Family £10.50. Group £8. Garden only: Adult £5.50, Child £2.80, Group £4.60/£2.30.

⬜ 🏵 📶 ♿ Ground floor & grounds. WC. 🍴 🐕 On leads in park.

LOUGHWOOD MEETING HOUSE

Dalwood, Axminster, Devon EX13 7DU

Tel: 01392 881691 **Fax:** 01392 881954

Owner: The National Trust   **Contact:** National Trust Devon Office

Around 1653 the Baptist congregation of the nearby village of Kilmington constructed this simple thatched building dug into the hillside. It still contains the original box pews.

Location: OS Ref. SY253993. 4m W of Axminster.

Open: All year, daily.

Admission: Free

ℹ️ Pushchairs and baby carriers admitted.

♿ Steep slope from the car park. Ground floor only.

🅿️ Very narrow country lanes. No parking for coaches. ✳️

LYDFORD CASTLE & SAXON TOWN ♯

Lydford, Okehampton, Devon

Tel: 01822 820320

Owner: English Heritage   **Contact:** The National Trust

Standing above the lovely gorge of the River Lyd, this 12th century tower was notorious as a prison. The earthworks of the original Norman fort are to the south. A Saxon town once stood nearby and its layout is still discernible.

Location. OS191 Castle Ref. SX510 848, Fort Ref. SX509 847. In Lydford off A386 8m SW of Okehampton.

Open: Any reasonable time, daylight hours.

Admission: Free.

🅿️ ♿ ✳️

MARKER'S COTTAGE

Broadclyst, Exeter, Devon EX5 3HR

Tel: 01392 461546

Owner: The National Trust   **Contact:** The Custodian

Thatched, medieval cob house containing a cross-passage screen decorated with a painting of St Andrew and his attributes.

Location: OS Ref. SX985 973. 1/4 E of B3181 in village of Broadclyst.

Open: 2 Apr - 29 Oct: Sun - Tue, 2 - 5pm. Last entry 1/2 hour before closing.

Admission: Adult £2.50, Child £1.25. Joint ticket with Clyston Mill: Adult £4, Child £2.

MARWOOD HILL

Barnstaple, Devon EX31 4EB

Tel: 01271 342528   **Contact:** Patricia Stout

20 acre garden with 3 small lakes. Extensive collection of camellias, bog garden. National collection of astilbes.

Location: OS Ref. SS545 375. 4m N of Barnstaple. 1/2 m W of B3230. Signs off A361 Barnstaple - Braunton road.

Open: All year: 10am - 5pm.

Admission: Adult £4, Child (under 12yrs) Free.

MORWELLHAM QUAY

Morwellham, Tavistock, Devon PL19 8JL

Tel: 01822 832766 **Fax:** 01822 833808

Owner: The Morwellham & Tamar Valley Trust   **Contact:** Anthony Power

Award-winning visitor centre at historic river port.

Location: OS Ref. SX446 697. Off A390 about 15 mins drive from Tavistock, Devon. 5m SW of Tavistock. 3m S of A390 at Gulworthy.

Open: Summer: daily, 10am - 5.30pm, last adm. 3.30pm. Winter: daily, 10am - 4.30pm, last adm. 2.30pm.

Admission: Adult £8.90, Child £6, OAP £7.80, Family (2+2) £26. Group rate please apply for details. Usual concessions. Prices may be subject to change.

OKEHAMPTON CASTLE ♯

Okehampton, Devon EX20 1JB

Tel: 01837 52844 **e-mail:** customers@english-heritage.org.uk

www.english-heritage.org.uk/okehampton

Owner: English Heritage   **Contact:** Visitor Operations Team

The ruins of the largest castle in Devon stand above a river surrounded by splendid woodland. There is still plenty to see, including the Norman motte and the jagged remains of the Keep. There is a picnic area and lovely woodland walks.

Location: OS Ref. SX584 942. 1m SW of Okehampton town centre off A30 bypass.

Open: 1 Apr - 30 Sept: daily, 10am - 5pm (6pm in July & Aug).

Admission: Adult £3, Child £1.50, Conc. £2.30. 15% discount for groups (11+).

📷 ♿ Access difficult for ambulant disabilities. Grounds. WC. 🎧 🅿️

🐕 In grounds, on leads. 🛡️ Tel. for details.

OLDWAY MANSION

Paignton, Devon

Tel: 01803 208979 **Fax:** 01803 207670

Owner: Torbay Council   **Contact:** Facilities Management Officer - Stuart Left

Built by sewing machine entrepreneur I M Singer in the 1870s.

Location: OS Ref. SX888 615. Off W side of A3022.

Open: All year: Mon - Sat, 9am - 5pm (except Christmas & New Year). Easter - Oct: Suns, 2 - 5pm. Visitors should note that not all rooms will always be open, access depends on other activities.

Admission: Free.

NTPL / Tony Murdoch

OVERBECK'S

SHARPITOR, SALCOMBE, SOUTH DEVON TQ8 8LW

www.nationaltrust.org.uk

Tel: 01548 842893 **e-mail:** overbecks@nationaltrust.org.uk

Owner: The National Trust   **Contact:** Property Manager

Elegant Edwardian house with diverse collections and luxuriant garden. The scientist Otto Overbeck lived here from 1928 to 1937 and the museum containing his collections of curios and nautical artefacts has an intimate atmosphere. Some of Overbeck's inventions are on show, including the intriguing 'rejuvenator' machine. The house is set in 2 3/4ha (7acres) of beautiful exotic gardens with spectacular views over the Salcombe estuary. It enjoys a sheltered microclimate and so is home to many rare plants. There is also a secret room for children with dolls, tin soldiers, other toys and a ghost hunt.

Location: OS Ref. SX728 374. 1 1/2 m SW of Salcombe. Signposted from Salcombe (single track lanes).

Open: Museum: 26 Mar - 16 July & 28 Aug - 29 Sept, Sun - Fri & Easter Sat, 11am - 5.30pm. 17 Jul - 27 August: daily, 11am - 5.30pm. 1 - 26 Oct: Sun - Thur, 11am - 4.30pm. Garden: All year: daily, 10am - 6pm.

Admission: Museum & Garden: Adult £5.50, Child £2.25, Family £13.75, 1-Adult Family £8.25. Garden only: Adult £5, Child £2.50.

ℹ️ No photography in house. 📷 ♿ Partial. 🛍️ 🎭 By arrangement.

🅿️ Limited. Charge refunded on admission. ▪️ 🐕 ✳️

POWDERHAM CASTLE ▥   *See page 215 for full page entry.*

special events
see page 571

PUSLINCH

YEALMPTON, PLYMOUTH, DEVON PL8 2NN

Tel: 01752 880555 **Fax:** 01752 880909

Owner/Contact: Sebastian Fenwick

A perfect example of a medium sized early Georgian house in the Queen Anne tradition with fine contemporary interiors. Built in 1720 by the Yonge family.

Location: OS Ref. SX570 509. Yealmpton.

Open: Groups only (min charge £30). All year, except Christmas & Boxing Day, by prior appointment only.

Admission: Adult £8.

ℹ️No photography. 🎦Obligatory. 🅿️ ✖️ ✳️

RHS GARDEN ROSEMOOR

GREAT TORRINGTON, DEVON EX38 8PH

www.rhs.org.uk/rosemoor

Tel: 01805 624067 **Fax:** 01805 624717 **e-mail:** rosemooradmin@rhs.org.uk

Owner/Contact: The Royal Horticultural Society

A beautiful garden mixing new gardens with Lady Anne's original garden. Something for all interests and tastes whatever the season, from formal gardens to a lake and Arboretum. The Rosemoor Plant Centre stocks a variety of hardy plants, the shop has books and gifts and, for refreshments, there is a café and restaurant.

Location: OS Ref. SS500 183. 1m S of Great Torrington on A3124.

Open: All year except Christmas Day; Apr - Sept: 10am - 6pm. Oct - Mar: 10am - 5pm.

Admission: Adult £5.50, Child (6 - 16yrs) £1.50, Child (under 6yrs) Free. Groups (10+) £4.50. Companion for disabled visitor Free. RHS member & 1 guest Free.

🖼️ ♿ ⬇️ 🍽️ 🍴Licensed. 🎦By arrangement. 🅿️ 🐕‍🦺Guide dogs only. ✳️ ⬛

©NTPL/Rupert Truman

©NTPL/Joe Cornish

SALTRAM ✿

PLYMPTON, PLYMOUTH, DEVON PL7 1JH

www.nationaltrust.org.uk

Tel: 01752 333500 **Fax:** 01752 336474 **e-mail:** saltram@nationaltrust.org.uk

Owner: The National Trust   **Contact:** Carol Murrin

Saltram stands high above the River Plym in a rolling and wooded landscaped park that now provides precious green space on the outskirts of Plymouth. The house, with its magnificent decoration and original contents, was largely created between the 1740s and 1820s by three generations of the Parker family. It features some of Robert Adam's finest rooms, exquisite plasterwork ceilings, original Chinese wallpapers and an exceptional collection of paintings including many by Sir Joshua Reynolds and Angelica Kauffman. The garden is predominantly 19th-century and contains an orangery and several follies, as well as beautiful shrubberies and imposing specimen trees.

The shop and art gallery offer work for sale from contemporary local artists, and National Trust gifts. The Park Restaurant offers refreshments for its visitors. Corporate business and special functions are very welcome.

Location: OS Ref. SX520 557. From A38, exit 3 miles north of Plymouth City Centre at Marsh Mill's roundabout. Take Plympton exit; continue in right hand lane to third set of traffic lights then turn right onto Cott Hill. At the top of the hill turn right into Merafield Road then right again after 200 yards..

Open: House: 25 Mar - 29 Oct: daily except Fris (open Good Fri), 12 noon - 4.30pm. Garden: Jan - 21 Dec: daily except Fri (open Good Fri), 11am - 4.30pm (4pm Nov - Mar). Gallery: 1 Mar - 21 Dec: daily except Fri (open Good Fri), 11am - 4.30pm (4pm Nov & Dec). Shop: 1 Mar - 21 Dec: daily except Fri, 11am - 5pm (4pm Nov & Dec). Restaurant: 1 Mar - 29 Oct: daily 11am - 5pm. 30 Oct - 21 Dec: daily (except Fri) 11am - 4pm. For details of all out-of-season opening times, please telephone.

Admission: House & Garden: Adult £8, Child £4, Family £20, 1-Adult Family £12. Groups (15+): £6.50. Garden only: Adult £4, Child £2.

🖼️ ♿ ⬇️ ♿WC. Braille guide. 🍽️ 🍴Licensed. 🎦 🐾 🅿️

🐕‍🦺On signed perimeter paths only, on leads. Guide dogs only in house & garden.

✳️ ⬛ Tel. for details.

SAND 🏛

SIDBURY, SIDMOUTH EX10 0QN

www.eastdevon.net/sand

Tel: 01395 597230   **e-mail:** sand@eastdevon.net

Contact: Mrs Stella Huyshe-Shires

Sand is one of East Devon's hidden gems. The beautiful valley garden extends to 6 acres and is the setting for the lived-in house, the 15th century Hall House, and the 17th century Summer House. The family, under whose unbroken ownership the property has remained since 1560, provide guided house tours.

Location: OS Ref. SY146 925. Well signed, 250 yards off A375 between Honiton and Sidmouth.

Open: House: BH Suns & Mons, 16/17 Apr, 30 Apr/1 May, 28/29 May & 27/28 Aug: 2 - 6pm. Garden: 2 Apr - 26 Sept: Sun - Tues. Last admission to house & garden: 5pm. Groups by appointment throughout the year.

Admission: House & Garden: Adult £5, Child/Student £1. Garden only: Adult £3, accompanied Child (under 16) Free.

ℹ️ No photography in house. 🅐 Partial. 🖥 ✘ Obligatory. 🅿 ◼
🐕 In grounds, on leads. ✳ 📺 Tel. for details.

TIVERTON CASTLE 🏛

TIVERTON, DEVON EX16 6RP

www.tivertoncastle.com

Tel: 01884 253200/255200   **Fax:** 01884 254200   **e-mail:** tiverton.castle@ukf.net

Owner: Mr and Mrs A K Gordon   **Contact:** Mrs A Gordon

Celebrating 900 years since original construction, few buildings evoke such immediate feelings of history. Inside it looks like a fairytale castle, with romantic ruins, Norman towers and gatehouse, and later additions. Beautiful walled gardens, including working kitchen garden. Civil War Armoury – try some on – interesting furniture, pictures. Superb holiday apartments.

Location: OS Ref. SS954 130. Just N of Tiverton town centre.

Open: Easter - end Oct: Sun, Thur, BH Mon, 2.30 - 5.30pm. Last admission 5pm. Open to groups (12+) by prior arrangement at any time.

Admission: Adult £4, Child (7-16yrs) £2, Child under 7 Free. Garden only: £1.50.

🖸 🅐 Partial. ✘ By arrangement. 🅿 🐕 📺 4 Apartments. ✳

SHOBROOKE PARK

Crediton, Devon EX17 1DG

Tel: 01363 775153   **Fax:** 01363 775153   **e-mail:** admin@shobrookepark.com

Owner: Dr J R Shelley   **Contact:** Clare Shelley

A classical English 180-acre park. The lime avenue dates from about 1800 and the cascade of four lakes was completed in the 1840s. Millennium amphitheatre built in the year 2000. The southern third of the Park is open to the public under the Countryside Commission Access Scheme. The 15 acre garden, created c1845 with Portland stone terraces, roses and rhododendrons is being restored.

Location: OS Ref. SS848 010. 1m E of Crediton. Access to park by kissing gate at SW end of park, just S of A3072. Garden access on A3072.

Open: South Park: daylight hours. Gardens: 22 Apr, 6 May & 17 Jun, 2 - 5pm.

Admission: Park: No charge. Gardens: NGS £3, accompanied child under 14 Free.
🐕 Guide dogs only in garden. Dogs welcome in the park. ✳

SHUTE BARTON 🌿

Shute, Axminster, Devon EX13 7PT

Tel: 01297 34692 (tenant)   **www.**nationaltrust.org.uk

Owner: The National Trust

One of the most important surviving non-fortified manor houses of the Middle Ages.

Location: OS Ref. SY253 974. 3m SW of Axminster, 2m N of Colyton, 1m S of A35.

Open: 1 Apr - 30 Sept: Weds & Sats, 2 - 5.30pm. Last admission 5pm. 4 - 28 Oct: Weds & Sats, 2 - 5pm. Last admission 4.30pm.

Admission: Adult £2.50, Child £1.30. No group reductions.

TAPELEY PARK & GARDENS

Instow, Bideford, Devon EX39 4NT

Tel: 01271 342558   **Fax:** 01271 342371

Owner: Tapeley Park Trust

Extensive gardens and park.

Location: OS Ref. SS478 291. Between Bideford and Barnstaple near Instow. Follow brown tourist signs from the A39 onto B3233.

Open: Good Fri - end Oct: daily except Sats, 10am - 5pm.

Admission: Adult £4, Child £2.50, OAP £3.50. Groups (5+): Adult £3.20, Child £2 (under 5s Free), OAP £2.80.

TOTNES CASTLE ⌗

Castle Street, Totnes, Devon TQ9 5NU

Tel/Fax: 01803 864406   **e-mail:** customers@english-heritage.org.uk

www.english-heritage.org.uk/totnes

Owner: English Heritage   **Contact:** Visitor Operations Team

By the North Gate of the hill town of Totnes you will find a superb motte and bailey castle, with splendid views across the roof tops and down to the River Dart. It is a symbol of lordly feudal life and a fine example of Norman fortification.

Location: OS202 Ref. SX800 605. In Totnes, on hill overlooking the town. Access in Castle St off W end of High St.

Open: 1 Apr - 31 Oct: daily 10am - 5pm (6pm in Jul & Aug; 4pm in Oct).

Admission: Adult £2.40, Child £1.20, Conc. £1.80. 15% discount for groups (11+).
🖸 🅐 Unsuitable. 🅿 Charged parking 64 metres (70 yds). 🐕 In grounds, on leads.
📺 Tel. for details.

education index
see page 564

Knightshayes Court, Devon.
©National Trust Photographic Library/Stephen Robson

MAP 2

Owner:
Patrick Cooke Esq

▶ **CONTACT**

Owen Davies /
Tracy Winder
Athelhampton House
Dorchester   DT2 7LG

Tel: 01305 848363
Fax: 01305 848135

e-mail: enquiry@
athelhampton.co.uk

▶ **LOCATION**

OS Ref. SY771 942

Off A35 (T) at
Puddletown
Northbrook junction,
5m E of Dorchester.

Rail: Dorchester.

ATHELHAMPTON 🏛
HOUSE & GARDENS

www.athelhampton.co.uk

Athelhampton is one of the finest 15th century manor houses and is surrounded by one of the great architectural gardens of England. The Great Hall was built by Sir William Martyn in 1485. The West wing is Elizabethan in period and contains the Great Chamber, Library and Wine Cellar. Athelhampton houses a fine collection of English furniture starting in the Jacobean period leading on to late Victorian. There is also a collection relating to A W Pugin and The Palace of Westminster. New for 2006: Gallery in the West Wing showing works by the Russian artist Marevna who lived at Athelhampton during the 1940s and 50s.

The glorious Grade I gardens, dating from 1891, contain the world-famous topiary pyramids, fountains and the River Piddle. Collections of tulips, magnolias, roses, clematis and lilies can be seen in season. Located in the gardens are a number of small buildings each with their own unique history. The two garden pavilions were used as water towers for the original fountain system. The Toll house was a collection point for the Wimborne turnpike trust between 1842 and 1878 and has now been restored along with its garden. The dovecote is one of the earliest in Dorset and with a capacity for 1200 birds would have supported a large household.

The Coach House contains all the facilities required for the comfort of daily visitors with private rooms available for visiting groups. The House and Gardens can be opened by appointment for evening visits and dinners. Fridays and Saturdays are available for wedding ceremonies and/or receptions.

▶ **OPENING TIMES**

March - October:
Daily (except Fri & Sat).

November - February:
Sun only.

10.30am - 5pm/dusk.
Last admission 4.30pm.

Coach House Restaurant
open as house & gardens.
Carvery on Suns.
Please book.

All facilities at Athelhampton are available for private hire outside our normal opening hours. We specialise in weddings on Fridays and Saturdays and dinners on any evening. Please contact Owen Davies, Manager.

Self catering cottage in the grounds – see website or telephone for details.

▶ **ADMISSION**

House & Gardens

Adult	£8.00
Child	Free
Conc.	£5.00
OAP	£7.50
Groups (12+)	
Adult	£6.00*

*£5.00 with pre-booked catering order.

CONFERENCE/FUNCTION

ROOM	SIZE	MAX CAPACITY
Coach House* Long Hall	13 x 6m	100
Conservatory*	16 x 11m	130
Main House* Great Hall	12 x 8m	70
Great* Chamber	10 x 6m	40
Garden Pavilions (2)	3 x 3m	6

*Licensed for Civil wedding ceremonies.

Great Hall

🏠 ❋ 🍸 By arrangement.
♿ Partial. WC.

🍽 Licensed. 🍴 Licensed.
🚶 By arrangement. **P** 🏠 🖼

🦌 Guide dogs only.

🖼 🔔 ❄

🎭 **SPECIAL EVENTS**

11 & 12 Feb
Antique carpet exhibition.

7 May
NCCPG Plant Sale.

11 - 15 June
Flower Festival.

11 July
Open Air Theatre.

BH Monday 28 August
Villiage Fête.

South West - England

MAP 2

FORDE ABBEY & GARDENS
www.fordeabbey.co.uk

Owner:
Mark Roper Esq

▶ **CONTACT**

Carolyn Clay
Forde Abbey
Chard
Somerset TA20 4LU

Tel: 01460 220231
e-mail:
info@fordeabbey.co.uk

▶ **LOCATION**
OS Ref. ST358 041

Just off the B3167
4m SE of Chard.

The magnificent Forde Abbey is set in spectacular gardens and grounds on the banks of the River Axe. The unspoilt rolling hills provide an unrivalled setting for this truly historic house.

Founded in 1140, Forde over the next 400 years became one of the most learned and wealthy monasteries in the land. Built of deep golden hamstone, the building survived the Dissolution and has evolved over the years into a beautiful country house of immense character and charm.

The house contains a collection of elaborately decorated plaster ceilings, exquisite pictures and fine furniture. In the Grand Saloon are some spectacular tapestries, woven from cartoons painted for the Sistine Chapel in Rome by Raphael, depicting scenes from the lives of St Peter and St Paul.

The 30 acres of world-famous gardens that surround the house date from the early 18th century, although much of the garden has been developed by the present occupiers. Highlights of the garden include: spectacular carpets of springtime bulbs, a magnificent Bog Garden, a unique living Beech House, sensational summer borders, a large working kitchen garden and the remarkable Centenary Fountain – the highest powered fountain in England. The garden has been described by Alan Titchmarsh as *"one of the greatest gardens of the West Country"*.

The Undercroft Restaurant serving morning coffee, lunches and cream teas, (using ingredients from the garden, estate, and local suppliers), together with the unique gift shop, plant centre, and pottery exhibition will complete a perfect day out.

▶ **OPENING TIMES**
House
2 April - 31 October
Tue - Fri, Sun & BH Mons
12 noon - 4pm.

Gardens
Daily all year:
10am - 4.30pm.

▶ **ADMISSION**
For current admission prices phone 01460 221290.

Available for wedding receptions. No photography in house.

Partial.

Licensed.

Licensed.

By arrangement.

On leads, in grounds.

Rupert Truman

MAP 3

KINGSTON LACY 🌿

www.nationaltrust.org.uk

Owner:
The National Trust

▶ **CONTACT**

The Property Manager
Kingston Lacy
Wimborne Minster
Dorset BH21 4EA

Tel: 01202 883402 /
842913 (Sat & Sun
11am - 5pm)

Infoline: 01202 880413
Fax: 01202 882402

Restaurant:
01202 889242

e-mail: kingstonlacy@
nationaltrust.org.uk

▶ **LOCATION**
OS Ref. ST980 019

On B3082 - Blandford /
Wimborne road, 1½ m
NW of Wimborne Minster.

Rail: Poole 8½ m.

Bus: Wilts & Dorset
132/3, 182/3 from
Bournemouth, Poole,
alight Wimbourne
Square 2½ m.

Kingston Lacy House lies at the heart of the 8,500 acre Bankes Estate. Opened to the public nearly twenty years ago, the 'secret estate' is still only slowly revealing itself. Lying a mile from Wimborne Minster and nine miles from the market town of Blandford Forum on the B3082, Kingston Lacy is the gateway to true, rural Dorset.

As the home of the Bankes family for 300 years, Kingston Lacy replaced the original family seat of Corfe Castle and is now presented by the National Trust as it was in its Edwardian heyday. This elegant country mansion contains an outstanding collection of fine works of art, including a Titian, a Sebastiano del Piombo and a Velázquez, as well as an unique group of Egyptian artefacts. Set in 32 acres of formal gardens, which include one of only two Egyptian obelisks in the UK (the other being Cleopatra's Needle), the house is surrounded

by hundreds of acres of park and woodland, crossed by way-marked walks and includes three child-friendly play areas.

In 2005 the restored Japanese Gardens opened for public viewing, part of a seven acre project funded by the Gordon Bulmer Charitable Trust, in the southern woodland shelter belt. In 2006 the magnificent Guido Reni detached fresco "Separation of Night from Day" will be remounted on the ceiling of 18th century Library. The painting is unique and important, the only known example in England of the artist's fresco work, and a significant achievement of The Trust's conservation work at the property.

Events and activities occur throughout the year including concerts, outdoor theatre, walks, talks, a children's holiday club, and the fabulous 'Enchanted Garden' evenings in October.

▶ **OPENING TIMES**

House
18 March - 29 October
Wed - Sun, 11am - 5pm.
Last admission 4pm.
(1hr to view the house thoroughly.)

Garden & Park
18 March - 29 October,
daily, 10.30am - 6pm.
3 November - 17 December,
Fri - Sun, 10.30am - 4pm.
3 February - 11 March 2007,
Sat & Sun, 10.30am - 4pm.
(12 - 16 February, Mon - Fri,
10.30am - 4pm.)

Shop & Restaurant
18 March - 29 October,
daily, 10.30am - 5.30pm.
3 November - 17 December,
Fri - Sun, 10.30am - 4pm.

Timed entry tickets may be issued on BHs and some weekends.

▶ **ADMISSION**

House & Gardens
Adult £9.00
Child £4.50
Family £22.00
Groups
House & Gardens... £7.50
Child (under 15yrs) ... £3.80

Park & Garden only
Adult £4.50
Child £2.30
Family £11.00

Garden only. Braille guide & Induction Loop system. WC. Less-abled access info: 01202 883402.

Licensed.

By arrangement.

On leads, in park & woodland walks only.

Tel: 01202 880413.

© National Trust Photographic Library

ABBOTSBURY SUB-TROPICAL GARDENS 🏛
ABBOTSBURY, WEYMOUTH, DORSET DT3 4LA

www.abbotsbury-tourism.co.uk   **www.abbotsburyplantsales.co.uk**

Tel: 01305 871387   **e-mail:** info@abbotsbury-tourism.co.uk

Owner: The Hon Mrs Townshend DL   **Contact:** Shop Manager

Established in 1765 by the first Countess of Ilchester. Developed since then into a 20-acre Grade I listed, magnificent woodland valley garden. World famous for its camellia groves, magnolias, rhododendron and hydrangea collections. In summer it is awash with colour. Since the restoration after the great storm of 1990 many new and exotic plants have been introduced. The garden is now a mixture of formal and informal, with charming walled garden and spectacular woodland valley views. Facilities include a Colonial Tea House for lunches, snacks and drinks, a plant centre and quality gift shop. Events such as Shakespeare and concerts are presented during the year. The floodlighting of the garden at the end of October should not be missed.

Location: OS Ref. SY564 851. Off A35 nr Dorchester, on B3157 between Weymouth & Bridport.

Open: Mar - Nov: daily, 10am - 6pm. Winter: daily, 10am - 4pm. Last admission 1 hr before closing.

Admission: Adult £9.50, Child £4.50, OAP £7.

Plants also for sale online. Partial. Licensed. By arrangement. Free. In grounds, on leads.

ATHELHAMPTON HOUSE & GARDENS 🏛
See page 228 for full page entry.

BROWNSEA ISLAND
Poole Harbour, Dorset BH13 7EE

Tel: 01202 707744 **Fax:** 01202 701635 **e-mail:** brownseaisland@nationaltrust.org.uk **www.**nationaltrust.org.uk/brownsea

Owner: The National Trust   **Contact:** NT Office

Atmospheric island of heath and woodland with wide variety of wildlife. The island is dramatically located at the entrance to Poole harbour, offering spectacular views across to Studland and the Purbeck Hills. Its varied and colourful history includes use as a coastguard station, Victorian pottery, Edwardian country estate, daffodil farm, and as a decoy in the Second World War. In 1907 it was the site of Baden-Powell's experimental camp from which Scouting and Guiding evolved. Home to important populations of red squirrel and seabirds, the island provides a safe and relaxing place for walks and picnics, ideal for families to explore. What's new in 2006: Cliff top walk, tracker packs for younger visitors, refurbished Visitor and Education Centre.

Location: OS Ref. SZ032 878. In Poole Harbour. Boats run from Poole Quay and Sandbanks every 30 mins. There is also a service from Bournemouth and Swanage.

Open: 25 Mar - 29 Oct: daily, 10am - 5pm (closes at 6pm 22 Jul - 3 Sept, 4pm in Oct).

Admission: Adult £4.40, Child: £2.20, Family (2+2) £11. Groups: Adult £3.80, Child £1.90, Family (1+3) £6.50.

Partial. Tel for details.

CHETTLE HOUSE
Chettle, Blandford Forum, Dorset DT11 8DB

Tel: 01258 830858

Owner/Contact: Mr & Mrs Peter Bourke

A fine Queen Anne manor house designed by Thomas Archer and a fine example of English baroque architecture. The house features a basement with the typical north-south passage set just off centre with barrel-vaulted ceilings and a magnificent oak staircase. Newly restored interiors. The house is set in 5 acres of peaceful gardens.

Location: OS Ref. ST952 132. 6m NE of Blandford NW of A354.

Open: Easter - end Sept: 1st Sun in each month. Other times by appointment.

Admission: Adult £3.50, Child Free (under 16yrs).

Wedding receptions and special events. Partial.

CHURCH OF OUR LADY & ST IGNATIUS
North Chideock, Bridport, Dorset DT6 6LF

Tel: 01308 488348   **email:** amyasmartelli40@hotmail.com

Owner: The Weld Family Trust   **Contact:** Mrs G Martelli

The Chapel dedicated to Our Lady Queen of Martyrs and St Ignatius was built on the site of an exisitng chapel-barn in 1872 by Charles Weld of Chideock Manor. He favoured the baroque style and oversaw much of the decoration himself. Several of the portraits of the 40 martyrs which surround the nave have been attributed to him. The chapel is a shrine to Our Lady and has been a centre of Catholicism since penal times. A Museum of village life is on view in the adjoining cloister.

Location: OS Ref. SY419 937. A30 from Bridport into Chideock. Right at St Giles' Church. Continue towards North Chideock for 1/2 m. The Chapel is on the right.

Open: All year: 10am - 4pm.

Admission: Donations welcome.

Moveable ramp in Church Porch. Limited.

Clouds Hill.

©National Trust Photographic Library/Dennis Gilbert.

CLOUDS HILL ✻
WAREHAM, DORSET BH20 7NQ
www.nationaltrust.org.uk

Tel: 01929 405616

Owner: The National Trust   **Contact:** The Custodian

A tiny isolated brick and tile cottage, bought in 1925 by T E Lawrence (Lawrence of Arabia) as a retreat. The austere rooms inside are much as he left them and reflect his complex personality and close links with the Middle East. An exhibition details Lawrence's extraordinary life.

Location: OS Ref. SY824 909. 9m E of Dorchester, $1^1/2$ m E of Waddock crossroads B3390.

Open: 23 Mar - 29 Oct: Thurs - Sun & BH Mons, 12 noon - 5pm or dusk if earlier; no electric light. Groups wishing to visit at other times must telephone in advance.

Admission: £3.50, no reduction for children or groups.

ⓘ No WC. 🅰 Braille guide. 🅿 No coaches. ◼ Small groups.

DEANS COURT 🏛
WIMBORNE, DORSET BH21 1EE

Tel: 01202 886116

Owner: Sir Michael & Lady Hanham   **Contact:** Wimborne Tourist Info Centre

13 peaceful acres. Specimen trees, lawns, borders, herb garden, long serpentine wall, kitchen and rose garden. Chemical-free produce usually for sale, also interesting herbaceous plants. Wholefood teas in garden or in Housekeeper's room (down steps).

Location: OS Ref. SZ010 997. 2 mins walk S from centre of Wimborne Minster. Entrance signed from Deans Court Lane.

Open: 16/17 & 30 Apr, 1 &, 28/29 May, 18 Jun, 27/28 Aug, 10 Sept: Suns, 2 - 6pm, BH Mons, 10am - 6pm.

Admission: Adult £3, Child (5-15yrs) £1, OAP £2. Groups by arrangement.

🏺 Garden produce sales. 🅲 🅿 Free in Garden. 🐕 Guide dogs only.

NTPL/Joe Cornish

CORFE CASTLE ✻
WAREHAM, DORSET BH20 5EZ
www.nationaltrust.org.uk

Tel: 01929 481294   **Fax:** 01929 477067   **e-mail:** corfecastle@nationaltrust.org.uk

Owner: The National Trust   **Contact:** The Property Manager

One of Britain's most majestic ruins, the Castle controlled the gateway through the Purbeck Hills and had been an important stronghold since the time of William the Conqueror. Defended during the Civil War by the redoubtable Lady Bankes, the Castle fell to treachery from within and was substantially destroyed afterwards by the Parliamentarians. Many fine Norman and early English features remain. Visitor Centre at Castle View. Seasonal regular Castle tours. New family guidebook. Improved on-sight interpretation.

Location: OS Ref. SY959 824. On A351 Wareham - Swanage Rd. NW of the village.

Open: All year: daily. Mar & Oct: 10am - 5pm; Apr - Sept: 10am - 6pm; Nov - Feb (Closed 25/26 Dec), 10am - 4pm.

Admission: Adult £5, Child £2.50, Family (2+3) £12.50, (1+3) £7.50. Groups: Adult £4.30, Child £2.15.

🅾 🅰 Limited. Braille guide. WC. 🅲 🎦 ◼ 🅿 🐕 On leads. ❄ 🅸 Tel for details.

EDMONDSHAM HOUSE & GARDENS 🏛
Cranborne, Wimborne, Dorset BH21 5RE

Tel: 01725 517207

Owner/Contact: Mrs Julia E Smith

Charming blend of Tudor and Georgian architecture with interesting contents. Organic walled garden, 6 acre garden with unusual trees and spring bulbs. 12th century church nearby.

Location: OS Ref. SU062 116. Off B3081 between Cranborne and Verwood, NW from Ringwood 9m, Wimborne 9m.

Open: House & Gardens: All BH Mons & Weds in Apr & Oct 2 - 5pm. Gardens: Apr - Oct, Suns & Weds 2 - 5pm.

Admission: House & Garden: Adult £4, Child £1 (under 5yrs Free). Garden only: Adult £2, Child 50p. Garden Season Ticket (incl. children) £5. Groups by arrangement, teas for groups.

🏺 🅰 🅲 Pre-booked (max 50). 🅸 Obligatory. 🐕 Car park only. ⬛ (max 50).

FORDE ABBEY & GARDENS 🏛   *See page 229 for full page entry.*

accommodation
see page 567

South West - England

HARDY'S COTTAGE ❧

HIGHER BOCKHAMPTON, DORCHESTER, DORSET DT2 8QJ

www.nationaltrust.org.uk

Tel: 01305 262366

Owner/Contact: The National Trust

A small cob and thatch cottage where the novelist and poet Thomas Hardy was born in 1840, and from where he would walk to school every day in Dorchester, six miles away. It was built by his great-grandfather and is little altered. Since the family left the interior has been furnished by the Trust (see also Max Gate). His early novels *Under the Green Wood Tree* and *Far From the Madding Crowd* were written here. Charming cottage garden.

Location: OS Ref. SY728 925. 3m NE of Dorchester, 1/2 m S of A35. 10 mins walk through the woods from car park.

Open: Please telephone 01297 561900 for opening arrangements. New Project.

Admission: Adult £3, Child £1.50.

ⓘ No WC. ⬚ ⬚ Partial. 🅿 No coach parking. ▣ ✖

HIGHER MELCOMBE

Melcombe Bingham, Dorchester, Dorset DT2 7PB

Tel: 01258 880251

Owner/Contact: Mr M C Woodhouse

Consists of the surviving wing of a 16th century house with its attached domestic chapel. A fine plaster ceiling and linenfold panelling. Conducted tours by owner.

Location: OS Ref. ST749 024. 1km W of Melcombe Bingham.

Open: May - Sept by appointment.

Admission: Adult £2 (takings go to charity).

⬚ Unsuitable. 🅺 By written appointment only. 🅿 Limited. 🅷 Guide dogs only.

KINGSTON LACY ❧

See page 230 for full page entry.

Sherborne Castle.

HIGHCLIFFE CASTLE 🏛

ROTHESAY DRIVE, HIGHCLIFFE-ON-SEA, CHRISTCHURCH BH23 4LE

www.highcliffecastle.co.uk

Tel: 01425 278807 **Fax:** 01425 280423 **e-mail:** enquiries@highcliffecastle.co.uk

Owner: Christchurch Borough Council **Contact:** The Manager

Built in 1830 in the Romantic and Picturesque style of architecture for Lord Stuart de Rothesay using his unique collection of French medieval stonework and stained glass. Recently repaired externally, it remains mostly unrepaired inside. Five State Rooms house a visitor centre, exhibitions, events and gift shop. Coastal grounds, village trail and nearby St Mark's church. Tea rooms in the Claretian's Wing.

Location: OS Ref. SZ200 930. Off the A337 Lymington Road, between Christchurch

and Highcliffe-on-Sea.

Open: 1 Feb - 23 Dec: daily, 11am - 5pm. Grounds: All year: daily from 7am. Access for coaches. Tearooms closed Christmas Day.

Admission: Adult £2, Child Free. Group (10+) rates available. Guided tours of unrestored areas (may be unsuitable for people with mobility problems - please ring for details): Adult £3.50, Child Free. Grounds: Free.

⬚ ⯆ ⬚ Partial. WC. ▣ 10am - 5pm. 🅺 By arrangement. 🅿 Limited. Parking charge. ▣ By arrangement. 🅷 In grounds, on leads. ⬚ ❈ ⬚ Tel for details.

Dave Penman

KINGSTON MAURWARD GARDEN

DORCHESTER, DORSET DT2 8PY

www.kmc.ac.uk/gardens

Tel: 01305 215003 **Fax:** 01305 215001 **e-mail:** events@kmc.ac.uk

Contact: Wendy Cunningham

Classical 18th century parkland setting, with majestic lawns sweeping down from the Grade I listed Georgian house to the lake. The Rainbow beds and beautiful herbaceous borders complement the series of 'rooms' within the formal Edwardian garden. National Collections of Penstemons and Salvias. Lakeside walks, animal park, shop, plant centre and refreshments.

Location: OS Ref. SY713 911. 1m E of Dorchester. Roundabout off A35 by-pass.

Open: 4 Jan - 21 Dec: daily, 10am - 5.30pm or dusk if earlier.

Admission: Adult £5, Child £3 (under 3yrs Free), Family £15.50. Groups (10+): Adult £3.50. Guided tours (by arrangement) (12+): £5pp.

ⓘConferences. 🅾 📶 🔲Wedding receptions. ⓺Partial. 💷Licensed. 🅘By arrangement. 🅿 🔳 🗙Guide dogs only. 🔺 ❄ 🔽 Tel for details.

KNOLL GARDENS & NURSERY

Stapehill Road, Hampreston, Wimborne BH21 7ND

Tel: 01202 873931 **Fax:** 01202 870842 **e-mail:** enquiries@knollgardens.co.uk

Owner: J & J Flude & N R Lucas **Contact:** Mr John Flude

Nationally acclaimed 6 acre gardens, with 6000+ named plants.

Location: OS Ref. SU059 001. Between Wimborne & Ferndown. Exit A31 Canford Bottom roundabout, B3073 Hampreston. Signposted 1^1/$_2$ m.

Open: 1 Feb - 31 Dec: Wed - Sun, 10am - 5pm or dusk if earlier. Closed Christmas & January.

Admission: Adult £4.25, Child (5-15yrs) £2.75, Conc £3.75. RHS Free. Groups: Adult £3.50, Family (2+2) £10.50.

Athelhampton House.

Lulworth Castle & Park

LULWORTH CASTLE & PARK AND LULWORTH CASTLE HOUSE

WAREHAM, DORSET BH20 5QS

www.lulworth.com

Tel: 0845 4501054 **Fax:** 01929 400563 **e-mail:** office@lulworth.com

Owner: The Weld Estate

Surrounded by beautiful parkland this 17th century hunting lodge was destroyed by fire in 1929 and has been restored by English Heritage. Steeped in history the Castle has remained in the same family since 1641. Features include a gallery on the Weld family, reconstructed kitchen, dairy and laundry rooms and a wine cellar. The Chapel is reputed to be one of the finest pieces of architecture in Dorset and houses an exhibition on vestments and recusant silver. **Lulworth Castle House:** Elegantly stands within the Park and has a stunning collection of pictures and furniture. The grounds also include the original kitchen garden to the Castle.

Lulworth Castle House

Location: OS Ref. SY853 822. In E Lulworth off B3070, 3m NE of Lulworth Cove.

Open: Castle & Park: All year (but closed 7 - 21 Jan & 24/25 Dec) Sun - Fri & Easter Sat: 10.30am - 6pm (closes 4pm autumn/winter). Also open some Sats for Special Events. Lulworth Castle House: Groups by appointment, tel 01929 400349.

Admission: Castle: Adult £7, Child (5 - 15yrs) £4 (under 5yrs free), Conc. £6, Family (2+3) £21, Family (1+3) £13.50. 10% discount for groups of 10+. Lulworth Castle House: Adult £3, Child Free. Prices may vary for special events including Summer Jousting Shows. Please see website or tel 0845 4501054 for details.

🅾 📶 ⓺Partial. WC. 💷Licensed. 🅘By arrangement. 🔳 🅿 🗙In ground, on leads. 🔳 5 holiday cottages, tel: 01929 400100. 🔺 ❄ 🔽See website or tel for details.

George Wright

MAPPERTON 🏠

BEAMINSTER, DORSET DT8 3NR

www.mapperton.com

Tel: 01308 862645   **Fax:** 01308 863348   **e-mail:** office@mapperton.com

Owner/Contact: The Earl & Countess of Sandwich

Jacobean 1660s manor with Tudor features and Georgian north front. Italianate upper garden with orangery, topiary and formal borders descending to fish ponds and shrub gardens. All Saints Church forms south wing opening to courtyard and stables. Area of outstanding natural beauty with fine views of Dorset hills and woodlands. House and Gardens featured in *Restoration*, *Emma* and *Tom Jones*.

Location: OS Ref. SY503 997. 1m S of B3163, 2m NE of B3066, 2m SE Beaminster, 5m NE Bridport.

Open: House: 29 May & 27 Jun - 5 Aug weekdays & 28 Aug: 2 - 4.30pm, last admission 4pm. Other times by appointment. Garden & All Saints Church: 1 Mar - 31 Oct: daily (exc. Sat) 11am - 5pm. Café: Mar - Sept: daily (exc. Sat) 11am - 5.30pm, for lunch and tea.

Admission: Gardens: £4, House: £3.50. Child (under 18yrs) £2, under 5yrs Free. Groups tours by appointment.

🖻 🖩 🖳Partial. 🖵Licensed. 🍽 🛠 By arrangement. ■ 🅿 Limited for coaches. 🐕 Guide dogs only. 🔺 💬Tel for details.

©National Trust Photographic Library

MAX GATE 🌸

ALINGTON AVENUE, DORCHESTER, DORSET DT1 2AA

www.thomas-hardy.connectfree.co.uk

Tel: 01305 262538   **e-mail:** heritage.venues@virgin.net

Owner: The National Trust   **Contact:** The Tenant

Novelist and poet Thomas Hardy designed and lived in this house from 1885 until his death in 1928. Here he wrote *Tess of the d'Urbervilles*, *Jude the Obscure* and *The Mayor of Casterbridge*, as well as much of his poetry. The house contains several pieces of his furniture.

Location: OS Ref. SY704 899. 1m E of Dorchester just N of the A352 to Wareham. From Dorchester follow A352 signs to the roundabout named Max Gate (at Jct. of A35 Dorchester bypass). Turn left and left again into cul-de-sac outside Max Gate.

Open: 27 Mar - 27 Sept: Mons, Weds & Suns, 2 - 5pm. Only hall, dining, drawing rooms & garden open. Private visits, tours & seminars by schools, colleges and literary societies at other times by prior appointment with the tenants, Mr & Mrs Andrew Leah.

Admission: Adult £2.80, Child £1.50.

ℹ️No WC. 🖳Partial. Braille guide. 🅿 ■ 🐕

MILTON ABBEY CHURCH

Milton Abbas, Blandford, Dorset DT11 0BZ

Tel: 01258 880215

Owner: Diocese of Salisbury   **Contact:** Chris Fookes

Abbey church dating from 14th century.

Location: OS Ref. ST798 024. 3½ m N of A354. Between Dorchester/Blandford Road.

Open: Abbey Church: daily 10am - 6pm. Groups by arrangement please.

Admission: By donation except Easter & mid-Jul - end Aug. Adult £2, Child Free.

MINTERNE GARDENS 🏠

Minterne Magna, Nr Dorchester, Dorset DT2 7AU

Owner/Contact: The Hon Mr & Mrs Henry Digby

Tel: 01300 341370   **Fax:** 01300 341747   **email:** enquiries@minterne.co.uk

www.minterne.co.uk

If you wish to wander peacefully through 20 wild woodland acres, where magnolias, rhododendrons, eucryphias, hydrangeas, water plants and water lilies provide a new vista at each turn, with small lakes and cascades landscaped in the 18th century, you will be welcome at Minterne, described by Simon Jenkins as 'a corner of paradise'. The home of the Churchill and Digby families for 350 years. The house, which contains magnificent Churchill tapestries and naval and other historical pictures, is open for organised groups only, which may be arranged by prior appointment.

Location: OS Ref. ST660 042. On A352 Dorchester/Sherborne Rd, 2m N of Cerne Abbas.

Open: 1 Mar - 31 Oct: daily, 10am - 6pm.

Admission: Adult £4, accompanied children Free.

🔲 🖳Unsuitable. 🐕 In grounds on leads. 🔺

English Heritage Photo Library

PORTLAND CASTLE ⛬

CASTLETOWN, PORTLAND, WEYMOUTH, DORSET DT5 1AZ

www.english-heritage.org.uk/portland

Tel: 01305 820539   **Fax:** 01305 860853   **e-mail:** customers@english-heritage.org.uk

Owner: English Heritage   **Contact:** Visitor Operations Staff

Discover one of Henry VIII's finest coastal fortresses. Perfectly preserved in a waterfront location overlooking Portland harbour, it is a marvellous place to visit for all the family whatever the weather. Explore the Tudor kitchen and gun platform, see ghostly sculptured figures from the past, enjoy the superb battlement views or picnic on the lawn in front of the Captain's House. An excellent audio tour, included in the admission charge, brings the castle's history and characters to life. Visit the 'Contemporary Heritage' Garden.

Location: OS Ref. SY684 743. Overlooking Portland harbour.

Open: 1 Apr - 30 Jun & Sept: daily, 10am - 5pm. 1 Jul - 31 Aug: daily, 10am - 6pm. 1 - 31 Oct: daily, 10am - 4pm.

Admission: Adult £3.70, Child £1.90, Conc. £2.80. 15% discount for groups (11+).

🖻 🔲 🖳Captain's House & ground floor. WCs. 🖵 🎧 🅿 🐕 🔺 💬Tel for details.

open all year
see page 557

SANDFORD ORCAS MANOR HOUSE

Sandford Orcas, Sherborne, Dorset DT9 4SB

Tel: 01963 220206

Owner/Contact: Sir Mervyn Medlycott Bt

Tudor manor house with gatehouse, fine panelling, furniture, pictures. Terraced gardens with topiary and herb garden. Personal conducted tour by owner.

Location: OS Ref. ST623 210. 2¹/2 m N of Sherborne, Dorset 4m S of A303 at Sparkford. Entrance next to church.

Open: Easter Mon, 10am - 5pm. May & Jul - Sept: Suns & Mons, 2 - 5pm.

Admission: Adult £4, Child £2. Groups (10+): Adult £3, Child £1.50.

🚫Unsuitable. ⓕObligatory. 🐕In grounds, on leads.

SHERBORNE CASTLE 🏛

SHERBORNE, DORSET DT9 5NR

www.sherbornecastle.com

Tel: 01935 813182   **Fax:** 01935 816727   **e-mail:** enquiries@sherbornecastle.com

Owner: Mr & Mrs John Wingfield Digby   **Contact:** Castle & Events Manager

Built by Sir Walter Raleigh in 1594, Sherborne Castle has been the home of the Digby family since 1617. Prince William of Orange was entertained here in 1688, and George III visited in 1789. Splendid interiors and collections of art, furniture and porcelain are on view in the Castle. Lancelot 'Capability' Brown created the lake in 1753 and gave Sherborne the very latest in landscape gardening, with magnificent vistas of the surrounding parklands. 40 acres of beautiful lakeside gardens and grounds open for public viewing.

Location: OS Ref. ST649 164. ³/4 m SE of Sherborne town centre. Follow brown signs from A30 or A352. ¹/2 m S of the Old Castle.

Open: Castle, Gardens, Shop & Tearoom: 1 Apr - 31 Oct: daily except Mon & Fri (open BH Mons), 11am - 4.30pm last admission. (Castle interior from 2.30pm Sats.) Groups (15+) by arrangement during normal opening hours.

Admission: Castle & Gardens: Adult £8, Child (0-15yrs) Free (max 4 per adult), OAP £7.50. Groups (15+): Adult/OAP £7, Child (0-15yrs) £3. Private views (15+): Adult/OAP £9, Child £4.50. Gardens only: Adult/OAP £4, Child (0-15yrs) Free (max 4 per adult), no concessions or group rates for gardens only.

📷 ☎ 🚹Partial. 🍽 ⓕBy arrangement. 🐕In grounds, on leads. 🅿 ⚲Tel for details.

SHERBORNE OLD CASTLE ⌗

Castleton, Sherborne, Dorset DT9 3SA

Tel/Fax: 01935 812730   **e-mail:** customers@english-heritage.org.uk

www.english-heritage.org.uk/sherborne

Owner: English Heritage   **Contact:** Visitor Operations Staff

The ruins of this early 12th century Castle are a testament to the 16 days it took Cromwell to capture it during the Civil War, after which it was abandoned. A gatehouse, some graceful arcading and decorative windows survive.

Location: OS Ref. ST647 167. ¹/2 m E of Sherborne off B3145. ¹/2 m N of the 1594 Castle.

Open: 1 Apr - 31 Oct: daily, 10am - 5pm (6pm in Jul & Aug, 4pm in Oct).

Admission: Adult £2.40, Child £1.20, Conc. £1.80. 15% discount for groups of 11+.

📷 🚹 Grounds. 🅿 Limited for cars. No coach parking. 🐕 ⚲Tel for details.

SMEDMORE HOUSE

Smedmore, Kimmeridge, Wareham BH20 5PG

Tel/Fax: 01929 480719

Owner: Dr Philip Mansel   **Contact:** Mr B Belsten

The home of the Mansel family for nearly 400 years nestles at the foot of the Purbeck hills looking across Kimmeridge Bay to Portland Bill.

Location: OS Ref. SY924 787. 15m SW of Poole.

Open: 28 May & 3 Sept: 2 - 5pm.

Admission: Adult £3.50, Child under 16 Free.

plant sales 🌸
see page 555

STOCK GAYLARD HOUSE

Stock Gaylard, Sturminster Newton, Dorset DT10 2BG

Tel: 01963 23215   **e-mail:** aclangmead@aol.com

Owner: Mrs J Langmead   **Contact:** Mrs J Langmead

A Georgian house overlooking an ancient deer park with the parish church of St Barnabas in the garden. The grounds and principal rooms of the house are open to the public for 28 days a year.

Location: OS Ref. ST722 130. 1 mile S of the junction of the A357 and the A3030 at the Lydlinch Common.

Open: 22 Apr - 1st May, 22 - 30 Jun & 22 - 30 Sept, 2 - 5pm. Access to the Park by arrangement, please telephone for information.

Admission: Adult £5, Child £2.

WHITE MILL

Sturminster Marshall, Nr Wimborne, Dorset BH21 4BX

Tel: 01258 858051   **www.**nationaltrust.org.uk

Owner: The National Trust   **Contact:** The Custodian

Rebuilt in 1776 on a site marked as a mill in the Domesday Book, this substantial corn mill was extensively repaired in 1994 and still retains its original elm and applewood machinery (now too fragile to be operative).

Location: OS Ref. ST958 006. On River Stour 1/2 m NE of Sturminster Marshall from the B3082 Blandford to Wimborne Rd, take road to SW signposted Sturminster Marshall. Mill is 1m on right. Car park nearby.

Open: 25 Mar - 29 Oct: Sats, Suns & BH Mons, 12 noon - 5pm. Admission by guided tour only.

Admission: Adult £3, Child £2. Groups by arrangement.

ℹ️No WC. ♿Ground floor. 👤Obligatory. 🅿️

🐕 Under close control in grounds and car park.

special events
see page 571

WOLFETON HOUSE 🏛

Nr Dorchester, Dorset DT2 9QN

Tel: 01305 263500   **Fax:** 01305 265090

e-mail: kthimbleby@wolfeton.freeserve.co.uk

Owner: Capt N T L Thimbleby   **Contact:** The Steward

A fine mediaeval and Elizabethan manor house lying in the water-meadows near the confluence of the rivers Cerne and Frome. It was much embellished around 1580 and has splendid plaster ceilings, fireplaces and panelling of that date. To be seen are the Great Hall, Stairs and Chamber, Parlour, Dining Room, Chapel and Cyder House. The mediaeval Gatehouse has two unmatched and older towers. There are good pictures and furniture.

Location: OS Ref. SY678 921. 1 1/2 m from Dorchester on the A37 towards Yeovil. Indicated by Historic House signs.

Open: June - end Sept: Mons, Weds & Thurs, 2 - 5pm. Groups by appointment throughout the year.

Admission: £5.

🍵By arrangement. ♿Ground floor. 💻By arrangement. 👤By arrangement. 🅿️ 🐕 ❄️

Hardy's Cottage.

MAP 6

BERKELEY CASTLE 🏛

www.berkeley-castle.com

Not many can boast of having their private house celebrated by Shakespeare nor of having held it in the possession of their family for nearly 850 years, nor having a King of England murdered within its walls, nor of having welcomed at their table the local vicar and Castle Chaplain, John Trevisa (1342-1402), reputed as one of the earliest translators of the Bible, nor of having a breach battered by Oliver Cromwell, which to this day it is forbidden by law to repair even if it was wished to do so. But such is the story of Berkeley.

This beautiful and historic Castle, begun in 1117, still remains the home of the famous family who gave their name to numerous locations all over the world, notably Berkeley Square in London, Berkeley Hundred in Virginia and Berkeley University in California. Scene of the brutal murder of Edward II in 1327 (visitors can see his cell and

nearby the dungeon) and besieged by Cromwell's troops in 1645, the Castle is steeped in history but twenty-four generations of Berkeleys have gradually transformed a Norman fortress into the lovely home it is today.

The State Apartments contain magnificent collections of furniture, rare paintings by primarily English and Dutch masters, and tapestries. Part of the world-famous Berkeley silver is on display in the Dining Room. Many other rooms are equally interesting including the Great Hall upon which site the Barons of the West Country met in 1215 before going to Runnymede to force King John to put his seal to the Magna Carta.

The Castle is surrounded by lovely terraced Elizabethan Gardens with a lily pond, Elizabeth I's bowling green, and sweeping lawns.

Owner:
Mr R J G Berkeley

▶ CONTACT
The Custodian
Berkeley Castle
Gloucestershire
GL13 9BQ

Tel: 01453 810332
Fax: 01453 512995
e-mail: info@berkeley-castle.com

▶ LOCATION
OS Ref. ST685 990

SE side of Berkeley village. Midway between Bristol & Gloucester, 2m W off the A38.

From motorway M5/J14 (5m) or J13 (9m).

📋

✿

ℹ️ Fashion shows and filming. Butterfly House. No photography inside the Castle.

🍽 Wedding receptions and corporate entertainment.

♿ Visitors may alight in the Outer Bailey.

🍴 Licensed. Serving lunches and home-made teas.

🚶 Free. Max. 120 people. Tour time: One hour. Evening groups by arrangement. Group visits must be booked.

🅿 Cars 150yds from Castle, 15 coaches 250yds away. Free.

🎒 Welcome. General and social history and architecture.

🚫

▶ OPENING TIMES

April - September*
Tues - Sat & BH Mons,
11am - 4pm,
Sun, 2 - 5pm.

October
Sundays only, 2 - 5pm.

The Butterfly House is closed in October.

Last admission 30 mins before closing.

* Except for weekends of 22/23 & 29/30 July: entry via the Joust Mediaeval Festival event only.

▶ ADMISSION

Global Ticket including Castle, Gardens & Butterfly House
Adult £7.50
Child (5-16yrs)....... £4.50
Child (under 5s)...... Free
OAP £6.00
Family (2+2) £21.00
Groups (25+ pre-booked)
Adult £7.00
Child (5-16yrs) £3.50
OAP £5.50

Gardens only
Adult £4.00
Child £2.00

Butterfly House
Adult.................. £2.00
Child (5-16yrs) £1.00
School groups £0.80
Family (2+2) £5.00

CONFERENCE/FUNCTION

ROOM	MAX CAPACITY
Great Hall	150
Long Drawing Rm	100

MAP 3

CHAVENAGE 🏛

www.chavenage.com

Chavenage is a wonderful Elizabethan house of mellow grey Cotswold stone and tiles which contains much of interest for the discerning visitor.

The approach aspect of Chavenage is virtually as it was left by Edward Stephens in 1576. Only two families have owned Chavenage; the present owners since 1891 and the Stephens family before them. A Colonel Nathaniel Stephens, MP for Gloucestershire during the Civil War was cursed for supporting Cromwell, giving rise to legends of weird happenings at Chavenage since that time.

Inside Chavenage there are many interesting rooms housing tapestries, fine furniture, pictures and many relics of the Cromwellian period. Of particular note are the Main Hall, where a contemporary screen forms a minstrels' gallery and two tapestry rooms where it is said Cromwell was lodged.

Recently Chavenage has been used as a location for TV and film productions including a Hercule Poirot story *The Mysterious Affair at Styles*, many episodes of the sequel to *Are you Being Served* now called *Grace & Favour*, a *Gotcha* for *The Noel Edmonds' House Party*, episodes of *The House of Elliot* and *Casualty*, in 1997/98 *Berkeley Square* and *Cider with Rosie* and in 2002 the US series *Relic Hunter* III. In 2005 it was one of the homes Jeremy Musson visited in the BBC's *The Curious House Guest*.

Chavenage is especially suitable for those wishing an intimate, personal tour, usually conducted by the owner, or for groups wanting a change from large establishments. Meals for pre-arranged groups have proved hugely popular. It also provides a charming venue for small conferences and functions.

Owner:
Mr David Lowsley-Williams

▶ **CONTACT**

D Lowsley-Williams or Caroline Lowsley-Williams
Chavenage
Tetbury
Gloucestershire
GL8 8XP

Tel: 01666 502329
Fax: 01453 836778
e-mail: info@chavenage.com

▶ **LOCATION**

OS Ref. ST872 952

Less than 20m from M4/J16/17 or 18. 1³/₄ m NW of Tetbury between the B4014 & A4135. Signed from Tetbury. Less than 15m from M5/J13 or 14. Signed from A46 (Stroud - Bath road)

Rail: Kemble Station 7m.

Taxi: SC Taxis 01666 504195.

Air: Bristol 35m. Birmingham 70m. Grass airstrip on farm.

▶ **OPENING TIMES**

Summer

May - September
Easter Sun, Mon & BHs, 2 - 5pm.

Thurs & Suns
2 - 5pm.

NB. Will open on any day and at other times by prior arrangement for groups.

Winter

October - March
By appointment only for groups.

▶ **ADMISSION**

Tours are inclusive in the following prices.

Summer

Adult £6.00
Child (5 - 16 yrs)....... £3.00

CONCESSIONS

By prior arrangement, concessions may be given to groups of 40+ and also to disabled and to exceptional cases.

Winter

Groups only:
Rates by arrangement.

CONFERENCE/FUNCTION

ROOM	SIZE	MAX CAPACITY
Ballroom	70' x 30'	120
Oak Room	25 'x 20'	30

ℹ️ Clay pigeon shooting, archery, cross-bows, pistol shooting, ATV driving, small fashion shows, concerts, plays, seminars, filming, product launching, photography. No casual photography in house.

🍽 Corporate entertaining. In-house catering for drinks parties, dinners, wedding receptions. Telephone for details.

♿ Partial. WC.

☕ Lunches, teas, dinners and picnics by arrangement.

🚶 By owner. Large groups given a talk prior to viewing. Couriers/group leaders should arrange tour format prior to visit.

🅿 Up to 100 cars. 2 - 3 coaches (by appointment). Coaches access from A46 (signposted) or from Tetbury via the B4014, enter the back gates for coach parking area.

🪑 Chairs can be arranged for lecturing.

🐕 In grounds on leads. Guide dogs only in house. ❄️

South West - England

Sabina Rüber

MAP 6

Owner:
Lady Ashcombe,
Henry and Mollie
Dent-Brocklehurst

CONTACT

The Secretary
Sudeley Castle
Winchcombe
Gloucestershire
GL54 5JD

Tel: 01242 602308
Fax: 01242 602959

e-mail: enquiries@
sudeley.org.uk

LOCATION

OS Ref. SP032 277

8m NE of Cheltenham,
at Winchcombe
off B4632.

From Bristol or
Birmingham M5/J9.
Take A46 then B4077
towards Stow-on-the-Wold.

Bus: Castleways to
Winchcombe.

Rail: Cheltenham
Station 8m.

Air: Birmingham or
Bristol 45m.

CONFERENCE/FUNCTION

ROOM	MAX CAPACITY
Chandos Hall	60
Banquet Hall & Pavilion	100
Marquee	Unlimited
Long Room	80
Library	50

SUDELEY CASTLE GARDENS & EXHIBITIONS

www.sudeleycastle.co.uk

Sitting proudly on the Cotswold escarpment, Sudeley Castle Gardens & Exhibitions not only celebrates its rich history but also explores the new. With many royal connections, it has played an important role in the turbulent and changing times of England's past. Sudeley is perhaps best known as the home of Queen Katherine Parr, who is entombed in St Mary's Church in the grounds.

Surrounding the Castle buildings and the ruins are 14 acres of stunning award-winning gardens. Highlights include the Queen's Garden, famous for its double yew hedges and collection of English roses, the semi-Mediterranean planting of the Secret Garden, the intricate Tudor Knot Garden and the bold planting surrounding the Tithe Barn Ruins.

A family home to the Dent-Brocklehursts since the early 19th Century, at which time an extensive and ambitious restoration programme was instigated, the family has remained devoted and enthused to the continued development of Sudeley. The Castle Apartments themselves are home to the three generations of the family, but at pre-arranged times are open to the public on an unmissable Connoisseur Tour (please telephone for further information).

The Contemporary Art exhibition staged in the grounds returns for its second year as part of a rolling three-year programme. World-renowned artists will provide either specifically commissioned pieces or recent works reacting to the landscape and history of Sudeley.

Also a Wildfowl & Pheasantry Area and varied exhibitions showcasing Sudeley's collection.

Summer
Please see website
for details.

Winter
Groups by appointment.

▶ **ADMISSION**

Adults	£7.20
Children (5 - 15yrs)	
	£4.20
Conc	£6.20

Group rates available.

Details may be subject
to change – please
telephone or visit our
website for updated
information.

ℹ️ Photographs and filming by prior arrangement. Concerts, corporate events and conferences. Product launches and activity days. Sudeley reserves the right to close any area and to amend information as necessary.

🛍️ 🌱

🍸 Corporate and private events, wedding receptions.

♿ Partial access to the grounds. WC.

☕ Licensed Coffee Shop.

🚶 Tours and talks by prior arrangement, including Connoisseur Tours of the Private Apartments.

🅿️ 1,000 cars. Meal vouchers, free access for coach drivers.

🚫

🏠 13 holiday cottages for 2 - 5 occupants.

🔔 🛡️ Tel for details.

BERKELEY CASTLE

See page 238 for full page entry.

CHAVENAGE

See page 239 for full page entry.

BLACKFRIARS PRIORY

Ladybellegate Street, Gloucester

Tel: 0117 9750700 **www**.english-heritage.org.uk/southwest

Owner: English Heritage   **Contact:** The South West Regional Office

A small Dominican priory church converted into a rich merchant's house at the Dissolution. Most of the original 13th century church remains, including a rare scissor-braced roof.

Location: OS Ref. SO830 186. In Ladybellegate St, Gloucester, off Southgate Street and Blackfriars Walk.

Open: Access by guided tour only (Jul & Aug: Sunday 3pm). Heritage Open Days: 9 - 10 Sept, free: 12.30pm & 3pm. Please contact the South West Regional Office.

Admission: Adult £3.50, Child £3.

P Nearby, not EH, charged.

CHEDWORTH ROMAN VILLA

Yanworth, Nr Cheltenham, Gloucestershire GL54 3LJ

Tel: 01242 890256   **Fax:** 01242 890909

e-mail: chedworth@nationaltrust.org.uk   **www**.nationaltrust.org.uk

Owner: The National Trust   **Contact:** The Property Manager

Discover one of the largest Romano-British sites in the country. Located within the beautiful Cotswolds scenery, a mile of walls survives along with several marvellous mosaics, two bathhouses, hypocausts, latrines and a water shrine. The site was first excavated in 1864 and retains a Victorian museum and atmosphere. A 15 minute introductory audio visual presentation is also available to visitors.

Location: OS Ref. SP053 135. 3m NW of Fossebridge on Cirencester - Northleach road (A429) via Yanworth or from A436 via Withington. Coaches must approach from Fossebridge.

Open: 1 - 25 Mar: Tues - Sun, 11am - 4pm. 26 Mar - 28 Oct: Tues - Sun, 10am - 5pm; 29 Oct - 12 Nov: Tues - Sun, 10am - 4pm. Open BH Mons. Shop open as Villa. Shop and reception close at above time.

Admission: Adult £5.50, Child £3, Family (2+3) £14. Booked group tours (max 30 per guide): Schools £20, others £40.

Partial. WC. By arrangement. P Adult £1.20, Child 80p. By arrangement. Tel for details.

© M B Paice

BOURTON HOUSE GARDEN

BOURTON-ON-THE-HILL GL56 9AE

www.bourtonhouse.com

Tel: 01386 700754   **Fax:** 01386 701081   **e-mail:** cd@bourtonhouse.com

Owner/Contact: Mr & Mrs Richard Paice

Exciting 3 acre garden surrounding a delightful 18th century Cotswold manor house and 16th century tithe barn. Featuring flamboyant borders, imaginative topiary, a unique shade house, a profusion of herbaceous and exotic plants and, not least, a myriad of magically planted pots. The mood is friendly and welcoming, the atmosphere tranquil yet inspiring. The garden... "positively fizzes with ideas". There are a further 7 of parkland where young trees progress apace. 'The Gallery' features contemporary art, craft and design in the tithe barn.

Location: OS Ref. SP180 324. 1³/₄ m W of Moreton-in-Marsh on A44.

Open: 24 May - 31 Aug: Wed - Fri; also 28/29 May & 27/28 Aug (BH Sun & Mon). Sept - Oct: Thur & Fri. 10am - 5pm.

Admission: Adult £5, Child Free.

Partial. By arrangement. P Limited for coaches.

NT Photographic Library: Ian Shaw

DYRHAM PARK

NR CHIPPENHAM, GLOUCESTERSHIRE SN14 8ER

www.nationaltrust.org.uk

Tel: 01179 372501   **Fax:** 01179 371353   **e-mail:** dyrhampark@nationaltrust.org.uk

Owner: The National Trust   **Contact:** The Property Manager

Dyrham Park was built between 1691 and 1702 for William Blathwayt, William III's Secretary at War and Secretary of State. The rooms have changed little since they were furnished by Blathwayt and their contents are recorded in his housekeeper's inventory. Many fine textiles and paintings, as well as items of blue-and-white Delftware. Restored Victorian domestic rooms open, including kitchen, bells passage, bakehouse, larders, tenants' hall and Delft-tiled dairy.

Location: OS Ref. ST743 757. 8m N of Bath, 12m E of Bristol. Approached from Bath - Stroud road (A46), 2m S of Tormarton interchange with M4/J18.

Open: House: 24 Mar - 29 Oct: Fri - Tue, 12 noon - 4pm, last admission 45 mins before closing. Garden: as house, 11am - 5pm. Park: daily (closed 25 Dec), 11am - 5pm (dusk if earlier). Contact property for winter opening times.

Admission: Adult £9, Child £4.50, Family £22.50. Garden & Park only: Adult £3.50, Child £1.80, Family £8. Park only (on days when house & garden closed): Adult £2.30, Child £1.10, Family £5.20.

Partial. No electric wheelchairs admitted. Licensed. Mons, 11.30am (max 20). House. P Only in dog-walking area. Tel for details.

accommodation
see page 567

FRAMPTON COURT
FRAMPTON ON SEVERN, GLOUCESTERSHIRE GL2 7EU
www.framptoncourtestate.co.uk

Tel: 01452 740267 **Fax:** 01452 740698 **e-mail:** clifford.fce@farming.co.uk

Owner: Mr & Mrs Rollo Clifford **Contact:** Jean Speed

Splendid Georgian family home of the Cliffords, who have lived in Frampton since the Norman Conquest. Built 1732, school of Vanbrugh, set in Grade I listed park and garden with fine views to extensive lake. Superb panelled interiors and period furniture. Also the famous 19th century "Frampton Flora" botanical watercolours. Principal bedrooms available for Bed and Breakfast.

Strawberry Hill Gothic Orangery with a Dutch ornamental canal is available for self catering holidays (tel: 01452 740698).

Location: OS Ref. SO750 078. In Frampton, 1/4 m SW of B4071, 3m NW of M5/J13.

Open: By arrangement for groups (10+).

Admission: House & Garden: £5.

[i] No photography in house. In Orangery walled garden. Pan Global Plants (tel: 01452 741641), rare plant nursery. Small. Garden only. Obligatory. Coaches limited. In grounds, on leads. B&B contact Gilian Keightley on 01452 740267. Orangery tel: 01452 740698.

FRAMPTON MANOR
Frampton-on-Severn, Gloucestershire GL2 7EP

Tel: 01452 740268 **Fax:** 01452 740698

Owner: Mr & Mrs Rollo Clifford **Contact:** Mrs Rollo Clifford

Medieval/Elizabethan timber-framed manor house with walled garden. Reputed 12th century birthplace of 'Fair Rosamund' Clifford, mistress of King Henry II. Wool Barn c1560 and 16th century dovecote.

Location: OS Ref. SO748 080. 3m M5/J13.

Open: House & Garden: open by appointment for groups (10+). Garden: 27 Apr - 21 Jul: Thur & Fri, 2.30 - 5pm.

Admission: House, Garden & Wool Barn: £5. Garden only: £3. Wool Barn only £1.

[i] No photography inside. Tearoom for groups. Obligatory. P Tel for details.

GLOUCESTER CATHEDRAL
Chapter Office, College Green, Gloucester GL1 2LR

Tel: 01452 508211 **Fax:** 01452 300469

e-mail: lin@gloucestercathedral.org.uk **www.**gloucestercathedral.org.uk

Contact: Mrs L Henderson

Daily worship and rich musical tradition continue in this abbey church founded 1300 years ago. It has a Norman nave with massive cylindrical pillars, a magnificent east window with medieval glass and glorious fan-vaulted cloisters. You can also find the tombs of King Edward II and Robert, Duke of Normandy.

Location: OS Ref. SO832 188. Off Westgate Street in central Gloucester.

Open: Daily, 8am until after Evensong. Groups must book via the Chapter Office.

Admission: £3 donation requested.

Partial. WC. By arrangement. PNone. In grounds, on leads.

special events
see page 571

HAILES ABBEY
Nr Winchcombe, Cheltenham, Gloucestershire GL54 5PB

Tel/Fax: 01242 602398 **e-mail:** customers@english-heritage.org.uk
www.english-heritage.org.uk/hailes

Owner: English Heritage & The National Trust **Contact:** Visitor Operations Staff

Seventeen cloister arches and extensive excavated remains in lovely surroundings of an abbey founded by Richard, Earl of Cornwall, in 1246. There is a small museum and covered display area.

Location: OS Ref. SP050 300. 2m NE of Winchcombe off B4632. 1/2 m SE of B4632.

Open: 1 Apr - 31 Oct: daily, 10am - 5pm. 1 Jul - 31 Aug: daily, 10am - 6pm. 1 - 31 Oct: daily, 10am - 4pm.

Admission: Adult £3.30, Child £1.70, Conc. £2.50.

Partial. WC. P In grounds, on leads. Tel for details.

© NTPL / Nick Meers

HIDCOTE MANOR GARDEN
HIDCOTE BARTRIM NR CHIPPING CAMPDEN, GLOUCESTERSHIRE GL55 6LR
www.nationaltrust.org.uk/hidcote

Tel: 01386 438333 **Fax:** 01386 438817 **e-mail:** hidcote@nationaltrust.org.uk

Owner: The National Trust **Contact:** Visitor Services Manager

One of the most delightful gardens in England, created in the early 20th century by the great horticulturist Major Lawrence Johnston; a series of small gardens within the whole, separated by walls and hedges of different species; famous for rare shrubs, trees, herbaceous borders, 'old' roses and interesting plant species.

Location: OS Ref. SP176 429. 4m NE of Chipping Campden, 1m E of B4632 off B4081. At Mickleton 1/4 m E of Kiftsgate Court. Coaches are not permitted through Chipping Campden High Street.

Open: 25 Mar - 29 Oct: Sat - Wed, 10.30am - 6pm (from 2 Oct closes at 5pm), last admission 1hr before closing. Open Good Fri.

Admission: Adult £7, Child £3.50, Family (2+3) £17. Groups (15+) Adult £6.20, Child £3.10.

Limited. WC. Licensed. P Send SAE for details.

© NTPL/Rupert Truman

Dyrham Park.

HOLST BIRTHPLACE MUSEUM
4 Clarence Road, Pittville, Cheltenham GL52 2AY
tel: 01242 524846
e-mail: holstmuseum@btconnect.com   **www.**holstmuseum.org.uk
Owner: Holst Birthplace Trust   **Contact:** Amelia Marriette - Curator
Birthplace of Gustav Holst (1874-1934), composer of The Planets, containing his piano and personal memorabilia. Holst's music is played. The museum is also a fine period house showing the 'upstairs – downstairs' way of life in Regency and Victorian times, including a working kitchen, elegant drawing room and charming nursery.
Location: OS163 Ref. SO955 237. 5mins walk from town centre, opposite Pittville Gates.
Open: Mid Feb - mid Dec: Tue - Sat, 10am - 4pm. Except for booked groups or guided tours who are welcome by appointment.
Admission: Adult £3.50, Child/Conc. £3, Family (2+3) £8. Groups pay same prices unless having a guided tour (6-15): Adult £4.50, Conc. £3.50. Special rates for school groups on request.
i Photography by prior permission only. ⬚ T ♿ Partial. ⟨ℐ⟩ By arrangement. P None. ▪ 🐕 Guide dogs only. ❋ ⦂ Tel for details.

HORTON COURT 🦋
Horton, Nr Chipping Sodbury, Bristol, South Gloucestershire BS37 6QR
Tel: 01179 372501   **www.**nationaltrust.org.uk
Owner: The National Trust   **Contact:** Dyrham Park
A Norman Hall and an exceptionally fine detached ambulatory are all that remain of what is probably the oldest rectory in England.
Location: OS Ref. ST766 849. 3m NE of Chipping Sodbury, ³/₄ m N of Horton, 1m W of A46 (Bath-Stroud road).
Open: 15 Apr - 28 Oct: Wed & Sat, 2 - 6pm or dusk if earlier. Other times by written appointment with tenant. Unsuitable for coach tours.
Admission: Adult £2.20, Child £1.10, Family (2+2) £5.60.
i No WC. ♿ Partial. P

Frampton Court.

Nigel Fisher

KELMSCOTT MANOR 🏚
KELMSCOTT, NR LECHLADE, GLOUCESTERSHIRE GL7 3HJ

www.kelmscottmanor.co.uk

Tel: 01367 252486   **Fax:** 01367 253754   **e-mail:** admin@kelmscottmanor.co.uk
Owner: Society of Antiquaries   **Contact:** Property Manager
Kelmscott Manor, a Grade I listed Tudor farmhouse adjacent to the River Thames, was the summer house of William Morris from 1871 until his death in 1896. Morris loved the house as a work of true craftsmanship, totally unspoilt and unaltered, and in harmony with the village and the surrounding countryside. He considered it so natural in its setting as to be almost organic, it looked to him as if it had 'grown up out of the soil', and with 'quaint garrets amongst great timbers of the roof where of old times the tillers and herdsmen slept'. The house contains an outstanding collection of the possessions and work of Morris and his associates, including furniture, original textiles, carpets and ceramics. The Manor is surrounded by beautiful gardens with barns, dovecote, a meadow and a stream. The garden was a constant source of inspiration for Morris and the images are reflected in his textile and wallpaper designs. William Morris called the village of Kelmscott: 'a heaven on earth'. His delight in its discovery can still be felt by the visitor today. The Manor is the most evocative of all the houses associated with William Morris.

Location: OS Ref. SU252 988. At SE end of the village, 2m due E of Lechlade, off the Lechlade - Faringdon Road.
Open: Apr - Sept: Weds, 11am - 5pm. 3rd Sat in Apr, May, Jun & Sept, also 1st & 3rd Sat in July & Aug, 2 - 5pm. Ticket sales start 30 mins prior to opening. Last entry 30 min prior to closing. No bookings on public open days. House has limited capacity; timed ticket system operates. Group bookings on Thurs & Fris.
Admission: Adult £8.50, Child/Student £4.25. Gardens only: £2.

⬚ T ♿ Grounds. WCs. ▣ Licensed. ⟨ℐ⟩ By arrangement. P Limited for coaches. ❋

South West - England

KIFTSGATE COURT GARDENS

CHIPPING CAMPDEN, GLOUCESTERSHIRE GL55 6LN

www.kiftsgate.co.uk

Tel/Fax: 01386 438777   **e-mail:** kiftsgte@aol.com

Owner: Mr and Mrs J G Chambers   **Contact:** Mr J G Chambers

Magnificently situated garden on the edge of the Cotswold escarpment with views towards the Malvern Hills. Many unusual shrubs and plants including tree peonies, abutilons, specie and old-fashioned roses. Winner HHA/Christie's Garden of the Year Award 2003.

Location: OS Ref. SP173 430. 4m NE of Chipping Campden. ¼ m W of Hidcote Garden.

Open: Apr, Aug & Sept: Sun, Mon & Wed, 2 - 6pm. May, June & July: daily except Thurs & Fri, 12 noon - 6pm. Coaches by appointment.

Admission: Adult £5.50, Child £1.50. Groups (20+) £5.

MILL DENE GARDEN

BLOCKLEY, MORETON-IN-MARSH, GLOUCESTERSHIRE GL56 9HU

www.milldenegarden.co.uk

Tel: 01386 700457, **Fax:** 01386 700526, **e-mail:** info@milldene.co.uk

Owner: Mr B S Dare   **Contact:** Mrs W V Dare

The Dares have created one of the most interesting gardens in the Cotswolds. It is personal, witty, surprising and of course, beautiful as well as horticulturally excellent.

Features of this 1 hectare garden include a misty grotto, a bog garden and stream. There are plenty of seats from which to enjoy the mill pond and its trout, kingfisher and ducks. It is an exercise in making the most of a difficult and steep sided site. It is also an exercise in creating something beautiful in which to meditate and to nourish the senses.

Location: OS Ref SP163 347. Off A44 from Bourton-on-the-Hill. Follow brown signs. 30 mins from Stratford-on-Avon and Cheltenham.

Open: Apr - Oct. Tues - Fri, 10am - 5.30pm. Occasional weekends for charity (see website).

Admission: Adult £4.50, Child £1 (under 15yrs), Conc £4. Groups (20+) £4 per head. RHS members welcome, free in Apr & Oct. Coaches and Groups welcome by appointment.

Partial. By arrangement. 2 ensuite (either kingsize doubles or twin) €

NTPL / Nadia MacKenzie

LODGE PARK & SHERBORNE ESTATE

SHERBORNE, NR CHELTENHAM, GLOUCESTERSHIRE GL54 3PP

www.nationaltrust.org.uk/lodgepark

Tel: 01451 844130   **Fax:** 01451 844131   **e-mail:** lodgepark@nationaltrust.org.uk

Owner: The National Trust   **Contact:** The Visitor Services Manager

Lodge Park is a rare example of a grandstand, situated on the picturesque Sherborne Estate in the Cotswolds, Lodge Park was created in 1634 by John 'Crump' Dutton. Inspired by his passion for gambling and banqueting, it is a unique survival of a Grandstand, Deer Course and Park. It was the home of Charles Dutton, 7th Lord Sherborne, until 1983 when he bequeathed his family's estate to The National Trust. The interior of the grandstand has been reconstructed to its original form and is the first project of its kind undertaken by the Trust that relies totally on archaeological evidence. The park behind was designed by Charles Bridgeman in 1725. The Sherborne Estate is 1650ha (4000 acres) of rolling Cotswold countryside with sweeping views down to the River Windrush. Much of the village of Sherborne is owned by the Trust, including the post office, shop, school and the social club. There are walks for all ages around the estate, which include the restored and working water meadows.

Location: OS Ref. SP146 123. 3m E of Northleach, approach only from A40. Bus: Swanbrook 53 Oxford-Gloucester, 1m walk from bus stop.

Open: Grandstand & Deer Park: 24 Mar - 2 June & 1 Sept - 29 Oct: Fri - Mon; 3 June - 29 Aug: daily except Wed & Thurs; 11am - 4pm (3pm Sats). Estate: All year: daily.

Admission: Adult £4.50, Child £2.50, Family £11. Estate: Free.

Video shows during the day. Civil ceremonies only. Partial. Dogs must be kept under close control. Tel for details.

MISARDEN PARK GARDENS

Stroud, Gloucestershire GL6 7JA

Tel: 01285 821303   **Fax:** 01285 821530   **e-mail:** estate.office@miserdenestate.co.uk

Owner/Contact: Major M T N H Wills

Historic garden dating from 17th century, standing 250m above sea level overlooking the 'Golden Valley'. Terraced lawns, long double herbaceous borders – important yew topiary (some by Lutyens). Fine trees, parterre with roses. Summerhouse and rill. Blue border and scented border. Good nursery adjacent.

Location: OS Ref. SO941 088. 6m NW Cirencester. Follow signs to Miserden from A417 or B4070.

Open: 4 Apr - 28 Sept: Tue - Thur, 10am - 5pm.

Admission: Adult £4 (guided tours extra), Child Free. 10% reduction for pre-arranged groups (20-55).

By arrangement. Limited for coaches.

© Mr David Lowsley-Williams

Tapestry, Chavenage.

© NTPL/Matthew Antrobus

NEWARK PARK 🌿

OZLEWORTH, WOTTON-UNDER-EDGE, GLOUCESTERSHIRE GL12 7PZ

www.nationaltrust.org.uk

Tel/Fax: 01453 842644 **e-mail:** newarkpark@nationaltrust.org.uk

Owner: The National Trust **Contact:** Michael Claydon

A Tudor hunting lodge converted into a castellated country house by James Wyatt. An atmospheric house, set in spectacular countryside with outstanding views.

Location: OS Ref172. ST786 934. 1½m E of Wotton-under-Edge, 1¼ m S of Junction of A4135 & B4058, follow signs for Ozleworth, House signposted from main road.

Open: House & Garden: 5 Apr - 31 May: Wed, Thurs & BH Mons; 1 Jun - 29 Oct: Wed, Thur, Sat, Sun & BH Mons, 11am - 5pm (last entry 4.30pm). Also open Easter: Good Fri - Mon, 11am - 5pm.

Admission: Adult £5, Child £2.50, Family (2+3) £13. Groups by appointment. No reduction for groups.

ℹ️No photography in house. ♿Partial. 📷By arrangement. 🅿️ ◼️
♿In grounds, on leads.

OWLPEN MANOR 🏠

NR ULEY, GLOUCESTERSHIRE GL11 5BZ

www.owlpen.com

Tel: 01453 860261 **Fax:** 01453 860819 **Restaurant:** 01453 860816
e-mail: sales@owlpen.com

Owner: Mr & Mrs Nicholas Mander **Contact:** Jayne Simmons

Romantic Tudor manor house, 1450-1616, with Cotswold Arts & Crafts associations. Remote wooded valley setting, with 16th and 17th century formal terraced gardens and magnificent yews. Contains unique painted cloth wall hangings, family and Arts & Crafts collections. Mill (1726), Court House (1620); licensed restaurant in medieval Cyder House. Victorian church. *"Owlpen - ah, what a dream is there!"* - Vita Sackville-West.

Location: OS Ref. ST801 984. 3m E of Dursley, 1m E of Uley, off B4066, by Old Crown pub.

Open: May - Sept: Tue, Thurs & Sun, 2 - 5pm. Restaurant 12 noon - 5pm.

Admission: Adult £5.25, Child (4-14yrs) £2.25, Family (2+4) £14.50. Gardens & Grounds: Adult £3.25, Child £1.25. Group rates available.

🎭♿Unsuitable. 🍴Licensed. 🅿️ 🏠Holiday cottages, all seasons, sleep 2 - 9.

OLD CAMPDEN HOUSE

Church St, Chipping Campden, Gloucestershire

Tel: 01628 825920/825925 (bookings) **e-mail:** bookings@landmarktrust.org.uk
www.landmarktrust.org.uk

Owner/Contact: The Landmark Trust

The site of Old Campden House, a Scheduled Ancient Monument, is owned and managed by the Landmark Trust, a building preservation charity. The main house was burnt to the ground during the Civil War but other buildings remain. The East and West Banqueting Houses and Almonry have been restored and are let for holidays throughout the year. Full details of Landmark's 183 historic buildings are featured in the Landmark Trust Handbook (price £11 refundable against first booking) from the Landmark Trust, Shottesbrooke, Maidenhead, Berkshire, SL6 3SW.

Location: OS Ref. SP156 394. Next to St James's Church in Church Street.

Open: Site open 30 days per year, with buildings open on 8 of these days. Contact the Landmark Trust for dates.

Admission: Free.

♿ 🏠Self catering for 6 & 5.

PAINSWICK ROCOCO GARDEN 🏠

PAINSWICK, GLOUCESTERSHIRE GL6 6TH

www.rococogarden.co.uk

Tel: 01452 813204 **Fax:** 01452 814888 **e-mail:** info@rococogarden.co.uk

Owner: Painswick Rococo Garden Trust **Contact:** P R Moir

Unique 18th century garden restoration situated in a hidden 6 acre Cotswold combe. Charming contemporary buildings are juxtaposed with winding woodland walks and formal vistas. Famous for its early spring show of snowdrops. Newly planted maze.

Location: OS Ref. SO864 106. ½ m NW of village of Painswick on B4073.

Open: 10 Jan - 31 Oct: daily, 11am - 5pm.

Admission: Adult £5, Child £2.50, OAP £4. Family (2+2) £13.
Free introductory talk for pre-booked groups (20+).

📷 ♿Partial. WC. 🍴Licensed. 🍴 🅿️ ◼️ ♿In grounds, on leads. 🔔 ✳️
🏠Tel for details.

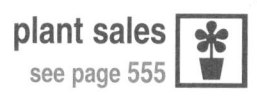

plant sales 🌱
see page 555

RODMARTON MANOR

CIRENCESTER, GLOUCESTERSHIRE GL7 6PF

www.rodmarton-manor.co.uk

Tel: 01285 841253 **Fax:** 01285 841298

e-mail: simon.biddulph@farming.co.uk

Owner: Mr & Mrs Simon Biddulph   **Contact:** Simon Biddulph

A Cotswold Arts and Crafts house, one of the last great country houses to be built in the traditional way and containing beautiful furniture, ironwork, china and needlework specially made for the house. The large garden complements the house and contains many areas of great beauty and character including the magnificent herbaceous borders, topiary, roses, rockery and kitchen garden. Available as a film location and for small functions.

Location: OS Ref. ST943 977. Off A433 between Cirencester and Tetbury.

Open: House & Garden: Easter Monday & May - Sept (Weds, Sats & BHs), 2 - 5pm

(Not guided tours). Garden only, for snowdrops,: 12, 16 & 19 Feb: from 1.30pm. Groups please book. Individuals need not book. Guided tours of the house (last about 1hr) may be booked for groups (15+) at any time of year (minimum group charge of £105 applies). Groups (5+) may book guided or unguided tours of the garden at other times.

Admission: House & Garden: £7, Child (5-15yrs) £3.50. Garden only: £4, Child (5-15yrs) £1. Guided tour of Garden: Entry fee plus £40 per group.

ⓘColour guidebook & postcards on sale. Available for filming. No photography in house. WCs in garden.

♿Garden & ground floor. ▣Most open days and groups by appointment. 𝐟By arrangement. 🅿 ▣ 🦮Guide dogs only. ✳

ST MARY'S CHURCH ⌗

Kempley, Gloucestershire

Tel: 0117 9750700 **www.**english-heritage.org.uk/southwest

Owner: English Heritage   **Contact:** The South West Regional Office

A delightful Norman church with superb wall paintings from the 12th - 14th centuries which were only discovered beneath whitewash in 1871.

Location: OS Ref. SO670 313. On minor road. 1½ m SE of Much Marcle, A449.

Open: 1 Mar - 31 Oct: daily, 10am - 6pm. Telephone for winter appointments

Admission: Free.

🦮

SEZINCOTE 🏠

Moreton-in-Marsh, Gloucestershire GL56 9AW

Tel: 01386 700444

Owner: Mr and Mrs D Peake   **Contact:** Mr E Peake

Exotic oriental water garden by Repton and Daniell. Large semi-circular orangery. House by S P Cockerell in Indian style was the inspiration for Brighton Pavilion.

Location: OS Ref. SP183 324. 2½ m SW of Moreton-in-Marsh. Turn W along A44 to Broadway and left into gateway just before Bourton-on-the-Hill (opposite the gate to Batsford Park, then 1m drive.

Open: Garden: Thurs, Fris & BH Mons, 2 - 6pm (dusk if earlier) throughout the year except Dec. House: May, Jun, Jul & Sept, Thurs & Fris, 2.30 - 6pm. Groups by written appointment.

Admission: House & Garden: Adult £6 (no children in house). Garden: Adult £4, Child £1.50 (under 5yrs Free).

♿Gravel paths. 🦮Guide dogs only. ✳

Hidcote Manor Garden.

open all year
see page 557

NTPL/ Nick Meers

SNOWSHILL MANOR

SNOWSHILL, NR BROADWAY, GLOUCESTERSHIRE WR12 7JU

www.nationaltrust.org.uk

Tel: 01386 852410 **Fax:** 01386 842822
e-mail: snowshillmanor@nationaltrust.org.uk

Owner: The National Trust **Contact:** The Property Manager

Snowshill Manor contains Charles Paget Wade's extraordinary collection of craftsmanship and design, including musical instruments, clocks, toys, bicycles, weavers' and spinners' tools and Japanese armour. Each room has something to interest or inspire the visitor. Run on organic principles, the intimate garden is laid out as a series of outdoor rooms, with terraces and ponds, and wonderful views across the Cotswold countryside.

The Snowshill Costume Collection can be viewed by appointment only at Berrington Hall, please tel: 01568 613720 on Thursdays or Fridays.

Location: OS Ref. SP096 339. 3m SW of Broadway, turning off the A44, by Broadway Green.

Open: House: 25 Mar - 29 Oct: Wed - Sun & BH Mons, 12 noon - 5pm. Garden: as House, 11am - 5.30pm. Restaurant & Shop: as Garden also 4 Nov - 10 Dec: Sat & Sun, 12 noon - 4pm.

Admission: House, Gardens, Shop & Restaurant: Adult £7.30, Child £3.65, Family £18.50. Garden, shop & Restaurant only: Adult £4, Child £2, Family £10. Visitors arriving by bicycle or on foot offered a voucher redeemable at Snowshill NT shop or tearoom. Coach & School groups by written appointment only.

Partial. Licensed. Tel for details.

STANWAY HOUSE & WATER GARDEN

STANWAY, CHELTENHAM, GLOS GL54 5PQ

www.stanwayfountain.co.uk

Tel: 01386 584528 **Fax:** 01386 584688 **e-mail:** stanwayhse@btopenworld.com

Owner: Lord Neidpath **Contact:** Debbie Lewis

"As perfect and pretty a Cotswold manor house as anyone is likely to see" (*Fodor's Great Britain 1998 guidebook*). Stanway's beautiful architecture, furniture, parkland and village are now complemented by the restored 18th century water garden and the magnificent fountain – 300 feet – making it the tallest garden fountain and gravity fountain in the world. Teas available. Beer for sale. Wedding reception venue.

Location: OS Ref. SP061 323. N of Winchcombe, just off B4077.

Open: House & Garden: June - Aug: Tue & Thur, 2 - 5pm. Garden: July & Aug, Sats only, 2 - 5pm. Private tours by arrangement at other times.

Admission: Adult £6, Child £1.50, OAP £4.50. Garden only: Adult £4, Child £1, OAP £3.

Film & photographic location. Wedding receptions. By arrangement.
In grounds on leads.
Grounds largely accessible. WCs. Tel for details.

©National Trust Photographic Library/Stephen Robson

WESTBURY COURT GARDEN ❧

WESTBURY-ON-SEVERN, GLOUCESTERSHIRE GL14 1PD

www.nationaltrust.org.uk

Tel: 01452 760461   **e-mail:** westburycourt@nationaltrust.org.uk

Owner: The National Trust   **Contact:** The Head Gardener

A Dutch water garden with canals and yew hedges, laid out between 1696 and 1705; the earliest of its kind remaining in England. Restored in 1971 and planted with species dating from pre-1700 including apple, pear and plum trees.

Location: OS Ref. SO718 138. 9m SW of Gloucester on A48.

Open: 8 Mar - 30 Jun & 30 Aug - 29 Oct: Wed - Sun, 10am - 5pm. 1 Jul - 29 Aug: daily, 10am - 5pm. Open BH Mons. Other times of year by appointment. Evening garden tours (book at garden): 10 May, 14 Jun, 12 Jul & 16 Aug.

Admission: Adult £4, Child £2, Family £10.

🖸 ⭒ Grounds largely accessible. WCs. 🅿 ⬚ Tel for details.

SUDELEY 🏛   *See page 240 for full page entry.*

WHITTINGTON COURT 🏛
Whittington, Cheltenham, Gloucestershire GL54 4HF

Tel: 01242 820556   **Fax:** 01242 820218

Owner: Mr & Mrs Jack Stringer   **Contact:** Mrs J Stringer

Elizabethan manor house. Family possessions including ceramics, antique and modern glass, fossils and fabrics.

Location: OS Ref. SP014 206. 4m E of Cheltenham on N side of A40.

Open: 15 - 30 April & 12 - 28 Aug: 2 - 5pm.

Admission: Adult £4, Child £1, OAP £3.

🖸 🅿

WESTONBIRT ARBORETUM

TETBURY, GLOUCESTERSHIRE GL8 8QS

www.forestry.gov.uk/westonbirt

Tel: 01666 880220   **Fax:** 01666 880559   **e-mail:** Westonbirt@forestry.gsi.gov.uk

Owner: The Forestry Commission   **Contact:** Helen Daniels

Westonbirt is a wonderful world of trees and is beautiful at any time of year. Set in 240 hectares of glorious Cotswold countryside, it has 17 miles of paths along which to stroll and over 17,000 trees and shrubs, including 130 British champions.

Spring is ablaze with colour from rhododendrons to bluebells, autumn brings brilliant reds, oranges and gold. Summer brings cool leafy glades and exciting events including The Classical Concert and The Festival of Wood. Add to this The Oak Hall,

shop, plant centre and a superb restaurant and you have a perfect day out.

Location: OS Ref. ST856 896. 3 miles SW of Tetbury on A433.

Open: All year, 10am - 8pm or dusk if earlier. Length of visit: 2 - 4 hours.

Admission: Depending on time of year: Adults £5 - £7.50, Child (under 14yrs) Free, Conc. £4 - £6.50, Families £10 - £15. Group rates available, please telephone for details.

🖸 ⭒ WC and parking on site. Wheelchairs on loan, booking necessary.

⬤ 🍴 🅿 ❋ ⬚ Tel for details.

Bath & North East Somerset Counci

MAP 2

MUSEUM OF COSTUME & ASSEMBLY ROOMS

www.museumofcostume.co.uk

The Assembly Rooms in Bath are open to the public daily (free of charge) and are also popular for dinners, dances, concerts, conferences and Civil weddings.

Originally known as the Upper Rooms, they were designed by John Wood the Younger and opened in 1771. The magnificent interior consists of a splendid Ball Room, Tea Room and Card Room, connected by two fine octagonal rooms. This plan was perfect for 'assemblies', evening entertainments popular in the 18th century, which included dancing, music, card-playing and tea drinking. They are now owned by The National Trust and managed by Bath & North East Somerset Council, which runs a full conference service.

The building also houses one of the largest and most comprehensive collections of fashionable dress in the world, the Museum of Costume. Its extensive displays cover the history of fashion from the late 16th century to the present day. Hand-held audioguides allow visitors to learn about the fashions on display while the lighting is kept to levels suitable for fragile garments. The 'Dress of the Year' collection traces significant moments in modern fashion history from 1963. For the serious student of fashion, the reference library and study facilities are available by appointment.

The museum shops sell publications and gifts associated with the history of costume and are open daily to all visitors.

Owner:
The National Trust

▶ CONTACT

For Room Hire:
Mr Tom Deller
Room Hire Manager
Stall Street
Bath BA1 1LZ

Tel: 01225 477173
Fax: 01225 477476

e-mail: tom_deller@
bathnes.gov.uk

Museum Enquiries:
Tel: 01225 477173
Fax: 01225 477743

▶ LOCATION

OS Ref. ST750 648

Near centre of Bath, 10m from M4/J18. Park & Ride or public car park.

Rail: Great Western from London Paddington (regular service) 90 mins approx.

Air: Bristol airport 45 mins.

▶ OPENING TIMES

All Year
January/February & November/December: 11am - 4pm.
March - October: 11am - 5pm.

Closed 25 & 26 December
Last exit 1hr after closing.

Special exhibitions:
'The Nureyev Style', until 31 December 2006.
'John Bates: Fashion Designer', 14 July - 28 August 2006.

▶ ADMISSION

Assembly Rooms ... Free
Museum of Costume:
Adult £6.50
Child* (summer).... £4.50
Conc. £5.50
Family (2+4) £18.00
Groups (20+)
Adult £5.25
Child* (summer).... £3.75
Child* (winter)....... £3.35

Joint Saver Ticket with Roman Baths
Adult £13.00
Child* £7.60
Conc. £11.00
Family (2+4) £36.00
Groups (20+)
Adult £8.80
Child* (summer).... £5.60
Child* (winter)....... £4.80

* Age 6 - 16yrs.
Child under 6yrs Free.

CONFERENCE/FUNCTION

ROOM	SIZE	MAX CAPACITY
Ballroom	103' x 40'	500/310
Octagon	47' x 47'	120/120
Tea Room	58' x 40'	260/170
Card Room	59' x 18'	80/60

ℹ️ Conference facilities.

📖 Extensive book & gift shops.

Ⴑ Corporate hospitality. Function facilities.

♿ Suitable. WC.

🚶 Hourly. Individual guided tours by arrangement.

🎧 English/Dutch/French/German/Italian/Japanese/Spanish.

🅿️ Charlotte Street car park.

📋 Teachers' pack.   🐕 Guide dogs only.

🔔 Civil Weddings/Receptions.

❄️

South West - England

Bath & North East Somerset Council

MAP 2

THE ROMAN BATHS & PUMP ROOM

www.romanbaths.co.uk

Owner:
Bath & North East
Somerset Council

▶ **CONTACT**
For Room Hire:
Mr Tom Deller
Stall Street
Bath BA1 1LZ
Tel: 01225 477734
Fax: 01225 477476
e-mail: tom_deller@
bathnes.gov.uk

**For visits to
Roman Baths:**
Tel: 01225 477785
Fax: 01225 477743

▶ **LOCATION**
OS Ref. ST750 648

Centre of Bath,
10m from M4/J18. Park
& Ride recommended.

Rail: Great Western
from London
Paddington,
half
hourly service,
1 hr 17 mins duration.

The first stop for any visitor to Bath is the Roman Baths surrounding the hot springs where the city began and which are still its heart. Here you'll see one of the country's finest ancient monuments – the great Roman temple and bathing complex built almost 2000 years ago. Discover the everyday life of the Roman spa and see ancient treasures from the Temple of Sulis Minerva. A host of new interpretive methods bring these spectacular buildings vividly to life and help visitors to understand the extensive remains.

The Grand Pump Room, overlooking the Spring, is the social heart of Bath. The elegant interior of

1795 is something every visitor to Bath should see. You can enjoy a glass of spa water drawn from the fountain, perhaps as an appetiser to a traditional Pump Room tea, morning coffee or lunch. The Pump Room Trio and resident pianists provide live music daily. The Roman Baths shop sells publications and gifts related to the site.

In the evening, the Pump Room is available for banquets, dances and concerts. Nothing could be more magical than a meal on the terrace which overlooks the Great Bath, or a pre-dinner drinks reception by torchlight around the Great Bath itself.

Bath & North East Somerset Council

🎁 Extensive gift shop.

ℹ️ Award-winning guide book in English, French and German.

🍽️ Comprehensive service for private and corporate entertainment. The Assembly Rooms, Guildhall, Victoria Art Gallery and Pump Room are all available for private hire, contact the Pump Room.

♿ Free access to terrace. Restricted access to the Museum, special visits for disabled groups by appointment. People with special needs welcome, teaching sessions available.

☕ Pump Room coffees, lunches and teas, no reservation needed. Music by Pump Room Trio or pianist.

🚶 Hourly. Private tours by appointment.

🎧 English, French, German, Italian, Japanese, Spanish, Dutch, Mandarin.

🅿️ City centre car parks available.

🏫 Teaching sessions available. Pre-booking necessary.

💒 Civil Weddings in two private rooms with photographs around the Great Bath.

❄️

▶ **OPENING TIMES**
January - February:
9.30am - 4.30pm.
March - June: 9am - 5pm.
July - August: 9am - 9pm.
September - October:
9am - 5pm.
November - December:
9.30am - 4.30pm.
Last exit 1 hour after closing.

Closed 25 & 26 December.

The Pump Room Trio plays 10am - 12 noon Mon - Sat and 3 - 5pm Sunday. During the summer it also plays from 3 - 5pm, Mon - Sat. Resident pianists play at lunch-time.

▶ **ADMISSION**
Roman Baths:
Adult £10.00
Child (6-16yrs) £6.00
Conc. £8.50
Family (2+4) £28.00
Groups (20+)
Adult £7.20
Child* (summer).... £4.50
Child* (winter)....... £4.20

Joint Saver Ticket with Museum of Costume
Adult £13.00
Child* £7.60
Conc. £11.00
Family (2+4) £36.00
Groups (20+)
Adult £8.80
Child* (summer).... £5.60
Child* (winter)....... £4.80

* Age 6 - 16yrs.
Child under 6yrs Free.

CONFERENCE/FUNCTION

ROOM	SIZE	MAX CAPACITY
Great Roman Bath		400 summer 200 winter
Pump Rm.	57' x 41'	180
Terrace overlooking Great Bath	83' x 11'	70
Reception Hall	56' x 44'	100
Smoking Rm & Drawing Rm	28' x 16'	40

NO 1 ROYAL CRESCENT

BATH BA1 2LR

www.bath-preservation-trust.org.uk

Tel: 01225 428126   **Fax:** 01225 481850

e-mail: no1museum@bptrust.org.uk

Owner: Bath Preservation Trust   **Contact:** Victoria Barwell - Curator

Take a look inside a sumptuous piece of Bath's unmatched architectural heritage and revel in the opulence of grand Georgian life. The exquisitely restored and lavishly furnished house is the epitome of elegant 18th century living, and a unique museum shop completes the experience.

Location: OS Ref. ST746 653. M4/J18. A46 to Bath. ¼ m NW of city centre.

Open: Mid Feb - end Nov: Tues - Sun, 10.30am - 5pm. BH Mons. Closes 4pm in Nov. Closed Good Fri. Last admission 30 mins before closing. Evening tours and other times by arrangement.

Admission: Adult £5, Child (5-16yrs) £2.50, Conc £3.50, Family £12. Groups: £3, Schools: £2.50 (Adults with school groups free).

⬜ ⬜ ♿Unsuitable. 🔧 **P** The Royal Crescent & Bath centre. ▦

Farleigh Hungerford Castle.

THE AMERICAN MUSEUM & GARDENS

CLAVERTON MANOR, BATH BA2 7BD

www.americanmuseum.org

Tel: 01225 460503   **Fax:** 01225 469160   **e-mail:** info@americanmuseum.org

Owner: The Trustees of the American Museum in Britain   **Contact:** Julian Blades

Claverton Manor was built in 1820 by Jeffry Wyattville. In the late 1950s it became the home of the American Museum in Britain. Inside the Manor there are 18 period rooms which show the development of American decorative arts from the 1680s to the 1860s. In addition there are galleries devoted to Folk Art, Native American Art, and our large collection of quilts and other textiles. The extensive grounds contain a replica of part of the garden at Mount Vernon, George Washington's house in Virginia, and an

Arboretum of North American trees and shrubs. Light lunches and teas are available.

Location: OS Ref. ST784 640. 2m SE of Bath city centre.

Open: 18 Mar - 29 Oct: Tues - Sun (open BH Mons and Mons in Aug) 12noon - 5pm. 18 Nov - 17 Dec: Tues - Sun, 12 - 4pm (Wed late night - 7.30pm).

Admission: Adult £6.50, Child £3.50, Conc. £6. Groups (20-100): Adult £5, OAP £5.

⬜ ⬜ ♿Partial. WC. 📷 🔧By arrangement. **P** ▦ 🐕In grounds, on leads.

📺Tel for details or visit website.

NTPL: Neil Campbell-Sharp

BARRINGTON COURT ❀

BARRINGTON, ILMINSTER, SOMERSET TA19 0NQ

www.nationaltrust.org.uk

Tel: 01460 241938 **Info:** 01460 242614
e-mail: barringtoncourt@nationaltrust.org.uk

Owner: The National Trust   **Contact:** Visitor Services Manager

The enchanting formal garden, influenced by Gertrude Jekyll, is laid out in a series of walled rooms, including the White Garden, the Rose and Iris Garden and the Lily Garden. The working Kitchen Garden has espaliered apple, pear and plum trees trained along high stone walls. The Tudor manor house was restored in the 1920s by the Lyle family. It is let to Stuart Interiors as showrooms with antique furniture for sale, thereby offering NT visitors a different kind of visit.

Location: OS Ref. ST395 181. In Barrington village, 5m NE of Ilminster, on B3168.

Open: House, Garden & Shop: 2 - 31 Mar & 1 - 31 Oct: daily except Weds, 11am - 4.30pm. 1 Apr - 30 Sept: daily except Weds, 11am - 5pm. 2 - 17 Dec: Sats & Suns, 11am - 4pm. Restaurant (weekdays: lunches only, weekends: lunch & teas): 2 - 31 Mar & 1 - 31 Oct: daily except Weds, 11am - 4pm. 1 Apr - 30 Sept: Mon, Tues, Thurs & Fri, 12 noon - 3pm. Sats & Suns, 12 - 5pm. 2 - 17 Dec: Sat & Suns, 11am - 4pm. Beagles café: 30 Mar - 1 Oct: daily except Weds, 11am - 5pm. 7 - 29 Oct: Sat & Suns, 11am - 4pm. NB. Café may close in poor weather (Oct) but restaurant will be open.

Admission: Adult £7, Child £3, Family (2+3) £17. Groups: £6.

🔲 🎫 ♿ Grounds. WC. 🍴 Licensed. **P** 🖼 🐾 Tel for details.

THE CHALICE WELL & GARDENS

CHILKWELL STREET, GLASTONBURY, SOMERSET BA6 8DD

www.chalicewell.org.uk

Tel: 01458 831154   **Fax:** 01458 835528   **e-mail:** info@chalicewell.org.uk

Owner/Contact: Chalice Well Trust

A jewel of a garden, nestling around one of Britain's oldest Holy Wells. Legend tells of the Well being visited by Joseph of Arimethea, bearing the Chalice of the Last Supper, and of King Arthur on his Grail Quest. Today, the beautifully landscaped grounds with the iron-rich waters are a haven of peace and tranquillity.

Location: OS Ref. ST507 384. On the A361 Glastonbury - Shepton Mallet road, at the foot of Glastonbury Tor.

Open: All year: Mar - Oct, 10am - 5.30pm. Nov - Feb, 10am - 4pm.

Admission: Adult £3, Child £1.50, Conc. £2.50.

ℹ️ No smoking in gardens. 🔲 ♿ 🐾 By arrangement. **P** Limited. At nearby Rural Life Museum. 🖼 🐕 Guide dogs only. ❄️ 🐾 Tel for details.

BECKFORD'S TOWER & MUSEUM
Lansdown Road, Bath BA1 9BH

Tel: 01225 460705   **Fax:** 01225 481850   **e-mail:** beckford@bptrust.org.uk

Owner: Bath Preservation Trust   **Contact:** The Administrator

Built in 1827 for eccentric William Beckford and recently restored by Bath Preservation Trust. The tower is a striking feature of the Bath skyline.

Location: OS Ref. ST735 676. Lansdown Road, 2m NNW of city centre.

Open: Easter weekend - end of October: Sats, Suns & BH Mons, 10.30am - 5pm.

Admission: Adult £3, Child/OAP £2, Family £7. BPT & NACF members: Free. Groups by arrangement.

BREAN DOWN ❀
Brean, North Somerset

Tel: 01934 844518   **www.nationaltrust.org.uk**

Owner: The National Trust   **Contact:** Property Manager

Brean Down, rich in wildlife and history, is one of the most striking landmarks of the Somerset coastline, extending 1¹/₂ m into the Bristol Channel. A Palmerston Fort built in 1865 and then re-armed in World War II, provides a unique insight into Brean's past.

Location: OS Ref. ST290 590. Between Weston-super-Mare and Burnham-on-Sea about 8m from M5/J22. Rail: Highbridge 5m.

Open: All year.

Admission: Free.

ℹ️ The cliffs are extremely steep. Please stay on the main paths and wear suitable footwear. 🔲 (Not NT.) ♿ Partial. WC. 🍴 (Not NT.) 🐾 Guided walks. **P** 🖼 🐕 On leads. ❄️

THE BUILDING OF BATH MUSEUM
**The Countess of Huntingdon's Chapel, The Vineyards,
The Paragon, Bath BA1 5NA**

Tel: 01225 333895 / 01225 445473   **e-mail:** amanda@bathmuseum.co.uk

Owner: Bath Preservation Trust   **Contact:** The Administrator

Discover the essence of life in Georgian Bath.

Location: OS Ref. ST751 655. 5 mins walk from city centre. Bath M4/J18.

Open: 14 Feb - 30 Nov: Tue - Sun & BH Mons, 10.30am - 5pm (last adm. 4.30pm).

Admission: Adult £4, Child £2.50, Conc. £3. Groups: £3.

CLEEVE ABBEY ⌗
Washford, Nr Watchet, Somerset TA23 0PS

Tel: 01984 640377   **Fax:** 01984 641348   **e-mail:** customers@english-heritage.org.uk
www.english-heritage.org.uk/cleeve

Owner: English Heritage   **Contact:** Visitor Operations Staff

There are few monastic sites where you will see such a complete set of cloister buildings, including the refectory with its magnificent timber roof. Built in the 13th century, this Cistercian abbey was saved from destruction at the Dissolution by being turned into a house and then a farm.

Location: OS Ref. ST047 407. In Washford, ¹/₄ m S of A39.

Open: 1 Apr - 30 Jun & Sept: daily, 10am - 5pm. 1 Jul - 31 Aug: daily, 10am - 6pm. 1 - 31 Oct: daily, 10am - 4pm.

Admission: Adult £3.40, Child £1.70, Conc. £2.60. 15% discount for groups (11+).

ℹ️ WC. 🔲 ♿ Partial. **P** 🐾 In grounds, on leads. 🐾 Tel for details.

NT Photographic Library: Magnus Rew

Dunster Castle.

CLEVEDON COURT ⚬

Tickenham Road, Clevedon, North Somerset BS21 6QU
Tel: 01275 872257 **www**.nationaltrust.org.uk
Owner: The National Trust   **Contact:** The
Administrator
Home of the Elton family since 1709, this 14th century manor house, once partly
fortified, has a 13th century hall and tower. Collections of Nailsea glass and Eltonware
ceramics. 18th century terraced garden.
Location: OS Ref. ST423 716. 1¹/₂ m E of Clevedon, on B3130, signposted from M5/J20.
Open: 2 Apr - 28 Sept: Wed, Thur, Sun & BH Mons, 2 - 5pm.
Admission: Adult £5.50, Child £2.50. Groups & coaches by arrangement.
♿No wheelchair access. **P** Limited. ▣ ✖

COLERIDGE COTTAGE ⚬

35 Lime Street, Nether Stowey, Bridgwater, Somerset TA5 1NQ
Tel: 01278 732662 **www**.nationaltrust.org.uk
Owner: The National Trust   **Contact:** The Custodian
The home of Samuel Taylor Coleridge for three years from 1797, with mementoes of
the poet on display. It was here that he wrote *The Rime of the Ancient Mariner,* part
of *Christabel, Frost at Midnight* and *Kubla Khan.*
Location: OS Ref. ST191 399. At W end of Nether Stowey, on S side of A39, 8m W of
Bridgwater.
Open: 1 Apr - 24 Sept: Thur - Sun, 2 - 5pm (open BH Mons).
Admission: Adult £3.50, Child £1.70, no reduction for groups, which must book.
ℹ️No WC. ♿ Braille guide. **P** 500yds (not NT). ✖

COMBE SYDENHAM COUNTRY PARK 🏛

Monksilver, Taunton, Somerset TA4 4JG
Tel: 0800 7838572
Owner: Theed Estates   **Contact:** John Burns
Built in 1580 on the site of a monastic settlement. Deer Park and woodland walks.
Location: OS Ref. ST075 366. Monksilver.
Open: Country Park: Easter - end Sept. House: All year by appointment only.
Admission: Country Park & car park Free. House & Gardens £5pp. Tel for details.

Christopher Simon Sykes

COTHAY MANOR

GREENHAM, WELLINGTON, SOMERSET TA21 0JR

Tel: 01823 672283 **Fax:** 01823 672345
Owner/Contact: Mr & Mrs Alastair Robb
It has been said that Cothay Manor is the finest example of a small classic,
medieval manor house in England. The manor has remained virtually untouched
since it was enlarged in 1480. The gardens, laid out in the 1920s have been
completely re-designed and replanted within the original framework of yew
hedges. A white garden, scarlet and purple garden, herbaceous borders and bog
garden are but a few of the delights to be found in this magical place.
Location: OS Ref. ST085 212. From M5 W J/27, take A38 dir Wellington. 3¹/₂ m left
to Greenham. From N/J26 take A38 dir. Exeter. 3¹/₂ m right to Greenham (1¹/₂ m).
On LH corner at bottom of hill turn right. Cothay 1m, always keeping left.
Open: May - Sept: Weds, Thurs, Suns & BHs, 2 - 6pm.
Admission: Garden: Adult £4.50, Child (under 12yrs) £2.50. House: Groups only
(20+): by arrangement throughout the year.
ℹ️No photography in house. ▨ ⊤ ♿ ▣ ℹ️By arrangement. **P** ✖ ✳

CROWE HALL

Widcombe Hill, Bath, Somerset BA2 6AR
Tel: 01225 310322
Owner/Contact: John Barratt Esq
Ten acres of romantic hillside gardens. Victorian grotto, classical Bath villa with good
18th century furniture and paintings.
Location: OS Ref. ST760 640. In Bath, 1m SE of city centre.
Open: Gardens only open 9 Apr, 14 May & 11 Jun, 2 - 6pm. House and Gardens by
appointment.
Admission: House & Gardens: Adult £5. Gardens only: Adult £3, Child £1.

DODINGTON HALL

Nr Nether Stowey, Bridgwater, Somerset TA5 1LF
Tel: 01278 741400
Owner: Lady Gass   **Contact:** P Quinn (occupier)
Small Tudor manor house on the lower slopes of the Quantocks. Great Hall with oak
roof. Semi-formal garden with roses and shrubs.
Location: OS Ref. ST172 405. ¹/₂ m from A39, 11m N of Bridgwater, 7m E of Williton.
Open: 3 - 13 Jun, 2 - 5pm.
Admission: Donations to charity.
ℹ️No inside photography. ♿Unsuitable. **P**Limited. No coach parking.

NTPL: Bill Batten

DUNSTER CASTLE ⚬

DUNSTER, NR MINEHEAD, SOMERSET TA24 6SL

www.nationaltrust.org.uk

Tel: 01643 821314 **Fax:** 01643 823000 **e-mail:** dunstercastle@nationaltrust.org.uk
Owner: The National Trust   **Contact:** The Property Manager
Dramatically sited on a wooded hill, a castle has existed here since at least Norman
times. The 15th century gatehouse survives, and the present building was
remodelled in 1868-72 by Antony Salvin for the Luttrell family, who lived here for
600 years. The fine oak staircase and plasterwork of the 17th century house he
adapted can still be seen. There is a sheltered terrace to the south which is home to
palms, sub-tropical plant species, and a varied collection of citrus. The terraced
gardens also house the National Collection of strawberry trees (arbutus) and there
is a pleasant riverside walk beside the River Avill.
Location: OS Ref. SS995 435. In Dunster, 3m SE of Minehead.
Open: Castle: 18 Mar - 29 Oct: daily except Thur & Fri (open Good Fri), 11am -
5pm; 30 Oct - 5 Nov: daily except Thur & Fri, 11am - 4pm. Garden & Park: 1 Jan
- 17 Mar & 30 Oct - 31 Dec: daily (closed 25/26 Dec), 11am - 4pm. 18 Mar - 29 Oct:
10am - 5pm. Varied events programme, please telephone for full details. Major roof repairs will be undertaken in 2006. Property open as normal. Access to
one or two rooms may be restricted. Please telephone for details.
Admission: Castle, Garden & Park: Adult £7.50, Child £3.80, Family (2+3) £18.50.
Groups (15+): £6.40. Garden & Park only: Adult £4.10, Child £2, Family £10.
▣ ▨ ♿Braille guide. ℹ️ Out of hours by arrangement. **P** ▣
✖In park, on leads. ☎ Tel for details (0870 2404068) or visit website.

DUNSTER WORKING WATERMILL

Mill Lane, Dunster, Nr Minehead, Somerset TA24 6SW

Tel: 01643 821759   **www**.nationaltrust.org.uk

Owner: The National Trust   **Contact:** The Tenant

Built on the site of a mill mentioned in the Domesday Survey of 1086. The mill is a private business and all visitors, including NT members, are asked to pay the admission charge.

Location: OS Ref. SS995 435. On River Avill, beneath Castle Tor, approach via Mill Lane or Castle gardens on foot.

Open: 2 Apr - 29 Jun & 1 Oct - 6 Nov: Daily except Fri, 11am - 4.45pm. 1 Jul - 30 Sept: Daily, 11am - 4.45pm.

Admission: Adult £2.60, Child £1.60, Senior Citizen £2.10, Family £6.60.

⬚ ♿ Ground floor. 🐕 🅿

ENGLISHCOMBE TITHE BARN

Rectory Farmhouse, Englishcombe, Bath BA2 9DU

Tel: 01225 425073   **e-mail:** jennie.walker@ukonline.co.uk

Owner/Contact: Mrs Jennie Walker

An early 14th century cruck-framed Tithe Barn built by Bath Abbey.

Location: OS172 Ref. ST716 628. Adjacent to Englishcombe Village Church. 1m SW of Bath

Open: BHs, 2 - 6pm. Other times by appointment or please knock at house. Closed 1 Dec - 1 Jan.

Admission: Free.

FAIRFIELD

Stogursey, Bridgwater, Somerset TA5 1PU

Tel: 01722 555131 / 01278 732251

Owner: Lady Gass   **Contact:** D W Barke FRICS

Elizabethan and medieval house (undergoing repairs). Occupied by the same family for over 800 years. Woodland garden. Views of Quantocks.

Location: OS Ref. ST187 430. 11m W of Bridgwater, 8m E of Williton. From A39 Bridgwater/Minehead turn North. House 1m W of Stogursey.

Open: 26 Apr - 29 May & 7 Jun - 7 July: Wed - Fri and BHs. Guided house tours at 2.30 & 3.30pm. Groups at other times by arrangement. Garden open for NGS and other charities on dates advertised in Spring. Advisable to contact to confirm dates.

Admission: £4 in aid of Stogursey Church.

ℹ️No inside photography. ♿ 🎥Obligatory. 🅿No coach parking.
🐕 Guide dogs only.

FARLEIGH HUNGERFORD CASTLE ⚏

Farleigh Hungerford, Bath, Somerset BA3 6RS

Tel/Fax: 01225 754026   **e-mail:** customers@english-heritage.org.uk

www.english-heritage.org.uk/farleighhungerford

Owner: English Heritage   **Contact:** Visitor Operations Staff

Extensive ruins of 14th century castle with a splendid chapel containing wall paintings, stained glass and the fine tomb of Sir Thomas Hungerford, builder of the castle.

Location: OS173, ST801 577. In Farleigh Hungerford 3¹/2 m W of Trowbridge on A366.

Open: 1 Apr - 31 Oct: daily, 10am - 5pm (6pm in Jul & Aug, 4pm in Oct). 1 Nov - 31 Mar: Sat & Sun, 10am - 4pm. Closed 24 - 26 Dec & 1 Jan.

Admission: Adult £3.50, Child £1.80, Conc. £2.60. 15% discount for groups of 11+.

ℹ️WCs. ⬚ ♿Grounds, Ground Floor & Virtual Reality Tour. 🅿 🎧
🐕 Guide dogs only. ❄ 🌳Tel for details.

GATCOMBE COURT

Flax Bourton, Somerset BS48 3QT

Tel: 01275 393141   **Fax:** 01275 394274

Owner/Contact: Mrs Charles Clarke

A Somerset manor house, dating from early 13th century, which has evolved over the centuries since. It is on the site of a large Roman village, traces of which are apparent. Rose and herb garden. Described in Simon Jenkins' book, *1000 Best Houses*.

Location: OS Ref. ST525 698. 5m W of Bristol, N of the A370, between the villages of Long Ashton and Flax Bourton. Close to Tyntesfield.

Open: May - July: for groups of 15 - 40 people by appointment.

♿Unsuitable. 🎥By arrangement. 🐕 🅿 🌳 ❄

THE GEORGIAN HOUSE

7 Great George Street, Bristol, Somerset BS1 5RR

Tel: 0117 921 1362

Owner: City of Bristol Museums & Art Gallery   **Contact:** Karin Walton

Location: OS172 ST582 730. Bristol.

Open: All year: Sat - Wed, 10am - 5pm.

Admission: Free.

© Christopher Simon Sykes

GLASTONBURY ABBEY

ABBEY GATEHOUSE, MAGDALENE ST, GLASTONBURY BA6 9EL

Tel/Fax: 01458 832267   **e-mail:** info@glastonburyabbey.com

Owner: Glastonbury Abbey Estate   **Contact:** F C Thyer - Deputy Custodian

Evocative and awe-inspiring ruined Abbey set amongst 36 acres of peaceful parkland, ponds, orchard and wildlife areas. Explore 2000 years of history and legend at what was once the largest and richest abbey in England. Legendary burial place of King Arthur. Traditionally the earliest Christian sanctuary in Britain.

Location: OS Ref. ST499 388. 50 yds from the Market Cross, in the centre of Glastonbury. M5/J23, then A39.

Open: Daily (except Christmas Day), 9.30am - 6pm or dusk if earlier. Jun, Jul & Aug: opens 9am. Dec, Jan & Feb: opens 10am.

Admission: Adult £4, Child £1.50, Conc. £3.50, Family (2+2) £10. Groups (booked, 10+): Adult £3.50, Child £1.50.

⬚ ♿ 🐕 🎥 🎧 🅿 🐕 ❄ 🌳 Tel for details.

GLASTONBURY TOR

Nr Glastonbury, Somerset

Tel: 01985 843600 / 01934 844518

Owner: The National Trust   **Contact:** The Regional Office

The dramatic and evocative Tor dominates the surrounding countryside and offers spectacular views over Somerset, Dorset and Wiltshire. At the summit of this very steep hill an excavation has revealed the plans of two superimposed churches of St Michael, of which only the 15th-century tower remains.

Location: OS Ref. ST512 386. Signposted from Glastonbury town centre, from where seasonal park-and-ride (not NT) operates.

Open: All year.

Admission: Free.

🅿 Park & ride from town centre Apr - Sept. Also free at Rural Life Museum. Tel 01458 831197.   🐕 On leads only. ❄

GLASTONBURY TRIBUNAL ⚏

Glastonbury High Street, Glastonbury, Somerset

Tel: 01458 832954   **e-mail:** glastonbury.tic@ukonline.co.uk

Owner: English Heritage   **Contact:** The TIC Manager

A well preserved medieval town house, reputedly once used as the courthouse of Glastonbury Abbey. Now houses Glastonbury Tourist Information Centre.

Location: OS182 Ref. ST499 390. In Glastonbury High Street.

Open: 1 Apr - 30 Sept: daily, 10am - 5pm (Fri & Sat, 5.30pm). 1 Oct - 31 Mar: daily, 10am - 4pm (Fri & Sat, 4.30pm). Closed 25 - 26 Dec & 1 Jan.

Admission: TIC Free. Museum areas: Adult £2, Child £1.50. Senior £1. Prices may be subject to change April 2006.

♿Partial. 🅿 Charge. ❄

THE WILLIAM HERSCHEL MUSEUM

19 New King Street, Bath BA1 2BL

Tel/Fax: 01225 446865

e-mail: debbie@herschelbpt.fsnet.co.uk

Owner: The Herschel House Trust   **Contact:** The Curator

Georgian town-house. Home to astronomer William Herschel and site of discovery of planet Uranus in 1781. Georgian garden. Audio tour. Star Vault Astronomy Auditorium.

Location: OS Ref. ST750 648. Bath, Somerset.

Open: 1 Feb - 15 Dec: daily except Weds, 1 - 5pm, Sats/Suns 11am - 5pm. School visits and group bookings by arrangement.

Admission: Adult £3.50, Child £2, Full Time Student £2.50, OAP £3, Family £7.50.

© Jason Ingram

HESTERCOMBE 🏛 GARDENS

CHEDDON FITZPAINE, TAUNTON, SOMERSET TA2 8LG

www.hestercombegardens.com

Tel: 01823 413923 **Fax:** 01823 413747
Email: info@hestercombegardens.com
Owner: Hestercombe Gardens Trust
Contact: Mr P White

Lose yourself in 40 acres of walks, streams and temples, vivid colours, formal terraces, woodlands, lakes, cascades and views that take your breath away. This is Hestercombe: a unique combination of three period gardens. The Georgian landscape garden was created in the 1750s by Copelstone Warre Bampfylde, whose vision was complemented by the addition of a Victorian terrace and shrubbery and the stunning Edwardian gardens designed by Sir Edwin Lutyens and Gertrude Jekyll. All once abandoned, now being faithfully restored to their former glory. Each garden has its own quality – tranquility, wonder, inspiration – refreshing the visitor, body and soul.

Location: OS Ref. ST241 287. 4m NE from Taunton, 1m NW of Cheddon Fitzpaine.

Open: All year: daily (except Christmas Day), 10am - 6pm (last admission 5pm). Groups & coach parties by arrangement.

Admission: Adult £6*, Conc. £5.50*, Student £3.50. Guided tour (20+): £7.90. *Prices include 2 children. Additional child £2.50.

🖼 🚻 ♿ Partial. WC. 🔊 Licensed.
🍴 Licensed. 🎦 By arrangement.
🅿 Limited for coaches. 🐕 On short leads. ❋

HOLBURNE MUSEUM OF ART

Great Pulteney Street, Bath BA2 4DB

Tel: 01225 466669   **Fax:** 01225 333121

Owner: Trustees   **Contact:** Katie Jenkins

This jewel in Bath's crown houses the treasures collected by Sir William Holburne: superb English and continental silver, porcelain, majolica, glass and Renaissance bronzes, and paintings by Turner, Guardi and Stubbs.

Location: OS Ref. ST431 545. Via A4 or A431, follow brown signs.

Open: Please telephone for details.

Admission: Varies with exhibitions - telephone for details.

HOLNICOTE ESTATE 🌿

Selworthy, Minehead, Somerset TA24 8TJ

Tel: 01643 862452   **Fax:** 01643 863011   **e-mail:** holnicote@nationaltrust.org.uk

Owner: The National Trust   **Contact:** The Estate Office

The Holnicote Estate covers 5042ha (12,500 acres) of Exmoor National Park. The Estate also covers 4 miles of coastline between Porlock Bay and Minehead. There are over 100 miles of footpaths to enjoy through the fields, woods, moors and villages.

Location: OS Ref. SS920 469. Off A39 Minehead - Porlock, 3m W of Minehead. Station: Minehead 5m.

Open: Estate Office: All year: Mon - Fri, 9am - 5pm.

Admission: Free.

🖼 ♿ 🔊(Not NT.) 🐕 ❋

KENTSFORD

Washford, Watchet, Somerset TA23 0JD

Tel: 01984 631307

Owner: Wyndham Estate   **Contact:** Mr R Dibble

Location: OS Ref. ST058 426.

Open: House open only by appointment with Mr R Dibble. Gardens: 7 Mar - 29 Aug: Tues & BHs.

Admission: House: £3, Gardens: Free.

♿ Gardens only. 🅿 Limited. 🐕 In grounds, on leads. ❋

KING JOHN'S HUNTING LODGE 🌿

The Square, Axbridge, Somerset BS26 2AP

Tel: 01934 732012   **www.**nationaltrust.org.uk

Owner/Contact: The National Trust

An early Tudor merchant's house, extensively restored in 1971. Note: the property is run as a local history museum by Axbridge & District Museum Trust in co-operation with Sedgemoor District Council, County Museum's Service and Axbridge Archaeological & Local History Society.

Location: OS Ref. ST431 545. In the Square, on corner of High Street, off A371.

Open: 1 Apr - 30 Sept: Daily, 1 - 4pm.

Admission: Free. Donations welcome.

♿ Ground floor. 🅿 🐕 By arrangement.

LOWER SEVERALLS

Crewkerne, Somerset TA18 7NX

Tel: 01460 73234   **e-mail:** mary@lowerseveralls.co.uk

Owner: Mrs Audrey Pring   **Contact:** Mary Pring

2½ acre garden, developed over the last 25 years including herb garden, mixed borders and island beds with innovative features, ie a giant living dogwood basket and a wadi.

Location: OS Ref. ST457 112. 1½ m NE of Crewkerne, between A30 & A356.

Open: Mar - Sept: Tue & Wed & Fri & Sat, 10am - 5pm.

Admission: Adult £3, Child (under 16yrs) Free.

education index
see page 564

LYTES CARY MANOR

Nr Charlton Mackrell, Somerset TA11 7HU

Tel: 01458 224471 (property)   **e-mail:** lytescarymanor@nationaltrust.org.uk
www.nationaltrust.org.uk

Owner: The National Trust   **Contact:** Visitor Services Manager

The house with its 14th century chapel and 15th century Great Hall was much added to in the 16th century. In the 20th century it was rescued from dereliction by Sir Walter Jenner who refurnished the interiors in period style. At the same time the garden was laid out in a series of 'rooms' with many contrasts, topiary, mixed borders, and a herbal border based on the famous 16th century Lytes Herbal, which can be seen in the house. Several walks through the wider estate show many features typical of farmed lowland England, including ancient hedges, rare arable weeds and farmland birds. Parts of Lytes Cary Manor may be under repair.

Location: OS Ref. ST529 269. 1m N of Ilchester bypass A303, signposted from Podimore roundabout at junction of A303. A37 take A372.

Open: 22 Mar - 29 Oct: Wed & Fri - Sun, 11am - 5pm. Closes dusk if earlier.

Admission: £5, Child £2. Family £12. Garden only: Adult £3.50, Child £1.50. Partial. Braille guide. By arrangement.

P Free. Small coaches only by arrangement. On leads in car park & river walk only. Tel 0870 4584000 or see website for details.

MAUNSEL HOUSE

NORTH NEWTON, Nr TAUNTON, SOMERSET TA7 0BU

www.maunselhouse.co.uk

Tel: 01278 661076   **Fax:** 01278 661074   **e-mail:** maunselhouse@btconnect.com

Owner: Sir Benjamin Slade   **Contact:** Alexa Plant

This imposing 13th century manor house offers the ideal location for wedding receptions, corporate events, private and garden parties, filming and family celebrations. The ancestral seat of the Slade family and home of the 7th baronet Sir Benjamin Slade, the house can boast such visitors as Geoffrey Chaucer, who wrote part of the *Canterbury Tales* whilst staying there. The beautiful grounds and spacious rooms provide both privacy and a unique atmosphere for any special event. Available for weekend/Christmas house parties, weddings, birthdays, dinner parties and conferences.

Location: OS Ref. ST302 303. Bridgwater 4m, Bristol 20m, Taunton 7m, M5/J24, A38 to North Petherton. 2½ m SE of A38 at North Petherton via North Newton.

Open: Coaches & groups welcome by appointment. Caravan rally field available.
Functions. Partial. In grounds, on leads.

MILTON LODGE GARDENS

Old Bristol Road, Wells, Somerset BA5 3AQ

Tel: 01749 672168

Owner/Contact: D Tudway Quilter Esq

"The great glory of the gardens of Milton Lodge is their position high up on the slopes of the Mendip Hills to the north of Wells … with broad panoramas of Wells Cathedral and the Vale of Avalon", (Lanning Roper). Charming, mature, Grade II listed terraced garden dating from 1909. Replanned 1962 with mixed shrubs, herbaceous plants, old fashioned roses and ground cover; numerous climbers; old established yew hedges. Fine trees in garden and in 7-acre arboretum across old Bristol Road.

Location: OS Ref. ST549 470. ½ m N of Wells from A39. N up Old Bristol Road. Free car park first gate on left.

Open: Garden & Arboretum: Easter - end Oct: Tues, Weds, Suns & BHs, 2 - 5pm Parties & coaches by prior arrangement.

Admission: Adult £3, Children under 14 Free.
Unsuitable.

MONTACUTE HOUSE

MONTACUTE, SOMERSET TA15 6XP

www.nationaltrust.org.uk

Tel: 01935 823289   **Fax:** 01935 826921   **e-mail:** montacute@nationaltrust.org.uk

Owner: The National Trust   **Contact:** The Property Manager

A glittering Elizabethan house, adorned with elegant chimneys, carved parapets and other renaissance features including contemporary plasterwork, chimney pieces and heraldic glass. The magnificent state rooms, including a long gallery which is the largest of its type in England, are full of fine 17th and 18th century furniture and Elizabethan and Jacobean portraits from the National Portrait Gallery.

Location: OS Ref. ST499 172. In Montacute village, 4m W of Yeovil, on S side of A3088, 3m E of A303.

Open: House: 22 Mar - 29 Oct: daily except Tue, 11am - 5pm. Garden: 1 Jan - 19 Mar & 1 Nov - 1 Mar 2006: Wed - Sun, 11am - 4pm; 22 Mar - 29 Oct: daily except Tue, 11am - 6pm. Shop: 1 - 19 Mar & 1 Nov - 17 Dec: Wed - Sun, 11am - 4pm; 22 Mar - 29 Oct: daily except Tue, 11am - 5.30pm. Restaurant: 5 - 19 Mar & 5 Nov - 17 Dec: Sun only, 11am - 4pm; 22 Mar - 29 Oct: daily except Tue, 12 noon - 3pm. Café: 4 - 19 Mar & 4 Nov - 17 Dec: Sat & Sun, 11am - 4pm; 22 Mar - 29 Oct: daily except Tue, 11am - 5.30pm.

Admission: House, Park & Garden: Adult £8, Child £4, Family £20. Groups (15+): Adult £7. Garden & Park only (22 Mar - 29 Oct): Adult £4.50, Child £2. 1 Nov - 17 Mar 2007: Adult £2, Child £1. Group organisers please book in writing to House Manager with a SAE.

Partial. Braille guide. WC. Licensed. Christmas lunches in Dec (must book). P In park, on leads.

MUCHELNEY ABBEY

Muchelney, Langport, Somerset TA10 0DQ

Tel: 01458 250664   **Fax:** 01458 253842   **e-mail:** customers@english-heritage.org.uk
www.english-heritage.org.uk/muchelney

Owner: English Heritage   **Contact:** Visitor Operations Staff

Well-preserved ruins of the cloisters, with windows carved in golden stone, and abbot's lodging of the Benedictine abbey, which survived by being used as a farmhouse after the Dissolution. Tactile displays and interactive video.

Location: OS193 Ref. ST428 248. In Muchelney 2m S of Langport.

Open: 1 Apr - 31 Oct: daily 10am - 5pm (6pm in Jul & Aug, 4pm in Oct).

Admission: Adult £3.20, Child £1.60, Conc. £2.40. 15% discount for groups (11+).
WCs. Partial. P Tel for details.

MUSEUM OF COSTUME & ASSEMBLY ROOMS

See page 249 for full page entry.

NUNNEY CASTLE

Nunney, Somerset

Tel: 0117 9750700   **e-mail:** customers@english-heritage.org.uk

Owner: English Heritage   **Contact:** Visitor Operations Staff

A small 14th century moated castle with a distinctly French style. Its unusual design consists of a central block with large towers at the angles.

Location: OS183 Ref. ST737 457. In Nunney 3½ m SW of Frome, 1m N of the A361.

Open: Any reasonable time.

Admission: Free.

ORCHARD WYNDHAM

Williton, Taunton, Somerset TA4 4HH

Tel: 01984 632309   **Fax:** 01984 633526

Owner: Wyndham Estate   **Contact:** Wyndham Estate Office

English manor house. Family home for 700 years encapsulating continuous building and alteration from the 14th to the 20th century.

Location: OS Ref. ST072 400. 1m from A39 at Williton.

Open: 3 Aug - 1 Sept: Thur & Fri, 2 - 5pm & Aug BH Mon, 2 - 5pm. Guided tours only. Last tour 4pm. Limited showing space within the house. To avoid disappointment please advance book places on tour by telephone or fax. Access only suitable for cars.

Admission: Adult £6, Child (under 12yrs) £2.

Obligatory & pre-booked. P Limited. No coach parking. In grounds, on leads.

PRIEST'S HOUSE

Muchelney, Langport, Somerset TA10 0DQ

Tel: 01458 253771 (Tenant) **www.nationaltrust.org.uk**

Owner: The National Trust **Contact:** The Administrator

A late medieval hall house with large gothic windows, originally the residence of priests serving the parish church across the road. Lived-in and recently repaired.

Location: OS Ref. ST429 250. 1m S of Langport.

Open: 26 Mar - 25 Sept: Sun & Mon, 2 - 5.30pm. Admission by guided tour. Last tour commences at 5pm.

Admission: Adult £3, Child £1.50. Not suitable for groups.

ⓘNo WC.

©NTPL/ David Noton

PRIOR PARK LANDSCAPE GARDEN

RALPH ALLEN DRIVE, BATH BA2 5AH

www.nationaltrust.org.uk

Tel: 01225 833422 **Infoline:** 09001 335242

e-mail: priorpark@nationaltrust.org.uk

Owner: The National Trust **Contact:** Visitor Services Manager

Beautiful and intimate 18th century landscape garden created by Bath entrepreneur Ralph Allen with advice from the poet Alexander Pope and 'Capability' Brown. Sweeping valley with magnificent views of the City of Bath, Palladian bridge and three lakes. The Wilderness Project, supported by the Heritage Lottery Fund, is the final phase of restoration of this sustainably managed garden. Access to the Bath Skyline Walk (NT) from the garden. Disabled parking only, telephone for a 'how to get there' leaflet. Prior Park College, a co-educational school, operates from the mansion (not NT).

Location: OS Ref. ST760 633. Frequent bus service from City Centre. First 2 & 4, City Sightseeing Skyline open top tour bus, every hour to the garden. Pick up from railway station & Abbey. Half price to NT members.

Open: 2 Feb - 30 Nov: Wed - Mon, 11am - 5.30pm or dusk if earlier. 1 Dec - 28 Jan 2007: Fri - Sun. 11am - dusk. Last adm. 1 hr before closing. Closed 25/26 Dec & 1 Jan.

Admission: Adult: £4.50, Child £2.50, Family £11.50.

Grounds. WC. Braille guide. Hearing Loop. By arrangement. Nov - Feb. Tel for details (0870 458 4000) or visit website.

THE ROMAN BATHS & PUMP ROOM

See page 250 for full page entry.

ROBIN HOOD'S HUT

Halswell, Goathurst, Somerset TA5 2EW

Tel: 01628 825925 **www.landmarktrust.org.uk**

Owner: The Landmark Trust

Robin Hood's Hut is an 18th century garden building with two distinct faces. On one side it is a small rustic cottage, with thatched roof and bark clad door while on the other is an elegant pavilion complete with umbrello (or stone canopy). In the 1740s, Charles Kemeys Tynte began to transform the landscape around Halswell House into one of the finest Georgian gardens in the south west. He built several follies including in 1767 Robin Hood's Hut. It is cared for by The Landmark Trust, a building preservation charity who let it for holidays. Full details of Robin Hood's Hut and 183 other historic and architecturally important buildings are featured in the Landmark Trust Handbook (price £11 refundable against a booking).

Location: OS Ref. ST255 333.

Open: Available for holidays for up to 2 people throughout the year. Appointments to view the building can be made when it is not booked for holidays through the Landmark Trust.

Admission: Please tel for details.

STEMBRIDGE TOWER MILL

High Ham, Somerset TA10 9DJ

Tel: 01935 823289 **www.nationaltrust.org.uk**

Owner: The National Trust **Contact:** The Administrator

The last thatched windmill in England, dating from 1822 and in use until 1910.

Location: OS Ref. ST432 305. 2m N of Langport, ½ m E of High Ham.

Open: 26 Mar - 24 Sept: Suns & BH Mons, 2 - 5pm.

Admission: Adult £2.50, Child £1.50. Arrangements may be made for school groups on 01935 827767.

ⓘNo WC. Ⓟ Limited.

special events
see page 571

© NTPL/Joe Cornish

Holnicote Estate.

STOKE-SUB-HAMDON PRIORY ❦

North Street, Stoke-sub-Hamdon, Somerset TA4 6QP

Tel: 01935 823289 www.nationaltrust.org.uk

Owner/Contact: The National Trust

A complex of buildings, begun in the 14th century for the priests of the chantry of St Nicholas, which is now destroyed. The Great Hall is open to visitors.

Location: OS Ref. ST473 174. 1/2 m S of A303. 2m W of Montacute between Yeovil and Ilminster.

Open: 26 Mar - 31 Oct: daily, 10am - 6pm or dusk if earlier. Not suitable for coaches.

Admission: Free.

ℹ️ No WC. 🅿️ Limited. ✖

TINTINHULL GARDEN ❦

Farm Street, Tintinhull, Somerset BA22 9PZ

Tel: 01935 823289 **e-mail:** tintinhull@nationaltrust.org.uk www.nationaltrust.org.uk

Owner: The National Trust   **Contact:** The Head Gardener

A delightful formal garden, created in the 20th century around a 17th century manor house. Small pools, varied borders and secluded lawns are neatly enclosed within walls and clipped hedges and there is also an attractive kitchen garden.

Location: OS Ref. ST503 198. 5m NW of Yeovil, 1/2m S of A303, on E outskirts of Tintinhull.

Open: 22 Mar - 29 Oct: Wed - Sun (open BH Mon) 11am - 5pm (Tearoom 11am - 4.30pm).

Admission: Adult £5, Child £2.50, Family £12.50. No reduction for groups.

♿ Grounds. Braille guide. ● 🎧 By arrangement. 🅿️ Limited. ✖

TREASURER'S HOUSE ❦

Martock, Somerset TA12 6JL

Tel: 01935 825015 www.nationaltrust.org.uk

Owner/Contact: The National Trust

A small medieval house, recently refurbished by The Trust. The two-storey hall was completed in 1293 and the solar block is even earlier.

Location: OS Ref. ST462 191. 1m NW of A303 between Ilminster and Ilchester.

Open: 26 Mar - 26 Sept: Sun - Tue, 2 - 5pm. Only medieval hall, wall paintings and kitchen are shown.

Admission: Adult £3, Child £1.50. Not suitable for groups.

ℹ️ No WC. 🅿️ Limited for cars. None for coaches & trailer caravans.

TYNTESFIELD ❦

Wraxall, North Somerset BS48 1NT

Tel: 01275 461900 www.nationaltrust.org.uk

Owner/Contact: The National Trust

Situated on a ridge overlooking the beautiful Land Yeo Valley, Tyntesfield was inspired and remodelled by John Norton in c1864 for William Gibbs, a successful merchant. The mansion is an extraordinary Gothic Revival extravaganza and survives intact with an unrivalled collection of Victorian decorative arts, an insight into life below stairs and a sumptuously decorated private chapel. Its surrounding 200ha (500 acres) of land includes formal gardens and a wonderful walled kitchen garden. Tyntesfield was saved for the nation by the National Trust in June 2002 with funding from the National Heritage Memorial Fund, other heritage partners and a £3 million public appeal. The property is now one of the most exciting projects of the National Trust due to its innovative approach to giving access to the ongoing conservation. Visitors should expect to see building and conservation work in progress and access to parts of the estate will be restricted for health and safety reasons.

Location: OS Ref. ST506 715. Off B3128.

Open: House, Chapel and Gardens: 9 Apr - 30 Oct, Sat, Sun, Mon & Wed. House: 11am - 5pm (last admission at 4pm by timed ticket). Chapel: 10.30am - 5pm. Garden/Shop/Kiosk: 10am - 5.30pm. Open Good Fri.

Admission: House, Chapel & Gardens: Adult £9, Child £4.50, Family £22.50. Gardens only: Adult £4.50, Child £2.30, Family £11.30. Groups by appointment (Tues only).

🖼️ ♿ Partial. ● 🎧 By arrangement. 🅿️ ✖

WELLS CATHEDRAL

Cathedral Green, Wells, Somerset BA5 2UE

Tel: 01749 674483   **Fax:** 01749 832210

Owner: The Chapter of Wells   **Contact:** Mr John Roberts

Fine medieval Cathedral. The West Front with its splendid array of statuary, the Quire with colourful embroidery and stained glass, Chapter House and 1392 astronomical clock should not be missed.

Location: OS Ref. ST552 458. In Wells, 20m S from both Bath & Bristol.

Open: Apr - Sept: 7am - 7pm; Oct - Mar: 7am - 6pm.

Admission: Suggested donation: Adult £5, Child/Student £2, OAP £3.50. Photo permit £2.

Robin Hood's Hut.

MAP 3

BOWOOD HOUSE & GARDENS

www.bowood.org

Owner:
The Marquis of
Lansdowne

▶ **CONTACT**

The Administrator
Bowood House and
Gardens
Calne
Wiltshire   SN11 0LZ

Tel: 01249 812102

Fax: 01249 821757

e-mail:
houseandgardens@
bowood.org

▶ **LOCATION**
OS Ref. ST974 700

From London M4/J17,
off the A4 in Derry Hill
village, midway
between Calne and
Chippenham.
Swindon 17m,
Bristol 26m,
Bath 16m.

Bus: to the gate,
1¹/₂ m through
park to House.

Rail: Chippenham
Station 5m.

Taxi: AA Taxis,
Chippenham 657777.

Bowood is the family home of the Marquis and Marchioness of Lansdowne. Begun c1720 for the Bridgeman family, the house was purchased by the 2nd Earl of Shelburne in 1754 and completed soon afterwards. Part of the house was demolished in 1955, leaving a perfectly proportioned Georgian home, over half of which is open to visitors. Robert Adam's magnificent Diocletian wing contains a splendid library, the laboratory where Joseph Priestley discovered oxygen gas in 1774, the orangery, now a picture gallery, the Chapel and a sculpture gallery in which some of the famous Lansdowne Marbles are displayed.

Among the family treasures shown in the numerous exhibition rooms are Georgian costumes, including Lord Byron's Albanian dress; Victoriana; Indiana (the 5th Marquess was Viceroy 1888-94); and superb collections of watercolours, miniatures and jewellery.

The House is set in one of the most beautiful parks in England. Over 2,000 acres of gardens and grounds were landscaped by 'Capability' Brown between 1762 and 1768, and are embellished with a Doric temple, a cascade, a pinetum and an arboretum. The Rhododendron Gardens are open for six weeks from late April to early June. All the walks have seats.

▶ **OPENING TIMES**

House & Garden
1 Apr - 31 October:
Daily, 11am - 6pm.
Last admission 5pm (or
1hr earlier after the
autumn clock change).

Rhododendron Walks
Off the A342 Chippenham
to Devizes road, midway
between Derry Hill and
Sandy Lane.

Open daily for 6 weeks
during the flowering
season, usually from late
April to early June,
11am - 6pm.
We recommend visitors
telephone or visit the
website to check the
progress of the
flowering season.

▶ **ADMISSION**

House & Garden
Adult	£7.50
Child (2-4yrs)	£3.80
Child (5-15yrs)	£5.00
Senior Citizen	£6.50
Family (2+2)	£22.50

Groups (20+)
Adult	£6.50
Child (2-4yrs)	£3.00
Child (5-15yrs)	£4.00
Senior Citizen	£5.50

Rhododendron Walks
Adult	£4.80
Senior Citizen	£4.30
Child (0-15yrs)	Free

Season Tickets available,
ask for details.
The charge for
Rhododendron Walks is
reduced by £1pp if
combined on the same day
with a visit to Bowood
House & Gardens.

Receptions, film location, 2,000 acre park, 40 acre lake, 18-hole golf course and Country Club, open to all players holding a current handicap.

Visitors may alight at the House before parking. WCs.

Self-service snacks, teas etc.

The Restaurant (waitress-service, capacity 85). Parties that require lunch or tea should book in advance.

On request, groups can be given introductory talk, or for an extra charge, a guided tour. Tour time 1¹/₄ hrs. Guide sheets in French, German, Dutch, Spanish & Japanese.

1,000 cars, unlimited for coaches, 400 yds from house. Allow 2-3 hrs to visit house, gardens and grounds.

Welcome. Special guide books. Picnic areas. Adventure playground.

Working assistance dogs only.

South West - England

MAP 3

CORSHAM COURT

www.corsham-court.co.uk

Owner:
J Methuen-
Campbell Esq

▶ **CONTACT**

Corsham Court
Corsham
Wiltshire SN13 0BZ

Tel/Fax: 01249 701610

▶ **LOCATION**

OS Ref. ST874 706

Corsham Court
is signposted
from the A4, approx.
4m W of Chippenham.
From Edinburgh, A1,
M62, M6, M5, M4,
8 hrs.
From London, M4,
2¼ hrs.
From Chester,
M6, M5, M4, 4 hrs.

Motorway: M4/J17 9m.

Rail: Chippenham
Station 6m.

Taxi: 01249 715959.

Corsham Court is an Elizabethan house of 1582 and was bought by Paul Methuen in the mid-18th century, to house a collection of 16th and 17th century Italian and Flemish master paintings and statuary. In the middle of the 19th century, the house was enlarged to receive a second collection, purchased in Florence, principally of fashionable Italian masters and stone-inlaid furniture.

Paul Methuen (1723-95) was a great-grandson of Paul Methuen of Bradford-on-Avon and cousin of John Methuen, ambassador and negotiator of the Methuen Treaty of 1703 with Portugal which permitted export of British woollens to Portugal and allowed a preferential 33⅓ percent duty discount on Portuguese wines, bringing about a major change in British drinking habits.

The architects involved in the alterations to the house and park were Lancelot 'Capability' Brown in the 1760s, John Nash in 1800 and Thomas Bellamy in 1845-9. Brown set the style by retaining the Elizabethan Stables and Riding School, but

rebuilding the Gateway, retaining the gabled Elizabethan stone front and doubling the gabled wings at either end and inside, by designing the East Wing as Stateroom Picture Galleries. Nash's work has now largely disappeared, but Bellamy's stands fast, notably in the Hall and Staircase.

The State Rooms, including the Music Room and Dining Room, provide the setting for the outstanding collection of over 150 paintings, statuary, bronzes and furniture. The collection includes work by such names as Chippendale, the Adam brothers, Van Dyck, Reni, Rosa, Rubens, Lippi, Reynolds, Romney and a pianoforte by Clementi.

GARDENS

'Capability' Brown planned to include a lake, avenues and specimen trees such as the Oriental Plane now with a 200-yard perimeter. The gardens, designed not only by Brown but also by Repton, contain a ha-ha, herbaceous borders, secluded gardens, lawns, a rose garden, a lily pool, a stone bath house and the Bradford Porch.

ℹ️ Souvenir desk. No umbrellas, no photography.

♿ Visitors may alight at the entrance to the property, before parking in the allocated areas.

🧍 For up to 55. If requested the owner may meet the group. Tour time 1hr.

🅿️ 120 yards from the house. Coaches may park in Church Square. Coach parties must book in advance. No camper vans, no caravans.

🏫 Available: rate negotiable.
A guide will be provided.

🐕 Must be kept on leads in the garden.

❄️

▶ **OPENING TIMES**
Summer

20 March - 30 September
Daily except Mons & Fris
but including BH Mons
2 - 5.30pm
Last admission 5pm.

Winter

1 October - 19 March
Weekends only
2 - 4.30pm
Last admission 4pm.

Closed December.

NB: Open throughout the year by appointment only for groups of 15+.

▶ **ADMISSION**
House & Garden

Adult £6.50
Child (5-15yrs)....... £3.00
OAP £5.00
Groups
(includes guided tour - 1 hr)
Adult £5.00

Garden only

Adult £2.50
Child (5-15yrs)....... £1.50
OAP £2.00

LONGLEAT 🏛

www.longleat.co.uk

MAP 2

Owner:
Marquess of Bath

▶ **CONTACT**

Longleat
Warminster
Wiltshire   BA12 7NW

Tel: 01985 844400
Fax: 01985 844885
e-mail: enquiries@
longleat.co.uk

▶ **LOCATION**

OS Ref. ST809 430

Just off the A36
between Bath -
Salisbury (A362
Warminster - Frome).
2hrs from London
following M3, A303,
A36, A362 or
M4/J18, A46, A36.

Rail: Warminster Station
(5m) on the
Cardiff/Portsmouth line.
Westbury Station (12m)
on the Paddington/
Penzance line.
Taxi rank at Warminster
& Westbury Stations.

Air: Bristol 30m.

CONFERENCE/FUNCTION

ROOM	SIZE	MAX CAPACITY
Great Hall	8 x 13m	120
Banqueting Suite	2 x (7 x 10m)	50
Green Library	7 x 13m	70
Wessex Pavilion	13 x 12m	200

Set within 900 acres of 'Capability' Brown landscaped grounds, Longleat House is widely regarded as one of the best examples of high Elizabethan architecture in Britain and one of the most beautiful stately homes open to the public.

Visited by Elizabeth I in 1574, Longleat House was built by Sir John Thynne from 1568 and is the current home of the 7th Marquess of Bath, Alexander Thynn. Many treasures are included within. The fine collection of paintings ranges from English portraits dating from the 16th century to hunting scenes by John Wootton c1736 (amongst his finest work) to Italian Old Masters.

Inspired by various Italian palace interiors, including the Ducal Palace in Venice, the ceilings are renowned for their ornate paintings and abundance of gilt with many made by the firm of John Dibblee Crace in the 1870s and 1880s. The furniture collection includes English pieces from as early as the 16th century, 17th century chairs from the Coromandel coast of India, fine French furniture of the 17th and 18th centuries and a

collection of major Italian pieces very unusual for an English country house.

The Murals in the private apartments in the West Wing have been painted by the present Marquess and are a fascinating and unique addition to the House. Incorporating a mixture of oil paints and sawdust, these private works of art offer a unique insight into Lord Bath's personality and beliefs. Mural Tours can be booked at the Front Desk of Longleat House on the date of a visit. They are subject to availability. Groups can enjoy a private tour of Longleat House or Gardens with a dedicated tour guide and a talk tailor-made to their interests, before enjoying a gourmet meal courtesy of the Longleat Banqueting Team.

Apart from the ancestral home, Longleat has a wonderland of attractions to suit all ages. Discover some of the world's most magnificent animals including lions, tigers and giraffe in the UK's original Safari Park; get lost in the Longleat Hedge Maze; voyage on the Safari Boats; journey on the Longleat Railway and much, much more!

🛍ⓘ Rooms in Longleat House can be hired for conferences, gala dinners and product launches. Extensive parkland for car launches, ride n' drives, company fun days, marquee based events, concerts, balloon festivals, equestrian events, caravan rallies & fishing. Film location.

🍴 Wessex Pavilion (200 capacity)

♿☕🍴 Cellar Café (capacity 80), licensed. Groups must book. From 3 course meals to cream teas, sandwiches & snacks. Traditional Wiltshire Fare. Not open all year.

🚶 Individuals & Groups (max 20; 15 for Murals). Booking essential.

🅿 Ample.

📷 Welcome with 1 teacher free entry per 8 children. GNVQ talks and packs available on request. Booking essential. Education sheets.

🐕 In grounds, on leads.

🔔 Orangery. ❄ 🛡 Tel for details.

▶ **OPENING TIMES**

House:
Open all year, daily (except Christmas Day). Easter - Sept: 10am - 5.30pm. Guided tours available 10 - 11am. Rest of year: 11am - 3pm. Guided tours only.

Guided tours may be subject to change - please telephone for up-to-date info.

Safari Park:
11 - 19 Feb & 1 Apr - 5 Nov: daily, 10am - 4pm (5pm on weekends, BHs & state school holidays). 25 Feb - 26 Mar: Sat/Sun only.

Other attractions:
11 - 19 Feb & 1 Apr - 5 Nov: daily, 11am - 5.30pm. 25 Feb - 26 Mar: Sat/Sun only.

Note: last admission times may be earlier in Mar & Sept - Nov.

▶ **ADMISSION**

House & Grounds
Adult £10.00
Child (3 -14yrs) £6.00
OAP £6.00

Longleat Passport
(see below)
Adult £19.00
Child (3 - 14yrs) £15.00
OAP £15.00

Groups (12+)
Adult £13.30
Child (3 - 16yrs) £10.50
OAP £10.50

LONGLEAT PASSPORT - includes:
Longleat House, Safari Park, Safari Boats, Longleat Hedge Maze, Pets Corner, Adventure Castle (including Blue Peter Maze)*, Longleat Railway, VirtuaScope Motion Ride, Butterfly Garden, Postman Pat Village*, Old Joe's mine, Grounds & Gardens.
*under 14yrs only

261

NTPL / Nick Meers

MAP 2

STOURHEAD

www.nationaltrust.org.uk

An outstanding example of the English landscape style of garden. Designed by Henry Hoare II and laid out between 1741 and 1780. Classical temples, including the Pantheon and Temple of Apollo, are set around the central lake at the end of a series of vistas, which change as the visitor moves around the paths and through the magnificent mature woodland with its extensive collection of exotic trees. The house, begun in 1721 by Colen Campbell, contains furniture by the younger Chippendale and fine paintings. King Alfred's Tower, an intriguing red-brick folly built in 1772 by Henry Flitcroft, is almost 50m high and gives breathtaking views over the estate. Art Gallery in Spread Eagle Courtyard (not NT). What's new in 2006: Exhibition area in basement of house.

Owner:
The National Trust

▶ **CONTACT**

The Estate Office
Stourton
Nr Warminster
BA12 6QD

Tel: 01747 841152

Fax: 01747 842005

e-mail: stourhead@
nationaltrust.org.uk

▶ **LOCATION**
OS Ref. ST780 340

At Stourton off the B3092, 3m NW of A303 (Mere), 8m S of A361 (Frome).

Rail: Gillingham 6¹/₂ m; Bruton 7m.

Bus: South West Coaches 80 Frome to Stourhead on Sat; First 58/0A.

NTPL

ⓘ Exhibition in Reception Buildings

❄

♿ Wheelchair accessible. Designated parking. Transfer available in main season to house & garden entrances. Powered mobility vehicles, recommended ground route map available. WCs. Braille guide.

☕🍴 Licensed.

🚶 Group tours, by arrangement.

🅿

🔫

🐕 Not in Tower or House. 1 Nov - 17 Mar only: on short fixed leads in landscape garden.

🔔

❄

 Tel for details.

▶ **OPENING TIMES**

Garden: All year: daily, 9am - 7pm or dusk if earlier.

House: 18 Mar - 31 Oct: Fri - Tue, 11.30am - 4.30pm. Last admission: 4pm.

King Alfred's Tower: 18 Mar - 31 Oct: daily, 11.30am - 4.30pm.

Restaurant: All year, daily (Closed 25 December), Mar & Oct: 10am - 5pm; Apr - Sept: 10am - 5.30pm; Nov - Feb: 10.30am - 4pm.

Shop & Plant Centre: All year, daily. (Closed 25 December) Mar & Oct: 10am - 5pm; Apr - Sept: 10am - 6pm; Nov - Feb: 10.30am - 4pm.

Closes dusk if earlier.

▶ **ADMISSION**

House & Garden:

Adult	£10.40
Child	£5.20
Family	£24.70
Groups (15+)	£9.90

House or Garden:

Adult	£6.20
Child	£3.40
Family	£14.90
Groups (15+)	£5.40

King Alfred's Tower:

Adult	£2.30
Child	£1.20
Family	£5.40
Groups (15+)	£2.00

NB. Groups must book.

MAP 3

Owner:
The Earl of Pembroke

▶ **CONTACT**

Duncan Leslie
The Estate Office
Wilton House
Wilton
Salisbury SP2 0BJ

Tel: 01722 746720
Fax: 01722 744447
e-mail:
tourism@
wiltonhouse.com

▶ **LOCATION**

OS Ref. SU099 311

3m W of Salisbury
along the A3.

Rail: Salisbury
Station 3m.

Bus: Every 10 mins
from Salisbury,
Mon - Sat.

Taxi: Sarum Taxi
01722 334477.

WILTON HOUSE 🏛

www.wiltonhouse.com

Wilton House has been the ancestral home of the Earl of Pembroke and his family for 460 years. In 1544 Henry VIII gave the Abbey and lands of Wilton to Sir William Herbert who had married Anne Parr, sister of Katherine, sixth wife of King Henry.

The Clock Tower, in the centre of the east front, is reminiscent of this part of the Tudor building which survived a fire in 1647. Inigo Jones and John Webb were responsible for the rebuilding of the house in the Palladian style, whilst further alterations were made by James Wyatt from 1801.

The chief architectural features are the magnificent 17th century state apartments (including the famous Single and Double Cube rooms) and the 19th century cloisters.

The house contains one of the finest art collections in Europe, with over 230 original paintings

on display, including works by Van Dyck, Rubens, Joshua Reynolds and Brueghel. Also on show are Greek and Italian statuary, a lock of Queen Elizabeth I's hair, Napoleon's despatch case, and Florence Nightingale's sash.

The Old Riding School houses a dynamic introductory film (narrated by Anna Massey), the reconstructed Tudor kitchen and the Estate's Victorian laundry. The house is set in magnificent landscaped parkland, bordered by the River Nadder which is the setting for the majestic Palladian Bridge. The 17th Earl of Pembroke was a keen gardener who created four new gardens since succeeding to the title in 1969 including the North Forecourt Garden, Old English Rose Garden, Water and Cloister Gardens.

ℹ️ Film location, fashion shows, product launches, equestrian events, garden parties, antiques fairs, concerts, vehicle rallies. No photography in house. French, German, Spanish, Italian, Japanese and Dutch information.

🍴 Exclusive banquets.

♿ Visitors may alight at the entrance. WCs.

☕ Licensed.

🚶 By arrangement.

🅿️ 200 cars and 12 coaches. Free coach parking. Group rates (min 15), meal vouchers, drivers' lounge.

📋 Teachers' handbook for National Curriculum. EFL students welcome. Free preparatory visit for group leaders.

🐕 Guide dogs only.

🔔

▶ **OPENING TIMES**

Summer
13 April - 30 September
Daily, 10.30am - 5.30pm

(House closed Saturdays except BH weekends).

Last admission 4.30pm.

Winter
Closed, except for private parties by prior arrangement.

▶ **ADMISSION**

Summer
**House, Grounds
& Exhibition**
Adult £9.75
Child (5 - 15yrs) £5.50
OAP/Student £8.00
Groups (15+)
Adult £7.00
Child £4.50
OAP £6.50

Membership
.... (from) £17.00

🎭 **SPECIAL EVENTS**

MAR 3 - 5
29th Annual Antiques Fair.
JUL 15
Classical Firework Concert.

CONFERENCE/FUNCTION

ROOM	SIZE	MAX CAPACITY
Double cube	60' x 30'	150
Exhibition Centre	50' x 40'	140
Film Theatre	34' x 20'	67

NTPL / David Norton

NT/Wessex region

AVEBURY MANOR & GARDEN, AVEBURY STONE CIRCLE ※ ♯
& ALEXANDER KEILLER MUSEUM

AVEBURY, Nr MARLBOROUGH, WILTSHIRE SN8 1RF

Tel: 01672 539250   **e-mail:** avebury@nationaltrust.org.uk

Owner: The National Trust   **Contact:** The Property Manager

Avebury Manor & Garden: A much-altered house of monastic origin, the present buildings date from the early 16th century, with notable Queen Anne alterations and Edwardian renovation by Col Jenner. The topiary and flower gardens contain medieval walls, ancient box and numerous 'rooms'. The Manor House is occupied and furnished by private tenants, who open a part of it to visitors. Owing to restricted space, guided tours will be in operation. Tours run every 40 mins from 2pm, last tour 4.40pm. Following periods of prolonged wet weather it may be necessary to close the house and garden.

Avebury Stone Circle (above left): One of the most important Megalithic monuments in Europe, this 28¹/₂ acre site with stone circle enclosed by a ditch and external bank, is approached by an avenue of stones.

Alexander Keiller Museum: The investigation of Avebury Stone Circle was largely the work of Alexander Keiller in the 1930s. He put together one of the most important prehistoric archaeological collections in Britain which can be seen at the Museum. The development of the Avebury landscape and the story of the people who discovered it is told, using interactive displays and CD ROMs, housed in the spectacular 17th century thatched barn.

Location: OS Ref. SU102 699 (Avebury Manor). OS Ref. SU102 699 (Stone Circle). OS Ref. SU100 699 (Alexander Keiller Museum). 6m W of Marlborough, 1m N of the A4 on A4361 & B4003.

Open: Avebury Manor & Stone Circle: Any reasonable time. Usual facilities may not be available around Summer Solstice 20 - 22 Jun. **Alexander Keiller Museum & Barn Gallery Exhibition** (above right): 1 Apr - 31 Oct: daily, 10am - 6pm; 1 Nov - 31 Mar: 10am - 4pm; close dusk if earlier. Closed 24 & 25 Dec.

Admission: Avebury Manor: House & Garden: Adult £4, Child £2. Garden only: Adult £3, Child £1.50. Groups (max 50): Adult £2.55, Child £1.30. **Stone Circle:** Free. **Alexander Keiller Museum:** (including Barn Gallery): Adult £4.20, Child £2.10, Family (2+3) £10.50, Family (1+3) £7.50. Groups (15+): Adult £3.60, Child £1.80. Discount when arriving by public transport or cycle. EH members Free.

⬜ Alexander Keiller Museum, Granary. ♿ Avebury Manor: ground floor with assistance & grounds; Avebury: ground floor fully accessible. WCs. Braille guide. ⬛ Avebury, licensed. 🅿 £2 (pay & display). ⬛

🐕 No dogs in house, guide dogs only in garden (Avebury Manor). On leads in Stone Circle. ❋ Stone Circle & Avebury Manor.

BOWOOD HOUSE & GARDENS ⬛   See page 259 for full page entry.

BRADFORD-ON-AVON TITHE BARN ♯

Bradford-on-Avon, Wiltshire

Tel: 0117 975 0700 **www.**english-heritage.org.uk/visits

Owner: English Heritage   **Contact:** South West Regional Office

A magnificent medieval stone-built barn with a slate roof and wooden beamed interior.

Location: OS Ref. ST824 604. ¹/₄ m S of town centre, off B3109.

Open: Daily, 10.30am - 4pm. Closed 25 Dec.

Admission: Free.

♿ 🅿 Charged. ⬛ ❋

BROADLEAS GARDENS

Devizes, Wiltshire SN10 5JQ

Tel: 01380 722035

Owner: Broadleas Gardens Charitable Trust   **Contact:** Lady Anne Cowdray

10 acres full of interest, notably The Dell, where the sheltered site allows plantings of magnolias, camellias, rhododendrons and azaleas.

Location: OS Ref. SU001 601. Signposted SW from town centre at S end of housing estate, (coaches must use this entrance) or 1m S of Devizes on W side of A360.

Open: Apr - Oct: Sun, Weds & Thurs, 2 - 6pm or by arrangement for groups.

Admission: Adult £5, Child (under 10yrs) £1.50, Groups (10+) £4.50.

CORSHAM COURT ⬛   See page 260 for full page entry.

open all year
see page 557 ❄

© NT Photographic Library/George Wright

THE COURTS ※

HOLT, BRADFORD-ON-AVON, WILTSHIRE BA14 6RR

Tel: 01225 782875 (opening hours) **Tel:** 01225 782340 (other times)

e-mail: courtsgarden@nationaltrust.org.uk

Owner: The National Trust   **Contact:** Head Gardener

One of Wiltshire's best-kept secrets, the English garden style at its best, full of charm and variety. There are many interesting plants and an imaginative use of colour surrounding water features, topiary and herbaceous borders. Complemented by an arboretum with natural planting of spring bulbs.

Location: OS Ref. ST861 618. 3m SW of Melksham, 3m N of Trowbridge, 2¹/₂ m E of Bradford-on-Avon, on S side of B3107.

Open: 25 Mar - 15 Oct: daily except Weds, 11am - 5.30pm. Open out of season by appointment only.

Admission: Adult £5, Child £2.50, Family (2+2) £12.80. Groups Adult £4.50, Child £2.30. Guided tours £2 extra per person.

ℹ️ No picnics. ♿ Adapted WC. 🔑 By appointment. 🅿 Limited. ⬛ ⬛

GREAT CHALFIELD MANOR
Nr Melksham, Wiltshire SN12 8NH

Tel: 01225 782239 **Fax:** 01225 783379 **www.**nationaltrust.org.uk

Owner: The National Trust   **Contact:** The Tenant

A charming manor house enhanced by a moat and gatehouse and with beautiful oriel windows and a great hall. Completed in 1480, the manor and gardens were restored earlier last century (c1905 - 1911) by Major R Fuller, whose family live here and manage the property. The garden, designed by Alfred Parsons, to complement the Manor, has been replanted.

Location: OS Ref. ST860 631. 3m SW of Melksham off B3107 via Broughton Gifford Common, sign for Atworth. Rail: Bradford-on-Avon 3m, Chippenham 10m.

Open: 2 Apr - 29 Oct: Tue - Thur, admission by guided tour only at 11.30am, 12.15, 2.15, 3 & 3.45pm, Sun 2 - 5pm only. The tours take 45 mins and numbers are limited to 25. Visitors arriving during a tour can visit the adjoining parish church and garden first. Note: Group visits are welcome on Fri & Sat (not BHs) by written arrangement with the tenant Mrs Robert Floyd, charge applies. Organisers of coach parties should allow 2 hrs because of limit on numbers in the house.

Admission: Adult £4.80, Child £2.40, Family (2+2) £12.20. Groups £4.30, Child £2.20. Garden only: Adult £3.

Ground floor with assistance. Limited access to Garden. WC. Obligatory. Limited.

HEALE GARDENS
HEALE HOUSE, MIDDLE WOODFORD, SALISBURY, WILTSHIRE SP4 6NT

Tel: 01722 782504

Owner: Mr & Mrs Guy Rasch   **Contact:** Miss Fiona Walmsley

First winner of Christie's/HHA Garden of the Year award. Grade I Carolean Manor House where King Charles II hid during his escape in 1651. In january great drifts of snowdrops and aconites bring early colour and the promise of spring. the garden provides a wonderfully varied collection of plants, shrub, musk and other roses, growing in the formal setting of clipped hedges and mellow stonework. Particularly lovely in spring and autumn is the water garden surrounding an authentic Japanese Tea House and Nikko Bridge which create an exciting focus in this part of the garden. The specialist Plant Centre has unusual and rare plants, also roses, hedging, trees, shrubs and herbaceous.

Location: OS Ref. SU125 365. 4m N of Salisbury on Woodford Valley road between A345 and A360.

Open: All year: daily except Mon (open BH Mons). Snowdrop Suns: 5 & 12 Feb.

Admission: Adult £4, Child (5-15yrs) £2 (under 5s Free). Booked groups (20-50): £3.75pp.

Partial. Guide dogs only. Tel for details.

© Skyscan. Taken from the book 'Historic Family Homes & Gardens from the Air'

HAMPTWORTH LODGE
HAMPTWORTH, LANDFORD, SALISBURY, WILTSHIRE SP5 2EA

Tel: 01794 390700 **Fax:** 01794 390644 **Email:** nda.hamptworth@btinternet.com

Contact: Mr N D Anderson

Rebuilt Jacobean manor house standing in woodlands on the edge of the New Forest. Grade II* family house with period furniture including clocks. The Great Hall has an unusual roof construction. There is a collection of prentice pieces and the Moffatt collection of contemporary copies. Room with late 17th century patterned wall hangings, believed unique in UK. Garden also open.

Location: OS Ref. SU227 195. 10m SE of Salisbury on road linking Downton on Salisbury/Bournemouth Road (A338) to Landford on A36, Salisbury - Southampton.

Open: 25 Mar - 29 Apr: Mon - Sat, 2.15 - 5pm. Closed 14 - 17 Apr. Coaches, by appointment only. 1 Apr - 30 Oct: Mon - Sat. House guided tours: daily except Sun, 2.15 & 3.30pm. Gardens: daily except Sun, 2.15 - 5pm.

Admission: £5, Child (under 11yrs) Free.

Ground floor & grounds. Obligatory.

THE KING'S HOUSE
Salisbury & South Wiltshire Museum
65 The Close, Salisbury, Wiltshire SP1 2EN

Tel: 01722 332151 **Fax:** 01722 325611 **www.**salisburymuseum.org.uk

e-mail: museum@salisburymuseum.org.uk

Owner: Occupied by Salisbury & South Wiltshire Museum Trust

                                              Contact: P R Saunders

Magnificent Grade 1 listed building, in the shadow of Salisbury Cathedral's glorious spire, which houses a museum with designated status for its archaeological collections. The museum also houses fine, Costume, Ceramics and local history galleries. Our fine art includes JMW Turner paintings. Also temporary exhibitions are held throughout the year.

Location: OS Ref. SU141 295. In Salisbury Cathedral Close, W side, facing Cathedral.

Open: All year: Mon - Sat: 10am - 5pm. Suns in Jul & Aug, 2 - 5pm.

Admission: Adult £4, Child £1.50, Conc. £3. Groups £3.

Ground floor only.

© Skyscan Balloon photography/English Heritage photo library

Old Sarum.

LACOCK ABBEY, FOX TALBOT MUSEUM & VILLAGE ❧

LACOCK, CHIPPENHAM, WILTSHIRE SN15 2LG

www.nationaltrust.org.uk

Tel: 01249 730459 (Visitor Reception)　**Fax:** 01249 730501 (Estate Office)

Owner: The National Trust　　　**Contact:** The Property Manager

Founded in 1232 and converted into a country house c1540, the fine medieval cloisters, sacristy, chapter house and monastic rooms of the abbey have survived largely intact. The handsome stable courtyard has half-timbered gables, a clockhouse, brewery and lubbahouse, surmounted with a medieval garden boasting a fine display of spring flowers and magnificent trees. The Fox Talbot Museum commemorates William Fox Talbot, a previous resident of the Abbey and inventor of the modern photographic negative. The village has many limewashed half-timbered and stone houses, featured in the TV and film productions of *Pride & Prejudice*, *Moll Flanders*, *Emma* and the recent *Harry Potter* films.

Location: OS Ref. ST919 684. In the village of Lacock, 3m N of Melksham, 3m S of Chippenham just E of A350.

Open: Museum, Cloisters & Garden: 25 Feb - 29 Oct: daily, 11am - 5.30pm (closed Good Fri). Only Museum open winter weekends (closed 25 Dec - 6 Jan), 11am - 4pm. Abbey: 25 Mar - 29 Oct: daily, 1 - 5.30pm (closed Tues & Good Fri).

Admission: Abbey, Museum, Cloisters & Grounds: Adult £7.80, Child £3.90, Family (2+2) £20. Groups: Adult £7, Child £3.50. Grounds, Cloisters & Museum only: Adult £4.80, Child £2.40, Family £12.20. Groups: Adult £4.30, Child £2.20. Abbey, Cloisters & Grounds only: Adult £6.30, Child £3.20, Family £16.10. Groups: Adult £5.70, Child £2.80. Museum (winter): Adult £3.40, Child £1.70, Family (2+2) £8.70. Groups: Adult £3, Child £1.50. Abbey guided tours £2 extra per person.

Braille guides. By arrangement. Tel or visit website for details.

LYDIARD PARK

LYDIARD TREGOZE, SWINDON, WILTSHIRE SN5 3PA

www.lydiardpark.org.uk

Tel: 01793 770401　**Fax:** 01793 770968　**e-mail:** lydiardpark@swindon.gov.uk

Owner: Swindon Borough Council　　　**Contact:** The Keeper

Lydiard Park, ancestral home of the Bolingbrokes, is Swindon's treasure. Set in rolling lawns and woodland, this beautifully restored Georgian mansion contains the family's furnishings and portraits, exceptional plasterwork, rare 17th century window and room devoted to 18th century society artist Lady Diana Spencer. Exceptional monuments such as the 'Golden Cavalier' in adjacent church. The historic grounds of Lydiard Park are part of a major restoration project.

Location: OS Ref. SU104 848. 4m W of Swindon, 1½ m N of M4/J16.

Open: House: Mon - Sat, 10am - 5pm, Sun, 2 - 5pm (4pm Nov - Feb). Grounds: all day, closing at dusk. Victorian Christmas decorations in December.

Admission: Adult £2.20, Child £1, Senior Citizen £2. Groups by appointment. Times & prices may change April 2006 - please telephone to confirm.

No photography in house. Open all year, but groups must book. By arrangement. In grounds on leads. Tel for details.

LARMER TREE GARDENS

Rushmore Estate, Tollard Royal, Salisbury, Wiltshire SP5 5PT

Tel: 01725 516228/516225　**Fax:** 01725 516321　**e-mail:** larmer.tree@rushmore-estate.co.uk　**www.**larmertreegardens.co.uk

Owner: Pitt Rivers Trustees　　　**Contact:** Sarah Hunter-Rodwell

General Augustus Pitt Rivers created these extraordinary 11-acre pleasure grounds in 1880. They contain a unique collection of buildings including a Roman temple, open-air theatre, colonial style tea pavilion and Nepalese rooms. Beautifully laid out gardens with mature trees, laurel hedges, rides and stunning views of the Cranborne Chase. The gardens are well suited to weddings and corporate events.

Location: OS Ref. ST943 169. 2m S Tollard Royal.

Open: 1 Apr - 31 Oct: daily, 11am - 4.30pm, closed Fri & Sat & Jul.

Admission: Adult £3.75, Child £2.50 (under 5yrs Free), Conc. £3, Family (2+4) £12.50. Groups (15+) £3.

Licensed for Sundays only. By arrangement. By arrangement. Tel for details.

LITTLE CLARENDON ❧

Dinton, Salisbury, Wiltshire SP3 5DZ

Tel: 01985 843600 (Regional Office)　**www.**nationaltrust.org.uk

Owner: The National Trust　　　**Contact:** The Regional Office

A Tudor house, altered in the 17th century and with a 20th century Catholic chapel. The three principal rooms on the ground floor are open to visitors and furnished with vernacular oak furniture.

Location: OS Ref. SU015 316. ¼ m E of Dinton Church. 9m W of Salisbury.

Open: 17 Apr, 1 & 29 May & 28 Aug: 2 - 5pm.

Admission: £2.

No WC, no pushchairs or prams, no coaches. Unsuitable. At Dinton Post Office.

LONGLEAT 🏛　　　*See page 261 for full page entry.*

THE MERCHANT'S HOUSE

132 HIGH STREET, MARLBOROUGH, WILTSHIRE SN8 1HN

www.themerchantshouse.co.uk

Tel/Fax: 01672 511491　**e-mail:** manager@merchantshousetrust.co.uk

Owner: Marlborough Town Council　　　**Contact:** Michael Gray

Situated in Marlborough's world-famous High Street, The Merchant's House is one of the finest middle-class houses in England. Its well-preserved Panelled Chamber was completed in 1656. Both the Dining Room and Great Staircase display recently uncovered 17th century wall paintings which have aroused much expert interest. Leased to the Merchant's House (Marlborough) Trust.

Location: OS Ref. SU188 691. N side of High Street, near Town Hall.

Open: Easter - end Sept: Fris & Sats, 11am - 4pm. All days for booked groups.

Admission: Adult £3, Child 50p. Booked groups (10-40): Adult £2.50, Child 50p.

Photography only by arrangement. Outside house, also in Hillier's Yard. Guide dogs only. Tel for details.

© NTPL/P3ter Cook

MOMPESSON HOUSE ✤

THE CLOSE, SALISBURY, WILTSHIRE SP1 2EL

www.nationaltrust.org.uk

Tel: 01722 335659 **Infoline:** 01722 420980 **Fax:** 01722 321559
e-mail: mompessonhouse@nationaltrust.org.uk

Owner: The National Trust   **Contact:** The Property Manager

An elegant and spacious 18th century house in the Cathedral Close. Featured in the award-winning film *Sense and Sensibility* and with magnificent plasterwork and a fine oak staircase. As well as pieces of good quality period furniture the house also contains the Turnbull collection of 18th century drinking glasses. Outside, the delightful walled garden has a pergola and traditional herbaceous borders.

Location: OS Ref. SU142 297. On N side of Choristers' Green in Cathedral Close, near High Street Gate.

Open: 25 Mar - 29 Oct: Sat - Wed, 11am - 5pm. Last admission 4.30pm. Open Good Fri.

Admission: Adult £4.40, Child £2.20, Family (2+2) £10.90. Groups: £3.90. Garden only: £1. Reduced rate when arriving by public transport.

🖸 🛇 Ground floor & grounds. Braille guide. WC. 🌑 🛣 By arrangement. 🔳 🗶

NORRINGTON MANOR

Alvediston, Salisbury, Wiltshire SP5 5LL
Tel: 01722 780367   **Fax:** 01722 780667

Owner/Contact: T Sykes

Built in 1377 it has been altered and added to in every century since, with the exception of the 18th century. Only the hall and the 'undercroft' remain of the original. It is currently a family home and the Sykes are only the third family to own it.

Location: OS Ref. ST966 237. Signposted to N of Berwick St John and Alvediston road (half way between the two villages).

Open: By appointment in writing.

Admission: A donation to the local churches is asked for.

🛇 Unsuitable. 🛣 By arrangement. 🅿 Limited for cars, none for coaches. 🗶 🏵

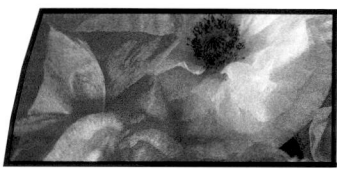

plant sales
see page 555 ❁

© English Heritage Photo Library/ Skyscan Balloon photography

NEWHOUSE 🏛

REDLYNCH, SALISBURY, WILTSHIRE SP5 2NX

Tel: 01725 510055   **Fax:** 01725 510284

Owner: George & June Jeffreys   **Contact:** Mrs Jeffreys

A brick, Jacobean 'Trinity' House, c1609, with two Georgian wings and a basically Georgian interior. Home of the Eyre family since 1633.

Location: OS184, SU218 214. 9m S of Salisbury between A36 & A338.

Open: 1 - 31 Mar, 3 - 10 Apr & 28 Aug: Mon - Fri, 2 - 5pm.

Admission: Adult £3.50, Child £2.50, Conc. £3.50. Groups (15+): Adult £3, Child £2.50, Conc. £3.

ℹ No photography in house, except at weddings. 🌑 🛣 By arrangement. 🅿 Limited for coaches. 🌑 Guide dogs only. ▲

OLD SARUM ⌗

CASTLE ROAD, SALISBURY, WILTSHIRE SP1 3SD

www.english-heritage.org.uk/oldsarum

Tel: 01722 335398   **Fax:** 01722 416037
e-mail: customers@english-heritage.org.uk

Owner: English Heritage   **Contact:** Visitor Operations Team

Built around 500BC by the Iron Age peoples, Old Sarum is the former site of the first cathedral and ancient city of Salisbury. A prehistoric hillfort in origin, Old Sarum was occupied by the Romans, the Saxons, and eventually the Normans who made it into one of their major strongholds, with a motte-and-bailey castle built at its centre. Old Sarum eventually grew into one of the most dramatic settlements in medieval England as castle, cathedral, bishop's palace and thriving township. When the new city we know as Salisbury was founded in the early 13th century the settlement faded away. With fine views of the surrounding countryside, Old Sarum is an excellent special events venue.

Location: OS184, SU138 327. 2m N of Salisbury off A345.

Open: 1 Apr - 30 Jun & Sept: Daily, 10am - 5pm. Jul & Aug: 9am - 6pm. 1 - 31 Oct: 10am - 4pm. Nov - Mar: 11am - 3pm (Mar, 10am - 4pm). Closed 24 - 26 Dec & 1 Jan.

Admission: Adult £2.90, Child £1.50, Conc. £2.20. 15% discount for groups (11+).

ℹ WCs. 🖸 🛇 Grounds. 🛣 Jul/Aug. 🅿 🌑 Grounds, on leads. 🏵 🐾 Tel for details.

OLD WARDOUR CASTLE ⌗

Nr TISBURY, WILTSHIRE SP3 6RR

www.english-heritage.org.uk/oldwardour

Tel/Fax: 01747 870487 **e-mail:** customers@english-heritage.org.uk

Owner: English Heritage **Contact:** Visitor Operations Team

In a picture-book setting, the unusual hexagonal ruins of this 14th century castle stand on the edge of a beautiful lake, surrounded by landscaped grounds which include an elaborate rockwork grotto.

Location: OS184, ST939 263. Off A30 2m SW of Tisbury.

Open: 1 Apr - 31 Oct: daily, 10am - 5pm (6pm Jul & Aug, 4pm Oct). 1 Nov - 31 Mar: Sats & Suns, 10am - 4pm. Closed 24 - 26 Dec & 1 Jan.

Admission: Adult £3.20, Child £1.60, Conc. £2.40. Groups (11+): 15% discount.

ℹ️WCs. 🖼 🕆 ♿Grounds. 🔂 🅿 ⛶Grounds, on leads. ▲ ❀ 📺 Tel for details.

PHILIPPS HOUSE & DINTON PARK ⚸

Dinton, Salisbury, Wiltshire SP3 5HH

Tel: 01722 716663 **www.**nationaltrust.org.uk

Owner: The National Trust **Contact:** The Regional Office

A neo-Grecian house by Jeffry Wyatville, completed in 1820. Lovely walks in surrounding parkland.

Location: OS Ref. SU004 319. 9m W of Salisbury, N side of B3089, 1/2 m W of Little Clarendon. Car park off St Mary's Road next to church.

Open: 8 Apr - 28 Oct: Sats, 10am - 1pm. 10 Apr - 30 Oct: Mons, 1 - 5pm. Park: all year.

Admission: House £3. Dinton Park Free.

ℹ️No WC. ♿House suitable, Park limited. Braille guide. ❀ Park.

special events
see page 571

THE PETO GARDEN AT IFORD MANOR 🏛

BRADFORD-ON-AVON, WILTSHIRE BA15 2BA

www.ifordmanor.co.uk

Tel: 01225 863146 **Fax:** 01225 862364

Owner/Contact: Mrs E A J Cartwright-Hignett

This unique Grade I Italian-style garden is set on a romantic hillside beside the River Frome. Designed by the Edwardian architect Harold A Peto, who lived at Iford Manor from 1899 - 1933, the garden has terraces, a colonnade, cloister, casita, statuary, evergreen planting and magnificent rural views. Renowned for its tranquillity and peace, the Peto Garden won the 1998 HHA/Christie's Garden of the Year Award.

Location: OS Ref. ST800 589. 7m SE of Bath via A36, signposted Iford. 1/2 m SW of Bradford-on-Avon via Westwood on B3109.

Open: Apr & Oct: Suns only & Easter Mon, 2 - 5pm. May - Sept: Tue - Thur, Sats, Suns & BH Mons, 2 - 5pm. Coaches by appointment at other times. Children under 10yrs welcome weekdays only for safety reasons.

Admission: Adult £4.50, Conc, Students & Children £4.00. Groups (10+) welcome outside normal opening hours, by appointment only, £5.

☕Teas (May-Aug: Sats, Suns & BHs, 2.30 - 5pm). ♿Partial. WCs. 📷By arrangement. 🅿 Limited for coaches. 🐕 On leads, in grounds.

SALISBURY CATHEDRAL

33 THE CLOSE, SALISBURY SP1 2EJ

www.salisburycathedral.org.uk

Tel: 01722 555120 **Fax:** 01722 555116 **e-mail:** visitors@salcath.co.uk

Owner: The Dean & Chapter **Contact:** Visitor Services

Salisbury Cathedral is a building of world importance. Set within the elegant splendour of the Cathedral Close. It is probably the finest medieval building in Britain. Built in one phase from 1220 to 1258. Britain's tallest spire (123m/404ft) was added a generation later. Discover nearly 800 years of history, the finest preserved Magna Carta (1215), Europe's oldest working clock and a unique 13th century frieze of bible stories in the beautiful Chapter House. Boy and girl choristers sing daily services which follow an historic tradition of worship. Explore the roof spaces on a tower tour, climbing 332 steps to the base of the spire, and marvel at the medieval craftsmanship and the magnificent views across Salisbury.

Location: OS Ref. SU143 295. S of City. M3, A303, A30 from London or A36.

Open: All year: Suns, 7.15am - 6.15pm. 1 Jan - 11 Jun, 27 Aug - 31 Dec: Mon - Sat, 7.15am - 6.15pm. 12 Jun - 26 Aug (excluding Sun): 7.15am - 7.15pm.

Admission: Donation: Adult £4, Child £2, Conc. £3.50, Family (2+2) £8.50.

🖼 🕆 ♿ ☕Licensed. 🍴 📷By arrangement. 🅿 In city centre. 🐕 In grounds, on leads. ❀ 📺 Tel for details.

STONEHENGE ⌗
AMESBURY, WILTSHIRE SP4 7DE

www.english-heritage.org.uk/stonehenge

Tel: 0870 3331181 (Customer Services) **Owner:** English Heritage

The mystical and awe-inspiring stone circle at Stonehenge is one of the most famous prehistoric monuments in the world, designated by UNESCO as a World Heritage Site. Stonehenge's orientation on the rising and setting sun has always been one of its most remarkable features. Whether this was simply because the builders came from a sun-worshipping culture, or because – as some scholars have believed – the circle and its banks were part of a huge astronomical calendar, remains a mystery. Visitors to Stonehenge can discover the history and legends which surround this unique stone circle, which began over 5,000 years ago, with a complimentary three part audio tour available in 9 languages (subject to availability).

Location: OS Ref. SU123 422. 2m W of Amesbury on junction of A303 and A344/ A360.

Open: 16 Mar - 31 May: daily 9.30am - 6pm. 1 Jun - 31 Aug: daily, 9am - 7pm. 1 Sept - 15 Oct: daily, 9.30am - 6pm. 16 Oct - 15 Mar: daily, 9.30am - 4pm. Closed 24 - 26 Dec & 1 Jan. Last recommended admission is 1/2 hr before advertised closing times and the site will be closed promptly 20 mins after the advertised closing times. Summer Solstice: 20 - 22 Jun, opening times may be amended.

Admission: Adult £5.90, Child £3, Conc £4.40, Family (2+3) £14.80. Groups (11+) 10% discount.

ℹ️WCs. 🔲 ♿ 💼 🎧 ♿ 🅿️ 🔀 ❄️ 🐕 Tel for details.

STONEHENGE HISTORIC LANDSCAPE ❀

Estate Office, 3/4 Stonehenge Cottages, Kings Barrows, Amesbury, Wiltshire SP4 7DD

Tel: 01980 664780 (Stonehenge Cottage) **Tel:** 0870 3331181 (EH Customer Services)

Owner: The National Trust **Contact:** NT Estate Office

The Trust own 850ha (2100 acres) of downland surrounding the famous monument, including some fine Bronze Age barrow groups and the Cursus, variously interpreted as an ancient racecourse or processional way. The Trust is now managing this historic landscape which encompasses the entire core zone of the Stonehenge World Heritage Site, to conserve archaeology, increase access and balance the needs of modern agricultural practice with natural conservation.

Location: OS Ref. SU120 420. 2m W of Amesbury on junction of A303 and A344/ A360.

Open: Tel for details. NT land N of visitor centre: All year, but parts may be closed at the Summer Solstice (21 Jun) for up to 2 days.

Admission: Free. A charge over the peak period (Jun - Oct) may apply. Refundable for NT members.

🔲 ♿ Partial. 🐕 Not on archaeological walks, under close control at all times. ❄️

STOURHEAD ❀ *See page 262 for full page entry.*

STOURTON HOUSE FLOWER GARDEN

Stourton, Warminster, Wiltshire BA12 6QF

Tel: 01747 840417

Owner/Contact: Mrs E Bullivant

Four acres of peaceful, romantic, plantsman's garden. Rare daffodils, camellias, rhododendrons, roses, hydrangeas and wild flowers.

Location: OS Ref. ST780 340. A303, 2m NW of Mere next to Stourhead car park. Follow blue signs.

Open: Apr - end Nov: Weds, Thurs, Suns, and BH Mons, 11am - 6pm. Plants & dried flowers for sale during the winter on weekdays. Groups any day.

Admission: Adult £3.50, Child 50p. Subject to increase Apr 2006.

WILTON HOUSE 🏛️ *See page 263 for full page entry.*

© NTPL/Ian Shaw

Stourhead.

Wrest Park, Bedfordshire.

bedfordshire   cambridgeshire   essex   hertfordshire

eastern region

East Anglia has magical coastal areas ranging from The Wash in Norfolk down to the Essex marshes. The Norfolk Broads is an area of inland waterways that attracts bird watchers from all over the world. The half timbered houses in Suffolk villages such as Lavenham contrast with the Norfolk flint found further north. Cambridge, with its colleges and riverside walks, merits a visit all to itself. Among the major properties that welcome visitors are Sandringham (Norfolk) the country home of HM The Queen, Woburn Abbey (Bedfordshire) and Hatfield House (Hertfordshire). But off the beaten track do find time for The Manor, Hemingford Grey (Cambridgeshire), reputedly one of the oldest continuously inhabited houses in Britain; or visit Copped Hall (Essex), the subject of a remarkable restoration programme by local residents.

norfolk   suffolk

WOBURN ABBEY 🏛

www.discoverwoburn.co.uk

MAP 7

Owner:
The Duke and Duchess
of Bedford &
The Trustees of Bedford
Estates

▶ **CONTACT**
William Lash
Woburn Abbey
Woburn
Bedfordshire MK17 9WA

Tel: 01525 290333
Fax: 01525 290271

e-mail: admissions@
woburnabbey.co.uk

▶ **LOCATION**
OS Ref. SP965 325

On A4012, midway
between M1/J13, 3m,
J14, 6m and
the A5 (turn off
at Hockliffe).
London approx. 1hr
by road (43m).

Rail: London Euston to
Leighton Buzzard,
Bletchley/Milton Keynes.
Kings Cross
Thameslink to Flitwick.

Air: Luton 14m.
Heathrow 39m.

CONFERENCE/FUNCTION

ROOM	SIZE	MAX CAPACITY
Sculpture Gallery	128' x 24'	300 250 (sit-down)
Lantern Rm	44' x 21'	60

Set in a beautiful 3,000 acre deer park, Woburn Abbey has been the home of the Dukes of Bedford for nearly 400 years, and is now occupied by the present Duke and Duchess and their family.

The Abbey houses one of the most important private art collections in the world, including paintings by Gainsborough, Reynolds, Van Dyck, Cuyp, and Canaletto, 21 of whose views hang in the Venetian Room.

The tour of the Abbey covers three floors, including the vaults, with 18th Century French and English furniture, silver and a wide range of porcelain on display. Amongst the highlights is the Sèvres dinner service presented to the 4th Duke by Louis XV of France.

The Deer Park is home to ten species of deer, including the Père David, descended from the Imperial Herd of China, which was saved from

extinction at Woburn and is now the largest breeding herd of this species in the world. In 1985 the 14th Duke gave 22 Père David deer to the People's Republic of China and the herd is now well established in its natural environment and numbers several hundred.

Woburn Abbey is also noted for its excellent and unique Antiques Centre with over 60 original 18th century shop fronts and show cases, and has an enviable reputation for its in-house catering. Woburn Abbey specialises in banqueting, conferences, receptions and company days; and the Sculpture Gallery overlooking the Private Gardens provides a splendid setting for weddings and wedding receptions.

There are a number of events in the Park each year including the Woburn Garden Show, Craft Fair and the ever popular de Havilland Moth Club annual fly-in.

ℹ Suitable for fashion shows, product launches and company 'days out'. Use of parkland and garden. No photography in House.

🛍 Two shops.

🍸 Conferences, exhibitions, banqueting, luncheons, dinners in the Sculpture Gallery, Lantern & Long Harness rooms.

☕ Group bookings in Sculpture Gallery. Flying Duchess Pavilion Coffee Shop.

🍽 Licensed.

🚶 £17.50, by arrangement, max 8. Tours in French, German & Italian available. Guide book available £5. Special interest tours can be arranged.

🅿 Ample.

🏫 Please telephone for details.

🐕 In park on leads, and guide dogs in house.

🔔 Civil Wedding Licence.

❄

🛡 Please telephone for details.

▶ **OPENING TIMES**
8 April - 1 October: daily.
Open during November
& December – please
telephone for
specific dates.

Abbey
Mon - Sat: 11am - 4pm
(last entry).

Deer Park
All year: Daily
10am - 5pm.
(except 24 - 26 December).

Antiques Centre
All year: Daily
10am - 5.30pm.
(except 24 - 26 December).

▶ **ADMISSION**
Woburn Abbey
(Prices incl. Private Apts)
Adult £10.50
Child (5 - 15yrs) £6.00
OAP £9.50
Group rates & family
tickets available.

**Car Park, Grounds &
Deer Park only**
.... £2.00pp

Reduced rates apply when
Private Apartments are in
use by the family.

BROMHAM MILL & GALLERY

Bridge End, Bromham, Bedfordshire MK43 8LP

Tel: 01234 824330 **email:** bromham.mill@bedscc.gov.uk

Owner: Bedfordshire County Council

Working water mill on River Ouse. Flour milling and changing contemporary art & craft exhibitions.

Location: OS Ref. TL010 506. Location beside the River Ouse bridge on N side of the former A428, 2$^{1}/_{2}$ m W of Bedford.

Open: Apr - Oct: Suns & BHs, 1 - 5pm. Other times for groups by arrangement.

Admission: Free. Group charges on application.

BUSHMEAD PRIORY ⚏

Colmworth, Bedford, Bedfordshire MK44 2LD

Tel: 01799 522842 **Regional Office:** 01223 582700

Owner: English Heritage   **Contact:** Visitor Operations Team

A rare survival of the medieval refectory of an Augustinian priory, with its original timber-framed roof almost intact and containing interesting wall paintings and stained glass.

Location: OS Ref. TL115 607. On unclassified road near Colmworth; off B660, 2m S of Bolnhurst. 5m W of St. Neots (A1).

Open: 1 May - 31 Aug. Pre-booked guided tours only, please call 01799 522842.

Admission: Adult £2 Child £1, Conc. £1.50.

P ✖

CECIL HIGGINS ART GALLERY

CASTLE LANE, BEDFORD MK40 3RP

www.cecilhigginsartgallery.org

Tel: 01234 211222 **Fax:** 01234 327149 **e-mail:** chag@bedford.gov.uk

Owner: Bedford Borough Council & Trustees of Gallery **Contact:** The Gallery

A recreation of an 1880s home, with superb examples of 19th century decorative arts. Room settings include items from the Handley-Read collection and the famous Gothic bedroom containing works by William Burges. Adjoining gallery housing renowned collections of watercolours, prints and drawings (exhibitions changed regularly), ceramics, glass and lace. Situated in pleasant gardens near the river embankment.

Location: OS Ref. TL052 497. Centre of Bedford, just off The Embankment. E of High St.

Open: Tue - Sat, 11am - 5pm (last admission 4.45pm). Sun & BH Mons, 2 - 5pm. Closed Mons, Good Fri, 25/26 Dec & 1 Jan.

Admission: Free.

ⓘ Photography in house by arrangement. ☐ ⊤ By arrangement. ♿
☕ Self-service coffee bar. ⚑ By arrangement. ▮ ✖ Guide dogs only. ✷
▧ Tel for details.

HOUGHTON HOUSE ⚏

Ampthill, Bedford, Bedfordshire

Tel: 01223 582700 (Regional Office)

Owner: English Heritage   **Contact:** East of England Regional Office

Reputedly the inspiration for "*House Beautiful*" in Bunyan's "*Pilgrim's Progress*", the remains of this early 17th century mansion still convey elements which justify the description, including work attributed to Inigo Jones.

Location: OS Ref. TL039 394. 1m NE of Ampthill off A421, 8m S of Bedford.

Open: Any reasonable time.

Admission: Free.

P ✖ ✷

MOGGERHANGER PARK

Park Road, Moggerhanger, Bedfordshire MK44 3RW

Tel: 01767 641007 **Fax:** 01767 641515

e-mail: enquiries@moggerhangerpark.com **www**.moggerhangerpark.com

Owner: Moggerhanger House Preservation Trust **Contact:** Mrs Jenny Cooper

Outstanding Georgian Grade I listed Country House, recently restored in keeping with the original design of architect, Sir John Soane and set in 33 acres of parkland originally landscaped by Humphry Repton.

Moggerhanger House has 25 en-suite bedrooms and 5 meeting rooms, making an ideal venue for conferences, promotions and corporate entertainment.

Location: OS Ref. TL048 475. On A603, 3m from A1 at Sandy, 6m from Bedford.

Open: House Tours: Jun - Sept: 11am - 4pm. Grounds, Tearooms & Visitors' Centre: All year.

Admission: Please telephone 01767 641007.

ⓘ No photography. No smoking. ☐ ⊤ ♿ ☕ Licensed. ▯ Licensed.
⚑ By arrangement. P Limited for coaches. ✖ In grounds, on leads.
▧ Double x 24, Single x 1, all en-suite. ✷.

SWISS GARDEN

Old Warden Park, Bedfordshire

Tel: 01767 627666

www.shuttleworth.org

Operated By: Bedfordshire County Council

The Swiss Garden, Old Warden Park, Bedfordshire, created in the 1820s by Lord Ongley, is a late Regency garden and an outstanding example of the Swiss picturesque. The Swiss Cottage provides the main element for this unusual and atmospheric garden. It provides the principal aspect for a number of contrived vistas which lead the eye towards this attractive thatched structure. Interesting things to see in the garden are, a grotto and fernery, a thatched tree shelter, an Indian Pavilion, two ponds and many fine specimens of shrubs and conifers, plus some remarkable trees.

Location: OS Ref. TL150 447. 1$^{1}/_{2}$ m W of Biggleswade A1 roundabout, signposted from A1 and A600.

Open: Apr - Oct: 10am - 5pm; Nov - Mar: 10am - 4pm. Closed Christmas week.

Admission: Adult £4, Child Free, Conc. £3. Special rates for groups, tours or private hire.

▯ ♿ ⊤ Catering. ☕ Refreshments adjacent. P ✖ ▲ ✷

WREST PARK ⚏

SILSOE, LUTON, BEDFORDSHIRE MK45 4HS

www.english-heritage.org.uk/visits

Tel: 01525 860152

Owner: English Heritage   **Contact:** Visitor Operations Team

Over 90 acres of enchanting gardens originally laid out in the early 18th century, and inspired by the great gardens of Versailles and the Loire Valley in France. Marvel at the magnificent collection of stone and lead statuary, the Bath House and the vast Orangery, built by the Earl de Grey, and dream of days gone by. The gardens form a delightful backdrop to the house which is built in the style of an 18th century French château.

Location: OS153, TL093 356. $^{3}/_{4}$ m E of Silsoe off A6, 10m S of Bedford.

Open: 1 Apr - 31 Oct: Sat, Sun & BHs, 10am - 6pm (5pm in Oct). Last admission 1hr before closing.

Admission: Adult £4.50, Child £2.30, Conc. £3.40. Family £11.30.

ⓘ WCs. Buggies available. ☐ ♿ ☐ P ✖ On leads. ▧ Tel for details.

ANGLESEY ABBEY, GARDENS & LODE MILL ❧
LODE, CAMBRIDGE, CAMBRIDGESHIRE CB5 9EJ
www.nationaltrust.org.uk/angleseyabbey

Tel/Fax: 01223 810080   **e-mail:** angleseyabbey@nationaltrust.org.uk

Owner: The National Trust   **Contact:** The Property Manager

Dating from 1600, the house, built on the site of an Augustinian priory, contains the famous Fairhaven collection of paintings and furniture. Surrounded by an outstanding 100 acre garden and arboretum, with a wonderful display of hyacinths in spring, magnificent herbaceous borders, a dahlia garden in summer, winter garden and woodland path. A watermill in full working order is demonstrated on the first and third Saturday each month.

Location: OS Ref. TL533 622. 6m NE of Cambridge on B1102, signs from A14.

Open: Summer: House & Mill: 22 Mar - 29 Oct: Wed - Sun & BH Mons: 1 - 5pm. Garden, Shop, Plant Centre & Restaurant: 22 Mar - 29 Oct: Wed - Sun & BH Mons; 10.30am - 5.30pm. Winter: Winter Garden, Shop, Plant Centre & Restaurant: 1 Nov - 22 Dec & 30 Dec - 20 Mar 2007: Wed - Sun, 10.30am - 4pm; Mill: Sat & Sun, 11am - 3.30pm. Gardens & Mill also open Tues in school holidays. Groups must book, no groups on Suns & BHs.

Admission: Summer: House & Garden: Adult £8, Child £4. Groups: Adult £6.95, Child £3.50. Garden only: Adult £4.50, Child £2.25. Groups: Adult £4, Child £2. Winter (garden only): Adult £4, Child £2. Groups: Adult £3.50, Child £1.75.

▣ ⛲ ♿ Partial. ⛏ Licensed. 🎟 🅿 ⛔ ❋ ♿ Tel for details.

©Nigel Luckhurst

CAMBRIDGE UNIVERSITY BOTANIC GARDEN
BATEMAN STREET, CAMBRIDGE CB2 1JF
www.botanic.cam.ac.uk

Tel: 01223 336265 **Fax:** 01223 336278 **e-mail:** enquiries@botanic.cam.ac.uk

Owner: University of Cambridge   **Contact:** Enquiries Desk

This 40 acre oasis of listed heritage landscape showcases over 8000 species, including alpines from every continent in the Rock Garden, nine national collections, the finest collection of trees in the Eastern Region, the historic Systematic Beds, the Dry Garden, the renowned Winter Garden and tropical forest in the Glasshouses.

Location: OS Ref. TL453 573. 3/4m S of Cambridge city centre; entrance on Bateman Street off A1309 (Trumpington Rd). 10mins walk from railway station.

Open: 3 Jan - 24 Dec: daily, 10am - 6pm; closes 5pm in autumn & spring and 4pm in winter.

Admission: Adult £3, Child (under 16yrs) Free, Conc. £2.50.

▣ Mar - Oct. ♿ ▣ 🎟 By arrangement. 🅿 Street/Pay & Display. ▣
🦮 Guide dogs only. ❋

OLIVER CROMWELL'S HOUSE
29 St Mary's Street, Ely, Cambridgeshire CB7 4HF

Tel: 01353 662062   **Fax:** 01353 668518   **e-mail:** tic@eastcambs.gov.uk

Owner: East Cambridgeshire District Council

The former home of the Lord Protector.

Location: OS Ref. TL538 803. N of Cambridge, 1/4 m W of Ely Cathedral.

Open: 1 Nov - 31 Mar: Sun - Fri, 11am - 4pm; Sats, 10am - 5pm. 1 Apr - 31 Oct: daily, 10am - 5.30pm.

Admission: Adult £3.85, Child £2.60, Conc. £3.35, Family £10.50 (Prices subject to change April 2006.)

DENNY ABBEY & THE FARMLAND MUSEUM ⚏
Ely Road, Chittering, Waterbeach, Cambridgeshire CB5 9TQ

Tel: 01223 860489   www.english-heritage.org.uk/visits

Owner: English Heritage/Managed by the Farmland Museum Trust

                               Contact: Visitor Operations Team

What at first appears to be an attractive stone-built farmhouse is actually the remains of a 12th century Benedictine abbey which, at different times, also housed the Knights Templar and Franciscan nuns. Founded by the Countess of Pembroke.

Location: OS Ref. TL495 684. 6m N of Cambridge on the E side of the A10.

Open: 1 Apr - 31 Oct: daily, 12 noon - 5pm.

Admission: Abbey & Museum: Adult £3.80, Child £1.70, Child under 5 Free, Conc. £3, Family £9.60, Members/OVP £2.40.

ℹ WC. ▣ ♿ ▣ Weekends only. 🅿 ⛔ On leads. ♿ Tel for details.

DOCWRA'S MANOR GARDEN 🏛
Shepreth, Royston, Hertfordshire SG8 6PS

Tel: 01763 261473 **Information:** 01763 260677

Owner: Mrs Faith Raven   **Contact:** Peter Rocket

Extensive garden around building dating from the 18th century.

Location: OS Ref. TL393 479. In Shepreth via A10 from Royston.

Open: All year: Weds & Fris, 10am - 4pm & 1st Sun in month from Apr - Oct: 2 - 5pm.

Admission: £4.

ELTON HALL
Nr PETERBOROUGH PE8 6SH
www.eltonhall.com

Tel: 01832 280468 **Fax:** 01832 280584 **e-mail:** office@eltonhall.com

Owner: Sir William Proby Bt **Contact:** The Administrator

Elton Hall, the home of the Proby family for over 350 years is a fascinating mixture of styles. Every room contains treasures, magnificent furniture and fine paintings. The library is one of the finest in private hands and includes Henry VIII's prayer book. The beautiful gardens have been carefully restored, with the addition of a new gothic Orangery to celebrate the Millennium.

Location: OS Ref. TL091 930. Close to A1 in the village of Elton, off A605 Peterborough - Oundle road.

Open: 28/29 May; June: Weds. Jul & Aug: Wed, Thur, Sun & BH Mon, 2 - 5pm. Private groups by arrangement Apr - Sept.

Admission: House & Garden: £6. Garden only: £4. Accompanied child under 16 Free. No photography in house. Garden suitable. Obligatory. Guide dogs in gardens only. Tel for details.

ELY CATHEDRAL
The Chapter House, The College, Ely, Cambridgeshire CB7 4DL

Tel: 01353 667735 ext.261 **Fax:** 01353 665658

Contact: Sally-Ann Ford (Visits & Tours Manager)

A wonderful example of Romanesque architecture. Octagon and Lady Chapel are of special interest. Superb medieval domestic buildings surround the Cathedral. Stained Glass Museum. Brass rubbing. Octagon and West Tower tours peak season.

Location: OS Ref. TL541 803. Via A10, 15m N of Cambridge City centre.

Open: Summer: 7am - 7pm. Winter: Mon - Sat, 7.30am - 6pm, Suns and week after Christmas, 7.30am - 5pm. Sun services: 8.15am, 10.30am and 3.45pm. Weekday services: 7.40am, 8am, and 5.30pm (Thurs only also 12.30pm).

Admission: Adult £4.80, Child Free, Conc. £4.40. Discounts for groups of 15+. Separate rates for school visits.

ISLAND HALL
GODMANCHESTER, CAMBRIDGESHIRE PE29 2BA

Tel: 01480 459676 **e-mail:** cvp@cvpdesigns.com

Owner: Mr Christopher & Lady Linda Vane Percy **Contact:** Mr C Vane Percy

An important mid 18th century mansion of great charm, owned and restored by an award-winning interior designer. This family home has lovely Georgian rooms, with fine period detail, and interesting possessions relating to the owners' ancestors since their first occupation of the house in 1800. A tranquil riverside setting with formal gardens and ornamental island forming part of the grounds in an area of Best Landscape. Octavia Hill wrote *"This is the loveliest, dearest old house, I never was in such a one before."*

Location: OS Ref. TL244 706. Centre of Godmanchester, Post Street next to free car park. 1m S of Huntingdon, 15m NW of Cambridge A14.

Open: Groups only, by arrangement: May - Jul & Sept.

Admission: (40+) Adult £4.50, (10-40 persons) Adult £5. Under 20 persons, min charge £100 per group (sorry but no children under 13yrs).

Home made teas.

plant sales
see page 555

KIMBOLTON CASTLE

Kimbolton, Huntingdon, Cambridgeshire PE28 0EA

Tel: 01480 860505 **Fax:** 01480 861763

www.kimbolton.cambs.sch.uk/castle_visits

Owner: Governors of Kimbolton School   **Contact:** Mrs N Butler

A late Stuart house, an adaptation of a 13th century fortified manor house, with evidence of Tudor modifications. The seat of the Earls and Dukes of Manchester 1615 - 1950, now a school. Katharine of Aragon died in the Queen's Room - the setting for a scene in Shakespeare's Henry VIII. 18th century rebuilding by Vanbrugh and Hawksmoor; Gatehouse by Robert Adam; the Pellegrini mural paintings on the Staircase, in the Chapel and in the Boudoir are the best examples in England of this gifted Venetian decorator.

Location: OS Ref. TL101 676. 7m NW of St Neots on B645.

Open: 5 Mar & 5 Nov, 1 - 4pm.

Admission: Adult £3.50, Child £2, OAP £2.50. Groups by arrangement throughout the year, including evenings.

🛠 ⅃ Unsuitable. 🔲 🗇 By arrangement. 🅿 🔳 🖿 On leads in grounds. ▲ ❋

THE MANOR, HEMINGFORD GREY

HUNTINGDON, CAMBRIDGESHIRE PE28 9BN

www.greenknowe.co.uk

Tel: 01480 463134 **Fax:** 01480 465026 **e-mail:** diana_boston@hotmail.com

Owner: Mrs D S Boston   **Contact:** Diana Boston

Built about 1130, it is one of the oldest continuously inhabited houses in Britain. Made famous as 'Green Knowe' by the author Lucy Boston. Her patchwork collection is also shown. Four acre garden with topiary, old roses and herbaceous borders.

Location: OS Ref. TL290 706. Off A14, 3m SE of Huntingdon. 12m NW of Cambridge. Access is by a small gate on the riverside footpath.

Open: House: All year (except May), to individuals or groups by prior arrangement. May only: guided tours at 11am & 2pm (booking advisable). Garden: All year, daily, 11am - 5pm (4pm in winter).

Admission: Adult £5, Child £1.50, OAP £4. Garden only: Adult £2, Child Free.

ℹ No photography in house. 🗇 🖄 🔲 Locally, by arrangement. 🗇 Obligatory. 🔳 🅿 Disabled only. 🖿 In garden, on leads. ❋

KING'S COLLEGE

KING'S PARADE, CAMBRIDGE CB2 1ST

www.kings.cam.ac.uk

Tel/Fax: 01223 331212 **e-mail:** derek.buxton@kings.cam.ac.uk

Owner: Provost and Fellows   **Contact:** Mr D Buxton

Visitors are welcome, but remember that this is a working college. Please respect the privacy of those who work, live and study here. The Chapel is sometimes used for services, recordings, broadcasts, etc, and ideally visitors should check before arriving.

Location: OS Ref. TL447 584.

Open: Out of term: Mon - Sat, 9.30am - 4.30pm. Sun, 10am - 5pm. In term: Mon - Fri: 9.30am - 3.30pm. Sat: 9.30am - 3.15pm. Sun: 1.15 - 2.30pm.

Admission: Adult £4.50, Child (12-17yrs)/Student (ID required)/OAP £3. Child (under 12 & accompanied) Free (only as part of family unit).

ℹ No photography inside Chapel. Conferences. 🗇 🛠 By arrangement. ⅃ 🗇 By arrangement. 🅿 None. 🖿 Guide dogs only. ❋

LONGTHORPE TOWER ⌗

Thorpe Rd, Longthorpe, Cambridgeshire PE1 1HA

Tel: 01799 522842 **www.english-heritage.org.uk/visits**

Owner: English Heritage   **Contact:** Visitor Operations Team

The finest example of 14th century domestic wall paintings in northern Europe showing a variety of secular and sacred objects. The tower, with the Great Chamber that contains the paintings, is part of a fortified manor house. Special exhibitions are held on the upper floor.

Location: OS Ref. TL163 983. 2m W of Peterborough just off A47.

Open: 1 May - 31 Aug: Pre-booked guided tours only, please call 01799 522842.

Admission: Adult £2.40, Child £1.20, Conc. £1.80.

ℹ No parking at site. 🗇 🗇 By arrangement. 🖿

Cambridge University Botanic Garden.

PECKOVER HOUSE & GARDEN ❦

NORTH BRINK, WISBECH, CAMBRIDGESHIRE PE13 1JR

www.nationaltrust.org.uk

Tel/Fax: 01945 583463   **e-mail:** peckover@nationaltrust.org.uk

Owner: The National Trust   **Contact:** The Property Manager

A town house, built c1722 and renowned for its very fine plaster and wood rococo decoration. The outstanding 2 acre Victorian garden includes an orangery, summer-houses, roses, herbaceous borders, fernery, croquet lawn and Reed Barn Restaurant.

Location: OS Ref. TF458 097. On N bank of River Nene, in Wisbech B1441.

Open: House, Garden, Shop & Restaurant: 25 Mar - 30 Apr, 2 Oct - 5 Nov: Sats & Suns. 2 May - 1 Oct: Sat/Sun & Tues/Wed. BH Mons, Good Fri, 29/30 Jun & Mons in Aug: 12 noon - 5pm (House 1 - 4pm).

Admission: Adult £5, Child £2.50, Family £15. Groups: £4.30.

▢ ▢ ▢ Partial. ▢ ▢ ▢ Signposted. ▢ ▢ ▢ ▢ Tel for details.

PETERBOROUGH CATHEDRAL

Chapter Office, Minster Precincts, Peterborough PE1 1XS

Tel: 01733 355300   **Fax:** 01733 355316

e-mail: a.watson@peterborough-cathedral.org.uk

www.peterborough-cathedral.org.uk   **Contact:** Andrew Watson

'An undiscovered gem.' With magnificent Norman architecture a unique 13th century nave ceiling, the awe-inspiring West Front and burial places of two Queens to make your visit an unforgettable experience. Exhibitions tell the Cathedral's story. Tours by appointment, of the cathedral, tower, Deanery Garden or Precincts. Freshly prepared meals and snacks at Beckets Restaurant (advance bookings possible). Cathedral gift shop and Tourist Information Centre in Precincts. Business meeting facilities.

Location: OS Ref. TL194 986. 4m E of A1, in City Centre.

Open: All year: Mon - Fri, 9am - 5.15pm. Sat, 9am - 5pm. Sun: services from 7.30am; visitors: 12 noon - 5pm.

Admission: No fixed charge – donations are requested.

ℹ Visitors' Centre. ▢ ▢ ▢ Mon - Sat. ▢ By arrangement. ▢ None. ▢
▢ Guide dogs only. ✳

special events
see page 571

WIMPOLE HALL & HOME FARM ❦

ARRINGTON, ROYSTON, CAMBRIDGESHIRE SG8 0BW

www.nationaltrust.org.uk   www.wimpole.org

Tel: 01223 206000   **Fax:** 01223 207838   **e-mail:** wimpolehall@nationaltrust.org.uk

Owner: The National Trust   **Contact:** The Property Manager

Wimpole is a magnificent country house built in 18th century style with a colourful history of owners. The Hall is set in restored formal gardens with parterres and a walled garden. Home Farm is a working farm and is the largest rare breeds centre in East Anglia.

Location: OS154. TL336 510. 8m SW of Cambridge (A603), 6m N of Royston (A1198).

Open: Hall: 25 Mar - 29 Oct: Sat - Wed (open Good Fri & BH Mon); Aug: Sat - Thur (open BH Mons); 5, 12, 19 & 26 Nov, Suns only; 1 - 5pm, BH Mon, 11am - 5pm, closes 4pm after 29 Oct. Garden: as Farm. Park: dawn - dusk. Farm: 25 Mar - 29 Oct: Sat - Wed (open Good Fri & BH Mon); Aug: Sat - Thur & BH Mon; Nov - Mar 2007: Sat & Sun (open Feb half-term week); 19 Mar - 29 Oct: 10.30am - 5pm; 4 Nov - Mar 2007, 11am - 4pm.

Admission: Hall: Adult £7.50, Child £4. Joint ticket with Home Farm: Adult £11, Child £6, Family £28. Garden: £3. Group rates (not Suns or BH Mons). Farm: Adult £6, Child (3yrs & up) £4. Discount for NT members (not Suns or BH Mons).

▢ ▢ ▢ ▢ Partial. ▢ ▢ Licensed. ▢ By arrangement. ▢ Limited for coaches. ▢
▢ In park, on leads. ▢ ✳ ▢ Tel for details.

UNIVERSITY OF CAMBRIDGE

Christ's College
St Andrew's Street
Cambridge CB2 3BU
Tel: 01223 334900
Fax: 01223 334967
Email: admissions@christs.cam.ac.uk
Founder: Lady Margaret Beaufort
Founded: 1505

Churchill College
Madingley Road, Cambridge CB3 0DS
Tel: 01223 336000
Fax: 01223 336180
Email: admissions@chu.cam.ac.uk
Founded: 1960

Clare College
Trinity Lane, Cambridge CB2 1TL
Tel: 01223 333200
Fax: 01223 333219
Email: admissions@clare.cam.ac.uk
        enquiries@clare.cam.ac.uk
Founded: 1326

Clare Hall
Herschel Road, Cambridge CB3 9AL
Tel: 01223 332360
Fax: 01223 332333
Email: receptionist@clarehall.cam.ac.uk
Founded: 1965

Corpus Christi College
King's Parade, Cambridge CB2 1RH
Tel: 01223 338000
Fax: 01223 338061
Email: admissions@corpus.cam.ac.uk
Founded: 1352

Darwin College
Silver Street, Cambridge CB3 9EU
Tel: 01223 335660
Fax: 01223 335667
Email: deanery@dar.cam.ac.uk
Founded: 1964

Downing College
Regent Street, Cambridge CB2 1DQ
Tel: 01223 334800
Fax: 01223 467934
Email: admissions@dow.cam.ac.uk
        college-secretary@dow.cam.ac.uk
Founded: 1800

Emmanuel College
St Andrew's Street, Cambridge CB2 3AP
Tel: 01223 334200
Fax: 01223 334426
Email: admissions@emma.cam.ac.uk
Founded: 1584

Fitzwilliam College
Huntingdon Road, Cambridge CB3 0DG
Tel: 01223 332000
Fax: 01223 464162
Email: admissions@fitz.cam.ac.uk
Founded: 1966

Girton College
Huntingdon Road, Cambridge CB3 0JG
Tel: 01223 338999
Fax: 01223 338896
Email: admissions@girton.cam.ac.uk
Founded: 1869

Gonville & Caius College
Trinity Street, Cambridge CB2 1TA
Tel: 01223 332400
Fax: 01223 332456
Email: admissions@cai.cam.ac.uk
Founded: 1348

Homerton College
Hills Road, Cambridge CB2 2PH
Tel: 01223 507111
Fax: 01223 507120
Email: admissions@homerton.cam.ac.uk
Founded: 1976

Hughes Hall
Wollaston Road, Cambridge CB1 2EW
Tel: 01223 334897
Fax: 01223 311179
Email: admissions@hughes.cam.ac.uk
        enquiries@hughes.cam.ac.uk
Founded: 1885

Jesus College
Jesus Lane, Cambridge CB5 8BL
Tel: 01223 339339
Fax: 01223 324910
Email: undergraduateadmissions@jesus.cam.ac.uk
Founded: 1496

King's College
King's Parade, Cambridge CB2 1ST
Tel: 01223 331100
Fax: 01223 331315
Email: undergraduate.admissions@kings.cam.ac.uk
graduate.admissions@kings.cam.ac.uk
Founded: 1441

Lucy Cavendish College
Lady Margaret Road, Cambs CB3 0BU
Tel: 01223 332190
Fax: 01223 332178
Email: lcc-admission@lists.cam.ac.uk
Founded: 1965

Magdalene College
Magdalene Street, Cambridge CB3 0AG
Tel: 01223 332100
Fax: 01223 363637
Email: magd-admissions@lists.cam.ac.uk
Founded: 1428

New Hall
Huntingdon Road, Cambridge CB3 0DF
Tel: 01223 762100
Fax: 01223 352941
Email: admissions@newhall.cam.ac.uk
Founded: 1954

Newnham College
Grange Road, Cambridge CB3 9DF
Tel: 01223 335700
Fax: 01223 359155/357898
Email: admissions@newn.cam.ac.uk
        enquiries@newn.cam.ac.uk
Founded: 1871

Pembroke College
Trumpington Street, Cambs B2 1RF
Tel: 01223 338100
Fax: 01223 338163
Email: admissions@pem.cam.ac.uk
        enquiries@pem.cam.ac.uk
Founded: 1347

Peterhouse
Trumpington Street, Cambs CB2 1RD
Tel: 01223 338200
Fax: 01223 337578
Email: admissions@pet.cam.ac.uk
Founder: The Bishop of Ely
Founded: 1284

Queens' College
Silver Street, Cambridge CB3 9ET
Tel: 01223 335511
Fax: 01223 335522 (General)
Email: admissions@quns.cam.ac.uk
        enquiries@quns.cam.ac.uk
Founder: Margaret of Anjou, Elizabeth Woodville
Founded: 1448

Robinson College
Grange Road, Cambridge CB3 9AN
Tel: 01223 339100
Fax: 01223 351794
Email: undergraduate admissions@robinson.cam.ac.uk
graduateadmissions@robinson.cam.ac.uk
Founded: 1979

St Catherine's College
King's Parade, Cambs CB2 1RL
Tel: 01223 338300
Fax: 01223 338340
Email: undergraduate.admissions@caths.cam.ac.uk
Founded: 1473

St Edmund's College
Mount Pleasant, Cambridge CB3 0BN
Tel: 01223 336086
Fax: 01223 336111
Email: admissions@st-edmunds.cam.ac.uk
college.office@st-edmunds.cam.ac.uk
Founded: 1896

St John's College
St John's Street, Cambridge CB2 1TP
Tel: 01223 338600
Fax: 01223 337720
Email: admissions@joh.cam.ac.uk
Founded: 1511

Selwyn College
Grange Road, Cambridge CB3 9DQ
Tel: 01223 335846
Fax: 01223 335837
Email: admissions@sel.cam.ac.uk
Founded: 1882

Sidney Sussex College
Sidney Street, Cambridge CB2 3HU
Tel: 01223 338800
Fax: 01223 338884
Email: admissions@sid.cam.ac.uk
        enquiries@sid.cam.ac.uk
Founded: 1596

Trinity College
Trinity Street, Cambridge CB2 1TQ
Tel: 01223 338400
Fax: 01223 338564
Email: admissions@trin.cam.ac.uk
        college.office@trin.cam.ac.uk
Founded: 1546

Trinity Hall
Trinity Lane, Cambridge CB2 1TJ
Tel: 01223 332500
Fax: 01223 332537
Email: admissions@trinhall.cam.ac.uk
Founded: 1350

Wolfson College
Grange Road, Cambridge CB3 9BB
Tel: 01223 335900
Fax: 01223 335908 (Porter's Lodge)
Email: ug-admissions@wolfson.cam.ac.uk
pg-admissions@wolfson.cam.ac.uk
Founded: 1965

Visitors wishing to gain admittance to the Colleges (meaning the Courts, not to the staircases & students' rooms) are advised to contact the Tourist Office for further information. It should be noted that Halls normally close for lunch (12 - 2pm) and many are not open during the afternoon. Chapels may be closed during services. Libraries are not normally open, and Gardens do not usually include the Fellows' garden. Visitors, and especially guided groups, should always call on the Porters Lodge first.

For further details contact: Cambridge Tourism, The Old Library, Wheeler Street, Cambridge CB2 3QB.
Tel: +44 (0)1223 464132   Infoline: 0906 5862526   Fax: +44 (0)1223 457549

English Heritage Photographic Library

AUDLEY END HOUSE & GDNS ⊞

www.english-heritage.org.uk/visits

MAP 7

Owner:
English Heritage

▶ **CONTACT**

Visitor Operations Team
Audley End House
Audley End
Saffron Walden
Essex CB11 4JF

Tel: 01799 522842
Fax: 01799 521276

Venue Hire and Hospitality:
Tel: 01799 529403

▶ **LOCATION**
OS Ref. TL525 382

1m W of Saffron Walden on B1383, M11/J8 & J10.

Rail: Audley End 1¼ m.

Audley End was a palace in all but name. Built by Thomas Howard, Earl of Suffolk, to entertain King James I. The King may have had his suspicions, for he never stayed there; in 1618 Howard was imprisoned and fined for embezzlement.

Charles II bought the property in 1668 for £50,000, but within a generation the house was gradually demolished, and by the 1750s it was about the size you see today. There are still over 30 magnificent rooms to see, each with period furnishings.

The house and its gardens, including a 19th century parterre and rose garden, are surrounded by an enchanting 18th century landscaped park laid out by 'Capability' Brown.

Visitors can also visit the working organic walled garden and purchase produce from its shop. Extending to nearly 10 acres the garden includes a 170ft long, five-bay vine house, built in 1802.

English Heritage Photographic Library

▶ **OPENING TIMES***

House
4 - 26 March, 7 - 29 October & 3 - 31 March 2007*: Sat & Sun: 10am - 4pm (Behind-the-Scenes Tours only).

April - June & 1 September - 1 October*, (Guided Historical Tours only). Also 1 Jul - 31 Aug: Wed - Sun, 11am - 5pm (Sats closes 3pm).

Last admission 1 hr before closing.

*At certain times of the year access to the house is by behind-the-scenes & guided historical tours only. Some rooms will not be open throughout the season. Please call for details. In some rooms, light levels are reduced to preserve vulnerable textiles and other collections. House may have to close at 4.30pm when events are booked.

Gardens
4 - 26 March, 1 - 29 October & 3 - 31 March: Sats & Suns, 10am - 5pm. 1 April - 1 Oct: Wed - Sun & BHs, 10am - 6pm.

▶ **ADMISSION**

House & Grounds
Adult	£8.95
Child (5 - 15yrs)	£4.50
Child (under 5yrs)	Free
Conc.	£6.70
Family (2+3)	£22.40

Grounds only
Adult	£4.80
Child (5 - 15yrs)	£2.40
Child (under 5yrs)	Free
Concessions	£3.60
Family (2+3)	£12.00
Groups (11+ 15% discount.

CONFERENCE/FUNCTION
ROOM	MAX CAPACITY
Grounds	Large scale events possible

🛍 ⊤ Private and corporate hire.

ⓘ Open air concerts and other events. WCs.

♿ Ground floor and grounds.

☕ ⊤⊤ Restaurant (max 50).

🏃 By arrangement for groups.

🅿 Coaches to book in advance, £5 per coach. Free entry for coach drivers and tour guides. One additional place for every extra 20 people.

 School visits free if booked in advance. Contact the Administrator or tel 01223 582700 for bookings.

🐕 On leads only. 🔔 ⊗ Tel for details.

BOURNE MILL

Bourne Road, Colchester, Essex CO2 8RT

Tel: 01206 572422   **www.**nationaltrust.org.uk

Owner: The National Trust   **Contact:** The Custodian

Originally a fishing lodge built in 1591. It was later converted into a mill with a 4 acre mill pond. Much of the machinery, including the waterwheel, is intact.

Location: OS Ref. TM006 238. 1m S of Colchester centre, in Bourne Road, off the Mersea Road B1025.

Open: June, Suns 2 - 5pm. July - August: Tues, Suns (& BH Mons), 2 - 5pm.

Admission: Adult £2.50, Child £1. No reduction for groups.

 Guide dogs only.

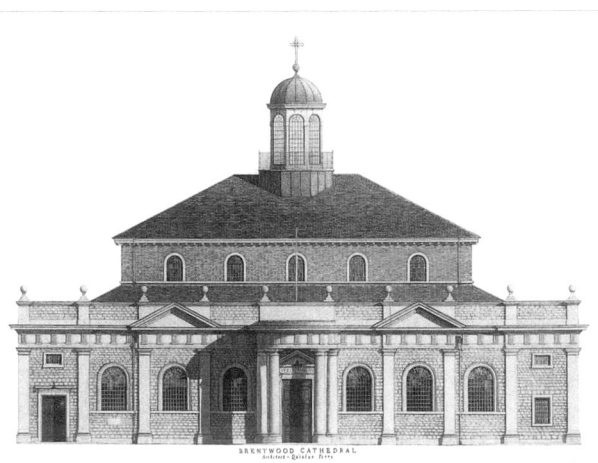

BRENTWOOD CATHEDRAL

INGRAVE ROAD, BRENTWOOD, ESSEX CM15 8AT

Tel: 01277 232266   **e-mail:** bishop@dioceseofbrentwood.org

Owner: Diocese of Brentwood   **Contact:** Rt Rev Thomas McMahon

The new (1991) Roman Catholic classical Cathedral Church of St Mary and St Helen incorporates part of the original Victorian church. Designed by distinguished classical architect Quinlan Terry with roundels by Raphael Maklouf. Architecturally, the inspiration is early Italian Renaissance crossed with the English Baroque of Christopher Wren. The north elevation consists of nine bays each divided by Doric pilasters. This is broken by a huge half-circular portico. The Kentish ragstone walls have a natural rustic look, which contrasts with the smooth Portland stone of the capitals and column bases. Inside is an arcade of Tuscan arches with central altar with the lantern above.

Location: OS Ref. TQ596 938. A12 & M25/J28. Centre of Brentwood, opposite Brentwood School.

Open: All year, daily.

Admission: Free.

 Limited. None for coaches.

CHELMSFORD CATHEDRAL

New Street, Chelmsford, Essex CM1 1TY

Tel: 01245 294489   **e-mail:** office@chelmsfordcathedral.org.uk

Contact: Mrs Bobby Harrington

15th century building became a Cathedral in 1914. Extended in 1920s, major refurbishment in 1980s and in 2000 with contemporary works of distinction and splendid new organs in 1994 and 1996.

Location: OS Ref. TL708 070. In Chelmsford.

Open: Daily: 8am - 5.30pm. Sun services: 8am, 9.30am, 11.15am and 6pm. Weekday services: 8.15am and 5.15pm daily. Holy Communion: Wed, 12.35pm & Thur, 10am. Tours by prior arrangement.

Admission: No charge but donation invited.

COGGESHALL GRANGE BARN

Grange Hill, Coggeshall, Colchester, Essex CO6 1RE

Tel: 01376 562226   **www.**nationaltrust.org.uk

Owner: The National Trust   **Contact:** The Custodian

One of the oldest surviving timber-framed barns in Europe, dating from around 1240, and originally part of a Cistercian Monastery. It was restored in the 1980s by the Coggeshall Grange Barn Trust, Braintree District Council and Essex County Council. Features a small collection of farm carts and wagons.

Location: OS Ref. TL848 223. Signposted off A120 Coggeshall bypass. West side of the road southwards to Kelvedon.

Open: 2 Apr - 8 Oct: Tues, Thurs, Suns & BH Mons, 2 - 5pm.

Admission: Adult £2.50, Child £1. Joint ticket with Paycocke's: Adult £4, Child £2.

 Coaches must book. Guide dogs only.

COLCHESTER CASTLE MUSEUM

14 Ryegate Road, Colchester, Essex CO1 1YG

Tel: 01206 282939   **Fax:** 01206 282925

Owner: Colchester Borough Council   **Contact:** Museum Resource Centre

The largest Norman Castle Keep in Europe with fine archaeological collections on show. Hands-on & interactive display brings history to life.

Location: OS Ref. TL999 253. In Colchester town centre, off A12.

Open: All year: Mon - Sat, 10am - 5pm, also Suns, 11am - 5pm.

Admission: Adult £4.90, Child (5-15yrs)/Conc. £3.50. Child under 5yrs Free. Saver ticket: £13.50. Prices may increase from April 2006.

COPPED HALL

CROWN HILL, EPPING, ESSEX CM16 5HH

www.coppedhalltrust.org.uk

Tel: 020 7267 1679   **Fax:** 020 7482 0557

Owner: The Copped Hall Trust   **Contact:** Alan Cox

Shell of 18th century Palladian mansion under restoration. Situated on ridge overlooking excellent landscaped park. Ancillary buildings including stables and small racquets court. Former elaborate gardens being rescued from abandonment. Large early 18th century walled garden – adjacent to site of 16th century mansion where 'A Midsummer Night's Dream' was first performed. Ideal film location.

Location: OS Ref. TL433 016. 4m SW of Epping, N of M25.

Open: By appointment only for groups (20+). Special open days.

Admission: Gardens: £3. Part of Mansion: £3, Child under 14yrs Free.

 Partial. Obligatory.   In grounds on leads.   Tel for details.

 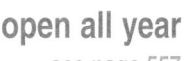 

open all year
see page 557

FEERINGBURY MANOR

Coggeshall Road, Feering, Colchester, Essex CO5 9RB
Tel: 01376 561946
Owner/Contact: Mrs Giles Coode-Adams
Location: OS Ref. TL864 215. 1¹/₂ m N of A12 between Feering & Coggeshall.
Open: From 1st Thur in Apr to last Fri in Jul: Thur & Fri only, 8am - 4pm.
Admission: Adult £3, Child Free. In aid of National Gardens Scheme.

Martin Sale

GARDENS OF EASTON LODGE 🏛

WARWICK HOUSE, EASTON LODGE, LITTLE EASTON, GT DUNMOW CM6 2BB

www.eastonlodge.co.uk

Tel/Fax: 01371 876979   **e-mail:** enquiries@eastonlodge.co.uk
Owner/Contact: Mr Brian Creasey
Beautiful gardens set in 23 acres. Horticultural associations from the 16th century to date. Visit the Italian gardens, currently undergoing restoration, designed by Harold Peto for 'Daisy' Countess of Warwick (Edward VII's mistress). In the dovecote, study the history of the house, garden and owners over 400 years. A peaceful and atmospheric haven! Millennium Project: Living yew and box sundial and Shakespeare border.
Location: OS Ref. TL593 240. 4m NW of Great Dunmow, off the B184 Dunmow to Thaxted road.
Open: Feb/Mar (snowdrops): daily. Easter - 31 Oct: Fri - Sun & BHs, 12 noon - 6pm or dusk if earlier. Groups at other times by appointment.
Admission: Adult £3.80, Child (3-12yrs) £1.50, Conc. £3.50. Group (20+): £3.50. Schools (20+) £1.50 per child, 1 teacher free per 10 children.
ℹ️ Exhibition & Study Centre in Dovecote. 🔧 🕤 🅰 Partial. WC. 📷 Picnics.
𝒦 By arrangement. 🅿 Limited for coaches. 🔳 🐕 In grounds on leads. ❋
📺 Tel for details. €

HARWICH REDOUBT FORT

Main Road, Harwich, Essex
Tel/Fax: 01255 503429   **e-mail:** theharwichsociety@quista.net
www.harwich-society.com
Owner: The Harwich Society   **Contact:** Mr Sheard
180ft diameter circular fort built in 1808 to defend the port against Napoleonic invasion. Being restored by Harwich Society and part is a museum. Eleven guns on battlements.
Location: OS Ref. TM262 322. Rear of 29 Main Road.
Open: 1 May - 31 Aug: daily, 10am - 4pm. Sept - Apr: Suns only, 10am - 4pm. Groups by appointment at any time.
Admission: Adult £2, Child Free (no unaccompanied children).
❋ €

plant sales 🌺
see page 555

HYLANDS HOUSE

HYLANDS PARK, LONDON ROAD, CHELMSFORD CM2 8WQ

www.chelmsfordbc.gov.uk/hylands

Tel: 01245 605500   **Fax:** 01245 605510
Owner: Chelmsford Borough Council   **Contact:** Nicki Jones
This beautiful Grade II* listed villa, with its neo-classical exterior, is set in 570 acres of historic landscaped parkland, including formal gardens. Following five phases of restoration, visitors can now enjoy spectacular rooms throughout the completed House. The Library, Drawing Room and Saloon which re-opened in 1999, have been restored to their early Victorian period. The Entrance Hall was restored to its Georgian origins in the 1995 restoration. April 2003 saw the opening of the West Wing, which includes the magnificent Victorian Banqueting Room and the Georgian Small Dining Room, as well as the original cellars, circa 1730. In September 2005, the final phase of restoration to the upper floors was completed, including the Victorian Grand Staircase and Repton Room, which offers stunning views over the park. Exhibition boards detail the history of the House, and guide books are available. The House hosts events and workshops throughout the year, and guided tours can be booked.
Location: OS Ref. TL681 054. 2m SW of Chelmsford. Signposted on A414 (formerly A1016) from J15 near Chelmsford.
Open: All year: Suns, Mons & BHs, 11am – 6pm (Oct – Apr: Mons, 11am – 4pm). Closed 25 Dec.
Admission: Adult £3.30, accompanied children under 16 Free. Conc. £2.30. Groups: £3.30pp or £85 (whichever greater).
ℹ️ No photography in house. 🔲 🔧 🕤 🅰 📷 Sun & Mon. 𝒦 By arrangement.
🅿 Limited for coaches. 🔳 🐕 In grounds. Guide dogs only in house. 🔺 ❋
📺 Tel for details.

INGATESTONE HALL 🏛

HALL LANE, INGATESTONE, ESSEX CM4 9NR

Tel: 01277 353010   **Fax:** 01245 248979

Owner: The Lord Petre   **Contact:** The Administrator
16th century mansion, set in 11 acres of grounds (formal garden and wild walk), built by Sir William Petre, Secretary of State to four Tudor monarchs, which has remained in the hands of his family ever since. The two Priests' hiding places can be seen, as well as the furniture, portraits and family memorabilia accumulated over the centuries.
Location: OS Ref. TQ653 986. Off A12 between Brentwood & Chelmsford. Take Station Lane at London end of Ingatestone High Street, cross level-crossing and continue for ¹/₂ m to SE.
Open: 15 Apr - 1 Oct: Sats, Suns & BH Mons. Plus 19 Jul - 1 Sept: Wed - Fri, 1 - 6pm.
Admission: Adult £4, Child £2 (under 5yrs Free), Conc. £3.50. 50p per head discount for groups (20+).
ℹ️ No photography in house. 🔲 🔧 🅰 Partial. 📷 𝒦 By arrangement. 🅿 🔳
🐕 Guide dogs only. 📺 Tel for details.

LAYER MARNEY TOWER

Nr COLCHESTER, ESSEX CO5 9US

www.layermarneytower.co.uk

Tel/Fax: 01206 330784   **e-mail:** info@layermarneytower.co.uk

Owner/Contact: Mr Nicholas Charrington

Built in the reign of Henry VIII, the tallest Tudor gatehouse in Great Britain. Lord Henry Marney clearly intended to rival Wolsey's building at Hampton Court, but he died before his masterpiece was finished. His son John died two years later, in 1525, and building work stopped. Layer Marney Tower has some of the finest terracotta work in the country, most probably executed by Flemish craftsmen trained by Italian masters. The terracotta is used on the battlements, windows, and most lavishly of all, on the tombs of Henry and John Marney. Visitors may climb the Tower, passing through the History Room, and enjoy the marvellous views of the Essex countryside. There are fine outbuildings, including the Long Gallery with its magnificent oak roof and the medieval barn which now houses some of the Home Farm's collection of Rare Breed farm animals. Function rooms available for receptions, conferences and corporate days.

Location: OS Ref. TL929 175. 7m SW of Colchester, signed off B1022.

Open: 9 Apr - 1 Oct: Sun - Thur, 12 noon (11am on BHs) - 5pm. Group visits/guided tours throughout the year by arrangement.

Admission: Adult £4, Child £2.50, Family £12. Groups (15+): Adult £3.75, Child £2.25. Guided tours (pre-booked) £5, min. charge £125. Schools by arrangement.

▢ ▢ ▢ ▢ Partial. WC. ▢ ▢ ▢ By arrangement. ▢ ▢ In grounds, on leads. ▢ 1 dble, 2 single. ▢ ▢ ▢ On BHs. Tel for details.

MARKS HALL GARDENS AND ARBORETUM

COGGESHALL, ESSEX CO6 1TG

www.markshall.org.uk

Tel: 01376 563796

Owner: The Thomas Philips Price Trust   **Contact:** Mrs G Nosworthy

Five individual gardens and a double long border, combining contemporary and traditional landscaping and planting, form the newly redesigned Walled Garden at Marks Hall. This unique garden is open on one side to a lake – on the opposite bank the Millennium Walk is designed to be at its best during the shortest days of the year. There is much to see in this Arboretum and Garden of over 100 acres on every day of the year.

Location: OS168 Ref. TQ840 252. Off B1024, 1½ m N of Coggeshall.

Open: Apr - Oct: Tues - Sun & BH Mons, 10.30am - 5pm. Winter weekends, 10.30am - dusk.

Admission: £4.20 per car.

▢ Transport for those with walking difficulties (must be booked in advance). ▢

Audley End House & Gardens.

MISTLEY TOWERS ⌗

Colchester, Essex

Tel: 01206 393884 / 01223 582700 (Regional Office)

Owner: English Heritage   **Contact:** The Keykeeper (Mistley Quay Workshops)

The remains of one of only two churches designed by the great architect Robert Adam. Built in 1776. It was unusual in having towers at both the east and west ends.

Location: OS Ref. TM116 320. On B1352, 1½ m E of A137 at Lawford, 9m E of Colchester.

Open: Please telephone for opening times.

Admission: Free.

Grounds only. Restricted areas.

PAYCOCKE'S

West Street, Coggeshall, Colchester, Essex CO6 1NS

Tel: 01376 561305   www.nationaltrust.org.uk

Owner: The National Trust   **Contact:** The Tenant

A merchant's house, dating from about 1500, with unusually rich panelling and wood carving. A display of lace, for which Coggeshall was famous, is on show. Delightful cottage garden.

Location: OS Ref. TL848 225. Signposted off A120.

Open: 2 Apr - 8 Oct. Tues, Thurs, Suns & BH Mons, 2 - 5pm.

Admission: Adult £3, Child £1.50. Groups (10+) by prior arrangement, no reduction for groups. Joint ticket with Coggeshall Grange Barn: Adult £4, Child £2.

Access to ground floor and garden. NT's at the Coggeshall Grange Barn.

PRIOR'S HALL BARN ⌗

Widdington, Newport, Essex

Tel: 01233 582700 (Regional Office)

Owner: English Heritage   **Contact:** East of England Regional Office

One of the finest surviving medieval barns in south-east England and representative of the group of aisled barns centred on north-west Essex.

Location: OS Ref. TL538 319. In Widdington, on unclassified road 2m SE of Newport, off B1383.

Open: 1 Apr - 30 Sept: Sats & Suns, 10am - 6pm.

Admission: Free.

SALING HALL GARDEN

Great Saling, Braintree, Essex CM7 5DT

Tel: 01371 850 243 **Fax:** 01371 850 274

Owner/Contact: Hugh Johnson Esq

Twelve acres including a walled garden dated 1698. Water garden and landscaped arboretum. The home of Tradescant's Diary in the Garden.

Location: OS Ref. TL700 258. 6m NW of Braintree, 2m N of B1256.

Open: May, Jun & Jul: Weds, 2 - 5pm.

Admission: Adult £3, Child Free.

TILBURY FORT ⌗

No. 2 Office Block, The Fort, Tilbury, Essex RM18 7NR

Tel: 01375 858489 www.english-heritage.org.uk

Owner: English Heritage   **Contact:** Visitor Operations Team

The best and largest example of 17th century military engineering in England, commanding the Thames. Learn more about the fascinating history of Tilbury Fort with a new interpretation scheme in the North East Bastion magazine passages. See new graphic panels and displays, new reproduction lamps and two fully restored charging stations.

There is also an interactive oral history programme to provide every visitor with a fascinating new insight to Tilbury.

Location: OS Ref. TQ651 751. ½ m E of Tilbury off A126 near Worlds End pub.

Open: 1 Apr - 31 Oct: daily, 10am - 5pm. 1 Nov - 31 Mar. Thur - Mon, 10am - 4pm. Closed 24 - 26 Dec & 1 Jan.

Admission: Adult £3.40, Child £1.70, Under 5s Free. Conc. £2.60, Family £8.50. EH Members/OVP Free.

WCs. Grounds only. On leads. Tel for details.

WALTHAM ABBEY GATEHOUSE & BRIDGE ⌗

Waltham Abbey, Essex

Tel: 01992 702200 / 01223 582700 (Regional Office)

Owner: English Heritage **Contact:** East of England Regional Office (01223 582700)

The late 14th century abbey gatehouse, part of the north range of the cloister and the medieval 'Harold's Bridge' of one of the great monastic foundations of the Middle Ages.

Location: OS Ref. TL381 008. In Waltham Abbey off A112. Just NE of the Abbey church.

Open: Any reasonable time.

Admission: Free.

Sensory trail guide. On leads.

RHS GARDEN HYDE HALL

BUCKHATCH LANE, RETTENDON, CHELMSFORD, ESSEX CM3 8ET

www.rhs.org.uk

Tel: 01245 400256   **Fax:** 01245 402100   **e-mail:** hydehall@rhs.org.uk

Owner: The Royal Horticultural Society   **Contact:** Visitor Services

RHS Hyde Hall is truly a garden of its time. Set on a hilltop amongst rolling hills of arable crops, the garden combines environmental and sustainable practices with the high standards of horticulture for which the RHS gardens are renowned. Highlights include the spectacular Dry Garden, colour themed Herbaceous Border, the Queen Mother's Garden, boldly planted Farmhouse Garden and ponds, garden for wildlife and, new for 2006, the Australian Border

Location: OS Ref. TQ782 995. SE of Chelmsford, signposted from A130.

Open: Jan - Mar & Oct - Dec (except Christmas Day): 10am - dusk; Apr - Sept: 10am - 6pm. Last entry 1 hour before closing.

Admission: Adult £5, Child (6-16yrs) £1, Companion/Carer of disabled person Free. RHS member and one guest Free. Pre-booked Groups (10+): £3.50.

Licensed. Guide dogs only. Tel for details.

Copped Hall.

Jerry Harpur

MAP 7

Owner:
The 7th Marquess
of Salisbury

▶ **CONTACT**

Director Visitors
Hatfield House
Hatfield
Hertfordshire AL9 5NQ

Tel: 01707 287010

Fax: 01707 287033

e-mail:
visitors@
hatfield-house.co.uk

▶ **LOCATION**

OS Ref. TL 237 084

21m N of London,
M25/J23 7m,
A1(M)/J4, 2m.

Bus: Local bus services
from St Albans and
Hertford.

Rail: From Kings Cross
every 30 mins.
Hatfield Station is
immediately opposite
entrance to Park.

Air: Luton (30 mins).
Stansted (45 mins).

HATFIELD HOUSE

www.hatfield-house.co.uk

This celebrated Jacobean house, which stands in its own park, was built between 1607 and 1611 by Robert Cecil, 1st Earl of Salisbury and Chief Minister to King James I. It has been the family home of the Cecils ever since.

The main designer was Robert Lyminge helped, it is thought, by the young Inigo Jones. The interior decoration was the work of English, Flemish and French craftsmen, notably Maximilian Colt.

The State Rooms are rich in famous paintings including The Rainbow Portrait of Queen Elizabeth I and The Ermine Portrait by Nicholas Hilliard. Other paintings include works by Hoefnagel, Mytens, John de Critz the Elder and Sir Joshua Reynolds. Fine furniture from the 16th, 17th and 18th centuries, rare tapestries and historic armour can be found in the State Rooms.

Within the delightful gardens stands the surviving wing of The Royal Palace of Hatfield (1485) where Elizabeth I spent much of her childhood and held her first Council of State in November 1558. Some of her possessions can be seen in the House.

GARDENS

John Tradescant the Elder, the celebrated plant hunter, was employed to plant and lay out the gardens after the completion of the house in 1611. Following the fashion for landscape gardening and some neglect in the 18th century, restoration of the garden started in earnest in Victorian times. Lady Gwendolen Cecil, younger daughter of Prime Minister Salisbury, designed the West Garden as it is today. The East Garden was laid out by the 5th Marquess of Salisbury. The present Dowager Lady Salisbury dedicated 30 years to the restoration and improvement of the garden that now bears her indelible imprint.

Jerry Harpur

▶ **OPENING TIMES**

15 April - end September
House
Wed - Sun & BHs.
12 noon - 4pm. Guided
tours on Thurs only
(except Aug).

**Park, West Garden,
Restaurant & Shop**
Daily, 11am - 5.30pm.

East Garden
Thurs only (except Aug).
11am - 5.30pm.

▶ **ADMISSION**

**House, Park
& West Garden**
Adult £8.00
Child (5 - 15yrs) £4.00
Family (2+4) £22.00
Groups (20+)
Adult £7.00
Park & West Garden
Adult £4.50
Child £3.50
Park only
Adult £2.00
Child (5 - 15yrs) £1.00
Thursdays
Park & Gardens £7.00
House tour .... £5 extra

RHS members free entry to
gardens daily (except on
Thurs and during special
events).

▷ **SPECIAL EVENTS**

MAY 4 - 7
Living Crafts.

JUNE 10 - 11
Flower Festival.

JULY 22
Battle Proms Concert.

AUG 4 - 6
National Pottery &
Ceramics Festival.

AUG 18 - 20
Hatfield House Country Show.

Please telephone for details of
other events. Separate charges
apply on Event days.

FUNCTION

ROOM	SIZE	MAX CAPACITY
The Old Palace	112' x 33'	280
Old Riding School	100' X 40'	180

ℹ️ No photography in house. National Collection of model soldiers, 5m of marked trails, children's play area.

🏛️ 🍷 Weddings, functions: tel 01707 287080. Banquets held in the Old Palace: tel 01707 262055.

♿ WCs. Parking next to house. Lift.

☕ 🍴 Seats 150. Pre-booked lunch and tea for groups 20+. Tel: 01707 262030.

🚶 Thur only. Group tours available in French, German, Italian, Spanish or Japanese by prior arrangement.

🅿️ Ample. Hardstanding for coaches.

📕 Resource books, play area & nature trails. Living History days throughout the school year: tel 01707 287042. KS2 & 3 groups not permitted in house.

🐕 In park. 🔔

Eastern - England

MAP 7

KNEBWORTH HOUSE

www.knebworthhouse.com

Owner: The Hon Henry Lytton Cobbold

▶ CONTACT

The Estate Office
Knebworth House
Knebworth
Hertfordshire SG3 6PY

Tel: 01438 812661
Fax: 01438 811908
e-mail: info@
knebworthhouse.com

▶ LOCATION

OS Ref. TL230 208

Direct access off the
A1(M) J7 (Stevenage
South A602).
28m N of London.
15m N of M25 J23.

Rail: Stevenage Station
2m (from Kings Cross).

Air: Luton Airport 15m
Landing facilities.

Taxi: 01438 811122.

CONFERENCE/FUNCTION

ROOM	SIZE	MAX CAPACITY
Banqueting Hall	26' x 41'	80
Dining Parlour	21' x 38'	50
Library	32' x 21'	40
Manor Barn	70' x 25'	250
Lodge Barn	75' x 30'	150

Home of the Lytton family since 1490, and still a lived-in family house. Transformed in early Victorian times by Edward Bulwer-Lytton, the author, poet, dramatist and statesman, into the unique high gothic fantasy house of today, complete with turrets, griffins and gargoyles.

Historically home to Constance Lytton, the Suffragette, and her father, Robert Lytton, the Viceroy of India who proclaimed Queen Victoria Empress of India at the Great Delhi Durbar of 1877. Visited by Queen Elizabeth I, Charles Dickens and Sir Winston Churchill.

The interior contains various styles including the magnificent Jacobean Banqueting Hall, a unique example of the 17th century change in fashion from traditional English to Italian Palladian. The high gothic State Drawing Room by John Crace contrasts with the Regency elegance of Mrs Bulwer-Lytton's bedroom and the 20th century designs of Sir Edwin Lutyens in the Entrance Hall, Dining Parlour and Library.

25 acres of beautiful gardens, simplified by Lutyens, including pollarded lime avenues, formal rose garden, maze, Gertrude Jekyll herb garden and newly designed Walled Garden. 250 acres of gracious parkland, with herds of red and sika deer, includes children's giant adventure playground and miniature railway. New Dino Trail with 72 life-size dinosaurs set grazing through the Wilderness Walk within the Formal Gardens. World famous for its huge open-air rock concerts, and used as a film location for *Batman*, *The Shooting Party*, *Wilde*, *Jane Eyre* and *The Canterville Ghost*, amongst others.

*The Jacobean
Banqueting Hall.*

📷 ✳ ℹ️ Suitable for fashion shows, air displays, archery, shooting, equestrian events, cricket pitch, garden parties, shows, rallies, filming, helicopter landing. No pushchairs, photography, smoking or drinking in House.

🍽 Indian Raj Evenings and Elizabethan Banquets with jousting. Full catering service.

♿ Parking. Ground floor accessible.

☕ Licensed tearoom. Special rates for advance bookings, menus on request.

🅿 Unlimited. Group visits must be booked in advance with Estate Office.

🚶 Daily at 30 min intervals or at booked times including evenings. Tour time 1hr. Shorter tours by arrangement. Room Wardens on duty on busy weekends. Themed tours available.

📋 National Curriculum based school activity days.

🐕 Guide dogs only in House. Park, on leads.

🔔 Licensed Garden Gazebo & Manor Barn.

🎭 Tel for details.

▶ OPENING TIMES

House, Park & Gardens
25/26 March, 6 - 21 May,
10 - 25 June & 9 - 24
September: Weekends
only.

1 -17 April, 27 May -
4 June & 1 July -
3 September: Daily.

22 April - 1 May:
Weekends & BHs only.

**Park, Gardens,
Dinosaurs, Playground
& Railway**
11am - 5.30pm.

**House & Indian
Exhibition**
12 noon - 5pm
(last adm. 4.30pm).

▶ ADMISSION

Including House

Adult £9.00
Child*/Conc £8.50
Family Day Ticket
(4 persons) £31.00
Groups (20+)
Adult £8.00
Child*/Conc £7.50

Excluding House

All Persons............. £7.00
Season Ticket £32.00
Family Day Ticket
(4 persons) £24.00
Groups (20+)
All persons £6.00

House Supplements
Adults £2.00
Child*/Conc £1.50

*Under 4s Free.

ASHRIDGE

Ringshall, Berkhamsted, Hertfordshire HP4 1LX

Tel: 01442 851227 **Fax:** 01442 850000 **e-mail:** ashridge@nationaltrust.org.uk
Owner: The National Trust **Contact:** The Visitor Centre
The Ashridge Estate comprises over 1800ha of woodlands, commons and downland. At the northerly end of the Estate the Ivinghoe Hills are an outstanding area of chalk downland which supports a rich variety of plants and insects.
Location: OS Ref. SP970 131. Between Northchurch & Ringshall, just off B4506.
Open: Visitor Centre & Shop: 18 Mar - 10 Dec: daily, 12 noon - 5pm. Monument: 18 Mar - 29 Oct: Sats & Suns, 12 noon - 5pm. Tearoom: 1 Jan - 12 Mar: Sats & Suns, 12 noon - 5pm. 18 Mar - 10 Dec: Tues - Sun, 12 noon - 5pm.
Admission: Monument: £1.30, Child 60p.
ℹ️Visitor Centre. 🖻 ♿Vehicles available. 🍴 🅿️Limited for coaches. ▮
🐕In grounds, on leads. 🎫Tel for details.

BENINGTON LORDSHIP GARDENS

Stevenage, Hertfordshire SG2 7BS

Tel: 01438 869668 **Fax:** 01438 869622 **e-mail:** rhbott@beningtonlordship.co.uk
www.beningtonlordship.co.uk
Owner: Mr R R A Bott **Contact:** Mr or Mrs R R A Bott
7 acre garden overlooking lakes in a timeless setting. Features include Norman keep and moat, Queen Anne manor house, James Pulham folly, walled vegetable garden, renowned herbaceous borders and snowdrops in February.
All location work welcome. Estate includes listed cottages, barns, buildings and airstrip.
Location: OS Ref. TL296 236. In village of Benington next to the church. 4m E of Stevenage.
Open: Gardens only: Snowdrops: 4 - 26 Feb. Easter & Spring/Summer BH weekends. Suns, 2 - 5pm. Mons, 12 noon - 5pm. Herbaceous Border week: 24 Jun - 2 Jul, 2 - 5pm. By request all year, please telephone. Coaches must book.
Admission: Adult £3.50 (Suns in Feb £4.50), Child Free.
♿Unsuitable. 🍴

BERKHAMSTED CASTLE ♯

Berkhamsted, St Albans, Hertfordshire

Tel: 01223 582700 (Regional Office)
Owner: English Heritage **Contact:** East of England Regional Office
The extensive remains of a large 11th century motte and bailey castle which held a strategic position on the road to London.
Location: OS Ref. SP996 083. Adjacent to Berkhamsted rail station.
Open: All year. Summer: daily, 10am - 6pm; Winter: daily, 10am - 4pm. Closed 25 Dec & 1 Jan.
Admission: Free.
🐕 ❋

THE BRITISH SCHOOLS MUSEUM, HITCHIN

41 - 42 Queen Street, Hitchin, Hertfordshire SG4 9TS

Tel/Fax: 01462 420144 **e-mail:** brsch@britishschools.freeserve.co.uk
www.hitchinbritishschools.org.uk
Owner: Hitchin British Schools Trust **Contact:** Mrs Rosie Pinhorn
Unique complex of school buildings dating from 1837 to 1905. Incorporates 1837 Lancasterian Schoolroom, believed to be the only surviving example, a rare 1853 galleried classroom (both Grade II*), Girls and Infants School 1857 and two Edwardian classrooms. Related displays, small museum and Family Trail with activities.
Location: OS Ref. TL186 289. Hitchin town centre.
Open: Feb - Nov: Tue, 10am - 4pm. Apr - Oct: Sat, 10am - 1pm, Sun, 2 - 5pm. Feb - Nov: School visits & groups by arrangement at other times.
Admission: Adult £3.25, Child £1.25. Education programme with teaching session £3.50 per child. Adult £1 .
🖻 ♿Partial. WC. 🍴 🎫
🅿️For 1 or 2 disabled only. Public parking (paid) nearby. ▮ 🐕Guide dogs only.

CATHEDRAL & ABBEY CHURCH OF ST ALBAN

St Albans, Hertfordshire AL1 1BY

Tel: 01727 860780 **Fax:** 01727 850944 **Contact:** Deputy Administrator
Abbey church of Benedictine Monastery founded 793AD commemorating Britain's first martyr.
Location: OS Ref. TL145 071. Centre of St Albans.
Open: All year: 9am - 5.45pm. Tel for details of services, concerts and special events Mon - Sat, 11am - 4pm.
Admission: Free of charge but donations welcomed.

CROMER WINDMILL

Ardeley, Stevenage, Hertfordshire SG2 7QA

Tel: 01279 843301
Owner: Hertfordshire Building Preservation Trust **Contact:** Cristina Harrison
17th century Post Windmill restored to working order.
Location: OS Ref. TL305 286. 4m NE of Stevenage on B1037. 1m SW of Cottered.
Open: Mid-May - mid-Sept: Sun, 2nd & 4th Sat & BHs, 2.30 - 5pm.
Admission: Adult £2, Child 25p. Groups (10+) by arrangement: Adult £1, Child 25p.

FORGE MUSEUM & VICTORIAN COTTAGE GARDEN

High Street, Much Hadham, Hertfordshire SG10 6BS

Tel/Fax: 01279 843301 **e-mail:** cristinaharrison@btopenworld.com
Owner: The Hertfordshire Building Preservation Trust **Contact:** The Curator
The garden reflects plants that would have been grown in 19th century.
Location: OS Ref. TL428 195. Village centre.
Open: Fri, Sat, Sun & BHs, 11am - 5pm (dusk in winter).
Admission: Adult £2, Child/Conc. 50p.

GORHAMBURY 🏛

St Albans, Hertfordshire AL3 6AH

Tel: 01727 854051 **Fax:** 01727 843675
Owner: The Earl of Verulam **Contact:** The Administrator
Late 18th century house by Sir Robert Taylor. Family portraits from 15th - 20th centuries.
Location: OS Ref. TL114 078. 2m W of St Albans. Access via private drive off A4147 at St Albans.
Open: May - Sept: Thurs, 2 - 5pm (last entry 4.15pm).
Admission: House & Gardens: Adult £6, Child £3, Conc £4. Visitors join guided tours. Special groups by arrangement (Thurs mornings preferred).
♿Partial. 🚫🅵Obligatory. 🅿️

HATFIELD HOUSE

See page 285 for full page entry.

HERTFORD MUSEUM

18 Bull Plain, Hertford

Tel: 01992 582686
Owner: Hertford Museums Trust **Contact:** Helen Gurney
Local museum in 17th century house, altered by 18th century façade, with recreated Jacobean knot garden.
Location: OS Ref. TL326 126. Town centre.
Open: Tue - Sat, 10am - 5pm.
Admission: Free.

KNEBWORTH HOUSE 🏛

See page 286 for full page entry.

OLD GORHAMBURY HOUSE ♯

St Albans, Hertfordshire

Tel: 01223 582700 (Regional Office)
Owner: English Heritage **Contact:** East of England Regional Office
The decorated remains of this Elizabethan mansion, particularly the porch of the Great Hall, illustrate the impact of the Renaissance on English architecture.
Location: OS Ref. TL110 077. On foot by permissive 2m path. By car, drive to Gorhambury Mansion and walk across the gardens.
Open: All year (except 1 Jun), any reasonable time.
Admission: Free.
🐕 ❋

THE WALTER ROTHSCHILD ZOOLOGICAL MUSEUM

Akeman Street, Tring, Hertfordshire HP23 6AP

Tel: 020 7942 6171 **Fax:** 020 7942 6150
Owner: The Natural History Museum **Contact:** General Organiser
The museum was opened to the public by Lord Rothschild in 1892. It houses his private natural history collection. Over 4,000 species of animal in a Victorian setting.
Location: OS Ref. SP924 111. S end of Akeman Street, $1/4$ m S of High Street.
Open: Mon - Sat, 10am - 5pm, Suns, 2 - 5pm. Closed 24 - 26 Dec.
Admission: Free.

ST PAULS WALDEN BURY

Hitchin, Hertfordshire SG4 8BP

Tel/Fax: 01438 871218 **e-mail:** spw@boweslyon.demon.co.uk
Owner/Contact: S and C Bowes Lyon
Formal woodland garden, covering about 60 acres, laid out 1730. Long rides lined with clipped beech hedges lead to temples, statues, lake and ponds, and to an outdoor theatre. Seasonal displays of snowdrops, daffodils, irises, magnolias, rhododendrons, woodland paeonies, lilies and shrub roses. Wild flower areas. Grade I listed.
Location: OS Ref. TL186 216. 30m N of London. 5m S of Hitchin on B651.
Open: Suns: 9, 23 April, 14 May & 4 June, 2 - 7pm. Other times by appointment.
Admission: Adult £3.50, Child 50p. Other times by appointment £6.

SCOTT'S GROTTO

Ware, Hertfordshire

Tel: 01920 464131
Owner: East Hertfordshire District Council **Contact:** J Watson
One of the finest grottos in England built in the 1760s by Quaker Poet John Scott.
Location: OS Ref. TL355 137. In Scotts Rd, S of the A119 Hertford Road.
Open: 1 Apr - 30 Sept: Sat & BH Mon, 2 - 4.30pm. Also by appointment.
Admission: Suggested donation of £1 for adults. Children Free. Please bring a torch.

SHAW'S CORNER ✤

AYOT ST LAWRENCE, WELWYN, HERTFORDSHIRE AL6 9BX

www.nationaltrust.org.uk

Tel/Fax: 01438 820307 **e-mail:** shawscorner@nationaltrust.org.uk

Owner: The National Trust   **Contact:** The Custodian

The fascinating home of playwright George Bernard Shaw until his death in 1950. The modest Edwardian villa contains many literary and personal relics, and the interior is still set out as it was in Shaw's lifetime. The garden, with its richly planted borders and views over the Hertfordshire countryside, contains the revolving summerhouse where Shaw retreated to write.

Location: OS Ref. TL194 167. At SW end of village, 2m NE of Wheathampstead, approximately 2m N from B653. A1(M)/J4, M1/J10.

Open: 18 Mar - 29 Oct: Wed - Sun & BH Mons (open Good Fri), House: 1 - 5pm; Garden: 12 noon - 5.30pm. Last admission to House & Garden 4.30pm. No large hand luggage inside house. Groups by prior appointment only.

Admission: Adult £4.20, Child £2.10, Family £10.50. Discounts for groups (15+).

ℹ WC. ♿ ⬇ Partial, ground floor, no WC. 🅿 ▪ 🐕 Car park only. 🎫 Tel 01438 829221 for details.

WALKERN HALL

STEVENAGE, HERTFORDSHIRE SG2 7JA

www.walkernhall.co.uk

Tel: 01438 869346

e-mail: deboinville@btconnect.com

Owner/Contact: David de Boinville

Walkern Hall is an early 18th century country house surrounded by extensive gardens, set in the medieval hunting park of Walkern Manor. Very secluded and only thirty miles north of London. The garden has extensive lawns, magnificent trees and a large functional walled garden. Suitable for wedding receptions, functions, launches and locations.

Location: OS Ref. TL300 249. Located ¹/₂ m SE of Walkern village.

Open: By appointment only. For events, functions, film & photography locations.

Admission: Prices on request. Telephone for information.

Ⓣ ⬇ Grounds only. 🅿 ▪ Farm tours availble. 🐕 Guide dogs only. ✤ 🎫 Tel for details. €

MAP 8

Owner:
The Earl of
Leicester CBE

▶ CONTACT

Promotions Manager
Laurane Herrieven
Holkham Estate Office
Wells-next-the-Sea
Norfolk   NR23 1AB

Tel: 01328 710227
Fax: 01328 711707
e-mail: l.herrieven@
holkham.co.uk

▶ LOCATION

OS Ref. TF885 428

From London 120m
Norwich 35m
King's Lynn 30m.

Rail: Norwich
Station 35m
King's Lynn
Station 30m.

Air: Norwich
Airport 32m.

HOLKHAM HALL 🏛
www.holkham.co.uk

Holkham Hall has been the home of the Coke family and the Earls of Leicester for almost 250 years. Built between 1734 and 1764 by Thomas Coke, 1st Earl of Leicester and based on a design by William Kent, this fine example of an 18th century Palladian style mansion reflects Thomas Coke's natural appreciation of classical art developed during his Grand Tour. The House is constructed of local yellow brick with a magnificent Entrance Hall of English alabaster.

The State Rooms occupy the first floor and contain Roman statuary, paintings by Rubens, Van Dyck, Claude, Gaspar Poussin and Gainsborough and original furniture.

On leaving the House, visitors pass Holkham Pottery and its adjacent shop, both under the supervision of the Countess of Leicester and where fine examples of local craftsmanship are for sale.

Beyond are the 19th century stables, now housing the Bygones Collection; some 4,000 items range from working steam engines, vintage cars and tractors to craft tools and kitchenware. The adjacent, free History of Farming Exhibition is aimed to help understand how a great Estate such as Holkham works and has evolved.

In the same courtyard, The Stables Café offers a variety of cakes, light snacks, hot and cold lunch dishes and delicious Holkham Ice Cream.

Holkham Hall is set in a stunning 3,000-acre park with a herd of 800 fallow deer. Boat trips are available in the summer months on the lake, which is home to many species of wildfowl. On the opposite side of the lake to the House, Holkham Gardens now occupy the former 19th century walled Kitchen Gardens.

🎞 ℹ Grounds for shows, rallies and filming. Photography allowed. No smoking in the Hall.

🍴 Hall & Grounds.

♿ Access to first floor in the Hall is suitable for most manual wheelchairs. Elsewhere, full disabled access.

🍽 🍴 Licensed. Menus for pre-booked groups on request.

🎧 Acoustiguide £2.

🚶 Private guided tours of Hall are available by arrangement when the Hall is not open to the public. Please tel for details.

Ⓟ Unlimited for cars, 12+ coaches. Parking, admission, refreshments free to coach drivers.

▦ Welcome. Areas of interest: Bygones Collection, History of Farming, three designated walks and a new Nature Trail.

🐕 No dogs in Hall, on leads in grounds.

❄ Deer Park, except Christmas Day at no charge.

▶ OPENING TIMES

Hall
15 - 17 & 29/30 Apr, 1 & 27 - 29 May, 26 - 28 Aug: 12 noon - 5pm.

4 - 26 May, daily except Tue & Wed. At 2pm prompt, Audio Tour on a "turn up and join in" basis (max 40).

1 Jun - 30 Sept: daily except Tue & Wed, 1 - 5pm.

Last admission 4.30pm.

The Libraries & Stranger's Wing form part of the private accommodation and are open at the family's discretion.

Terraces around the Hall open Mon (not BH Mons): Thur & Fri.

The Stables' Café & Pottery Shop
15 - 17, 29 & 30 Apr, 1 & 4 May - 30 Sept: daily except Wed, 10am - 5.30pm. 1 - 31 Oct: daily except Wed, 11am - 4.30pm.

Bygones Museum & History of Farming
15 - 17 & 29/30 Apr, 1 & 27 - 29 May, 26 - 28 Aug: 12 noon - 5pm.

4 May - 30 Sept: daily except Tue & Wed, 12 noon - 5pm.
Last admission 4.30pm.

▶ ADMISSION

Hall
Adult £6.50
Child (5-16yrs) £3.25
Acoustiguide hire £2pp

Bygones Museum
Adult £5.00
Child (5-16yrs) £2.50

**Combined Ticket
(Hall & Bygones)**
Adult £10.00
Child (5-16yrs) £5.00
Family (2+2, 5-16yrs) ...£25.00

Audio Tour (May)......... £8.00
Groups (20+) ... 10% discount
Private Guided Tours....£14.00
Boat trips on the lake:
Adult £2.50
Child (5-16yrs) £2.00

HM Queen Elizabeth II

MAP 7

Owner:
H M The Queen

▶ **CONTACT**

The Public Enterprises
Manager
The Estate Office
Sandringham
Norfolk PE35 6EN

Tel: 01553 612908
Fax: 01485 541571

e-mail: visits@
sandringhamestate.co.uk

▶ **LOCATION**

OS Ref. TF695 287

8m NE of King's Lynn
on B1440 off A148.

Rail: King's Lynn.

Air: Norwich.

SANDRINGHAM

www.sandringhamestate.co.uk

Sandringham House is the charming country retreat of Her Majesty The Queen, hidden in the heart of 60 acres of beautiful wooded gardens. Still maintained in the style of Edward and Alexandra, Prince and Princess of Wales (later King Edward VII and Queen Alexandra), all the main ground floor rooms used by The Royal Family, full of their treasured ornaments, portraits and furniture, are open to the public.

More family possessions are displayed in the Museum housed in the old stables and coach houses, including vehicles ranging in date from the first car owned by a British monarch, a 1900 Daimler, to a half-scale Aston Martin used by Princes William and Harry. A display tells the mysterious tale of the Sandringham Company who fought and died at Gallipolli in 1915, and a

photographic exhibition in the Museum shows the history of Sandringham House from 1870 to the present day.

The 60-acre gardens include the formal North Garden, the Stream Walk and Queen Alexandra's Summerhouse, perched above the lake; the formal planting of the Edwardian age has given way to great sweeping glades, bordered by splendid specimen trees and shrubs, to create an informal garden full of colour and interest throughout the year. Guided garden tours take place on Fridays and Saturdays. There are also 600 acres of the Country Park open to all, with tractor tours running daily; a free Land Train from within the entrance will carry passengers less able to walk through the gardens to the House and back.

HM Queen Elizabeth II

▶ **OPENING TIMES**

House, Museum & Gardens
15 April - late July & early Aug - 29 Oct.

▶ **ADMISSION**

House, Museum & Gardens

Adult	£8.00
Child (5-15yrs)	£5.00
Conc.	£6.50
Family	£21.00

Museum & Gardens

Adult	£5.50
Child (5-15yrs)	£3.50
Conc.	£4.50
Family	£14.50

Groups (20+):
10% discount.

🛍

ℹ No photography in house.

✿ Plant Centre.

⊤ Visitor Centre only.

♿ Licensed. 🍴 Licensed.

👤 By arrangement. Private evening tours.

🅿 Ample.

🐕 Guide dogs only.

⊡ Tel for details.

CONFERENCE/FUNCTION

ROOM	MAX CAPACITY
Restaurant	200
Tearoom	60

BERNEY ARMS WINDMILL ⌗

c/o 8 Manor Road, Southtown, Gt Yarmouth NR31 0QA

Tel: 01799 522842

Owner: English Heritage   **Contact:** Visitor Operations Team

A wonderfully situated marsh mill, one of the best and largest remaining in Norfolk, with seven floors, making it a landmark for miles around. It was in use until 1951.

Location: OS Ref. TG465 051. 3^1/$_2$ m NE of Reedham on N bank of River Yare, 5m from Gt. Yarmouth. Accessible by boat from Yarmouth or by footpath from Halvergate (3^1/$_2$ m).

Open: 1 May - 31 Aug. Pre-booked guided tours only.

Admission: Adult £2.40, Child £1.20, Conc. £1.80.

BINHAM PRIORY ⌗

Binham-on-Wells, Norfolk

Tel: 01328 830362/ 01223 582700 (Regional Office)

Owner: English Heritage (Managed by Binham Parochial Church Council)

     Contact: East of England Regional Office

Extensive remains of a Benedictine priory, of which the original nave of the church is still in use as the parish church.

Location: OS Ref. TF982 399. ^{1}/$_4$ m NW of village of Binham-on-Wells, on road off B1388.

Open: Any reasonable time.

Admission: Free.

BIRCHAM WINDMILL

Snettisham Road, Great Bircham, Norfolk PE31 6SJ

Tel: 01485 578393

Owner/Contact: Mr & Mrs S Chalmers

One of the last remaining complete windmills. Tearoom, bakery, windmill museum, gift shop, cycle hire, regular events and holiday cottage.

Location: OS Ref. TF760 326. ^{1}/$_2$ m W of Bircham. N of the road to Snettisham.

Open: Easter - end Sept: Daily 10am - 5pm.

Admission: Adult £3, Child £1.75, Retired £2.75.

BRADENHAM HALL GARDENS

Bradenham, Thetford, Norfolk IP25 7QP

Tel: 01362 687243   **Fax:** 01362 687669   **e-mail:** info@bradenhamhall.co.uk

www.bradenhamhall.co.uk

Owner: Chris & Panda Allhusen   **Contact:** Chris Allhusen

A plant-lover's garden for all seasons. The house and garden walls are covered with unusual climbers. Flower gardens, formal rose gardens, paved garden, herbaceous and shrub borders. Arboretum of over 800 different trees, all labelled. Traditional walled kitchen gardens, mixed borders, and two glasshouses. Massed daffodils in spring.

Location: OS Ref. TF921 099. Off A47, 6m of Swaffham. 3m W of E Dereham. S on Dale Road, then S 2m to Bradenham.

Open: Apr - Sept: 2nd & 4th Suns of each month, 2 - 5.30pm. Groups by appointment at other times.

Admission: Adult £4, Child Free. Group discounts available.

ⓘNo commercial photography. House not open. ⬚ ⬚Partial. ⬚ ⓘBy arrangement. ⓟAmple. Limited for coaches. ⬚Guide dogs only.

BURGH CASTLE ⌗

Breydon Water, Great Yarmouth, Norfolk

Tel: 01223 582700 (Regional Office)

Owner: English Heritage   **Contact:** East of England Regional Office

Impressive walls, with projecting bastions, of a Roman fort built in the late 3rd century as one of a chain to defend the coast against Saxon raiders.

Location: OS Ref. TG475 046. At far W end of Breydon Water, on unclassified road 3m W of Great Yarmouth. SW of the church.

Open: Any reasonable time.

Admission: Free.

open all year
see page 557

BLICKLING HALL ✿

BLICKLING, NORWICH, NORFOLK NR11 6NF

www.nationaltrust.org.uk

Tel: 01263 738030   **Fax:** 01263 738035   **e-mail:** blickling@nationaltrust.org.uk

Owner: The National Trust   **Contact:** The Property Manager

Built in the early 17th century and one of England's great Jacobean houses. Blickling is famed for its spectacular long gallery, superb library and fine collections of furniture, pictures and tapestries.

Location: OS133 Ref. TG178 286. 1^1/$_2$ m NW of Aylsham on B1354. Signposted off A140 Norwich (15m) to Cromer.

Open: House: 25 Mar - 1 Oct: Wed - Sun & BH Mons, 1 - 4.30pm (last admission, house closes at 5pm). 4 - 29 Oct: 1 - 3.30pm (last admission, house closes at 4pm). Also open Mons during local school holidays. Garden: Same days as house, 10.15am - 5.15pm. 3 Nov - end Mar 2007: Thurs - Suns, 11am - 4pm. Park & Woods: daily, dawn - dusk.

Admission: Hall & Gardens: £8. Garden only: £5. Groups must book.

⬚ Open as garden. Cycle hire available in Orchard, ring for details. ⬚ ⬚ ⬚Mostly suitable. ⬚ ⬚Open as garden. Licensed. ⓘBy arrangement. ⓟ ⬚ ⬚In park, on leads. ⬚ ⬚ ⬚ Tel for details.

©National Trust Photographic Library

CAISTER CASTLE CAR COLLECTION

Caister-on-sea, Great Yarmouth, Norfolk NR30 5SN

Tel: 01572 787251

Owner/Contact: Mr J Hill

Large collection of historic motor vehicles from 1893 to recent. Moated Castle built by Sir John Falstaff in 1432. Car park free.

Location: OS Ref. TG502 122. Take A1064 out of Caister-on-sea towards Filby, turn left at the end of the dual carriageway.

Open: Mid May - End Sept: Sun - Fri (closed Sats), 10.30am - 4pm.

Admission: Contact property for details.

ⓘNo photography. ♿ Partial. WCs. ▣ ℙ 🔲

CASTLE ACRE PRIORY ♯

Stocks Green, Castle Acre, King's Lynn, Norfolk PE32 2XD

Tel: 01760 755394 **www.**english-heritage.org.uk/visits

Owner: English Heritage **Contact:** Visitor Operations Team

Explore the romantic ruins of this 12th century Cluniac priory, set in the picturesque village of Castle Acre. The impressive Norman façade, splendid prior's lodgings and chapel, and delightful recreated medieval herb garden should not be missed.

Location: OS Ref. TF814 148. ¼ m W of village of Castle Acre, 5m N of Swaffham.

Open: 1 Apr - 30 Sept: daily, 10am - 6pm. 1 Oct - 31 Mar: Thur - Mon, 10am - 4pm. Closed 24 - 26 Dec & 1 Jan. EH Members/OVP free.

Admission: Adult £4.50, Child £2.30, Conc. £3.40. Family £11.30.

▣ ♿ Ground floor & grounds. ⌕ ℙ ▣ 🔲 On leads. ✲ 🍷 Tel for details.

CASTLE RISING CASTLE

CASTLE RISING, KING'S LYNN, NORFOLK PE31 6AH

Tel: 01553 631330 **Fax:** 01553 631724

Owner: Greville Howard **Contact:** The Custodian

Possibly the finest mid-12th century Keep left in England: it was built as a grand and elaborate palace. It was home to Queen Isabella, grandmother of the Black Prince. Still in surprisingly good condition, the Keep is surrounded by massive ramparts up to 120 feet high. Picnic area adjacent tearoom. Free audio tour.

Location: OS Ref. TF666 246. Located 4m NE of King's Lynn off A149.

Open: 1 Apr - 1 Nov: daily, 10am - 6pm. 2 Nov - 31 Mar: Wed - Sun, 10am - 4pm. Closed 24 - 26 Dec & 1 Jan.

Admission: Adult £3.85, Child £2.20, Conc. £3.10, Family £11.50. 15% discount for groups (11+). Prices include VAT.

ⓘPicnic area. ▣ ♿Grounds. WC. ⌕ ⌕ ℙ ✲

corporate hospitality
see page 568

DRAGON HALL

115 - 123 KING ST, NORWICH, NORFOLK NR1 1QE

www.dragonhall.org

Tel: 01603 663922 **e-mail:** info@dragonhall.org

Owner: Norfolk & Norwich Heritage Trust **Contact:** Stephanie Potts

Magnificent medieval merchant's trading hall c1430 and one of Norwich's most important buildings. The modest exterior conceals a stunning Great Hall with impressive crown post roof and intricately carved dragon. Fascinating displays on three floors tell the story of this unique legacy of medieval life and the importance of trade in the creation of England's second city.

Location: OS Ref. TG235 084. Riverside location, 5 minutes from city centre, 10 minutes from railway station.

Open: Easter - 16 Dec: Mon - Sat, 10am - 5pm. Last admission 4pm.

Admission: Adult £4.95, Child (5 - 16) £2.95 (under 5yrs free). Conc. £4.25, Family £12 . Pre-booked groups (10+) receive a 10% discount.

ⓘ ▣ 🍷 Except cellars. 🎟 Groups only. ⌕ Free. ▣ 🔲 Guide dogs only. ⛿ ✲ 🍷 Tel for details.

FAIRHAVEN WOODLAND & WATER GARDEN

School Road, South Walsham NR13 6DZ

Tel/Fax: 01603 270449

Owner: The Fairhaven Garden Trust **Contact:** George Debbage, Manager

Delightful natural woodland and water garden with private broad in the beautiful Norfolk Broads. 3 miles of scenic paths. Boat trips on our private broad: April - end October.

Location: OS Ref. TG368 134. 9m NE of Norwich. Signed on A47 at junction with B1140.

Open: Daily (except 25 Dec), 10am - 5pm, also May - Aug: Wed & Thurs evenings until 9pm.

Admission: Adult £4, Child £1.50 (under 5yrs Free), OAP £3.50. Group reductions.

NTPL / Nick Meers

Blickling Hall.

FELBRIGG HALL ❧

FELBRIGG, NORWICH, NORFOLK NR11 8PR

www.nationaltrust.org.uk

Tel: 01263 837444 **Fax:** 01263 837032 **e-mail:** felbrigg@nationaltrust.org.uk

Owner: The National Trust **Contact:** The Property Manager

One of the finest 17th century country houses in East Anglia. The hall contains its original 18th century furniture and one of the largest collections of Grand Tour paintings by a single artist. The library is outstanding. The Walled Garden has been restored and features a series of pottager gardens, a working dovecote and the National Collection of Colchicums. The Park, through which there are way-marked walks, is well known for its magnificent and aged trees. There are also walks to the church and lake and through the 500 acres of woods.

Location: OS133 Ref. TG193 394. Nr Felbrigg village, 2m SW of Cromer, entrance off B1436, signposted from A148 and A140.

Open: House: 25 Mar - 29 Oct: daily except Thur & Fri, 1 - 5pm. (Open Good Fri.) Gardens: 25 Mar - 22 Oct: Daily except Thur & Fri (open Good Fri) 11am - 5pm. Some additional opening, telephone for details.

Admission: House & Garden: Adult £7, Child £3.50, Family £17.50. Garden only: Adult £3, Child £1.50. Groups (except BHs), £6. Groups please telephone property to pre-book.

⬜ 01263 837040. ▮ ▯ 01263 838237. ⬜ Partial. ◼ Licensed. ⬜ Licensed. ✦ By arrangement. ℗ ⬜ In grounds, on leads. ⬜ Tel 01263 837444 for details.

NT Photographic Library / Bill Batten

GREAT YARMOUTH ROW HOUSES ⌗

South Quay, Great Yarmouth, Norfolk NR30 2RQ

Tel: 01493 857900

Owner: English Heritage **Contact:** Visitor Operations Team

Two immaculately presented 17th century Row Houses, a type of building unique to Great Yarmouth. Row 111 House was almost destroyed by bombing in 1942/3 and contains items rescued from the rubble. Old Merchant's House boasts magnificent plaster-work ceilings and displays of local architectural fittings. Visitors can also visit Greyfriars' Cloisters, the remains of a 13th century friary of Franciscan 'grey friars', with wall paintings dating from c1300.

Location: OS134, TG525 072. In Great Yarmouth, make for Historic South Quay, by riverside and dock, ½ m inland from beach. Follow signs to dock and south quay.

Open: 1 Apr - 30 Sept: daily, 12 noon - 5pm. Free guided tours of the Greyfriars' Cloisters on the first Wed on the month throughout the season.

Admission: Adult £3.40. Child £1.70, Conc. £2.60.

⬜ ⬜

GRIME'S GRAVES ⌗

Lynford, Thetford, Norfolk IP26 5DE

Tel: 01842 810656

Owner: English Heritage **Contact:** Visitor Operations Team

These remarkable Neolithic flint mines, unique in England, comprise over 300 pits and shafts. The visitor can descend some 30 feet by ladder into one excavated shaft, and look along the radiating galleries, from where the flint used for making axes and knives was extracted.

Location: OS 144, TL818 898. 7m NW of Thetford off A134.

Open: 3 - 31 Mar & 6 - 31 Oct: Thur - Mon, 10am - 5pm. 1 Apr - 30 Sept: daily, 10am - 6pm. Last visit to site 30 mins before close. No entry to the mines for children under 5 yrs. Closed 24 & 25 Dec and 1 Jan.

Admission: Adult £2.70, Child £1.40, Conc. £2, (Child under 5yrs free), Family £6.80. EH Members/OVP free.

⬜ ⬜ Exhibition area only. ℗ ⬜ Restricted areas. ⬜ Tel for details.

HOLKHAM HALL ⬜   *See page 289 for full page entry.*

Oxburgh Hall.

HOUGHTON HALL

HOUGHTON, KING'S LYNN, NORFOLK PE31 6UE

www.houghtonhall. com

Tel: 01485 528569 **Fax:** 01485 528167 **e-mail:** enquiries@houghtonhall.com

Owner: The Marquess of Cholmondeley   **Contact:** Susan Cleaver

Houghton Hall is one of the finest examples of Palladian architecture in England. Built in the 18th century by Sir Robert Walpole, Britain's first prime minister. Original designs by James Gibbs & Colen Campbell, interior decoration by William Kent. The House has been restored to its former grandeur, containing many of its original furnishings. The spectacular 5-acre walled garden is divided into areas devoted to fruit and vegetables, elegant herbaceous borders, and a formal rose garden with over 150 varieties – full of colour throughout the summer. The unique Model Soldier Collection contains over 20,000 models arranged in various battle formations.

Location: OS Ref. TF792 287. 13m E of King's Lynn, 10m W of Fakenham 1½ m N of A148.

Open: Easter Sun - 28 Sept: Weds, Thurs, Suns & BH Mons. House: 1.30 - 5pm (last admission 4.30pm). Gates, Garden, Soldier Museum, Restaurant & Gift Shop: 11am - 5.30pm (last admission 5pm).

Admission: Adult £7, Child (5-16) £3, Family £16. Excluding House: Adult £4.50, Child £2. Group (20+) discounts available, please tel for details.

ⓘ ▣ ▣ ⓖ ▣ Licensed. ⑪ Licensed. ✗ By arrangement. Ⓟ ▣ ▣ On leads, in grounds.

HOVETON HALL GARDENS

Wroxham, Norwich, Norfolk NR12 8RJ

Tel: 01603 782798 **Fax:** 01603 784564 **e-mail:** info@hovetonhallgardens.co.uk

Owner: Mr & Mrs Andrew Buxton   **Contact:** Mrs Buxton

15 acres of rhododendrons, azaleas, woodland and lakeside walks, walled herbaceous and vegetable gardens. Traditional tearooms and plant sales. The Hall (which is not open to the public) was built 1809 - 1812. Designs attributed to Humphry Repton.

Location: OS Ref. TG314 202. 8m N of Norwich. 1½ m NNE of Wroxham on A1151. Follow brown tourist signs.

Open: Easter Sun - 17 Sept: Weds, Fris, Suns & BH Mons, also Thurs in May & June, 10.30am - 5pm.

Admission: Adult £4, Child (4-16yrs) £1.50, Senior £4, Wheelchair pusher and user £2pp. Season Ticket: Adult £10.50, Family £22.

▣

KIMBERLEY HALL

WYMONDHAM, NORFOLK NR18 0RT

www.kimberleyhall.co.uk

Tel/Fax: 01603 759447 **e-mail:** events@kimberleyhall.co.uk

Owner/Contact: R Buxton

Magnificent Queen Anne house built in 1712 by William Talman for Sir John Wodehouse, an ancestor of P G Wodehouse. Towers added after 1754 and wings connected to the main block by curved colonnades in 1835. Internal embellishments in 1770s include some very fine plasterwork by John Sanderson and a 'flying' spiral staircase beneath a coffered dome. The park, with its picturesque lake, ancient oak trees and walled gardens was laid out in 1762 by 'Capability' Brown.

Location: OS Ref. TG091 048. 10m SW of Norwich, 3m from A11.

Open: House & Park not open to the public. Grounds, certain rooms and extensive cellars available for corporate hospitality and weddings (licensed for Civil ceremonies) as well as product launches, film and fashion shoots.

Admission: Please telephone for details.

▣ ⓖ ▣

Holkham Hall.

LETHERINGSETT WATERMILL

Riverside Road, Letheringsett, Holt, Norfolk NR25 7YD

Tel: 01263 713153   **e-mail:** watermill@ic24.net

Owner/Contact: M D Thurlow

Water-powered mill producing wholewheat flour from locally grown wheat. Built in 1802.

Location: OS Ref. TG062 387. Riverside Road, Letheringsett, Holt, Norfolk.

Open: Whitsun - Oct: Mon - Fri, 10am - 5pm, Sat 9am - 1pm. Working demonstration, Tue - Fri, 2 - 4.30pm. Viewing may take place at any other time. Oct - Whitsun: Mon - Fri, 9am - 4pm. Sat, 9am - 1pm. Winter working demonstration times: ring for details.

Admission: Adult £2.50, Child £1.50. When demonstrating: Adult £3.50, Child £2.50, OAP £3, Family (2+2) £10.

MANNINGTON GARDENS & COUNTRYSIDE

MANNINGTON HALL, NORWICH NR11 7BB

www.manningtongardens.co.uk

Tel: 01263 584175   **Fax**: 01263 761214

Owner: The Lord & Lady Walpole   **Contact:** Lady Walpole

The gardens around this medieval moated manor house feature a wide variety of plants, trees and shrubs in many different settings. Throughout the gardens are thousands of roses especially classic varieties. The Heritage Rose and 20th Century Rose Gardens have roses in areas with designs reflecting their date of origin from the 15th century to the present day.

Location: OS Ref. TG144 320. Signposted from Saxthorpe crossroads on the Norwich - Holt road B1149. 1½ m W of Wolterton Hall.

Open: Gardens: May - Sept: Suns 12 - 5pm. Jun - Aug: Wed - Fri, 11am - 5pm, and at other times by prior appointment. Walks: daily from 9am. Medieval Hall open by appointment. Grounds & Park open all year.

Admission: Adult £4, Child (under 16yrs) Free, Conc. £3. Groups by arrangement. 🔲🖼️♿️ 🅿️ ⭤ ♿️ Grounds. WCs. 🦽 Licensed. 🎟️ By arrangement. 🅿️ £2 car park fee (walkers only). 🔲 🖼️ In park only. ❄️ Park. 🐕 Tel for details. €

NORWICH CASTLE MUSEUM & ART GALLERY

Norwich, Norfolk NR1 3JU

Tel: 01603 493625   **Fax:** 01603 493623   **e-mail:** museums@norfolk.gov.uk

Norman Castle Keep, housing displays of art, archaeology and natural history.

Location: OS Ref. TG233 085. City centre.

Open: All year: Mon - Fri, 10.30am - 4.30pm. Sat, 10am - 5pm. Sun, 1 - 5pm.

Admission: Adult £5.95, Child (4-16yrs) £4.45, Conc. £4.95. 2005 prices.

special events
see page 571

©National Trust Photographic Library

OXBURGH HALL & ESTATE

OXBOROUGH, KING'S LYNN, NORFOLK PE33 9PS

www.nationaltrust.org.uk

Tel: 01366 328258   **Fax:** 01366 328066   **e-mail:** oxburghhall@nationaltrust.org.uk

Owner: The National Trust   **Contact:** The Property Secretary

A moated manor house built in 1482 by the Bedingfeld family, who still live here. The rooms show the development from medieval austerity to Victorian comfort and include an accessible Priest's Hole and an outstanding display of embroidery by Mary Queen of Scots. The attractive gardens include a French parterre, kitchen garden and orchard and woodland walks.

Location: OS143, TF742 012. At Oxborough, 7m SW of Swaffham on S side of Stoke Ferry road.

Open: House: 25 Mar - 27 Sept: Sat - Wed, 1 - 5pm. 1 - 31 Aug: daily, 1- 5pm. 30 Sept - 29 Oct: Sat - Wed, 1 - 4pm. Garden: 7 Jan - 19 Mar: Sat & Sun only, 11am - 4pm; 25 Mar - 31 July & 2 - 27 Sept: Sat - Wed. Aug: daily, 11am - 5.30pm; 4 Nov - 17 Dec & 6 Jan - 25 Feb 07: Sat & Sun only, 11am - 4pm.

Admission: House & Garden: Adult £6.50, Child £3.25. Garden & Estate only: Adult £3.25, Child £1.65. Groups must book with SAE to the Property Secretary.

🔲 🍴 Licensed. ♿️ Partial. 🎟️ By arrangement. 🔲 🅿️ 🖼️ 🐕 Send SAE for details.

RAVENINGHAM GARDENS

RAVENINGHAM, NORWICH, NORFOLK NR14 6NS

www.raveningham.com

Tel: 01508 548152 **Fax**: 01508 548958

e-mail: info@raveningham.com

Owner: Sir Nicholas Bacon Bt   **Contact:** Mrs Janet Woodard

Superb herbaceous borders, 18th century walled kitchen garden, Victorian glass-house, herb garden, Edwardian rose garden, contemporary sculptures, 14th century church and much more. Also house guided tours.

Location: OS Ref. TM399 965. Between Norwich & Lowestoft off A146 then B1136/B1140.

Open: 12 - 19 Feb (closed Sat 18), 15, 16, 31 Apr, 1 & 26 May - 12 Jun (closed Sats), & 27/28 Aug. Suns & BH Mons, 2 - 5pm, Mon - Fri, 1 - 4pm.

Admission: Garden only: Adult £4, Child (under 16yrs) Free, OAP £3. Garden & House tour: Adult £7.50, Child £3, OAP £6.50. Groups by prior arrangement.

Teas on Suns & BH Mons. House tours by arrangement.

ST GEORGE'S GUILDHALL

29 King Street, King's Lynn, Norfolk PE30 1HA

Tel: 01553 765565 **www.west-norfolk.gov.uk**

Owner: The National Trust   **Contact:** The Administrator

The largest surviving English medieval guildhall and now converted into an arts centre, but with many interesting surviving features.

Location: OS132, TF616 202. On W side of King Street close to the Tuesday Market Place.

Open: Please telephone for details of opening dates and times. Closed Good Fri, BHs & 24 Dec - 1st Mon in Jan). The Guildhall is not usually open on days when there are performances in the theatre, tel box office 01553 764864 for details.

Admission: Free.

Access to galleries. Licensed.

SANDRINGHAM   *See page 290 for full page entry.*

SHERINGHAM PARK

Upper Sheringham, Norfolk NR26 8TL

Tel: 01263 820550 **e-mail:** sheringhampark@nationaltrust.org.uk

www.nationaltrust.org.uk

Owner: The National Trust   **Contact:** Visitor Centre

One of Humphry Repton's most outstanding achievements, the landscape park contains fine mature woodlands, and the large woodland garden is particularly famous for its spectacular show of rhododendrons and azaleas (mid May-June). There are stunning views of the coast and countryside from the viewing towers and many delightful waymarked walks.

Location: OS133, TG135 420. 2m SW of Sheringham, access for cars off A148 Cromer - Holt road; 5m W of Cromer, 6m E of Holt.

Open: All year: weekends, Mar - Sept, daily, dawn - dusk.

Admission: Pay & Display: Cars £3 (NT members Free - display card in car). Coaches £9 (must book for May & Jun visits).

Partial. WC. Easter - end Sept. Limited for coaches. In grounds, on leads. Tel. for details.

WALSINGHAM ABBEY GROUNDS & SHIREHALL MUSEUM

Little Walsingham, Norfolk NR22 6BP

Tel: 01328 820259 **Fax:** 01328 820098 **e-mail:** walsingham.estate@farmline.com

Owner: Walsingham Estate Company   **Contact:** Estate Office

Set in the picturesque medieval village of Little Walsingham, a place of pilgrimage since the 11th century, the grounds contain the remains of the famous Augustinian Priory with attractive gardens and river walks. The Shirehall Museum includes a Georgian magistrates' court and displays on the history of Walsingham.

Location: OS Ref. TF934 367. B1105 N from Fakenham - 5m.

Open: 18 Mar - 29 Oct: daily, 10am - 4.30pm. Also daily during snowdrop season (February) 10am - 4pm. Abbey Grounds: many other times, please telephone for details.

Admission: Combined ticket: Adult £3, Conc. £1.50.

Partial. By arrangement. In grounds, on leads. Tel for details.

WOLTERTON PARK

NORWICH, NORFOLK NR11 7LY

www.manningtongardens.co.uk

Tel: 01263 584175 **Fax:** 01263 761214

Owner: The Lord and Lady Walpole   **Contact:** The Lady Walpole

18th century Hall. Historic park with lake.

Location: OS Ref. TG164 317. Situated near Erpingham village, signposted from Norwich - Cromer Rd A140.

Open: Park: daily from 9am. Hall: 21 Apr - 27 Oct: Fridays, 2 - 5pm (last entry 4pm) and by appointment.

Admission: £5. £2 car park fee only for walkers. (Groups by application: from £4.)

Partial. WC. In park, on leads. Park. Tel for details. €

Felbrigg Hall.

NTPL / Rupert Truman

Houghton Hall - The Great Staircase.

HOUSES OPEN IN 2006

The Abbey, Coggeshall
The Abbey, Eye
Barsham Old Hall
Bawdsey Manor
Bedfield Hall
Bruisyard Hall
Bull's Hall, Yaxley
Butley Priory
Buxlow Manor
Chippenham Park
Columbine Hall
Cupola House
Euston Hall
Glemham Hall
The Great Lodge
Haughley House
Heath Farm House
Hemingstone Hall
High Hall

Hintlesham Hall
Ingatestone Hall
Island Hall
The Jockey Club
Kentwell Hall
Layer Marney Tower
Linden House, Eye
North Cove Hall
Otley Hall
Playford Hall Gardens
Polstead Hall
Read Hall, Mickfield
Roos Hall, Beccles
St Andrew's Church
Saxham Hall
South Elmham Hall
Spencers Garden
Tannington Hall
Yaxham Park
Yaxley Hall

These are not your normal, impersonal stately home tours. For a start, most of you will be shown round by the owners; then many of our houses are too small to open regularly so you will be special guests. But all, from C18 Palladian country houses to C15 farmhouses, from C14 priories to 1880s piles, are part of East Anglia's history.

INVITATION TO VIEW

Invitation to View has a cult following in Suffolk after eight years and, in 2006, it spreads into East Anglia with a record 39 properties. Visitors can view by appointment on specific days. Our brochure and website list all properties together with days and times of opening. Virtually all of us also welcome group bookings.

Tel: 01284 827087 Website: www.invitationtoview.co.uk

THE ANCIENT HOUSE

Clare, Suffolk CO10 8NY

Tel: 01628 825920 or 825923 (bookings) **www**.landmarktrust.org.uk

Owner: Leased to the Landmark Trust by Clare PC   **Contact:** The Landmark Trust

A 14th century house extended in the 15th and 17th centuries, decorated with high relief pargetting. Half of the building is managed by the Landmark Trust, which lets buildings for self-catering holidays. The other half of the house is run as a museum. Full details of The Ancient House and 183 other historic buildings available for holidays are featured in The Landmark Handbook (price £11 refundable against booking), from The Landmark Trust, Shottesbrooke, Maidenhead, Berkshire SL6 3SW.

Location: OS Ref. TL769 454. Village centre, on A1092 8m WNW of Sudbury.

Open: House: 7 Open Days a year and at other times by appointment. Museum: Easter & May - Sept: Thur, Fri & Sun, 2 - 5pm, Sat & BHs 11.30am - 5pm.

Admission: Please contact the Landmark Trust for details.

COCKFIELD HALL

YOXFORD, SUFFOLK   IP17 3ET

www.cockfieldhall.com

Tel: 01728 668076   **Fax:** 01728 668078   **e-mail:** enquiries@cockfieldhall.com

Owner: Mr and Mrs Owen Roberts   **Contact:** Anne Roberts

Majestic, Grade I Listed Tudor and Jacobean Manor set in 36 acres of tranquil, historic parkland. Built by Sir Arthur Hopton, said to have accompanied Henry VIII on the Field of the Cloth of Gold in 1520. Magnificent, vaulted Great Hall and fine plasterwork ceilings. Picturesque walled gardens, working dovecote and topiary yew hedges.

Location: OS Ref. TM395 692. Cockfield Hall N of Yoxford is on A12, 17 m N of Woodbridge. Directions can be found on the website.

Open: By appointment for groups only: All year.

Admission: Contact property for details.

ℹ️No smoking in the house. Film location. T️Licensed. 🔥Partial. WC. ●️By arrangement. 🅵By arrangement. 🅿️Ample. 🐕Guide dogs only. 🛏️3 ensuite doubles. 5 Diamonds & Gold Award - VisitBritain. 🔺 🅴Tel for details.€

BELCHAMP HALL

BELCHAMP WALTER, SUDBURY, SUFFOLK CO10 7AT

www.belchamphall.com

Tel: 01787 881961   **Fax:** 01787 466778

Owner/Contact: Mr C F V Raymond

Superb Queen Anne house on a site belonging to the Raymond family since 1611. Historic portraits and period furniture. Suitable for receptions and an ideal film location, often seen as 'Lady Jane's house' in *Lovejoy*. Gardens including a cherry avenue, follies, a sunken garden, walled garden and lake. Medieval church with 15th century wall paintings.

Location: OS Ref. TL827 407. 5m SW of Sudbury, opposite Belchamp Walter Church.

Open: By appointment only: May - Sept: Tues, Thurs & BHs, 2.30 - 6pm.

Admission: Adult £5, Child £2. No reduction for groups.

ℹ️No photography in house. Conference facilities. T️ ●️By arrangement. 🅵Obligatory. 🅿️ 🐕Guide dogs only.

EAST BERGHOLT PLACE GARDEN

East Bergholt, Suffolk CO7 6UP

Tel/Fax: 01206 299224   **e-mail:** sales@placeforplants.co.uk

Owner: Mr & Mrs R L C Eley   **Contact:** Sara Eley

Fifteen acres of garden and arboretum originally laid out at the beginning of the last century by the present owner's great-grandfather. A wonderful collection of fine trees and shrubs, many of which are rarely seen growing in East Anglia and originate from the famous plant hunter George Forrest. Particularly beautiful in the spring when the rhododendrons, magnolias and camellias are in flower.

Location: OS Ref. TM084 343. 2m E of A12 on B1070, Manningtree Rd, on the edge of East Bergholt.

Open: Mar - Sept: daily, 10am - 5pm. Closed Easter Sun.

Admission: Adult £3, Child Free. (Proceeds to garden up-keep).

🌱Specialist Plant Centre in the Victorian walled garden. 🅵By arrangement. 🐾

CHRISTCHURCH MANSION

Christchurch Park, Ipswich, Suffolk IP4 2BE

Tel: 01473 433554   **Fax:** 01473 433564

Owner/Contact: Ipswich Borough Council

A fine Tudor house set out as a museum.

Location: OS Ref. TM165 450. Christchurch Park, near centre of Ipswich.

Open: All year: Tue - Sat, 10am - 5pm (4pm in winter). Suns, 2.30 - 4.30pm (4pm in winter). Also open BH Mons. Closed 24 - 26 Dec, 1/2 Jan & Good Fri.

Admission: Free.

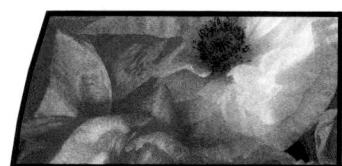

plant sales
see page 555

© English Heritage Photo Library

EUSTON HALL 🏛

ESTATE OFFICE, EUSTON, THETFORD, NORFOLK IP24 2QP

www.eustonhall.co.uk

Tel: 01842 766366 **Fax:** 01842 766764 **e-mail:** lcampbell@euston-estate.co.uk

Owner: The Duke of Grafton **Contact:** Mrs L Campbell

Euston Hall has been home to the Dukes of Grafton for over 300 years. It contains a collection of paintings of the Court of Charles II by Van Dyck and Lely, also "Mares and Foals" by George Stubbs. The gardens were laid out by the diarist John Evelyn and his walk through the Pleasure Grounds can still be enjoyed today. The park and river layout was designed by William Kent and is considered one of his greatest works. The project was completed by 'Capability' Brown. The 18th century watermill has been restored recently. The church is one of only four country churches built during the reign of Charles II.

Location: OS Ref. TL897 786. 12m N of Bury St Edmunds, on A1088. 2m E of A134.

Open: 15 Jun - 14 Sept: Thurs only. Also 25 Jun, 16 July & 3 Sept: 2.30 - 5pm.

Admission: Adult £5, Child £2, OAP £4. Groups (12+): £4pp.

FRAMLINGHAM CASTLE ⚔

FRAMLINGHAM, SUFFOLK IP13 9BT

www.english-heritage.org.uk/visits

Tel: 01728 724189

Owner: English Heritage **Contact:** Visitor Operations Team

A magnificent 12th century castle which, from the outside, looks almost the same as when it was built. From the continuous curtain wall linking 13 towers, there are excellent panoramic views of Framlingham and the charming reed-fringed Mere. Throughout its colourful history the castle has been a fortress, an Elizabethan prison, a poor house and a school. The many alterations over the years have led to a pleasing mixture of historic styles.

Location: OS Ref. TM287 637. In Framlingham on B1116. NE of town centre.

Open: 1 Apr - 30 Sept: daily, 10am - 6pm. 1 Oct - 31 Mar: Thur - Mon, 10am - 4pm. Closed 24 - 26 Dec & 1 Jan.

Admission: Adult £4.50, Child £2.30, Children under 5s Free. Conc. £3.40, Family £11.30. Members/OVP Free.

Ground floor & grounds. WCs. Tel for details.

FLATFORD BRIDGE COTTAGE

Flatford, East Bergholt, Colchester, Essex CO7 6OL

Tel: 01206 298260 **Fax:** 01206 297212 **www.nationaltrust.org.uk**

Owner: The National Trust **Contact:** The Property Manager

Just upstream from Flatford Mill, the restored thatched cottage houses a display about John Constable, several of whose paintings depict this property. Facilities include a tea garden, shop, boat hire, an Information Centre and countryside walks.

Location: OS Ref. TM077 332. On N bank of Stour, 1m S of East Bergholt B1070.

Open: Mar & Apr: Wed - Sun, 11am - 5pm. May - end Sept: daily, 10.30am - 5.30pm. Oct: daily, 11am - 4pm. Nov & Dec: Wed - Sun, 11am - 3.30pm. Jan & Feb: Sats & Suns only, 11am - 3.30pm. Closed Christmas & New Year.

Admission: Guided walks (when guide available) £2.50, accompanied child Free.

Tea garden & shop. WC. Charge applies. Guide dogs only.

FRESTON TOWER

Nr Ipswich, Suffolk IP9 1AD

Tel: 01628 825925 **www.landmarktrust.org.uk**

Owner: The Landmark Trust

An Elizabethan six-storey tower overlooking the estuary of the River Orwell. The tower was built in 1578 by a wealthy Ipswich merchant called Thomas Gooding, perhaps to celebrate the recent grant of his coat of arms. Freston Tower is cared for by The Landmark Trust, a building preservation charity who let it for holidays. Full details of Freston Tower and 183 other historic and architecturally important buildings are featured in the Landmark Trust Handbook (price £11 refundable against a booking).

Location: OS Ref. TM177 397.

Open: Available for holidays for up to 4 people throughout the year. Please contact the Landmark Trust for details. Open Days on 8 days a year.

Admission: Free on Open Days, contact Landmark Trust for details.

© National Trust

Sutton Hoo.

GAINSBOROUGH'S HOUSE

46 GAINSBOROUGH ST, SUDBURY, SUFFOLK CO10 2EU

www.gainsborough.org

Tel: 01787 372958   **Fax:** 01787 376991   **e-mail:** mail@gainsborough.org
Owner: Gainsborough's House Society   **Contact:** Rosemary Woodward
Birthplace of Thomas Gainsborough RA (1727-88). Historic house dating back to the 16th century with attractive walled garden. The outstanding collection is shown together with 18th century furniture and displays more of Gainsborough's work than any other gallery. Varied programme of exhibitions on both historic British art and contemporary arts and crafts.
Location: OS Ref. TL872 413. 46 Gainsborough Street, Sudbury town centre.
Open: All year: Mon - Sat, 10am - 5pm. Closed: Suns, Good Fri and Christmas to New Year.
Admission: Adult £3.50, Child/Student £1.50, Conc £2.80, Family Ticket £8.
ℹ️No photography. 🄯 ♿WCs. 🅿 None. ▣ ❄

HELMINGHAM HALL GARDENS

HELMINGHAM, SUFFOLK IP14 6EF

www.helmingham.com

Tel: 01473 890799   **Fax:** 01473 890776   **e-mail:** events@helmingham.com
Owner: The Lord & Lady Tollemache   **Contact:** Mrs Sarah Harris
The Tudor Hall surrounded by its wide moat is set in a 400 acre deer park. Two superb gardens, one surrounded by its own moat and walls extends to several acres and has wide herbaceous borders and an immaculate kitchen garden. The second enclosed within yew hedges, has a special rose garden with a herb and knot garden containing plants grown in England before 1750. Coach bookings welcome.
Location: OS Ref. TM190 578. B1077, 9m N of Ipswich, 5m S of Debenham.
Open: Gardens only: 7 May - 17 Sept: Suns & Weds, 2 - 6pm.
Admission: Adult £4.50, Child (5-15yrs) £2.50. Groups (30+) £4.
🄯 ⚘ 🍴 ♿Grounds. WCs. 🅿 In grounds, on leads. Tel for details.

HADLEIGH GUILDHALL

Hadleigh, Suffolk IP7 5DT
Tel: 01473 827752
Owner: Hadleigh Market Feoffment Charity   **Contact:** Jane Haylock
Fine timber framed guildhall, one of the least known medieval buildings in Suffolk.
Location: OS Ref. TM025 425. S side of churchyard.
Open: mid Jun - end Sept: Building: Thurs & Suns; Garden: Sun - Fri, 2 - 5pm.
Admission: Free. Donations welcome.

HAUGHLEY PARK

Stowmarket, Suffolk IP14 3JY
Tel: 01359 240701   **www.**haughleyparkbarn.co.uk
Owner/Contact: Mr & Mrs Robert Williams
Mellow red brick manor house of 1620 set in gardens, park and woodland. Original five-gabled east front, north wing re-built in Georgian style, 1820. 6 acres of well tended gardens including walled kitchen garden. 17th century brick and timber barn restored as meeting rooms. Woodland walks with bluebells (special Sun opening), lily-of-the-valley (May), rhododendrons and azaleas.
Location: OS Ref. TM005 618. 4m W of Stowmarket signed off A14.
Open: Garden only: May - Sept: Tues & last Sun in Apr & 1st Sun in May, 2 - 5.30pm. House visits and groups by appointment (even outside normal times). Barn bookable for special lunches, teas, dinners, lectures etc. (capacity 120).
Admission: House: £2. Garden: £3. Child under 16 Free.
ℹ️ Picnics allowed. ⚘ Bluebell Sun. 🍴 ♿ 🐕 Bluebell Sun. 🎟 By arrangement. 🅿
On leads only. ▣ ❄

NT Photographic Library: Rupert Truman

ICKWORTH HOUSE & PARK

THE ROTUNDA, HORRINGER, BURY ST EDMUNDS IP29 5QE

www.nationaltrust.org.uk

Tel: 01284 735270   **Fax:** 01284 735175   **e-mail:** ickworth@nationaltrust.org.uk
Owner: The National Trust   **Contact:** The Property Manager
One of the most unusual houses in East Anglia. The huge Rotunda of this 18th century Italianate house dominates the landscape. Inside are collections of Georgian silver, Regency furniture, Old Master paintings and family portraits.
Location: OS155 Ref. TL816 611. In Horringer, 3m SW of Bury St Edmunds on W side of A143.
Open: House: 20 Mar - 5 Nov: daily except Wed & Thur, 1 - 5pm, last admission 4.30pm (closes 4.30pm in Oct/Nov). Garden: 2 Jan - 19 Mar & 2 Oct - 18 Mar 07, 11am - 4pm. 20 Mar - 1 Oct, 10am - 5pm. Park open all year dawn to dusk except Christmas day.
Admission: Adult £7, Child £3. Family discounts. Park & Garden only (includes access to shop & restaurant): Adult £3.40, Child 90p. Group discounts on pre-booked visits, no group discounts on Suns & BH Mons.
🄯 ♿Partial. 🍴 Licensed. 🎟 By arrangement. ▣ In park, on leads.
Tel for details.

special events
see page 571

KENTWELL HALL & GARDENS
LONG MELFORD, SUFFOLK CO10 9DA
www.kentwell.co.uk

Tel: 01787 310207 **Fax:** 01787 379318 **e-mail:** info@kentwell.co.uk

Owner: Patrick Phillips Esq   **Contact:** The Estate Office

Heritage Building of the Year 2001. Atmospheric moated Tudor Hall with rare service building of c1500. Interior 'improved' by Thomas Hopper in 1820s. Still a lived-in family home. Famed for the long-time, long term, ongoing restoration works.

Re-Creations: Kentwell is renowned for its award-winning Re-Creations of Everyday Tudor Life. It has now added occasional Re-Creations of WW2 Life. Re-Creations take place on selected weekends. Telephone for dates.

Gardens: Over 30 years endeavour has resulted in Gardens which are a joy in all seasons. Moats predominate with massed spring bulbs, extensive wild flowers; ancient fruit blossom and clipped yews to large Herb Garden & Potager.

Corporate: Any sort of function including authentic Tudor Banquets.

Schools: Half a million school children have now visited a Tudor Re-Creation, recognized by teachers to be an unequalled educational resource.

Filming: Much used for medieval and Tudor periods for its wide range of perfectly equipped locations inside and out and access to Kentwell's 700 Tudors as extras.

Location: OS Ref. TL864 479. Off the A134. 4m N of Sudbury, 14m S of Bury St. Edmunds 1m NNW of Long Melford off A134.

Open: BHs, Sat - Mon (+Fri, Easter & Aug): 11am - 6pm. 12 Feb - 26 Mar, half term daily & Suns, Gardens only, 11am - 4pm. 2 Apr - 17 Jun: Sun - Wed, school holidays & half term, daily: 12noon - 5pm. 18 Jun - 9 Jul: Great Annual Re-Creation of Tudor Life only (booked schools on weekdays, public on Sat, Sun & 5 Jul). 12 Jul - 24 Sept: daily (check for Sats) 12 noon - 5pm. Oct: Suns & half term, daily, 12 noon - 5pm.

Admission: House & Gardens: Adult £7.50, Child (5-15yrs) £4.75, OAP £6.50. Special prices apply BH w/ends and for Special Events, tel for details.

ⓘNo photography in house. 🏠Home-made food. Tel for details.

LANDGUARD FORT ⌘
Felixstowe, Suffolk

Tel: 07749 695523

Owner: English Heritage   **Contact:** Visitor Operations Team
(Manged by Languard For Trrust)

Impressive 18th century fort with later additions built on a site originally fortified by Henry VIII and in use until after World War II. Existing guided tours and audio tours of the fort will be supplemented in 2006 by a DVD presetatiuon of the site's history and by guided tours of the substantial outside batteries.

Location: OS Ref. TM284 318. 1m S of Felixstowe town centre - follow brown tourist signs to Landguard Point and Nature Reserve from A14.

Open: 1 Apr - 27 Oct: daily, 10am - 6pm (5pm Oct). Last admission 1hr before closing. Telephone 07749 695523 for Battery & Group tour bookings.

Admission: Adult £3, Child £1, Conc. £2.50. Free entry for children under 5yrs and wheelchair users. No unaccompanied children.

Contact David Tolliday or David Wood for details of tours of the outer batteries & charges for special events.

LAVENHAM: THE GUILDHALL OF CORPUS CHRISTI
THE MARKET PLACE, LAVENHAM, SUDBURY CO10 9QZ
www.nationaltrust.org.uk

Tel: 01787 247646 **e-mail:** lavenhamguildhall@nationaltrust.org.uk

Owner: The National Trust   **Contact:** The Property Manager

This splendid 16th century timber-framed building dominates the Market Place of the picturesque town of Lavenham with its many historic houses and wonderful church. Inside are exhibitions on local history, farming and industry, as well as the story of the medieval woollen cloth trade. There is also a walled garden with dye plants.

Location: OS155, TL915 942. 6m NNE of Sudbury. Village centre. A1141 & B1071.

Open: 1 - 30 Mar: Sat & Sun, 11am - 4pm. 1 - 30 Apr: Wed - Sun, 11am - 5pm. 1 May - 31 Oct: daily, 11am - 5pm. 1 - 30 Nov: Sat & Sun, 11am - 4pm. Open BH Mon, closed Good Fri. Parts of the building may be closed occasionally for community use.

Admission: Adult £3.50, accompanied child £1.50. Groups: £3. School parties (by arrangement) £1 per child.

Shop & tearoom.

LEISTON ABBEY ⌘
Leiston, Suffolk

Tel: 01223 582700 (Regional Office)

Owner: English Heritage   **Contact:** The East of England Regional Office

The remains of this abbey for Premonstratensian canons, including a restored chapel, are amongst the most extensive in Suffolk.

Location: OS Ref. TM445 642. 1m N of Leiston off B1069.

Open: Any reasonable time.

Admission: Free.

MANOR HOUSE MUSEUM
Honey Hill, Bury St Edmunds, Suffolk IP33 1RT

Tel: 01284 757076 **Fax:** 01284 747231 **e-mail:** manor.house@stedsbc.gov.uk

Owner: St Edmundsbury Borough Council   **Contact:** The Manager

A Georgian town house displaying a stunning array of costume, clocks, paintings and furniture.

Location: OS Ref. TL858 640. Bury town centre off A14. Just S of Abbey grounds.

Open: All year: Wed - Sun, 11am - 4pm.

Admission: Adult £2.60, Conc £2.10. Free to residents of the Borough.

©National Trust Photographic Library

MELFORD HALL ❦

LONG MELFORD, SUDBURY, SUFFOLK CO10 9AA

www.nationaltrust.org.uk

Tel/Fax: 01787 379228   **Info:** 01787 376395
e-mail: melford@nationaltrust.org.uk
Owner: The National Trust   **Contact:** Stephen Bennett - Property Manager

Set in the unspoilt villiage of Long Melford, the house has changed little externally since 1578 when Queen Elizabeth I was entertained here, and retains its original panelled banqueting hall. It has been the home of the Hyde Parker family since 1786. There is a Regency Library, Victorian bedrooms, good collections of furniture and porcelain and a small display of items connected with Beatrix Potter, who was related to the family. The garden contains some spectacular specimen trees and a banqueting house, and there is an attractive walk through the park.

Location: OS Ref. TL867 462. In Long Melford off A134, 14m S of Bury St Edmunds, 3m N of Sudbury.

Open: Apr: Sat & Sun only (also open 19, 20 & 21 Apr). 1 May - 30 Sept: Wed - Sun. 1 - 29 Oct: Sat & Sun only. Open BH Mons. 1.30 - 5pm. Last admission 4.30pm.

Admission: Adult £5, Child (under 16yrs) £2.50, Family £12.50. Groups (15+): Adult £4, Child £2. Phone, e-mail or write with SAE to Property Manager.

ℹ️No photography in house. 🚻 ♿Suitable. WC. 🐕 🅿️In car park & park walk only, on leads. 📶 Tel Infoline for details.

© English Heritage Photo Library. © Skyscan Balloon Photography

ORFORD CASTLE ⚜

ORFORD, WOODBRIDGE, SUFFOLK IP12 2ND

www.english-heritage.org.uk/visits

Tel: 01394 450472
Owner: English Heritage   **Contact:** Visitor Operations Team

An enchanting royal castle built by Henry II for coastal defence in the 12th century. A magnificent keep survives almost intact with three immense towers offering beautiful views over Orford Ness and the surrounding countryside.

Location: OS169, TM419 499. In Orford on B1084, 20m NE of Ipswich.

Open: 1 Apr - 30 Sept: daily, 10am - 6pm. 1 Oct - 31 Mar: Thur - Mon, 10am - 4pm. Closed 24 - 26 Dec & 1 Jan.

Admission: Adult £4.50, Child £2.30, Under 5s Free, Conc. £3.40, Family £11.30. Members/OVP Free.

🏠 🎧 🅿️ ♿ ✳️ 📶 Tel for details.

OTLEY HALL

OTLEY, IPSWICH, SUFFOLK IP6 9PA

www.otleyhall.co.uk

Tel: 01473 890264   **Fax:** 01473 890803   **e-mail:** enquiries@otleyhall.co.uk
Owner: Dr Ian & Mrs Catherine Beaumont   **Contact:** Kat Pennington

A stunning medieval Moated Hall (Grade I) frequently described as "one of England's loveliest houses". Noted for its richly carved beams, superb linenfold panelling and 16th century wall paintings, Otley Hall was once the home of the Gosnold family and is still a family home. Bartholomew Gosnold voyaged to the New World in 1602 and named Cape Cod and Martha's Vineyard, (an account of the voyage is believed to have inspired Shakespeare's *Tempest*). Gosnold returned in 1607 and founded the Jamestown colony, the first English-speaking settlement in the US. The unique 10 acre gardens include historically accurate Tudor recreations designed by Sylvia Landsberg (author of *The Medieval Garden*).

Location: OS Ref. TM207 563. 7m N of Ipswich, off the B1079.

Open: BH Suns (30 Apr, 28 May, 27 Aug), 2 - 6pm. Afternoon teas available. Coach parties welcome all year by appointment for private guided tours.

Admission: BHs: Adult £5, Child £2.50.

🍽 ♿Partial. 🐕 📷By arrangement. 🅿️ ✳️ 📶 Tel for details.

ST EDMUNDSBURY CATHEDRAL

Angel Hill, Bury St Edmunds, Suffolk IP33 1LS

Tel: 01284 754933 **Fax:** 01284 768655 **e-mail:** cathedral@burycathedral.fsnet.co.uk
www.stedscathedral.co.uk

Owner: The Church of England **Contact:** Sarah Friswell

Be among the first to see the magnificent Millennium Tower, which now completes the last unfinished Anglican cathedral in England. Built over the past five years of English limestone, brick and lime mortar, the 150ft Lantern Tower, along with new chapels, cloisters and North Transept, completes nearly fifty years of development in a style never likely to be repeated.

Location: OS Ref. TL857 642. Bury St Edmunds town centre.

Open: All year: daily 8.30am - 6pm.

Admission: Donation invited.

▨ ⓖPartial. WC. ☞ Ⓘ ▥ ✳

SAXTEAD GREEN POST MILL ♯

Post Mill Bungalow, Saxtead Green, Woodbridge, Suffolk IP13 9QQ

Tel: 01728 685789 **www**.english-heritage.org.uk/visits

Owner: English Heritage **Contact:** Visitor Operations Team

The finest example of a Suffolk Post Mill. Still in working order, you can climb the wooden stairs to the various floors, full of fascinating mill machinery. Ceased production in 1947.

Location: OS Ref. TM253 645. 2¹/₂ m NW of Framlingham on A1120.

Open: 1 Apr - 30 Sept: Fri & Sat, 12 noon - 5pm.

Admission: Adult £2.60, Child £1.30, Conc. £2.

SHRUBLAND PARK GARDENS

Ipswich, Suffolk IP6 9QQ

Tel: 01473 830221 **Fax:** 01473 832202

Owner/Contact: Lord de Saumarez

One of the finest examples of an Italianate garden in England, designed by Sir Charles Barry.

Location: OS Ref. TM125 525. 6m N of Ipswich to the E of A14/A140.

Open: Jun: Suns only, (Jul - Aug, Wed & Sun), BH Suns & Mons from Easter, 2 - 5pm.

Admission: Adult £3, Child/OAP £2.

Orford Castle.

SOMERLEYTON HALL & GARDENS 🏛

SOMERLEYTON, LOWESTOFT, SUFFOLK NR32 5QQ

www.somerleyton.co.uk

Tel: 08712 224244 (office) **Fax:** 01502 732143 **e-mail:** enquiries@somerleyton.co.uk

Owner: Hon Hugh Crossley **Contact:** Cathy Hatt

Splendid early Victorian mansion built in Anglo-Italian style by John Thomas, with lavish architectural features, magnificent carved stonework and fine state rooms. Paintings by Landseer, Wright of Derby and Stanfield, wood carvings by Willcox of Warwick and Grinling Gibbons. Somerleyton's 12-acre gardens are justly renowned with beautiful borders, specimen trees and the 1846 yew hedge maze which ranks amongst the finest in the country. Special features include glasshouses by Paxton, 300ft pergola, walled garden, Vulliamy tower clock, Victorian ornamentation. Film location for BBC drama *The Lost Prince* (2002).

Location: OS134 Ref. TM493 977. 5m NW of Lowestoft on B1074, 7m SW of Great Yarmouth off A143.

Open: 2 Apr- 29 Oct: Thurs, Suns, BH Fri & Mons. Jul & Aug: Tue - Thur, Suns & BH Mons. Gardens: 10am - 5pm. Hall: 12 noon - 4pm (guided tours only every half hour). Tearoom: 10am - 5pm.

Admission: Hall Tour & Gardens : Adult £7.50, Child £3.50, Conc. £6.50. Gardens only: Adult £4.50, Child £2.50, Conc. £3.50, Family £20.

ⓘ No photography in house. ▨ ✳

Ⓣ Receptions/functions/conferences/weddings. ⓖ ☞ Ⓘ Obligatory. Ⓟ ▥ ✖

▲ ✳

SOUTH ELMHAM HALL

ST CROSS, HARLESTON, NORFOLK IP20 0PZ

www.southelmham.co.uk   www.batemansbarn.co.uk

Tel: 01986 782526 **Fax:** 01986 782203 **e-mail:** enquiries@southelmham.co.uk

Owner/Contact: John Sanderson

A Grade I listed medieval manor house set inside moated enclosure. Originally built by the Bishop of Norwich around 1270. Much altered in the 16th century. Self guided trail through former deer park to South Elmham Minster, a ruined Norman chapel with Saxon origins.

Location: OS30 Ref. TM778 324. Between Harleston and Bungay from the A143 take the B1062.

Open: Minster, Walks (Café: 1 May - 3 Sept: Thurs, Fris & BH Mons). 1 Oct - 30 Apr: Suns only, 10am - 5pm. Hall: Guided tours only: 1 May - 30 Sept: Thurs, 2pm, Sun & BH Mons, 3pm.

Admission: House: Adult £6.50, Child £3. Groups (15-50): Adult £4.50, Child £2.50. Walks (free).

⬜ 🔲 ♿ WC. 🔲 🅵 Obligatory. ■ 🅿 🔲 In grounds, on leads. ▲ ❋

SUTTON HOO ❧

TRANMER HOUSE, SUTTON HOO, WOODBRIDGE, SUFFOLK IP12 3DJ

www.nationaltrust.org.uk

Tel: 01394 389700 **Fax:** 01394 389702 **e-mail:** suttonhoo@nationaltrust.org.uk

Owner: The National Trust   **Contact:** The Property Manager

Anglo-Saxon royal burial site where priceless treasure was discovered in a ship grave in 1939. Given to the National Trust in 1998, the 99ha site has an exhibition hall with reconstruction of the burial chamber, burial site and estate walks. Original gold buckle returns to Sutton Hoo in 2006 as part of summer treasury exhibition.

Location: OS Ref. TM288 487. Off B1083 Woodbridge to Bawdsey road. Follow signs from A12. Train ½ m Melton. Bus: First 83 Ipswich - Bawdsey (passing Melton train station).

Open: Exhibition Hall, shop & restaurant: 25 Mar - 2 Apr: Wed - Sun, 11am - 5pm. 3 - 17 Apr: daily, 11am - 5pm. 18 Apr - 2 Jul: Wed - Sun, 11am - 5pm. 3 Jul - 4 Sept: daily, 11am - 5pm. 5 Sept - 29 Oct: Wed - Sun, 11am - 5pm. 30 Oct - 22 Dec: Wed - Sun, 11am - 4pm. 27 - 31 Dec: Wed - Sun, 11am - 4pm. 1 Jan - 25 Mar 07: Sat & Sun, 11am - 4pm. Open BH Mons & daily during half terms. Closed 23 - 26 Dec.

Admission: NT members free. Adult £5.50, Child £2.50. Family £13.50. Groups: Adult £4, School groups £2. Discount for visitors arriving by cycle or on foot.

⬜ 🔲 ♿ Licensed. 🔲 Licensed. 🅵 By arrangement. 🅿 ■ 🔲 In grounds, on leads. ❋ 🔲 Programme of events, tel for details.

THE TIDE MILL

Woodbridge, Suffolk IP12 4SR

Tel: 01728 746959

Contact: Terina Booker

First recorded in 1170, now fully restored, machinery demonstrated at low tide. Ring for wheel turning times.

Location: OS Ref. TM275 487. By riverside ¼ m SE of Woodbridge town centre. 1¼ m off A12.

Open: Easter & May - Sept: daily. Apr & Oct: Sats & Suns only, 11am - 5pm.

Admission: Adult £2, Child Free, Conc. £1.50.

WYKEN HALL GARDENS

STANTON, BURY ST EDMUNDS, SUFFOLK IP31 2DW

www.wykenvineyards.co.uk

Tel: 01359 250287 **Fax:** 01359 253420

Owner: Sir Kenneth & Lady Carlisle   **Contact:** Mrs Barbara Hurn

The Elizabethan manor house is surrounded by a romantic, plant-lover's garden with maze, knot and herb garden and rose garden featuring old roses. A walk through ancient woodlands leads to Wyken Vineyards, winner of EVA Wine of the Year. In the 16th century barn, the Vineyard Restaurant serves our wines along with a varied menu from fresh local produce. It is a 'Bib Gourmand' in the *Michelin Guide* and features also in *The Good Food Guide*.

Location: OS Ref. TL963 717. 9m NE of Bury St. Edmunds 1m E of A143. Follow brown tourist signs to Wyken Vineyards from Ixworth.

Open: 5 Jan - 24 Dec: daily, 10am - 6pm. Garden: 26 Mar - 1 Oct: daily except Sat, 2 - 6pm. Open for dinner from 7pm Fri & Sat (advisable to book).

Admission: Gardens: Adult £3, Child (under 12yrs) Free, Conc. £2.50. Groups by appointment.

⬜ 🔲 🔲 🔲 ♿ Suitable. WC. 🔲 Licensed. 🅿 🔲 In grounds, on leads. ❋

Haughley Park.

Tissington Hall, Derbyshire. © Heritage House Group Limited

east midlands

Britain's heartland: from the rolling grass pastureland of Northamptonshire, Leicestershire and Rutland, through Nottinghamshire to the more rugged countryside of Derbyshire. This is a part of Britain that is sadly often overlooked, but it is well worth further investigation. The industrial coalfields of Nottinghamshire and Derbyshire may have closed for good, but Sherwood Forest, the haunt of the legendary Robin Hood, remains. Pay a visit to Rockingham Castle (Northamptonshire), built by William the Conqueror, with its dramatic views over five counties. Further north, Chatsworth and Haddon Hall (Derbyshire) are two very different examples of stately homes. Contrast them with the charming manor house of Eyam Hall (Derbyshire) and the stunning gardens of Coton Manor (Northamptonshire).

northamptonshire   nottinghamshire

Gary Rogers Hamburg

Owner: Trustees of the Chatsworth Settlement. Home of the Devonshire family

▶ CONTACT

Mr John Oliver
Chatsworth
Bakewell
Derbyshire   DE45 1PP

Tel: 01246 582204
01246 565300
Fax: 01246 583536

e-mail: visit@chatsworth.org

▶ LOCATION

OS Ref. SK260 703

From London
3 hrs M1/J29,
signposted via
Chesterfield.

3m E of Bakewell,
off B6012,
10m W of Chesterfield.

Rail: Chesterfield
Station, 11m.

Bus: Chesterfield -
Baslow, 1¹/₂ m.

CONFERENCE/FUNCTION	
ROOM	MAX CAPACITY
Hartington Rm.	70
Coffee Rm.	24

CHATSWORTH
www.chatsworth.org

The great treasure house of Chatsworth was first built by Bess of Hardwick in 1552 and has been lived in by the Cavendish family, the Dukes of Devonshire, ever since. The House was rebuilt by the 1st Duke at the end of the 17th century, while the 6th Duke added a wing 130 years later. Visitors see the grandest rooms in the house, including the magnificent 17th century State Rooms, which are being re-presented in 2006 to reflect the taste and era of their creator, the 1st Duke, with furniture and gold and silver pieces never seen by visitors before. The Library, Great Dining Room and Sculpture Gallery reflect the taste of the 6th Duke, and the latter was used to great effect as Pemberley in the new *Pride and Prejudice* film. Among the treasures on view, there are painted ceilings by Verrio, Thornhill and Laguerre, tapestry, silk and leather wall hangings, furniture and decorative arts by the greatest British and European makers, classical and neo-classical sculpture, including four works by Antonio Canova and paintings by Rembrandt, Tintoretto, Veronese, Reynolds, Gainsborough, Landseer and Sargent. In 2006, we open a new exhibition in eight rooms of the house, to celebrate the life and collecting of Andrew, the 11th Duke, including important 20th century works of art collected by him, ranging from William Nicholson to Lucian Freud. Chatsworth has won many awards as the country's favourite stately home.

GARDEN
The 105 acre garden was created during three great eras in garden and landscape design. The 200 metre Cascade, the Willow Tree fountain and the Canal survive from the 1st Duke's formal garden. 'Capability' Brown landscaped the garden and park in the 1760s. The 6th Duke's gardener, Sir Joseph Paxton, built rockeries and designed a series of glasshouses. He also created the Emperor fountain, one of the tallest gravity-fed fountains in the world. More recent additions include the Rose, Cottage and Kitchen gardens, the Serpentine Hedge, the Maze, and a new Sensory garden.

Farmyard and Adventure Playground. Guide book translations and audio guides in French, German, Italian, Spanish and Japanese.

Wheelchairs in part of the house, and welcome in garden (3 electric, 7 standard available). WCs. Special leaflet.

Rooms available for conferences and private functions. Contact Head of Catering.

Restaurant (max 300); home-made food. Menus on request.

Private tours of house or Greenhouses and Behind the Scenes Days, by arrangement only (extra charges apply). Groups please pre-book.

Cars 100 yds, Coaches 25 yds from house.

Guided tours, packs, trails and school room. Free preliminary visit recommended.

▶ OPENING TIMES

15 March - 20 December.
Daily: 11am - 4.30pm.
The Park is open free throughout the year.

▶ ADMISSION

House & Garden
Adult	£9.75
Child	£3.50
OAP/Student	£7.75
Family	£23.00

Pre-booked groups (12+)
Adult	£8.25
OAP/Student	£6.75

Garden only
Adult	£6.00
Child	£2.75
OAP/Student	£4.50
Family	£14.50

House, Garden & 11th Duke Exhibition Scots Rooms
Adult	£12.00
Child	£4.50
OAP	£10.00
Family	£28.50

Groups
Adult	£10.50
OAP/Student	£9.00

Farmyard & Adventure Playground
All	£4.50
Groups (5+)	£3.90
OAP/School groups	£3.25
Child under 3yrs	Free

Family pass for all attractions | £42.00

Rates differ during Christmas season (4 Nov - 20 Dec).

▶ SPECIAL EVENTS
Tel for details.

MAP 6

Owner:
Lord Edward Manners

▶ CONTACT

Janet O'Sullivan
Estate Office
Haddon Hall
Bakewell
Derbyshire
DE45 1LA

Tel: 01629 812855
Fax: 01629 814379

e-mail: info@
haddonhall.co.uk

▶ LOCATION

OS Ref. SK234 663

From London 3 hrs
Sheffield ¹/₂ hr
Manchester 1 hr
Haddon is on the
E side of A6 1¹/₂ m
S of Bakewell.
M1/J30.

Rail: Chesterfield
Station, 12m.

Bus: Chesterfield
Bakewell.

HADDON HALL 🏛

www.haddonhall.co.uk

Haddon Hall sits on a rocky outcrop above the River Wye close to the market town of Bakewell, looking much as is would have done in Tudor times. There has been a dwelling here since the 11th century but the house we see today dates mainly from the late 14th century with major additions in the following 200 years and some alterations in the early 17th century including the creation of the Long Gallery.

William the Conqueror's illegitimate son Peverel, and his descendants, held Haddon for 100 years before it passed to the Vernon family. In the late 16th century the estate passed through marriage to the Manners family, in whose possession it has remained ever since.

When the Dukedom of Rutland was conferred on the Manners family in 1703 they moved to Belvoir Castle, and Haddon was left deserted for 200 years. This was Haddon's saving grace as the Hall thus escaped the major architectural changes of the 18th and 19th centuries ready for the great restoration at the beginning of the 20th century by the 9th Duke of Rutland. Henry VIII's elder brother Arthur, who was a frequent guest of the Vernons, would be quite familiar with the house as it stands today.

Haddon Hall is a popular location for film and television productions. Recent films include *Jane Eyre* and *Elizabeth*.

GARDENS

Magnificent terraced gardens with over 150 varieties of rose and clematis, many over 70 years old, provide colour and scent throughout the summer.

▶ OPENING TIMES

Summer
Easter: 14 - 18 April
April & October:
Sat - Mon.
May - September:
Daily, 12 noon - 5pm
Last admission 4pm.

▶ ADMISSION

Summer
Adult £7.75
Child (5 -15yrs) £4.00
Conc £6.75
Family (2+3) £20.00

Regular Visitor Pass:
.... £14.00

Groups (15+)
Adult £6.75
Child (5 -15yrs) £3.50
Conc £5.75

🏠 ℹ Haddon Hall is ideal as a film location due to its authentic and genuine architecture requiring little alteration. Suitable locations are also available on the Estate.

♿ Unsuitable, steep approach, varying levels of house.

☕🍴 Self-service, licensed (max 75). Home-made food.

🎫 Special tours £30 extra for groups of 15, 7 days' notice.

🅿 Ample, 450 yds from house. £1 per car.

🎭 Tours of the house bring alive Haddon Hall of old. Costume room also available, very popular!

🐕 Guide dogs only. 💍 Tel for details.

East Midlands - England

MAP 6

Owner: High Peak Borough Council

▶ CONTACT

Leanne Holmes
Pavilion Gardens
St John's Road
Buxton
Derbyshire SK17 6XN

Tel: 01298 23114
Fax: 01298 27622

e-mail:
paviliongardens@
highpeak.gov.uk

▶ LOCATION

OS Ref. SK055 734

Situated on the A6 in the Peak District, within easy reach of Manchester, Sheffield and the East Midlands.

Rail: Buxton station $^1/_2$ m.

PAVILION GARDENS

www.paviliongardens.co.uk

PAVILION

With Grade II listed buildings dating from 1871 and 23 acres of beautiful Victorian landscaped gardens in the centre of Buxton on the River Wye, there are attractions to suit all tastes and ages.

The Pavilion hosts a range of fairs and events such as Antique, Book and Toy fairs to Classic Car Auctions, Tea Dances and Farmers' Markets.

There are facilities for conferences, seminars and meetings with a capacity to cater for up to 400 people with a full meal menu.

Visitors can also use the Restaurant, Café and Coffee Lounge or browse in the Food and Gift Shop, which specialises in locally produced goods.

GARDENS

Over the last 125 years, various changes have been made to the Gardens (they hosted the only Open Tennis Championships in the UK outside Wimbledon). The Gardens, originally designed by the eminent landscape gardener Edward Milner, have recently been restored to their original Victorian splendour, following a £4.5 million Heritage Lottery grant.

The bandstand is used on most summer Sundays, with brass bands playing from 2 - 4pm, when deckchairs are available on the terrace promenade.

There is also a colourful and relaxing Conservatory, housing an extensive range of flowers and plants, and which adjoins the renowned, Frank Matcham designed, Buxton Opera House.

▶ OPENING TIMES

Every day except Christmas Day.

Opens: 10am.

▶ ADMISSION

Free entry into building.

Charges vary for different events and fairs.

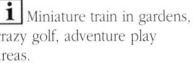 Miniature train in gardens, crazy golf, adventure play areas.

Food & gift shops.

Wedding receptions, banquets, functions & conferences.

Partial.

Licensed.

P Charge applies

In gardens on leads. Guide dogs only in Pavilion.

Tel for details.

English Heritage Photo Library/Jonathan Bailey

BOLSOVER CASTLE ⌗

CASTLE STREET, BOLSOVER, DERBYSHIRE S44 6PR

www.english-heritage.org.uk/visits

Tel: 01246 822844

Owner: English Heritage   **Contact:** Visitor Operations Team

An enchanting and romantic spectacle, situated high on a wooded hilltop dominating the surrounding landscape. Built on the site of a Norman castle, this is largely an early 17th century mansion. Most delightful is the 'Little Castle', with intricate carvings, panelling and wall painting. See the restored interiors of the Little Castle including the only remaining copies of Titian's Caesar Paintings, and the Venus Fountain and statuary. There is also an impressive 17th century indoor Riding House built by the Duke of Newcastle. Enjoy the Visitor and Discovery Centre. Exciting recent interpretation scheme includes Audio/Visual and scale model of Little Castle. Also contemporary Visitor Centre with information about Bolsover town's development. Picnickers are welcome. (Bolsover is now available for Civil weddings, receptions and corporate hospitality.)

Location: OS120, SK471 707. Signposted from M1/J29, 6m from Mansfield. In Bolsover 6m E of Chesterfield on A632.

Open: Apr, Oct & Nov - Mar: Thur - Mon, 10am - 5pm (Nov - Mar 4pm). 1 May - 30 Sept: daily, 10am - 6pm. Closes 4pm on Sats all year. Closed 24 - 26 Dec & 1 Jan. May close earlier for evening events.

Admission: Adult £6.60, Child £3.30, Conc. £5, Family £16.50. 15% discount for groups (11+).

▢ ☎ ♿Grounds. WC. ◼Airconditioned café. 𝕂 ▢Free with admission. ▣ ▥ ✖ ▲ ✳ ♿ Tel for details.

NT Photographic Library; Rupert Truman

NT Photographic Library; Andreas von Einsiedel

CALKE ABBEY ✿

TICKNALL, DERBYSHIRE DE73 1LE

www.nationaltrust.org.uk

Tel: 01332 863822   **Fax:** 01332 865272   **e-mail:** calkeabbey@nationaltrust.org.uk

Owner: The National Trust   **Contact:** The Property Manager

The house that time forgot, this baroque mansion, built 1701 - 3 for Sir John Harpur, is set in a landscaped park. Little restored, Calke is preserved by a programme of conservation as a graphic illustration of the English country house in decline; it contains the family's collection of natural history, a magnificent 18th century state bed and interiors that are virtually unchanged since the 1880s. Walled garden, pleasure grounds and orangery. Early 19th century Church. Historic parkland with Portland sheep and deer. Staunton Harold Church is nearby.

Location: OS128, SK356 239. 10m S of Derby, on A514 at Ticknall between Swadlincote and Melbourne.

Open: House, Garden & Church: 18 Mar - 29 Oct: Sat - Wed; House: 12.30 - 5.30pm (ticket office opens 11am). Closed 10 - 12 Aug for concert. Garden & Church: 11am - 5.00pm. Park: most days until 8pm or dusk. Shop & Restaurant: 18 Mar - 29 Oct: as house, 10.30am - 5.00pm. 4 - 26 Nov & Jan - Mar 2007: Sat & Sun, 11am - 4pm; also 27 Nov - 17 Dec: Sat - Wed, 11am - 4pm.

Admission: All sites: Adult £6.80, Child £3.40, Family £17. Garden only: Adult £4.20, Child £2.10, Family £10.50. Discount for pre-booked groups.

▢ ♿House. Braille guide. Wheelchairs. WCs. ⁋Licensed. 𝕂By arrangement. ✖In park, on leads only. ✳

CARNFIELD HALL

South Normanton, Nr Alfreton, Derbyshire DE55 2BE

Tel: 01773 520084

Owner/Contact: J B Cartland

Unspoilt Elizabethan manor house. Panelled rooms and two Jacobean staircases. Since 1502 home of the Revell, Wilmot, Radford and Cartland families. 300 years of fascinating contents. Old walled garden and deer park in course of restoration. (Adjoining garden centre/café.)

Location: OS Ref. SK425 561. 1 1/2 m W of M1/J28 on B6019. Alfreton Station 5 mins walk.

Open: By appointment. Groups 8 - 25.

Admission: £5. Evening visits £7.

No photography in Hall. Park available for events. Grounds. Obligatory. In grounds, on leads only.

CATTON HALL

CATTON, WALTON-ON-TRENT, SOUTH DERBYSHIRE DE12 8LN

www.catton-hall.com

Tel: 01283 716311 **Fax:** 01283 712876 **e-mail:** kneilson@catton-hall.com

Owner/Contact: Robin & Katie Neilson

Catton, built in 1745, has been in the hands of the same family since 1405 and is still lived in by the Neilsons as their private home. This gives the house, with its original collection of 17th and 18th century portraits, pictures and antique furniture, a unique, relaxed and friendly atmosphere. With its spacious reception rooms, luxurious bedrooms and delicious food and wine, Catton is centrally located for residential or non-residential business meetings, product launches and team-building activities, as well as for accommodation for those visiting Birmingham, the NEC, the Belfry, the Potteries and Dukeries – or just for a weekend celebration of family and friends. The acres of parkland alongside the River Trent are ideal for all types of corporate and public events.

Location: OS Ref. SK206 154. 2m E of A38 at Alrewas between Lichfield & Burton-on-Trent (8m from each). Birmingham NEC 20m.

Open: By prior arrangement all year for corporate hospitality, shooting parties, wedding receptions, private groups. Guided tours: 3 Apr - 9 Oct. Mons, 2pm (Groups 15+ by prior arrangemnet)).

Conference facilities. By arrangement. By arrangement for groups. 3 x four posters, 5 twin, all en-suite.

CHATSWORTH

See page 308 for full page entry.

CROMFORD MILL

MILL LANE, CROMFORD DE4 3RQ

www.arkwrightsociety.org.uk

Tel: 01629 823256 **e-mail:** smcleod@arkwrightsociety.org.uk

Owner: The Arkwright Society **Contact:** The Visitor Services Dept.

Built in 1771, Cromford Mill is the world's first successful water powered cotton spinning mill, set in the beautiful Derwent Valley surrounded by limestone tors and rolling hills. There is a wholefood restaurant on site with shops, free car parking and friendly staff. A tour guide will explain the story of this important historic site and describe the development plans for the future.

Location: OS Ref. SK296 569. 3m S of Matlock, 17m N of Derby just off A6.

Open: All year except Christmas Day, 9am - 5pm.

Admission: Free entry. Guided tours: Adult £2, Conc. £1.50.

Partial. WCs. In grounds, on leads.

ELVASTON CASTLE COUNTRY PARK

Borrowash Road, Elvaston, Derbyshire DE72 3EP

Tel: 01332 571342 **Fax:** 01332 758751

Owner: Derbyshire County Council **Contact:** The Park Manager

200 acre park landscaped in 19th century by William Barron. Walled garden.

Location: OS Ref. SK407 330. 5m SE of Derby, 2m from A6 or A52.

Open: Please contact park for details.

Admission: Park and Gardens Free. Car park: Midweek 80p, weekends/BHs £1.40, Coaches £8.

Ground floor & grounds. WCs. By arrangement. In grounds, under close control.

Pavilion Gardens, Buxton.

EYAM HALL

EYAM, HOPE VALLEY, DERBYSHIRE S32 5QW

www.eyamhall.com

Tel: 01433 631976   **Fax:** 01433 631603   **e-mail:** nicola@eyamhall.com

Owner: Mr R H V Wright   **Contact:** Mrs N Wright

This small but charming manor house in the famous plague village of Eyam has been the home of the Wright family since 1671 and it retains the intimate atmosphere of a much-loved private home. The restoration of the beautiful walled garden is nearing completion. A Craft Centre in the historic farmyard houses crafts people at work. Licensed for Civil wedding ceremonies, Eyam Hall is ideal for both intimate in-house and larger marquee receptions.

Location: OS119, SK216 765. Approx 10m from Sheffield, Chesterfield and Buxton. Eyam is off A623 between Stockport and Chesterfield. Eyam Hall is in the centre of the village, past the church.

Open: House & Garden: Easter Sun & Mon, 2 July - 31 Aug: Wed, Thur, Sun & BH Mon, 12 noon - 4pm. (Booked parties May - Sept.) Craft Centre: Tel for details.

Admission: Adult £6.25, Child £4, Conc. £5.75. Family (2+4) £19. Group rates available. Craft Centre: Free.

ℹ️ Craft Centre. 📷 📺 ♿ Partial. 🍴 Licensed. 👤 Obligatory. 🅿️ 🖼️
🐕 In grounds, on leads. Guide dogs only in house. ▲ ❄️ 🛡️ Tel for details.

HADDON HALL 🏠   *See page 309 for full page entry.*

HARDSTOFT HERB GARDEN

Hall View Cottage, Hardstoft, Chesterfield, Derbyshire S45 8AH

Tel: 01246 854268

Owner: Mr Stephen Raynor/L M Raynor   **Contact:** Mr Stephen Raynor

Consists of four display gardens with information boards and well labelled plants.

Location: OS Ref. SK436 633. On B6039 between Holmewood & Tibshelf, 3m from J29 on M1.

Open: Gardens, Nursery & Tearoom: 15 Mar - 15 Sept: Wed - Sun, 10am - 5pm. Closed Mon & Tue except Easter and BHs when open throughout.

Admission: Adult £1.50, Child Free.

corporate hospitality
see page 568

HARDWICK HALL, GARDENS, PARK & STAINSBY MILL 🌿

DOE LEA, CHESTERFIELD, DERBYSHIRE S44 5QJ

www.nationaltrust.org.uk

Tel: 01246 850430   **Fax:** 01246 858424   **Shop/Restaurant:** 01246 858409
e-mail: hardwickhall@nationaltrust.org.uk

Owner: The National Trust   **Contact:** The Property Manager

Hardwick Hall: A late 16th century 'prodigy house' designed by Robert Smythson for Bess of Hardwick. The house contains outstanding contemporary furniture, tapestries and needlework including pieces identified in an inventory of 1601; a needlework exhibition is on permanent display. Walled courtyards enclose fine gardens, orchards and a herb garden. The country park contains Whiteface Woodland sheep and Longhorn cattle.

Location: OS120, SK456 651. 7½ m NW of Mansfield, 9½ m SE of Chesterfield: approach from M1/J29 via A6175.

Open: Hall: 25 Mar - 29 Oct: Wed, Thur, Sat, Sun, BH Mon & Good Fri: 12 noon - 4.30pm. Gardens: as Hall, Wed - Sun, 11am - 5.30pm. Parkland: daily. Shop: As Hall, 11am - 5pm. Restaurant: As Shop. Stone centre: 25 Mar - 29 Oct Weds, Thur, Sat, Sun, 11am - 1pm, 2 - 4pm.

Admission: Hall & Garden: Adult £7.80, Child £3.90, Family £19.50. Garden only: Adult £4, Child £2, Family £10. Joint ticket for Hall (NT) and Old Hall (EH): Adult £10.60, Child £5.30, Family £26.50 (NT members Free). Pre-booking for groups essential, discount for groups of 15+. Timed tickets on busy days.

Hardwick Estate - Stainsby Mill is an 18th century water-powered corn mill in working order.

Location: OS120, SK455 653. From M1/J29 take A6175, signposted to Clay Cross then first left and left again to Stainsby Mill.

Open: 25 Mar - 29 Jun & 2 Sept - 29 Oct: Wed, Thur, Sat, Sun, BH Mons & Good Fri; 1 Jul - 31 Aug: Wed - Sun & BH Mons plus 26 Dec & 1 Jan 2007, 11am - 4.30pm.

Admission: Adult £2.60, Child £1.30, Family £6.50. No discounts for groups, suitable for school groups. For information send SAE to Property Manager at Hardwick Hall.

📷 ♿ Garden, Hall: 3 display rooms only. 🍴 Licensed. 🖼️ 🐕 In park, on leads.

HARDWICK OLD HALL ⌗

DOE LEA, Nr CHESTERFIELD, DERBYSHIRE S44 5QJ

www.english-heritage.org.uk/visits

Tel: 01246 850431

Owner: National Trust, managed by English Heritage

Contact: Visitor Operations Team

This large ruined house, finished in 1591, still displays Bess of Hardwick's innovative planning and interesting decorative plasterwork. New graphics panels will focus on the rich interiors Bess created. The views from the top floor over the country park and 'New' Hall are spectacular. Picnickers are welcome.

Location: OS120, SK463 638. $7^1/_2$ m NW of Mansfield, $9^1/_2$ m SE of Chesterfield, off A6175, from M1/J29.

Open: 1 Apr - 30 Sept: Wed, Thur, Sat & Sun, 10am - 6pm.

Admission: Adult £3.50, Child £1.80, Conc. £2.60, Family £8.80. 15% discount for groups (11+).

⬜ ⬜Free with admission. ⬛ 🅿 ♿On leads.

Bolsover Castle.

KEDLESTON HALL ✻

DERBY DE22 5JH

www.nationaltrust.org.uk

Tel: 01332 842191   **Fax:** 01332 844059   **e-mail:** kedlestonhall@nationaltrust.org.uk

Owner: The National Trust

Contact: The Property Manager

Experience the age of elegance in this neo-classical house built between 1759 and 1765 for the Curzon family and little altered since. Set in 800 acres of parkland with an 18th century pleasure ground, garden and woodland walks – a day at Kedleston is truly an experience to remember. The influence of the architect Robert Adam is everywhere, from the Park buildings to the decoration of the magnificent state rooms. Groups are welcome and an introductory talk from the 18th century housekeeper can be arranged. Guided tours of the Hall, gardens, stables and fishing pavilion. Tel for times and prices.

Location: OS Ref. SK312 403. 5m NW of Derby, signposted from roundabout where A38 crosses A52 Derby ring road.

Open: House: 11 Mar - 29 Oct: Sat - Wed (open Good Fri), 12 noon - 4.30pm.

Garden: as house: daily, 10am - 6pm. Park: as garden and 30 Oct - 9 Mar: daily, 10am - 4pm. Occasional day restrictions may apply in Dec 2006 & Jan 2007. Shop: 11 Mar - 29 Oct: Sat - Wed, 11.30am - 5.30pm (27 Jul - 1 Sept: daily, 12 noon - 4pm) 4 Nov - 4 Mar 07: Sat & Sun, 12 noon - 4pm. Restaurant: 11 Mar - 29 Oct: Sat - Wed, 11am - 5pm; 27 Jul - 1 Sep: daily, 12 noon - 4pm; 4 Nov - 4 Mar 07: Sat & Sun, 12 noon - 4pm. Church 11 Mar - 29 Oct: Sat - Wed, 11am - 5pm. Closed 25/26 Dec.

Admission: Adult £6.90, Child £3.30, Family £17. Garden & Park: Adult £3.10, Child £1.55, Family £7.70. (Park & garden ticket refundable against tickets for house). Winter admission for Park only, £3.00 per vehicle.

⬜ ♿Wheelchairs are available on the State floor, tel for details. Access to the basement and comprehensive book with photographs and descriptions of the State floor. 🍴 Licensed. 🐕 ♿In park (but not Long Walk), on leads. 🔔 📺Tel for details.

MELBOURNE HALL & GARDENS 🏛

MELBOURNE, DERBYSHIRE DE73 8EN

www.melbournehall.com

Tel: 01332 862502   **Fax:** 01332 862263

Owner: Lord & Lady Ralph Kerr   **Contact:** Mrs Gill Weston

This beautiful house of history, in its picturesque poolside setting, was once the home of Victorian Prime Minister William Lamb. The fine gardens, in the French formal style, contain Robert Bakewell's intricate wrought iron arbour and a fascinating yew tunnel. Upstairs rooms available to view by appointment.

Location: OS Ref. SK389 249. 8m S of Derby. From London, exit M1/J24.

Open: Hall: Aug only (not first 3 Mons) 2 - 5pm. Last admission 4.15pm. Gardens: 1 Apr - 30 Sept: Weds, Sats, Suns, BH Mons, 1.30 - 5.30pm. Additional open days possible in August, please telephone for details.

Admission: Hall: Adult £3.50, Child £2, OAP £3. Gardens: Adult £3, Child/OAP £2. Hall & Gardens: Adult £5.50, Child £3.50, OAP £4.50.

ℹ️ Crafts. No photography in house. 📷 ♿ Partial. 🐕 👤 Obligatory in house. 🅿️ Limited. No coach parking. 🦮 Guide dogs only.

RENISHAW HALL GARDENS 🏛

SHEFFIELD, DERBYSHIRE S21 3WB

www.sitwell.co.uk

Tel: 01246 432310   **Fax:** 01246 430760   **e-mail:** info2@renishaw-hall.co.uk

Owner: Sir Reresby Sitwell Bt DL   **Contact:** The Administrator

Home of Sir Reresby and Lady Sitwell. Eight acres of Italian style formal gardens stand in 300 acres of mature parkland, encompassing statues, shaped yew hedges, herbaceous borders, a water garden and lakes. The Sitwell museum and art galleries are located in Georgian stables alongside craft workshops and Gallery café, furnished with contemporary art. Beautiful camellias and carpets of daffodils in April.

Location: OS Ref. SK435 786. On A6135 3m from M1/J30, equidistant from Sheffield and Chesterfield.

Open: 30 Mar - 1 Oct: Thurs - Sun & BHs, 10.30am - 4.30pm. Hall is not open to the general public, private groups (25+) only by prior arrangement. Hall tours may be booked.

Admission: Garden, Museum & Galleries: Adult £5, Conc. £4.20, Under 10s Free.

📷 👥 🍴 ♿ 🐕 👤 By arrangement. 🅿️ 🦮 In grounds, on leads. 🔺 🌸 Bluebell fortnight (27 Apr - 14 May).

PAVILION GARDENS   *See page 310 for full page entry.*

PEVERIL CASTLE ⌗

Market Place, Castleton, Hope Valley S33 8WQ

Tel: 01433 620613   **www.**english-heritage.org.uk/visits

Owner: English Heritage   **Contact:** Visitor Operations Team

There are breathtaking views of the Peak District from this castle, perched high above the pretty village of Castleton. The great square tower of Henry II stands almost to its original height. A walkway opens up new areas and views from the first floor of the Keep. Peveril Castle is one of the earliest Norman castles to be built in England. The new Peveril Castle Visitor Centre has displays which tell the story of Peveril as the focal point of the Royal Forest of the Peak as well as improved access and facilities. Picnickers are welcome.

Location: OS110, SK150 827. S side of Castleton, 15m W of Sheffield on A6187.

Open: 1 Apr - 31 Oct: daily, 10am - 5pm (6pm May - Aug). 1 Nov - 31 Mar: Thur - Mon, 10am - 4pm. Closed 24 - 26 Dec & 1 Jan.

Admission: Adult £3.50, Child £1.80, Conc. £2.60, Family £8.80. 15% discount for groups (11+).

ℹ️ WCs 📷 ◼ 🦮 ✳️ 🌸 Tel for details.

SUTTON SCARSDALE HALL ⌗

Chesterfield, Derbyshire

Tel: 01604 735400 (Regional Office)   **www.**english-heritage.org.uk/visits

Owner: English Heritage   **Contact:** The East Midlands Regional Office

The dramatic hilltop shell of a great early 18th century baroque mansion.

Location: OS Ref. SK441 690. Between Chesterfield & Bolsover, 1½ m S of Arkwright Town.

Open: Daily in summer: 10am - 6pm (4pm rest of year). Closed 24 - 26 Dec & 1 Jan.

Admission: Free.

♿ 🅿️ ✳️

Tissington Hall.

Derbyshire Countryside Ltd

TISSINGTON HALL

ASHBOURNE, DERBYSHIRE DE6 1RA

www.tissington-hall.com

Tel: 01335 352200 **Fax:** 01335 352201 **e-mail:** tisshall@dircon.co.uk

Owner/Contact: Sir Richard FitzHerbert Bt

Home of the FitzHerbert family for over 500 years. The Hall stands in a superbly maintained estate village, and contains wonderful panelling and fine old masters. A 10 acre garden and arboretum. Schools very welcome. Award-winning Old Coach House Tearoom, open Apr - Oct: daily; Nov - Mar, Thurs - Sun, 11am - 5pm for coffees, lunch and tea.

Location: OS Ref. SK175 524. 4m N of Ashbourne off A515 towards Buxton.

Open: 17 - 21 Apr, 29 May - 2 Jun: daily. 25 Jul - 25 Aug: Tue - Fri.

Admission: Hall & Gardens: Adult £6.50, Child (10-16yrs) £3.50, Conc. £5, Gardens only: Adult £3, Child £2, Conc. £3.

ℹ️ No photography in house. 🇹 🅢 Partial. WCs at tearooms. 🅟 Tearoom adjacent to Hall. 🇫 Obligatory. 🅟 Limited. 🅜 🅴 Guide dogs only. 🅐 ✳️ 🅥 Tel for details.

Chatsworth.

BELVOIR CASTLE

www.belvoircastle.com

MAP 7

Owner:
Their Graces The Duke & Duchess of Rutland

▶ CONTACT
Mary McKinlay
Castle Opening Office
Belvoir Castle
Grantham
Leicestershire NG32 1PE

Tel: 01476 871002
Fax: 01476 871018
e-mail: info@
belvoircastle.com

▶ LOCATION
OS Ref. SK820 337
A1 from London 110m
Grantham Junction
York 100m. Leicester 30m
Grantham 7m.
Nottingham 20m.

Air: Nottingham
& Robin Hood Airports.
Helicopter Landing Pad.

Rail: Grantham Stn 7m

Bus: Melton Mowbray -
Vale of Belvoir via
Castle Car Park.

Taxi: Grantham Taxis
01476 563944 / 563988.

CONFERENCE/FUNCTION

ROOM	SIZE	MAX CAPACITY
State Dining Room	52' x 31'	130
Regents Gallery	131' x 16'	220
Old Kitchen	45' x 22'	100
Ballroom		90
Guards Room		175
Stewards Restaurant		100

Belvoir Castle, home of the Duke and Duchess of Rutland, commands a magnificent view over the Vale of Belvoir. The name Belvoir, meaning beautiful view, dates back to Norman times, when Robert de Todeni, Standard Bearer to William the Conqueror, built the first castle on this superb site. Destruction caused by two Civil Wars and by a catastrophic fire in 1816 have breached the continuity of Belvoir's history. The present building owes much to the inspiration and taste of Elizabeth, 5th Duchess of Rutland and was built after the fire.

Inside the Castle are notable art treasures including works by Poussin, Holbein, Rubens, and Reynolds, Gobelin and Mortlake tapestries, Chinese silks, furniture, fine porcelain and sculpture.

The Queen's Royal Lancers' Museum at Belvoir has a fascinating exhibition of the history of the Regiment, as well as a fine collection of weapons, uniforms and medals.

GARDENS
A remarkable survival of English garden history that are being sensitively restored to their former glory. The Spring Gardens, opened to all day visitors in 2005, contain a collection of Victorian daffodils planted sympathetically with primroses and bluebells, against a background of rhododendrons and azaleas. There are also rare specimen trees, many the largest of their type in the British Isles.

Belvoir Castle is available for exclusive hire as a film location and for conferences, weddings and special events. It is also possible to put on events in conjunction with the open season.

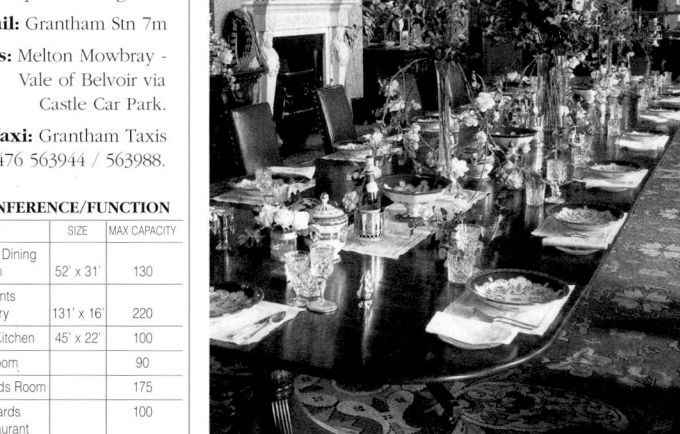

Suitable for exhibitions, product launches, conferences, filming, photography welcomed (permit £2).

Banquets, private room available.

Ground floor and restaurant accessible. Please telephone for advice. WC.

Licensed. Groups catered for (100 max).

Tue - Thur, twice daily. Tour time: 1¼ hrs. Specialist picture and costume tours.

Ample. £1 per car at weekends. Coaches can take passengers to entrance by arrangement but should report to the main car park and ticket office on arrival.

Guided tours. Teacher's pack. Education room. Picnic area and adventure playground.

Guide dogs only.

Belvoir Castle is a day out for all the family and hosts different events every weekend from jousting to medieval re-enactments. Tel for details.

▶ OPENING TIMES
Summer
1 April - 30 September:
Tues - Thurs, Sats & Suns,
(open BH Mon &
Good Fri).

Winter
October: Suns only;
3 - 8 December.
11am - 5pm.
Last entry 4pm.

Groups welcome by appointment.

▶ ADMISSION
Adult	£10.00
Child (5-16yrs)	£5.00
Conc.	£9.00
Family (2+2/3)	£26.00

Groups (15+)
Adult	£8.00
Child (5-16yrs)	£4.50
Conc.	£7.00
School	£4.50

Grounds only
Adult/Conc.	£5.00
Child (5-16yrs)	Free

Spring Garden Tours (15+)
Adult	£7.50
Conc.	£6.50

MAP 7

Owner:
Mr Frederick de Lisle

▶ **CONTACT**

Mrs F de Lisle
Quenby Hall
Hungarton
Nr Leicester LE7 9JF

Tel/Fax: 0116 2595224

e-mail: enquiries@
quenbyhall.co.uk

▶ **LOCATION**
OS Ref. SK702 065

7m E of Leicester,
20 mins from M1/J21A,
40 mins A1.

Air: East Midlands
International 25 mins.

Rail: Market
Harborough.

QUENBY HALL

www.quenbyhall.co.uk

Quenby Hall lies seven miles east of Leicester and is a perfect and unspoiled example of a Jacobean country house. It was built by George Ashby in 1627. Amidst ancient cedars and beeches, it commands magnificent views of the countryside, in the secluded setting of 1400 acres of gardens, parkland and farm.

Stilton cheese was invented by the housekeeper at Quenby Hall. It was sold by her daughter who lived at the popular staging inn at Stilton, on the Great North Road: hence its name.

It is the private home of the de Lisle family and has been extensively restored, making it exceptionally warm and comfortable whilst remaining true to its Jacobean style, with beautiful panelling, plaster and stonework and other architectural features. It is not open to the public and is available for exclusive hire as a film location and for conferences, weddings and special events. The Old Dairy, with its old beams, stone floor and more 'country' ambience, is also available for hire.

Full exclusive use of the rooms can be made by groups numbering up to 150. Dinners can be held for up to 80 in the house with dancing in the old Dairy, or up to 300 in a marquee on the back lawn. Four beautiful ensuite bedrooms, two with four posters, available by special arrangement.

▶ **OPENING TIMES**

Not open to the public. Available for exclusive hire as a film location and for conferences, weddings and special events.

▶ **ADMISSION**

Please contact property for details.

 Banquets, private room available.

By arrangement.

Ample.

By arrangement.

Tel for details.

MAP 7

Owner:
Nicholas Fothergill Esq

▶ **CONTACT**

Robert Thomas or
Sarah Maughan
Stanford Hall
Lutterworth
Leicestershire
LE17 6DH

Tel: 01788 860250
Fax: 01788 860870

e-mail: enquiries@
stanfordhall.co.uk

▶ **LOCATION**

OS Ref. SP587 793

M1/J18 6m,
M1/J19 (from/to
the N only) 2m,
M6 exit/access at
A14/M1(N)J 2m,
A14 2m.
Follow Historic
House signs.

Rail: Rugby Stn 7^1/$_2$ m.

Air: Birmingham
Airport 27m.

Taxi: Fone-A-Car.
01788 543333.

STANFORD HALL ⛫

www.stanfordhall.co.uk

Stanford has been the home of the Cave family, ancestors of the present owner, since 1430. In the 1690s, Sir Roger Cave commissioned the Smiths of Warwick to pull down the old Manor House and build the present Hall, which is an excellent example of their work and of the William and Mary period.

As well as over 5000 books, the handsome Library contains many interesting manuscripts, the oldest dating from 1150. The splendid pink and gold Ballroom has a fine coved ceiling with four *trompe l'oeil* shell corners. Throughout the house are portraits of the family and examples of

furniture and objects which they collected over the centuries. There is also a collection of Royal Stuart portraits, previously belonging to the Cardinal Duke of York, the last of the male Royal Stuarts. An unusual collection of family costumes is displayed in the Old Dining Room, which also houses some early Tudor portraits and a fine Empire chandelier.

The Hall and Stables are set in an attractive Park on the banks of Shakespeare's Avon. There is a walled Rose Garden behind the Stables. An early ha-ha separates the North Lawn from the mile-long North Avenue.

▶ **OPENING TIMES**

Summer
16 April - 24 September:
Sun & BH Mons,
1.30 - 5.30pm,
last admission 5pm.

NB. Grounds open
12 noon on BH Suns &
Mons and earlier on event
days.

House open any day or
evening (except Saturdays)
for pre-booked groups.

Winter
25 September - 7 April
2007: Closed to public.
Available during October
for corporate events.

▶ **ADMISSION**

House & Grounds
Adult £5.00
Child (5-15yrs) £2.00
Groups (20+)
Adult £4.75
Child (5-15yrs) £1.80

Grounds only
Adult £3.00
Child (5-15yrs) £1.00

CONFERENCE/FUNCTION

ROOM	SIZE	MAX CAPACITY
Ballroom	39' x 26'	100
Old Dining Rm	30' x 20'	20
Crocodile Room	39' x 20'	60

ℹ️ Craft centre (most Suns). No photography in house. Corporate days, clay pigeon shoots, filming, photography, small conferences and fashion shows. Parkland, helicopter landing area, lecture room, Blüthner piano.

🛍️

🍽️ Lunches, dinners & wedding receptions (outside caterers).

♿ Visitors may alight at the entrance. WC.

☕ Teas, lunch & supper. Groups must book (70 max.)

🚶 Tour time: ^{3}/$_4$ hr in groups of approx 25.

🅿️ 1,000 cars and 6 - 8 coaches. Free meals for coach drivers, coach parking on gravel in front of house.

🐕 In Park, on leads.

♿ Tel for details.

ASHBY DE LA ZOUCH CASTLE ⚔

South Street, Ashby de la Zouch, Leicestershire LE65 1BR

Tel: 01530 413343 **www.**english-heritage.org.uk/visits

Owner: English Heritage **Contact:** Visitor Operations Team

The impressive ruins of this late medieval castle are dominated by a magnificent tower, over 80 feet high, which was split in two during the Civil War. Panoramic views. Explore the tunnel linking the kitchens to the Hastings Tower.

Location: OS128, SK363 167. In Ashby de la Zouch, 12m S of Derby on A511. SE of town centre.

Open: 1 Apr - 30 Jun: Thur - Mon, 10am - 5pm. 1 Jul - 31 Aug: daily, 10am - 6pm. 1 Sept - 31 Mar: Thur - Mon, 10am - 5pm (4pm Nov - Mar). Closed 24 - 26 Dec & 1 Jan.

Admission: Adult £3.40, Child £1.70, Conc. £2.60, Family £8.50. 15% discount for groups (11+).

ℹ️WC. 📷 ♿Grounds. 🎧Free with admission. 🅿️Restricted.■ 🐕On leads. ❋ 🛡️Tel for details.

BELVOIR CASTLE 🏛

See page 317 for full page entry

BRADGATE PARK & SWITHLAND WOOD COUNTRY PARK

Bradgate Park, Newtown Linford, Leics

Tel: 0116 2362713

Owner: Bradgate Park Trust **Contact:** M H Harrison

Includes the ruins of the brick medieval home of the Grey family and childhood home of Lady Jane Grey. Also has a medieval deer park.

Location: OS Ref. SK534 102. 7m NW of Leicester, via Anstey & Newtown Linford. Country Park gates in Newtown Linford. 1¼ m walk to the ruins.

Open: All year during daylight hours.

Admission: No charge. Car parking charges.

DONINGTON-LE-HEATH MANOR HOUSE

Manor Road, Donington-le-Heath, Leicestershire LE67 2FW

Tel: 01530 831259 / 0116 2658326

Owner/Contact: Leicestershire County Council

Medieval manor c1280 with 16th-17th century alterations.

Location: OS Ref. SK421 126. ½ m SSW of Coalville. 4½ m W of M1/J22, by A511.

Open: Mar - Nov: daily, 11am - 4pm. Dec - Feb: Sat & Sun only, 11am - 4pm. (Plus occasional weekdays. Tel for details.)

Admission: Free.

KIRBY MUXLOE CASTLE ⚔

Kirby Muxloe, Leicestershire LE9 9MD

Tel: 01604 735400 **www.**english-heritage.org.uk/visits

Owner: English Heritage **Contact:** East of England Regional Office (01223 528700)

Picturesque, moated, brick built castle begun in 1480 by William Lord Hastings. The castle is presently closed subject to the completion of major conservation work and is due to re-open in 2007.

Location: OS140, SK524 046. 4m W of Leicester off B5380.

Open: Closed for conservation work until 2007.

LYDDINGTON BEDE HOUSE ⚔

Blue Coat Lane, Lyddington, Uppingham, Rutland LE15 9LZ

Tel: 01572 822438 **www.**english-heritage.org.uk/visits

Owner: English Heritage **Contact:** Visitor Operations Team

Located in this picturesque 'Cotswold' village of honey coloured stone cottages and public houses lies the splendid former 'palace' of the powerful medieval Bishops of Lincoln. In the 1600s the building was converted into an almshouse.

Location: OS141, SP875 970. In Lyddington, 6m N of Corby, 1m E of A6003.

Open: 1 Apr - 31 Oct: Thur - Mon, 10am - 5pm.

Admission: Adult £3.40, Child £1.70, Conc. £2.60, Family £8.50. 15% group discount (11+).

📷 ♿Ground floor only. 🅿️ ■ 🛡️Tel for details.

OAKHAM CASTLE

Castle Lane (off Market Place), Oakham, Rutland LE15 6DF

Tel: 01572 758440 **www.**rutnet.co.uk/rcccastle

Owner: Rutland County Council **Contact:** Rutland County Museum

Exceptionally fine Norman Great Hall of a late 12th century fortified manor house, with contemporary musician sculptures. Bailey earthworks and remains of earlier motte. The hall contains over 200 unique horseshoes forfeited by royalty and peers of the realm to the Lord of the Manor from Edward IV onwards.

Location: OS Ref. SK862 088. Near town centre, E of the church. Off Market Place, Oakham.

Open: All year: Mon - Sat, 10.30am - 1pm & 1.30 - 5pm; Sun, 2 - 4pm. Closed Good Fri, Christmas and New Year.

Admission: Free.

📷 ♿Great Hall. 🅿️For disabled, on request. ■ ▲ ❋

QUENBY HALL

See page 318 for full page entry.

STANFORD HALL 🏛

See page 319 for full page entry.

STAUNTON HAROLD CHURCH ⛪

Staunton Harold Church, Ashby-de-la-Zouch, Leicestershire

Tel: 01332 863822 **Fax:** 01332 865272

One of the very few churches to be built during the Commonwealth, erected by Sir Robert Shirley, an ardent Royalist. The interior retains its original 17th century cushions and hangings and includes fine panelling and painted ceilings.

Location: OS Ref. SK379 208. 5m NE of Ashby-de-la-Zouch, W of B587.

Open: 7 Jun - 1 Sept: Wed - Sun, 1 - 4.30pm. 1 Apr - 29 Oct: Sat & Sun, 1 - 4.30pm.

Admission: £1 donation.

♿Partial. ■ At hall.

WARTNABY GARDENS

Melton Mowbray, Leicestershire LE14 3HY

Tel: 01664 822549 **Fax:** 01664 822231 **www.**wartnabygardenlabels.co.uk

Owner: Lady King

This garden has delightful little gardens within it, including a white garden and a sunken garden. There are good herbaceous borders, climbers and old fashioned roses, and a series of pools, woodland walks with primulas, ferns and several varieties of lily. There is an arboretum with a good collection of trees and shrub roses, and alongside the drive is a beech hedge in a Grecian pattern. Greenhouses, a fruit and vegetable garden with rose arches and cordon fruit.

Location: OS Ref. SK709 228. 4m NW of Melton Mowbray. From A606 turn W in Ab Kettleby for Wartnaby.

Open: 26 Feb "Promise of Spring" plants and bulbs for sale: 11am - 3pm. 4 Apr - 25 Jul: Tues, 9.30am - 12.30pm. 30 Apr (Plants for sale) & 18 Jun (Plant Fair): 11am - 4pm. Groups by appointment at other times.

Admission: Adult £2.50, Child Free. 26 Feb "Promise of Spring" £2.

🚻 26 Feb, 30 Apr & 18 June. ♿ ● 🅵By arrangement. 🅿️ Limited for coaches. 🐕In grounds on leads. ❋ 🛡️Tel for details.

Quenby Hall.

BURGHLEY HOUSE

www.burghley.co.uk

MAP 7

Owner:
Burghley House
Preservation Trust Ltd

▶ CONTACT

The House Manager
Burghley House
Stamford
Lincolnshire PE9 3JY

Tel: 01780 752451
Fax: 01780 480125

e-mail: burghley@
burghley.co.uk

▶ LOCATION

OS Ref. TF048 062

Burghley House
is 1m SE of Stamford.
From London, A1 2hrs.

Visitors entrance
is on B1443.

Rail: London -
Peterborough 1hr
(GNER).
Stamford Station
1 1/2 m, regular service
to Peterborough.

Taxi: Direct Line:
01780 481481.

CONFERENCE/FUNCTION

ROOM	SIZE	MAX CAPACITY
Great Hall	70' x 30'	150
Orangery	100' x 20'	120

Burghley House, home of the Cecil family for over 400 years, was built as a country seat during the latter part of the 16th century by Sir William Cecil, later Lord Burghley, principal adviser and Lord Treasurer to Queen Elizabeth.

The House was completed in 1587 and there have been few alterations to the architecture since that date thus making Burghley one of the finest examples of late Elizabethan design in England. The interior was remodelled in the late 17th century by John, 5th Earl of Exeter who was a collector of fine art on a huge scale, establishing the immense collection of art treasures at Burghley. Burghley is truly a 'Treasure House', containing one of the largest private collections of Italian art, unique examples of Chinese and Japanese porcelain and superb items of 18th century furniture. The remodelling work of the 17th century means that examples of the work of

the principal artists and craftsmen of the period are to be found at Burghley: Antonio Verrio, Grinling Gibbons and Louis Laguerre all made major contributions to the beautiful interiors.

PARK AND GARDENS

The house is set in a 300-acre deer park landscaped by 'Capability' Brown. A lake was created by him and delightful avenues of mature trees feature largely in his design. The park is home to a large herd of Fallow deer, established in the 16th century. The Sculpture Garden contains many specimen trees and shrubs and is a display area for a number of dramatic art works by contemporary sculptors. The sculptures are varied in style, but their placement is designed to provoke thought and accentuate the beauty of the surroundings. The private gardens around the house are open in April for the display of spring bulbs. Please telephone for details.

🛍️ ℹ️ Suitable for a variety of events, large park, golf course, helicopter landing area, cricket pitch. No photography in house.

♿ Visitors may alight at entrance. WC. Chair lift to Orangery Restaurant, house tour has two staircases one with chairlift.

🍴 Restaurant/tearoom. Groups can book in advance.

🧍 Available.

🅿️ Ample. Free refreshments for coach drivers.

📖 Welcome. Guide provided.

🚫🐕 No dogs in house. In park on leads.

🔔 Civil Wedding Licence.

🎭 Tel for details.

▶ OPENING TIMES

Summer
1 April - 29 October
(closed 8 September)
Daily (except Fridays)
11am - 5pm
(last admission 4.30pm).

Specialist, VIP and Twilight Tours available. Please telephone for details. Access to the Private Apartments is available by appointment.

Orangery Restaurant & Gift Shop
1 February - 1 April
Wed - Sun, 10am - 4pm.

1 April - 29 October
Daily (except Fridays),
10am - 6pm
(Gift Shop, 11am - 6pm).

South Gardens
April: Daily, 11am - 4pm.

Park
All year. Admission is free except on event days.

▶ ADMISSION

Adult	£9.00
Child (5 - 15yrs)	£4.00
Conc.	£8.00
Family	£22.00

Groups (20+)

Adult	£7.80
School (up to 14yrs)	£4.00

The Sculpture Garden
All year, 11am - 5pm. Free entry with house ticket otherwise:

Adult	£3.20
Child (5 - 15yrs)	£1.00

Season ticket

Adult	£10.00
Family (2+2)	£22.00

MAP 7

GRIMSTHORPE CASTLE, PARK & GARDENS

www.grimsthorpe.co.uk

Owner:
Grimsthorpe and
Drummond Castle
Trust Ltd

▶ CONTACT

Ray Biggs
Grimsthorpe Estate
Office
Grimsthorpe
Bourne, Lincolnshire
PE10 0LY

Tel: 01778 591205
Fax: 01778 591259

e-mail: ray@
grimsthorpe.co.uk

▶ LOCATION

OS Ref. TF040 230

TF040 230. 4m NW of
Bourne on A151, 8m E
of Colsterworth
roundabout off A1.

Home of the Willoughby de Eresby family since 1516. Examples of 13th century architecture and building styles from the Tudor period. The dramatic 18th century North Front is Sir John Vanbrugh's last major work. State Rooms and picture galleries with magnificent contents including tapestries, furniture and paintings. Unusual collection of thrones, fabrics and objects from the old House of Lords, associated with the family's hereditary Office of Lord Great Chamberlain.

The Grounds and Gardens

3,000 acre landscaped park with lakes, ancient woods, woodland walk with all-weather footpath, adventure playground, red deer herd. Family cycle trail. Park tours in a vehicle with the Ranger.

Unusual ornamental vegetable garden and orchard, created in the 1960s by the Countess of Ancaster and John Fowler. Intricate parterres lined with box hedges. Herbaceous border with yew topiary framing views across to the lake. Woodland garden.

Groups can explore the park from the comfort of their coach by booking a one-hour, escorted park tour, with opportunities to discover more about the site of the Cistercian Abbey, the ancient deer parks and extensive series of early tree-lined avenues.

ℹ️ No photography in house.

🛍️

🍸 Conferences (up to 50), inc catering.

♿ Partial. WC.

☕ Licensed.

🔑 Obligatory except Suns.

🅿️ Ample.

🖼️

🐕 In grounds, on leads.

🎭 Tel for details.

▶ OPENING TIMES

Castle
April - September: Suns, Thurs & BH Mons.

August: Sun - Thur.
1 - 4.30pm.

Park & Gardens
April, May & September: Suns, Thurs & BH Mons.
June - August: Sun - Thur.
11am - 6pm (Gardens open 12 noon).

Groups: Apr - Sept: by arrangement. Also evening candlelight supper tours.

▶ ADMISSION

Castle, Park & Garden
Adult £8.00
Child £3.50
Conc. £7.00
Family (2+2) £18.50

Park & Gardens
Adult £3.50
Child £2.00
Conc. £3.00
Family (2+2) £9.00

Special charges may be made for special events. Group rates on application.

AYSCOUGHFEE HALL MUSEUM & GARDENS

CHURCHGATE, SPALDING, LINCOLNSHIRE PE11 2RA

www.sholland.gov.uk

Tel: 01775 761161 **e-mail:** museum@sholland.gov.uk
Owner: South Holland District Council **Contact:** Museum Manager

Ayscoughfee Hall, a magnificent Grade II* listed building, of great architectural importance, was built in the 1450s. The Hall is set in extensive landscaped grounds, which include, amongst other impressive features, a memorial designed by Edward Lutyens. The building and gardens, combined, reflect the slendour of the Medieval, Georgian and Victorian ages.

Ayscoughfee Hall Museum re-opens to the public in Easter 2006 following an extensive restoration project, which has uncovered some very important and rare features. The Museum will explain the history of the Hall, and feature the lives of the people who lived there and in the surrounding Fens.

Location: OS Ref. TF249 223. E bank of the River Welland, 5 mins walk from Spalding town centre.
Open: Summer: Mon - Fri, 10.30am - 5pm (7pm Thurs). Sats & Suns, 9.30am - 4pm. Winter: 12 noon - 5pm. Sats & Suns, 9.30am - 4pm.
Admission: Free.

◻ T 🔾 Suitable. 🔾 ⚥ By arrangement. ◻ P Limited for cars. ◼ ✕ ✳

BURGHLEY HOUSE 🏛   *See page 321 for full page entry*

Thunder storm during Burghley Horse Trials 2005. Photograph by Tony Parkes. e-mail tonyparkes@eircom.net

BELTON HOUSE 💥
GRANTHAM, LINCOLNSHIRE NG32 2LS

www.nationaltrust.org.uk

Tel: 01476 566116 **Fax:** 01476 579071 **e-mail:** belton@nationaltrust.org.uk

Owner: The National Trust **Contact:** The Property Manager

Belton, considered by many to be the perfect English Country House, with stunning interiors, fine silver and furniture collections and the remnants of a collection of Old Masters. There are also huge garden scenes by Melchior d'Hondecoeter acquired by the last Earl. The 17th century saloon in the centre of the house is panelled and decorated with intricate limewood carvings of the Grinling Gibbons school. The virtually unaltered north-facing chapel has a baroque plaster ceiling by Edward Gouge. Built in 1685 - 88, Belton offers you a great day out whether you are looking for peace and tranquillity or lots to do. With magnificent formal gardens, Orangery, landscaped park with lakeside walk, woodland adventure playground and Bellmount Tower. Fine church with family monuments. Winners of "Excellence in Tourism" and Sandford Heritage Education awards 2002.

Location: OS Ref. SK929 395. 3m NE of Grantham on A607. Signed off the A1.

Open: House: 25 Mar - 29 Oct: Wed - Sun (open BH Mons & Good Fri), 12.30 - 5pm. Garden & Park: as house, 11am - 5.30pm (Aug: daily, 10.30am - 5.30pm). Garden only: 3 Nov - 17 Dec: Fri - Sun, 12 noon - 4pm. Shop & Restaurant: 25 Mar - 29 Oct: 11am - 5.15pm. 3 Nov - 17 Dec: Fri - Sun, 12 noon - 4pm.

Admission: Adult £8, Child £4.50, Family £22.50. Discount for groups. Grounds only: Adult £6, Child £3.50, Family £15.50.

▢ ▧ Partial. Please telephone for arrangements. ⊞ Licensed. 🅿 ▣ ▲

DODDINGTON HALL & GARDENS 🏛
LINCOLN LN6 4RU

www.doddingtonhall.com

Tel: 01522 694308 **Fax:** 01522 682584 **e-mail:** info@doddingtonhall.com

Owner: Mr & Mrs J J C Birch **Contact:** The Estate Office

Magnificent Smythson mansion which stands today as it was completed in 1600 with its walled gardens and gatehouse. The Hall has an elegant Georgian interior with a fine collection of porcelain, paintings and textiles, representing 400 years of unbroken family occupation. The five acres of beautiful gardens contain a superb layout of box-edged parterres, sumptuous borders that provide colour in all seasons, and a wild garden with a marvellous succession of spring bulbs and flowering shrubs set amongst mature trees. Nature trail into the nearby countryside. Private group visits and specialist tours welcomed. Special facilities for disabled and visually impaired visitors; please ring for details. Free children's activity trail with prize. Special interest group tours; textiles, porcelain, furniture etc. Choice of refreshments and meals available in charming restaurant. Please call the Estate Office to discuss your requirements. Innovative schools programme. Civil weddings in Doddington Hall and in the adjoining Littlehouse.

Location: OS Ref. SK900 710. 5m W of Lincoln on the B1190, signposted off the A46 bypass and A57.

Open: Gardens only: 19 Feb - 23 Apr: Suns & Easter Mon, 1 - 5pm. House & Gardens: 30 Apr - 27 Sept: Weds, Suns & BH Mons, 1 - 5pm. Gardens open 12 - 5pm & House 1 - 5pm.

Admission: House & Gardens: Adult £5.50, Child £2.75, Family £15.50. Gardens only: Adult £3.80, Child £1.90. Groups (20+): exclusive House opening and guided tour £7. Exclusive Head Gardener tour of Gardens £5.50. Discounts for groups on regualr opening days. RHS and HHA members Free.

ⓘ No photography in Hall. No stilettos. ▢▧⌨Gardens & ground floor. WC (please call for assistance). ▣ ⊞ ✍By arrangement. ⌨ Free. 🅿 ▣ ⌨ Guide dogs only. ▲ ⌨ Tel for details.

EASTON WALLED GARDENS

THE GARDEN OFFICE, EASTON, GRANTHAM, LINCOLNSHIRE NG33 5AP

www.eastonwalledgardens.co.uk

Tel: 01476 530063 **Fax:** 01476 530063 **e-mail:** info@eastonwalledgardens.co.uk

Owner: Sir Fred & Lady Cholmeley   **Contact:** Kate Kingston

President Franklin Roosevelt described these gardens as a *'Dream of Nirvana … almost too good to be true'*. 50 years later, the house was pulled down and the gardens abandoned. 100 years later see the ongoing revival of these magnificent gardens. Funded privately and with the support of visitors, this garden experience is like no other. Alongside the recovery of these 400 year old gardens are: fantastic snowdrops, David Austin Roses, Daffodil and Iris Collections, a cut flower garden, cottage garden and 80m of poppies. Teas and light lunches are served overlooking the garden. Groups can book out of hours if wished.

Location: OS Ref. SK938 274. 1m from A1 (between Stamford and Grantham) N of the Colsterworth roundabout. Right onto B6403 and follow signs.

Open: 11 - 19 Feb for snowdrops, 11am - 3pm. 2 Apr - 29 Sept: BH Mons, Weds, Fris & Suns, 11am - 4pm.

Admission: Adult £4, Child Free.

⬜ ⬛ ⬛ ⬛ Partial. WCs. ⬛ ⬛By arrangement. 🅿 Ample. ⬛ ⬛ Guide dogs only. ⬛

FULBECK MANOR

Fulbeck, Grantham, Lincolnshire NG32 3JN

Tel: 01400 272231 **Fax:** 01400 273545 **e-mail:** fane@fulbeck.co.uk

Owner/Contact: Mr Julian Francis Fane

Built c1580. 400 years of Fane family portraits. Open by written appointment. Guided tours by owner approximately 1¼ hours. Tearooms at Craft Centre, 100 yards, for light lunches and teas.

Location: OS Ref. SK947 505. 11m N of Grantham. 15m S of Lincoln on A607. Brown signs to Craft Centre & Tearooms and Stables.

Open: By written appointment.

Admission: Adult £6. Groups (10+) £5.

ℹ️No photography. ⬛Unsuitable. WCs. ⬛ ⬛ ⬛Obligatory. 🅿Ample. Limited for coaches. ⬛ Guide dogs only. ⬛ € .

GAINSBOROUGH OLD HALL ⬛

Parnell Street, Gainsborough, Lincolnshire DN21 2NB

Tel: 01427 612669 **www.english-heritage.org.uk/visits**

Owner: English Heritage   **Contact:** Visitor Operations Team

A large medieval manor house with a magnificent Great Hall and suites of rooms. A collection of historic furniture and a re-created medieval kitchen are on display.

Location: OS121, SK815 895. In centre of Gainsborough, opposite library.

Open: 2 Apr - 29 Oct: Sun 1 - 4.30pm, Mon - Sat, 10am - 5pm. 30 Oct - 7 Mar: Mon - Sat 10am - 5pm. Closed 24 - 26 & 31 Dec/1 Jan.

Admission: Adult £3.70, Child (5-15yrs) £2.50 (Under 5yrs Free), Conc. £2.50, Family (2+3) £9.99.

ℹ️WC. ⬛ ⬛ ⬛ ⬛

GRIMSTHORPE CASTLE, ⬛   *See page 322 for full page entry*
PARK & GARDENS

GUNBY HALL ⬛

Gunby, Spilsby, Lincolnshire PE23 5SS

Tel: 01909 486411 **Fax:** 01909 486377 **www**.nationaltrust.org.uk

Owner: The National Trust   **Contact:** Regional Office

A red brick house with stone dressings, built in 1700 and extended in 1870s. Within the house, there is good early 18th century wainscoting and a fine oak staircase, also English furniture and portraits by Reynolds. Also of interest is the contemporary stable block, a walled kitchen and flower garden, sweeping lawns and borders and an exhibition of Field Marshal Sir Archibald Montgomery-Massingberd's memorabilia. Gunby was reputedly Tennyson's 'haunt of ancient peace'.

Location: OS122, TF466 672. 2½ m NW of Burgh Le Marsh, 7m W of Skegness. On S side of A158 (access off roundabout).

Open: Ground floor of house & garden: 29 Mar - 27 Sept: Weds, 2 - 6pm. Last admission 5.30pm. Closed BHs. Garden also open Thurs, 2 - 6pm. House & garden also open Tues, Thurs & Fris by written appointment to J D Wrisdale at above address.

Admission: House & Garden: Adult £4.50, Child £2.30, Family £11.30. Garden only: Adult £3.30, Child £1.70, Family £8.30. No reduction for groups. Access roads unsuitable for coaches which must park in layby at gates ½ m from Hall.

⬛Grounds. ⬛In grounds, on leads.

HECKINGTON WINDMILL

Hale Road, Heckington, Sleaford, Lincolnshire NG34 9JW

Tel: 01529 461919   **Contact:** Derek James

Britain's last surviving eight sail windmill. Now in full working order.

Location: OS Ref. TF145 437. W side of B1394, S side of Heckington village.

Open: Contact property for details.

Admission: Ground floor & Shop: Free. Mill: Adult £1.50, Child 75p.

LEADENHAM HOUSE

Leadenham House, Lincolnshire LN5 0PU

Tel: 01400 273256 **Fax:** 01400 272237

Owner: Mr P Reeve   **Contact:** Mr and Mrs P Reeve

Late eighteenth century house in park setting.

Location: OS Ref. SK949 518. Entrance on A17 Leadenham bypass (between Newark and Sleaford).

Open: 1 - 5, 8 - 12 May, 11 - 15 & 18 - 22 & 25 - 30 Sept & Spring & Aug BHs: 2 - 5pm.

Admission: £3.50. Groups by prior arrangement only.

ⓘNo photography. 🅐 ✖

LINCOLN CASTLE

Castle Hill, Lincoln LN1 3AA

Tel: 01522 511068 **e-mail:** lincoln_castle@lincolnshire.gov.uk

Contact: The Manager

Built by William the Conqueror in 1068. Informative exhibition of the 1215 Magna Carta.

Location: OS Ref. SK975 718. Opposite west front of Lincoln Cathedral.

Open: BST: Sats, 9.30am - 5.30pm, Suns, 11am - 5.30pm. GMT: Mon - Sat: 9.30am - 4pm, Suns, 11am - 4pm. Closed Christmas Day, Boxing Day & New Year's Day. Opening times are subject to change.

Admission: Adult £4.50, Child £3.00, Family £13.50. Prices are subject to change.

LINCOLN CATHEDRAL

Lincoln LN2 1PZ

Tel: 01522 544544 **Fax:** 01522 511307   **Contact:** Communications Office

One of the finest medieval buildings in Europe.

Location: OS Ref. SK978 718. At the centre of Uphill, Lincoln.

Open: All year: Summer, 7.15am - 8pm. Winter, 7.15am - 6pm. Sun closing 6pm in Summer & 5pm in Winter. Tours of the floor, roof & tower available. Pre-booked groups welcome.

Admission: £4, Child (5-16yrs) £1, Child (under 5s) Free, Conc. £3, Family £10. Optional guided tours & photography Free. No charge on Sun or for services.

LINCOLN MEDIEVAL BISHOPS' PALACE ⌗

Minster Yard, Lincoln LN2 1PU

Tel: 01522 527468 **www.**english-heritage.org.uk/visits

Owner: English Heritage   **Contact:** Visitor Operations Team

Constructed in the late 12th century, the medieval bishops' palace was once one of the most important buildings in England. Built on hillside terraces, it has views of the cathedral and the Roman, medieval and modern city. See a virtual tour of the Palace, explore the grounds and see the award winning Contemporary Heritage Garden and Vineyard (most northerly exposed vineyard in Europe).

Location: OS121 Ref. SK981 717. S side of Lincoln Cathedral, in Lincoln.

Open: 1 Apr - 31 Oct: daily, 10am - 5pm (6pm Jul - Aug). 1 Nov - 31 Mar: Thur - Mon, 10am - 4pm. Closed 24 - 26 Dec & 1 Jan. Open daily for Lincoln Christmas Market.

Admission: Adult £3.70, Child £1.90, Conc. £2.80, Family £9.30. 15% discount for groups (11+).

🔲 ⌂ 🅿 Limited disability parking only. ✖ ✳ ⊻ Tel for details.

MARSTON HALL

Marston, Grantham NG32 2HQ

Tel/Fax: 07812 356237 **e-mail:** thorold@fsworld.co.uk

Owner/Contact: J R Thorold

The ancient home of the Thorold family. The building contains Norman, Plantaganet, Tudor and Georgian elements through to the modern day. Marston Hall is undergoing continuous restoration some of it which may be disruptive. Please telephone in advance of intended visits.

Location: OS Ref. SK893 437. 5m N of Grantham and about 1m E of A1.

Open: 25 - 27 Feb, 18 - 21 Mar, 13 - 17 & 29/30 Apr, 1, 13 - 15 & 29 May, 8 - 10 Jul, 26 - 28 Aug & 9 - 11 Sept, 1 - 6pm.

Admission: Adult £3.50, Child £1.50. Groups must book.

ⓘNo photography.

SIBSEY TRADER WINDMILL ⌗

Sibsey, Boston, Lincolnshire PE22 0SY

Tel: 01205 750036 **www.**english-heritage.org.uk/visits

Owner: English Heritage   **Contact:** The East Midlands Regional Office

An impressive old mill built in 1877, with its machinery and six sails still intact. Flour milled on the spot can be bought here.

Location: OS Ref. TF345 511. ¹/₂ m W of village of Sibsey, off A16, 5m N of Boston.

Open: 1 Apr - 31 Oct: Suns 11am - 6pm. Sat, Tues & BHs, 10am - 6pm. 1 Nov - 31 Mar: Sats only, 11am - 5pm. Closed 24 - 26 Dec & 1 Jan.

Admission: Adult £2, Child £1 (under 5yrs Free), Conc. £1.50. Members OUP Free.

ⓘWC. 🅐 Exterior only. 🍴 🅿 ✖

© NTPL / Andrew Butler

TATTERSHALL CASTLE ⚘

TATTERSHALL, LINCOLN LN4 4LR

www.nationaltrust.org.uk

Tel: 01526 342543 **e-mail:** tattershallcastle@nationaltrust.org.uk

Owner: The National Trust   **Contact:** The Property Manager

A vast fortified tower built c1440 for Ralph Cromwell, Lord Treasurer of England. The Castle is an important example of an early brick building, with a tower containing state apartments, rescued from dereliction and restored by Lord Curzon 1911-14. Four great chambers, with ancillary rooms, contain late gothic fireplaces and brick vaulting. There are tapestries and information displays in turret rooms.

Location: OS122 Ref. TF209 575. On S side of A153, 15m NE of Sleaford, 10m SW of Horncastle.

Open: 4 - 19 Mar & 4 Nov - 10 Dec: Sat & Sun, 12 noon - 4pm. 25 Mar - 27 Sept: Sat, Sun - Wed, 11am - 5.30pm. 30 Sept - 1 Nov: Sat - Wed, 11am - 4pm.

Admission: Adult £4, Child £2, Family £10. Group discounts.

🅐 Ground floor. WC. ⌂ Free. ✖ Car park only. ⬤

© NTPL / Nick Meers

WOOLSTHORPE MANOR ⚘

23 NEWTON WAY, WOOLSTHORPE-BY-COLSTERWORTH, GRANTHAM NG33 5NR

www.nationaltrust.org.uk

Tel: 01476 860338 **Fax:** 01476 862826

e-mail: woolsthorpemanor@nationaltrust.org.uk

Owner: The National Trust   **Contact:** The Property Manager

This small 17th century farmhouse was the birthplace and family home of Sir Isaac Newton. Some of his major work was formulated here, during the Plague years (1665 - 67); an early edition of the Principia is on display. The orchard has a descendant of the famous apple tree. Science Discovery Centre and exhibition of Sir Isaac Newton's work.

Location: OS130 Ref. SK924 244. 7m S of Grantham, ¹/₂ m NW of Colsterworth, 1m W of A1.

Open: House & Science Discovery Centre: 4 - 26 Mar: Sat & Sun, 1 - 5pm; 29 Mar - 1 Oct: Wed - Sun (open BH Mons & Good Fri), 1 - 5pm. 7 - 29 Oct: Sat & Sun, 1 - 5pm.

Admission: Adult £4.50, Child £2.20, Family £11.20, 1-Adult Family £6.70, no reduction for groups which must book in advance.

🅐 Ground floor. 🅿 Limited. ✖ Car park only.

East Midlands - England

The Stable Block.

MAP 7

ALTHORP

www.althorp.com

The history of Althorp is the history of a family. The Spencers have lived and died here for nearly five centuries and twenty generations.

Since the death of Diana, Princess of Wales, Althorp has become known across the world, but before that tragic event, connoisseurs had heard of this most classic of English stately homes on account of the magnificence of its contents and the beauty of its setting.

Next to the mansion at Althorp lies the honey-coloured stable block, a truly breathtaking building which at one time accommodated up to 100 horses and 40 grooms. The stables are now the setting for the Exhibition celebrating the life of Diana, Princess of Wales and honouring her memory after her death. The freshness and modernity of the facilities are a unique tribute to a woman who captivated the world in her all-too-brief existence.

All visitors are invited to view the House, Exhibition and Grounds as well as the Island in the Round Oval where Diana, Princess of Wales is laid to rest.

Owner:
The Earl Spencer

▶ **CONTACT**

Visitor Manager
Althorp
Northampton NN7 4HQ

Tel: 01604 770107
Fax: 01604 770042

Book online
www.althorp.com

e-mail:
mail@althorp.com

▶ **LOCATION**
OS Ref. SP682 652

From the M1/J16, 7m
J18, 10m.
Situated on A428
Northampton - Rugby.
London on average 85
mins away.

Rail: 5m from
Northampton station.
14m from Rugby
station.

▶ **OPENING TIMES**
Summer

1 July - 30 August
Daily, 11am - 5pm.

Last admission 4pm.

Winter
Closed.

▶ **ADMISSION**
House & Garden
  Adult £12.00
  Child* (5-17yrs)........ £6.00
  OAP/Student £10.00
  Family (2+3) £29.50

£1 discount on all tickets
for advanced internet
bookings.

Groups (by arrangement
only, tel 01604 772110):
  Adult £10.00
  Child* (5-17yrs)........ £5.00
  OAP £10.00
* under 5yrs Free.

Carers accompanying
visitors with disabilities are
admitted free.

There is a supplement to
view the upstairs rooms
of the House of £2.50pp.

Please check website for
up to date information.

The Picture Gallery.

 Information leaflet issued to all ticket holders who book in advance. No indoor photography with still or video cameras.

Visitor Centre & ground floor of house accessible. WCs.

Café.

Limited for coaches.

Guide dogs only.

MAP 7

BOUGHTON HOUSE

www.boughtonhouse.org.uk

Boughton House, a Buccleuch Historic Home, is the Northamptonshire home of the Duke of Buccleuch and Queensberry KT and his Montagu ancestors since 1528. A 500 year old Tudor monastic building gradually enlarged around seven courtyards until the French style addition of 1695, which has lead to Boughton House being described as 'England's Versailles'.

The house contains an outstanding collection of 17th and 18th century French and English furniture, tapestries, 16th century carpets, porcelain, painted ceilings and notable works of art. There is an incomparable Armoury and Ceremonial Coach.

Beautiful parkland with historic avenues, lakes, picnic area, gift shop, adventure woodland play area, plant centre and tearoom. Boughton House is administered by The Living Landscape Trust, which was created by the present Duke of Buccleuch to show the relationship between the historic Boughton House and its surrounding, traditional, working estate.

For information on the group visits programme or educational services, please contact The Living Landscape Trust. Our interactive internet website gives information on Boughton House and The Living Landscape Trust, including a 'virtual' tour, together with full details of our schools' educational facilities (Sandford Award winner 1988, 1993, 1998 and 2003).

Silver Award winner of the 1st Historic House Awards, given by AA and NPL, in co-operation with the Historic Houses Association, for the privately-owned historic house open to the public which has best preserved its integrity, character of its architecture and furniture, while remaining a lived-in family home.

Owner:
His Grace The Duke of Buccleuch & Queensberry KT

▶ CONTACT
Charles Lister
The Living
Landscape Trust
Boughton House
Kettering
Northamptonshire
NN14 1BJ

Tel: 01536 515731
Fax: 01536 417255

e-mail:
llt@boughtonhouse.
org.uk

▶ LOCATION
OS Ref. SP900 815

3m N of
Kettering on
A43 - junction 7
from A14.

Signposted through
Geddington.

CONFERENCE/FUNCTION	
ROOM	MAX CAPACITY
Lecture	100
Seminar Rm	25
Conference facilities available in stable block adjacent to House	

Parkland available for film location and other events. Stableblock room contains 100 seats. No inside photography. No unaccompanied children. Browse our website for a 'virtual' tour of the house

Access to ground floor and all facilities. Virtual tour of first floor.

Tearoom seats 80, groups must book. Licensed.

By arrangement.

P

Heritage Education Trust Sandford Award winner 1988, 1993, 1998 & 2003. School groups free.

No dogs in house and garden, welcome in Park on leads.

By arrangement.

▶ OPENING TIMES
Summer

House
1 August - 1 September
Daily, 2 - 5pm.
Last entry 4pm.
(Monday & Friday:
Guided Tours only.)

Grounds
1 May - 1 September
Daily: (except Fris, May -
July) 1 - 5pm.

During August opening
Guided Tours will operate
on Mondays & Fridays.

Opening of the Woodland
Adventure Play Area is
subject to weather
conditions for reasons of
health and safety.

Winter

Daily by appointment
throughout the year for
educational groups -
contact for details.

▶ ADMISSION
Summer
House & Grounds
Adult £6.00
Child/Conc. £5.00

Grounds
Adult £1.50
Child/Conc. £1.00

Wheelchair visitors Free.
HHA Friends are admitted
Free in August.

Winter
Group rates available –
contact for further details.

MAP 7

DEENE PARK 🏛

www.deenepark.com

A most interesting house, occupied and developed by the Brudenell family since 1514, from a mediaeval manor around a courtyard into a Tudor and Georgian mansion. Visitors see many rooms of different periods, providing an impressive yet intimate ambience of the family home of many generations. The most flamboyant member of the family to date was the 7th Earl of Cardigan, who led the charge of the Light Brigade at Balaklava and of whom there are many historic relics and pictures on view.

Mr Edmund Brudenell, the current owner, has taken considerable care in restoring the house after the Second World War. The gardens have also been improved during the last thirty years or so, with long, mixed borders of shrubs, old-fashioned roses and flowers, together with a parterre designed by David Hicks and long walks under fine old trees by the water. The car park beside the main lake is a good place for visitors to picnic.

Owner:
E Brudenell Esq

▶ CONTACT

The House Keeper
Deene Park
Corby
Northamptonshire
NN17 3EW

Tel: 01780 450278
or 01780 450223

Fax: 01780 450282

e-mail: admin@
deenepark.com

▶ LOCATION
OS Ref. SP950 929

6m NE of
Corby off A43.
From London via
M1/J15 then A43.
or via A1, A14,
A43 - 2 hrs.

From Birmingham
via M6, A14, A43, 90
mins.

Rail: Kettering
Station
20 mins.

CONFERENCE/FUNCTION

ROOM	MAX CAPACITY
Great Hall	150
Tapestry Rm	75
East Room	18

🎒 ℹ️ Suitable for indoor and outdoor events, filming, specialist lectures on house, its contents, gardens and history. No photography in house.

🍽 Including buffets, lunches and dinners.

♿ Partial. Visitors may alight at the entrance, access to ground floor and garden. WC.

☕ Special rates for groups, bookings can be made in advance, menus on request.

🍴 By arrangement.

🚶 Tours inclusive of admittance, tour time 90 mins. Owner will meet groups if requested.

🅿 Unlimited for cars, space for 3 coaches 10 yds from house.

🐕 In car park only.

🛏 Residential conference facilities by arrangement.

❄️ 🛏 Tel for details.

▶ OPENING TIMES
Summer

Open Suns & Mons of Easter - August BH weekends.
Also, June - August Suns, 2 - 5pm

Open at all other times by arrangement, including pre-booked parties.

Winter
Gardens only
Suns 12 & 19 Feb:
11am - 4pm for snowdrops. Refreshments available in the Old Kitchen.

Otherwise House and Gardens closed to casual visitors. Open at all other times by arrangement for groups.

▶ ADMISSION
Public Open Days
House & Gardens

Adult	£6.50
Child (10-14yrs)	£2.50
Conc.	£5.50

Gardens only

Adult	£4.00
Child (10-14yrs)	£1.50

Groups (20+)
by arrangement:

Weekdays	£5.50
(Min £110)	
Weekends & BHs	£6.00
(Min £120)	

* Child up to 10yrs free with an accompanying adult.

Winter
Groups visits only by prior arrangement.

ROCKINGHAM CASTLE

www.rockinghamcastle.com

MAP 7

Owner:
James Saunders Watson

▶ **CONTACT**

Andrew Norman
Operations Manager
Rockingham Castle
Market Harborough
Leicestershire
LE16 8TH

Tel: 01536 770240

e-mail: estateoffice@
rockinghamcastle.com

▶ **LOCATION**
OS Ref. SP867 913.

1m N of Corby on A6003.
9m E of Market
Harborough. 14m SW of
Stamford on A427.

Rockingham Castle stands on the edge of an escarpment with dramatic views over five counties and the Welland Valley below. Built by William the Conqueror, the Castle was a royal residence for 450 years. In the 16th century Henry VIII granted it to Edward Watson, and for 450 years it has remained a family home. The predominantly Tudor building, within Norman walls, has architecture, furniture and works of art from practically every century including, unusually, a remarkable collection of 20th century pictures. Charles Dickens was a regular visitor to the Castle and based *Chesney Wolds* in *Bleak House*

on Rockingham.

Surrounding the Castle are some 12 acres of gardens largely following the foot print of the medieval castle. The vast 400 year old "Elephant Hedge" dissects the formal 17th century terraced gardens. The circular yew hedge stands on the site of the motte and bailey and provides shelter for the rose garden. Below the Castle is the beautiful 19th century "Wild Garden" replanted with advice from Kew Gardens during the early 1960s. Included in the gardens are many specimen trees and shrubs including the remarkable Handkerchief Tree.

▶ **OPENING TIMES**

Easter (16 April) -
end May: Suns &
BH Mons.

June - September:
Tues, Suns & BH Mon.

Grounds: 12 noon - 5pm.

Castle opens at 1pm, last
entrance: 4.30pm.

▶ **ADMISSION**
House & Grounds

Adult £7.50
Child (5-16yrs). £4.50
OAP £6.50
Family (2+2) £19.50

Groups (20+, Can be
accommodated on most
days by arrangement)
Adult £6.50
Adult (private tour). £8.50
Child (5-16yrs) £3.25
School* £3.25
*1 Adult free with every 15
children.

**Grounds only (including
Gardens, Salvin's Tower,
Gift Shop & Tea Room)**
(Not available when special
events are held in grounds.)
Adult £4.50
Child (5-16yrs). £4.50

▶ **SPECIAL EVENTS**

16/17 APRIL
Children's Easter Egg Hunt &
family fun quiz.

22/23 APRIL
Scarecrows at Rockingham.

4 JUNE
Medieval Jousting.

27/28 AUGUST
Vikings! Of Middle England.

  No photography in Castle.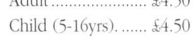
Licensed. Partial. WC. By arrangement. In grounds, on leads.

East Midlands - England

NTPL/ Andrew Butler

78 DERNGATE

82 DERNGATE, NORTHAMPTON NN1 1UH

www.78 derngate.org.uk

Tel: 01604 603407 **Fax:** 01604 603408
e-mail: info@78derngate.org.uk

Owner: 78 Derngate Northampton Trust   **Contact:** House Manager

Charles Rennie Mackintosh transformed a typical terraced house into a startlingly modern home. It was his last major commission and his only work in England. The house is a testament to a partnership of designer and patron, combining striking interiors with practical solutions to living in a small terrace house.

Location: OS Ref. SP759 603. In the heart of Northampton close to the rear of the Derngate Theatre. Follow Derngate road out of the centre of town

Open: 10 Apr - Nov: Wed - Sun & BH Mons: 10.30am - 5pm. Strictly pre-booked tours only.

Admission: Adult £5.50, Conc. £4. Family (2+2): £13.50.

ⓘNo indoor photography. ◻ ♿Partial. 🎧Obligatory. 🅿None. ▨
🐕Guide dogs only.

CANONS ASHBY ❧

CANONS ASHBY, DAVENTRY, NORTHAMPTONSHIRE NN11 3SD

www.nationaltrust.org.uk

Tel: 01327 861900   **Fax:** 01327 861909   **e-mail:** canonsashby@nationaltrust.org.uk

Owner: The National Trust   **Contact:** The Property Manager

Home of the Dryden family since the 16th century, this Elizabethan manor house was built c1550, added to in the 1590s, and altered in the 1630s and c1710; largely unaltered since. Within the house, Elizabethan wall paintings and outstanding Jacobean plasterwork are of particular interest. A formal garden includes terraces, walls and gate piers of 1710. There is also a medieval priory church and a 70 acre park.

Location: OS Ref. SP577 506. Access from M40/J11, or M1/J16. Signposted from A5 2m S of Weedon crossroads. Then 7m to SW.

Open: House: 25 Mar - 30 Sept: Sat - Wed, 1 - 5.30pm. Park & Church (as House): 11am - 5.30pm (Oct - 5 Nov, 11am - 4.30pm). Gardens: 11am - 5.30pm (Oct: 11am - 4.30pm). Shop & Tearoom: 12 noon - 5pm (1 Oct - 5 Nov: 12 noon - 4.30pm). Gardens, Shop, Tearoom, Park & Church: 11 Nov - 17 Dec: Sats & Suns, 12 noon - 4pm.

Admission: Adult £6.10, Child £3.10, Family £15.20. Garden only: £2.20. Discount for booked groups, contact Property Manager.

◻ ♿Some steps. WC. ☕🐕In Home Paddock, on leads.

ALTHORP   *See page 327 for full page entry.*

BOUGHTON HOUSE ⬚   *See page 328 for full page entry.*

© English Heritage Photographic Library

Kirby Hall.

COTON MANOR GARDEN

GUILSBOROUGH, NORTHAMPTONSHIRE NN6 8RQ

www.cotonmanor.co.uk

Tel: 01604 740219   **Fax:** 01604 740838
e-mail: pasleytyler@cotonmanor.fsnet.co.uk

Owner: Ian & Susie Pasley-Tyler   **Contact:** Sarah Ball

Traditional English garden laid out on different levels surrounding a 17th century stone manor house. Many herbaceous borders, with extensive range of plants, old yew and holly hedges, rose garden, water garden and fine lawns set in 10 acres. Also wild flower meadow and bluebell wood.

Location: OS Ref. SP675 716. 9m NW of Northampton, between A5199 (formerly A50) and A428.

Open: 1 Apr - 30 Sept: Tue - Sat & BH weekends; also Suns Apr - May: 12 noon - 5.30pm.

Admission: Adult £4.50, Child £2, Conc. £4. Groups: £4.

◻ 🚻 ♿Grounds. WC. ⧉ ☕ 🎧By arrangement. 🅿 ✦

COTTESBROOKE HALL & GARDENS 🏛

COTTESBROOKE, NORTHAMPTONSHIRE NN6 8PF

www.cottesbrookehall.co.uk

Tel: 01604 505808 **Fax:** 01604 505619 **e-mail:** enquiries@cottesbrooke.co.uk

Owner: Mr & Mrs A R Macdonald-Buchanan   **Contact:** The Administrator

This magnificent Queen Anne house dating from 1702 is set in delightful rural Northamptonshire. Reputed to be the pattern for Jane Austen's *Mansfield Park*, the Hall's beauty is matched by the magnificence of the gardens and views and by the excellence of the picture, furniture and porcelain collections it houses. The Woolavington collection of sporting pictures at Cottesbrooke is possibly one of the finest of its type in Europe and includes paintings by Stubbs, Ben Marshall and many other artists renowned for works of this genre, from the mid 18th century to the present day. Portraits, bronzes, 18th century English and French furniture and fine porcelain are also among the treasures of Cottesbrooke Hall.

In the formal gardens huge 300-year-old cedars set off magnificent double herbaceous borders, pools and lily-ponds. In midsummer, visitors enjoy the splendid array of planters, a sight not to be missed. The Wild Garden is a short walk across the Park and is planted along the course of a stream with its small cascades and arched bridges.

Winner of the *HHA/Christie's Garden of the Year* award in 2000.

Location: OS Ref. SP711 739. 10m N of Northampton near Creaton on A5199 (formerly A50). Signed from Junction 1 on the A14.

Open: 1 May - end of Sept. May & Jun: Wed & Thur, 2 - 5.30pm. Jul - Sept: Thur, 2 - 5.30pm. Open BH Mons (May - Sept), 2 - 5.30pm.

Admission: House & Gardens: Adult £7.50, Child £3.50, Conc £6. Gardens only: Adult £5, Child £2.50, Conc £4. RHS members Free access to gardens. Group & private bookings by arrangement.

ℹ️No photography in house. Filming & outside events. ❈Unusual plants. 🍽
♿Gardens. WC. Parking. 🍰Home-made cakes. 🚶Hall guided tours obligatory. 🅿 ✖

DEENE PARK 🏛   *See page 329 for full page entry.*

ELEANOR CROSS ♯

Geddington, Kettering, Northamptonshire

Tel: 01604 735400 (Regional Office)   **www.**english-heritage.org.uk/visits

Owner: English Heritage   **Contact:** The East Midlands Regional Office

One of a series of famous crosses, of elegant sculpted design, erected by Edward I to mark the resting places of the body of his wife, Eleanor, when brought for burial from Harby in Nottinghamshire to Westminster Abbey in 1290. Picnickers are welcome.

Location: OS Ref. SP896 830. In Geddington, off A43 between Kettering and Corby.

Open: Any reasonable time.

🚶 ❈

HADDONSTONE SHOW GARDENS

The Forge House, East Haddon, Northampton NN6 8DB

Tel: 01604 770711 **Fax:** 01604 770027

e-mail: info@haddonstone.co.uk **www.**haddonstone.co.uk

Owner: Haddonstone Ltd   **Contact:** Marketing Director

See Haddonstone's classic garden ornaments in the beautiful setting of the walled manor gardens – including urns, troughs, fountains, statuary, bird baths, sundials and balustrading. The garden is on different levels with shrub roses, conifers, clematis and climbers. The Jubilee garden features a pavilion, temple and Gothic grotto. An Orangery was opened in 2002.

Location: OS Ref. SP667 682. 7m NW of Northampton off A428. Signposted.

Open: Mon - Fri, 9am - 5.30pm. Closed weekends, BHs & Christmas period.

Admission: Free. Groups by appointment only. Not suitable for coach groups.

📷 ♿ 🚶By arrangement. 🅿Limited. 🚶Guide dogs only.

HOLDENBY HOUSE GARDENS 🏛 & FALCONRY CENTRE

HOLDENBY, NORTHAMPTONSHIRE NN6 8DJ

www.holdenby.com

Tel: 01604 770074 **Fax:** 01604 770962 **e-mail:** enquiries@holdenby.com

Owner: James Lowther Esq   **Contact:** The Commercial Manager

Built by Sir Christopher Hatton as the largest house in England, Holdenby became the palace and prison of Charles I. Now you can visit the beautiful gardens and watch flying displays of birds from our Falconry Centre. The historic Arches Field makes a romantic site for marquee weddings. Holdenby is also a superb venue for corporate functions, from elegant private dinners or lunches, to meetings and conferences, to lavish outdoor events and company staff days. It is also a perfect location for TV, film and video productions.

Location: OS Ref. SP693 681. M1/J15a. 7m NW of Northampton off A428 & A5199.

Open: Gardens & Falconry: Apr - Sept inclusive: Sundays 1-5pm, BH Suns & Mons 11am - 6pm (with event) 1 - 5pm (no event), House 17 April & 29 May only and by appointment. Events: Victorian Easter - 16/17 April; Plant Fair - 28/29 May.

Admission: Gardens & Falconry: Adult £4.50, Child (3-15) £3, OAPs £4, Family (2+2) £12. Different tariffs apply for events.

ℹ️Children's play area. 📷 ❈ 🍽 ♿ Partial. WC.
🍽Home-made teas. Groups must book. 🚶By arrangement. 🅿
🏅Sandford Award-winner. 🚶In grounds, on leads. 🔺 🛏 Tel for details.

KELMARSH HALL 🏛

KELMARSH, NORTHAMPTONSHIRE NN6 9LT

www.kelmarsh.com

Tel: 01604 686543   **Fax:** 01604 686437   **e-mail:** administrator@kelmarsh.com

Owner: The Kelmarsh Trust   **Contact:** Administrator

Built in 1732 to a James Gibbs design, Kelmarsh Hall is surrounded by its working estate, grazed parkland and beautiful gardens. In 1928 Ronald and Nancy Tree rented the Palladian house from the Lancaster family and decorated the rooms in the manner that has become known as the English country house look. In the 1950s she returned to Kelmarsh as Nancy Lancaster and continued to develop her style both in the house and in the gardens. Additional schemes and designs by Geoffrey Jellicoe and Norah Lindsay have created a remarkable garden. Gifted to the Kelmarsh Trust by the Lancaster family the house, gardens and estate are now available for study, group and general visits.

Location: OS Ref. SP736 795. ⅓m N of A14-A508 jct. Rail & Bus: Mkt Harborough.

Open: House & Garden: 16/17 & 30 Apr, 1 & 28/29 May, 27/28 Aug, 4 June, 2 Jul, 6 Aug, 3 Sept & Thurs May - Aug, 2 - 5.30pm. Gardens: 16 Apr - 28 Sept, Tues - Thurs & Suns, 2 - 5.30pm.

Admission: House & Garden: Adult £4.50, Child (5-16yrs) £2.50, Conc. £4. Access to house by guided tour only. Garden only: Adult £3.50, Child (5-16yrs) £2, Child under 5yrs Free, Conc £3.

ⓘNo photography in house. 🚻 ⊤Conferences & functions ♿Partial. WC. 🍴Licensed. 🎦Obligatory. 🅿 🚻 🐕In grounds, on leads. 🔔 ❋ For group visits. 📅Please check website for events to avoid disappointment.

KIRBY HALL ⊞

DEENE, CORBY, NORTHAMPTONSHIRE NN17 1AA

www.english-heritage.org.uk/visits

Tel: 01536 203230

Owner: The Earl of Winchilsea & Nottingham (Managed by English Heritage)

                                          Contact: Visitor Operations Team

The peaceful partial ruins of a large, stone-built Elizabethan mansion, begun in 1570 with 17th century alterations. The richly carved decoration is exceptional, full of amazing Renaissance detail. There are fine gardens with topiary, home to peacocks. Jane Austen's *Mansfield Park* was filmed at Kirby Hall. Newly restored Elizabethan decorative schemes in the Great Hall, Billiard Room, Library & Best Bedchamber. Located in beautiful countryside close to both Rockingham Castle & Deene Park.

Picnickers are welcome.

Location: OS Ref. SP926 927. On unclassified road off A43, Corby to Stamford road, 4m NE of Corby. 2m W of Deene Park.

Open: 1 Apr - 30 Jun: Thur - Mon, 10am - 5pm. 1 Jul - 31 Aug: daily, 10am - 6pm. 1 Sept - 31 Mar 2007: Thur - Mon, 10am - 5pm (4pm Nov - Mar). Closed 24 - 26 Dec & 1 Jan.

Admission: Adult £4.50, Child £2.30, Conc. £3.40, Family £11.30. 15% discount for groups (11+).

ⓘWC. 📷 ♿ Grounds, gardens & ground floor only. 📷 Free with admission. 🅿 🚻 🐕 Restricted areas. ❋ 📅Tel for details.

LAMPORT HALL & GARDENS 🏛

LAMPORT, NORTHAMPTONSHIRE NN6 9HD

www.lamporthall.co.uk

Tel: 01604 686272 **Fax:** 01604 686224 **e-mail:** admin@lamporthall.co.uk

Owner: Lamport Hall Trust   **Contact:** Executive Director

Home of the Isham family from 1560 to 1976. The 17th and 18th century façade is by John Webb and the Smiths of Warwick. The Hall contains an outstanding collection of furniture, china and paintings including portraits by Van Dyck, Kneller and Lely. The Library contains books dating back to the 16th century and the Cabinet Room houses rare Venetian cabinets. The first floor includes a replicated 17th century bedchamber and a photographic record of Sir Gyles Isham, a Hollywood actor, who initiated the restoration. The gardens owe much to the 10th Baronet who, in the mid 19th century, created the famous rockery.

Location: OS Ref. SP759 745. Entrance on A508. 8m N of Northampton, 3m S of A14 J2. Bus: Limited Stagecoach from Northampton and Leicester.

Open: 8 April - 15 Oct. Tours: Suns, 2.30 & 3.30pm; Mon - Fri in Aug, 2.30pm. All fair days from 2.15pm with Room Stewards. Group visits on other days by arrangement.

Admission: Adult £5.50, Child (5-16yrs) £2, OAP. £5. Groups (max 60): £5.50, min £150.

ℹ️No photography in house. 📷 📺Conferences & functions ♿Partial. WC. 🍽Licensed. 🎫Obligatory other than Fair Days. 🅿Cars free. Limited for coaches. 🐾 🐕In grounds, on leads.🔼 ❄️

LYVEDEN NEW BIELD ✿

NR OUNDLE, PETERBOROUGH PE8 5AT

www.nationaltrust.org.uk

Tel: 01832 205358 **Fax:** 01327 861909

e-mail: lyvedennewbield@nationaltrust.org.uk

Owner: The National Trust   **Contact:** The Property Manager

An incomplete Elizabethan garden house and moated garden. Begun in 1595 by Sir Thomas Tresham to symbolise his Catholic faith, Lyveden remains virtually unaltered since work stopped when Tresham died in 1605. Fascinating Elizabethan architectural detail; remains of one of the oldest garden layouts; set amongst beautiful open countryside.

Location: OS141, SP983 853. 4m SW of Oundle via A427, 3m E of Brigstock, off Harley Way. Access by foot along a ¹/₂ m farm track.

Open: House, Elizabethan water garden & visitor information room: 24 Mar - 29 Oct: Wed - Sun (open BH Mons & Good Fri), 10.30am - 5pm (Aug: daily); 4 - 26 Nov & 3 Feb - 25 Mar 2007: Sat & Sun, 10.30am - 4pm. Groups by arrangement with Property Manager.

Admission: Adult £3.50, Child Free, Family £7.

🅿Limited. 🐕On leads. ❄️

NORTHAMPTON CATHEDRAL

Catholic Cathedral House, Primrose Hill, Northampton NN2 6AG

Tel: 01604 714556   **Contact:** Father J Udris

Partly 19th century Pugin.

Location: OS Ref. SP753 617. ³/₄ m N of town centre on A508.

Open: Apply at house: Services: Sat 7pm; Sun 8.30am, 10.30am & 5.15pm; weekday 9.30am & 7pm.

Admission: Guided visits by prior application.

THE PREBENDAL MANOR

Nassington, Peterborough PE8 6QG

Tel: 01780 782575 **e-mail:** info@prebendal-manor.co.uk

www.prebendal-manor.co.uk

Owner/Contact: Mrs J Baile

Grade I listed, dating from the early 13th century, it retains many fine original medieval features and included in the visit are the 15th century dovecote, tithe barn museum and medieval fish ponds. Encompassing 6 acres are the largest 14th century re-created medieval gardens in Europe.

Location: OS Ref. TL063 962. 6m N of Oundle, 9m W of Peterborough, 7m S of Stamford.

Open: Easter Monday - end Sept: Sun & Wed, also BH Mons, 1 - 5.30pm. Closed Christmas.

Admission: Adult £5.50, Child £2.50, OAP £5. Groups (20 - 50) outside normal opening times by arrangement: Adult £5, Child £2.

ℹ️No photography. 📺 ♿Partial. 🍽Home-made teas. 🅿Limited. 🎫 📷Free. 🐕Guide dogs only.

ROCKINGHAM CASTLE 🏛   *See page 330 for full page entry.*

RUSHTON TRIANGULAR LODGE ⊞
Rushton, Kettering, Northamptonshire NN14 1RP
Tel: 01536 710761 **www**.english-heritage.org.uk/visits
Owner: English Heritage   **Contact:** Visitor Operations Team
This extraordinary building, completed in 1597, symbolises the Holy Trinity. It has three sides, 33 ft wide, three floors, trefoil windows and three triangular gables on each side. Picnickers are welcome.
Location: OS141, SP830 831. 1m W of Rushton, on unclassified road 3m from Desborough on A6.
Open: 1 Apr - 31 Oct: Thurs - Mon, 10am - 5pm.
Admission: Adult £2.40, Child £1.20, Conc. £1.80.
⬜ P Nearby lay-by. Restricted areas.

SOUTHWICK HALL 🏛
Nr Oundle, Peterborough PE8 5BL
Tel: 01832 274064 **www**.southwickhall.co.uk
Owner: Christopher Capron Esq   **Contact:** G Bucknill
A family home since 1300, retaining medieval building dating from 1300, with Tudor rebuilding and 18th century additions. Exhibitions: Victorian and Edwardian Life, collections of agricultural and carpentry tools and local archaeological finds.
Location: OS152, TL022 921. 3m N of Oundle, 4m E of Bulwick.
Open: BH Suns & Mons: 16/17 Apr, 30 Apr & 1, 28/29 May, 27/28 Aug: 2 - 5pm. Last admission 4.30pm. Groups at other times by arrangement.
Admission: House & Grounds: Adult £5, Child £2.50.
♿ Partial. WC. 🖼 By arrangement. P In grounds on leads.

STOKE PARK PAVILIONS
Stoke Bruerne, Towcester, Northamptonshire NN12 7RZ
Tel: 01604 862172
Owner: A S Chancellor Esq   **Contact:** Mrs C Cook
The two Pavilions, dated c1630 and attributed to Inigo Jones, formed part of the first Palladian country house built in England by Sir Francis Crane. The central block, to which the Pavilions were linked by quadrant colonnades, was destroyed by fire in 1886. The grounds include extensive gardens and overlook the former park, now farmland.
Location: OS Ref. SP740 488. 7m S of Northampton.
Open: Aug: daily, 3 - 6pm. Other times by appointment only.
Admission: Adult £3, Child £1.50.
♿ Grounds. P Limited. In grounds, on leads.

SULGRAVE MANOR
MANOR ROAD, SULGRAVE, BANBURY, OXON OX17 2SD

www.sulgravemanor.org.uk

Tel: 01295 760205 **Fax:** 01295 768056 **e-mail:** enquiries@sulgravemanor.org.uk
A delightful 16th century Manor House that was the home of George Washington's ancestors. Today it presents a typical wealthy man's home and gardens of Elizabethan times. Restored with scholarly care and attention to detail that makes a visit both a pleasure and an education. A herb garden has been developed by the Herb Society, now based at Sulgrave Manor. The Courtyard buildings house fine visitor/education/wedding and function facilities.
Location: OS152, SP561 457. Off Banbury - Northampton road 5m from M40/J11. 15m from M1/J15A.

Open: 1 Apr - 29 Oct: Weekends, 12 noon - 4.30pm (last entry). 2 May - 26 Oct: Tues - Thurs, 2 - 4.30pm (last entry). Open for booked groups on any day or evening throughout the year (except Jan). Access to house may be restricted during private wedding ceremonies.
Admission: Adult £5.75, Child (2-16) £2.50. Garden only: £2.50. Special rates for booked groups (15+). Prices vary for Special Event Days - please contact for details. All visitors on non-event days are taken round the Manor House on regularly organized guided tours.
ℹ No photography in house. ⬜ 🍴 T ♿ Partial. 🖼 Obligatory. P ■
In grounds, on leads. Various. Send for details.

WAKEFIELD LODGE
Potterspury, Northamptonshire NN12 7QX
Tel: 01327 811395 **Fax:** 01327 811051
Owner/Contact: Mrs J Richmond-Watson
Georgian hunting lodge with deer park.
Location: OS Ref. SP739 425. 4m S of Towcester on A5. Take signs to farm shop for directions.
Open: House: 18 Apr - 31 May: Mon - Fri (closed BHs), 12 noon - 4pm. Appointments by telephone. Access walk open Apr & May.
Admission: £5.
ℹ No photography. ⬜ ♿ Unsuitable. 🖼 Obligatory. P Guide dogs only.

open all year
see page 557

CARLTON HALL

Carlton-on-Trent, Nottinghamshire NG23 6LP
Tel: 01636 821421   **Fax:** 01636 821554
Owner/Contact: Lt Col & Mrs Vere-Laurie
Mid 18th century house by Joseph Pocklington of Newark. Stables attributed to Carr of York. Family home occupied by the same family since 1832.
Location: OS Ref. SK799 640. 7m N of Newark off A1. Opposite the church.
Open: 1 Apr - 30 Sept: Weds only, 2 - 5pm. Other dates and times by appointment.
Admission: Hall and Garden: £8. Groups (10+) £5pp.
⊤Conferences. 🅴Unsuitable. 🅸Obligatory.
🅷In grounds, on leads. Guide dogs in house. ✳

HODSOCK PRIORY GARDEN

Blyth, Nr Worksop, Nottinghamshire S81 0TY
Tel: 01909 591204   **Fax:** 01909 591578
Owner: Sir Andrew & Lady Buchanan   **Contact:** Kate Garton - 07860 329815
Sensational snowdrops, winter flowering plants and shrubs, woodland walk.
Location: OS Ref. SK612 853. W of B6045 Worksop/Blyth road, 1m SW of Blyth, less than 2m from A1.
Open: 28 Jan - 5 Mar: daily, 10am - 4pm. Please telephone for details.
Admission: Adult £4, accompanied Child (6-16yrs) £1.

CLUMBER PARK ✿

CLUMBER PARK, WORKSOP, NOTTINGHAMSHIRE S80 3AZ

www.nationaltrust.org.uk

Tel: 01909 476592   **Fax:** 01909 500721
Owner: The National Trust   **Contact:** Property Manager
Historic parkland with peaceful woods, open heath and rolling farmland around a serpentine lake.
Location: OS120 Ref SK626 746. 4 1/2 m SE of Worksop, 6 1/2 m SW of Retford, just off A1/A57 via A614. 11m from M1/J30.
Open: Park: All year except 8 Jul & 19 Aug & 25 Dec. Walled Kitchen Garden: 1 Apr - 1 Oct: daily (open BH Mons), 10am - 5pm (6pm on Sats & Suns). Chapel: 1 Apr - 1 Oct: daily, 10am - 6pm. 2 Oct - 11 Jan 2007: daily, 10am - 4pm. Closed 12 Jan - end Mar for conservation cleaning.
Admission: Pedestrians, Cyclists & Coaches: Free, NT Members Free, Cars & Motorbikes £4.30, Minibuses & caravans £5.50. Walled Kitchen Garden £2.
🅾🅸⊤🅴Partial. Wheelchairs available. 🅲🅿🅻🅷In grounds on leads. ✳

©National Trust Photographic Library/ Andrew Butler

HOLME PIERREPONT HALL 🏛

HOLME PIERREPONT, Nr NOTTINGHAM NG12 2LD

www.holmepierreponthall.com

Tel: 0115 933 2371
Owner: Mr & Mrs Robin Brackenbury   **Contact:** Robert Brackenbury
This charming late medieval manor house is set in 30 acres of Park and Gardens with regional furniture and family portraits. The Ball Room, Drawing Room and Long Gallery are available to hire for functions on an exclusive basis. Filming welcome.
Location: OS Ref. SK628 392. 5m ESE of central Nottingham. Follow signs to the National Water Sports Centre and continue for 1 1/2 m.
Open: 1 Feb - 22 Mar, Mon - Wed; 12 Feb, 19 Mar, 9 & 11 Apr & 20 Jun: 2 - 5pm. Corporate/private and wedding venue. Functions at other times by arrangement.
Admission: Adult £4.50, Child £1.50. Gardens only £2.50.
ℹNo photography or video recording in house when open to the public.
⊤Business & charity functions, wedding receptions. 🅴Please ring for details.
🅷In grounds on leads. 🅰🅿 Tel for details.

Patrick Lane.

Wollaton Hall Natural History Museum, Nottinghamshire.

D H LAWRENCE HERITAGE

Durban House Heritage Centre, Mansfield Road, Eastwood, Nottinghamshire NG16 3DZ
Tel: 01773 717353   **Fax:** 01773 713509   **e-mail:** Durban@broxbcl.demon.co.uk
www.broxtowe.gov.uk
Owner: Broxtowe Borough Council   **Contact:** Sally Rose
Durban House and the D H Lawrence Birthplace Museum bring to life the world of the famous novelist and artist D H Lawrence, author of *Lady Chatterley's Lover.*
Location: OS Ref. SK466 469 From the M1/J26 take the A610 towards Eastwood and follow the brown tourism signs. Or from M1/J27 take the A608 through Brinsley towards Eastwood.
Open: Daily, 10am - 5pm (4pm Nov - Mar). Closed 24 Dec - 3 Jan.
Admission: Mon - Fri Free. Sat/Sun & BHs charges apply: Single site: Adult £2, Conc. £1.20, Family (2+2) £5.80; Joint site: Adult £3.50, Conc. £1.80, Family (2+2) £8. Groups welcome. (2005 prices, subject to change.)
🅾⊤🅴Partial. WCs. 🅲🅸By arrangement. 🅿Limited. 🅻
🅷Guide dogs only. In grounds, on leads. 🅰✳

NEWARK TOWN HALL

Market Place, Newark, Nottinghamshire NG24 1DU
Tel: 01636 680333   **Fax:** 01636 680350
Owner: Newark Town Council   **Contact:** The Curator
A fine Georgian Grade I listed Town Hall containing a museum of the town's treasures. Disabled access – lift and WC.
Location: OS Ref. SK570 395. Close to A46 and A1.
Open: All year: Mon - Fri, 11am - 4pm. Sats, 12 noon - 4pm. Closed BHs.
Admission: Free.

NEWSTEAD ABBEY

Newstead Abbey Park, Nottinghamshire NG15 8NA
Tel: 01623 455900   **Fax:** 01623 455904   **www.**newsteadabbey.org.uk
                                         Contact: Gillian Crawley
Historic home of the poet, Lord Byron, set in extensive formal gardens with lakes and grounds of 300 acres. See Byron's private apartments, period rooms and the medieval cloisters. The West Front of the Priory Church was recently featured as part of the BBC's *Restoration* series.
Location: OS Ref. SK540 639. 12m N of Nottingham 1m W of the A60 Mansfield Rd.
Open: House: 1 Apr - 30 Sept: 12 noon - 5pm, last adm. 4pm. Grounds: All year: 9am - dusk except for the last Friday in November and 25 Dec.
Admission: House & Grounds: Adult £6, Child £2.50, Conc. £4, Family (2+3) £16. Groups (10+) £4. Grounds only: Adult £3, Child £1.50, Conc. £2.50, Family £8.50. Groups (10+) £2.50. (Oct - Mar: Adult £2, Conc. £1.50).
🖰 🕿 🖅 🅿 🄑 🄰 🖻 Tel for details.

NOTTINGHAM CASTLE

Nottingham NG1 6EL
Tel: 0115 9153700   **Fax:** 0115 9153653   **e-mail:** castle@ncmg.demon.co.uk
17th century mansion built on the site of the original medieval Castle, with spectacular views of the city. A vibrant museum and art gallery housing collections of paintings, silver, Wedgwood and armour, 15 centuries of Nottingham history plus exhibitions of contemporary and historical art. Tour the underground caves system.
Location: OS Ref. SK569 395. Just SW of the city centre on hilltop.
Open: Daily, 10am - 5pm (4pm during winter). Closed 24 - 26 Dec & 1 Jan.
Admission: Weds Free. Weekends & BHs: Adult £3, Child/Conc. £1.50, Family (2+3) £5. (Prices likely to change in 2006.)
🖰 🕿 🕭 🖅 🄵 Caves. 🄑 🖾 🗯 🖻 Tel for details.

PAPPLEWICK HALL

Papplewick, Nottinghamshire NG15 8FE
Tel: 0115 963 3491
Owner/Contact: J R Godwin-Austen
A beautiful stone built classical house set in a park with woodland garden laid out in the 18th century. The house is notable for its very fine plasterwork and elegant staircase. Grade I listed.
Location: OS Ref. SK548 518. Halfway between Nottingham & Mansfield, 3m E of M1/J27. A608 & A611 towards Hucknall. Then A6011 to Papplewick and B683 N for ¹/₂ m.
Open: 1st, 3rd & 5th Wed in each month, 2 - 5pm, by appointment.
Admission: Adult £7. Groups (10+): £4.
🄸 No photography. 🄵 Obligatory. 🅿 Limited for coaches. 🖅 In grounds on leads. 🗯

RUFFORD ABBEY ♯

Ollerton, Nottinghamshire NG22 9DF
Tel: 01623 822944   **www.**english-heritage.org.uk/visits
Owner: English Heritage   **Contact:** Nottinghamshire County Council
The remains of a 17th century country house; built on the foundations of a 12th century Cistercian Abbey, set in Rufford Country Park. Picnickers welcome.
Location: OS120, SK645 646. 2m S of Ollerton off A614.
Open: Easter - 1 Jan: daily, 10am - 5pm. 2 Jan - Easter 2007: daily, 10.30am - 4pm. Closed 25 Dec.
Admission: Free - parking charge applies.
🄸 WC. 🖰 🕭 🖐 🅿 🖾 🗯

THRUMPTON HALL 🏠

THRUMPTON, NOTTINGHAM NG11 0AX
www.thrumptonhall.com

Tel: 01159 830333   **e-mail:** mirandaseymour@btinternet.com
Owner: Miranda Seymour   **Contact:** The Hon Mrs R Seymour
Magnificent Jacobean house, built in 1607 incorporating an earlier manor house. Priest's hiding hole, carved Charles II staircase, carved and panelled saloon. Other fine rooms containing beautiful 17th and 18th century furniture and Byron memorabilia. Large lawns separated from landscaped park by ha-ha and by lake in front of the house. The house is still lived in as a home and tours are led by family members. Dining room with capacity for 50 silver service or buffet for 100. Free access and meal for coach drivers.
Location: OS Ref. SK508 312. 7m S of Nottingham, 3m E M1/J24, 1m from A453.
Open: By appointment throughout the year. Groups of (20+) 10.30am - 6pm.
Admission: Adult £7, Child £3.50.
🖰 🕿 Wedding receptions. 🕭 Ground floor & grounds. WC. 🍴
🖅 In grounds on leads. 🗯

UPTON HALL 🏠

Upton, Newark, Nottinghamshire NG23 5TE
Tel: 01636 813795   **Fax:** 01636 812258   **www.**bhi.co.uk
Owner: British Horological Institute   **Contact:** The Museum Manager
A fine country house dating from the 16th century, but extensively altered in the 19th century, set within its own grounds. Since 1972, it has been the headquarters of the British Horological Institute and its fascinating museum containing a large historic collection of public and domestic clocks and watches.
Location: OS Ref. SK735 544. A612 between Newark and Southwell.
Open: All year, groups by appointment only.
Admission: £5pp.
🄵 Obligatory. 🅿 🗯

WINKBURN HALL

Winkburn, Newark, Nottinghamshire NG22 8PQ
Tel: 01636 636465   **Fax:** 01636 636717
Owner/Contact: Richard Craven-Smith-Milnes Esq
A fine William and Mary house.
Location: OS Ref. SK711 584. 8m W of Newark 1m N of A617.
Open: Throughout the year by appointment only.
Admission: £5.50.

WOLLATON HALL & PARK

Wollaton, Nottingham NG8 2AE
Tel: 0115 915 3900   **e-mail:** wollatonhall@ncmg.demon.co.uk
                                         Contact: The Manager
Standing on a natural hill 3 miles west of Nottingham City Centre, Wollaton Hall is a flamboyant 16th century Robert Smythson building set in a scenic 500-acre historic park. Wollaton houses a Natural History Museum, Industrial Museum and The Yard gallery with constantly changing exhibitions linked to the theme of Natural History.
The park is home to herds of free-roaming red and fallow deer. Visitors have the choice of a variety of walks or can simply stroll around the lake or relax in the formal gardens. Due to ongoing refurbishment some areas of the Hall may be closed. Please call in advance if you are interested in seeing a particular part of the Hall.
Location: OS Ref. SK532 392. Wollaton Park, Nottingham. 3m W of city centre.
Open: Hall: Summer, 11am - 5pm; Winter, 11am - 4pm. Park: All year, 9am - dusk.
Admission: Weekdays Free. Weekends & BHs: Joint ticket for all museums: Adult £2.50, Child £1.50. Grounds £2/car (free for disabled badge holders). Yard Gallery Free.
🖰 🕿 🖅 🕭 🄵 🅿 🗯 🖻 Tel for details.

Witley Court, Worcestershire. © English Heritage Photo Library/Paul Highnam

herefordshire   shropshire   staffordshire   warwickshire

west midlands

The counties of the West Midlands are among some of Britain's best kept secrets. Shakespeare's birthplace of Stratford-upon-Avon justly receives thousands of visitors each year, but travel further west too, into the gloriously unspoilt counties of Herefordshire and Worcestershire. The Wye Valley remains a haven of green fields, cider orchards and a meandering river. Surrounded by the Malvern Hills, the fairytale Eastnor Castle (Herefordshire) has something to interest all visitors, whilst Warwick Castle (Warwickshire) provides exciting living history to entertain all ages within its medieval walls. A network of canals, with boats to hire, offers an alternative way to explore this fascinating area.

west midlands   worcestershire

© National Trust Photographic Library

MAP 6

Owner:
The National Trust

▶ **CONTACT**

The Property
Manager
Berrington Hall
Nr Leominster
Herefordshire
HR6 0DW

Tel: 01568 615721
Fax: 01568 613263

Restaurant:
01568 610134

Shop:
01568 610529

Costume Curator:
01568 613720

e-mail: berrington
@nationaltrust.org.uk

▶ **LOCATION**
OS137 SP510 637

3m N of Leominster,
7m S of Ludlow on
W side of A49.

Rail: Leominster 4m.

BERRINGTON HALL 🌿

www.nationaltrust.org.uk/berrington

Berrington Hall is the creation of Thomas Harley, the 3rd Earl of Oxford's remarkable son, who made a fortune from supplying pay and clothing to the British Army in America and became Lord Mayor of London in 1767 at the age of thirty-seven. The architect was the fashionable Henry Holland. The house is beautifully set above the wide valley of a tributary of the River Lugg, with views west and south to the Black Mountains and Brecon Beacons. This was the site chosen by 'Capability' Brown who created the lake with its artificial island. The rather plain neo-classical exterior with a central portico

gives no clue to the lavishness of the interior. Plaster ceilings decorated in muted pastel colours adorn the principal rooms. Holland's masterpiece is the staircase hall rising to a central dome. The rooms are set off with a collection of French furniture, including pieces which belonged to the Comte de Flahault, natural son of Talleyrand, and Napoleon's step-daughter Hortense.

In the dining room, vast panoramic paintings of battles at sea, three of them by Thomas Luny, are a tribute to the distinguished Admiral Rodney.

NT Photographic Library

▶ **OPENING TIMES**

House
4 - 19 March: Sats & Suns,
20 March - 1 November:
Sat - Wed (open Good Fri).
1 - 4.30pm.

Garden
4 - 19 March: Sats & Suns,
20 March - 1 November:
Sat - Wed,
4 November - 17 December:
Sats & Suns.
12 noon - 5pm
(closes 4.30pm in Nov
& Dec).

Park Walk
17 June - 1 November:
Sat - Wed,
4 November - 17 December:
Sats & Suns.
12 noon - 5pm
(closes 4.30pm in Nov
& Dec).

Shop & Restaurant
As Garden.

▶ **ADMISSION**

Adult £5.30
Child (5-12yrs) £2.65
Family (2+3).......... £13.25
Groups (15-25)*
Adult £4.40
Child £2.20

Garden Ticket £3.70

Groups must pre-book.
Two groups can visit at a time.

Joint Ticket for Berrington
& Croft Castle £7.50

📷 ℹ️ No photography in the house. Groups by arrangement only.

♿ Single seater batricar for use outdoors; pre-booking essential. Audio tours for the visually impaired.

🍴 Licensed restaurant: open as house: 12 noon - 5pm (4.30pm in Oct & Nov).

🚶 By arrangement only. Tour time: 1 hr.

🅿 Ample for cars. Parking for coaches limited; instructions given when booking is made.

🖼 Children's quizzes. Play area in walled garden.

🐕 Guide dogs only. 🎭 Tel for details.

MAP 6

Owner:
Mr J Hervey-Bathurst

▶ CONTACT

Simon Foster
Portcullis Office
Eastnor Castle
Nr Ledbury
Herefordshire HR8 1RL

Tel: 01531 633160
Fax: 01531 631776
e-mail: enquiries@
eastnorcastle.com

▶ LOCATION

OS Ref. SO735 368

2m SE of Ledbury on
the A438 Tewkesbury
road. Alternatively
M50/J2 & from Ledbury
take the A449/A438.

Tewkesbury 20 mins,
Malvern 20 mins, Gloucester
25 mins, Hereford 25 mins,
Worcester 30 mins,
Cheltenham 30 mins,
B'ham 1 hr, London 2¼ hrs.

Taxi: Richard James
07836 777196.

EASTNOR CASTLE 🏛

www.eastnorcastle.com

In the style of a medieval Welsh-border fortress, Eastnor Castle was built in the early 19th century by John First Earl Somers and is a good example of the great Norman and Gothic revival in architecture of that time. The Castle is dramatically situated in a 5000 acre estate in the Malvern Hills and remains the family home of the Hervey-Bathursts, his direct descendants.

This fairytale home is as dramatic inside as it is outside. A vast, 60' high Hall leads to a series of State Rooms including a Gothic Drawing Room designed by Pugin, with its original furniture, and a Library in the style of the Italian Renaissance, with views across the Lake.

The Hervey-Bathursts have lovingly restored the interiors and many of the Castle's treasures which have been buried away in the cellars and attics since the Second World War – early Italian Fine Art, medieval armour, 17th century Venetian furniture, Flemish tapestries and paintings by Van Dyck, Reynolds, Romney and Watts and early photographs by Julia Margaret Cameron.

GARDENS

Castellated terraces descend to a 21 acre lake with a restored lakeside walk. The arboretum holds a famous collection of mature specimen trees. There are spectacular views of the Malvern hills across a 300 acre deer park, once part of a mediaeval chase and now designated a Site of Special Scientific Interest.

🛈 Tree trail, maze, assault course, off-road driving, clay-pigeon shooting, quad bikes, archery and falconry. Survival training, team building activity days. Product launches, fashion shows, concert, charity events, craft fairs, television and feature films. No photography in Castle.

🍽 Wedding receptions. Catering for booked events.

♿ Wheelchair stairclimber to main State Rooms. DVD tour of first floor rooms. Visitors may alight at the Castle. Priority parking.

☕ By arrangement.

Ⓟ Ample 10 - 200 yds from castle. Coaches phone in advance to arrange parking & catering. Tea Room voucher for drivers/courier.

Welcome. Guides available if required. Children's fun worksheets.

🐕 On leads in grounds.

Luxury accommodation within castle for small groups (min. 10 guests). 1 single room, 11 double. Ensuite available.

▶ OPENING TIMES

Easter 13, 14, 16, 17

Every Sunday & Bank Holiday Monday from 23 April - 1 October

17 July - 31 August: daily (except Saturdays)

11am - 5pm.

▶ ADMISSION

Summer
Castle & Grounds

Adult	£7.00
Child (5-15yrs)	£4.00
OAP	£6.00
Family (2+3)	£18.00

Groups (20+)
(with guide)

Adult	£9.00

Groups (20+)
(without guide)

Adult	£5.50

Grounds only

Adult	£3.00
Child (5-15yrs)	£1.00
OAP	£2.00

🎭 SPECIAL EVENTS

16/17 APR
Easter Treasure Hunt.

30 APR - 1 MAY
Arms & Armour.

28/29 MAY
Steam & Woodland Festival.

21 JULY
'A Midsummer Night's Dream'

6 AUG
Birds of Prey Displays with Hawkeye Falconry.

14 - 18 AUG
Children's Fun Week.

27/28 AUG
Knight's Treasure Hunt.

1 OCT
Victorian Eastnor.

3 DEC
Christmas at Eastnor.

CONFERENCE/FUNCTION

ROOM	SIZE	MAX CAPACITY
Great Hall	16 x 8m	150
Dining Rm	11 x 7m	80
Gothic Rm	11 x 7m	80
Octagon Rm	9 x 9m	50

ABBEY DORE COURT GARDEN
Abbey Dore, Herefordshire HR2 0AD

Tel/Fax: 01981 240419

Owner/Contact: Mrs C L Ward

6 acres of new and established garden with a wild river walk leading to a meadow planted with a variety of interesting trees.
Location: OS Ref. SO387 309. 3 m W of A465 midway Hereford - Abergavenny.
Open: Apr - Sept: Sat, Sun, Tue, Thur & BH Mons, 11am - 5.30pm. Other times by appointment.
Admission: Adult £3.50, Child 50p.

BERRINGTON HALL

See page 340 for full page entry.

BROCKHAMPTON ESTATE
Bringsty, Worcestershire WR6 5TB

Tel: 01885 488099/482077   **www**.nationaltrust.org.uk/brockhampton

Owner: The National Trust   **Contact:** The Property Manager
Wood and parkland estate with waymarked walks including Lower Brockhampton, a 14th century moated manor house with timber framed gatehouse.
Location: OS Ref. SO682 546. 2m E of Bromyard on A44.
Open: Lower Brockhampton: 4 - 26 Mar: Sats & Suns, 12 noon - 4pm; 1 Apr - 29 Oct: Wed - Sun & BHs, 12 noon - 5pm (closes at 4pm in Oct). Woodland walks: All year: daily during daylight hours.
Admission: Lower Brockhampton: Adult £4, Child £2, Family £10. Groups (15+) £3.50. Estate Car Park: £2.
Partial. Dogs in woodland walks, on leads.

CROFT CASTLE
Leominster, Herefordshire HR6 9PW

Tel: 01568 780246   **e-mail:** croftcastle@nationaltrust.org.uk
www.nationaltrust.org.uk

Owner: The National Trust   **Contact:** The Property Manager
Home of the Croft family since Domesday. Walls and corner towers date from 14th and 15th centuries, interior mainly 18th century.
Location: OS Ref. SO455 655. 5m NW of Leominster, 9m SW of Ludlow, approach from B4362.
Open: House: 4 - 26 Mar: Sat & Sun, Apr - Sept: Wed - Sun & BH Mons, 1 - 5pm. 1 - 29 Oct: Sat & Sun, 1 - 4.30pm. Gardens & Tearoom: 4 - 26 Mar: Sat & Sun; Apr - Sept: Wed - Sun, 12 noon - 5pm. 1 Oct - 26 Nov: Sat & Sun, 11am - 4pm. Park: All year.
Admission: House & Garden: Adult £5, Child £2.50, Family £12.50, Group (15+) £4.20, outside normal hours £8.50. Garden only: Adult £3.50, Child £1.70.

CWMMAU FARMHOUSE
Brilley, Whitney-on-Wye, Herefordshire HR3 6JP

Tel: 01981 590509

Owner: The National Trust   **Contact:** The Property Manager
A wonderful timber-framed and stone tiled traditional Welsh farmhouse restored from dereliction. There is an informal atmosphere with free guided tours by volunteers and access to all parts of the house.
Location: OS Ref. SO267 514. SW of Kington between A4111 and A438.
Open: 14 - 17 Apr, 27 - 29 May & 26 - 28 Aug: 2 - 5pm. Remainder of year available as holiday cottage.
Admission: Adult £3.40, Child £1.70, Family £8.
Picnics in garden. Ground floor. Not suitable for coaches. On leads, only in grounds.

EASTNOR CASTLE

See page 341 for full page entry.

English Heritage Photo Library

GOODRICH CASTLE
ROSS-ON-WYE, HEREFORDSHIRE HR9 6HY

www.english-heritage.org.uk/visits

Tel: 01600 890538

Owner: English Heritage   **Contact:** Visitor Operations Team
This magnificent red sandstone castle is remarkably complete with a 12th century keep and extensive remains from 13th & 14th centuries. From the battlements there are fine views over the Wye Valley to Symonds Yat. Marvel at the maze of small rooms and the 'murder holes'.
Location: OS162 Ref. SO577 200. 5m S of Ross-on-Wye, off A40.
Open: 1 Apr - 31 Oct: daily, 10am - 5pm (6pm Jun - Aug). 1 Nov - 28 Feb: Thur - Mon, 10am - 4pm. 1 - 31 Mar: daily, 10am - 5pm. Closed 24 - 26 Dec & 1 Jan.
Admission: Adult £4.50, Child £2.30, Conc. £3.40, Family £11.30. 15% discount for groups (11+).
WC. Tel for details.

©NTPL

Croft Castle.

HELLENS

MUCH MARCLE, LEDBURY, HEREFORDSHIRE HR8 2LY

Tel: 01531 660504   **Fax:** 01531 660501

Owner: Pennington-Mellor-Munthe Charity Trust   **Contact:** The Administrator

Built as a monastery and then a stone fortress in 1292 by Mortimer, Earl of March, with Tudor, Jacobean and Stuart additions and lived in ever since by descendants of the original builder. Visited by the Black Prince, Bloody Mary and the 'family ghost'. Family paintings, relics and heirlooms from the Civil War and possessions of the Audleys, Walwyns and Whartons as well as Anne Boleyn. Also beautiful 17th century woodwork carved by the 'King's Carpenter', John Abel. All those historical stories incorporated into guided tours, revealing the loves and lives of those who lived and died here. Goods and chattels virtually unchanged.

Location: OS Ref. SO661 332. Off A449 at Much Marcle. Ledbury 4m, Ross-on-Wye 4m.

Open: Easter Sun - 3 October: Wed, Thur, Sun & BH Mons. Guided tours only at 2pm, 3pm & 4pm. Other times by arrangement with the Administrator throughout the year.

Admission: Adult £5, Child £2.50, OAP £4, Family ticket £10.

ℹ️No photography inside house. 🈺 ♿Partial. 📷Obligatory. 🏠 🅿
🐕In grounds, on leads. 📺Tel for details.

HEREFORD CATHEDRAL

Mappa Mundi and Chained Library Exhibition.

Hereford HR1 2NG   www: herefordcathedral.org

Tel: 01432 374202   **Fax:** 01432 374220   **e-mail:** visits@herefordcathedral.org

Contact: Mrs C Quinto - The Visits Manager

Location: OS Ref. SO510 398. Hereford city centre on A49.

Open: Cathedral: Daily, 9.15am - Evensong. Exhibition: Easter - Oct: Mon - Sat, 10am - 4.15pm, Sun, 11am - 3.15pm; Nov - Easter: Mon - Sat, 11am - 3.15pm.

Admission: Admission only for Mappa Mundi and Chained Library Exhibition: Adult £4.50, OAP/Student/Unemployed £3.50, Child under 5yrs Free. Family (2+3) £10.

🏠 🍵 ♿ 🈺 🍴 📷 🏠 ✳ 📺Tel for details.

HERGEST COURT

c/o Hergest Estate Office, Kington HR5 3EG

Tel: 01544 230160   **Fax:** 01544 232031   **e-mail:** gardens@hergest.co.uk

Owner/Contact: W L Banks

The ancient home of the Vaughans of Hergest, dating from the 13th century.

Location: OS Ref. SO283 554. 1m W of Kington on unclassified road to Brilley.

Open: Strictly by appointment only through Estate Office.

Admission: Adult £4, Child £1.50. Groups: Adult £3.50, Child £1.

♿Unsuitable. 🅿Limited. 🐕Guide dogs only. ✳

HERGEST CROFT GARDENS

KINGTON, HEREFORDSHIRE HR5 3EG

www.hergest.co.uk

Tel: 01544 230160   **Fax:** 01544 232031   **e-mail:** gardens@hergest.co.uk

Owner: W L Banks   **Contact:** Melanie Lloyd

From spring bulbs to autumn colour, this is a garden for all seasons. An old-fashioned kitchen garden has spring and summer borders and roses. Over 59 Champion trees and shrubs grow in one of the finest collections in the British Isles. Holds National Collection of birches, maples and zelkovas. Park Wood is a hidden valley with rhododendrons up to 30 ft tall.

Location: OS Ref. SO281 565. On W side of Kington. 1/2 m off A44, left at Rhayader end of bypass. Turn right and gardens are 1/4 m on left. Signposted from bypass.

Open: Mar: Sats & Suns. 1 Apr - 29 Oct: daily, 12.30 - 5pm. May & June: daily, 12 noon - 6pm. Season tickets and groups by arrangement throughout the year. Winter by appointment.

Admission: Adult £5, Child (under 16yrs) Free. Pre-booked groups (20+) £4. Pre-booked guided groups (20+) £6pp. Season ticket £17.

ℹ️Gift sales. ✳Rare plants. ♿Limited. 🈺 🐕In grounds, on leads. ✳
📺Tel for details.

special events
see page 571

LANGSTONE COURT

Llangarron, Ross on Wye, Herefordshire HR9 6NR

Tel: 01989 770254

Owner/Contact: R M C Jones Esq

Mostly late 17th century house with older parts. Interesting staircases, panelling and ceilings.

Location: OS Ref. SO534 221. Ross on Wye 5m, Llangarron 1m.

Open: 20 May - 31 Aug: Wed & Thur, 11am - 2.30pm, also spring & summer BHs.

Admission: Free.

LONGTOWN CASTLE ♯

Abbey Dore, Herefordshire

Tel: 0121 625 6820 (Regional Office)

Owner: English Heritage   **Contact:** The West Midlands Regional Office

An unusual cylindrical keep, perched atop a large earthen motte, built c1200, with walls 15ft thick. There are magnificent views of the nearby Black Mountains.

Location: OS161 Ref. SO321 291. 4m WSW of Abbey Dore.

Open: Any reasonable time.

Admission: Free.

MOCCAS COURT ▥

Moccas, Herefordshire HR2 9LH

Tel: 01981 500019   **Fax:** 01981 500095   **e-mail:** bencmaster@btconnect.com

Owner: Trustees of the Baunton Trust   **Contact:** Ben & Mimi Chester-Master

18th century Adam interiors, 'Capability' Brown park.

Location: OS Ref. SO359 434. 1m N of B4352, 3^1/$_2$ m SE of Bredwardine.

Open: Apr - Sept: Thurs, 2 - 6pm. Last admission 5.15pm.

Admission: £4.

OLD SUFTON

Mordiford, Hereford HR1 4EJ

Tel: 01432 870268/850328   **Fax:** 01432 850381   **e-mail:** jameshereford@aol.com

Owner: Trustees of Sufton Heritage Trust   **Contact:** Mr & Mrs J N Hereford

A 16th century manor house which was altered and remodelled in the 18th and 19th centuries and again in this century. The original home of the Hereford family (see Sufton Court) who have held the manor since the 12th century.

Location: OS Ref. SO575 384. Mordiford, off B4224 Mordiford - Dormington road.

Open: By written appointment to Sufton Court or by fax.

Admission: Adult £3, Child 50p.

Partial. Obligatory. Small school groups. No special facilities.

ROTHERWAS CHAPEL ♯

Hereford

Tel: 0121 625 6820 (Regional Office)

Owner: English Heritage   **Contact:** The West Midlands Regional Office

This Roman Catholic chapel, dating from the 14th and 16th centuries, is testament to the past grandeur of the Bodenham family and features an interesting mid-Victorian side chapel and High Altar.

Location: OS149 Ref. SO536 383. 1^1/$_2$ m SE of Hereford 500yds N of B4399.

Open: Any reasonable time. Keykeeper at nearby filling station.

Admission: Free.

SUFTON COURT ▥

Mordiford, Hereford HR1 4LU

Tel: 01432 870268/850328   **Fax:** 01432 850381   **e-mail:** jameshereford@aol.com

Owner: J N Hereford   **Contact:** Mr & Mrs J N Hereford

Sufton Court is a small Palladian mansion house. Built in 1788 by James Wyatt for James Hereford. The park was laid out by Humphrey Repton whose 'red book' still survives. The house stands above the rivers Wye and Lugg giving impressive views towards the mountains of Wales.

Location: OS Ref. SO574 379. Mordiford, off B4224 on Mordiford to Dormington road.

Open: 16 - 29 May & 15 - 28 Aug. 2 - 5pm. Guided tours. 2, 3 and 4pm.

Admission: Adult £5, Child 50p.

Obligatory. Only small coaches. Small school groups. No special facilities. In grounds, on leads.

THE WEIR ✿

Swainshill, Hereford HR4 7QF

Tel: 01981 590509   **www.**nationaltrust.org.uk

Owner: The National Trust   **Contact:** Property Manager

Delightful riverside garden particularly spectacular in early spring, with fine views over the River Wye and Black Mountains.

Location: OS Ref. SO435 421. 5m W of Hereford on S side of A438.

Open: 21/22 & 28/29 Jan: 11 - 4pm. 1 - 26 Feb: Wed - Sun, 11 - 4pm. 27 Feb - 30 Apr: daily, 11 - 5pm. 3 May - 1 Oct: Wed - Sun, 11am - 5pm. 7 - 29 Oct: Sats & Suns, 11am - 4pm. Open BH Mons.

Admission: Adult £3.80, Child £1.90, Family £9.

WCs. Unsuitable. Unsuitable for coaches.

Eastnor Castle, Gothic Drawing Room.

MAP 6

Owner:
Mr & Mrs F Fisher

▶ **CONTACT**

Mrs Ann E Fisher
Oakley Hall
Market Drayton
Shropshire TF9 4AG

Tel: 01630 653472
Fax: 01630 653282

▶ **LOCATION**

OS Ref. SJ701 367

From London 3hrs:
M1, M6/J14, then A5013
to Eccleshall, turn right
at T-junction, 200 yards,
then left onto B5026.
Mucklestone is 1¾ m
from Loggerheads on
B5026. 3m NE of
Market Drayton
N of the A53,
1½ m W of
Mucklestone,
off B5145.

OAKLEY HALL

Oakley Hall is situated in magnificent countryside on the boundary of Shropshire and Staffordshire. The present Hall is a fine example of a Queen Anne mansion house and was built on the site of an older dwelling mentioned in the Domesday Survey of 1085. Oakley Hall was the home of the Chetwode family until it was finally sold in 1919.

GARDENS

Set in 100 acres of rolling parkland, the Hall commands superb views over the surrounding countryside and the gardens include wild areas in addition to the more formal parts.

Oakley Hall is a privately owned family house and since it is not open to the general public it provides a perfect location for exclusive private or corporate functions. The main hall can accommodate 100 people comfortably and has excellent acoustics for concerts. Four double bedrooms are available for those attending functions. The secluded location and unspoilt landscape make Oakley an ideal setting for filming and photography.

The surrounding countryside is rich in historical associations. St Mary's Church at Mucklestone, in which parish the Hall stands, was erected in the 13th century and it was from the tower of this Church that Queen Margaret of Anjou observed the Battle of Blore Heath in 1459. This was a brilliant victory for the Yorkist faction in the Wars of the Roses and the blacksmith at Mucklestone was reputed to have shod the Queen's horse back to front in order to disguise her escape.

▶ **OPENING TIMES**

All Year
Not open to the public. The house is available all year round for private or corporate events.

▶ **ADMISSION**

Please telephone for details.

 Concerts, conferences (see left for rooms available). Fashion shows, product launches, seminars, clay pigeon shooting, garden parties and filming. Grand piano, hard tennis court, croquet lawn, horse riding. No stiletto heels.

Wedding receptions, buffets, lunches and dinners can be arranged for large or small groups, using high quality local caterers.

Visitors may alight at the entrance to the Hall, before parking in allocated areas. WCs.

By prior arrangement groups will be met and entertained by members of the Fisher family.

 100 cars, 100 yds from the Hall.

 4 double with baths.

CONFERENCE/FUNCTION		
ROOM	SIZE	MAX CAPACITY
Hall	50' x 30'	100
Dining Rm	40' x 27'	60
Ballroom	40' x 27'	60

MAP 6

Owner:
The Weston Park
Foundation

▶ **CONTACT**

Kate Thomas
Weston Park
Weston-under-Lizard
Nr Shifnal
Shropshire TF11 8LE

Tel: 01952 852100
Fax: 01952 850430
e-mail: enquiries@
weston-park.com

▶ **LOCATION**

OS Ref. SJ808 107

Birmingham 40 mins.
Manchester 1 hr.
Motorway access
M6/J12 or M54/J3.
House situated on A5 at
Weston-under-Lizard.

Rail: Nearest Railway
Stations: Wolverhampton,
Stafford or Telford.

Air: Birmingham,
West Midlands,
Manchester.

CONFERENCE/FUNCTION

ROOM	SIZE	MAX CAPACITY
Dining Rm	52' x 23'	90
Orangery	51' x 20'	120
Music Rm	50' x 20'	80
The Stables	58' x 20'	60
Conference Room	40' x 7'6"	60

WESTON PARK

www.weston-park.com

Weston Park is a magnificent Stately Home and Parkland situated on the Staffordshire/Shropshire border. The former home of the Earls of Bradford, the Park is now held in trust for the nation by The Weston Park Foundation.

Built in 1671 by Lady Elizabeth Wilbraham, this warm and welcoming house boasts a superb collection of paintings, including work by Van Dyck, Gainsborough and Stubbs, furniture and *objéts d'art*, providing continued interest and enjoyment for all of its visitors.

Step outside to enjoy the 1,000 acres of glorious Parkland, take one of a variety of woodland and wildlife walks, all landscaped by the legendary 'Capability' Brown in the 18th Century. Then browse through the Gift Shop before relaxing in The Stables Restaurant and Bar.

With the exciting Woodland Adventure Playground and Deer Park, as well as the Miniature Railway, there is so much for children to do. New for 2006, Yew Hedge Maze and Orchard.

Weston Park has a long-standing reputation for staging outstanding events. The exciting and varied programme of entertainment includes Music Festivals, Model Air Shows and Game Fairs.

ℹ️ House available on an exclusive use basis. Conferences, product launches, outdoor concerts and events, filming location. Helipad and airstrip. Sporting activities organised for private groups eg. clay pigeon shooting, archery, hovercrafts, rally driving. Interior photography by prior arrangement only.

🛍️ Gift Shop.

🍸 Full event organisation service. Residential parties, special dinners, wedding receptions. Dine and stay arrangements in the house on selected dates.

♿ House and part of the grounds. WCs.

☕🍴 The Stables Bar and Restaurant provide meals and snacks. Licensed.

🅿️ Ample 100 yds away. Private booked groups may park vehicles at front door.

Award-winning educational programme available during all academic terms. Private themed visits aligned with both National Curriculum and QCA targets.

🐕 In grounds, on leads.

🛏️ Weston Park offers 28 delightful bedrooms with bathrooms (24 doubles & 4 singles).

🔔 Tel for details.

▶ **OPENING TIMES**

15 - 23, 29/30 Apr. May -
June: Sats, Suns & BHs.

July & August:
Most days (except 29 July,
17 - 23 August) &
1 - 3 Sept.

House: 1 - 5pm
Last admission 4.30pm.

Park & Gardens:
11am - 6.30pm
Last admission 5pm.

▶ **ADMISSION**

House, Park & Gardens

Adult £7.00
Child (3 - 14yrs) £4.50
OAP £6.00
Family (2+3 or 1+4) .. £17.00
Groups
Adult £4.50
Child (3 - 14yrs) £3.50
OAP £4.00

Park & Gardens

Adult £4.00
Child (3 - 14yrs) £2.50
OAP £3.50
Family
(2+3 or 1+4) £12.00
Groups
Adult £3.00
Child (3 - 14yrs) £2.00
OAP £2.50

Privilege Pass

Adult £18.00
Child (3 - 14yrs) £12.00
OAP £15.00
Family
(2+3 or 1+4) £50.00

NB. Visitors are advised
to telephone to confirm
opening times and
admission prices.

ACTON BURNELL CASTLE
Acton Burnell, Shrewsbury, Shropshire
Tel: 0121 625 6820 (Regional Office)
Owner: English Heritage   **Contact:** The West Midlands Regional Office
The warm red sandstone shell of a fortified 13th century manor house.
Location: OS126, SJ534 019. In Acton Burnell, on unclassified road 8m S of Shrewsbury.
Open: Any reasonable time.
Admission: Free.

NT Photographic Library

NTPL - James Mortimer

ATTINGHAM PARK ✤
SHREWSBURY, SHROPSHIRE SY4 4TP

Infoline: 01743 708123   **Tel:** 01743 708162   **Fax:** 01743 708175
Owner: The National Trust   **Contact:** The Property Manager
Late 18th century house, sitting in 500 acres of wonderful parkland. Built for the 1st Lord Berwick, the Georgian house contains some beautiful Italian furniture and a large silver collection. Lord Berwick, and subsequently his two elder sons, had a passion for art and music and this is seen in the Picture Gallery with fine paintings and a Samuel Green organ, which is occasionally played for visitors' enjoyment during the season. Woodland walks along the River Tern and through the Deer Park take in picturesque views of the Wrekin and Shropshire Hills. Costumed guided tours of the House are on offer every day the house is open. Events planned for 2006 include

Easter Egg Trail, Spring Plant Fair, Food Fayre and Apple Weekend.
Location: OS127, SJ837 083. 4m SE of Shrewsbury on N side of B4380 in Atcham village.
Open: 25 Mar - 29 Oct (weekends only 4 - 19 Mar): daily (closed Wed & Thur), 1 - 5pm, last admission to house 4pm. Timed Taster tours only 12 noon - 1pm.
Admission: House & Grounds: Adult £6.50, Child £3.25, Family £16.25. Booked groups (15+): Adult £5.50, Child £2.75. Grounds only: Adult £3.30, Child £1.65. Family £8.20.
ⓘNo photography in house. Licensed. By arrangement. In grounds on leads. Tel for details.

© NTPL/James Mortimer

BENTHALL HALL ✤
Benthall, Nr Broseley, Shropshire TF12 5RX
Tel: 01952 882159
Owner: The National Trust   **Contact:** The Custodian
A 16th century stone house with mullioned windows and moulded brick chimneys.
Location: OS Ref. SJ658 025. 1m NW of Broseley (B4375), 4m NE of Much Wenlock, 1m SW of Ironbridge.
Open: House & Garden: 16 Apr - 28 Jun: Tues & Weds; 2 Jul - 27 Sept: Tues, Weds & Suns, 2 - 5.30pm. Open BH Suns & Mons.
Admission: House & Garden: Adult: £4.40, Child: £2.20. Garden: Adults £2.75, Child £1.35. Groups outside normal times £5.30 (NT members £2.65).
Partial. Ground floor. WC. By arrangement. Limited.

Attingham Park.

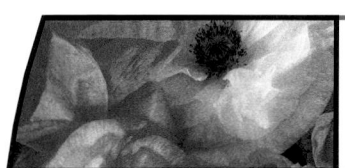

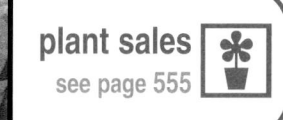
plant sales ✲
see page 555

West Midlands - England

English Heritage Photo Library

BOSCOBEL HOUSE & THE ROYAL OAK ⬢

BREWOOD, BISHOP'S WOOD, SHROPSHIRE. ST19 9AR

www.english-heritage.org.uk

Tel: 01902 850244

Owner: English Heritage   **Contact:** Visitor Operations Team

This 17th century hunting lodge was destined to play a part in Charles II's escape from the Roundheads. A descendant of the Royal Oak, which sheltered the fugitive King from Cromwell's troops after the Battle of Worcester in 1651, still stands in the fields near Boscobel House. The timber-framed house where the King slept in a tiny 'sacred hole' has been fully restored and furnished in Victorian period and there are panelled rooms and secret hiding places. There is an exhibition in the house as well as the farmyard and smithy.

Location: OS127, SJ838 082. On unclassified road between A41 & A5. 8m NW of Wolverhampton.

Open: 1 Apr - 31 May & 1 Sept - 31 Oct: Thur - Mon, 10am - 5pm. 1 Jun - 31 Aug: daily, 10am - 6pm. Last entry 1hr before closing.

Admission: Adult £4.80, Child £2.40, Conc. £3.60, Family £12. Grounds only: Adult £1.50, Child 80p, Conc. £1.10.

▢ ♿Grounds. WC. 🅟 🕱Obligatory. 🅟 🚌 ⛛ ⛛Tel for details.

BUILDWAS ABBEY ⬢

Iron Bridge, Telford, Shropshire TF8 7BW

Tel: 01952 433274 **www.**english-heritage.org.uk

Owner: English Heritage   **Contact:** Visitor Operations Team

Extensive remains of a Cistercian abbey built in 1135, set beside the River Severn against a backdrop of wooded grounds. The remains include the church which is almost complete except for the roof.

Location: OS127, SJ643 043. On S bank of River Severn on A4169, 2m W of Ironbridge.

Open: 1 Apr - 31 May & 1 - 30 Sept: Thur - Mon, 10am - 5pm. 1 Jun - 31 Aug: daily, 10am - 6pm.

Admission: Adult £2.70, Child £1.40, Conc. £2.

▢ ♿ 🅟 🚌

CLUN CASTLE ⬢

Clun, Ludlow, Shropshire

Tel: 0121 625 6820 (Regional Office)

Owner: English Heritage   **Contact:** The West Midlands Regional Office

Remains of a four-storey keep and other buildings of this border castle are set in outstanding countryside, near the Welsh border. Built in the 11th century.

Location: OS137, SO299 809. In Clun, off A488, 18m W of Ludlow. 9m W of Craven Arms.

Open: Any reasonable time.

Admission: Free.

🚌 ⛛

COLEHAM PUMPING STATION

Longden Coleham, Shrewsbury, Shropshire SY3 7DN

Tel: 01743 361196 **Fax:** 01743 358411

e-mail: museums@shrewsbury.gov.uk **www.**shrewsburymuseums.com

Owner: Shrewsbury & Atcham Borough Council   **Contact:** Mary White

Two Renshaw beam engines of 1901 now restored to steam by members of Shrewsbury Steam Trust.

Location: OS Ref. SJ497 122. Shrewsbury town centre, near the River Severn.

Open: Apr - July & Sept: 4th Sun in each month, 10am - 4pm. Plus occasional other days. Details: 01743 361196.

Admission: Adult £1, Child 50p, Student £1.

♿ Partial. 🕱 By arrangement. 🅟 No parking. 🕯 🚌 Guide dogs only.

COMBERMERE ABBEY

Whitchurch, Shropshire SY13 4AJ

Tel: 01948 662880 **Fax:** 01948 871604

e-mail: estate@combermereabbey.co.uk **www.**combermereabbey.co.uk

Owner: Mrs S Callander Beckett   **Contact:** Administrator

Combermere Abbey, originally a Cistercian monastery, remodelled as a Tudor manor house and in 1820 as a Gothic house, sits in a magnificent 1000 acre parkland designed by Webb, in front of a large natural mere. The Walled Gardens have been restored and a unique Fruit Tree Maze created. Tours can now include the gardens. Excellent accommodation is available on the Estate.

Location: OS Ref. SJ590 440. 5m E of Whitchurch, off A530. Manchester, Liverpool and Birmingham airports 1hr.

Open: 6 Apr - 28 Sept: Thurs only for tours, 2 - 4pm. Advance bookings necessary. Group visits (20 - 60) by arrangement. Available for corporate hospitality, meetings, location shoots, wedding and naming ceremonies. Please look at Whats On/Abbey section on website for full events schedule.

Admission: On open days: Adult £5, Child (under 15yrs) £3. Group tours: £7.50 - £10 per person inclusive of refreshments.

ℹNo photography. 🅣 ♿Unsuitable. 🕯 By arrangement. 🕱By arrangement. 🅟 Limited. 🈺 🏠 ⛣ For groups. ⛛ Tel for details.

COUND HALL

Cound, Shropshire SY5 6AH

Tel: 01743 761721 **Fax:** 01743 761722

Owner: Mr & Mrs D R Waller   **Contact:** Mrs J Stephens

Queen Anne red brick Hall.

Location: OS Ref. SJ560 053.

Open: 10 - 14 July: 10am - 4pm.

Admission: Adult £4.50, Child £2.30, Conc. £3.40, Family £11.30.

ℹNo photography. ♿Partial. 🅟 Limited. 🚌

Michael Caldwell

DUDMASTON ❦

QUATT, BRIDGNORTH, SHROPSHIRE WV15 6QN

Tel: 01746 780866 **Fax:** 01746 780744 **e-mail:** dudmaston@nationaltrust.org.uk

Owner: The National Trust   **Contact:** The House & Visitor Services Manager

Late 17th century manor house. Contains furniture and china, Dutch flower paintings, watercolours, botanical art and modern pictures and sculpture, family and natural history. 9 acres of lakeside gardens and Dingle walk. Two estate walks 5¹/₂ m and 3¹/₂m starting from Hampton Loade car park.

Location: OS Ref. SO748 888. 4m SE of Bridgnorth on A442.

Open: House & Garden: 2 Apr - 27 Sept, Tues, Weds, Suns & BH Mons, 2 - 5.30pm. Last admission to house 5pm. Garden: Mon - Wed, Suns & BH Mons, 12 noon - 6pm.

Admission: House & Garden: Adult £5, Child £2.50, Family £12.50, Group £4. Garden only: Adult £4, Child £2, Family £9, Group £3. Free tours Mon afternoons (except BHs).

ℹCountryside walks. ▢ ♿ 🕯 🚌In parkland and estate, on leads, not garden.

HAUGHMOND ABBEY ⌗

Upton Magna, Uffington, Shrewsbury, Shropshire SY4 4RW

Tel: 01743 709661   **www**.english-heritage.org.uk

Owner: English Heritage   **Contact:** Visitor Operations Team

Extensive remains of a 12th century Augustinian abbey, including the Chapter House which retains its late medieval timber ceiling, and including some fine medieval sculpture.

Location: OS126, SJ542 152. 3m NE of Shrewsbury off B5062.

Open: 1 Apr - 31 May : Thur - Mon, 10am - 5pm. 1 Jun - 31 Aug: daily, 10am - 6pm. Sept: Thur - Mon, 10am - 5pm.

Admission: Adult £2.70, Child £1.40, Conc. £2.

▢ ⓰ 🅿 🐕 ⓥ Tel for details.

HAWKSTONE HALL & GARDENS

Marchamley, Shrewsbury SY4 5LG

Tel: 01630 685242   **Fax:** 01630 685565

Owner: The Redemptorists   **Contact:** Guest Mistress

Grade I Georgian mansion and restored gardens set in spacious parkland.

Location: OS Ref. SJ581 299. Entrance 1m N of Hodnet near A442.

Open: Closed until 2007.

HODNET HALL GARDENS 🏛

Hodnet, Market Drayton, Shropshire TF9 3NN

Tel: 01630 685786   **Fax:** 01630 685853

email: secretary@heber-percy.freeserve.co.uk

Owner: Mr and the Hon Mrs A Heber-Percy   **Contact:** Mrs M Revie

The 60+ acres are renowned as amongst the finest in the country. Forest trees provide a wonderful backdrop for formal gardens planted to give delight during every season, with extensive woodland walks amongst wild flowers and unusual flowering shrubs along the banks of a chain of ornamental pools.

Location: OS Ref. SJ613 286. 12m NE of Shrewsbury on A53; M6/J15, M54/J3.

Open: Groups only welcome by appointment, please contact the Secretary.

Admission: £4 per person.

⌕ For groups. 🅿 ▣ Educational package linked to Key stages 1 & 2 of National Curriculum. 🐕 On leads.

IRON BRIDGE ⌗

Ironbridge, Shropshire

Tel: 0121 625 6820 (Regional Office)

Owner: English Heritage   **Contact:** The West Midlands Regional Office

The world's first iron bridge and Britain's best known industrial monument. Cast in Coalbrookdale by local ironmaster, Abraham Darby, it was erected across the River Severn in 1779. Iron Bridge is a World Heritage Site. Visit the recently refurbished Toll House on the Bridge, with interpretation displays.

Location: OS127, SJ672 034. In Ironbridge, adjacent to A4169.

Open: Any reasonable time.

Admission: Free crossing.

🐕 ✳

LANGLEY CHAPEL ⌗

Acton Burnell, Shrewsbury, Shropshire

Tel: 0121 625 6820 (Regional Office)

Owner: English Heritage   **Contact:** The West Midlands Regional Office

A delightful medieval chapel, standing alone in a field, with a complete set of early 17th century wooden fittings and furniture.

Location: OS126, SJ538 001. 1½ m S of Acton Burnell, on unclassified road 4m E of the A49, 9½ m S of Shrewsbury.

Open: Any reasonable time.

Admission: Free.

🐕 ✳

LILLESHALL ABBEY ⌗

Oakengates, Shropshire

Tel: 0121 625 6820 (Regional Office)

Owner: English Heritage   **Contact:** The West Midlands Regional Office

Extensive ruins of an abbey of Augustinian canons including remains of the 12th and 13th century church and the cloister buildings. Surrounded by green lawns and ancient yew trees.

Location: OS127, SJ738 142. On unclassified road off the A518, 4m N of Oakengates.

Open: 1 Apr - 30 Sept: daily, 10am - 5pm.

Admission: Free.

🐕

LONGNER HALL 🏛

Uffington, Shrewsbury, Shropshire SY4 4TG

Tel: 01743 709215

Owner: Mr R L Burton   **Contact:** Mrs R L Burton

Designed by John Nash in 1803, Longner Hall is a Tudor Gothic style house set in a park landscaped by Humphry Repton. The home of one family for over 700 years. Longner's principal rooms are adorned with plaster fan vaulting and stained glass.

Location: OS Ref. SJ529 110. 4m SE of Shrewsbury on Uffington road, ¼ m off B4380, Atcham.

Open: Apr - Oct: Tues & BH Mons, 2 - 5pm. Tours at 2pm & 3.30pm. Groups at any time by arrangement.

Admission: Adult £5, Child/OAP £3.

ⓘ No photography in house. ✦ ⓰ Partial. ▣ By arrangement for groups. 𝍖 Obligatory. 🅿 Limited for coaches. ▣ By arrangement. 🐕 Guide dogs only. ✳

LUDLOW CASTLE

CASTLE SQUARE, LUDLOW, SHROPSHIRE SY8 1AY

www.ludlowcastle.com

Tel: 01584 873355

Owner: The Earl of Powis & The Trustees of the Powis Estate

          Contact: Helen J Duce

900 year old castle of the Marches, dates from 1086 and extended over the centuries to a fortified Royal Palace. Seat of government for the Council for Wales and the Marches. Privately owned by the Earls of Powis since 1811. A magnificent ruin set in the heart of medieval Ludlow.

Location: OS Ref. SO509 745. Shrewsbury 28m, Hereford 26m. A49 centre of Ludlow.

Open: Jan: weekends only, 10am - 4pm, Feb - Mar & Oct - Dec: 10am - 4pm. Apr - Jul & Sept: 10am - 5pm. Aug: 10am - 7pm. Last adm. 30mins before closing. Closed 25 Dec.

Admission: Adult £4, Child £2, Conc. £3.50, Family £11. 10% reduction for groups (10+).

▢ ⓰ Partial. 𝍖 By arrangement. ▢ 🅿 None. ▣ 🐕 ✳ ⓥ Tel for details.

Weston Park.

MAWLEY HALL

CLEOBURY MORTIMER, DY14 8PN

www.mawley.com

Tel: 020 7495 6702 **Fax:** 020 7409 1810 **e-mail:** administration@mawley.com

Owner: R Galliers-Pratt Esq   **Contact:** Mrs R Sharp

Built in 1730 and attributed to Francis Smith of Warwick, Mawley is set in 18th century landscaped parkland with extensive gardens and walks down to the River Rea. Magnificent plasterwork and a fine collection of English and Continental furniture and porcelain.

Location: OS137, SO688 753. 1m N of Cleobury Mortimer on the A4117 and 7m W of Bewdley.

Open: 17 Apr - 20 Jul: Mons & Thurs, 3 - 5pm and throughout the year by appointment.

Admission: Adult £8, Child/OAP £5.

⊤ 𝒦 By arrangement. **P** ▣ ▤ In grounds, on leads. ✳

MORETON CORBET CASTLE ♯

Moreton Corbet, Shrewsbury, Shropshire

Tel: 0121 625 6820 (Regional Office)

Owner: English Heritage   **Contact:** The West Midlands Regional Office

A ruined medieval castle with the substantial remains of a splendid Elizabethan mansion, captured in 1644 from Charles I's supporters by Parliamentary forces.

Location: OS126, SJ561 231. In Moreton Corbet off B5063, 7m NE of Shrewsbury.

Open: Any reasonable time.

Admission: Free.

♿ **P** ▤ ✳

MORVILLE HALL ⚘

Bridgnorth, Shropshire WV16 5NB

Tel: 01746 780838

Owner: The National Trust   **Contact:** Dr & Mrs C Douglas

An Elizabethan house of mellow stone, converted in the 18th century and set in attractive gardens.

Location: OS Ref. SO668 940. Morville, on A458 3m W of Bridgnorth.

Open: By written appointment only with the tenants.

Admission: £3. NT members free.

OAKLEY HALL   *See page 345 for full page entry.*

PREEN MANOR GARDENS

Church Preen, Church Stretton, Shropshire SY6 7LQ

Tel: 01694 771207

Owner/Contact: Mrs P Trevor-Jones

Six acre garden on site of Cluniac monastery, with walled, terraced, wild, water, kitchen and chess gardens. 12th century monastic church.

Location: OS Ref. SO544 981. 10m SSE of Shrewsbury. 7m NE of Church Stretton, 6m SW of Much Wenlock.

Open: 30 Apr & 1 Oct: 2 - 5pm. 1 Jun & 27 Jul: 2 - 6pm. Groups by arrangement in Jun & Jul.

Admission: Adult £3.50, Child 50p.

SHIPTON HALL 🏛

Much Wenlock, Shropshire TF13 6JZ

Tel: 01746 785225 **Fax:** 01746 785125

Owner: Mr J N R Bishop   **Contact:** Mrs M J Bishop

Built around 1587 by Richard Lutwyche who gave the house to his daughter Elizabeth on her marriage to Thomas Mytton. Shipton remained in the Mytton family for the next 300 years. The house has been described as *'an exquisite specimen of Elizabethan architecture set in a quaint old fashioned garden, the whole forming a picture which as regards both form and colour, satisfies the artistic sense of even the most fastidious'*. The Georgian additions by Thomas F Pritchard include some elegant rococo interior decorations. There is some noteworthy Tudor and Jacobean panelling. Family home. In addition to the house visitors are welcome to explore the gardens, the dovecote and the parish church which dates back to Saxon times.

Location: OS Ref. SO563 918. 7m SW of Much Wenlock on B4378. 10m W of Bridgnorth.

Open: Easter - end Sept: Thurs, 2.30 - 5.30pm. Also Suns and Mons of BH, 2.30 - 5.30pm. Groups of 20+ at any time of day or year by prior arrangement.

Admission: Adult £4.50, Child (under 14yrs) £2.25. 10% Discount for groups (20+). ♿ Unsuitable. ▣ By arrangement for groups (20+). 𝒦 Obligatory. ▤ Guide dogs only.

SHREWSBURY ABBEY

Shrewsbury, Shropshire SY2 6BS

Tel: 01743 232723 **Contact:** William Hayes

Benedictine Abbey founded in 1083, tomb of Roger de Montgomerie and remains of tomb of St Winefride, 7th century Welsh saint. The Abbey was part of the monastery and has also been a parish church since the 12th century.

Location: OS Ref. SJ499 125. Signposted from Shrewsbury bypass (A5 and A49). 500yds E of town centre, across English Bridge.

Open: All year. Summer: 10am - 4.30pm. Winter: 10.30am - 3pm.

Admission: Donation. For guided tours, please contact Abbey.

SHREWSBURY CASTLE &
THE SHROPSHIRE REGIMENTAL MUSEUM

Castle Street, Shrewsbury SY1 2AT

Tel: 01743 358516 **Fax:** 01743 358411 **e-mail:** museums@shrewsbury.gov.uk
www.shrewsburymuseums.com

Owner: Shrewsbury & Atcham Borough Council   **Contact:** Mary White

Norman Castle with 18th century work by Thomas Telford. Free admission to attractive floral grounds. The main hall houses The Shropshire Regimental Museum and displays on the history of the castle. Open-air theatre, music and events throughout the summer.

Location: OS Ref. SJ495 128. Town centre, adjacent BR and bus stations.

Open: Main building & Museum: Late May BH - mid Sept: Mon - Sat, 10am - 5pm; Suns, 10am - 4pm. Winter: Please call for details. Grounds: Mon - Sat, 10am - 5pm & Suns as above.

Admission: Museum: Adult £2.50, OAP £1.25, Shrewsbury residents, under 18s, Students & members of the regiments Free. Grounds: Free.

ℹ No photography. ▣ ♿ **P** None. ▣ ▤ Guide dogs only. ▲ ☏ Tel for details.

SHREWSBURY MUSEUM & ART GALLERY

Barker Street, Shrewsbury, Shropshire SY1 1QH

Tel: 01743 361196 **Fax:** 01743 358411

e-mail: museums@shrewsbury.gov.uk **www**.shrewsburymuseums.com

Owner: Shrewsbury and Atcham Borough Council   **Contact:** Mary White

Impressive timber-framed building and attached 17th century brick mansion with archaeology and natural history, geology, social history and special exhibitions, including contemporary art.

Location: OS Ref. SJ490 126. Barker Street.

Open: Late May BH - mid Sept: Mon - Sat, 10am - 5pm; Suns, 10am - 4pm. Rest of year: Tue - Sat, 10am - 4pm. Closed Christmas/New Year.

Admission: Free.

ℹ No photography. ▣ ♿ Ground floor only. **P** Adjacent public. ▣
▤ Guide dogs only. ✳

©English Heritage Photo Library

STOKESAY CASTLE ⌗

Nr CRAVEN ARMS, SHROPSHIRE SY7 9AH

www.english-heritage.org.uk

Tel: 01588 672544

Owner: English Heritage   **Contact:** Visitor Operations Team

This perfectly preserved example of a 13th century fortified manor house gives us a glimpse of the life and ambitions of a rich medieval merchant. Lawrence of Ludlow built this country house to impress the landed gentry. The magnificent Great Hall, almost untouched since medieval times, was used for feasting. The family's private quarters were in the bright, comfortable solar on the first floor. From the outside the castle forms a picturesque grouping of castle, parish church and timber-framed Jacobean gatehouse set in the rolling Shropshire countryside.

Location: OS148, SO446 787. 7m NW of Ludlow off A49. 1m S of Craven Arms off A49.

Open: 1 - 30 Apr & 1 Sept - 31 Oct: Thur - Mon, 10am - 5pm. 1 May - 30 Jun: daily, 10am - 5pm. 1 Jul - 31 Aug: daily, 10am - 6pm. 1 Nov - 28 Feb: Fri - Mon, 10am - 4pm. Closed 24 - 26 Dec & 1 Jan.

Admission: Adult £4.80, Child £2.40, Conc. £3.60, Family £12. 15% discount for groups (11+).

◻ ⑤ Great Hall & gardens. WC. ▣ ◻ P ✖ ✳ ▣ Tel for details.

SUNNYCROFT ✻

200 Holyhead Road, Wellington, Telford, Shropshire TF1 2DR

Tel: 01952 242884

Owner: The National Trust   **Contact:** The Custodian

Late Victorian gentleman's suburban villa. The grounds amount to a 'mini-estate', with pigsties, stables, kitchen garden, orchards, conservatory, flower garden and superb Wellingtonia avenue.

Location: OS Ref. SJ652 109. M54 exit 7, follow B5061 towards Wellington.

Open: House & Garden: 26 Mar - 29 Oct: Mons, Fris & Suns.

Admission: House & Garden: Adult £5, Child £2.50, Family £12.50. Garden only: Adult £2.50, Child £1.25, Family £6.30. Groups at other times £10.

⑤ Ground Floor, Adapted WC. ⒧ By arrangement. P

WENLOCK GUILDHALL

Much Wenlock, Shropshire TF13 6AE

Tel: 01952 727509

Owner/Contact: Much Wenlock Town Council

16th century half-timbered building has an open-arcade market area.

Location: OS Ref. SJ624 000. In centre of Much Wenlock, next to the church.

Open: 1 Apr - 31 Oct: Mon - Sat, 10.30am - 1pm & 2 - 4pm. Suns: 2 - 4pm.

Admission: Adult 50p, Child Free.

WENLOCK PRIORY ⌗

Much Wenlock, Shropshire TF13 6HS

Tel: 01952 727466   www.english-heritage.org.uk

Owner: English Heritage   **Contact:** Visitor Operations Team

A prosperous, powerful priory at its peak in the Middle Ages. A great deal of the structure still survives in the form of high, romantic ruined walls and it is the resting place of St Milburga the first Abbess. A monastery was first founded at Wenlock in the 7th century, and little more is known of the site until the time of the Norman Conquest when it became a Cluniac monastery. These majestic ruins of the priory church are set in green lawns and topiary, and there are substantial remains of the early 13th century church and Norman Chapter House.

Location: OS127, SJ625 001. In Much Wenlock.

Open: Apr, Sept & Oct: Thur - Mon, 10am - 5pm. 1 May - 30 Jun: daily, 10am - 5pm. 1 Jul - 31 Aug: daily, 10am - 6pm. 1 Nov - 28 Feb: Thur - Sun, 10am - 4pm. Closed 24 - 26 Dec & 1 Jan.

Admission: Adult £3.30, Child £1.70, Conc. £2.50.

ⓘ WC. ◻ ◻ P ✖ ✳ ▣ Tel for details.

WESTON PARK 🏠   *See page 346 for full page entry.*

WOLLERTON OLD HALL GARDEN

Wollerton, Market Drayton, Shropshire TF9 3NA

Tel: 01630 685760   **Fax:** 01630 685583

Owner: Mr & Mrs J D Jenkins   **Contact:** Mrs Di Oakes

Three acre plantsman's garden created around a 16th century house (not open).

Location: OS Ref. SJ623 296. 14m NE of Shrewsbury off A53 between Hodnet and Market Drayton.

Open: Easter Good Fri - end Sept: Fris, Suns & BHs, 12 noon - 5pm. Groups (25+) by appointment at other times.

Admission: Adult £4, Child £1.

WROXETER ROMAN CITY ⌗

Wroxeter, Shrewsbury, Shropshire SY5 6PH

Tel: 01743 761330   www.english-heritage.org.uk

Owner: English Heritage   **Contact:** Visitor Operations Team

The part-excavated centre of the fourth largest city in Roman Britain, originally home to some 6,000 men and several hundred houses. Impressive remains of the 2nd century municipal baths. There is a site museum in which many finds are displayed, including those from recent work by Birmingham Field Archaeological Unit.

Location: OS126, SJ565 087. At Wroxeter, 5m E of Shrewsbury, on B4380.

Open: 1 Mar - 31 Oct: daily, 10am - 5pm (6pm Jun - Aug). 1 Nov - 28 Feb: Wed - Sun, 10am - 4pm. Closed 24 - 26 Dec & 1 Jan.

Admission: Adult £4, Child £2, Conc. £3, Family £10.

ⓘ WC. ◻ ⑤ ◻ P ▣ ✖ ✳ ▣ Tel for details.

© English Heritage/Andrew Tryner

Boscobel House.

THE ANCIENT HIGH HOUSE
Greengate Street, Stafford ST16 2JA

Tel: 01785 619131 **Fax:** 01785 619132 **e-mail:** ahh@staffordbc.gov.uk
www.staffordbc.gov.uk

Owner: Stafford Borough Council　　　　　**Contact:** Mark Hartwell

Over four hundred years of history are waiting to be discovered within the walls of Stafford's Ancient High House – England's largest timber-framed town house and one of the finest Tudor buildings in the country. Now fully restored, the superb period room settings reflect its fascinating story.

Location: OS Ref. SJ922 232. Town centre.

Open: All year: Tues - Sat, 10am - 4pm.

Admission: Free. Check for events, charges may apply.

⬜ 🚻 Unsuitable. 🍴 By arrangement. 🏫 School tours by arrangement.
🐕 Guide dogs only. ❄ 📺 Tel for details.

CHILLINGTON HALL 🏛
CODSALL WOOD, WOLVERHAMPTON, STAFFORDSHIRE WV8 1RE
www.chillingtonhall.co.uk

Tel: 01902 850236 **Fax:** 01902 850768
e-mail: mrsplod@chillingtonhall.co.uk

Owner/Contact: Mr & Mrs J W Giffard

Home of the Giffards since 1178. Built during 18th century by Francis Smith of Warwick and John Soane. Park designed by 'Capability' Brown. Smith's Staircase, Soane's Saloon and the Pool (a lake of 70 acres) are splendid examples of the days of the Georgian landowner.

Location: OS Ref. SJ864 067. 2m S of Brewood off A449. 4m NW of M54/J2.

Open: House: BHs, Easter; May & Jul: Suns. Aug: Wed - Fri, Suns & BH, 2 - 5pm. Grounds: as House, also Suns Easter - end May.

Admission: Adult £4, Child £2. Grounds only: half price.

🚻 Partial. 🍴 Obligatory. 🅿 🐕 In grounds, on leads. €

NTPL / Ian Shaw

BIDDULPH GRANGE GARDEN 🌺
GRANGE ROAD, BIDDULPH, STOKE-ON-TRENT ST8 7SD

Tel: 01782 517999 **Fax:** 01782 510624

Owner: The National Trust　　　　　**Contact:** The Garden Office

A rare and exciting survival of a High Victorian garden, restored by the National Trust. The garden is divided into a series of themed gardens within a garden, with a Chinese temple, Egyptian court, pinetum, dahlia walk, glen and many other settings. Difficult uneven levels, unsuitable for wheelchairs.

Location: OS Ref. SJ891 592. E of A527, 3¹⁄₂ m SE of Congleton, 8m N of Stoke-on-Trent.

Open: 25 Mar - 29 Oct: Wed - Sun, 11.30am - 5.30pm. BH Mons, 11.30am - 5.30pm or dusk. 4 Nov - 17 Dec: Sats & Suns, 11am - 3pm.

Admission: Adult £5.30, Child £2.60, Family (2+3) £13.00. Booked guided tours: Groups (15+): £7.50. Nov & Dec: Adult £2, Child £1, Family £5. Voucher to visit Little Moreton Hall at a reduced fee when purchasing Adult ticket.

⬜ 🍴 🚻 Unsuitable for wheelchairs and people with mobility problems. 🍽
🐕 In car park, on leads.

THE DOROTHY CLIVE GARDEN
WILLOUGHBRIDGE, MARKET DRAYTON, SHROPSHIRE TF9 4EU
www.dorothyclivegarden.co.uk

Tel: 01630 647237 **Fax:** 01630 647902

Owner: Willoughbridge Garden Trust　　　　　**Contact:** Garden Office

The Dorothy Clive Garden accommodates a wide range of choice and unusual plants providing year round interest. Features include a quarry with spectacular waterfall, flower borders, a scree and water garden. Tearoom serving home-baked hot and cold snacks throughout the day.

Location: OS Ref. SJ753 400. A51, 2m S of Woore, 3m from Bridgemere.

Open: 11 Mar - 29 Oct: daily, 10am - 5.30pm.

Admission: Adult £4.20, Child (11-16yrs) £1, (under 16yrs Free), OAP £3.60. Pre-booked Groups (20+) £3.60.

🚻 🍽 🅿 🐕 In grounds on leads.

CASTERNE HALL 🏛
Ilam Nr Ashbourne, Derbyshire DE6 2BA

Tel: 01335 310489 **e-mail:** mail@casterne.co.uk **www.**casterne.co.uk

Owner/Contact: Charles & Susannah Hurt

Small manor house in beautiful location.

Location: OS Ref. SK123 523. Take first turning on left N of Ilam and continue past 'Casterne Farms only' sign.

Open: 2 May - 8 Jun (closed 1 May): weekdays only. Tours on the hour: 2, 3, & 4pm.

Admission: £4.

🚻 Partial. 🍴 Obligatory. 🍽 🏠 €

DUNWOOD HALL

Longsdon, Nr Leek, Stoke-on-Trent, Staffordshire ST9 9AR

Tel: 01538 372978   **e-mail:** info@dunwoodhall.co.uk

www.dunwoodhall.co.uk

Owner: Dr R V Kemp/C Lovatt   **Contact:** Camilla Lovatt

This fine, unspoiled example of Victorian Gothic Revival architecture was built in 1871 as the country home for Thomas Hulme, Mayor of Burslem, the local Potteries' town and birthplace of Josiah Wedgwood. It features carved stonework, decorative wrought iron and an impressive three-storey, galleried hall over an extensive Minton encaustic-tile floor.

Location: OS Ref. SJ947 544. On the A53 between Stoke-on-Trent and Leek, 3 miles West of Leek. Regular bus service on A53.

Open: Groups (15 - 50), by arrangement only.

Admission: Please telephone for details.

🕎 🖬 🇹 🖺 Partial. ☎ 🎦 Obligatory. 🅿 Limited for cars, arrangements for coaches. 🐕 Guide dogs only. 🛏 3 doubles.

ERASMUS DARWIN HOUSE 🏛

Beacon Street, Lichfield, Staffordshire WA13 7AD

www.erasmusdarwin.org

Tel: 01543 306260   **e-mail:** enquiries@erasmusdarwin.org

Owner: The Erasmus Darwin Foundation   **Contact:** Alison Wallis

Grandfather of Charles Darwin and a founder member of the Lunar Society, Erasmus Darwin (1731-1802) was a leading doctor, scientist, inventor and poet. This elegant Georgian house was his home and contains an exhibition of his life, theories, and inventions. There is also an 18th century herb garden.

Location: OS Ref. SK115 098. Situated at the W end of Lichfield Cathedral Close.

Open: All year. Please telephone for details.

Admission: Adult £2.50, Child/Conc. £2, Family £6. Groups (10-50) £2.

🗗 🕎 🖬 🖺 🎦 By arrangement. 🔊 🅿 Disabled only. ☎ 🐕 Guide dogs only. ❄

FORD GREEN HALL

Ford Green Road, Smallthorne, Stoke-on-Trent ST6 1NG

Tel: 01782 233195   **Fax:** 01782 233194

e-mail: ford.green.hall@stoke.gov.uk   **www**.stoke.gov.uk/fordgreenhall

Owner: Stoke-on-Trent City Council   **Contact:** Angela Graham

A 17th century house, home to the Ford family for two centuries. The hall has been designated a museum with an outstanding collection of original and reproduction period furniture, ceramics and textiles. There is a Tudor-style garden. The museum has an award-winning education service and regular events. Children's parties available.

Location: OS Ref. SJ887 508. NE of Stoke-on-Trent on B505, signposted from A500.

Open: All year: (closed 25 Dec - 1 Jan), Sun - Thurs, 1 - 5pm.

Admission: Charge applies. Special group packages and packages with other visitor attractions (must book, min 10).

🗗 🕎 🖺 Partial. WC. ☎ 🅿 ☎ 🐕 In grounds, on leads. 🛏 ❄ 🖵 Tel for details.

THE HEATH HOUSE

Tean, Stoke-on-Trent, Staffordshire ST10 4HA

Tel: 01538 722212/01386 792110

e-mail: philips@heathhouse1.freeserve.co.uk   **www**.theheathhouse.co.uk

Owner/Contact: Mr John Philips

The Heath House is an early Victorian mansion designed and built 1836 - 1840 in the Tudor style for John Burton Philips. The collection of paintings is a rare survival and has remained undisturbed since its acquisition. It is still a Philips family home. Large attractive formal garden.

Location: OS Ref. SK030 392. A522 off A50 at Uttoxeter 5m W, at Lower Tean turn right.

Open: 25 Apr - 30 Sept: Tues & BHs, by appointment, 2 - 5pm.

Admission: Adult £3.50, Conc £3. No reductions for groups.

ⓘ No photography or video recording. 🖺 🎦 Obligatory. 🅿 🐕 In grounds, on leads. 🛏

IZAAK WALTON'S COTTAGE

Worston Lane, Shallowford, Nr Stafford ST15 0PA

Tel/Fax: 01785 760278

e-mail: ahh@staffordbc.gov.uk   **www**.staffordbc.gov.uk/heritage

Owner: Stafford Borough Council   **Contact:** Mark Hartwell

Stafford's rural heritage is embodied in the charming 17th century cottage owned by the celebrated author of *The Compleat Angler*. Izaak Walton's Cottage gives a fascinating insight into the history of angling and the life of a writer whose work remains 'a unique celebration of the English countryside.'

Location: OS Ref. SJ876 293. M6/J14, A5013 towards Eccleshall, signposted on A5013.

Open: May - Aug: Sat & Sun, 1 - 5pm.

Admission: Free. Check for events, charges may apply.

🗗 🖺 Partial. WCs. ☎ 🅿 Limited for cars. 🐕 Guide dogs only. 🛏

MOSELEY OLD HALL 🌿
FORDHOUSES, WOLVERHAMPTON WV10 7HY

Tel: 01902 782808   **e-mail:** moseleyoldhall@nationaltrust.org.uk

Owner: The National Trust   **Contact:** The Property Manager

An Elizabethan timber-framed house encased in brick in 1870; with original interiors. Charles II hid here after the Battle of Worcester. The bed in which he slept is on view as well as the hiding place he used. An exhibition retells the story of the King's dramatic escape from Cromwell's troops, and there are optional, free guided tours. The garden has been reconstructed in 17th century style with formal box parterre, only 17th century plants are grown. The property is a Sandford Education Award Winner.

Location: OS Ref. SJ932 044. 4m N of Wolverhampton between A449 and A460.

Open: 18 Mar - 29 Oct: Sats, Suns, Weds, BH Mons & following Tues 1- 5pm, BH Mons 11am - 5pm. 5 - 19 Nov: Suns, 1 - 4pm (guided tours only). 26 Nov - 17 Dec: Christmas activites, ground floor of the house only. Last admission to the house 30 minutes before closing. Shop, Tearoom & Garden: Open 12 noon.

Admission: Adult £5, Child £2.50, Family £12.50. Groups (15+) £4.30pp. Private visits in closing times £5.70pp (Min £114). NT members free with valid membership card.

🗗 🕎 🖺 Ground floor & grounds. WC. ☎ Tearoom in 18th century barn. 🎦 🅿 ☎ 🐕 On leads. 🛏 🖵 Tel for details.

SANDON HALL

SANDON, STAFFORDSHIRE ST18 0BZ

www.sandonhall.co.uk

Tel/Fax: 01889 508004   **e-mail:** info@sandonhall.co.uk

Owner: The Earl of Harrowby   **Contact:** Michael Bosson

Ancestral seat of the Earls of Harrowby, conveniently located in the heart of Staffordshire. The imposing neo-Jacobean house was rebuilt by William Burn in 1854. Set amidst 400 acres of glorious parkland, Sandon, for all its grandeur and elegance, is first and foremost a home. The family museum which opened in 1994 has received considerable acclaim, and incorporates several of the State Rooms. The 50 acre landscaped gardens feature magnificent trees and are especially beautiful in May and autumn.

Location: OS Ref. SJ957 287. 5m NE of Stafford on the A51, between Stone and Lichfield, easy access from M6/J14.

Open: All year for events, functions and for pre-booked visits to the museum and gardens. Evening tours by special arrangement.

Admission: Museum: Adult £4, Child £3, OAP £3.50. Gardens: Adult £1.50, Child £1, OAP £1. NB. Max group size 22 or 45 if combined Museum and Gardens.

⊤ 🔲 🄳 By arrangement. 🎦 Obligatory. 🄿 Limited for coaches.
🔙 In grounds, on leads. ▣ ✳ 🛈 Tel for details.

STAFFORD CASTLE & VISITOR CENTRE
Newport Road, Stafford ST16 1DJ

Tel/Fax: 01785 257698   **e-mail:** ahh@staffordbc.gov.uk

Owner: Stafford Borough Council   **Contact:** Mark Hartwell

Stafford Castle has dominated the Stafford landscape for over 900 years. William the Conqueror first built Stafford Castle as a fortress to subdue the local populace. The visitor centre – built in the style of a Norman guardhouse – features an audio-visual area that brings its turbulent past to life.

Location: OS Ref. SJ904 220. On N side of A518, 1½ m WSW of town centre.

Open: Apr - Oct: Tue - Sun, 10am - 5pm (open BHs). Nov - Mar: Sat & Sun, 10am - 4pm.

Admission: Free (admission charges may apply for events).

🎦 By arrangement. ✳

WALL ROMAN SITE (Letocetum)   ⌗ ⚔
Watling Street, Nr Lichfield, Staffordshire WS14 0AW

Tel: 01543 480768   **www.**english-heritage.org.uk

Owner: English Heritage   **Contact:** Visitor Operations Team

The remains of a staging post alongside Watling Street. Foundations of an Inn and a Bath House can be seen and there is a display of finds in the site museum.

Location: OS139, SK098 066. Off A5 at Wall, nr Lichfield.

Open: 1 Mar - 30 Jun & 1 Sept - 31 Oct. Wed - Sun, 10am - 5pm. 1 Jul - 31 Aug: daily, 10am - 6pm.

Admission: Adult £3, Child £1.50, Conc. £2.30.

🛈 WC. 🔲 🄿 🔙 🛈 Tel for details.

education index
see page 564

SHUGBOROUGH ⚔

MILFORD, STAFFORD ST17 0XB

www.shugborough.org.uk

Tel: 01889 881388   **Fax:** 01889 881323
e-mail: info@shugborough.org.uk

Owner: The National Trust (Managed and financed by Staffordshire County Council.   **Contact:** Sales and Marketing Office

With evocative sounds, real smells and the true taste of a complete working historic estate, immerse yourself in a world of days gone by in a variety of sensory experiences that bring your visit to life. With its magnificent 18th century Mansion House, authentic Servants' Quarters and Georgian park farm with rare breeds, Shugborough provides a full day out with history, guides and living costumed characters ready to share a powerful set of stories from the past.

Location: OS Ref. SJ992 225. 10mins from M6/J13 on A513 Stafford/Lichfield Rd.

Open: 17 March – 27 Oct. Daily 11am - 5pm.

Admission: Adults £10, Concessions £7, Children £6, Family £25, Group Rate £6. (National Trust Members consult handbook.)

🛈 🔲 ⊤ 🄳 Suitable. ▣ By arrangement. ⑪ 🎦 🄿 Limited for coaches. ▣
🔙 On leads. ▣ 🛈 Tel for details.

WHITMORE HALL 🏛

WHITMORE, NEWCASTLE-UNDER-LYME ST5 5HW

Tel: 01782 680478   **Fax:** 01782 680906

Owner: Mr Guy Cavenagh-Mainwaring   **Contact:** Mr Michael Cavenagh-Thornhill

Whitmore Hall is a Grade I listed building, designated as a house of outstanding architectural and historical interest, and is a fine example of a small Carolinian manor house, although parts of the hall date back to a much earlier period. The hall has beautifully proportioned light rooms, curving staircase and landing. There are some good family portraits to be seen with a continuous line, from 1624 to the present day. It has been the family seat, for over 900 years, of the Cavenagh-Mainwarings who are direct descendants of the original Norman owners. The interior of the hall has recently been refurbished and is in fine condition. The grounds include a beautiful home park with a lime avenue leading to the house, as well as landscaped gardens encompassing an early Victorian summer house. One of the outstanding features of Whitmore is the extremely rare example of a late Elizabethan stable block, the ground floor is part cobbled and has nine oak-carved stalls.

Location: OS Ref. SJ811 413. On A53 Newcastle - Market Drayton Road, 3m from M6/J15.

Open: 1 May - 31 Aug: Tues, Weds, 2 - 5pm (last tour 4.30pm).

Admission: Adult £4, Child 50p.

🄳 Ground floor & grounds.
▣ Afternoon teas for booked groups (15+), May - Aug. 🎦 🄿 🔙

West Midlands - England

MAP 7

Owner:
The Viscount Daventry

▶ CONTACT

Miss Brenda Newell
Arbury Hall
Nuneaton
Warwickshire
CV10 7PT

Tel: 024 7638 2804
Fax: 024 7664 1147
e-mail: brenda.newell@
arburyhall.net

▶ LOCATION

OS Ref. SP335 893

London, M1, M6/J3
(A444 to Nuneaton),
2m SW of Nuneaton.
1m W of A444.

Chester A51, A34, M6
(from J14 to J3),
2¹/₂ hrs.
Nuneaton 10 mins.

London 2 hrs,
Birmingham ¹/₂ hr,
Coventry 20 mins.

Bus: Nuneaton 3m.

Rail: Nuneaton
Station 3m.

Air: Birmingham
International 17m.

CONFERENCE/FUNCTION

ROOM	SIZE	MAX CAPACITY
Dining Room	35' x 28'	120
Saloon	35' x 30'	70
Long Gallery	48' x 11'	40
Stables Tearooms	31' x 18'	80

ARBURY HALL 🏛

Arbury Hall has been the seat of the Newdegate family for over 400 years and is the ancestral home of Viscount Daventry. This Tudor/Elizabethan House was gothicised by Sir Roger Newdegate in the 18th century and is regarded as the 'Gothic Gem' of the Midlands. The Hall contains a fine collection of both oriental and Chelsea porcelain, portraits by Lely, Reynolds, Devis and Romney and furniture by Chippendale and Hepplewhite. The principal rooms, with their soaring fan vaulted ceilings and plunging pendants and filigree tracery, stand as a most breathtaking and complete example of early Gothic Revival architecture and provide a unique and fascinating venue for corporate entertaining, product launches, receptions, fashion shoots and activity days. Exclusive use of this historic Hall, its gardens and parkland is offered to clients. The Hall stands in the middle of beautiful parkland with landscaped gardens of rolling lawns, lakes and winding wooded walks. Spring flowers are profuse and in June rhododendrons, azaleas and giant wisteria provide a beautiful environment for the visitor.

George Eliot, the novelist, was born on the estate and Arbury Hall and Sir Roger Newdegate were immortalised in her book *'Scenes of Clerical Life'*.

🏛 ℹ Corporate hospitality, film location, small conferences, product launches and promotions, marquee functions, clay pigeon shooting, archery and other sporting activities, grand piano in Saloon, helicopter landing site. No cameras or video recorders indoors.

🍴 Exclusive lunches and dinners for corporate parties in dining room, max. 50, buffets 120.

♿ Visitors may alight at the Hall's main entrance. Parking in allocated areas. Ramp access to main hall.

☕ By arrangement for groups.

🚶 Obligatory. Tour time: 1hr.

🅿 200 cars and 3 coaches 250 yards from house. Follow tourist signs. Approach map available for coach drivers.

🚌 Welcome, must book. School room available.

🐕 In gardens on leads. Guide dogs only in house.

❄ 🎭 Tel for details.

▶ OPENING TIMES

All Year

Open all year on Tues, Weds & Thurs only, for corporate events.

Pre-booked visits to the Hall and Gardens for groups of 25+ on Tues, Weds & Thurs (until 4pm) from Easter to the end of September.

Hall & Gardens open 2 - 5pm on BH weekends only (Suns & Mons) Easter - September.

▶ ADMISSION

Summer

Hall & Gardens

Adult £6.50
Child (up to 14 yrs.).. £4.00
Family (2+2) £18.00

Gardens Only

Adult £5.00
Child (up to 14 yrs.)... £3.50

Groups (25+)

Adult £6.50

West Midlands - England

MAP 6

BADDESLEY CLINTON

www.nationaltrust.org.uk

Owner:
The National Trust

▶ CONTACT

The Estate Office
Baddesley Clinton Hall
Rising Lane
Baddesley Clinton
Knowle
Solihull B93 0DQ

Tel: 01564 783294
Fax: 01564 782706

e-mail:
baddesleyclinton@
nationaltrust.org.uk

▶ LOCATION
OS Ref. SP199 715

³/₄m W of A4141
Warwick/Birmingham
road at Chadwick End.

Enjoy a day at Baddesley Clinton, the medieval moated manor house with hidden secrets! One of the most enchanting properties owned by the National Trust, Baddesley Clinton has seen little change since 1633 when Henry Ferrers 'the Antiquary' died. He was Squire at Baddesley for almost seventy years and remodelled the house over a long period of time, introducing much of the panelling and chimney pieces. Henry was proud of his ancestry and began the tradition at Baddesley of armorial glass, which has continued until the present day. Henry let the house in the 1590s when it became a refuge for Jesuit priests, and hiding places, called 'priest holes', created for their concealment, survive from this era. Pictures painted by Rebecca, wife of Marmion Edward Ferrers, remain to show how the romantic character of Baddesley was enjoyed in the late 19th century when the family also re-created a sumptuously furnished Chapel.

The garden, which surrounds the house, incorporates many features including stewponds; a small lake (the 'Great Pool'); a walled garden with thatched summer house, and a lakeside walk with nature trail and wildflower meadow. Make a day of it! Complementary opening times and substantial discounts on joint ticket prices make a combined visit to Baddesley Clinton and Packwood House even more attractive, especially since both properties are only two miles apart.

▶ OPENING TIMES
House
1 Mar - 5 Nov:
Wed - Sun, Good Friday
& BH Mons.

Mar, Apr, Oct & Nov:
1.30 - 5pm;

May - end Sept:
1.30 - 5.30pm.

Grounds
1 Mar - 10 Dec:
Wed - Sun, Good Friday
& BH Mons.

Mar, Apr, Oct & 1 - 5 Nov:
12 noon - 5pm;

May - end Sept:
12 noon - 5.30pm;

8 Nov - 10 Dec:
12 noon - 4.30pm.

▶ ADMISSION
Adult...................... £6.80
Child £3.40
Family £17.00
Groups..................... £5.80
Guided tours
(out of hours) £11.60

Grounds only
Adult £3.40
Child £1.70

Combined Ticket with Packwood House
Adult £9.80
Child £4.90
Family £24.50
Groups £8.40

Gardens only
Adult £4.90
Child £2.45

  Partial. WC. Licensed. By arrangement. ■ 🐕 Guide dogs only. Tel for details.

©Coughton Court

MAP 6

COUGHTON COURT 🏛 🌿

www.coughtoncourt.co.uk

Owner:

The National Trust but the Throckmorton family lease, part fund and manage.

▶ CONTACT

Sales Office
Coughton Court
Alcester
Warwickshire B49 5JA

Tel: 01789 400777
Fax: 01789 765544

Visitor Information:
01789 762435

e-mail:
coughtoncourt@
nationaltrust.org.uk

▶ LOCATION

OS Ref. SP080 604

Located on A435,
2m N of Alcester,
8m NW of
Stratford-on-Avon.
18m from Birmingham
City Centre.

Rail: Birmingham
International.

Air: Birmingham
International.

Coughton Court has been the home of the Throckmortons since the 15th century and the family still live here today. The magnificent Tudor gatehouse was built around 1530 with the north and south wings completed 10 or 20 years later. The gables and the first storey of these wings are of typical mid-16th century half-timbered work.

Of particular interest to visitors is the Throckmorton family history from Tudor times to the present generation. On view are family portraits through the centuries, memorabilia, furniture, tapestries and porcelain.

A long-standing Roman Catholic theme runs through the family history which is maintained to the present day. The house has strong connections with the Gunpowder plot and also suffered damage in the Civil War.

GARDENS

The house stands in 25 acres of gardens and grounds along with two churches and a lake. The Gardens include a Formal Garden, Elizabethan Knot Garden, Orchard, Bog Garden and a 1 acre Walled Garden, now considered to be one of Britain's finest walled gardens, which features a spectacular Rose Labyrinth. These beautiful Gardens have been created and financed by the Throckmorton family over the past decade. They are the inspiration and treasured project of Mrs Clare Throckmorton, translated into reality by her daughter Christina Williams, garden designer.

ℹ️ Wedding receptions, special occasion dinners, business meetings, filming, fairs and corporate activity days. The acoustics of the Saloon make it ideal for live theatre and musical concerts. Marquees can be erected in the grounds. No photography or stiletto heels in house.

🎁 ✳️

🍴 Private dinners can be provided by arrangement in the Dining Room, Saloon and Tudor Rooms. Licensed for Civil Marriage ceremonies.

♿ Ground floor of house, gardens & restaurant. WC.

☕🍴 Licensed restaurant, 11am - 5.30pm. Capacity: 100 inside, 60 outside.

👤 By arrangement. Ask for group organisers brochure.

🅿️ Unlimited for cars plus 4 coaches.

📕 Teacher's pack available.

🐕 Car park only.

🔔   🎭 Tel for details.

©Coughton Court

©Coughton Court

▶ OPENING TIMES

House
April - September:
Wed - Sun plus
BH Mons & Tues

October
Sats & Suns only

11.30am - 5pm.

Closed Good Friday.

House may close early some Sats due to functions and events, check prior to your visit: 01789 762435. Closed Sats 24 June & 15 July.

Gardens, Restaurant, Shop & Plant Sales:
Dates as house,
11am - 5.30pm.

Walled Garden
Dates as house,
11.30am - 4.30pm.

Last admissions are $^1/_2$ hr before closing times.

▶ ADMISSION

House & Gardens

Adult	£8.60
Child* (5-15yrs)	£4.30
Family (2+2)	£24.80
Family (2+3)	£28.75
Groups (15+)**	£7.50

Gardens only

Adult	£5.90
Child* (5-15yrs)	£2.95
Family (2+2)	£17.00
Family (2+3)	£19.50
Groups (15+)**	£5.15

Parking ...... All cars £1.00

*Under 5yrs free.
**Paying visitors.

CONFERENCE/FUNCTION

ROOM	SIZE	MAX CAPACITY
Dining Rm	45' x 27'	60
Saloon	60' x 36'	100

The Saloon, which has particularly good acoustics, is often used for music recording.

West Midlands - England

MAP 6

Owner:
The National Trust

▶ **CONTACT**

The Estate Office
Packwood House
Lapworth
Solihull B94 6AT

Tel: 01564 783294
Fax: 01564 782706

e-mail:
packwoodhouse@
nationaltrust.org.uk

▶ **LOCATION**
OS Ref. SP174 722

2m E of Hockley Heath
(on A3400), 11m SE of
central Birmingham.

PACKWOOD HOUSE

www.nationaltrust.org.uk

Packwood lies in the pleasantly wooded Forest of Arden and was, for many years, the home of the Fetherstons, who allowed Cromwell's General, Henry Ireton, to stay overnight before the Battle of Edgehill in 1642. There is also a tradition that Charles II was given refreshment at Packwood after his defeat at Worcester in 1651. Many of Packwood's interiors were designed in the 1920s and 30s in idealised Elizabethan or Jacobean styles for Graham Baron Ash. They offer a wonderful insight into the taste, rich decoration and way of life of a wealthy connoisseur in the period between the wars. Packwood still retains the intimate atmosphere of a real home, with lavishly furnished rooms containing French and Flemish tapestries and fine 17th & 18th century furniture. The oak panelled bedrooms with their sumptuous four-poster beds give you a glimpse of what it was like to stay the night as Baron Ash's

guest. Queen Mary, another regal guest who took refreshment here, visited in August 1927. Look out for several reminders of that historic visit throughout the house.

The house is surrounded by its own delightful, tranquil grounds. A large flower garden complete with long terraced herbaceous borders, enclosed by red brick walls with a gazebo in each corner, is a blend of the traditional country house garden and the Carolean Garden of the Fetherstons. The famous 17th century Yew Garden is traditionally said to represent 'The Sermon on the Mount' and is a highly unusual and attractive feature. Make a day of it! Complementary opening times and substantial discounts on joint ticket prices make a combined visit to Packwood House and Baddesley Clinton even more attractive, especially since both properties are only two miles apart.

▶ **OPENING TIMES**

House
1 March - 5 November:
Wed - Sun, Good Friday
& BH Mons:
12 noon - 4.30pm.

Garden
1 March - 5 November:
Wed - Sun, Good Friday
& BH Mons;

March , April, October &
November:
11am - 4.30pm;

May - end September:
11am - 5.30pm.

Park & Woodland Walks
All year: daily.

▶ **ADMISSION**

Adult	£6.20
Child	£3.10
Family	£15.50
Groups	£5.30
Guided tours (out of hours)	£10.60

Garden only

Adult	£3.20
Child	£1.60

Combined Ticket with Baddesley Clinton

Adult	£9.80
Child	£4.90
Family	£24.50
Groups	£8.40

Gardens only

Adult	£4.90
Child	£2.45

Partial. By arrangement. Guide dogs only. Parkland only. Tel for details.

MAP 6

RAGLEY HALL & GARDENS 🏛

www.ragleyhall.com

Ragley Hall, the family home of the Marquess and Marchioness of Hertford, was designed by Robert Hooke, the inventive genius, in 1680 and is one of the earliest and loveliest of England's great Palladian Houses. The perfect symmetry of the architecture of Ragley remains unchanged save for the spectacular portico by Wyatt added in 1780.

The majestic Great Hall, soaring two storeys high, is adorned with some of England's finest and most exquisite baroque plasterwork by James Gibbs, dated 1750.

Ragley houses a superb collection of 18th century and earlier paintings, china, and furniture and wonderful ceilings decorated with Grisaille panels and insets by Angelica Kauffman.

A most striking feature of Ragley is the breathtaking mural "The Temptation" by Graham Rust in the south staircase hall, that was painted between 1969 and 1983.

Ragley is a working estate with more than 6000 acres of land. The house is set in 400 acres of picturesque parkland landscaped by Lancelot "Capability" Brown and 27 acres of fascinating gardens including the enchanting rose garden, richly planted borders and mature woodland.

Near to the Hall the working stables, designed by James Gibbs in 1751, house a collection of carriages dating back to 1760 and equestrian equipment.

For children there is an exciting woodland adventure playground, 3D maze and an extensive lakeside play and picnic area, and for walkers the delightful woodland walk.

Owner:
The Marquess of Hertford

▶ **CONTACT**
Bryan McDonald
General Manager
Ragley Hall
Alcester
Warwickshire B49 5NJ

Tel: 01789 762090
Fax: 01789 764791

e-mail:
bryanmcdonald@
ragleyhall.com

▶ **LOCATION**
OS Ref. SP073 555

Off A46/A435 1m SW of Alcester. From London 100m, M40 via Oxford and Stratford-on-Avon.

Rail: Evesham Station 9m.

Air: Birmingham International 20m.

Taxi: 007 Taxi 01789 414007

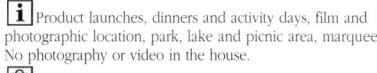
ℹ Product launches, dinners and activity days, film and photographic location, park, lake and picnic area, marquee. No photography or video in the house.

⬛ Wedding ceremonies and receptions, private and corporate entertainment, conferences and seminars.

♿ Visitors may alight at entrance. Parking in allocated areas. WCs. Lifts. Coffee House & Restaurant on ground floor. Electric scooter for visiting the gardens may be available. Please enquire.

🍴 Tearoom in the Park and Hooke's Coffee-House & Restaurant. Groups please book.

🏃 By arrangement.

🅿 Coach drivers admitted free and receive info pack and voucher. Please advise of group visits.

🎒 Welcome. Teachers' packs and work modules available. Adventure Wood and Woodland Walk.

🐕 In grounds, on leads.

🔔 😀 Please visit website or telephone for details.

CONFERENCE/FUNCTION

ROOM	SIZE	MAX CAPACITY
Great Hall	70' x 40'	150
Red Saloon	30' x 40'	40
Hertford	45' x 22'	60
Seymour	25' x 23'	30

▶ **OPENING TIMES**

Summer: House
25 March - 1 October:
Thur - Sun & BH Mons
12 noon - 5.30pm (last admission 4.30pm).

Garden, Park, Adventure Playground & Jerwood Sculpture Park
Thur - Sun & BH Mons, also daily in school holidays: 10 - 23 April, 29 May - 2 June & 21 July - 3 September, 10am - 6pm (last admission 4.30pm).

Winter:
October: Saturdays & Sundays only - November - March: closed.

Open by special arrangement with the General Manager.

▶ **ADMISSION**

House, Garden, Park, Adventure Playground & Jerwood Sculpture Park incl.
Adult £7.50
Child (5-16yrs)...... £4.50
Conc. £6.50
Family (2+4) £25.00
Groups
Adult/Conc. £6.00
Child £3.50

Season Tickets:
Family(2+4) £75.00
Individual £25.00

Garden, Park & Adventure Playground
Adult £6.00
Child (5-16yrs)...... £4.50
Conc. £5.50
Family (2+4) £22.00
Groups
Adult/Conc. £5.00
Child £3.50

West Midlands - England

Hall's Croft

Anne Hathaway's Cottage

MAP 6

THE SHAKESPEARE HOUSES

www.shakespeare.org.uk

Owner:
The Shakespeare
Birthplace Trust

▶ **CONTACT**

The Shakespeare
Birthplace Trust
Henley Street
Stratford-upon-Avon
CV37 6QW

Tel: 01789 204016
(General enquiries)
Tel: 01789
201806/201836
(Group Visits)
01789 201808
(Special/Evening Visits).
Fax: 01789 263138

e-mail: info@
shakespeare.org.uk

groups@
shakespeare.org.uk

▶ **LOCATION**

OS Refs:
Birthplace - SP201 552
New Place - SP201 548
Hall's Croft - SP200 546
Hathaway's - SP185 547
Arden's - SP166 582

Rail: Direct service
from London
(Paddington)

2 hrs from London
45 mins from
Birmingham by car.

4m from M40/J15
and well signed from
all approaches.

These five Shakespeare Houses, all authentic and directly linked to William Shakespeare and his family, offer a great insight into the world of the famous writer, his life and his work. Experience and enjoy the architectural character, period furniture, special collections, attractive gardens, grounds and walks, and craft displays.

In Town: Shakespeare's Birthplace: The half-timbered house, where William Shakespeare was born in 1564, continued as the family home until the 19th century and has welcomed visitors for well over 250 years. The house offers a fascinating insight into life as it was when Shakespeare was a child. Includes Shakespeare Exhibition – an introduction to his life, work and times, and a beautiful traditional English garden.

Nash's House and New Place: Once owned by Thomas Nash, who married Shakespeare's granddaughter Elizabeth. In addition to exceptional furnishings of Shakespeare's time, from May 2006 there will be a special exhibition devoted to 'Shakespeare's Complete Works' from the first collected plays of 1623 to the present day. Outside lies the site of Shakespeare's final Stratford home – discover why it was demolished. Stroll in the Elizabethan-style knot garden and rest awhile in Shakespeare's Great Garden.

Hall's Croft: Named after Dr John Hall who

married Shakespeare's daughter Susanna. This impressive 16th century house, with Jacobean additions, includes outstanding furniture and paintings. See the exhibition of medicine in Shakespeare's time with references to remedies and potions mentioned in the plays. The large peaceful garden is home to an ancient mulberry tree and a herbal bed.

Out of Town: Anne Hathaway's Cottage: This world famous, picturesque thatched cottage, childhood home of Shakespeare's wife, continued to be owned by Anne Hathaway's descendants until the late 19th century. It still contains the Hathaway bed. Outside lies a beautiful cottage garden and a tree and sculpture garden including a maze and romantic willow cabin. There are many pleasant walks leading from the cottage.

Mary Arden's House and The Shakespeare Countryside Museum: Great for a family day out, the site includes the home of Shakespeare's mother before she married John Shakespeare. The site today, with its many farm buildings, activities and rare breeds of farm animals, brings to life for visitors the work and traditions of the countryside around Stratford-upon-Avon from Shakespeare's time to the early 20th century. The grounds also feature rare livestock, a falconry with displays throughout the day, and adventure playground.

Shakespeare's Birthplace.

ℹ️ City Sightseeing guided bus tour service connecting the town houses with Anne Hathaway's Cottage and Mary Arden's House. No photography inside houses.

🛍️ Shops at Shakespeare's Birthplace, Hall's Croft, Anne Hathaway's Cottage and Mary Arden's House.

🍴 Available, tel for details.

♿ WCs. Naturally difficult levels but much for disabled to enjoy at Mary Arden's House, ground floor & gardens accessible. Virtual reality tour at Shakespeare's Birthplace &

Anne Hathaway's Cottage.

🅿️ Available on site or close by.

🚶 By special arrangement.

🅿️ The Trust provides a free coach terminal for delivery and pick-up of groups, maximum stay 30 mins at Shakespeare's Birthplace. Parking at Anne Hathaway's Cottage and Mary Arden's House.

Available for all houses. For information 01789 201804.

🐕 Guide dogs only.

✱

▶ **OPENING TIMES**

Mid Season:
Apr - May & Sept - Oct.

**Birthplace &
Mary Arden's House**
Mon - Sun: 10am - 5pm.

**Hall's Croft &
Nash's House &
New Place**
Daily: 11am - 5pm.

Anne Hathaway's
Mon - Sat: 9.30am - 5pm.
Suns: 10am - 5pm.

Summer Season:
Jun - Aug.

**Birthplace &
Anne Hathaway's**
Mon - Sat: 9am - 5pm.
Suns: 9.30am - 5pm.

**Hall's Croft &
Nash's House &
New Place**
Mon - Sat: 9.30am - 5pm.
Suns: 10am - 5pm.

Mary Arden's House
Daily: 9.30am - 5pm.

Winter Season:
Nov - Mar.

**Birthplace &
Anne Hathaway's House**
Mon - Sat: 10am - 4pm.
Suns: 10.30am - 4pm.
(Anne Hathaway's
10am - 4pm)

**Hall's Croft &
Nash's House**
Daily: 11am - 4pm.

Closed 23 - 26 Dec.
All times are for
admission to last entry.

▶ **ADMISSION**

Multiple house tickets for all five houses and the three in-town houses and single house tickets are available. Please tele 01789 204016 for further information or visit www.shakespeare.org.uk

STONELEIGH ABBEY

www.stoneleighabbey.org

MAP 6

Owner:
Stoneleigh Abbey Ltd

▶ CONTACT

Enquiry Office
Stoneleigh Abbey
Kenilworth
Warwickshire CV8 2LF

Tel: 01926 858535

Fax: 01926 850724

e-mail: enquire
@stoneleighabbey.org

▶ LOCATION
OS Ref. SP318 712

Off A46/B4115,
2m W of Kenilworth.
From London 100m,
M40 to Warwick.

Rail: Coventry station
5m, Leamington Spa
station 5m.

Air: Birmingham
International 20m.

Stoneleigh Abbey was founded in the reign of Henry II and after the Dissolution was granted to the Duke of Suffolk. The estate then passed into the ownership of the Leigh family who remained for 400 years. The estate is now managed by a charitable trust.

Visitors will experience a wealth of architectural styles spanning more than 900 years: the magnificent state rooms and chapel of the 18th century Baroque West Wing contain original pieces of furniture including a set of library chairs made by William Gomm in 1763; a medieval Gatehouse; the Gothic Revival-style Regency Stables. Jane Austen was a distant relative of the Leigh family and in her description of 'Sotherton' in *Mansfield Park* she recalls her stay at Stoneleigh Abbey. Parts of *Northanger Abbey* also use Stoneleigh for inspiration.

The River Avon flows through the estate's 690 acres of grounds and parkland which displays the influences of Humphry Repton and other major landscape architects. In June 1858 Queen Victoria and Prince Albert visited Stoneleigh Abbey. During their stay Queen Victoria planted an oak tree and Prince Consort planted a Wellington Gigantia. While Prince Albert's tree flourished it is thought that the oak did not survive.

Stoneleigh Abbey has been the subject of a major restoration programme funded by the Heritage Lottery Fund, English Heritage and the European Regional Development Fund.

▶ OPENING TIMES

Good Fri - end October

Tue - Thur, Suns & BHs:
House tours at
11am, 1pm & 3pm.

Grounds: 10am - 5pm.

▶ ADMISSION

House Tour & Grounds

Adult...................... £6.00
1 Child Free
with each adult

Additional Child £2.50
OAP £4.00

Discounts for Groups (20+).

Grounds only £2.50

Parking .... Free

Groups are welcome during the published opening times or at other times by arrangement. Please telephone.

 Available for public and commercial hire.

House only. WCs.

Obligatory.

Schools welcome.

 In grounds, on leads.

Tel for details.

CONFERENCE/FUNCTION

ROOM	SIZE	MAX CAPACITY
Saloon	14 x 9m	100
Gilt Hall	7 x 7m	60
Servants' Hall	14 x 8m	100
Riding School	12 x 33m	490
Conservatory	19 x 6m	100

MAP 6

UPTON HOUSE & GARDEN

www.nationaltrust.org.uk

Owner:
The National Trust

▶ **CONTACT**

The Visitor Services
Manager
Upton House
Banbury
Oxfordshire OX15 6HT

Tel: 01295 670266
Fax: 01295 671144

e-mail: uptonhouse
@nationaltrust.org.uk

▶ **LOCATION**
OS Ref. SP371 461

On A422, 7m NW
of Banbury. 12m SE of
Stratford-upon-Avon

Rail: Banbury
Station, 7m.

Upton House stands less than a mile to the south of the battlefield of Edgehill and there has been a house on this site since the Middle Ages. The present house was built at the end of the 17th century and remodelled 1927 - 29 for the 2nd Viscount Bearsted.

He was a great collector of paintings, china and many other valuable works of art, and adapted the building to display them. The paintings include works by El Greco, Bruegel, Bosch, Canaletto, Guardi, Hogarth and Stubbs. The rooms provide an admirable setting for the china collection which includes Chelsea figures and superb examples of beautifully decorated Sèvres porcelain. The set of 17th century Brussels tapestries depict the Holy Roman Emperor Maximilian I's boar and stag hunts.

Artists and Shell Exhibition of Paintings and Posters commissioned by Shell for use in its publicity 1921 - 1949, while the 2nd Viscount Bearsted was chairman of the company, founded by his father.

GARDEN

The outstanding garden is of interest throughout the season with terraces descending into a deep valley from the main lawn. There are herbaceous borders, the national collection of asters, over an acre of kitchen garden, a water garden laid out in the 1930s and pools stocked with ornamental fish.

An 80-seat licensed restaurant in the grounds serves full lunches and afternoon teas. It is available for hire throughout the year for dinners, conferences and functions by arrangement.

▶ **OPENING TIMES**

Spring & Summer
18 March - 1 November
House: Sat - Wed
including BH Mons &
Good Fri: 1 - 5pm (last
admission to house 4.30pm).
(shop open until 5.15pm).

Garden & Restaurant:
Sat, Sun & BHs: 11am - 5pm.
Mon - Wed: 12 noon - 5pm.

Winter
Garden, Restaurant & Shop:
4 Nov - 17 Dec, Sat & Sun,
12 noon - 4pm.
House: 2 - 17 Dec, Sat &
Sun, 12 noon - 4pm.

▶ **ADMISSION**

House & Garden
Adult £7.00
Child £3.70
Family £17.00
Groups (15+) £5.60

Garden only
Adult £4.20
Child £2.10
Groups (15+) £3.50

Garden Only:
4 Nov - 17 Dec
Adult £2.00
Child £1.00
House & Garden:
2 Nov - 17 Dec
Adult £3.00
Child £2.00

ℹ️ Parent & baby room. No indoor photography.

📷 ❀ ☂

♿ Ground floor. Wheelchair available. Virtual tour. WC.
Motorised buggy to/from reception/lower garden on request.

🍴 Licensed. Self-service.

🏃 Tour time 1½ - 2hrs. Groups (15+) must pre-book.
Evening tours by written appointment (no reduction).

🅿 350 yds from House. 🐕 In car park, on leads. ❄

SPECIAL EVENTS

ALL YEAR
Art tours, conservation demonstrations, concerts and other events, please send SAE or telephone.

MAP 7

WARWICK CASTLE

www.warwick-castle.co.uk

Bursting to the towers with tales of treachery and torture, passion and power and above all fascinating people, times and events, Warwick Castle is so much more than simply a castle. Experience preparations for battle, feel the weight of a sword and get a solider's eye view from beneath a battle helmet, see lavishly decorated State Rooms, watch as a household prepares for a Victorian party and discover how electricity was generated over 100 years ago to light up the castle.

With 60 acres of landscaped grounds and gardens, there is plenty to see outside as well as in. Wander around the beautiful Peacock Garden and enter the 18th century Conservatory, filled with an array of exotic plants. There is also the Victorian Rose Garden to explore.

See the world's largest trebuchet, a mighty siege machine similar to a catapult, measuring 18 metres high, weighing in at 22 tonnes and capable of shooting missiles up to 300 metres.

Throughout the year there is a programme of fantastic special events including opportunities to see the trebuchet in action. Visit www.warwick-castle.co.uk for further information.

▶ CONTACT

Warwick Castle
Warwick   CV34 4QU

Tel: 0870 442 2000

Fax: 0870 442 2394

e-mail:
customer.information@
warwick-castle.com

▶ LOCATION
OS Ref. SP284 648

2m from M40/J15.
Birmingham 35 mins
Leeds 2 hrs 5 mins
London, 1 hr 30 mins
Vehicle entrance from
A429 ¹/₂ m SW of town
centre.

Rail: Intercity from
London Euston to
Coventry. Direct
service from
Marylebone &
Paddington to Warwick.

▶ OPENING TIMES

Every day except 25 Dec
10am - 6pm
(closes 5pm during
October - March).

▶ ADMISSION

Adult .... from £13.50
Child .... from £8.25
Student .... from £9.95
OAP .... from £9.75
Family (2+2) from £38.00

Groups (15+)
Adult .... from £9.95
Child .... from £6.50
Student .... from £8.75
OAP .... from £7.95

**Please visit
www.warwick-castle.co.uk
for further information.**

**Admission prices are
subject to change
without prior notice.**

CONFERENCE/FUNCTION

ROOM	SIZE	MAX CAPACITY
Great Hall	61' x 34'	130
State Dining Room	40' x 25'	30
Undercroft	46' x 26'	120
Coach House	44' x 19'	80
Marquees		2000

ℹ Corporate events, receptions, Kingmaker's Feasts and Highwayman's Suppers. Guide books available in English, French, German, Japanese and Spanish.

🛍 Three shops.

♿ Parking spaces in Stables Car Park. Telephone for details.

🍽 Available, ranging from cream teas to three-course hot meals. During the summer there is an open air barbecue and refreshment pavilion in the grounds (weather permitting).

🛈 For groups (pre-booked). Guides in most rooms.

🅿 A charge is made for car parking. Free coach parking, free admission and refreshment voucher for coach driver.

🏰 Ideal location, being a superb example of military architecture dating back to the Norman Conquest and with elegant interiors up to Victorian times. Group rates apply. To qualify for group rates, groups must book in advance. Education packs available.

🐕 Registered assistance dogs only.  Tel for details.

ARBURY HALL 🏛 *See page 355 for full page entry.*

BADDESLEY CLINTON 🌿 *See page 356 for full page entry.*

NT Photographic Library

NT Severn SWT / D Sellman

CHARLECOTE PARK 🌿

WARWICK CV35 9ER

www.nationaltrust.org.uk

Tel: 01789 470277 **Fax:** 01789 470544 **Events (info & booking):** 07788 658495 **e-mail:** charlecote.park@nationaltrust.org.uk

Owner: The National Trust

Owned by the Lucy family since 1247, Sir Thomas Lucy built the house in 1558. Now, much altered, it is shown as it would have been a century ago, complete with Victorian kitchen, brewhouse and family carriages in the coach house and two bedrooms, a dressing room and the main staircase. A video of Victorian life can be viewed. The formal gardens and informal parkland lie to the north and west of the house. Jacob Sheep were brought to Charlecote in 1756 by Sir Thomas Lucy. It is reputed that William Shakespeare was apprehended for poaching c1583 and Sir Thomas Lucy is said to be the basis of Justice Shallow in Shakespeare's *'Merry Wives of Windsor'*.

Location: OS151, SP263 564. 1m W of Wellesbourne, 5m E of Stratford-upon-Avon.

Open: Please telephone or see our website for opening times, dates, and details of regular events and activities.

Admission: NT members and those joining at Charlecote Park: Free. Adult £6.90, Child (5-16yrs) £3.50, Family £17. Grounds only: Adult £3.50, Child £1.85.

🖼ⓘ Children's play area. 🍴 ♿ 🛍 🍽Licensed. 🎫For booked groups. 🅿Limited for coaches. 🎦By arrangement. 🐕On leads, in car park only. ♿Tel for details.

© NTPL/Stephen Robson

Upton House & Garden.

COMPTON VERNEY
COMPTON VERNEY, WARWICKSHIRE CV35 9HZ
www.comptonverney.org.uk

Tel: 01926 645500   **Fax:** 01926 645501   **e-mail:** info@comptonverney.org.uk

Owner: Compton Verney House Trust   **Contact:** Ticketing Desk

Set in a restored 18th century Robert Adam mansion, Compton Verney offers a unique art gallery experience. Surrounded by 120 acres of 'Capability' Brown landscape, the gallery houses a diverse permanent collection, complemented by temporary exhibitions, events and activities.

Location: OS Ref. SP312 529. 7m E of Stratford-upon-Avon, 10 mins from M40/J12, on B4086 between Wellesbourne and Kineton.

Open: 31 Mar - 5 Nov: Tues - Sun & BH Mons, 10am - 5pm. Last entry to Gallery 4.30pm. Groups welcome, please book in advance.

Admission: Adult £6, Child (5-16yrs) £2, Conc. £4, Family £14. Tuesdays half price. Groups (15+): Adult £5.40, Conc. £3.60, group rate with tour, Adult £10, Conc. £8.

ⓘNo photography in the Gallery. ⬛ ♿ 🍽Licensed. 🍴Licensed.
🎟By arrangement. 🅿Ample. 🔲 🦮 Assistance dogs only. ❄ 📺Tel for details.

COUGHTON COURT 🏛 ❧   *See page 357 for full page entry.*

FARNBOROUGH HALL ❧
BANBURY, OXFORDSHIRE OX17 1DU
www.nationaltrust.org.uk

Tel: 01295 690002 (information line)

Owner: The National Trust

A classical mid-18th century stone house, home of the Holbech family for 300 years; notable plasterwork, the entrance hall, staircase and 2 principal rooms are shown; the grounds contain charming late 17th century temples, a ²/₃ mile terrace walk and an obelisk.

Location: OS151, SP430 490. 6m N of Banbury, ¹/₂ m W of A423.

Open: House, Garden & Terrace Walk: 1 Apr - 30 Sept: Weds & Sats, 2 - 5.30pm. 30 April/1 May: Sun & Mon, 2 - 5.30pm.

Admission: House, Garden & Terrace Walk: Adult £4.20, Child £2.10, Family £11.50. Garden & Terrace Walk only: £2.10.

♿House & grounds, but steep terrace walk. 🦮In grounds, on leads.

THE HILLER GARDEN
Dunnington Heath Farm, Alcester, Warwickshire B49 5PD

Tel: 01789 491342 **Fax:** 01789 490439

Owner: A H Hiller & Son Ltd   **Contact:** Mr Jeff Soulsby

2 acre garden of unusual herbaceous plants and over 200 rose varieties.

Location: OS Ref. SP066 539. 1¹/₂ m S of Ragley Hall on B4088 (formerly A435).

Open: All year: daily 10am - 5pm.

Admission: Free.

Ragley Hall.

HONINGTON HALL

SHIPSTON-ON-STOUR, WARWICKSHIRE CV36 5AA

Tel: 01608 661434 **Fax:** 01608 663717

Owner/Contact: Benjamin Wiggin Esq

This fine Caroline manor house was built in the early 1680s for Henry Parker in mellow brickwork, stone quoins and window dressings. Modified in 1751 when an octagonal saloon was inserted. The interior was also lavishly restored around this time and contains exceptional mid-Georgian plasterwork. Set in 15 acres of grounds.

Location: OS Ref. SP261 427. 10m S of Stratford-upon-Avon. 1¹/₂ m N of Shipston-on-Stour. Take A3400 towards Stratford, then signed right to Honington.

Open: Guided tours by appointment only.

Admission: Telephone for details.

Obligatory.

LORD LEYCESTER HOSPITAL

HIGH STREET, WARWICK CV34 4BH

www.lordleycester.com

Tel/Fax: 01926 491422

Owner: The Governors   **Contact:** The Master

This magnificent range of 14th century half-timbered buildings was adapted into almshouses by Robert Dudley, Earl of Leycester, in 1571. The Hospital still provides homes for ex-servicemen and their wives. The Guildhall, Great Hall, Chapel, Brethren's Kitchen and galleried Courtyard are still in everyday use. The Queen's Own Hussars regimental museum is here. The historic Master's Garden, featured in BBC TV's *Gardener's World*, has been restored.

Location: OS Ref. 280 648. 1m N of M40/J15 on the A429 in town centre.

Open: All year: Tue - Sun & BHs (except Good Fri & 25 Dec), 10am - 5pm (4pm in winter). Garden: Apr - Sept: 10am - 4.30pm.

Admission: Adult £4.90, Child £3.90, Conc. £4.40. Garden only £2. 5% discount for adult groups (20+).

Partial. By arrangement. Limited. Guide dogs only.

© English Heritage Photo Library

KENILWORTH CASTLE

KENILWORTH, WARWICKSHIRE CV8 1NE

www.english-heritage.org.uk/kenilworthcastle

Tel: 01926 852078

Owner: English Heritage   **Contact:** Visitor Operations Team

Kenilworth is the largest castle ruin in England, the former stronghold of great Lords and Kings. Its massive walls of warm red stone tower over the peaceful Warwickshire landscape. The Earl of Leicester entertained Queen Elizabeth I with 'Princely Pleasures' during her 19 day visit. He built a new wing for the Queen to lodge in and organised all manner of lavish and costly festivities. The Great Hall, where Gloriana dined with her courtiers, still stands and John of Gaunt's Hall is second only in width and grandeur to Westminster Hall. Climb to the top of the tower beside the hall and you will be rewarded by fine views over the rolling wooded countryside. Exhibition, interactive castle model and café in Leicester's Barn. Recreated Tudor garden and atmospheric audio tour. New in 2006: The newly conserved and renovated Leicester's Gatehouse will be open to the public for the first time in many decades. New visitor admissions building and shop. Recreation of the castle's original Tudor gardens continues.

Location: OS140, SP278 723. In Kenilworth, off A452, W end of town.

Open: 1 Apr - 31 Mar: daily, 10am - 5pm (4pm Nov - Feb & 6pm Jun - Aug). Closed 24 - 26 Dec & 1 Jan.

Admission: Adult £5.90, Child £3, Conc. £4.40, Family £14.80. 15% discount for groups (11+)

WC. Tel for details.

MIDDLETON HALL

Middleton, Tamworth, Staffordshire B78 2AE

Tel: 01827 283095 **Fax:** 01827 285717 **e-mail:** middletonhall@btconnect.com

Owner: Middleton Hall Trust   **Contact:** Carol Sullivan

Hall (1285 - 1824). Former home of Hugh Willoughby (Tudor explorer), Francis Willughby and John Ray (17th century naturalists).

Location: OS Ref. SP193 982. A4091, S of Tamworth.

Open: Easter - 25 Sept: Suns, 2 - 5pm, BH Mons, 11am - 5pm.

Admission: £2.50, OAP £1.50. BHs & Special Events: Adult £5, Child £1, OAP £3.50.

PACKWOOD HOUSE   *See page 358 for full page entry.*

RAGLEY HALL   *See page 359 for full page entry.*

education index

see page 564

RYTON ORGANIC GARDENS

COVENTRY, WARWICKSHIRE CV8 3LG

www.gardenorganic.org.uk

Tel: 024 7630 3517 **Fax:** 024 7663 9229 **e-mail:** enquiry@hdra.org.uk

Owner: HDRA - The Organic Organisation   **Contact:** Angela Bull

Ten glorious acres of organic gardening on the human scale. Come for information and inspiration whether your interest is ornamentals, herbs, vegetables, fruit or a bit of everything. Also visit our Vegetable Kingdom exhibition and enjoy our famous organic restaurant. Events throughout the year. Wonderful shop for organic food, gifts and plants.

Location: OS Ref. SP400 745. 5m SE of Coventry off A45 on the road to Wolston.

Open: Daily (closed Christmas week): 9am - 5pm.

Admission: Adult £5, accompanied Child £2.50, Conc. £4.50.

▢ ▤ ⊤ ⧖ ▣ Licensed. ⊞ Licensed. 𝑓 By arrangement. P ▥
✖ Dog shelter available. ❅ ▽ Tel for details.

THE SHAKESPEARE HOUSES   *See page 360 for full page entry.*

STONELEIGH ABBEY   *See page 361 for full page entry.*

UPTON HOUSE ✄   *See page 362 for full page entry.*

WARWICK CASTLE   *See page 363 for full page entry.*

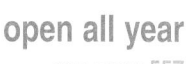 

open all year
see page 557 ❄

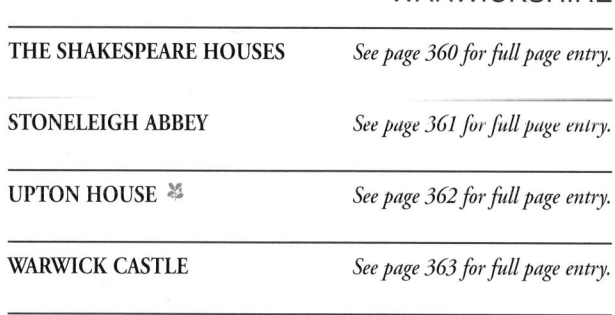

© Compton Verney

Compton Verney.

Ragley Hall. © Derek Littlewood

CJB Photography

MAP 6

HAGLEY HALL

www.hagleyhall.com

This elegant Palladian house, completed in 1760, contains some of the finest examples of Italian plasterwork. Hagley's rich rococo decoration is a remarkable tribute to the artistic achievement of great 18th century architects and designers. Hagley Hall was designed by Sanderson Miller and built for George, the First Lord Lyttelton, who was private secretary to The Prince of Wales in 1732, was made Lord of the Treasury in 1744 and Cofferer to the Royal Household in 1754. George was raised to the peerage in 1756 when he was created Baron of Frankley. The house is set in a 350 acre landscaped park and is still the much loved, privately owned home of the 11th Viscount Cobham.

Owner:
Viscount Cobham

▶ **CONTACT**

Mrs Joyce Purnell
Hagley Hall
Hagley
Worcestershire DY9 9LG

Tel: 01562 882408
Fax: 01562 882632

e-mail: contact@
hagleyhall.info

▶ **LOCATION**

OS Ref. SO920 807

Easily accessible from all areas of the country. ¹/₄ m S of A456 at Hagley.

Close to the M42, M40, M6 and only 5m from M5/J3/J4.

Birmingham City Centre 12m.

Rail: Railway Station and the NEC 25 mins.

Air: Birmingham International Airport 25 mins.

▶ **OPENING TIMES**

House

9 - 31 January,
1 February - 1 March,
17 - 21 April
29 May - 2 June,
28 August - 1 September.

Daily except Sats.
2 - 5pm Guided tours.

Please telephone prior to visit to ensure the house is open.

▶ **ADMISSION**

House

Adult	£5.00
Child (under 14 yrs)	£2.00
Conc.	£2.50
Student	£2.50

ℹ️ Available on an exclusive basis for conferences, presentations, lunches, dinners, product launches, concerts, small wedding receptions, country sporting days, team-building activities, off-road driving and filming. Please telephone for details.

🍽️

♿ Visitors may alight at the entrance. No WC.

☕ Teas available during opening times.

🚶 Obligatory. Please book groups (8+) in advance, guided tour of house time: 1hr. Colour guidebook.

🅿️ Unlimited for coaches and cars.

🐾 By arrangement.

🦮 Guide dogs only.

🔔

CONFERENCE/FUNCTION

ROOM	SIZE	MAX CAPACITY
Crimson Rm	23' x 31'	40
The Saloon	34' x 27'	70
Westcote	31' x 20'	60

THE BIRMINGHAM BOTANICAL GARDENS AND GLASSHOUSES

WESTBOURNE ROAD, EDGBASTON, BIRMINGHAM B15 3TR

www.birminghambotanicalgardens.org.uk

Tel: 0121 454 1860   **Fax:** 0121 454 7835
e-mail: admin@birminghambotanicalgardens.org.uk
Owner: Birmingham Botanical & Horticultural Society   **Contact:** Mrs L Keen
Tropical, Mediterranean and Arid Glasshouses contain a wide range of exotic and economic flora. 15 acres of beautiful gardens with the finest collection of plants in the Midlands. Home of the National Bonsai Collection. Children's adventure playground, aviaries, gallery and sculpture trail.
Location: OS Ref. SP048 855. 2m W of city centre. Follow signs to Edgbaston then brown tourist signs.
Open: Daily: 9am - Dusk (7pm latest except pre-booked groups). Suns opening time 10am. Closed Christmas Day.
Admission: Adult £5.90 (£6.20 on summer Suns & BHs), Conc. £3.50, Family £17 (£18 on summer Suns & BHs). Groups (10+): Adult £4.80, Conc. £3.10.
⬚ 🍴 ♿ 🍴Licensed. 🅿 Guide dogs only. ▲ ❋ ☷Tel for details.

CASTLE BROMWICH HALL GARDENS

CHESTER ROAD, CASTLE BROMWICH, BIRMINGHAM B36 9BT

www.cbhgt.colebridge.net

Tel/Fax: 0121 749 4100   **e-mail:** admin@cbhgt.colebridge.net
Owner: Castle Bromwich Hall & Gardens Trust   **Contact:** Sue Brain
A unique example of 17th and 18th century formal garden design within a 10 acre walled area, comprising historic plants, vegetables, herbs and fruit, with a 19th century holly maze. Classical patterned parterres can be seen at the end of the holly walk, together with restored green house and summer house. RHS Silver Medal NEC 2004.
Location: OS Ref. SP142 898. Off B4114, 4m E of Birmingham city centre, 1m from M6/J5 (exit northbound only). Southbound M6/J6 and follow A38 & A452.
Open: 1 Apr - 1 Oct: Wed - Fri, 1.30 - 4.30pm. Sats, Suns & BH Mon 1.30 - 5.30pm. Please telephone or visit website for winter opening times.
Admission: Adult £3.50, Child 50p, OAP £3. Groups & guided tours by appointment.
⬚ 🍴 ♿ 🍴 🅿 Limited for coaches. ▣ In grounds, on leads.
❋ ☷ Tel. for details.

COVENTRY CATHEDRAL

1 Hill Top, Coventry CV1 5AB
Tel: 024 7652 1200   **Fax:** 024 7652 1220
e-mail: information@coventrycathedral.org.uk   **www.**coventrycathedral.org.uk
Owner: Dean & Canons of Coventry Cathedral   **Contact:** The Visits Secretary
The remains of the medieval Cathedral, bombed in 1940, stand beside the new Cathedral by Basil Spence, consecrated in 1962. Modern works of art include a huge tapestry by Graham Sutherland, a stained glass window by John Piper and a bronze sculpture by Epstein. *'Reconciliation'* statue by Josefina de Vasconcellos.
Location: OS Ref. SP336 790. City centre.
Open: Cathedral: All year: 9am - 5pm. Benedict Coffee Room, shops & video presentation: opening times vary, please call for details. Groups must book in advance.
Admission: Free - donations welcomed.
ℹ Photo permit required. ⬚♿ Partial.WC. ▣ 🍴 𝑖 By arrangement.
🅿None. ▣ Guide dogs only. ❋

HAGLEY HALL 🏛   *See page 369 for full page entry.*

RYTON ORGANIC GARDENS

Ryton on Dunsmore, Coventry, West Midlands CV8 3LG
Tel: 024 7630 3517   **Fax:** 024 7663 9229
Owner: HDRA - The Organic Organisation   **Contact:** Angela Bull
Beautiful and informative gardens including herbs, shrubs, flowers, rare and unusual vegetables, all organically grown.
Location: OS Ref. SP400 745. 5m SE of Coventry off A45 on the road to Wolston.
Open: Daily (closed Christmas week): 9am - 5pm.
Admission: Adult £4.50, Child £2.50, Conc £4.. Groups (14+) £2.50 plus 50p for garden tour.

special events
see page 571

Birmingham Botanical Gardens, Loudon Terrace.

West Midlands - England

National Trust Photographic Library

SELLY MANOR

MAPLE ROAD, BOURNVILLE, WEST MIDLANDS B30 2AE

www.bvt.org.uk/sellymanor

Tel/Fax: 0121 472 0199 **e-mail:** sellymanor@bvt.org.uk

Owner: Bournville Village Trust **Contact:** Gillian Ellis

A beautiful half-timbered manor house in the heart of the famous Bournville village. The house has been lived in since the 14th century and was rescued from demolition by George Cadbury. It houses furniture dating back several centuries and is surrounded by a delightful typical Tudor garden.

Location: OS Ref. SP045 814. N side of Sycamore Road, just E of Linden Road (A4040). 4m SSW of City Centre.

Open: All year: Tue - Fri, 10am - 5pm. Apr - Sept: Sats, Suns & BHs, 2 - 5pm. Closed Mons.

Admission: Adult £3, Child £1, Conc. £2, Family £6.50.

🗎 🔲Partial. WC. 🗓By arrangement. 🄿Limited. 🔳 ⛔In grounds, on leads.
🔺 ❋

WIGHTWICK MANOR ❧

WIGHTWICK BANK, WOLVERHAMPTON, WEST MIDLANDS WV6 8EE

Tel: 01902 761400 **Fax:** 01902 764663

Owner: The National Trust **Contact:** The Property Manager

Begun in 1887, the house is a notable example of the influence of William Morris, with many original Morris wallpapers and fabrics. Also of interest are pre-Raphaelite pictures, Kempe glass and De Morgan ware. The 17 acre Victorian/Edwardian garden designed by Thomas Mawson has formal beds, pergola, yew hedges, topiary and terraces, woodland and two pools.

Location: OS Ref. SO869 985. 3m W of Wolverhampton, up Wightwick Bank (A454), beside the Mermaid Inn.

Open: 2 Mar - 23 Dec: Thur - Sat, 12.30 - 5pm (last entry 4.30pm). Admission by timed ticket. Guided groups through ground floor, freeflow upstairs (min. tour time approx. 1 hr). Also open BH Sats, Suns & Mons, 12.30 - 5pm (last entry 4.30pm) - ground floor only, no guided tours. Booked groups Tues & Weds. Garden: Wed - Sat, 11am - 6pm; BH Suns & Mons, 11am - 6pm.

Admission: Adult £6.60, Child £3.30. Garden only: £3.30, Child Free.

🗎 ♿ Ground floor & grounds. 🔳 🄿400 yds. ⛔In grounds, on leads.

© David Lawson

Ryton Organic Gardens - purple flowers entitled Diversity in Landscape.

BROADWAY TOWER

BROADWAY, WORCESTERSHIRE WR12 7LB

www.broadwaytower.co.uk

Tel: 01386 852390 **Fax:** 01386 858038 **e-mail:** broadwaytower1@aol.com

Owner: Broadway Tower Country Park Ltd **Contact:** Annette Gorton

Broadway Tower is a unique historic building on top of the Cotswold ridge, having been built by the 6th Earl of Coventry in the late 1790s. Its architecture, the fascinating views as well as its exhibitions on famous owners and occupants (including William Morris) make the Tower a "must" for all visitors to the Cotswolds. The Tower is surrounded by 35 acres of parkland, picnic/ BBQ facilities. A complete family day out.

Location: OS Ref. SP115 362. $^1/_2$ m SW of the A44 Evesham to Oxford Rd. $1^1/_2$ m E of Broadway.

Open: 1 Apr – 31 Oct: daily, 10.30am - 5pm. Nov - Mar: Sats & Suns (weather permitting), 11am - 3pm.

Admission: Adult £3.50, Child £2, Conc. £3. Group rate on request.

⬜ 🅣 Wedding receptions. ♿ WC. 🅿 ♿ 🅗 Licensed. ■ ⬛ In grounds, on leads. ✳

National Trust

CROOME PARK ✤

SEVERN STOKE, WORCESTERSHIRE WR8 9JS

www.nationaltrust.org.uk

Tel: 01905 371006 **Fax:** 01905 371090 **e-mail:** croomepark@nationaltrust.org.uk

Owner: The National Trust **Contact:** The Property Manager

Croome was 'Capability' Brown's first complete landscape, making his reputation and establishing a new parkland aesthetic which became universally adopted over the next fifty years. The elegant park buildings and other structures are mostly by Robert Adam and James Wyatt. 2006 will see the completion of the first phase of restoration – a 10 year Heritage Lottery Funded programme that has replanted over 14 acres of shrubbery and thousands of trees, dredged the lake and river, reinstated miles of paths and restored elegant parkland buildings.

Location: OS150, SO878 448. 8m S of Worcester and E of A38 and M5, 6m W of Pershore and B4084.

Open: Park & Church: 3 Mar - Apr & 6 Sept - Oct: Wed - Sun, 10am - 5.30pm. May - Aug: daily, 10am - 5.30pm. Nov - 17 Dec: Wed - Sun, 10am - 4pm. Open BH Mons. Last admission 30 min before park closes. Church open in association with the Churches Conservation Trust.

Admission: Adult £3.90, Child £1.90, Family £9.50.

♿ Partial. ⬛ 🅘 🅿 ⬛ ⬛ Tel for details.

THE GREYFRIARS 🐾

Worcester WR1 2LZ

Tel: 01905 23571 **e-mail:** greyfriars@nationaltrust.org.uk **www.**nationaltrust.org.uk

Owner: The National Trust **Contact:** The Custodian

Built about 1480 next to a Franciscan friary in the centre of medieval Worcester, this timber-framed house has 17th and late 18th century additions. It was rescued from demolition at the time of the Second World War and was carefully restored. The panelled rooms have noteworthy textiles and interesting furniture. An archway leads through to a delightful walled garden.

Location: OS150, SO852 546. Friar Street, in centre of Worcester.

Open: 1 Mar - 16 Dec: Wed - Sat (also Suns 2 Jul - 27 Aug), 1 - 5pm.

Admission: Adult £3.60, Child £1.90, Family £9. Booked Groups (8+) £3.

HANBURY HALL 🐾

DROITWICH, WORCESTERSHIRE WR9 7EA

www.nationaltrust.org.uk

Tel: 01527 821214 **Fax:** 01527 821251 **e-mail:** hanburyhall@nationaltrust.org.uk

Owner: The National Trust **Contact:** The Property Manager

In its beautiful setting of Worcestershire parkland, this delightful William and Mary style country house retains its lived in and friendly atmosphere. With its superb staircase murals by Thornhill, and the unique Watney collection of fine porcelain, Hanbury Hall also boasts tranquil 18th century formal gardens including a playable bowling green and a stunning Orangery and working mushroom house.

Location: OS150, SO943 637. $4^1/_2$ m E of Droitwich, 4m SE M5/J5.

Open: 4 - 12 Mar: Sat & Sun; 18 Mar - 1 Nov: Sat - Wed. Grounds/Tearoom/Shop: 4 Nov - 10 Dec, Sats & Suns, 11am - 4pm.

Admission: House & Garden: Adult £6, Child £3, Family £15. Garden & Grounds only: Adult £4, Child £2, Family £10. Groups (15+) £5.20. Weekends (Nov - Dec): Adult £2, Child £1, Family £5.

⬜ 🅘 🅣 ♿ Partial. WC. ⬛ 🅘 For pre-booked groups. 🅿 ⬛ Guide dogs only. ▲ ⬛ Tel for details.

Witley Court.

HARTLEBURY CASTLE

HARTLEBURY, NR KIDDERMINSTER DY11 7XZ

Tel: 01299 250416 **Fax:** 01299 251890 **e-mail:** museum@worcestershire.gov.uk

Owner: The Church Commissioners   **Contact:** The County Museum

Hartlebury Castle has been home to the Bishops of Worcester for over a thousand years. The three principal State Rooms - the medieval Great Hall, the Saloon and the unique Hurd Library - contain period furniture, fine plasterwork and episcopal portraits. In the Castle's North Wing the Worcestershire County Museum brings the county's past to life through a wide variety of exhibitions and a regular events programme.

Location: OS Ref. SO389 710. N side of B4193, 2m E of Stourport, 4m S of Kidderminster.

Open: 1 Feb - 21 Dec: Tue - Fri, 10am - 5pm. Sat, Sun & BHs, 11am - 5pm. Closed Mons & Good Friday.

Admission: Adults £3, Conc. £1.50, Family (2+3) £8. (2005 prices.)

⬜ ♿ ▣ ⚹ For pre-booked groups. 🅿 ▣ 🐕 Guide dogs only.
▣ Tel for details.

HARVINGTON HALL 🏛

HARVINGTON, KIDDERMINSTER, WORCESTERSHIRE DY104LR

www.harvingtonhall.com

Tel: 01562 777846 **Fax:** 01562 777190

e-mail: thehall@harvington.fsbusiness.co.uk

Owner: Roman Catholic Archdiocese of Birmingham   **Contact:** The Hall Manager

Harvington Hall is a moated, medieval and Elizabethan manor house. Many of the rooms still have their original Elizabethan wall paintings and the Hall contains the finest series of priest hides in the country. A full programme of events throughout the year including outdoor plays, craft fairs, living history weekends and a pilgrimage is available.

Location: OS Ref. SO877 745. On minor road, ¹/₂ m NE of A450/A448 crossroads at Mustow Green. 3m SE of Kidderminster.

Open: Mar & Oct: Sats & Suns; Apr - Sept: Wed - Sun & BH Mons (closed Good Fri), 11.30am - 5pm. Open throughout the year for pre-booked groups and schools. Occasionally the Hall may be closed for a private function.

Admission: Adult £4.50, Child £3, OAP £3.80, Family £12.50. Garden: £1.

⬜ ▣ ♿ Partial. 🅿 Limited for coaches. ▣ 🐕 Guide dogs only. ✳
▣ Tel for details.

HAWFORD DOVECOTE

Hawford, Worcestershire

Tel: 01743 708100 (Regional Office) www.nationaltrust.org.uk

Owner: The National Trust   **Contact:** Regional Office

A 16th century half-timbered dovecote.

Location: OS Ref. SO846 607. 3m N of Worcester, ¹/₂ m E of A449.

Open: 1 Apr - 31 Oct: daily, 9am - 6pm or sunset if earlier. Other times by prior appointment with the Regional Office.

Admission: £1.

LEIGH COURT BARN

Worcester

Tel: 0121 625 6820 - Regional Office

Owner: English Heritage   **Contact:** The West Midlands Regional Office

Magnificent 14th century timber-framed barn built for the monks of Pershore Abbey. It is the largest of its kind in Britain.

Location: OS150 Ref. SO783 535. 5m W of Worcester on unclassified road off A4103.

Open: 1 Apr - 30 Sept: Thur - Sun & BH Mons, 10am - 6pm.

Admission: Free.

LITTLE MALVERN COURT

Nr Malvern, Worcestershire WR14 4JN

Tel: 01684 892988   **Fax:** 01684 893057

Owner: Trustees of the late T M Berington   **Contact:** Mrs T M Berington

Prior's Hall, associated rooms and cells, c1480, of former Benedictine Monastery. Formerly attached to, and forming part of the Little Malvern Priory Church which may also be visited. It has an oak-framed roof, 5-bay double-collared roof, with two tiers of cusped windbraces. Library. Collections of religious vestments, embroideries and paintings. Gardens: 10 acres of former monastic grounds with spring bulbs, blossom, old fashioned roses and shrubs. Access to Hall only by flight of steps.

Location: OS Ref. SO769 403. 3m S of Great Malvern on Upton-on-Severn Rd (A4104).

Open: 19 Apr - 20 Jul: Weds & Thurs, 2.15 - 5pm. 26 Mar & 1 May for NGS: 2.15 - 5pm. Last admission 4.30pm.

Admission: House & Garden: Adult £5.50, Child £2, Garden only: Adult £4.50, Child £1. Groups must book, max 35.

MADRESFIELD COURT

Madresfield, Malvern WR13 5AU

Tel: 01684 573614   **Fax:** 01684 569197   **e-mail:** madresfield@clara.co.uk

Owner: The Trustees of Madresfield Estate   **Contact:** Mr Peter Hughes

Elizabethan and Victorian house with medieval origins. Fine contents. Extensive gardens and arboretum.

Location: OS Ref. SO809 474. 6m SW of Worcester. 1¹/₂ m SE of A449. 2m NE of Malvern.

Open: Guided tours: 12 Apr - 27 Jul: mostly Wed & Thur, also Sats 22 Apr, 20 May, 10 Jun & 15 Jul: 10.45am & 2.30pm. Numbers are restricted and prior booking, by telephone to The Estate Office (01684 573614), is strongly recommended to avoid disappointment.

Admission: £8.

Obligatory.

SPETCHLEY PARK GARDENS

SPETCHLEY PARK, WORCESTER WR5 1RS

www.spetchleygardens.co.uk

Tel: 01453 810303   **Fax:** 01453 511915   **e-mail:** hb@spetchleygardens.co.uk

Owner: Spetchley Gardens Charitable Trust   **Contact:** Mr R J Berkeley

This lovely 30 acre private garden contains a large collection of trees, shrubs and plants, many rare or unusual. A garden full of secrets, every corner reveals some new vista, some treasure of the plant world. The exuberant planting and the peaceful walks make this an oasis of beauty, peace and quiet. Deer Park close by.

Location: OS Ref. SO895 540. 3m E of Worcester on A44. Leave M5/J6/J7.

Open: 21 Mar- 30 Sept: Wed - Sun & BHs, 11am - 6pm. Oct: Sats & Suns, 11am - 4pm. (last admission 1hr before closing).

Admission: Adult £5, Child (under 16yrs) Free. Groups (25+): Adult £4.50. Adult Season Ticket £25.

THE TUDOR HOUSE

16 Church Street, Upton-on-Severn, Worcestershire WR8 0HT

Tel: 01684 592447/592754

Owner: Mrs Lavender Beard   **Contact:** Mrs Wilkinson

Upton past and present, exhibits of local history.

Location: OS Ref. SO852 406. Centre of Upton-on-Severn, 7m SE of Malvern by B4211.

Open: Apr - Oct: daily, 2 - 5pm (4pm on Suns). Winter Suns only, 2 - 4pm. Groups by arrangement.

Admission: Adult £1, Conc. 50p, Family £2.

WICHENFORD DOVECOTE

Wichenford, Worcestershire

Tel: 01743 708100 (Regional Office) www.nationaltrust.org.uk

Owner: The National Trust   **Contact:** Regional Office

A 17th century half-timbered black and white dovecote.

Location: OS Ref. SO788 598. 5¹/₂ m NW of Worcester, N of B4204.

Open: 1 Apr - 31 Oct: daily, 9am - 6pm or sunset if earlier. Other times by appointment with Regional Office.

Admission: £1.

English Heritage Photo Library

WITLEY COURT ⊞

GREAT WITLEY, WORCESTER WR6 6JT

www.english-heritage.org.uk

Tel: 01299 896636

Owner: English Heritage   **Contact:** Visitor Operations Team

The spectacular ruins of a once great house. An earlier Jacobean manor house, converted in the 19th century into an Italianate mansion, with porticoes by John Nash. The adjoining church, by James Gibbs, has a remarkable 18th century baroque interior. The gardens, William Nesfield's 'Monster Work' were equally elaborate and contained immense fountains, which survive today. The largest is the Perseus and Andromeda Fountain which has been restored and now fires daily throughout the summer, contact the site for details and timings. The landscaped grounds, parterres, fountains and woodlands have recently been restored to their former glory. The Woodland Walks in the North Park include various species of tree and shrub acquired from all over the world and the new garden in "The Wilderness" is part of the Contemporary Heritage Garden project.

Location: OS150, SO769 649. 10m NW of Worcester off A443.

Open: 1 Apr - 31 Oct: daily, 10am - 5pm (6pm Jun - Aug). 1 Nov - 28 Feb: Thur - Mon, 10am - 4pm. Closed 24 - 26 Dec & 1 Jan.

Admission: Adult £5.20, Child £2.60, OAP £3.90, Family £13. 15% discount for groups (11+).

ⓘVisitor welcome point. ⬚ ⬚ Grounds. WC. ⬚ ⬚ ⬚ ⬚ ⬚ ⬚ Tel for details.

©The National Trust Photographic Library.

Croome Park.

Whitby Abbey. © English Heritage Photo Library

yorkshire & the humber

Yorkshire is Britain's largest county, with countryside to match – with its wild North York Moors, the softer Yorkshire Dales, and the flatter landscape of the Humber estuary. York contains constant reminders of its medieval origins, but is as well known for its elegant Jacobean and Georgian architecture. The Jorvik Centre brings back to life the Viking occupation of York, together with sights, sounds and even smells! Within easy reach of York are grand palaces such as Castle Howard, designed by Sir John Vanbrugh in 1699, and Harewood House, home of HM the Queen's cousin, the Earl of Harewood. But there are also more modest gems to be seen such as Sion Hill Hall, and the gardens at the RHS Harlow Carr are amongst the finest in Britain.

BRAMHAM PARK

www.bramhampark.co.uk

Bramham Park is the stunning family home of the Lane Fox family, who are direct descendants of Robert Benson, the founder of Bramham over 300 years ago. The gardens extend to some 66 acres and, with the Pleasure Grounds, extend to over 100 acres.

The focus at Bramham has always been the landscape (the house was merely built as a 'villa' from which to admire it). Inspiration for the design of the Garden at Bramham was French and formal, but the manner in which it was adapted to the national landscape is relaxed and entirely English. It is completely original and few other parks of this period survive; none on

the scale and complexity of Bramham. It is a rare and outstanding example of the formal style of the late 17th century and early 18th century.

Bramham is a garden of walks and vistas, architectural features and reflecting water. A broad vista stretches away at an angle from the house and a number of other allées have focal points – temples and vistas. This creates an experience of anticipation when walking around the grounds.

The house, gardens and surrounding parkland make an ideal venue for events, private dinners, corporate entertaining, product launches and filming.

Owner:
George Lane Fox

▶ CONTACT

The Estate Office
Bramham Park
Wetherby
West Yorkshire
LS23 6ND

Tel: 01937 846000
Fax: 01937 846007
e-mail: enquiries@
bramhampark.co.uk

▶ LOCATION
OS Ref. SE410 416

A1/M1 1m,
Wetherby 5m,
Leeds 7m,
Harrogate 12m,
York 14m.

Rail: Leeds or York.

Bus: 770; Bus stop
1/2 m.

Air: Leeds/Bradford
15m.

CONFERENCE/FUNCTION

ROOM	SIZE	MAX CAPACITY
Gallery	80' x 20'	110
Hall	30' x 30'	50
North Room	27' x 48'	100
East Room	20' x 18'	14
Old Kitchen	22' x 23'	50

▶ OPENING TIMES

House
For groups of 10+ by appointment only (separate fee).

Gardens
1 April - 30 September: daily, 11.30am - 4.30pm. Closed 5 - 11 June & 14 August - 1 September.

▶ ADMISSION
Gardens only

Adult	£4.00
Child (under 16yrs)	£2.00
Child (under 5yrs)	Free
OAP	£2.00

♿ Grounds. WC.
🐕 Dogs on leads.

🎭 SPECIAL EVENTS

JUN 8 - 11
Bramham International 3-Day Event.

AUG 25 - 27
Leeds Festival.

© English Heritage

MAP 11

BRODSWORTH HALL ⊞ & GARDENS

www.english-heritage.org.uk/yorkshire

This once opulent Victorian Hall offers a fascinating insight into the changing fortunes of a previously wealthy Victorian family, with many original fixtures and fittings still in place.

The 15 acres of garden, a rare survival from the Victorian Age, have been restored to their 1860s heyday. Against a backdrop of enchanting features like the summerhouse, pleasure grounds, fernery, pet cemetery and fountain centre-piece, the pathways wind through carpets of spring snowdrops, the dazzling laburnum arch, rainbows of period summer bedding and the seasonal delight of winter evergreens, all revealing the fashions and desires of the Victorian country gentry.

Owner:
English Heritage

▶ CONTACT
Visitor Operations Team
Brodsworth Hall
Brodsworth
Nr Doncaster
Yorkshire DN5 7XJ

Tel: 01302 722598

Fax: 01302 337165

e-mail: customers@
english-heritage.org.uk

▶ LOCATION
OS Ref. SE507 071

In Brodsworth, 5m NW
of Doncaster off A635.
Use A1(M)/J37.

Rail: Doncaster.

© English Heritage Photo Library / John Critchley

▶ OPENING TIMES
Summer

House

1 April - 29 September
Tue - Sun & BHs,
1 - 5pm.

30 September - 29 October
Sats & Suns,
12 noon - 4pm.

Gardens & Tea Rooms

1 April - 29 October
Daily,
10am - 5.30pm.

Winter

**Gardens, Tea Rooms,
Shop & Servants' Wing**

30 October - 31 March
Sats & Suns, 10am - 4pm.

Closed 24 - 26 December
& 1 January.

Last admission $^1/_2$ hr
before closing.

▶ ADMISSION*
House & Gardens
Adult £6.60
Child (5-15yrs) £3.30
Child (under 5yrs) ...... Free
Conc. £5.00

Groups (11+) 15% discount

*Free admission for tour
leaders and coach drivers.

Gardens only
Adult £4.60
Child (5-15yrs) £2.30
Child (under 5yrs) ...... Free
Conc. £3.50

ℹ️ Exhibitions about the family, the servants and the gardens. WCs.

🛗❄️

♿ Most of house is accessible. WCs.

☕ Seating for 70.

🎎 Groups must book. Booked coach parties: 10am - 1pm.

🅿️ 220 cars and 3 coaches. Free.

🎒 Education Centre. Free if booked in advance.

♿

❄️

🎭 Tel for details.

CASTLE HOWARD

www.castlehoward.co.uk

In a dramatic setting between two lakes with extensive gardens and impressive fountains, this 18th century Palace was designed by Sir John Vanbrugh in 1699. Undoubtedly the finest private residence in Yorkshire, it was built for Charles Howard, 3rd Earl of Carlisle, whose descendants still live here.

With its painted and gilded dome reaching 80ft into the Yorkshire sky, this impressive house has collections of antique furniture, porcelain and sculpture, while its fabulous collection of paintings is dominated by the famous Holbein portraits of Henry VIII and the Duke of Norfolk.

Designed on a heroic scale covering 1,000 acres. The gardens include memorable sights such as the Temple of the Four Winds and the Mausoleum, the New River Bridge and the restored waterworks of the South Lake, Cascade, Waterfall and Prince of Wales Fountain. The walled garden has collections of old and modern roses.

Ray Wood, acknowledged by the Royal Botanic Collection, Kew, as a "rare botanical jewel" has a unique collection of rare trees, shrubs, rhododendrons, magnolias and azaleas.

Owner:
The Hon Simon Howard

▶ CONTACT
Visitor Services
Castle Howard
York, North Yorks
YO60 7DA

Tel: 01653 648333
Fax: 01653 648529

e-mail:
house@
castlehoward.co.uk

▶ LOCATION
OS Ref. SE716 701

Approaching from S, A64 to Malton, on entering Malton, take Castle Howard road via Coneysthorpe village. Or from A64 following signs to Castle Howard via the Carrmire Gate 9' wide by 10' high.

York 15m (20 mins), A64. From London: M1/J32, M18 to A1(M) to A64, York/Scarborough Road, 3¹/₂ hrs.

Train: London Kings Cross to York 1hr. 50 mins. York to Malton Station 30 mins.

Bus: Service and tour buses from York Station.

▶ OPENING TIMES
Summer
1 March - 5 November
Daily, 10am - 4pm
(last admission).

Winter
Grounds only
November - mid February, it is recommended that you telephone before setting off.

Stable Courtyard (gift shops, farm shop, chocolate shop, plant centre, café) open year round.

Access to Pretty Wood Pyramid is available from 1 July to 31 August. Special tours to newly restored rooms in the house are available by arrangement.
For more information please contact Castle Howard Estate Office on 01653 648444.

▶ ADMISSION
Summer

House & Garden
Adult	£9.50
Child (4-16yrs)	£6.50
Under 4yrs	Free
Conc	£8.50

Garden only
Adult	£7.00
Child (4-16yrs)	£5.00
Under 4yrs	Free
Conc	£6.50

CONFERENCE/FUNCTION

ROOM	SIZE	MAX CAPACITY
Long Gallery	197' x 24'	280
Grecian Hall	40' x 40'	160

Outdoor tours, events, concerts, theatre, exhibitions, historical character guides, adventure playground, plant centre, farm shop, chocolate shop, gift & book shops. Gift fairs, product launches, garden parties, firework displays, banqueting and other events. Suitable for helicopter landing. Used as a film location. No photography in the House unless prior permission is granted.

Booked private parties and receptions, min. 25.

Transport equipped for wheelchairs. Wheelchair lift in House to main floor. WCs.

Two cafeterias (third open Jul - Sept). Stable Courtyard Café open year round.

Guides posted throughout House. Private tours and lectures by arrangement covering architecture, history, art, collections, House including tours of recently refurbished rooms.

400 cars, 20 coaches.

1:10 teacher/pupil ratio required. KS2&3 education pack. Special interest: architecture, art, history, wildlife, horticulture.

FAIRFAX HOUSE

www.fairfaxhouse.co.uk

Fairfax House was acquired and fully restored by the York Civic Trust in 1983/84. The house, described as a classic architectural masterpiece of its age and certainly one of the finest townhouses in England, was saved from near collapse after considerable abuse and misuse this century, having been converted into a cinema and dance hall.

The richly decorated interior with its plasterwork, wood and wrought-iron, is now the home for a unique collection of Georgian furniture, clocks,

paintings and porcelain.

The Noel Terry Collection, gift of a former treasurer of the York Civic Trust, has been described by Christie's as one of the finest private collections formed in the 20th century. It enhances and complements the house and helps to create that special 'lived-in' feeling, providing the basis for a series of set-piece period exhibitions which bring the house to life in a very tangible way.

Owner:
York Civic Trust

▶ CONTACT

Mr Peter Brown
Fairfax House
Castlegate
York   YO1 9RN

Tel: 01904 655543
Fax: 01904 652262

e-mail: peterbrown@
fairfaxhouse.co.uk

▶ LOCATION

OS Ref. SE605 515

In centre of York between Castle Museum and Jorvik Centre.

London 4 hrs by car, 2 hrs by train.

Rail: York Station, 10 mins walk.

Taxi: Station Taxis 01904 623332.

▶ OPENING TIMES

Summer
11 February - 31 December
Mon - Thur: 11am - 5pm.
Fridays: Guided tours only at 11am and 2pm.
Saturdays: 11am - 5pm.
Sundays: 1.30 - 5pm.
Last admission 4.30pm.

Winter
Closed
1 January - 10 February & 24 - 26 December.

▶ ADMISSION

Adult......................£4.50
Child......... Free with full paying adult.
Conc. £3.75
Groups*
Adult......................£4.00
Child.....................£1.00
Conc. £3.25

* Min payment 15 persons.

i Suitable for filming. No photography in house. Liveried footmen, musical & dancing performances can be arranged.

Max. 28 seated. Groups up to 50: buffet can be provided.

Visitors may alight at entrance prior to parking. No WCs except for functions.

A guided tour can be arranged at a cost of £6. Evening and daytime guided tours, telephone for details. Available in French and German. Tour time: 1¹/2 hrs. Special connoisseur tours available - contact the Director to discuss.

P 300 cars, 50 yds from house. Coach park is ¹/2 m away, parties are dropped off; drivers please telephone for details showing the nearest coach park and approach to the house.

▶ SPECIAL EVENTS

MAR 4 - DEC 31
The John Butler Collection of Georgian Glass.

DEC 1 - 31
Keeping of Christmas.

Yorkshire & The Humber - England

Mike Williams

MAP 10

Owner:
The National Trust

▶ **CONTACT**

The National Trust
Fountains Abbey
and Studley Royal
Ripon
North Yorkshire
HG4 3DY

Tel: 01765 608888
Fax: 01765 601002
e-mail:
fountainsenquiries@
nationaltrust.org.uk

▶ **LOCATION**
OS Ref. SE275 700

Abbey entrance;
4m W of Ripon off
B6265.
8m W of A1.

Rail: Harrogate 12m.

Bus: Regular
season service
tel: 0870 608 2608
for details.

FOUNTAINS ABBEY
& STUDLEY ROYAL

One of the most remarkable sites in Europe, sheltered in a secluded valley, Fountains Abbey and Studley Royal, a World Heritage Site, encompasses the spectacular remains of a 12th century Cistercian abbey with one of the finest surviving monastic watermills in Britain, an Elizabethan mansion, and one of the best surviving examples of a Georgian green water garden. Elegant ornamental lakes,

avenues, temples and cascades provide a succession of unforgettable eye-catching vistas in an atmosphere of peace and tranquillity. St Mary's Church, built by William Burges in the 19th century, provides a dramatic focal point to the medieval deer park with over 500 deer.

Small museum near to the Abbey. Exhibitions in Fountains Hall, Swanley Grange and the Mill.

▶ **OPENING TIMES**

March - October
Daily: 10am - 5pm.

November - February
Daily: 10am - 4pm.

Closes early on
special event days.

Closed 24/25 December,
& Fridays from Nov - Jan.

Deer Park: All year,
daily during daylight
(closed 24/25 December).

▶ **ADMISSION**

Adult £6.50
Child* (5-16yrs)........ £3.50
Family £17.50

Groups (15+)
Adult £5.50
Child* (5-16yrs)........ £3.00

Groups (31+)
Adult £5.00
Child* (5-16yrs)........ £2.50

Group discount
applicable only with
prior booking.

Group visits and disabled
visitors, please telephone
in advance, 01765 643197.

* NT, EH Members &
Under 5s Free.

The Abbey is owned by
the National Trust and
maintained by English
Heritage.
St Mary's Church is owned
by English Heritage and
managed by the
National Trust.

ℹ️ Events held throughout the year. Exhibitions. Seminar facilities. Outdoor concerts, meetings, activity days, walks.

🛍️ Two shops.

🍽️ Dinners and dances.

♿ Free Batricars & wheelchairs, please book, tel. 01765 643185. 3-wheel Batricars not permitted due to terrain. Tours for visually impaired, please book. WC.

🍴 Groups please book, discounted rates. Licensed.

🍴 Licensed.

🚶 Free, but seasonal. Groups (please book on 01765 643197), please use Visitor Centre entrance.

🅿️ Drivers must book groups.

🐕 In grounds, on leads.

🔔 Fountains Hall, an Elizabethan Mansion is an ideal setting for weddings. For details or a Wedding pack tel: 01765 643196/643198.

✳️ Tel for details.

Harewood House

HAREWOOD HOUSE

www.harewood.org

Harewood House is the magnificent Yorkshire home of the Queen's cousin, the Earl of Harewood. Nestling in 'Capability' Brown landscaped surrounds, Harewood is one of the great Treasure Houses of England and is renowned for its magnificent architecture and outstanding art collections. Designed by John Carr and completed in 1772, the House features exquisite interiors by Robert Adam, was furnished throughout by Thomas Chippendale, contains world-class art collections, including watercolours by J M W Turner, who stayed at Harewood under the patronage of Edward Lascelles; family portraits by Gainsborough and Sir Joshua Reynolds; and Renaissance masterpieces.

Steeped in history, Royal Family memorabilia recalls Lord Harewood's mother, HRH Princess Mary, the Princess Royal, who lived at Harewood from 1929 until her death in 1965. A permanent exhibition, 'Below stairs: Harewood's Hidden Collections', includes many items from throughout Princess Mary's life, as well as giving public access to previously unseen corridors and rooms, providing a fascinating glimpse into the hidden world of the servants' domain.

Harewood's stunning gardens enfold lakeside and woodland walks, a Rock Garden, Walled Garden and the restored Parterre Terrace. The Lakeside Bird Garden contains around 100 species of threatened and exotic birds as well as popular favourites, penguins and flamingos.

Throughout the season Harewood plays host to many special events, including concerts, craft festivals and car rallies, and features a programme of exhibitions within the House.

Owner:
The Earl of Harewood

▶ CONTACT

Harewood House Trust
Moor House
Harewood
Leeds
West Yorkshire
LS17 9LQ

Tel: 0113 2181010
Fax: 0113 2181002
e-mail: info@
harewood.org

▶ LOCATION

OS Ref. SE311 446

A1 N or S to Wetherby.

A659 via Collingham, Harewood is on A61 between Harrogate and Leeds. Easily reached from A1, M1, M62 and M18. Half an hour from York,

15 mins from centre of Leeds or Harrogate.

Rail: Leeds Station 7m.

Bus: No. 36 from Leeds or Harrogate.

CONFERENCE/FUNCTION

ROOM	SIZE	MAX CAPACITY
State Dining Rm.		32
Gallery		96
Courtyard		120

Harewood House

🛍️ 🎭 ℹ️ Marquees can be accommodated, concerts and product launches. No photography in the House.

🍽️ Ideal for corporate entertaining including drinks receptions, buffets and wedding receptions. Specific rooms available for corporate entertaining.

♿ Visitors may alight at entrance. Parking in allocated areas. Most facilities accessible. Wheelchair available at House and Bird Garden. WC. Special concessions apply to disabled groups. Some steep inclines.

🍷 Licensed. 🍴 Licensed.

🅿️ Cars 400 yds from house. 50+ coaches 500 yds from house. Drivers to verify in advance.

🚶 🎧 By arrangement. Audio tour of house available. Lectures by arrangement. Daily free talks.

🏫 Sandford Award for Education.

🐕 Dogs on leads in grounds, guide dogs only in house.

💍 Civil Wedding Licence.

▶ OPENING TIMES

House & Grounds
24 March - 29 October:
Daily, 10am - 6pm.

**Grounds only –
winter weekends**
7 November - 17 December:
Sats & Suns only.

Please call for opening times of specific areas.

▶ ADMISSION

All attractions*

Adult	£11.00
Child/Student	£6.50
OAP	£10.00
Family	£37.50

Bird Garden, Grounds, & Adventure Playground

Adult	£8.75
Child/Student	£5.75
OAP	£7.75
Family	£32.00

Groups (15+):
please telephone for details.

* Prices are for Mon - Fri. Prices on weekends & BH Mons are slightly higher.

🎭 SPECIAL EVENTS

MAY 27 - 29
Noddy's Here Again!

JUN 18
Harewood Vintage & Classic Vehicle Rally.

AUG 27/28
Steam Rally.

Please telephone for details of other events.

Yorkshire & The Humber - England

NEWBY HALL & GARDENS

www.newbyhall.com

Owner:
Mr Richard Compton

▶ CONTACT

The Administrator
Newby Hall
Ripon
North Yorkshire
HG4 5AE

Tel: 01423 322583
Information Hotline:
0845 450 4068

Fax: 01423 324452

e-mail:
info@newbyhall.com

▶ LOCATION
OS Ref. SE348 675

Midway between
London and Edinburgh,
4m W of A1, towards
Ripon. S of Skelton 2m
NW of (A1)
Boroughbridge.
4m SE of Ripon.

Taxi: Ripon Taxi Rank
01765 601283.

Bus: On Ripon - York
route.

The home of Richard and Lucinda Compton, Newby Hall was built in the 1690s by Sir Christopher Wren's number two, John Etty. In the 1760s William Weddell, an ancestor of the Comptons, acquired a magnificent collection of Ancient Roman sculpture and Gobelins tapestries. He commissioned Robert Adam to alter the interior of the house and Thomas Chippendale to make furniture. The result is a perfect example of the Georgian 'Age of Elegance'.

GARDENS
25 acres of glorious award-winning gardens contain rare and beautiful shrubs and plants, including the National Collection of the Genus Cornus. Newby's famous double herbaceous borders, flanked by great bastions of yew hedges, sweep down to the River Ure. Formal gardens such as the Autumn and Rose Gardens – each with splashing fountains – a Victorian rock garden, the tranquillity of Sylvia's Garden, pergolas and even a tropical garden, make Newby a 'Garden for all Seasons'. The gardens incorporate an exciting children's adventure garden and miniature railway. There is also an unusual exhibition of contemporary sculptures, set in ornamental woodland.

▶ OPENING TIMES
Summer

House
1 April - 1 October

April, May, June &
September:
Tues - Sun & BH Mons;
July - August: Daily
12 noon - 5pm.
Last admission 4.30pm.

Garden
Dates as House,
11am - 5.30pm.
Last admission 5pm.

Winter
October - end March
Closed.

▶ ADMISSION
House & Garden
Adult £9.20
Child/Disabled £6.40
OAP £8.20
Group (15+)
Adult/OAP £7.50
Child/Disabled £6.00

Garden only
Adult £6.90
Child/Disabled £5.20
OAP £5.90
Group (15+)
Adult £5.90
Child (4-16yrs) £4.70

Suitable for filming and for special events, craft and country fairs, vehicle rallies etc, promotions and lectures. No indoor photography. Allow a full day for viewing house and gardens.

Wedding receptions & special functions.

6 wheelchairs available. Access to ground floor of house and key areas in gardens. WC.

Garden restaurant, teas, hot and cold meals. Booked groups in Grantham Room. Menus/rates on request.

Ample. Hard standing for coaches.

Welcome. Rates on request. Grantham Room for use as wet weather base subject to availability. Woodland discovery walk, adventure gardens and train rides on 10¹/₄" gauge railway.

Guide dogs only. Tel for details.

CONFERENCE/FUNCTION

ROOM	SIZE	MAX CAPACITY
Grantham Room	90' x 20'	200

RIPLEY CASTLE

www.ripleycastle.co.uk

Owner:
Sir Thomas Ingilby Bt

▶ CONTACT

Tours: Anneliese Ford
Meetings/Dinners:
Rachel Terry
Ripley Castle
Ripley
Harrogate
North Yorkshire
HG3 3AY

Tel: 01423 770152
Fax: 01423 771745
e-mail: enquiries@
ripleycastle.co.uk

▶ LOCATION

OS Ref. SE283 605

W edge of village. Just
off A61, 3¹/₂ m N of
Harrogate, 8m S of Ripon.
M1 18m S, M62 20m S.

Rail: London -
Leeds/York 2hrs.
Leeds/York - Harrogate
30mins.

Taxi: Blueline taxis
Harrogate
(01423) 503037.

CONFERENCE/FUNCTION

ROOM	SIZE	MAX CAPACITY
Morning Rm	27' x 22'	80
Large Drawing Rm	30' x 22'	80
Library	31 x 19'	70
Tower Rm	33' x 21'	70
Map Rm	19' x 14'	20
Dining Rm	23' x 19'	20
Long Gallery	19' x 6.5'	150
Amcotts Suite	10.2' x 6.6' 7.3' x 6'	120

Ripley Castle has been the home of the Ingilby family for twenty-six generations and Sir Thomas and Lady Ingilby together with their five children continue the tradition. The guided tours are amusing and informative, following the lives and loves of one family for over 670 years and how they have been affected by events in English history. The Old Tower dates from 1555 and houses splendid armour, books, panelling and a Priest's Secret Hiding Place, together with fine paintings, china, furnishings and chandeliers collected by the family over the centuries. The extensive Victorian Walled Gardens have been transformed and are a colourful delight through every season. In the Spring you can appreciate 150,000 flowering bulbs which create a blaze of colour through the woodland walks, and also the National Hyacinth Collection whose scent is breathtaking. The restored Hot Houses have an extensive tropical plant collection, and in the Kitchen Gardens you can see an extensive collection of rare vegetables from the Henry Doubleday Research Association.

Ripley village on the Castle's doorstep is a model estate village with individual charming shops, an art gallery, delicatessen and Farmyard Museum.

No photography inside Castle unless by prior written consent. Parkland for outdoor activities & concerts. Murder mystery weekends.

VIP lunches & dinners (max. 120): unlimited in marquees. Full catering service, wedding receptions, banquets, meetings and activity days.

5/7 rooms accessible. Gardens accessible (not Tropical Collection). WCs. Parking 50 yds.

The Castle Tearooms (seats 54) in Castle courtyard. Licensed. Pub lunches or dinner at hotel (100 yds). Groups must book.

Obligatory. Tour time 75 mins.

290 cars - 300 yds from Castle entrance. Coach park 50 yds. Free.

Welcome by arrangement, between 10.30am - 7.30pm.

Guide dogs only.

Boar's Head Hotel (RAC***) 100 yds. Owned and managed by the estate.

Civil Wedding Licence.

Open all year.

▶ OPENING TIMES

Summer
Castle & Gardens
June - September: Daily.
April/May/October:
Tues, Thurs, Sat & Sun.
10.30am - 3pm.

Winter
November, February &
March: Tues, Thurs,
Sats & Suns.

December & January:
Weekends only.
10.30am - 3pm.

Gardens
Daily, 10am - 5pm.

▶ ADMISSION

All Year
Castle & Gardens
Adult £6.50
Child (5-16yrs) £4.00
OAP £5.50
Groups (15+)
Adult £5.50
Child (5-16yrs) £3.50

Gardens only
Adult £4.00
Child (5-16yrs) £2.50
OAP £3.50
Groups (15+)
Adult £3.5

▶ SPECIAL EVENTS

JUN 8 - 11
Grand Summer Sale.

JUL 22
Last Night of the Proms.

SKIPTON CASTLE

www.skiptoncastle.co.uk

▶ CONTACT

Judith Parker
Skipton Castle
Skipton
North Yorkshire
BD23 1AW

Tel: 01756 792442

Fax: 01756 796100

e-mail: info@
skiptoncastle.co.uk

▶ LOCATION

OS Ref. SD992 520

In the centre of
Skipton, at the N end
of High Street.

Skipton is 20m W of
Harrogate on the A59
and 26m NW
of Leeds on A65.

Rail: Regular services
from Leeds & Bradford.

Guardian of the gateway to the Yorkshire Dales for over 900 years, this unique fortress is one of the most complete and well-preserved medieval castles in England. Standing on a 40-metre high crag, fully-roofed Skipton Castle was founded around 1090 by Robert de Romille, one of William the Conqueror's Barons, as a fortress in the dangerous northern reaches of the kingdom.

Owned by King Edward I and Edward II, from 1310 it became the stronghold of the Clifford Lords withstanding successive raids by marauding Scots. During the Civil War it was the last Royalist bastion in the North, yielding only after a three-year siege in 1645. 'Slighted' under the orders of Cromwell, the castle was skilfully restored by the redoubtable Lady Anne Clifford and today visitors can climb from the depths of the Dungeon to the top of the Watch Tower, and explore the Banqueting Hall, the Kitchens, the Bedchamber and even the Privy!

Every period has left its mark, from the Norman entrance and the Medieval towers, to the beautiful

Tudor courtyard with the great yew tree planted by Lady Anne in 1659. Here visitors can see the coat of arms of John Clifford, the infamous 'Bloody' Clifford of Shakespeare's *Henry VI*, who fought and died in the Wars of the Roses whereupon the castle was possessed by Richard III. Throughout the turbulent centuries of English history, the Clifford Lords fought at Bannockburn, at Agincourt and in the Wars of the Roses. The most famous of them all was George Clifford, 3rd Earl of Cumberland, Champion to Elizabeth I, Admiral against the Spanish Armada and conqueror of Puerto Rico in 1598.

In the castle grounds visitors can see the Tudor wing built as a royal wedding present for Lady Eleanor Brandon, niece of Henry VIII, the beautiful Shell Room decorated in the 1620s with shells and Jamaican coral and the ancient medieval chapel of St John the Evangelist. The Chapel Terrace, with its delightful picnic area, has fine views over the woods and Skipton's lively market town.

▶ OPENING TIMES

All Year
(closed 25 December)

Mon - Sat: 10am - 6pm
Suns: 12 noon - 6pm
(October - February 4pm)

▶ ADMISSION

Adult	£5.40
Child (0-4yrs)	Free
Child (5-17yrs)	£2.90
OAP	£4.80
Student (with ID)	£4.80
Family (2+3)	£15.90
Groups (15+)	
Adult	£4.40
Child (0-17yrs)	£2.90

Includes illustrated tour sheet in a choice of nine languages, plus free badge for children.

Groups welcome:
Guides available for booked groups at no extra charge.

Unsuitable.

Tearoom. Indoor and outdoor picnic areas.

By arrangement.

Large public coach and car park off nearby High Street. Coach drivers' rest room at Castle.

Welcome. Guides available. Teachers free.

In grounds on leads.

 Tel for details.

 €

ALDBOROUGH ROMAN SITE ⌗
Main Street, Aldborough, Boroughbridge, North Yorkshire YO51 9EP
Tel: 01423 322768 **e mail:** customers@english heritage.org.uk
www.english heritage.org.uk/yorkshire
Owner: English Heritage   **Contact:** Visitor Operations Team
Aldborough succeeded Stanwick as the tribal capital of Britian's largest Roman tribe, the Brigantes. Parts of the town's defences, now lying in the peaceful surroundings of a Victorian arboretum, are clearly visible, along with two spectacular mosaic pavements, still in their original position.
Location: OS Ref. SE405 661. Close to Boroughbridge off A1.
Open: 1 Apr - 30 Jun & Sept: Sats & Suns, 11am - 5pm. 1 Jul - 31 Aug: Thur - Mon, 10am - 5pm.
Admission: Adult £3, Child £1.50, Conc. £2.30. 15% discount for groups (11+).
ⓘWC. ▣ ◪ ⊠

ASKE HALL ⌂
Richmond, North Yorkshire DL10 5HJ
Tel: 01748 822000 **Fax:** 01748 826611 **e-mail:** office@aske.co.uk
www.aske.co.uk
Owner: The Marquess of Zetland   **Contact:** The Secretary
A good, predominantly Georgian collection of paintings, furniture and porcelain in house which has been the seat of the Dundas family since 1763.
Location: OS Ref. NZ179 035. 4m SW of A1 at Scotch Corner, 2m from the A66, on the B6274.
Open: 5 Apr, 3 & 17 May, 7 & 21 June, 5 & 19 Jul, 2 Aug & 6 & 13 Sept. Tours at 10 & 11am & 12 noon. Booking essential. Other times by arrangement.
Admission: House & grounds: Adult £7.
ⓕObligatory. ⓟLimited. ⊠In grounds on leads.

BAGSHAW MUSEUM
Wilton Park, Batley, West Yorkshire WF17 0AS
Tel: 01924 326155 **Fax:** 01924 326164
Owner: Kirklees Cultural Services   **Contact:** Amanda Daley
A Victorian Gothic mansion set in Wilton Park.
Location: OS Ref. SE235 257. From M62/J27 follow A62 to Huddersfield. At Birstall, follow tourist signs.
Open: Mon - Fri, 11am - 5pm. Sat & Sun, 12 noon - 5pm. Pre-booked groups and school parties welcome.
Admission: Free.

BENINGBROUGH HALL & GARDENS ✿
Beningbrough, North Yorkshire YO30 1DD
Tel: 01904 470666 **Fax:** 01904 470002 **e-mail:** beningbrough@nationaltrust.org.uk
Owner: The National Trust   **Contact:** The Visitor Services Manager
Imposing 18th century house with over 100 portraits from the National Portrait Gallery.
Location: OS Ref. SE516 586. 8m NW of York, 3m W of Shipton, 2m SE of Linton-on-Ouse, follow signposted route.
Open: Grounds only: 1 Apr - 31 May: Daily except Thur & Fris, 11am - 5.30pm. House, New Galleries & Grounds: 3 June - 29 Oct: Daily except Thurs & Fris, but open Fris during Jul & Aug, 12 noon - 5pm (last admission for house 4.30pm).
Admission: House & Grounds: Adult £7, Child £3.50, Family £16. Groups: £6.50. Grounds & Galleries: Adult £4.50, Child £2.50, Family £10. Groups £4.
▣ ◪ ⓺Partial. WC. �‖ⓟReduced rates for groups (15+), not Suns or BHs. ◼ ⊠ ▲

Whitby Abbey - view of the Abbey from the harbour.

BOLTON ABBEY
SKIPTON, NORTH YORKSHIRE BD23 6EX
www.boltonabbey.com
Tel: 01756 718009 **Fax:** 01756 710535 **e-mail:** tourism@boltonabbey.com
Owner: Chatsworth Settlement Trustees   **Contact:** Visitor Manager
Wordsworth, Turner and Landseer were inspired by this romantic and varied landscape. The Estate, centred around Bolton Priory (founded 1154), is the Yorkshire home of the Duke and Duchess of Devonshire and provides 80 miles of footpaths to enjoy some of the most spectacular landscape in England.
Location: OS Ref. SE074 542. On B6160, N from the junction with A59 Skipton - Harrogate road, 23m from Leeds.
Open: All year.
Admission: £5.00 per car, £3.50 for disabled (occupants free).
▣ ⓣ ⓺ ▣Licensed. ‖Licensed. ⓕBy arrangement. ⓟ ◼
⊠In grounds, on leads. ▤Devonshire Arms Country House Hotel & Devonshire Fell Hotel nearby. ✱

BOLTON CASTLE ⌂
LEYBURN, NORTH YORKSHIRE DL8 4ET
www.boltoncastle.co.uk
Tel: 01969 623981 **Fax:** 01969 623332 **e-mail:** harry@boltoncastle.co.uk
Owner/Contact: Lord Bolton or Sarah Penty
A fine medieval castle which overlooks beautiful Wensleydale. Bolton Castle celebrated its 600th anniversary in 1999. Set your imagination free as you wander around this fascinating castle, which once held Mary Queen of Scots prisoner for 6 months and succumbed to a bitter Civil War siege. Don't miss the beautiful medieval garden and vineyard.
Location: OS Ref. SE034 918. Approx 6m W of Leyburn. 1m NW of Redmire.
Open: Mar - Nov: daily, 10am - 5pm. Please telephone for winter opening times.
Admission: Adult £5, Child/OAP £3.50, Family £12.
▣ ⓣWedding receptions. ⓺Partial. ● ⓟ ◼ ⊠In grounds, on leads. ▲ ✱

387

BRAMHAM PARK 🏛   *See page 378 for full page entry.*

BROCKFIELD HALL 🏛
Warthill, York YO19 5XJ
Tel: 01904 489362   **e-mail:** simon@brockfieldhall.co.uk
Owner/Contact: Mr & Mrs Simon Wood

A fine late Georgian house designed by Peter Atkinson, assistant to John Carr of York, for Benjamin Agar Esq. Begun in 1804, its outstanding feature is an oval entrance hall with a fine cantilevered stone staircase curving past an impressive Venetian window. It is the family home of Mr and Mrs Simon Wood. Mrs Wood is the daughter of the late Lord and of Lady Martin Fitzalan Howard. He was the brother of the 17th Duke of Norfolk and son of the late Baroness Beaumont of Carlton Towers, Selby. There are some interesting portraits of her old Roman Catholic family, the Stapletons, and some good English furniture. Permanent exhibition of paintings by Staithes Group Artists (by appointment outside August).

Location: OS Ref. SE664 550. 5m E of York off A166 or A64.
Open: Aug: daily except Mons (open Aug BH Mon), 1 - 4pm. Other times by appt.
Admission: Adult £5, Child £2.
♿Partial. 🚶Obligatory. 🅿 🐕Guide dogs only.

BRODSWORTH HALL 🏛   *See page 379 for full page entry.*
& GARDENS

BRONTË PARSONAGE MUSEUM
Church St, Haworth, Keighley, West Yorkshire BD22 8DR
Tel: 01535 642323   **Fax:** 01535 647131   **e-mail:** bronte@bronte.org.uk
www.bronte.info
Owner: The Brontë Society   **Contact:** The Administrator

Georgian parsonage, former home of the Brontë family, now a museum with rooms furnished as in the sisters' day and displays of their personal treasures as seen on BBC1's "In Search of the Brontës".

Location: OS Ref. SE029 373. 8m W of Bradford, 3m S of Keighley.
Open: Apr - Sept: 10am - 5pm, Oct - Mar: 11am - 4.30pm. Daily except 24 - 27 Dec & 3 - 31 Jan 2006.
Admission: Adult £5, Child (5-16yrs) £2, Conc. £3.80, Family £12. Discounts for booked groups.
📷 ♿Limited. 🍴🐕Guide dogs only. ❄ 💷Tel for details.

Beningbrough Hall Gardens.

BROUGHTON HALL
SKIPTON, NORTH YORKSHIRE BD23 3AE

www.broughtonhall.co.uk   www.ruralsolutions.co.uk

Tel: 01756 799608   **Fax:** 01756 700357
e-mail: tempest@broughtonhall.co.uk   **e-mail:** info@ruralsolutions.co.uk
Owner: The Tempest Family   **Contact:** The Estate Office

Stephen Tempest built Broughton Hall in 1597 and it was extended in the 18th and 19th centuries into the handsome and graceful form we see today. It is the private home of the Tempest family and is a Grade I listed building, the rooms containing fine Gillow furniture and interesting family portraits. Groups may visit for tours by prior arrangement. A 3,000 acre parkland setting and Italianate gardens which include a stunning conservatory, make Broughton Hall a desirable location for film makers and for corporate and promotional events, the owners being very experienced in successfully meeting the needs of such clients.

Nearby Estate buildings have been skilfully converted into the Broughton Hall Business Park. Here forty companies employ over five hundred people in quality offices in unspoilt historic buildings and peaceful surroundings, thanks to the innovative approach of Rural Solutions, the rural regeneration specialists (01756 799955) who conceived and completed the project.

Location: OS Ref. SD943 507. On A59, 3m W of Skipton midway between the Yorkshire and Lancashire centres. Good air and rail links.
Open: Tours by arrangement.
Admission: £8.

♿ 🍴 🚶By arrangement. 🅿 ❄

BURTON AGNES HALL 🏛

DRIFFIELD, EAST YORKSHIRE YO25 0ND

www.burton-agnes.com

Tel: 01262 490324 **Fax:** 01262 490513

Owner: Burton Agnes Hall Preservation Trust Ltd **Contact:** Mrs Susan Cunliffe-Lister

A lovely Elizabethan Hall containing treasures collected by the family over four centuries from the original carving and plasterwork to modern and Impressionist paintings. The Hall is surrounded by lawns and topiary yew. The old walled garden contains a maze, potager, jungle garden, campanula collection and colour gardens incorporating giant game boards. Children's corner.

Location: OS Ref. TA103 633. Off A614 between Driffield and Bridlington.

Open: 1 Apr - 31 Oct: daily, 11am - 5pm.

Admission: House & Gardens: Adult £5.50, Child £2.75, OAP £5. Gardens only: Adult £2.75, Child £1.30, OAP £2.50. 10% reduction for groups of 30+.

▢ ⚐ ♿ Ground floor & grounds. ◙ Café. Ice-cream parlour.

🐕 In grounds, on leads. ♟

Burton Constable Hall.

BURTON CONSTABLE HALL 🏛

SKIRLAUGH, EAST YORKSHIRE HU11 4LN

www.burtonconstable.com

Tel: 01964 562400   **Fax:** 01964 563229   **e-mail:** via www.burtonconstable.com

Owner: Burton Constable Foundation   **Contact:** Mrs Helen Dewson

One of the most fascinating country houses to survive with its historic collections, Burton Constable is a large Elizabethan mansion set in a 300 acre park with nearly 30 rooms open. The interiors of faded splendour are filled with fine furniture, paintings and sculpture, a library of 5,000 books and a remarkable 18th century 'cabinet of curiosities'. Occupied by the Constable family for over 400 years, the house still maintains the atmosphere of a home. Pleasure grounds with a delightful orangery, a stable block, woodland and lakeside walks in park landscaped by 'Capability' Brown in the 1770s.

Location: OS Ref. TA193 369. From Beverley (14 miles) take A1079 Bridlington road and turn right at White Cross roundabout then follow A165 towards Hull. From Hull (10 miles) follow A1033 towards Hedon, turn left at Saltend roundabout and then follow signs to Preston and Sproatley or A165 towards Bridlington and follow Historic House signs from Skirlaugh.

Open: Hall, Grounds & Tearoom: Easter Sat - 31 Oct: Sat - Thur. Grounds & Tearoom: 12.30 - 5pm. Hall: 1 - 5pm. Last admission 4pm.

Admission: Hall & Grounds: Adult £5.50, Child £2.50, OAP £5, Family £12.50. Grounds only: Adult £1.50, Child 75p. Groups (15-80): £4.50. Connoisseur Study Visits: prices on request.

ℹ No photography in house. ▢ ♿ Suitable. WCs. ◙ 🅿 ◼ 🐕 In grounds on leads. ♟ Sunday 16 Apr (Easter Sunday) - Easter Egg Hunt. Sunday 16 Jul - Burton Constable Country Fair. 31 Oct - Halloween Ghost Tours.

Yorkshire & The Humber - England

BYLAND ABBEY ⌗
Coxwold, Thirsk, North Yorkshire YO61 4BD

Tel: 01347 868614 **e-mail:** customers@english-heritage.org.uk
www.english-heritage.org.uk/yorkshire

Owner: English Heritage **Contact:** Visitor Operations Team
This beautiful ruin was once one of the great northern monasteries, second only to Rievaulx and Fountains. Its design, a mixture of Romanesque and Gothic, proclaimed the arrival of a new architectural style, which Byland pioneered. The Abbey's splendid collection of medieval floor tiles is a testament to its earlier magnificence.
Location: OS Ref. SE549 789. 2m S of A170 between Thirsk and Helmsley, NE of Coxwold village.
Open: 1 Apr - 30 Sept: Thur - Mon (Aug: daily), 10am - 5pm.
Admission: Adult £3, Child £1.50, Conc. £2.30. 15% discount for groups (11+).
ⓘWC. ⬚ 🅿Limited. 🔳 On leads.

CANNON HALL MUSEUM, PARK & GARDENS
Cawthorne, Barnsley, South Yorkshire S75 4AT

Tel: 01226 790270 **Fax:** 01226 792117 **e-mail:** cannonhall@barnsley.gov.uk
www.barnsley.gov.uk

Owner: Barnsley Metropolitan Borough Council **Contact:** The Museum Manager
Set in 70 acres of historic parkland and gardens, Cannon Hall now houses collections of fine furniture, old master paintings, stunning glassware and colourful pottery, much of which is displayed in period settings. Plus 'Charge', the Regimental museum of the 13th/18th Royal Hussars (QMO). Events and education programme and an ideal setting for conferences and Civil wedding ceremonies.
Location: OS Ref. SE272 084. 6m NW of Barnsley of A635. M1/J38.
Open: Nov, Dec & Mar: Sun, 12 noon - 4pm; closed Jan & Feb. Apr - Oct: Wed - Fri, 10.30am - 5pm; Sat & Sun, 12 noon - 5pm. Last admission 4.15pm for 5pm. Open all year for weddings, school visits and corporate hospitality.
Admission: Free except for some events. Charge for car parking.
ⓞ ⊤ ⬚Partial. WC. ⬛Weekends. 🅿 🔳 🔄In grounds, on leads. 🔺 ❋
🔲Tel for details.

CASTLE HOWARD 📞
See page 380 for full page entry.

CAWTHORNE VICTORIA JUBILEE MUSEUM
Taylor Hill, Cawthorne, Barnsley, South Yorkshire S75 4HQ

Tel: 01226 790545/ 790246

Owner: Cawthorne Village **Contact:** Mrs Mary Herbert
A quaint and eccentric collection in a half-timbered building. Museum has a ramp and toilet for disabled visitors. School visits welcome.
Location: OS Ref. SE285 080. 4m W of Barnsley, just off the A635.
Open: Palm Sun - end Oct: Sats, Suns & BH Mons, 2 - 5pm. Groups by appointment throughout the year.
Admission: Adult 50p, Child 20p.

CLIFFE CASTLE
Keighley, West Yorkshire BD20 6LH

Tel: 01535 618231

Owner: City of Bradford Metropolitan District Council **Contact:** Daru Rooke
Victorian manufacturer's house of 1878 with tall tower and garden. Now a museum.
Location: OS Ref. SE057 422. ¾ m NW of Keighley off the A629.
Open: All year: Tues - Sat & BH Mons, 10am - 5pm. Suns, 12 noon - 5pm. Closed 25/26 Dec.
Admission: Free.

CLIFFORD'S TOWER ⌗
Tower Street, York YO1 9SA

Tel: 01904 646940 **e-mail:** customers@english-heritage.org.uk
www.english-heritage.org.uk/yorkshire

Owner: English Heritage **Contact:** Visitor Operations Team
Visit this proud symbol of the might of our medieval kings – originally built by William the Conqueror to subdue the rebellious north, it was rebuilt by Henry III in the 13th century. Fantastic panoramic views of York and the surrounding countryside from the top of the Tower show why it played such a key role in the control of northern England.
Location: OS Ref. SE 605 515. York city centre.
Open: 1 Apr - 30 Sept: daily, 10am - 6pm; 1 - 31 Oct: daily, 10am - 5pm. 1 Nov - 31 Mar: daily, 10am - 4pm. Closed 24-26 Dec & 1 Jan.
Admission: Adult £3, Child £1.50, Conc. £2.30. Family ticket £7.50. 15% discount available for groups (11+).
ⓞ ⬚Unsuitable. 🅿Charged. 🔄 ❋ 🔲Tel for details.

CLIFTON PARK MUSEUM
Clifton Lane, Rotherham, South Yorkshire S65 2AA

Tel: 01709 336633 **e-mail:** cliftonparkmuseum@rotherham.gov.uk

Owner: Rotherham Metropolitan Borough Council **Contact:** Steve Blackbourn
Recently restored 18th century house by John Carr, in parkland setting. Displays include local Rockingham pottery.
Location: OS Ref. SK435 926.
Open: All year: Mon - Thur & Sat, 10am - 5pm. Suns, 1.30 - 4.30pm. Closed over Christmas and New Year.
Admission: Free.
❋

CONISBROUGH CASTLE ⌗
Castle Hill, Conisbrough, South Yorkshire DN12 3BU

Tel: 01709 863329 **e-mail:** customers@english-heritage.org.uk
www.english-heritage.org.uk/yorkshire

Owner: English Heritage **Contact:** The Administrator
The white, cylindrical keep of this 12th century castle is a spectacular structure. Built of magnesian limestone, it is the only example of its kind in England, and was one of the inspirations for Sir Walter Scott's "Ivanhoe". Managed by The Ivanhoe Trust.
Location: OS Ref. SK515 989. ½ m SW of Doncaster.
Open: 1 Apr - 30 Sept: daily, 10am - 5pm (last admission 4.20pm). 1 Oct - 31 Mar: daily, 10am - 4pm (last admission 3.20pm). Closed 24 - 26 Dec & 1 Jan.
Admission: Adult £4, Child £2.15, Conc. £2.75, Family £10 (valid to 31 Mar 2006).
ⓞ ⬚Limited access. 🅿 🔄 ❋

CONSTABLE BURTON HALL GARDENS 📞
LEYBURN, NORTH YORKSHIRE DL8 5LJ

www.constableburtongardens.co.uk

Tel: 01677 450428 **Fax:** 01677 450622

Owner/Contact: M C A Wyvill Esq

A delightful terraced woodland garden of lilies, ferns, hardy shrubs, roses and wild flowers, attached to a beautiful Palladian house designed by John Carr (not open). Garden trails and herbaceous borders. Stream garden with large architectural plants and reflection ponds. Impressive spring display of daffodils and tulips.
Location: OS Ref. SE164 913. 3m E of Leyburn off the A684.
Open: Garden only: 18 Mar - 15 Oct: daily, 9am - 6pm.
Admission: Adult £3, Child (5-16yrs) 50p, OAP £2.50.
❋ ⬚Partial. 🔳Group tours of house & gardens by arrangement.
🅿Limited for coaches. 🔄In grounds, on leads. 🔲Tel for details.

open all year
see page 557

Skyscan/William Cross

DUNCOMBE PARK

HELMSLEY, NORTH YORKSHIRE YO62 5EB

www.duncombepark.com

Tel: 01439 770213 **Fax:** 01439 771114

e-mail: liz@duncombepark.com

Owner/Contact: Lord & Lady Feversham

Lord and Lady Feversham's restored family home in the North York Moors National Park. Built on a virgin plateau overlooking Norman Castle and river valley, it is surrounded by 35 acres of beautiful 18th century landscaped gardens and 400 acres of parkland with national nature reserve and veteran trees.

Location: OS Ref. SE604 830. Entrance just off Helmsley Market Square, signed off A170 Thirsk - Scarborough road.

Open: 30 Apr - 29 Oct: Sun - Thur. House by guided tour only: 12.30, 1.30, 2.30 & 3.30pm. Gardens & Parkland Centre: 11am - 5.30pm.

Admission: House & Gardens: Adult £6.50, Child (10-16yrs) £3, Conc. £5, Family (2+2) £13.50 Groups (15+): £4.75. Gardens & Parkland: Adult £3.50, Child (10-16yrs) £1.75, Conc £3. Parkland: Adult £2, Child (10-16yrs) £1. Season ticket (2+2) £25.

Country walks, nature reserve, orienteering, conferences. Banqueting facilities. Partial. Licensed. Obligatory. In park on leads. Tel for details.

EAST RIDDLESDEN HALL

BRADFORD ROAD, KEIGHLEY, WEST YORKSHIRE BD20 5EL

www.nationaltrust.org.uk

Tel: 01535 607075 **Fax:** 01535 691462 **e-mail:** eastriddlesden@ntrust.org.uk

Owner: The National Trust **Contact:** Property Manager

Homely 17th century merchant's house with beautiful embroideries and textiles, Yorkshire carved oak furniture and fine ceilings. Delightful garden with lavender and herbs. Also wild garden with old varieties of apple trees. Magnificent oak framed barn. Handling collection, children's play area. Costumed tours July and August. Events.

Location: OS Ref. SE079 421. 1m NE of Keighley on S side of B6265 in Riddlesden. 50yds from Leeds/Liverpool Canal. Bus: Frequent services from Skipton, Bradford and Leeds. Railway station at Keighley 2m.

Open: 1 Apr - 3 Aug & 2 Sept - 5 Nov: Tues, Wed, Sat & Sun (also Mons 3 Jul - 3 Aug), 12 noon - 5pm. Shop/Tearoom: 1 Apr - 5 Nov: as house. 11 Nov - 17 Dec, 12 noon - 4pm. Also BHs & Good Fri, Mother's Day and additional days during school hols.

Admission: Adult £4, Child £2, Family £10. Booked groups (15+): Adult £3.50, Child £1.80. £1 off when arriving by Keighley & District transport buses.

Partial. By arrangement. Limited for coaches, please book. In grounds, on leads. Tel for details.

FAIRFAX HOUSE *See page 381 for full page entry.*

FOUNTAINS ABBEY & STUDLEY ROYAL *See page 382 for entry.*

THE GEORGIAN THEATRE ROYAL

Victoria Road, Richmond, North Yorkshire DL10 4DW

Tel: 01748 823710 **Box Office:** 01748 825252

e-mail: admin@georgiantheatreroyal.co.uk

Owner: Georgian Theatre Royal Trust **Contact:** Judith Clark

The most complete Georgian playhouse in Britain. Built in 1788 by actor/manager, Samuel Butler and restored to its Georgian grandeur in 2003.

Location: OS Ref. NZ174 013. 4m from the A1 (Scotch Corner) on the A6108.

Open: All year: Mon - Sat, 10am - 7.30pm (5pm on non-performance nights, 4pm until curtain up on performance Suns). Guided tours: On the hour, 10am - 4pm.

Admission: Donation £3. Child Free.

HAREWOOD HOUSE *See page 383 for full page entry.*

HELMSLEY CASTLE

CASTLEGATE, HELMSLEY, NORTH YORKSHIRE YO62 5AB

www.english-heritage.org.uk/yorkshire

Tel: 01439 770442 **e-mail:** customers@english-heritage.org.uk

Owner: English Heritage **Contact:** Visitor Operations Team

Originally a medieval castle, a Tudor mansion was added in the 1600s, before Cromwell's men blew up the great keep, slicing it in half. The changing fortunes of the castle over 900 years are explored in an audio tour and interactive displays, including original artefacts excavated from the site.

Location: OS Ref. SE611 836. In Helmsley town.

Open: 1 Apr - 31 Oct: daily, 10am - 6pm (Oct 5pm). 1 Nov - 31 Mar: Thur - Mon, 10am - 4pm. Closed 24 - 26 Dec & 1 Jan.

Admission: Adult £4, Child £2, Conc £3, Family £10. 15% discount for groups (11+).

Tourist information located within Castle Visitor Centre. Charged. Dogs welcome on leads. Tel for details.

HELMSLEY WALLED GARDEN

Cleveland Way, Helmsley, North Yorkshire YO62 5AH

Tel/Fax: 01439 771427

Owner: Helmsley Walled Garden Ltd **Contact:** Paul Radcliffe/Lindsay Tait

A 5 acre walled garden under restoration. Orchid house restored. Plant sales area and café conservatory.

Location: OS Ref. SE611 836. 25m N of York, 15m from Thirsk. In Helmsley follow signs to Cleveland Way.

Open: 1 Apr - 31 Oct: daily, 10.30am - 5pm. Nov - Mar: Sats/Suns, 12 noon - 4pm.

Admission: Adult £3.50, Child Free, Conc. £2.50.

HOVINGHAM HALL
YORK, NORTH YORKSHIRE YO62 4LU

www.hovingham.co.uk

Tel: 01653 628771 **Fax:** 01653 628668 **e-mail:** office@hovingham.co.uk

Owner: William Worsley   **Contact:** Mrs Lamprey

This attractive Palladian family home, in its beautiful parkland setting, was designed and built by Thomas Worsley, Surveyor General to King George III. It is still lived in by his descendants and was the childhood home of Katharine Worsley, the Duchess of Kent.

Hovingham Hall is unique in being entered through a huge riding school and features halls with vaulted ceilings and a beautiful collection of pictures and furniture.

The house has attractive gardens with magnificent Yew hedges and the cricket ground in front of the house is reputed to be the oldest private cricket ground in England.

Location: OS Ref. SE666 756. 18m N of York on Malton/Helmsley Road (B1257).

Open: 5 Jun - 8 Jul except Suns. 1.15 - 4.30pm (last tour 3.30pm)

Admission: Adult £6, Conc. £5.50, Child £3. Gardens only: £3.50.

ⓘNo photography in house. 🚇 ♿Partial. 💷 🎫Obligatory. 🅿Limited. 🦮Guide dogs only.

JERVAULX ABBEY
Ripon, North Yorkshire HG4 4PH

Tel: 01677 460226

Owner/Contact: Mr I S Burdon

Extensive ruins of a former Cistercian abbey.

Location: OS Ref. SE169 858. Beside the A6108 Ripon - Leyburn road, 5m SE of Leyburn and 5m NW of Masham.

Open: Daily during daylight hours. Tearoom: Mar - 1 Nov (all home baking, staff permitting).

Admission: Adult £2, Child £1.50 in honesty box at Abbey entrance.

KIPLIN HALL 🏛
KIPLIN, NR SCORTON, RICHMOND, NORTH YORKSHIRE DL10 6AT

www.kiplinhall.co.uk www.herriotdaysout.com

Tel/Fax: 01748 818178 **e-mail:** info@kiplinhall.co.uk

Owner: Kiplin Hall Trustees   **Contact:** The Administrator

A Grade I Listed Jacobean house built in 1620 by George Calvert, 1st Lord Baltimore, founder of the State of Maryland, USA, containing paintings and furniture collected by four families over four centuries. Continuing major restoration has brought the Hall back to life as a comfortable Victorian family home. New exhibition for 2006: 'Georgian Life in a Yorkshire Country House'.

Location: OS Ref. SE274 976. Signposted from Scorton - Northallerton road (B6271).

Open: Good Friday, Easter Sat & Sun 16 Apr - 31 Oct, Sun - Wed 2 - 5pm. Open at other times by appointment with the administrator.

Admission: Adult £4.50, Child £2.50, Conc. £3.50. Family (2+3) £12.75. Groups (15-50) by arrangement.

📷 ♿Partial. 💷 🎫By arrangement. 🅿Limited. 💷

🦮In grounds, on leads. Guide dogs only in house. 🏨 🛏Tel for details.

Nunnington Hall.

KIRKHAM PRIORY ⌗

Kirkham, Whitwell-on-the-Hill, North Yorkshire YO60 7JS
Tel: 01653 618768   **e-mail:** customers@english-heritage.org.uk
www.english-heritage.org.uk/yorkshire
Owner: English Heritage   **Contact:** Visitor Operations Team
The ruins of this Augustinian priory include a magnificent carved gatehouse, declaring to the world the Priory's association with the rich and powerful. However, the site also has more modern associations including a secret visit by the then Prime Minister Winston Churchill during the Second World War.
Location: OS Ref. SE735 657. 5m SW of Malton on minor road off A64.
Open: 1 Apr - 31 Aug: daily, 10am - 6pm. 1 - 30 Sept: Thur - Mon, 10am - 4pm. 1 - 31 Oct: Sats & Suns, 10am - 4pm.
Admission: Adult £3, Child £1.50, Conc. £2.30. 15% discount for groups (11+).
ⓘWC. 🅾 🅻 🅿 Limited. ▣ 🚻 On leads.

KNARESBOROUGH CASTLE & MUSEUM

Knaresborough, North Yorkshire HG5 8AS
Tel: 01423 556188   **Fax:** 01423 556130
Owner: Duchy of Lancaster   **Contact:** Ceryl Evans
Ruins of 14th century castle standing high above the town. Local history museum housed in Tudor Courthouse. Gallery devoted to the Civil War.
Location: OS Ref. SE349 569. 5m E of Harrogate, off A59.
Open: Good Friday - 1 Oct: daily, 10.30am - 5pm.
Admission: Adult £2.50, Child £1.30, OAP £1.50, Family £6.50, Groups (10+) £2.

LEDSTON HALL

Hall Lane, Ledston, Castleford, West Yorkshire WF10 2BB
Tel: 01423 523423   **Fax:** 01423 521373   **e-mail:** james.hare@carterjonas.co.uk
Contact: James Hare
17th century mansion with some earlier work.
Location: OS Ref. SE437 289. 2m N of Castleford, off A656.
Open: Exterior only: May - Aug: Mon - Fri, 9am - 4pm. Other days by appointment.
Admission: Free.

LINDLEY MURRAY SUMMERHOUSE

The Mount School, Dalton Terrace, York YO24 4DD
Tel: 01904 667506   www.mount.n-yorks.sch.uk
Owner/Contact: The Mount School
Location: OS Ref. SE593 510. Dalton Terrace, York.
Open: By prior arrangement: Mon - Fri, 9am - 4.30pm all the year (apart from BHs).
Admission: Free.
🅻 🅿 🚻 Guide dogs only. ✳

LING BEECHES GARDEN

Ling Lane, Scarcroft, Leeds, West Yorkshire LS14 3HX
Tel: 0113 2892450
Owner/Contact: Mrs A Rakusen
A 2 acre woodland garden designed by the owner.
Location: OS Ref. SE354 413. Off A58 midway between Leeds & Wetherby. At Scarcroft turn into Ling Lane, signed to Wike on brow of hill.
Open: By appointment, please telephone for details.
Admission: Adult £3, Child Free.

LONGLEY OLD HALL

Longley, Huddersfield, West Yorkshire HD5 8LB
Tel: 01484 430852   **e-mail:** gallagher@longleyoldhall.co.uk
www.longleyoldhall.co.uk
Owner: Christine & Robin Gallagher   **Contact:** Christine Gallagher
This timber framed Grade II* manor house dates from the 14th century. It was owned by the Ramsden family, the former Lords of the Manors of Almondbury and Huddersfield, for over 400 years. It is included in Simon Jenkins' *England's Thousand Best Houses*.
Location: OS Ref. SE154 150. 1¹/² m SE of Huddersfield towards Castle Hill, via Dog Kennel Bank.
Open: Easter, Summer BH weekends and 27 - 30 Dec for pre-booked guided tours. Group viewings by appointment (min 12 max 25 in winter and 50 in the summer; smaller groups by arrangement).
Admission: £6 for open days - £10 for groups.
🅾 🅻Unsuitable. ⓘObligatory. 🅿 Limited for coaches. ✖ ✳

special events
see page 571

LOTHERTON HALL & GARDENS

ABERFORD, LEEDS, WEST YORKSHIRE LS25 3EB

www.leeds.gov.uk/lothertonhall

Tel: 0113 2813259   **e-mail:** lotherton@leeds.gov.uk
Owner: Leeds City Council   **Contact:** The Supervisor
Charming Edwardian country home rich in collections of paintings, furniture, silver, china, costume and oriental art. Beautiful formal, wildflower and wooded grounds, red deer park and one of the country's most impressive and important collections of rare and endangered birds.
Location: OS92, SE450 360. 2¹/² m E of M1/J47 on B1217 the Towton Road.
Open: 1 Apr - 31 Oct: Tue - Sat, 10am - 5pm, Suns, 1 - 5pm. 1 Nov - 31 Dec & Mar: Tue - Sat, 10am - 4pm, Sun, 12 noon - 4pm. Last adm. ³/⁴ hr before closing. Closed Jan & Feb.
Admission: Adult £3, Child £1, Conc/Groups: £1.50. Car parking: £5 per day or £15 per year (including one year free admission to house for driver). Coach parking £16 per day.
🅾 ♿ 🍴 🅿 ▣ 🚻 🐕 Tel for details.

MARKENFIELD HALL 🏛

Nr Ripon, North Yorkshire HG4 3AD
Tel: 01765 692303   **Fax:** 01765 607195
e-mail: markenfieldhall@btinternet.com   **www.**markenfield.com
Owner: Lady Deirdre Curteis   **Contact:** The Administrator
"This wonderfuly little-altered building is the most complete surviving example of the mediam-sized C14th country house in England" John Martin Robinson *The Architecture of Northern England*. Tucked privately away, fortified, completely moated, and still privately owned – Markenfield has been called Yorkshire's Best Kept Secret.
Location: OS Ref. SE294 672. Access from W side of A61. 2¹/²miles S of the Ripon bypass.
Open: 1 - 14 May & 18 Jun - 1 Jul: daily, 2 - 5pm. Groups all year round by appointment.
Admission: Adult £4, Conc £3. Booked groups (min charge £80).
🍴 🍴 🅿 ▲ ✳ 🐕Tel for details.

MIDDLEHAM CASTLE ⌗

Castle Hill, Middleham, Leyburn, North Yorkshire DL8 4QR
Tel: 01969 623899   **e-mail:** customers@english-heritage.org.uk
www.english-heritage.org.uk/yorkshire
Owner: English Heritage   **Contact:** Visitor Operations Team
This was the childhood and favourite home of Richard III, where he learnt the military skills and the courtly manners appropriate for a future king. The massive keep, one of the largest in England, was both a defensive building and a self-contained residence for the Lords of Middleham.
Location: OS Ref. SE128 875. At Middleham, 2m S of Leyburn on A6108.
Open: 1 Apr - 30 Sept: daily, 10am - 6pm. 1 Oct - 31 Mar: Thur - Mon, 10am - 4pm. Closed 24 - 26 Dec & 1 Jan.
Admission: Adult £3.50, Child £1.80, Conc. £2.60. 15% discount for groups (11+).
ⓘExhibition. 🅾 🅻 Partial. ▣ In grounds, on leads. ✳
🐕 Tel for details.

MOUNT GRACE PRIORY ⌗
Staddlebridge, Nr Northallerton, North Yorkshire DL6 3JG
Tel: 01609 883494 **e-mail:** customers@english-heritage.org.uk
www.english-heritage.org.uk/yorkshire
Owner: English Heritage **Contact:** Visitor Operations Team
This 3-in-1 site is enchanting: the monastery ruins are the best-preserved of any in Britain; the manor-house is a rare building of the Commonwealth period; and the gardens, re-modelled in the Arts & Crafts style, are a haven for the famous 'Priory Stoats'.
Location: OS Ref. SE449 985. 12m N of Thirsk, 7m NE of Northallerton on A19.
Open: 1 Apr - 30 Sept: Thur - Mon, 10am - 6pm. 1 Oct - 31 Mar: Thur - Sun, 10am - 4pm. Closed 24 - 26 Dec & 1 Jan.
Admission: Adult £4, Child £2, Conc. £3, Family £10. 15% discount for groups (11+).
ⅰ WCs. ▣ 🅟 ▣ Tel for details.

THE MUSEUM OF SOUTH YORKSHIRE LIFE
Cusworth Hall & Park, Cusworth Lane, Doncaster, South Yorkshire DN5 7TU
Tel: 01302 782342
Owner: Doncaster Metropolitan Borough Council **Contact:** Mr F Carpenter, Curator
A magnificent Grade I country house set in a landscaped parkland and built in 1740, with a chapel and other rooms designed by James Paine, the house is now the home of a museum showing the changing home, work and social conditions of the region over the last 250 years. Regular events and activities.
Location: OS Ref. SE547 039. A1(M)/J37, then A635 and right into Cusworth Lane.
Open: The building will be closed due to extensive renovation during 2006. Please telephone for more information.

NATIONAL CENTRE FOR EARLY MUSIC
St Margaret's Church, Walmgate, York YO1 9TL
Tel: 01904 632220 **Fax:** 01904 612631 **e-mail:** info@ncem.co.uk
www.ncem.co.uk
Owner: York Early Music Foundation **Contact:** Mrs G Baldwin
The National Centre for Early Music is based in the medieval church of St Margaret's York. The church boasts a 12th century Romanesque doorway and a 17th century brick tower of considerable note. The Centre hosts concerts, music education activities, conferences, recordings and events.
Location: OS Ref. SE609 515. Inside Walmgate Bar, within the city walls, on the E side of the city.
Open: Mon - Fri, 10am - 4pm. Also by appointment. Access is necessarily restricted when events are taking place.
Admission: Free, donations welcome.
By arrangement. 🅟 Limited. No coaches. Guide dogs only. ▣

NEWBY HALL & GARDENS ▦ *See page 384 for full page entry.*

Burton Agnes Hall - The Staircase.

NEWBURGH PRIORY
COXWOLD, NORTH YORKSHIRE YO61 4AS
Tel: 01347 868435
Owner/Contact: Sir George Wombwell Bt
Originally 1145 with major alterations in 1568 and 1720, it has been the home of the Earls of Fauconberg and of the Wombwell family since 1538. Tomb of Oliver Cromwell (3rd daughter Mary married Viscount Fauconberg) is in the house. Extensive grounds contain a water garden, walled garden, topiary yews and woodland walks.
Location: OS Ref. SE541 764. 4m E of A19, 18m N of York, ½ m E of Coxwold.
Open: 2 Apr - 28 Jun: Wed & Sun (open Easter Sun & Mon). House: 2.30 - 4.45pm. Garden: 2 - 6pm. Tours every ½ hour, take approximately 50mins. Booked groups by arrangement.
Admission: House & Grounds: £5.50. Child £1.50. Gardens only: £3, Child Free. Special tours of Private Apartment in addition to the above (Easter Sun & Mon and Weds & Suns 2 Apr - 30 Apr) £6pp.
ⅰ No photography in house. Partial. Obligatory. 🅟 Limited for coaches. In grounds, on leads.

NORTON CONYERS ▦
NR RIPON, NORTH YORKSHIRE HG4 5EQ
Tel/Fax: 01765 640333 **e-mail:** norton.conyers@bronco.co.uk
Owner: Sir James and Lady Graham **Contact:** Lady Graham
Visited by Charlotte Brontë in 1839, Norton Conyers is an original of 'Thornfield Hall' in *Jane Eyre*, and a family legend was an inspiration for the mad Mrs Rochester. House and garden have a friendly, quiet and unspoilt atmosphere. They have been in the Grahams' possession for 382 years. Family pictures, furniture, costumes and ceramics on display. 18th century walled garden near house, with Orangery and herbaceous borders. Small plants sales area specialising in unusual hardy plants. Pick your own fruit in season.
Location: OS Ref. SE319 763. 4m N of Ripon. 3½m from the A1.
Open: House and Garden: Easter Sun & Mon (16/17 Apr), BHs Suns & Mons (30 Apr - 1 May; 28/29 May; 27/28 Aug), Sun from 23 Apr - 20 Aug, 3 - 8 Jul: daily, 2 - 5pm (last adm. 4.40pm). Garden is also open every Thur 10am - 4pm. Please check beforehand. Groups by appointment.
Admission: House: Adult £5.50, Child (under 16yrs) free, OAP £4. Garden: Admission is free; donations welcome. A charge is made when the garden is open for charity. Groups by arrangement.
ⅰ No interior photography. No high-heeled shoes. Partial. WC. Garden charity openings only. By arrangement. 🅟 Dogs, other than guide dogs, are not allowed in the house and must be on a lead in the grounds. Tel for details.

NOSTELL PRIORY

Doncaster Road, Wakefield, West Yorkshire WF4 1QE

Tel: 01924 863892 **Fax:** 01924 866846 **www.**nationaltrust.org.uk

Owner: The National Trust **Contact:** Visitor Services Manager

Nostell Priory, one of Yorkshire's finest jewels, is an 18th century architectural masterpiece by James Paine.

Location: OS Ref. SE403 175. 6m SE of Wakefield, off A638.

Open: Conservation Tour: 13 - 19 Feb: daily, 12 noon - 4pm. House: 1 Apr - 5 Nov: Wed - Sun, 1 - 5pm. 9 - 17 Dec: daily 12 noon - 4pm. Grounds: 13 - 19 Feb: daily 11am - 4pm. 4 - 26 Mar: Sats & Suns, 11am - 5pm. 1 Apr - 5 Nov: Wed - Sun, 11am - 6pm.

Admission: House & Garden: Adult £6.50, Child £3.25, Family (2+4) £16. Groups (20+) £6. Groups outside normal opening times £12. Garden only: Adult £4, Child £1.75.

ℹ Baby facilities. 🚽 📷 ♿ Partial. WC. 🐕 🌳 By arrangement. 🅿 ▣ 🐕 In grounds, on leads. ▲ ⚘ Send SAE for details.

NUNNINGTON HALL

Nunnington, North Yorkshire YO62 5UY

Tel: 01439 748283 **Fax:** 01439 748284

Owner: The National Trust **Contact:** The Property Manager

17th century manor house with magnificent oak-panelled hall, nursery, haunted room, and attics, with their fascinating Carlisle collection of miniature rooms fully furnished to reflect different periods.

Location: OS Ref. SE670 795. In Ryedale, 4^1/$_2$ m SE of Helmsley, 1^1/$_2$ m N of B1257.

Open: 18 Mar - 30 Apr: Wed - Sun, 1.30 - 5pm; 3 - 31 May & Sept: Wed - Sun, June - Aug: Tues - Sun 1.30 - 5.30pm; 1 Oct - 5 Nov: Wed - Sun, 1.30 - 5pm.

Admission: House & Garden: Adult £5.20, Child £2.60, Family £13. Groups: £4.70 (outside hours £5.20). Garden only: Adult £2.60, Child Free.

📷 ♿ Ground floor and grounds.WC. 🐕 🌳 Guide dogs only. ⚘ Tel for details.

ORMESBY HALL

Ladgate Lane, Ormesby, Middlesbrough TS7 9AS

Tel: 01642 324188 **Fax:** 01642 300937 **e-mail:** ormesbyhall@nationaltrust.org.uk

Owner: The National Trust **Contact:** The House Manager

A mid 18th century house with opulent decoration inside, including fine plasterwork by contemporary craftsmen.

Location: OS Ref. NZ530 167. 3m SE of Middlesbrough.

Open: 1 Apr - 29 Oct: Sats & Suns, 1.30 - 5pm. Shop/Tearoom: as House, 12.30 - 5pm.

Admission: House, grounds & railway: Adult £4, Child £2.50, Family £10.50. Groups £3.50pp. Grounds, railway & exhibition only: Adult £2.90, Child £1.30.

📷 ♿ Ground floor & grounds. WC. 🐕

PARCEVALL HALL GARDENS

Skyreholme, Skipton, North Yorkshire BD23 6DE

Tel:/Fax: 01756 720311 **e-mail:** info@parcevallhallgardens.co.uk

Contact: Phillip Nelson (Head Gardener)

Owner: Walsingham College (Yorkshire Properties) Ltd.

Location: OS Ref. SE068 613. E side of Upper Wharfedale, 1^1/$_2$ m NE of Appletreewick. 12m NNW of Ilkley by B6160 and via Burnsall.

Open: 1 Apr - 31 Oct: 10am - 6pm.

Admission: £4, Child 75p. RHS Free access May - Aug.

PICKERING CASTLE ⌗

Castlegate, Pickering, North Yorkshire YO18 7AX

Tel: 01751 474989 **e-mail:** customers@english-heritage.org.uk

www.english-heritage.org.uk/yorkshire

Owner: English Heritage **Contact:** Visitor Operations Team

An excellent example of a motte and bailey castle, built by William the Conqueror, with much of the original keep, towers and walls remaining, and offering superb views over North York Moors. It was used by a succession of medieval kings as a hunting lodge, holiday home and even stud farm.

Location: OS Ref. SE800 845. In Pickering, 15m SW of Scarborough.

Open: 1 Apr - 30 Sept: daily, 10am - 6pm. 1 - 31 Oct: Thur - Mon, 10am - 5pm. Closed 1 Nov - 31 Mar.

Admission: Adult £3, Child £1.50, Conc. £2.30, Family £7.50. 15% discount for groups (11+).

ℹ WCs. 📷 ♿ Partial. 🅿 Limited. ▣ 🐕 In grounds, on leads. ⚘ Tel for details.

PLUMPTON ROCKS

Plumpton, Knaresborough, North Yorkshire HG5 8NA

Tel: 01289 386360 **www.**plumptonrocks.co.uk

Owner: Edward de Plumpton Hunter **Contact:** Robert de Plumpton Hunter

Grade II* listed garden extending to over 30 acres including an idyllic lake, dramatic millstone grit rock formation, romantic woodland walks winding through bluebells and rhododendrons. Declared by English Heritage to be of outstanding interest. Painted by Turner. Described by Queen Mary as 'Heaven on earth'.

Location: OS Ref. SE355 535. Midway between Harrogate and Wetherby on the A661, 1m SE of A661 junction with the Harrogate southern bypass.

Open: Mar - Oct: Sat, Sun & BHs, 11am - 6pm.

Admission: Adult £2, Child/OAP £1.

♿ Unsuitable. 🌳 By arrangement. 🅿 Limited for coaches. ▣ 🐕 In grounds, on leads.

RHS GARDEN HARLOW CARR

CRAG LANE, HARROGATE, NORTH YORKSHIRE HG3 1QB

www.rhs.org.uk

Tel: 01423 565418 **Fax:** 01423 530663 **e-mail:** admin-harlowcarr@rhs.org.uk

Owner/Contact: Royal Horticultural Society

One of Yorkshire's most relaxing yet inspiring locations! Highlights of the beautiful garden include spectacular new contemporary herbaceous borders, *Gardens through Time*, streamside garden, alpines, scented and kitchen gardens, woodland and wildflower meadow, extensive Shop and Plant Centre, new Betty's Café Tea Rooms and free parking. Events include outdoor theatre, festivals, workshops and children's activities.

Location: OS Ref. SE285 543. 1^1/$_2$ m W from town centre on B6162.

Open: Daily: 9.30am - 6pm (4pm Nov - Feb). Last entry 1 hour before closing.

Admission: Adult £6, Child (6-16yrs) £1.60, Child (under 6yrs) Free. Groups (10+): £4.60. Groups must book in advance. RHS Members: free.

ℹ Picnic area. 📷 🌳 ♿ Partial. WC. 🐕 Licensed. 🍴 Licensed. 🌳 By arrangement. 🅿 ▣ 🐕 Guide dogs only. ✿ ⚘

Brodsworth Hall, the kitchen.

plant sales
see page 555

RICHMOND CASTLE

TOWER ST, RICHMOND, NORTH YORKSHIRE DL10 4QW

www.english-heritage.org.uk/yorkshire

Tel: 01748 822493 **e-mail:** customers@english-heritage.org.uk

Owner: English Heritage **Contact:** Visitor Operations Team

Built shortly after 1066 on a rocky promontory high above the River Swale, this is the best preserved castle of such scale and age in Britain. The magnificent Keep, with breathtaking views, is reputed to be the place where the legendary King Arthur sleeps. An exhibition and contemporary garden reflect the castle's military history from the 11th to 20th centuries.

Location: OS Ref. NZ174 006. In Richmond.

Open: 1 Apr - 30 Sept: daily, 10am - 6pm. 1 Oct - 31 Mar: Thur - Mon, 10am - 4pm. Closed 24 - 26 Dec & 1 Jan .

Admission: Adult £3.60, Child £1.80, Conc. £2.70, Family £9. 15% discount for groups (11+).

ⓘ Interactive exhibition. WCs. ▣ ⓺ Partial. ▣ ⓱ In grounds, on leads. ✲ ▨ Tel for details.

RIEVAULX TERRACE & TEMPLES ⚜

Rievaulx, Helmsley, North Yorkshire YO62 5LJ

Tel: 01439 748283 **Fax:** 01439 748284

Owner: The National Trust **Contact:** The Property Manager

A ½ m long grass-covered terrace and adjoining woodlands with vistas over Rievaulx Abbey and Rye valley. There are two mid-18th century temples. Note: no access to property Nov - end Mar.

Location: OS Ref. SE579 848. 2½ m NW of Helmsley on B1257. E. of the Abbey.

Open: 18 Mar - 30 Sept: daily, 10.30am - 6pm (5pm Oct - 5 Nov).

Admission: Adult £4, Child (5-16yrs) £2.10, Family (2+3) £10. Groups (15+): £3.40.

▣ ⓺ Grounds. Batricar available. ⓱ In grounds, on leads. ▨ Tel for details.

Sledmere House.

RIEVAULX ABBEY

RIEVAULX, NR HELMSLEY, NORTH YORKSHIRE YO62 5LB

www.english-heritage.org.uk/yorkshire

Tel: 01439 798228 **e-mail:** customers@english-heritage.org.uk

Owner: English Heritage **Contact:** Visitor Operations Team

Rievaulx was the first Cistercian Abbey to be founded in the North of England in the 12th century. Set in the Rye Valley, just a short drive from Helmsley, it is a place of beauty and calm. The atmospheric ruins were once home to the greatest spiritual writer of the Medieval Ages, St Aelred, who described it as *"everywhere peace, everywhere serenity, and a freedom from the tumult of the world"*. A special exhibition, "The Work of God and Man", looks at the commercial activities of the monks and shows how religion blended with business.

Location: OS Ref. SE577 849. 2¼ m W of Helmsley on minor road off B1257.

Open: 1 Apr - 30 Sept: daily, 10am - 6pm. 1 Oct - 31 Mar: Thur - Mon, 10am - 4pm (5pm Oct). Closed 24- 26 Dec & 1 Jan.

Admission: Adult £4.20, Child £2.10, Conc. £3.20. 15% discount for groups (11+).

ⓘ WCs. ▣ ⓱ ⓺ Partial. ▣ ⓺ ⓹ ▣ ⓱ On leads. ✲ ▨ Tel for details.

RIPLEY CASTLE 🏛   *See page 385 for full page entry.*

RIPON CATHEDRAL
Ripon, North Yorkshire HG4 1QR
Tel: 01765 604108 (information on tours etc.)   **Contact:** Canon Keith Punshon
One of the oldest crypts in Europe (672). Marvellous choir stalls and misericords (500 years old). Almost every type of architecture. Treasury.
Location: OS Ref. SE314 711. 5m W signposted off A1, 12m N of Harrogate.
Open: All year: 8am - 6pm.
Admission: Donations; £3. Pre-booked guided tours available.

ROCHE ABBEY ⌗
Maltby, Rotherham, South Yorkshire S66 8NW
Tel: 01709 812739 **e-mail:** customers@english-heritage.org.uk
www.english-heritage.org.uk/yorkshire
Owner: English Heritage   **Contact:** Visitor Operations Team
Set in a beautiful, secluded valley landscaped by 'Capability' Brown in the 18th century, the early Gothic transepts of this 'miniature Fountains Abbey' still survive to their original height.
Location: OS Ref. SK544 898. 1m S of Maltby off A634.
Open: 1 Apr - 30 Sept: Thur - Mon (daily in Aug), 10am - 5pm.
Admission: Adult £3, Child £1.50, Conc. £2.30. 15% discount for groups (11+).
ℹ WCs. 🔲 ♿ Partial. 🅿 Limited. 🔳 🐕 In grounds, on leads.

RYEDALE FOLK MUSEUM
Hutton le Hole, York, North Yorkshire YO62 6UA
Tel: 01751 417367 **e-mail:** info@ryedalefolkmuseum.co.uk
Owner: The Crosland Foundation
13 historic buildings showing the lives of ordinary folk from earliest times to the present day.
Location: OS Ref. SE705 902. Follow signs from Hutton le Hole. 3m N of Kirkbymoorside.
Open: 20 Jan - 20 Dec: 10am - 5.30pm (last adm. 4.30pm) or dusk during winter months.
Admission: Adult £4.50, Child £3, Conc. £4. Family (2+2) £12 (Season Ticket £25).

THE WALLED GARDEN AT SCAMPSTON
SCAMPSTON HALL, MALTON, NORTH YORKSHIRE YO17 8NG

www.scampston.co.uk

Tel: 01944 759111   **Fax:** 01944 758700   **e-mail:** info@scampston.co.uk
Owner: Sir Charles Legard Bt   **Contact:** Maggie Cochrane
An exciting new garden designed by Piet Oudolf, winner of Gold and 'Best in Show' at Chelsea. The contemporary layout in the 4½ acre walled garden includes perennial meadow planting and grasses in Oudolf's signature style, and a 21st century prospect mount in 17th century manner offers visitors a delightful overview. Described by Stephen Anderton in *The Times* as *"A gem"*.
Location: OS Ref. SE865 755. 4m E of Malton, off A64.
Open: 15 Apr - 15 Oct: daily (closed Mons except BHs), 10am - 5pm.
Admission: Adult £5, Child (12-16yrs) £3, Senior £4.50. Child (11yrs & under) Free. Groups by arrangement. Combined Ticket: Adult £9.50, Child (12-16yrs) £5.
♿ 🚻 ♿ 🍴 🅿 🐕

©Tim Imrie-Tait/Country Life Picture Library

SCAMPSTON HALL 🏛
SCAMPSTON, MALTON, NORTH YORKSHIRE YO17 8NG

www.scampston.co.uk

Tel: 01944 759111/758224   **Fax:** 01944 758700   **e-mail:** info@scampston.co.uk
Owner: Sir Charles Legard Bt   **Contact:** Maggie Cochrane
Scampston is among the best examples of the English country house, combining fine architecture with a wealth of art treasures in a beautiful parkland setting in Yorkshire. Recently restored to its former glory, the house was voted *Country Life* "House of the Year". Restaurant and other facilities in the Walled Garden (see top right).
Location: OS Ref. SE865 755. 4m E of Malton, off A64.
Open: 22 Jun - 23 Jul: daily except Mons, 1.30 - 5pm (last adm. 4pm).
Admission: Adult £6, Child (12-16yrs) £3. Child (11yrs & under) Free. Groups by arrangement. Combined Ticket: Adult £9.50, Child (12-16yrs) £5.
🚶 🅿 🐕

English Heritage Photo Library

SCARBOROUGH CASTLE ⌗
CASTLE ROAD, SCARBOROUGH, NORTH YORKSHIRE YO11 1HY

www.english-heritage.org.uk/yorkshire

Tel: 01723 372451   **e-mail:** customers@english-heritage.org.uk
Owner: English Heritage   **Contact:** Visitor Operations Team
This 12th century castle conceals over 2,500 years of history encompassing the Roman army, Saxon monks, Viking invaders, Civil War besiegers and even First World War German naval guns. With wonderful views over the East Coast and a new exhibition giving further insight into the Castle's fascinating history, including artefacts excavated from the site.
Location: OS Ref. TA050 893. Castle Road, E of town centre.
Open: 1 Apr - 30 Sept: daily, 10am - 6pm. 1 Oct - 31 Mar: Thur - Mon, 10am - 4pm (5pm Oct). Closed 24 - 26 Dec & 1 Jan.
Admission: Adult £3.50, Child £1.80, Conc. £2.60, Family £8.80. 15% discount for groups (11+).
ℹ WCs. 🔲 ♿ Partial. 🎧 Inclusive. 🔳 🐕 In grounds, on leads. ❄
📞 Tel for details.

SHANDY HALL
COXWOLD, NORTH YORKSHIRE YO61 4AD

www.

Tel/Fax: 01347 868465

Owner: The Laurence Sterne Trust   **Contact:** Mr P Wildgust

Here in 1760-1767 the witty and eccentric parson Laurence Sterne wrote *Tristram Shandy* and *A Sentimental Journey*. Shandy Hall was built as a timber-framed open-hall in the 15th century and added to by Sterne in the 18th. It houses the world's foremost collection of editions of Sterne's work, and is surrounded by a walled garden full of old-fashioned roses and cottage garden plants. Also an acre of wild garden in the adjoining old quarry. It is a lived-in house where you are sure of a personal welcome. May - Sept: exhibitions.

Location: OS Ref. SE531 773. W end of Coxwold village, 4m E of A19 between Easingwold and Thirsk. 20m N of York.

Open: 1 May - 30 Sept: Weds, 2 - 4.30pm. Suns, 2.30 - 4.30pm. Garden: 1 May - 30 Sept: Sun - Fri, 11am - 4.30pm. Other times by appointment.

Admission: Hall & Garden: Adult £4.50, Child £1.50. Garden only: Adult £2.50, Child £1.

ℹ️ No photography in house. 📷 ♿ Partial. 🍴 In nearby village. 📷 Obligatory. 🅿️ ✖️

SHIBDEN HALL
Lister's Road, Halifax, West Yorkshire HX3 6XG

Tel: 01422 352246   **Fax:** 01422 348440   **www.**calderdale.gov.uk

Owner: Calderdale MBC   **Contact:** Valerie Stansfield

A half-timbered manor house, the home of Anne Lister, set in a landscaped park. Oak furniture, carriages and an array of objects make Shibden an intriguing place to visit.

Location: OS Ref. SE106 257. 1½ m E of Halifax off A58.

Open: 1 Mar - 30 Nov: Mon - Sat, 10am - 5pm (last admission 4.30pm), Suns, 12 noon - 5pm (last admission 4.30pm). Dec - Feb: Mon - Sat, 10am - 4pm, Suns, 12 noon - 4pm (last admission 3.30pm).

Admission: Adult £3.50, Child/Conc. £2.50, Family £10. Prices subject to change April 2006.

📷 ♿ Ground floor & grounds. 🍴 🅿️ 🛏️ Guide dogs only. ✖️

SKIPTON CASTLE   *See page 386 for full page entry.*

Scampston Walled Garden.

SION HILL HALL 🏛️
KIRRY WISKE, THIRSK, NORTH YORKSHIRE YO7 4EU

www.sionhillhall.co.uk

Tel: 01845 587206   **Fax:** 01845 587486   **e-mail:** sionhill@btconnect.com

Owner: H W Mawer Trust   **Contact:** R M Mallaby

Designed in 1912 by the renowned York architect Walter H Brierley, 'the Lutyens of the North', receiving an award from the Royal Institute of British Architects as being of 'outstanding architectural merit'. Sion Hill contains the H W Mawer collection of fine furniture, porcelain, paintings and clocks in superb settings.

Location: OS Ref. SE373 844. 6m S of Northallerton off A167, signposted. 4m W of Thirsk, 6m E of A1 via A61.

Open: Jun - Sept: Weds only, 1 - 5pm, last entry 4pm. Also Easter Sun and all BH Mons. Guided tours during public opening times/Connoisseur tours at any time May - Oct by arrangement.

Admission: House: Adult £4.50, Child 12-16yrs, £2, Child under 12yrs £1, Conc. £4. Guided tours during public opening times: £5.75ea. Connoisseur Tours: £8.50. Grounds: £1.50.

♿ Partial. WC. 🍴 📷 🅿️

SLEDMERE HOUSE 🏛️
SLEDMERE, DRIFFIELD, EAST YORKSHIRE YO25 3XG

www.sledmerehouse.com

Tel: 01377 236637   **Fax:** 01377 236560

Owner: Sir Tatton Sykes Bt   **Contact:** Mrs Charlotte Dixon

Sledmere House is often described as one of Yorkshire's best kept secrets. At the heart of the picturesque rolling Wolds countryside and surrounded by its renowned quintessential English Estate Village, it provides a fascinating day out for all the family.

Home of Sir Tatton Sykes the 8th Baronet, Sledmere House is a wonderful country house in the finest tradition, containing a fantastic series of beautifully decorated 'Georgian' interiors. Sympathetically restored in the early 1900's following a disastrous fire, visitors will have a chance to see how magnificently the restoration was achieved. Many comment on the wonderful 'lived-in' feel of this fine house. Gardeners will delight in exploring the many different aspects of the grounds at Sledmere; including the 18th Century walled garden, and the parterre.

Round off your visit with a stroll in the Capability Brown Parkland and a visit the exhibition centre including a fine museum, café and gift shop.

Location: OS Ref. SE931 648. Off the A166 between York & Bridlington. ½ hr drive from York, Bridlington & Scarborough.

Open: House & Grounds: 14 - 17 Apr: Fri - Mon & 29 Apr - 17 Sept: Wed - Fri, Suns & BH Sats & Mons. Grounds: Apr - Sept: Wed - Sun.

Admission: House & Grounds: Adult £6, Child £2, Conc. £5.50. Grounds: Adult £4, Child £1. Groups (15+) £4.50pp. RHS members £3 (Gardens & Grounds only).

ℹ️ No photography in house. 📷 ♿ Licensed. 📷 By arrangement: Garden Tour & Park, Estate & Outbuildings Tour. Tel for arrangements. 🅿️ 🛏️ In grounds on leads. Guide dogs in house. 🚻

Yorkshire & The Humber - England

STOCKELD PARK

WETHERBY, NORTH YORKSHIRE LS22 4AW

Tel: 01937 586101 **Fax:** 01937 580084

Owner: Mr and Mrs P G F Grant   **Contact:** Mrs L A Saunders

Stockeld is a beautifully proportioned Palladian villa designed by James Paine in 1763, featuring a magnificent cantilevered staircase in the central oval hall. The much loved home to the same family for 150 years, Stockeld houses a fine collection of 18th and 19th century furniture and paintings. The house is surrounded by stunning gardens of formal clipped hedges and topiary mixed with flowing herbaceous and shrub plantings. It is fringed by ancient woodland and set in over 100 acres of magnificent parkland in the midst of an extensive farming estate. A beautiful and fascinating house which is a popular location for filming and photography. Perfect parkland setting for exclusive outdoor activities.

Location: OS Ref. SE376 497. York 12m, Harrogate 5m, Leeds 12m.

Open: Privately booked events only. Please contact the Estate Office: 01937 586101.

Admission: Prices on application.

House only.

SUTTON PARK

SUTTON-ON-THE-FOREST, NORTH YORKSHIRE YO61 1DP

www.statelyhome.co.uk

Tel: 01347 810249/811239 **Fax:** 01347 811251 **e-mail:** suttonpark@fsbdial.co.uk

Owner: Sir Reginald & Lady Sheffield   **Contact:** Administrator

The Yorkshire home of Sir Reginald and Lady Sheffield. Charming example of early Georgian architecture. Magnificent plasterwork by Cortese. Rich collection of 18th century furniture, paintings, porcelain, needlework, beadwork. All put together with great style to make a most inviting house. Award winning gardens attract enthusiasts from home and abroad.

Location: OS Ref. SE583 646. 8m N of York on B1363 York - Helmsley Road.

Open: House: 2 Apr - 28 Sept: Wed, Sun & BH Mons, 1.30 - 5pm. Gardens: Apr - Sept: daily, 11am - 5pm. Tearoom: Apr - end Sept: Wed - Sun, 11am - 5pm. Private groups any other day by appointment. House open Oct - Mar for private parties (15+) only.

Admission: House & Garden: Adult £6, Child £3.50, Conc. £5. Coaches £5.50. Private Groups (15+): £6.50. Gardens only: Adult £3.50, Child £1, Conc. £2.50. Coaches £3. Caravans: £7 per unit per night. Electric hookup: £9 per unit per night.

No photography. Lunches & dinners in Dining Room. Partial. WCs. Home-baked fayre. Obligatory. Limited for coaches.

RHS Garden Harlow Carr.

TEMPLE NEWSAM

LEEDS LS15 0AE

www.leeds.gov.uk/templenewsam

Tel: 0113 2647321 **e-mail:** temple.newsam@leeds.gov.uk

Owner: Leeds City Council   **Contact:** Denise Lawson

One of the great country houses of England, this Tudor-Jacobean mansion was the birthplace of Lord Darnley, husband of Mary Queen of Scots and home to the Ingram family for 300 years. Rich in newly restored interiors, paintings, furniture (including Chippendale), textiles, silver and ceramics; an ever-changing exhibitions programme, audio-tours, family activities and children's trails are also on offer along with one of the largest working rare breed farms in Europe. Temple Newsam sits within 1500 acres of grand and beautiful 'Capability' Brown parkland with formal and wooded gardens as well as national plant collections.

Location: OS Ref. SE358 321. 5m E of city centre, off A63 Selby Road. M1/J46.

Open: 27 Mar - 30 Oct: Tue - Sun and BHs. House: 10.30am - 5pm. Farm: 10am - 5pm. 31 Oct - 26 Mar: Tue - Sun and BHs. House: 10.30am - 4pm. Farm, 10am - 4pm. Last admission ¾ hour before closing. Estate open free, dawn to dusk.

Admission: House only: Adult £3.50, Child £2.50, Family £9. House and Home Farm: Adult £5, Child £3.50, Family £14, special rates for educational groups. Parking £3.50 (car), £15 (coach), annual parking pass £10.

Tel for details.

THORP PERROW ARBORETUM, WOODLAND GARDEN & FALCONRY CENTRE

Bedale, North Yorkshire DL8 2PR

Tel/Fax: 01677 425323   **e-mail:** enquiries@thorpperrow.com
www.thorpperrow.com

Owner: Sir John Ropner Bt   **Contact:** Louise McNeill

85 acres of woodland walks. One of the largest collections of trees and shrubs in the north of England, including a 16th century spring wood and 19th century pinetum, and holds four National Collections - Ash, Lime, Walnut and Laburnum. The Falcons of Thorp Perrow is a captive breeding and conservation centre. Three flying demonstrations daily throughout the season.

Location: OS Ref. SE258 851. Bedale - Ripon road, S of Bedale, 4m from Leeming Bar on A1.

Open: All year: dawn - dusk. Telephone for winter opening times.

Admission: Arboretum & Falcons: Adult £5.95, Child £3.10, OAP £4.60, Family (2+2) £17.50, (2+4) £23. Groups prices available.

ⓘPicnic area. Children's playground. 🖼 🍴 ♿Partial. WCs. 🍽Licensed. 🎦By arrangement. 🅿 Limited for coaches. 🐾 🐕In grounds, on leads. ✳ ♨Tel for details.

TREASURER'S HOUSE 🌿

Minster Yard, York, North Yorkshire YO1 7JL

Tel: ~~01904 624247~~   Fax: ~~01904 647372~~   e-mail: ~~~~

Owner: The National Trust   **Contact:** The Property Manager

Named after the Treasurer of York Minster and built over a Roman road, the house is not all that it seems! Nestled behind the Minster, the size and splendour and contents of the house are a constant surprise to visitors – as are the famous ghost stories. Free trails for children and free access to the National Trust tearoom.

Location: OS Ref. SE604 523. The N side of York Minster. Entrance on Chapter House St.

Open: 18 Mar - 5 Nov: daily except Fri, 11am - 4.30pm.

Admission: Adult £5, Child £2.50, Family £12.50. Booked groups (15+): Adult £4.20, Child £2.10. House & Cellar: Adult £7, Child £4. Groups: Adult £6.20, Child £3.50.

🍴 ♿Partial. WC. 🍽Licensed. 🍴Licensed. 🅿 None. 🐾 🐕In grounds, on leads. 🔦

UNDERGROUND (RAF) BUNKER

RAF Holmpton, Withernsea, East Yorkshire HU19 2QR

Tel: 01964 630208 (24hr infoline)   **Fax:** 01964 630972

e-mail: info@holmpton.com   **www.**holmpton.com

Owner: Secure Facilities Establishment   **Contact:** Mike Lea

Guided tours take you through over 50 years history of this massive RAF Command Bunker still in full use today.

Location: OS Ref. TA380 231. 19m from Hull, 3m S of Withernsea. (Follow the brown Bunker signs.)

Open: 4 Mar - 29 Oct: weekends. Easter, Summer & BH Hols: daily, gates open 2.15pm & tours depart at 3pm.

Admission: Adult £5, Child £3.50, OAP £4.50, Family (2+3) £15.

ⓘPhotography permitted. 🖼 🍴 ♿Unsuitable. 🍽 🅿Ample. 🐾 🐕In grounds on leads.

accommodation
see page 567

WASSAND HALL

SEATON, HULL, EAST YORKSHIRE HU11 5RJ

www.wassand.co.uk

Tel: 01964 534488   **Fax:** 01964 533334   **email:** wassand@tiscali.co.uk

Owner/Contact: R E O Russell - Resident Trustee

Fine Regency house 1815 by Thomas Cundy the Elder. Beautifully restored walled gardens, woodland walks, Parks and vistas over Hornsea Mere, part of the Estate since 1580. The Estate was purchased circa 1539 by Dame Joan Constable and has remained in the family to the present day, Mr Rupert Russell being the great nephew of the late Lady Strickland-Constable. The house contains a fine collection of 18/19th century paintings, English and Continental silver, furniture and porcelain. Wassand is very much a family home and retains a very friendly atmosphere. Homemade afternoon teas are served in the conservatory on weekend Open Days.

Location: OS Ref. TA174 460. On the B1244 Seaton - Hornsea road. Approximately 2m from Hornsea.

Open: 26 - 29 May; 8 - 12 & 22 - 26 Jun; 14/15 Jul; 4, 6/7, 10 - 14 & 25 - 28 Aug: 2 - 5pm.

Admission: Hall, all grounds & walks: Adult £5, Child (11-15yrs) £3. Hall: Adult £3, Child (11-15yrs) £1.50. Grounds & Garden: Adult £3, Child (11-15yrs) £1.50. Child under 10yrs Free.

♿Limited. 🍽 🎦By arrangement. 🅿Ample for cars, limited for coaches. 🐕In grounds, on leads. ♨Victorian carriage rides and wood turning demonstrations on certain weekends.

WENTWORTH CASTLE GARDENS

Lowe Lane, Stainborough, Barnsley, South Yorkshire S75 3ET

Tel: 01226 776040 **Fax:** 01226 776042

Owner: Barnsley MBC **Contact:** Richard Evans - Heritage Director

This historic 18th century parkland estate features over 26 listed monuments and a magnificent 60-acre pleasure garden open on selected days from spring to autumn.

Location: OS Ref. SE320 034. 5km W of Barnsley, M1/J36 via Birdwell & Rockley Lane then Lowe Lane.

Open: Gardens open on selected days while a programme of restoration takes place. Please telephone the gardens direct for details of opening times.

Admission: Garden: Adult £2.50, Conc. £2. Guided tours: Adult £3.50, Conc. £2.50.

© English Heritage

WHITBY ABBEY ⌗

WHITBY, NORTH YORKSHIRE YO22 4JT

www.english-heritage.org.uk/yorkshire

Tel: 01947 603568 **e-mail:** customers@english-heritage.org.uk

Owner: English Heritage **Contact:** Visitor Operations Team

Since pre-history, successive generations have been drawn to this headland location. Founded by St Hilda in AD657, Whitby Abbey soon acquired great influence, before being ransacked by the invading Viking army. It was to be 200 years before the monastic tradition was revived, but yet again the Abbey was plundered, this time following the Dissolution. Following detailed archaelogical investigation of the site, an interactive History Gallery recreates images of the Abbey over time and includes "Talking Heads" of personalities from the past.

Location: OS Ref. NZ904 115. On cliff top E of Whitby.

Open: 1 Apr - 31 Oct: daily, 10am - 6pm (5pm in Oct). 1 Nov - 31 Mar: Thur - Mon, 10am - 4pm. Closed 24 - 26 Dec & 1 Jan.

Admission: Adult £4.20, Child £2.10, Conc. £3.20, Family £10.50. 15% discounts for groups (11+).

WCs. Ground floor. Managed by the YHA. Charged. In grounds, on leads. Tel for details.

WILBERFORCE HOUSE

25 High Street, Hull, East Yorkshire HU1 1NQ

Tel: 01482 613902 **Fax:** 01482 613710

Owner: Hull City Council **Contact:** S R Green

Birthplace of William Wilberforce – slavery abolitionist. Displays include costume gallery, the history of slavery, clocks and the Hull Silver Collection.

Location: OS Ref. TA102 286. High Street, Hull.

Open: Mon - Sat, 10am - 5pm. Suns, 1.30 - 4.30pm. Closed Good Fri, Christmas Day & 1 Jan.

Admission: Free.

THE WORKHOUSE MUSEUM OF POOR LAW

Allhallowgate, Ripon, North Yorkshire HG1 4LE

Tel: 01765 690799 **Contact:** The Curator

"Vacancies for Vagrants: bath, 2 nights' bed and board; payment - stone breaking & wood chopping".

Location: OS Ref. SE312 712 Close to Market Square.

Open: 1 Apr - 31 Oct: daily except Weds, 1 - 4pm. During local school holidays open 11am - 4pm. Groups anytime by appointment.

Admission: Adult £2.50, Child under 6yrs Free, Conc/Student £2.

WORTLEY HALL

Wortley, Sheffield, South Yorkshire S35 7DB

Tel: 0114 2882100 **Fax:** 0114 2830695

Owner: Labour, Co-operative & Trade Union Movement **Contact:** Marc Mallender

15 acres of formal Italianate gardens surrounded by 11 acres of informal pleasure grounds.

Location: OS Ref. SK313 995. 10kms S of Barnsley in Wortley on A629.

Open: Gardens: Mar - Oct. 4 Jun & 27 Aug: Specialist Plant Fairs.

Admission: Free. Garden tours with Head Gardener for groups (15+) £2.

YORK GATE GARDEN

BACK CHURCH LANE, ADEL, LEEDS, WEST YORKSHIRE LS16 8DW

www.perennial.org.uk

Tel: 0113 2678240

Owner: Perennial **Contact:** The Garden Co-ordinator

Inspirational one acre garden renowned for its outstanding design and exquisite detail. A series of smaller gardens, separated by hedges and stone walls, are linked by a succession of delightful vistas. One of many highlights is the famous herb garden with topiary.

Location: OS Ref. 275 403. 2¹/₄m SE of Bramhope. ¹/₂m E of A660.

Open: Apr - Sept: Thur, Sun & BH Mons, 2 - 5pm. Also Thur 22, 29 Jun and 6 Jul, 6:30 - 9pm.

Admission: Adult £3.50, Child (16yrs & under) Free. Season Ticket £8.50. Free access for RHS Members in Apr, May and Sept.

Groups must book. When available. Tea & Biscuits: Jun - Sept & BH w/ends. By arrangement. Limited. Guide dogs only.

YORK MINSTER

Deangate, York YO1 7HH

Tel: 01904 557216 **Fax:** 01904 557218 **e-mail:** visitors@yorkminster.org

Owner: Dean and Chapter of York **Contact:** Stephen Hemming

Large gothic church housing the largest collection of medieval stained glass in England.

Location: OS Ref. SE603 522. Centre of York.

Open: All year: Mon - Sat, 9.30am - 5pm, Sun: 12 noon - 5pm.

Admission: Adult £5, Child (under 16yrs) Free, Conc. £4. Groups: Adult £4.50, Child (under 16yrs) Free, Conc. £3.50.

Formby Point © National Trust Photographic Library/Joe Cornish

cheshire   cumbria

north west

Four very disparate counties make up the North West Region. Cheshire has two strikingly different faces; the East, more industrial and more rugged where it adjoins the Peak District National Park, and the West, the flatter 'Cheshire Plain', more densely farmed and with easily recognisable red brick buildings. The Lake District National Park was one of the first National Parks to be created in Britain (in 1951) and covers 880 sq. miles. No trip to this area would be complete without a visit to Dove Cottage and for children, the Beatrix Potter Gallery (Cumbria) is a must. On the edge of the Lake District is Levens Hall (Cumbria), with its Topiary Garden and to the west, at Ravenglass is Muncaster Castle (Cumbria), and its fascinating Owl Centre. The Eskdale and Ravenglass Railway is a wonderful way to get up the valley before a long downhill walk back to the sea.

lancashire   merseyside

MAP 6

ADLINGTON HALL

www.adlingtonhall.com

Owner:
Mrs C J C Legh

▶ CONTACT

Corporate Enquiries:
The Estate Office
Adlington Hall
Macclesfield
Cheshire SK10 4LF

Tel: 01625 829206
Fax: 01625 828756

e-mail: enquiries@
adlingtonhall.com

Hall Tours:
The Guide
Tel: 01625 820875

▶ LOCATION

OS Ref. SJ905 804

5m N of
Macclesfield, A523,
13m S of Manchester.
London 178m.

Rail: Macclesfield
& Wilmslow
stations 5m.

Air: Manchester
Airport 8m.

Adlington Hall, the home of the Leghs of Adlington from 1315 to the present day, was built on the site of a Hunting Lodge which stood in the Forest of Macclesfield in 1040. Two oaks, part of the original building, remain with their roots in the ground and support the east end of the Great Hall, which was built between 1480 and 1505.

The Hall is a manor house, quadrangular in shape, and was once surrounded by a moat. Two sides of the Courtyard and the east wing were built in the typical 'Black and White' Cheshire style in 1581. The south front and west wing (containing the Drawing Room and Dining Room) were added between 1749 and 1757 and are built of red brick with a handsome stone portico with four Ionic columns on octagonal pedestals. Between the trees in the Great Hall stands an organ built by

'Father' Bernard Smith (c1670-80). Handel subsequently played on this instrument and, now fully restored, it is the largest 17th century organ in the country.

GARDENS

The gardens were landscaped in the style of 'Capability' Brown in the middle of the 18th century. Visitors may walk round the 'wilderness' area; among the follies to be seen are 'Temple to Diana', a 'Shell Cottage', Chinese bridge and T'ing house. There is a fine yew walk and a lime avenue planted in 1688. An old fashioned rose garden and yew maze have recently been planted. In this continually evolving garden, the 'Father Tiber' water garden was created in 2002 and the Penstemon garden in 2003.

▶ OPENING TIMES

June - August
Wed only, 2 - 5pm.

Also by prior arrangement
for groups weekdays
throughout the year.
Please contact for details.

▶ ADMISSION

Hall & Gardens

Adult £6.00
Child £3.00
Student £3.00
Groups of 20+ £5.50

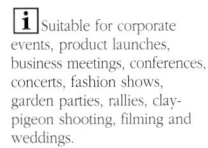

| ⓘ | Suitable for corporate events, product launches, business meetings, conferences, concerts, fashion shows, garden parties, rallies, clay-pigeon shooting, filming and weddings. |

The Great Hall and Dining Room are available for corporate entertaining. Catering can be arranged.

Visitors may alight at entrance to Hall. WCs.

Tearoom.

By arrangement.

For 100 cars and 4 coaches, 100 yds from Hall.

Schools welcome. Guide can be provided.

No dogs.

Tel for details.

CONFERENCE/FUNCTION

ROOM	SIZE	MAX CAPACITY
Great Hall	11 x 8m	80
Dining Rm	10.75 x 7m	80
Courtyard	27 x 17m	200

MAP 6

ARLEY HALL & GARDENS

www.arleyhallandgardens.com

Owned by the same family for over 500 years, Arley is a delightful estate. The gardens, described as one of the 50 best in Europe, offer a wide range of plant interest throughout the season. Particular features are the renowned double herbaceous border (c1846), the Quercus Ilex and Pleached Lime Avenues, yew hedges, two walled gardens and shrub rose collection. The Grove (a woodland garden) contains a large collection of rhododendrons, azaleas and other shrubs and exotic trees. The Victorian Jacobean Hall (Grade II*), with family pictures and furniture, is ideal for weddings and other receptions. Chapel by Salvin. Plant Nursery, Restaurant and Gift Shop.

Owner:
Viscount & Viscountess
Ashbrook

▶ **CONTACT**

Estate Secretary
Arley
Nr Northwich
Cheshire CW9 6NA

Tel: 01565 777353
Fax: 01565 777465
e-mail: enquiries@
arleyhallandgardens
.com

▶ **LOCATION**

OS117, OS Ref. SJ675

5m W Knutsford,
6m NE Norwich,
5m from M6/J20
and M56 J10.

▶ **OPENING TIMES**

1 April - 2 October &
October weekends.

Hall:
Tuesdays, Sundays & BHs
12 noon - 4.30pm.

**Gardens, Grounds &
Chapel:**
Tuesday - Sunday & BHs,
11am - 5pm.

▶ **ADMISSION**

**Gardens, Grounds
& Chapel:**

Adult	£5.00
Child (5-15yrs)	£2.00
Concession	£4.50
Family	£12.00
Season ticket	£25.00
Family Season Ticket (2+2)	£58.00

Group discounts available

Hall & Gardens

Adult	£7.50
Child (5-15yrs)	£3.00
Concession	£6.50
Family	£18.50

Group discounts available

▶ **SPECIAL EVENTS**

27/28 MAY
Arley Horse Trials &
Country Fair.

24/25 JUNE
Arley Garden Festival.

1 JULY
Blues on the Park.

2 - 9 DECEMBER
Christmas Floral Extravaganza.

 Photography in garden only.

Partial.

 By arrangement.

P 🏠

In grounds on leads.

MAP 6

CAPESTHORNE HALL

www.capesthorne.com

Owner:
Mr & Mrs
Bromley-Davenport

▶ CONTACT

Gwyneth Jones
Hall Manager
Capesthorne Hall
Siddington
Macclesfield
Cheshire SK11 9JY

Tel: 01625 861221
Fax: 01625 861619
e-mail: info@
capesthorne.com

▶ LOCATION

OS Ref. SJ840 727

5m W of Macclesfield.
30 mins S of
Manchester on A34.
Near M6, M63 and M62.

Air: Manchester
International 20 mins.

Rail: Macclesfield 5m
(2 hrs from London).

Taxi: 01625 533464.

Capesthorne Hall, set in 100 acres of picturesque Cheshire parkland, has been touched by nearly 1,000 years of English history - Roman legions passed across it, titled Norman families hunted on it and, during the Civil War, a Royalist ancestress helped Charles II to escape after the Battle of Worcester. The Jacobean-style Hall has a fascinating collection of fine art, marble sculptures, furniture and tapestries. Originally designed by the Smiths of Warwick it was built between 1719 and 1732. It was altered by Blore in 1837 and partially rebuilt by Salvin in 1861 following a disastrous fire.

The present Squire is William Bromley-Davenport, Lord Lieutenant of Cheshire, whose ancestors have owned the estate since Domesday times when they were appointed custodians of the Royal Forest of Macclesfield.

In the grounds near the family Chapel the 18th century Italian Milanese Gates open onto the herbaceous borders and maples which line the beautiful lakeside gardens. But amid the natural spectacle and woodland walks, Capesthorne still offers glimpses of its man-made past... the remains of the Ice House, the Old Boat House and the curious Swallow Hole.

Facilities at the Hall can be hired for corporate occasions and family celebrations including Civil wedding ceremonies.

ℹ️ Available for corporate functions, meetings, product launches, promotions, exhibitions, presentations, seminars, activity days, Civil weddings and receptions, family celebrations, still photography, clay shooting, car rallies, garden parties, barbecues, concerts, antique, craft, country and game fairs. No photography in Hall.

🍽️ Catering can be provided for groups (full menus on request). Function rooms available for wedding receptions, corporate hospitality, meetings and other special events.

'The Butler's Pantry' serves tea, coffee and ices.

♿ Compacted paths, ramps. WCs.

👥 For up to 50. Tours are by staff members or Hall Manager. Tour time 1 hr.

🅿️ 100 cars/20 coaches on hard-standing and unlimited in park, 50 yds from house.

🐕 Guide dogs in Hall. Under control in Park.

🔔 Civil Wedding Licence. 🎭 Tel for details.

▶ OPENING TIMES

Summer
April - Oct
Weds, Suns & BHs.

Hall
1.30 - 4pm.
Last admission 3.30pm.

Gardens & Chapel
12 noon - 5pm.

Groups welcome by appointment.

Caravan Park also open Easter - end October.

Corporate enquiries: March - December.

▶ ADMISSION

Sundays & BHs only
Hall, Gardens & Chapel

Adult	£6.00
Child (5-16yrs)	£3.00
OAP	£5.00
Family*	£15.00

*Parents and children aged up to 16yrs in the same car.

Gardens & Chapel only

Adult	£4.00
Child (5-16yrs)	£2.00
OAP	£3.00

Transfers from Gardens & Chapel to Hall

Adult/OAP	£3.50
Child (5-16yrs)	£1.50

Wednesdays only: Hall, Chapel & Gardens
Car
(up to 4 pass.) £10.00
Additional person... £2.50
Minibus
(up to 12 pass)...... £25.00
Coach
(up to 50 pass) £50.00

Caravan Park
Up to 2 people £15.00 pn
Over 2 people .. £18.00 pn

CONFERENCE/FUNCTION

ROOM	SIZE	MAX CAPACITY
Theatre	45' x 19'	150
Garden Room	52' x 20'	80
Saloon	40' x 25'	80
Queen Anne Room	34' x 25'	80

ADLINGTON HALL *See page 404 for full page entry.*

ARLEY HALL AND GARDENS *See page 405 for full page entry.*

BEESTON CASTLE

Chapel Lane, Beeston, Tarporley, Cheshire CW6 9TX
Tel: 01829 260464   **e-mail:** customers@english-heritage.org.uk
www.english-heritage.org.uk/northwest
Owner: English Heritage   **Contact:** Visitor Operations Team
Standing majestically on a sheer rocky crag, Beeston has perhaps the most stunning views of any castle in England. It also has a long history from Bronze Age settlement to Iron Age hillfort, to impregnable royal fortress. This 4,000 year history is outlined in the "Castle of the Rock" exhibition.
Location: OS Ref. SJ537 593. 11m SE of Chester on minor road off A49, or A41. 2m SW of Tarporley.
Open: 1 Apr - 30 Sept: daily, 10am - 6pm. 1 Oct - 31 Mar: Thur - Mon, 10am - 4pm. Closed 24 - 26 Dec & 1 Jan.
Admission: Adult £4, Child £2, Conc. £3. 15% discount for groups (11+).
Exhibition. WCs. Unsuitable. In grounds on leads. Tel for details.

CAPESTHORNE HALL *See page 406 for full page entry.*

CHESTER CATHEDRAL

Werburgh Street, Chester, Cheshire
Tel: 01244 500958   **Fax:** 01244 341110   **e-mail:** fry@chestercathedral.com
Owner: Church of England   **Contact:** Nicholas Fry
Medieval monastic complex.
Location: OS Ref. SJ406 665. Chester city centre.
Open: Mon - Sat: 9am - 5pm. Sun 1 - 5pm.
Admission: Adult £4, Child (5-16) £1.50, Senior Citizens/Groups £3, Family Ticket £10.

CHESTER ROMAN AMPHITHEATRE

Vicars Lane, Chester, Cheshire
Tel: 01244 402466   **e-mail:** enquiries@chesteramphitheatre.co.uk
www.chesteramphitheatre.co.uk
Owner: Managed by English Heritage and Chester City Council
                                        Contact: Chester City Council
The largest Roman amphitheatre in Britain, the site is in the process of being excavated. Work carried out over 2004/05 indicates that there were two stone-built amphitheatres, one very similar to those in Pompeii, emphasising the great importance of Chester during the Roman era.
Location: OS Ref. SJ404 660. On Vicars Lane beyond Newgate, Chester.
Open: Any reasonable time.
Admission: Free.
Partial On leads.

plant sales
see page 555

CHOLMONDELEY CASTLE GARDEN
MALPAS, CHESHIRE SY14 8AH

Tel: 01829 720383   **Fax:** 01829 720877   **email:** penny@cholmondeleycastle.co.uk
Owner: The Marchioness of Cholmondeley   **Contact:** The Secretary
Extensive ornamental gardens dominated by romantic Gothic Castle built in 1801 of local sandstone. Visitors can enjoy the beautiful Temple Water Garden, Rose Garden and many mixed borders. Lakeside picnic area, children's play areas, rare breeds of farm animals, including llamas, children's corner with rabbits, chickens and free flying aviary birds. Private chapel in the park.

Location: OS Ref. SJ540 515. Off A41 Chester/Whitchurch Rd. & A49 Whitchurch/ Tarporley Road. 7m N of Whitchurch.
Open: 2 Apr - 28 Sept: Weds, Thurs, Suns & BHs, 11.30am - 5pm. Also possible Oct opening for Autumn Tints, tel for details. Groups (25+): other days by prior arrangement at reduced rates. Castle not open to the public
Admission: Adult £4, Child £1.50, no concessions.
Limited. WCs. In grounds on leads only.

DORFOLD HALL

ACTON, Nr NANTWICH, CHESHIRE CW5 8LD

Tel: 01270 625245 **Fax:** 01270 628723

Owner/Contact: Richard Roundell

Jacobean country house built in 1616 for Ralph Wilbraham. Family home of Mr & Mrs Richard Roundell. Beautiful plaster ceilings and oak panelling. Attractive woodland gardens and summer herbaceous borders.

Location: OS Ref. SJ634 525. 1m W of Nantwich on the A534 Nantwich - Wrexham road.

Open: Apr - Oct: Tue only and BH Mons, 2 - 5pm.

Admission: Adult £5, Child £3.

Obligatory. Limited. Narrow gates with low arch prevent coaches. In grounds on leads.

GAWSWORTH HALL

MACCLESFIELD, CHESHIRE SK11 9RN

www.gawsworthhall.com

Tel: 01260 223456 **Fax:** 01260 223469 **e-mail:** enquiries@gawsworthhall.com

Owner: Mr and Mrs T Richards **Contact:** Mr T Richards

Fully lived-in Tudor half-timbered manor house with Tilting Ground. Former home of Mary Fitton, Maid of Honour at the Court of Queen Elizabeth I, and the supposed 'Dark Lady' of Shakespeare's sonnets. Pictures, sculpture and furniture. Open air theatre with covered grandstand - June, July and August, please telephone for details. Situated halfway between Macclesfield and Congleton in an idyllic setting close to the lovely medieval church.

Location: OS Ref. SJ892 697. 3m S of Macclesfield on the A536 Congleton to Macclesfield road.

Open: Easter weekend then 29 Apr - 24 Sept: Sun - Wed and for Special Events & BHs. Jul - Aug: daily, 2 - 5pm.

Admission: Adult £6, Child £3. Groups (20+): £5.

Guide dogs in garden only. Tel for details.

HARE HILL

Over Alderley, Macclesfield, Cheshire SK10 4QB

Tel: 0161 928 0075 (Regional Office) 01625 584412/828836 (Countryside Office)
www.nationaltrust.org.uk

Owner: The National Trust **Contact:** The Head Gardener

A woodland garden surrounding a walled garden with pergola, rhododendrons, hollies and hostas. Parkland.

Location: OS Ref. SJ875 765. Between Alderley Edge and Macclesfield (B5087). Turn off N onto Prestbury Road, continue for 3/4 m.

Open: 5 Apr - 7 May, 31 May - 29 Oct: Wed, Thur, Sat, Sun 10am - 5pm. 8 - 28 May: daily 10am - 5pm

Admission: Adult £2.70, Child £1.25. Car park fee £1.50 (refundable on entry to garden). Groups by written appointment c/o Garden Lodge at address above. Gravel paths - strong companion advisable. On leads in park.

HOLMSTON HALL BARN

Little Budworth, Tarporley, Cheshire CW6 9AY

Tel: 01829 760366/07778 510287 **Fax:** 01829 760366

Owner/Contact: Mr Richard & Dr Yvonne Hopkins

Newly restored 15th century oak framed barn. Sandstone base and floors, with twelve exterior oak doors.

Open: All year by appointment only.

Admission: Free.

LITTLE MORETON HALL

Congleton, Cheshire CW12 4SDN

Tel: 01260 272018 **www**.nationaltrust.org.uk

Owner: The National Trust **Contact:** The Property Manager

Begun in 1450 and completed 160 years later, Little Moreton Hall is regarded as the finest example of a timber-framed moated manor house in the country.

Location: OS Ref. SJ833 589. 4m SW of Congleton on E side of A34.

Open: 1 - 24 Mar: Wed - Sun, 11.30am - 4pm. 25 Mar - 5 Nov: Wed - Sun & BH Mons, 11.30am - 5pm. 11 Nov - 17 Dec: Sats & Suns, 11.30am - 4pm.

Admission: Adult £5.50, Child £2.80, Family £13. Groups: £4.70 (must book).

Braille guide, wheelchair. WCs. Car park only. Tel. for details.

LYME PARK

Disley, Stockport, Cheshire SK12 2NX

Tel: 01663 762023 **Fax:** 01663 765035 **www**.nationaltrust.org.uk

Owner: The National Trust **Contact:** The Property Manager

Legh family home for 600 years. Part of the original Elizabethan house survives with 18th and 19th century additions by Giacomo Leoni and Lewis Wyatt. Mortlake tapestries, Grinling Gibbons carvings, unique collection of English clocks.

Location: OS Ref. SJ965 825. Off the A6 at Disley. 6 1/2 m SE of Stockport. M60 J1.

Open: House: 29 Mar - 30 Oct: Fri - Tue, 1 - 5pm (last adm 4.30pm) (BH Mons & Good Fri, 11am - 5pm). Park: 1 Apr - 31 Oct: daily, 8am - 8.30pm; Nov - Mar: 8am - 6pm. Gardens: 29 Mar - 30 Oct: Fri - Tue, 11am - 5pm.

Admission: House & Garden: £5.80. House only: £4.20. Garden only: £2.70. Park only: car £3.80 (refundable on purchase of adult house & garden ticket), motorbike £2, coach/minibus £6. Booked coach groups Park admission Free. NT members Free.

No photography in house. Partial. WC. Licensed. By arrangement. In park, close control. Guide dogs only in house & garden.

NESS BOTANIC GARDENS

Ness, Neston, Cheshire CH64 4AY

Tel: 0151 353 0123 **Fax:** 0151 353 1004

Owner: University of Liverpool **Contact:** Dr E J Sharples

New Visitors Centre and Garden Entrance for 2006.

Location: OS Ref. SJ302 760 (village centre). Off A540. 10m NW of Chester. 1 1/2 m S of Neston.

Open: Mar - Oct: daily, 9.30am - 5pm. Nov - Feb: 9.30am - 4pm.

Admission: Adult £5, Conc £4.50, Child (under 18yrs) Free. 10% discount for groups. Please telephone for details.

NETHER ALDERLEY MILL

Congleton Rd, Nether Alderley, Macclesfield SK10 4TW

www.nationaltrust.org.uk
Tel: 01625 527468 (Quarry Bank Mill Reception)
e-mail: quarrybankmill.recep@nationaltrust.org.uk

Owner: The National Trust **Contact:** Property Manager

15th century mill beside a tranquil millpond. Heavy framework, low beams and floors connected by wooden ladders, all set beneath an enormous sloping stone roof, help to create this wonderful corn mill.

Location: OS Ref. SJ844 763. 1 1/2 m S of Alderley Edge, on E side of A34.

Open: 1 Apr - 30 Oct: Thur, 1 - 5pm. Sun & BH Mons, 11am - 5pm.

Admission: Adult £2.50, Child £1.20, Family £8. Groups by prior arrangement (max 20).

By arrangement. Limited. Coaches must book. By arrangement.

NORTON PRIORY MUSEUM & GARDENS

TUDOR ROAD, MANOR PARK, RUNCORN WA7 1SX

www.nortonpriory.org

Tel: 01928 569895   **e-mail:** info@nortonpriory.org

Owner/Contact: The Norton Priory Museum Trust

Discover the 800 year old priory range, excavated priory remains, museum gallery, the St Christopher statue – one of the great treasures of medieval Europe – exciting sculpture trail and award winning Walled Garden. Set in 38 acres of tranquil, woodland gardens, Norton Priory also has a coffee shop, retail area and temporary exhibitions gallery.

Location: OS Ref. SJ545 835. 3m from M56/J11. 2m E of Runcorn.

Open: All year: daily, from 12 noon. Telephone for details.

Admission: Adult £4.75, Child/Conc. £3.45, Family £12.50. Groups £3.

▣ ⚑ ⚫Wheelchairs, braille guide, audio tapes & WC. ⚫ ⚑By arrangement. ▣ ▣ ⚑In grounds, on leads. ❄ ⚑Tel for details.

QUARRY BANK MILL & STYAL ESTATE ⚘

Styal, Wilmslow SK9 4LA

Tel: 01625 527468   **Fax:** 01625 539267

e-mail: quarrybankmill.reception@nationaltrust.org.uk   **www.**nationaltrust.org.uk

Owner: The National Trust   **Contact:** Nikky Braithwaite

Unique Georgian Cotton Mill with working machinery, daily demonstrations and fascinating living history. See the steam engines and mighty watermill in action. Experience the grim conditions in the Apprentice House. Enjoy the beautiful 300 acre Styal Estate.

Location: OS Ref. SJ835 835. 1¹/₂ m N of Wilmslow off B5166. 2¹/₂ m from M56/J5. Styal Shuttle Bus, Airport 2¹/₂ m.

Open: Mill: Apr - Sept: daily, 10.30am - 5.30pm, last adm. 4pm. Oct - Mar: daily except Mon, 10.30am - 5pm, last adm. 3.30pm. Apprentice House & Garden: Tue - Fri, 2 - 4.30pm, Sat/Sun, 11am - 4.30pm.

Admission: Adult £7.30, Child/Conc. £4.50, Family £15 (2+3). Mill only: Adult £5.20, Child/Conc. £3.50. Booked Groups (20+) at child rate.

▣ ⚑ ⚫Partial. ⚫ ⚑Licensed. ⚑By arrangement. ▣ ▣ ⚑In grounds on leads. ▲ ❄ ⚑Tel for details.

open all year
see page 557

PEOVER HALL ⛪

OVER PEOVER, KNUTSFORD WA16 9HW

Tel: 01565 632358

Owner: Randle Brooks   **Contact:** I Shepherd

An Elizabethan house dating from 1585. Fine Carolean stables. Mainwaring Chapel, 18th century landscaped park. Large garden with topiary work, also walled and herb gardens.

Location: OS Ref. SJ772 734. 4m S of Knutsford off A50 at Whipping Stocks Inn.

Open: Apr - Oct: House, Stables & Gardens: Mons except BHs, 2 - 5pm. Tours of the House at 2.30 & 3.30pm. Stables & Gardens only: Thur, 2 - 5pm.

Admission: House, Stables & Gardens: Adult £4.50, Child £3. Stables & Gardens only: Adult £3, Child £2.

⚫Mondays only. ⚑Obligatory. ⚑

RODE HALL ⛪

CHURCH LANE, SCHOLAR GREEN, CHESHIRE ST7 3QP

www.rodehall.co.uk

Tel: 01270 873237   **Fax:** 01270 882962   **e-mail:** rodehall@scholargreen.fsnet.co.uk

Owner/Contact: Sir Richard Baker Wilbraham Bt

The Wilbraham family have lived at Rode since 1669; the present house was constructed in two stages, the earlier two storey wing and stable block around 1705 and the main building was completed in 1752. Later alterations by Lewis Wyatt and Darcy Braddell were undertaken in 1812 and 1927 respectively. The house stands in a Repton landscape and the extensive gardens include a woodland garden, with a terraced rock garden and grotto, which has many species of rhododendrons, azaleas, hellebores and climbing roses following snowdrops and daffodils in the early spring. The formal rose garden was designed by W Nesfield in 1860 and there is a large walled kitchen garden which is at its best from the middle of June. The icehouse in the park has recently been restored.

Location: OS Ref. SJ819 573. 5m SW of Congleton between the A34 and A50. Kidsgrove railway station 2m NW of Kidsgrove.

Open: 5 Apr - 27 Sept: Weds & BHs and by appointment. Garden only: Tues & Thurs, 2 - 5pm. Snowdrop Walk: 4 - 26 Feb daily - closed Mondays.

Admission: House, Garden & Kitchen Garden: Adult £5, Conc £4. Garden & Kitchen Garden: Adult £3, Concession £2.50. Snowdrop Walk: £3.

⚑ ⚫Home-made teas. ⚑On leads.

TABLEY HOUSE

KNUTSFORD, CHESHIRE WA16 0HB

www.tableyhouse.co.uk

Tel: 01565 750151 **Fax:** 01565 653230 **e-mail:** inquiries@tableyhouse.co.uk

Owner: The University of Manchester   **Contact:** The Assistant Administrator
The finest Palladian House in the North West, Tabley a Grade I listing, was designed by John Carr of York for the Leicester family. Set in landscaped parkland it contains the first collection of English paintings, including works of art by Turner, Reynolds, Lawrence and Lely. Furniture by Chippendale, Bullock and Gillow and fascinating family memorabilia adorn the rooms. Interesting Tea Room and 17th century Chapel adjoin.

Location: OS Ref. SJ725 777. M6/J19, A556 S on to A5033. 2m W of Knutsford.

Open: Apr - end Oct inclusive: Thurs, Fris, Sats, Suns & BHs, 2 - 5pm.

Admission: Adult £4. Child/Student £1.50. Groups by arrangement.

▣ ⬥ ⬤ **P**
⬥ Civil Wedding Licence plus Civil Naming Ceremonies & Re-affirmation of Vows.
⬥ Tel for details.

TATTON PARK ✄

Tatton, Knutsford, Cheshire WA16 6QN

Tel: 01625 534400   **info:** 01625 534435   **Fax:** 01625 534403

Owner: The National Trust   **Contact:** Mr Robinson, The Curator
A neo-classical mansion by Wyatt, set in 50 acres of garden and 1000 acres of parkland.

Location: OS Ref. SJ745 815. From M56/J7 follow signs. From M6/J19, signed on A56 & A50.

Open: 25 Mar - 1 Oct, Mansion: Tues - Sun, 1 - 5pm, Park: daily, 10am - 7pm, Gardens: Tues - Sun, 10am - 6pm. 3 Oct - 23 Mar 2007, Park & Gardens: Tues - Sun, 11am - 5pm (Gardens close 4pm).

Admission: Mansion, Gardens, Tudor Old Hall and Farm: Adult £3.50, Child £2, Family £9.

WOODHEY CHAPEL

Faddiley, Nr Nantwich, Cheshire CW5 8JH

Tel: 01270 524215

Owner: The Trustees of Woodhey Chapel   **Contact:** Mr Robinson, The Curator
Small private chapel that has been recently restored.

Location: OS Ref. NJ574 530. Proceeding W from Nantwich on A534, turn left 1m W of the Faddiley - Brindley villages onto narrow lane, keep ahead at next turn, at road end obtain key from farmhouse.

Open: Apr - Oct: Sats & BHs, 2 - 5pm, or apply for key at Woodhey Hall.

Admission: Donation box.

Lyme Park.

MAP 10

ABBOT HALL ART GALLERY

www.abbothall.org.uk

Abbot Hall is a jewel of a building in a beautiful setting on the banks of the River Kent, surrounded by a park and overlooked by the ruins of Kendal Castle. This is one of Britain's finest small art galleries and a wonderful place in which to see and enjoy changing exhibitions in the elegantly proportioned rooms of a Grade I Listed Georgian building. The collection includes works by Romney, Ruskin, Turner and Freud. The adjacent Museum of Lakeland Life is a popular family attraction with a Victorian street scene, farmhouse rooms, Arthur Ransome room and displays of Arts and Crafts Movement furniture and fabrics.

Owner:
Lakeland Arts Trust

▶ CONTACT
Hannah Neale
Abbot Hall Art Gallery
Kendal
Cumbria LA9 5AL

Tel: 01539 722464

Fax: 01539 722494

e-mail: info@
abbothall.org.uk

▶ LOCATION
OS Ref. SD516 922

10 mins from M6/J36. Follow brown museum signs to South Kendal.

Rail: Oxenholme.

Air: Manchester.

▶ OPENING TIMES

12 January - 24 December
Mon - Sat
10.30am - 5pm
(4pm, Jan - Mar, Nov/Dec.)

Closed Sun.

▶ ADMISSION

Exhibition incl. free entry
to collection £5.00
Collection only £4.00

All ages welcome.

ℹ️ No photography. No mobile phones.

🛍️ Bookshop.

♿ Chairlifts in split level galleries. WCs.

☕ Licensed.

🅿️ Ample. Free.

🎭

♿ By arrangement.

🐕 Guide dogs only.

❄️

BLACKWELL -
THE ARTS & CRAFTS HOUSE

www.blackwell.org.uk

Owner:
Lakeland Arts Trust

▶ CONTACT

Harvey Wilkinson
Blackwell
The Arts & Crafts House
Bowness on
Windermere
Cumbria   LA23 3JR

Tel: 01539 446139

Fax: 01539 488486

e-mail: info@
blackwell.org.uk

▶ LOCATION
OS Ref. SD400 945

1¹/₂ m S of Bowness
just off the A5074 on
the B5360.

Rail: Windermere.

Air: Manchester.

Blackwell is a superb house situated in the Lake District. Completed in 1900, it sits in an elevated position overlooking Lake Windermere. Blackwell is the most important, and the largest, surviving early example of work by the architect Mackay Hugh Baillie Scott. Changing exhibitions of the highest quality applied arts and crafts can be seen in the setting of the Arts and Crafts Movement architecture itself.

In this treasure trove of 1890s Arts and Crafts design are fine examples of the decorative arts, drawn from natural forms. Lakeland birds and local wild flowers, trees and berries can be seen in the many original stained glass windows, pristine oak panelling and plasterwork. These rooms were designed for relaxation and everywhere you turn you will find inglenooks and places to sit and enjoy the views and garden terraces.

▶ OPENING TIMES

13 February - 24 December
Daily, 10.30am - 5pm,
(4pm, Feb/Mar, Nov/Dec.).

▶ ADMISSION

Adult £5.45

All ages welcome.

Lakeland Arts Trust/Jonathan Lynch

  No photography. No mobile phones.  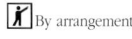   By arrangement.   **P** Limited for cars and coaches.

Ground floor & part of 1st floor. WCs.   Licensed.   Guide dogs only.   ✳

© C H Bagot

MAP 10

Owner: C H Bagot

▶ CONTACT
Peter Milner
Levens Hall
Kendal
Cumbria LA8 0PD

Tel: 01539 560321

Fax: 01539 560669

e-mail:
houseopening@
levenshall.co.uk

▶ LOCATION
OS Ref. SD495 851

5m S of Kendal on the
A6. Exit M6/J36.

Rail: Oxenholme 5m.

Air: Manchester.

LEVENS HALL 🏛
www.levenshall.co.uk

Levens Hall is an Elizabethan mansion built around a 13th century pele tower. The much loved home of the Bagot family, visitors comment on the warm and friendly atmosphere. Fine panelling and plasterwork, period furniture, Cordova leather wall coverings, paintings by Rubens, Lely and Cuyp, the earliest English patchwork and Wellingtoniana combine with other beautiful objects to form a fascinating collection.

The world famous Topiary Gardens were laid out by Monsieur Beaumont from 1694 and his design has remained largely unchanged to this day. Over ninety individual pieces of topiary, some over nine metres high, massive beech hedges and colourful seasonal bedding provide a magnificent visual impact. *"Considered to be in the top ten UK gardens"* – Monty Don.

On Sundays and Bank Holidays 'Bertha', a full size Showman's Engine, is in steam. Delicious home-made lunches and teas are available, together with the award-winning Levens beer 'Morocco Ale', in the Bellingham Buttery.

© C H Bagot

▶ OPENING TIMES
Summer
2 April - 12 October
Sun - Thur
(closed Fris & Sats).

House: 12 noon - 5pm
Last admission 4.30pm.

Gardens, Plant Centre,
Gift Shop & Tearoom:
10am - 5pm.

Winter
Closed.

▶ ADMISSION
House & Gardens
Adult £9.00
Child £4.00
Family (2+3*)........ £23.00
Groups (20+)
Adult £7.50
Child £3.80

Gardens
Adult £6.00
Child £3.00
Family (2+3*)........ £17.50
Groups (20+)
Adult £5.50
Child £2.70
*Additional Children at
Group rate.

Evening Tours
House & Garden, for
groups (20+) by prior
arrangement only
(Mon - Thur) £9.50

Gardens guided tour by
the Head Gardener or his
Assistant for groups (20+)
by prior arrangement
only £7.00

Morning Tours
House tours starting
between 10 - 10.30am
for pre-arranged groups
(20+/min charge £170)
.... £8.50

No admission charge for gift shop, tearoom and plant centre.

 No indoor photography. Partial. WC. Electric buggy hire. DVD of interior.
 Licensed. By arrangement.  Schools welcome. P Guide dogs only.

MAP 10

MUNCASTER CASTLE 🏛

GARDENS, OWL CENTRE & MEADOWVOLE MAZE

www.muncaster.co.uk

Owner: Mrs Phyllida
Gordon-Duff-
Pennington

▶ CONTACT

Peter Frost-Pennington
Muncaster Castle
Ravenglass
Cumbria   CA18 1RQ
Tel: 01229 717614
Fax: 01229 717010

e-mail: info@
muncaster.co.uk

▶ LOCATION

OS Ref. SD103 965

On the A595 1m S of
Ravenglass, 19m S of
Whitehaven.

From London 6 hrs,
Chester 2¹/₂ hrs,
Edinburgh 3¹/₂ hrs,
M6/J36, A590,
A595 (from S). M6/J40,
A66, A595 (from E).
Carlisle, A595 (from N).

Rail: Ravenglass
(on Barrow-in-Furness-
Carlisle Line) 1¹/₂ m.

Air: Manchester 2¹/₂ hrs.

**Top Attraction (up to 100,000 visitors)
Northwest Awards for Excellence 2004.**

Muncaster Castle, set in 77 acres of gardens with
spectacular views of the Lakeland Fells, has been
home to the Pennington family since at least 1208.

The Castle, complete with an impressive library,
beautiful barrel-vaulted drawing room and
exquisite dining room, is a treasure trove of
paintings, silver, tapestries, and much more.

'Ghost tours' are possible by appointment, and up
to 8 brave guests can book an overnight 'Ghost
Sit' in the 'haunted' Tapestry Room.

The extensive, wild woodland gardens include
glorious rhododendrons, camellias, azaleas,
magnolias and many other interesting and rare
trees and shrubs.

The World Owl Centre, HQ of the World Owl
Trust, is home to one of the largest collections of
these fascinating birds.

Most Saturday and Sunday evenings in winter,
(closed January) *Darkest Muncaster* transforms the
gardens with hundreds of multi-coloured lights, as
well as music, sound and other special effects.

In the *MeadowVole Maze* visitors young and old
help Max MeadowVole safely find his way home
through this innovative, indoor attraction, with a
strong conservation message. *Muncaster
Interactive* gives visitors free access to computers
with games and quizzes, as well as facts and
figures on the Castle, gardens, owls and the
surrounding area. It also provides access to on-
site cameras.

Muncaster is the perfect place to entertain in style
and frequently hosts weddings, dinner parties and
similar family celebrations or corporate events.

Accommodation is available in the 'Coachman's
Quarters' in the gardens of the Castle and in three
houses on the wider estate.

📷🚫 ℹ️ Church. Garden parties, film location, clay pigeon
shooting. No photography inside the Castle.

🍽 For wedding receptions, catering, & functions, tel: 01229 717614.

♿ By arrangement visitors can alight near Castle. Wheelchairs
for loan. WCs. Audio tour tapes for partially sighted/those with
learning difficulties. Allocated parking.

🍴 Creeping Kate's Kitchen (licensed) (max 80) – full
menu. Groups can book: 01229 717614 to qualify for discounts.

🚶🎧 Individual audio tour (40mins) included in price.
Private tours with a personal guide (family member possible)
can be arranged at additional fee. Ghost Sits our speciality.

🅿️ 500 cars 800 yds from House; coaches may park closer.
Free.

📖 Guides available. Historical subjects, horticulture, conservation,
owl tours.

🐕 In grounds, on leads. 🏨🛏🎭 Tel for details.

CONFERENCE/FUNCTION

ROOM	MAX CAPACITY
Drawing Rm	100
Dining Rm	50
Family Dining Rm	60
Great Hall	100
Old Laundry	100
Library	48
Guard Room	30

▶ OPENING TIMES

Castle
12 February - 5 November
Daily (closed Sat),
12 noon - 5pm.

Gardens & Owl Centre
All year except January:
Daily, 10.30am - 6pm
or dusk if earlier.

'Meet the Birds'
12 February - 5 November
Daily at 2.30pm.

**Watch the wild herons
feeding during the
'Heron Happy Hour'.**
Daily at 4.30pm (3.30pm
in winter).

Winter
Castle closed. Open by
appointment for groups.

Darkest Muncaster
A Winter Evening of Magic
– see website for details.

▶ ADMISSION

**Castle, Gardens,
Owl Centre &
MeadowVole Maze**
Adult £9.00
Child (5-15yrs) £6.00
Under 5yrs .... Free
Family (2+2) £25.00
Groups
Adult £7.50
Child (5-15yrs) £4.50

**Gardens, Owl Centre
& MeadowVole Maze**
Adult £6.50
Child (5-15yrs) £4.50
Under 5yrs .... Free
Family (2+2) £20.00
Groups
Adult £6.00
Child (5-15yrs) £3.50

ABBOT HALL ART GALLERY

See page 411 for full page entry.

ACORN BANK GARDEN & WATERMILL

Temple Sowerby, Penrith, Cumbria CA10 1SP
Tel: 01768 361893 **e-mail:** acornbank@nationaltrust.org.uk
www.nationaltrust.org.uk
Owner: The National Trust **Contact:** The Custodian
Seventeenth century walls enclose a herb garden with over 250 varieties of medicinal and culinary plants and orchards with traditional fruit trees surrounded by mixed borders. Beyond the walls, paths lead through woodland to a partially restored watermill. House not open.
Location: Gate: OS Ref. NY612 281. Just N of Temple Sowerby, 6m E of Penrith on A66.
Open: 25 Mar - 29 Oct: daily except Mon and Tue, 10am - 5pm. Last admission 4.30pm. Tearoom: 11am - 4.30pm.
Admission: Adult £3.20, Child £1.60, Family £8. Pre-arranged groups £2.70.
WCs. Woodland walks only.

BEATRIX POTTER GALLERY

Main Street, Hawkshead, Cumbria LA22 0NS
Tel: 01539 436355 **Fax:** 01539 436187
e-mail: beatrixpottergallery@nationaltrust.org.uk
www.nationaltrust.org.uk
Owner: The National Trust **Contact:** Ticket Office / House Steward
An annually changing exhibition of original sketches and watercolours painted by Beatrix Potter for her children's stories. *The Tale of Mr Jeremy Fisher* features for his 100th birthday. The gallery was once the office of Beatrix Potter's husband, William Heelis. It is ideally matched with a visit to Beatrix Potter's house, Hill Top, two miles away, where she wrote and illustrated many of her children's stories. Quizzes for children.
Location: OS Ref. SD352 982. 5m SSW of Ambleside. In the Square.
Open: 1 Apr - 29 Oct: Sat - Wed and Good Fri plus Thur in Aug 10.30am - 4.30pm. Last admission 4pm. Admission is by timed ticket (incl. NT members). Shop: daily.
Admission: Adult £3.60, Child £1.80, Family £9. No reduction for groups. Discount for Hill Top ticket holders (not groups). Group booking essential.
No photography inside. Assistance dogs only.

BLACKWELL - THE ARTS & CRAFTS HOUSE

See page 412 for full page entry.

BRANTWOOD

Coniston, Cumbria LA21 8AD
Tel: 01539 441396 **Fax:** 01539 441263 **e-mail:** enquiries@brantwood.org.uk
www.brantwood.org.uk
Owner: The Brantwood Trust
Brantwood, the former home of John Ruskin, is the most beautifully situated house in the Lake District. Explore Brantwood's estate and gardens or experience contemporary art in the Severn Studio. Brantwood's bookshop, the Jumping Jenny restaurant and Coach House Craft Gallery combine for a perfect day out.
Location: OS Ref. SD313 959. 2 1/2 m from Coniston village on the E side of Coniston Water.
Open: Mid Mar - mid Nov: daily, 11am - 5.30pm. Mid Nov - mid Mar: Wed - Sun, 11am - 4.30pm.
Admission: Adult £5.50, Child £1, Student £4, Family (2+3) £11.50. Garden only: Adult £3.75, Family (2+3) £8. Groups: Adult £4.50, Child £1, Student £3, Garden only: £3.
No photography in the house. Partial. Licensed. Licensed.
By arrangement. Ample. Limited for coaches. In grounds, on leads.

BROUGH CASTLE

Brough, Cumbria
Tel: 01228 591922
Owner: English Heritage **Contact:** Visitor Operations Manager
This ancient site dates back to Roman times. The 12th century keep replaced an earlier stronghold destroyed by the Scots in 1174.
Location: OS Ref. NY791 141. 8m SE of Appleby S of A66. South part of the village.
Open: Any reasonable time.
Admission: Free.
On leads.

BROUGHAM CASTLE

Penrith, Cumbria CA10 2AA
Tel: 01768 862488
Owner: English Heritage **Contact:** Visitor Operations Team
These impressive ruins on the banks of the River Eamont include an early 13th century keep and later buildings. You can climb to the top of the keep and survey the domain of its eccentric one-time owner Lady Anne Clifford. Exhibition about the Roman fort, medieval castle and Lady Anne Clifford.
Location: OS Ref. NY537 290. 1 1/2 m SE of Penrith, between A66 & B6262.
Open: 1 Apr - 30 Sept: daily, 10am - 5pm. 1 - 31 Oct: Thur - Mon, 10am - 4pm.
Admission: Adult £2.70, Child £1.40, Conc. £2. 15% discount for groups (11+).
WCs. Grounds. Limited. In grounds, on leads. Tel for details.

© English Heritage Photo Library

CARLISLE CASTLE

CARLISLE, CUMBRIA CA3 8UR

Tel: 01228 591922
Owner: English Heritage **Contact:** Visitor Operations Team
This impressive medieval castle, where Mary Queen of Scots was once imprisoned, has a long and tortuous history of warfare and family feuds. A portcullis hangs menacingly over the gatehouse passage, there is a maze of passages and chambers, endless staircases to lofty towers and you can walk the high ramparts for stunning views. There is also a medieval manor house in miniature: a suite of medieval rooms furnished as they might have been when used by the castle's former constable. The castle includes the King's Own Royal Border Regimental Museum.
Location: OS Ref. NY397 563. In Carlisle town, at N end of city centre.
Open: 1 Apr - 30 Sept: daily, 9.30am - 5pm. 1 Oct - 31 Mar: daily, 10am - 4pm. Closed 24 - 26 Dec & 1 Jan.
Admission: Adult £4.10, Child £2.10, Conc £3.10. 15% discount for groups (11+).
Partial, wheelchairs available. By arrangement. Disabled parking only. Dogs on leads. Tel for details.

CARLISLE CATHEDRAL

Carlisle, Cumbria CA3 8TZ
Tel: 01228 548151 **Fax:** 01228 547049 **Contact:** Ms C Baines
Fine sandstone Cathedral, founded in 1122. Medieval stained glass.
Location: OS Ref. NY399 559. Carlisle city centre, 2m from M6/J43.
Open: Mon - Sat: 7.40am - 6.15pm, Suns, 7.40 - 5pm. Closes 4pm between Christmas Day & New Year. Sun services: 8am, 10.30am & 3pm. Weekday services: 8am, 5.30pm & a 12.30 service on Weds and Fris.
Admission: Donation.

special events
see page 571

education index
see page 564

CONISHEAD PRIORY & BUDDHIST TEMPLE
Ulverston, Cumbria LA12 9QQ
Tel: 01229 584029 **Fax:** 01229 580080 **e-mail:** info@manjushri.org
Owner: Manjushri Kadampa Meditation Centre **Contact:** Geoffrey Roe
A Victorian gothic mansion. Special features include decorative ceilings, a vaulted great hall with fine stained glass and a 177 feet long cloister corridor.
Location: OS Ref. SD305 757. 2m S of Ulverston on A5087 Coast Road.
Open: Easter - Oct: Sat, Sun & BHs, 2 - 5pm. Closed 20 May - 4 Jun & 15 Jul - 13 Aug. Opening times sometimes vary, please telephone to confirm and for weekday details.
Admission: Free. Guided Tours: Adult £2.50, Conc: £2, Under 12yrs free.

DALEMAIN 🏛
PENRITH, CUMBRIA CA11 0HB
www.dalemain.com

Tel: 017684 86450 **Fax:** 017684 86223 **e-mail:** admin@dalemain.com
Owner: Robert Hasell-McCosh Esq **Contact:** Jayne Pickles - General Manager
Dalemain is a fine mixture of mediaeval, Tudor and early Georgian architecture. The imposing Georgian façade strikes the visitor immediately but in the cobbled courtyard the atmosphere of the north country Tudor manor is secure. The present owner's family have lived at Dalemain since 1679 and have collected china, furniture and family portraits.

Delightful and fascinating 5 acre plantsman's gardens set against the picturesque splendour of the Lakeland Fells and Parkland. Richly planted herbaceous borders. Rose Walk with over 100 old-fashioned roses and ancient apple trees of named varieties. Magnificent Abies Cephalonica and Tulip Tree. Tudor Knot Garden. Wild Garden with profusion of flowering shrubs and wild flowers and in early summer the breathtaking display of blue Himalayan Poppies.

Location: OS Ref. NY477 269. On A592 1m S of A66. 4m SW of Penrith. From London, M1, M6/J40: 5 hrs. From Edinburgh, A73, M74,M6/J40: 2¹/₂ hrs.

Open: 26 Mar - 29 Oct: Sun - Thur. House: 11am - 4pm. Gardens/restaurant/tearoom/gift shop/plant sales/museums: 10.30am - 5pm. Groups (10+) please book. Winter: Gardens, restaurant & tearoom open for homemade food: 30 Oct - mid Mar: Sun - Thur, 11am - 4pm.

Admission: House & Garden: Adult £6.50, Accompanied Child Free. Groups £4.50. Gardens only: Adult £4, Accompanied Child Free. Groups £3.50. Visitors in wheelchairs Free. All prices include VAT.

ℹ️ No photography in house. Moorings available on Ullswater. 📷♿⊤
♿ Visitors may drive into the Courtyard and alight near the gift shop. Electric scooter. WCs. ●🍴 Licensed. Groups must book for lunches/high teas.
🎟 1hr tours. German and French translations. Garden tour for groups extra. 🅿 50 yds.
🐕 Guide dogs in house only. No dogs in garden, allowed in grounds. 📧 Tel for details.

Holker Hall.

©The Wordsworth Trust

DOVE COTTAGE
& THE WORDSWORTH MUSEUM
GRASMERE, CUMBRIA LA22 9SH
www.wordsworth.org.uk

Tel: 01539 435544 **Fax:** 01539 435748
e-mail: bookings@wordsworth.org.uk
Owner: The Wordsworth Trust **Contact:** Bookings Officer
Situated in the heart of the English Lake District, Dove Cottage is the beautifully preserved Grasmere home of England's finest poet William Wordsworth. Visitors are offered fascinating guided tours of his world-famous home. The award-winning Museum displays priceless Wordsworth manuscripts and memorabilia. Onsite tearooms and book and gift shop.
Location: OS Ref. NY342 070. Immediately S of Grasmere village on A591. Main car/coach park next to Dove Cottage Tea Rooms and Restaurant.
Open: All year: daily, 9.30am - 5.30pm (last admission 5pm). Closed 9 Jan - 6 Feb.
Admission: Adult £6.20, Child £3.90, OAP £5.60, Family tickets available. Pre-arranged groups (10-60): Adult £4.90. Reciprocal discount ticket with Rydal Mount and Wordsworth House.
ⓘNo photography. 🗐 🛇Partial. WC. 🖰 🍴 𝒻Obligatory. 🅿Limited. 🖿 🐕Guide dogs only. ✲ ▾Tel for details.

FELL FOOT PARK 🌿
Newby Bridge, Cumbria LA12 8NN
Tel: 01539 531273 **Fax:** 01539 539926 **e-mail:** fellfootpark@nationaltrust.org.uk
Owner: The National Trust **Contact:** Park Manager
Come and explore this lakeshore Victorian park on the edge of Windermere. A great place for the family, with boat hire, tearoom, play area, family activity sheets and wildlife room showing birds and bats who live around the park. Fantastic views of the Lakeland fells. Wonderful colour in spring.
Location: OS Ref. SD381 869. S end of Lake Windermere on E shore, entrance from A592. Near Aquarium of the Lakes and Haverthwaite Steam Railway.
Open: Daily, 9am - 5pm (except Christmas Day and Boxing Day).
Admission: Car park: 2hrs £3, 4hrs £5, all day £6.50. Coaches by arrangement.
🗐 🛇Partial. 🖰 🅿Charge. 🖿On leads. ✲ ▾Tel for details.

FURNESS ABBEY ⌗
Barrow-in-Furness, Cumbria LH13 0TJ
Tel: 01229 823420
Owner: English Heritage **Contact:** Visitor Operations Staff
Hidden in a peaceful green valley are the beautiful red sandstone remains of the wealthy abbey founded in 1123 by Stephen, later King of England. This abbey first belonged to the Order of Savigny and later to the Cistercians. There is a museum and exhibition.
Location: OS Ref. SD218 717. 1½ m NE of Barrow-in-Furness.
Open: 1 Apr - 30 Sept: daily, 10am - 5pm. 1 Oct - 31 Mar: Thur - Mon, 10am - 4pm. Closed 24 - 26 Dec & 1 Jan.
Admission: Adult £3.40, Child £1.70, Conc. £2.60. 15% discount for groups (11+).
ⓘWC. 🗐 🛇Grounds. 🖰Inclusive. 🅿 🖿 🖿In grounds, on leads. ✲ ▾Tel for details.

HARDKNOTT ROMAN FORT ⌗
Ravenglass, Cumbria
Tel: 0161 242 1400
Owner: English Heritage **Contact:** The North West Regional Office
This fort, built between AD120 and 138, controlled the road from Ravenglass to Ambleside.
Location: OS Ref. NY219 015. At the head of Eskdale. 9m NE of Ravenglass, at W end of Hardknott Pass.
Open: Any reasonable time. Access may be hazardous in winter.
Admission: Free.
🅿 🖿On leads. ✲

HERON CORN MILL & MUSEUM OF PAPERMAKING
Beetham Trust, Waterhouse Mills, Beetham, Milnthorpe LA7 7AR
Tel: 015395 65027 **Fax:** 015395 65033 **e-mail:** info@heronmill.org
Owner: Heron Corn Mill Beetham Trust **Contact:** Audrey Steeley
A fascinating visitor attraction. An 18th century corn mill and museum of papermaking offers hand-made paper demonstrations and art workshops for visitors.
Location: OS Ref. SD497 800. At Beetham. 1m S of Milnthorpe on the A6.
Open: Mar - Oct: Daily except Mons (open BH Mons), 11am - 5pm.
Admission: Adult £2, Child £1, OAP £1.50. Schools and groups welcome.

©National Trust Photographic Library/Geoffrey Frosh

HILL TOP 🌿
NEAR SAWREY, AMBLESIDE, CUMBRIA LA22 0LF
www.nationaltrust.org.uk

Tel: 01539 436269 **Fax:** 01539 436811 **e-mail:** hilltop@nationaltrust.org.uk
Owner: The National Trust **Contact:** Ticket Office/Visitor Services Manager
Beatrix Potter wrote and illustrated many of her famous children's stories in this little 17th century house, which contains her furniture and china. There is a traditional cottage garden attached. A selection of the original illustrations may be seen at the Beatrix Potter Gallery in Hawkshead. Shop specialises in Beatrix Potter items.
Location: OS Ref. SD370 955. 2m S of Hawkshead, in hamlet of Near Sawrey, behind the Tower Bank Arms.
Open: 1 Apr - 29 Oct: Sat - Wed & Good Fri, plus Thur in Aug & 21/22 Dec, 10.30am - 4.30pm. Garden & Shop: 30 Oct - 20 Dec, 10am - 4pm. Admission by timed ticket (incl. NT members). Group booking essential.
Admission: Adult £5.10, Child £2.30, Family £12.50. No reduction for groups. Discount for Beatrix Potter Gallery ticket holders (not groups). Garden: Free on Thur & Fri.
ⓘNo photography in house. 🗐 🛇Partial. 🅿None for coaches. 🖿Assistance dogs only. ▾Tel for details.

HOLEHIRD GARDENS
Patterdale Road, Windermere, Cumbria LA23 1NP
Tel: 01539 446008
Owner: Lakeland Horticultural Society
Contact: The Hon Secretary/Publicity Officer
Over 10 acres of hillside gardens overlooking Windermere, including a wide variety of plants, specimen trees and shrubs, extensive rock and heather gardens, a walled garden, alpine houses and herbaceous borders. The all year garden also is home to the national collections of Astilbe, Hydrangea and Polystichum ferns. Managed and maintained entirely by volunteers.
Location: OS Ref. NY410 008. On A592, ¾ m N of junction with A591. ½ m N of Windermere. 1m from Townend.
Open: All year: dawn till dusk. Groups by arrangement. Reception: Apr - Oct, 10am - 5pm.
Admission: Free. Donation appreciated (at least £3 suggested).

HOLKER HALL & GARDENS 🏠

CARK-IN-CARTMEL, GRANGE-OVER-SANDS, CUMBRIA LA11 7PL

www.holker-hall.co.uk

Tel: 01539 558328 **Fax:** 01539 558378 **e-mail:** publicopening@holker.co.uk

Owner: Lord Cavendish of Furness **Contact:** Elizabeth Ward

Holker Hall, home of Lord and Lady Cavendish, shows the confidence, spaciousness and prosperity of Victorian style on its grandest scale. The New Wing was designed by architects Paley and Austin and built by the 7th Duke of Devonshire during 1871-4. Despite this grand scale, Holker is very much a family home with visitors able to wander freely throughout the New Wing. Varying in period and style, Louis XV pieces happily mix with the Victorian, including an early copy of the famous triple portrait of Charles I by Van Dyck. The award-winning gardens include formal and woodland areas covering 25 acres. Designated 'amongst the best in the world in terms of design and content' by the *Good Gardens Guide*. This inspiring garden includes a limestone cascade, fountain, the Sunken Garden, the Elliptical and Summer Gardens and many rare plants and shrubs. Newly created Labyrinth designed by Lady Cavendish and international designer Jim Buchanen. Winner 2004 'Cumbria in Bloom Award for Creative & Adventurous Horticultural Development'.

Location: OS Ref. SD359 773. Close to Morecambe Bay, 5m W of Grange-over-Sands by B5277. From Kendal, A6, A590, B5277, B5278: 16m. Motorway: M6/J36.

Open: Hall & Gardens: 26 Mar - 29 Oct: daily except Sat, Hall: 11am - 4pm. Gardens: 10.30am - 5.30pm. Food Hall/Courtyard Café/Gift Shop: open daily from 1 Mar - 22 Dec, 10.30am - 5.30pm (30 Oct - 22 Dec: closes at 4pm). Motor Museum open daily from Mar - 17 Dec, 10.30am - 4.45pm.

Admission: Hall, Gardens & Lakeland Motor Museum: Adult £10.50, Child £6, Conc £9.75, Family £29. Gardens/Park: Adult £5.70, Child £3, Conc £5, Family £15.50.

ℹ️ No photography in house. 📷 Holker Food Hall – produce from the estate. ✴️ ▼ ♿ Visitors alight at entrance. WCs. ● Licensed. 🍽 ✏️ By arrangement. 🅿️ 75 yds from Hall. ■ 🐾 In grounds, on leads (not formal gardens).

HUTTON-IN-THE-FOREST 🏠

PENRITH, CUMBRIA CA11 9TH

www.hutton-in-the-forest.co.uk

Tel: 017684 84449 **Fax:** 017684 84571 **e-mail:** info@hutton-in-the-forest.co.uk

Owner: Lord Inglewood **Contact:** Edward Thompson

The home of Lord Inglewood's family since 1605. Built around a medieval pele tower with 17th, 18th and 19th century additions. Fine collections of furniture, paintings, ceramics and tapestries. Outstanding grounds with terraces, topiary, walled garden, dovecote and woodland walk through magnificent specimen trees.

Location: OS Ref. NY460 358. 6m NW of Penrith & 2 ½ m from M6/J41 on B5305.

Open: 12 Apr - 1 Oct: Weds, Thurs, Suns & BH Mons, 12.30 - 4pm (last entry). Tearoom: As house: 11am - 4.30pm. Gardens & Grounds: Apr - Oct, daily except Sats, 11am - 5pm.

Admission: House, Gardens & Grounds: Adult £5.50, Child £3.50, Family £15. Gardens & Grounds: Adult £3.50, Child £1.

ℹ️ Picnic area. 📷 Gift stall. ▼ By arrangement. ♿ Partial. ● ✏️ Obligatory (except Jul/Aug & BHs). 🅿️ ■ 🐾 On leads. ☎️ Tel for details.

LANERCOST PRIORY ⚌
Brampton, Cumbria CA8 2HQ
Tel: 01697 73030
Owner: English Heritage   **Contact:** Visitor Operations Team
This Augustinian priory was founded c1166. The nave of the church, which is intact and in use as the local parish church, contrasts with the ruined chancel, transepts and priory buildings. Free audio tour.
Location: OS Ref. NY556 637. 2m NE of Brampton. 1m N of Naworth Castle.
Open: 1 Apr - 30 Sept: daily, 10am - 5pm. 1 - 31 Oct: Thur - Mon, 10am - 4pm.
Admission: Adult £2.60, Child £1.30, Conc. £2. Groups (11+): 15% discount.
⬚ ♿ Ground floor. 🅾Inclusive. 🅿Limited. ■ ■ ♿ Tel for details.

LEVENS HALL 🏠   *See page 413 for full page entry.*

MIREHOUSE 🏠
KESWICK, CUMBRIA CA12 4QE
www.mirehouse.com

Tel: 017687 72287   **e-mail:** info@mirehouse.com
Owner: James Fryer-Spedding   **Contact:** Janaki Spedding
Melvyn Bragg described Mirehouse as '*Manor from Heaven*'. Hunter Davies wrote '*Not to be missed*' and Simon Jenkins in *The Times* said '*It is the Lake District with its hand on its heart*'. Literary house linked with Tennyson and Wordsworth. Natural playgrounds and lakeside walk.
Location: OS Ref. NY235 284. Beside A591, 3¹/₂ m N of Keswick. Good bus service.
Open: Apr - Oct: Gardens & Tearoom: daily, 10am - 5.30pm. House: Suns & Weds (also Fris in Aug), 2 - 5pm (4.30pm last entry). Groups (20+) welcome by appointment.
Admission: House & Garden: Adult £4.80, Child £2.40, Family (2+4) £14.40. Gardens only: Adult £2.40, Child £1.20. Pre-booked 10% discount for groups (20+).
ⓘNo photography in house. ♿ ⬛ 🅵By arrangement. 🅿Limited. ■
🐕Dogs on leads only.

MUNCASTER CASTLE 🏠   *See page 414 for full page entry.*

PENRITH CASTLE ⚌
Penrith, Cumbria
Tel: 0161 242 1400
Owner: English Heritage   **Contact:** The North West Regional Office
This 14th century castle, set in a park on the edge of the town, was built to defend Penrith against repeated attacks by Scottish raiders.
Location: OS Ref. NY513 299. Opposite Penrith railway station. W of the town centre. Fully visible from the street.
Open: Park: 7.30am - 9pm (4.30pm winter).
Admission: Free.
ⓘWC 🐕On leads.

RYDAL MOUNT & GARDENS
RYDAL, CUMBRIA LA22 9LU
www.rydalmount.co.uk

Tel: 01539 433002 **Fax:** 01539 431738 **e-mail:** info@rydalmount.co.uk
Owner: Rydal Mount Trustees   **Contact:** Peter & Marian Elkington
Nestling in the beautiful fells between Lake Windermere and Rydal Water, lies the 'most beloved home' of William Wordsworth from 1813 - 1850. *Experience* the splendid historic home of Wordsworth's descendants; *Enjoy* the beautiful terraced gardens landscaped by the poet; *Feel* the peaceful relaxed 'romantic' atmosphere; *The freedom* of wandering through this 'spot of more perfect and enjoyable beauty' as wrote Dr Thomas Arnold.
Location: OS Ref. NY364 063. 1¹/₂ m N of Ambleside on A591 Grasmere Road.
Open: Mar - Oct: daily, 9.30am - 5pm. Nov - Feb: daily except Tues, 10am - 4pm.
Admission: House & Garden: Adult £5, Child £2, Student £3.75, OAP £4, Family £12. Garden only: £2.50. Free parking. Reciprocal discount ticket with Dove Cottage & Wordsworth House (on full paying admission only).
ⓘNo inside photography. ⬚ ♿Partial. 🅵By arrangement. 🅿Limited. ■
🐕In grounds, on leads. Guide dogs only in house. ❋

SIZERGH CASTLE & GARDEN 🍃
NR KENDAL, CUMBRIA LA8 8AE
www.nationaltrust.org.uk

Tel/Fax: 01539 560951   **e-mail:** sizergh@nationaltrust.org.uk
Owner: The National Trust   **Contact:** Property Administrator
The Strickland family has lived here for more than 750 years. The impressive 14th century tower was extended in Tudor times, with some of the finest Elizabethan carved overmantels in the country. Contents include good English and French furniture and family portraits. A visit culminates in the important and impressive Inlaid Chamber. The castle is surrounded by gardens of beauty and interest, including the Trust's largest limestone rock garden; good autumn colour. Large estate; walks leaflet available in shop.
Location: OS Ref. SD498 878. 3¹/₂ m S of Kendal, NW of the A590/A591 interchange.
Open: Castle: 2 Apr - 29 Oct: Sun - Thur & BHs except Good Fri, 1 - 5pm. Tearoom as Castle. Garden/Shop: 12 noon - 5pm. Last admission 5pm.
Admission: Adult £6.20, Child £3.10, Family £15.50, Family (1 + 3). Groups (15+): £5.20 by arrangement (not on BHs). Garden only: Adult £4, Child £2.
⬚ 🅵 ♿ Partial. ⬛ 🅿Limited for coaches. ■ ♿ Tel for details.

STAGSHAW GARDEN

Ambleside, Cumbria LA22 0HE

Tel /Fax: 015394 46027 **e-mail:** stagshaw@nationaltrust.org.uk

Owner: The National Trust

This woodland garden contains a fine collection of azaleas and rhododendrons, planted to give good blends of colour under thinned oaks on the hillside; also magnolias, camellias and embothriums. Adjacent to the woods are Skelghyll Woods which offer delightful walks and access to the fells beyond.

Location: OS Ref. NY380 029. ½ m S of Ambleside on A591. Ferry Waterhead ½ m.

Open: 1 Apr - 30 Jun: daily, 10am - 6.30pm. Colours best Apr - Jun. Jul - end Oct: by appointment through the property office at St Catherines, Patterdale Road, Windermere LA23 1NH.

Admission: £2, by honesty box.

♿ Unsuitable. **P** Limited. ✉

STOTT PARK BOBBIN MILL ⌗

Low Stott Park, Nr Newby Bridge, Cumbria LA12 8AX

Tel: 01539 531087

Owner: English Heritage **Contact:** Visitor Operations Team

When this working mill was built in 1835 it was typical of the many mills in the Lake District which grew up to supply the spinning and weaving industry in Lancashire but have since disappeared. A remarkably opportunity to see a demonstration of the machinery and techniques of the Industrial Revolution. Steam days: Tues - Thurs.

Location: OS Ref. SD373 883. Near Newby Bridge on A590.

Open: 1 Apr - 30 Sept: daily, 10am - 5pm (Steam days, Mon - Thurs). 1 - 31 Oct: Tue - Sat, 10am - 5pm (Steam days Tue - Thur). Last admission 1hr before closing.

Admission: Adult £4.10, Child £2.10, Conc. £3.10, Family £10.30. Groups: discount for groups (11+).

▣ ♿ Ground floor. WC. Ⓕ Free. **P** ✉ ✉

HELENA THOMPSON MUSEUM

Park End Road, Workington, Cumbria CA14 4DE

Tel: 01900 326254 **Fax:** 01900 326320 **e-mail:** helena.thompson@allerdale.gov.uk

Owner: Allerdale Borough Council **Contact:** Heritage & Arts Unit

The museum is housed in a fine listed mid-Georgian building. Displays include pottery, silver, glass, furniture and dress collection.

Location: OS Ref. NY007 286. Corner of A66, Ramsey Brow & Park End Road.

Open: All year: Mon - Wed, 10am - 4pm. Sat & Sun, 12 noon - 4pm.

Admission: Free.

WORDSWORTH HOUSE

Main Street, Cockermouth, Cumbria CA13 9RX

Tel: 01900 824805 **Opening Info:** 01900 820884 **Fax:** 01900 820883

e-mail: wordsworthhouse@nationaltrust.org.uk

www: nationaltrust.org.uk

Owner: The National Trust **Contact:** The Custodian

This Georgian town house was the birthplace of William Wordsworth. Imaginatively presented as the home of the Wordsworth family in the 1770s, the house offers a lively and participative visit with costumed living history. The garden, with terraced walk overlooking the River Derwent, has been restored to its 18th century appearance.

Location: OS Ref. NY118 307. Main Street, Cockermouth.

Open: 28 Mar - 28 Oct: Tues - Sat, open BHs Mons and Mons in Jul and Aug. 11am - 4.30pm. Last entry 4pm. Shop: 6 Mar - 23 Dec: Mon - Sat, 10am - 5pm.

Admission: Adult £4.70, Child £2.60, Family £13.50. Pre-booked groups (15+): Adult £3.70, Child £1.60.

ℹ No photography. ▣ ♿ Partial. WCs. Ⓕ By arrangement only. ✉ ✉ Guide dogs only.

civil wedding venues
see page 562

TOWNEND

TROUTBECK, WINDERMERE, CUMBRIA LA23 1LB

www.nationaltrust.org.uk

Tel: 01539 432628 **e-mail:** townend@nationaltrust.org.uk

Owner: The National Trust **Contact:** The Custodian

An exceptional relic of Lake District life during past centuries. Originally a 'statesman' (wealthy yeoman) farmer's house, built about 1626. Townend contains carved woodwork, books, papers, furniture and fascinating implements of the past which were accumulated by the Browne family who lived here from 1626 until 1943.

Location: OS Ref. NY407 023. 3m SE of Ambleside at S end of Troutbeck village. 1m from Holehird, 3m N of Windermere.

Open: 25 Mar - 29 Oct: Wed - Sun & BH Mons, 1 - 5pm or dusk if earlier. Last entry 4.30pm.

Admission: Adult £3.60, Child £1.80, Family £9. No reduction for groups which must be pre-booked.

♿ Unsuitable for wheelchairs. ✉ Ⓧ Tel for details.

Hill Top Garden.

NT Photographic Library: Matthew Antrobus

English Life Publication Ltd

LEIGHTON HALL 🏛

www.leightonhall.co.uk

MAP 10

Owner:
Richard Gillow
Reynolds Esq

▶ **CONTACT**

Mrs C S Reynolds
Leighton Hall
Carnforth
Lancashire LA5 9ST

Tel: 01524 734474
Fax: 01524 720357

e-mail: info@
leightonhall.co.uk

▶ **LOCATION**

OS Ref. SD494 744

9m N of Lancaster,
10m S of Kendal,
3m N of Carnforth.
1¹/₂ m W of A6.
3m from M6/A6/J35,
signed from J35A.

Rail: Carnforth
Station 3m.

Bus: The Carnforth
Connect (line 1) bus
from Carnforth Railway
Station stops at the
gates of Leighton Hall
(info 01524 734311).

Air: Manchester
Airport 65m.

Taxi: Carnforth Radio
Taxis, 01524 732763.

CONFERENCE/FUNCTION

ROOM	SIZE	MAX CAPACITY
Music Room	24' x 21'6'	80
Dining Rm		30
Other		80

Leighton Hall is one of the most beautifully sited houses in the British Isles, situated in a bowl of parkland, with the whole panorama of the Lakeland Fells rising behind. The Hall's neo-gothic façade was superimposed on an 18th century house, which, in turn, had been built on the ruins of the original medieval house. The present owner is descended from Adam d'Avranches who built the first house in 1246.

The whole house is, today, lived in by the Reynolds family whose emphasis is put on making visitors feel welcome in a family home.

Mr Reynolds is also descended from the founder of Gillow and Company of Lancaster. Connoisseurs of furniture will be particularly interested in the many 18th century Gillow pieces, some of which are unique. Fine pictures, clocks, silver and *objéts d'art* are also on display.

Leighton Hall is home to a varied collection of Birds of Prey. These birds are flown daily during opening hours, weather permitting.

GARDENS

The main garden has a continuous herbaceous border with rose covered walls, while the Walled Garden contains flowering shrubs, a herb garden, and an ornamental vegetable garden with a caterpillar maze. Beyond is the Woodland Walk where wild flowers abound from early spring.

🖼 ❋ ℹ No photography in house. Gifts & unusual plants for sale.

▼ Product launches, conferences, seminars, filming, garden parties. Outdoor events include: overland driving, archery and clay pigeon shooting. Wedding receptions, buffets, lunches and dinners.

♿ Partial. WC. Visitors may alight at the entrance to the Hall. Ground floor only.

🍴 Booking essential for group catering, menus on request.

👤 Obligatory. By prior arrangement owner may meet groups. The 45 minute tour includes information on the property, its gardens and history. House and flying display tour time: 2 hrs.

🅿 Ample for cars and coaches.

🏫 School programme: all year round. Choice of Countryside Classroom, Victorian Leighton or Local History. Sandford Award for Heritage Education winner in 1983 and 1989.

🐕 In Park, on leads.

❋ For booked groups & functions.

🔔 An unusual, but spectacular venue, Leighton Hall is a fairytale choice.

🛡 Visit website for details.

▶ OPENING TIMES

Summer

May - September
Tue - Fri (also
BH Sun & Mon)
2 - 5pm.

August only:
Tue - Fri and Sun
(also BH Mon)
12.30 - 5pm.

NB. Booked groups (25+) at any time, all year by arrangement.

Winter

1 October - 30 April
Open to booked groups (25+).

▶ ADMISSION

Summer

House, Garden & Birds
  Adult £5.50
  Child (5-12yrs)....... £4.00
  Student/OAP £5.00
  Family (2+3) £17.00
Grounds & Birds....... £3.50
Groups (25+)
  Adult £4.50
  Child (5-12yrs)....... £3.50
  Family (2+3) £17.00

Child under 5yrs, Free

Grounds only
(after 4.30pm)
  Per person £1.50

Winter

As above but groups by appointment only.

Pre-booked Candlelit Tours Nov - Jan.

Note: The owners reserve the right to close or restrict access to the house and grounds for special events, or at any other time without prior notice.

BLACKBURN CATHEDRAL

Cathedral Close, Blackburn, Lancashire BB1 5AA

Tel: 01254 503090 **Fax:** 01254 689666   **Contact:** Pauline Rowe

On an historic Saxon site in town centre. The 1826 Parish Church dedicated as the Cathedral in 1977 with new extensions to give a spacious and light interior.

Location: OS Ref. SD684 280. 9m E of M6/J31, via A59 and A677. City centre.

Open: Daily, 9am - 5pm. Sun services: at 8am, 9am, 10.30am and 4pm. Catering: Tues - Fri, 10am - 2.30pm or Sat by arrangement.

Admission: Free. Donations invited.

BROWSHOLME HALL 🏠

Clitheroe, Lancashire BB7 3DE

Tel: 01254 827160 **Fax:** 01254 827161 **e-mail:** rrp@browsholme.co.uk **www.**browsholme.co.uk

Owner/Contact: Robert Parker

Ancestral home of the Parker Family, with a major collection of oak furniture and portraits, arms and armour, stained glass and many unusual antiquities from the civil war to a fragment of a Zeppelin. Browsholme, pronounced 'Brusom', lies in the Forest of Bowland, 4miles north west of Clitheroe and was built in 1507 by Edmund Parker. The façade stills remains the 'H' shape of the original house with later Queen Anne and Regency additions when the house was refurbished by Thomas Lister Parker a noted antiquarian and patron of artists such as Turner and Northcote, and remodelled by Webster.

Location: OS Ref. SD683 452. 5m NW of Clitheroe off B6243.

Open: 17 Apr, 21 May with Garden and Craft Fair. 27 - 30 May, 24 June - 7 July & 19 - 30 Aug: Tues - Sun (open BH Mons). Groups welcome by appointment.

Admission: Adult £4.50, Child £1.50, OAP £4.

GAWTHORPE HALL 🍂

Padiham, Nr Burnley, Lancashire BB12 8UA

Tel: 01282 771004 **Fax:** 01282 776663 **e-mail:** gawthorpehall@nationaltrust.org.uk

Owner: The National Trust   **Contact:** Property Office

The house was built in 1600-05, and restored by Sir Charles Barry in the 1850s. Barry's designs have been re-created in the principal rooms. Gawthorpe was the home of the Shuttleworth family, and the Rachel Kay-Shuttleworth textile collections are on display in the house, private study by arrangement. Collection of portraits on loan from the National Portrait Gallery.

Location: OS Ref. SD806 340. M65/J8. On E outskirts of Padiham, ³/₄ m to house on N of A671. Signed to Clitheroe, then signed from 2nd set of traffic lights.

Open: Hall & Tearoom: 1 Apr - 29 Oct: daily except Mons & Fris, open Good Fri & BH Mons, 1 - 5pm. Last adm. 4.30pm. Garden: All year: daily, 10am - 6pm.

Admission: Hall: Adult £3, Conc. £1.50, accompanied Child Free (prices may change). Garden: Free. Groups must book. Prices subject to confirmation in Mar 2006.
♿ Please ring in advance. 📷 🐕 In grounds on leads. ❋

HALL I'TH'WOOD

off Green Way, off Crompton Way, Bolton BL1 8UA

Tel: 01204 332370

Owner: Bolton Metropolitan Borough Council   **Contact:** Liz Shaw

Late medieval manor house with 17/18th century furniture, paintings and decorative art.

Location: OS Ref. SD724 116. 2m NNE of central Bolton. 1/4 m N of A58 ring road between A666 and A676 crossroads.

Open: Apr - Oct: Wed - Sun, 11am - 5pm. Nov - Mar: Sats & Suns, 11am - 5pm.

Admission: Adult £2, Child/Conc. £1, Family £5.

Rufford Old Hall.

HEATON HALL

HEATON PARK, MANCHESTER M25 2SW

www.manchestergalleries.org

Tel: 0161 773 1085/235 8888 **Fax** 0161 235 8899

Owner: Manchester City Council

Heaton Hall is a magnificent James Wyatt house, built for Sir Thomas Egerton in 1772, and is one of Manchester's most impressive and important buildings. It is set in the middle of Heaton Park's rolling landscape, designed by William Eames and John Webb, much of which has recently been restored with the help of a Heritage Lottery Fund grant. The principal rooms of the Hall have been beautifully restored and are used to display furniture, paintings and other decorative arts appropriate to the late 18th century.

Location: OS Ref. SD833 044. NW Manchester, close to M60/J19. Main entrance off St Margaret's Road, off Bury Old Road - A665.

Open: 8 Apr - 1 Oct: Wed - Sun & BH Mons (Closed Good Friday), 11am - 5.30pm.

Admission: Free.

ⓘNo photography. Ⓣ ⒼPartial. WCs. ⓔ ⒡By arrangement.
ⓅAmple, but limited for coaches. ⬛ ⒽIn grounds, on leads. ▲

HOGHTON TOWER ⓐ

HOGHTON, PRESTON, LANCASHIRE PR5 0SH

www.hoghtontower.co.uk

Tel: 01254 852986 **Fax:** 01254 852109 **e-mail:** mail@hoghtontower.co.uk

Owner: Sir Bernard de Hoghton Bt **Contact:** Office

Hoghton Tower, home of 14th Baronet, is one of the most dramatic looking houses in northern England. Three houses have occupied the hill site since 1100 with the present house re-built by Thomas Hoghton between 1560 - 1565. Rich and varied historical events including the Knighting of the Loin 'Sirloin' by James I in 1617.

Location: OS Ref. SD622 264. M65/J3. Midway between Preston & Blackburn on A675.

Open: Jul, Aug & Sept: Mon - Thur, 11am - 4pm. Suns, 1 - 5pm. BH Suns & Mons excluding Christmas & New Year. Group visits by appointment all year.

Admission: Gardens & House tours: Adult £6, Child/Conc. £5, Family £18. Gardens, Shop & Tearoom only: £3. Children under 5yrs Free. Private tours by arrangement (25+) £6, OAP £5.

🄾 ⓉConferences, wedding receptions. ⓖUnsuitable. ⓔ ⒡Obligatory. Ⓟ ⬛ ✳

LEIGHTON HALL ⓐ *See page 421 for full page entry.*

MANCHESTER CATHEDRAL

Manchester M3 1SX

Tel: 0161 833 2220 **Fax:** 0161 839 6218 **www**.manchestercathedral.co.uk

In addition to regular worship and daily offices, there are frequent professional concerts, day schools, organ recitals, guided tours and brass-rubbing. The cathedral contains a wealth of beautiful carvings and has the widest medieval nave in Britain. Visitor Centre and restaurant.

Location: OS Ref. SJ838 988. Manchester.

Open: Daily. Visitor Centre: Mon - Sat, 10am - 4.30pm.

Admission: Donations welcome.

ⓘVisitor Centre. ✳

MARTHOLME

Great Harwood, Blackburn, Lancashire BB6 7UJ

Tel: 01254 886463

Owner: Mr & Mrs T H Codling **Contact:** Miss P M Codling

Part of medieval manor house with 17th century additions and Elizabethan gatehouse.

Location: OS Ref. SD753 338. 2m NE of Great Harwood off A680 to Whalley.

Open: Please telephone for details.

Admission: £5.

RUFFORD OLD HALL ✤
RUFFORD, Nr ORMSKIRK, LANCASHIRE L40 1SG
www.nationaltrust.org.uk

Tel: 01704 821254   **Fax:** 01704 823823   **e-mail:** ruffordhall@nationaltrust.org.uk

Owner: The National Trust   **Contact:** The Property Manager

One of the finest 16th century buildings in Lancashire. The magnificent Great Hall contains an intricately carved movable screen and suits of armour, and is believed to have hosted Shakespeare. Collections of weapons, tapestries and oak furniture are found in the Carolean Wing and attractive gardens contain sculptures and topiary.

Location: OS Ref. SD463 160. 7m N of Ormskirk, in village of Rufford on E side of A59.

Open: 25 Mar - 29 Oct: Mon - Wed, Sat, Sun. Also Garden, Shop and Restaurant, 1 Nov - 17 Dec: Wed - Fri, Sat, Sun, with free entry to all visitors (except for special events). Grounds, Shop & Restaurant: 11 - 5pm . House: 1 - 5pm. Last adm. 4.30pm.

Admission: House & Garden: Adult £4.90, Child £2.50, Family £12.00. Garden only: Adult £2.80, Child £1.30. Booked groups (15+) by arrangement: Adult £3.10, Child £1.30.

ℹ No photography in house. ◻ ⊤ ♿ Partial. ⬛ Licensed. 🎭 By arrangement. 🎧 ℗ Limited for coaches. ⬛ ⬛ In grounds, on leads. ⬛ ⬛ Tel for details.

SAMLESBURY HALL
Preston New Road, Samlesbury, Preston PR5 0UP

Tel: 01254 812010 **Fax:** 01254 812174

Owner: Samlesbury Hall Trust   **Contact:** Mrs S Jones - Director

Built in 1325, the hall is an attractive black and white timbered manor house set in extensive grounds. Weddings & events welcome. Antiques & crafts all year.

Location: OS Ref. SD623 305. N side of A677, 4m WNW of Blackburn.

Open: All year: daily except Sats: 11am - 4.30pm.

Admission: Adult £3, Child £1. Free entry to Restaurant and Police Museum.

SMITHILLS HALL HISTORIC HOUSE
Smithills Dean Road, Bolton BL7 7NP

Tel: 01204 332377   **e-mail:** office@smithills.org

Owner: Bolton Metropolitan Borough Council   **Contact:** Michelle Monks

14th century manor house with Tudor panelling. Stuart furniture. Stained glass.

Location: OS Ref. SD699 119. 2m NW of central Bolton, ½ m N of A58 ringroad.

Open: Apr - Sept: Tue - Sat, 11am - 5pm, Sun, 2 - 5pm. Last adm. 4.15pm. Closed Mon except BH Mons.

Admission: Adult £3, Conc. £1.75, Family (2+3) £7.75.

TOWNELEY HALL ART GALLERY & MUSEUMS
Burnley BB11 3RQ

Tel: 01282 424213   **Fax:** 01282 436138   **www.**towneleyhall.org.uk

Owner: Burnley Borough Council   **Contact:** Miss Susan Bourne

House dates from the 14th century with 17th and 19th century modifications. Collections include oak furniture, 18th and 19th century paintings. There is a Museum of Local Crafts and Industries.

Location: OS Ref. SD854 309. ½ m SE of Burnley on E side of Todmorden Road (A671).

Open: All year: daily except Fris, 12 noon - 5pm. Closed Christmas - New Year.

Admission: Small charge. Guided tours: Tues - Thur afternoons or as booked for groups.

◻ ♿ WC. 🎭 ⬛ ⬛ Tel for details.

TURTON TOWER
Chapeltown Road, Turton BL7 0HG

Tel: 01204 852203   **Fax:** 01204 853759   **e-mail:** turtontower@mus.lancscc.gov.uk

Owner: The Trustees of Turton Tower (run by Lancashire County Museums Service)

Contact: Fiona Jenkins

Country house based on a medieval tower, extended in the 16th, 17th and 19th centuries.

Location: OS Ref. SD733 153. On B6391, 4m N of Bolton.

Open: Feb & Nov: Suns, 1 - 4pm. May - Sept: Mon - Thur, 11am - 5pm; Sat & Sun, 1 - 5pm. Apr: Sat - Wed, 1 - 5pm. Mar & Oct: Mon - Wed, 1 - 5pm. Sats & Suns 1 - 4pm.

Admission: Adult £3, Child Free, OAP £1.50.

VICTORIA BATHS
MANCHESTER'S WATER PALACE, HATHERSAGE ROAD, Nr LONGSIGHT, MANCHESTER M13 0FE
www.victoriabaths.org.uk

Tel: 0161 224 2020   **Fax:** 0161 224 0707   **e-mail:** info@victoriabaths.org.uk

Owner: Manchester City Council (licensed to Victoria Baths Trust)

Contact: Diana Terry

Victoria Pool and Turkish Baths is the most ornate Edwardian Baths in the country and won the first BBC *Restoration* series. See its period splendour for yourself before work begins; guided tours tell you about its history, the campaign to save the building and the plans for its future.

Location: OS Ref. SD857 959. 1½ m S of Manchester City Centre, near Manchester Royal Infirmary and St. Mary's Hospitals. Hathersage Road crosses A34, Upper Brook Street & B5117 Oxford Road.

Open: Public Open Days are held on the first Sunday of each month from Apr - Sept: 12 noon - 4pm. Heritage Open Days: 7 - 10 Sept incl.: 11am - 5pm (admission free).

Admission: £1. Group tours can be arranged at any time. £3 - £5 per head.

◻ ⊤ ♿ Partial. ⬛ Tearoom/Café. 🎭 ℗ ⬛ ⬛ Guide dogs only.

WARTON OLD RECTORY ⌗
Warton, Carnforth, Lancashire

Tel: 0161 242 1400

Owner: English Heritage   **Contact:** The North West Regional Office

A rare medieval stone house with remains of the hall, chambers and domestic offices.

Location: OS Ref. SD499 723. At Warton, 1m N of Carnforth on minor road off A6.

Open: 1 Apr - 31 Mar: daily, 10am - 6pm (5pm Oct & 4pm Nov - Mar). Closed 24 - 26 Dec & 1 Jan.

Admission: Free.

⬛ On leads. ✳

special events
see page 571

The Courtyard at Speke Hall by Joseph Nash.

©National Trust Photographic Library/John Hammond

CROXTETH HALL & COUNTRY PARK

Liverpool, Merseyside L12 0HB

Tel: 0151 228 5311 Fax: 0151 228 2817

Owner: Liverpool City Council   **Contact:** Mrs Irene Vickers

Ancestral home of the Molyneux family. 500 acres country park. Special events and attractions most weekends.

Location: OS Ref. SJ408 943. 5m NE of Liverpool city centre.

Open: Parkland: daily throughout the year. Hall, Farm & Garden: Easter - Sept: daily, 10.30am - 5pm. Telephone for exact dates.

Admission: Parkland: Free. Hall, Farm & Garden: prices on application.

LIVERPOOL CATHEDRAL

Liverpool, Merseyside L1 7AZ

Tel: 0151 709 6271 Fax: 0151 702 7292

Owner: The Dean and Chapter   **Contact:** Jenny Moran

Sir Giles Gilbert Scott's greatest creation. Built last century from local sandstone with superb glass, stonework and major works of art, it is the largest cathedral in Britain.

Location: OS Ref. SJ354 893. Central Liverpool, ¹/₂ S of Lime Street Station.

Open: All year: daily, 8am - 6pm. Sun services: 8am, 10.30am, 3pm, 4pm. Weekdays: 8am & 5.30pm, also 12.05pm on Fri. Sats: 8am & 3pm.

Admission: Donation. Lift to Tower and Embroidery Exhibition: £4.25 (concessions available). Family Ticket (2+3) £10.

LIVERPOOL METROPOLITAN
CATHEDRAL OF CHRIST THE KING

Liverpool, Merseyside L3 5TQ

Tel: 0151 709 9222 Fax: 0151 708 7274 e-mail: enquiries@metcathedral.org.uk
www.liverpoolmetrocathedral.org.uk

Owner: Roman Catholic Archdiocese of Liverpool   **Contact:** Rt Rev P Cookson

Modern circular cathedral with spectacular glass by John Piper and numerous modern works of art. Extensive earlier crypt by Lutyens. Grade II* listed.

Location: OS Ref. SJ356 903. Central Liverpool, ¹/₂ m E of Lime Street Station.

Open: 8am - 6pm (closes 5pm Suns in Winter). Sun services: 8.30am, 10am, 11am & 7pm. Weekday services: 8am, 12.15pm & 5.15pm. Sats, 9am & 6.30pm. Gift Shop & Restaurant: Mon - Sat, 10am - 5pm; Sun, 11am - 4pm.

Admission: Donation.

🖥 ♿ Except crypt. WCs. 🍴 🅉 By arrangement. 🅿 Ample for cars. ▦
🐕 Guide dogs only. ✳

MEOLS HALL 🏛

Churchtown, Southport, Merseyside PR9 7LZ

Tel: 01704 228326 Fax: 01704 507185 e-mail: events@meolshall.com
www.meolshall.com

Owner: The Hesketh Family   **Contact:** Pamela Whelan

17th century house with subsequent additions. Interesting collection of pictures and furniture. Tithe Barn available for wedding ceremonies and receptions all year.

Location: OS Ref. SD365 184. 3m NE of Southport town centre in Churchtown. SE of A565.

Open: 14 Aug - 14 Sept: daily, 2 - 5pm.

Admission: Adult £4, Child £1. Groups only (25+) £9 (inclusive of full afternoon tea). ▼ Wedding ceremonies and receptions now available in the Tithe Barn.

♿ ♥ 🅿 ▲ ▦

SPEKE HALL GARDEN & ESTATE 🌿

The Walk, Liverpool L24 1XD

Tel: 0151 427 7231 Fax: 0151 427 9860 Info Line: 08457 585702
www.spekehall.org.uk www.nationaltrust.org.uk

Owner: The National Trust   **Contact:** The Property Manager

One of the most famous half-timbered houses in the country.

Location: OS Ref. SJ419 825. North bank of the Mersey, 6m SE of city centre. Follow signs for Liverpool John Lennon airport.

Open: House: 22 Mar - 29 Oct: Daily except Mons & Tues (open BH Mons), 1 - 5pm; 4 Nov - 3 Dec: Sats & Suns only, 1 - 4.30pm. Grounds: Daily, 11am - 5.30pm. Check for winter opening.

Admission: Adult £6.50, Child £3.50, Family £19.50. Grounds only: Adult £3.50, Child £1.80, Family £10.

Warkworth Castle, Northumberland © English Heritage Photo Library/Graeme Peacock

co.durham

northumberland

north east

Rugged and Roman – the North East region of Britain offers the visitor a wealth of history going back to the Roman occupation. But it does not just live in the past – 'The Angel of the North', the huge sculpture alongside the A1 at Gateshead, the regeneration of Tyneside, and the Millennium Garden Project at Alnwick Castle are evidence of the area's enthusiasm for the modern alongside the ancient. As well as visiting the magnificent fortress castles at Alnwick, Bamburgh and Chillingham, time should be set aside to explore properties such as Wallington, with its exceptional murals depicting Northumbrian history, and The Lady Waterford Murals at Ford, with its 1860 biblical murals.

tyne and wear

© www.mikekipling.com

MAP 10

THE BOWES MUSEUM

www.bowesmuseum.org.uk

Owner:
The Bowes Museum
Charitable Trust

▶ **CONTACT**

Barnard Castle
Co. Durham
DL12 8NP

Tel: 01833 690606
Fax: 01833 637163

e-mail: info@
bowesmuseum.org.uk

▶ **LOCATION**
OS Ref. NZ055 164

¼ m E of Market Place
in Barnard Castle,
just off A66.

John and Joséphine Bowes had a passion for collecting beautiful works of art which led to the opening of The Bowes Museum in 1892.

The wonderful 19th century building was purposefully designed as a museum. Its spacious galleries, flooded with natural light, house one of the finest collections in the country.

The outstanding collection contains over 30,000 items of art, ceramics, furniture and textiles and many other treasures, covering a wide range of European styles and periods. Included within the collection are works by Canaletto, El Greco and Goya. However the most loved piece is the magical Silver Swan automaton which continues to perform each day.

The romantic museum story is retold as you wander through over twenty fascinating galleries. An audio guide and variety of interactive elements are available to inform and entertain as you go on a journey of discovery through the house of treasures.

The world class art is complemented by a series of major exhibitions. Highlights for 2006 include 'Turner: Tours of Durham & Richmondshire' which runs from the 28 January to 14 May'.

The Bowes Museum is situated in the historic market town of Barnard Castle in the heart of picturesque Teesdale. Set in large grounds of beautiful parkland and garden, you can enjoy a quiet stroll or explore the unusual tree trail whatever the season.

Open all year, The Bowes Museum also offers the acclaimed Café Bowes, Museum Shop, and Coffee Bar, making this wonderful attraction a great day out for all.

▶ **OPENING TIMES**

All year
Daily
11am - 5pm.

Closed 25/26 December &
1 January.

▶ **ADMISSION**

Adult £7.00
Child (under 16yrs) .... Free
Conc. £6.00
Disabled carers .... Free

Groups (15+)
Adult £6.00
Conc. £5.00

Palatial rooms and acres of parkland. Individual tailored packages for wedding or corporate function.

Access to most of the Museum including gift shop, café and WCs. Wheelchair facility is available. Signposted disabled parking and entrance.

Licensed.

By arrangement.

Ample.

In grounds.

Tel for details.

© Heritage House Group Ltd

MAP 10

RABY CASTLE

www.rabycastle.com

The magnificent Raby Castle, in the beautiful North Pennines, has been home to Lord Barnard's family since 1626 when it was purchased by his ancestor, Sir Henry Vane the Elder, the eminent statesman and politician. The Castle was built mainly in the 14th century by the Nevill family on the site of an earlier manor house. The Nevills continued to live at Raby until 1569 when, after the failure of the Rising of the North, the Castle and its land were forfeited to the Crown.

The impressive Entrance Hall (below) was created into its present dramatic form by John Carr for the 2nd Earl of Darlington, to celebrate the coming of age of his heir in 1787. The roof was raised to enable carriages to pass through the Hall and the result is a stunning interior in the Gothic Revival

style. Raby's treasures include an important collection of Meissen porcelain, fine furniture and artworks, including paintings by Munnings, De Hooch, Reynolds, Van Dyck, Batoni, Teniers, Amigoni, Vernet and De Vos.

There is a 200-acre Deer Park with two lakes and a beautiful walled garden with formal lawns, ancient yew hedges and an ornamental pond. The 18th century stable block contains a horse-drawn carriage collection including the State Coach last used by the family for the Coronation of Edward VII in 1902.

Part of the Stables has been converted into a gift shop and tearooms, where the former stalls have been incorporated to create an atmospheric setting. A Woodland Adventure Playground is close to the picnic area.

Owner:
The Lord Barnard

▶ **CONTACT**
Clare Owen/
Catherine Turnbull
Raby Castle
Staindrop
Darlington
Co. Durham DL2 3AH

Tel: 01833 660202
Fax: 01833 660169

e-mail: admin@
rabycastle.com

▶ **LOCATION**
OS Ref. NZ129 218

On A688, 1m N of Staindrop. 8m NE of Barnard Castle, 12m WNW of Darlington.

Rail: Darlington Station, 12m.

Air: Durham Tees Valley Airport, 20m.

© Heritage House Group Ltd

   Film locations, product launches, corporate events, fairs & concerts. Raby Estates venison & game sold in tearooms. Soft fruit when in season. Lectures on Castle, its contents, gardens & history. No photography or video filming is permitted inside. Colour illustrated guidebook and DVD on sale. Christmas Shop in Stable Yard throughout December.

Partial. WC.

Licensed.

By arrangement for groups (20+) or min charge. VIP & Standard Castle Tours available. Tour time 1½ hrs.

P By arrangement (20+), weekday am. Primary & junior £3; Secondary £3.50.

Guide dogs welcome. On leads in park only.

 Throughout Summer. Tel for details or see website.

▶ **OPENING TIMES**

Castle
May, June & September Weds & Suns. July & August: Daily except Sats. BHs (incl. Easter): Sat - Mon. 1- 5pm.

Park & Gardens
May - Sept: Sun - Fri & BH Sats, 11am - 5.30pm (5pm in Sept).

▶ **ADMISSION**

Castle, Park & Gardens
Adult £9.00
Child (5-15yrs) £4.00
OAP/Student £8.00
Family (2+3) £25.00
Groups (12+)
Adult £8.00
Child (5-15yrs). £3.00
OAP/Student £7.00

Park & Gardens
Adult £4.00
Child (5-15yrs) £2.50
OAP/Student £3.50
Family (2+3) £12.50
Groups (12+)
Adult £3.50
Child (5-15yrs). £2.50
OAP/Student £3.00

Season Tickets available.

Guided Tours*
VIP Private Guided Tour (incl. reception, tea/coffee in entrance hall) Easter - Sept, Mon - Fri mornings.
20+ £12.00
or min charge £240.00

Standard Guided Tours*
Castle, Park & Gardens (min group 20+ or £160). Easter - Sept, Mon - Fri.
Adult £8.00
Child (5 - 15) £3.00
OAP/Student £7.00
*Please book in advance.

Free RHS access.

AUCKLAND CASTLE 🏛

BISHOP AUCKLAND, CO. DURHAM DL14 7NR

www.auckland-castle.co.uk

Tel: 01388 601627 **Fax:** 01388 609323 **e-mail:** auckland.castle@zetnet.co.uk

Owner: Church Commissioners   **Contact:** The Manager

Principal country residence of the Bishops of Durham since Norman times and now the official residence of the present day Bishops. The Chapel, reputedly one of the largest private chapel in Europe, was originally the 12th century banquet hall. Chapel and State Rooms including the Throne Room, Long Dining Room and King Charles Dining Room are open to the public. Access to the adjacent Bishop's Park with its 18th century Deer House.

Location: OS Ref. NZ214 303. Bishop Auckland, N end of town centre.

Open: Easter Mon - 30 Sept: Suns & Mons (plus Weds in August) , 2 - 5pm. Last admission 4.30pm. The managment reserves the right to close the castle to visitors.

Admission: Adult £4, Child/Conc. £3. Child (up to 12yrs) Free. Special openings for groups (25+).

ⓘExhibitions. No indoor photography. 🖾 🎊Wedding receptions, functions. ♿ Wheelchair access to chapel, ground floor. WC. Stairwalker available for upstairs staterooms by prior arrangement. 🍴 🅿 🔲 🐕Guide dogs only.

AUCKLAND CASTLE DEER HOUSE ⌗

Bishop Auckland, Durham

Tel: 0191 2691200

Owner: English Heritage   **Contact:** The Regional Office

A charming building erected in 1760 in the Park of the Bishops of Durham so that the deer could shelter and find food.

Location: OS Ref. NZ216 305. In Bishop Auckland Park, just N of town centre on A689. About 500 yds N of the castle.

Open: Park: 1 Apr - 28 Mar: 10am - 6pm (4pm Oct - Mar). Closed 24 - 26 Dec & 1 Jan.

Admission: Free.

🐕On leads.

BARNARD CASTLE ⌗

Barnard Castle, Castle House, Durham DL12 9AT

Tel: 01833 638212

Owner: English Heritage   **Contact:** Visitor Operations Team

The substantial remains of this large castle stand on a rugged escarpment overlooking the River Tees. Parts of the 14th century Great Hall and the cylindrical 12th century tower, built by the Baliol family can still be seen. Sensory garden.

Location: OS92, NZ049 165. In Barnard Castle.

Open: 1 Apr - 30 Sept: daily, 10am - 6pm. 1 - 31 Oct: daily, 10am - 4pm. 1 Nov - 31 Mar: Thur - Mon, 10am - 4pm. Closed 24 - 26 Dec & 1 Jan.

Admission: Adult £3.40, Child £1.70, Conc. £2.60. 15% discount for groups (11+).

ⓘWCs in town. 🖾 ♿Grounds. 🐕In grounds, on leads. ✳

🛡Tel for details.

BINCHESTER ROMAN FORT

Bishop Auckland, Co. Durham

Tel: 01388 663089 / 0191 3834212 (outside opening hours)

Owner: Durham County Council   **Contact:** Deborah Anderson

Once the largest Roman fort in Co Durham, the heart of the site has been excavated.

Location: OS92 Ref. NZ210 312. 1¹/₂ m N of Bishop Auckland, signposted from A690 Durham - Crook and from A688 Spennymoor - Bishop Auckland roads.

Open: 15 Apr - 30 Sept: daily, 11am - 5pm.

Admission: Adult £2, Child/Conc. £1.

THE BOWES MUSEUM   *See page 428 for full page entry.*

CROOK HALL & GARDENS

Sidegate, Durham DH1 5SZ

Tel: 0191 3848028

Owner: Keith & Maggie Bell   **Contact:** Mrs Maggie Bell

Medieval manor house set in rural landscape on the edge of Durham city.

Location: OS Ref. NZ274 432. ¹/₂ m N of city centre.

Open: 28 May - 10 Sept, Easter weekend & BHs: Wed - Sun, 1 - 5pm.

Admission: Adult £4.50, Conc. £4, Family £12.

DERWENTCOTE STEEL FURNACE ⌗

Newcastle, Durham

Tel: 0191 2691200 (Mon - Fri)

Owner: English Heritage   **Contact:** Regional Office

Built in the 18th century it is the earliest and most complete authentic steel making furnace to have survived.

Location: OS Ref. NZ131 566. 10m SW of Newcastle N of the A694 between Rowland's Gill and Hamsterley.

Open: By arrangement.

Admission: Free.

🅿 🐕On leads in restricted areas.

DURHAM CASTLE

Palace Green, Durham DH1 3RW

Tel: 0191 3343800 **Fax:** 0191 3343801   **Contact:** Mrs Julie Marshall

Durham Castle, founded in the 1070s, with the Cathedral is a World Heritage Site.

Location: OS Ref. NZ274 424. City centre, adjacent to cathedral.

Open: Mar - Sept: 10am - 12 noon & 2 - 4.30pm. Oct - Mar: Mon, Wed, Sat & Sun 2 - 4pm.

Admission: Adult £5, OAP £2.50, Family (2+2) £10. Guide book £2.50.

DURHAM CATHEDRAL
Durham DH1 3EH
Tel: 0191 3864266 **Fax:** 0191 3864267 **e-mail:** enquiries@durhamcathedral.co.uk
                                                Contact: Miss A Heywood
A World Heritage Site. Norman architecture. Burial place of St Cuthbert and the Venerable Bede.
Location: OS Ref. NZ274 422. Durham city centre.
Open: Summer: 12 June 3 Sept: 9.30am - 8pm. Open only for worship and private prayer: All year: Mon - Sat, 7.30am - 9.30am and Suns, 7.45am - 12.30pm. The Cathedral is closed to visitors during evening recitals and concerts. Visitors welcome Mon - Sat, 9.30 - 5pm, Suns 12.30 - 3.30pm.
Admission: Cathedral: Request a donation of min. £4. Tower: Adult £2.50, Child (under 16) £1.50, Family £7. Monk's Dormitory: Adult £1, Child 30p, Family £2.10. AV: Adult £1.10, Child 30p, Family £2.

EGGLESTONE ABBEY ♯
Durham
Tel: 0191 2691200
Owner: English Heritage   **Contact:** The Regional Office
Picturesque remains of a 12th century abbey, located in a bend of the River Tees. Substantial parts of the church and abbey buildings remain.
Location: OS Ref. NZ062 151. 1½ m SE of Barnard Castle on minor road off B6277.
Open: Daily, 10am - 6pm.
Admission: Free.
🅿 🐕 On leads.

ESCOMB CHURCH
Escomb, Bishop Auckland DL14 7ST
Tel: 01388 602861
Owner: Church of England   **Contact:** Mrs E Kitching (01388 662265)
Saxon church dating from the 7th century built of stone from Binchester Roman Fort.
Location: OS Ref. NZ189 302. 3m W of Bishop Auckland.
Open: Summer: 9am - 8pm. Winter: 9am - 4pm. Key available from 22 Saxon Green, Escomb.
Admission: Free.

FINCHALE PRIORY ♯
Finchdale Priory, Brasside, Newton Hall DH1 5SH
Tel: 0191 269 1200/386 6528
Owner: English Heritage   **Contact:** Regional Office
These beautiful 13th century priory remains are located beside the curving River Wear.
Location: OS Ref. NZ297 471. 4½ m NE of Durham.
Open: Telephone key keeper on 0191 386 6528.
Admission: Free.
ℹ WC. 🚻 (Not managed by EH.) 🅿 (charge) on S side of river. 🐕 On leads.

RABY CASTLE 🏛
See page 429 for full page entry.

THE WEARDALE MUSEUM & HIGH HOUSE CHAPEL
Ireshopeburn, Co. Durham DL13 1EY
Tel: 01388 517433 **e-mail:** dtheatherington@ormail.co.uk
                                                Contact: D T Heatherington
Small folk museum and historic chapel. Includes 1870 Weardale cottage room, John Wesley room and local history displays.
Location: OS Ref. NZ872 385. Adjacent to 18th century Methodist Chapel.
Open: Easter & May - Sept: Wed - Sun & BH, 2 - 5pm. Aug: daily, 2 - 5pm.
Admission: Adult £1.50, Child 50p.

special events
see page 571

Kite flying at Raby Castle.

MAP 14

ALNWICK CASTLE 🏛

www.alnwickcastle.com

Set in a stunning landscape designed by Capability Brown, Alnwick Castle was voted one of Britain's Finest Castles in 2003 and is the family home of the Duke of Northumberland.

Owned by his family since 1309, this beautiful castle originally built to defend England from the Scots now appeals to visitors of all ages from across the world.

Considered to be one of the finest castles in England, and known as the 'Windsor of the North', this has been the home of the Percy family for nearly 700 years. In the 1760s it was transformed from a fortification into a family home for the First Duke and Duchess. Today it is a tourist attraction of real significance, full of historical facts, fun and entertainment.

Visitors walking through the gates, set in massive stone walls, enter one of the most stunning castles in Europe. The Keep sits magnificently in the spacious grounds, with its medieval towers housing the castle's 14th century dungeon and the entrance to the remarkable State Rooms. Decorated and furnished by the Fourth Duke in the mid 19th century, the rooms are a splendid example of Italian Renaissance design, with beautiful carved and gilded ceilings, marble fireplaces, and walls hung with original paintings by Canaletto, Van Dyck and Titian.

Within the grounds are the museums and towers that tell the story of the Northumberland Fusiliers from 1674 to the present day, local archaeology of the area, the Percy Tenantry Volunteers and a new exhibition on siege craft.

Adding to the magic of this castle and making it so popular for children [of all ages!] is the fact that the castle was used as a film location and was portrayed as "Hogwarts" for the films 'Harry Potter and the Philosopher's Stone' and 'Harry Potter and the Chamber of Secrets'.

Owner:
His Grace the Duke of Northumberland

▶ **CONTACT**

Alnwick Castle
Estate Office
Alnwick
Northumberland
NE66 1NQ

Tel: 01665 510777
Info: 01665 511100
Group bookings:
01665 510777
Fax: 01665 510876
e-mail: enquiries@
alnwickcastle.com

▶ **LOCATION**

OS Ref. NU187 135

In Alnwick 1¹/₂ m
W of A1.
From London 6hrs,
Edinburgh 2hrs,
Chester 4hrs,
Newcastle 40mins
North Sea ferry
terminal 30mins.

Bus: From bus station
in Alnwick.

Rail: Alnmouth
Station 5m.
Kings Cross, London
3¹/₂hrs.

Air: Newcastle 40mins.

▶ **OPENING TIMES**

5 April - 29 October
Daily, 10am - 5pm.
State Rooms open
at 11am (last admission to
State Rooms 4.30pm).

▶ **ADMISSION**

Castle

Adult	£8.50
Child (6-15yrs)	£3.50
Child (under 5yrs)	Free
Conc.	£7.50

Booked Groups
(14+, tel 01665 510777)

Adult	£7.50
Child	£1.50

Weekly & Season
Tickets available.

HHA members free access
to Castle only.

CONFERENCE/FUNCTION

ROOM	SIZE	MAX CAPACITY
The Guest Hall	100' x 30'	300

ℹ️ Conference facilities. Fashion shows, fairs, filming, parkland for hire. No photography inside the castle. No unaccompanied children.

👜 Wedding receptions.

♿ Unsuitable.

☕ Coffee, light lunches and teas.

🅿️ 500 cars and 12 coaches.

📖 Guidebook and worksheet, special rates for children and teachers.

🐕 Guide dogs only. 🎭 Tel for details.

Jarrold Colour Publications

MAP 14

BAMBURGH CASTLE

www.bamburghcastle.com

Bamburgh Castle is the home of the Armstrong family. The earliest reference to Bamburgh shows the craggy citadel to have been a royal centre by AD 547. Recent archaeological excavation has revealed that the site has been occupied since prehistoric times.

The Norman Keep has been the stronghold for nearly nine centuries, but the remainder has twice been extensively restored, initially by Lord Crewe in the 1750s and subsequently by the 2nd Lord Armstrong at the beginning of the 20th century. This Castle was the first to succumb to artillery fire – that of Edward IV.

The public rooms contain many exhibits,

including the loan collections of armour from HM Tower of London, the John George Joicey Museum, Newcastle-upon-Tyne and other private sources, which complement the castle's armour. Porcelain, china, jade, furniture from many periods, oils, water-colours and a host of interesting items are all contained within one of the most important buildings of Britain's national heritage.

VIEWS

The views from the ramparts are unsurpassed and take in Holy Island, the Farne Islands, one of Northumberland's finest beaches and, landwards, the Cheviot Hills.

Owner:
Trustees Lord Armstrong
dec'd.

▶ CONTACT

The Administrator
Bamburgh Castle
Bamburgh
Northumberland
NE69 7DF

Tel: 01668 214515

Fax: 01668 214060

e-mail: bamburghcastle
@aol.com

▶ LOCATION
OS Ref. NU184 351

42m N of
Newcastle-upon-Tyne.
20m S of Berwick upon
Tweed. 6m E of Belford
by B1342 from
A1 at Belford.

Bus: Bus service
200 yards.

Rail: Berwick-upon-
Tweed 20m.

Taxi: J Swanston
01289 306124.

Air: Newcastle-upon-
Tyne 45m.

▶ OPENING TIMES

11 March -
31 October
Daily, 11am - 5pm.
Last entry 4.30pm.

Tours by arrangement
at any time.

▶ ADMISSION
Summer
Adult £6.00
Child (6 - 15yrs) £2.50
OAP £5.00
Groups *
Adult £4.50
Child (6 - 15yrs) £2.00
OAP £3.50

Winter
Group rates only quoted.

ℹ️ Filming. No photography in house.

📷

♿ Limited access. WC.

Tearooms for light refreshments. Groups can book.

By arrangement at any time, min charge out of hours £150.

🅿️ 100 cars, coaches park on tarmac drive at entrance.

Welcome. Guide provided if requested, educational pack.

🐕 Guide dogs only.

🔔

❄️

MAP 14

CHILLINGHAM CASTLE

www.chillingham-castle.com

Owner:
Sir Humphry
Wakefield Bt

▶ CONTACT

Administrator
Chillingham Castle
Northumberland
NE66 5NJ

Tel: 01668 215359
Fax: 01668 215463

e-mail: enquiries@
chillingham-castle.com

▶ LOCATION
OS Ref. NU062 258

45m N of Newcastle
between A697 & A1.
2m S of B6348
at Chatton.
6m SE of Wooler.

Rail: Alnmouth
or Berwick.

Rated 4-star (amongst the top 100!) in Simon Jenkins' *England's Thousand Best Houses*.

This remarkable castle, the home of Sir Humphry Wakefield Bt, with its alarming dungeons has, as now and since the 1200s, been continuously owned by the family of the Earls Grey and their relations. You will see active restoration of complex masonry, metalwork and ornamental plaster as the great halls and state rooms are gradually brought back to life with tapestries, arms and armour as of old and even a torture chamber.

At first a 12th century stronghold, Chillingham became a fully fortified castle in the 14th century (see the original 1344 Licence to Crenellate). Wrapped in the nation's history it occupied a strategic position as a fortress during Northumberland's bloody border feuds, often besieged and at many times enjoying the patronage

of royal visitors. In Tudor days there were additions but the underlying medieval character has always been retained. The 18th and 19th centuries saw decorative extravagances including the lake, garden and grounds laid out by Sir Jeffrey Wyatville, fresh from his triumphs at Windsor Castle. These contrast the prehistoric Wild Cattle in the park beyond (a separate tour).

GARDENS

With romantic grounds, the castle commands breathtaking views of the surrounding countryside. As you walk to the lake you will see, according to season, drifts of snowdrops, daffodils or bluebells and an astonishing display of rhododendrons. This emphasises the restrained formality of the Elizabethan topiary garden, with its intricately clipped hedges of box and yew. Lawns, the formal gardens and woodland walks are all fully open to the public.

▶ OPENING TIMES
Summer

Easter
1 May - 30 September
Daily except some Sats,
Castle, 1 - 5pm,
Grounds & Tearoom,
12 noon - 5pm

Winter

October - April: Groups
any time by appointment.
All function activities
available.

▶ ADMISSION
Summer

Adult	£6.75
Child (under 16yrs)	£3.00
Child (under 5yrs)	£1.00
Conc	£5.50

Groups (10+)

Per person	£6.00
Tour	£25.00

Corporate entertainment, lunches, drinks, dinners, wedding ceremonies and receptions.

Partial.

Booked meals for up to 100 people.

By arrangement.

Avoid Lilburn route, coach parties welcome by prior arrangement. Limited for coaches.

Apartments.

Civil Wedding Licence.

CONFERENCE/FUNCTION

ROOM	MAX CAPACITY
King James I Room	
Great Hall	100
Minstrels' Hall	60
2 x Drawing Room	
Museum	
Tea Room	35
Lower Gallery	
Upper Gallery	

ALNWICK CASTLE 🏰   *See page 432 for full page entry.*

AYDON CASTLE ⌗

Corbridge, Northumberland NE45 5PJ

Tel: 01434 632450

Owner: English Heritage   **Contact:** Visitor Operations Team

One of the finest fortified manor houses in England, dating from the late 13th century. Its survival, intact, can be attributed to its conversion to a farmhouse in the 17th century.

Location: OS Ref. NZ002 663. 2m NE of Corbridge, on minor road off B6321 or A68.

Open: 14 Apr - 30 Sept: Thur - Mon, 10am - 5pm.

Admission: Adult £3.40, Child £1.70, Conc. £2.60. 15% discount for groups (11+).

ⓘ WC. 🖻 ♿ Ground floor & grounds. 🅿 ❚ 🐕 In grounds, on leads. ⓥ Tel for details.

BAMBURGH CASTLE 🏰   *See page 432 for full page entry.*

Belsay Hall.
© English Heritage

© English Heritage Photo Library

© English Heritage Photo Library

BELSAY HALL, CASTLE & GARDENS ⌗

BELSAY, Nr PONTELAND, NORTHUMBERLAND NE20 0DX

www.english-heritage.org.uk/visits

Tel: 01661 881636   **Fax:** 01661 881043

Owner: English Heritage   **Contact:** Visitor Operations Team

Belsay is one of the most remarkable estates in Northumberland's border country. The buildings, set amidst 30 acres of magnificent landscaped gardens, have been occupied by the same family for nearly 600 years. The gardens, created largely in the 19th century, are a fascinating mix of the formal and the informal with terraced gardens, a rhododendron garden, magnolia garden, mature woodland and even a winter garden. The buildings comprise a 14th century castle, a manor house and Belsay Hall, an internationally famous mansion designed by Sir Charles Monck in the 19th

century in the style of classical buildings he had encountered during a tour of Greece.

Location: OS87, NZ088 785. In Belsay 14m (22.4 km) NW of Newcastle on SW of A696. 7m NW of Ponteland. Nearest airport and station is Newcastle.

Open: 1 Apr - 31 Oct: daily, 10am - 5pm (4pm Oct). 1 Nov - 31 Mar: Thur - Mon, 10am - 4pm. Closed 24 - 26 Dec and 1 Jan.

Admission: Adult £5.50, Child £2.80, Conc. £4.10, Family £13.80. 15% discount for groups (11+).

🖻 ♨ 🍴 ♿ Partial. WC. 🍴 During summer & weekends Apr - Oct. 🅿 ❚ 🐕 In grounds, on leads. ✳ ⓥ Tel for details.

BERWICK BARRACKS ⌗

The Parade, Berwick-upon-Tweed, Northumberland TD15 1DF

Tel: 01289 304493

Owner: English Heritage   **Contact:** Visitor Operations Team

Among the earliest purpose built barracks, these have changed very little since 1717. They house an exhibition 'By Beat of Drum', which recreates scenes such as the barrack room from the life of the British infantryman, the Museum of the King's Own Scottish Borderers and the Borough Museum with fine art, local history exhibition and other collections.

Location: OS Ref. NT994 535. On the Parade, off Church Street, Berwick town centre.

Open: 1 Apr - 30 Sept: daily, 10am - 5pm. 1 - 31 Oct: daily, 10am - 4pm. 1 Nov - 31 Mar: telephone for details. Closed 24 - 26 Dec and 1 Jan.

Admission: Adult £3.30, Child £1.70, Conc. £2.50. 15% discount for groups (11+).

🖻 🅿 In town. ❚ 🐕 In grounds, on leads. ✳ ⓥ Tel for details.

BERWICK RAMPARTS ⌗

Berwick-upon-Tweed, Northumberland

Tel: 0191 269 1200

Owner: English Heritage   **Contact:** The Regional Office

A remarkably complete system of town fortifications consisting of gateways, ramparts and projecting bastions built in the 16th century.

Location: OS Ref. NT994 535. Surrounding Berwick town centre on N bank of River Tweed.

Open: Any reasonable time.

Admission: Free.

✳

BRINKBURN PRIORY

Long Framlington, Morpeth, Northumberland NE65 8AF

Tel: 01665 570628

Owner: English Heritage   **Contact:** Visitor Operations Staff

This late 12th century church is a fine example of early gothic architecture, almost perfectly preserved, and is set in a lovely spot beside the River Coquet.

Location: OS Ref. NZ116 984. 4$^{1}/_{2}$ m SE of Rothbury off B6344 5m W of A1.

Open: 14 Apr - 30 Sept: Thur - Mon, 10am - 5pm.

Admission: Adult £2.70, Child £1.40, Conc. £2. 15% discount for groups (11+).

On leads. Tel for details.

CAPHEATON HALL

Newcastle-upon-Tyne NE19 2AB

Tel/Fax: 01830 530253

Owner/Contact: J Browne-Swinburne

Built for Sir John Swinburne in 1668 by Robert Trollope, an architect of great and original talent.

Location: OS Ref. NZ038 805. 17m NW of Newcastle off A696.

Open: By written appointment only.

CHERRYBURN – THOMAS BEWICK BIRTHPLACE

Station Bank, Mickley, Stocksfield, Northumberland NE43 7DD

Tel: 01661 843276   www.nationaltrust.org.uk

Owner: The National Trust   **Contact:** The Administrator

Birthplace of Northumbria's greatest artist, wood engraver and naturalist, Thomas Bewick, b1753. The Museum explores his famous works. Farmyard animals, picnic area, garden.

Location: OS Ref. NZ075 627. 11m W of Newcastle on A695 (400yds signed from Mickley Square). 1$^{1}/_{2}$ m W of Prudhoe.

Open: 18 Mar - 29 Oct: daily except Weds, 11am - 5pm. Last admission 4.30pm. Booked groups 20 Mar - 27 Oct, Mon - Fri, 10am - 4pm.

Admission: Adult £3.50, Child £1.75. Child under 5yrs Free. Groups (20+): £3.

Some steps. WC. Morning coffee for booked groups. Tel for details.

© English Heritage Photo Library

CHESTERS ROMAN FORT & MUSEUM

CHOLLERFORD, Nr HEXHAM, NORTHUMBERLAND NE46 4EP

Tel: 01434 681379

Owner: English Heritage   **Contact:** Visitor Operations Team

The best preserved example of a Roman cavalry fort in Britain, including remains of the bath house on the banks of the River North Tyne. The museum houses a fascinating collection of Roman sculpture and inscriptions.

Location: OS87, NY913 701. 1$^{1}/_{2}$ m from Chollerford on B6318.

Open: 1 Apr - 30 Sept: daily, 9.30am - 6pm. 1 Oct - 31 Mar: daily, 10am - 4pm. Closed 24 - 26 Dec and 1 Jan.

Admission: Adult £3.80, Child £1.90, Conc. £2.90. 15% discount for groups (11+).

Grounds. WC. Summer only. In grounds, on leads. Tel for details.

CHILLINGHAM CASTLE

See page 434 for full page entry.

CHIPCHASE CASTLE

Wark, Hexham, Northumberland NE48 3NT

Tel: 01434 230203   **Fax:** 01434 230740

Owner/Contact: Mrs P J Torday

The castle overlooks the River North Tyne and is set in formal and informal gardens. One walled garden is used as a nursery specialising in unusual perennial plants.

Location: OS Ref. NY882 758. 10m NW of Hexham via A6079 to Chollerton. 2m SE of Wark.

Open: Castle: 1 - 28 Jun: daily, 2 - 5pm. Tours by arrangement at other times. Castle Gardens & Nursery: Easter - 31 Jul, Thur - Sun & BH Mons, 10am - 5pm.

Admission: Castle £5, Garden £3, concessions available. Nursery Free.

Unsuitable. Obligatory.

CORBRIDGE ROMAN TOWN

Corbridge, Northumberland NE45 5NT

Tel: 01434 632349

Owner: English Heritage   **Contact:** Visitor Operations Team

A fascinating series of excavated remains, including foundations of granaries with a grain ventilation system. From artefacts found, which can be seen in the site museum, we know a large settlement developed around this supply depot.

Location: OS Ref. NY983 649. $^{1}/_{2}$ m NW of Corbridge on minor road, signposted for Corbridge Roman Site.

Open: 1 Apr - 30 Sept: daily, 10am - 5.30pm. 1 - 31 Oct: daily, 10am - 4pm. 1 Nov - 31 Mar: Sat & Sun, 10am - 4pm. Closed 24 - 26 Dec and 1 Jan.

Admission: Adult £3.80, Child £1.90, Conc. £2.90. 15% discount for groups (11+).

Partial. Inclusive. Limited for coaches. In grounds, on leads. Tel for details.

CRAGSIDE

Rothbury, Morpeth, Northumberland NE65 7PX

Tel: 01669 620150   **Fax:** 01669 620066   www.nationaltrust.org.uk

Owner: The National Trust   **Contact:** Property Manager

Revolutionary home of Lord Armstrong, Victorian inventor and landscape genius, Cragside sits on a rocky crag high above the Debdon Burn. Crammed with ingenious gadgets, it was the first house in the world lit electrically. Armstrong constructed 5 lakes, one of Europe's largest rock gardens and planted over 7 million trees and shrubs. Today, this magnificent estate can be explored on foot and by car and provides one of the last shelters for the endangered red squirrel. Children will love the tall trees, tumbling streams, adventure play area and labyrinth.

Location: OS Ref. NU073 022. $^{1}/_{2}$ m NE of Rothbury on B6341.

Open: Estate & Gardens: 1 Apr - 29 Oct & BH Mons, Tue - Sun, 10.30am - 7pm; 1 Nov - 17 Dec, Wed - Sun: 11am - 4pm. House closed in 2006.

Admission: Estate & Gardens: Adult £6.50, Child (5-17yrs) £3, Family (2+3) £16. Groups (15+) £5.50.

Partial. In grounds, on leads. Tel for details.

DUNSTANBURGH CASTLE

c/o Grieves Garage, Embleton, Northumberland NE66 3TT

Tel: 01665 576231

Owner: The National Trust   **Guardian:** English Heritage

    Contact: Visitor Operations Team

An easy, but bracing, coastal walk leads to the eerie skeleton of this wonderful 14th century castle sited on a basalt crag, rearing up more than 100 feet from the waves crashing on the rocks below. The surviving ruins include the large gatehouse, which later became the keep, and curtain walls.

Location: OS75, NU258 220. 8m NE of Alnwick.

Open: 1 Apr - 30 Sept: daily, 10am - 5pm. 1 - 31 Oct, daily, 10am - 4pm. 1 Nov - 31 Mar: Thur - Mon, 10am - 4pm. Dates & times may vary, please tel property for details.

Admission: Adult £2.70, Child £1.40, Conc. £2. 15% discount for groups (11+).

None. In grounds, on leads.

EDLINGHAM CASTLE

Edlingham, Alnwick, Northumberland

Tel: 0191 269 1200

Owner: English Heritage   **Contact:** The Regional Office

Set beside a splendid railway viaduct this complex ruin has defensive features spanning the 13th and 15th centuries.

Location: OS Ref. NU115 092. At E end of Edlingham village, on minor road off B6341 6m SW of Alnwick.

Open: Any reasonable time.

Admission: Free.

In grounds, on leads.

ETAL CASTLE ⌗

Cornhill-on-Tweed, Northumberland

Tel: 01890 820332

Owner: English Heritage   **Contact:** Visitor Operations Team

A 14th century castle located in the picturesque village of Etal. Award-winning exhibition about the castle, Border warfare and the Battle of Flodden.

Location: OS75, NT925 394. In Etal village, 10m SW of Berwick.

Open: 14 Apr - 30 Sept: daily, 11am - 4pm.

Admission: Adult £3.40, Child £1.70, Conc. £2.60, Family £8.50. 15% discount for groups (11+).

ℹ️WC in village. 🅾️ ♿Partial. WC. 🔊Inclusive. 🅿️ ⬛ 🐕In grounds, on leads. 🎫Tel for details.

HERTERTON HOUSE GARDENS

Hartington, Cambo, Morpeth, Northumberland NE61 4BN

Tel: 01670 774278

Owner/Contact: C J "Frank" Lawley

One acre of formal garden in stone walls around a 16th century farmhouse, including a small topiary garden, physic garden, flower garden, fancy garden and gazebo.

Location: OS Ref. NZ022 881. 2m N of Cambo, just off B6342, Signposted (brown).

Open: 1 Apr - 30 Sept: Mons, Weds, Fri - Sun, 1.30 - 5.30pm.

Admission: Adult £2.80, Child (5-15yrs) £1. Groups by arrangement.

♿ ♿Unsuitable. 📷By arrangement. 🅿️ Limited for coaches. ⬛ Guided tours for adult students only. 🐕

HOUSESTEADS ROMAN FORT ⌗ 🌿

NR HAYDON BRIDGE, NORTHUMBERLAND NE47 6NN

Tel: 01434 344363

Owner: The National Trust   **Guardian:** English Heritage
                              Contact: Visitor Operations Team

Perched high on a ridge overlooking open moorland, this is the best known part of the Wall. The fort covers five acres and there are remains of many buildings, such as granaries, barrack blocks and gateways. A small exhibition displays altars, inscriptions and models.

Location: OS Ref. NY790 687. 2m NE of Bardon Mill.

Open: 1 Apr - 30 Sept: daily, 10am - 6pm. 1 Oct - 31 Mar: daily, 10am - 4pm. Closed 24 - 26 Dec and 1 Jan. (Subject to confirmation by English Heritage, see www.english-heritage.org.uk.)

Admission: Adult £3.60, Child £1.80, Conc. £2.70, Family £9. 15% discount for groups (11+).

🅾️ 🅿️Charge. ⬛ 🐕In grounds, on leads. 🐕

HOWICK HALL GARDENS

Howick, Alnwick, Northumberland NE66 3LB

Tel: 01665 577285   **e-mail:** estateoffice@howickuk.com

www.howickhallgardens.org

Owner: Howick Trustees Ltd   **Contact:** Mrs D Spark

Romantically landscaped grounds surrounding the house in a little valley, with rare rhododendrons and flowering shrubs and trees. New Arboretum for 2006.

Location: OS Ref. NU249 175. 6m NE of Alnwick. 1m E of B1339.

Open: 1 Apr - 31 Oct: daily 12 noon - 6pm.

Admission: Adult £4, Child (under 16yrs) Free, OAP £3. Season tickets available.

♿ Grounds partial. WC. ⬛ 🅿️ New car park. 🐕Guide dogs only.

KIRKLEY HALL GARDENS

Ponteland, Northumberland NE20 0AQ

Tel: 01670 841200   **Fax:** 01661 860047   **Contact:** Reception

Over 9 acres of beautiful gardens incorporating a Victorian walled garden, woodland walks, sunken garden and wildlife areas and ponds.

Location: OS Ref. NZ150 772. 10m from the centre of Newcastle upon Tyne. 2½ m N of Ponteland on byroad to Morpeth.

Open: All year: daily, 10am - 4pm.

Admission: Free.

🌿

THE LADY WATERFORD HALL & MURALS

Ford, Berwick-upon-Tweed TD15 2QA

Tel: 01890 820503   **Fax:** 01890 820384

Owner: Ford & Etal Estates   **Contact:** Dorien Irving

Commissioned in 1860 the walls of this beautiful building are decorated with beautiful murals depicting Bible stories.

Location: OS Ref. NT945 374. On the B6354, 9m from Berwick-upon-Tweed, midway between Newcastle-upon-Tyne and Edinburgh, close to the A697.

Open: 27 Mar - 29 Oct: daily, 10.30am - 12.30pm & 1.30 - 5.30pm. By arrangement with the caretaker during winter months. Note: the Hall may be closed on occasion for private functions. Please telephone prior to travelling.

Admission: Adult £2, Child 75p, Child (under 12yrs) Free, Conc. £1.50. Groups by arrangement.

LINDISFARNE CASTLE 🌿

Holy Island, Berwick-upon-Tweed, Northumberland TD15 2SH

Tel: 01289 389244   **www.**nationaltrust.org.uk

Owner: The National Trust   **Contact:** Property Manager

Built in 1550 to protect Holy Island harbour from attack, the castle was restored and converted into a private house for Edward Hudson by Sir Edwin Lutyens in 1903.

Location: OS Ref. NU136 417. On Holy Island, ¾ m E of village, 6m E of A1 across causeway. Usable at low tide.

Open: 18 - 26 Feb & 17 - 25 Feb 2007: daily (incl BH Mons). 18 Mar - 29 Oct: daily except Mon. 26 - 29 Dec: Tue - Fri. Times vary.

Admission: Adult £5, Child £2.50, Family £12.50. Garden only: Adult £1, Child Free. Out of hours group tours (10+) by arrangement £6pp.

🅾️ NT Shop (in Main St). 🐕In grounds, on leads.

Wallington – The Kitchen.

© English Heritage Photo Library

LINDISFARNE PRIORY ⌗
HOLY ISLAND, BERWICK-UPON-TWEED TD15 2RX

Tel: 01289 389200

Owner: English Heritage   **Contact:** Visitor Operations Team

The site of one of the most important early centres of Christianity in Anglo-Saxon England. St Cuthbert converted pagan Northumbria, and miracles occurring at his shrine established this 11th century priory as a major pilgrimage centre. The evocative ruins, with the decorated 'rainbow' arch curving dramatically across the nave of the church, are still the destination of pilgrims today. The story of Lindisfarne is told in an exhibition which gives an impression of life for the monks, including a reconstruction of a monk's cell.

Location: OS Ref. NU126 418. On Holy Island, check tide times.

Open: 1 Apr - 30 Sept: daily, 9.30am - 5pm. 1 - 31 Oct: daily, 9.30am - 4pm. 1 Nov - 31 Mar: Sat - Mon, 10am - 2pm. Closed 24 - 26 Dec and 1 Jan.

Admission: Adult £3.70, Child £1.90, Conc. £2.80. 15% discount for groups (11+).

▢ Partial. Disabled parking. **P** Charge. ▦ ✖ Restricted. ❉ ♨ Tel for details.

NORHAM CASTLE ⌗
Norham, Northumberland

Tel: 01289 304493

Owner: English Heritage   **Contact:** Visitor Operations Team

Set on a promontory in a curve of the River Tweed, this was one of the strongest of the Border castles, built c1160.

Location: OS75, NT907 476. 6m SW of Berwick.

Open: Please telephone for details.

Admission: Free.

♿ Partial. ✖ On leads.

PRESTON TOWER 🏠
Chathill, Northumberland NE67 5DH

Tel: 01665 589227

Owner/Contact: Major T Baker-Cresswell

The Tower was built by Sir Robert Harbottle in 1392 and is one of the few survivors of 78 pele towers listed in 1415. The tunnel vaulted rooms remain unaltered and provide a realistic picture of the grim way of life under the constant threat of "Border Reivers". Two rooms are furnished in contemporary style and there are displays of historic and local information. Visitors are welcome to walk in the grounds which contain a number of interesting trees and shrubs. A woodland walk to the natural spring from which water is now pumped up to the Tower for the house and cottages.

Location: OS Ref. NU185 253. Follow Historic Property signs on A1 7m N of Alnwick.

Open: 14 Apr - 30 Sept: Thurs - Mon, 10am - 6pm.

Admission: Adult £1.50, Child 50p, Conc. £1. Groups £1.

♿ Grounds. ✖ ❉

PRUDHOE CASTLE ⌗
Prudhoe, Northumberland NE42 6NA

Tel: 01661 833459

Owner: English Heritage   **Contact:** Visitor Operations Team

Set on a wooded hillside overlooking the River Tyne are the extensive remains of this 12th century castle including a gatehouse, curtain wall and keep. Small exhibition and video presentation.

Location: OS88 Ref. NZ092 634. In Prudhoe, on minor road N from A695.

Open: 14 Apr - 30 Sept: Thur - Mon, 10am - 5pm.

Admission: Adult £3.40, Child £1.70, Conc. £2.60. 15% discount for groups (11+).

ℹ WC. ▢ ♿ Partial. ☕ **P** ▦ ✖ In grounds, on leads. ♨ Tel for details.

SEATON DELAVAL HALL 🏠
SEATON SLUICE, WHITLEY BAY, NORTHUMBERLAND NE26 4QR

Tel: 0191 237 1493 / 0191 237 0786   **e-mail:** lordhastings@onetel.net.uk

Owner: Lord Hastings   **Contact:** Mrs Mills

The home of Lord and Lady Hastings, half a mile from Seaton Sluice, is the last and most sensational mansion designed by Sir John Vanbrugh, builder of Blenheim Palace and Castle Howard. It was erected 1718 - 1728 and comprises a high turreted block flanked by arcaded wings which form a vast forecourt. The centre block was gutted by fire in 1822, but was partially restored in 1862 and again in 1959 - 1962 and 1999 - 2000. The remarkable staircases are a visual delight, and the two surviving rooms are filled with family pictures and photographs and royal seals spanning three centuries as well as various archives. This building is used frequently for concerts and charitable functions. The East Wing contains immense stables in ashlar stone of breathtaking proportions. Nearby are the Coach House with farm and passenger vehicles, fully documented, and the restored ice house with explanatory sketch and description. There are beautiful gardens with herbaceous borders, rose garden, rhododendrons, azaleas, laburnum walk, statues, and a spectacular parterre by internationally famous Jim Russell, also a unique Norman Church.

Location: OS Ref. NZ322 766. 1/2m from Seaton Sluice on A190, 3m from Whitley Bay.

Open: May & Aug BH Mons; Jun - Sept: Weds & Suns, 2 - 6pm.

Admission: Adult £4, Child £1, OAP £3.50, Student £2. Groups (20+): Adult £3, Child/Student £1.

▢ ♿ Partial. WC. ☕ **P** Free. ▦ ✖ In grounds, on leads.

NT Photographic Library/Andrea Jones

WALLINGTON ❦

CAMBO, MORPETH, NORTHUMBERLAND NE61 4AR

www.nationaltrust.org.uk

Tel: 01670 773600 **Fax** 01670 774420 **e-mail:** wallington@nationaltrust.org.uk

Owner: The National Trust **Contact:** The Estate Office

Dating from 1688, the much-loved home of the Trevelyan family contains magnificent rococco plasterwork, fine ceramics and a collection of doll's houses. The Pre-Raphaelite Central Hall depicts floral wall paintings and a series of scenes of Northumbrian history by William Bell Scott.

There are extensive walks through a variety of lawns, shrubberies, lakes and woodland to the exuberant walled garden, which remain open throughout the year.

Location: OS Ref. NZ030 843. Near Cambo, 6m NW of Belsay (A696).

Open: House & Restaurant: 5 Apr - 29 Oct: daily except Tue, 1 - 5.30pm (closes 4.30pm from 4 Sep). Last admissions 1 hr (House)/30 min (Restaurant) prior to closing times. Walled garden: 1 Apr - 31 Oct: daily, 10am - 7pm. 1 Nov - 31 Mar: daily, 10am - 4pm. Shop: 1 Mar - 28 May: daily except Tue, 10.30am - 4.30pm; 29 May - 3 Sept: daily, 10.30am - 5.30pm; 4 Sep - 29 Oct: daily except Tue, 10.30am - 4.30pm; 1 Nov - 11 Feb: Wed - Sun, 10.30am - 4.30pm. Restaurant as shop. Farm shop: 1 Apr - 24 Dec: daily, 10.30am - 5pm; 28 Dec - 31 Mar (outside turnstile): 10.30am - 4pm. Grounds: All year: daily in daylight hours.

Admission: House, garden & grounds: Adult £8, Child £4, Family £20, Groups £6.80. Garden & grounds only: Adult £5.50, Child £2.75, Family £14, Groups £4.70.
⬚ ⬚ ⬚ ⬚ Partial. ⬚ ⬚ By arrangement. **P** ⬚ ⬚ In grounds on leads. ⬚ ⬚ ⬚ Tel for details.

© English Heritage Photo Library

WARKWORTH CASTLE ⌗

WARKWORTH, ALNWICK, NORTHUMBERLAND NE66 0UJ

Tel: 01665 711423

Owner: English Heritage **Contact:** Visitor Operations Team

The great towering keep of this 15th century castle, once the home of the mighty Percy family, dominates the town and River Coquet. Warkworth is one of the most outstanding examples of an aristocratic fortified residence. Upstream by boat from the castle lies Warkworth Hermitage, cutting into the rock of the river cliff (separate charge applies).

Location: OS Ref. NU247 057. 7m S of Alnwick on A1068.

Open: 1 Apr - 30 Sept: daily, 10am - 5pm. 1 - 31 Oct: daily, 10am - 4pm. 1 Nov - 31 Mar: Sat - Mon, 10am - 4pm. Closed 24 - 26 Dec and 1 Jan.

Admission: Adult £3.40, Child £1.70, Conc. £2.60, Family £8.50. 15% discount for groups (11+).
ⓘ WC. ⬚ ⬚ Grounds. ⬚ Inclusive. **P** ⬚ ⬚ On leads. ⬚ ⬚ Tel for details.

WARKWORTH HERMITAGE ⌗

Warkworth, Northumberland

Tel: 01665 711423

Owner: English Heritage **Contact:** Visitor Operations Team

Upstream by boat from the castle this curious hermitage cuts into the rock of the river cliff.

Location: OS Ref. NU247 057. 7 1/2 m SE of Alnwick on A1068.

Open: 1 Apr - 30 Sept: Weds, Suns & BHs, 11am - 5pm.

Admission: Adult £2.40, Child £1.20, Conc. £1.80.
⬚ ⬚ Grounds. **P** At Castle. ⬚ ⬚ On leads.

NTPL/Derrick E Witty

Cragside - 1st Lord Armstrong of Cragside.

Souter Lighthouse. ©NTPL/Matthew Antrobus.

ARBEIA ROMAN FORT

Baring Street, South Shields, Tyne & Wear NE33 2BB

Tel: 0191 456 1369 **Fax:** 0191 427 6862

Owner: South Tyneside Metropolitan Borough Council **Contact:** The Curator

Managed by: Tyne & Wear Museums

More than 1,500 years on, the remains at Arbeia represent the most extensively excavated example of a military supply base anywhere in the Roman Empire. Museum includes weapons, jewellery and tombstones.

Location: OS Ref. NZ365 679. Near town centre and Metro Station.

Open: Easter - Sept: Mon - Sat: 10am - 5.30pm, Suns, 1 - 5pm. Open BH Mons. Oct - Easter: daily except Suns, 10am - 3.30pm. Closed 25/26 Dec, 1 Jan & Good Friday.

Admission: Free, except for Time Quest Gallery: Adult £1.50, Child/Conc. 80p.

BEDE'S WORLD MUSEUM

Church Bank, Jarrow, Tyne & Wear NE32 3DY

Tel: 0191 489 2106 **Fax:** 0191 428 2361

Managed by: Bede's World **Contact:** Visitor Services

A museum telling the story of the Venerable Bede and Anglo-Saxon Northumbria. Anglo Saxon demonstration farm with animals and reconstructed timber buildings.

Location: OS Ref. NZ339 652. Just off A19, S end of Tyne Tunnel. 300yds N of St Paul's.

Open: Apr - Oct: Mon - Sat, 10am - 5.30pm, Suns, 12 noon - 5.30pm. Nov - Mar: Mon - Sat, 10am - 4.30pm, Suns, 12 noon - 4.30pm. Also open BH Mons but closed Good Fri. Tel for Christmas opening times.

Admission: Adult £4.50, Conc. £3, Family £10. Groups by arrangement.

BESSIE SURTEES HOUSE

41 - 44 Sandhill, Newcastle, Tyne & Wear

Tel: 0191 269 1200

Owner: English Heritage **Contact:** Reception

Two 16th and 17th century merchants' houses stand on the quayside near the Tyne Bridge. One is a rare example of Jacobean domestic architecture. 3 rooms open.

Location: OS Ref. NZ252 639. 41 - 44 Sandhill, Newcastle. Riverside. City centre.

Open: All year: Mon - Fri: 10am - 4pm. Closed BHs & 24 Dec – 2 Jan.

Admission: Free.

WC.

GIBSIDE

Nr Rowlands Gill, Burnopfield, Newcastle-upon-Tyne NE16 6BG

Tel: 01207 541820 **e-mail:** gibside@nationaltrust.org.uk **www**.nationaltrust.org.uk

Owner: The National Trust **Contact:** The Property Manager

Gibside is one of the finest 18th century designed landscapes in the north of England. The Chapel was built to James Paine's design soon after 1760. Outstanding example of Georgian architecture approached along a terrace with an oak avenue. Walk along the River Derwent through woodland.

Location: OS Ref. NZ172 583. 6m SW of Gateshead, 20m NW of Durham. Entrance on B6314 between Burnopfield and Rowlands Gill.

Open: 6 Mar - 22 Oct: daily, 10am - 6pm. 23 Oct - 4 Mar: daily, 10am - 4pm.

Admission: Adult £5, Child £3, Family (2+4) £15, Family (1+3) £10. Booked groups £4.50.

Partial. By arrangement. Limited for coaches. On leads, in grounds. Tel for details.

NEWCASTLE CASTLE KEEP

Castle Keep, Castle Garth, Newcastle-upon-Tyne NE1 1RQ

Tel: 0191 232 7938

Owner: Newcastle City Council **Contact:** Paul MacDonald

The Keep originally dominated the castle bailey. The 'new' castle was founded in 1080.

Location: OS Ref. NZ251 638. City centre between St Nicholas church and the High Level bridge.

Open: All year: daily, 9.30am - 5.30pm (4.30pm winter).

Admission: Adult £1.50, Child/Conc. 50p.

ST PAUL'S MONASTERY

Jarrow, Tyne & Wear

Tel: 0191 489 7052

Owner: English Heritage **Contact:** The Regional Office – 0191 269 1200

The home of the Venerable Bede in the 7th and 8th centuries, partly surviving as the chancel of the parish church. It has become one of the best understood Anglo-Saxon monastic sites.

Location: OS Ref. NZ339 652. In Jarrow, on minor road N of A185. 300yds S of Bede's World.

Open: Any reasonable time.

Admission: Free.

SOUTER LIGHTHOUSE

Coast Road, Whitburn, Sunderland, Tyne & Wear SR6 7NH

Tel: 0191 529 3161 **Fax:** 0191 529 0902 **e-mail:** souter@nationaltrust.org.uk **www**.nationaltrust.org.uk

Owner: The National Trust **Contact:** The Property Manager

Dramatic red and white lighthouse tower on rugged coast. Built in 1871, the first to be powered by alternating electric current.

Location: OS Ref. NZ408 641. 2$^1/_2$m S of South Shields on A183. 5m N of Sunderland.

Open: 1 Apr - 5 Nov: daily except Fri (open Good Fri), 11am - 5pm. Last adm 4.30pm.

Admission: Adult £4, Child £2.50, Family £10.50. Booked Groups (10+): Adult £3.50, Child £2. NT members Free: membership available from shop.

Partial. WCs. By arrangement. In grounds, on leads.

TYNEMOUTH PRIORY & CASTLE

North Pier, Tynemouth, Tyne & Wear NE30 4BZ

Tel: 0191 257 1090

Owner: English Heritage **Contact:** Visitor Operations Team

The castle walls and gatehouse enclose the substantial remains of a Benedictine priory founded c1090 on a Saxon monastic site. Their strategic importance has made the castle and priory the target for attack for many centuries. In World War I, coastal batteries in the castle defended the mouth of the Tyne.

Location: OS Ref. NZ374 695. In Tynemouth.

Open: 1 Apr - 30 Sept: daily, 10am - 5pm. 1 - 31 Oct: daily, 10am - 4pm. 1 Nov - 31 Mar: Thur - Mon, 10am - 4pm. Closed 24 - 26 Dec & 1 Jan.

Admission: Adult £3.40, Child £1.70, Conc. £2.60, Family £8.50. 15% discount for groups (11+).

Grounds. By arrangement. In grounds, on leads. Tel for details.

WASHINGTON OLD HALL

The Avenue, Washington Village, District 4, Washington, Tyne & Wear NE38 7LE

Tel: 0191 416 6879 **Fax:** 0191 419 2065 **www**.nationaltrust.org.uk

Owner: The National Trust **Contact:** The Property Manager

Jacobean manor house incorporating portions of 12th century house of the Washington family. Small Jacobean knot garden.

Location: OS Ref. NZ312 566. In Washington on E side of The Avenue. 5m W of Sunderland (2m from A1), S of Tyne Tunnel, follow signs for Washington District 4 and then village.

Open: House: 2 Apr - 29 Oct: Sun - Wed, 11am - 5pm. Garden: 2 Apr - 29 Oct: 10am - 5pm. Last admission 4.30pm. Open Good Fri.

Admission: Adult £4, Child £2.50, Family £10.50. Booked groups (15+): Adult £3.50, Child £2. Membership available from reception.

Conferences. Ground floor and grounds. By arrangement.
Limited. In grounds, on leads.

© English Heritage

Tynemouth Castle.

Drummond Castle, Perthshire.

X Scotland

Drummond Castle, Perthshire.

borders | south west scotland | edinburgh city, coast & countryside
greater glasgow & the clyde valley | perthshire, angus & dundee & the kingdom of fife
west highlands & islands, loch lomond, stirling & trossachs

scotland

Scotland is loosely divided into the Highlands and the Lowlands. The cattle and sheep reared on Lowland pastures produce meat of the highest quality which is sought after worldwide. The Highlands, in their turn, provide wonderfully romantic scenery; mountains and moorlands, lochs and glens. This is the home of red deer, wild cats and golden eagles. First time visitors to Scotland can only scratch the surface of its cultural and social history. Edinburgh Castle is, of course, Scotland's most famous castle but there are so many others which merit a visit: fairytale Dunrobin on the east coast, Dunvegan on the Isle of Skye, Cawdor, home of the Thanes of Cawdor from the 14th century – the list is endless. No visit to Scotland would be complete without a trip to a distillery. The soft water of the Highlands produces the finest malt whisky in the world.

grampian highlands, aberdeen & the north east coast
highlands & skye
outer islands, western isles, orkney & shetland

'The Pink Boy' - Sir Josh... Reynolds

MAP 13

Owner: His Grace the
Duke of Buccleuch &
Queensberry KT

▶ **CONTACT**

Buccleuch Heritage
Trust
Bowhill House &
Country Park
Bowhill
Selkirk TD7 5ET

Tel: 01750 22204

Fax: 01750 23893

e-mail:
bht@buccleuch.com

▶ **LOCATION**

OS Ref. NT426 278

3m W of Selkirk off
A708 Moffat Road,
A68 from Newcastle,
A7 from Carlisle
or Edinburgh.

Bus: 3m Selkirk.

Taxi: 01750 20354.

BOWHILL HOUSE & 🏛 COUNTRY PARK

Scottish Borders home of the Duke and Duchess of Buccleuch, dating mainly from 1812 and christened 'Sweet Bowhill' by Sir Walter Scott in his *Lay of the Last Minstrel.*

Many of the works of art were collected by earlier Montagus, Douglases and Scotts or given by Charles II to his natural son James, Duke of Monmouth and Buccleuch. Paintings include Canaletto's *Whitehall*, works by Guardi, Claude, Ruysdael, Gainsborough, Raeburn, Reynolds, Van Dyck and Wilkie.   Superb French furniture, Meissen and Sèvres porcelain, silver and tapestries.

Historical relics include Monmouth's saddle and execution shirt, Sir Walter Scott's plaid and some

proof editions, Queen Victoria's letters and gifts to successive Duchesses of Buccleuch, her Mistresses of the Robes.

There is also a completely restored Victorian Kitchen, 19th century horse-drawn fire engine, 'Bowhill Theatre', a lively centre for the performing arts and where, prior to touring the house, visitors can see 'The Quest for Bowhill', a 20 minute audio-visual presentation by Dr Colin Thompson. James Hogg Exhibition.

Conference centre, arts courses, literary lunches, education service, visitor centre. Shop, tearoom, adventure playground, woodland walks, nature trails, picnic areas. Garden and landscape designed by John Gilpin.

'Winter' - Sir Joshua Reynolds

🎨 ❄ ℹ Fashion shows, air displays, archery, clay pigeon shooting, equestrian events, charity garden parties, shows, rallies, filming, lecture theatre. House is open by appointment outside public hours to groups led by officials of a recognised museum, gallery or educational establishment. No photography inside house.

🍽 Inside caterers normally used but outside caterers considered.

♿ Visitors may alight at entrance. WC. Wheelchair visitors free.

🍴 Groups can book in advance (special rates), menus on request.

🚶 For groups. Tour time 1¼ hrs.

🅿 60 cars and 6 coaches within 50yds of house.

📷 Welcome. Projects in Bowhill House and Victorian kitchen, Education Officers (service provided free of charge), schoolroom, ranger-led nature walks, adventure playground. Heritage Education Trust Sandford Award winner '93, '98 & '04.

🐕 On leads. ❄

▶ **OPENING TIMES**

House

1 - 31 July:
Daily, 1 - 5pm.

Outwith stated times to educational groups by appointment.

Country Park

1 - 17 April: Daily
May - June: weekends
& BHs
July: Daily with House.
August: Daily, 11am - 5pm.

▶ **ADMISSION**

Summer

House & Country Park

Adult	£7.00
Child (5-16yrs)	£2.00
OAP	£5.00

Country Park only

All ages	£2.00
Child (under 5yrs) & Wheelchair visitors	Free

Family tickets and group tickets available.

CONFERENCE/FUNCTION

ROOM	MAX CAPACITY
Bowhill Little Theatre	72

Skyscan Photo Library

MAP 14

Owner: His Grace the
Duke of Roxburghe

▶ **CONTACT**

Judy Potts
Sales & Events
Organiser
Roxburghe Estates
Office
Kelso
Roxburghshire
Scotland TD5 7SF

Tel: 01573 223333

Fax: 01573 226056

e-mail:
jpotts@floorscastle.com

▶ **LOCATION**

OS Ref. NT711 347

From South A68, A698.

From North A68,
A697/9
In Kelso follow signs.

Bus: Kelso Bus Station
1m.

Rail: Berwick 20m.

FLOORS CASTLE
www.floorscastle.com

Floors Castle, home of the Duke and Duchess of Roxburghe, is situated in the heart of the Scottish Border Country. It is reputedly the largest inhabited castle in Scotland. Designed by William Adam, who was both masterbuilder and architect, for the first Duke of Roxburghe, building started in 1721.

It was the present Duke's great-great-grand-father James, the 6th Duke, who embellished the plain Adam features of the building. In about 1849 Playfair, letting his imagination and talent run riot, transformed the castle, creating a multitude of spires and domes.

The apartments now display the outstanding collection of French 17th and 18th century furniture, magnificent tapestries, Chinese and European porcelain and many other fine works of art. Many of the treasures in the castle today were collected by Duchess May, American wife of the 8th Duke.

The castle has been seen on cinema screens worldwide in the film *Greystoke*, as the home of Tarzan, the Earl of Greystoke.

GARDENS
The extensive parkland and gardens overlooking the River Tweed provide a variety of wooded walks. The garden centre and walled gardens contain splendid herbaceous borders and in the outer walled garden a parterre to commemorate the Millennium can be seen. An excellent children's playground and picnic area are very close to the castle.

 Gala dinners, conferences, product launches, 4 x 4 driving, incentive groups, highland games and other promotional events. Extensive park, helicopter pad, fishing, clay pigeon and pheasant shooting. No photography inside the castle.

Visitors may alight at the entrance. WC.

Self-service, licensed, seats 125 opens 11am.

By arrangement. Tour time 1 hr.

Unlimited for cars, 100 yds away, coach park 50 yds. Coaches can be driven to the entrance, waiting area close to restaurant exit. Lunch or tea for coach drivers.

Welcome, guide provided. Playground facilities.

On leads, in grounds.

▶ **OPENING TIMES**

Summer

1 April - 29 October:
Daily: 11am - 5pm.

Last admission 4.30pm.

Winter

November - March
Closed to the general public, available for events.

▶ **ADMISSION**

Summer

Adult £6.00
Child* (5 - 15yrs) £3.25
OAP/Student £5.00
Family £16.00
Groups (20+)
Adult £5.00
Child* (5 - 15yrs) £2.00
OAP/Student £4.50

*Under 5yrs Free.

▶ **SPECIAL EVENTS**

APRIL 16
Easter Eggstravaganza.

MAY 9
Tapestry Trail Day.

MAY 20 - 22
Horse Trials.

JULY 8/9
Gardeners' Festival.

AUG 10
Shakespeare – The Merry Wives of Windsor.

AUG 27
Massed Pipe Bands Family Day.

DEC 9/10
Christmas Winter Wonderland.

CONFERENCE/FUNCTION		
ROOM	SIZE	MAX CAPACITY
Dining Rm	18m x 7m	150
Ballroom	21m x 8m	150

MAP 14

MANDERSTON

www.manderston.co.uk

Manderston, together with its magnificent stables, stunning marble dairy and 56 acres of immaculate gardens, forms an ensemble which must be unique in Britain today.

The house was completely rebuilt between 1903 and 1905, with no expense spared.

Visitors are able to see not only the sumptuous State rooms and bedrooms, decorated in the Adam manner, but also all the original domestic offices, in a truly 'upstairs downstairs' atmosphere. Manderston boasts a unique and recently restored silver staircase.

There is a special museum with a nostalgic display of valuable tins made by Huntly and Palmer from 1868 to the present day. Winner of the AA/NPI Bronze Award UK 1994.

GARDENS

Outside, the magnificence continues and the combination of formal gardens and picturesque landscapes is a major attraction unique amongst Scottish houses.

The stables, still in use, have been described by *Horse and Hound* as 'probably the finest in all the wide world'.

Manderston has often been used as a film location, most recently it was the star of Channel 4's *'The Edwardian Country House'*.

Owner:
The Lord Palmer

▶ CONTACT
The Lord or Lady
Palmer
Manderston
Duns
Berwickshire
Scotland   TD11 3PP

Tel: 01361 883450
Secretary: 01361 882636
Fax: 01361 882010
e-mail: palmer@
manderston.co.uk

▶ LOCATION
OS Ref. NT810 544

From Edinburgh
47m, 1hr.
1¹/₂ m E of Duns on
A6105.
Bus: 400 yds.
Rail: Berwick
Station 12m.
Taxi: Chirnside 818216.
Airport: Edinburgh or
Newcastle both
60m or 80 mins.

Corporate & incentives venue. Ideal retreat: business groups, think-tank weekends. Fashion shows, air displays, archery, clay pigeon shooting, equestrian events, garden parties, shows, rallies, filming, product launches and marathons. Two airstrips for light aircraft, approx 5m, grand piano, billiard table, pheasant shoots, sea angling, salmon fishing, stabling, cricket pitch, tennis court, lake. Nearby: 18-hole golf course, indoor swimming pool, squash court. No photography in house.

Available. Buffets, lunches and dinners. Wedding receptions.

Special parking available outside the House.

Tearoom (open as house) with waitress service. Can be booked in advance, menus on request.

Included. Available in French. Guides in rooms. If requested, the owner may meet groups. Tour time 1¹/₄ hrs.

400 cars 125yds from house, 30 coaches 5yds from house. Appreciated if group fees are paid by one person.

Welcome. Guide can be provided. Biscuit Tin Museum of particular interest.

Grounds only, on leads.

6 twin, 4 double.

▶ OPENING TIMES
Summer

Mid-May - end September
Thurs & Sun, 1.30 - 5pm
Last entry 4.15pm.
Gardens: 11.30am - dusk.

BH Mons, late May
& late August, 2 - 5pm.
Gardens open until dusk.

Groups welcome all year
by appointment.

Winter

September - May
Group visits welcome
by appointment.

▶ ADMISSION
House & Grounds
Adult £7.00
Child (under 12yrs) ... Free
Conc. £6.50

Groups (20+) £6.50
(£7 other than open days)

Grounds only
Including Stables &
Marble Dairy............ £3.50

On days when the house is closed to the public, groups viewing by appointment will have personally conducted tours. The Gift Shop will be open. On these occasions reduced party rates (except for school children) will not apply. Group visits (20+) other than open days are £6.50 (minimum £130). Edwardian teas on open days only.

CONFERENCE/FUNCTION

ROOM	SIZE	MAX CAPACITY
Dining Rm	22' x 35'	100
Ballroom	34' x 21'	150
Hall	22' x 38'	130
Drawing Rm	35' x 21'	150

ABBOTSFORD 🏠

MELROSE, ROXBURGHSHIRE TD6 9BQ

www.scottsabbotsford.co.uk

Tel: 01896 752043 **Fax:** 01896 752916 **Email:** enquiries@scottsabbotsford.co.uk

Contact: Jacqui Wright

The Home of Sir Walter Scott. A wonderfully interesting house with fascinating collections. Garden, including walled garden, woodland walk, stunning grounds leading down to the River Tweed. Gift Shop. Tea Shop in grounds for light refreshments. Tours of the private apartments by arrangement.

Location: OS Ref. NT508 343 35 mins S of Edinburgh. Melrose 3m, Galashiels 2m. On B6360.

Open: 20 Mar - 31 Oct: Mon - Sat, 9.30am - 5pm. Mar - May & Oct: Sun, 2 - 5pm. Jun - Sept: Sun, 9.30am - 5pm. Other dates by arrangement.

Admission: Adult £5, Child £2.50, Groups £3.90

🗔 🖼 🗍 By arrangement. 🅿 €

AYTON CASTLE 🏠

AYTON, EYEMOUTH, BERWICKSHIRE TD14 5RD

Tel: 018907 81212 **Fax:** 018907 81550

Owner: D I Liddell-Grainger of Ayton   **Contact:** The Curator

Built in 1846 by the Mitchell-Innes family and designed by the architect James Gillespie Graham. Over the last ten years it has been fully restored and is now a family home. It is a unique restoration project and the quality of the original and restored workmanship is outstanding. The castle stands on an escarpment surrounded by mature woodlands containing many interesting trees and has been a film-making venue due to this magnificent setting.

Location: OS Ref. NT920 610. 7m N of Berwick-on-Tweed on Route A1.

Open: 14 May - 10 Sept: by telephone appointment.

Admission: Adult £3, Child (under 15yrs) Free.

🗍 🗍 Partial. 🗍 Obligatory. 🅿 🖼 In grounds, on leads. ✳

BOWHILL HOUSE
& COUNTRY PARK 🏠   *See page 446 for full page entry.*

DAWYCK BOTANIC GARDEN

Stobo, Peeblesshire EH45 9JU

Tel: 01721 760254 **Fax:** 01721 760214 **e-mail:** dawyck@rbge.org.uk

Contact: The Curator

Renowned historic arboretum. Amongst mature specimen trees – some over 40 metres tall – are a variety of flowering trees, shrubs and herbaceous plants. Explore the world's first Cryptogamic Sanctuary and Reserve for 'non-flowering' plants.

Location: OS Ref. NT168 352. 8m SW of Peebles on B712.

Open: Feb - Nov: daily, 10am - 6pm (closes 4pm Feb & Nov, 5pm Mar & Oct). Last admission 1 hr before closing.

Admission: Adult £3.50, Child £1, Conc. £3, Family £8. Group discounts & membership programme available.

DRYBURGH ABBEY 🏛

St Boswells, Melrose

Tel: 01835 822381

Owner: Historic Scotland   **Contact:** The Steward

Remarkably complete ruins of Dryburgh Abbey.

Location: OS Ref. NT591 317. 5m SE of Melrose off B6356. 11/2 m N of St Boswells.

Open: 1 Apr - 30 Sept: daily, 9.30am - 6.30pm, last ticket 6pm. 1 Oct - 31 Mar: daily, 9.30am - 4.30pm, last ticket 4pm.

Admission: Adult £4, Child £1.60, Conc. £3.

🗔🗍Partial. 🗍By arrangement. 🅿 🖼 €

DUNS CASTLE

DUNS, BERWICKSHIRE TD11 3NW

www.dunscastle.co.uk

Tel: 01361 883211 **Fax:** 01361 882015 **e-mail:** aline_hay@lineone.net

Owner: Alexander Hay of Duns   **Contact:** Mrs Aline Hay

This historical 1320 pele tower has been home to the Hay family since 1696, and the current owners Alexander and Aline Hay offer it as a welcoming venue for individuals, groups and corporate guests to enjoy. They have renovated it to produce high standards of comfort while retaining all the character of its rich period interiors. Wonderful lakeside and parkland setting.

Location: OS Ref. NT777 544. 10m off A1. Rail: Berwick station 16m. Airports: Newcastle & Edinburgh, 1 hr.

Open: Available all year by reservation for individuals, groups, parties and companies for day visits or residential stays, on an exclusive use basis. Not open to the general public.

Admission: Rates for private and corporate visits, wedding receptions, filming on application.

🛏 4 x 4-poster, 4 x double, 3 x twin (all with bathrooms), 1 single plus 6 cottages in grounds. ✳

FERNIEHIRST CASTLE
JEDBURGH, ROXBURGHSHIRE TD8 6NX

Tel: 01835 862201 **Fax:** 01835 863992
Owner: The Ferniehirst Trust
Contact: Mrs J Fraser

Ferniehirst Castle – Scotland's Frontier Fortress. Ancestral home of the Kerr family. Restored (1984/1987) by the 12th Marquess of Lothian. Unrivalled 16th century Border architecture. Grand Apartment and Turret Library. A 16th century Chamber Oratory. The Kerr Chamber – Museum of Family History. A special tribute to Jedburgh's Protector to Mary Queen of Scots – Sir Thomas Kerr. Riverside walk by Jed Water. Archery Field opposite the Chapel where sheep of Viking origin still graze as they did four centuries ago.

Location: OS Ref. NT653 181. 2m S of Jedburgh on the A68.

Open: 1 June - 6 August: Tue - Sun, 11am - 4pm. (Closed Mons).

Admission: Adult £3, Child £1.50. Groups (max. 50) by prior arrangement (01835 862201).

🅿 🔲 Suitable. WCs.
🔎 Guided tours only, groups by arrangement.
🅿 Ample for cars and coaches.
🐕 In grounds, on leads.

FLOORS CASTLE 🏛   *See page 447 for full page entry.*

HALLIWELL'S HOUSE MUSEUM
Halliwell's Close, Market Place, High Street, Selkirk

Tel: 01750 20096 **Fax:** 01750 23282
Owner: Scottish Borders Council   **Contact:** Jane Petrie
Re-creation of buildings, formerly used as a house and ironmonger's shop.
Location: OS Ref. NT472 286. In Selkirk town centre.
Open: Apr - Sept: Mon - Sat, 10am - 5pm, Sun, 10am - 12 noon. Jul & Aug: 10 am - 1pm. Closed for Selkirk Common Riding. Please telephone in advance to confirm opening times.
Admission: Free.

HERMITAGE CASTLE 🏛
Liddesdale, Newcastleton

Tel: 01387 376222
Owner: In the care of Historic Scotland   **Contact:** The Steward
Eerie fortress at the heart of the bloodiest events in the history of the Borders. Mary Queen of Scots made her famous ride here to visit her future husband.
Location: OS Ref. NY497 961. In Liddesdale 5¹/₂ m NE of Newcastleton, B6399.
Open: 1 Apr - 30 Sept: daily, 9.30am - 6.30pm, last ticket 6pm.
Admission: Adult £3, Child £1.30, Conc. £2.30.

🅸🔲🛒🅿🐕 €

THE HIRSEL GARDENS, COUNTRY PARK 🏛
& HOMESTEAD MUSEUM
Coldstream, Berwickshire TD12 4LP

Tel: 01573 224144 **Fax:** 01573 226313 **e-mail:** rogerdodd@btconnect.com
www.hirselcountrypark.co.uk
Owner: Lord Home of the Hirsel   **Contact:** Roger G Dodd
Wonderful spring flowers and rhododendrons. Homestead museum and crafts centre. The Cottage Tearoom. Displays of estate life and adaptation to modern farming.
Location: OS Ref. NT838 393. Immediately W of Coldstream off A697.
Open: All year during daylight hours.
Admission: £2 per car, coaches by appointment.

🅿 🛒 🔲WCs. 🅿 Limited for coaches. 🐕In grounds, on leads. ❄

JEDBURGH ABBEY 🏛
4/5 ABBEY BRIDGEND, JEDBURGH TD8 6JQ

Tel: 01835 863925
Owner: In the care of Historic Scotland   **Contact:** The Steward
Founded by David I c1138 for Augustinian Canons. The church is mostly in the Romanesque and early Gothic styles and is remarkably complete. The award-winning visitor centre contains the priceless 12th century 'Jedburgh Comb' and other artefacts found during archaeological excavations.
Location: OS Ref. NT650 205. In Jedburgh on the A68.
Open: Apr - Sept: daily, 9.30am - 6.30pm. Oct - Mar: daily, 9.30am - 4.30pm. Last ticket 30 mins before closing. 10% discount for groups (10+).
Admission: Adult £4.50, Child £2, Conc. £3.50.

🅸 Picnic area. 🅿 🔲 Partial to visitor centre. WC. 🅿 🔲 🐕 Free when booked.
🐕 Guide dogs only. ❄ €

MANDERSTON *See page 448 for full page entry.*

©Historic Scot and Photographic Library

MELLERSTAIN HOUSE

MELLERSTAIN, GORDON, BERWICKSHIRE TD3 6LG

www.mellerstain.com

Tel: 01573 410225   **Fax:** 01573 410636   **e-mail:** enquiries@mellerstain.com

Owner: The Earl of Haddington   **Contact:** Rosemary Evans

One of Scotland's great Georgian houses and a unique example of the work of the Adam family; the two wings built in 1725 by William Adam, the large central block by his son, Robert 1770-78. Rooms contain fine plasterwork, colourful ceilings and marble fireplaces. The library is considered to be Robert Adam's finest creation. Many fine paintings and period furniture.

Location: OS Ref. NT648 392. From Edinburgh A68 to Earlston, turn left 5m, signed.

Open: Easter weekend, 1 May - 30 Sept: Sun/Mon and Wed/Thur. Oct: Sun only. House: 12.30 - 5pm. Last ticket 4.15pm. Groups any time by appointment. Tearoom, shop & gardens: 11.30am - 5pm.

Admission: Adult £6, Child (under 16yrs) with adult Free. Groups (20+) £5.50 (outside normal hours £6.50). Grounds only: £3.50.

ℹ️No photography or video cameras. 🅾 🐾 🇹 🦽Partial. 🍽Licensed. 🍴Licensed. 🍷By arrangement. 🅿

🐕In grounds, on leads. Guide dogs only in house. 📹 Tel for details.

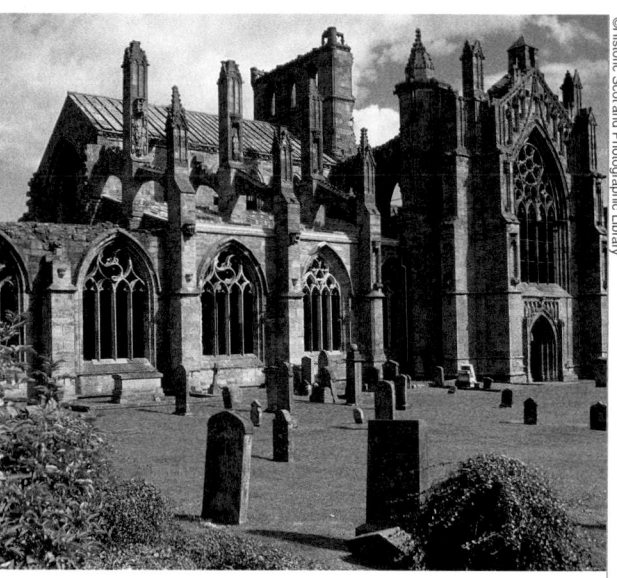

MELROSE ABBEY

MELROSE, ROXBURGHSHIRE TD6 9LG

Tel: 01896 822562

Owner: Historic Scotland   **Contact:** The Steward

The abbey was founded about 1136 by David I as a Cistercian abbey and at one time was probably the richest in Scotland. Richard II's English army largely destroyed it in 1385 but it was rebuilt and the surviving remains are mostly 14th century. Burial place of Robert the Bruce's heart. Local history displays.

Location: OS Ref. NT549 342. In the centre of Melrose off the A68 or A7.

Open: Apr - Sept: daily, 9.30am - 6.30pm. Oct - Mar: daily, 9.30am - 4.30pm. Last ticket 30 mins before closing.

Admission: Adult £4.50, Child £2, Conc. £3.50. 10% discount for groups (10+).

ℹ️Picnic area. 🅾 🦽Tape for visitors with learning difficulties. 🔂 🅿 🖼Pre-booked visits free. 🐕Guide dogs only. ✳ €

MERTOUN GARDENS

St Boswells, Melrose, Roxburghshire TD6 0EA

Tel: 01835 823236   **Fax:** 01835 822474

Owner: His Grace the Duke of Sutherland **Contact:** Angela Dodds/Susan Murdoch

26 acres of beautiful grounds. Walled garden and well-preserved circular dovecote.

Location: OS Ref. NT617 318. Entrance off B6404 2m NE of St Boswells.

Open: Apr - Sept: Fri - Mon, 2 - 6pm. Last admission 5.30pm.

Admission: Adult £2.50, Child 50p, OAP £1.50. Groups by arrangement: 10% reduction.

🍷By arrangement. 🅿 🐕

Thirlestane Castle.

MONTEVIOT HOUSE GARDENS
JEDBURGH, ROXBURGHSHIRE TD8 6UQ

Tel: 01835 830380 (mornings only) / 01835 830704 **Fax:** 01835 830288

Owner: The Marquess of Lothian   **Contact:** The Administrator

The river garden planted with herbaceous shrub borders, has a beautiful view of the River Teviot. A semi-enclosed rose garden with a collection of hybrid teas, floribunda and shrub roses. The pinetum is full of unusual trees and nearby a water garden of islands is linked by bridges.

Location: OS Ref. NT648 247. 3m N of Jedburgh. S side of B6400 (to Nisbet). 1m E of A68.

Open: House: 3 - 16 Jul: 12 noon - 4.15pm. Garden: Apr - Oct: daily, 12 noon - 5pm. Coach parties by prior arrangement.

Admission: House or Garden only: Adult £2.50. House & Garden: Adult £4.50. Under 16yrs Free.

⚑ ♿Partial. Parking & WCs. 🅵By arrangement. 🅿

Duns Castle.

OLD GALA HOUSE
Scott Crescent, Galashiels TD1 3JS

Tel: 01750 20096   **Fax:** 01750 23282

Owner: Scottish Borders Council

Dating from 1583, the former house of the Lairds of Gala. Particularly memorable is the painted ceiling dated 1635.

Location: OS Ref. NT492 357. S of town centre, signed from A7.

Open: Apr, May & Sept: Tue - Sat, 10am - 4pm. Jun - Aug: Mon - Sat, 10am - 4pm, Sun, 1 - 4pm. Oct: Tue - Fri, 1 - 4pm, Sat, 10am - 4pm.

Admission: Free.

PAXTON HOUSE, GALLERY & COUNTRY PARK 🏛
BERWICK-UPON-TWEED TD15 1SZ
www.paxtonhouse.com

Tel: 01289 386291   **Fax:** 01289 386660   **e-mail:** info@paxtonhouse.com

Owner: The Paxton Trust   **Contact:** The Director

Award winning Palladian country house built 1758 to the design of John Adam. 12 period rooms contain the finest collections of Chippendale and Regency furniture. Magnificent picture gallery and restored Georgian kitchen. Enjoy the grounds and gardens, riverside and woodland walks, red squirrel and bird hides plus the salmon net fishing museum. Visit the shops, tearoom and our ever changing exhibition programme.

Location: OS Ref. NT931 520. 3m off the A1 Berwick-upon-Tweed bypass on B6461.

Open: 1 Apr - 31 Oct: House: 11am - 5pm. Last house tour 4pm. Grounds: 10am - sunset. Open to groups/schools all year by appointment.

Admission: Adult £6, Child £3. Groups (pre-arranged, 12+). Adult £5, Child £2.50. Grounds only: Adult £3, Child £1.50.

ⓘNo photography. 📷 ⚑ ☕Conferences, weddings. ♿ Partial. ⬛ 🍴Licensed. 🅵Obligatory. 🅿 ⬛ 🐕In grounds, on leads. ❋ 🦽Tel for details.

SMAILHOLM TOWER 🏛
Smailholm, Kelso

Tel: 01573 460365

Owner: In the care of Historic Scotland   **Contact:** The Steward

Set on a high rocky knoll this well preserved 16th century tower houses an exhibition of tapestries and costume dolls depicting characters from Sir Walter Scott's Minstrelsy of the Scottish Borders.

Location: OS Ref. NT638 347. Nr Smailholm Village, 6m W of Kelso on B6937 then B6404.

Open: 1 Apr - 30 Sept: daily, 9.30am - 6.30pm. Oct: Sat - Wed, 9.30am - 4.30pm. Nov - Mar: Sats & Suns only, 9.30am - 4.30pm. Last tickets 30 mins before closing.

Admission: Adult £3, Child £1.30, Conc. £2.30.

⬛🅿❋€

THIRLESTANE CASTLE

LAUDER, BERWICKSHIRE TD2 6RU

www.thirlestanecastle.co.uk

Tel: 01578 722430   **Fax:** 01578 722761   **e-mail:** admin@thirlestanecastle.co.uk

Owner: Thirlestane Castle Trust   **Contact:** Ian Garner

Thirlestane Castle was the ancient seat of the Earls and Duke of Lauderdale and is still home to the Maitlands. Standing in beautiful Border countryside, Thirlestane has exquisite 17th century plasterwork ceilings, a fine portrait collection, historic toys, kitchens and country life exhibitions. Facilities include free parking, audio visual display, gift shop, café, adventure playground, and woodland picnic tables. Four star STB award; Registered Museum. The state rooms are available for banquets, dinners and receptions. Non-destructive events can be held in the grounds which overlook the Leader Valley and Lammermuir Hills.

Location: OS Ref. NT540 473. Off A68 at Lauder, 28m S of Edinburgh.

Open: Good Fri & Easter Sun/Mon; 14 Apr - 24 Sept: Sun, Mon, Wed & Thurs (Jul - Aug: Sat - Thur), 10am - 3pm (last admission). Private parties may be arranged outwith opening times by contacting the administrator.

Admission: Castle & Grounds: Adult £5.50, Child £3, Senior £5, Family (2+3) £15. Lauder Residents Seasonal Ticket £15. Grounds only: Adult £2, Child £1. Groups (18+): Adult £4.50, Child £1.50.

ⓘ Woodland walk, children's adventure playground, country life display area. ⌷ ⊤ ⑤ Unsuitable. ⚫ 𝑓 By arrangement. 𝐏 ▣ ⛬ In grounds, on leads.

Floors Castle.

TRAQUAIR

INNERLEITHEN, PEEBLESSHIRE EH44 6PW

www.traquair.co.uk

Tel: 01896 830323   **Fax:** 01896 830639   **e-mail:** enquiries@traquair.co.uk

Contact: Ms C Maxwell Stuart

Traquair, situated amidst beautiful scenery and close by the River Tweed, is the oldest inhabited house in Scotland - visited by twenty-seven kings. Originally a Royal hunting lodge, it was owned by the Scottish Crown until 1478 when it passed to a branch of the Royal Stuart family whose descendants still live in the house today. Nearly ten centuries of Scottish political and domestic life can be traced from the collection of treasures in the house. It is particularly rich in associations with the Catholic Church in Scotland, Mary Queen of Scots and the Jacobite Risings. There is an 18th century working brewery in one of the wings of the house where the famous Traquair House Ales are produced. Maze, Craft Workshops, Children's Adventure Playground. 1745 cottage restaurant, gift shop, brewshop and museum.

Location: OS Ref. NY330 354. On B709 near junction with A72. Edinburgh 1hr, Glasgow 1½ hrs, Carlisle 1½ hrs, Newcastle 1½ hrs.

Open: 8 Apr - 29 Oct: daily. House: 12 noon - 5pm; Jun - Aug: 10.30am - 5pm (last admission 4pm); Oct: 11am - 4pm. Nov: w/ends only, 12 noon - 4pm (guided tours). Guided tours also available in Apr and outside normal opening hrs. They must be booked in advance.

Admission: House & Grounds: Adult £6.20, Child £3.30, Senior £5.60, Family (2+3) £17.50. Grounds only: Adult £3.50, Child £2. Groups (20+). House & Grounds: Adult £5.50, Child £2.60, Senior £5.30. Guided tours (must pre-book, 20+): £7pp; Personal guided tours by Catherine Maxwell Stuart, 21st Lady of Traquair, £10pp; Reception in the High Drawing Room or Dining Room with Traquair House Ales/Cuvée Catherine/Sherry £4pp, with canapés £5pp, coffee & shortbread £3.50pp.

⌷ⓘ No photography in house. ⊤ Exclusive lunches/dinners (max 30) in the Dining Room. ⑤ ⚫ Licensed, self-service. 𝖋 Home cooked meals (max 50) at 1745 Cottage Restaurant. 𝑓 Apr & outside opening hours. 𝐏 Coaches please book. ⛬ In grounds on leads. 🛏 3 en-suites. B&B. ⊡

South West Scotland, Dumfries & Galloway, Ayrshire and the Isle of Arran

His Grace the Duke of Buccleuch & Queensberry KT

MAP 13

DRUMLANRIG CASTLE

www.drumlanrig.com

Owner: His Grace the Duke of Buccleuch & Queensberry KT

▶ **CONTACT**

Claire Oram
Drumlanrig Castle
Thornhill
Dumfriesshire
DG3 4AQ

Tel: 01848 331555
Fax: 01848 331682

e-mail: bre@
drumlanrigcastle.org.uk

▶ **LOCATION**
OS Ref. NX851 992

18m N of Dumfries,
3m NW of Thornhill
off A76.
16m from M74 at
Elvanfoot.
Approx. 1¹/₂ hrs
by road from
Edinburgh, Glasgow
and Carlisle.

Drumlanrig Castle, Gardens and Country Park, Dumfriesshire home of the Duke of Buccleuch and Queensberry KT was built between 1679 and 1691 by William Douglas, 1st Duke of Queensberry. Drumlanrig is rightly recognised as one of the first and most important buildings in the grand manner in Scottish domestic architecture. James Smith, who made the conversion from a 15th century castle, made a comparable transformation at Dalkeith a decade later.

The Castle, of local pink sandstone, offers superb views across Nithsdale. It houses a renowned art collection, cabinets made for Louis XIV's Versailles, relics of Bonnie Prince Charlie and a 300 year old silver chandelier.

The story of Sir James Douglas, killed in Spain while carrying out the last wish of Robert Bruce, pervades the Castle in the emblem of a winged heart. Douglas family historical exhibition. Other attractions include craft workshops, mountain bike trails and bike hire, Cycle Museum, working forge and adventure play area. The gardens, now being restored to the plan of 1738, include a plant centre and add to the overall effect. The fascination of Drumlanrig as a centre of art, beauty and history is complemented by its role in the Queensberry Estate, a model of dynamic and enlightened land management.

ℹ️ No photography inside the Castle.

🔌 ♿ Suitable. WC. Please enquire about facilities before visit.

☕ Licensed.

🍴 Snacks, lunches and teas during opening hours.

🚶

🅿️ Adjacent to the castle.

🎒 Children's quiz and worksheets. Ranger-led activities, including woodlands and forestry. Adventure playground. School groups welcome throughout the year by arrangement.

🐕 In grounds on leads.

❄️

🛡️ Tel for details.

▶ **OPENING TIMES**
Summer

Castle
1 May - 28 August: daily.

May & June: 12 noon - 4pm (last tour).

July & August: 11am - 4pm (last tour).

Country Park, Gardens & Adventure Woodland
3 April - 1 October: daily, 11am - 5pm.

Winter
By appointment only.

▶ **ADMISSION***

Castle and Country Park
Adult £7.00
Child (5-15yrs)....... £3.00
OAP/Student £5.00
Family (2+4) £20.00
Disabled in
wheelchairs............. Free
Pre-booked groups (20+)
Adult £5.00
Child (5-15yrs)....... £2.00
Outside normal
opening times........... £8.00

Country Park only
Adult £3.00
OAP/Child (5-15yrs).. £2.00
Family (2+4) £10.50

Season Ticket.......... £25.00

*All visitors to the Castle must sign the visitor book as a condition of entry.

CONFERENCE/FUNCTION

ROOM	SIZE	MAX CAPACITY
Visitors' Centre	6m x 13m	50

South West Scotland, Dumfries & Galloway, Ayrshire and the Isle of Arran

ARDWELL GARDENS
Ardwell, Nr Stranraer, Dumfries and Galloway DG9 9LY
Tel: 01776 860227
Owner: Mr Francis Brewis   **Contact:** Mrs Terry Brewis
The gardens include a formal garden, wild garden and woodland.
Location: OS Ref. NX102 455. A716 10m S of Stranraer.
Open: 1 Apr - 30 Sept: daily, 10am - 5pm.
Admission: Adult £3, Children under 14 free.

AUCHINLECK HOUSE
Ochiltree, Ayrshire
Tel: 01628 825920 or 825925   **Fax:** 01628 825417
e-mail: bookings@landmarktrust.org.uk   **www**.landmarktrust.org.uk
Owner/Contact: The Landmark Trust
One of the finest examples of an 18th century Scottish country house, the importance of which is further enhanced by its association with James Boswell, author of *The Life of Samuel Johnson*. The house has been restored by the Landmark Trust and is let for holidays for up to 13 people. Full details of staying at Auchinleck House and 183 other historic buildings are featured in the Landmark Trust Handbook (price £11 refundable against booking).
Location: OS Ref. NS507 230. Ochiltree, Ayrshire.
Open: Parts of the house will be open to the public Easter - Oct: Wed afternoons. Grounds: dawn - dusk in the Spring & Summer season.
Admission: By appointment only. Tickets £3 from 01628 825920.
🐕In grounds, on leads. 🛏Up to 13 people, self-catering.

BARGANY GARDENS
Girvan, Ayrshire KA26 9QL
Tel: 01465 871249   **Fax:** 01465 871282
Owner/Contact: Mr John Dalrymple Hamilton
Lily pond, rock garden and a fine collection of hard and softwood trees.
Location: OS Ref. NX851 992. 18m N of Dumfries, 3m NW of Thornhill off A76. 16m from M74 at Elvanfoot.
Open: May: daily, 1 - 5pm.
Admission: £2pp, Child Free. Buses by arrangement.

BRODICK CASTLE 🏰
Isle of Arran KA27 8HY
Tel: 0131 243 9300
Owner: The National Trust for Scotland
Castle built on the site of a Viking fortress with interesting contents.
Location: OS Ref. NX684 509. Off A711 /A755, in Kirkcudbright, at 12 High St.

BURNS' COTTAGE
Alloway, Ayrshire KA7 4PY
Tel: 01292 441215   **Fax:** 01292 441750   **Contact:** J Manson
Thatched cottage, birthplace of Robert Burns in 1759, with adjacent museum.
Location: OS Ref. NS335 190. 2m SW of Ayr. Two separate sites, 600yds apart.
Open: Apr - Sept: daily, 9.30am - 5.30pm. Oct - Mar: daily, 10am - 5pm. Closed 25/26 Dec & 1/2 Jan.
Admission: Adult £3, Child/OAP £2, Family £9. Prices may change in Apr 2006.

Threave Castle.

CAERLAVEROCK CASTLE 🏰
GLENCAPLE, DUMFRIES DG1 4RU
Tel: 01387 770244
Owner: In the care of Historic Scotland   **Contact:** Valerie Bennett
One of the finest castles in Scotland on a triangular site surrounded by moats. Its most remarkable features are the twin-towered gatehouse and the Renaissance Nithsdale lodging. The site of two famous sieges. Exhibition with video presentation, children's park, replica siege engines and nature trail to site of earlier castle.
Location: OS84 NY025 656. 8m S of Dumfries on the B725.
Open: Apr - Sept: daily, 9.30am - 6.30pm; Oct - Mar: daily, 9.30am - 4.30pm. Last ticket sold 30 mins before closing.
Admission: Adult £4.50, Child £2, Conc. £3.50. 10% discount for groups (10+).
ℹ️🖼 ♿Partial. WCs. 🎧 🅿 Limited for coaches. ■ Free if pre-booked. 🐕 In grounds, on leads. ✳ €

CARDONESS CASTLE 🏰
Gatehouse of Fleet
Tel: 01557 814427
Owner: In the care of Historic Scotland   **Contact:** The Steward
Well preserved ruin of a four storey tower house of 15th century standing on a rocky platform above the Water of Fleet. Ancient home of the McCullochs. Very fine fireplaces.
Location: OS Ref. NX591 553. 1m SW of Gatehouse of Fleet, beside the A75.
Open: 1 Apr - 30 Sept: daily, 9.30am - 6.30pm. Last ticket 6pm. Oct: daily except Thurs & Fri; Nov - Mar: Sats & Suns only, 9.30am - 4.30pm. Last ticket 4pm.
Admission: Adult £3, Child £1.30, Conc. £2.30.
ℹ️🖼 🅿 🐕 ✳ €

CASTLE KENNEDY GARDENS
Stair Estates, Rephad, Stranraer, Dumfries and Galloway DG9 8BX
Tel: 01776 702024 / 01581 400225 (Gardens) **Fax:** 01776 706248
e-mail: info@castlekennedygardens.co.uk
Owner: The Earl & Countess of Stair   **Contact:** The Earl of Stair
75 acres of gardens, originally laid out in 1730, includes rhododendrons, pinetum, walled garden and circular lily pond.
Location: OS Ref. NX109 610. 3m E of Stranraer on A75.
Open: Apr - Sept: daily, 10am - 5pm.
Admission: Adult £4, Child £1, OAP £3.

CRAIGDARROCH HOUSE
Moniaive, Dumfriesshire DG3 4JB
Tel: 01848 200202
Owner/Contact: Mr Alexander Sykes
Location: OS Ref. NX741 909. S side of B729, 2m W of Moniaive, 19m WNW of Dumfries.
Open: Jul: daily, 2 - 4pm. Please note: no WCs.
Admission: £2.

CRAIGIEBURN GARDEN

Craigieburn House, Nr Moffat, Dumfriesshire DG10 9LF

Tel: 01683 221250

Owner/Contact: Janet Wheatcroft

A plantsman's garden with a huge range of rare and unusual plants surrounded by natural woodland.

Location: OS Ref. NT117 053. NW side of A708 to Yarrow & Selkirk, 2¹/₂ m E of Moffat.

Open: 13 Apr - Oct: Thur - Sun (open for charity).

Admission: Adult £2.50, Child Free.

CROSSRAGUEL ABBEY

Maybole, Strathclyde

Tel: 01655 883113

Owner: In the care of Historic Scotland   **Contact:** The Steward

Founded in the early 13th century by the Earl of Carrick. Remarkably complete remains include church, cloister, chapter house and much of the domestic premises.

Location: OS Ref. NS275 083. 2m S of Maybole on the A77.

Open: 1 Apr - 30 Sept: daily, 9.30am - 6.30pm. Last ticket 6pm.

Admission: Adult £3, Child £1.30, Conc. £2.30.

CULZEAN CASTLE

Maybole KA19 8LE

Tel: 0131 243 9300

Owner: The National Trust for Scotland

Romantic 18th century Robert Adam clifftop mansion.

Location: OS Ref. NS240 100. 12m SW of Ayr, on A719, 4m W of Maybole.

DALGARVEN MILL MUSEUM

Dalgarven, Dalry Road, Nr Kilwinning, Ayrshire KA13 6PL

Tel/Fax: 01294 552448   **e-mail:** admin@dalgarvenmill.org.uk

Owner: Dalgarven Mill Trust   **Contact:** The Administrator

Museum of Ayrshire Country Life and Costume.

Location: OS Ref. NS295 460. On A737 2m from Kilwinning.

Open: All year: Summer: Easter - end Oct: Tue - Sat, 10am - 5pm, Suns, 11am - 5pm. Winter: Tue - Fri, 10am - 4pm, Sat 10am -5pm, Sun, 11am - 5pm.

Admission: Charges.

DEAN CASTLE COUNTRY PARK

Dean Road, Kilmarnock, East Ayrshire KA3 1XB

Tel: 01563 522702   **Fax:** 01563 572552

Owner: East Ayrshire Council   **Contact:** Andrew Scott-Martin

Set in 200 acres of Country Park. Visits to castle by guided tour only.

Location: OS Ref. NS437 395. Off A77. 1¹/₄ m NNE of town centre.

Open: Country Park: All year: dawn - dusk. Please telephone for Castle opening details.

Admission: Free (group charge on application).

DRUMLANRIG CASTLE 🏰   *See page 454 for full page entry.*

DUNDRENNAN ABBEY

Kirkcudbright

Tel: 01557 500262

Owner: Historic Scotland   **Contact:** The Steward

Mary Queen of Scots spent her last night on Scottish soil in this 12th century Cistercian abbey founded by David I. The abbey stands in a small and secluded valley.

Location: OS Ref. NX749 4750. 6¹/₂ m SE of Kirkcudbright on the A711.

Open: 1 Apr - 30 Sept: daily, 9.30am - 6.30pm. Last ticket 6pm. Oct: Sat - Wed; Nov - Mar: Sats & Suns only, 9.30am - 4.30pm. Last ticket 4pm.

Admission: Adult £2.50, Child £1, Conc. £2.

GILNOCKIE TOWER

Hollows, Canonbie, Dumfriesshire

Tel: 01387 371876   **e-mail:** ted.armclan@btinternet.com

Owner/Contact: Edward Armstrong

16th century tower house, occupied by the Clan Armstrong Centre.

Location: OS Ref. NY383 787. 2m N of Canonbie on minor road E of A7 just N of Hollows.

Open: Summer months by guided tour at 2.30pm sharp (1 tour daily). Winter months open by appointment. Tours to be booked in advance by telephone.

Admission: Adult £5, Child (under 14yrs) £2.50.

GLENLUCE ABBEY

Glenluce

Tel: 01581 300541

Owner/Contact: In the care of Historic Scotland

A Cistercian abbey founded in 1190. Remains include a 16th century chapter house.

Location: OS Ref. NX185 587. 2m NW of Glenluce village off the A75.

Open: 1 Apr - 30 Sept: daily 9.30am - 6.30pm. Last ticket 6pm. Oct: daily; Nov - Mar: Sats & Suns only, 9.30am - 4.30pm. Last ticket 4pm.

Admission: Adult £2.50, Child £1, Conc. £2.

GLENWHAN GARDENS

Dunragit, Stranraer, Wigtownshire DG9 8PH

Tel/Fax: 01581 400222   **Contact:** Tessa Knott

Beautiful 12 acre garden overlooking Luce Bay and the Mull of Galloway. Licensed tearoom, groups catered for.

Location: OS Ref. NX150 580. N side of A75, 6m E of Stranraer.

Open: 1 Apr - 30 Sept: daily, 10am - 5pm or by appointment at other times. Tearoom open from 30 Apr.

Admission: Adult £4, Child £1.50, Conc. £3.50, Family £10. Honesty box runs until end of October.

special events
see page 571

Auchinleck House.

South West Scotland, Dumfries & Galloway, Ayrshire and the Isle of Arran

KELBURN CASTLE & COUNTRY CENTRE 🏛
FAIRLIE, BY LARGS, AYRSHIRE KA29 0BE
www.kelburncountrycentre.com

For Country Park and Castle tours:- Earl of Glasgow
Tel: 01475 568685   **Fax:** 01475 568121   **e-mail:** admin@kelburncountrycentre.com
For functions in the Castle:- Countess of Glasgow
Tel: 01475 568204   **e-mail:** isabelglasgow@aol.com
Owner/Contact: The Earl of Glasgow
Kelburn is the home of the Earls of Glasgow and has been in the Boyle family for over 800 years. It is notable for its waterfalls, historic family gardens, romantic glen and unique trees, including two of the hundred most important in Scotland, and its outstanding views over the Firth of Clyde.
The Country Centre includes exhibitions, gift shop, licensed café, riding school, pottery workshop, falconry centre, full ranger service, stockade, new indoor

playbarn, pet's corner and Scotland's most unusual attraction – The Secret Forest. The Castle is open for guided tours in July and August and available for weddings, conferences, dinner parties and other functions all the year round.
Location: OS Ref NS210 580. A78 to Largs, 2m S of Largs.
Open: Country Centre: Easter - Oct: daily. Castle: July & Aug. Open by arrangement for groups at other times of the year.
Admission: Country Centre: Adult £7, Child/Conc. £4.50, Family £22. Groups (10+): Adult: £4.50, Conc. £3.50. Castle: £1.75 extra pp.
🏠 ⊤ 🛇 Partial. 🖤 🍴 Licensed.
🎦 July & August. By arrangement at other times of the year. 🅿 🖩
🐕 In grounds on leads. 🕸

LOGAN BOTANIC GARDEN
Port Logan, Stranraer, Wigtownshire DG9 9ND
Tel: 01776 860231 **Fax:** 01776 860333 **e-mail:** logan@rbge.org.uk
Owner: Royal Botanic Garden Edinburgh   **Contact:** The Curator
Scotland's most exotic garden. Take a trip to the south west of Scotland and experience the southern hemisphere!
Location: OS Ref. NX097 430. 14m S of Stranraer on B7065, off A716.
Open: 1 Mar - 31 Oct: daily, 10am - 5pm (Apr - Sept: closes 6pm).
Admission: Adult £3.50, Child £1, Conc. £3, Family £8. Group discount and membership programme available.

MACLELLAN'S CASTLE 🛡
Kirkcudbright
Tel: 01557 331856
Owner: In the care of Historic Scotland   **Contact:** The Steward
Castellated mansion, built in 1577 using stone from an adjoining ruined monastery by the then provost. Elaborately planned with fine architectural details, it has been a ruin since 1752.
Location: OS Ref. NX683 511. Centre of Kirkcudbright on the A711.
Open: 1 Apr - 30 Sept: daily, 9.30am - 6.30pm. Last ticket 6pm.
Admission: Adult £3, Child £1.30, Conc. £2.30.
ⓘ 🏠 🛇 Partial. 🖤 🐕 €

NEW ABBEY CORN MILL 🛡
New Abbey Village
Tel: 01387 850260
Owner: Historic Scotland   **Contact:** The Custodian
This carefully renovated 18th century water-powered oatmeal mill is in full working order and regular demonstrations are given for visitors in the summer.
Location: OS Ref. NX962 663. 8m S of Dumfries on the A710. Close to Sweetheart Abbey.
Open: 1 Apr - 30 Sept: daily, 9.30am - 6.30pm. Last ticket 6pm. 1 Oct - 31 Mar: Sat - Wed, 9.30am - 4.30pm. Last ticket 4pm.
Admission: Adult £3.50, Child £1.50, Conc. £2.50.
ⓘ 🏠 🖤 🕸 €

RAMMERSCALES 🏛
Lockerbie, Dumfriesshire DG11 1LD
Tel: 01387 810229 **e-mail:** malcolm@rammerscales.co.uk
Owner/Contact: Mr M A Bell Macdonald
Georgian house, with extensive library and fine views over Annandale.
Location: OS Ref. NY080 780. W side of B7020, 3m S of Lochmoben.
Open: Last week in Jul, 1st three weeks in Aug: daily (excluding Sat), 2 - 5pm.
Admission: Adult £5, Conc. £2.50.

SORN CASTLE 🏛
Ayrshire KA5 6HR
Tel: 01290 551555
Owner/Contact: Mrs R G McIntyre
Dating from the 14th century, the Castle stands on a cliff overlooking the River Ayr, surrounded by wooded grounds. It has been enlarged throughout the centuries, most recently in 1908. Sorn contains many fine Scottish paintings and artifacts.
Location: OS Ref. NS555 265. 4m E of Mauchline on B743.
Open: 15 Jul - 12 Aug: daily, 2 - 4pm and by appointment.
Admission: Adult £4.
🎦 🐕

STRANRAER CASTLE
Stranraer, Galloway
Tel: 01776 705088   **Fax:** 01776 705835
Owner: Dumfries & Galloway Council   **Contact:** John Picken
Also referred to as the Castle of St John. A much altered 16th century L-plan tower house, now a museum.
Location: OS Ref. NX061 608. In Stranraer, towards centre, ¼ m short of the harbour.
Open: Easter - mid Sept: Mon - Sat, 10am - 1pm & 2 - 5pm.
Admission: Free.

SWEETHEART ABBEY 🔔

New Abbey Village

Tel: 01387 850397

Owner: In the care of Historic Scotland   **Contact:** The Steward
Cistercian abbey founded in 1273 by Devorgilla, in memory of her husband John Balliol.
A principal feature is the well-preserved precinct wall enclosing 30 acres.

Location: OS Ref. NX965 663. In New Abbey Village, on A710 8m S of Dumfries.

Open: 1 Apr - 30 Sept: daily, 9.30am - 6.30pm. Last ticket 6pm. 1 Oct - 31 Mar: Sat -
Wed, 9.30am - 4.30pm. Last ticket 4pm.

Admission: Adult £3.50, Child £1.50, Conc. £2.50.

ℹ️ 🅿️ ✳️ €

THREAVE CASTLE 👑 🔔

Castle Douglas

Tel: 07711 223101

Owner: The National Trust for Scotland   **Contact:** Historic Scotland
Built by Archibald the Grim in the late 14th century, early stronghold of the Black
Douglases. Around its base is an artillery fortification built before 1455 when the
castle was besieged by James II. Ring the bell and the custodian will come to ferry
you over. Long walk to property. Owned by The National Trust for Scotland but
under the guardianship of Historic Scotland.

Location: OS Ref. NX739 623. 2m W of Castle Douglas on the A75.

Open: 1 Apr - 30 Sept: daily, 9.30am - 6.30pm. Last ticket 6pm.

Admission: Adult £3.50, Child £1.50, Conc. £2.50. Charges include ferry trip.

WHITHORN PRIORY & MUSEUM 🔔

Whithorn

Tel: 01988 500508

Owner: In the care of Historic Scotland   **Contact:** The Project Manager
The site of the first Christian church in Scotland. Founded as 'Candida Casa' by
St Ninian in the early 5th century it later became the cathedral church of Galloway.
Visitors can now see the collection of early Christian carved crosses in a newly
refurbished museum.

Location: OS Ref. NX445 403. At Whithorn on the A746. 18m S of Newton Stewart.

Open: 21 Mar - 31 Oct: daily, 10.30am - 5pm.

Admission: Adult £3, Child £1.50, Conc. £2. Joint ticket gives entry to Priory, Priory
Museum and 'The Story of Whithorn'.

ℹ️ 📷 ♿ 💼 🅿️ €

education index
see page 564

Caerlaverock Castle, Dumfriesshire.

MAP 13

DALMENY HOUSE

www.dalmeny.co.uk

Owner:
The Earl of Rosebery

▶ **CONTACT**

The Administrator
Dalmeny House
South Queensferry
Edinburgh
EH30 9TQ

Tel: 0131 331 1888
Fax: 0131 331 1788

e-mail: events@
dalmeny.co.uk

▶ **LOCATION**
OS Ref. NT167 779

From Edinburgh A90,
B924, 7m N, A90 ½ m.

On south shore
of Firth of Forth.

Bus: From St Andrew
Square to Chapel Gate
1m from House.

Rail: Dalmeny
station 3m.

Taxi: Call us Cabs
0131 331 3232.

Dalmeny House rejoices in one of the most beautiful and unspoilt settings in Great Britain, yet it is only seven miles from Scotland's capital, Edinburgh, fifteen minutes from Edinburgh airport and less than an hour's drive from Glasgow. It is an eminently suitable venue for group visits, business functions, meetings and special events, including product launches. Outdoor activities, such as off-road driving, can be arranged.

Dalmeny House, the family home of the Earls of Rosebery for over 300 years, boasts superb collections of porcelain and tapestries, fine paintings by Gainsborough, Raeburn, Reynolds and Lawrence, together with the exquisite Mentmore Rothschild collection of 18th century French furniture. There is also the Napoleonic collection, assembled by the 5th Earl of Rosebery, Prime Minister, historian and owner of three Derby winners.

The Hall, Library and Dining Room will lend a memorable sense of occasion to corporate receptions, luncheons and dinners. A wide range of entertainment can also be provided, from a clarsach player to a floodlit pipe band Beating the Retreat.

▶ **OPENING TIMES**

Summer
July and August
Sun - Tue, 2 - 5.30pm.
Last admission 4.30pm.

Winter
Open at other times by
appointment only.

▶ **ADMISSION**

Summer
Adult £5.00
Child (10-16yrs) £3.00
OAP £4.00
Student £4.00
Groups (20+) £4.00

ℹ️ Fashion shows, product launches, archery, clay pigeon shooting, shows, filming, background photography, small meetings and special events. Lectures on House, contents and family history. Helicopter landing area. House is centre of a 4½ m shore walk from Forth Rail Bridge to small foot passenger ferry at Cramond (ferry 9am - 1pm, 2 - 7pm in summer, 2 - 4pm winter, closed Fri). No fires, picnics or photography.

🍽️ Conferences and functions, buffets, lunches, dinners.

♿ Partially suitable. Visitors may alight at entrance. WC.

☕ Teas, groups can book in advance.

🚶 Obligatory. Special interest tours can be arranged outside normal opening hours.

🅿️ 60 cars, 3 coaches. Parking for functions in front of house.

Edinburgh City, Coast & Countryside

MAP 13

Owner:
Hopetoun House
Preservation Trust

▶ CONTACT

Mhairi MacDougall
Hopetoun House
South Queensferry
Edinburgh
West Lothian
EH30 9SL

Tel: 0131 331 2451
Fax: 0131 319 1885

e-mail: marketing@
hopetounhouse.com

▶ LOCATION

OS Ref. NT089 790

2¹/₂ m W of Forth Road
Bridge.

12m W of Edinburgh
(25 mins. drive).

34m E of Glasgow
(50 mins. drive).

HOPETOUN HOUSE 🏛

www.hopetounhouse.com

Hopetoun House is a unique gem of Europe's architectural heritage and undoubtedly 'Scotland's Finest Stately Home'. Situated on the shores of the Firth of Forth, it is one of the most splendid examples of the work of Scottish architects Sir William Bruce and William Adam. The interior of the house, with opulent gilding and classical motifs, reflects the aristocratic grandeur of the early 18th century, whilst its magnificent parkland has fine views across the Forth to the hills of Fife. The house is approached from the Royal Drive, used only by members of the Royal Family, notably King George IV in 1822 and Her Majesty Queen Elizabeth II in 1988.

Hopetoun is really two houses in one, the oldest part of the house was designed by Sir William Bruce and built between 1699 and

1707. It shows some of the finest examples in Scotland of carving, wainscotting and ceiling painting. In 1721 William Adam started enlarging the house by adding the magnificent façade, colonnades and grand State apartments which were the focus for social life and entertainment in the 18th century.

The house is set in 100 acres of rolling parkland including fine woodland walks, the red deer park, the spring garden with a profusion of wild flowers, and numerous picturesque picnic spots.

Hopetoun has been home of the Earls of Hopetoun, later created Marquesses of Linlithgow, since it was built in 1699 and in 1974 a charitable trust was created to preserve the house with its historic contents and surrounding landscape for the benefit of the public for all time.

▶ OPENING TIMES

Summer
13 April - 24 September:
Daily, 11am - 5.30pm.
Last admission 4.30pm.

Winter
By appointment only
for Groups (20+).

▶ ADMISSION

House & Grounds
Adul	£8.00
Child (5-16yrs)*	£4.25
Conc/Student	£7.00
Family (2+2)	£22.00
Additional Child	£3.00
Groups...................	£7.00

Grounds only
Adult	£3.70
Child (5-16yrs)*	£2.20
Conc/Student	£3.20
Family (2+2)	£10.00
Groups...................	£3.20

School Visits
Child	£5.25
Teachers.................	Free

*Under 5yrs Free.

Winter group rates on request.

Admission to Tearoom Free.

CONFERENCE/FUNCTION

ROOM	SIZE	MAX CAPACITY
Ballroom	92' x 35'	300
Tapestry Rm	37' x 24'	100
Red Drawing Rm	44' x 24'	100
State Dining Rm	39' x 23'	20
Stables	92' x 22'	200

📷 ℹ️ Private functions, special events, antiques fairs, concerts, Scottish gala evenings, conferences, wedding ceremonies and receptions, grand piano, helicopter landing. No smoking or flash photography in house.

🍸 Receptions, gala dinners.

♿ 🍷 Licensed.

🍴 Licensed. Groups (up to 250) can book in advance,

menus on request tel: 0131 331 4305.

🧍 By arrangement.

🅿️ Close to the house for cars and coaches. Book if possible, allow 1-2hrs for visit (min).

▪️ Special tours of house and/or grounds for different age/ interest groups.

🐕 No dogs in house, on leads in grounds. ❄️

Edinburgh City, Coast & Countryside

John Freeman/ The Royal Collection © 2006 HM Queen Elizabeth II

MAP 21

Owner:
Official Residence of
Her Majesty The Queen

▶ **CONTACT**
Ticket Sales &
Information Office
Buckingham Palace
London SW1A 1AA

Tel: 0131 556 5100
Groups (15+):
020 7766 7321

Fax: 020 7930 9625

e-mail: bookinginfo@
royalcollection.org.uk

▶ **LOCATION**
OS Ref. NT269 739

Central Edinburgh,
end of Royal Mile.

PALACE OF HOLYROODHOUSE
& THE QUEEN'S GALLERY

www.royalcollection.org.uk

The Palace of Holyroodhouse, the official residence in Scotland of Her Majesty The Queen, stands at the end of Edinburgh's Royal Mile against the spectacular backdrop of Arthur's Seat. This fine baroque palace is closely associated with Scotland's rich history. Today the Royal Apartments are used by The Queen for State ceremonies and official entertaining. They are finely decorated with magnificent works of art from the Royal Collection.

The Palace is perhaps best known as the home of Mary, Queen of Scots and was the setting for the many dramatic episodes in her short and turbulent reign. She witnessed the brutal murder of her secretary, Rizzio, by her jealous second husband, Lord Darnley, in her private apartments at Holyrood. Many of her personal belongings are on display in the Palace.

The Queen's Gallery, Edinburgh

The Gallery provides purpose-built facilities and state-of-the-art environmental controls, which enable exhibitions of the most delicate works from the Royal Collection to be shown.

Unfolding Pictures
(9 December 2005 - 29 May 2006)
The first exhibition of fans from the Royal Collection brings together over 80 samples, ranging from the early 17th century to the 1930s. Among the highlights will be a leather fan said to have belonged to Charles I, three fans by Fabergé and a vast ostrich feather fan presented to Her Majesty Queen Elizabeth The Queen Mother by the Worshipful Company of Fan Makers at the time of the Coronation in 1937.

Canaletto in Venice
(16 June 2006 - 7 January 2007)
His dazzling paintings and lively drawings have fixed the 18th century city of canals, palaces, churches and squares in the popular imagination. Fourteen luminous paintings of the Grand Canal will form the centrepiece of the exhibition and will be displayed with the largest group of Canaletto's drawings ever shown.

▶ **OPENING TIMES**

Palace of Holyroodhouse
April - October:
Daily (closed 14 April and during Royal Visits),
9.30am - 6pm.
Last admission 5pm.

November - February:
Daily (closed 25/26 December and during Royal Visits),
9.30am - 4.30pm.
Last admission 3.30pm.

Opening times are subject to change at short notice. Please check before planning a visit.

Private tours of the Palace and The Queen's Gallery are available for pre-booked groups (15+).
Tel: 020 7766 7322.

The Queen's Gallery
Daily (closed 14 April, 30 May - 15 June, 25/26 December). Opening times as Palace.

Each exhibition is priced separately. Timed admission may operate during peak periods.

▶ **ADMISSION**
(Price incl. audio tour)
For admission prices please call the Ticket Sales & Information Office.
Groups (15+) discounts available.

Information correct at time of going to print.

The Royal Collection © 2006 HM Queen Elizabeth II

The Royal Collection © 2006 HM Queen Elizabeth II

📷 ♿ Please book in advance. ☕ 🎧 Palace. 🅿️ 🖼 🐕 Guide dogs only. ❄

461

AMISFIELD MAINS
Nr Haddington, East Lothian EH41 3SA
Tel: 01875 870201 **Fax:** 01875 870620
Owner: Wemyss and March Estates Management Co Ltd   **Contact:** M Andrews
Georgian farmhouse with gothic barn and cottage.
Location: OS Ref. NT526 755. Between Haddington and East Linton on A199.
Open: Exterior only: By appointment, Wemyss and March Estates Office, Longniddry, East Lothian EH32 0PY.
Admission: Please contact for details.

ARNISTON HOUSE
GOREBRIDGE, MIDLOTHIAN EH23 4RY
www.arniston-house.co.uk

Tel/Fax: 01875 830515   **e-mail:** arnistonhouse@btconnect.com
Owner: Mrs A Dundas-Bekker   **Contact:** Miss H Dundas-Bekker
Magnificent William Adam mansion started in 1726. Fine plasterwork, Scottish portraiture, period furniture and other fascinating contents. Beautiful country setting beloved by Sir Walter Scott.
Location: OS Ref. NT326 595. Off B6372, 1m from A7, Temple direction.
Open: Apr, May & Jun: Tue & Wed; 2 Jul - 15 Sept: Sun - Fri, guided tours at 2pm & 3.30pm. Pre-arranged groups (10 - 50) accepted throughout the rest of the year.
Admission: Adult £5, Child £2, Conc. £4.
[i] No inside photography. WC. Obligatory. P In grounds, on leads.

BEANSTON
Nr Haddington, East Lothian EH41 3SB
Tel: 01875 870201 **Fax:** 01875 870620
Owner: Wemyss and March Estates Management Co Ltd   **Contact:** M Andrews
Georgian farmhouse with Georgian orangery.
Location: OS Ref. NT546 763. Between Haddington and East Linton on A199.
Open: Exterior only: By appointment, Wemyss and March Estates Office, Longniddry, East Lothian EH32 0PY.
Admission: Please contact for details.

BLACKNESS CASTLE
Blackness
Tel: 01506 834807
Owner: In the care of Historic Scotland   **Contact:** The Steward
One of Scotland's most important strongholds. Built in the 14th century and massively strengthened in the 16th century as an artillery fortress, it has been a royal castle and a prison armaments depot and film location for *Hamlet*. It was restored by the Office of Works in the 1920s. It stands on a promontory in the Firth of Forth.
Location: OS Ref. NT055 803. 4m NE of Linlithgow on the Firth of Forth, off the A904.
Open: 1 Apr - 30 Sept: daily, 9.30am - 6.30pm. Last ticket 6pm. 1 Oct - 31 Mar: daily, 9.30am - 4.30pm. Last ticket 4pm. Closed Thur & Fri in winter.
Admission: Adult £3.50, Child £1.50, Conc. £2.50.

CRAIGMILLAR CASTLE
Edinburgh
Tel: 0131 661 4445
Owner: In the care of Historic Scotland   **Contact:** The Steward
Mary, Queen of Scots fled to Craigmillar after the murder of Rizzio. This handsome structure with courtyard and gardens covers an area of one and a quarter acres. Built around an L-plan tower house of the early 15th century including a range of private rooms linked to the hall of the old tower.
Location: OS Ref. NT285 710. 22½ m SE of Edinburgh off the A68.
Open: 1 Apr - 30 Sept: daily, 9.30am - 6.30pm. Last ticket 6pm. 1 Oct - 31 Mar: daily, 9.30am - 4.30pm. Last ticket 4pm. Closed Thur & Fri in winter.
Admission: Adult £3.50, Child £1.50, Conc. £2.50.

CRICHTON CASTLE
Pathhead
Tel: 01875 320017
Owner: In the care of Historic Scotland   **Contact:** The Steward
A large and sophisticated castle with a spectacular façade of faceted stonework in an italian style added by the Earl of Bothwell between 1581 and 1591 following a visit to Italy. Mary Queen of Scots attended a wedding here.
Location: OS Ref. NT380 612. 3½ m SW of Pathhead off the A68.
Open: 1 Apr - 30 Sept: daily, 9.30am - 6.30pm, last ticket 6pm.
Admission: Adult £3, Child £1.30, Conc. £2.30.

DALMENY HOUSE
See page 459 for full page entry.

©Historic Scotland Photographic Library.

DIRLETON CASTLE & GARDEN
DIRLETON, EAST LOTHIAN EH39 5ER

Tel: 01620 850330
Owner: In the care of Historic Scotland   **Contact:** The Steward
The oldest part of this romantic castle dates from the 13th century, when it was built by the De Vaux family. The renowned gardens, first laid out in the 16th century, now include a magnificent Arts and Crafts herbaceous border (the longest in the world) and a re-created Victorian Garden. In the picturesque village of Dirleton.
Location: OS Ref. NT516 839. In Dirleton, 2m W of North Berwick on the A198.
Open: Apr - Sept: daily, 9.30am - 6.30pm. Oct - Mar: daily, 9.30am - 4.30pm. Last ticket 30 mins before closing.
Admission: Adult £4, Child £1.60, Conc. £3. 10% discount for groups (10+).
Partial. P Free if booked.

special events
see page 571

DUNGLASS COLLEGIATE CHURCH

Cockburnspath

Tel: 0131 668 8800

Owner: In the care of Historic Scotland

Founded in 1450 for a college of canons by Sir Alexander Hume. A handsome cross-shaped building with vaulted nave, choir and transepts.

Location: OS67 NT766 718. 1m NW of Cockburnspath. SW of A1.

Open: All year.

Admission: Free.

GOSFORD HOUSE

LONGNIDDRY, EAST LOTHIAN EH32 0PX

Tel: 01875 870201   **Owner/Contact:** The Earl of Wemyss

Though the core of the house is Robert Adam, the family home is in the South Wing built by William Young in 1890. This contains the celebrated Marble Hall and a fine collection of paintings and works of art. The house is set in extensive policies with an 18th century Pleasure Garden and Ponds. Greylag geese and swans abound.

Location: OS Ref. NT453 786. Off A198 2m NE of Longniddry.

Open: 11 Jun - 11 Aug: Fri - Sun, 2 - 5pm.

Admission: Adult £6, Child £1.

In grounds, on leads.

EDINBURGH CASTLE

CASTLEHILL, EDINBURGH EH1 2NG

Tel: 0131 225 9846   **Fax:** 0131 220 4733

Owner: Historic Scotland   **Contact:** The Stewards

Scotland's most famous castle, dominating the capital's skyline and giving stunning views of the city and countryside. Home to the Scottish crown jewels, the Stone of Destiny and Mons Meg. Other highlights include St Margaret's Chapel, the Great Hall and the Scottish National War Memorial.

Location: OS Ref. NT252 736. At the top of the Royal Mile in Edinburgh.

Open: Apr - Sept: daily, 9.30am - 6pm. Oct - Mar: daily, 9.30am - 5pm. Last ticket 45 mins before closing.

Admission: Adult £10.30, Child £4.50, Conc. £8.50. Pre-booked school visits available free, except May - Aug.

Private evening hire. Partial. WCs. Courtesy vehicle. Licensed. In 6 languages. (except Jun-Oct). Guide dogs.

THE GEORGIAN HOUSE

7 Charlotte Square, Edinburgh EH2 4DR

Tel: 0131 243 9300

Owner: The National Trust for Scotland

A good example of the neo-classical 'palace front'. Three floors are furnished as they would have been around 1796. There is an array of china and silver, pictures and furniture, gadgets and utensils.

Location: OS Ref. NT247 738. In Charlotte Square.

GLADSTONE'S LAND

477b Lawnmarket, Royal Mile, Edinburgh EH1 2NT

Tel: 0131 243 9300

Owner: The National Trust for Scotland

Gladstone's Land was the home of a prosperous Edinburgh merchant in the 17th century. Decorated and furnished to give visitors an impression of life in Edinburgh's Old Town some 300 years ago.

Location: OS Ref. NT255 736. In Edinburgh's Royal Mile, near the castle.

GREYWALLS

MUIRFIELD, GULLANE, EAST LOTHIAN EH31 2EG

www.greywalls.co.uk

Tel: 01620 842144   **Fax:** 01620 842241   **e-mail:** hotel@greywalls.co.uk

Owner: Giles Weaver   **Contact:** Mrs Sue Prime

Stunning Edwardian Country House Hotel only 30 minutes from the centre of Edinburgh. Close to wonderful golf courses and beaches. Designed by Sir Edwin Lutyens with secluded walled gardens attributed to Gertrude Jekyll. Greywalls offers the delights of an award-winning menu and an excellent wine list in this charming and relaxed environment (non residents welcome).

Location: OS Ref. NT490 835. Off A198, 5m W of North Berwick, 30 mins from Edinburgh.

Open: Apr - Oct.

Edinburgh City, Coast & Countryside

HAILES CASTLE

East Linton

Tel: 0131 668 8800

Owner: In the care of Historic Scotland

Beautifully-sited ruin incorporating a fortified manor of the 13th century. It was extended in the 14th and 15th centuries. There are two vaulted pit prisons.

Location: OS Ref. NT575 758. 1¹/₂ m SW of East Linton. 4m E of Haddington. S of A1.

Open: All year.

Admission: Free.

HARELAW FARMHOUSE

Nr Longniddry, East Lothian EH32 0PH

Tel: 01875 870201 **Fax:** 01875 870620

Owner: Wemyss and March Estates Management Co Ltd   **Contact:** M Andrew

Early 19th century 2-storey farmhouse built as an integral part of the steading. Dovecote over entrance arch.

Location: OS Ref. NT450 766. Between Longniddry and Drem on B1377.

Open: Exteriors only: By appointment, Wemyss and March Estates Office, Longniddry, East Lothian EH32 0PY.

Admission: Please contact for details.

HOPETOUN HOUSE

See page 460 for full page entry.

HOUSE OF THE BINNS

Linlithgow, West Lothian EH49 7NA

Tel: 0131 243 9300

Owner: The National Trust for Scotland

17th century house, home of the Dalyells, one of Scotland's great families, since 1612.

Location: OS Ref. NT051 786. Off A904, 15m W of Edinburgh. 3m E of Linlithgow.

LENNOXLOVE HOUSE

Haddington, East Lothian EH41 4NZ

Tel: 01620 823720 **Fax:** 01620 825112 **e-mail:** enquiries@lennoxlove.com

Owner: Lennoxlove House Ltd   **Contact:** Events Manager

Location: OS Ref. NT515 721. 18m E of Edinburgh, 1m S of Haddington.

Open: Lennoxlove House will be closed until summer 2007 for refurbishment.

LIBERTON HOUSE

73 Liberton Drive, Edinburgh EH16 6NP

Tel: 0131 467 7777 **Fax:** 0131 467 7774 **e-mail:** mail@ngra.co.uk

Owner/Contact: Nicholas Groves-Raines

Built around 1600 for the Littles of Liberton, this harled L-plan house has been carefully restored by the current architect owner using original detailing and extensive restoration of the principal structure. Public access restricted to the Great Hall and Old Kitchen. The restored garden layout suggests the original and there is a late 17th century lectern doocot by the entrance drive.

Location: OS Ref. NT267 694. 73 Liberton Drive, Edinburgh.

Open: 1 Mar - 31 Oct: 10am - 4.30pm, by prior appointment only.

Admission: Free.

Unsuitable. Limited.

Hopetoun House.

LINLITHGOW PALACE

LINLITHGOW, WEST LOTHIAN EH49 7AL

Tel: 01506 842896

Owner: Historic Scotland   **Contact:** The Steward

The magnificent remains of a great royal palace set in its own park and beside Linlithgow Loch. A favoured residence of the Stewart monarchs, James V and his daughter Mary, Queen of Scots were born here. Bonnie Prince Charlie stayed here during his bid to regain the British crown.

Location: OS Ref. NT003 774. In the centre of Linlithgow off the M9.

Open: Apr - Sept: daily, 9.30am - 6.30pm. Oct - Mar: Daily, 9.30am - 4.30pm. Last ticket 30 mins before closing.

Admission: Adult £4.50, Child £2, Conc. £3.50. 10% discount for groups (10+).

Picnic area. Private evening hire. Partial. Free if booked. Cars only. In grounds, on leads. Tel for details.

NEWLISTON

Kirkliston, West Lothian EH29 9EB

Tel: 0131 333 3231

Owner/Contact: Mrs Caroline Maclachlan

Late Robert Adam house. 18th century designed landscape, rhododendrons, azaleas and water features. On Sundays tea is in the Edinburgh School of Food and Wine in the William Adam Coach House. Also on Sundays there is a ride-on steam model railway from 2pm to 5pm.

Location: OS Ref. NT110 735. 8m W of Edinburgh, 3m S of Forth Road Bridge, off B800.

Open: 3 May - 4 Jun: Wed - Sun, 2 - 6pm. Also by appointment.

Admission: Adult £2, Conc. £1.

Grounds. In grounds, on leads.

NIDDRY CASTLE

By Winchburgh, West Lothian EH52 6RP

Tel: 01506 891751

Owner/Contact: Richard Nairn

Niddry Castle is a late 15th/early 16th century L -plan tower built by George, 3rd Lord Seton. In 1676 it was sold to John Hope whose family lived there for around 30 years until Hopetoun House was built and the castle subsequently abandoned. It was ruined for almost 300 years until the mid-1980s when it was partially restored.

Location: OS Ref. NT095 734 . 1km S of Winchburgh, towards A89

Open: 3 May - 4 Jun: Wed - Sun, 1.30 - 4.30pm. Limited access to interior pending restoration.

Admission: Adult £3, Child £1.50

Unsuitable. Limited. No coaches. Guide dogs only.

PALACE OF HOLYROODHOUSE
& THE QUEEN'S GALLERY

See page 461 for full page entry.

PRESTON MILL

East Linton, East Lothian EH40 3DS

Tel: 0131 243 9300

Owner: The National Trust for Scotland   **Contact:** Property Manager

For centuries there has been a mill on this site and the present one operated commercially until 1957.

Location: OS Ref. NT590 770. Off the A1, in East Linton, 23m E of Edinburgh.

©Historic Scotland Photographic Library

Edinburgh City, Coast & Countryside

RED ROW

Aberlady, East Lothian

Tel: 01875 870201   **Fax:** 018/5 8/0620

Owner: Wemyss & March Estates Management Co Ltd   **Contact:** M Andrews
Terraced Cottages.

Location: OS Ref. NT464 798. Main Street, Aberlady, East Lothian.

Open: Exterior only. By appointment, Wemyss & March Estates Office, Longniddry, East Lothian EH32 0PY.

Admission: Please contact for details.

ROYAL BOTANIC GARDEN EDINBURGH

20A Inverleith Row, Edinburgh EH3 5LR

Tel: 0131 552 7171   **Fax:** 0131 248 2901   **e-mail:** info@rbge.org.uk

Contact: Press Office

Scotland's premier garden. Discover the wonders of the plant kingdom in over 70 acres of beautifully landscaped grounds.

Location: OS Ref. NT249 751. Off A902, 1m N of city centre.

Open: Daily (except 25 Dec & 1 Jan): open 10am, closing: Nov - Feb: 4pm; Mar & Oct: 6pm; Apr - Sept: 7pm.

Admission: Free, with an admission charge on the Glasshouses.

ST MARY'S EPISCOPAL CATHEDRAL

Palmerston Place, Edinburgh EH12 5AW

Tel: 0131 225 6293   **Fax:** 0131 225 3181

                                        Contact: Cathedral Secretary

Neo-gothic grandeur in the classical new town. Designed by G Gilbert Scott.

Location: OS Ref. NT241 735. $^1/_2$ m W of west end of Princes Street.

Open: Mon - Fri, 7.30am - 6pm; Sat & Sun, 7.30am - 5pm. Sun services: 8am, 10.30am & 3.30pm. Services: Weekdays, 7.30am, 1.30pm & 5.30pm; Thurs, 11.30am, Sat, 7.30am.

Admission: Free.

SCOTTISH NATIONAL PORTRAIT GALLERY

1 Queen Street, Edinburgh EH2 1JD

Tel: 0131 624 6200

Unique visual history of Scotland.

Location: OS Ref. NT256 742. At E end of Queen Street, 300yds N of Princes Street.

Open: All year to permanent collection: daily, 10am - 5pm (Thurs closes 7pm). Closed 25 & 26 Dec. Open 1 Jan, 12 noon - 5pm.

Admission: Free

TANTALLON CASTLE 🛡

BY NORTH BERWICK, EAST LOTHIAN EH39 5PN

Tel: 01620 892727

Owner: In the care of Historic Scotland   **Contact:** The Steward

Set on the edge of the cliffs, looking out to the Bass Rock, this formidable castle was a stronghold of the powerful Douglas family. The castle has earthwork defences and a massive 80-foot high 14th century curtain wall. Interpretive displays include a replica gun.

Location: OS67 NT595 850. 3m E of North Berwick off the A198.

Open: Apr - Sept: daily, 9.30am - 6.30pm. Last ticket 6pm. Oct - Mar: Sat - Wed, 9.30am - 4.30pm. Last ticket 4pm.

Admission: Adult £4, Child £1.60, Conc. £3. 10% discount for groups (11+).

ⓘPicnic area. ⬚ ♿Partial. ▣ 🅿 ▣ Booked school visits free.
🐕In grounds, on leads. ✳ €

Tantallon Castle.

Greater Glasgow and Clyde Valley

BURRELL COLLECTION

Pollok Country Park, 2060 Pollokshaws Road, Glasgow G43 1AT

Tel: 0141 287 2550   **Fax:** 0141 287 2597

Owner: Glasgow Museums

An internationally renowned, outstanding collection of art.

Location: OS Ref. NS555 622. Glasgow 15 min drive.

Open: All year: Mon - Thur & Sats, 10am - 5pm, Fri & Sun, 11am - 5pm. Closed 25/26 Dec, 31 Dec (pm) & 1/2 Jan.

Admission: Free. Small charge may apply for temporary exhibitions.

COLZIUM HOUSE & WALLED GARDEN

Colzium-Lennox Estate, off Stirling Road, Kilsyth G65 0RZ

Tel/Fax: 01236 828156

Owner: North Lanarkshire Council   **Contact:** Charlie Whyte

A walled garden with an extensive collection of conifers, rare shrubs and trees, curling pond, picnic tables, woodland walks.

Location: OS Ref. NS722 786. Off A803 Banknock to Kirkintilloch Road. 1/2 m E of Kilsyth.

Open: Walled garden: Apr - Sept: daily, 12 noon - 7pm; Oct - Mar: Sats & Suns, 12noon - 4pm. House closed for refurbishment 2006.

Admission: Free

COREHOUSE

Lanark ML11 9TQ

Tel: 0131 667 1514

Owner: The Trustees of the late Lt Col A J E Cranstoun MC   **Contact:** Estate Office

Designed by Sir Edward Blore and built in the 1820s, Corehouse is a pioneering example of the Tudor Architectural Revival in Scotland.

Location: OS Ref. NS882 416. On S bank of the Clyde above the village of Kirkfieldbank.

Open: 8 - 31 May & 9 - 17 Sept: Sat - Wed. Guided tours: weekdays: 1 & 2pm, weekends: 3 & 4pm. Closed Thurs & Fri.

Admission: Adult £5, Child (under 14yrs)/OAP £2.50.

Obligatory.

CRAIGNETHAN CASTLE

Lanark, Strathclyde

Tel: 01555 860364

Owner: Historic Scotland   **Contact:** The Steward

In a picturesque setting overlooking the River Nethan and defended by a wide and deep ditch with an unusual caponier, a stone vaulted artillery chamber, unique in Britain.

Location: OS Ref. NS815 463. 5 1/2 m WNW of Lanark off the A72. 1/2 m footpath to W.

Open: 1 Apr - 30 Sept: daily, 9.30am - 6.30pm. Oct: Sat - Wed; Nov - Mar: Sats & Suns only, 9.30am - 4.30pm.

Admission: Adult £3, Child £1.30, Conc. £2.30.

Picnic area. WC. €

Colzium Walled Garden.

GLASGOW CATHEDRAL

Castle Street, Glasgow

Tel: 0141 552 6891

Owner: Historic Scotland   **Contact:** The Steward

The only Scottish mainland medieval cathedral to have survived the Reformation complete. Built over the tomb of St Kentigern. Notable features in this splendid building are the elaborately vaulted crypt, the stone screen of the early 15th century and the unfinished Blackadder Aisle.

Location: OS Ref. NS603 656. E end of city centre. In central Glasgow.

Open: 1 Apr - 30 Sept: Mon - Sat, 9.30am - 6pm, Sun, 1 - 5pm; 1 Oct - 31 Mar: Mon - Sat, 9.30am - 4pm, Sun 1 - 4pm.

Admission: Free.

Partial. Tel for details.

MOTHERWELL HERITAGE CENTRE

High Road, Motherwell ML1 3HU

Tel: 01698 251000

Owner: North Lanarkshire Council   **Contact:** The Manager

Multimedia exhibition and other displays of local history. STB 4-Star attraction.

Location: OS Ref. NS750 570. In High Road, 200yds N of A723 (Hamilton Road).

Open: All year. Wed - Sat, 10am - 5pm. Sun, 12 noon - 5pm. (Closed 25/26 Dec & 1/2 Jan). Closed Mon & Tue.

Admission: Free.

John Soury

NEW LANARK WORLD HERITAGE SITE

NEW LANARK MILLS, LANARK, S. LANARKSHIRE ML11 9DB

www.newlanark.org

Tel: 01555 661345   **Fax:** 01555 665738   **e-mail:** visit@newlanark.org

Owner: New Lanark Conservation Trust   **Contact:** Rachael Love

Surrounded by native woodlands and close to the famous Falls of Clyde, this cotton mill village was founded in 1785 and became famous as the site of Robert Owen's radical reforms. Now beautifully restored as both a living community and attraction, the fascinating history of the village is interpreted in an award-winning Visitor Centre. Accommodation is available in the New Lanark Mill Hotel and Waterhouses, a stunning conversion from an original 18th century mill. New Lanark is now a World Heritage Site.

Location: OS Ref. NS880 426. 1m S of Lanark.

Open: All year: daily, 10.30am - 5pm (11am - 5pm Sept - May). Closed 25 Dec & 1 Jan.

Admission: Visitor Centre: Adult £5.95, Child/Conc. £4.95. Groups: 1 free/10 booked.

Conference facilities. Partial. WC. Visitor Centre wheelchair friendly. By arrangement. 5 min walk. In grounds, on leads. Tel for details. €

NEWARK CASTLE

Port Glasgow, Strathclyde

Tel: 01475 741858

Owner: In the care of Historic Scotland   **Contact:** The Steward

The oldest part of the castle is a tower built soon after 1478 with a detached gatehouse, by George Maxwell. The main part was added in 1597 - 99 in a most elegant style. Enlarged in the 16th century by his descendent, the wicked Patrick Maxwell who murdered two of his neighbours.

Location: OS Ref. NS329 744. In Port Glasgow on the A8.

Open: 1 Apr - 30 Sept: daily, 9.30am - 6.30pm. Last ticket 6pm.

Admission: Adult £3, Child £1.30, Conc. £2.30.

WC. €

Patrick Lane

POLLOK HOUSE ♘

Pollok Country Park, Pollokshaws Road, Glasgow G43 1AT

Tel: 0131 243 9300

Owner: The National Trust for Scotland

The house contains an internationally famed collection of paintings as well as porcelain and furnishings appropriate to an Edwardian house.

Location: OS Ref. NS550 616. In Pollok Country Park, off M77/J1, follow signs for Burrell Collection.

ST MARY'S EPISCOPAL CATHEDRAL

300 Great Western Road, Glasgow G4 9JB

Tel: 0141 339 6691   **Fax:** 0141 334 5669   **Contact:** The Office

Newly restored, fine Gothic Revival church by Sir George Gilbert Scott, with outstanding contemporary murals by Gwyneth Leech. Regular concerts and exhibitions.

Location: OS Ref. NS578 669. 1/4 m after the Dumbarton A82 exit from M8 motorway.

Open: All year. Tue - Thur, 5.30 - 7.30pm, Sat, 9.30 - 10am. Sun services: 8.30am, 10am, 12 noon & 6.30pm.

SUMMERLEE HERITAGE PARK

Heritage Way, Coatbridge, North Lanarkshire ML5 1QD

Tel: 01236 431261

Owner: North Lanarkshire Council   **Contact:** The Manager

STB 4-star attraction. 22 acres of industrial heritage including Scotland's only remaining electric tramway; a re-created addit mine and mine workers' cottages. Please note that all or part of Summerlee may be closed at times during 2006. This is due to a major redevelopment of the exhibition hall. If planning a visit, please phone for full details.

Location: OS Ref. NS729 655. 600yds NW of Coatbridge town centre.

Open: All year. Summer: 10am - 5pm. Winter: 10am - 4pm (closed 25/26 Dec & 1/2 Jan).

Admission: Free. Tram ride: Adult 80p, Child 45p.

❄

THE TENEMENT HOUSE ♘

145 Buccleuch Street, Glasgow G3 6QN

Tel: 0131 243 9300

Owner: The National Trust for Scotland

A typical Victorian tenement flat of 1892, and time capsule of the first half of the 20th century.

Location: OS Ref. NS583 662. Garnethill (three streets N of Sauchiehall Street, near Charing Cross), Glasgow.

THE TOWER OF HALLBAR

Braidwood Road, Braidwood, Lanarkshire ML8 5RD

Tel: 0845 090 0194   **Fax:** 0845 090 0174   **e-mail:** enquiries@vivat.org.uk

www.vivat.org.uk

Owner: The Vivat Trust   **Contact:** Miss Ellen Jordan

A 16th century defensive tower and Bothy set in ancient orchards and meadowland. Converted into self-catering holiday accommodation by The Vivat Trust and furnished and decorated in keeping with its history. Hallbar sleeps up to seven people, including facilities for a disabled person and their carer.

Location: OS Ref. NS842 471. S side of B7056 between Crossford Bridge & Braidwood.

Open: All year. Sats, 2 - 3pm, or by appointment. Also four open days a year.

Admission: Free.

♿ Partial. 🎬 By arrangement. 🅿 Limited. 🐕 In grounds, on leads.
🛏 3 single, 1 twin & 1 double. ❄

special events
see page 571

New Lanark World Heritage Site.

Perthshire, Angus & Dundee and The Kingdom of Fife

MAP 13

Owner: Blair
Charitable Trust

▶ CONTACT

Administration Office
Blair Castle
Blair Atholl
Pitlochry
Perthshire PH18 5TL

Tel: 01796 481207
Fax: 01796 481487
e-mail: office@
blair-castle.co.uk

▶ LOCATION

OS Ref. NN880 660

From Edinburgh 80m,
M90 to Perth, A9,
follow signs for Blair
Castle, 1¹/₂ hrs.
Trunk Road A9 2m.

Bus: Bus stop 1m
in Blair Atholl.

Train: 1m, Blair Atholl
Euston-Inverness line.

Taxi: Elizabeth Yule,
01796 472290.

FUNCTION

ROOM	SIZE	MAX CAPACITY
Ballroom	88' x 36'	400
Ballroom Dining	36' x 25'	220
Exhibition Hall	55' x 27'	90

BLAIR CASTLE

www.blair-castle.co.uk

Perthshire's 5 star historic home. Blair Castle has been the ancient home and fortress of the Earls and Dukes of Atholl for over 725 years. Its central location makes it easily accessible from all major Scottish centres in less than two hours.

The castle has known the splendour of Royal visitations, submitted to occupation by opposing forces on no less than four occasions, suffered siege and changed its architectural appearance to suit the taste of successive generations.

Today 30 rooms of infinite variety display fine furniture, paintings, arms, armour, china, costumes, lace and embroidery, and Jacobite relics.

The Duke of Atholl has the unique distinction of having the only remaining private army in Europe – The Atholl Highlanders.

GARDENS

Blair Castle is set in extensive and beautiful grounds. Hercules Garden is a walled garden of some 9 acres, which has recently been restored. Diana's Grove is a two acre plantation, which includes some of the tallest trees in the UK. A picnic area and a deer park are readily accessible from the car park and castle.

Fashion shows, equestrian events, shows, rallies, filming, highland and charity balls, piping championships, grand piano, helicopter pad, cannon firing by Atholl Highlanders, resident piper, needlework displays. No smoking.

Civil and religious weddings may be held in the castle and receptions for up to 220 guests can be held in the ballroom. Banquets, dinners and private functons are welcome.

May alight at entrance. WC & wheelchair facilities. Limited mobility scooter available for hire.

Non-smoking. Seats up to 125. Private group lunches for up to 35 can be arranged in the Garry Room.

Audio visual presentation.

In English, German and French at no extra cost. Tour time 1¹/₂ hrs (max). Illustrated guide books (English, German, French and Italian) £3.50.

200 cars, 20 coaches. Coach drivers/couriers free, plus free meal and shop voucher, information pack.

Nature walks, deer park, ranger service & pony trekking, children's play area.

Grounds only. ❄

Event programme available on application.

▶ OPENING TIMES

Summer
1 April - 27 October
Daily, 9.30am - 4.30pm
(Last admission).

Winter
Tuesday and Saturday mornings and for groups by arrangement.

▶ ADMISSION

House & Grounds
Adult £7.20
Child (5-16yrs)....... £4.50
Senior £6.20
Student (with ID) .. £5.90
Family £18.50
Disabled £2.30
Groups* (12+)
(Please book)
Adult £5.80
Child(5-16yrs)........ £4.25
Primary School £3.25
Senior £5.35
Student (with ID) .. £4.80
Disabled £2.10

Grounds only
(with access to restaurant,
gift shop & WC)
Adult £2.30
Child (5-16yrs)....... £1.20
Senior/Student....... £2.30
Family £5.40
Disabled .... Free
Scooter Hire £3.20
Groups* (12+)
(Please book)
Adult £2.10
Child (5-16yrs).......£1.10
Primary School £1.00
Senior/Student....... £2.10
Disabled .... Free

* Group rates only apply when all tickets bought by the Driver, Courier or Group Leader at one time.

MAP 13

Owner: Grimsthorpe & Drummond Castle Trust

▶ **CONTACT**

The Caretaker
Drummond Castle
Gardens
Muthill
Crieff
Perthshire PH7 4HZ

Tel: 01764 681433
Fax: 01764 681642
e-mail:
thegardens@drummond
castle.sol.co.uk

▶ **LOCATION**

OS Ref. NN844 181

2m S of Crieff off the A822.

DRUMMOND CASTLE GARDENS

www.drummondcastlegardens.co.uk

Scotland's most important formal gardens, among the finest in Europe. A mile of beech-lined avenue leads to a formidable ridge top tower house. The magnificent Italianate parterre is revealed from a viewpoint at the top of the terrace, celebrating the saltaire and family heraldry that surrounds the famous multiplex sundial by John Milne, master mason to Charles I. First laid out in the early 17th century by John Drummond, 2nd Earl of Perth and renewed in the early 1950s by Phyllis Astor, Countess of Ancaster. The gardens contain ancient yew hedges and two copper beech trees planted by Queen Victoria during her visit in 1842. Shrubberies are planted with many varieties of Maple and other individual ornamental trees including purple-leaf oaks, whitebeam, weeping birch and a tulip tree, *Liriodendron tulipifera*. The tranquility of the gardens makes them the perfect setting to stroll amongst the well-manicured plantings or sit and absorb the atmosphere of this special place.

▶ **OPENING TIMES**

Easter weekend & 1 May -
31 October
Daily, 1 - 6pm

Last admission 5pm.

▶ **ADMISSION**

Adult	£4.00
Child	£1.50
Conc.	£3.00

Groups (20+)
10% discount.

Prices subject to change.

Partial. Viewing platform. WC.   By arrangement.   On leads.   Tel for details.

MAP 13

Owner: The Earl of Strathmore & Kinghorne

▶ **CONTACT**

Mr David Adams
Castle Administrator
Estates Office
Glamis
by Forfar
Angus   DD8 1RJ

Tel: 01307 840393
Fax: 01307 840733

e-mail: enquiries@
glamis-castle.co.uk

▶ **LOCATION**

OS Ref. NO386 480

From Edinburgh M90,
A94, 81m.
From Forfar A94, 6m.
From Glasgow 93m.
Motorway: M90.

Rail: Dundee
Station 12m.

Air: Dundee
Airport 12m.

Taxi: K Cabs
01575 573744.

GLAMIS CASTLE 🏛

www.glamis-castle.co.uk

Glamis Castle is the family home of the Earls of Strathmore and Kinghorne and has been a royal residence since 1372. It was the childhood home of Her Majesty Queen Elizabeth The Queen Mother, the birthplace of Her Royal Highness The Princess Margaret and the legendary setting of Shakespeare's play *Macbeth*. Although the castle is open to visitors it remains a family home lived in and loved by the Strathmore family.

The castle, a five-storey 'L' shaped tower block, was originally a royal hunting lodge. It was remodelled in the 17th century and is built of pink sandstone. It contains the Great Hall, with its

magnificent plasterwork ceiling dated 1621, a beautiful family Chapel constructed inside the Castle in 1688, an 18th century billiard room housing what is left of the extensive library once at Glamis, a 19th century dining room containing family portraits and the Royal Apartments which have been used by Her Majesty Queen Elizabeth The Queen Mother.

The castle stands in an extensive park, landscaped towards the end of the 18th century, and contains the beautiful Italian Garden and the Pinetum which reflect the peace and serenity of the castle and grounds.

▶ **OPENING TIMES**

Mid March - December
Daily, 10am - 6pm.

Last admission 4.30pm.

Groups welcome. Out of hours visits can also be arranged.

▶ **ADMISSION**

Castle & Grounds

Adult	£7.30
Child (5-16yrs)	£4.10
OAP/Student	£6.10
Family	£21.00

Groups (20+)

Adult	£6.20
Child (5-16yrs)	£3.60
OAP/Student	£5.50

Grounds only ticket available.

ℹ Fashion shoots, archery, equestrian events, shows, rallies, filming, product launches, highland games, new shopping development, grand piano. Photography allowed during special events and private tours.

🛍 Shopping pavilion.   ❋

🍸 The State Rooms are available for grand dinners, lunches and wedding receptions.

♿ Disabled visitors may alight at entrance. Those in wheelchairs will be unable to tour the castle but may visit the two exhibitions. WC.

☕🍴 Morning coffees, light lunches, afternoon teas. Self-service, licensed restaurant.

🚶 All visits are guided, tour time 50 - 60 mins. Tours leave every 10 - 15 mins. Tours in French, German, Italian and Spanish by appointment at no additional cost. Three exhibitions.

🅿 500 cars and 20 coaches 200 yds from castle. Coach drivers and couriers admitted free. Beware narrow gates; they are wide enough to take buses (10ft wide).

📖 One teacher free for every 10 children. Nature trail, family exhibition rooms, dolls' house, play park. Glamis Heritage Education Centre in Glamis village. Education pack. Winner of Sandford Award in 1997. Children's Quest.

🐕 In grounds, on leads.    Tel for details.   €

CONFERENCE/FUNCTION

ROOM	SIZE	MAX CAPACITY
Dining Rm	84 sq.m	90
Restaurant	140 sq.m	100
16th century Kitchens		40

MAP 13

SCONE PALACE & GROUNDS

www.scone-palace.co.uk

Owner: The Earl of Mansfield

▶ CONTACT

The Administrator
Scone Palace
Perth   PH2 6BD

Tel: 01738 552300
Fax: 01738 552588

e-mail: visits@
scone-palace.co.uk

▶ LOCATION

OS Ref. NO114 266

From Edinburgh
Forth Bridge M90,
A93 1hr.

Bus: Regular buses
from Perth.

Rail: Perth Station 3m.

Motorway: M90 from
Edinburgh.

Taxi: 01738 636777.

Scone Palace is the home of the Earl and Countess of Mansfield and is built on the site of an ancient abbey. 1500 years ago it was the capital of the Pictish kingdom and the centre of the ancient Celtic church. In the intervening years, it has been the seat of the parliaments and crowning place of kings, including Macbeth, Robert the Bruce and Charles II. The State Rooms house a superb collection of *objets d'art*, including items of Marie Antoinette, bought by the 2nd Earl of Mansfield. Notable works of art are also on display, including paintings by Sir David Wilkie, Sir Joshua Reynolds, and Johann Zoffany. The Library boasts one of Scotland's finest collections of porcelain, including Sèvres, Ludwigsburg and Meissen, whilst the unique 'Vernis Martin' *papier mâché* may be viewed in the Long Gallery.

Gardens

The grounds of the Palace house magnificent collections of shrubs, with woodland walks through the pinetum containing David Douglas' original fir and the unique Murray Star Maze. There are Highland cattle and peacocks to admire and an adventure play area for children. The 100 acres of mature Policy Parks, flanked by the River Tay, are available for a variety of events, including corporate and private entertaining.

▶ OPENING TIMES

Summer
24 March - 31 October
Daily: 9.30am - 6pm.

Last admission 5pm.

Evening tours by appointment.

Winter
By appointment.

Grounds only: Fri,
11am - 4pm.

▶ ADMISSION

Summer
Palace & Grounds
Adult £7.20
Child (under 16yrs)... £4.20
Senior/Student....... £6.20
Family £23.00
Groups (20+)
Adult £6.00
Child (5-16yrs) £4.00
Senior/Student....... £5.30

Grounds only
Adult £3.50
Child (5-16yrs) £2.20
Senior/Student....... £3.00

Under 5s Free
Private Tour £40 supplement.

Winter
On application.

Receptions, fashion shows, war games, archery, clay pigeon shooting, equestrian events, garden parties, shows, rallies, filming, shooting, fishing, floodlit tattoos, product launches, highland games, parkland, cricket pitch, helicopter landing, croquet, racecourse, polo field, firework displays, adventure playground. No photography in state rooms. Gift shop & food shop.

Grand dinners in state rooms, buffets, receptions, wedding receptions, cocktail parties.

All state rooms on one level, wheelchair access to restaurants. Stairlift in gift shop.

Licensed. Teas, lunches & dinners, can be booked, menus upon request, special rates for groups.

By arrangement. Guides in rooms, tour time 45 mins. French and German guides available by appointment.

Welcome.

300 cars and 15 coaches, groups please book, couriers and coach drivers free meal and admittance.

In grounds on leads.

 €

▶ SPECIAL EVENTS

Please telephone for details.

CONFERENCE/FUNCTION

ROOM	SIZE	MAX CAPACITY
Long Gallery	140' x 20'	200
Queen Victoria's Rm	20' x 20'	20
Drawing Rm	48' x 25'	80

ABERDOUR CASTLE

Aberdour, Fife

Tel: 01383 860519

Owner: In the care of Historic Scotland   **Contact:** The Steward

A 14th century castle built by the Douglas family. The gallery on the first floor gives an idea of how it was furnished at the time. The castle has a 14th century tower extended in the 16th and 17th centuries, a delightful walled garden and a circular dovecote.

Location: OS Ref. NT193 854. In Aberdour 5m E of the Forth Bridge on the A921.

Open: 1 Apr - 30 Sept: daily, 9.30am - 6.30pm, last ticket 6pm. 1 Oct - 31 Mar: daily, 9.30am - 4.30pm, last ticket 4pm. Closed Thurs & Fri in winter.

Admission: Adult £3.50, Child £1.50, Conc. £2.50.

ⓘ Picnic area. WCs. ♿WC ⬛🅿❄ €

ARBROATH ABBEY

Arbroath, Tayside

Tel: 01241 878756

Owner: In the care of Historic Scotland   **Contact:** The Steward

The substantial ruins of a Tironensian monastery, notably the gate house range and the abbot's house. Arbroath Abbey holds a very special place in Scottish history. Scotland's nobles swore their independence from England in the famous 'Declaration of Arbroath' in 1320. New visitor centre.

Location: OS Ref. NO611 414. In Arbroath town centre on the A92.

Open: 1 Apr - 30 Sept: daily 9.30am - 6.30pm, last ticket 6pm. 1 Oct - 31 Mar: daily, 9.30am - 4.30 pm, last ticket 4pm.

Admission: Adult £4, Child £1.60, Conc. £3.

ⓘ WCs. ⬛ ♿WC. 🅿❄ €

BALCARRES

Colinsburgh, Fife KY9 1HL

Tel: 01333 340206

Owner: Balcarres Trust   **Contact:** The Earl of Crawford

16th century tower house with 19th century additions by Burn and Bryce. Woodland and terraced gardens.

Location: OS Ref. NO475 044. ¹/₂ m N of Colinsburgh.

Open: Woodland & Gardens: 1 - 20 Feb & 3 Apr - 19 Jun, 2 - 5pm. House not open except by written appointment and 10 - 26 Apr, excluding Sun.

Admission: Adult £5. Garden only: £3.

🅇 By arrangement.

BALGONIE CASTLE

Markinch, Fife KY7 6HQ

Tel: 01592 750119   **Fax:** 01592 753103   **e-mail:** sbalgonie@yahoo.co.uk

Owner/Contact: The Laird of Balgonie

14th century tower, additions to the building up to 1702. Still lived in by the family. 14th century chapel for weddings.

Location: OS Ref. NO313 006. ¹/₂ m S of A911 Glenrothes - Leven road at Milton of Balgonie on to B921.

Open: All year: daily, 10am - 5pm.

Admission: Adult £3, Child £1.50, OAP £2.

BALHOUSIE CASTLE (BLACK WATCH MUSEUM)

Hay Street, North Inch Park, Perth PH1 5HR

Tel: 0131 310 8530

Owner: MOD   **Contact:** Major Proctor

Regimental museum housed in the castle.

Location: OS Ref. NO115 244. ¹/₂ m N of town centre, E of A9 road to Dunkeld.

Open: May - Sept: Mon - Sat, 10am - 4.30pm. Oct - Apr: Mon - Fri, 10am - 3.30pm. Closed 23 Dec - 5 Jan & last Sat in Jun.

Admission: Free.

BLAIR CASTLE 🏛   *See page 468 for full page entry.*

BRECHIN CASTLE

Brechin, Angus DD9 6SG

Tel: 01356 624566   **e-mail:** fay@dalhousieestates.co.uk

www.dalhousieestates.co.uk

Owner: Dalhousie Estates   **Contact:** Fay Clark

Dating from 1711 the Castle contains many family pictures and artefacts. Beautiful gardens.

Location: OS Ref. NO593 602. Off A90 on A935.

Open: 8 Jul - 6 Aug: guided tours only.

Admission: Adult £5. Child under 12yrs Free.

ⓘ No photography. ♿Unsuitable. 🅇Obligatory. ❖

CAMBO GARDENS

Cambo Estate, Kingsbarns, St Andrews, Fife KY16 8QD

Tel: 01333 450054   **Fax:** 01333 450987   **e-mail:** cambo@camboestate.com

www.camboestate.com

Owner: Mr & Mrs T P N Erskine   **Contact:** Catherine Erskine

Victorian walled garden with burn, willow, waterfall and rose-clad bridges. Naturalistic plantings of rare and interesting herbaceous perennials, spectacular bulbs, including acres of woodland walks leading to sea carpeted in snowdrops, roses, September borders, woodland garden with colchicum meadow. "All seasons plantsman's paradise."

Location: OS Ref. NO603 114. 3m N of Crail. 7m SE of St Andrews on A917.

Open: All year: daily, 10am - dusk.

Admission: Adult £3.50, Child Free. RHS access.

ⓘ Conferences. 🅇 ❄ Mail order snowdrops in the green plus interesting and unusual herbaceous plants throughout the year at potting shed. 🍴 ♿
🅿 Limited for coaches. 🐕 In grounds, on leads.
🛏 2 doubles & self-catering apartments/cottages. ❄

CASTLE CAMPBELL ♛

Dollar Glen, Central District

Tel: 0131 243 9300

Owner: The National Trust for Scotland   **Contact:** Historic Scotland

Known as 'Castle Gloom' this spectacularly sited 15th century fortress was the lowland stronghold of the Campbells. Stunning views from the parapet walk.

Location: OS Ref. NS961 993. At head of Dollar Glen, 10m E of Stirling on the A91.

Open: 1 Apr - 30 Sept: daily, 9.30am - 6.30pm, last ticket 6pm. 1 Oct - 31 Mar: daily, 9.30am - 4.30pm. Closed Thurs & Fri, last ticket 4pm.

Admission: Adult £4, Child £1.60, Conc. £3.

❄ €

CHARLETON HOUSE

Colinsburgh, Leven, Fife KY9 1HG

Tel: 01333 340249   **Fax:** 01333 340583

Location: OS Ref. NO464 036. Off A917. 1m NW of Colinsburgh. 3m NW of Elie.

Open: Sept: daily, 12 noon - 3pm. Admission every ¹/₂ hr with guided tours only.

Admission: £10.

🅇 Obligatory.

CORTACHY ESTATE

Cortachy, Kirriemuir, Angus DD8 4LX

Tel: 01575 570108   **Fax:** 01575 540400

e-mail: office@airlieestates.com   **www**.airlieestates.com

Owner: Trustees of Airlie Estates   **Contact:** Estate Office

Countryside walks including access through woodlands to Airlie Monument on Tulloch Hill with spectacular views of the Angus Glens and Vale of Strathmore. Footpaths are waymarked and colour coded.

Location: OS Ref. NO394 596. Off the B955 Glens Road from Kirriemuir.

Open: Woodland Walks: all year. Gardens: 14 - 17 Apr; 1 May & 15 May - 4 Jun; 7 & 28 Aug: 10am - 4pm, last admission 3.30pm. Castle not open.

Admission: Please contact estate office for details.

♿Not suitable. 🅿Limited. ❖ ❄

CULROSS PALACE ♛

Tel: 0131 243 9300

Owner: The National Trust for Scotland   **Contact:** Property Manager

Relive the domestic life of the 16th and 17th centuries at this Royal Burgh fringed by the River Forth. Enjoy too the Palace, dating from 1597 and the medieval garden.

Location: OS Ref. NS985 860. Off A985. 12m W of Forth Road Bridge and 4m E of Kincardine Bridge, Fife.

DRUMMOND CASTLE GARDENS 🏛   *See page 469 for full page entry.*

DUNFERMLINE ABBEY & PALACE

Dunfermline, Fife

Tel: 01383 739026

Owner: In the care of Historic Scotland   **Contact:** The Steward

The remains of the Benedictine abbey founded by Queen Margaret in the 11th century. The foundations of her church are under the 12th century Romanesque-style nave. Robert the Bruce was buried in the choir. Substantial parts of the abbey buildings remain, including the vast refectory.

Location: OS Ref. NY090 873. In Dunfermline off the M90.

Open: 1 Apr - 30 Sept: daily, 9.30am - 6.30pm, last ticket 6pm. 1 Oct - 31 Mar: Mon - Sat, 9.30am - 4.30pm, Sun, 2 - 4.30pm, last ticket 4pm. Closed Thurs pm and Fri in winter.

Admission: Adult £3, Child £1.30, Conc. £2.30.

ⓘ ⬛ 🐕 ❄ €

DUNNINALD

Montrose, Angus DD10 9TD
Tel: 01674 674842 **Fax:** 01674 674860
www.dunninald.com
Owner/Contact: J Stansfeld
This house, the third Dunninald built on the estate, was designed by James Gillespie Graham in the gothic Revival style, and was completed for Peter Arkley in 1824. It has a superb walled garden and is set in a planned landscape dating from 1740. It is a family home.
Location: OS Ref. NO705 543 2m S of Montrose, between A92 and the sea.
Open: 29 Jun - 30 Jul: Tue - Sun, 1 - 5pm. Garden: from 12.30pm.
Admission: Adult £5, Child (under 12) Free, Conc. £4. Garden only: £2.50.
No photography in house. Unsuitable. Obligatory. In grounds, on leads. €

EDZELL CASTLE AND GARDEN

Edzell, Angus
Tel: 01356 648631
Owner: In the care of Historic Scotland   **Contact:** The Steward
The beautiful walled garden at Edzell is one of Scotland's unique sights, created by Sir David Lindsay in 1604. The 'Pleasance' is a delightful formal garden with walls decorated with sculptured stone panels, flower boxes and niches for nesting birds. The fine tower house, now ruined, dates from the last years of the 15th century. Mary, Queen of Scots held a council meeting in the castle in 1562 on her way north as her army marched against the Gordons.
Location: OS Ref. NO585 691. At Edzell, 6m N of Brechin on B966. 1m W of village.
Open: 1 Apr - 30 Sept: daily, 9.30am - 6.30pm, last ticket 6pm. 1 Oct - 31 Mar: daily, 9.30am - 4.30pm, last ticket 4pm. Closed Thur and Fri in winter.
Admission: Adult £4, Child £1.60, Conc. £3.
Tel for details. €

ELCHO CASTLE

Perth
Tel: 01738 639998
Owner: In the care of Historic Scotland   **Contact:** The Steward
This handsome and complete fortified mansion of 16th century date has four projecting towers. The original wrought-iron grilles to protect the windows are still in place.
Location: OS Ref. NO164 211. On the Tay, 3m SE of Perth.
Open: 1 Apr - 30 Sept: daily, 9.30am - 6.30pm, last ticket 6pm.
Admission: Adult £2.50, Child £1, Conc. £2.
€

FALKLAND PALACE

Falkland KY15 7BU
Tel: 0131 243 9300
Owner: The National Trust for Scotland
Built between 1502 and 1541, the Palace is a good example of Renaissance architecture. Surrounded by gardens, laid out in the 1950s.
Location: OS Ref. NO253 075. A912, 11m N of Kirkcaldy.

GLAMIS CASTLE

See page 470 for full page entry.

GLENEAGLES

Auchterarder, Perthshire PH3 1PJ
Tel: 01764 682388
Owner: Gleneagles 1996 Trust   **Contact:** J Martin Haldane of Gleneagles
Gleneagles has been the home of the Haldane family since the 12th century. The 18th century pavilion is open to the public by written appointment.
Location: OS Ref. NS931 088. ¾m S of A9 on A823. 2½m S of Auchterarder.
Open: By written appointment only.

HILL OF TARVIT MANSIONHOUSE

Cupar, Fife KY15 5PB
Tel: 0131 243 9300
Owner: The National Trust for Scotland
House rebuilt in 1906 by Sir Robert Lorimer, the renowned Scottish architect, for a Dundee industrialist, Mr F B Sharp.
Location: OS Ref. NO379 118. Off A916, 2½ m S of Cupar, Fife.

HOUSE OF DUN

Montrose, Angus DD10 9LQ
Tel: 0131 243 9300
Owner: The National Trust for Scotland
Georgian house, overlooking the Montrose Basin, designed by William Adam and built in 1730 for David Erskine, Lord Dun.
Location: OS Ref. NO670 599. 3m W Montrose on A935.

HUNTINGTOWER CASTLE

Perth
Tel: 01738 627231
Owner: In the care of Historic Scotland   **Contact:** The Steward
The splendid painted ceilings are especially noteworthy in this castle, once owned by the Ruthven family. Scene of a famous leap between two towers by a daughter of the house who was nearly caught in her lover's room. The two towers are still complete, one of 15th - 16th century date, the other of 16th century origin. Now linked by a 17th century range.
Location: OS Ref. NO084 252. 3m NW of Perth off the A85.
Open: 1 Apr - 30 Sept: daily, 9.30am - 6.30pm, last ticket 6pm. 1 Oct - 31 Mar: daily, 9.30am - 4.30pm, last ticket 4pm. Closed Thur & Fris in winter.
Admission: Adult £3.50, Child £1.50, Conc. £2.50.
By arrangement. €

INCHCOLM ABBEY

Inchcolm, Fife
Tel: 01383 823332
Owner: In the care of Historic Scotland   **Contact:** The Steward
Known as the 'Iona of the East'. This is the best preserved group of monastic buildings in Scotland, founded in 1123. Includes a 13th century octagonal chapter house.
Location: OS Ref. NT190 826. On Inchcolm in the Firth of Forth. Reached by ferry from South Queensferry (30 mins), or Newhaven (45 mins). Tel. 0131 331 5000 for times/charges.
Open: 1 Apr - 30 Sept: daily, 9.30am - 6.30pm, last ticket 6pm.
Admission: Adult £4, Child £1.60, Conc. £3. Additional charge for ferries.
Visitor Centre. €

KELLIE CASTLE & GARDEN

Pittenweem, Fife KY10 2RF
Tel: 0131 243 9300
Owner: The National Trust for Scotland
Good example of domestic architecture in Lowland Scotland dates from the 14th century and was sympathetically restored by the Lorimer family in the late 19th century.
Location: OS Ref. NO519 051. On B9171, 3m NW of Pittenweem, Fife.

LOCHLEVEN CASTLE

Loch Leven, Kinross
Tel: 07778 040483
Owner: In the care of Historic Scotland   **Contact:** The Steward
Mary Queen of Scots endured nearly a year of imprisonment in this 14th century tower before her dramatic escape in May 1568. During the First War of Independence it was held by the English, stormed by Wallace and visited by Bruce.
Location: OS Ref. NO138 018. On island in Loch Leven reached by ferry from Kinross off the M90.
Open: Last sailing 5.15pm. Open summer only.
Admission: Adult £4, Child £1.60, Conc. £3. Prices include ferry trip.
€

MEGGINCH CASTLE GARDENS

Errol, Perthshire PH2 7SW
Tel: 01821 642222 **Fax:** 01821 642708   **Email:** catherine.herdman@gmail.com
Owner: Captain Drummond of Megginch & The Hon Mrs Herdman
15th century castle, 1,000 year old yews, flowered parterre, double walled kitchen garden, topiary, astrological garden, pagoda dovecote in courtyard. Part used as a location for the film *Rob Roy*.
Location: OS Ref. NO241 245. 8m E of Perth on A90.
Open: Apr - Oct: Wed. Aug: daily, 2.30 - 6pm.
Admission: Adult £4, Child £1.
Partial. By arrangement. Limited for coaches. In grounds, on leads.

MONZIE CASTLE

Crieff, Perthshire PH7 4HD
Tel: 01764 653110
Owner/Contact: Mrs C M M Crichton
Built in 1791. Destroyed by fire in 1908 and rebuilt and furnished by Sir Robert Lorimer.
Location: OS Ref. NN873 244. 2m NE of Crieff.
Open: 13 May - 11 Jun: daily, 2 - 5pm. By appointment at other times.
Admission: Adult £3, Child £1. Group rates available, contact property for details.

NORTHFIELD

Colinsburgh, Fife KY9 1HQ

Tel: 01333 340214 **e-mail:** enquiries@andersonofnorthfield.net
www.andersonofnorthfield.net

Owner: Margaret Aynscough   **Contact:** Mrs M E Aynscough
"Andersons of Northfield", formerly of St Germains and Bourhouse. Display of family portraits from late 1600s to present day, including Dewar, Naesmyth, Murray, Findlay, Seton and other branches of the family tree. Holiday accommodation available all year.
Location: OS Ref. NO468 033. East Neuk of Fife. 10m from St Andrews, 2m from Elie, 31m from Forth Road Bridge.
Open: 26 May - 4 Jun: 10am - 4pm.
Admission: Free - Donation for charity.
👞Partial. 👥 PLimited. 🐾In grounds, on leads. 📷All year.

ST ANDREWS CASTLE ⚖

THE SCORES, ST ANDREWS, KY16 9AR

Tel: 01334 477196

Owner: Historic Scotland   **Contact:** David Eaton
This was the castle of the bishops of St Andrews and has a fascinating mine and counter-mine, rare examples of medieval siege techniques. There is also a bottle dungeon hollowed out of solid rock. Cardinal Beaton was murdered here and John Knox was sent to the galleys when the ensuing siege was lifted.
Location: OS Ref. NO513 169. In St Andrews on the A91.
Open: Apr - Sept: daily, 9.30am - 6.30pm. Oct - Mar: daily, 9.30am - 4.30pm. Last ticket 30 mins before closing.
Admission: Adult £4.50, Child £2, Conc. £3.50. 10% discount for groups (10+). Joint ticket available with cathedral: Adult £6, Child £2.70 Conc. £4.50.
🛈Visitor centre. 📷 👞Partial. WCs. ✓By arrangement. POn street. 📷Free if booked. 🐾Guide dogs. ✺ €

ST ANDREWS CATHEDRAL ⚖

St Andrews, Fife

Tel: 01334 472563

Owner: Historic Scotland   **Contact:** Alison Sullivan
The remains still give a vivid impression of the scale of what was once the largest cathedral in Scotland along with the associated domestic ranges of the priory.
Location: OS Ref. NO514 167. In St Andrews.
Open: 1 Apr - 30 Sept: daily, 9.30am - 6.30pm, last ticket 5.45pm. 1 Oct - 31 Mar: daily, 9.30am - 4.30pm, last ticket 3.45pm.
Admission: Adult £3.50, Child £1.50, Conc. £2.50. Joint entry ticket with St Andrews Castle available: Adult £6, Child £2.70 Conc. £4.50.
✺ €

SCONE PALACE & GROUNDS 🏛   *See page 471 for full page entry.*

STOBHALL 🏛

Stobhall, Cargill, Perthshire PH2 6DR

Tel: 01821 640332 **www.**stobhall.com

Owner: Viscount Strathallan
Original home of the Drummond chiefs from the 14th century. Romantic cluster of small-scale buildings around a courtyard in a magnificent situation overlooking the River Tay, surrounded by formal and woodland gardens. 17th century painted ceiling in Chapel depicts monarchs of Europe and North Africa on horse (or elephant) back.
Location: OS Ref. NO132 343. 8m N of Perth on A93.
Open: 3 Jun - 2 Jul: Tues - Sun, (closed Mons). Open by tour only. Tours at 2, 3 & 4pm of the Chapel, Drawing Room and Folly. Explore the garden at leisure after the tour. Library by prior appointment.
Admission: Adult £4, Child £2, Conc. £3. Large group visits must be booked.
👞 Partial. Please see website or ring for details. ✓Obligatory.
P Limited. Coaches please book.

STRATHTYRUM HOUSE & GARDENS

St Andrews, Fife

Tel: 01334 473600

Owner: The Strathtyrum Trust   **Contact:** George or Carol Woodhouse
Location: OS Ref. NO490 172. Entrance from the St Andrews/Guardbridge Road which is signposted when open.
Open: 1 - 6 May, 5 - 10 Jun, 3 - 8 Jul, 7 - 12 Aug and 4 - 9 Sept: 2 - 4pm.
Admission: Adult £5, Child £2.50.
P Free. 🐾 Guide dogs only.

TULLIBOLE CASTLE

Crook of Devon, Kinross KY13 0QN

Tel: 01577 840236 **e-mail:** visit@tulbol.demon.co.uk
www.tulbol.demon.co.uk/visit.htm

Owner: Lord & Lady Moncreiff   **Contact:** Lord Moncreiff
Recognised as a classic example of the Scottish tower house. Completed in 1608, the Moncreiff family have lived here since 1747. The Castle is in a parkland setting with ornamental fishponds (moat), a roofless lectarn doocot, with a short walk to a 9th century graveyard and a ruined church.
Location: OS Ref. NO540 888. Located on the B9097 1m E of Crook of Devon.
Open: Last week in Aug - 30 Sept: Tue - Sun, 1 - 4pm. Admission every 1/2 hr with guided tours only.
Admission: Adult £3.50, Child/Conc. £2.50. Free as part of "Doors Open Day" (last weekend of Sept).
👞Unsuitable. ✓Obligatory. PAmple but limited for coaches. 📷
🐾Guide dogs only. 🛌Twin x 1.

Stobhall.

West Highlands & Islands, Loch Lomond, Stirling and Trossachs

© Historic Scotland.

© Historic Scotland.

MAP 13

Owner: Historic Scotland

ARGYLL'S LODGING

This attractive townhouse, sitting at the foot of Stirling Castle, is decorated as it would have been during the 9th Earl of Argyll's occupation around 1680. Before coming into Historic Scotland's care the building was a youth hostel, but restoration revealed hidden secrets from the lodging's past. Perhaps the best of these was a section of 17th century *trompe l'oeil* panelling in the dining room, created by painter David McBeath.

Visitors to Argyll's Lodging might wonder at the highly decorated walls and rich materials and colours used but the restoration relied on a household inventory of 1680 found among the then Duchess's papers. But no matter how rich the decoration, it cannot match the colourful lives of Argyll Lodging's inhabitants.

The 9th Earl, Archibald Campbell, was sentenced to death for treason and imprisoned in Edinburgh Castle. However he escaped when his stepdaughter smuggled him out dressed as her page. Archibald escaped to Holland, but his stepdaughter was arrested and placed in public stocks – a major humiliation. He didn't cheat death a second time, however. Joining plots over the succession following Charles II's death, he was captured and beheaded in 1685.

An earlier inhabitant of Argyll's Lodging, Sir William Alexander, was tutor to James VI's son, Prince Henry and in 1621 he attempted to colonise Nova Scotia in Canada. Great wealth eluded him all his life, however, and he died a bankrupt in 1640, leading to the town council taking over the lodging and selling it to the Earl of Argyll in the 1660s.

▶ CONTACT

The Steward
Argyll's Lodging
Castle Wynd
Stirling   FK8 1EJ

Tel: 01786 431319
Fax: 01786 448194

▶ LOCATION

OS Ref. NS793 938

At the top and on E side of Castle Wynd in Stirling. One way route from town centre from Albert Street.

Rail: Stirling.

Air: Edinburgh or Glasgow.

▶ OPENING TIMES

April - September
Daily, 9.30am - 6pm.

October - March
Daily, 9.30am - 5pm.

▶ ADMISSION

Adult £4.00
Child* £1.60
Conc** £3.00

Joint entry
Adult £8.50
Child* £3.50
Conc** £6.50

* up to 16 years.
Under 5yrs free.
** (60+ & unemployed)

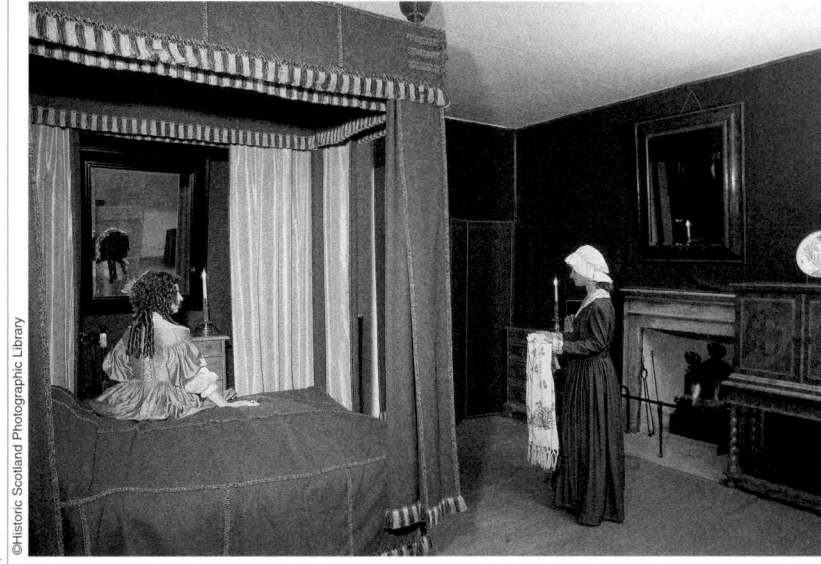
©Historic Scotland Photographic Library

FUNCTION

ROOM	SIZE	MAX CAPACITY
Laigh Hall	11 x 6m	60 for receptions
High Dining Room	11 x 6m	26 for dinner
Both rooms:	120 for receptions	

ℹ️🛍️ Interpretation scheme includes computer animations; joint ticket with Stirling Castle available.

🍷 Evening receptions/dinners.

♿ Partial. No wheelchair access to upper floor.

🅿️ Ample parking for coaches and cars on Stirling Castle Esplanade.

🏫 Free pre-booked school visits scheme.

🐕 Guide dogs only. ❄️ 🛡️ Tel for details.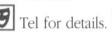

West Highlands & Islands, Loch Lomond, Stirling and Trossachs

MAP 13

INVERARAY CASTLE 🏛

www.inveraray-castle.com

The Duke of Argyll's family have lived in Inveraray since the early 15th century. The present Castle was built between 1745 and 1790.

The ancient Royal Burgh of Inveraray lies about 60 miles north west of Glasgow by Loch Fyne in an area of spectacular natural beauty combining the ruggedness of highland scenery with the sheltered tidal loch 90 miles from the open sea.

The Castle is the home of the Duke and Duchess of Argyll. Its fairytale exterior belies the grandeur of its gracious interior. The building was designed by Roger Morris and decorated by Robert Mylne, the clerk of works being William Adam, father of Robert and John, who did much of the laying out of the present Royal Burgh, an unrivalled example of an early planned town.

Visitors may see the famous Armoury Hall containing some 1300 pieces, French tapestries made especially for the Castle, fine examples of Scottish, English and French furniture together with a wealth of other works of art including china, silver and family artifacts, all of which form a unique collection spanning the generations which are identified by a magnificent genealogical display in the Clan Room.

Owner:
Duke of Argyll

▶ CONTACT

The Factor
Dept HHD
Argyll Estates Office
Cherry Park
Inveraray
Argyll   PA32 8XE

Tel: 01499 302203
Fax: 01499 302421

e-mail: enquiries@
inveraray-castle.com

▶ LOCATION
OS Ref. NN100 090

From Edinburgh
2¹/₂ - 3hrs via Glasgow.

Just NE of Inveraray
on A83. W shore
of Loch Fyne.

Bus: Bus route
stopping point within
¹/₂ m.

▶ OPENING TIMES

Summer

1st Sat in April - Last Sun
in October

April, May & October:
Mon - Thurs & Sat:
10am - 1pm & 2 - 5.45pm
Fridays: closed.
Sun: 1 - 5.45pm.
Last admissions
12.30 & 5pm.

June, July, August &
September:
Daily: 10am - 5.45pm
(including Friday)
Sun: 1 - 5.45pm.
Last admission 5pm.

Winter
Closed.

▶ ADMISSION
House only
Adult £6.30
Child (under 16yrs) .. £4.10
OAP/Student £5.20
Family (2+2).......... £17.00

Groups of
(20+) .... 20% discount

No photography. Guide books in French, Italian, Japanese and German translations.

Visitors may alight at the entrance. 2 wheelchair ramps to castle. All main public rooms suitable but two long flights of stairs to the smaller rooms upstairs. WCs.

Seats up to 50. Licensed. Menus available on request. Groups book in advance. Tel: 01499 302112.

Available for up to 100 people at no additional cost. Groups please book. Tour time: 1 hr.

P 100 cars. Separate coach park close to Castle

£2.10 per child. A guide can be provided. Areas of interest include a nature walk.

In grounds, on leads. Guide dogs only inside Castle.

West Highlands & Islands, Loch Lomond, Stirling and Trossachs

ANGUS'S GARDEN
Barguillean, Taynuilt, Argyll, West Highlands PA35 1HY
Tel: 01866 822335 **Fax:** 01866 822539   **Contact:** Sean Honeyman
Memorial garden of peace, tranquillity and reconciliation.
Location: OS Ref. NM978 289. 4m SW on Glen Lonan road from A85.
Open: All year: daily, 9am - 5pm (dusk during summer months).
Admission: Adult £2, Child Free.

ARDENCRAIG GARDENS
Ardencraig, Rothesay, Isle of Bute, West Highlands PA20 9BP
Tel: 01700 505339   **Fax:** 01700 502492
Owner: Argyll and Bute Council   **Contact:** Allan Macdonald
Walled garden, greenhouses, aviaries. Woodland walk from Rothesay 1 mile (Skippers Wood.)
Location: OS Ref. NS105 645. 2m from Rothesay.
Open: May - Sept: Mon - Fri, 10am - 4.30pm, Sat & Sun, 1 - 4.30pm.
Admission: Free.

ARDKINGLAS ESTATE
CAIRNDOW, ARGYLL PA26 8BH
www.ardkinglas.com

Tel: 01499 600261   **Fax:** 01499 600241   **e-mail:** ardkinglas@btinternet.com
Contact: The Estate Manager
Ardkinglas House, a superb neo-baronial house near the head of Loch Fyne was built by Sir Robert Lorimer in 1907 and has retained many original features. Although not generally open to the public, group visits can be arranged. The house is available for weddings, corporate days or as a film location. The Woodland Gardens, which are open to the public, are part of a designed landscape and are of outstanding horticultural and scenic significance and include many champion trees.
Location: OS Ref. NN179 106. Head of Loch Fyne, just off the A83 at Cairndow, 10m W of Arrochar. About 1hr from Glasgow.
Open: Woodland Garden & woodland trails: All year, dawn - dusk.
Admission: Garden admission charge for adults.
🖳 Tree shop. 🌣 🖳 Partial. 🖤 🍴 🎨 By arrangement. 🅿 Limited. 🐾 In grounds, on leads. ✳ €

BARCALDINE CASTLE
Benderloch, Oban, Argyll PA37 1SA
Tel: 01631 720598   **email:** enquiries@barcaldinecastle.co.uk
www.barcaldinecastle.co.uk
Owner: Roderick Campbell   **Contact:** Caroline Campbell
Argyll's only ancient castle offering bed and breakfast accommodation. 16th century home of the Campbells of Barcaldine. Spectacular locaton. Visit Scotland 4 star graded.
Location: OS Ref. SY419 937. 10m N of Oban & 4m S of Appin.
Open: Open for booked functions and accommodation only.
🖳 🅿 Ample parking for cars. 🛏 2 x double, 1 x ensuite.

BENMORE BOTANIC GARDEN
Dunoon, Argyll PA23 8QU
Tel: 01369 706261   **Fax:** 01369 706369   **Contact:** The Curator
A botanical paradise. Enter the magnificent avenue of giant redwoods and follow trails through the Formal Garden and hillside woodlands with its spectacular outlook over the Holy Loch and the Eachaig Valley.
Location: OS Ref. NS150 850. 7m N of Dunoon on A815.
Open: 1 Mar - 31 Oct: daily, 10am - 6pm. Closes 5pm in Mar & Oct.
Admission: Adult £3.50, Child £1, Conc. £3, Family £8. Group discounts available.

BONAWE IRON FURNACE 🏛
Taynuilt, Argyll
Tel: 01866 822432
Owner: In the care of Historic Scotland   **Contact:** The Steward
Founded in 1753 by Cumbrian iron masters this is the most complete remaining charcoal fuelled ironworks in Britain. Displays show how iron was once made here.
Location: OS Ref. NN005 310. By the village of Taynuilt off the A85.
Open: 1 Apr - 30 Sept: daily, 9.30am - 6.30pm, last ticket 6pm.
Admission: Adult £3.50, Child £1.50, Conc. £2.50.
ℹ 📷 🎨 🅿 €

CASTLE STALKER
Portnacroish, Appin, Argyll PA38 4BA
Tel: 01883 622768   **Fax:** 01883 626238   **www.**castlestalker.com
Owner: Mrs M Allward   **Contact:** Messrs R & A Allward
Early 15th century tower house and ancient seat of the Stewarts of Appin. Picturesquely set on a rocky islet approx 400 yds off the mainland on the shore of Loch Linnhe. Reputed to have been used by James IV as a hunting lodge. Garrisoned by Government troops during the 1745 rising. Restored from a ruin by the late Lt Col Stewart Allward following acquisition in 1965 and now retained by his family.
Location: OS Ref. NM930 480. Approx. 20m N of Oban on the A828. On islet ¼ m offshore.
Open: 8 - 12 & 15 - 19 May, 21 - 25 & 28 Aug - 1 Sept & 18 - 22 Sept. Telephone for appointments. Times variable depending on tides and weather.
Admission: Adult £8, Child £4.
ℹ Not suitable for coach parties. ♿ Unsuitable.

DOUNE CASTLE 🏛
Doune
Tel: 01786 841742
Owner: Earl of Moray (leased to Historic Scotland)   **Contact:** The Steward
A formidable 14th century courtyard castle, built for the Regent Albany. The striking keep-gatehouse combines domestic quarters including the splendid Lord's Hall with its carved oak screen, musicians' gallery and double fireplace.
Location: OS Ref. NN720 020. In Doune, 8m S of Callander on the A84.
Open: 1 Apr - 30 Sept: daily, 9.30am - 6.30pm. 1 Oct - 31 Mar: Mon - Wed, Sat & Sun, 9.30am - 4.30pm, last admission 30 mins before closing.
Admission: Adult £3.50, Child £1.50, Conc. £2.50.
ℹ 📷 🅿 ✳ €

ARGYLL'S LODGING 🏛
See page 475 for full page entry.

BALLOCH CASTLE COUNTRY PARK
Balloch, Dunbartonshire G83 8LX
Tel: 01389 722199   **Fax:** 01389 720922
Contact: Loch Lomond & The Trossachs National Park
A 200 acre country park on the banks of Loch Lomond.
Location: OS Ref. NS390 830. SE shore of Loch Lomond, off A82 for Balloch or A811 for Stirling.
Open: Visitor Centre: Easter - Oct: variable hours, please phone for details. Country Park: All year: dawn - dusk.
Admission: Free for both Visitor Centre and Country Park.

corporate hospitality
see page 568

West Highlands & Islands, Loch Lomond, Stirling and Trossachs

DUART CASTLE

ISLE OF MULL, ARGYLL PA64 6AP

www.duartcastle.com

Tel: 01680 812309 or 01577 830311 **e-mail:** duartguide@isle-of-mull.demon.co.uk

Owner/Contact: Sir Lachlan Maclean Bt

Duart is a fortress, one of a line of castles stretching from Dunollie in the east to Mingary in the north, all guarding the Sound of Mull. The earliest part of the Castle was built in the 12th century, the keep was added in 1360 by the 5th Chief Lachlan Lubanach and the most recent alterations were completed in 1673. The Macleans were staunchly loyal to the Stuarts. After the rising of 1745 they lost Duart and their lands were forfeited. Sir Fitzroy Maclean, 25th Chief, restored the Castle in 1910. Duart remains the family home of the Chief of the Clan Maclean.

Location: OS Ref. NM750 350. Off A849 on the east point of the Isle of Mull.

Open: 1 - 30 Apr: Sun - Thurs, 11am - 4pm. 1 May - 9 Oct: daily, 10.30am - 5.30pm.

Admission: Adult: £4.50, Child £2.25, Conc. £4, Family £11.25.

⬜ ⬚ ♿ Unsuitable. ⬛ 👤 By arrangement. 🅿 🐕 In grounds, on leads.

accommodation
see page 567

©Historic Scotland Photographic Library

DUMBARTON CASTLE

Dumbarton, Strathclyde

Tel: 01389 732167

Owner: Historic Scotland   **Contact:** The Steward

Location: OS Ref. NS401 744. 600yds S of A84 at E end of Dumbarton.

Open: 1 Apr - 30 Sept: daily, 9.30am - 6.30pm, last ticket 5.45pm. 1 Oct - 31 Mar: Sat - Wed, 9.30am - 4.30pm, last ticket 3.45pm.

Admission: Adult £3.50, Child £1.50, Conc £2.50.

⬜ ⬚ ⬛ 🅿 🐕 ❄ 🚻 Tel for details. €

DUNBLANE CATHEDRAL

Dunblane

Tel: 01786 823388

Owner: Historic Scotland   **Contact:** The Steward

One of Scotland's noblest medieval churches. The lower part of the tower is Romanesque but the larger part of the building is of the 13th century. It was restored in 1889 - 93 by Sir Rowand Anderson.

Location: OS Ref. NN782 015. In Dunblane.

Open: All year: Mon - Sat, 9.30am - 6pm, Sun 2 - 6pm. Closed daily 12.30 - 1.30pm.

Admission: Free.

❄

DUNSTAFFNAGE CASTLE

BY OBAN, ARGYLL PA37 1PZ

Tel: 01631 562465

Owner: In the care of Historic Scotland   **Contact:** The Steward

A very fine 13th century castle built on a rock with a great curtain wall. The castle's colourful history stretches across the Wars of Independence to the 1745 rising. The castle was briefly the prison of Flora Macdonald. Marvellous views from the top of the curtain wall. Close by are the remains of a chapel with beautiful architectural detail.

Location: OS49 NM882 344. 3½ m NE of Oban off A85.

Open: Apr - Sept: daily, 9.30am - 6.30pm, last ticket 30 mins before closing. Oct - Mar: daily, 9.30am - 4.30pm. Closed Thurs & Fri.

Admission: Adult £3, Child £1.30, Conc. £2.30. 10% discount for groups (11+).

⬜ ♿ Partial. 👤 By arrangement. 🅿 ■ Free pre-booked school visits. 🐕 In grounds, on leads. ❄ €

THE HILL HOUSE

Upper Colquhoun Street, Helensburgh G84 9AJ

Tel: 0131 243 9300

Owner: The National Trust for Scotland

Charles Rennie Mackintosh set this 20th century masterpiece high on a hillside overlooking the Firth of Clyde. Mackintosh also designed furniture, fittings and decorative schemes to complement the house.

Location: OS Ref. NS300 820. Off B832, between A82 & A814, 23m NW of Glasgow.

INCHMAHOME PRIORY

Port of Menteith

Tel: 01877 385294

Owner: In the care of Historic Scotland   **Contact:** The Steward

A beautifully situated Augustinian priory on an island in the Lake of Menteith founded in 1238 with much of the building surviving. The five year old Mary, Queen of Scots was sent here for safety in 1547.

Location: OS Ref. NN574 005. On an island in Lake of Menteith. Reached by ferry from Port of Menteith, 4m E of Aberfoyle off A81.

Open: 1 Apr - 30 Sept: daily, 9.30am - 6.30pm, last ticket 6pm.

Admission: Adult £4, Child £1.60, Conc. £3. Charge includes ferry trip.

ℹ️ 📷 €

INVERARAY CASTLE   *See page 476 for full page entry.*

INVERARAY JAIL

Church Square, Inveraray, Argyll PA32 8TX

Tel: 01499 302381   **Fax:** 01499 302195   **e-mail:** info@inverarayjail.co.uk

www.inverarayjail.co.uk

Owner: Visitor Centres Ltd   **Contact:** J Linley

A living 19th century prison! Uniformed prisoners and warders, life-like figures, imaginative exhibitions, sounds, smells and trials in progress, bring the 1820 courtroom and former county prison back to life. See the 'In Prison Today' exhibition.

Location: OS Ref. NN100 090. Church Square, Inveraray, Argyll.

Open: Apr - Oct: 9.30am - 6pm, last admission 5pm. Nov - Mar: 10am - 5pm, last admission 4pm.

Admission: Adult £6.25, Child £3.15, OAP £4.15, Family £17.20. Groups (10+): Adult £4.95, OAP £3.45.

📷 ♿ Partial (FOC). ▮ 🐕 ❄️

IONA ABBEY & NUNNERY

Iona, Argyll

Tel/Fax: 01681 700512   **e-mail:** hs.ionaabbey@scotland.gov.uk

www.historic-scotland.gov.uk

Owner: In the care of Historic Scotland   **Contact:** The Steward

One of Scotland's most historic and venerated sites, Iona Abbey is a celebrated Christian centre and the burial place for many Scottish kings. The abbey and nunnery grounds house one of the most comprehensive collections of Christian carved stones in Scotland, dating from 600AD to the 1600s. Includes the Columba Centre, Fionnphort exhibition and giftshop.

Location: OS Ref. NM270 240. Ferry service from Fionnphort, Mull.

Open: All year: daily.

Admission: Adult £4, Child (under 16yrs) £1.60, Conc. £3. Columba Centre, exhibition & giftshop: Free.

📷 ♿ Partial. ▮ 🍴 ▮ 🐕 In grounds. ❄️ €

KILBRYDE CASTLE
DUNBLANE, PERTHSHIRE FK15 9NF
www.kilbrydecastle.com

Tel: 01786 824897   **e-mail:** kilbryde1@aol.com

Owner/Contact: Sir James Campbell

Kilbryde Castle, situated in the centre of Scotland, is available for weddings, private parties and other corporate functions either in Kilbryde Castle or in a marquee in the gardens. There is aso a chapel available for weddings, christenings etc.

Location: OS Ref. NN756 037.

Open: By appointment (other than Scotland's Gardens' scheme).

Admission: Negotiated per event.

📶 ♿ Partial. 🅿️ Ample for cars, limited for coaches. ✈️

KILCHURN CASTLE

Loch Awe, Dalmally, Argyll

Tel: 01786 431323

Owner: In the care of Historic Scotland   **Contact:** Neil Young

A square tower, built by Sir Colin Campbell of Glenorchy c1550, it was much enlarged in 1693 to give the building, now a ruin, its present picturesque outline. Spectacular views of Loch Awe.

Location: OS Ref. NN133 276. At the NE end of Loch Awe, 2$^{1}/_{2}$ m W of Dalmally.

Open: Ferry service operates in the summer. Tel: 01838 200440 for times & prices.

Admission: Please telephone for details.

Stirling Castle.

West Highlands & Islands, Loch Lomond, Stirling and Trossachs

MOUNT STUART
ISLE OF BUTE PA20 9LR

www.mountstuart.com

Tel: 01700 503877 **Fax:** 01700 505313 **e-mail:** contactus@mountstuart.com
Owner: Mount Stuart Trust **Contact:** Donna Chisholm

Spectacular High Victorian gothic house, ancestral home of the Marquess of Bute. Splendid interiors, art collection and architectural detail. Set in 300 acres of stunning woodlands, mature Victorian pinetum, arboretum and exotic gardens.

Location: OS Ref. NS100 600. SW coast of Scotland, 5m S of Rothesay. Local bus service to House, frequent ferry service from Wemyss Bay, Renfrewshire and Colintraive, Argyll.

Open: Easter & 1 May - 30 Sept. Please telephone for detailed opening times.

Admission: Adult £7.50, Child £3.50, Conc. £6, Family £18. Groups (12+) discount available.

ℹ️No photography. 🅾️ 👶 🍴 ♿ ⭐Licensed. 🍴Licensed. 🎫Obligatory. 🅿️Ample. ⬛ 🦮Guide dogs only. 🛏️ Tel for details. €

STIRLING CASTLE
CASTLE WYND, STIRLING FK8 1EJ

Tel: 01786 450000 **Fax:** 01786 464678
Owner: Historic Scotland

Stirling Castle has played a key role in Scottish history, dominating the north–south and east–west routes through Scotland. The battles of Stirling Bridge and Bannockburn were fought in its shadow and Mary, Queen of Scots lived here as a child. Renaissance architecture, restored Great Hall and tapestry weaving.

Location: OS Ref. NS790 941. At the top of Castle Wynd in Stirling.

Open: Apr - Sept: 9.30am - 6pm. Oct - Mar: 9.30am - 5pm. Last ticket 45 mins before closing.

Admission: Adult £8.50, Child £3.50, Conc. £6.50. 10% discount for groups (10+). Free booked school visits, except May - August.

ℹ️Picnic area. Joint ticket with Argyll's Lodging. 🅾️ 🍴Private hire. ♿Partial. WC. ⭐Licensed. 🎫 🎧 🅿️ ⬛ 🦮 Guide dogs only. 🛏️ Tel for details. €

ROTHESAY CASTLE 🏛️
Rothesay, Isle of Bute
Tel: 01700 502691

Owner: In the care of Historic Scotland **Contact:** The Steward

A favourite residence of the Stuart kings, this is a wonderful example of a 13th century circular castle of enclosure with 16th century forework containing the Great Hall. Attacked by Vikings in its earlier days.

Location: OS Ref. NS088 646. In Rothesay, Isle of Bute. Ferry from Wemyss Bay on the A78.

Open: 1 Apr - 30 Sept: daily, 9.30am - 6.30pm, last ticket 6pm. 1 Oct - 31 Mar: Sat - Wed, 9.30am - 4.30pm, last ticket 4pm.

Admission: Adult £3.50, Child £1.50, Conc. £2.50.

🅾️ ♿ Partial. 🦮 On leads. 🛏️ €

ST BLANE'S CHURCH 🏛️
Kingarth, Isle of Bute
Tel: 0131 668 8800

Owner: In the care of Historic Scotland

This 12th century Romanesque chapel stands on the site of a 12th century Celtic monastery.

Location: OS Ref. NS090 570. At the S end of the Isle of Bute.

Open: All year: daily.

Admission: Free.

🛏️ €

TOROSAY CASTLE & GARDENS 🏛️
CRAIGNURE, ISLE OF MULL PA65 6AY

www.torosay.com

Tel: 01680 812421 **Fax:** 01680 812470 **e-mail:** torosay@aol.com
Owner/Contact: Mr Chris James

Torosay Castle and Gardens set on the beautiful Island of Mull, was completed in 1858 by the eminent architect David Bryce in the Scottish baronial style, and is surrounded by 12 acres of spectacular gardens which offer a dramatic contrast between formal terraces, impressive statue walk and informal woodland, also rhododendron collection, alpine, walled, water and oriental gardens. The house offers family history, portraits, scrapbooks and antiques in an informal and relaxed atmosphere.

Location: OS Ref. NM730 350. 1½ m SE of Craignure by A849.

Open: House: 1 Apr - 31 Oct: daily, 10.30am - 5pm. Gardens: All year: daily, 9am - 7pm or daylight hours in winter.

Admission: Adult £5.50, Child £2.25, Conc. £5, Family £14.

ℹ️Children's adventure playground. 🅾️ 👶 🍴 ♿WC. ⬛ 🅿️ 🦮 Holiday cottages. 🛏️ Tel for details. €

open all year
see page 557 ❄️

ALTYRE ESTATE
Altyre Estate, Forres, Moray IV36 2SH
Tel: 01463 796050   **Fax:** 01463 798246   **e-mail:** acampbell@bidwells.co.uk
Contact: Bidwells - Managing Agent
Altyre Estate comprises architecturally interesting buildings including Italianate farm buildings, standing stones and access to areas of natural and ornithological interest. Altyre Estate may interest scientific groups, students, and the general public.
Location: OS Ref. NJ028 552. Details given on appointment.
Open: Visitors are welcome by appointment on the first working day of Apr, May Jun, Jul & Aug.
Admission: Free.

ARBUTHNOTT HOUSE
Arbuthnott, Laurencekirk AB30 1PA
Tel: 01561 361226   **e-mail:** keith@arbuthnott.co.uk   **www.**arbuthnott.co.uk
Owner: The Viscount of Arbuthnott   **Contact:** The Master of Arbuthnott
Arbuthnott family home for 800 years with formal 17th century walled garden on unusually steep south facing slope. Well maintained grass terraces, herbaceous borders, shrubs and greenhouses.
Location: OS Ref. NO796 751. Off B967 between A90 and A92, 25m S of Aberdeen.
Open: House: 30 Apr, 1, 28 & 29 May, 30/31 Jul, 6/7 & 27/28 Aug and by prior arrangement. Guided tours: 2 - 5pm. Garden: All year: 9am - 5pm.
Admission: House: £4.50. Garden: £2.
🚶Ground floor. 🎧Obligatory. 🅿 ✖ ❋

BALFLUIG CASTLE
Alford, Aberdeenshire AB33 8EJ
Tel: 020 7624 3200
Owner/Contact: Mark Tennant of Balfluig
Small 16th century tower house in farmland, restored in 1967.
Location: OS Ref. NJ586 151. Alford, Aberdeenshire.
Open: Please write to M I Tennant Esq, 30 Abbey Gardens, London NW8 9AT. Occasionally let by the week for holidays.
🚶Unsuitable. ✖ 🛏1 single, 4 double. ❋

BALMORAL CASTLE (GROUNDS & EXHIBITIONS)
Balmoral, Ballater, Aberdeenshire AB35 5TB
Tel: 013397 42534   **Fax:** 013397 42034   **e-mail:** info@balmoralcastle.com
www.balmoralcastle.com
Owner: Her Majesty The Queen   **Contact:** Garry Marsden
Scottish home to The Royal Family. Ballroom, grounds and exhibitions, large café seating 120, quality gift shop. Excellent for coaches and groups. Holiday cottages, pony trekking and salmon fishing.
Location: OS Ref. NO256 951. Off A93 between Ballater and Braemar. 50m W of Aberdeen.
Open: 1 Apr - 31 Jul: daily, 10am - 5pm, last admission 4.30pm. Nov - 20 Dec: Guided tours every Wed, 11am - 2pm.
Admission: Adult £6, Child £1, OAP £5 (Audio tour included). Discounts for groups (20+).
📷 💷 📹 🛏

BALVENIE CASTLE 🏛
Dufftown
Tel: 01340 820121
Owner: In the care of Historic Scotland   **Contact:** The Steward
Picturesque ruins of 13th century moated stronghold originally owned by the Comyns. Visited by Edward I in 1304 and by Mary Queen of Scots in 1562. Occupied by Cumberland in 1746.
Location: OS Ref. NJ326 408. At Dufftown on A941.
Open:1 Apr - 30 Sept: daily, 9.30am - 6.30pm, last ticket 6pm.
Admission: Adult £3, Child £1.30, Conc. £2.30.
€

BRODIE CASTLE 🏛
Forres, Moray IV36 0TE
Tel: 0131 243 9300
Owner: The National Trust for Scotland
The lime harled building is a typical 'Z' plan tower house with ornate corbelled battlements and bartizans, with 17th & 19th century additions.
Location: OS Ref. NH980 577. Off A96 4¹/₂ m W of Forres and 24m E of Inverness.

accommodation
see page 567

CAIRNESS HOUSE
Lonmay, Fraserburgh, Aberdeenshire AB43 8XP
Tel/Fax: 01346 582078   **e-mail:** cairnesshouse@hotmail.com
www: cairnesshouse.co.uk
Owners: Mr J Soriano-Ruiz / Mr K H Khairallah   **Contact:** Property Manager
Scotland's most extraordinary neo-classical house: James Playfair's architectural masterpiece built in 1790s. Largely neglected and forgotten for 60 years. Magnificent and unique semi-circular service wing, icehouse, and earliest Egyptian room in Britain. Elaborate plasterwork and finest private collection of Regency furniture and paintings in Buchan. House and grounds undergoing restoration.
Location: OS Ref. NK038 609. Off A90, 4m SE of Fraserburgh, ¹/₄ m W of B9033 about 2m S of St Comb's.
Open: All year by written appointment only.
Admission: Adult £7, OAP/Student £6.
ℹNo photography. No smoking. 🎧Obligatory. 🅿 Limited. ✖ ❋

CASTLE FRASER & GARDEN 🏛
Sauchen, Inverurie AB51 7LD
Tel: 0131 243 9300
Owner: The National Trust for Scotland
Begun in 1575, the two low wings contribute to the scale and magnificence of the towers rising above them, combining to make this the largest and most elaborate of the Scottish castles built on the 'Z' plan.
Location: OS Ref. NJ723 125. Off A944, 4m N of Dunecht & 16m W of Aberdeen.

CORGARFF CASTLE 🏛
Strathdon
Tel: 013398 83635
Owner: In the care of Historic Scotland   **Contact:** The Steward
A 16th century tower house converted into a barracks for Hanoverian troops in 1748.
Location: OS Ref. NJ255 086. 8m W of Strathdon on A939. 14m NW of Ballater.
Open: 1 Apr - 30 Sept: daily, 9.30am - 6.30pm. 1 Oct - 31 Mar: Sat & Sun, 9.30am - 4.30pm. Last admission 30 mins before closing.
Admission: Adult £4, Child £1.60, Conc. £3.
❋ €

CRAIG CASTLE
Rhynie, Huntly, Aberdeenshire AB54 4LP
Tel: 01464 861705   **Fax:** 01464 861702
Owner: Mr A J Barlas   **Contact:** The Property Manager
The Castle is built round a courtyard and consists of a 16th century L-shaped Keep, a Georgian house (architect John Adam) and a 19th century addition (architect Archibald Simpson of Aberdeen). The Castle was a Gordon stronghold for 300 years. It has a very fine collection of coats-of-arms.
Location: OS Ref. NJ472 259. 3m W of Rhynie and Lumsden on B9002.
Open: May - Sept: Wed & every 2nd weekend in each month, 2 - 5pm.
Admission: Adult £5, Child £1.
📹 🚶Unsuitable. 🎧By arrangement. 🅿Limited for coaches. 🐕Guide dogs only.

CRAIGSTON CASTLE
Turriff, Aberdeenshire AB53 5PX
Tel: 01888 551228/551640
Owner: William Pratesi Urquhart   **Contact:** Mrs Fiona Morrison
Built in 1607 by John Urquhart Tutor of Cromarty, Craigston bears the marks of a client's brief rather than an architect's whim, which seems to belong to that strange slightly Gothic world. Few changes have been made to its exterior in its 400 years. A sculpted balcony unique in Scottish architecture depicts a piper, two grinning knights and David and Goliath. The interior dates from the early 19th century. Remarkable carved oak panels of Scottish kings' biblical heroes, mounted in doors and shutters of the early 17th century. 18th century Craigston dinner service is on display until 2007 to mark the castle's 400th anniversary.
Location: OS Ref. NJ762 550. On B9105, 4¹/₂ m NE of Turriff.
Open: 13 - 21 May; 17 - 25 Jun; 29 Jul - 6 Aug: daily, 11am - 3pm. Throughout the year by appointment.
Admission: Adult £6, Child £2, Conc. £4. Groups: Adult £5, Child/School £1.
🚶Unsuitable. 🎧Obligatory. 🅿 🐕In grounds on leads. ❋

CRATHES CASTLE & GARDEN 🏛
Banchory AB31 3QJ
Tel: 0131 243 9300
Owner: The National Trust for Scotland
The building of the castle began in 1553 and took 40 years to complete. Just over 300 years later, Sir James and Lady Burnett began developing the walled garden.
Location: OS Ref. NO733 969: On A93, 3m E of Banchory and 15m W of Aberdeen.

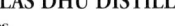

Grampian – Highlands, Aberdeen and North East Coast

CRUICKSHANK BOTANIC GARDEN
St Machar Drive, Aberdeen AB24 3UU
Tel: 01224 272704 **Fax:** 01224 272703
Owner: University of Aberdeen   **Contact:** R B Rutherford
Extensive collection of shrubs, herbaceous and alpine plants and trees. Rock and water gardens.
Location: OS Ref. NJ938 084. In old Aberdeen. Entrance in the Chanonry.
Open: All year: Mon - Fri, 9am - 4.30pm. Also May - Sept: Sat & Sun, 2 - 5pm.
Admission: Free.

DALLAS DHU DISTILLERY
Forres
Tel: 01309 676548
Owner: In the care of Historic Scotland   **Contact:** The Steward
A completely preserved time capsule of the distiller's craft. Wander at will through this fine old Victorian distillery then enjoy a dram. Visitor centre, shop and audio-visual theatre.
Location: OS Ref. NJ035 566. 1m S of Forres off the A940.
Open: 1 Apr - 30 Sept: daily, 9.30am - 6.30pm, last ticket 6pm. 1 Oct - 31 Mar: daily, 9.30am - 4.30pm, last ticket 4pm. Closed Thurs and Fri in winter.
Admission. Adult £4.50, Child £2, Conc. £3.50.
Visitor centre. WC.

DELGATIE CASTLE
TURRIFF, ABERDEENSHIRE AB53 5TD
www.delgatiecastle.com
Tel/Fax: 01888 563479 **e-mail:** jjohnson@delgatie-castle.freeserve.co.uk
Owner: Delgatie Castle Trust   **Contact:** Mrs Joan Johnson
Dating from 1030 the Castle is steeped in Scottish history yet still has the atmosphere of a lived in home. It has some of the finest painted ceilings, Mary Queen of Scots' bed-chamber, armour, Victorian clothes, fine furniture and paintings are displayed. Widest turnpike stair of its kind in Scotland. Clan Hay Centre.
Location: OS Ref. NJ754 506. Off A947 Aberdeen to Banff Road.
Open: 2 Apr - 25 Oct: daily, 10am - 5pm. Winter: daily, 10am - 4pm. Closed Christmas & New Year.
Admission: Adult £5, Child £3, Conc. £4, Family £10. Groups (10+): £3.
No photography. Ground floor. WC. Home-baking and lunches. By arrangement. 6 x houses for self catering.

DRUM CASTLE & GARDEN
Drumoak, by Banchory AB31 3EY
Tel: 0131 243 9300
Owner: The National Trust for Scotland
Owned for 653 years by one family, the Irvines. The combination over the years of a 13th century square tower, a very fine Jacobean mansion house and the additions of the Victorian lairds make Drum Castle unique among Scottish castles.
Location: OS Ref. NJ796 004. Off A93, 3m W of Peterculter and 10m W of Aberdeen.

DRUMMUIR CASTLE
Drummuir, by Keith, Banffshire AB55 5JE
Tel: 01542 810332 **Fax:** 01542 810302
Owner: The Gordon-Duff Family   **Contact:** Joy Hoffman
Castellated Victorian Gothic-style castle built in 1847 by Admiral Duff. 60ft high lantern tower with fine plasterwork. Family portraits, interesting artefacts and other paintings.
Location: OS Ref. NJ372 442. Midway between Keith (5m) and Dufftown, off the B9014.
Open: 19/20 & 26/27 Aug and 4 - 22 Sept (incl.): tours 2pm - 5pm.
Admission: Adult £2, Child £1.50. Pre-arranged groups: Adult £2, Child £1.50.
Obligatory. In grounds on leads.

DUFF HOUSE
Banff AB45 3SX
Tel: 01261 818181 **Fax:** 01261 818900   **Contact:** The Chamberlain
One of the most imposing and palatial houses in Scotland, with a strong classical façade and a grand staircase leading to the main entrance.
Location: OS Ref. NJ691 634. Banff. 47m NW of Aberdeen on A947.
Open: All year: Thur - Sun, 11am - 5pm (closes 4pm 1 Nov - 31 Mar).
Admission: Adult £5.50, Conc. £4.50, Family £14. Groups (10+): £4.50. Free admission to shop, tearoom, grounds & woodland walks.

DUNNOTTAR CASTLE
Dunnottar Castle Lodge, Stonehaven, Kincardineshire AB39 2TL
Tel: 01569 762173   **e-mail:** info@dunechtestates.co.uk
www.dunechtestates.co.uk   **Contact:** P McKenzie
Spectacular ruined cliff top fortress, home to the Earls Marischals of Scotland. The Crown Jewels of Scotland were hidden at this site, then smuggled away during the dark days of Cromwell's occupation.
Location: OS Ref. NO881 839. Just off A92. 1½ m SE of Stonehaven.
Open: Easter Mon - 17 Jun & 24 Sep - 15 Oct: Mon - Sat, 9am - 6pm, Sun, 2 - 5pm. 18 Jun - 23 Sep: daily, 9am - 7pm. 24 Sep - Good Fri: Fri - Mon, 10.30am - sunset. Last ticket 30 mins before closing.
Admission: Adult £4, Child £1.

ELGIN CATHEDRAL
Elgin
Tel: 01343 547171
Owner: Historic Scotland   **Contact:** The Steward
When entire this was perhaps the most beautiful of Scottish cathedrals, known as the Lantern of the North. 13th century, much modified after almost being destroyed in 1390 by Alexander Stewart, the infamous 'Wolf of Badenoch'. The octagonal chapterhouse is the finest in Scotland. You can see the bishop's home at Spynie Palace, 2m north of the town.
Location: OS Ref. NJ223 630. In Elgin on the A96.
Open: 1 Apr - 30 Sept: daily, 9.30am - 6.30pm, last ticket 6pm. 1 Oct - 31 Mar: daily, 9.30am - 4.30pm, last ticket 4pm. Closed Thurs & Fris in winter.
Admission: Adult £4, Child £1.60, Conc. £3. Joint entry ticket with Spynie Palace: Adult £5, Child £2.10, Conc. £3.80.

FYVIE CASTLE
Turriff, Aberdeenshire AB53 8JS
Tel: 0131 243 9300
Owner: The National Trust for Scotland
The five towers of the castle bear witness to the five families who have owned it. Fyvie Castle has a fine wheel stair and a collection of arms and armour and paintings.
Location: OS Ref. NJ763 393. Off A947, 8m SE of Turriff, and 25m N of Aberdeen.

HADDO HOUSE
Tarves, Ellon, Aberdeenshire AB41 0ER
Tel: 0131 243 9300
Owner: The National Trust for Scotland
Designed by William Adam in 1731 for William, 2nd Earl of Aberdeen. Much of the interior is 'Adam Revival' carried out about 1880 for John, 7th Earl and 1st Marquess of Aberdeen and his Countess, Ishbel.
Location: OS Ref. NJ868 348. Off B999, 4m N of Pitmedden, 10m NW of Ellon.

HUNTLY CASTLE
Huntly
Tel: 01466 793191
Owner: In the care of Historic Scotland   **Contact:** The Steward
Known also as Strathbogie Castle, this glorious ruin stands in a beautiful setting on the banks of the River Deveron. Famed for its fine heraldic sculpture and inscribed stone friezes.
Location: OS Ref. NJ532 407. In Huntly on the A96. N side of the town.
Open: 1 Apr - 30 Sept: daily, 9.30am - 6.30pm, last ticket 6pm. 1 Oct - 31 Mar: daily, 9.30am - 4.30pm, last ticket 4pm. Closed Thurs & Fri in winter.
Admission: Adult £4, Child £1.60, Conc £3.

KILDRUMMY CASTLE
Alford, Aberdeenshire

Tel: 01975 571331

Owner: In the care of Historic Scotland   **Contact:** The Steward
Though ruined, the best example in Scotland of a 13th century castle with a curtain wall, four round towers, hall and chapel of that date. The seat of the Earls of Mar, it was dismantled after the first Jacobite rising in 1715.
Location: OS Ref. NJ455 164. 10m W of Alford on the A97. 16m SSW of Huntley.
Open: 1 Apr - 30 Sept: daily, 9.30am - 6.30pm, last ticket 6pm.
Admission: Adult £3, Child £1.30, Conc. £2.30.
i WC. ⬛ & WC P €

KILDRUMMY CASTLE GARDEN
Kildrummy, Aberdeenshire

Tel: 01975 571203 / 571277   **Contact:** Alastair J Laing
Ancient quarry, shrub and alpine gardens renowned for their interest and variety. Water gardens below ruined castle.
Location: OS Ref. NJ455 164. On A97 off A944 10m SW of Alford. 16m SSW of Huntly.
Open: Apr - Oct: daily, 10am - 5pm.
Admission: Adult £3, Child Free.

LEITH HALL
Huntly, Aberdeenshire AB54 4NQ

Tel: 0131 243 9300

Owner: The National Trust for Scotland   **Contact:** The Property Manager
This mansion house, built around a courtyard was the home of the Leith family for almost 300 years.
Location: OS Ref. NJ541 298. B9002, 1m W of Kennethmont, 7m S of Huntley.

LICKLEYHEAD CASTLE
Auchleven, Insch, Aberdeenshire AB52 6PN

Tel: 01464 821359

Owner: The Leslie family   **Contact:** Zoë Knowles
A beautifully restored Laird's Castle, Lickleyhead was built by the Leslies c1450 and extensively renovated in 1629 by John Forbes of Leslie, whose initials are carved above the entrance. It is an almost unspoilt example of the transformation from 'Chateau-fort' to 'Chateau-maison' and boasts many interesting architectural features.
Location: OS Ref. NJ628 237. Auchleven is 2m S of Insch on B992. Twin pillars of castle entrance on left at foot of village.
Open: 1 - 13 May: daily and thereafter on Sats 12 noon - 3pm until 5 Aug.
Admission: Free.
& Unsuitable. P Limited. No coaches. ⬛ In grounds, on leads.

PITMEDDEN GARDEN
Ellon, Aberdeenshire AB41 0PD

Tel: 0131 243 9300

Owner: The National Trust for Scotland
The centrepiece of this property is the Great Garden which was originally laid out in 1675 by Sir Alexander Seton, 1st Baronet of Pitmedden.
Location: OS Ref. NJ885 280. On A920 1m W of Pitmedden village & 14m N of Aberdeen.

PLUSCARDEN ABBEY
Nr Elgin, Moray IV30 8UA

Tel: 01343 890257   **Fax:** 01343 890258
e-mail: monks@pluscardenabbey.org   **Contact:** Brother Michael
Valliscaulian, founded 1230.
Location: OS Ref. NJ142 576. On minor road 6m SW of Elgin. Follow B9010 for first mile.
Open: All year: 4.45am - 8.30pm. Shop: 8.30am - 5pm.
Admission: Free.

PROVOST SKENE'S HOUSE
Guestrow, off Broad Street, Aberdeen AB10 1AS

Tel: 01224 641086   **Fax:** 01224 632133

Owner: Aberdeen City Council   **Contact:** Christine Rew
Built in the 16th century, Provost Skene's House is one of Aberdeen's few remaining examples of early burgh architecture. Splendid room settings include a suite of Georgian rooms, an Edwardian nursery, magnificent 17th century plaster ceilings and wood panelling.
Location: OS Ref. NJ943 064. Aberdeen city centre, off Broad Street.
Open: Contact property for details.
Admission: Free.

ST MACHAR'S CATHEDRAL TRANSEPTS
Old Aberdeen

Tel: 0131 668 8800

Owner: In the care of Historic Scotland
The nave and towers of the Cathedral remain in use as a church, and the ruined transepts are in care. In the south transept is the fine altar tomb of Bishop Dunbar (1514 - 32).
Location: OS Ref. NJ939 088. In old Aberdeen. 1/2 m N of King's College.
Admission: Free.
✱

SPYNIE PALACE
Elgin

Tel: 01343 546358

Owner: In the care of Historic Scotland   **Contact:** The Steward
Spynie Palace was the residence of the Bishops of Moray from the 14th century to 1686. The site is dominated by the massive tower built by Bishop David Stewart (1461-77) and affords spectacular views across Spynie Loch.
Location: OS Ref. NJ231 659. 2m N of Elgin off the A941.
Open: 1 Apr - 30 Sept: daily, 9.30am - 6.30pm. 1 Oct - 31 Mar: Sat & Sun, 9.30am - 4.30pm. Last ticket 30 mins before closing.
Admission: Adult £3, Child £1.30, Conc. £2.30. Joint entry ticket with Elgin Cathedral: Adult £5, Child £2.10, Conc. £2.30.
i Picnic area ⬛ & WC P ✱ €

TOLQUHON CASTLE
Aberdeenshire

Tel: 01651 851286

Owner: In the care of Historic Scotland   **Contact:** The Steward
Tolquhon was built for the Forbes family. The early 15th century tower was enlarged between 1584 and 1589 with a large mansion around the courtyard. Noted for its highly ornamented gatehouse and pleasance.
Location: OS Ref. NJ874 286. 15m N of Aberdeen on the A920. 6m N of Ellon.
Open: 1 Apr - 30 Sept: daily, 9.30am - 6.30pm. 1 Oct - 31 Mar: Sat & Sun, 9.30am - 4.30pm. Last ticket 30 mins before closing.
Admission: Adult £3, Child £1.30, Conc. £2.30.
i Picnic area ⬛ & WC P ✱ €

DAVID WELCH WINTER GARDENS – DUTHIE PARK
Polmuir Road, Aberdeen, Grampian Highlands AB11 7TH

Tel: 01224 585310   **Fax:** 01224 210532
e-mail: wintergardens@aberdeencity.gov.uk.   **www.**aberdeencity.gov.uk
Owner: Aberdeen City Council   **Contact:** Alan Findlay
One of Europe's largest indoor gardens with many rare and exotic plants on show from all around the world.
Location: OS Ref. NJ97 044. Just N of River Dee, 1m S of city centre.
Open: All year: daily from 9.30pm.
Admission: Free.
✱

open all year
see page 557

Elgin Cathedral.

MAP 16

Owner: The Dowager
Countess Cawdor

CAWDOR CASTLE 🏛

www.cawdorcastle.com

This splendid romantic castle dating from the late 14th century was built as a private fortress by the Thanes of Cawdor, and remains the home of the Cawdor family to this day. The ancient medieval tower was built around the legendary holly tree.

Although the house has evolved over 600 years, later additions mainly of the 17th century were all built in the Scottish vernacular style with slated roofs over walls and crow-stepped gables of mellow local stone. This style gives Cawdor a strong sense of unity, and the massive, severe exterior belies an intimate interior that gives the place a surprisingly personal, friendly atmosphere.

Good furniture, fine portraits and pictures, interesting objects and outstanding tapestries are arranged to please the family rather than to echo fashion or impress. Memories of Shakespeare's *Macbeth* give Cawdor an elusive, evocative quality that delights visitors.

GARDENS
The flower garden also has a family feel to it, where plants are chosen out of affection rather than affectation. This is a lovely spot between spring and late summer. The walled garden has been restored with a holly maze, paradise garden, knot garden and thistle garden. The wild garden beside its stream leads into beautiful trails through a spectacular mature mixed woodland, through which paths are helpfully marked and colour-coded. New are the Tibetan garden and traditional Scottish vegetable garden at Auchindoune.

▶ CONTACT

The Secretary
Cawdor Castle
Nairn
Scotland IV12 5RD

Tel: 01667 404401

Fax: 01667 404674

e-mail: info@
cawdorcastle.com

▶ LOCATION
OS Ref. NH850 500

From Edinburgh
A9, 3¹/₂ hrs,
Inverness 20 mins,
Nairn 10 mins.
Main road: A9, 14m.

Rail: Nairn
Station 5m.

Bus: Inverness to Nairn
bus route 200 yds.

Taxi: Cawdor Taxis
01667 404315.

Air: Inverness
Airport 5m.

▶ OPENING TIMES
Summer
1 May - 8 October
Daily: 10am - 5.30pm.
Last admission 5pm.

Winter
October - April
Groups by appointment,
admission prices on
application.

Auchindoune Garden
May - July: Tue & Thurs,
10am - 4.30pm.
Otherwise by
appointment.

▶ ADMISSION
Summer
House & Garden

Adult	£7.00
Child (5-15yrs)	£4.30
OAP/Student	£6.00
Family (2+5)	£22.00

Groups (20+)

Adult	£6.10
Child (5-15yrs)	£3.70
OAP/Student	£6.00

Garden only
Per person £3.70

RHS Access ....
Free admission to gardens
May, June, September &
October.

CONFERENCE/FUNCTION

ROOM	MAX CAPACITY
Cawdor Hall	40

ℹ️ 9 hole golf course, putting green, golf clubs for hire, Conferences, whisky tasting, musical entertainments, specialised garden visits. No photography, video taping or tripods inside.

🛍 Gift, book and wool shops.

🍷 Lunches, sherry or champagne receptions.

♿ Visitors may alight at the entrance. WC. Only ground floor accessible.

🍴 Licensed buttery, May-Oct, groups should book.

🅿 250 cars and 25 coaches. Two weeks' notice for group catering, coach drivers/couriers free.

📖 £3.70 per child. Room notes, quiz and answer sheet can be provided.

🐕 Guide dogs only.

▶ SPECIAL EVENTS

JUN 3/4
Special Gardens Weekend:
Guided tours of gardens.

JUN 24
RHS Lecture on "Plant Magic"
by Sue Hoy, 11am in Cawdor
Village Hall. Booking required.

MAP 15

DUNVEGAN CASTLE

www.dunvegancastle.com

Dunvegan is unique. It is the only Great House in the Western Isles of Scotland to have retained its family and its roof. It is the oldest home in the whole of Scotland continuously inhabited by the same family – the Chiefs of the Clan Macleod. A Castle placed on a rock by the sea - the curtain wall is dated before 1200 AD – its superb location recalls the Norse Empire of the Vikings, the ancestors of the Chiefs.

Dunvegan's continuing importance as a custodian of the Clan spirit is epitomised by the famous Fairy Flag, whose origins are shrouded in mystery but whose ability to protect both Chief and Clan is unquestioned. To enter Dunvegan is to arrive at a place whose history combines with legend to make a living reality.

GARDENS

The gardens and grounds extend over some ten acres of woodland walks, peaceful formal lawns and a water garden dominated by two spectacular natural waterfalls. The temperate climate aids in producing a fine show of rhododendrons and azaleas, the chief glory of the garden in spring. One is always aware of the proximity of the sea and many garden walks finish at the Castle Jetty, from where traditional boats make regular trips to view the delightful Seal Colony.

Owner: John Macleod
of Macleod

▶ CONTACT

The Administrator
Dunvegan Castle
Isle of Skye
Scotland IV55 8WF

Tel: 01470 521206
Fax: 01470 521205
Seal Tel: 01470 521500

e-mail: info@
dunvegancastle.com

▶ LOCATION

OS Ref. NG250 480

1m N of village. NW corner of Skye.

From Inverness A82 to Invermoriston, A887 to Kyle of Lochalsh 82m. From Fort William A82 to Invergarry, A87 to Kyle of Lochalsh 76m.

Kyle of Lochalsh to Dunvegan 45m via Skye Bridge (toll).

Ferry: To the Isle of Skye, 'roll-on, roll-off', 30 minute crossing.

Rail: Inverness to Kyle of Lochalsh 3 - 4 trains per day - 45m.

Bus: Portree 25m, Kyle of Lochalsh 45m.

ℹ️ Gift and craft shop. Boat trips to seal colony. Pedigree Highland cattle. No photography in castle.

♿ Visitors may alight at entrance. WC.

🍴 Licensed restaurant, (cap. 70) special rates for groups, menus upon request. Tel: 01470 521310. Open late peak season for evening meals.

🚶 By appointment in English or Gaelic at no extra charge. If requested owner may meet groups, tour time 45mins.

🅿️ 120 cars and 10 coaches. Do not attempt to take passengers to Castle Jetty (long walk). If possible please book. Seal boat trip dependent upon weather.

🏫 Welcome by arrangement. Guide available on request.

🐕 In grounds only, on lead. Guide Dogs allowed in Castle.

🛏️ 4 self-catering units, 3 of which sleep 6 and 1 of which sleeps 7.

▶ OPENING TIMES

Summer
20 March - 31 October
Daily: 10am - 5.30pm.
Last admission 5pm.

Winter
1 November - mid March
Daily: 11am - 4pm.
Last admission 3.30pm.

Closed Christmas Day, Boxing Day, New Year's Day and 2 January.

▶ ADMISSION

Summer
Castle & Gardens

Adult	£7.00
Child (5 -15yrs)	£4.00
OAP/Student	£6.00
Groups (10+)	£6.00

Gardens only

Adult	£5.00
Child (5 -15yrs)	£3.00
Senior/Student	£3.50

Seal Boats

Adult	£6.00
Child (5 -12yrs)	£3.50
Child (under 5yrs)	£1.50

Winter (2005 prices)

Adult	£5.00
Child* (5 -15yrs)	£2.50
Conc.	£3.50
Groups (10+)	£3.50

CASTLE LEOD

Strathpeffer IV14 9AA

Tel/Fax: 01997 421264   **e-mail:** cromartie@castle-leod.freeserve.co.uk

Owner/Contact: The Earl of Cromartie

Turreted 15th century tower house of rose-pink stone. Lived in by the Mackenzie family, chiefs of the clan, for 500 years and still very much a home where the family ensure a personal welcome. Magnificent setting below Ben Wyvis and amongst some of the finest trees in Scotland.

Location: OS Ref. NH485 593. 1km E of Strathpeffer on the A834 Strathpeffer to Dingwall road.

Open: 13 - 16 Apr, 18 - 21 May, 8 - 11 Jun, 29 Jun - 2 Jul, 31 Aug - 3 Sept & 27 Sept - 1 Oct: 2 - 5.30pm (last admission 4.45pm).

Admission: Adult £5, Child £2, OAP/Student £4.

i No coaches. T & Grounds only. WC. f By arrangement, all year. P No coach parking. Guide dogs only. Tel for details.

THE DOUNE OF ROTHIEMURCHUS

By Aviemore PH22 1QH

Tel: 01479 812345   **e-mail:** info@rothie.co.uk   **www.**rothiemurchus.net

Owner: J P Grant of Rothiemurchus   **Contact:** Rothiemurchus Visitor Centre

The family home of the Grants of Rothiemurchus was nearly lost as a ruin and has been under an ambitious repair programme since 1975. This exciting project may be visited on selected Mondays throughout the season and on other days by arrangement by email. Book with the Visitor Centre for a longer 2hr 'Highland Lady' tour which explores the haunts of Elizabeth Grant of Rothiemurchus, born 1797, author of *Memoirs of a Highland Lady*, who vividly described the Doune and its surroundings from the memories of her childhood.

Location: OS Ref. NH900 100. 2m S of Aviemore on E bank of Spey river.

Open: House: selected Mons. Grounds: May - Aug: Mon, 10am - 12.30pm & 2 - 4.30pm, also 1st Mon in the month during winter.

Admission: House only £1. Tour (booking essential, 4+) £10pp.

i Visitor Centre. f Obligatory. P Limited. In grounds, on leads.

CASTLE OF MEY

THURSO, CAITHNESS KW14 8XH

www.castleofmey.org.uk

Tel: 01847 851473   **Fax:** 01847 851475   **e-mail:** castleofmey@totalise.co.uk

Owner: The Queen Elizabeth Castle of Mey Trust   **Contact:** James Murray

The home of The Queen Mother in Caithness and the only property in Britain that she owned. She bought the Castle in 1952, saved it from becoming a ruin and developed the gardens. It became her ideal holiday home because of the beautiful surroundings and the privacy she was always given.

Location: OS Ref. ND290 739. On A836 between Thurso and John O'Groats, just outside the village of Mey. 12m Thurso station, 18m Wick airport.

Open: 13 May - 27 Jul & 9 Aug - 28 Sept: daily (closed Fris), 10.30am - 4pm.

Admission: Adult £7, Child (16yrs and under) Free, Conc. £6. Booked groups (20+): £6. Gardens & grounds only: Adult £3.

i No photography in the Castle. & Partial. f By arrangement. P In grounds, on leads.

The Queen Elizabeth Castle of Mey Trust

DUNROBIN CASTLE

GOLSPIE, SUTHERLAND KW10 6SF

www.highlandescape.com

Tel: 01408 633177   **Fax:** 01408 634081   **e-mail:** info@dunrobincastle.net

Owner: The Sutherland Trust   **Contact:** Scott Morrison

Dates from the 13th century with additions in the 17th, 18th and 19th centuries. Wonderful furniture, paintings, library, ceremonial robes and memorabilia. Victorian museum in grounds with a fascinating collection including Pictish stones. Set in fine woodlands overlooking the sea. Magnificent formal gardens, one of few remaining French/Scottish formal parterres. Falconry display.

Location: OS Ref. NC850 010. 50m N of Inverness on A9. 1m NE of Golspie.

Open: 1 Apr - 15 Oct: Mon - Sat, 10.30am - 4.30pm, Suns, 12 noon - 4.30pm. 1 Jun - 30 Sept: Mon - Sat, 10.30am - 5.30pm, Suns, 12 noon - 5.30pm (Jul & Aug: Suns, opens at 10.30am.)

Admission: Adult £6.80, Child £4.70, Student £6, Conc. £5.80, Family (2+2) £18. Booked groups: Adult £5.60, OAP. £5.

T & Unsuitable for wheelchairs. f By arrangement. P

CASTLE OF OLD WICK

Wick

Tel: 01667 460232

Owner/Contact: Historic Scotland

Essential work to safeguard the future of Scotland's best-preserved Norse castle has been completed and it has now reopened to the public. Visitors can now enjoy visiting this dramatically located castle once again. One of the oldest keeps in Scotland, the castle is a simple square keep of at least three storeys. In addition to the tower the site contains the low-lying ruins of other buildings. These have never been excavated and are largely covered by turf in order to protect them from damage.

Location: OS Ref. ND368 487. 1m S of Wick on Shore Road, E of A9.

Open: All year.

Admission: Free.

CAWDOR CASTLE

See page 484 for full page entry.

DUNVEGAN CASTLE

See page 485 for full page entry.

EILEAN DONAN CASTLE

Dornie, Kyle of Lochalsh, Wester Ross IV40 8DX

Tel: 01599 555202   **Fax:** 01599 555262   **e-mail:** info@donan.f9.co.uk

www.eileandonancastle.com   **Contact:** Rod Stenson – Castle Keeper

Location: OS Ref. NG880 260. On A87 8m E of Skye Bridge.

Open: Mar & Nov: 10am - 3.30pm. Apr - Oct: 10am - 5.30pm.

Admission: Adult £4.75, Conc. £3.75.

©Historic Scotland Photographic Library

FORT GEORGE 🏛

ARDERSIER BY INVERNESS IV1 2TD

Owner: In the care of Historic Scotland   **Contact:** Brian Ford

Tel/Fax: 01667 460232

Built following the Battle of Culloden to subdue the Highlands, Fort George never saw a shot fired in anger. One of the most outstanding artillery fortifications in Europe with reconstructed barrack room displays. The Queen's Own Highlanders' Museum.

Location: OS Ref. NH762 567. 11m NE of Inverness off the A96 by Ardersier.

Open: Apr - Sept: daily, 9.30am - 6.30pm. Oct - Mar: daily, 9.30am - 4.30pm. Last ticket sold 45 mins before closing.

Admission: Adult £6.50, Child £2.50, Conc. £5. 10% discount for groups (11+).

ℹ️Picnic tables. 🖼🎭Private evening hire. ♿Wheelchairs available. WCs. 🔲🎧🅿️🔳 Free if pre-booked. 🐕In grounds, on leads. ❋ 🏵 Tel for details. €

©Historic Scotland Photographic Library

URQUHART CASTLE 🏛

DRUMNADROCHIT, LOCH NESS

Tel: 01456 450551

Owner: In the care of Historic Scotland   **Contact:** Euan Fraser

The remains of one of the largest castles in Scotland dominate a rocky promontory on Loch Ness. Most of the existing buildings date from the 16th century. New visitor centre with original artefacts, audio-visual presentation, shop and café.

Location: OS Ref. NH531 286. On Loch Ness, 1 1/2m S of Drumnadrochit on A82.

Open: 1 Apr - 30 Sept: daily, 9.30am - 6.30pm. Last ticket 5.45pm. 1 Oct - 31 Mar: daily, 9.30am - 4.30pm. Last ticket 3.45pm.

Admission: Adult £6.50, Child £2.50, Conc. £5.

🔲🎭♿Partial. WCs. 🔲🅿️🎧🔳Free if pre-booked. 🐕Guide/hearing dogs ❋€

Heritage House Group/Nick McCann

The Castle & Gardens of Mey - seascape.

BALFOUR CASTLE

Shapinsay, Orkney Islands KW17 2DY

Tel: 01856 711282   **Fax:** 01856 711283

Owner/Contact: Mrs Lidderdale

Built in 1848.

Location: OS Ref. HY475 164 on Shapinsay Island, 3^1/$_2$ m NNE of Kirkwall.

Open: May - Sept: Suns only, 2.15 - 5.30pm.

Admission: Admission includes boat fare, guided tour, gardens & afternoon tea. Bookings essential. Contact property for details.

BISHOP'S & EARL'S PALACES

Kirkwall, Orkney

Tel: 01856 875461

Owner: In the care of Historic Scotland   **Contact:** The Steward

The Bishop's Palace is a 12th century hall-house with a round tower built by Bishop Reid in 1541-48. The adjacent Earl's Palace built in 1607 has been described as the most mature and accomplished piece of Renaissance architecture left in Scotland.

Location: Bishop's Palace: OS Ref. HY447 108. Earl's Palace: OS Ref. HY448 108. In Kirkwall on A960.

Open: 1 Apr - 30 Sept: daily, 9.30am - 6.30pm, last ticket 6pm.

Admission: Adult £3, Child £1.30, Conc. £2.30. Joint entry ticket available for all the Orkney monuments: Adult £11, Child £3.50, Conc. £8.

€

BLACK HOUSE

Arnol, Isle of Lewis

Tel: 01851 710395

Owner: In the care of Historic Scotland   **Contact:** The Steward

A traditional Lewis thatched house, fully furnished, complete with attached barn, byre and stockyard. A peat fire burns in the open hearth. New visitor centre open and restored 1920s croft house.

Location: OS Ref. NB320 500. In Arnol village, 11m NW of Stornoway on A858.

Open: 1 Apr - 30 Sept: Mon - Sat, 9.30am - 6.30pm, last ticket 6pm. 1 Oct - 31 Mar: Mon - Thur & Sat, 9.30am - 4.30pm, last ticket 4pm.

Admission: Adult £4.50, Child £2, Conc. £3.50.

❋ €

BROCH OF GURNESS

Aikerness, Orkney

Tel: 01831 579478

Owner: In the care of Historic Scotland   **Contact:** The Steward

Protected by three lines of ditch and rampart, the base of the broch is surrounded by Iron Age buildings.

Location: OS Ref. HY383 268. At Aikerness, about 14m NW of Kirkwall on A966.

Open: 1 Apr - 30 Sept: daily, 9.30am - 6.30pm, last ticket 6pm.

Admission: Adult £4, Child £1.60, Conc. £3. Joint entry ticket available for all Orkney monuments: Adult £11, Child £3.50, Conc. £8.

€

CARRICK HOUSE

Carrick, Eday, Orkney KW17 2AB

Tel: 01857 622260

Owner: Mr & Mrs Joy   **Contact:** Mrs Rosemary Joy

17th century house built by John Stewart, Lord Kinclaven, Earl of Carrick younger brother of Patrick, 2nd Earl of Orkney in 1633. Scene of Pirate Gow's capture.

Location: OS Ref. NT227 773. N of island of Eday on minor roads W of B9063 just W of the shore of Calf Sound. Regular ferry service.

Open: Jun - Sept: occasional Suns by appointment only.

Admission: No fee. Donations to charity.

🎦 Obligatory.

JARLSHOF PREHISTORIC & NORSE SETTLEMENT
Shetland

Tel: 01950 460112

Owner: In the care of Historic Scotland   **Contact:** The Steward

Over 3 acres of remains spanning 3,000 years from the Stone Age. Oval-shaped Bronze Age houses, Iron Age broch and wheel houses. Viking long houses, medieval farmstead and 16th century laird's house.

Location: OS Ref. HY401 096. At Sumburgh Head, 22m S of Lerwick on the A970.

Open: 1 Apr - 30 Sept: daily, 9.30am - 6.30pm. Last ticket 30mins before closing.

Admission: Adult £4, Child £1.60, Conc. £3.

€

MAESHOWE

Orkney

Tel: 01856 761606

Owner: In the care of Historic Scotland   **Contact:** The Steward

This world-famous tomb was built in Neolithic times, before 2700 BC. The large mound covers a stone-built passage and a burial chamber with cells in the walls. Runic inscriptions tell of how it was plundered of its treasures by Vikings.

Location: OS Ref. NY318 128. 9m W of Kirkwall on the A965.

Open: 1 Apr - 30 Sept: daily, 9.30am - 6.30pm. 1 Oct - 31 Mar: daily, 9.30am - 4.30pm.

Admission: Adult £4.50, Child £2, Conc. £3.50. Joint entry ticket for all Orkney monuments available. Timed ticketing in place - please telephone for details, and to book. Admission and shop at nearby Tormiston Mill.

🖻 🎦 🅿 Limited. ❂ ❋ €

RING OF BRODGAR STONE CIRCLE & HENGE

Stromness, Orkney

Tel: 0131 668 8800

Owner/Contact: In the care of Historic Scotland

A magnificent circle of upright stones with an enclosing ditch spanned by causeways. Of late Neolithic date.

Location: OS Ref. HY294 134. 5m NE of Stromness.

Open: Any reasonable time.

Admission: Free.

❋

©Historic Scotland Photographic Library

SKARA BRAE & SKAILL HOUSE
SANDWICK, ORKNEY

Tel: 01856 841815

Owner: Historic Scotland/Major M R S Macrae   **Contact:** The Steward

Skara Brae is one of the best preserved groups of Stone Age houses in Western Europe. Built before the Pyramids, the houses contain stone furniture, hearths and drains. Visitor centre and replica house with joint admission with Skaill House – 17th century home of the laird who excavated Skara Brae.

Location: OS6 HY231 188. 19m NW of Kirkwall on the B9056.

Open: Apr - Sept: daily, 9.30am - 6.30pm. Oct - Mar: daily, 9.30am - 4.30pm. Last ticket 45 mins before closing.

Admission: Apr - Sept: Adult £6.50, Child £2.50, Conc. £5. Oct - Mar: Adult £5.50, Child £2, Conc. £4.50. 10% discount for groups (10+). Joint ticket with other Orkney sites available.

ℹ Visitor centre. 🖻 ♿ Partial. WCs. 🍴 Licensed. 🅿
✉ Free school visits when booked. 🐕 Guide dogs only. ❋ €

TANKERNESS HOUSE

Broad Street, Kirkwall, Orkney

Tel: 01856 873535   **Fax:** 01856 871560

Owner: Orkney Islands Council   **Contact:** Steve Callaghan

A fine vernacular 16th century town house contains The Orkney Museum.

Location: OS Ref. HY446 109. In Kirkwall opposite W end of cathedral.

Open: Oct - Apr: Mon - Sat, 10.30am - 12.30pm & 1.30 - 5pm. May - Sept: Mon - Sat, 10.30am - 5pm, Sun, 2 - 5pm. Gardens always open.

Admission: Free.

Carreg Cennen Castle, South Wales.

Wales

Caernarfon Castle, North Wales. © Cadw:Welsh Historic Monuments. Crown Copyright.

north wales

south wales

wales

The traditional border between Wales and England is Offa's Dyke, built by King Offa between 757 and 796AD. North Wales is a holiday area attracting lovers of coast and countryside alike. To the west lies Snowdon (Eryri as it is known in Welsh), the highest peak in England and Wales, a popular destination for climbers and walkers. The Snowdonia National Park offers mountain walks, forest trails and miles of golden sandy beaches. To the east, in contrast, is a gentler landscape of moorlands, valleys and the hills of the Welsh Borders. Further south, the Gower Peninsula, a haven for wildlife, was the first place in Britain to be designated an Area of Outstanding Natural Beauty.

ABERCONWY HOUSE

Castle Street, Conwy LL32 8AY

Tel: 01492 592246   **Fax:** 01492 564818

Owner: The National Trust

Dating from the 14th century, this is the only medieval merchant's house in Conwy to have survived the turbulent history of this walled town for nearly six centuries. Furnished rooms and an audio-visual presentation show daily life from different periods in its history.

Location: OS Ref. SH781 777. At junction of Castle Street and High Street.

Open: 25 Mar - 29 Oct: Wed - Mon, 11am - 5pm. Last adm. 30 mins before close. Shop: 1 Mar - 31 Dec: daily (closed 25/26 Dec), 10am - 5pm (5.30pm 25 Mar - 29 Oct). Jan - Feb 2007: Wed - Sun, 11am - 5pm. Suns open at 11am.

Admission: Adult £3, Child £1.50, Family (2+2) £7.50. Pre-booked groups (15+) Adult £2.50, Child £1. National Trust members Free.

ⓘNo indoor photography. ◻All year. ✗By arrangement. ◠
ⓅIn town car parks only. ▣ ♿Guide dogs only.

BEAUMARIS CASTLE ✚

BEAUMARIS, ANGLESEY LL58 8AP

www.cadw.wales.gov.uk

Tel: 01248 810361

Owner: In the care of Cadw   **Contact:** The Custodian

The most technically perfect medieval castle in Britain, standing midway between Caernarfon and Conwy, commanding the old ferry crossing to Anglesey. A World Heritage Listed Site.

Location: OS Ref. SH608 762. 5m NE of Menai Bridge (A5) by A545. 7m from Bangor.

Open: 1 Apr - 31 May & Oct: daily, 9.30am - 5pm. 1 Jun - 30 Sept: daily, 9.30am - 6pm. 1 Nov - 31 Mar: Mon - Sat, 9.30am - 4pm, Suns 11am - 4pm.

Admission: Adult £3, Child (under 16 yrs)/Conc. £2.50, Child under 5yrs free, Family (2+3) £8.50. (Prices subject to review Mar 2006).

◻ ♿ ✗ Ⓟ ♿Guide dogs only. ❊

BODELWYDDAN CASTLE

Bodelwyddan, Denbighshire LL18 5YA

Tel: 01745 584060   **Fax:** 01745 584563   **e-mail:** enquiries@bodelwyddan-castle.co.uk
www.bodelwyddan-castle.co.uk

Owner: Bodelwyddan Castle Trust   **Contact:** Kevin Mason

Set within 200 acres of historical parkland, Bodelwyddan Castle is the Welsh home of the National Portrait Gallery, displaying works from its 19th century collection. Complementary collection of sculpture and furniture in a period setting. Victorian games gallery. Temporary exhibitions and events.

Location: OS Ref. SH999 749. Follow signs off A55 expressway. 2m W of St Asaph, opposite Marble Church.

Open: Easter - end Oct: daily except Fri: 10.30am - 5pm. Winter: Thurs, Sats & Suns, 10.30am - 4pm.

Admission: Adult £5, Child (5-16yrs) £2 (under 4yrs free), Conc. £4.50, Family (2+2) £12. Discounts for schools, groups & disabled. Season ticket available.

◻ ⏣ ♿Partial. WCs. ● ✗By arrangement. ◠ Free. Ⓟ ▣ ♿Guide dogs only. ❊ ⌂
⌘ Tel for details.

BODNANT GARDEN

Tal-y-Cafn, Colwyn Bay LL28 5RE

Tel: 01492 650460   **Fax:** 01492 650448   **e-mail:** office@bodnantgarden.co.uk
www.bodnantgarden.co.uk

Owner: The National Trust

Bodnant Garden is one of the finest gardens in the country not only for its magnificent collections of rhododendrons, camellias and magnolias but also for its idyllic setting above the River Conwy with extensive views of the Snowdonia range.

Location: OS Ref. SH801 723. 8 miles S of Llandudno and Colwyn Bay, off A470. Signposted from A55, exit at Junction 19.

Open: 11 Mar - 5 Nov: daily, 10am - 5pm (Tearoom from 11am).

Admission: Adult £6, Child £3. Groups (20+) £5. RHS members free.

◻ ⏣ ♿Partial. WCs. ● Ⓟ ♿Guide dogs only.

BODRHYDDAN 🏠

Rhuddlan, Clwyd LL18 5SB

Tel: 01745 590414   **Fax:** 01745 590155   **e-mail:** bodrhyddan@hotmail.com
www.bodrhyddan.co.uk

Owner/Contact: Colonel The Lord Langford OBE DL

The home of Lord Langford and his family, Bodrhyddan is basically a 17th century house with 19th century additions by the famous architect, William Eden Nesfield, although he not at its earliest building much. The house has been in the hands of the same family since it was built over 500 years ago. There are notable pieces of armour, pictures, period furniture, a 3,000 year old mummy, a formal parterre, a woodland garden and attractive picnic areas. Bodrhyddan is a Grade I listing, making it one of few in Wales to remain in private hands.

Location: OS Ref. SJ045 788. On the A5151 midway between Dyserth and Rhuddlan, 4m SE of Rhyl.

Open: Jun - Sept inclusive: Tues & Thurs, 2 - 5.30pm.

Admission: House & Gardens: Adult £4, Child £2. Gardens only: Adult £2, Child £1.

♿Partial. ● ✗Obligatory. Ⓟ ⌂

BRYN BRAS CASTLE

LLANRUG, CAERNARFON, GWYNEDD LL55 4RE

www.brynbrascastle.co.uk

Tel/Fax: 01286 870210   **e-mail:** holidays@brynbrascastle.co.uk

Owner: Mr & Mrs N E Gray-Parry   **Contact:** Marita Gray-Parry

Built in the Neo-Romanesque style in c1830, on an earlier structure, and probably designed by Thomas Hopper, it stands in the Snowdonian Range. The tranquil garden includes a hill-walk with fine views of Mt Snowdon, Anglesey and the sea. Bryn Bras, a much loved home, offers a delightful selection of apartments for holidays for twos within the Grade II* listed castle. Many local restaurants, inns.

Location: OS Ref. SH543 625. ¹/₂ m off A4086 at Llanrug, 4¹/₂ m E of Caernarfon.

Open: Only by appointment.

Admission: By arrangement. No children please.

⬚ ⬚Self-catering Apartments for twos within castle. ❊

CAERNARFON CASTLE ✠

CASTLE DITCH, CAERNARFON LL55 2AY

www.cadw.wales.gov.uk

Tel: 01286 677617

Owner: In the care of Cadw   **Contact:** The Custodian

The most famous, and perhaps the most impressive castle in Wales. Taking nearly 50 years to build, it proved the costliest of Edward I's castles. A World Heritage Listed Site.

Location: OS Ref. SH477 626. In Caernarfon, just W of town centre.

Open: 1 Apr - 31 May & Oct: daily, 9.30am - 5pm. 1 Jun - 30 Sept: daily, 9.30am - 6pm. 1 Nov - 31 Mar: Mon - Sat, 9.30am - 4pm, Suns 11am - 4pm.

Admission: Adult £4.75, Child (under 16 yrs)/Conc. £3.75, Child under 5yrs free, Family (2+3) £13.25. (Prices subject to review Mar 2006.)

⬚ 🅿 ♿ Guide dogs only. ✳

CONWY CASTLE ✠

CONWY LL32 8AY

www.cadw.wales.gov.uk

Tel: 01492 592358

Owner: In the care of Cadw   **Contact:** The Custodian

Taken together the castle and town walls are the most impressive of the fortresses built by Edward I, and remain the finest and most impressive in Britain. A World Heritage Listed Site.

Location: OS Ref. SH783 774. Conwy by A55 or B5106.

Open: 1 Apr - 31 May & Oct: daily, 9.30am - 5pm. 1 Jun - 30 Sept: daily, 9.30am - 6pm. 1 Nov - 31 Mar: Mon - Sat, 9.30am - 4pm, Suns 11am - 4pm.

Admission: Adult £4, Child (under 16yrs)/Conc. £3.50, Child under 5yrs free, Family (2+3) £11.50. Joint ticket for entry to Conwy Castle and Plas Mawr: Adult £6.50, Conc. £5.50, Family (2+3) £18.50. (Prices subject to review Mar 2006.)

⬚ 𝑖 By arrangement. 🅿 ♿ Guide dogs only. ✳

CHIRK CASTLE ⚜

Chirk LL14 5AF

Tel: 01691 777701   **Fax:** 01691 774706   **e-mail:** chirkcastle@nationaltrust.org.uk

Owner: The National Trust

700 year old Chirk Castle, a magnificent marcher fortress, commands fine views over the surrounding countryside. Rectangular with a massive drum tower at each corner, the castle has beautiful formal gardens with clipped yews, roses and a variety of flowering shrubs. Voted best National Trust garden in 1999. The dramatic dungeon is a reminder of the castle's turbulent history, whilst later occupants have left elegant state rooms, furniture, tapestries and portraits. The castle was sold for five thousand pounds to Sir Thomas Myddelton in 1595, and his descendants continue to live in part of the castle today.

Location: OS Ref. SJ275 388. 8m S of Wrexham off A483, 2m from Chirk village.

Open: Castle & Shop: 25 Mar - 29 Oct, Wed - Sun & BH Mons (+Tues Jul - Aug), 12 noon - 5pm (4pm in Oct), last admission 1/2 hr before closing. Garden: as Castle, 10am - 6pm (5pm in Oct), last admission 1hr before closing. Tearoom: as Castle, 10am - 5pm (4pm in Oct). Farm Shop: As Tearoom (6pm Jul - Aug). Home Farm & Estate: as Garden.

Admission: House & Garden: Adult £7, Child £3.50, Family £17.50. Pre-booked groups (15+): Adult £5, Child £2.50. Garden only: Adults £4.50, Child £2.20, Family £11.20. Pre-booked groups: Adult £3.20, Child £1.60.

𝑖 No indoor photography. ⬚ ♿ 🅿 🍴 Licensed. 𝑖 By arrangement. 🅿 ▣ ♿ Guide dogs only. ▲ ♿ Tel for details

COCHWILLAN OLD HALL

Talybont, Bangor, Gwynedd LL57 3AZ

Tel: 01248 355853

Owner: R C H Douglas Pennant   **Contact:** Miss M D Monteith

A fine example of medieval architecture with the present house dating from about 1450. It was probably built by William Gryffydd who fought for Henry VII at Bosworth. Once owned in the 17th century by John Williams who became Archbishop of York. The house was restored from a barn in 1971.

Location: OS Ref. SH606 695. 3 1/2 m SE of Bangor. 1m SE of Talybont off A55.

Open: By appointment.

Admission: Please telephone for details.

✳

CRICCIETH CASTLE ✠

Castle Street, Criccieth, Gwynedd LL52 0DP

Tel: 01766 522227   **www**.cadw.wales.gov.uk

Owner: In the care of Cadw   **Contact:** The Custodian

Overlooking Cardigan Bay, Criccieth Castle is the most striking of the fortresses built by the native Welsh Princes. Its inner defences are dominated by a powerful twin-towered gatehouse.

Location: OS Ref. SH500 378. A497 to Criccieth from Porthmadog or Pwllheli.

Open: 1 Apr - 31 May & Oct : daily, 10am - 5pm. 1 June - 30 Sept: daily, 10am - 6pm. (Open and unstaffed at all other times with no admission charge at all other times.)

Admission: Adult £2.90, Child (under 16yrs)/Conc. £2.40, Child under 5yrs free, Family (2+3) £8.20. (Prices subject to review Mar 2006.)

⬚ 🅿 ♿ Guide dogs only. ✳

North Wales

DENBIGH CASTLE ♣

Denbigh, Clwyd

Tel: 01745 813385   **www**.cadw.wales.gov.uk

Owner: In the care of Cadw   **Contact:** The Custodian

Crowning the summit of a prominent outcrop dominating the Vale of Clwyd, the principal feature of this spectacular site is the great gatehouse dating back to the 11th century. Some of the walls can still be walked by visitors.

Location: OS Ref. SJ052 658. Denbigh via A525, A543 or B5382.

Open: 1 Apr - 30 Sept: Mon - Fri, 10am - 5.30pm, Sats & Suns, 9.30am - 5.30pm. (Open and unstaffed at all other times with no admission charge.)

Admission: Castle: Adult £2.50, Child (under 16yrs)/Conc. £2, Child under 5 yrs free, Family (2+3) £7. (Prices subject to review Mar 2006.)

🅿 Guide dogs only. ✳

DOLBELYDR

Trefnant, Denbighshire LL16 5AG

Tel: 01628 825925   **www**.landmarktrust.org.uk

Owner/Contact: The Landmark Trust

A 16th century, Grade II* listed building, a fine example of a 16th century gentry house and has good claim to be the birthplace of the modern Welsh language. It was at Dolbelydr that Henry Salesbury wrote his *Grammatica Britannica*. Dolbelydr is cared for by The Landmark Trust, a building preservation charity who let it for holidays. Full details of Dolbelydr and 183 other historic and architecturally important buildings are featured in the Landmark Trust Handbook (£11 refundable against a booking).

Location: OS Ref. SJ031 709.

Open: Available for holidays for max 6 people throughout the year. Open Days on 8 days throughout the year. Contact the Landmark Trust for details.

Admission: Free on Open Days.

✳

DOLWYDDELAN CASTLE ♣

Blaenau Ffestiniog, Gwynedd

Tel: 01690 750366   **www**.cadw.wales.gov.uk

Owner: In the care of Cadw   **Contact:** The Custodian

Standing proudly on a ridge, this stern building remains remarkably intact and visitors cannot fail to be impressed with the great solitary square tower, built by Llewelyn the Great in the early 13th century.

Location: OS Ref. SH722 522. A470(T) Blaenau Ffestiniog to Betws-y-Coed, 1m W of Dolwyddelan.

Open: All Year: Mon - Sat, 10am - 6pm (4pm, 1 Oct - 31 Mar). Suns 11am - 4pm.

Admission: Adult £2, Child (under 16yrs)/Conc. £1.50, Child under 5 yrs free, Family (2+3) £5.50. (Subject to review Mar 2006).

🅿 Guide dogs only. ✳

ERDDIG ※

Nr Wrexham LL13 0YT

Tel: 01978 355314   **Fax:** 01978 313333   **Info Line:** 01978 315151

Owner: The National Trust

One of the most fascinating houses in Britain, not least because of the unusually close relationship that existed between the family of the house and their servants. The beautiful and evocative range of outbuildings includes kitchen, laundry, bakehouse, stables, sawmill, smithy and joiner's shop, while the stunning state rooms display most of their original 18th & 19th century furniture and furnishings, including some exquisite Chinese wallpaper.

Location: OS Ref. SJ326 482. 2m S of Wrexham.

Open: House: 25 Mar - 29 Oct: Sat - Wed (+Thur Jul - Aug), 12 noon - 5pm (Mar/Apr & Oct closes 4pm). Garden: 25 Mar - 28 Jun & 2 - 30 Sept: Sat - Wed, 11am - 6pm; 1 Jul - 31 Aug: Sat - Thur, 10am - 6pm; Oct: Sat - Wed, 11am - 5pm; 4 Nov - 17 Dec: Sats & Suns, 11am - 4pm. Restaurant & Shop/Plants: As Garden, Mar - Sept, 11am - 5.15pm

Admission: All-inclusive ticket: Adult £8, Child £4, Family (2+3) £20. Pre-booked group (15+) £6.80, Child £3.40. Garden: Adult £5, Child £2.50, Family £12.50. Groups, Adult £4.20, Child £2.10. NT members Free.

🔲 ♿ Partial. WCs. 🍴 Licensed. 📷 AV presentation. 🅿 Guide dogs only.

FFERM

Pontblyddyn, Mold, Flintshire

Tel/Fax: 01352 770217

Owner/Contact: Dr M Jones-Mortimer

17th century farmhouse. Viewing is limited to 7 persons at any one time. Prior booking is recommended. No toilets or refreshments.

Location: OS Ref. SJ279 603. Access from A541 in Pontblyddyn, 3½ m SE of Mold.

Open: 2nd Wed in every month, 2 - 5pm. Pre-booking is recommended.

Admission: £4.

✉ ✳

GWYDIR CASTLE

LLANRWST, GWYNEDD LL26 0PN

www.gwydircastle.co.uk

Tel/Fax: 01492 641687   **e-mail:** info@gwydircastle.co.uk

Owner/Contact: Mr & Mrs Welford

Gwydir Castle is situated in the beautiful Conwy Valley and is set within a Grade I listed, 10 acre garden. Built by the illustrious Wynn family c1500, Gwydir is a fine example of a Tudor courtyard house, incorporating re-used medieval material from the dissolved Abbey of Maenan. Further additions date from c1600 and c1826. The important 1640s panelled Dining Room has now been reinstated, following its repatriation from the New York Metropolitan Museum.

Location: OS Ref. SH795 610. ½ m W of Llanrwst on B5106.

Open: 1 Mar - 31 Oct: daily, except Sats 10am - 4.30pm. Limited openings at other times. Please telephone for details.

Admission: Adult £3.50, Child £1.50. Group discount 10%.

🍴 ♿ Partial. 📷 By arrangement. ⓘ By arrangement. 🅿 🛏 2 doubles. 🔔

HARLECH CASTLE ♣

Harlech LL46 2YH

Tel: 01766 780552   **www**.cadw.wales.gov.uk

Owner: In the care of Cadw   **Contact:** The Custodian

Set on a towering rock above Tremadog Bay, this seemingly impregnable fortress is the most dramatically sited of all the castles of Edward I. A World Heritage Listed Site.

Location: OS Ref. SH581 312. Harlech, Gwynedd on A496 coast road.

Open: 1 Apr - 31 May & Oct: daily, 9.30am - 5pm. 1 Jun - 30 Sept: daily, 9.30am - 6pm. 1 Nov - 31 Mar: Mon - Sat, 9.30am - 4pm, Suns 11am - 4pm.

Admission: Adult £3, Child (under 16yrs)/Conc. £2.50, Child under 5 yrs free, Family (2+3) £8.50. (Prices subject to review Mar 2006.)

🔲 🅿 Guide dogs only. ✳

HARTSHEATH 🏛

Pontblyddyn, Mold, Flintshire

Tel/Fax: 01352 770217

Owner/Contact: Dr M Jones-Mortimer

18th and 19th century house set in parkland. Viewing is limited to 7 persons at any one time. Prior booking is recommended. No toilets or refreshments.

Location: OS Ref. SJ287 602. Access from A5104, 3½ m SE of Mold between Pontblyddyn and Penyffordd.

Open: 1st, 3rd & 5th Wed in every month, 2 - 5pm.

Admission: £4.

✉ ✳

ISCOYD PARK

Nr Whitchurch, Shropshire SY13 3AT

Owner/Contact: Mr P C Godsal

18th century Grade II* listed redbrick house in park.

Location: OS Ref. SJ504 421. 2m W of Whitchurch on A525.

Open: By written appointment only.

🍴 ✳

PENRHYN CASTLE

Bangor LL57 4HN

Tel: 01248 353084   **Infoline:** 01248 371337   **Fax:** 01248 371281

Owner: The National Trust

This dramatic neo-Norman fantasy castle sits between Snowdonia and the Menai Strait. Built by Thomas Hopper between 1820 and 1845 for the wealthy Pennant family, who made their fortune from Jamaican sugar and Welsh slate. The castle is crammed with fascinating things such as a 1-ton slate bed made for Queen Victoria.

Location: OS Ref. SH602 720. 1m E of Bangor, at Llandygai (J11, A55).

Open: Castle: 25 Mar - 29 Oct, daily (except Tues), 12 noon - 5pm (11am Jul - Aug). Grounds & Tearoom: as Castle (10am Jul - Aug). Shop & Museums: 23 Mar - 29 Oct, daily (except Tues), 11am - 5pm.

Admission: Adult £8, Child £4, Family (2+2) £20. Pre-booked groups (15+) £6.50. Garden & Stableblock Exhibitions only: Adult £5.40, Child £2.70. Audio tour: £1 (including NT members). NT members Free.

🖾 🖵 Licensed. ⊞ 🛈 🖼 Guide dogs only. ▣

PLAS BRONDANW GARDENS 🏚

Plas Brondanw, Llanfrothen, Gwynedd LL48 6SW

Tel: 01743 241181/07880 766741

Owner: Trustees of the Second Portmeirion Foundation.

Italianate gardens with topiary.

Location: OS Ref. SH618 423. 3m N of Penrhyndeudraeth off A4085, on Croesor Road.

Open: All year: daily, 9am - 5pm. Coaches accepted, please book.

Admission: Adult £3, Subsequent adult £2pp, Child Free if accompanied by an adult.

Cadw: Welsh Historic Monuments. Crown Copyright

PLAS MAWR ✦

HIGH STREET, CONWY LL32 8EF

www.cadw.wales.gov.uk

Tel: 01492 580167

Owner: In the care of Cadw   **Contact:** The Custodian

The best preserved Elizabethan town house in Britain, the house reflects the status of its builder Robert Wynn. A fascinating and unique place allowing visitors to sample the lives of the Tudor gentry and their servants, Plas Mawr is famous for the quality and quantity of its decorative plasterwork.

Location: OS Ref. SH781 776. Conwy by A55 or B5106 or A547.

Open: 1 Apr - 31 May, Sept & Oct: Tues - Suns & BH Mons, 9.30am - 5pm (4pm in Oct). 1 Jun - 31 Aug: Tues - Suns & BH Mons, 9.30am - 6pm.

Admission: Adult £4.50, Child (under 16yrs)/Conc. £3.50, Child under 5yrs free, Family (2+3) £12.50. Joint ticket for entry to Conwy Castle and Plas Mawr: Adult £6.50, Conc. £5.50, Family (2+3) £18.50. (Prices subject to review Mar 2006.)

🖾 🅿 Limited. 🖾 🖼 Guide dogs only.

PLAS NEWYDD 🌿

Llanfairpwll, Anglesey LL61 6DQ

Tel: 01248 714795   **Infoline:** 01248 715272   **Fax:** 01248 713673

Owner: The National Trust

Set amidst breathtaking beautiful scenery and with spectacular views of Snowdonia. Fine spring garden and Australasian arboretum with an understorey of shrubs and wildflowers. Summer terrace, and, later, massed hydrangeas and Autumn colour. A woodland walk gives access to a marine walk on the Menai Strait. Rhododendron garden open April - early June only. Elegant 18th century house by James Wyatt, famous for its association with Rex Whistler whose largest painting is here. Military museum contains relics of 1st Marquess of Anglesey and Battle of Waterloo. A historic cruise, a boat trip on the Menai Strait operates from the property weather and tides permitting (additional charge). 5 seater buggy to rhododendron garden and woodland walk.

Location: OS Ref. SH521 696. 2m S of Llanfairpwll and A5.

Open: 1 Apr - 1 Nov: Sat - Wed & Good Fri. House: 12 noon - 5pm. Garden: 11am - 5.30pm. Last admission 4.30pm. Shop & Tearoom: 1 Apr - 1 Nov, Sat - Wed, 10.30am - 5.30pm, 4 Nov - 17 Dec, 11am - 4pm, Sats & Suns.

Admission: House & Garden: Adult £6, Child £3 (under 5yrs free), Family (2+3) £15. Groups (15+) £5.40. Garden only: Adult £4, Child £2. NT members Free.

🛈 No indoor photography. 🖾 🖼 Partial. WCs. Minibus from car park to house. 🖵 Licensed. ⊞ 🎔 By arrangement. 🅿 ▣ 🖼 Guide dogs only. ▤ Tel for details.

PLAS YN RHIW 🌿

Rhiw, Pwllheli LL53 8AB

Tel/Fax: 01758 780219

Owner: The National Trust

A small manor house, with garden and woodlands, overlooking the west shore of Porth Neigwl (Hell's Mouth Bay) on the Llyn Peninsula. The house is part medieval, with Tudor and Georgian additions, and the ornamental gardens have flowering trees and shrubs, divided by box hedges and grass paths, rising behind to the snowdrop wood.

Location: OS Ref. SH237 282. 16m SW of Pwllheli, 3m S of the B4413 to Aberdaron. No access for coaches.

Open: 1 Apr - 29 May: Thur - Mon; 31 May - 30 Sept: daily except Tues 12 noon - 5pm.; 1 - 22 Oct: Sats & Suns; 23 - 29 Oct: daily, 12 noon - 4pm.

Admission: Adult £3.40, Child £1.70, Family (2+3) £8.50. Groups: £2.80, Child £1.40. Gardens only: Adult £2.20, Child £1.10, Family (2+3) £5.50. Groups £1.70.

🖾 🎔 🖼 Partial. WCs. 🎔 By arrangement. 🅿 Limited. 🖼 Guide dogs only.

PORTMEIRION

Portmeirion, Gwynedd LL48 6ET

Tel: 01766 770000   **Fax:** 01766 771331   **e-mail:** info@portmeirion-village.com

Owner: The Portmeirion Foundation   **Contact:** Mr R Llywelyn

Built by Clough Williams-Ellis as an 'unashamedly romantic' village resort.

Location: OS Ref. SH590 371. Off A487 at Minffordd between Penrhyndeudraeth and Porthmadog.

Open: All year: daily, 9.30am - 5.30pm. Closed 25 Dec.

Admission: Adult £6.50, Child £3.50, OAP £5, Family (2+2) £16.

civil wedding venues
see page 562 🔔

POWIS CASTLE & GARDEN ※

Nr Welshpool SY21 8RF

Tel: 01938 551929   **Infoline:** 01938 551944   **Fax:** 01938 554336
e-mail: powiscastle@nationaltrust.org.uk

Owner: The National Trust   **Contact:** Visitor Services Manager

The world-famous garden, overhung with enormous clipped yew trees, shelters rare and tender plants in colourful herbaceous borders. Laid out under the influence of Italian and French styles, the garden retains its original lead statues and, an orangery on the terraces. Perched on a rock above the garden terraces, the medieval castle contains one of the finest collections of paintings and furniture in Wales.

Location: OS Ref. SJ216 064. 1m W of Welshpool, car access on A483.

Open: Castle & Museum: 6 Apr - 29 Oct: Thur - Mon (+Wed Jul - Aug), 1 - 5pm (4pm 18 Sept - Oct). Coach House, Shop & Restaurant: as Castle, Apr - 17 Sept 11am - 5.30pm. 18 Sept - Oct, 11am - 4.30pm. Garden: 25/26 Mar & 1/2 Apr, 11am - 5pm. 6 Apr - 29 Oct: Thur - Mon (+ Wed Jul - Aug), 11 - 6pm (5pm 18 Sept - Oct). Last entry 45 mins before closing.

Admission: Castle & Garden: Adult £9.60, Child £4.80, Family (2+3) £24. Groups (15+ booked): £8.60. Garden only: Adult £6.60, Child £3.30, Family (2+3) £16. Groups (15+ booked): £5.60. No groups rates on Suns or BHs. NT members & under 5s Free.

ⓘ No indoor photography. 🖼 🎁 🖥 Partial. 🍴 Licensed. 🍴 By arrangement. 🅿 Limited for coaches. ✠ Guide dogs only.

RHUDDLAN CASTLE ✚

Castle Gate, Castle Street, Rhuddlan LL18 5AD

Tel: 01745 590777   www.cadw.wales.gov.uk

Owner: In the care of Cadw   **Contact:** The Custodian

Guarding the ancient ford of the River Clwyd, Rhuddlan was the strongest of Edward I's castles in North-East Wales. Linked to the sea by an astonishing deep water channel nearly 3 miles long, it still proclaims the innovative genius of its architect.

Location: OS Ref. SJ025 779. SW end of Rhuddlan via A525 or A547.

Open: 1 Apr - 30 Sept: daily, 10am - 5pm. Last adm. 4.30pm. Closed at all other times.

Admission: Adult £2.75, Child (under 16yrs)/Conc. £2.25, Child under 5 yrs free, Family (2+3) £7.75. (Prices subject to review Mar 2006.)

🖼 🅿 ✠ Guide dogs only.

RUG CHAPEL & LLANGAR CHURCH ✚

c/o Coronation Cottage, Rug, Corwen LL21 9BT

Tel: 01490 412025   www.cadw.wales.gov.uk

Owner: In the care of Cadw   **Contact:** The Custodian

Prettily set in a wooded landscape, Rug Chapel's exterior gives little hint of the wonders within. Nearby the attractive medieval Llangar Church still retains its charming early Georgian furnishings.

Location: Rug Chapel: OS Ref. SJ065 439. Off A494, 1m N of Corwen. Llangar Church: OS Ref. SJ064 423. Off B4401, 1m S of Corwen (obtain key at Rug).

Open: **Rug** – 1 Apr - 30 Sept: Wed - Sun (but open BH Mons & Tues), 10am - 5pm.
Llangar – 1 Apr - 30 Sept: Wed - Sun (but open BH Mons & Tues). Access is arranged daily at 2pm through Custodian at Rug Chapel; please telephone 01490 412025 for details.

Admission: Adult £2.50, Child (under 16yrs)/Conc. £2, Child under 5 yrs free, Family (2+3) £7. (Prices subject to review Mar 2006.)

🅿 ✠ Guide dogs only.

ST ASAPH CATHEDRAL

St Asaph, Denbighshire LL17 0RL

Tel: 01745 583429   **Contact:** Chapter Office

Britain's smallest ancient cathedral founded in 560AD by Kentigern, a religious community enclosed in a 'llan', hence Llanelwy.

Location: OS Ref. SJ039 743. In St Asaph, S of A55.

Open: Summer: 9am - 6pm. Winter: 9am - dusk. Sun services: 8am, 11am, 3.30pm. Morning Prayer: 9am.

✠

TOWER

Nercwys, Mold, Flintshire CH7 4EW

Tel: 01352 700220   **e-mail:** enquiries@towerwales.co.uk   www.towerwales.co.uk

Owner/Contact: Charles Wynne-Eyton

This Grade I listed building is steeped in Welsh history and bears witness to the continuous warfare of the time. A fascinating place to visit or for overnight stays.

Location: OS Ref. SJ240 620. 1m S of Mold.

Open: 1 - 15 & 19 - 31 May & 27/28 Aug: 2 - 4.30pm. Groups also welcome at other times by appointment.

Admission: Adult £3, Child £2.

✠

TREWERN HALL

Trewern, Welshpool, Powys SY21 8DT

Tel: 01938 570243

Owner: Chapman Family   **Contact:** M Chapman

Trewern Hall is a Grade II* listed building standing in the Severn Valley. It has been described as 'one of the most handsome timber-framed houses surviving in the area'. The porch contains a beam inscribed RF1610, though it seems likely that parts of the house are earlier. The property has been in the ownership of the Chapman family since 1918.

Location: OS Ref. SJ269 113. Off A458 Welshpool - Shrewsbury Road, 4m from Welshpool.

Opening: Last week in Apr, 1 - 31 May: Mon - Fri, 2 - 5pm.

Admission: Adult £2, Child/Conc. £1.

🖥 Unsuitable. 🅿 Limited. None for coaches. ✠

TŶ MAWR WYBRNANT ※

Penmachno, Betws-y-Coed, Conwy LL25 0HJ

Tel: 01690 760213

Owner: The National Trust

Situated in the beautiful and secluded Wybrnant valley, Tŷ Mawr was the birthplace of Bishop William Morgan, first translator of the entire Bible into Welsh. The house has been restored to its probable late 16th century appearance and houses a display of Welsh Bibles. A footpath leads from the house through woodland and the surrounding fields, which are traditionally managed.

Location: OS Ref. SH770 524. From A5 3m S of Betws-y-Coed, take B4406 to Penmachno. House is 2¹/₂ m NW of Penmachno by forest road.

Open: 30 Mar - 30 Oct: Thur - Sun, 12 noon - 5pm (4pm in Oct).

Admission: Adult £3, Child £1.50, Family £7.50. Booked groups (15+): Adult £2.50, Child £1. NT members Free.

🖥 Ground floor. 🅿 ✠ Guide dogs only.

VALLE CRUCIS ABBEY ✚

Llangollen, Clwyd

Tel: 01978 860326   www.cadw.wales.gov.uk

Owner: In the care of Cadw   **Contact:** The Custodian

Set in a beautiful valley location, Valle Crucis Abbey is the best preserved medieval monastery in North Wales, enhanced by the only surviving monastic fish pond in Wales.

Location: OS Ref. SJ205 442. B5103 from A5, 2m NW of Llangollen, or A542 from Ruthin.

Open: 1 Apr - 30 Sept: daily, 10am - 5pm. Last adm. 4.30pm. Unstaffed with no admission charge during winter, generally between 10am - 4pm.

Admission: Adult £2, Child (under 16yrs)/Conc. £1.50, Child under 5 yrs free, Family (2+3) £5.50. (Prices subject to review Mar 2006.)

🖼 🅿 ✠ Guide dogs only. ✠

WERN ISAF

Penmaen Park, Llanfairfechan LL33 0RN

Tel: 01248 680437

Owner/Contact: Mrs P J Phillips

This Arts and Crafts house was built in 1900 by the architect H L North as his family home and it contains much of the original furniture and William Morris fabrics. It is situated in a woodland garden and is at its best in the Spring. It has extensive views over the Menai Straits and Conwy Bay. One of the most exceptional houses of its date and style in Wales.

Location: OS Ref. SH685 75. Off A55 midway between Bangor and Conwy.

Open: 3 - 31 Mar: daily, except Mons.

Admission: Free.

accommodation
see page 567

ABERCAMLAIS

Brecon, Powys LD3 8EY

Tel: 01874 636206 **Fax:** 01874 636964 **e-mail:** info@abercamlais.co.uk
www.abercamlais.co.uk
Owner/Contact: Mrs S Ballance

Splendid Grade II* mansion dating from middle ages, altered extensively in early 18th century with 19th century additions, in extensive grounds beside the river Usk. Still in same family ownership and occupation since medieval times. Exceptional octagonal pigeon house, formerly a privy.

Location: OS Ref. SN965 290. 5m W of Brecon on A40.
Open: Apr - Oct: by appointment.
Admission: Adult £5, Child Free.
ⓘNo photography in house. ⬛ 🚻Obligatory. 🅿 ✸

ABERDULAIS FALLS 🌿

Aberdulais, Vale of Neath SA10 8EU

Tel: 01639 636674 **Fax:** 01639 645069

Owner: The National Trust   **Contact:** The Property Warden

For over 300 years this famous waterfall has provided the energy to drive the wheels of industry, from the first manufacture of copper in 1584 to present day remains of the tinplate works. It has also been visited by famous artists such as J M W Turner in 1796. You can today harness a unique hydro-electrical scheme which has been developed to harness the waters of the Dulais river.

Location: OS Ref. SS772 995. On A4109, 3m NE of Neath. 4m from M4/J43, then A465.
Open: 4 Mar - 3 Apr: Fri - Sun, 11am - 4pm. 4 Apr - 30 Oct: Mon - Fri, 10am - 5pm; Sats & Suns & BH Mons, 11am - 6pm. 4 Nov - 18 Dec: Fri - Sun, 11am - 4pm; 19 - 21 Dec: 11am - 4pm.
Admission: Adult £3.20, Child £1.60, Family £8. Groups (15+): Adult £2.40, Child £1.20. Children must be accompanied by an adult.
⬛ ⬛Light refreshments (summer only). 🅿 Limited. ⬛

BLAENAVON IRONWORKS ♣

Nr Brecon Beacons National Park, Blaenavon, Gwent

Tel: 01495 792615 **Winter Bookings:** 01633 648082 **www.**cadw.wales.gov.uk
Owner: In the care of Cadw   **Contact:** The Custodian

The famous ironworks at Blaenavon were a milestone in the history of the Industrial Revolution. Visitors can view much of the ongoing conservation work as well as 'Stack Square' - a rare survival of housing built for pioneer ironworkers. Part of a World Heritage Site.

Location: OS Ref. SO248 092. Via A4043 follow signs to Big Pit Mining Museum and Blaenavon Ironworks. Abergavenny 8m. Pontypool 8m. From car park, cross road, then path to entrance gate.
Open: 5 Apr - 31 Oct: Mon - Fri, 9:30am - 4:30pm. Sat, 10am - 5pm. Sun, 10am - 4.30pm. For other times, telephone Torfaen County Borough Council, 01633 648081.
Admission: Adult £2, Child (under 16 yrs)/Conc. £1.50, Child under 5yrs free, Family (2+3) £5.50. (Prices subject to review March 2005.)
⬛ ⬛Partial. 🚻By arrangement. 🅿 ⬛Guide dogs only.

CAE HIR GARDENS

Cae Hir, Cribyn, Lampeter, Cardiganshire SA48 7NG

Tel: 01570 470839

Owner/Contact: Mr W Akkermans

This transformed ten acre smallholding offers a succession of pleasant surprises and shows a quite different approach to gardening.

Location: OS Ref. SN521 520. NW on A482 from Lampeter, after 5m turn S on B4337. Cae Hir is 2m on left.
Open: Open daily, 1 - 6pm.
Admission: Adult £4.50, Child 50p, OAP £4. Free to RHS members.

ABERGLASNEY GARDENS

LLANGATHEN, CARMARTHENSHIRE SA32 8QH

www.aberglasney.org

Tel/Fax: 01558 668998 **e-mail:** info@aberglasney.org.uk

Owner: Aberglasney Restoration Trust   **Contact:** Booking Department

Aberglasney is one of the most remarkable restoration projects of recent years. When acquired in 1995 the Mansion and grounds were so derelict they were considered by most to be beyond restoration. It was not until the undergrowth was cleared and extensive archaeological surveys undertaken, that the importance of this historical garden was realised. The parapet walkway, dating from 1600, is the only example that survives in the United Kingdom. The nine acre garden is already planted with many rare and unusual plants, giving interest throughout the year. Aberglasney is destined to become one of the most fascinating gardens in the country.

Location: OS Ref. SN581 221. 4m W of Llandeilo. Follow signs from A40.
Open: All year: daily (except Christmas Day). Apr - Sept: 10am - 6pm, last entry 5pm. Oct - Mar: 10.30am - 4pm.
Admission: Adult £6, Child £3, Senior £5, Disabled £3. Booked groups (10+): Adult £5.50, Child £3, Senior £4.50.
⬛ ⬛ ⬛ ⬛Licensed. 🍽Licensed. 🚻Daily: 11.30am & 2.30pm.
🅿Limited for coaches. ⬛ ⬛Guide dogs only. ⬛ ✸

CAERLEON ROMAN BATHS & AMPHITHEATRE ✤

High Street, Caerleon NP6 1AE

Tel: 01633 422518   **www**.cadw.wales.gov.uk

Owner: In the care of Cadw   **Contact:** The Custodian

Caerleon is the most varied and fascinating Roman site in Britain – incorporating fortress and baths, well-preserved amphitheatre and a row of barrack blocks, the only examples currently visible in Europe.

Location: OS Ref. ST340 905. 4m ENE of Newport by B4596 to Caerleon, M4/J25 (westbound), M4/J26 (eastbound).

Open: 1 Apr - 31 Oct: daily, 9.30am - 5pm. Last admission 4.30pm. 1 Nov - 31 Mar: Mon - Sat, 11 - 4pm. Sun 12 noon - 5pm.

Admission: Adult £2.50, Child (under 16 yrs)/Conc. £2, Child under 5yrs free, Family (2+3) £7. (Prices subject to review March 2005.)

▢ ℙ ♿ Guide dogs only. ❋

CAERPHILLY CASTLE ✤

Caerphilly CF8 1JL

Tel: 029 2088 3143

www.cadw.wales.gov.uk

Owner: In the care of Cadw   **Contact:** The Custodian

Often threatened, never taken, this vastly impressive castle is much the biggest in Wales. 'Red Gilbert' de Clare, Anglo-Norman Lord of Glamorgan, flooded a valley to create the 30 acre lake, setting his fortress on 3 artificial islands. Famous for its leaning tower, its fortifications are scarcely rivalled in Europe.

Location: OS Ref. ST156 871. Centre of Caerphilly, A468 from Newport, A470, A469 from Cardiff.

Open: 1 Apr - 31 May & Oct: daily, 9.30am - 5pm. 1 Jun - 30 Sept: daily, 9.30am - 6pm. 1 Nov - 31 Mar: Mon - Sat, 9.30am - 4pm, Sun 11am - 4pm.

Admission: Adult £3, Child (under 16 yrs)/Conc. £2.50, Child under 5yrs free, Family (2+3 under 16 yrs) £8.50. (Prices subject to review March 2006.)

▢ ▢ ℙLimited. ♿Guide dogs only. ▲ ❋

CALDICOT CASTLE & COUNTRY PARK

Church Road, Caldicot, Monmouthshire NP26 4HU

Tel: 01291 420241   **Fax:** 01291 435094

e-mail: caldicotcastle@monmouthshire.gov.uk   **www**.caldicotcastle.co.uk

Owner: Monmouthshire County Council   **Contact:** Castle Development Officer

Caldicot's magnificent castle is set in fifty acres of beautiful parkland. Founded by the Normans, developed in royal hands in the Middle Ages and restored as a Victorian home. Discover the Castle's past with an audio tour. Visitors can relax in tranquil gardens, explore medieval towers, discover children's activities and play giant chess.

Location: OS Ref. ST487 887. From M4 take J23a and B4245 to Caldicot. From M48 take J2 and follow A48 & B4245. Castle signposted from B4245.

Open: Mar - Oct: daily, 11am - 5pm. Please telephone for winter opening times.

Admission: Adult £3.50, Child/Conc £2. Groups (10 - 100): Adult £2.50, Child/Conc £1.50.

▢ Ⓣ ♿Partial. WCs. ▣ ⒤By arrangement. ▢ ℙ
▥ Free for formal educational visits. ♿In Castle, on leads. ▲ ▽ Tel for details.

CARDIFF CASTLE

Castle Street, Cardiff CF10 3RB

Tel: 029 2087 8100   **Fax:** 029 2023 1417

Owner: City and County of Cardiff   **Contact:** Booking Office

2000 years of history, including Roman Walls, Norman Keep and Victorian interiors.

Location: OS Ref. ST181 765. Cardiff city centre, signposted from M4.

Open: 1 Mar - 31 Oct: daily, 9.30am - 6pm. Tours 10am - 5pm, last entry 5pm; 1 Nov - 28 Feb: daily, 9.30am - 5pm. Tours 10am - 4pm, last entry 4pm. Closed 25/26 Dec & 1 Jan.

Admission: Full Tour: Adult £6.30, Child/OAP £3.90. Short Tour: Adult £3.90, Child/OAP £2.40. Grounds only: Adult £3.20, Child/OAP £2. Curator Tours: Adult/OAP £11.50.

CARMARTHEN CASTLE

Carmarthen, South Wales

Tel: 0126 7224923   **e-mail:** clgriffiths@carmarthenshire.gov.uk

Owner/Contact: The Conservation Department, Carmarthenshire County Council

The fortress, originally founded by Henry I in 1109, witnessed several fierce battles, notably in the 15th century when the Welsh hero Owain Glyndwr burnt the town and took the castle from the English.

Location: OS Ref. SN413 200. In the town centre.

Open: Throughout the year.

Admission: Free (guided tours while archaeologists continue to work at the site).

special events see page 571

CARREG CENNEN CASTLE ✤

Tir-y-Castell Farm, Llandeilo

Tel: 01558 822291   **www**.cadw.wales.gov.uk

Owner: In the care of Cadw   **Contact:** The Custodian

Spectacularly crowning a remote crag 300 feet above the River Cennen, the castle is unmatched as a wildly romantic fortress sought out by artists and visitors alike. The climb from Rare Breeds Farm is rewarded by breathtaking views and the chance to explore intriguing caves beneath.

Location: OS Ref. SN668 190. Minor roads from A483(T) to Trapp village. 5m SE of A40 at Llandeilo.

Open: All Year: daily, 9.30am - 6.30pm (dusk, 1 Nov - 31 Mar). Only closed 25 Dec.

Admission: Adult £3, Child (under 16 yrs)/Conc. £2.50, Child under 5yrs free, Family (2+3) £8.50. (Prices subject to review March 2006.)

▢ ▣ ▢ ℙ ♿Guide dogs only. ❋

CADW: Welsh Historic Monuments. Crown Copyright

CASTELL COCH ✤

TONGWYNLAIS, CARDIFF CF4 7JS

www.cadw.wales.gov.uk

Tel: 029 2081 0101

Owner: In the care of Cadw   **Contact:** The Custodian

A fairytale castle in the woods, Castell Coch embodies a glorious Victorian dream of the Middle Ages. Designed by William Burges as a country retreat for the 3rd Lord Bute, every room and furnishing is brilliantly eccentric, including paintings of Aesop's fables on the drawing room walls.

Location: OS Ref. ST131 826. M4/J32, A470 then signposted. 5m NW of Cardiff city centre.

Open: Apr - May & Oct: daily, 9.30am - 5pm. 1 Jun - 30 Sept: daily, 9.30am - 6pm. Nov - Mar: Mon - Sat, 9.30am - 4pm, Sun 11am - 4pm.

Admission: Adult £3, Child (under 16 yrs)/Conc. £2.50, Child under 5yrs free, Family (2+3) £8.50. (Prices subject to review March 2006.)

▢ ♿ ▣ ▢ ℙ ♿Guide dogs only. ▲ ❋

CHEPSTOW CASTLE ✤

Chepstow, Gwent

Tel: 01291 624065   **www**.cadw.wales.gov.uk

Owner: In the care of Cadw   **Contact:** The Custodian

This mighty fortress has guarded the route from England to South Wales for more than nine centuries. So powerful was this castle that it continued in use until 1690, being finally adapted for cannon and musket after an epic Civil War siege. This huge, complex, grandiosely sited castle deserves a lengthy visit.

Location: OS Ref. ST533 941. Chepstow via A466, B4235 or A48. 1¹⁄₂ m N of M48/J22.

Open: 1 Apr - 31 May & Oct: daily, 9.30am - 5pm. 1 Jun - 30 Sept: daily, 9.30am - 6pm. 1 Nov - 31 Mar: Mon - Sat, 9.30am - 4pm, Sun 11am - 4pm.

Admission: Adult £3, Child (under 16 yrs)/Conc. £2.50, Child under 5yrs free, Family (2+3) £8.50. (Prices subject to review March 2006.)

▢ ♿Partial. ℙ ♿Guide dogs only. ❋

CILGERRAN CASTLE

Cardigan, Dyfed

Tel: 01239 615007 **www.**cadw.wales.gov.uk

Owner: In the care of Cadw   **Contact:** The Custodian

Perched high up on a rugged spur above the River Teifi, Cilgerran Castle is one of the most spectacularly sited fortresses in Wales. It dates from the 11th - 13th centuries.

Location: OS Ref. SN195 431. Main roads to Cilgerran from A478 and A484. 3¹/₂ m SSE of Cardigan.

Open: All year: daily, 9.30am - 6.30pm (4pm, 1 Nov - 31 Mar).

Admission: Adult £2.50, Child (under 16 yrs)/Conc. £2, Child under 5yrs free, Child under 5yrs free, Family (2+3) £7. (Prices subject to review March 2006.)

Guide dogs only.

CLYNE GARDENS

Mill Lane, Blackpill, Swansea SA3 5BD

Tel: 01792 401737

Owner: City and County of Swansea   **Contact:** Steve Hopkins

50 acre spring garden, large rhododendron collection, 4 national collections, extensive bog garden, native woodland.

Location: OS Ref. SS614 906. S side of Mill Lane, 300yds W of A4067 Mumbles Road, 3m SW of Swansea.

Open: All year.

Admission: Free.

COLBY WOODLAND GARDEN

Amroth, Narbeth, Pembrokeshire SA67 8PP

Tel: 01834 811885   **Fax:** 01834 831766

Owner: The National Trust

This 3¹/₂ ha (8 acre) garden has a fine display of colour in spring, with rhododendrons, magnolias, azaleas and camellias, underplanted with bluebells. Later highlights are the summer hydrangeas and autumn foliage. Open and wooded pathways through the valley offer lovely walks.

Location: OS Ref. SN155 080. ¹/₂ m inland from Amroth beside Carmarthen Bay. Signs from A477.

Open: 26 Mar - 29 Oct: daily. Woodland Garden: 10am - 5pm; Walled Garden: 11am - 5pm.

Admission: Adult £4, Child £2, Family £10. Groups (15+): Adult £3.40, Child £1.70.

Gallery events.

CORNWALL HOUSE

58 Monnow St, Monmouth NP25 3EN

Tel/Fax: 01600 712031

Owner/Contact: Ms Jane Harvey

Town house, dating back to at least the 17th century. Red brick garden façade in Queen Anne style, dating from 1752. Street façade remodelled in Georgian style (date unknown). Many original features, including fine staircase. Delightful town garden with original walled kitchen garden.

Location: OS Ref. SO506 127. Half way down main shopping street in Monmouth.

Open: 25/26 Mar; 1/2, 8/9, 15 -17, 22/23, 29/30 Apr; 1 May; 26 - 28 Aug; 2/3, 9/10, 16/17, 23/24 Sept: 2 - 5pm.

Admission: Adult £4, Conc. £2.

Grounds only. Obligatory. Public car park nearby. Guide dogs only. €

CRESSELLY

Kilgetty, Pembrokeshire SA68 0SP

Fax: 01646 687045   **e-mail:** hha@cresselly.org.uk   **www.**cresselly.org.uk

Owner/Contact: H D R Harrison-Allen Esq MFH

Home of the Allen family for 250 years. The house is of 1770 with matching wings of 1869 and contains good plasterwork and fittings of both periods. The Allens are of particular interest for their close association with the Wedgwood family of Etruria and a long tradition of foxhunting. Grade II listed holiday cottages nearby on river.

Location: OS Ref. SN065 065. W of the A4075.

Open: Mon - Fri only. 12 - 16, 19 - 23, 26 - 30 Jun; 3 - 7, 10 - 14, 17 - 21 Jul: 10am - 1pm. Guided tours only, on the hour. Coaches and at other times by arrangement.

Admission: Adult £4, no children under 12.

Ground floor only. Obligatory. Coaches by arrangement. Holiday cottages.

CYFARTHFA CASTLE MUSEUM

Brecon Road, Merthyr Tydfil, Mid Glamorgan CF47 8RE

Tel/Fax: 01685 723112   **e-mail:** cyfarthacastle@fsmail.net

Owner: Merthyr Tydfil County Borough Council   **Contact:** Scott Reid

Castle originates from 1824/1825, now a museum and school.

Location: OS Ref. SO041 074. NE side of A470 to Brecon, ¹/₂ m NW of town centre.

Open: 1 Apr - 30 Sept: Mon - Sun, 10am - 5.30pm. Winter: Tue - Fri, 10am - 4pm Sats & Suns, 12 noon - 4pm. Closed between Christmas and New Year.

Admission: Free.

DINEFWR

Llandeilo SA19 6RT

Tel: 01558 650177   **Fax:** 01558 650707   **e-mail:** dolaucothi@nationaltrust.org.uk

Owner: The National Trust   **Contact:** The House Manager

Historic site with particular connections to the medieval Princes of Wales.

Location: OS Ref. SN625 225. On outskirts of Llandeilo.

Open: House: 1 Jul - 30 Oct: Thurs - Mon, 11am - 5pm. Park: 25 Mar - 30 Oct, Thur - Mon, 11am - 5pm. During the school holidays the park and house will be open daily. House opens in July following refurbishment. Please telephone in advance if you plan to to visit in early July.

Admission: House & Park: Adult £5, Child £2.50, Family £12.50. Groups (15+): £4.20. Park only: Adult £3, Child £1.50, Family £7.50. Groups: £2.60.

By arrangement. Limited for coaches. In grounds on leads.

Aberglasney Gardens.

DYFFRYN GARDENS AND ARBORETUM 🏛

ST NICHOLAS, NR CARDIFF CF5 6SU

www.dyffryngardens.org.uk

Tel: 029 2059 3328 **Fax:** 029 2059 1966

Owner: Vale of Glamorgan Council   **Contact:** Ms G Donovan

Dyffryn Gardens is a beautiful Grade I registered Edwardian garden, set in the heart of the Vale of Glamorgan countryside. The 55-acre gardens are the result of a unique collaboration between the eminent landscape architect, Thomas Mawson, and the passionate plant collector, Reginald Cory. The garden includes great lawns, herbaceous borders, many individual themed garden 'rooms' and a well established Arboretum including 14 champion trees. The gardens are being restored with grant assistance from the Heritage Lottery Fund. The gardens remain open throughout the restoration and there is an extensive events programme planned for 2006 to celebrate the garden's centenary year.

Location: OS Ref. ST095 723. 3m NW of Barry, J33/M4. 1½ m S of St Nicholas on A48.

Open: Easter - Sept: daily, 10am - 6pm. Oct: daily, 10am - 5pm.

Admission: Adult £3.50, Child/Conc. £2.50. Discount available for groups (15+).

▢ 🔆 ♿ ⬛ 🅕 🅿 ▦ 🐴 ⬛ ❋ ♿ Tel for details.

Skyscan

FONMON CASTLE 🏛

RHOOSE, BARRY, SOUTH GLAMORGAN CF62 3ZN

Tel: 01446 710206 **Fax:** 01446 711687 **e-mail:** sophie@fonmoncastle.fsnet.co.uk

Owner: Sir Brooke Boothby Bt   **Contact:** Sophie Katzi

Occupied as a home since the 13th century, this medieval castle has the most stunning Georgian interiors and is surrounded by extensive gardens. Available for weddings, concerts, corporate entertainment and multi-activity days.

Location: OS Ref. ST047 681. 15m W of Cardiff, 1m W of Cardiff airport.

Open: 1 Apr - 30 Sept: Tue & Wed, 2 - 5pm (last tour 4pm). Other times by appointment. Groups: by appointment.

Admission: Adult £5, Child Free.

ℹ Conferences. 🅣 By arrangement (up to 120). ♿ WC. 🅿
🐴 Guide dogs only. ⬛ ❋

THE JUDGE'S LODGING

BROAD STREET, PRESTEIGNE, POWYS LD8 2AD

www.judgeslodging.org.uk

Tel: 01544 260650 **Fax:** 01544 260652 **e-mail:** info@judgeslodging.org.uk

Owner: Powys County Council   **Contact:** Gabrielle Rivers

Explore the fascinating world of the Victorian judges, their servants and felonious guests at this award-winning, totally hands-on historic house. From the stunning restored judge's apartments to the gas lit servants' quarters below. Follow an 'eavesdropping' audio tour featuring actor Robert Hardy. Damp cells, vast courtroom and local history rooms included.

Location: OS Ref. SO314 644. In town centre, off A44 and A4113. Easy reach from Herefordshire and mid-Wales.

Open: 1 Mar - 31 Oct: daily, 10am - 6pm. 1 Nov - 22 Dec: Wed - Sun, 10am - 4pm. Bookings by arrangement accepted all year.

Admission: Adult £4.95, Child £3.95, Conc. £4.50. Groups (10-80): Adult £4.50, Child/Conc. £3.95, Family £15.

▢ 🅣 ♿ Partial (access via lift). 🅕 By arrangement. 🅘 🅿 In town. ▦
🐴 Guide dogs only. ⬛ ♿ Tel for details.

KIDWELLY CASTLE ✤
Kidwelly, West Glamorgan SA17 5BG
Tel: 01554 890104   **www**.cadw.wales.gov.uk
Owner: In the care of Cadw   **Contact:** The Custodian
A chronicle in stone of medieval fortress technology this strong and splendid castle developed during more than three centuries of Anglo-Welsh warfare. The half-moon shape stems from the original 12th century stockaded fortress, defended by the River Gwendraeth on one side and a deep crescent-shaped ditch on the other.
Location: OS Ref. SN409 070. Kidwelly via A484. Kidwelly Rail Station 1m.
Open: 1 Apr - 31 May & Oct: daily, 9.30am - 5pm. 1 Jun - 30 Sept: daily, 9.30am - 6pm. 1 Nov - 31 Mar: Mon - Sat, 9.30am - 4pm, Sun 11am - 4pm.
Admission: Adult £2.50, Child (under 16 yrs)/Conc. £2, Child under 5yrs free, Family (2+3) £7. (Prices subject to review March 2006)

LAMPHEY BISHOP'S PALACE ✤
Lamphey, Dyfed
Tel: 01646 672224   **www**.cadw.wales.gov.uk
Owner: In the care of Cadw   **Contact:** The Custodian
Lamphey marks the place of the spectacular Bishop's Palace but it reached its height of greatness under Bishop Henry de Gower who raised the new Great Hall. Today the ruins of the comfortable manor reflect the power enjoyed by the medieval bishops.
Location: OS Ref. SN018 009. A4139 from Pembroke or Tenby. N of village (A4139).
Open: 1 Apr - 31 Mar: daily, 10am - 5pm. Closed at all other times.
Admission: Adult £2.50, Child (under 16 yrs)/Conc. £2, Child under 5yrs free, Family (2+3) £7. (Prices subject to review March 2006.)

LAUGHARNE CASTLE ✤
King Street, Laugharne SA33 4SA
Tel: 01994 427906   **www**.cadw.wales.gov.uk
Owner: In the care of Cadw   **Contact:** The Custodian
Picturesque Laugharne Castle stands on a low ridge overlooking the wide Taf estuary, one of a string of fortresses controlling the ancient route along the South Wales coast.
Location: OS Ref. SN303 107. 4m S of A48 at St Clears via A4066.
Open: 1 Apr - 30 Sept: daily, 10am - 5pm. Closed at all other times.
Admission: Adult £2.75, Child (under 16 yrs)/Conc. £2.25, Child under 5yrs free, Family (2+3) £7.75. (Prices subject to review March 2006.)

LLANCAIACH FAWR MANOR
Nelson, Treharris CF46 6ER
Tel: 01443 412248   **Fax:** 01443 412688
Owner: Caerphilly County Borough Council   **Contact:** The Administrator
Tudor fortified manor dating from 1530 with Stuart additions. Costumed guides.
Location: OS Ref. ST114 967. S side of B4254, 1m N of A472 at Nelson, in the county borough of Caerphilly.
Open: All year: weekdays, 10am - 5pm. weekends, 10am - 6pm. Last admission 1½ hours before closing. Nov - Feb: closed Mons. Closed Christmas week.
Admission: Adult £4.95, Child £3.50, Conc. £3.75, Family £14.

LLANVIHANGEL COURT
Nr Abergavenny, Monmouthshire NP7 8DH
Tel: 01873 890217   **Fax:** 01873 890380   **www**.llanvihangel-court.co.uk
Owner/Contact: Julia Johnson
A Grade I Tudor Manor. The home in the 17th century of the Arnolds who built the imposing terraces and stone steps leading up to the house. The interior has a fine hall, unusual yew staircase and many 17th century moulded plaster ceilings. Delightful grounds. Includes 17th century features, notably Grade I stables.
Location: OS Ref. SO433 139. 4m N of Abergavenny on A465.
Open: 27 Apr - 7 May, 11 - 20 & 25 - 28 Aug: 2.30 - 5.30pm. Last tour 5pm.
Admission: Adult £4, Child £2, Conc. £4.

MUSEUM OF WELSH LIFE
St Fagans, Cardiff CF5 6XB
Tel: 029 2057 3500   **Fax:** 029 2057 3490
St Fagans Castle, a 16th century building built within the walls of a 13th century castle.
Location: OS Ref. ST118 772. 4m W of city centre, 1½ m N of A48, 2m S of M4/J33. Entrance drive is off A4232 (southbound only).
Open: All year: daily, 10am - 5pm. Closed 24 - 26 Dec & 1 Jan.
Admission: Free.

THE NATIONAL BOTANIC GARDEN OF WALES
CARMARTHENSHIRE SA32 8HG
www.gardenofwales.org.uk
Tel: 01558 667148   **Fax:** 01558 668933   **e-mail:** info@gardenofwales.org.uk
Owner: The National Botanic Garden of Wales   **Contact:** Helen Edwards
Four years after opening, the first national botanic garden of the new Millennium is blossoming into one of the most beautiful and stimulating gardens in the UK. Created within a 568 acre Regency parkland it is home to a unique and large collection of plants. The centrepiece is the awe inspiring largest single span glasshouse in the world, which houses Mediterranean plants from across the globe. The recently restored double walled garden is a major new feature displaying the family tree of plants. Visitors can also enjoy a large variety of themed outdoor gardens including the award winning Japanese and Apothecaries' Gardens, exhibitions, multi-media theatre, water features, adventure playground, mini-farm, restaurant, shop and plant sales. Further information is available at www.gardenofwales.org.uk
Location: OS159 Ref. SN518 175. ¼m from the A48 midway between Crosshands and Carmarthen. Clearly signposted from A48 and Carmarthen. Train & Bus in Carmarthen (7m).
Open: British Summer Time: 10am - 6pm. British Winter Time: 10am - 4.30pm. Closed Christmas Day.
Admission: Adult £7.50, Child £2.50, OAP/Students £5.50, Family (2+4) £16.50. Groups (10+): Adult £6.50, Child £2, OAP/Student £4.50.

OXWICH CASTLE ✿

c/o Oxwich Castle Farm, Oxwich SA3 1NG

Tel: 01792 390359 **www**.cadw.wales.gov.uk

Owner: In the care of Cadw   **Contact:** The Custodian

Beautifully sited in the lovely Gower peninsula, Oxwich Castle is a striking testament to the pride and ambitions of the Mansel dynasty of Welsh gentry.

Location: OS159 Ref. SS497 864. A4118, 11m SW of Swansea, in Oxwich village.

Open: 1 Apr - 30 Sept: daily, 10am - 5pm. Closed at all other times.

Admission: Adult £2, Child (under 16 yrs)/Conc. £1.50, Child under 5yrs free, Family (2+3) £5.50. (Prices subject to review March 2006.)

⬛ 🅿 ♿ Guide dogs only.

PEMBROKE CASTLE

PEMBROKE SA71 4LA

www.pembrokecastle.co.uk

Tel: 01646 681510 **Fax:** 01646 622260 **e-mail:** pembroke.castle@talk21.com

Owner: Trustees of Pembroke Castle   **Contact:** Mr D Ramsden

Pembroke Castle is situated within minutes of beaches and the breathtaking scenery of the Pembrokeshire Coastal National Park. This early Norman fortress, birthplace of the first Tudor King, houses many fascinating displays and exhibitions. Enjoy a picnic in the beautifully kept grounds, or on the roof of St. Anne's Bastion and take in the views along the estuary. Events every weekend in July and August.

Location: OS Ref. SM983 016. W end of the main street in Pembroke.

Open: All year. 1 Apr - Sept: daily, 9.30am - 6pm. Mar & Oct: daily, 10am - 5pm. Nov - Feb: daily, 10am - 4pm. Closed 24 - 26 Dec & 1 Jan. Brass rubbing centre open Summer months and all year by arrangement.

Admission: Adult £3.50, Child/Conc. £2.50, Groups (20+): Adult £3, OAP/Student £2.

⬛ ♿ ♨ Easter - Oct. 🎬 End of May - Sept by arrangement. ▮

♿ In grounds on leads. ❄ ♨ Tel for details.

Tintern Abbey.

Cadw/Welsh Historic Monuments. Crown Copyright.

PICTON CASTLE 🏛

HAVERFORDWEST, PEMBROKESHIRE SA62 4AS

www.pictoncastle.co.uk

Tel/Fax: 01437 751326 **e-mail:** pct@pictoncastle.freeserve.co.uk

Owner: The Picton Castle Trust   **Contact:** Mr D Pryse Lloyd

Built in the 13th century by Sir John Wogan, his direct descendants still use the Castle as their family home. The medieval castle was modernised in the 1750s, above the undercroft and extended around 1790 with fine Georgian interiors. The 40 acres of woodland and walled gardens are part of The Royal Horticultural Society access scheme for beautiful gardens. There is a unique collection of rhododendrons and azaleas, mature trees, unusual shrubs, wild flowers, fern walk, fernery, maze, restored dewpond, a herb collection labelled with medicinal remedies and a children's nature trail. The Picton Gallery is used for nationally acclaimed exhibitions. Events include spring and autumn plant sales.

Location: OS Ref. SN011 135. 4m E of Haverfordwest, just off A40.

Open: 1 Apr - 30 Sept: daily except Mon (open BH Mons), 10.30am - 5pm. Entrance to Castle by guided tours only, between 12 noon - 4pm. Oct: Gardens only, daily, 10.30am - dusk.

Admission: Castle, Garden & Gallery: Adult £5.95, Child £2.50, OAP £5.75. Garden & Gallery: Adult £4.95, Child £2.50, OAP £4.75. Groups (20+): reduced prices by prior arrangement.

ℹ No indoor photography. ⬛ ♨ 🚻 ♿ 🍴 Licensed. 🎬 Obligatory. 🅿

♿ In grounds, on leads. ▲ ❄ Tel or email for details.

RAGLAN CASTLE ✿

RAGLAN NP5 2BT

www.cadw.wales.gov.uk

Tel: 01291 690228

Owner: In the care of Cadw   **Contact:** The Custodian

Undoubtedly the finest late medieval fortress-palace in Britain, it was begun in the 1430s by Sir William ap Thomas who built the mighty 'Yellow Tower'. His son William Lord Herbert added a palatial mansion defended by a gatehouse and many towered walls. The high quality is still obvious today.

Location: OS Ref. SO415 084. Raglan, NE of Raglan village off A40 (eastbound) and signposted.

Open: 1 Apr - 31 May & Oct: daily, 9.30am - 5pm. 1 Jun - 30 Sept: daily, 9.30am - 6pm. 1 Nov - 31 Mar: Mon - Sat, 9.30am - 4pm, Sun 11am - 4pm.

Admission: Adult £2.75, Child (under 16 yrs)/Conc. £2.25, Child under 5yrs free, Family (2+3) £7.75. (Prices subject to review March 2006.)

⬛ 🅿 ♿ Guide dogs only. ❄

ST DAVIDS BISHOP'S PALACE ✤

St Davids, SA62 6PE

Tel: 01437 720517 **www.**cadw.wales.gov.uk

Owner: In the care of Cadw   **Contact:** The Custodian

The city of St Davids boasts not only one of Britain's finest cathedrals but also the most impressive medieval palace in Wales. Built in the elaborate 'decorated' style of gothic architecture, the palace is lavishly encrusted with fine carving.

Location: OS Ref. SM750 254. A487 to St Davids, minor road past the Cathedral.

Open: 1 Apr - 31 May & Oct: daily, 9.30am - 5pm. 1 Jun - 30 Sept: daily, 9.30am - 6pm. 1 Nov - 31 Mar: Mon - Sat, 9.30am - 4pm, Sun 11am - 4pm.

Admission: Adult £2.50, Child (under 16 yrs)/Conc. £2, Child under 5yrs free, Family (2+3) £7. (Prices subject to review March 2006.)

⬚ ⬚ Partial. **P** 🐕 Guide dogs only. ❄

ST DAVIDS CATHEDRAL

St Davids, Pembs SA62 6QW

Tel: 01437 720691 **Fax:** 01437 721885   **Contact:** Mr R G Tarr

Over eight centuries old. Many unique and 'odd' features.

Location: OS Ref. SM751 254. 5-10 mins walk from car/coach parks: signs for pedestrians.

Open: Daily: 8.30am - 5.30pm. Sun: 12.30 - 5.30pm, may be closed for services in progress. Evensong Mon (spoken), Tues - Sun 6pm, Monday - Saturday services. Weds extra service: 10am.

Admission: Donations. Guided tours (Adult £3, Child £1.20) must be booked.

STRATA FLORIDA ABBEY ✤

Ystrad Meurig, Pontrhydfendigaid SY25 6BT

Tel: 01974 831261 **www.**cadw.wales.gov.uk

Owner: In the care of Cadw   **Contact:** The Custodian

Remotely set in the green, kite-haunted Teifi Valley with the lonely Cambrian mountains as a backdrop, the ruined abbey has a wonderful doorway with Celtic spiral motifs and preserves a wealth of beautiful medieval tiles.

Location: OS Ref. SN746 658. Minor road from Pontrhydfendigaid 14m SE of Aberystwyth by the B4340.

Open: 1 Apr - 30 Sept: Wed - Sun, 10am – 5pm. The monument will be open and unstaffed on Mon & Tue (except BH Mons). Open at all other times generally between 10am - 4pm, but unstaffed and with no admission charge.

Admission: Adult £2.25, Child (under 16 yrs)/Conc. £1.75, Child under 5yrs free, Family (2+3) £6.25. (Prices subject to review March 2006.)

⬚ ⬚ **P** 🐕 Guide dogs only. ❄

TINTERN ABBEY ✤

TINTERN NP6 6SE

www.cadw.wales.gov.uk

Tel: 01291 689251

Owner: In the care of Cadw   **Contact:** The Custodian

Tintern is the best preserved abbey in Wales and ranks among Britain's most beautiful historic sites. Elaborately decorated in 'gothic' architecture style this church stands almost complete to roof level. Turner sketched and painted here, while Wordsworth drew inspiration from the surroundings.

Location: OS Ref. SO533 000. Tintern via A466, from M4/J23. Chepstow 6m.

Open: 1 Apr - 31 May & Oct: daily, 9.30am - 5pm. 1 Jun - 30 Sept: daily, 9.30am - 6pm. 1 Nov - 31 Mar: Mon - Sat, 9.30am - 4pm, Sun 11am - 4pm.

Admission: Adult £3.25, Child (under 16 yrs)/Conc. £2.75, Child under 5yrs free, Family (2+3) £9.25. (Prices subject to review March 2006.)

⬚ ⬚ ⬚ **P** 🐕 Guide dogs only. ❄

TREBERFYDD

Bwlch, Powys LD3 7PX

Tel: 01874 730205 **e-mail:** david.raikes@btinternet.com

www: treberfydd.net

Owner: David Raikes   **Contact:** David Garnons-Williams

Treberfydd is a Victorian country house, built in the Gothic style in 1847 - 50. The house was designed by J L Pearson, and the garden and grounds by W A Nesfield.

Location: From A40 in Bwlch take road to Llangors, after ¼m turn left, follow lane for 2m until white gates and Treberfydd sign.

Open: 1 - 28 Aug. Guided tours of the House: 2 & 4pm, telephone or e-mail to secure a place on a tour. Grounds: 2 - 6pm.

Admission: Adult £2.50 (inc. tour), Child (under 12yrs) Free. Grounds: £2.50.

⬚ Partial. ⬚ Obligatory. **P** Limited. None for coaches. 🐕 On leads, in grounds.

TREBINSHWN

Nr Brecon, Powys LD3 7PX

Tel: 01874 730653 **Fax:** 01874 730843

Owner/Contact: R Watson

16th century mid-sized manor house. Extensively rebuilt 1780. Fine courtyard and walled garden.

Location: OS Ref. SO136 242. 1½m NW of Bwlch.

Open: Easter - 31 Aug. Mon - Tue, 10am - 1.30pm.

Admission: Free.

P

TREDEGAR HOUSE & PARK 🏛

NEWPORT, SOUTH WALES NP1 9YW

Tel: 01633 815880 **Fax:** 01633 815895 **e-mail:** tredegar.house@newport.gov.uk

Owner: Newport City Council   **Contact:** The Manager

South Wales' finest country house, ancestral home of the Morgan family. Parts of a medieval house remain, but Tredegar owes its reputation to lavish rebuilding in the 17th century. Visitors have a lively and entertaining tour through 30 rooms, including glittering State Rooms and 'below stairs'. Set in 90 acres of parkland with formal gardens. Winner of Best Public Park and Garden in Great Britain 1997. Craft workshops.

Location: OS Ref. ST290 852. M4/J28 signposted. From London 2½hrs, from Cardiff 20 mins. 2m SW of Newport town centre.

Open: Easter - Sept: Wed - Sun & BHs, 11.30am - 4pm. Evening tours & groups by appointment. Oct - Mar: Groups only by appointment.

Admission: Adult £5.40, Child Free (when accompanied by paying adult), Conc. £3.95. Special discounts for Newport residents. (2005 prices.)

ℹ Conferences. No photography in house. ⬚ ⬚ ⬚ Partial. WC. ⬚ ⬚ Obligatory. **P** ⬚ 🐕 In grounds, on leads. ⬚ ⬚ Tel for details.

open all year
see page 557

TREOWEN 🏠

Wonastow, Nr Monmouth NP25 4DL

Tel/Fax: 01600 712031   **e-mail:** john.wheelock@virgin.net   **www**.treowen.co.uk
Owner: R A & J P Wheelock   **Contact:** John Wheelock
Early 17th century mansion built to double pile plan with magnificent well-stair to four storeys.
Location: OS Ref. SO461 111. 3m WSW of Monmouth.
Open: May, Jun Aug & Sept: Fri, 10am - 4pm. Also 18/19 & 25/26 Mar; 1/2 Apr; 16/17 & 23/24 Sept: 2 - 5pm. HHA Friends Free on Fri only.
Admission: £5 (£3 if appointment made). Groups by appointment only.
🖥 🖼 Entire house let, self-catering. Sleeps 24+. 🔼

TRETOWER COURT & CASTLE ✤

Tretower, Crickhowell NP8 2RF

Tel: 01874 730279   **www**.cadw.wales.gov.uk
Owner: In the care of Cadw   **Contact:** The Custodian
A fine fortress and an outstanding medieval manor house, Tretower Court and Castle range around a galleried courtyard, now further enhanced by a beautiful recreated medieval garden.
Location: OS Ref. SO187 212. Signposted in Tretower Village, off A479, 3m NW of Crickhowell.
Open: 22 - 31 Mar & Oct: daily, 10am - 4pm (5pm, 1 Apr - 30 Sept). Closed at all other times.
Admission: Adult £2.50, Child (under 16 yrs)/Conc. £2, Child under 5yrs free, Family (2+3) £7. (Prices subject to review March 2006.)
📷 📷 🅿 🖼 Guide dogs only.

TUDOR MERCHANT'S HOUSE 🌿

Quay Hill, Tenby SA70 7BX

Tel/Fax: 01834 842279
Owner: The National Trust   **Contact:** The Custodian
A late 15th century town house, characteristic of the area at the time when Tenby was a thriving trading port. The house is furnished to recreate family life from the Tudor period onwards. There is access to the small herb garden.
Location: OS Ref. SN135 004. Tenby. W of alley from NE corner of town centre square.
Open: 27 Mar - 27 Oct: daily (closed Sats), 11am - 5pm.
Admission: Adult £2.50, Child £1.20, Family £6.20. Groups: Adult £2, Child £1.
ℹ️No indoor photography. 🅿No parking. 🖥 🖼Guide dogs only.

TYTHEGSTON COURT

Tythegston, Bridgend CF32 0NE

e-mail: cknight@tythegston.com   **www**.tythegston.com
Owner/Contact: C Knight
Location: OS Ref. SS857 789. 2m E of Porthcawl on Glamorgan coast.
Open: By written appointment (no telephone calls please).
Admission: Adult £10, Child £2.50, Conc. £5.
🖥 🚹Partial. 📷Obligatory. 🅿Limited. No coaches. 🖼Guide dogs only.

USK CASTLE

Usk, Monmouthshire NP5 1SD

Tel: 01291 672563   **e-mail:** info@uskcastle.co.uk   **www**.uskcastle.com
Owner/Contact: J H L Humphreys
Romantic, ruined castle overlooking the picturesque town of Usk. Inner and outer baileys, towers and earthwork defences. Surrounded by enchanting gardens (open under NGS) incorporating The Castle House, the former medieval gatehouse.
Location: OS Ref. SO376 011. Up narrow lane off Monmouth road in Usk, opposite fire station.
Open: Castle ruins: daily, 11am - 5pm. Groups by appointment. Gardens: private visits welcome & groups by arrangement. House: Jun & BHs: 2 - 5pm (closed 24/25 Jun), small groups & guided tours only.
Admission: Castle ruins: Adult £2, Child Free. Gardens: Adult £3. House: Adult £6, Child £3.
🖥 🚹Partial. 📷 By arrangement. 🖥 🅿 No coaches. 🖼 In grounds, on leads. ✳

WEOBLEY CASTLE ✤

Weobley Castle Farm, Llanrhidian SA3 1HB

Tel: 01792 390012   **www**.cadw.wales.gov.uk
Owner: In the care of Cadw   **Contact:** The Custodian
Perched above the wild northern coast of the beautiful Gower peninsula, Weobley Castle was the home of the Knightly de Bere family. Its rooms include a fine hall and private chamber as well as numerous 'garderobes' or toilets and an early Tudor porch block.
Location: OS Ref. SN477 928. B4271 or B4295 to Llanrhidian Village, then minor road for 1¹/2 m.
Open: 1 Apr - 31 Oct: daily, 9.30am - 6pm (5pm, Nov - Mar).
Admission: Adult £2, Child (under 16 yrs)/Conc. £1.50, Child under 5yrs free, Family (2+3) £5.50. (Prices subject to review March 2006.)
📷 🅿 🖼 Guide dogs only. ✳

WHITE CASTLE ✤

Llantillio Crossenny, Gwent

Tel: 01600 780380   **www**.cadw.wales.gov.uk
Owner: In the care of Cadw   **Contact:** The Custodian
With its high walls and round towers reflected in the still waters of its moat, White Castle is the ideal medieval fortress. It was rebuilt in the mid-13th century by the future King Edward I to counter a threat from Prince Llywelyn the Last.
Location: OS Ref. SO380 167. By minor road 2m NW from B4233 at A7 Llantilio Crossenny. 8m ENE of Abergavenny.
Open: 1 Apr - 30 Sept: Wed - Sun, 10am – 5pm. The monument will be open and unstaffed on Mon & Tue (except BH Mons). Open at all other times generally between 10am - 4pm, but unstaffed and with no admission charge.
Admission: Adult £2, Child (under 16 yrs)/Conc. £1.50, Child under 5yrs free, Family (2+3 under 16 yrs) £5.50. (Prices subject to review March 2006.)
📷 🅿 🖼 Guide dogs only. ✳

CADW.

Caerphilly Castle.

White Park Bay, Northern Ireland

Crom Estate © NTPL/Joe Cornish

northern ireland

ireland

Northern Ireland's industrial past centres on its world-famous linen production and on the shipyards of Belfast. The ill-fated 'Titanic' was built here. Today, visitors to the province come largely to enjoy the countryside and what it has to offer. Fishing (both river and sea) and golf are two of the most popular attractions. The waters of Lough Erne and Lough Neagh encourage visiting sailors and the Mourne Mountains are a magnet for walkers. There are many heritage properties both in private ownership and owned by the National Trust for Ireland that have fascinating histories, among them Mount Stewart, once the home of Lord Castlereagh, which played host to many prominent political figures. Its magnificent gardens have been nominated as a World Heritage Site.

ANTRIM CASTLE GARDENS
Randalstown Road, Antrim BT41 4LH

Tel: 028 9448 1338   **Fax:** 028 9448 1344   **e-mail:** clotworthyarts@antrim.gov.uk

Owner: Antrim Borough Council   **Contact:** Philip Magennis

Situated adjacent to Antrim Town, the Sixmilewater River and Lough Neagh's shore, these 17th century Anglo-Dutch water gardens are maintained in a manner authentic to the period. The gardens comprise of ornamental canals, round pond, ancient motte and a parterre garden planted with 17th century plants - many with culinary or medicinal uses. An interpretative display introducing the history of the gardens and the process of their restoration is located in the reception of Clotworthy Arts Centre.

Location: Outside Antrim town centre off A26 on A6.

Open: All year: Mon - Fri, 9.30am - 9.30pm (dusk if earlier). Sats, 10am - 5pm. Jul & Aug: also open Suns, 2 - 5pm.

Admission: Free. Charge for guided group tours (by arrangement only).

ARDRESS HOUSE
64 Ardress Road, Portadown, Co Armagh BT62 1SQ

Tel/Fax: 028 8778 4753   **e-mail:** ardress@nationaltrust.org.uk   **www**.ntni.org.uk

Owner: The National Trust   **Contact:** The Custodian

A 17th century farmhouse with elegant 18th century additions by owner-architect George Ensor. Includes a display of antique farming implements in the farmyard.

Location: On B28, 5m from Moy, 5m from Portadown, 3m from M1/J13.

Open: 17 Mar: 2 - 6pm. 1 Apr - 30 Sept: Sats, Suns & BH/PHs, 2 - 6pm.

Admission: House tour: Adult £3.40, Child £1.80, Family £8.60. Groups £3.10 (outside normal hours £5.10).

Ground floor. WC. Obligatory. On leads.

THE ARGORY
Moy, Dungannon, Co Tyrone BT71 6NA

Tel: 028 8778 4753   **Fax:** 028 8778 9598

e-mail: argory@nationaltrust.org.uk   **www**.ntni.org.uk

Owner: The National Trust   **Contact:** The Property Manager

The Argory is a handsome 19th century Victorian house furnished as it was in 1900, providing an excellent illustration of Victorian/Edwardian interior taste and interests.

Location: On Derrycaw road, 4m from Moy, 3m from M1/J13 or J14 (coaches J13).

Open: House: 17 Mar - 29 May: Sats, Suns & BH/PH (incl. 14 - 23 Apr daily): Jun - Aug: daily; 2 - 30 Sept: Sats & Suns, 1 - 6pm. Grounds: Oct - Apr: daily, 10am - 4pm; May - Sept: daily, 10am - 7pm (2 - 7pm on Event Days). Tearoom: as House, open at 2pm. Shop: as House. Last admission 1 hr before closing.

Admission: House tour: Adult £4.70, Child £2.50, Family £11.90. Groups: £4.20 (outside normal hours £5). Grounds only: Car £2.60.

Ground floor. WC. Obligatory. On leads.

BALLYWALTER PARK
Nr Newtownards, Co Down BT22 2PP

Tel: 028 4275 8264   **Fax:** 028 4275 8818

e-mail: enquiries@dunleath-estates.co.uk   **www**.ballywalterpark.com

Owner: Lord Dunleath   **Contact:** The Secretary, The Estate Office

Victorian mansion, situated in 40 acres of landscaped grounds, built in the mid-19th century by Charles Lanyon, with Edwardian additions by W J Fennell. Restoration of conservatory in 2006. Self-catered (4 star) listed gatelodge overlooking beach available for holiday lets (sleeps four).

Location: 1km S of Ballywalter village.

Open: By appointment, please telephone the Estate Office.

Admission: House or Gardens: Adult £6. House and gardens: Adult £10. Groups (max 50): Adult £6.

No photography indoors. Pick-your-own, Jun - Aug. By prior arrangement. Obligatory. Self-catering. Tel for details. €

BARONS COURT
Newtownstewart, Omagh, Co Tyrone BT78 4EZ

Tel: 028 8166 1683   **Fax:** 028 8166 2059   **Contact:** The Agent

The home of the Duke and Duchess of Abercorn, Barons Court was built between 1779 and 1782, and subsequently extensively remodelled by John Soane (1791), William and Richard Morrison (1835-1839), Sir Albert Richardson (1947-49) and David Hicks (1975-76).

Location: 5km SW of Newtownstewart.

Open: By appointment only.

Admission: Adult £5. Groups max. 50.

Partial. WCs. By arrangement. €

CASTLE COOLE
Enniskillen, Co Fermanagh BT74 6JY

Tel: 028 6632 2690   **Fax:** 028 6632 5665   **e-mail:** castlecoole@nationaltrust.org.uk   **www**.ntni.org.uk

Owner: The National Trust   **Contact:** The Property Manager

One of the finest neo-classical houses in Ireland, built by James Wyatt in the late 18th century, and sited in a rolling landscape park right on the edge of Enniskillen.

Location: On A4, 1.5m from Enniskillen on A4, Belfast - Enniskillen road.

Open: House: 17 - 19 Mar, 1 - 6pm. 1 Apr - 29 May: Sats, Suns & BH/PHs 1 - 6pm. 14 - 23 Apr, 1 Jun - 31 Aug: daily (Jun closed Thur), 1 - 6pm (from 12 noon Jul - Aug). 2 - 30 Sept: Sat & Sun, 1 - 6pm. Estate: 1 Apr - 29 Oct, daily, 10am - 4pm (8pm Apr - Oct). Tea Room & Shop: as House, closes 5pm. Last tour 1 hr before closing.

Admission: House Tour & Grounds: Adult £4.50, Child £2, Family £11. Groups: £3.50 (outside normal hours £5). Grounds: Car £2 (Honesty Box).

Partial. WC. In grounds, on leads.

Castle Ward.

CASTLE WARD & STRANGFORD LOUGH WILDLIFE CENTRE 😾
Strangford, Downpatrick, Co Down BT30 7LS

Tel: 028 4488 1204 **Fax:** 028 4488 1729 **e-mail:** castleward@nationaltrust.org.uk
www.ntni.org.uk
Owner: The National Trust   **Contact:** The Property Manager
Castle Ward is a beautiful 820 acre walled estate in a stunning location overlooking Strangford Lough. The mid-Georgian mansion is one of the architectural curios of its time, built inside and out in two distinct architectural styles.
Location: On A25, 7m from Downpatrick and 1¹/₂ m from Strangford.
Open: Grounds: All year: daily, 10am - 4pm (8pm May - Sept). Last tour 1 hr before closing. House: 17 Mar, 1 Apr - 25 Jun: Sats, Suns & BH/PHs (inc. 14 - 23 Apr), Jul & Aug: daily, 2 - 30 Sep. Sats & Suns, 1 - 6pm. Last tour 1hr before closing.
Admission: Grounds & Wildlife Centre only: Adult £3.80, Child £1.80, Family £9.40. Groups: £3.20.
⬜ 🔲 ♿ Ground floor & grounds. 🔲 🎥 Obligatory. 🅿 ♿ In grounds, on leads.
🏕 Caravan park, holiday cottages, basecamp. ⬆ ✳

CROM DEMESNE 😾
Newtownbutler, Co Fermanagh BT92 8AP

Tel/Fax: 028 6773 8118 (Visitor Centre) 028 6773 8174 (Estate)

e-mail: crom@nationaltrust.org.uk **www**.ntni.org.uk
Owner: The National Trust   **Contact:** The Visitor Facilities Manager
Crom is one of Ireland's most important nature conservation areas. It is set in 770 hectares of romantic and tranquil islands, woodland and ruins on the shores of Upper Lough Erne.
Location: 3m from A34, well signposted from Newtownbutler. Jetty at Visitor Centre.
Open: Grounds: 11 Mar - Jun & Sept: daily, 10am - 6pm; Jul & Aug: daily, 10am - 7pm; 1 - 15 Oct: Sats & Suns, 12 noon - 6pm. All Suns: 12 noon - 6pm. Visitor Centre: 11 Mar - 30 Apr: Sats, Suns & BH/PHs, 14 - 23 Apr & May - Sept: daily, 10am - 6pm. All Suns: 12 noon - 6pm. Last admission 1 hr before closing.
Admission: Demesne & Visitor Centre: Car/Boat £4.80. Minibus £13.50, Coach £17, Motorbike £2.
🔲 🍴 🅿 🏕 7 x 4-star holiday cottages & play-area. ⬆

DERRYMORE HOUSE 😾
Bessbrook, Newry, Co Armagh BT35 7EF

Tel: 028 8778 4753 **www**. ntni.org.uk
Owner: The National Trust
An elegant late 18th century thatched cottage, built by Isaac Corry, who represented Newry in the Irish House of Commons. Park laid out in the style of 'Capability' Brown.
Location: On A25, 2m from Newry on road to Camlough.
Open: Grounds: May - Sep: daily, 10am - 7pm. Oct - Apr: daily, 10am - 4pm.
Admission: Treaty Room Tour: Adult £3.10.
🅿 ♿ On leads.

FLORENCE COURT 😾
Enniskillen, Co Fermanagh BT92 1DB

Tel: 028 6634 8249 **Fax:** 028 6634 8873 **e-mail:** florencecourt@nationaltrust.org.uk
www.ntni.org.uk
Owner: The National Trust   **Contact:** The Property Manager
Florence Court is a fine mid-18th century house and estate set against the stunning backdrop of the Cuilcagh Mountains. House tour includes service quarters popular with all ages. Beautiful walled garden and lots of walks in grounds.
Location: 8m SW of Enniskillen via A4 and then A32 to Swanlinbar.
Open: House: 17 - 19 Mar: 1 Apr - 29 May: Sats, Suns & BH/PHs; 14 - 23 Apr: daily, 1 - 6pm. Jun: daily except Tues, 1 - 6pm; Jul & Aug: daily, 12 noon - 6pm. 2 - 30 Sept: Sat & Sun, 1 - 6pm. Estate & Gardens: All Year, daily, 10am - 4pm (8pm Apr - Oct). Last tour 1hr before closing. Tea Room & Shop: as house, closes at 5.30pm.
Admission: House tour: Adult £4.25, Child £2, Family £10.50. Groups: £3.50 (outside normal hours £5). Grounds only: Car £3, Minibus £15, Coach £20.
⬜ 🔲 ♿ Ground floor. WC. 🔲 🎥 Obligatory. 🅿 ♿ In grounds, on leads.
🏕 Holiday cottage. ⬆

GRAY'S PRINTING PRESS 😾
49 Main Street, Strabane, Co Tyrone BT82 8AU

Tel: 028 7188 0055 **www**.ntni.org.uk
Owner: The National Trust   **Contact:** The Administrator
Historic printworks, featuring 18th century printing press and 19th century hand-printing machines. Tour includes audio-visual presentation.
Location: In the centre of Strabane.
Open: 1 Apr - 27 May & 2 - 30 Sept: Sats; 3 - 30 Jun & Jul - Aug: Tue - Sat, 2 - 5pm (from 11am Jul/Aug).
Admission: Press Tour: Adult £2.80, Child £1.70, Family £7.30. Group £2.40 (outside normal hours £3.70).
🎥 🔲

HEZLETT HOUSE 😾
107 Sea Road, Castlerock, Coleraine, Co Londonderry BT51 4TW

Tel/Fax: 028 8778 4753 **e-mail:** downhillcastle@nationaltrust.org.uk
www.ntni.org.uk
Owner: The National Trust   **Contact:** The Custodian
Charming 17th century thatched house with 19th century furnishings. One of only a few pre-18th century Irish buildings still surviving.
Location: 5m W of Coleraine on Coleraine - Downhill coast road, A2.
Open: Jul - Aug, Wed - Sun, 12 noon - 5pm.
Admission: House Tour: Adult £2.80, Child £1.80, Family £7.40. Groups £2.20. (£4.70 outside normal hours.)
♿ Ground floor. 🎥 Obligatory. 🅿 ♿ In grounds, on leads.

KILLYLEAGH CASTLE
Killyleagh, Downpatrick, Co Down BT30 9QA

Tel/Fax: 028 4482 8261 **e-mail:** gatehouses@killyleagh.plus.com
www.killyleaghcastle.com
Owner/Contact: Mrs G Rowan-Hamilton
Oldest occupied castle in Ireland. Self-catering towers available to sleep 4-15. Swimming pool and tennis court available. Access to garden.
Location: At the end of the High Street.
Open: By arrangement. Groups (30-50): by appointment.
Admission: Adult £3.50, Child £2. Groups: Adult £2.50, Child £1.50.
ℹ No photography in house. 🍴 Wedding receptions. ♿ Unsuitable. 🎥 Obligatory.
🅿 🏕 ⬆ ✳

NT Photographic Library, Joe Cornish

MOUNT STEWART 😾
NEWTOWNARDS, Co DOWN BT22 2AD

www.ntni.org.uk

Tel: 028 4278 8387 **Fax:** 028 4278 8569 **e-mail:** mountstewart@nationaltrust.org.uk
Owner: The National Trust   **Contact:** The Property Manager
Home of the Londonderry family since the early 18th century, Mount Stewart was Lord Castlereagh's house and played host to many prominent political figures. The magnificent gardens planted in the 1920s have made Mount Stewart famous and earned it a World Heritage Site nomination. They feature a series of formal outdoor 'rooms', vibrant parterres, and formal and informal vistas, some with Strangford Lough views. Many rare and unusual plants thrive in the mild climate of the Ards, including eucalyptus, beschorneria, mimosa, and cordyline. The garden is also home to national collections of phormium and libertia. The house includes the famous painting 'Hambletonian', as well as the full set of chairs used at Congress of Vienna. The Temple of the Winds, a 1785 banqueting hall, is in the grounds. Café-bistro restaurant, gift shop and exhibition areas.
Location: On A20, 5m from Newtownards on the Portaferry road.
Open: House: 11 Mar - 30 Apr: Sats, Suns & BH/PHs; 14 - 23 Apr: daily; 12 - 6pm. May - Jun: daily (closed Tues May), 1 - 6pm (12 noon: Sats, Suns & BH/PHs). Jul - Aug: daily & BH/PHs, 12 - 6pm. Lakeside Gardens: All year, daily, 10am - sunset. Formal Gardens: 11 - 26 Mar: Sats, Suns & BH/PHs, 10am - 4pm; Apr - Oct: daily, 10am - 6pm (8pm May - Sept).
Admission: House Tour, Gardens & Temple of Winds: Adult £5.50, Child £2.80, Family £13.80. Group: £5 (outside normal hours £6). Gardens only: Adult £4.50, Child £2.40, Family £11.40. Group: £4.
⬜ 🔲 🍴 🍴 ♿ 🔲 🎥 Obligatory. 🅿 🔲 ♿ In grounds, on leads. ⬆ ✳ Lakeside area.
🍴 Tel for details. €

MUSSENDEN TEMPLE ❧

Castlerock, Co. Londonderry

Tel/Fax: 028 2073 1582 **e-mail:** downhillcastle@nationaltrust.org.uk
www.ntni.org.uk

Owner: The National Trust

Set on a stunning and wild headland with fabulous views over Ireland's north coast is the landscaped demesne of Downhill.

Location: 1m W of Castlerock.

Open: Temple: 1 May - 30 Jun: Sats, Suns & BH/PH, 11am - 5pm. Jul & Aug: daily, 11am - 5pm. 2 - 30 Sept: Sats & Suns, 1 - 5pm. Demesne & Downhill Ruins: All year, dawn - dusk.

Admission: Car park charge at Lion's Gate during Temple opening: Car £3.80, Minibus £7.50, Motorbike £2.40.

⊤ P ⊠ On leads. ◫

ROWALLANE GARDEN ❧

Saintfield, Ballynahinch, Co Down BT24 7LH

Tel: 028 9751 0721 **Fax:** 028 9751 1242

e-mail: rowallane@nationaltrust.org.uk **www**.ntni.org.uk

Owner: The National Trust   **Contact:** Head Gardener

Rowallane is a natural landscape of some 21 hectares, planted with an outstanding collection of trees, shrubs and other plants from many parts of the world, creating a beautiful display of form and colour throughout the year.

Location: On A7, 1m from Saintfield on road to Downpatrick.

Open: All year: daily, 10am - 4pm (8pm 15 Apr - 17 Sept). Closed 25/26 Dec & 1 Jan.

Admission: Adult £3.80, Child £1.80, Family £9.40. Groups £3.20 (outside normal hours £3.70).

⊠ Grounds. WC. ◨ Apr - Aug. ⊠ In grounds, on leads. ✲

Visitors at Mount Stewart.

SEAFORDE GARDENS 🏛

Seaforde, Co Down BT30 8PG

Tel: 028 44811 225   **Fax:** 028 44811 370   **e-mail:** plants@seafordegardens.com
www.seafordegardens.com

Owner/Contact: Patrick Forde

18th century walled garden and adjoining pleasure grounds, containing many rare and beautiful trees and shrubs; many of them tender. There are huge rhododendrons and the National Collection of Eucryphias. The oldest maze in Ireland is in the centre of the walled garden, which can be viewed from the Mogul Tower. The tropical butterfly house contains hundreds of beautiful highly coloured butterflies; also a collection of parrots, insects and reptiles. The nursery garden contains many interesting plants for sale.

Location: 20m S of Belfast on the main road to Newcastle.

Open: Easter - end Sept: Mon - Sat, 10am - 5pm; Suns, 1 - 6pm. Gardens only: Oct - Mar: Mon - Fri, 10am - 5pm.

Admission: Butterfly House or Gardens: Adult £3, Child £2. Groups (10+): Adult £2.40, Child £1.50. Butterfly House & Gardens: Adult £5.50, Child £3. Groups: Adult £4.50, Child £2.70, Family (2+2) £15. RHS members Free access: Apr - Jun.

🖼 ⊤ ⊠ 🍴 📷By arrangement. P ⊞ ⊠ ✲ €

SPRINGHILL HOUSE & COSTUME COLLECTION ❧

20 Springhill Road, Moneymore, Co Londonderry BT45 7NQ

Tel/Fax: 028 8674 8210 **e-mail:** springhill@nationaltrust.org.uk **www**.ntni.org.uk

Owner: The National Trust   **Contact:** The Property Manager

A charming and atmospheric 17th century 'plantation' house, said by many to be one of the prettiest houses in Ulster. It was home to ten generations of the Conyngham family, originally from Ayr. 50 minutes drive from Belfast or Londonderry, 35 minutes from Coleraine.

Location: 1m from Moneymore on B18 to Coagh, 5m from Cookstown.

Open: 17 Mar, 14 - 23 Apr & Jul - Aug: daily; 1 Apr - 25 Jun: Sats, Suns & BH/PHs; 2 - 30 Sept: Sat & Sun; 1 - 6pm. Last admission 1hr before closing.

Admission: House & Costume Collection Tour: Adult £4.30, Child £2.30, Family £10.90. Group £3.70 (outside normal hours £5.20).

🖼 ⊤ ⊠ Partial. WC. ◨ 📷 P ⊠ In grounds, on leads. ◫

WELLBROOK BEETLING MILL ❧

20 Wellbrook Road, Corkhill, Co. Tyrone BT80 9RY

Tel: 028 8674 8210/8675 1735 **e-mail:** wellbrook@nationaltrust.org.uk
www.ntni.org.uk

Owner: The National Trust   **Contact:** The Custodian

Wellbrook is an 19th century water-powered beetling mill with the only working beetling engines on show in Northern Ireland. New exhibition on the history of linen and its importance to Ireland.

Location: 4m from Cookstown, following signs from A505 Cookstown - Omagh road.

Open: 17 Mar, 14 - 23 Apr & Jul - Aug: daily; 1 Apr - 25 Jun: Sats, Suns & BH/PHs; 2 - 30 Sept: Sat & Sun; 1 - 6pm.

Admission: Mill Tour: Adult £3.10, Child £1.80, Family £8. Group: £2.60 (outside normal hours £3.70).

🖼 P

Florence Court.

Opening Arrangements at Properties grant-aided by English Heritage

ENGLISH HERITAGE

I am very pleased to introduce this year's list of opening arrangements at properties grant-aided by English Heritage. Over half the properties are open free, but we give details of admission charges where appropriate. There is also a brief description of each property, information on parking and access for people with disabilities.

The extent of public access varies from one property to another. The size of the building or garden, their nature and function are all taken into account. Some buildings, such as town halls, museums or railway stations, are of course open regularly. For other properties, especially those which are family homes or work places, access may need to be arranged in a way that also recognises the vulnerability of the building or the needs of those who live or work in it. Usually this will mean opening by appointment or on an agreed number of days each year. This is made clear by each entry.

Some properties are open by written appointment only. In most cases you should still be able to make initial contact by telephone, but you will be asked to confirm your visit in writing. This is to confirm the seriousness of your interest just as you would for example when making a hotel booking. It also provides a form of identification, enabling owners to feel more confident about inviting strangers into their house.

It has always been a condition of grant-aid from English Heritage that the public should have a right to see the buildings to whose repair they have contributed. We therefore welcome feedback from visitors on the quality of their visit to grant-aided properties. In particular, please let us know if you are unable to gain access to any of the buildings on the list on the days or at the times specified, or if you have difficulty in making an appointment to visit and do not receive a satisfactory explanation from the owner. Please contact English Heritage Customer Services at PO Box 569, Swindon SN2 2YP (telephone: 0870 3331181; e-mail: customers@english-heritage.org.uk).

Information about public access is also included on our website (www.english-heritage.org.uk). The website is updated regularly to include new properties, any subsequent changes that have been notified to us or any corrections. We suggest that you consult our website for up-to-date information before visiting. If long journeys or special requirements are involved, we strongly recommend that you telephone the properties in advance, even if no appointment is required.

Finally, may I use this introduction to thank all those owners with whom we work. Their support for the access arrangements has been hugely encouraging. That the public can enjoy a visit to a grant-aided property is not only good in itself, it demonstrates that the historic environment is in a very real sense a common wealth, part of the richness and diversity that makes the English landscape – both urban and rural – so special. It also illustrates how crucially important the private owner is in maintaining that quality and distinctiveness.

I very much hope you enjoy the sites and properties you find in this list - from the famous to the many lesser-known treasures. They are all worth a visit - I hope we have helped you to find, and enjoy, them.

Neil Cossons.

Sir Neil Cossons
Chairman

BEDFORDSHIRE

OLD WARDEN PARK

Old Warden nr. Biggleswade, Bedfordshire SG18 9EA

Built in 1872 by Joseph Shuttleworth in a Jacobean design by Henry Clutton. Still housing original Gillows furniture, oak panelling and carvings, and a collection of 18th century paintings. The park was laid out by landscape architect Edward Milner.

www.shuttleworth.org

Grant Recipient: The Shuttleworth Trust

Access contact: Ms Amanda McBrayne

T: 01767 626230

Open: Exterior of the building daily May - Sept, 9am - 5pm. Access to interior by appointment. Occasionally the site will be closed for private events, please call in advance: 01767 626200. Heritage Open Days: No.

P Spaces: 15.

Partial ramps. WC for the disabled. Guide Dogs allowed.

£ Free, except on event days.

BERKSHIRE

WELFORD PARK

Welford, Newbury, Berkshire RG20 8HU

Red brick country house c1652 and remodelled in 1702, when a third storey was added and the front façade was decorated with Ionic columns. Other alterations were made in the Victorian period.

Grant Recipient: Mr J H L Puxley

Access Contact: Mr J H L Puxley

T: 01488 608691   **F:** 01488 608853

Open: 5 June - 7 July (except 17 June & Suns): exterior only 11am - 5pm. Interior of house (4 principal rooms) by arrangement.

P Spaces: 40. 80 more spaces within ¼ mile walk.

Full wheelchair access. No WC for the disabled. Guide Dogs allowed.

£ £5 (interior of house). Free entry to garden and grounds, except on occasional charity days. Child: Free except on occasional charity days.

BUCKINGHAMSHIRE

CLIVEDEN MANSION & CLOCK TOWER

Cliveden, Taplow, Maidenhead, Bucks SL6 0JA

Built by Charles Barry in 1851, once lived in by Lady Astor now let as an hotel. Series of gardens, each with its own character, featuring roses, topiary, water gardens, a formal parterre, informal vistas, woodland and riverside walks.

www.nationaltrust.org.uk

Grant Recipient: The National Trust

Access Contact: Property Manager

T: 01628 605069   **F:** 01628 669461

E-mail: cliveden@nationaltrust.org.uk

Open: House (main ground floor rooms) and Octagon Temple: 2 Apr - 29 Oct, Thur & Sun 3 - 5.30pm. Estate & garden: 15 Mar - 22 Dec, daily 11am - 6pm (closes at 4pm from 30 Oct).

P Spaces: 300. Woodlands car park: open all year, daily 11am - 5.30pm (closes at 4pm Nov - Mar). Overflow car park with 1000 spaces.

Full wheelchair access. WC for the disabled. Guide dogs allowed.

£ Adult: £1 extra (house), £7.50 (grounds), £3 (woodlands car park). Child: 50p extra (house), £3.70 (grounds), £1.50 (woodlands car park). Family: £18.70 (grounds), £7.50 (woodlands car park).

HALL BARN GOTHIC TEMPLE

Beaconsfield, Buckinghamshire HP9 2SG

Garden building in existence by 1740 but possibly c1725 and by Colen Campbell. Gothic Revival style hexagonal-shaped garden building. Situated in landscaped garden, laid out in 1680s.

Grant Recipient: 5th Baron Burnham's Will Trust

Access Contact: J A C Read

T: 01494 673 020

Open: By written application to Mrs Farncombe, Hall Barn, Windsor End, Beaconsfield, Buckinghamshire HP9 2SG.

P Spaces: 10.

Full wheelchair access. No WC for the disabled. Guide Dogs allowed.

£ No.

HUGHENDEN MANOR DISRAELI MONUMENT

High Wycombe, Buckinghamshire HP14 4LA

The home of Prime Minister Benjamin Disraeli from 1848-1881. Hughenden has a red brick 'gothic' exterior. Much of his furniture, books and paintings remain. The garden has been recreated in the spirit of his wife, Mary Anne, with colourful designs. Park and woodland walks.

www.nationaltrust.org.uk

Grant Recipient: The National Trust

Access Contact: Property Manager

T: 01494 755573   **F:** 01494 474284

E-mail: hughenden@nationaltrust.org.uk

Open: House: 1 Mar - 5 Nov, Wed - Sun 1 - 5pm. Good Fri & BH Mons 1 - 5pm. House Tours: 1 Mar - 5 Nov, Wed - Sun 11am - 1pm. 2 - 17 Dec, Sat & Sun 12 - 3pm. Gardens: as house 11am - 5pm. 2 - 17 Dec Sat and Sun 12 - 3pm. Park and woodlands all year. Note: long and steep walk to house entrance if arriving by public transport.

P Spaces: 100.

Wheelchair access to ground floor of house, terrace, stable yard restaurant and shop. WC for the disabled. Guide Dogs allowed.

£ Adult: £6, £2.50 (garden only). Child: £3, £1.80 (garden only). Family: £15. Parks and woods free.

STOWE HOUSE

Buckingham, Buckinghamshire MK18 5EH

Mansion built in 1680 and greatly altered and enlarged in the 18th century, surrounded by important 18th century gardens which are owned by the National Trust (see entry for Stowe Landscape Gardens). House and gardens variously worked on by Vanbrugh, Gibbs, Kent and Leoni and is one of the most complete neo-classical houses in Europe. The House is now occupied by the Preservation Trust's tenant, Stowe School.

www.shtp.co.uk

Grant Recipient: The Stowe House Preservation Trust

Access Contact: Ms Anna McEvoy

T: 01280 818186 (Mon-Fri)   **F:** 01280 818186

E-mail: amcevoy@stowe.co.uk

Open: 15 - 19 Feb, 29 Mar - 16 Apr, 31 May - 4 June & 25 - 29 Oct: Wed - Sun 12 noon - 5pm, 2pm tours. 28 and 29 May: 12 noon - 5pm, 2pm tours. 21 & 22 Jan, 11 and 12 Mar, 6 and 7 May, 13 - 15 Oct, 18 & 19 Nov and 16 & 17 Dec: 2pm tours only. Sat & Sun only for Heritage Open Days, please check times. Group visits by arrangement throughout the year (tel: 01280 818229).

P Spaces: 15.

Full wheelchair access. WC for the disabled. Guide Dogs allowed.

£ Adult £3, £4 (with tour). Child: £2, £2.50 (with tour). Other: 15% discount for group tours of 15+.

STOWE LANDSCAPE GARDENS

Buckingham, Buckinghamshire MK18 5EH

Extensive and complex pleasure grounds and park around a country mansion. Begun late 17th century but substantially developed in the 18th and 19th centuries by, among others, Charles Bridgeman, Sir John Vanbrugh, James Gibbs, William Kent and Lancelot 'Capability' Brown (Brown was originally head gardener here before leaving to set up his landscape practice). The park and gardens contain over 30 buildings, many of great architectural importance. Stowe was supremely influential on the English landscape garden during the 18th century.

www.nationaltrust.org.uk

Grant Recipient: The National Trust

Access Contact: Property Manager

T: 01280 822850   **F:** 01280 822437

E-mail: stowegarden@nationaltrust.org.uk

Open: 1 Jan - 26 Feb and 4 Nov - 31 Dec: Sat and Sun 10am - 4pm (last adm. 3pm). 1 Mar - 29 Oct: daily, except BH Mons and Tues, 10am - 5.30pm (last adm. 4pm). Open BH Mons and closed 27 May, 24 & 25 Dec.

P Spaces: 100.

Partial Wheelchair Access. Self-drive battery cars available. WC for the disabled. Guide Dogs allowed.

£ Adult: £6. Child: £3. Family: £15.

WEST WYCOMBE PARK (WEST PORTICO)

West Wycombe, Buckinghamshire HP14 3AJ

House built early 18th century, extensively remodelled between 1750 and 1780 by Sir Francis Dashwood (creator of

the Hell-Fire Club). Porticoes were added to the east and west fronts by Nicholas Revett (his work is relatively rare), and on the south, linking the wings, John Donovell added a two storey colonnade. Although the latter is based on Renaissance prototypes, it too is a rare feature. Frescoes were painted on the ceiling of the West Portico by one of the Borgnis.

www.nationaltrust.org.uk

Grant Recipient: The National Trust

Access Contact: Property Manager

T: 01494 755573

Open: Grounds only: 2 Apr - 31 May, daily 2 - 6pm except Fri and Sat (open BH Mons). House & Grounds: 1 June - 31 August: daily 2 - 6pm except Fri and Sat. Weekdays: entry by guided tour every 20 minutes (approx). Last admission 5.15pm.

P Spaces: 30. Parking on site.

Wheelchair access to ground floor only. No WC for the disabled. Guide Dogs allowed.

£ Adult: £5.70 (house & grounds), £3 (grounds only). Child: £2.80 (house & grounds), £1.50 (grounds only). Family: £14.50.

WIDMERE FARM CHAPEL

Widmere, nr. Marlow, Buckinghamshire SL7 3DF

Chapel attached to farmhouse, early 13th century with traces of 14th century windows and later alterations. Grade II*. 11th or 12th century crypt and medieval roof.

Grant Recipient: Mr G J White

Access Contact: Mr G J White

T: 01628 484204

Open: By arrangement.

P Spaces: 6.   No Access.   £ No.

CAMBRIDGESHIRE

BUCKDEN TOWERS

High Street, Buckden, Cambridgeshire PE19 5TA

Former ecclesiastical palace set in 15 acres of gardens and parkland. Buildings include the Great Tower and the Inner Gatehouse (both constructed in the late 15th century) and the Victorian mansion. The grounds include an Elizabethan knot garden. Famous occupants include St Hugh of Lincoln (12th century) and Katherine of Aragon (1533-4).

Grant Recipient: The Claretian Missionaries

Access Contact: Mrs Margaret Caulfield

T: 01480 810344   **Fax:** 01480 811284

E-mail: claret_centre@claret.org.uk

Open: Guided tours by arrangement. Grounds open throughout the year. Heritage Open Days.

P Spaces: 50.

Full wheelchair access. WC for the disabled. Guide Dogs allowed.

£ No.

ELTON HALL

Elton, nr. Peterborough, Cambs PE8 6SH

Grade I historic building and country house. Late 15th century gatehouse and chapel built by Sapcote family. Main entrance façade built by Sir Thomas Proby in the 17th century and remodelled by Henry Ashton for 3rd Earl of Carysfort in the 19th century. South Garden façade built between 1789 and 1812 in Gothic style.

www.eltonhall.com

Grant Recipient: Sir William Proby Bt

Access Contact: Sir William Proby Bt

T: 01832 280468   **F:** 01832 280584

E-mail: whp@eltonhall.com

Open: 30 May. June: Weds. July and Aug: Weds, Thurs and Suns plus Aug BH Mon 2 - 5pm. Private groups by arrangement Apr - Oct.

P Spaces: 500. 300 metres from the Hall.

Full wheelchair access to garden. Access to house is difficult. Please tel 01832 280468. WC for the disabled. Guide Dogs allowed.

£ Adult: £6 (house), £3 (garden). Child: Free if accompanied.

MADINGLEY POST MILL

Mill Farm, Madingley Road, Coton, Cambridgeshire CB3 7PH

Historic post mill with machinery intact.

Grant Recipient: Mr Matthew Mortlock

Access Contact: Mr Matthew Mortlock

T: 01954 211047   **F:** 01954 210752

E-mail: mattcb37ph@aol.com
Open: Weekdays & Sats 11am - 4pm by telephone arrangement.
P Spaces: 5. Parking available at American Cemetery (next door).
Wheelchair access around base of Windmill only. No WC for the disabled. Guide Dogs allowed.
£ No.

MINSTER PRECINCTS

Peterborough Cathedral, Peterborough, Cambridgeshire PE1 1XS
The Minster Precincts incorporate many remains from the medieval monastery of which the Cathedral church was a part. These include the richly decorated 13th century arcades of the former infirmary, the originally 13th century Little Prior's Gate and the 15th century Table Hall.
www.peterborough-cathedral.org.uk
Grant Recipient: The Dean & Chapter of Peterborough Cathedral
Access Contact: The Chapter of Peterborough Cathedral
T: 01733 343342 **F:** 01733 552465
E-mail: a.watson@peterborough-cathedral.org.uk
Open: All year, exterior only. Heritage Open Days.
P City centre car parks (nearest 5 minute walk).
Full wheelchair access. WC in Cathedral restaurant, Tourist Information Centre and Cathedral Education Centre. Guide Dogs allowed.
£ Guided Tours: Adult: £3.50. Conc: £2.50. Schools £1.50. Otherwise, donations welcome from Cathedral visitors.

PRIOR CRAUDEN'S CHAPEL

The College, Ely, Cambridgeshire CB7 4DL
Private chapel built by Prior Crauden in 1524-5 of Barnack stone ashlar with clunch carved interior, over a 13th century vaulted undercroft. Has windows in the "Decorated" style, octagonal entrance and tower with spiral staircase, richly carved interior and a 14th century mosaic tile floor.
www.cathedral.ely.anglican.org
Grant Recipient: The Dean & Chapter of Ely Cathedral
Access Contact: Mr Stephen Wikner
T: 01353 667735 **F:** 01353 665658
E-mail: stephen.wikner@cathedral.ely.anglican.org
Open: By written arrangement with the Bursar, The Chapter House, The College, Ely, Cambs CB7 4DL. Heritage Open Days.
P In town centre car parks. Parking for the disabled in Cathedral car park by arrangement.
Wheelchair access to the undercroft only. WC for the disabled in Cathedral. Guide Dogs allowed.
£ No.

QUEEN'S HALL

The Gallery, Ely, Cambridgeshire CB7 4DL
Built by Prior Crauden c1330 of Carr stone rubble with Barnack, or similar, stone dressings and much brick patching. Has original undercroft with ribbed vaulting, 14th century pointed arched windows with curvilinear tracery and corbels carved in the shape of crouching figures. Reputedly constructed for entertaining Queen Philippa, wife of Edward III.
Grant Recipient: The Dean & Chapter of Ely Cathedral
Access Contact: The Assistant Bursar
T: 01353 660700 **F:** 01353 662187
E-mail: NigelC@kings-ely.cambs.sch.uk
Open: By written arrangement with the Assistant Bursar, the King's School, Ely, Cambs CB7 4DN.
P Spaces: 5. In town centre car parks. Parking for the disabled in Cathedral car park by arrangement.
Wheelchair access to ground floor only. WC for the disabled in Cathedral. Guide Dogs allowed.
£ No.

SIR JOHN JACOB'S ALMSHOUSE CHAPEL

Church Street, Gamlingay, Cambs SG19 3JH
Built 1745 of Flemish bond red brick with plain tiled roof, in keeping with adjoining terrace of ten almshouses constructed 80 years before. Now used as parish council offices.
Grant Recipient: The Trustees of Sir John Jacob's Almshouses
Access Contact: Mrs K Rayner and Mrs L Bacon
T: 01767 650310 **F:** 01767 650310
E-mail: gamlingaypc@lineone.net
Open: The office is generally open on Mon, Wed and Fri between 9.15am and 3.00pm. Heritage Open Days.
P On-street parking.
Full wheelchair access. WC for the disabled. Guide Dogs allowed.
£ No.

SULEHAY HOUSE

32 Old Market, Wisbech, Cambs PE13 1NF
Grade II* town house, built 1723, with fine original staircase.
Grant Recipient: Cambridgeshire Historic Buildings Preservation Trust
Access Contact: Richard Miers
T: 01945 461 873
Open: By arrangement. Heritage Open Days.
P No. No access. Guide Dogs allowed. £ No.

THE ALMONRY

High Street, Ely, Cambridgeshire CB7 4JU
The Almonry (now a restaurant) is part of a long range of buildings which back onto the High Street on the north side of the Cathedral. Originally built by Alan of Walsingham soon after he became Sacrist in 1322, but mainly rebuilt in the 19th century.
www.cathedral.ely.anglican.org
Grant Recipient: The Dean & Chapter of Ely
Access Contact: Mr Stephn Wikner
T: 01353 667735 **F:** 01353 665658
E-mail: stephen.wikner@cathedral.ely.anglican.org
Open: Mon - Sat 10am - 5pm, Sun 11am - 5pm Heritage Open Days.
P In town centre car parks. Parking for the disabled in Cathedral car park by arrangement.
Wheelchair access to ground floor only. WC for the disabled. Guide Dogs allowed.
£ No.

THE BLACK HOSTELRY

The College, Ely, Cambridgeshire CB7 4DL
Built c1291-2 of Carr stone rubble with Barnack, or similar, stone dressings, upper storey is timber-framed and plastered on the south and east sides with stone on the west side. Has early 13th century undercroft with ribbed vaults, 13-14th century King Post roof, and 15th century red brick chimney and doorway. Constructed to accommodate visiting monks from other Benedictine monasteries.
www.cathedral.ely.anglican.org
Grant Recipient: The Dean & Chapter of Ely
Access Contact: Mr Stephen Wikner
T: 01353 667735 **F:** 01353 665658
E-mail: stephen.wikner@cathedral.ely.anglican.org
Open: By written arrangement with the Bursar, The Chapter House, The College, Ely, Cambs CB7 4DL. Heritage Open Days.
P In town centre car parks. Parking for the disabled in Cathedral car park by arrangement.
Wheelchair access to rear entrance hall only. WC for the disabled in Cathedral. Guide Dogs allowed.
£ No.

THE CHAPTER HOUSE

The College, Ely, Cambridgeshire CB7 4DL
Originally part of the chapel of the Infirmary, now the remains of this house the Deanery and the Chapter Office. Contains part of the arch, ribbed vaulting and arcade of the 12th century chancel.
www.cathedral.ely.anglican.org
Grant Recipient: The Dean & Chapter of Ely
Access Contact: Mr Stephen Wikner
T: 01353 667735 **F:** 01353 665658
E-mail: stephen.wikner@cathedral.ely.anglican.org
Open: By written arrangement with the Bursar, The Chapter House, The College, Ely, Cambs CB7 4DL. Heritage Open Days.
P In town centre car parks. Parking for the disabled in Cathedral car park by arrangement.
Wheelchair access to ground floor only. WC for the disabled in Cathedral. Guide Dogs allowed.
£ No.

THE MANOR

Hemingford Grey, Huntingdon, Cambridgeshire PE28 9BN
Built c1130 and one of the oldest continuously inhabited houses in Britain. Made famous as Green Knowe by the author Lucy Boston. Her patchwork collection is also shown. Four acre garden with topiary, old roses and herbaceous borders.
www.greenknowe.co.uk
Grant Recipient: Mrs Diana Boston
Access Contact: Mrs Diana Boston
T: 01480 463134 **Fax:** 01480 465026

E-mail: diana_boston@hotmail.com
Open: House: all year (except May) to individuals or groups by arrangement. May: guided tours at 11am and 2pm (booking advisable). Garden: all year, daily 11am - 5pm (4pm in winter).
P Spaces: 2. Parking for disabled adjacent to property.
Wheelchair access to garden and dining room only. WC for the disabled. Guide Dogs allowed.
£ Adult: £5, £2 (garden only). Child: £1.50, free (garden only). Other: £4, £2 (garden only).

THE OLD PALACE

Sue Ryder Care, Palace Green, Ely, Cambridgeshire CB7 4EW
Grade I listed building formerly a bishops palace opposite cathedral, with an Elizabethan promenading gallery, bishops chapel and monks' room. Two acre garden contains the oldest plane tree in Europe. Used as a neurological centre for the physically disabled.
www.suerydercare.org/theoldpalace
Grant Recipient: The Sue Ryder Care
Access Contact: Mrs Mavis Garner
T: 01353 667686 **F:** 01353 669425
E-mail: mavis.garner@suerydercareely.org.uk
Open: By arrangement for access to the Long Gallery and Chapel. Gardens: open during the Open Gardens Scheme May - June. Other events held throughout the year, contact Mrs Garner for details.
P Nearest car parks: St Mary's St and Barton Rd.
Wheelchair access to garden and Long Gallery only. WC for the disabled. Guide Dogs allowed.
£ Charge on garden open days: Adult £3, Child 50p.

THORPE HALL HOSPICE

Sue Ryder Care, Longthorpe, Peterborough, Cambridgeshire PE3 6LW
Built in the 1650s by Peter Mills for Oliver St John, Oliver Cromwell's Lord Chief Justice. Ground floor retains many original features.
Grant Recipient: Sue Ryder Care
Access Contact: Mr Bruce Wringe
T: 01733 330060 **F:** 01733 269078
E-mail: bruce.wringe@sueryderthorpe.fsnet.co.uk
Open: Access to the Hall by arrangement. Gardens: open all year. Heritage Open Days.
P Spaces: 150.
Wheelchair access WC for the disabled. Guide Dogs allowed.
£ Donations welcome.

CHESHIRE

ADLINGTON HALL

Mill Lane, Adlington, Macclesfield, Cheshire SK10 4LF
Tudor/Elizabethan/Georgian manor house built around a Medieval hunting lodge. The Great Hall houses a 17th century organ, the most important of its type in the country, once played by Handel.
www.adlingtonhall.com
Grant Recipient: Mrs C J C Legh
Access Contact: Mrs C J C Legh
T: 01625 829 206 **F:** 01625 828 756
E-mail: camilla@adlingtonhall.com
Open: June - Aug: Weds only 2 - 5pm. Open to groups on weekdays throughout the year by arrangement.
P Areas for parking at North front and East front.
Wheelchair access to ground floor and some areas of gardens. WC for the disabled. No Guide Dogs.
£ Adult: £6. Child: £3. Groups: £5.50.

BACHE HOUSE FARM

Chester Road, Hurleston, Nantwich, Cheshire CW5 6BO
A timber-framed house with slate roof dating from 17th century with an 18th century extension. The house is a four square house with two gables at the rear. The interior shows timbers in the house walls and an oak staircase.
Grant Recipient: P R Posnett
Access Contact: Mrs E A Posnett
T: 01829 260251
Open: By arrangement at all reasonable times.
P Spaces: 10. No access. £ No.

BELMONT HALL

Great Budworth, Northwich, Cheshire CW9 6HN
Country house, built 1755, initial design by James Gibbs, with fine plasterwork interiors. Set in parkland. Now a private day school with family apartments in the East Wing. Also accessible is surrounding farmland, woods and medieval moat.
Grant Recipient: The Trustees of Belmont Hall
Access Contact: Mr R C Leigh
T: 01606 891235 **Fax:** 01606 892349
E-mail: asmleigh@hotmail.com
Open: Guided tours during the school holidays and on weekends by arrangement with the Estate Manager, Belmont Hall, Great Budworth, Northwich, Cheshire CW9 6HN (tel: 01606 891235). Please note: the property and adjacent area are also open by way of a Countryside Stewardship Educational Access Agreement for schools as well as adult parties.
P Spaces: 100. Unlimited free parking on site.
No wheelchair access or WC for the disabled. Guide Dogs allowed.
£ Adult: £5.

BRAMALL HALL

Bramhall Park, Stockport, Cheshire SK7 3NX
Black and white timber-framed manor house dating back to the 14th century, with several subsequent renovations (many during the Victorian period). Contains 14th century wallpaintings, an Elizabethan plaster ceiling and Victorian kitchen and servants quarters.
www.stockport.gov.uk/tourism/bramall
Grant Recipient: Stockport Metropolitan Borough Council
Access Contact: Ms Caroline Egan
T: 0161 485 3708 **F:** 0161 486 6959
E-mail: bramall.hall@stockport.gov.uk
Open: Good Fri - end September: Mon - Sun 1 - 5pm. Bank Holidays 11am - 5pm. Oct - 1 Jan: Tues- Sun 1 - 4pm. Bank Holidays 11am - 4pm. 2 Jan - Easter: weekends only 1 - 4pm.
P Spaces: 60. Pay parking.
Wheelchair access to ground floor only. WC for the disabled. Guide Dogs allowed.
£ Adult: £3.95. Child: £2.50. Conc: £2.50.

CAPESTHORNE HALL

Macclesfield, Cheshire SK11 9JY
Jacobean style hall with a collection of fine art, sculpture, furniture, tapestry and antiques from Europe, America and the Far East. The Hall dates from 1719 when it was originally designed by the Smith's of Warwick. Altered in 1837 by Blore and rebuilt by Salvin in 1861 following a disastrous fire.
www.capesthorne.com
Grant Recipient: Mr William Arthur Bromley-Davenport
Access Contact: Mrs Gwyneth Jones
T: 01625 861221 **F:** 01625 861619
E-mail: info@capesthorpe.com
Open: Apr - Oct: Sun, Wed and Bank Holidays. Gardens and Chapel 12 noon - 5pm, Hall from 1.30 - 4pm (last adm. 3.30pm). Parties on other days by arrangement.
P Spaces: 2000.
Wheelchair access to ground floor and butler's pantry. WC for the disabled. Guide Dogs allowed.
£ Adult: £6 (Suns & BHs), £4 (garden & chapel only). Child: £3 (5-18 yrs), £2 (garden & chapel). Senior: £5, £3 (garden & chapel). Family: £15. Wed only: £10 (Car: 4 people) £25 (minibus) £50 (coach).

DIXON'S ALMSHOUSES

1-6 The Pit, Little Heath Lane, Christleton, Chester, Cheshire CH3 7AN
Originally six almshouses, built in 1868 by J. Oldrid Scott in Tudor style in memory of James Dixon of Littleton. A good, early example of Victorian timber framing. Order of Malta Homes carried out a major refurbishment in 1998 which won a council award for design.
Grant Recipient: Order of Malta Homes Trust
Access Contact: Mrs Beth Harding
T: 01522 813120 **F:** 01522 810 009
E-mail: b.harding@osjct.co.uk
Open: Property can be viewed from the outside with access to the interior by arrangement with the Reverend Peter Lee (tel: 01244 335663).
P On-street parking. No access. £ No.

HIGHFIELDS

Audlem, nr. Crewe, Cheshire CW3 0DT
Small half-timbered manor house dating back to c1600.
Grant Recipient: Mr J B Baker
Access Contact: Mrs Susan Baker
T: 01630 655479
Open: Guided tour of hall, drawing room, dining room, parlour, bedrooms and gardens by written arrangement.
P Spaces: 20.
Wheelchair access to ground floor only. WC for the disabled with assistance (down 2 steps). Guide Dogs allowed.
£ Adult/conc: £5. Child: £2.50.

LYME PARK

Disley, Stockport, Cheshire SK12 2NX
Home to the Legh family for 600 years, Lyme Park comprises a 1400 acre medieval deer park, a 17 acre Victorian garden and a Tudor hall which was transformed into an Italianate palace in the 18th century. Location for 'Pemberley' in the BBC TV's production of Pride and Prejudice.
www.nationaltrust.org.uk
Grant Recipient: Stockport Metropolitan Borough Council
Access Contact: Mr Philip Burt
T: 01663 762023 **F:** 01663 765035
E-mail: lymepark@nationaltrust.org.uk
Open: Hall: 27 Mar - 31 Oct, daily except Wed and Thurs 1 - 5pm. Garden: 27 Mar - 31 Oct, daily 11am - 5pm. 1 Nov - 18 Dec: weekends 12 - 4pm. Park: 1 Apr - 15 Oct, daily 8am - 8.30pm. 15 Oct - 31 Mar: daily 8am - 6pm.
P Spaces: 1500. Park entry £4.50 per car.
Wheelchair access to garden, first floor of house, parts of park, shop and restaurant. WC for the disabled. Guide Dogs allowed.
£ Adult: £6.50 (House & Garden), £5 (House only). Child: £3.30 (House & Garden), £2.50 (House only). National Trust members free.

RODE HALL

Church Lane, Scholar Green, Cheshire ST7 3QP
Country house built early – mid 18th century, with later alterations. Set in a parkland designed by Repton. Home to the Wilbraham family since 1669.
www.rodehall.co.uk
Grant Recipient: Sir Richard Baker Wilbraham Bt
Access Contact: Sir Richard Baker Wilbraham Bt
T: 01270 873237 **F:** 01270 882962
E-mail: rodehall@scholargreen.fsnet.co.uk
Open: Hall and Gardens: 1 Apr - 30 Sept, Weds and Bank Holidays (closed Good Fri) 2 - 5pm. Gardens only: Daily except Tues 2 - 5pm. Snowdrop Walks: 4 - 26 Feb 12 - 4pm.
P Spaces: 200. Parking for the disabled available adjacent to entrance by arrangement.
Wheelchair access with assistance to ground floor. WC for the disabled. Guide Dogs allowed.
£ Adult: £5 (house & garden), £3 (garden only). Child: £4 over 12s (house & garden), £2.50 (garden only). Seniors: £4 (house & garden), £2.50 (garden only).

ST CHAD'S CHURCH TOWER

Wybunbury, Nantwich, Cheshire CW5 7NA
Grade II* listed 15th or 16th century church tower, rest of Church demolished in 1977. 96ft high and containing six restored bells, spiral staircase, charity boards, monuments and affords panoramic views over the South Cheshire plain. Bells are rung every Thursday evening.
www.wybunburytower.org.uk
Grant Recipient: Wybunbury Tower Preservation Trust
Access Contact: Mrs D Lockhart
T: 01270 841481
Open: Sat 10 June 'Fig Pie Wakes' (local race and festival) 1 - 5pm. Heritage Open Days 11am - 4pm. At other times by arrangement with Mrs D Lockhart (tel: 01270 841481) or Mr John Colbert (tel: 01270 841158).
P Spaces: 20.
Wheelchair access to ground floor only. No WC for the disabled. Guide Dogs allowed.
£ Adult: £2. Child: £1.

CLEVELAND

MARSKE HALL

Marske by the Sea, Redcar & Cleveland TS11 6AA
Country house built by Sir William Pennyman in 1625. 2 storeys with 3-storey projecting towers in a 9-bay range forming a symmetrical front approx. 115ft long. Altered in the late 19th and 20th centuries. Varied uses during 20th century include as quarters for the Royal Flying Corps in WWI, Army quarters in WWII, school 1948-58 and since 1963 a Cheshire Foundation nursing home.
Grant Recipient: Teesside Cheshire Homes
Access Contact: Mrs Sue O'Brien
T: 01642 482672 **F:** 01642 759973
E-mail: marske@ney.leonard-cheshire.org.uk
Open: Hall by arrangement. Grounds open to public at all fund raising events such as the Summer Fete.
P Spaces: 20.
Full wheelchair access. WC for the disabled. Guide Dogs allowed.
£ No.

CO DURHAM

BARNARD CASTLE MARKET CROSS

Barnard Castle, Durham DL12 8EL
Two-storey building dating from 1747 with a colonnaded ground floor and enclosed upper storey. Two slate roofs crowned by a bell tower and gilded weather vane with two bullet holes from 1804. Formerly used as Town Hall, butter market, lock-up, Court room and fire station.
Grant Recipient: Teesdale District Council
Access Contact: Mr James Usher
T: 01833 696209 **F:** 01833 637269
E-mail: j.usher@teesdale.gov.uk
Open: Colonnaded area (ground floor) is open to the public at all times. The first floor is only accessible through organised tours with keys available from Teesdale House, Galgate, Barnard Castle, Co. Durham DL12 8EL by special arrangement.
P On-street parking. No access. £ No.

CROXDALE HALL

Durham DH6 5JP
18th century re-casing of an earlier Tudor building, containing comfortably furnished mid-Georgian rooms with Rococo ceilings. There is also a private chapel in the north elevation, walled gardens, a quarter-of-a-mile long terrace, an orangery and lakes which date from the mid-18th century.
Grant Recipient: Captain G M Salvin
Access Contact: Mr W H T Salvin
T: 01833 690100 **F:** 01833 637004
E-mail: whtsalvin@aol.com
Open: By arrangement on Tues and Weds from the first Tues in May to the second Wed in July, 10am - 1pm. Heritage Open Days.
P Spaces: 20.
Partial Wheelchair Access. WC for the disabled. No Guide Dogs.
£ Adult: £7.50. Child: Free (under 16s).

DURHAM CASTLE

Palace Green, Durham DH1 3RW
Dating from 1072, the Castle was the seat of the Prince Bishops until 1832. Together with the Cathedral, the Castle is a World Heritage site. It now houses University College, the Foundation College of Durham University, and is a conference, banqueting and holiday centre in vacations.
www.durhamcastle.com
Grant Recipient: University of Durham
Access Contact: University of Durham
T: 0191 374 4682
Open: Easter - end of Sept: guided tours daily from 10am - 4pm. 1 Oct - Easter Mon: Wed, Sat and Sun (afternoons only). Tours may not take place when the Castle is being used for functions. Heritage Open Days.
P Parking in city car parks.
Wheelchair access to courtyard only. WC for the disabled inaccessible to wheelchairs. Guide Dogs allowed.
£ Adult: £5, £3 (group rate 10+). Child: £2.50 (3-14), £2 (group rate 10+). Senior: £2.50. Family £10.

FORMER STOCKTON & DARLINGTON RAILWAY BOOKING OFFICE

48 Bridge Road, Stockton-on-Tees, Durham TS18 3AX
Original booking office of the Stockton and Darlington Railway. Cottage of plain brick with slate roof facing railway line. A bronze tablet on the gable ends "Martin 1825 the Stockton and Darlington Company booked first passenger, thus marking an epoch in the history of mankind". The first rail of the Railway was laid outside the building. Now used as an administration office and accommodation for single homeless men.
Grant Recipient: Stockton Church's Mission to the Single Homeless
Access Contact: Ms Margaret McCarthy
T: 01642 800322　**F:** 01642 800322
Open: Mon - Fri: 9am - 3pm.
P Spaces: 50. Parking on opposite side of the road.
Limited wheelchair access to ground floor only. No WC for the disabled. Guide Dogs allowed.
£ No.

HAMSTEELS HALL

Hamsteels Lane, Quebec, Durham DH7 9RS
Early 18th century farmhouse with 19th century alterations. Panelled window shutters; ground-floor room with full early 18th century panelling; similar panelling and cupboards in first-floor room. Good quality dogleg stair with turned balusters.
Grant Recipient: Mr G F Whitfield
Access Contact: Mrs June Whitfield
T: 01207 520 388　**F:** 01207 520 388
E-mail: june@hamsteelshall.co.uk
Open: By arrangement.
P Spaces: 8.
Wheelchair access to Dining Room and Front Parlour only. No WC for the disabled. No Guide Dogs.
£ No.

LOW BUTTERBY FARMHOUSE

Croxdale & Hett, Durham DH6 5JN
Stone built farmhouse constructed on medieval site incorporating elements of 17th, 18th and 19th century phases of development.
Grant Recipient: The Trustees of Captain GM Salvin's 1983 Settlement
Access Contact: Mr W H T Salvin
T: 01833 690100　**F:** 01833 637004
E-mail: whtsalvin@aol.com
Open: By prior written or telephone arrangement with Mr W H T Salvin, The Estate Office, Egglestone Abbey, Barnard Castle, Co. Durham DL12 9TN. Heritage Open Days.
P Spaces: 2.
Limited wheelchair access with assistance (some changes in floor level). No WC for the disabled. No Guide Dogs.
£ No.

RECTORY FARM BARN

Hall Walks, Easington, Peterlee, Durham SR8 3BS
Barn, possibly 13th century with extensive alterations. May originally have been an oratory connected with Seaton Holme. Limestone rubble construction; first floor contains medieval windows. Purchased by Groundwork in 1997 and recently renovated. Listed Grade II*.
Grant Recipient: Groundwork East Durham
Access Contact: Mr Peter Richards
T: 0191 5273333　**F:** 0191 5273665
E-mail: peter.richards@groundwork.org.uk
Open: Access to the exterior at all reasonable times.
P Parking available.
Full wheelchair access. WC for the disabled. Guide Dogs allowed.
£ No.

SHOTLEY HALL

Shotley Bridge, Consett, Durham DH8 9TE
Grade II* listed building designed in 1862 by Edward Robson in a Gothic style. Exceptionally complete and unaltered interior with stained glass tiles and interior elements designed by Edward Burne-Jones and made by William Morris.
Grant Recipient: Mr Martell
Access Contact: A Martell
T: 01207 582285　**E-mail:** shelaghmartell@aol.com
Open: 1 May - 1 June: daily except Suns 10am - 4pm.
Advisable to telephone before visiting. By appointment only at other times 1 Apr - 30 Sept to scholars, researchers and enthusiasts of William Morris and Edward Burne-Jones.
P Spaces: 5.
Wheelchair access to ground floor only. No WC for the disabled. Guide Dogs allowed.
£ No.

UNTHANK HALL

Stanhope, Durham DL13 2PQ
Jacobean farmhouse dating from 1520s. Many original features still remain.
Grant Recipient: Alan Morton
Access Contact: Mr Alan Morton
T: 01388 526025　**F:** 01388 527 390
E-mail: alanunthank@aol.com
Open: 9, 16, 23 & 30 Jan, 6 and 13 Feb, 6, 13 & 20 Mar, 8, 15 & 22 May, 12, 19 & 26 June, 11, 18 & 25 July, 8, 15 & 22 Aug, 5, 12, 19 & 26 Sept, 3, 10, 17 & 24 Oct, 6, 13, 20 & 27 Nov, 4, 11 & 18 Dec: 10am - 3pm. Heritage Open Days.
P Parking by river.
No wheelchair access or WC for the disabled. Guide Dogs allowed.
£ No.

CORNWALL

CAERHAYS CASTLE & GARDENS

Gorran, St Austell, Cornwall PL26 6LY
Built by John Nash in 1808. Set in 60 acres of informal woodland gardens created by J C Williams, who sponsored plant hunting expeditions to China at the turn of the 19th century.
www.caerhays.co.uk
Grant Recipient: The Trustees of Charles Williams (Caerhays Estate)
Access Contact: Mrs M Kemp
T: 01872 501144/501310　**F:** 01872 501870
E-mail: estateoffice@caerhays.co.uk
Open: House: 13 Mar - 31 May (incl BHs), Mon - Fri 12 - 4pm. Conducted tours every 45 mins. Gardens: 13 Feb - 31 May, daily 10am - 5pm (last entry 4pm).
P Spaces: 500.
Limited wheelchair access to gardens (area around castle). Access to ground floor of castle with assistance, please tel 01872 501144 or 01872 501310 to check. WC for the disabled. Guide Dogs allowed.
£ Adult: £9.50 (garden & house), £5.50 (house tour only), £5.50 (gardens). Child: £3.50 (garden & house), £2.50 (house tour only), £2.50 (gardens). Under 5s free. Groups (15+) £5 (house tour), £6.50 (garden tour), £4 (garden without tour).

COTEHELE

St Dominick, Saltash, Cornwall PL12 6TA
Cotehele, situated on the west bank of the River Tamar, was built mainly between 1485-1627. Home of the Edgcumbe family for centuries. Its granite and slatestone walls contain intimate chambers adorned with tapestries, original furniture and armour.
www.nationaltrust.org.uk
Grant Recipient: The National Trust
Access Contact: Mr Toby Fox
T: 01579 351346　**F:** 01579 351222
E-mail: cotehele@nationaltrust.org.uk
Open: House and restaurant: 19 Mar - 29 Sept daily except Fri (but open Good Fri) 11am - 4.30pm. 1 - 31 Oct 11am - 4pm. Mill: 19 Mar - 30 June daily except Fri (but open Good Fri) 1 - 5.30pm. 1 July - 31 Aug open daily. 1 Sept - 30 Sept daily except Fri 1 - 5.30pm. 1 - 31 Oct daily except Fri 1 - 4.30pm. Garden: daily all year 10.30am - dusk.
P Spaces: 100. Space available for pre-booked coaches.
Wheelchair access to house (hall, kitchen and Edgcumbe Room only), garden, area around house, restaurant and shop. Ramps available. Woodland walks: some paths accessible. WC for the disabled. Guide Dogs allowed.
£ Adult: £8 (house, garden & mill), £4.80 (garden & mill). Child: £4 (house, garden & mill), £2.40 (garden & mill). Family: (house, garden & mill): 1 Adult £12, 2 Adults £20. Family: (garden & mill): 1 Adult £7.20, 2 Adults £12. Pre-booked groups £7.40.

CULLACOTT FARMHOUSE

Werrington, Launceston, Cornwall PL15 8NH
Grade I listed medieval hall house, built in the 1480s as a long house, and extended 1579. Contains wall paintings of fictive tapestry, Tudor arms, St James of Compostella and remains of representation of St George and the Dragon. Extensively restored 1995-7 but still retains many original features. Now used as holiday accommodation.
www.cullacottholidays.co.uk
Grant Recipient: Mr & Mrs J Cole
Access Contact: J Cole
T: 01566 772631
E-mail: marycole@cullacottholidays.co.uk
Open: By arrangement.
P Spaces: 20.
Wheelchair access to Great Hall, through passage WC for the disabled. Guide Dogs allowed.
£ Adult £4, child free.

GODOLPHIN HOUSE

Godolphin Cross, Helston, Cornwall, TR13 9RE
Tudor-Stuart mansion of granite round a courtyard. For many generations seat of the Godolphin family who were courtiers from the 16th to the 18th century, the 1st Earl (who was born here) rose to be Queen Anne's Lord Treasurer. Has late Elizabethan stables with wagon collection and large medieval and other gardens.
www.godolphinhouse.com
Grant Recipient: Mrs L M P Schofield
Access Contact: Mrs Joanne Schofield
T: 01736 763194　**F:** 01736 763194
E-mail: godo@euphony.net
Open: Easter Mon - 30 Sept: daily except Mon & Sat, 11am - 5pm. Groups all year by arrangement.
P Spaces: 100. Parking for 3 coaches.
Wheelchair access to all of the house except one room. No access to the stables, and gardens may be difficult. WC for the disabled. Guide Dogs allowed.
£ Adult: £6 (house and gardens). Child: £1.50 (5-15 years). Senior: £5, £2 (gardens only).

PENCARROW

Washaway Bodmin, North Cornwall, Cornwall PL30 3AG
A Georgian house, completed in c1771, set in 50 acres of formal woodland gardens. Owned and lived in by the Molesworth-St Aubyn Family. Gardens include a sunken Italian Garden, Ice House, lake and many specimen trees.
www.pencarrow.co.uk
Grant Recipient: Trustees of Pencarrow House
Access Contact: Mr Jonathon Riley
T: 020 7849 2857　**F:** 020 7831 9607
E-mail: jonathon.riley@macfarlanes.com
Open: Gardens: 1 Mar - 31 Oct. House: 2 Apr - 26 Oct.
P Spaces: 100. Main car park is 50 yards from house, also overflow car park with 220 spaces.
Wheelchair access to ground floor only. If visitor cannot walk upstairs, admission price is halved. Tape recording of the upstairs tour is provided. WC for the disabled. Guide Dogs allowed.
£ Adult: £7.50 (house & garden), £4 (garden only). Child: £3.50 (house & garden), £1 (garden only).

PORTH-EN-ALLS LODGE

Prussia Cove, St Hilary, Cornwall TR20 9BA
Originally a chauffeur's lodge, built c1910-1914 and designed by Philip Tilden. It is built into the cliff and sits in close proximity to the main house. The Chauffeur's lodge is one of a number of historic houses on the Porth-en-Alls Estate.
www.prussiacove.com
Grant Recipient: Trustees of Porth-en-Alls Estate
Access Contact: Mr P Tunstall-Behrens
T: 01736 762 014　**F:** 01736 762 014
E-mail: penapc@dial.pipex.com
Open: Available as self-catering holiday lets throughout the year. Members of the public may view the property by arrangement, but only if it is unoccupied at the time.
P Spaces: 50. Public car park approximately 1/2 mile from the Lodge, off the A394 (near Rosudgeon village).
Wheelchair access to the lodge is very difficult. No WC for the disabled. Guide Dogs allowed.
£ No.

TREGREHAN

Par, Cornwall PL24 2SLJ
Mid 19th century gardens and pleasure grounds designed by W A Nesfield together with significant 19th and 20th century plant collections. Concentrating on genera from warm temperate regions. An important green gene bank of known source plants. 1846 glasshouse range in walled garden. Set in 18th and 19th century parkland.
www.tregrehan.org
Grant Recipient: T C Hudson
Access Contact: Mr T C Hudson
T: 01726 814 389 **F:** 01726 814389
E-mail: greengene@tregrehan.org
Open: Mid Mar - mid June: Wed - Sun & BHs (closed Easter Sun) 10.30am - 5pm. Mid June - end Aug: Weds only 2 - 5pm.
P Spaces: 50.
Wheelchair access to 10 acres of garden. WC for the disabled. Guide Dogs allowed.
£ Adult: £4. Child: Free.

TRESCO ABBEY GARDENS

Tresco Estate, Isles of Scilly, Cornwall TR24 0QQ
25 acre garden with plants mainly from the Mediterranean region. Plant groups include protea, aloe from South Africa, succulents from Canary Isles and palms from Mexico. All grown outside all year round. Unique, frost-free climate.
www.tresco.co.uk
Grant Recipient: Tresco Estate
Access Contact: Mr Michael Nelhams
T: 01720 424105 **F:** 01720 422868
E-mail: mikenelhams@tresco.co.uk
Open: Daily 10am - 4pm.
P No.
Wheelchair access to all garden areas but some gravel slopes which may be difficult. WC for the disabled. Guide Dogs allowed.
£ Adult: £8.50. Child: Free (under 14). Weekly ticket: £12.50.

TREVELVER FARMHOUSE

St Minver, Wadebridge, Cornwall PL27 6RJ
Remains of manor house now farmhouse. Dining room with 17th century painted panelling, a painted frieze and an over-mantle painted picture.
Grant Recipient: Mr Wills
Access Contact: Miss Melanie Wills
T: 01208 816 982
E-mail: melanie@pawtondairy.com
Open: By arrangement with Melanie Wills at any reasonable time. Access to dining room only.
P Spaces: 4. No access. £ No.

CUMBRIA

BRANTWOOD

Coniston, Cumbria LA21 8AD
Brantwood, situated on Coniston Water, was the former home of Victorian writer and artist, John Ruskin, from 1872 to 1900. Displays a collection of paintings by Ruskin and his circle, his furniture, books and personal items. Video, bookshop, craft gallery and restaurant on site. Gardens include the Harbour Walk and Professor's Garden where Ruskin experimented with native flowers and fruit.
www.brantwood.org.uk
Grant Recipient: Brantwood Education Trust Ltd
Access Contact: Mr Howard Hull
T: 015394 41396 **F:** 015394 41263
E-mail: enquiries@brantwood.org.uk
Open: All year: mid Mar - mid Nov, daily 11am - 5.30pm. Mid Nov - mid Mar, Wed - Sun 11am - 4.30pm (closed Christmas Day and Boxing Day).
P Spaces: 50.
Wheelchair access to house, toilets and restaurant only. WC for the disabled. Guide Dogs allowed.
£ Adult: £5.50. Child: £1. Student: £4.

CROWN & NISI PRIUS COURT

The Courts, English Street, Carlisle, Cumbria CA3 8NA
Former Crown Court in Carlisle situated at southern entrance to the city. One of a pair of sandstone towers built in the early 19th century as replicas of the medieval bastion. The towers were built to house the civil and criminal courts,
used until the 1980s.
Grant Recipient: Cumbria Crown Court
Access Contact: Mr Mike Telfer
T: 01228 606116
Open: Guided Tours July & Aug, Mon - Fri 1pm & 2.30pm (excl Aug BH Mon).
P Town centre car parks.
Wheelchair access to Grand Jury Room, Court No.2 and Public Area Crown Court Room. WC for the disabled. Guide Dogs allowed.
£ Adult £3. Child: £2 (age 5-15. Other: £2.50.

DIXON'S CHIMNEY

Shaddongate, Carlisle, Cumbria CA2 5TZ
270ft chimney, formerly part of Shaddongate Mill. Built in 1836 by Peter Dixon. At its original height of 306ft the chimney was the tallest cotton mill chimney to have been constructed. Structural problems meant that the decorative stone capping had to be removed in the 1950s.
Grant Recipient: Carlisle City Council
Access Contact: Mr Peter Messenger
T: 01228 871195 **F:** 01228 817199
E-mail: PeterMe@carlisle-city.gov.uk
Open: Chimney can be viewed from Shaddongate and Junction Street.
P No parking. No access. £ No.

DRAWDYKES CASTLE

Brampton Old Road, Carlisle, Cumbria CA6 4QE
Pele tower, probably 14th century, converted to house 1676 by William Thackery and John Aglionby. Original tower with Classical Revival facade. Grade II* listed.
Grant Recipient: Mr J M Milbourn
Access Contact: Mr J M Milbourn
T: 01228 525 804
Open: By arrangement.
P No parking. No access. £ No.

KIRKBY HALL WALLPAINTINGS

Kirkby-in-Furness, Cumbria LA17 7UX
Chapel in west wing, accessible only from trap door in dairy passage. Wallpaintings in red ochre and black consisting of panels with stylised trees, animals and birds with texts above of the Lord's Prayer, Creed, Ten Commandments and Galations 5, 16-21 from the Great Bible of 1541.
Grant Recipient: Holker Estates Company Ltd
Access Contact: Mr D P R Knight
T: 015395 58313 **F:** 015395 58966
E-mail: estateoffice@holker.co.uk
Open: By written arrangement with the Holker Estate Office, Cark-in-Cartmel, Grange-over-Sands, Cumbria LA11 7PH
P Spaces: 3. No access. £ No.

LEVENS HALL

Kendal, Cumbria LA8 0PD
Elizabethan house built around a 13th century pele tower, containing fine furniture, panelling, plasterwork and an art collection. The gardens, which include much topiary, were laid out in the late 17th century by Monsieur Beaumont for Colonel James Grahme and are of national importance.
www.levenshall.co.uk
Grant Recipient: Mr C H Bagot
Access Contact: Mr P E Milner
T: 01539 560321 **F:** 01539 560669
E-mail: houseopening@levenshall.co.uk
Open: House: 2 Apr - 12 Oct, Sun - Thurs 12 noon - 5pm (last adm. 4.30). Garden: as house 10am - 5pm. Admission prices are under review at time of publication, please check with Mr Milner at the Estate Office for current information.
P Spaces: 80.
House unsuitable for wheelchair users due to stairs and narrow doorways but all other facilities (topiary garden, plant centre, gift shop, and tea room) are accessible. DVD tour of the House is available in the Buttery during opening hours. A mobility buggy is available for hire. WC for the disabled. Guide Dogs allowed.
£ Adult: £8 (House & Garden), £5.90 (Garden only). Child: £3.80 (House & Garden), £2.70 (Garden only).

MUNCASTER CASTLE

Ravenglass, Cumbria CA18 1RQ
Large house incorporating medieval fortified tower, remodelled by Anthony Salvin for the 4th Lord Muncaster in 1862-66. Ancestral home of the Pennington family for 800
years containing a panelled Hall and octagonal library. Headquarters of the World Owl Trust. Woodland garden, Lakeland setting. World-famous rhododendrons, camelias and magnolias with a terrace walk along the edge of the Esk valley.
www.muncastercastle.co.uk
Grant Recipient: Mrs P R Gordon-Duff-Pennington
Access Contact: Mrs Iona Frost-Pennington
T: 01229 717614 **F:** 01229 717010
E-mail: info@muncaster.co.uk
Open: Castle: 13 Feb - 6 Nov, daily (except closed Sat) 12 noon - 5pm (or dusk if earlier). Gardens, Owl Centre and Maze: open all year (closed Jan) 10.30am - 6.30pm (or dusk if earlier). Refreshments available.
P Spaces: 150.
Wheelchair access to ground floor of Castle only but other attractions and facilities accessible. The hilly nature of the site can create access difficulties so please ask for further information on arrival. WC for the disabled. Guide Dogs allowed.
£ Adult: £9 (Castle, Gardens, Owls & Maze), £6 (Gardens, Owls & Maze). Child: £6.50 (Castle, Gardens, Owls & Maze), £4.50 (Gardens, Owls & Maze). Under 5s free. Family: £25 (Castle, Gardens, Owls & Maze), £20 (Gardens, Owls & Maze).

ORTHWAITE HALL BAR

Uldale, Wigton, Cumbria CA7 1HL
Grade II* listed agricultural barn. Former house adjoining later Hall, probably late 16th or early 17th century, now used for storage and housing animals.
Grant Recipient: Mrs S Hope
Access Contact: Mr Jonathan Hope
T: 016973 71344
Open: By prior telephone arrangement.
P Spaces: 3.
No wheelchair access or WC for the disabled. Guide Dogs allowed.
£ No.

PERCY HOUSE

38-42 Market Place, Cockermouth, Cumbria CA13 9NG
Built in 1598 by Henry Pery the 9th Earl of Northumberland. Many of the original features of the building still remain, including carved plaster ceiling, Percy coat of arms, Tudor fireplace, oak plank and muslin screen and flag stone and oak floors.
www.percyhouse.co.uk
Grant Recipient: Mr R E Banks
Access Contact: Mr R E Banks
T: 01900 85643/ 07710 800973 **F:** 01900 85543
E-mail: banksrothersyke@aol.com
Open: Mon - Sat 10am - 5pm.
P Spaces: 150. On street parking in Market Place and public car park off Market Place.
Wheelchair access to ground floor only. Disabled WC available in nearby car park. Guide Dogs allowed.
£ No.

PRIOR SLEE GATEHOUSE

Carlisle Cathedral, Carlisle, Cumbria CA3 8TZ
Dated 1528, the Gatehouse would have replaced an earlier one. It has a large chamber over the gate, with two Tudor fireplaces. Graffiti carved in the stonework is believed to include merchants' marks. One of two integral lodges survives on the north-east side of the building. Now used as residential accommodation.
Grant Recipient: The Chapter of Carlisle Cathedral
Access Contact: Mr T I S Burns
T: 01228 548151 **F:** 01228 547049
E-mail: office@carlislecathedral.org.uk
Open: By arrangement with Mr T I S Burns, The Chapter of Carlisle Cathedral, 7 The Abbey, Carlisle, Cumbria CA3 8TZ.
P Parking in nearby City centre car parks. 2 parking spaces for the disabled in Cathedral grounds.
No wheelchair access. WC for the disabled is nearby (approx. 200 yards). Guide Dogs allowed.
£ No.

PRIOR'S TOWER

The Abbey, Carlisle, Cumbria CA3 8TZ
This Grade I listed three storey pele tower type building was constructed c1500. It formed part of the Prior's Lodgings and until relatively recently was part of the Deanery. Of special interest is the magnificent ceiling of 45 hand-painted panels

dating from c1510 and associated with Prior Senhouse.

Grant Recipient: The Chapter of Carlisle Cathedral

Access Contact: Mr T I S Burns

T: 01228 548151   **F:** 01228 547049

E-mail: office@carlislecathedral.org.uk

Open: By arrangement with Mr T I S Burns, The Chapter of Carlisle Cathedral, 7 The Abbey, Carlisle, Cumbria CA3 8TZ. Heritage Open Days.

P In nearby City centre car parks. 2 parking spaces for the disabled in Cathedral grounds.

No wheelchair access. WC for the disabled is nearby (approx. 100 yards). Guide Dogs allowed.

£ No.

SIZERGH CASTLE

Kendal, Cumbria LA8 8AE

Sizergh Castle has been the home of the Strickland family for [over 760 years. Its core is the 14th century pele tower later] extended and containing some fine Elizabethan carved wooden chimney-pieces and inlaid chamber. The Castle is surrounded by gardens, including a rock garden.

www.nationaltrust.org.uk

Grant Recipient: The National Trust

Access Contact: Property Manager

T: 01539 560 951

E-mail: sizergh@nationaltrust.org.uk

Open: Castle: 2 Apr - 29 Oct, daily except Fri and Sat 1 - 5pm. Garden: 2 Apr - 29 Oct, daily except Fri and Sat 12 - 5pm. Closed Good Fri. Winter building work may delay planned Apr opening, please telephone or check website if visiting in Spring.

P Spaces: 250. Parking for the disabled near the house.

Wheelchair access to Castle Lower Hall and garden gravel paths only. WC for the disabled. Guide Dogs allowed.

£ Adult: £6.20, £4 (garden only). Child: £3.10, £2 (garden only). Family: £15.50, £5.80pp (pre-booked parties, min 15 persons, not BHs).

SMARDALE GILL VIADUCT

Kirkby Stephen, Cumbria

Rail overbridge, built 1860-1 by Sir Thomas Bouch for the South Lancashire and Durham Union Railway. 550ft long with 14 arches spanning Scandal Beck at Smardale Gill, a National Nature Reserve. A well-preserved example of a large road bridge on this line.

Grant Recipient: The Trustees of the Northern Viaduct Trust

Access Contact: Mr Michael Sewell

T: 01768 371456

Open: All year, access by footpaths only from Newbiggin-on-Lune or Smardale. Path along former railway.

P Spaces: 8. Parking at Smardale.

Wheelchair access from Smardale only. No WC for the disabled. Guide Dogs allowed.

£ No.

ST ANNE'S HOSPITAL

Boroughgate, Appleby, Cumbria

17th century almshouses. There are 13 dwellings and a chapel set round a cobbled courtyard. Founded by Lady Anne Clifford in 1653.

Grant Recipient: The Trustees of St Anne's Hospital

Access Contact: Lord Hothfield

T: 017683 51487   **F:** 017683 53259

E-mail: lulieant@aol.com

Open: All year: daily 9am - 5pm.

P Spaces: 50. On-street parking.

No wheelchair access or WC for the disabled. Guide Dogs allowed.

£ No.

WRAY CASTLE

Low Wray, Ambleside, Cumbria

A large Gothic mock castle and arboretum. Built in the 1840s over looking the western shore of Lake Windermere.

www.nationaltrust.org.uk

Grant Recipient: The National Trust

Access Contact: Property Manager

T: 015394 36269   **F:** 015394 36811

E-mail: Hawkshead@nationaltrust.org.uk

Open: Castle (entrance hall only): by arrangement. Further public access under review at time of publication, please check the English Heritage website or with the access contact for current information. Garden and grounds all year.

Telephone the property manager for further details (tel: 015394 36269).

P Spaces: 20.   No access.   £ No.

DERBYSHIRE

ASSEMBLY ROOMS

The Crescent, Buxton, Derbyshire SK17 6BH

The Crescent was designed by John Carr of York and built by the Fifth Duke of Devonshire between 1780-89. It provided hotels, lodgings and a suite of elaborately decorated Assembly Rooms. The front elevation of three storeys is dominated by Doric pilasters over a continuous rusticated ground floor arcade.

Grant Recipient: Derbyshire County Council

Access Contact: Mr Allan Morrison

T: 01629 533190   **F:** 01629 533143

E-mail: allan.morrison@derbyshire.gov.uk

Open: Exterior accessible from public highway. No interior access until refurbishment works completed, other than special agreement.

P On-street pay and display parking.   No access.   £ No.

BARLBOROUGH HALL

Barlborough, Chesterfield, Derbyshire S43 4TL

Built by Sir Francis Rhodes in the 1580s, the Hall is square in plan and stands on a high basement with a small internal courtyard to provide light. Contains Great Chamber, now a chapel, bearing a date of 1584 on the overmantel whilst the porch is dated 1583. Now a private school.

Grant Recipient: The Governors of Barlborough Hall School

Access Contact: Mr C F A Bogie

T: 01246 435138   **F:** 01246 435090

Open: By arrangement only 29 Mar - 11 Apr, 31 May - 5 June, 4 July - 3 Sept and most weekends all year. External visits (without guide) after 6pm or weekends.

P Spaces: 50.

No wheelchair access or WC for the disabled. Guide Dogs allowed.

£ No.

BENNERLEY VIADUCT

Erewash Valley, Ilkeston, Derbyshire

Disused railway viaduct over the Erewash valley, c1878-9, and approximately 500 yards long with 15 piers. It is one of two remaining wrought iron lattice-girder bridges in the British Isles.

Grant Recipient: Railway Paths Ltd

Access Contact: Mr Simon Ballantine

T: 01548 550 331   **F:** 01548 550 331

E-mail: simonb@sustrans.org.uk

Open: Access to the viaduct by a public footpath running underneath it, but the deck itself is inaccessible.

P No.   No access.   £ No.

CALKE ABBEY

Ticknall, Derbyshire DE73 1LE

Baroque mansion, built 1701-3 for Sir John Harpur and set in a landscaped park. Little restored, Calke is preserved by a programme of conservation as a graphic illustration of the English house in decline. It contains the natural history collection of the Harpur Crewe family, an 18th century state bed and interiors that are essentially unchanged since the 1880s.

www.nationaltrust.org.uk

Grant Recipient: The National Trust

Access Contact: Property Manager

T: 01332 863822   **F:** 01332 865272

E-mail: calkeabbey@nationaltrust.org.uk

Open: House: 18 Mar - 29 Oct: daily except Thurs & Fri 12.30 - 5pm (ticket office opens 11am). Garden & Church: 18 Mar - 29 Oct: daily except Thurs & Fri 11am - 5pm, 29 June - 1 Sept: daily 11am - 5pm. Park: most days until 8pm or dusk if earlier. Timed ticket system. All visitors (inc NT members) require a ticket.

P Spaces: 75.

Wheelchair access to ground floor of house, stables, shop and restaurant. Garden and park partly accessible. WC for the disabled. Guide Dogs allowed.

£ Adult: £6.80, £4.20 (garden only).   Child: £3.40, £2.10 (garden only).   Family: £17, £10.50 (garden only).

CATTON HALL,

Catton, Walton-on-Trent, Derbyshire DE12 8LN

Country house built c1741 by Smith of Warwick for Christopher Horton. Property owned by the same family since 1405. Contains an interesting collection of 17th and 18th century pictures, including Royal and Family portraits; also Byron and Napoleon memorabilia. Gardens, which run down to the River Trent, include a family chapel.

www.catton-hall.com

Grant Recipient: Mr R Neilson

Access Contact: Mrs C Neilson

T: 01283 716311   **F:** 01283 712876

E-mail: kneilson@catton-hall.com

Open: 3 Apr - 9 Oct: including tour of the house, chapel and gardens every Mon at 2pm. Group tours (15+) at any time by arrangement.

P Unlimited parking.

Wheelchair access by separate entrance to all rooms. No WC for the disabled. Guide Dogs allowed.

£ Adult: £4.   Conc: £3.

CROMFORD MILL

Mill Lane, Cromford, nr. Matlock, Derbyshire DE4 3RQ

Grade 1 listed mill complex established by Sir Richard Arkwright in 1771. The world's first successful water powered cotton spinning mill situated in the Derwent Valley Mills World Heritage Site. Currently being conserved by the Arkwright Society, an educational charity. The Mill is permanently home to five shops and a restaurant.

www.arkwrightsociety.org.uk

Grant Recipient: The Arkwright Society

Access Contact: Mr Jon Charlton

T: 01629 823256   **F:** 01629 824297

E-mail: dburridge@arkwrightsociety.org.uk

Open: Daily 9am - 5pm, closed Christmas Day. Free entry to main site, charges for guided tours.

P Spaces: 100.

Wheelchair access to shops, WCs and restaurant only. Guide Dogs allowed.

£ Guided tours: Adult: £2.   Child: £1.50.   Other: £1.50.

HARDWICK HALL

Doe Lea, Chesterfield, Derbyshire S44 5QJ

A late 16th century 'prodigy house' designed by Robert Smythson for Bess of Hardwick. Contains an outstanding collection of 16th century furniture, tapestries and needlework. Walled courtyards enclose gardens, orchards and herb garden.

www.nationaltrust.org.uk

Grant Recipient: The National Trust

Access Contact: Property Manager

T: 01246 850430   **F:** 01246 854200

E-mail: hardwickhall@nationaltrust.org.uk

Open: 25 Mar - 29 Oct: daily. except Mon, Tues & Fri (but open BH Mons & Good Fri) 12 noon - 4.30pm. Garden: Wed - Sun 11am - 5.30pm. Parkland: daily. 8am - 6pm (closes at dusk in winter).

P Spaces: 200.

Partial wheelchair access. WC for the disabled. Guide Dogs allowed.

£ Adult: £7.80, £4 (garden only). Child: £3.90, £2 (garden only). Family: £19.50, £4 (garden only). Joint ticket with Hardwick Old Hall, EH property £10.60.

KEDLESTON HALL

Derby, Derbyshire DE22 5JH

A classical Palladian mansion built 1759-65 for the Curzon family and little altered since. Robert Adam interior with state rooms retaining their collection of paintings and original furniture. The Eastern museum houses a range of objects collected by Lord Curzon when Viceroy of India (1899-1905). Set in 800 acres of parkland and 18th century pleasure ground, garden and woodland walks.

www.nationaltrust.org.uk

Grant Recipient: The National Trust

Access Contact: Property Manager

T: 01332 842191   **F:** 01332 841972

E-mail: kedlestonhall@nationaltrust.org.uk

Open: Hall: 11 Mar - 29 Oct: daily except Thurs & Fri 12 noon - 4.30pm. Garden: 11 Mar - 29 Oct: daily, 10am - 6pm. Park: all year (restrictions may apply in Dec & Jan 2007); 11 Mar - 29 Oct 10am - 6pm; 30 Oct - 4 Mar 2007 10am - 4pm.

P Winter admission for park only, parking charge of £2.70.
Wheelchair access to ground floor of house via stairclimber, garden, restaurant and shop. WC for the disabled. Guide Dogs allowed.
£ Adult: £6.90, £3.10 (park & garden only). Child: £3.30, £1.55 (park & garden only). Family: £15.50, £7.70 (park & garden only).

MASSON MILLS (SIR RICHARD ARKWRIGHT'S)

Derby Road, Matlock Bath, Derbyshire DE4 3PY
Sir Richard Arkwright's 1783 showpiece Masson Mills are the finest surviving example of one of Arkwright's cotton mills. The "Masson Mill pattern" of design was an important influence in nascent British and American mill development. Museum with historic working textile machinery. Part of the Derwent Valley Mills World Heritage Site.
www.massonmills.co.uk
Grant Recipient: Mara Securities Ltd
Access Contact: Museum Reception
T: 01629 581001   **F:** 01629 581001
Open: All year except Christmas Day & Easter Day: Mon - Fri 10am - 4pm, Sat 11am - 5pm & Sun 11am - 4pm.
P Spaces: 200.
Wheelchair access to most areas. WC for the disabled. No Guide Dogs.
£ Adult: £2.50. Child: £1.50. Conc: £2. School groups £1 per child.

NORTH LEES HALL

Birley Lane, Outseats, Hathersage, Derbyshire S30 1BR
Tower House built c1590 in the Peak District National Park and designed by the architect Robert Smythson. The Hall's tenants were the Eyre family. They were visited by Charlotte Bronte who is thought to have based Thornfield Hall on North Lees Hall.
www.vivat.org.uk
Grant Recipient: Ms Frances Lloyd The Vivat Trust
Access Contact: Miss Lisa Simm
T: 0845 090 2212   **F:** 0845 090 0174
E-mail: enquiries@vivat.org.uk
Open: Heritage Open Days in Sept 10am - 5pm. Other times by arrangement with Miss Lisa Simm. The Vivat Trust, 70 Cowcross Street, London, EC1M 6EJ.
P Spaces: 7.
Wheelchair access to ground floor rooms by arrangement. No WC for the disabled. Guide Dogs allowed.
£ No.

ST ANN'S HOTEL

The Crescent, Buxton, Derbyshire SK17 6BH
The Crescent was designed by John Carr of York and built by the Fifth Duke of Devonshire between 1780-89. It provided hotels, lodgings and a suite of elaborately decorated Assembly Rooms. The front elevation of three storeys is dominated by Doric pilasters over a continuous rusticated ground floor arcade.
Grant Recipient: High Peak Borough Council
Access Contact: Mr Richard Tuffrey
T: 01457 851653   **F:** 01457 860290
E-mail: richard.tuffrey@highpeak.gov.uk
Open: Exterior accessible from public highway. No interior access until refurbishment works completed.
P On-street parking available.   No access.   £ No.

SUDBURY HALL

Sudbury, Ashbourne, Derbyshire DE6 5HT
17th century house with rich interior decoration including wood carvings by Laguerre. The Great Staircase (c1676) with white-painted balustrade with luxuriantly carved foliage by Edward Pierce, is one of the finest staircases of its date in an English house. 19th century service wing houses the National Trust Museum of Childhood.
www.nationaltrust.org.uk
Grant Recipient: The National Trust
Access Contact: Property Manager
T: 01283 585305   **F:** 01283 585139
E-mail: sudburyhall@nationaltrust.org.uk
Open: Hall and Museum: 11 Mar - 29 Oct: Wed - Sun (but open BH Mons & Good Fri) 1 - 5pm. Grounds: as House to 29 Oct 11am - 6pm.
P Spaces: 100. Car park is a short distance from the Hall; six-seater volunteer driven buggy available.
Wheelchair access to lake, tea room and shop. Ground floor access to museum. Access to Hall difficult – please

contact the Property Manager in advance. WC for the disabled. Guide Dogs allowed.
£ Adult: £5.50, £6.50 (peak/off peak) (house & garden), £6, £7 (museum), £10, £12 (hall & museum) £1 (garden only). Child: £2.50, £3 (peak/off peak) (house & garden), £4, £4.50 (museum), £5.50, £6.50 (hall & museum) 50p (garden only). Other: £13, £16 (peak/off peak). Family: £16 (house & garden), £18.50 (museum), £25, £27 (hall & museum); £2.50 (garden only).

TISSINGTON HALL

Tissington, Ashbourne, Derbyshire DE6 1RA
Grade II* listed Jacobean manor house altered in the 18th century and extended in the 20th. Contains fine furniture, pictures and interesting early 17th century panelling. Home of the FitzHerbert family for over 500 years.
www.tissington-hall.com
Grant Recipient: Sir Richard FitzHerbert Bt
Access Contact: Sir Richard FitzHerbert Bt
T: 01335 352200   **F:** 01335 352201
E-mail: tisshall@dircon.co.uk
Open: 17 Apr - 21 Apr, 29 May - 2 June and 25 July - 25 Aug inc: Tues - Fri 1.30 - 4pm. Heritage Open Days.
P Spaces: 100.
Wheelchair access to gardens and various rooms. Guide Dogs by arrangement. WC for the disabled.
£ Adult: £6.50 (house & garden), £3 (garden). Child: £3.50 age 10-16 (house & garden), £1 (garden). Other: £5 (house & garden), £3 (garden).

DEVON

21 THE MINT

Exeter, Devon EX4 3BL
The refectory range of St Nicholas Priory, converted into a substantial town house in the Elizabethan period and later into tenements. Features include medieval arch-braced roof, traces of the Norman priory and later Elizabethan panelling. Recently restored, now dwellings and meeting room.
Grant Recipient: Exeter Historic Buildings Trust
Access Contact: Ms Katharine Chant
T: 01392 436000 / 496653   **F:** 01392 496653
E-mail: the-chants@tiscali.co.uk
Open: Every Mon all year 2 - 4pm (except BHs). Also Spring BH (27 - 29 May), Festival of Exeter weekend in July and Heritage Open Days 11am - 4pm. Redcoat guided tour 'Catacomb and The Mint' starting from Cathedral Close, Mar - Oct every Wed 2pm.
P No.
Wheelchair access to ground floor and courtyard garden only. No WC for the disabled. Guide Dogs allowed.
£ Meeting room available for hire.

ANDERTON HOUSE/RIGG SIDE

Goodleigh, North Devon, Devon
Anderton House also known as Rigg Side. 1970-1 to the designs of Peter Aldington and John Craig for Mr and Mrs Anderton. The inspiration for its profile is taken from the longhouses of Devon. Timber frame, forming a two-row grid of double posts and beams with a tent roof, set half proud of concrete block walls and glazed clerestory and stained tiled gabled roof. Timber linings and ceilings internally, with tiled floors. Its sliding doors give views of the Devon countryside.
www.landmarktrust.org.uk
Grant Recipient: The Landmark Trust
Access Contact: Mrs Victoria O'Keeffe
T: 01628 825920   **F:** 01628 825417
E-mail: vokeeffe@landmarktrust.org.uk
Open: The Landmark Trust is an independent charity, which rescues small buildings of historic or architectural importance from decay or unsympathetic improvement. Landmark's aim is to promote the enjoyment of these historic buildings by making them available to stay in for holidays. Anderton House can be rented by anyone, at all times of the year, for periods ranging from a weekend to three weeks. Bookings can be made by telephoning the Booking Office on 01628 825925. As the building is in full-time use for holiday accommodation, it is not normally open to the public. However the public can view the building by arrangement by telephoning the access contact (Victoria O'Keeffe on 01628 825920) to make an appointment. Potential visitors will be asked to write to confirm the details of their visit. Heritage Open Days.
P At local playing fields.

Wheelchair access to kitchen, bedrooms and dining room. No WC for the disabled. Guide Dogs allowed.
£ No.

AYSHFORD CHAPEL

Ayshford, Burlescombe, Devon
Grade I listed private medieval chapel with a simple medieval screen. Distinctive stained glass of 1848 and 17th century monuments to the Ashford family.
www.friendsoffriendlesschurches.org.uk
Grant Recipient: Friends of Friendless Churches
Access Contact: Mr & Mrs Kelland
T: 01884 820271
Open: At any reasonable time. Keyholder lives nearby. Heritage Open Days.
P Spaces: 2. On-street parking.
Wheelchair access with help, through field and up one step.

BROOMHAM FARM

King's Nympton, Devon EX37 9TS
Late medieval Grade II* listed Devon long-house of stone and cob construction with thatched roof. Contains a smoking room. Currently undergoing renovation.
Grant Recipient: Mr Clements
Access contact: Miss J Clements
T: 01769 572322
Open: By telephone arrangement. Heritage Open Days: No
P Spaces: 3.
No wheelchair access. Guide dogs not allowed.
£ No.

COLDHARBOUR MILL

Uffculme, Devon EX15 3EE
Woollen mill built by Thomas Fox between 1797-1799. Grade II* listed building. Now a working textile mill museum with demonstrations of textile machinery. Exhibition gallery, picnic area, café, waterside walks and shop.
www.coldharbourmill.org.uk
Grant Recipient: The Coldharbour Mill Trust
Access Contact: Mr Ashley Smart
T: 01884 840960   **F:** 01884 840858
E-mail: info@coldharbourmill.org.uk
Open: Mar - Oct: daily, 10.30am - 5.30pm. Nov - Feb: please telephone for opening times.
P Spaces: 100.
Wheelchair access to the mill via lift. Café not accessible but planning to relocate. WC for the disabled. Guide Dogs allowed.
£ Adult: £5.95. Child: £2.95. Family: £16.

COOKWORTHY MUSEUM OF RURAL LIFE IN SOUTH DEVON

The Old Grammar School, 108 Fore Street, Kingsbridge, Devon TQ7 1AW
17th century schoolroom with 19th century annex in Tudor style. Original entrance arch. Now a local museum with Victorian kitchen, Edwardian pharmacy and walled garden.
www.devonmuseums.net
Grant Recipient: William Cookworthy Museum Society
Access Contact: Miss Margaret Lorenz
T: 01548 853235
E-mail: wcookworthy@talk21.com
Open: 3 Apr - 28 Oct: Mon - Sat 10.30am - 5pm (Oct 10.30am - 4pm). Pre-booked groups all year (contact Mr Clifford Peach at the Cookworthy Museum). Local History Resource Centre open all year.
P Spaces: 100. Public car park on Fore Street, 100 metres from Museum.
Wheelchair access with assistance to Victorian kitchen and scullery, Farm Gallery, walled garden, shop and Local Heritage Resource Centre. Ground floor viewing gallery with 'Virtual Museum Tour' DVD. WC for the disabled. Guide Dogs allowed.
£ Adult: £2. Child: £1. Senior: £1.50. Family £5.

DARTINGTON HALL

Dartington, Totnes, Devon TQ9 6EL
Medieval mansion and courtyard built 1388-1399 by John Holland, Earl of Huntingdon and later Duke of Exeter, half brother to Richard II. Set in a landscaped garden and surrounded by a 1200 acre estate. The Champernowne family owned Dartington for 400 years before selling the estate to Leonard and Dorothy Elmhirst who founded the

Dartington Hall Trust.
www.dartingtonhall.org.uk
Grant Recipient: The Dartington Hall Trust
Access Contact: Mrs K Hockings
T: 01803 847002 **F:** 01803 847007
E-mail: trust@dartingtonhall.org.uk
Open: All year for courses, events and activities. The Hall, courtyard and gardens are accessible for external viewing all year. Access to the interior by arrangement. Coach parties by arrangement.
P Spaces: 250.
Wheelchair access to Great Hall, courtyard and top garden paths. WC for the disabled. Guide Dogs allowed.
£ Some activities have an entry fee.

EXETER CUSTOM HOUSE

The Quay, Exeter, Devon EX1 1NN
Located on the historic quayside, the Custom House was constructed in 1680-1 and is the earliest purpose-built customs house in Britain. Contains many original fittings and three exceptionally ornamental plaster ceilings by John Abbot of Frithelstock (amongst the finest such work of this date in the south west).
www.exeter.gov.uk/visiting/attractions
Grant Recipient: Exeter City Council
Access Contact: Tourism Promotions Officer
T: 01392 265136 **F:** 01392 265695
E-mail: guidedtours@exeter.gov.uk
Open: Daily (except 25 & 26 Dec): tours mornings, afternoons and some evenings. Please call for times of tours (01392 265136). Heritage Open Days.
P Spaces: 400. Cathedral and Quay car park (75 metres). 5 public spaces for the disabled in front of Custom House.
Wheelchair access to ground floor stair area only. WC for the disabled in car park. No Guide Dogs.
£ No.

FINCH FOUNDRY

Sticklepath, Okehampton, Devon EX20 2NW
19th century water-powered forge, which produced agricultural and mining hand tools. Still in working order with regular demonstrations. The foundry has three water-wheels driving the huge tilt hammer and grindstone.
www.nationaltrust.org.uk
Grant Recipient: The National Trust
Access Contact: Mr Roger Boney
T: 01837 840046 **F:** 01837 840046
E-mail: rboney@nationaltrust.org.uk
Open: 25 Mar - 29 Oct: daily except Tues 11am - 5.30pm (last adm. 5pm). Tea room/shop as Foundry.
P Spaces: 50. Access to car park is narrow and unsuitable for coaches and wide vehicles.
Wheelchair access to museum and workshop is difficult, Foundry can be viewed through shop window. No WC for the disabled. Guide Dogs allowed.
£ Adult: £3.70. Child: £1.85.

KILWORTHY FARM COW HOUSES & GRANARY

Tavistock Hamlets, Devon PL9 0JN
Kilworthy Farm was part of the Duke of Bedford's Devon estates. The farm buildings, dated 1851, consist of three parallel ranges of cowhouses situated over an undercroft of granite construction. A two storey granary adjoins the cowhouses to the east and a stableyard of single storey buildings lies separately to the west. An unusually large and complete example of a planned farmyard covering all functions of the farm for dairy and arable. The cowhouses with underground dung pit are of exceptional interest.
Grant Recipient: Mesdames Coren, Dennis & Edworthy
Access Contact: Mrs Sandra Vallance
T: 01822 614477/ 07792645589 **F:** 01822 614477
Open: 25 July - 20 Aug: daily except Suns, and Thurs during Aug; Easter Sat & Easter Mon, May & Aug BH weekends. Other times by arrangement with Mr & Mrs A Vallance 10am - 5pm. Guided tour start at 11am & 2pm or by special arrangement. Heritage Open Days.
P Spaces: 4. Please ensure access for farm traffic is not obstructed.
Wheelchair access to the ground floor of the granary and the lengthwise walkways of the cowhouses. The undercroft is cobbled and the central passages are passable but rough. Guide dogs are welcome but as a working farm care is requested. No WC for the disabled.
£ Adult £3 (includes leaflet & guided tour). Child £1 (under 10).

LAWRENCE CASTLE HALDON BELVEDERE

Higher Ashton, nr. Dunchideock, Exeter, Devon EX6 7QY
Grade II* listed building built in 1788 as the centrepiece to a 11,600 acre estate. Stands 244 metres above sea level overlooking the cathedral city of Exeter, the Exe estuary and the surrounding countryside. Contains a spiral staircase and miniature ballroom.
www.haldonbelvedere.co.uk
Grant Recipient: Devon Historic Buildings Trust
Access Contact: Mr Ian Turner
T: 01392 833668 **F:** 01392 833668
E-mail: turner@haldonbelvedere.co.uk
Open: Feb - 29 Oct: Suns & BHs 1.30 - 5.30pm. Other times by arrangement. Grounds open all year.
P Spaces: 15. Parking for the disabled adjacent to building.
Wheelchair areas to ground floor only. WC for the disabled. Guide Dogs allowed.
£ Adult: £2. Child: Free. Free for wheelchair bound visitors.

LYNTON TOWN HALL

Lee Road, Lynton, Devon EX35 6HT
Grade II* listed Town Hall. Cornerstone laid 1898, opened by the donor Sir George Newnes, 15 Aug 1900. Neo-Tudor design with Art Nouveau details. In use as Town Hall and community facility.
www.lyntonandlynmouth.org.uk/towncouncil
Grant Recipient: Lynton & Lynmouth Town Council
Access Contact: Mr Dwyer
T: 01598 752384 **F:** 01598 752677
E-mail: ltc@northdevon.gov.uk
Open: Mon - Fri 9.30 - 11am. Other times by arrangement.
P No.
Partial wheelchair access. No WC for the disabled. Guide Dogs allowed.
£ No.

OLD QUAY HEAD

The Quay, Ilfracombe, Devon EX34 9EQ
Grade II* listed quay originally constructed early in the 16th century by William Bourchier, Lord Fitzwarren. The Quay was paved with stone in the 18th century and extended further in the 19th. This extension is marked by a commemorative stone plaque at its southern end. The Quay separates the inner harbour basin from the outer harbour.
Grant Recipient: North Devon District Council
Access Contact: Lieutenant Commander R Lawson
T: 01271 862108 **F:** 01271 862 108
E-mail: harbour_master@northdevon.gov.uk
Open: At all times.
P Spaces: 144. Charges apply from Mar - Oct. Disabled parking available.
Full wheelchair access. WCs for the disabled immediately adjacent to the Old Quay Head. Guide Dogs allowed.
£ No.

SALEM CHAPEL

East Budleigh, Budleigh Salterton, Devon EX9 7EF
Dating from 1719, built as a Presbyterian Chapel which later became congregational. Three galleries added later in 1836 when the façade was re-designed.
www.hct.org.uk
Grant Recipient: Historic Chapels Trust
Access Contact: Ms Kathy Moyle
T: 01395 445 236
Open: At any reasonable time by arrangement with the key holder, Kathy Moyle, 4 Collins Park, East Budleigh, Budleigh Salterton, Devon EX9 7EG.
P 2 spaces for the disabled. Public parking close by.
Wheelchair access to ground floor only. WC for the disabled. Guide Dogs allowed.
£ Donations invited.

SALTRAM HOUSE

Plympton, Plymouth, Devon PL7 1UH
A remarkable survival of a George II mansion, complete with its original contents and set in a landscaped park. Robert Adam worked here on two occasions to create the state rooms and produced what are claimed to be the finest such rooms in Devon. These show his development as a designer, from using the conventional Rococo, to the low-relief kind of Neo-Classical detail that became his hallmark and with which he broke new ground in interior design.
www.nationaltrust.org.uk
Grant Recipient: The National Trust
Access Contact: Carol Murrin
T: 01752 333500 **F:** 01752 336474
E-mail: saltram@nationaltrust.org.uk
Open: House: 25 Mar - 29 Oct daily except Fri (but open Good Fri) 12 noon - 4.30pm. Garden: 1 Mar - 29 Oct daily except Fri (but open Good Fri) 11am - 4.30pm. 30 Oct - 28 Feb daily except Fri 11am - 4pm.
P Spaces: 250. 500 metres from house, 30 marked spaces on tarmac, remainder on grass.
Wheelchair access to first floor via lift (66cm wide by 86.5cm deep), restaurant, tearoom, ticket offices over cobbles. Wheelchairs available. WC for the disabled. Guide Dogs allowed.
£ Adult: £8 (house & garden), £4 (garden only). Child: £4 (house & garden), £2 (garden only). Under 5s Free. Other: £12 (family: 1 adult), £20 (family: 2 adults). £6.50 (groups 15+).

SMEATON'S TOWER

The Hoe, Plymouth, Devon PL1 2NZ
Re-sited upper part of the former Eddystone Lighthouse. Built 1759 by John Smeaton, erected here on new base in 1882. Circular tapered tower of painted granite with octagonal lantern. When this lighthouse was first constructed it was considered to be an important technical achievement.
www.plymouthdome.info
Grant Recipient: Plymouth City Museum & Art Gallery
Access Contact: Mr Andrew Gater
T: 01752 304386 **F:** 01752 256361
E-mail: andrew.gater@plymouth.gov.uk
Open: Easter - end Oct: daily 10am - 4pm. Nov - Easter: Tues - Sat 10am - 3pm. Heritage Open Days.
P Spaces: 40. On-street parking.
No access.
£ Adult: £2.25. Child: £1.25.

SOUTH MOLTON TOWN HALL AND PANNIER MARKET

South Molton, Devon EX36 3AB
Guild Hall, dating from 1743 and Grade I listed. Incorporates Court Room, Old Assembly Room and Mayors Parlour with Museum on ground floor. Adjacent to Pannier Market and New Assembly Room.
Grant Recipient: South Molton Town Council
Access Contact: Mr Malcolm Gingell
T: 01769 572501 **F:** 01769 574008
E-mail: smtc@northdevon.gov.uk
Open: Museum open Mar - Oct: Mon, Tues, Thurs and Sat. All other rooms used for meetings, functions etc as and when required. Constable Room rented by Devon County Council.
P In Pannier Market except Thurs & Sats.
Wheelchair access to all areas except Court Room, Mayor's Parlour and Old Assembly Room. WC for the disabled. Guide Dogs allowed.
£ No.

UGBROOKE PARK

Chudleigh, Devon TQ13 0AD
House and chapel built c1200 and redesigned by Robert Adam in the 1760s for the 4th Lord Clifford. Chapel and library wing in Adam's characteristic castle style. Set in 'Capability' Brown landscaped park with lakes and 18th century Orangery. Home of the Lords Clifford of Chudleigh for 400 years.
www.ugbrooke.co.uk
Grant Recipient: Clifford Estate Company Ltd
Access Contact: Lord Clifford
T: 01626 852179 **F:** 01626 853322
E-mail: cliffordestate@btconnect.com
Open: 9 July - 14 Sept: Tues, Wed, Thurs, Sun and Aug Bank Holiday Mon 1 - 5.30pm. Group tours and private functions by arrangement.
P Spaces: 200.
Full wheelchair access. WC for the disabled. Guide Dogs allowed.
£ Adult: £5.50 (house & garden), £3 (garden). Child: £3 (house & garden), £2 (garden). Senior: £5 (house & garden).

DORSET

BLANDFORD FORUM TOWN HALL & CORN EXCHANGE

Market Place, Blandford Forum, Dorset DT1 7PY
The Town Hall built by the Bastard Brothers and completed in 1734, has a Portland stone facade. On the ground floor is a loggia with 3 semi-circular arches enclosed by iron gates. The former magistrates room and the mid 20th century Council Chamber sit at 1st floor level. Attached to the rear of the building is the Corn Exchange, built in 1858, with interesting elliptical roof-trusses.
www.blandford-tc.co.uk
Grant Recipient: Blandford Forum Town Council
Access Contact: The Town Clerk
T: 01258 454500   **F:** 01258 454432
E-mail: admin@blandford-tc.co.uk
Open: All year for markets, civic functions and other events. Other times by telephone arrangement with The Town Clerk, Mon - Fri 9.30am - 12.30pm. Heritage Open Days.
P Spaces: 20. On-street meter parking, except on market days (Thurs & Sats). Other parking is available in the town.
♿ Wheelchair access to ground floor only. WC for the disabled. Guide Dogs allowed.
£ No.

HIGHCLIFFE CASTLE

Rothesay Drive, Highcliffe-on-Sea, Christchurch, Dorset BH23 4LE
Cliff-top mansion built in the 1830s by Charles Stuart. Constructed in the romantic, picturesque style, much of its stonework is medieval coming from France. Exterior has been restored, interior houses changing exhibitions and the 16th century stained glass Jesse window. Gift shop and tea rooms on site with 14 acre cliff-top park.
www.highcliffecastle.co.uk
Grant Recipient: Christchurch Borough Council
Access Contact: Mr David Hopkins
T: 01425 278807   **F:** 01425 280423
E-mail: d.hopkins@christchurch.gov.uk
Open: 1 Feb - 23 Dec: daily 11am - 5pm. Also some evenings for special events. Tea rooms open all year 10am - late afternoon; grounds all year from 7am. Heritage Open Days.
P Spaces: 120. Charged parking in Council car park Apr - Sept (free Oct - Mar) with additional parking in Highcliffe Village (1 mile from Castle).
♿ No wheelchair access to the building. WC for the disabled. Guide Dogs allowed.
£ Adult: £2. Child: Free. Other: HHA/Season Ticket holders free.

THE CHANTRY

128 South Street, Bridport, Dorset DT6 3PA
14th or 15th century two-storey stone rubble house, originally situated on a promontory of the River Brit. At one time known as the "Prior's House", more probably the house of a chantry priest. Interesting internal details including fragments of 17th century domestic wall paintings.
www.vivat.org.uk
Grant Recipient: The Vivat Trust Ltd
Access Contact: Miss Lisa Simm
T: 0845 090 2212   **F:** 0845 090 0174
E-mail: enquiries@vivat.org.uk
Open: Heritage Open Days in Sept 10am - 5pm. At other times by arrangement with The Vivat Trust (tel: 0845 090 2212, fax: 0845 090 0174, email: enquiries@vivat.co.uk).
P Spaces: 1. Additional on-street parking.
♿ Wheelchair access with difficulty through back entrance to kitchen and sitting room on ground floor. No WC for the disabled. Guide Dogs allowed.
£ No.

EAST RIDING OF YORKSHIRE

CONSTABLE MAUSOLEUM

Halsham, Kingston-upon-Hull, East Riding of Yorkshire
The Constable Mausoleum was commissioned by Edward Constable in 1792, built by Atkinson and York and completed in 1802 at a cost of £3,300. It comprises a central domed rotunda of stone, internally lined with black marble and surrounded by heraldic shields. The external raised and railed podium is part of a vaulted ceiling to the crypt below, in which various generations of the Constable family are interred.

Grant Recipient: Mr John Chichester-Constable
Access Contact: Mr John Chichester-Constable
T: 01964 562316   **F:** 01964 563283
E-mail: info@burtonconstable.co.uk
Open: By written arrangement with Mr John Chichester-Constable, South Wing - Estate Office, Burton Constable Hall, nr Kingston-upon-Hull, East Riding of Yorkshire HU11 4LN.
P Spaces: 1. On street parking.
♿ No wheelchair access. WC for the disabled at Halsham Arms approximately 300 metres. No Guide Dogs.
£ No.

MAISTER HOUSE

160 High Street, Kingston-upon-Hull, East Riding of Yorkshire HU1 1NL
Rebuilt in 1743 during Hull's heyday as an affluent trading centre, this house is a typical but rare survivor of a contemporary merchant's residence. The restrained exterior belies the spectacular plasterwork staircase inside. The house is now let as offices.
www.nationaltrust.org.uk
Grant Recipient: The National Trust
Access Contact: Property Manager
T: 01482 324114/ 01723 870423   **F:** 01482 227003
Open: Daily except Sat & Sun (closed Good Fri & all BHs) 10am - 4pm. Access is to entrance hall and staircase only. Unsuitable for groups.
P No parking.
♿ No wheelchair access or WC for the disabled. Guide Dogs allowed.
£ Donations welcome.

STAMFORD BRIDGE VIADUCT

Stamford Bridge, East Riding of Yorkshire
Built 1847 for the York & North Midland Railway Company, East Riding lines. Mainly red brick with 10 unadorned round brick arches. The railway line was closed in the mid 1960s and is now repaired as part of a circular pedestrian walkway around the village.
Grant Recipient: East Riding of Yorkshire Council
Access Contact: Mr Chris Chatten
T: 01482 391678   **F:** 01482 391660
E-mail: chris.chatten@eastriding.gov.uk
Open: The site is permanently open as a footpath.
P Informal parking for approx. 20 cars near sports hall.
♿ Access to viaduct, but some large wheelchairs may be restricted. No WC for the disabled. Guide Dogs allowed.
£ No.

ESSEX

HARWICH REDOUBT FORT

behind 29 Main Road, Harwich, Essex CO12 3LT
180ft diameter circular fort commanding the harbour entrance built in 1808 to defend the port against a Napoleonic invasion. Surrounded by a dry moat, there are 11 guns on the battlements. 18 casements which originally sheltered 300 troops in siege conditions now house a series of small museums.
www.harwich-society.com
Grant Recipient: The Harwich Society
Access Contact: Mr A Rutter
T: 01255 503429   **F:** 01255 503429
E-mail: info@harwich-society.com
Open: 1 May - 31 Aug: daily 10am - 4pm. Rest of year: Suns only 10am - 4pm. Heritage Open Days.
P No.
♿ No wheelchair access or WC for the disabled. Guide Dogs allowed.
£ Adult: £1. Accompanied children free.

HYLANDS HOUSE

Hylands Park, London Road, Widford, Chelmsford, Essex CM2 8WQ
Grade II* listed building, surrounded by 600 acres of landscaped parkland, partly designed by Humphry Repton. Built c1730, the original house was a red brick Queen Anne style mansion, subsequent owners set about enlarging the property, which produced a neo-classical style house. Internal inspection of the house reveals its Georgian and Victorian features.
www.chelmsfordbc.gov.uk/hylands
Grant Recipient: Chelmsford Borough Council
Access Contact: Mrs Linda Palmer

T: 01245 605 500   **F:** 01245 605 510
E-mail: linda.palmer@chelmsfordbc.gov.uk
Open: All year: Suns and BHs (except Christmas Day) 11am - 6pm. Apr - end Sept: Mons 11am - 6pm. Oct - end Mar: Mons 11am - 4pm. Tea room: Suns throughout the year 11am - 4.30pm. Apr - end Sept: Mons 11am - 4.30pm. Oct - end Mar: Mons 11am - 4.30pm. Group visits by arrangement with Mrs Ceri Lowen, Assistant Hylands House Manager, Leisure Services, Chelmsford Borough Council, Civic Centre, Duke Street, Chelmsford, Essex CM1 1JE (tel:01245 496800). Also events programme.
P Spaces: 84. 4 spaces for the disabled, coaches by arrangement. Please note that during construction work this will be reduced with alternative parking nearby.
♿ Full wheelchair access. WC for the disabled. Guide Dogs allowed.
£ Adult: £3.30. Child: Free (under 16). Other: £2.30.

JOHN WEBB'S WINDMILL

Fishmarket Street, Thaxted, Essex CM6 2PG
Brick tower mill built in 1804 consisting of five floors. Has been fully restored as a working mill. On two floors there is a museum of rural and domestic bygones. There is also a small picture gallery of early photographs of the mill and the surrounding countryside.
Grant Recipient: Thaxted Parish Council
Access Contact: Mr L A Farren
T: 01371 830285   **F:** 01371 830285
Open: May - Sept: Sat - Sun & BHs 2 - 6pm. Groups during weekdays by special arrangement. For further information please contact Mr L A Farren, Borough Hill, Bolford Street, Thaxted, Essex CM6 2PY. Heritage Open Days.
P Spaces: 80. Public parking in Thaxted.
♿ Wheelchair access to ground floor only. WC for disabled in public car park in Margaret St. Guide Dogs allowed.
£ Donations welcome.

OLD FRIENDS MEETING HOUSE

High Street, Stebbing, Essex CM6 3SG
The Stebbing Meeting House is the earliest Quaker meeting House in Essex. Built c1674 it is a particularly fine and complete example of an early Quaker meeting house and its historical importance is recognised by its Grade II* listing.
Grant Recipient: The Trustees of the Old Friends Meeting House
Access Contact: Mr R T Guyer
T: 01371 856155   **E-mail:** clareguyer@aol.com
Open: By telephone or written arrangement with Mr R T Guyer, Fermoy Cottage, The Downs, Stebbing, Essex CM6 3RD (tel: 01371 856155). Heritage Open Days.
P Spaces: 10.
♿ Wheelchair access to ground floor. WC for the disabled. Guide Dogs allowed.
£ No.

THE GREAT DUNMOW MALTINGS

Mill Lane, Great Dunmow, Essex CM6 1BD
Grade II* maltings complex (listed as Boyes Croft Maltings, White Street), early 16th century and later, timber-framed and plastered, part weatherboarding and brick. The building exhibits the entire floor malting process whilst the Great Dunmow Museum Society occupies the ground floor with displays of local history. The first floor is available for community use.
www.greatdunmowmaltings.co.uk
Grant Recipient: Great Dunmow Maltings Preservation Trust
Access Contact: Mr David A Westcott
T: 01371 873958   **F:** 01371 873958
E-mail: david.westcott2@btinternet.com
Open: All year: Sat, Sun and BHs 11am - 4pm. Groups at any reasonable time by arrangement. Closed Christmas/New Year holiday week.
P Spaces: 100. Public car park nearby (pay and display, free on Suns and Bank Holidays).
♿ Full wheelchair access. WC for the disabled. Guide Dogs allowed.
£ Adult: £1. Child/Senior: 50p.

VALENTINES MANSION

Emerson Road, Ilford, Essex IG1 4XA
Valentines Mansion is a late 17th century house, largely Georgian in appearance with Regency additions. Of particular interest is the unusual curved early 19th century porte cochere. The exterior was extensively repaired and restored in 2000.

www.valentinesmansion.org.uk
Grant Recipient: London Borough of Redbridge
Access Contact: Mr Nigel Burch
T: 020 8708 3619   **F:** 020 8708 3178
E-mail: nigel.burch@redbridge.gov.uk
Open: 20 May for annual May Fair and for London Open House weekend in Sept. At other times by arrangement with Nigel Burch, Chief Leisure Officer, London Borough of Redbridge, Lynton House, 255/259 High Road, Ilford, Essex IG1 1NY (tel:020 8708 3619).
P On-street parking, Emerson Road, Tillotson Road, Bethell Avenue and Holcombe Road.
Wheelchair access to ground floor only. No WC for the disabled. Guide Dogs allowed.
£ No.

GLOUCESTERSHIRE

ACTON COURT
Latteridge Road, Iron Acton,
South Gloucestershire BS37 9TJ
Seat of the Poyntzes, an influential courtier family who occupied the house until 1680 when it was converted into a farm house. A Tudor range, constructed in 1535 to accommodate King Henry VIII and Queen Anne Boleyn survives along with part of the North range. The rooms are unfurnished but contain important traces of original decoration.
www.actoncourt.com
Grant Recipient: Rosehill Corporation
Access Contact: Ms Lisa Kopper
T: 01454 228224   **F:** 01454 227256
E-mail: actonct@dircon.co.uk or info@actoncourt.com
Open: Guided tours and events 13 June - 20 Aug. Closed Mons. Pre-booking essential. Ring information line for details 01454 228 224.
P Spaces: 40.
Wheelchair access to ground floor only. WC for the disabled. Guide Dogs allowed.
£ Adult: £5.50. Child: £4. Seniors & the disabled: £4. Exclusive groups tours (max 25) £100. Special events priced separately.

CHASTLETON HOUSE
Chastleton, Moreton-in-Marsh, Glos GL56 0SU
Jacobean house filled with a mixture of rare and everyday objects, furniture and textiles collected since 1612. Continually occupied for 400 years by the same family. Emphasis lies on conservation rather than restoration.
www.nationaltrust.org.uk
Grant Recipient: The National Trust
Access Contact: The Custodian
T: 01608 674355   **F:** 01608 674355
E-mail: chastleton@nationaltrust.org.uk
Open: 29 Mar - 30 Sept: Wed - Sat 1 - 5pm (last adm. 4pm). 4 Oct - 28 Oct: Wed - Sat 1 - 4pm (last adm. 3pm). Visitor numbers limited, pre-booking advised. Groups by written arrangement with the Custodian.
P Spaces: 50.
Wheelchair access to ground floor with assistance and parts of garden only. WC for the disabled. Guide Dogs allowed.
£ Adult: £6.50. Child: £3.30. Family: £16.30. Private View £7.50. NT Members £2.50.

CHAVENAGE
Tetbury, Gloucestershire GL8 8XP
Elizabethan Manor House (c1576), contains tapestry rooms, furniture and relics from the Cromwellian Period. Has been the home of only two families since the time of Elizabeth I. Used as a location for television and film productions.
www.chavenage.com
Grant Recipient: Trustees of the Chavenage Settlement
Access Contact: Miss Caroline Lowsley-Williams
T: 01666 502329   **F:** 01453 836778
E-mail: info@chavenage.com
Open: May - Sept: Thurs, Sun & BHs plus Easter Sun & Mon 2 - 5pm. Groups at other times by arrangement. Heritage Open Days.
P Spaces: 40.
Wheelchair access to ground floor only. Parking for the disabled by front door. WC for the disabled. Guide Dogs allowed.
£ Adult: £6. Child: £3

DYRHAM PARK
Dyrham, nr. Chippenham, Gloucestershire SN14 8ER
17th century house set within an ancient deer park, woodlands and formal garden. The house was furnished in the Dutch style and still has many original contents including paintings, ceramics, furniture and 17th century tapestries. The Victorian domestic rooms include the kitchen, larder, bakehouse, dairy and tenants' hall.
www.nationaltrust.org.uk
Grant Recipient: The National Trust
Access Contact: Visitor Services Manager
T: 01179 372501   **F:** 01179 371353
E-mail: dyrhampark@nationaltrust.org.uk
Open: House: 24 Mar - 29 Oct, daily except Wed & Thurs 12 noon 4pm (last adm. to house 3.15pm). Garden: as for house 11am - 5pm or dusk if earlier. Park: all year (closed 25 Dec) 11am - 5pm or dusk if earlier. BH Mons & Good Fri 11am - 5pm.
P Spaces: 250. Free shuttle bus from car park to house.
Wheelchair access to all but four upstairs rooms. A photograph album of these rooms is available. WC for the disabled. Guide Dogs allowed.
£ Adult: £8.80, £3.40 (grounds only), £2.25 (park only when house & garden closed). Child: £4.35, £1.70 (grounds only), £1.10 (park only when house & garden closed). Family: £21.75 (house & grounds), £7.75 (grounds only).

EAST BANQUETING HOUSE
Calf Lane, Chipping Campden, Gloucestershire
The East Banqueting House stands opposite the West Banqueting House across a broad terrace that ran in front of Sir Baptist Hick's mansion, which was deliberately destroyed by the Royalists in 1645 only 30 years after it had been built. It is elaborately decorated with spiral chimney stacks, finials and ebullient strapwork parapets. Steep staircases.
www.landmarktrust.org.uk
Grant Recipient: The Landmark Trust
Access Contact: Mrs Victoria O'Keeffe
T: 01628 825920   **F:** 01628 825417
E-mail: vokeeffe@landmarktrust.org.uk
Open: The Landmark Trust is an independent charity, which rescues small buildings of historic or architectural importance from decay or unsympathetic improvement. Landmark's aim is to promote the enjoyment of these historic buildings by making them available to stay in for holidays. East Banqueting House can be rented by anyone, at all times of the year, for periods ranging from a weekend to three weeks. Bookings can be made by telephoning the Booking Office on 01628 825925. The public can also view the building on eight Open Days throughout the year (dates to be set) or by arrangement; telephone the access contact Victoria O'Keeffe on 01628 825920 to make an appointment. Potential visitors will be asked to write to confirm the details of their visit. Heritage Open Days.
P Parking available in town only.
No wheelchair access or WC for the disabled. Guide Dogs allowed.
£ No.

EBLEY MILL
Westward Road, Stroud, Gloucestershire GL5 4UB
19th century riverside textile mill, now restored and converted into offices occupied by Stroud District Council. Has Gothic-style clock tower and block designed by George Bodley.
www.stroud.gov.uk
Grant Recipient: Stroud District Council
Access Contact: Mr D Marshall
T: 01453 754646   **F:** 01453 754942
E-mail: information@stroud.gov.uk
Open: Mon - Thurs 8.45am - 5pm; Fris 8.45am - 4.30pm. Closed BHs. Tours by arrangement. Heritage Open Days.
P Spaces: 30.
Full wheelchair access. WC for the disabled. Guide Dogs allowed.
£ No.

ELMORE COURT ENTRANCE GATES
Elmore, Gloucestershire GL2 3NT
Early 18th century carriage and pedestrian gateway, with 19th century flanking walls. By William Edney, blacksmith of Bristol for Sir John Guise at Rendcomb. Gateway was removed from Rendcomb and re-erected here in early 19th century.

Grant Recipient: Trustees of the Elmore Court Estate
Access Contact: Trustees of the Elmore Court Estate
T: 01452 720293
Open: Visible at all times from public highway.
P Spaces: 5. Off-road parking on forecourt in front of Gates.
Full wheelchair access. No WC for the disabled. Guide Dogs allowed.
£ No.

FRAMPTON MANOR BARN
(THE WOOL BARN, MANOR FARM)
The Green, Frampton-on-Severn, Glos GL2 7EP
Grade I listed timber framed barn built c1560. Re-used worked stones in ashlar plinth wall were found during repair works.
www.framptoncourtestate.com
Grant Recipient: Mr P R H Clifford
Access Contact: Mr P R H Clifford
T: 01452 740698   **F:** 01452 740698
E-mail: clifford@framptoncourt.wanadoo.co.uk
Open: Mon - Fri, 8.30am - 4.30pm. Other times by arrangement.
P Spaces: 30.
Full wheelchair access. WC for the disabled. Guide Dogs allowed.
£ Adult: £1. Child: Free (special rates for school parties).

NEWARK PARK
Ozleworth, Wotton-under-Edge, Glos GL12 7PZ
Tudor hunting lodge built c1550 for one of Henry VIII's courtiers, Sir Nicholas Poyntz (who married into the equally wealthy Berkeley family), reputedly with stone from the destroyed Kingswood Abbey. Enlarged in early 17th century and then remodelled into a castellated country house by James Wyatt in the late 18th century. Retains many original features and is located on the edge of a 40ft cliff with outstanding views of the surrounding countryside.
www.nationaltrust.org.uk
Grant Recipient: The National Trust
Access Contact: Visitor Services Manager
T: 01453 842644   **F:** 01453 842644
E-mail: newarkpark@nationaltrust.org.uk
Open: 5 Apr - 31 May: Wed & Thurs 11am - 5pm. 1 June - 29 Oct: Wed, Thurs, Sat & Sun 11am - 5pm. Open BH Mons, Good Fri, and Easter Sat & Sun 11am - 5pm.
P Spaces: 10.
No wheelchair access or WC for the disabled. Guide Dogs allowed.
£ Adult: £5. Child: £2.50. Family: £13.

REGAN HOUSE
23 Lansdowne Terrace, Cheltenham, Gloucestershire
Regency house, now flats. Richly detailed stone façade with portico. Mews arch between No. 22 and Regan House.
Grant Recipient: Abel Developments/Forward Construction
Access Contact: Mr Mark Davis ARICS
T: 01242 260266
Open: Access to the exterior only at all times.
P Spaces: 2.
No wheelchair access or WC for the disabled. Guide Dogs allowed.
£ No.

STANCOMBE PARK TEMPLE
Dursley, Gloucestershire GL11 6AU
One in a series of buildings in the folly gardens at Stancombe Park, in the form of a Greek temple. Built in approximately 1815.
www.thetemple.info
Grant Recipient: Mr N D Barlow
Access Contact: Mrs G T Barlow
T: 01453 542815   **E-mail:** nicb@nicbarlow.com
Open: All year by telephone arrangement. To the exterior only during Heritage Open Days. Heritage Open Days.
P Spaces: 10.
No wheelchair access or WC for the disabled. Guide Dogs allowed.
£ Adult £3 (charity donation for visits to garden). No charge for anyone specifically wishing to see the temple only.

STANLEY MILL
King's Stanley, Stonehouse, Gloucestershire GL10 3HQ
Built 1813, with large addition c1825, of Flemish bond red brick with ashlar dressings and Welsh slate roof. Early example of fireproof construction (which survived a major

fire in 1884).

Grant Recipient: Stanley Mills Ltd

Access Contact: Mr Mark Griffiths/ Jill May

T: 01453 821800 **F:** 01453 791 167

Open: By written arrangement as the Mill is used by various manufacturing companies.

P Spaces: 30. By written arrangement as the Mill is used by various manufacturing companies.

No access.

£ No.

TANHOUSE FARM TITHE BARN

Frampton-on-Severn, Gloucestershire GL2 7EH

17th century Tithe Barn with cattle Byre.

Grant Recipient: M A & C R Williams

Access Contact: M R & C A Williams

T: 01452 741 072

E-mail: tanhouse.farm@lineone.net

Open: By arrangement.

P Spaces: 20. Parking within 100 metres.

Wheelchair access to main areas. No WC for the disabled. Guide Dogs allowed.

£ No.

WEST BANQUETING HOUSE

Chipping Campden, Gloucestershire

The West Banqueting House stands opposite the East Banqueting House across a broad terrace. It is elaborately decorated with spiral chimney stacks, finials and strapwork parapets.

www.landmarktrust.org.uk

Grant Recipient: The Landmark Trust

Access Contact: Mrs Victoria O'Keeffe

T: 01628 825920 **F:** 01628 825417

E-mail: vokeeffe@landmarktrust.org.uk

Open: The Landmark Trust is an independent charity, which rescues small buildings of historic or architectural importance from decay or unsympathetic improvement. Landmark's aim is to promote the enjoyment of these historic buildings by making them available to stay in for holidays. West Banqueting House can be rented by anyone, at all times of the year, for periods ranging from a weekend to three weeks. Bookings can be made by telephoning the Booking Office on 01628 825925. The public can also view the building on eight Open Days throughout the year (dates to be set) or by arrangement; telephone the access contact Victoria O'Keeffe on 01628 825920 to make an appointment. Potential visitors will be asked to write to confirm the details of their visit. Heritage Open Days.

P In town only.

No wheelchair access or WC for the disabled. Guide Dogs allowed.

£ No.

WICK COURT

Overton Lane, Arlingham, Gloucestershire GL2 7JJ

Medieval, 16th and 17th century Grade II* listed manor house with a range of farm buildings enclosed by a moat. The house is now a Farms for City Children centre.

www.farmsforcitychildren.co.uk

Grant Recipient: Farms for City Children

Access Contact: Ms Heather Tarplee

T: 01452 741023 **F:** 01452 741366

E-mail: wickcourt@yahoo.co.uk

Open: 4 - 20 Jan, 10 - 19 Feb, 31 Mar - 20 Apr & 21 July - 3 Sept. Other times by arrangement with Heather Tarplee, Farm School Manager (tel: 01452 741023).

P Spaces: 20.

Wheelchair access to ground floor of manor house only. WC for the disabled. Guide Dogs allowed.

£ £2.50 (guided tour).

WOODCHESTER PARK MANSION

Nympsfield, Stonehouse, Gloucestershire GL10 3TS

Grade I listed Victorian mansion, abandoned incomplete in 1870. One of the most remarkable houses of its period and uniquely exhibiting its construction process. Set in a large landscaped park (possibly by 'Capability' Brown). The building is also a site of special scientific interest housing two nationally important populations of endangered bats.

www.woodchestermansion.org.uk

Grant Recipient: Woodchester Mansion Trust

Access Contact: Mr Steven Woodman

T: 01453 861541 **F:** 01453 861337

E-mail: office@woodchestermansion.org.uk

Open: Easter - End of Oct: every Sun, first Sat in month and

BH weekends. July - Aug: Sat & Sun, 14 Apr and 2, 9 and 16 Aug 11am - 5.30pm (last adm. to house at 4pm). Groups and private visits welcome by arrangement. Heritage Open Days.

P Spaces: 60. Parking 1 mile from Mansion, access via woodland walk. Minibus service available.

Wheelchair access to ground floor only. No WC for the disabled. Guide Dogs allowed.

£ Adult: £5. Child: Free with parents. English Heritage & N T members, Seniors & NUS card holders: £4.

GREATER MANCHESTER

1830 WAREHOUSE
THE MUSEUM OF SCIENCE & INDUSTRY IN MANCHESTER

Liverpool Road, Castlefield, Manchester, Greater Manchester M3 4FP

Former railway warehouse, c1830, originally part of the Liverpool Road Railway Station (the oldest surviving passenger railway station in the world) which was the terminus of the Liverpool and Manchester Railway built by George Stephenson and his son Robert. Now part of The Museum of Science and Industry in Manchester.

www.msim.org.uk

Grant Recipient: The Museum of Science & Industry in Manchester

Access Contact: Mr Robin Holgate

T: 0161 832 2244 **F:** 0161 606 0186

E-mail: collections@msim.org.uk

Open: Daily (except 24 - 26 Dec &1 Jan) 10am - 5pm.

P Spaces: 50.

Full wheelchair access. WC for the disabled. Guide Dogs allowed.

£ Free entry to main museum building. Charge for special exhibitions.

DAM HOUSE

Astley Hall Drive, Astley, Tyldesley, Greater Manchester M29 7TX

17th century house with extensive additions in the 19th century. Formerly a hospital, now a community facility. Retains many original and Regency features.

www.damhouse.net

Grant Recipient: Morts Astley Heritage Trust

Access Contact: Mrs Helen Bolton

T: 01942 876417 **F:** 01942 876417

E-mail: info@damhouse.net

Open: Daily 9am - 5pm. Heritage Open Days.

P Spaces: 50. Parking at rear/front of building

Full wheelchair access. WC for the disabled. Guide Dogs allowed.

£ No.

HALL I' TH' WOOD MUSEUM

Green Way, Bolton, Greater Manchester BL1 8UA

Grade I listed manor house, early 16th century, where Samuel Crompton invented his spinning mule in 1779. Part of the Hall is timber-framed and shows the development of a house in the 16th and 17th centuries. Now a museum.

www.boltonmuseums.org.uk

Grant Recipient: Bolton Metropolitan Borough Council

Access Contact: Miss Elizabeth Shaw

T: 01204 332370 **F:** 01204 332215

E-mail: hallithwood@bolton.gov.uk

Open: 8 Jan - 9 Apr: Sat & Sun 11am - 5pm. 12 Apr - 30 Oct: Wed - Sun 11am - 5pm (last adm. 4.15pm). 31 Oct - end Mar 2007: Sat & Sun 11am - 5pm (last adm. 4.15pm). Heritage Open Days.

P Spaces: 10.

No access.

£ Adult: £2. Child: £1. Senior: £1.

HEATON PARK TEMPLE

Prestwich, Greater Manchester M25 2SW

Grade II* listed ornamental temple. Probably late 18th century, by James Wyatt. Situated on a hill in Heaton Park near Heaton Hall. The form is a simple, small rotunda of Tuscan columns with domed roof and lantern. It is said that Sir Thomas Egerton may have used the structure as an observatory.

www.manchester.gov.uk/leisure/parks/heaton.htm

Grant Recipient: Manchester City Council

Access Contact: Mr Stephen Downey, Operations Manager

T: 0161 773 1085 **F:** 0161 798 0107

E-mail: s.downey@manchester.gov.uk

Open: The temple can be viewed externally 365 days a year. Access to the interior by arrangement or when local artist is in residence (usually during summer months). Internal access also available in the winter through the park warden's team: please phone for details (tel: 0161 773 1085 x207).

P Spaces: 500.

External viewing only possible: pathway to the temple on a steep incline. WC for the disabled. Guide Dogs allowed.

£ No.

MANCHESTER LAW LIBRARY

14 Kennedy Street, Manchester M2 4BY

Built in Venetian Gothic style in 1885 to a design by Manchester architect, Thomas Hartas. Has stained glass windows by Evans of Birmingham.

www.manchester-law-library.co.uk

Grant Recipient: The Manchester Incorporated Law Library Society

Access Contact: Mrs Jane Riley

T: 0161 236 6312 **F:** 0161 236 6119

E-mail: librarian@manchester-law-library.co.uk

Open: By prior telephone or written arrangement. Heritage Open Days.

P No.

No wheelchair access or WC for the disabled. Guide Dogs allowed.

£ No.

OLD GRAMMAR SCHOOL

Boarshaw Road, Middleton, Greater Manchester M24 6BR

Endowed by Elizabeth I in 1572, completed in 1584 with house added 1830s. Restored in 1998. Grade II* listed building with fine original oak beams and items of historical and local interest. An important early example of a building type for which there was little architectural precedent.

Grant Recipient: The Old Grammar School Trust

Access Contact: Mr David Brenan, Trustee

T: 0161 643 2693 **F:** 0161 643 2693

E-mail: davebrennan@tinyworld.co.uk

Open: All year except Christmas/New Year period: Tues, Wed and Thurs 2 - 4pm. Parties by arrangement on 0161 643 7442 or 0161 653 4526. Regular programme of events and use by community groups. Heritage Open Days.

P Spaces: 17.

Full wheelchair access. WC for the disabled. Guide Dogs allowed.

£ No.

STAIRCASE HOUSE

30a/31 Market Place, Stockport, Greater Manchester SK1 3XE

Timber framed town house. Dating from 1460, enlarged in 16th and 17th centuries and altered in 18th, 19th and 20th centuries. Early panelled rooms and an important 17th century caged newel staircase from which the house takes its name. Damaged by fire, but restored by Stockport Council. Interpretation charts the history of the house and its evaluation to WWII. The house is fully interactive with visitors invited to touch all objects and furniture.

Grant Recipient: Stockport Metropolitan Borough Council

Access Contact: Mrs Angela Stead

T: 0161 474 3279

E-mail: Angela.Stead@Stockport.Gov.UK

Open: Daily 1 - 5pm, closed Christmas Day & Boxing Day.

P Town centre car parks and street parking.

Full wheelchair access. WC for the disabled. Guide Dogs allowed.

£ Adult: £2.50. Child: Free to under 5s. £1.25 with leisure key.

VICTORIA BATHS

Hathersage Road, Manchester, Greater Manchester M13 0FE

Swimming pool complex built 1903 - 1906, with 2 pools, Turkish and Russian Bath suite, Aeratone and extensive stained glass and tilework.

www.victoriabaths.org.uk

Grant Recipient: The Manchester Victoria Baths Trust

Access Contact: Ms Diana Terry

T: 0161 224 2020   F: 0161 224 0707

E-mail: info@victoriabaths.org.uk

Open: Apr - Oct: first Sun in each month 12 - 4pm. Additional opening days include Heritage Open Days in Sept, but please ring to confirm. At other times by arrangement with Ms Gill Wright of the Manchester Victoria Baths Trust, Studio 20, Longsight Business Park, Hamilton Road, Longsight, Manchester M13 0PD (tel: 0161 224 2020).

P On-street parking during the week. Use of large adjacent car park at weekends.

♿ Wheelchair access to ground floor with assistance. Most of the building can be seen from the ground floor. No WC for the disabled. Guide Dogs allowed.

£ Adult: £1 (proposed). Child: Free. Admission charges may be increased in 2006, please ring to confirm.

HAMPSHIRE

AVINGTON PARK

Winchester, Hampshire SO21 1DB

Palladian mansion dating back to the 11th century, enlarged in 1670 by the addition of two wings and a classical Portico surmounted by three statues. Visited by Charles II and George IV. Has highly decorated State rooms and a Georgian church in the grounds.

www.avingtonpark.co.uk

Grant Recipient: Mrs Sarah Bullen

Access Contact: Mrs Sarah Bullen

T: 01962 779260   F: 01962 779202

E-mail: enquiries@avingtonpark.co.uk

Open: May - Sept: Suns & BHs (and Mons in Aug) 2.30 - 5.30pm. Other times by arrangement. Heritage Open Days.

P Spaces: 150.

♿ Wheelchair access to ground floor only. Church with assistance (one step to interior). WC for the disabled. Guide Dogs allowed.

£ Adult: £4. Child: £2.

BOATHOUSE NO. 6

Portsmouth Naval Base, Portsmouth PO1 3LJ

Large Victorian naval boathouse constructed 1845. Designed by Captain James Beatson of the Royal Engineers, it is one of the first examples of a brick building constructed around a metal frame. Its massive cast iron beams are inscribed with their load-bearing capacity.

www.actionstations.org

Grant Recipient: Portsmouth Naval Base Property Trust

Access Contact: Mr Mark Meacher

T: 023 9282 0921   F: 023 9286 2437

E-mail: mm@pnbpt.com

Open: All year except Christmas Eve, Christmas Day and Boxing Day 10am - 5.30pm (Apr - Oct) & 10am - 5pm (Nov - Mar). Groups by arrangement. Heritage Open Days.

P Spaces: 150. Additional parking 500 metres from the site.

♿ Full wheelchair access. WC for the disabled. Guide Dogs allowed.

£ Adult: £9.70. Child: £8. Family: £33.

BREAMORE HOME FARM TITHE BARN

Breamore, nr. Fordingbridge, Hampshire SP6 2DD

Late 16th century tithe barn with dwarf walls supporting a timber-frame and external cladding under a tiled roof with massive timber aisle posts, double doors in the centre of each side and an area of threshing boards.

Grant Recipient: Breamore Ancient Buildings Conservation Trust

Access Contact: Mr Michael Hulse

T: 01725 512858   F: 01725 512858

Open: Weekdays by arrangement with Mr Michael Hulse of Breamore House.

P Spaces: 10.

♿ Full wheelchair access. No WC for the disabled. Guide Dogs allowed.

£ No.

CALSHOT

(Activities Main Hanger, Games Hanger & FFF Hanger), Calshot, Fawley, Hampshire SO45 1BR

Part of the most outstanding group of early aircraft structures of this type in Britain and the largest hanger built for use by fixed-wing aircraft during World War I. Now an activities centre.

www.calshot.com

Grant Recipient: Hampshire County Council

Access Contact: Mr Peter Davies

T: 01962 841841   F: 01962 841326

E-mail: arccpd@pbrs.hants.gov.uk

Open: Daily except Christmas Day, Boxing Day and New Year's Day.

P Spaces: 150. Ample free parking on-site.

♿ Full wheelchair access. WC for the disabled. Guide Dogs allowed.

£ No.

HIGHCLERE CASTLE & PARK

Highclere, Newbury, Hampshire RG20 9RN

Early Victorian mansion rebuilt by Sir Charles Barry in 1842, surrounded by 'Capability' Brown parkland with numerous listed follies including Heavens Gate, an 18th century eye-catching hill-top landscape feature and The Temple, c1760, altered by Barry in mid 19th century, a regular classical circular structure. Family home of the 8th Earl and Countess of Carnarvon.

www.highclerecastle.co.uk

Grant Recipient: Executors of the 7th Earl of Carnarvon & Lord Carnarvon

Access Contact: Mr Alec Tompson

T: 01223 351421   F: 01223 324554

E-mail: agent@hwdean.co.uk

Open: 1 June - 31 Aug: Mon - Fri, plus Easter Sun and Mon, May BH & Aug BH 11am - 4pm (gates open 10am). Last admission 3pm. Temple: permissive path on days when Castle is open. Other times by arrangement with Estate Office, Highclere Park (T: 01635 255401).

P Spaces: 200. Unlimited parking.

♿ Wheelchair access to ground floor only. WC for the disabled. Guide Dogs allowed.

£ Adult: £7.50. Child: £4. Senior: £6.

HOUGHTON LODGE GARDENS

Stockbridge, Hampshire SO20 6LQ

Landscaped pleasure grounds and a park laid out c1800 with views from higher ground over informal landscape (Grade II*) surrounding the 18th century Cottage Ornee (Grade II*). Chalk cob walls enclose ancient espaliers, greenhouses and herb garden. Formal topiary 'Peacock' Garden, snorting topiary dragon and wild flowers. A popular TV Film location. 14 acres of Meadow Walks through river valley.

www.houghtonlodge.co.uk

Grant Recipient: Capt M W Busk

Access Contact: Capt. M W Busk

T: 01264 810502   F: 01264 810063

E-mail: info@houghtonlodge.co.uk

Open: All year: Sats, Suns & BHs 10am - 5pm. Mon, Tues, Thurs & Fri 2 - 5pm. Closed Dec 22 - 4 Jan.

P Spaces: 100.

♿ Full wheelchair access. WC for the disabled. Guide Dogs allowed.

£ Adult: £5. Child: Free. Groups: £4.50.

MANOR FARMHOUSE

Hambledon, Hampshire PO7 4RW

12th century stone built house with later medieval wing. 17th and 18th century re-fronting of part and minor renovation.

Grant Recipient: Mr Stuart Mason

Access Contact: Mr Stuart Mason

T: 023 92632433

Open: By arrangement only.

P Spaces: 2.

♿ Full wheelchair access. No WC for the disabled. Guide Dogs allowed.

£ No.

ST MICHAEL'S ABBEY

Farnborough, Hampshire GU14 7NQ

Grade I listed church and Imperial Mausoleum crypt of Napoleon III and his family. Abbey Church also built for the Empress Eugenie so the monks could act as custodians of the tombs. Now a Benedictine priory, raised to Abbey status in 1903.

www.farnborughabbey.org

Grant Recipient: Empress Eugenie Memorial Trust

Access Contact: Fr Magnus Wilson

T: 01252 894211/546105   F: 01252 372822

E-mail: prior@farnboroughabbey.org

Open: Sats & BHs at 3.30pm. Contact Fr Magnus Wilson, Bursar, or Fr D C Brogan, Prior, for further information.

P Spaces: 10. ♿ No access.   £ No.

WHITCHURCH SILK MILL

28 Winchester Street, Whitchurch, Hampshire RG28 7AL

Grade II* watermill built c1800 and has been in continuous use as a silk weaving mill since the 1820s. Now a working museum, the winding, warping and weaving machinery installed between 1890 and 1927 produces traditional silks for theatrical costume, historic houses, fashion and artworks.

www.whitchurchsilkmill.org.uk

Grant Recipient: Hampshire Buildings Preservation Trust

Access Contact: General Manager

T: 01256 892065   F: 01256 893882

E-mail: silkmill@btinternet.com

Open: Mill and shop: Tues - Sun 10.30am - 5pm (last adm. 4.15pm). Mill and shop closed Mons (except BHs) and between Christmas and New Year. Heritage Open Days.

P Spaces: 20. Free parking next to Mill, 2 spaces for the disabled next to shop and to adjacent car park

♿ Wheelchair access to ground floor, shop and gardens. Stairlift to first floor and two steps to tea room. WC for the disabled. Guide Dogs allowed.

£ Adult: £3.50. Child: £1.75. Other: £3. Family: £8.75.

HEREFORDSHIRE

CHANDOS MANOR

Rushall, Ledbury, Herefordshire HR8 2PA

Farmhouse, probably late 16th century with 18th century extensions. Timber-frame, partly rendered.

Grant Recipient: Mr Richard White

Access Contact: Mr Richard White

T: 01531 660208

Open: Easter - Sept: Suns by arrangement.

P Spaces: 12.

♿ No wheelchair access or WC for the disabled. Guide Dogs allowed.

£ Donations to charity welcome.

EASTNOR CASTLE

Ledbury, Herefordshire HR8 1RL

Norman-style castellated mansion set in the western slopes of the Malvern Hills. Constructed 1812 - 1820 and designed by Sir Robert Smirke, the castle has 15 state and other rooms fully-furnished and open to visitors. The decoration includes tapestries, paintings, armour and a drawing room by Augus Pugin.

www.eastnorcastle.com

Grant Recipient: Mr J Hervey-Bathurst

Access Contact: Mr S Foster

T: 01531 633160   F: 01531 631776

E-mail: enquiries@eastnorcastle.com

Open: Easter - end Sept: Suns & BH Mons 11am - 5pm. 17 July - 31 Aug: Daily except Sats 11am - 5pm.

P Spaces: 150.

♿ Wheelchair access to grounds and ground floor with assistance (always available). WC for the disabled. Guide Dogs allowed.

£ Adult: £7, Child: £4, Senior: £6.

HERGEST COURT

Kington, Herefordshire HR5 3EG

House dates back to 1267 and was the ancestral home of the Clanvowe and Vaughan families. It is an unusual example of a fortified manor in the Welsh Mares. It has literary associations with Sir John Clanvowe and Lewis Glyn Cothi.

Grant Recipient: Mr W L Banks

Access Contact: Mr W L Banks

T: 01544 230160   F: 01544 232031

E-mail: gardens@hergest.co.uk

Open: By arrangement with the Hergest Estate Office, Kington, Herefordshire HR5 3EG. Bookings by phone or fax with five days' notice.

P Spaces: 5.

♿ Wheelchair access to ground floor only. No WC for the disabled. Guide Dogs allowed.

£ Adult: £4. Child: Free. Groups: £3.50.

THE PAINTED ROOM

Town Council Offices, Church Street, Ledbury, Herefordshire HR8 1DH

The wall paintings, discovered here in 1989, are a unique example of domestic wall painting dating from the Tudor period. They are clearly the work of a commoner, created to imitate the rich tapestries or hangings that would have been

found in the homes of the gentry.

Grant Recipient: Ledbury Town Council

Access Contact: Ms T Wildermoth

T: 01531 632306   **F:** 01531 631193

E-mail: ledburytowncouncil@ledbury.net

Open: Easter - end Sept: guided tours Mon - Fri 11.00am - 1pm and 2 - 4pm. Sun 2 - 5pm (from end of May - end Sept). Rest of year: Mon, Tues, Wed & Fri 10am - 2pm, if member of staff available. Tours may be arranged out of these hours at a cost of £1 per adult (min 10). Children's groups are free. Heritage Open Days.

P Town centre car parks nearby.

♿ No wheelchair access. Guides are aware of the location of the nearest WC for the disabled. Guide Dogs allowed.

£ No charge when open normally (£1 for adults on out of hours tours) but donations welcome.

THE WATERWORKS MUSEUM - HEREFORD

(formerly Broomy Hill Pumping Station), Broomy Hill, Hereford, Herefordshire

Set in the Victorian water pumping station of Hereford with working pumping engines telling the story of drinking water. Oldest triple-expansion steam engine working in Britain plus beam, gas and diesel engines and overshot waterwheel.

www.waterworksmuseum.org.uk

Grant Recipient: Herefordshire Waterworks Museum Ltd

Access Contact: Dr Noel Meeke

T: 01600 890 118   **F:** 01600 890 009

E-mail: info@waterworksmuseum.org.uk

Open: Apr - Oct: every Tues and second and last Suns in month when engines are working plus Easter, Spring & Aug BHs 2 - 5pm (last adm. 4.30pm).

P Spaces: 30. Additional 50 spaces nearby, disabled parking in courtyard. Space for one full size coach.

♿ Full wheelchair access. WC for the disabled. Guide Dogs allowed.

£ Adult £3. Child: £1. Senior: £2.

HERTFORDSHIRE

ALL SAINTS PASTORAL CENTRE

Shenley Lane, London Colney, St Albans, Hertfordshire AL2 1AF

Grade II* listed building, designed by architect Leonard Stokes. Chapel begun in 1927 by Ninian Comper and finished in 1964 by his son Sebastian Comper.

www.allsaintspc.org.uk

Grant Recipient: Diocese of Westminster

Access Contact: Diocese of Westminster

Open: Daily 9am - 5pm except last week of Dec.

P Spaces: 130.

♿ Full wheelchair access. WC for the disabled. Guide Dogs allowed.

£ No.

BERKHAMSTED TOWN HALL

196 High Street, Berkhamsted, Hertfordshire HP4 3AP

Berkhamsted Town Hall and Market House, built in 1859, also housed the Mechanics' Institute. It has a gothic façade and retains much of the original stonework. There are three rooms: the Great Hall, Clock Room, Sessions Hall. In the Great Hall many of the original features have been preserved, including the fireplace and barrel vaulted ceiling.

Grant Recipient: Berkhamsted Town Hall Trust

Access Contact: Mrs Angela Smith

T: 01442 862288

E-mail: bthtmanager@tiscali.co.uk

Open: Mon - Fri 10am - 1pm. Other times the Town Hall is let for functions. Additional opening by arrangement with the Town Hall Manager (tel: 01442 862288). Heritage Open Days.

P Nearby public car parks.

♿ Full wheelchair access. WC for the disabled. Guide Dogs allowed.

£ No.

BRIDGEWATER MONUMENT

Ashbridge Estate, Aldbury, Hertfordshire HP4 1LT

The monument was erected in 1832 to commemorate the Duke of Bridgewater. It is the focal point of Ashridge Estate which runs across the borders of Hertfordshire and Buckinghamshire along the main ridge of the Chilterns.

www.nationaltrust.org.uk

Grant Recipient: The National Trust

Access Contact: Property Manager

T: 01442 851227   **F:** 01442 850000

E-mail: ashridge@nationaltrust.org.uk

Open: Monument: 18 Mar - 29 Oct: Sat, Sun & BH Mons 12 noon - 5pm. Mon - Fri by arrangement, weather permitting. Estate: open all year. Visitor Centre: 18 Mar - 10 Dec, daily Mon - Fri 12 - 5pm. Sat, Sun, BH Mons & Good Fri 12 noon - 5pm.

P Spaces: 100.

♿ Wheelchair access to monument area, monument drive and visitor centre. WC for the disabled. Guide Dogs allowed.

£ Adult: £1.30. Child: 60p.

CROMER WINDMILL

Ardeley, Stevenage, Hertfordshire SG2 7QA

Grade II* postmill dated 1674, last surviving postmill in Hertfordshire. Restored to working order (but not actually working). Houses displays about Hertfordshire's lost windmills, television and video display on the history of Cromer Mill and audio sound effects of a working mill.

www.hertsmuseums.org.uk

Grant Recipient: Hertfordshire Building Preservation Trust

Access Contact: Ms Cristina Harrison

T: 01279 843301/07949 577760   **F:** 01279 843301

E-mail: cristinaharrison@ btopenworld.com

Open: 13 May - 10 Sept, open Sat before National Mill Day, i.e. second Sun in May. Then Suns & BHs, and second and fourth Sats, until Heritage Open Days, 2.30 - 5pm. 30 minute video for schools and other groups. Guided tours. Special groups by arrangement with Ms Cristina Harrison, The Forge Museum, High Street, Much Hadham, Hertfordshire SG10 6BS. Refreshments available.

P Spaces: 20.

♿ Wheelchair access to ground floor only but video of upper floors showing all the time. No WC for the disabled. Guide Dogs allowed.

£ Adult: £1.50. Child: 25p.

DUCKLAKE HOUSE WALLPAINTING

Springhead, Ashwell, Baldock, Hertfordshire SG7 5LL

16th century wall painting, located on the ground floor, containing classical grotesques holding cartouches.

Grant Recipient: Mr P W H Saxton

Access Contact: Mr P W H Saxton

T: 01462 742 491

Open: By written arrangement to view the wall painting only.

P Spaces: 1. ♿ No access. **£** No.

FOLLY ARCH

Hawkshead Road, Little Heath, Potters Bar, Hertfordshire EN6 1NN

Grade II* listed gateway and folly, once the entrance to Gobions estate. Circa 1740 for Sir Jeremy Sambrooke, probably by James Gibbs. Red brick with large round-headed arch and thin square turrets.

Grant Recipient: Mr R J Nicholas

Access Contact: Mr and Mrs Nicholas

T: 01707 663553   **E-mail:** robnic@mac.com

Open: The Arch is on the boundary between public open space and a private garden and can be viewed from public ground at any time.

P On street parking.

♿ Full wheelchair access. No WC for the disabled. Guide Dogs allowed.

£ No.

KNEBWORTH HOUSE

Knebworth, Stevenage, Hertfordshire SG3 6PY

Originally a Tudor manor house, rebuilt in gothic style in 1843. Contains rooms in various styles, which include a Jacobean banqueting hall. Set in 250 acres of parkland with 25 acres of formal gardens. Home of the Lytton family since 1490.

www.knebworthhouse.com

Grant Recipient: Knebworth House Education & Preservation Trust

Access Contact: Mrs Christine Smith

T: 01438 812661   **F:** 01438 811908

E-mail: info@knebworthhouse.com

Open: Daily: 1 Apr - 17 Apr, 27 May - 4 June, 1 July - 5 Sept. Weekends & BHs: 25 - 26 Mar, 22 Apr - 1 May, 10 - 25 June, 9 - 24 Sept. Gardens, Park & Playground: 11.00am - 5.30pm. House: 12 noon- 5.00pm (last adm. 4.15pm).

P 50-75 spaces on gravel, unlimited space on grass.

♿ Wheelchair access to ground floor of House only. Gravel

paths around gardens and House but level route from car park to House entrance. WC for the disabled. Guide Dogs allowed.

£ Adult: £9 (£8 group). Child: £8.50 (£7.50 group). Senior: £8.50 (£7.50 group).

THE OLD CHURCH TOWER OF ALL SAINTS

Chapel Lane, Long Marston, Hertfordshire HP23 4QT

Grade II* listed 15th century tower. The only remnant of a Chapel of Ease dating back to the 12th century, the rest of the church was demolished in 1883.

Grant Recipient: Tring PCC Tower Conservation

Access Contact: Dr Noakes

T: 01296 660 072

Open: Exterior (churchyard) open at all times. Interior by arrangement and under supervision only.

P Parking in nearby village, 200 metre walk.

♿ Wheelchair access to churchyard only. No WC for the disabled. Guide Dogs allowed.

£ No.

THE OLD CLOCKHOUSE

Cappell Lane, Stanstead Abbots, Herts SG12 8BU

Grammar school, now private residence, c1636 also used for Sun services in 17th century.

Grant Recipient: Mr Michael Hannon

Access Contact: Mr Michael Hannon

T: 01920 871495

Open: Access to exterior at all times; Bell Tower can only be viewed from High Street.

P Public car park in Stansted Abbots High Street.

♿ No access. **£** No.

TORILLA

11 Wilkins Green Lane, Nast Hyde, Hatfield, Hertfordshire AL10 9RT

'Torilla' (house at Nast Hyde) was built by F R S Yorke in 1935 in the international style and features a flat roof, 2 balconies and a large double height living room. Constructed of concrete with large steel framed windows. F R S Yorke was a key figure in the evolution of modern architecture in Britain.

Grant Recipient: Mr Alan Charlton

Access Contact: Mr Alan Charlton

T: 01707 259582

Open: By arrangement (written or telephone) 11am - 5pm on Sun 14 May & Sun 13 Aug. Other times by written arrangement.

P Spaces: 5.

♿ Wheelchair access to ground floor only. No WC for the disabled. Guide Dogs allowed.

£ No.

WOODHALL PARK

Watton-at-Stone, Hertfordshire SG14 3NF

Country house, now school. Designed and built by Thomas Leverton in 1785 in neo-Classical style. Normally associated with London houses, this is one of his few country houses. Highly decorated interiors which include the Print Room with walls covered in engraved paper, reproductions of paintings with frames, ribbons, chains, busts, candelabra and piers with vases.

Grant Recipient: The Trustees of R M Abel Smith 1991 Settlement

Access Contact: The Trustees of R M Abel Smith 1991 Settlement

T: 01920 830286   **F:** 01920 830162

E-mail: woodhallest@dial.pipex.com

Open: At all reasonable times, preferably school holidays, by arrangement with the Trustees.

P Spaces: 30. Limited to 10 spaces in termtime.

♿ Wheelchair access to ground floor only. No WC for the disabled. Guide Dogs allowed.

£ No.

KENT

AYLESFORD PRIORY

The Friars, Aylesford, Kent ME20 7BX

Home of a community of Carmelite Friars and a popular centre of pilgrimage. Chapels contain modern religious art created by Adam Kossowski.

Grant Recipient: Church of England

Access Contact: Father Prior

T: 01622 717272   **F:** 01622 715575

E-mail: jkemsley@carmelnet.org
Open: At all times. Heritage Open Days.
P Spaces: 1500.
Full wheelchair access. WC for the disabled. Guide Dogs allowed.
£ No.

CHIDDINGSTONE CASTLE

Chiddingstone, nr. Edenbridge, Kent TN8 7AD

Tudor mansion subsequently twice remodelled by the Streatfeilds whose seat it was. William Atkinson "Master of the picturesque" is responsible for the romantic design, c1805, of the building as it is today. Rescued from dereliction by Denys Bower in the 20th century, now managed by a charitable trust.

www.chiddingstone-castle.org.uk
Grant Recipient: Trustees of the Denys Eyre Bower Bequest
Access Contact: Mr N Birrini
T: 01892 870347
Open: Apr and May: Easter and Spring BHs only. June - Sept: Thurs, Sun & BHs. Weekdays: 2 - 5.30pm. Sun and BHs: 11.30am - 5.30pm (last admittance 5pm). Groups (20+), including school groups, throughout the year by arrangement. No mobile phones.
P Spaces: 50. Parking for the disabled available at entrance.
Wheelchair access to ground floor (includes everything except the Egyptian collection) and tea room. WC for the disabled. Guide Dogs allowed.
£ Adult: £5. Child: £3 (5-15, under 5 free when accompanied by an adult).

CHURCH HOUSE

72 High Street, Edenbridge, Kent TN8 5AR

Late 14th century timber-framed farmhouse, Tudor additions include fireplace and 18th century brick frontage. Now houses the Eden Valley Museum which illustrates economic and social changes during the 14th to 20th centuries.
www.evmt.org.uk
Grant Recipient: Edenbridge Town Council
Access Contact: Mrs Jane Higgs
T: 01732 868102   **F:** 01732 867866
E-mail: curator@evmt.org.uk
Open: Feb - Dec (until Christmas): Wed & Fri 2 - 4.30pm, Thurs & Sat 10am - 4.30pm. Apr - Sept: Suns 2 - 4.30pm. Heritage Open Days.
P Spaces: 150. Free parking in town centre car park, 200 yards from House.
Wheelchair access to ground floor only (visual computer link to upstairs). WC for the disabled. Guide Dogs allowed.
£ No.

COBHAM HALL AND DAIRY

Cobham, Kent DA12 3BL

Gothic-style dairy in grounds of Cobham Hall, built by James Wyatt c1790.
www.cobhamhall.com
Grant Recipient: Cobham Hall Heritage Trust
Access Contact: Mr N G Powell
T: 01474 823371   **F:** 01474 825904
E-mail: enquiries@cobhamhall.com
Open: Easter - July / Aug: Hall open Wed & Sun 2 - 5pm (last tour 4.30pm). Please tel to confirm. At other times (and coach groups) by arrangement. Self-guided tour of Gardens and Parkland (historical/conservation tour by arrangement).
P Spaces: 100.
Wheelchair access to ground floor, manual assistance required for first floor access. WC for the disabled. Guide Dogs allowed.
£ Adult: £4.50. Child: £3.50. Conc: £3.50.

CRABBLE CORN MILL

Lower Road, River, nr. Dover, Kent CT17 0UY

Georgian watermill with millpond, cottages and gardens. Guided and non-guided tours and demonstrations of milling techniques. Flour produced and sold on site. Cafeteria and art gallery. Available for group tours, functions and events.
www.ccmt.org.uk
Grant Recipient: Crabble Corn Mill Trust
Access Contact: Mr Anthony Skaveley
T: 01304 823292   **F:** 01304 823292
E-mail: miller@ccmt.org.uk
Open: Feb - Apr: Suns 11am - 5pm. Apr - Sept: Daily 11am - 5pm. Open to group visits all year by arrangement (contact Alan Davis, Tony Staveley, Anne Collins or Anthony Reid, tel: 01304 823292).

P Spaces: 32. Parking in recreation ground opposite site.
Wheelchair access to ground and first floor, art gallery, cafeteria and milling floor. No WC for the disabled. Guide Dogs allowed.
£ Mill Tour: Adult: £4. Child: £3 (age 5-15). Senior/Student: £3). Family £9.

DOVER TOWN HALL

Biggin Street, Dover, Kent CT16 1DL

The Town Hall incorporates the remains of a medieval hospital, 14th century chapel tower, 19th century prison, town hall and assembly rooms. The Maison Dieu Hall of c1325 was originally part of a hospital founded by Hubert de Burgh in the early 13th century. The Town Hall designed by Victorian Gothic architect William Burges was built in 1881 on the site of the hospital.
Grant Recipient: Dover District Council
Access Contact: Mr Jelmo Piotro
T: 01843 296111 (Admin)
E-mail: dover@leisureforce.co.uk
Open: Normally open during the week for functions and other bookings. Guided tours to be organised on two Suns per month June - Sept and one Sun per month Oct - May. To ensure access please telephone (tel: 01843 296111).
P Parking at the rear of the building.
Full wheelchair access. WC for the disabled. Guide Dogs allowed.
£ No.

HERNE WINDMILL

Mill Lane, Herne Bay, Kent CT6 7DR

Kentish smock mill built 1789, worked by wind until 1952 and then by electricity until 1980. Bought by Kent County Council in 1985, which carried out some restoration. Now managed by Friends of Herne Mill on behalf of the County Council. Much of the original machinery is in place, some is run for demonstration and the sails are used when the wind conditions permit.
www.kentwindmills.co.uk
Grant Recipient: Kent County Council
Access Contact: Mr Ken Cole
T: 01227 361326
Open: Easter - end Sept: Sun & BHs, plus Thurs in Aug 2 - 5pm. National Mills Weekend, Sat & Sun, 2 - 5pm. For further information contact Ken Cole, Secretary, Friends of Herne Mill (tel: 01227 361326) or John Fishpool (Chairman, tel: 01227 366863). Heritage Open Days.
P Spaces: 6, in Mill grounds. Free on-street parking (Windmill Road).
Wheelchair and guide dog access to ground floor of Mill and meeting room. WC for the disabled. Guide Dogs allowed.
£ Adult: £1. Child: 25p (accompanied by adult).

IGHTHAM MOTE

Ivy Hatch, Sevenoaks, Kent TN15 0NT

Moated manor house covering 650 years of history from medieval times to 1960s. Extended visitor route now includes the newly refurbished north-west quarter with Tudor Chapel, Billiards Room and Drawing Room, South West Quarter and apartments of Charles Henry Robinson, the American donor of Ightham Mote to the National Trust. Interpretation displays and special exhibition featuring conservation in action.
www.nationaltrust.org.uk
Grant Recipient: The National Trust
Access Contact: Property Manager
T: 01732 810378   **F:** 01732 493 310
E-mail: ighthammote@nationaltrust.org.uk
Open: 18 Mar - 30 Oct, daily except Tues & Sat. House: 10.30am - 5.30pm; Garden 10am - 5.30pm. Estate open all year Dawn - Dusk.
P Spaces: 420.
Wheelchair access to ground floor with assistance and part of the exterior only. WC for the disabled. Guide Dogs allowed.
£ Adult: £7. Child: £3.50. Family: £17.50. Groups £5.50, no reduction on Sun or BHs.

PENSHURST PLACE PARK

Tonbridge, Kent TN11 8DG

Open parkland, formerly a medieval deer park, circa 80 hectares. Scattered mature trees, lake with a small island and Lime Avenue originally planted in 1730s.
www.penshurstplace.com
Grant Recipient: Lord De L'Isle
Access Contact: Mr Ian R Scott

T: 01892 870307   **F:** 01892 870866
E-mail: ianscott@penshurstplace.com
Open: Footpaths through parkland open 365 days a year.
P Spaces: 50.
No wheelchair access or WC for the disabled. Guide Dogs allowed.
£ No.

THE ARCHBISHOPS' PALACE

Mill Street, Maidstone, Kent ME15 6YE

14th century Palace built by the Archbishops of Canterbury. Much altered and extended over the centuries, the interior contains 16th century panelling and fine wood or stone fireplaces. Now used as Kent County Council's Register Office.
Grant Recipient: Maidstone Borough Council
Access Contact: Mrs Maggie Taylor
T: 01622 701920
E-mail: maidstone.registeroffice@kent.gov.uk
Open: All year for weddings and at other times by arrangement with the Registrar. Heritage Open Days.
P Spaces: 100. In town centre car parks (pay and display).
No wheelchair access or WC for the disabled. Guide Dogs allowed.
£ No.

LANCASHIRE

GAWTHORPE HALL

Padiham, nr. Burnley, Lancashire BB12 8UA

An Elizabethan property in the heart of industrial Lancashire. Restored and refurbished in the mid 19th century by Sir Charles Barry. There are many notable paintings on display loaned to the National Trust by the National Portrait Gallery, and a collection of needlework, assembled by the last family member to live there, Rachel Kay-Shuttleworth.
www.nationaltrust.org.uk
Grant Recipient: The National Trust
Access Contact: Property Manager
T: 01282 771004   **F:** 01282 770178
E-mail: gawthorpehall@nationaltrust.org.uk
Open: Hall: 25 Mar - 2 Nov, daily except Mon & Fri (but open Good Fri & BH Mons) 1 - 5pm. Garden: all year 10am - 6pm. Heritage Open Days.
P Spaces: 50.
Wheelchair access to garden only. WC for the disabled. Guide Dogs allowed.
£ Adult £3 (provisional). Child: Free when accompanied by an adult. Conc: £1.50, garden free (provisional).

GRAND THEATRE

33 Church Street, Blackpool, Lancashire FY1 1HT

Grade II* 1200-seat theatre designed by Frank Matcham, 1894. Major restoration ongoing.
www.blackpoolgrand.co.uk
Grant Recipient: Blackpool Grand Theatre Trust Ltd
Access Contact: Mr David Fletcher
T: 01253 290111   **F:** 01253 751767
E-mail: geninfo@blackpoolgrand.co.uk
Open: Daily. Tours take place on a semi-regular basis. Shows in the auditorium once or twice a day. Contact David Fletcher (tel: 01253 290111) for more information. Heritage Open Days.
P Spaces: 200. Parking in West St car park (2 minute walk).
Wheelchair access to stalls and bar. WC for the disabled. Guide Dogs allowed.
£ Adult: £5 (guided tour). Child: £3.50. Charges made for performances. Free on open days.

HOGHTON TOWER

Hoghton, Preston, Lancashire PR5 0SH

16th century fortified manor house, ancestral home of the de Hoghton family since William the Conqueror. Associated with many kings and queens (the Banqueting Hall is where James I knighted the Loin of Beef 'Sirloin') and William Shakespeare. Various staterooms open to the public, as well as a Tudor horse-drawn well, dungeons and underground passages.
www.hoghtontower.co.uk
Grant Recipient: Hoghton Tower Preservation Trust
Access Contact: Mr John Graver
T: 01254 852986   **F:** 01254 852109
E-mail: mail@hoghtontower.co.uk
Open: July - Sept: Mon - Thurs 11am - 4pm (Suns 1 - 5pm). Guided tours: BH Suns/Mons (excl Christmas & New Year); Private tours throughout the year by arrangement.

P Spaces: 250.
⬧ Wheelchair access to Gardens, Banqueting Hall and Kings Hall. WC for the disabled. Guide Dogs allowed.
£ Adult: £5.   Child: £4.   Senior/Student: £4.   Family: £16.

INDIA MILL CHIMNEY

Bolton Road, Darwen, Blackburn, Lancashire BB3 1AE
Chimney, 1867, built as part of cotton spinning mill. Brick with ashlar base. Square section, 300 feet high, in the style of an Italian campanile. Rests on foundation stone said to have been the largest single block quarried since Cleopatra's Needle. Listed Grade II*.
Grant Recipient: Brookhouse Managed Properties Ltd.
Access Contact: Mr John M Fryer
T: 01254 777 788   F: 01254 777 799
Open: Visible from public highway (no interior access).
P On-street parking.
⬧ Full wheelchair access. No WC for the disabled. Guide Dogs allowed.
£ No.

LEIGHTON HALL

Carnforth, Lancashire LA5 9ST
Country House, 1765, probably by Richard Gillow, with earlier remains. Gothic south-east front early 19th century, possibly by Thomas Harrison. Tower at west end of the façade 1870 by Paley and Austin. Ancestral home of the Gillow family with fine furniture, paintings and *objets d'art*.
www.leightonhall.co.uk
Grant Recipient: Mr Richard Reynolds
Access Contact: Mr & Mrs Richard Reynolds
T: 01524 734474   F: 01524 720357
E-mail: leightonhall@yahoo.co.uk
Open: May - Sept: Tues- Fri (also BH Suns & Mons) 2 - 5pm. Aug only: Tues- Fri & Sun (also BH Mon) 12.30 - 5pm. Groups (25+) all year by arrangement. The owner reserves the right to close or restrict access to the Hall and grounds for special events (please see our website for up to date information).
P Spaces: 100.
⬧ Wheelchair access to ground floor, shop and tea rooms. WC for the disabled. Guide Dogs allowed.
£ Adult: £5.50. Child: £4 (age 5-12).   Senior/student: £5, Family: £17. Groups £4.50 (adults 25+), £3.50 (child group).

QUEEN STREET MILL

Harle Syke, Burnley, Lancashire BB10 2HX
Built in 1894, containing much of its original 19th century equipment including over 300 Lancashire looms and steam engine.
www.lanesmuseums.goc.uk
Grant Recipient: Lancashire County Council
Access Contact: Lancashire County Council
Open: Mar and Nov: Tues - Thurs 12 - 4pm. Apr and Oct: Tues - Fri 12 - 5pm. May - Sept: Tues - Sat 12 - 5pm. Open Sun and Mons on BH weekends only. Closed Dec, Jan & Feb. Heritage Open Days.
P Spaces: 40. Free.
⬧ Full wheelchair access. WC for the disabled. Guide Dogs allowed.
£ Adult: £2.50. Child: Free if accompanied. Conc: £1.25.

SAMLESBURY HALL

Preston New Road, Samlesbury, Preston, Lancs PR5 0UP
Built in 1325, the hall is an attractive black and white timbered manor house set in extensive grounds. Independently owned and administered since 1925 by The Samlesbury Hall Trust whose primary aim is to maintain and preserve the property for the enjoyment and pleasure of the public. Currently open to the public as an antiques/craft centre.
www.samlesburyhall.co.uk
Grant Recipient: Samlesbury Hall Trust
Access Contact: Ms Sharon Jones
T: 01254 812010/01254 812229   F: 01254 812174
E-mail: samlesburyhall@btconnect.com
Open: Daily except Sats, 11am - 4.30pm. Open Bank Holidays. For Christmas closing times please contact the Hall. Heritage Open Days.
P Spaces: 70. Additional parking for 100 cars in overflow car park.
⬧ Wheelchair access to ground floor of historical part of Hall. WC for the disabled. Guide Dogs allowed.
£ Adult: £3. Child: £1 (ages 4-16).

STONYHURST COLLEGE

Stonyhurst, Clitheroe, Lancashire BB7 9PZ
16th century manor house, now home to a Catholic independent co-education boarding and day school. Contains dormitories, library, chapels, school-rooms and historical apartments.
www.stonyhurst.ac.uk
Grant Recipient: Stonyhurst College
Access Contact: Miss Frances Ahearne
T: 01254 826345   F: 01254 826732
E-mail: domestic-bursar@stonyhurst.ac.uk
Open: House: 17 July - 28 Aug: daily (except Fri), plus Aug BH Mon 1 - 5pm. Gardens: 1 July - 28 Aug: daily (except Fri), plus Aug BH Mon 1 - 5pm. Coach groups by arrangement.
P Spaces: 200.
⬧ Wheelchair access limited but assistance is available by arrangement. WC for the disabled. Guide Dogs allowed.
£ Adult: £6. Child: £5. Other: £5.

TODMORDEN UNITARIAN CHURCH

Honey Hole Road, Todmorden, Lancashire OL14 6LE
Grade I church with a large wooded burial ground and ornamental gardens designed by John Gibson, 1865-69. Victorian Gothic style with tall tower and spire. Detached smaller burial ground nearby and listed lodge in churchyard. Lavish interior with highly decorated fittings and furnishings. One of the most elaborate Non conformist churches of the High Gothic Revival.
www.hct.org.uk
Grant Recipient: Historic Chapels Trust
Access Contact: Mr Rob Goldthorpe
T: 01706 815648
E-mail: rob.goldthorpe@btinternet.com
Open: At all reasonable times by application to the keyholder, Mr Rob Goldthorpe, 14 Honey Hole Close, Todmorden, Lancashire OL14 6LH or by calling at the caretaker's house, Todmorden Lodge, at the entrance to the churchyard. Heritage Open Days.
P Spaces: 10. Parking for disabled and elderly adjacent. Safeway Supermarket by agreement with Historic Chapels Trust.
⬧ Full wheelchair access. WC for the disabled. Guide Dogs allowed.
£ Donations invited.

LEICESTERSHIRE

7 KING STREET

Melton Mowbray, Leicestershire LE13 1XA
Dating from 1330, this is the oldest secular building in Melton Mowbray. The building has Medieval roof timbers, a 16th century timber-framed extension and has been modified and gentrified through the centuries. Listed Grade II*, the building was at risk for many years. Restoration by Melton Mowbray Borough Council was completed in 2004 and is the Council's Tourist Information Centre.
Grant Recipient: Melton Borough Council
Access Contact: Mr Richard Spooner MA IHBC
T: 01664 502387   F: 01664 410283
E-mail: rspooner@melton.gov.uk
Open: Mon - Sat (hours to be determined). Access to the upper floors by arrangement.
P Public car park adjacent (Pay and Display).
⬧ Wheelchair access to ground floor rooms. WC for the disabled. Guide Dogs allowed.
£ No.

REARSBY PACKHORSE BRIDGE

Rearsby, Leicestershire LE7 4YE
Low narrow medieval bridge, perhaps 16th century, comprising seven arches of random granite masonry and brick coping. On the upstream side there are four cutwaters, three of granite and one of brick. The bridge has recently been restored.
Grant Recipient: Leicestershire County Council
Access Contact: Mr P Steer
T: 0116 265 7151   F: 0116 265 7135
E-mail: psteer@leics.gov.uk
Open: In use as a public highway.
P Street parking.
⬧ Full wheelchair access. No WC for the disabled. Guide Dogs allowed.
£ No.

STANFORD HALL

Lutterworth, Leicestershire LE17 6DH
William and Mary house, built by the Smiths of Warwick (begun 1697), for Sir Roger Cave, ancestor of present owner, whose family home it is. Visitors see every room on the ground floor (except modern kitchen & small dining room), the "flying staircase" and two bedrooms. Contents include collection of Royal Stuart paintings.
www.stanfordhall.co.uk
Grant Recipient: Lady Braye
Access Contact: Mr Robert Thomas
T: 01788 860250   F: 01788 860870
E-mail: enquiries@stanfordhall.co.uk
Open: 16 Apr - 24 Sept: Sun & BH Mons 1.30 - 5.30pm (last adm. 5pm). On BH Suns & Mons Grounds open at 12noon and earlier on Event Days. Open any day or evenings during the Season (except Sats) for pre-booked groups (20+).
P Spaces: 1500. Parking for disabled adjacent to house.
⬧ Wheelchair access to Park, Gardens, the 1898 Flying Machine and the ground floor of Hall (entrance steps can be negotiated). WC for the disabled. Guide Dogs allowed.
£ Adult: £5 (house and grounds), £3 (grounds only). Child: £2 (house & grounds), £1 (grounds only). Other: £4.75 (groups 20+, adult), £1.80 (group 20+, child).

TOMB OF ANDREW LORD ROLLO

St Margaret's Church, Canning Place, Leicester
Grade II* listed tomb of 1765. Each face has a large rectangular plaque with ornate carved pilaster panels. The west front has a long inscription on the slate plaque recording the life and exploits of Andrew Lord Rollo, who died in 1765. The remaining three fronts each have a shallow carved relief of Lord Rollo's arms and military trophies.
Grant Recipient: The Abbey Parish PCC
Access Contact: Mr Jack Adams
T: 0116 2897432
Open: The churchyard is open at all times.
P Spaces: 3.
⬧ Full wheelchair access. No WC for the disabled. Guide Dogs allowed.
£ No.

LINCOLNSHIRE

HEGGY'S COTTAGE

Hall Road, Haconby, nr. Bourne, Lincolnshire PE10 0UY
Built c1500 of mud and stud construction, a good example of early conversion to two storeys. Restored to its original state in 1995.
Grant Recipient: J E Atkinson & Son
Access Contact: Mrs J F Atkinson
T: 01778 570790
Open: By written arrangement with Mrs J F Atkinson, Haconby Hall, nr. Bourne, Lincolnshire PE10 0UY.
P Spaces: 1   ⬧ No access.   £ No.

JEWS' COURT

(the Society for Lincolnshire History & Archaeology),
2/3 Steep Hill, Lincoln, Lincolnshire LN2 1LS
Grade I two storey stone building, c12th century, with cellar and attic. Traditionally the medieval synagogue. Now used by the Society for Lincolnshire History & Archaeology and for worship.
www.lincolnshirepast.org.uk
Grant Recipient: Jews' Court Trust
Access Contact: Ms Pearl Wheatley
T: 01522 521337   F: 01522 521337
E-mail: slha@lincolnshirepast.org.uk
Open: Daily except Suns, 10am - 4pm. Closed over the Christmas period
P Ample public parking within 300 yards.
⬧ Access for wheelchairs is not possible. Electric stair-lift available for access to first floor. Several days notice is required as two trained staff members need to be in attendance. No WC for the disabled. Guide Dogs allowed.
£ No.

KYME TOWER

Manor Farm, South Kyme, Lincoln, Lincs LN4 4JN
23.5m high tower with one storey and a stair turret. Remainder of a fortified medieval manor house, built on the site of an Auginian priory, itself built on an Anglo-Saxon religious establishment. There are also visible earthworks of

the former moat and fishponds.

Grant Recipient: The Crown Estate Commissioners

Access Contact: Mr W B Lamyman

T: 01526 860603

Open: By telephone arrangement with Mr W B Lamyman of Manor Farm (tel: 01526 860603). At least one week's notice required.

P Spaces: 3. No access. £ No.

LINCOLN CASTLE

Castle Hill, Lincoln, Lincolnshire LN1 3AA

Lincoln Castle was begun by William the Conqueror in 1068. For 900 years the castle has been used as a court and prison. Many original features still stand and the wall walks provide magnificent views of the cathedral, city and surrounding countryside.

www.lincolnshire.gov.uk/lincolncastle

Grant Recipient: Lincolnshire County Council

Access Contact: Mr Peter Allen

T: 01522 511068   **F:** 01522 512150

E-mail: allenp@lincolnshire.gov.uk

Open: Mon - Sat: 9.30am - 5.30pm. Sun 11am - 5.30pm (4pm in winter). Closed 24 - 26 Dec, 31 Dec & 1 Jan.

P Paid parking available in the Castle / Cathedral area.

Wheelchair access to grounds, Magna Carta exhibition, audio visual presentation and café. WC for the disabled. Guide Dogs allowed.

£ Adult: £3.70. Child: £2.15 (under 5s free). Conc: £2.15. Family £9.60.

MONKSTHORPE CHAPEL

Spilsby, East Lindsey, Lincolnshire

Resembling a brick barn, this remote chapel with outdoor baptistery was used by local Baptists as a secluded place of worship and is one of the two best surviving examples in England. It was substantially altered to its present appearance in the early 19th century.

Grant Recipient: The National Trust

Access Contact: The National Trust

T: 01909 486411   **F:** 01909 486377

Open: 29 Mar - 28 Sept: Wed & Thurs 2 - 5pm. Stewarded some Sats: 15 Apr, 20 May, 17 June, 15 July, 19 Aug & 16 Sept. Services: 1 Apr, 6 May, 3 June, 1 July, 29 July, 2 Sept, 7 Oct and 16 Dec. At other times key collected from Gunby Hall, £10 returnable deposit required.

P No. No access. £ No.

ST PETER

Sotby, Lincolnshire

Grade II* listed church dating from early 12th and 13th centuries.

Grant Recipient: Mr B F Cotton

Access Contact: Ms Sandra Meaking

T: 01507 343662 (evenings)

Open: Key available by telephone or written arrangement with Sandra Meaking, Chapel Cottage, Moor Lane, Sotby, Lincolnshire.

P Roadside parking.

Grass entry to building and small step. No WC for the disabled. Guide Dogs allowed.

£ No.

TATTERSHALL CASTLE

Tattershall, Lincoln, Lincolnshire LN4 4LR

A vast fortified and moated red-brick tower, built c1440 for Ralph Cromwell, Treasurer of England. The building was rescued from becoming derelict by Lord Curzon 1911-14 and contains four great chambers with enormous Gothic fireplaces, tapestries and brick vaulting. Gatehouse with museum room.

www.nationaltrust.org.uk

Grant Recipient: The National Trust

Access Contact: Property Manager

T: 01526 342543   **F:** 01526 342543

E-mail: tattershallcastle@nationaltrust.org.uk

Open: 4 Mar - 19 Mar & 4 Nov - 10 Dec: Sat & Sun 12 noon - 4pm; 25 Mar - 27 Sept: Sat - Wed 11am - 5.30pm. 30 Sept - 1 Nov: Sat - Wed 11am - 4pm. Ground floor of Castle may occasionally be closed for functions or events.

P Spaces: 40.

Wheelchair access to ground floor via ramp. Photograph album of inaccessible parts of Castle. WC for the disabled. Guide Dogs allowed.

£ Adult: £4. Child: £2. Family: £10.

WESTGATE HOUSE

Westgate, Louth, Lincolnshire LN11 9YQ

Grade II* Georgian town house in brick and stone, with 1775 neo-classical additions and proto-Regency remodelling c1799 on the Westgate façade. Interior contains fine plasterwork, mahogany doors, Carrara fireplaces and other fine details. Used as a school 1937-1980s but now in course of restoration as a residence by the present owners, after dereliction.

Grant Recipient: Professor P Byrne

Access Contact: Professor Byrne & Mrs Byrne

T: 01507 354388

Open: Ground floor only. Guided visits 11.30am - 4pm, by arrangement. Evening group visits for societies, etc., by arrangement all year.

P Public parking in town centre (5 mins walk).

No wheelchair access or WC for the disabled. Guide Dogs allowed.

£ Adult £3. Child: Free (when accompanied by an adult). Evening group visits: £5 pp (max 30) including wine and canapés.

13/13A MINSTER YARD

Lincoln, Lincolnshire LN2 1PW

Houses, mid-18th century, with late 18th and 19th century alterations.

Grant Recipient: Dean & Chapter of Lincoln Cathedral

Access Contact: Mrs Carol Heidschuster

T: 01522 527637   **F:** 01522 575 688

E-mail: worksmanager@lincolncathedral.com

Open: By written arrangement with the Works Manager, Lincoln Cathedral, 28 Eastgate, Lincoln LN2 4AA.

P No.

No wheelchair access or WC for the disabled. Guide Dogs allowed.

£ No.

18/18A MINSTER YARD

Lincoln, Lincolnshire LN2 1PX

13th and 14th century building with 17th century additions. Remodelled and extended in 1827 and re-fronted 1873 by J L Pearson.

Grant Recipient: Dean & Chapter of Lincoln Cathedral

Access Contact: Mrs Carol Heidschuster

T: 01522 527637   **F:** 01522 575 688

E-mail: worksmanager@lincolncathedral.com

Open: By written arrangement with the Works Manager, Lincoln Cathedral, 28 Eastgate, Lincoln LN2 4AA.

P No.

No wheelchair access or WC for the disabled. Guide Dogs allowed.

£ No.

ARABELLA AUFRERE TEMPLE

Brocklesby Park, Grimsby, Lincolnshire DN41 8PN

Garden Temple of ashlar and red brick with coupled doric columns on either side of a central arch leading to a rear chamber. Built c1787 and attributed to James Wyatt. Inscription above inner door: "Dedicated by veneration and affection to the memory of Arabella Aufrere."

Grant Recipient: The Earl of Yarborough

Access Contact: Mr H A Rayment

T: 01469 560214   **F:** 01469 561346

E-mail: office@brocklesby-estate.co.uk

Open: 1 Apr - 31 Aug: viewable from permissive paths through Mausoleum Woods at all reasonable times.

P Spaces: 10. Free parking in village or walks car park, 1 mile from site.

No wheelchair access or WC for the disabled. Guide Dogs allowed.

£ No.

BROCKLESBY MAUSOLEUM

Brocklesby Park, Grimsby, Lincolnshire DN41 8PN

Family Mausoleum designed by James Wyatt and built between 1787 and 1794 by Charles Anderson Pelham, who subsequently became Lord Yarborough, as a memorial to his wife Sophia who died at the age of 33. The classical design is based on the Temples of Vesta at Rome and Tivoli.

Grant Recipient: The Earl of Yarborough

Access Contact: Mr H A Rayment

T: 01469 560214   **F:** 01469 561346

E-mail: office@brocklesby-estate.co.uk

Open: Exterior: 1 Apr - 31 Aug: viewable from permissive paths through Mausoleum Woods at all reasonable times. Interior (excluding private crypt) by arrangement with the Estate Office. Admission charge for interior.

P Spaces: 10. Free parking in village or walks car park, ¼ mile from site.

No wheelchair access or WC for the disabled. Guide Dogs allowed.

£ Interior: Adult: £2. Child: £2. Other: £2.

BURGHLEY HOUSE

Stamford, Lincolnshire PE9 3JY

Large country house built by William Cecil, Lord High Treasurer of England, between 1555 and 1587, and still lived in by descendants of his family. Eighteen State Rooms, many decorated by Antonio Verrio in the 17th century, housing a collection of artworks including 17th century Italian paintings, Japanese ceramics, European porcelain and wood carvings by Grinling Gibbons and his followers There are also four State Beds, English and continental furniture and tapestries and textiles. 'Capability' Brown parkland.

www.burghley.co.uk

Grant Recipient: Burghley House Preservation Trust Ltd

Access Contact: Mr Philip Gompertz

T: 01780 761 974   **F:** 01780 480125

E-mail: philip.gompertz@burghley.co.uk

Open: 1 Apr - 29 Oct: daily (except Fris & 9 Sept) 11am - 4.30pm. Guided tours available at certain times.

P Spaces: 500. Parking for the disabled close to entrance.

Full wheelchair access. Please tel Property Manager for information on wheelchair access. WC for the disabled. Guide Dogs allowed.

£ Adult: £9. Child: £4. Senior/Student: £8. Groups (20+) £7.80pp. Schools £4. Family £22.

FYDELL HOUSE GATES, PIERS & RAILINGS

South Street, Boston, Lincolnshire PE21 6HU

Fronted by renewed, grant-aided gate, gate piers and railings, Fydell House was built in 1726 with minor 19th century alterations. Example of a small 18th century stately home. It contains links between Boston England and Boston Mass and houses the adult educational Pilgrim College Ltd.

Grant Recipient: Boston Preservation Trust Ltd

Access Contact: Boston Preservation Trust Ltd

Open: Access to the exterior at all reasonable times. Open all year (except BHs) but in term-time access to rooms is limited.

P Public car park nearby.

Full wheelchair access. WC for the disabled. Guide Dogs allowed.

£ No.

HARDING HOUSE

48-54 Steep Hill, Lincoln, Lincolnshire LN2

Grade II listed house of the 16th century, remodelled in the 18th and restored in the 20th. Built of coursed rubble and brick with a pantile roof. The building is divided up into several studios predominately used for a variety of craft uses.

Grant Recipient: Lincoln City Council

Access Contact: Mr Mark Wheater

T: 01522 873464   **F:** 01522 542589

E-mail: mark.wheater@lincoln.gov.uk

Open: During normal shop opening hours.

P No.

No wheelchair access or WC for the disabled. Guide Dogs allowed.

£ No.

HARLAXTON MANOR

Harlaxton, Grantham, Lincolnshire NG32 1AG

Grade I listed country house 1832-1844. Elizabethan, Revival style, now a university. The owner, Gregory Gregory, acted largely as his own architect, in collaboration with Anthony Salvin 1832-1838. The interior decoration, c1837-1854, incorporates important plasterwork probably by Bernasconi.

www.ueharlax.ac.uk

Grant Recipient: University of Evansville-Harlaxton College

Access Contact: Mr Ian Welsh

T: 01476 403000   **F:** 01476 403030

E-mail: iwelsh@ueharlax.ac.uk

Open: 1 - 13 Aug: 11am - 5pm open house. Guided tours (20+). Other times by arrangement.

P Spaces: 150.

Full wheelchair access. WC for the disabled. Guide Dogs allowed.

£ Adult: £5. Child: £2. Conc: £4, £10 (guided tours, including refreshments).

LONDON

BENJAMIN FRANKLIN'S HOUSE

36 Craven Street, London WC2N 5NF

A 1730s terraced house with c1792 alterations. Part of the Craven family's 18th century development of their Brewhouse estate, laid out by Flitcroft. Listed Graded I for historical associations. The world's only remaining home of the diplomat, scientist, inventor, writer, and philosopher Benjamin Franklin. Due to open to the public in Jan 2006, in time for Franklin's 300th 'birthday'. The house will feature a 'museum as theatre' historical experience that reveals the role Franklin and the house played on the eve of the American Revolution and Age of Enlightenment. A student science centre featuring hands-on experimentation with Franklin's London science, and a scholarship centre for promoting Anglo-American research and understanding.

www.thersa.org/Franklin

Grant Recipient: Friends of Benjamin Franklin House
Access Contact: Dr Marcia Balisciano
T: 020 7930 9121   **F:** 020 7930 9124
E-mail: BenjaminFranklinHouse@msn.com
Open: Limited viewing by arrangement until building work completed when the house will open to the public. London Open House: No
P None.
& No wheelchair access. No WC for the disabled. Guide Dogs allowed.
£ After opening there will be admission charges.

BRIXTON ACADEMY

211 Stockwell Road, Lambeth, London SW9 9SL

Built in 1929 as the largest of the four "Astoria" theatres. Retains many original features including elaborate presenium arch over stage and art deco interior. Presently used as a music venue.

www.brixton-academy.co.uk

Grant Recipient: McKenzie Group Ltd (Ex Magstack Ltd)
Access Contact: Mr Nigel Downs
T: 020 7787 3131   **F:** 020 7738 4427
E-mail: nigel@brixton-academy.co.uk
Open: Academy Open Day: 2 Aug 12 noon - 4pm. Performances throughout the year. London Open House: Yes
P Spaces: 300. NCP car park (Popes Road). Restricted parking around Brixton Academy.
& Wheelchair access to ground floor and auditorium. WC for the disabled. Guide Dogs allowed.
£ Charge applies to events at the venue.

BRUCE CASTLE MUSEUM (HARINGEY LIBRARIES ARCHIVES & MUSEUM SERVICE)

Lordship Lane, London N17 8NU

Once a 16th century manor house, Bruce Castle has been modified over the 17th, 18th and 19th centuries. Past owners include Sir Rowland Hill, the postal reformer, who ran a school here. Now a museum, set in parkland, it houses displays about the building, local history & art, and an archive.

www.haringey.gov.uk/leisure

Grant Recipient: London Borough of Haringey
Access Contact: Ms Deborah Hedgecock
T: 020 8808 8772   **F:** 020 8808 4118
E-mail: museum.services@haringey.gov.uk
Open: Museum: Wed - Sun 1 - 5pm plus Easter Mon, May Day, late May BH and Aug BH. Closed Good Fri, Christmas Day, Boxing Day & New Year's Day. Groups at other times by arrangement. Archive: Wed & Sat 1 - 5pm, Thurs & Fri 9am - 5pm. Visitors to the archive are advised to book. London Open House: No
P Spaces: 15.
& Full wheelchair access. WC for the disabled. Guide Dogs allowed.
£ No.

BRUNSWICK SQUARE GARDENS

Brunswick Square, London, WC1

A public park originally part of the grounds of the Foundling Hospital, founded by Sir Thomas Coram.

www.camden.gov.uk

Grant Recipient: London Borough of Camden
Access Contact: Mr Martin Stanton
T: 020 7974 1693   **F:** 020 7974 1543
E-mail: martin.stanton@camden.gov.uk
Open: From 7.30am until dusk all year.

London Open House: No.
P On street parking.
& Full wheelchair access. No WC for the disabled. Guide Dogs allowed.
£ No.

BUILDING 40

Royal Military Academy, Woolwich, London SE18 6ST

Building 40 is a Grade II* listed building on the historic Royal Arsenal site. Constructed in 1718 and 1723 of red brown stock brick with a slate roof, attributed to Nicholas Hawsmoor. One of four buildings now housing the Royal Artillery Museum called Firepower.

www.firepower.org.uk

Grant Recipient: Royal Artillery Museums Ltd
Access Contact: Mrs Eileen Noon
T: 020 8855 7755   **F:** 020 88557100
E-mail: eileen@firepower.org.uk
Open: Building 40: used for corporate events and temporary exhibitions. Museum: Wed - Sun 10:30am - 5pm, closed Mon and Tues. London Open House: Yes.
P Spaces: 400.
& Wheelchair access through the rear of the building to the ground floor only. WC for the disabled. Guide Dogs allowed.
£ Charging varies according to event.

CHAPEL OF THE HOSPITAL OF ST JOHN AND ST ELIZABETH

60 Grove End Road, London NW8 9NH

Built in 1864 and designed by George Goldie, a leading Catholic architect of the day in the Italian Baroque style.

Grant Recipient: Trustees of the Hospital Chapel
Access Contact: Ms Christine Malcolmson, Matron
T: 0207 806 4000 (ext.4294)   **F:** 0207 806 4001
E-mail: christine.malcolmson@hje.org.uk
Open: All year. Mass said in Chapel on Suns between 11am - 12pm and other times during the week.
P NCP Car Park.
& Via the balconies on the 1st floor. WC for the disabled. Guide Dogs allowed.
£ No.

CLISSOLD HOUSE

Stoke Newington Church Street, London N16

House built c1770 for Jonathan Hoare, a Quaker banker. Located in middle of Clissold park, a late 18th Century park, developed in 1880s into a public park.

Grant Recipient: London Borough of Hackney
Access Contact: Ms Carole Stewart
T: 020 8356 7476   **F:** 020 8356 7575
E-mail: carole.stewart@hackney.gov.uk
Open: Café is open all year, daily 9am - 7pm. Heritage Open Days: guided tours for small groups. London Open House: Yes.
P On street parking.
& No wheelchair access or WC for the disabled. Guide Dogs allowed.
£ No.

COLLEGE OF ARMS

Queen Victoria Street, London EC4V 4BT

Built in 1670s/1680s to the design of Francis Sandford and Morris Emmett to house the Heralds' offices, on the site of their earlier building, Derby Place, which was destroyed in the Great Fire of 1666. The principal room is Earl Marshal's Court, which is two floors high with gallery, panelling and throne. New record room added 1842 and portico and terrace in 1867.

www.college-of-arms.gov.uk

Grant Recipient: College of Arms
Access Contact: The Bursar
T: 020 7248 2762   **F:** 020 7248 6448
E-mail: enquiries@college-of-arms.gov.uk
Open: Earl Marshal's Court only: all year (except BHs, State and Special Occasions), Mon - Fri 10am - 4pm. Group tours of Record Room (max 20) and lecture after 6pm by arrangement with Officer-in-Waiting (tel: 020 7248 2762). London Open House: Yes.
P No.
& No wheelchair access or WC for the disabled. Guide Dogs allowed.
£ No.

COUNTESS OF DERBY'S ALMSHOUSES

Church Hill, Harefield, London UB9 6DU

16th century range, established in 1636 for poor women of good character in the Parish of Harefield, known as the Countess of Derby Almshouses. Four stacks of paired or tripled diagonal brick chimney stacks. Originally housed six residents in 'one up one down' 'apartments' each with their own front door and staircase, hence the windows at first floor level. Converted to accommodate four on the ground floor only in the 1950s and underwent conversion again in 2003/4 into two self-contained flats. Listed Grade II*. There is a memorial by Maximilian Colt to Lady Alice, the Dowager Countess of Derby, who bequeathed the Almshouses in her Will dated 1636, in Grade I listed St Mary's Parish Church, Harefield (100 metres from the Almshouses).

www.harefieldcharities.co.uk

Grant Recipient: Harefield Parochial Charities
Access Contact: Mrs Joyce Willis/ Mr John Ross
T: 01895 822657 / 01895 823058   **F:** 01895 823644
E-mail: hpc@harefieldcharities.co.uk
Open: Access to the exterior from the main road, Church Hill, Harefield, London Open House: No.
P On street parking.   **&** No access.   **£** No.

DISSENTERS' CHAPEL

Kensal Green Cemetery, Harrow Road, London W10 4RA

Grade II* listed building within Grade II* Registered cemetery. Cemetery dates from 1832 and is London's oldest. The Chapel was designed in Greek Revival style by John Griffith in 1834. It is now used by the Friends of Kensal Green Cemetery as a headquarters, exhibition space and art gallery and as a centre for their guided walks, lectures and special events.

www.hct.org.uk or www.kensalgreen.co.uk

Grant Recipient: Historic Chapels Trust
Access Contact: Mr Tom Bolton
T: 020 8671 0801 **E-mail:** teabolton@hotmail.com
Open: Cemetery: daily. Dissenters' Chapel: Sun afternoons , other times by arrangement. Guided tours of chapels and cemetery for modest charge, also tours of the Catacombs 1st and 3rd Sun in every month. London Open House: Yes.
P Parking in adjacent streets, parking for the disabled in cemetery.
& Full wheelchair access. WC for the disabled. Guide Dogs allowed.
£ £5 (donation requested for guided tours only).

DR JOHNSON'S HOUSE

17 Gough Square, London EC4A 3DE

Fine 18th century town house in the heart of the City of London. Here Dr Johnson compiled his dictionary (published 1755). Original staircase and woodwork throughout and collection of prints, paintings and Johnson memorabilia.

www.drjohnsonshouse.org

Grant Recipient: Dr Johnson's House Trust
Access Contact: The Curator Dr Johnson's House Trust
T: 020 7353 3745   **F:** 020 7353 3745
E-mail: curator@drjohnsonshouse.org
Open: Mon - Sat: May - Sept: 11am - 5.30pm, Oct - Apr: 11am - 5pm. Closed Suns & BHs. London Open House: Yes.
P On-street meter parking.
& No wheelchair access. WC for the disabled. Guide Dogs allowed.
£ Adult: £4.50. Child: £1.50. Conc: £3.50.

DULWICH COLLEGE

College Road, Dulwich, London SE21 7LD

Dulwich College was founded in 1619; the main buildings date from 1866-70 by the younger Charles Barry and are listed Grade II*. Three blocks lined by arcades in ornate Northern Italian Renaissance style. Close to Dulwich Village.

www.dulwich.org.uk

Grant Recipient: Dulwich College
Access Contact: Ms Julia Field
T: 020 8299 9284   **F:** 020 8299 9262
E-mail: borns@dulwich.org.uk
Open: Exterior visible from South Circular. Interior by arrangement with the Bursar. London Open House: Yes.
P Spaces: 50. 200 parking spaces during school holidays.
& Wheelchair access with assistance (a few steps at entrance). WC for the disabled. Guide Dogs allowed.
£ Adult: £4, £6 (tour & archives). Child: £4, £6 (tour & archives). Other: £4, £6 (tour & archives).

FULHAM PALACE STABLEYARD WALL

Bishop's Avenue, London SW6

Home to the Bishops of London for over a thousand years to 1973. The two storey medieval west court is red brick with terracotta roof tiles. The mainly three storey Georgian east court is brown and yellow brick with parapets and slate roofs. Set in historic grounds near the river.

Grant Recipient: London Borough of Hammersmith & Fulham

Access Contact: Dr Scott Cooper

T: 020 7736 8140   **F:** 020 7751 0164

E-mail: scott.cooper@lbhf.gov.uk

Open: The Palace grounds open throughout year during daylight hours, admission is free. Museum of Fulham Palace: Mar - Oct: Wed - Sun 2 - 5pm; Nov - Feb: Thurs - Sun 1 - 4pm. Tours of principal rooms and gardens every 2nd & 4th Sun. Restoration works will affect access to the Museum and Palace: please check for current information. London Open House: Yes.

Ⓟ Pay parking on Bishop's Avenue, next to Palace.

♿ Prior notice is required for wheelchair users wishing to visit the ground floor rooms to enable the ramp to be installed. Gardens accessible. WC for the disabled. Guide Dogs allowed.

£ No.

GARRICK'S TEMPLE

Hampton Court Road, Richmond-upon-Thames, London TW12 2EN

The actor-manager David Garrick built the Temple in 1756 to celebrate the genius of William Shakespeare. The Temple was restored between 1997-1999 and now houses an exhibition of Garrick's acting career and life at Hampton, while the grounds have been landscaped to echo their original 18th century layout.

www.hampton-online.co.uk

Grant Recipient: London Borough of Richmond-upon-Thames

Access Contact: Mark De Novellis / Sara Bird

T: 020 8831 6000   **F:** 020 8744 0501

E-mail: m.denovellis@richmond.gov.uk

Open: Temple: Apr - Sept: Suns, 2 - 5pm. Also pre-arranged visits for small groups throughout the year (tel: 020 8831 6000). Lawn: open all year 7.30am - dusk. London Open House: Yes.

Ⓟ Public parking on Molesey Hurst from where Temple access is via Ferry which runs all day throughout the summer.

♿ Wheelchair access to lawn gardens only. No WC for the disabled. Guide Dogs allowed.

£ No.

GUNNERSBURY PARK TEMPLE

Gunnersbury Park, Popes Lane, Acton, London W3 8LQ

Grade II* listed temple. Built before 1760. Red brick with stone Doric portico. Situated in Gunnersbury Park, the estate of Princess Amelia in the 18th century. The 185 acre park became a public park in 1926.

www.hounslow.info/gunnersburypark

Grant Recipient: London Borough of Hounslow

Access Contact: Ms Jill Draper

T: 020 8992 1612   **F:** 020 8752 0686

E-mail: gp-museum@cip.org.uk

Open: Park open daily 8am - dusk. The interior will be open for London Open House and at other times by arrangement. The Temple is used for events throughout the year and is available for hire.

Ⓟ Spaces: 120.

♿ Wheelchair access to the exterior only. There are two toilets for the disabled in park, but not in close proximity to the Temple. Guide Dogs allowed.

£ No.

HACKNEY EMPIRE

291 Mare Street, London E8 1EJ

Hackney Empire, designed and built by Frank Matcham in 1901, is one of the finest surviving variety theatres in Britain. Restoration and renovation completed 2004, providing modern facilities and access for all.

www.hackneyempire.co.uk

Grant Recipient: Hackney Empire Ltd

Access Contact: Mr S Thomsett

T: 020 8510 4500   **F:** 020 8510 4530

E-mail: info@hackneyempire.co.uk

Open: Performances all year. London Open House: Yes.

Ⓟ On-street parking.

♿ Full wheelchair access. WC for the disabled. Guide Dogs allowed.

£ Charges for performances and some organised tours.

HIGHPOINT

North Hill, Highgate, London N6 4BA

Two blocks of flats built in 1935 and 1938 by Lubetkin and Tecton. Constructed of reinforced concrete with decorative features.

Grant Recipient: Mantra Ltd

Access Contact: Mr Stephen Ellman

T: 0870 702 2700   **F:** 0870 702 2701

E-mail: stephen.ellman@grossfine.com

Open: By arrangement with Mr Stephen Ellman Gross Fine, Saffron House, Saffron Way, London EC1N 8YB. London Open House: Yes.

Ⓟ No Parking.

♿ No wheelchair access or WC for the disabled. Guide Dogs allowed.

£ No.

HIMALAYA PALACE CINEMA (FORMERLY LIBERTY CINEMA)

14 South Road, Southall, London UB1 1RT

Former cinema, later market hall. 1928. An early work by George Coles; the only known example of cinema built in the Chinese style. Street elevation faced with coloured glazed tiles with red pantiled pagoda roofs. Interior badly fire damaged. Repaired and returned to use as a three screen cinema showing Bollywood, Tamil, Telugu and Afganistan movies.

Grant Recipient: Himalaya Carpets Ltd

Access Contact: Mr S Pandher

T: 020 8574 6193   **F:** 020 8574 2317

E-mail: himalayacarpets@tiscali.co.uk

Open: Daily, 10.30am - 11.30pm. Non-public areas by arrangement. London Open House: No.

Ⓟ Council car park at rear of cinema.

♿ Full wheelchair access. No WC for the disabled. No Guide Dogs.

£ Adult: £3.95 (before 2pm), £5.95 other times. Child: £3.95 (all times). Senior: £3.95.

KEW BRIDGE STEAM MUSEUM

Kew Bridge Pumping Station, Green Dragon Lane, Brentford, London TW8 0EN

19th century Victorian waterworks with original steam pumping engines which are operated every weekend. "Water for Life" gallery exploring 2000 years of London's water.

www.kbsm.org

Grant Recipient: Kew Bridge Engines Trust & Water Supply Museum Ltd

Access Contact: Kew Bridge Engines Trust & Water Supply Museum Ltd

T: 020 8568 4757   **F:** 020 8569 9978

E-mail: info@kbsm.org

Open: Daily, 11am - 5pm. Closed Good Fri & 23 Dec - 2 Jan. Subject to change. Contact the Museum for up-to-date information. London Open House: Yes.

Ⓟ Spaces: 45.

♿ Partial wheelchair access. WC for the disabled. Guide Dogs allowed.

£ Adult: £5.75. Child: Free. Other: £4.75.

LANDMARK ARTS CENTRE

Ferry Road, Teddington, London TW11 9NN

Grade II* former church, c1889, in French-Gothic style by architect William Niven. A number of intended architectural features were never in the end built, due to insufficient funds (hence the incomplete flying buttresses for example). Redundant as a church in 1977. Following renovation now used as an Arts Centre with a variety of arts events, classes and private events.

www.landmarkartscentre.org

Grant Recipient: London Diocesan Fund

Access Contact: Mr Graham Watson

T: 020 8614 8036   **F:** 020 8614 8080

E-mail: grahamgwatson@aol.com

Open: Mon - Fri 10am - 5pm (shorter hours on public event weekends), contact James West at the Landmark Arts Centre (tel: 020 8977 7558, fax: 020 8977 4830, e-mail: info@landmarkartscentre.org) to check. Visits at other times by arrangement with James West, subject to staff availability. London Open House: No

Ⓟ Spaces: 4. Additional on-street parking nearby.

♿ Full access. WC for the disabled. Guide Dogs allowed.

£ Admission charges for some public events.

LSO ST LUKE'S

161 Old Street, London EC1V 9NG

Former Church of St Luke, 1727-33. The west tower, spire and flanking staircase wings by Nicholas Hawksmoor. Listed Grade I. Restored to become the home of the London Symphony Orchestra's music education and community programme. Its conversion began in 2000 and the building combines external restoration with a contemporary interior.

www.lso.co.uk/lsostlukes

Grant Recipient: St Luke Management Company Ltd

Access Contact: St Luke Management Company Ltd

Open: By arrangement only. London Open House: Yes

Ⓟ Spaces: 5. Strictly limited to people attending events at the site, by arrangement.

♿ Full wheelchair access. WC for the disabled. Guide Dogs allowed.

£ Charges according to event.

MAPPIN TERRACE CAFÉ

London Zoo, Regents Park, London NW1 4RY

The café was designed by John James Joass and built between 1914-20. It was funded by John Newton Mappin. It is a single story red-brick building with a pantiled roof. It is characterised by paired Tuscan columns, French windows, bracketed eaves and pavilion towers at three angles.

Grant Recipient: Zoological Society of London

Access Contact: Zoological Society of London

Open: On view to visitors to London Zoo (daily except 25 Dec). London Open House: No.

Ⓟ Spaces: 300. Car park £7, 250 yards away.

♿ Full wheelchair access. Guide Dogs are housed and a personal guide provided. WC for the disabled.

£ Adult: £13. Child: £9.75. Other: £11.

ORLEANS HOUSE GALLERY

Riverside, Twickenham, London TW1 3DJ

Orleans House Gallery comprises the Octagon Room (1721) with its fine Baroque interior, and the surviving wing/orangery of the 18th century Orleans House, the rest having been demolished in 1926. Overlooking the Thames and residing in preserved natural woodland, the Gallery presents a programme of temporary exhibitions, organises educational projects/activities and is responsible for the Richmond Borough Art Collection.

www.richmond.gov.uk/orleanshouse

Grant Recipient: London Borough of Richmond-upon-Thames

Access Contact: Mr Mark De Novellis

T: 020 8831 6000   **F:** 020 8744 0501

E-mail: m.denovellis@richmond.gov.uk

Open: All year: Tues - Sat 1 - 5.30pm. Suns 2 - 5.30pm. Oct - Mar, closes 4.30pm. Grounds: daily from 9am until dusk. For BH and Christmas opening hours please telephone. London Open House: Yes.

Ⓟ Spaces: 60.

♿ Wheelchair access to ground floor only. WC for the disabled. Guide Dogs allowed.

£ No.

PITZHANGER MANOR HOUSE & GALLERY

Walpole Park, Mattock Lane, London W5 5EQ

Pitzhanger Manor House is set in Walpole Park, Ealing and was owned and rebuilt by architect and surveyor Sir John Soane (1753-1837). Much of the house has been restored to its early 19th century style and a Victorian wing houses a collection of Martinware Pottery (1877-1923). Pitzhanger Manor Gallery opened in 1996 in a 1940s extension and exhibitions of professional contemporary art in all media are shown in both the House and Gallery.

www.ealing.gov.uk/pmgallery&house

Grant Recipient: London Borough of Ealing

Access Contact: Pitzhanger Manor House and Gallery

T: 020 8567 1227   **F:** 020 8567 0596

E-mail: pmgallery&house@ealing.gov.uk

Open: Tues - Fri 1pm - 5pm, Sat 11am - 5pm. Summer Sun openings (ring for details). Closed BHs, Christmas and Easter. London Open House: Yes.

Ⓟ Parking for orange badge holders. 2 parking meters.

♿ Access for certain types of wheelchair only with assistance (domestic lift and some steps), please phone in advance for further information. WC for the disabled. Guide Dogs allowed.

£ No.

PRIORY CHURCH OF THE ORDER OF ST JOHN

St John's Square, Clerkenwell, London EC1M

Remains of the Priory Church of the Knights Hospitallers' London headquarters, including choir and 12th century crypt. Museum in adjacent St John's Gate presents information on the Order of St John and conducts guided tours.

www.sja.org.uk/history

Grant Recipient: The Order of St John of Jerusalem

Access Contact: Ms Pamela Willis

T: 020 7324 4071   **F:** 020 7336 0587

E-mail: museum@nhq.sja.org.uk.

Open: Guided tours: Tues, Fri & Sat 11am & 2.30pm. Other days and times by arrangement with the Museum. London Open House: Yes.

P Metered parking available in St John's Square.

& Wheelchair access to Church with assistance, but not the crypt. WC for the disabled at St John's Gate. Guide Dogs allowed.

£ Donations requested for guided tours.

RAINHAM HALL

The Broadway, Rainham, Havering, London RM13 9YN

Georgian house built in 1729 to a symmetrical plan and with fine wrought iron gates, carved porch and interior panelling plasterwork.

www.nationaltrust.org.uk

Grant Recipient: The National Trust

Access Contact: Property Manager

T: 01708 555 360

Open: Limited access on BH weekends, please check with the Hall before visiting. London Open House: No.

P On-street pay-and-display parking nearby.

& Wheelchair access to ground floor only. Guide dogs by arrangement. WC for the disabled.

£ No.

RICHMOND WEIR & LOCK

Riverside, Richmond-upon-Thames, London

The lock and weir are important examples in the history of hydraulic engineering. Constructed in 1894 to control river levels between Richmond and Teddington at half-tide level, the weir was engineered to ensure that the river remained navigable at all times. Operated and maintained by the Port of London Authority since its establishment in 1909, the machinery was designed and built by Ransomes & Rapier.

www.portoflondon.co.uk

Grant Recipient: Port of London Authority

Access Contact: Mr James Trimmer

T: 020 7743 7900   **F:** 020 7743 7998

E-mail: james.trimmer@pola.co.uk

Open: The lock and weir are open at all times for passage by river except for 3 weeks in Nov/Dec for major maintenance undertaken by the Port of London Authority. The footbridge over the lock is open 6.30am - 9.30pm BST and 6.30am - 7.30pm GMT. London Open House: Yes.

P No.   **&** No access.   **£** No.

ST ANDREWS OLD CHURCH

Old Church Lane, Kingsbury, Brent, London

Possibly of Saxon origin, now of 15th century appearance with 19th century restoration work. Considered to be the oldest building in Brent. Contains brasses and memorials to well-known local families dating from the 16th to the 19th centuries.

Grant Recipient: The Churches Conservation Trust

Access Contact: Ms Chloe Cockerill

T: 020 7213 0660   **F:** 020 7213 0678

Open: 29 May (Welsh Harp Day) and London Open House, at other times by arrangement.

P On-street parking.

& Full wheelchair access. No WC for the disabled. Guide Dogs allowed.

£ No.

ST ETHELBURGA'S CENTRE FOR RECONCILIATION AND PEACE

78 Bishopgate, London EC2N 4AG

Church of St Ethelburga the Virgin built in the late 14th and early 15th centuries. Devastated by a terrorist bomb in Apr 1993 and re-opened in Nov 2002, after restoration, for use as a Centre for Reconciliation and Peace.

www.stethelburgas.org

Grant Recipient: St Ethelburga's Centre for Reconciliation & Peace

Access Contact: Mr Simon Keyes

T: 020 7496 1610   **F:** 020 7638 1440

E-mail: enquiries@stethelburgas.org

Open: Every Wed 11am - 3pm. Groups may visit at other times by arrangement. Details of services, public lectures and other events available from the website or by telephone. London Open House: Yes.

P No.

& Full wheelchair access. WC for the disabled. Guide Dogs allowed.

£ No.

ST MATTHIAS OLD CHURCH COMMUNITY CENTRE

113 Poplar High Street, Poplar, London E14 0AE

Built by in 1650-54 by the East India Company, St Matthias Old Church is the oldest building in Docklands. Declared redundant in 1977, the building became derelict. In 1990 the building was restored and is now used as a community arts/cultural centre.

Grant Recipient: London Diocesan Fund

Access Contact: Mr Nizam Uddin

T: 020 7987 0459   **F:** 020 7531 9973

E-mail: niz_68@hotmail.com

Open: Mon - Fri: 10am - 3pm. London Open House: No.

P Car park for limited number of cars.

& Full wheelchair access. WC for the disabled. Guide Dogs allowed.

£ No.

ST PAUL'S STEINER PROJECT

1 St Paul's Road, London N1 2QH

Grade II* listed church, 1826-28 by Sir Charles Barry. Perpendicular in style. Converted to a 'cradle to grave' education and cultural centre, including a Steiner school, multi use community performance space, adult education and information centre.

Grant Recipient: St Paul's Steiner Project

Access Contact: Ms Jane Gerhard

T: 020 7226 4454   **F:** 102 7226 2062

E-mail: st.pauls.school@btinternet.com

Open: 3 Feb, 10 Mar, 19 May, 16 June and 15 Nov. Other times by arrangement with 2 days notice. London Open House: Yes.

P Pay and display.

& Wheelchair access to ground floor. WC for the disabled. Guide Dogs allowed.

£ No.

THE HOUSE MILL

Three Mill Lane, Bromley-by-Bow, London E3 3DU

Industrial water mill, originally built 1776 as part of a distillery. Contains four floors with remains of un-restored machinery, four water wheels and gearing. Originally had 12 pairs of millstones and has unique survival of Fairbairn-style "silent millstone machinery".

Grant Recipient: River Lea Tidal Mill Trust

Access Contact: Ms Patricia Wilkinson

T: 020 8539 6726   **F:** 020 8539 2317

E-mail: RLTMT@bcos.demon.co.uk

Open: Sun of National Mills Week, Heritage Open Days and the first Sun of each month Apr - Dec: 11am - 4pm. Other Suns May - Oct: 2 - 4pm. Groups by arrangement with Ms Patricia Wilkinson, 1B Forest Drive East, Leytonstone, London E11 1JX. For further info tel: 020 8539 6726. London Open House: Yes.

P Car park nearby.

P Full wheelchair access. WC for the disabled. Guide Dogs allowed.

£ Adult £3. Child: Free. Other: £1.50.

THE QUEEN'S CHAPEL OF THE SAVOY

Savoy Hill, Strand, London WC2R 0DA

Originally part of a hospital founded in 1512 by Henry VII. Rebuilt by Robert Smirke after a fire in 1864, from which time the ceiling covered with heraldic emblems dates. Recently restored.

Grant Recipient: Duchy of Lancaster

Access Contact: Mr Phillip Chancellor

T: 020 7836 7221   **F:** 020 7379 8088

E-mail: pdc46@mailcity.com

Open: All year except Aug & Sept: Tues- Fri 11.30am - 3.30pm; Sun for Morning Service only. Closed for a week after Christmas Day & Easter Day. London Open House: No.

P No.

& Partial wheelchair access. No WC for the disabled. Guide Dogs allowed.

£ No.

THE ROUND CHAPEL

(Clapton Park United Reformed Church), 1d Glenarm Road, London E5 0LY

Grade II* listed United Reformed Church, c1871. Horseshoe-shaped plan with roof and gallery supported by iron pillars. Detailed columns form a continuous iron arcade at roof level with latticework effects. Contemporary pulpit with double flight of stairs, organ and organ case.

Grant Recipient: Hackney Historic Buildings Trust

Access Contact: Dr Ann Robey

T: 020 8525 0706   **F:** 020 8986 0029

E-mail: roundchapel@pop3.poptel.org.uk

Open: Many events take place in the Round Chapel which the public can attend. Also available to hire for private events, otherwise access by arrangement. London Open House: Yes.

P Spaces: 3.

& Wheelchair access to ground floor only. WC for the disabled. Guide Dogs allowed.

£ No.

WALPOLE'S HOUSE

St Mary's College, Strawberry Hill, Waldegrave Road, Twickenham, London TW1 4SX

Bought by Horace Walpole in 1749 and over the next half century converted into his own vision of a 'gothic' fantasy with 14 rooms open to the public containing chimneypieces based on Medieval tombs and a collection of 16th century painted glass roundels. Reputedly the first substantial building of the Gothic Revival.

Grant Recipient: St Mary's, Strawberry Hill

Access Contact: Head of Catering and Conference Services

T: 020 8240 4044   **F:** 020 8255 4255

E-mail: gallaghs@smuc.ac.uk

Open: 7 May - 24 Sept: Sun only 2 - 3.30pm. Guided group tours (10+) by arrangement on any day except Sat. London Open House: Yes.

P Spaces: 60.

& Wheelchair access to ground floor and grounds with difficulty - doorways are small. WC for the disabled. Guide Dogs allowed.

£ Adult: £5.50, Child: £4.75, Senior: £4.75.

WAPPING HYDRAULIC POWER PUMPING STATION

Wapping Wall, London E1W 3ST

The Wapping Hydraulic Power Station was built by the London Hydraulic Power Company in 1890. One of the five London Stations of its kind, it harnessed Thames water to provide power throughout the central London area. The showcase building of the LHPC, it was used as a model for power stations in Argentina, Australia, New York and Europe. Now houses an art gallery and restaurant.

www.thewappingproject.com

Grant Recipient: Women's Playhouse Trust

Access Contact: Women's Playhouse Trust

T: 020 7680 2080   **F:** 020 7680 2081

E-mail: jules@wapping-wpt.com

Open: All year except 23 Dec - 4 Jan: Mon - Fri: 12 noon - Midnight. Sat 10am - Midnight & Sun 10am - 6pm. London Open House: No.

P Spaces: 30.

& Full wheelchair access. WC for the disabled. Guide Dogs allowed.

£ No.

WHITECHAPEL ART GALLERY

Whitechapel High Street, London E1 7QX

Grade II* listed Arts and Crafts building constructed in the late 1890s by C H Townsend. Occupied by the Whitechapel Art Gallery, which was founded in 1901 by the Revd Canon Barnett 'to bring great art to the people of the East End'.

www.whitechapel.org

Grant Recipient: Trustees of the Whitechapel Art Gallery

Access Contact: Mr Tom Wilcox

T: 020 7522 7865   **F:** 020 7377 1685

E-mail: TomWilcox@whitechapel.org

Open: All year: Tues - Sun 11am - 6pm, Thurs 11am - 9pm. Various exhibitions. London Open House: No.

P Paid parking in Spreadeagle Yard to the left of the gallery off Whitechapel High Street.

& Full wheelchair access. WC for the disabled. Guide Dogs allowed.

£ No, but one exhibition per year will have entrance fee.

WILTONS MUSIC HALL

Graces Alley, Tower Hamlets, London E1 8JB
The world's oldest surviving grand Victorian music hall now listed Grade II*. John Wilton built the theatre behind his public house 'The Prince of Denmark' in 1858, in Graces Alley and it continued as a music hall until 1884. Hall now open with regular performances and shows.
www.wiltons.org.uk
Grant Recipient: Wiltons Music Hall Trust
Access Contact: Frances Mayhen, House Manager
T: 020 7702 9555   **F:** 020 7702 1414
E-mail: info@wiltons.org.uk
Open: Mon - Fri 10am - 4pm, pre-booked guided tours only. Other public events/productions in evenings. London Open House. fee.
P Parking facilities near by.
access to main building and [illegible] WC for the disabled. Guide Dogs allowed.
£ £4 (guided tour).

MERSEYSIDE

BROUGHTON HALL CONSERVATORY

Convent of Mercy, Yew Tree Lane, West Derby, Liverpool, Merseyside L12 9HH
Victorian conservatory of rectangular shape with an entrance porch at one end and an access bay to main building, at the other. The cast iron structure is mounted on a stone plinth. The elevations are divided into a series of panels with decorated cast iron circular columns. From the capitols spring semi-circular arches. These form the bases of the frieze moulding which runs round the periphery of the building. The flooring is of quarry tiles.
Grant Recipient: The Institute of Our Lady of Mercy
Access Contact: Sister Superior
T: 0151 228 9232   **F:** 0151 259 0677
Open: By written arrangement only, Mon - Sat 10am - 4pm. No access on Suns or BHs.
P Spaces: 4.
Full wheelchair access. WC for the disabled. Guide Dogs allowed.
£ No.

FORMBY HALL

Southport Old Road, Formby, Merseyside L37 0AB
Built c1620 with 18th century extensions and later alterations.
Grant Recipient: Mr Michael McComb
Access Contact: Mr Michael McComb
T: 01704 878 999   **F:** 01704 572 436
Open: Access to the exterior by arrangement with Mr McComb, 8 Victoria Road, Formby, Liverpool L37 7AG. Telephone: 01704 878 999.
P Spaces: 1.   No access.   £ No.

LIVERPOOL COLLEGIATE APARTMENTS

Shaw Street, Liverpool, Merseyside L6 1NR
Grade II* former school built 1843 of red sandstone in Tudor Gothic style, gutted by fire and now converted into residential block.
Grant Recipient: Urban Splash Ltd
Access Contact: Mr Bill Maynard
T: 0161 839 2999   **F:** 0161 839 8999
E-mail: billmaynard@urbansplash.co.uk
Open: Exterior only, visible from Shaw Street.
P No.
Full wheelchair access. No WC for the disabled. No Guide Dogs.
£ No.

SEFTON PARK

Liverpool, Merseyside L18 3JD
108 hectare public park, designed in 1867, the first to introduce French influence to the design of parks through the designer Edouard André who had worked on the design of major Parisian parks. Sefton Park is Grade II* registered and contains several listed statues and other features. The Grade II* listed Palm House, 1896 by Mackenzie and Moncur, is an octagonal iron frame structure which appears as 3 domed roofs, one above the other.
www.palmhouse.org.uk
Grant Recipient: Liverpool City Council
Access Contact: Ms Emma Reid
T: 0151 726 9304   **F:** 0151 726 2419
E-mail: info@palmhouse.org.uk
Open: Park open at all times. Palm House: 1 Apr - 31 Oct: Mon - Sat 10.30am - 5pm, Sun 10.30am - 4pm, may be closed on Tues and Thurs & from 4pm for events; 1 Nov - 31 Mar: Mon - Sun 10.30am - 4pm, may be closed on Tues and Thurs for events. The Trust reserves the right to shut the Palm House on other occasions and will endeavour to give as much notice as possible on the website and information line (tel: 0151 726 2415). Heritage Open Days.
P On-street parking available on edge of park.
Full wheelchair access. No WC for the disabled. Guide Dogs allowed.
£ No.

SPEKE HALL

The Walk, Liverpool, Merseyside L24 1XD
One of the most important timber framed manor houses in the country, dating from 1530. The interior spans many periods: the Great Hall and great tudor room, the Oak Parlour and smaller rooms, some with William Morris wallpapers, show the Victorian desire for privacy and comfort. There is some Jacobean plasterwork and intricately carved furniture. Restored garden and woodland walks.
www.nationaltrust.org.uk
Grant Recipient: The National Trust
Access Contact: Property Manager
T: 0151 427 7231   **F:** 0151 427 9860
E-mail: spekehall@nationaltrust.org.uk
Open: House: 22 Mar - 29 Oct, Wed - Sun (open BH); Nov and Dec, Sat & Sun only. Mar - mid Oct 1 - 5.30pm; mid Oct - Dec 1 - 4.30pm. Woodland & garden: open daily all year, closed 24 - 26 & 31 Dec, 1 Jan. Times: Mar - mid Oct 11am - 5.30pm; mid Oct 2006 - mid Mar 2007 11am - dusk.
P Spaces: 400.   500 yards from the property. Courtesy shuttle service.
Wheelchair access to ground floor of house. WC for the disabled. Guide Dogs allowed.
£ Adult: £6.50, £3.50 (grounds only). Child: £3.50, £1.80 (grounds only). Family: £19.50, £10 (grounds only).

WALLASEY UNITARIAN CHURCH

Manor Road, Liscard, Wallasey, Merseyside CH44
'Arts & Crafts' chapel interior dating from 1899 with fittings by Bernard Sleigh and craftsmen associated with Bromsgrove Guild.
www.hct.org.uk
Grant Recipient: Historic Chapels Trust
Access Contact: Mr Terry Edgar
T: 0151 639 9707
E-mail: terryedgar@hotmail.com
Open: At all reasonable times by arrangement with key holder, Terry Edgar, 5 Mere Lane, Wallasey Village CH45 3HY. Heritage Open Days.
P Spaces: 10.
Full wheelchair access. WC for the disabled. Guide Dogs allowed.
£ Donations invited.

WEST DERBY COURTHOUSE

Almonds Green, Liverpool L12 5HP
Mid 17th century sandstone Courthouse. Its interior, lit by four mullioned windows contains original court furniture such as stewards and jury benches as well as muniment cupboards for rolls of parchment documents produced by the Manor and Hundred Courts.
Grant Recipient: Liverpool City Council
Access Contact: Ms Irene Vickers
T: 0151 228 5311
E-mail: croxtethcountrypark@liverpool.gov.uk
Open: 1 Apr - 31 Oct: Suns 2 - 4pm. Other times by arrangement, 7 days notice required. Heritage Open Days.
P No.
No wheelchair access or WC for the disabled. Guide Dogs allowed.
£ No.

NORFOLK

CHURCH OF ST MARY THE VIRGIN

Houghton-on-the-Hill, Norfolk PE37 8DP
Ancient church at least 900 years old. Many original features remain including double splay windows, keyhole chancel, Roman brick arch, 12th century North door and early wall paintings. All areas open.
www.saintmaryschurch.org.uk
Grant Recipient: Norfolk County Council

Access Contact: Mr & Mrs R Davey
T: 01760 440470
Open: All year at any reasonable time. Heritage Open Days.
P Spaces: 40.
Full wheelchair access. No WC for the disabled. Guide Dogs allowed.
£ No.

FELBRIGG HALL

Felbrigg, Norwich, Norfolk NR11 8PR
17th century house containing its original 18th century furniture and paintings. The walled garden has been restored and features a working dovecote, small orchard and the national collection of Colchicum. The park is renowned for its fine and aged trees.
www.nationaltrust.org.uk
Grant Recipient: The National Trust
Access Contact: Property Manager
T: 01263 837 444   F: 01263 837 032
E-mail: felbrigg@nationaltrust.org.uk
Open: House: 25 Mar - 29 Oct: daily except Thurs & Fri 1 - 5pm. Garden: 25 Mar - 22 Oct: daily except Thurs & Fri 11am to 5pm (21 July - 2 Sept: daily 11am - 5pm).
P Spaces: 200. Separate parking for disabled and drop-off point.
Wheelchair access to ground floor, photograph album of first floor. Garden, shop & bookshop (ramp), tea room & restaurant accessible. WC for the disabled. Guide Dogs allowed.
£ Adult: £7. Child: £3.50. Family: £17.50, £3 (adult) £1.50 (child) gardens only.

HALES HALL BARN

Loddon, Norfolk NR14 6QW
Late 15th century brick and thatch barn 180ft long, built by James Hobart, Henry VII's Attorney General. Queen post roof, and crown post roof to living accommodation, and richly patterned brickwork. The Barn and similar sized gatehouse, ranged around defended courtyards, are all that remains of the house that once stood on this site. Large garden with topiary and yew hedges, and national collections of citrus, grapes and figs.
www.haleshall.com
Grant Recipient: Mr & Mrs Terence Read
Access Contact: Mr & Mrs Terence Read
T: 01508 548507   **F:** 01508 548040
E-mail: judy@haleshall.com
Open: All year, Tues - Sat 10am - 5pm (or dusk if earlier); plus Easter - Oct, Sun afternoons & BH Mons 11am - 4pm. Closed 25 Dec - 5 Jan and Good Fri. Garden with yew and box topiary included charge. Groups and guided tours by arrangement with Mr or Mrs Terence Read, Hales Hall, Loddon, Norfolk NR14 6QW (tel: 01508 548507). Barn and garden available for wedding receptions, particularly Sat afternoon: telephone to ensure access.
P Spaces: 40.
Full wheelchair access. WC for the disabled. Guide Dogs allowed.
£ Adult: £2 (including guide). Child: Free. Other: £1.50, £3 (guided tours by arrangement).

HOLKHAM HALL VINERY

Wells-next-the-Sea, Norfolk NR23 1AB
Range of late 19th century Glasshouses. Six houses in the range, three of which have been repaired, the fourth is being repaired.
www.holkham.co.uk
Grant Recipient: Coke Estates Ltd
Access Contact: The Estate Office
T: 01328 710227   **E-mail:** enquiries@holkham.co.uk
Open: Exterior can be viewed when the gardens are open to the public during the summer months. (Please check with Estate Office for current opening times). Access to the interior by appointment.
P Spaces: 25.   No access.   £ No.

KING'S LYNN CUSTOM HOUSE

Purfleet Quay, King's Lynn, Norfolk PE30 1HP
Built 1683 as a merchants exchange, became official Custom House in 1703. Building purchased by the Crown in 1717 for £800 and was used by HM Customs until 1989. The Borough Council of King's Lynn and West Norfolk obtained a lease of the building in 1995 and restored it.
Grant Recipient: King's Lynn & West Norfolk Council
Access Contact: Mrs Karen Cooke
T: 01553 763044   **F:** 01553 819441
E-mail: kings-lynn.tic@west-norfolk.gov.uk
Open: Mon - Sat 10.30am - 4pm & Suns 12 - 4pm. Longer during summer months, check with the access contact for

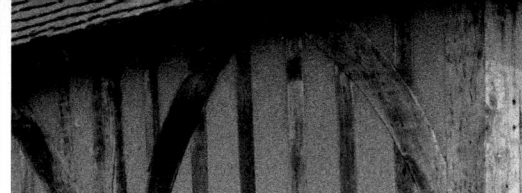

current information

🅿 Parking in public car parks, plus many pay and display spaces within 10 minute walk.

🚻 Wheelchair access to ground floor only. No WC for the disabled. Guide Dogs allowed.

£ No.

OLD BUCKENHAM CORNMILL

Green Lane, Old Buckenham, Norfolk NR17

Mill with the largest diameter tower in England, which had five sets of stones when it was working. Once owned by the Colmans of Norwich and Prince Duleep Singh. Built by John Burlingham in 1818.

www.norfolkwindmills.co.uk

Grant Recipient: Norfolk Windmills Trust

Access Contact: Mrs A L Rix

T: 01603 222708   **F:** 01603 224413

E-mail: amanda.rix@norfolk.gov.uk

Open: Apr - Sept: second Sun of each month 2 - 5pm. Groups at other times by arrangement with Mrs A L Rix, Conservation Officer, Building Conservation Section, Dept of Planning & Transportation, Norfolk County Council, County Hall, Martineau Lane, Norwich, Norfolk NR1 2SG.

🅿 Spaces: 6.   🚻 No access.   £ Adult: £2. Child: Free.

OLD HALL

Norwich Road, South Burlingham, Norfolk NR13 4EY

Small Elizabethan manor house with a painted stucco fireplace, painted stucco mermaids and scrollwork on the front porch, and a long gallery of hunting scenes in grisaille, c1600.

Grant Recipient: Mr P Scupham

Access Contact: Mr P Scupham

T: 01493 750804

E-mail: margaret@moonshinecat.fsnet.co.uk

Open: By tel arrangement with Mr P Scupham or Ms M Steward. No access for guide dogs to the Long Gallery. Heritage Open Days.

🅿 Spaces: 8. 12 extra parking spaces available in small attached meadow.

🚻 Wheelchair access to ground floor and garden, painted gallery inaccessible. No WC for the disabled. Guide Dogs allowed.

£ No.

OXBURGH HALL

Oxborough, King's Lynn, Norfolk PE33 9PS

Moated manor house with Tudor gatehouse, was built in 1482 by the Bedingfeld family who still live there. The rooms show the development from medieval austerity to Victorian comfort, and include a display of embroidery by Mary, Queen of Scots and Bess of Hardwick. Gardens include a French Parterre and woodland walks, as well as a Catholic chapel.

www.nationaltrust.org.uk

Grant Recipient: The National Trust

Access Contact: Property Manager

T: 01366 328258   **F:** 01366 328066

E-mail: oxburghhall@nationaltrust.org.uk

Open: House: 19 Mar - 30 Oct: daily except Thurs & Fri, 1 - 5pm. BHs 11am - 5pm (last adm. 4.30pm). Garden: 8 Jan - 13 Mar, 5 Nov - 18 Dec & 7 Jan - 26 Feb: Sat & Sun 11am - 4pm. 19 Mar - 31 July & 3 Sept - 30 Oct: daily except Thurs & Fri, 11am - 5.30pm. Aug: daily, 11am - 5.30pm.

🅿 Spaces: 100.

🚻 Wheelchair access to 4 ground floor rooms (shallow ramp), difficult stairs to upper floors. Garden largely accessible, restaurant and shop accessible. WC for the disabled. Guide Dogs allowed.

£ Adult: £6.50. Child: £3.25. Family: £17, £3.25 (garden & estate only).

RUINED CHURCH OF ST PETER

Wiggenhall St Peter with Wigge, Norfolk

Former parish church, largely 15th century, now ruined. South aisle was demolished in 1840.

Grant Recipient: Wiggenhall St Peter PCC

Access Contact: Mrs Yeoman

T: 01553 617518

Open: To the exterior at all reasonable times.

🅿 Spaces: 2.   🚻 No access.   £ No.

ST ANDREW'S HALL

St Andrew's Plain, Norwich, Norfolk NR3 1AU

Remains of medieval friary, including the nave (St Andrew's Hall), choir (Blackfriars Hall), crypt, cloisters, private chapel

(Beckets) and chapter house. Hammerbeam roof in nave, medieval bosses in choir and a 13th century 7-light East Window. A civic hall in use since 1540.

www.norwich.gov.uk

Grant Recipient: Norwich City Council

Access Contact: Mr Russell Wilson

T: 01603 628477   **F:** 01603 762182

E-mail: TheHalls@norwich.gov.uk/ russellwilson@norwich.gov.

Open: Mon - Sat ,9am - 4pm. Subject to events. Heritage Open Days.

🅿 Multi-storey car park in city centre. Blue Badge on site, Orange Badge if space is available.

🚻 Wheelchair access to ground floor only. WC for the disabled. Guide Dogs allowed.

£ No.

ST BENET'S LEVEL MILL

Ludham, Norfolk

Typical example of a Broadland drainage mill with tapering red brick tower, white boat shaped cap, sails and fantail. Built in 18th century and altered over the years, it became redundant in the 1940s. Ground and first floors accessible. Information boards on site.

Grant Recipient: Crown Estates Commissioners

Access Contact: Mr D L Ritchie

T: 01692 678232   **E-mail:** Laurie@ludhamhall.co.uk

Open: Second Sun in May and first Sun in Aug. At other times by arrangement with Mr D L Ritchie at Hall Farm, Ludham, Great Yarmouth, Norfolk NR29 5NU (tel: 01692 678232) or Mrs Jenny Scaff, Carter Jonas, 6-8 Hills Road, Cambridge CB2 1NH (tel: 01223 346628).

🅿 No.

🚻 No wheelchair access. Guide dog access possible to ground floor only. No WC for the disabled.

£ No.

ST CLEMENT

Colegate, Norwich, Norfolk NR3 1BQ

15th century church, now a pastoral care and counselling centre. Has a slender tower decorated with lozenges of flushwork (patterns made from flint and stone).

Grant Recipient: Norwich Historic Churches Trust

Access Contact: Reverend Jack Burton

T: 01603 622747

Open: Daily, 10am - 4pm (sometimes longer). Occasionally closed when steward on leave. Heritage Open Days.

🅿 In city centre car parks.

🚻 Wheelchair access to Nave at street level. No WC for the disabled. Guide Dogs allowed.

£ No.

ST LAWRENCE

The Street, South Walsham, Norfolk NR13 6DQ

Medieval church destroyed by fire and rebuilt in 1832 as a parish church and used for worship until c1890. Formerly redundant but now re-licensed for worship. Now houses St Lawrence Centre for Training and the Arts, open to the public and used for exhibitions, classes and concerts. Access to Sacristans Garden.

www.st-lawrence.org.uk

Grant Recipient: South Walsham Parochial Church Council

Access Contact: Mrs Caroline Linsdell

T: 01603 270522

Open: Daily, 9am - 6pm or dusk in winter.

🅿 Spaces: 8.

🚻 Full wheelchair access. WC for the disabled. Guide Dogs allowed.

£ No.

ST MARTIN AT OAK

Oak Street, Norwich, Norfolk

15th century former church, now redundant.

Grant Recipient: Norwich Historic Churches Trust

Access Contact: Mrs J Jones

T: 07867 801995   **F:** 01603 722008

E-mail: hall.farm@btinternet.com

Open: By arrangement with the tenant. Please telephone 07867 801995 for details.

🅿 Parking meters in St Martin Lane and city centre car parks.

🚻 No access.

£ No.

ST MARTIN AT PALACE

Norwich, Norfolk NR3 1RW

Medieval former church, now housing the Norfolk Association for the Care and Resettlement of Offenders (NACRO). Has a fine 16th century tomb for Lady Elizabeth Calthorpe.

Grant Recipient: Norwich Historic Churches Trust

Access Contact: Ms Amanda Payne

T: 01603 763555   **E-mail:** Richard@norfolkacro.org

Open: By written arrangement. Heritage Open Days.

🅿 City centre car parks.

🚻 Wheelchair access to ground floor only, by arrangement. WC for the disabled. Guide Dogs allowed.

£ No.

ST MARY

Fordham, Downham Market, Norfolk

Medieval aisleless church in rural landscape, now redundant. Listed Grade II*.

Grant Recipient: Fordham St Mary Preservation Trust

Access Contact: Mr Robert Bateson

T: 01366 388399   **F:** 01366 385859

E-mail: bateson@rannerlow.co.uk

Open: By arrangement or key may be available from farm opposite church.

🅿 Spaces: 12.

🚻 No wheelchair access or WC for the disabled. Guide Dogs allowed.

£ No.

ST MARY'S ABBEY

West Dereham, Norfolk

The present six bay house is the remains of the service block of Sir Thomas Dereham's Renaissance style mansion, which he built after 1689 incorporating the surviving parts of a Premonstratensian Abbey founded in 1188 by Hubert Walter. Had become a ruin and was only recently restored, with the building re-roofed and a first floor and stair tower added. The house is now a private residence.

Grant Recipient: Mr G Shropshire

Access Contact: Mrs Ann King

T: 01353 727200   **F:** 01353 727325

E-mail: ann.king@gs-marketing.com

Open: By arrangement with Mrs Ann King, G's Marketing Ltd, Barway, Ely, Cambridgeshire CB7 5TZ (tel: 01353 727200, Mon-Fri only). Up to one month's notice may be required. Heritage Open Days.

🅿 Spaces: 20.

🚻 Full wheelchair access. WC for the disabled available on request, although they are not specifically designed for such use. Guide Dogs allowed.

£ No.

ST PETER & ST PAUL

Tunstall, Norfolk

Chancel and ruined nave and tower of medieval church.

Grant Recipient: Tunstall (Norfolk) Church Preservation Trust

Access Contact: The Secretary

T: 01493 700279   **F:** 01493 700279

Open: Normally all year. If locked, it is due to severe weather. Key available at the Manor House in Tunstall.

🅿 Spaces: 6.

🚻 Full wheelchair access. Access is across uneven path. No WC for the disabled. Guide Dogs allowed.

£ No.

THE DEANERY

56 The Close, Norwich, Norfolk NR1 4EG

13th century with later additions, originally the Prior's lodgings. It remains the residence of the Dean of Norwich. The interior is closed to the public.

www.cathedral.org.uk

Grant Recipient: The Chapter of Norwich Cathedral

Access Contact: Mr Tim Cawkwell

T: 01603 218300   **F:** 01603 766032

E-mail: chapter@cathedral.org.uk

Open: Exterior visible from The Close which is open to visitors during daylight hours throughout the year.

🅿 No.

🚻 Full wheelchair access. No WC for the disabled. No Guide Dogs.

£ No.

THURNE DYKE DRAINAGE MILL

Thurne Staithe, Thurne, Norfolk
Broadland drainage mill c1820 with classic 'hained' appearance and turbine pump. Originally 2 storey tapering circular whitewashed brick tower but raised to 3 storeys in mid 19th century, with timber weatherboarded boat shaped cap, sails and fan.
www.norfolkwindmills.co.uk
Grant Recipient: Norfolk Windmills Trust
Access Contact: Mrs A Rix
T: 01603 222705   **F:** 01603 224413
Open: Apr - Sept: 2nd & 4th Sun of each month; National Mills weekend (second weekend in May) 2 - 5pm and at other times by arrangement.
P Spaces: 4. Parking at parish staithe, approx. 100 yds. Pub also allows parking for visitors.
No access.
No conditions noted.

WAXHAM GREAT BARN

Sea Palling, Norfolk NR1 2DH
Grade I listed barn, 1570s-80s, with later additions. Flint with ashlar dressings and thatched roof. Much of its fabric is reused material from dissolved monasteries.
Grant Recipient: Norfolk County Council
Access Contact: Ms Caroline Davison
T: 01603 222706   **F:** 01603 224413
E-mail: caroline.davison@norfolk.gov.uk
Open: Provisional: 19 Mar - 30 Oct, daily 10.30am - 4.30pm. Visitors should ring nearer the time to confirm opening times.
P Spaces: 100. Free parking.
Wheelchair access with assistance (gravel path from car park to Barn). WC for the disabled. Guide Dogs allowed.
£ Adult: £2.50. Child: Free.

NORTH YORKSHIRE

AISKEW WATER CORNMILL

Bedale, North Yorkshire DL8 1AW
Grade II* watermill, late 18th and early 19th century. Sold in 1918 in a major dispersal of estate properties. Roof and main structure restored. Restoration of interior with original wooden machinery is planned.
www.farmattraction.co.uk
Grant Recipient: David Clark
Access Contact: Jared, Duncan & Carol Clark
T: 01677 422125   **F:** 01677 425205
E-mail: enquiries@farmattraction.co.uk
Open: Access to the exterior at all reasonable times. Guided tours available by arrangement.
P Spaces: 40.
Full wheelchair access. WC for the disabled. Guide Dogs allowed.
£ No.

BENINGBROUGH HALL

Shipton-by-Beningbrough, North Yorkshire Y030 1DD
Country house, c1716, contains an impressive Baroque interior exhibiting over one hundred 18th century portraits in partnership with the National Portrait Gallery. A very high standard of craftsmanship is displayed throughout, most of the original work surviving with extremely fine woodcarving and other ornate decoration, and an unusual central corridor running the full length of the house. There is a fully equipped Victorian laundry and walled garden.
www.nationaltrust.org.uk
Grant Recipient: The National Trust
Access Contact: Property Manager
T: 01904 470666   **F:** 01904 470002
E-mail: beningbrough@nationaltrust.org.uk
Open: House: 3 - 28 June: daily except Thurs & Fri 12 noon - 5pm. 1 July - 1 Sept: daily except Thurs 12 noon - 5pm. 2 Sept - 29 Oct: daily except Thurs & Fri 12 noon - 5pm. Grounds & shop: 25 Mar - 28 June: daily except Thurs & Fri 11am - 5.30pm. 1 July - 1 Sept: daily except Thurs & Fri 11am - 5.30pm. 4 Nov - 17 Dec: Sats & Suns 11am - 3.30pm. Restaurant: as grounds.
P Spaces: 250.
Wheelchairs available on all floors, and seating. Steps to entrance with handrail or lift available as well as alternative entrance. Access to ground floor and stairs with handrail or lift to other floors. WC for the disabled. Guide Dogs allowed.
£ Adult: £7 (house & grounds). Child: £3.50 (house &

grounds). Family: £16 (2+3 or 1+4). Group: £6.50 (adult), £4 (child). Reduced rate when arriving by cycle.

CASTLE HOWARD

York, North Yorkshire YO60 7DA
Large stately home dating from the beginning of the 18th century and designed by Sir John Vanbrugh. Situated in 10,000 acres of landscaped grounds, which includes numerous monuments.
www.castlehoward.co.uk
Grant Recipient: The Hon. Simon Howard
Access Contact: Mr D N Peake
T: 01653 648444   **F:** 01653 648529
E-mail: estatemanager@castlehoward.co.uk
Open: 1 Mar - 5 Nov: daily 11am - 4pm (Grounds only from 10am); Nov - mid-Mar: grounds open most days but please tel for confirmation in Nov, Dec and Jan. Access to interior of Temple of the Four Winds by arrangement.
P Spaces: 888.
Wheelchair access to all but chapel and first floor of exhibition wing. WC for the disabled. Guide Dogs allowed.
£ Adult: £9.50. Child: £7. Other: £8.50 (provisional).

DUNCOMBE PARK

Helmsley, York, North Yorkshire YO62 5EB
Recently restored family home of Lord and Lady Feversham. Originally built in 1713 and then rebuilt after a fire in 1879 largely to the original design. Early 18th century gardens.
www.duncombepark.com
Grant Recipient: Lord Feversham
Access Contact: Duncombe Park Estate Office
T: 01439 770213   **F:** 01439 771114
E-mail: liz@duncombepark.com
Open: Easter Sun 16 Apr & Easter Mon 17 Apr 10am -5pm. 1 May-Oct: Sun - Thurs, House & Garden 12noon-5.30pm (tours hourly 12.30 - 3.30pm lasting 1 1/4 hours. Last adm. to gardens & parkland 4.30pm), parkland Centre Tea room, shop & parkland walks 11am - 5.30pm (last orders in tearoom 5.15pm). Special Events all year. Duncombe Park reserve the right to alter opening arrangements without prior notice - please telephone to check.
P Spaces: 200.
Wheelchair access to ground and first floor only. WC for the disabled. Guide Dogs allowed.
£ Adult: £6.50 (house & gardens), £3.50 (gardens & parkland), £2 (parkland). Child: £3 (10-16, house & garden), £2 (10-16, gardens & parkland), £1 (10-16, parkland). Other: £5 (concessions, house & garden), £13.50 (family, house & garden), £4.75 (groups, house & garden), £25 (family season ticket).

FOUNTAINS HALL

Ripon, North Yorkshire HG4 3DY
Elizabethan mansion, built between 1589 and 1604 for Stephen Proctor. Three rooms; the Stone Hall, the Arkell Room, and the Reading Room, all unfurnished, are open to the public. The conservation of a fourth room, the Great Chamber, has recently been completed. This upper room features an ornate chimney piece depicting the Biblical story of the Judgement of Solomon. The mansion is situated within a World Heritage Site which also includes the ruins of a 12th century Cistercian Abbey, monastic water mill and Georgian water garden.
www.fountainsabbey.org.uk
Grant Recipient: The National Trust
Access Contact: Property Manager
T: 01765 608888   **F:** 01765 601002
E-mail: fountainsenquiries@nationaltrust.org.uk
Open: As part of the Fountain's Abbey and Studley Royal Estate. Jan - Feb: 10am - 4pm. Mar - Oct 10am - 5pm. Nov - Dec 10am - 4pm. Estate closed 24, 25 Dec and Fris in Jan, Nov and Dec.
P Spaces: 500.
Full wheelchair access. WC for the disabled. Guide Dogs allowed.
£ Adult: £6.50. Child: £3.50. Other: £17.50 (family). £5.50 (adult, groups 15 - 30), £3 (child, groups 15-30). £5 (adult, groups 31+), £2.50 (child, 31+). EH Members free.

GIGGLESWICK SCHOOL CHAPEL

Giggleswick, Settle, North Yorkshire BD24 0DE
Built 1897-1901 by T G Jackson for Walter Morrison as a gift to the school to commemorate the Diamond Jubilee of Queen Victoria. Constructed of Gothic banded rockfaced millstone grit sandstone and limestone, with lead hipped roof

to nave and copper covered terracotta dome to chancel. Contains Italian sgrafitto work throughout.
www.giggleswick.org.uk
Grant Recipient: The Governors of Giggleswick School
Access Contact: The Bursar and Clerk to the Governors
T: 01729 893000/893012   **F:** 01729 893150
E-mail: bursar@giggleswick.org.uk
Open: Mon - Fri 9am - 5pm, closed BHs. Other times by arrangement. Visitors must report to reception to obtain the key to the Chapel. Heritage Open Days.
P Spaces: 25.
Wheelchair access to ground floor only. WC for the disabled in main school premises. Guide Dogs allowed.
£ No.

HACKFALL

Grewelthorpe, North Yorkshire
Developed as a wild gothic woodland landscape in the 18th century, remains of a number of man-made features can still be seen. The woodland is known to have existed since at least 1600 and the ground flora is characteristic of ancient woodland. Beech, oak, ash and wild cherry can also be seen together with spindle, an unusual tree found in chalk and limestone. The site is very steep and paths can sometimes be narrow and difficult to negotiate.
www.woodland-trust.org.uk
Grant Recipient: The Woodland Trust
Access Contact: Mr Mark Brown
T: 01476 581 112
Open: The site is open to the public at all times. For further information contact Mark Brown.
P Spaces: 6. Visitor parking on opposite side of road courtesy of Swinton Estate.
No access.
£ No.

HOVINGHAM HALL

Hovingham, York, North Yorkshire YO62 4LU
Palladian house built c1760 by Thomas Worsley to his own design. Unique entry through huge riding school. Extensive gardens in a parkland setting. The private cricket ground in front of the house is reported to be the oldest in England.
www.hovingham.co.uk
Grant Recipient: Mr William Worsley
Access Contact: Mrs Kathryn Lamprey
T: 01653 628771   **F:** 01653 628668
E-mail: office @hovingham.co.uk
Open: 5 June - 8 July: Mon - Sat 1.15 - 4.30pm (closed Sun). Last tour 3.30pm.
P Spaces: 80.
Wheelchair access to ground floor. WC for the disabled in adjacent village hall. Guide Dogs allowed.
£ Adult: £6.   Child: £3. Other: £5.50 (concessions), £3.50 (gardens).

JERVAULX ABBEY

Ripon, North Yorkshire HG4 4PH
Ruins of Cistercian Abbey moved to this site in 1156, built of sandstone ashlar in Early English style. Remains of nave, transepts and choir, with a cloister on the south side of the nave, flanked by a chapter house to the east and a kitchen and dorter to the south.
Grant Recipient: Mr Ian Burdon
Access Contact: Mr Ian Burdon
T: 01677 460391/01677 460226
E-mail: ba123@btopenworld.com
Open: At any reasonable time throughout the year.
P Spaces: 55.
Wheelchair access to church, infirmary, frater and cloisters. Uneven terrain and steps on other parts of site. WC for the disabled. Guide Dogs allowed.
£ Adult: £2 (honesty box). Child: £1.50 (honesty box).

MARKENFIELD HALL

Ripon, North Yorkshire HG4 3AD
Fortified moated manor house, built 1310-1323 for John de Markenfield (Chancellor of the Exchequer to Edward II), with further additions and alterations in the 16th, 18th and 19th centuries. Restored 1981 - 1984 and 2001 - 2003.
www.markenfield.com
Grant Recipient: Lady Deirdre Curteis
Access Contact: The Administrator
T: 01765 692303   **F:** 01765 607195

E-mail: markenfieldhall@btinternet.com

Open: 1 - 14 May & 18 June - 1 July 2 - 5pm. Groups with guided tour by appointment all year round.

℗ Spaces: 25.

♿ Wheelchair access to ground floor only. No WC for the disabled. Guide Dogs allowed.

£ Adult: £4. Child: £3. Senior: £3, £60 (min charge groups out of opening times).

MOWBRAY POINT

The Ruin, Hackfall, Harrogate, North Yorkshire

Folly, built c1750, standing in the Grade 1 registered remains of the 18th century garden at Hackfall. It is a small pavilion above a steep wooded gorge.

www.landmarktrust.org.uk

Grant Recipient: The Landmark Trust

Access Contact: Ms Victoria O'Keeffe

T: 01628 825920   **F:** 01628 825417

E-mail: vokeeffe@landmarktrust.org.uk

Open: The Landmark Trust is an independent charity, which rescues small buildings of historic or architectural importance from decay or unsympathetic improvement. Landmark's aim is to promote the enjoyment of these historic buildings by making them available to stay in for holidays. Mowbray Point can be rented by anyone, at all times of the year, for periods ranging from a weekend to three weeks. Bookings can be made by telephoning the Booking Office on 01628 825925. As the building is in full-time use for holiday accommodation, it is not normally open to the public. However the public have access to and across the terrace all year 11am - 4pm and to the interior by arrangement by telephoning the access contact (Victoria O'Keeffe on 01628 825920) to make an appointment. Potential visitors will be asked to write to confirm the details of their visit.

℗ Spaces: 2.

♿ No wheelchair access or WC for the disabled. Guide Dogs allowed.

£ No.

NATIONAL CENTRE FOR EARLY MUSIC

**St Margaret's Church, Walmgate, York,
North Yorkshire YO1 9TL**

14th century church with highly decorated 12th century Romanesque doorway (removed from chapel of the ruined hospital of St Nicholas, probably during 1684-5 rebuilding of church (orange-red brick tower of same date) occasioned by Civil War damage). Now houses the National Centre for Early Music and used for concerts, music educational activities, conferences, recordings and events.

www.ncem.co.uk

Grant Recipient: York Early Music Foundation

Access Contact: Mrs G Baldwin

T: 01904 632220   **F:** 01904 612631

E-mail: info@ncem.co.uk

Open: All year: Mon - Fri 10am - 4pm. Also by arrangement. Access is necessarily restricted when events are taking place.

℗ Spaces: 9. 2 parking places for the disabled.

♿ Full wheelchair access. WC for the disabled. Guide Dogs allowed.

£ No.

NORTON CONYERS

Ripon, North Yorkshire HG4 5EQ

Medieval house with Stuart and Georgian additions. 18th century walled garden nearby. Family pictures, furniture and costumes. Visited by Charlotte Bronte in 1839; a family legend of a mad woman confined in an attic room contributed towards the mad Mrs Rochester in 'Jane Eyre' and the house was a model for 'Thornfield Hall'.

Grant Recipient: Sir James Graham Bt

Access Contact: Sir James Graham Bt

T: 01765 640333   **F:** 01765 640333

E-mail: norton.conyers@bronco.co.uk

Open: House & Garden: Easter Sun and Mon, BH Suns and Mons, & Suns 23 Apr - 20 Aug. 3 July - 8 July daily. House: 2 - 5pm (last adm. 4.40pm). Garden open on Thurs all year 10am - 4pm (please check beforehand). Groups by arrangement.

℗ Spaces: 60. Free car park approx. 50m from the house; disabled parking available near front door by arrangement.

♿ Wheelchair access to ground floor of house only. Some gravelled paths in garden may be difficult. WC for the disabled. Guide Dogs allowed.

£ Adult: £5.50. Child: Free (16 and under). Senior: £4.

ORMESBY HALL

**Church Lane, Ormesby, Middlesbrough,
North Yorkshire TS7 9AS**

A mid-18th century Palladian mansion, notable for its fine plasterwork and carved wood decoration. The Victorian laundry and kitchen with scullery and game larder are interesting. 18th century stable block, attributed to Carr of York, is leased to the Cleveland Mounted Police. Large model railway and garden with holly walk.

www.nationaltrust.org.uk

Grant Recipient: The National Trust

Access Contact: Property Manager

T: 01642 324188   **F:** 01642 300937

E-mail: ormesbyhall@nationaltrust.org.uk

Open: Hall: 1 Apr - 29 Oct, Sats & Suns only (and BH Mons) 1.30 - 5pm (last adm. 4.30pm). Tea room: as Hall 12.30 - 5pm.

℗ Spaces: 100. 100 metres from House.

♿ Wheelchair access to ground floor of Hall (shallow step at entrance), shop, tea room and garden. No WC for the disabled. Guide Dogs allowed.

£ Adult: £4. Child: £2.50. Family: £10.50. Groups: £3.50.

RIBBLEHEAD VIADUCT

Ribblehead, North Yorkshire

Railway viaduct, 1870-74, rockfaced stone and brick. 104 feet high at highest point. Largest and most impressive of the viaducts of the Settle - Carlisle line of the Midland Railway.

Grant Recipient: British Rail

Access Contact: Mr Simon Brooks

T: 0161 228 8584   **F:** 0161 228 8790

E-mail: simon.brooks@networkrail.co.uk

Open: Viewing from ground level only. Strictly no access from Network Rail property.

℗ On-street parking in Cave.   ♿ No access.   £ No.

SCAMPSTON HALL

Scampston, Malton, North Yorkshire YO17 8NG

Late 17th century country house, extensively remodelled in 1801 by Thomas Leverton. Contains Regency interiors and an art collection. Set in a parkland designed by 'Capability' Brown with 10 acres of lakes and a Palladian bridge.

www.scampston.co.uk

Grant Recipient: Sir Charles Legard Bt

Access Contact: Sir Charles Legard Bt

T: 01944 758224   **F:** 01944 758700

E-mail: info@scampton.co.uk

Open: 22 June - 23 July (closed Mons) 1.30 - 5.00pm

℗ Spaces: 50.

♿ Wheelchair access to ground floor only. WC for the disabled. Guide Dogs allowed.

£ Adult: £6 (house, garden & park). Child: £3 (12-16yrs). Free for 11 & under.

ST PAULINUS

Brough Park, Richmond, North Yorkshire DL10 7PJ

Catholic neo-Gothic chapel designed by Bonomi with priest's accommodation and school room in undercroft.

Grant Recipient: Mr Greville Worthington

Access Contact: Mr Greville Worthington

T: 01748 812127   **E-mail:** grev@saintpaulinus.co.uk

Open: By arrangement.

℗ Spaces: 2.

♿ Wheelchair access to downstairs. No WC for the disabled. Guide Dogs allowed.

£ No.

ST SAVIOUR'S CHURCH
(ARCHAEOLOGICAL RESOURCE CENTRE)

St Saviourgate, York, North Yorkshire YO1 8NN

Church on site by late 11th century, present building dates from the 15th and extensively remodelled in 1845. Now promotes access to archaeological material through hands-on displays.

www.yorkarchaeology.co.uk

Grant Recipient: York Archaeological Trust

Access Contact: Mrs Christine McDonnell

T: 01904 663022 (until 3/06)   **F:** 01904 663024

E-mail: cmcdonnell@yorkarchaeology.co.uk

Open: School terms, from Apr: Mon - Sun (except Christmas Day) 10am - 5pm. By arrangement (tel: 01904 543403). Visitors who simply want to view the building should contact the information line (tel: 01904 543403). Sensory garden on

architectural theme.

℗ On-street parking for disabled visitors outside entrance; public car parks nearby.

♿ Full wheelchair access. WC for the disabled. Guide Dogs allowed.

£ Adult: £4.50 (ARC). Child: £4. Family: £15. Carers / enablers free when helping disabled person.

THE MOUNT SCHOOL LINDLEY MURRAY SUMMERHOUSE

Dalton Terrace, York, North Yorkshire YO24 4DD

Grade II* listed summerhouse built c1774, formerly situated in the grounds of Holgate House, York. Octagonal timber structure on raised stepped circular base with lead ogee roof and decorated with Doric columns. Restored in 1997.

Grant Recipient: The Mount School

Access Contact: Ms Anne Bolton

T: 01904 667506   **F:** 01904 667524

E-mail: abolton@mount.n-yorks.sch.uk

Open: By arrangement Mon - Fri all year (except BHs) 9am - 4.30pm.

℗ Spaces: 3.

♿ Full wheelchair access. WC for the disabled. Guide Dogs allowed.

£ Donations welcome.

THOMPSON MAUSOLEUM

**Little Ouseburn Churchyard, Little Ouseburn,
North Yorkshire YO26 9TS**

18th century Mausoleum in magnesian limestone. It is a rotunda encircled by 13 Tuscan columns, above which a frieze and cornice support a plain drum and ribbed domed roof. Listed Grade II*. Built for the use of the Thompson family of Kirby Hall.

Grant Recipient: Little Ouseburn Mausoleum Ltd

Access Contact: Mr H Hibbs

T: 01423 330414   **E-mail:** helier1@talktalk.net

Open: Always available to view from the outside, interior visible through a replica of the original wrought iron gate. Access to interior by arrangement. Contact Mr Hibbs, Little Ouseburn Mausoleum Ltd, Hilltop Cottage, Little Ouseburn, North Yorks YO26 9TD (tel: 01423 330414) for current information. Heritage Open Days.

℗ Spaces: 8.

♿ Wheelchair access with assistance (gravel path and grass). No WC for the disabled. Guide Dogs allowed.

£ No.

NORTHAMPTONSHIRE

BOUGHTON PARK

Boughton, Northamptonshire NN16 9UP

Extensive remains of formal gardens of late 17th and early 18th century around a country house rebuilt at the same time, set in a park developed from a late medieval deer park. Beyond the park are avenues and rides, also part of the landscape of the late 17th and early 18th centuries. The grant aided Lily pool is approximately 100 meters south of the House.

www.boughtonhouse.org.uk

Grant Recipient: Boughton Estates Ltd

Access Contact: Mr Christopher B Sparrow MRICS

T: 01536 482308   **F:** 01536 410 452

E-mail: csparrow@boughtonestate.co.uk

Open: 1 May - 1 Sept daily (except Fridays May - July) 1 - 5pm.

℗ Spaces: 100.

♿ Wheelchair access to ground floor fully accessible, first floor viewable on virtual tour in gift shop. No WC for the disabled. Guide Dogs allowed.

£ Adult: £1.50 (grounds), £6 (house and grounds). Child: £1 (grounds), £5 (house and grounds). Other: £1 (grounds), £5 (house and grounds).

HARROWDEN HALL GARDEN STATUES

Wellingborough, Northamptonshire NN9 5AD

Early 18th century Harrowden Hall retains its surprisingly unaltered contemporary garden containing a number of garden features, including statues by the Dutch sculptor Van Nost, of which one has recently been repaired.

Grant Recipient: Wellingborough Golf Club

Access Contact: Mr Roy Tomlin

T: 01933 677234   **F:** 01933 67937

E-mail: secretary@wellingboroughgolfclub.com

Open: 27 Mar to 2 Oct: Mondays.

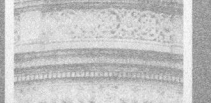

P Spaces: 100.
Full wheelchair access. WC for the disabled. Guide Dogs allowed.
£ No.

LAXTON HALL

Corby, Northamptonshire NN17 3AU
Stone built 18th century manor house, enlarged and modified in 19th century and set in 60 acres of parkland. Stable block by Repton. Formerly a boys school, now a residential home for elderly Poles.
Grant Recipient: Polish Benevolent Housing Association Ltd
Access Contact: Mr Z S Lis
T: 020 7359 8863   **F:** 020 7226 7677
E-mail: pbf.pmk@ukonlinke.co.uk
Open: By written arrangement with Mr Z S Lis, PBF Housing Association, 2 Devonia Road, London N1 8JJ, access will be arranged through the manager of the residential home.
P Spaces: 10.
Wheelchair access to ground floor only. WC for the disabled. Guide Dogs allowed.
£ No.

NORTHUMBERLAND

27/28 MARKET PLACE

Hexham, Northumberland NE46 3PB
Grade II* listed 4 storey house built 1749. Ground floor is a shop and the upper floors have been converted into flats. Imposing rear elevation to Back Row.
Grant Recipient: Two Castles Housing Association
Access Contact: Ms Julie Cuthbert
T: 0191 261 4774   **F:** 0191 2619629
E-mail: julie.cuthbert@twocastles.org.uk
Open: Exterior only.
P No. No access. £ No.

ALNWICK TOWN HALL

Market Place, Alnwick, Northumberland NE66 1HS
Situated in Alnwick Market Place. Property includes the Hall, the Freemen's Council Room and the Clock Tower. The 18th century building houses the Freemen's Shields and various items of Freemen's History.
Grant Recipient: The Freemen's Common Council
Access Contact: Mr Dennis Nixon, Clerk to the Freemen
T: 01665 603 517   **F:** 01665 603 517
Open: To the exterior at all times; to the interior by arrangement.
P No. No access. £ No.

BELFORD HALL

Belford, Northumberland NE70 7EY
Palladian Country House by James Paine, 1754-56, Wings & North Front added 1818 by John Dobson. Derelict for 40 years until restored and converted into private apartments by North East Civic Trust and Monument Trust, 1984-87. The Saloon, Staircase, Portico and Wine Cellar are open to the public.
Grant Recipient: North East Civic Trust
Access Contact: Mr John Harris
T: 01668219 716/01968673693
E-mail: jhharris@dircon.co.uk
Open: Interior and exterior: any day, excl Christmas and Easter 10am - 4.30pm (3pm in winter months) by arrangement with Ms Fairburn (tel: 01668 213794) or Lady Graham (tel: 01668 213140). No public toilets. Heritage Open Days.
P Spaces: 8. Free parking.
Wheelchair access to ground floor by ramp (three steps to main entrance). No WC for the disabled. Guide Dogs allowed.
£ No.

COANWOOD FRIENDS MEETING HOUSE

Coanwood, nr. Haltwhistle, Northumberland NE49
Built in 1760, remaining relatively unchanged. Located in a remote valley south of Hadrian's Wall.
www.hct.org.uk
Grant Recipient: Historic Chapels Trust
Access Contact: Dr Jennifer Freeman
T: 020 7481 0533   **E-mail:** chapels@hct.org.uk
Open: At all reasonable times. Heritage Open Days.
P Spaces: 20.

Full wheelchair access. No WC for the disabled. Guide Dogs allowed.
£ Donations invited.

HIGH STAWARD FARM

Langley-on-Tyne, Hexham, Northumberland NE47 5NS
Georgian farmhouse standing inside a walled garden surrounded by the farm steading. Has a ging gang, threshing machine, pig stys with stone troughs and a blacksmiths shop. Most of the house and buildings are of dressed stone and the house has flagged floors, ceiling hooks, cheeseboard and rail, large pantry and servants staircase. Still a working hill farm.
Grant Recipient: Mr R J Coulson
Access Contact: Mr R J Coulson
T: 01434 683619
Open: By arrangement.
P Spaces: 4.
No wheelchair access or WC for the disabled. Guide Dogs allowed.
£ No.

LADY'S WELL

Holystone, Harbbottle, Northumberland
The Lady's Holy Well is considered to be of Roman origin and is located on a halting place along the Roman road. The main feature of the well today is a rectangular stone tank which is fed by a natural spring.
www.nationaltrust.org.uk
Grant Recipient: The National Trust
Access Contact: Mr John O'Brien
T: 01669 620333 ext. 101   **F:** 01669 620066
Open: At all times.
P No.
No wheelchair access or WC for the disabled. Guide Dogs allowed.
£ No.

LAMBLEY VIADUCT

Lambley, Tynedale, Northumberland
17 arch stone viaduct, 100ft high and 1650ft long, spanning the South Tyne river. Originally carried single track, now used as a footpath.
www.npht.com
Grant Recipient: British Rail Property Board/North Pennines Heritage Trust
Access Contact: Mr David Flush, Chief Executive
T: 01434 382 294   **F:** 01434 382 294
E-mail: trust@npht.com
Open: At all times as part of the South Tyne Trail between Featherstone Park and Alston.
P Spaces: 30.
Full wheelchair access. No WC for the disabled. Guide Dogs allowed.
£ No.

LINDISFARNE CASTLE

Holy Island, Berwick-upon-Tweed, Northumberland TD15 2SH
Built in 1550 to protect Holy Island harbour from attack, the castle was converted into a private house for Edward Hudson by Sir Edwin Luytens in 1903. Small walled garden was designed by Gertrude Jekyll. 19th century lime kilns in field by the castle.
www.nationaltrust.org.uk
Grant Recipient: Ms Helen Clarke, Communication & Productions Officer
Access Contact: Property Manager
T: 01289 389244   **F:** 01289 389349
E-mail: lindisfarne@nationaltrust.org.uk
Open: Castle: 18 Feb - 26 Feb daily. 18 Mar - 29 Oct: daily except Mon (open Scottish and English BH Mons). Open for 4½ hours either 10.30am - 3pm or 12 noon - 4.30pm, depending on the tide. Garden: all year 10am - dusk.
P Local authority car park 1 mile from site.
No wheelchair access or WC for the disabled. Guide Dogs allowed.
£ Adult: £5.20 (castle), £1 (garden only). Child: £2.60. Family: £13. NT members free. £6 (groups 10+ out-of-hours by arrangement).

LITTLE HARLE TOWER

Kirkwhelpington, Newcastle-upon-Tyne, Northumberland NE19 2PD
Medieval tower with 17th century range and a Victorian wing which contains a recently restored 1740s drawing room. It has been one family's home since 1830 though part is now let.
Grant Recipient: Mr J P P Anderson
Access Contact: Mr Simon Rowarth
T: 01434 609000   **F:** 01434 606900
E-mail: simon.rowarth@youngscs.com
Open: By arrangement (at least two weeks notice required) with Mr Simon Rowarth of Youngs, 3 Wentworth Place, Hexham, Northumberland NE46 1XB.
P Spaces: 6.
Wheelchair access to the ground floor only. No WC for the disabled. Guide Dogs allowed.
£ Donations to the church requested.

MITFORD HALL CAMELLIA HOUSE

Morpeth, Northumberland NE61 3PZ
East wing and conservatory of country house built c1820 by John Dobson, detached from main house by demolition of north-east wing in the 20th century. The conservatory houses a superb specimen of a red flowering camellia dating to c1826.
Grant Recipient: Shepherd Offshore plc
Access Contact: Mr B Shepherd
T: 01670 512637   **F:** 0191 2639872
Open: By written arrangement during the summer.
P Spaces: 3.
Wheelchair access by arrangement. Ordinary WC on site may be accessible for some disabled persons, please contact Hall for further information. Guide Dogs allowed.
£ No.

NETHERWITTON HALL

Morpeth, Northumberland NE61 4NW
Grade I listed mansion house built c1685 by Robert Trollope for Sir Nicholas Thornton. Access to main ground floor rooms and external elevations. Built as a family home and remains the current family home.
Grant Recipient: Mr J H T Trevelyan
Access Contact: Mr J H T Trevelyan
T: 01670 772 249   **F:** 01670 772 510
Open: By arrangement at least 24 hours in advance. 1 May - 29 May & 5 - 13 June: Mon - Fri 11am - 2pm by compulsory tour. Groups at other times by arrangement.
P Spaces: 20.
Full wheelchair access. Use of ramps up external steps. No WC for the disabled. Guide Dogs allowed.
£ Adult: £5. Child: £1.

POTTERGATE TOWER

Pottergate, Alnwick, Northumberland
Built as part of the town's defences, Pottergate Tower was one of the many gates providing access into Alwick. Rebuilt in 1768 to a design by Mr Henry Bell with a crown spire (removed in 1812). Above the archway is a St Michael and Dragon (the symbol of the Town), a blank roundel (formerly with a clock) and a memorial tablet: 'This tower was rebuilt at the expense of the Borough of Alnwick and the new foundation laid Apr 28 AD. 1768.' The Tower is approximately 50 feet in height and has a spiral stone staircase leading on an inner room. Listed Grade II*.
Grant Recipient: The Freemen of Alnwick
Access Contact: Mr Dennis Nixon
T: 01665 603517   **F:** 01665 603517
Open: To the exterior at all times; to the interior by arrangement. Heritage Open Days.
P No.
Guide dogs and wheelchair access to the exterior only. No WC for the disabled. No Guide Dogs.
£ No.

SEATON DELAVAL HALL

Seaton Sluice, Whitley Bay, Northumberland NE26 4QR
Country house, 1718-29 by Sir John Vanbrugh for Admiral George Delaval. Listed Grade I. The house comprises a centre block between two arcaded pedimented wings. In 1822 the centre block was gutted by fire and was partially restored in 1862-63, and again in 1959-62 and 1999-2000. Extensive gardens with statues and also a Norman church.

Grant Recipient: The Lord Hastings
Access Contact: Mrs Mills
T: 0191 2371493   E-mail: lordhastings@onetel.com
Open: 1 June - 30 Sept: May and Aug BH Mons, Weds and Suns 2 - 6pm.
℗Spaces: 50.
♿Wheelchair access to Stables, Tea Room, Coach House, Ice House, Norman Church and gardens. WC for the disabled. Guide Dogs allowed.
£Adult: £4. Child: £1. Senior: £3.50. Student £1. Groups (20+) £3 per adult.

ST CUTHBERT'S CHAPEL
Farne Islands, Northumberland
St Cuthbert's Chapel was completed in 1370. By the early 19th century it was in a ruinous condition. Restored in 1840 by Archdeacon Thorp it includes some fine 17th century woodwork from Durham Cathedral and a memorial to Grace Darling. Remains of an original window.
www.nationaltrust.org.uk
Grant Recipient: The National Trust
Access Contact: Mr John Walton
T: 01665 720651   F: 01665 720651
E-mail: john.walton@nationaltrust.org.uk
Open: 1 - 30 Apr & 1 Aug - 30 Sept: daily 10.30am - 6pm. 1 May - 31 July (breeding season) daily Staple Island 10.30am - 1.30pm, Inner Farne 1.30 - 5pm.
℗Public parking in Seahouses (nearest mainland village).
♿Inner Farne is accessible for wheelchairs (telephone the Property Manager in advance). Staple Island is not accessible. WC for the disabled on Inner Farne. Guide dogs are allowed on boat but not on islands.
£Adult: £5.20 (breeding season), £4.20 (outside breeding season), Child: £2.60 (breeding season), £2.10 (outside breeding season). Other: £2.60 (booked school parties, breeding season, per island), £2.10 (outside breeding season, per island). Admission fees do not include boatmen's charges.

ST MICHAEL'S PANT
Alnwick, Northumberland
St Michael's Pant (drinking fountain) was built in 1765 by Matthew Mills, designed by Mr Bell. St Michael and Dragon (the symbol of the Town) on top of an octagonal drum, gargoyle for the water spout with large square trough which measures approximately ten square metres. Listed Grade II*.
Grant Recipient: The Freemen of Alnwick
Access Contact: Mr D Nixon
T: 01665 603517   F: 01665 603517
Open: To the exterior at all times. Heritage Open Days.
℗No.
♿Full wheelchair access. No WC for the disabled. Guide Dogs allowed.
£No.

SWINBURNE CASTLE
Hexham, Northumberland NE48 4DQ
Kitchen range 1600-1650, incorporating earlier fabric and with later alterations, stands at right angles to the footprint of the now demolished (1966) mid 18th century house which stood on the site of the medieval castle. East (laundry) wing 1770, restored in 2000. Orangery early 19th century.
Grant Recipient: Trustees of R W Murphy
Access Contact: Major R P Murphy
T: 01434 681610
Open: 3 - 7, 10 - 13, 17 - 21, 24 - 28 Apr; 1 - 5, 8 - 9, 29 May; 28 August: 12 noon - 4.30pm.
℗Spaces: 6.
♿Wheelchair access to East Wing ground floor only. No WC for the disabled. No Guide Dogs.
£No.

THE TOWER
Elsdon, Northumberland NE19 1AA
14th century Tower House, residence of the Rector until 1961 and originally used as a refuge from the Border Reivers. Fine example of a medieval tower house and listed Grade I.
Grant Recipient: Dr J F Wollaston
Access Contact: Dr J F Wollaston
F: 01830 520904
Open: 1 Apr - 30 Oct: By previously arranged guided visit, weekends only.
℗Spaces: 30.
♿No wheelchair access or WC for the disabled. Guide Dogs allowed.
£Adult: £5.

VINDOLANDA ROMAN FORT
Bardon Mill, Hexham, Northumberland NE47 7NJ
Roman Fort and civilian settlement in central sector of Hadrian's Wall with active excavation and education programmes. The site is owned and administered by the Vindolanda Charitable Trust and has an on-site museum, with full visitor services, reconstructed Roman buildings and gardens.
www.vindolanda.com
Grant Recipient: Vindolanda Trust
Access Contact: Mrs Patricia Birley
T: 01434 344277   F: 01434 344060
E-mail: info@vindolanda.com
Open: 14 Feb - 14 Nov. Feb - Mar and Oct - Nov: daily 10am - 5pm. Apr - Sept: daily 10am - 6pm. Winter opening to be decided.
℗Spaces: 60. Coach parking available on-site.
♿Wheelchair access to parts of the archaeological site and all of the museums, gardens and open air museum. WC for the disabled. Guide Dogs allowed.
£Adult: £4.95. Child: £3. Other: £4.10. 10% reduction for EH members.

WALLINGTON HALL & CLOCK TOWER
Cambo, Morpeth, Northumberland NE61 4AR
Dating from 1688, the house was home to many generations of the Blackett and Trevelyan family. Contains Rococo plasterwork, fine ceramics, paintings and a doll's house collection. Pre-Raphaelite central hall with scenes from Northumbrian history. Hall, Clock Tower and stable buildings set among lawns, lakes and woodland with walled garden.
www.nationaltrust.org.uk
Grant Recipient: Ms Helen Clarke, Communication & Production Officer
Access Contact: Property Manager
T: 01670 773600   F: 01670 774420
E-mail: wallington@nationaltrust.org.uk
Open: House: daily except Tuesday. 5 Apr - 3 Sept 1 - 5.30pm. 4 Sept - 29 Oct 1- 4.30pm. Walled garden: daily, 1 Apr - 30 Sept 10am - 7pm. 1 Oct - 31 Oct 10am - 6pm. 1 Nov - 31 Mar 10am - 4pm. Grounds: daily in daylight hours.
℗Spaces: 500.
♿Lift to first floor for visitors with mobility problems. WC for the disabled. Guide Dogs allowed.
£Adult: £8 (house & gardens), £5.50 (gardens only). Child: £4 (house & gardens), £2.75 (gardens only). Other: £20 (family, house & gardens), £13 (family, gardens only). Groups (15+): £6.80 (house & gardens), £4.70 (gardens only).

NOTTINGHAMSHIRE

UPTON HALL
(THE BRITISH HOROLOGICAL INSTITUTE)
Upton, Newark, Nottinghamshire NG23 5TE
Grade II* listed house in Greek revival style, 1832, incorporating the earlier 17th century house. Large addition and interior remodelled in 1895. During the Second World War the house was a school for partially-sighted children. Now houses the British Horological Institute watch and clock museum featuring clocks from the 17th - 20th centuries.
www.bhi.co.uk/tour/start.htm
Grant Recipient: British Horological Institute
Access Contact: British Horological Institute
T: 01636 813795   F: 01636 812258
E-mail: clocks@bhi.co.uk
Open: Museum: 26 Mar and 29 Oct 11am - 5pm. Groups and guided tours (10+) by appointment. Further public access under review at time of publication, please check the English Heritage website or with the access contact for current information.
℗Spaces: 50. Coach parking available.
♿Wheelchair access to ground floor only. No WC for the disabled. Guide Dogs allowed.
£Adult: £3.50, (guided tours £5 pp). Child: £2 (under 10s free). Senior: £3. Family £10.

CHURCH OF ST MARY
New Road, Colston Bassett, Rushcliffe, Nott NG12 3FP
Grade I listed and scheduled monument dating from 1130, now ruined in isolated hill-top position.
Grant Recipient: St Mary's Church Repair Fund Committee
Access Contact: Mr A J M Alcock
T: 01949 81248
Open: Access at all times.
℗Spaces: 7. Unlimited on-street parking on New Road.

♿Full wheelchair access. No WC for the disabled. Guide Dogs allowed.
£No.

KILN WAREHOUSE
Mather Road, Newark, Nottinghamshire NG24 1FB
Grade II* former warehouse. Early example of the use of massed concrete construction. Interior completely destroyed by fire in the early 1990s, the exterior walls have been restored and warehouse converted into offices.
Grant Recipient: British Waterways Midlands & South West
Access Contact: Mrs Karen Tivey
T: 0115 950 7577   F: 0115 950 7688
E-mail: karen@fhp.co.uk
Open: The exterior walls for which the property is notable can be viewed without arrangement. Access to the internal courtyard is by arrangement with Karen Tivey of Fisher Hargreaves Proctor, Chartered Surveyors, 10 Oxford Street, Nottingham NG1 5BG (tel:0115 950 7577).
℗Parking is available on adjacent land.
♿Full wheelchair access. WC for the disabled. Guide Dogs allowed.
£No.

OXFORDSHIRE

ASTON MARTIN HERITAGE TRUST
Drayton St Leonard, Wallingford, Oxon OX10 7BG
15th century tithe barn, 6 bays. Constructed of elm with hipped roof. Listed Grade II*.
www.amheritrust.org
Grant Recipient: Aston Martin Owners Club
Access Contact: Mr Robert Ellis
T: 01865 400414   F: 01865 400200
E-mail: secretary@amheritrust.org
Open: Wednesdays: 2 - 5pm. Other times by arrangement.
℗Spaces: 30.
♿Wheelchair access to ground floor only. WC for the disabled. Guide Dogs allowed.
£No.

BAPTIST CHAPEL
Shifford Road, Cote, Oxfordshire OX18 2EG
Built around 1739-40 on earlier site and enlarged in 1756.
www.hct.org.uk
Grant Recipient: Historic Chapels Trust
Access Contact: Mr Ray Sale
T: 01993 850 421
Open: At all reasonable times by arrangement with key holder, Ray Sale, Elm Barn, Shilford Road, Cote, Oxon OX18 2EG. Heritage Open Days.
℗Spaces: 30. On-street parking.
♿Full wheelchair access. WC for the disabled. Guide Dogs allowed.
£Donations invited.

BLENHEIM PALACE & PARK
Woodstock, Oxfordshire OX20 1PX
Ancestral home of the Dukes of Marlborough and birthplace of Winston Churchill. Built between 1705-22 for John Churchill, the 1st Duke, in recognition of his victory at the Battle of Blenheim in 1704. Designed by Sir John Vanbrugh, the house contains in its many state rooms a collection of paintings, furniture, bronzes and the Marlborough Victories tapestries. A five-room Churchill Exhibition includes his birth room. 'Capability' Brown park and gardens.
www.blenheimpalace.com
Grant Recipient: Duke of Marlborough
Access Contact: Mrs Heather Carter
T: 01993 810531   F: 01993 813527
E-mail: hcarter@blenheimpalace.com
Open: Palace: 11 Feb - 10 Dec, daily 10.30am - 5.30pm (last adm. 4.45pm). Nov & Dec closed Mon & Tues. Park: daily (except Christmas Day) 9am - 6pm (last adm. 4.45pm).
℗Spaces: 10,000.
♿Full wheelchair access. WC for the disabled. Guide Dogs allowed.
£Adult: £12 off peak, £14 peak. Child: £6.50 off peak, £8.50 peak. Senior: £9.50 off peak, £11.50 peak.

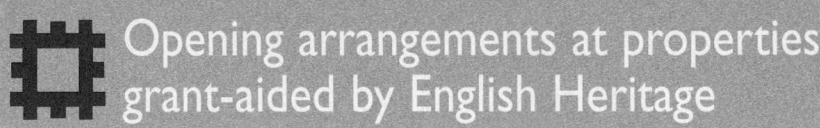
CLATTERCOTE PRIORY FARM
Claydon, Banbury, Oxfordshire OX17 1QB
Founded c1150, the Priory is now a family house - part farmhouse, part tenanted. A rare example of a Gilbertine Priory with cellars and 'chapel', probably medieval.
Grant Recipient: Mr Adrian Taylor
Access Contact: Mr Adrian Taylor
T: 01295 690476   **F:** 01295 690476
E-mail: clattercote1@aol.com
Open: By written arrangement.
P Spaces: 4
No wheelchair access or WC for the disabled. Guide Dogs allowed.
£ Adult: £5 (to cancer charity).

CORNBURY PARK
Charbury, Oxford, Oxfordshire OX7 3EH
400 acre deer park adjacent to Wychwood forest containing newly restored/replanted beech avenues, ancient English oak trees and several ancient monuments.
www.cornburypark.co.uk
Grant Recipient: The Lord Rotherwick
Access Contact: Helen Spearman/ Richard Watkins/Lindsey Sculter
T: 01608 811276   **F:** 01608 811252
E-mail: estate@cpark.co.uk
Open: 1 Mar - 31 Oct: Tues & Thurs 10am - 4pm. Please note that a permit is required for access to the Park; permit must be applied for in advance. Organised educational access walks for groups by arrangement.
P Spaces: 20.   No access.   £ No.

CULHAM MANOR DOVECOTE
The Green, Culham, Oxfordshire OX14 4LZ
Dovecote constructed from brick and stone, with a datestone above the door of 1685. Reputed to be the second largest dovecote in England, formed of two large cells each with an entry lantern for dove access. In total, it has over 3,000 nesting boxes.
Grant Recipient: Mr James Wilson MacDonald
Access Contact: Mr James Wilson MacDonald
T: 01235 527009   **F:** 01865 744520
E-mail: wil.mac@virgin.net
Open: By arrangement (tel: evenings, fax/e-mail: anytime).
P Spaces: 20. On Green by Church.
No wheelchair access or WC for the disabled. Guide Dogs allowed.
£ No.

FARNBOROUGH HALL
Farnborough, Banbury, Oxfordshire OX17 1DU
Mid-18th century honey-coloured stone built home of the Holbech family for over 300 years, contains impressive plasterwork. Set in grounds with 18th century temples, a terrace walk and an obelisk.
www.nationaltrust.org.uk
Grant Recipient: The National Trust
Access Contact: Mr & Mrs G Holbech
T: 01295 690002
E-mail: farnboroughhall@nationaltrust.org.uk
Open: House and garden: 1 Apr - 30 Sept, Wed and Sat 2 - 5.30pm. 30 Apr and 1 May: Sun and Mon 2 - 5.30pm. Terrace walk: same days as house.
P Spaces: 10. Additional free parking, 200 yds.
Wheelchair access to ground floor of house and garden. Terrace walk may be difficult as it is very steep. No WC for the disabled. Guide Dogs allowed.
£ Adult: £4.20, £2.10 (terrance walk only). Child: £2.10. Family: £11.50.

FREEMAN MAUSOLEUM
St Mary's Churchyard, Fawley, nr Henley-on-Thames, Oxfordshire RG9 6HZ
Built in 1752 for the Freeman family who owned the Fawley Estate. Design by John Freeman based on the mausoleum of Cecilia Metella on the Appian Way in Rome, which he visited while on his Grand Tour. It contains 30 coffin slots with 12 being filled by the Freemans before they sold the Estate in 1850.
Grant Recipient: St Mary's Parochial Church Council
Access Contact: Mrs Dorothea Giddy
T: 01491 572686
Open: By arrangement with the key holder, Mrs D Giggy (tel:01491 572686).

P On-street parking adjacent to church.
Full wheelchair access. No WC for the disabled. Guide Dogs allowed.
£ No.

MARTYRS' MEMORIAL
St. Giles, Oxford, Oxfordshire OX1
Erected in 1841-3 and designed by Sir George Gilbert Scott, in commemoration of Protestant martyrs, Archbishop Cranmer, Bishops Ridley and Latimer who were burnt to death in 1555 and 1556. The memorial is hexagonal in plan and takes the form of a steeple of three stages reaching a height of 21 metres.
Grant Recipient: Oxford City Council
Access Contact: Mr Nick Worlledge
T: 01865 252147   **F:** 01865 252144
E-mail: nworlledge@oxford.gov.uk
Open: Accessible at all times
P No.
Full wheelchair access. No WC for the disabled. Guide Dogs allowed.
£ No.

SHOTOVER PARK
Wheatley, Oxfordshire OX33 1QS
Early 18th century garden follies. The Gothic Temple (designer unknown) lies east of the house at the end of a long canal vista. Has a battlemented gable with a central pinnacle and a rose-window, below which is an open loggia of three pointed arches. The other Temple west of the house, designed by William Kent, is of a domed octagonal construction.
Grant Recipient: Sir John Miller
Access Contact: Sir John Miller
T: 01865 872450 or 874095
Open: Access to Temples at all reasonable times (lie close to public rights of way). Parking for a few cars at the Gothic Temple, otherwise other arrangements can be made in advance with Sir John Miller on 01865 872450 or Mrs Price on 01865 874095.
P Spaces: 50.
Wheelchair access to the Gothic Temple with assistance. WC for the disabled. Guide Dogs allowed.
£ No.

SWALCLIFFE TITHE BARN
Shipston Road, Swalcliffe, Banbury, Oxfordshire OX15 5DR
15th century barn built for the Rectorial Manor of Swalcliffe by New College, who owned the Manor. Constructed between 1400 and 1409, much of the medieval timber half-cruck roof remains intact. It is now a museum.
www.oxfordshire.gov.uk
Grant Recipient: Oxfordshire Historic Building Trust Ltd
Access Contact: Mr Raj Pal
T: 01993 814114   **F:** 01993 813239
E-mail: raj.pal@oxfordshire.gov.uk
Open: Easter - end of Sept: Sun & BHs 2 - 5pm. Other times by arrangement (contact Jeff Demmar tel: 01295 788278).
P Spaces: 10.
Full wheelchair access. WC for the disabled. Guide Dogs allowed.
£ No.

THE OLD RECTORY DOVECOTE
Mill Street, Kidlington, Oxford, Oxfordshire OX5 2EE
Large round medieval dovecote.
Grant Recipient: Ms Felicity Duncan
Access Contact: Ms Felicity Duncan
T: 01865 513816
Open: Daily, 10am - 5.30pm.
P No.
No wheelchair access or WC for the disabled. Guide Dogs allowed.
£ No.

SHROPSHIRE

2/3 MILK STREET
Shrewsbury, Shropshire SY1 1SZ
Timber-framed two and a half storey building dating from the 15th century with later alterations and additions. Medieval shop front to rear. Still a shop.

Grant Recipient: Mr M J Cockle
Access Contact: Mr H Carter
T: 01743 276633   **F:** 01743 242140
E-mail: htc@pooks.co.uk
Open: Ground floor shop open 6 days a week all year. Mon - Sat 9.30am - 5.30pm. Upper floor flats can be visited only by arrangement with Mr H Carter, Pooks, 26 Claremont Hill, Shrewsbury, Shropshire SY1 1RE.
P No.
Wheelchair access to ground floor only. No WC for the disabled. Guide Dogs allowed.
£ No.

ATTINGHAM PARK
Atcham, Shrewsbury, Shropshire SY4 4TP
Built 1785 by George Steuart for the 1st Lord Berwick, with a picture gallery by John Nash. Contains Regency interiors, [...] landscaped by Repton in 1797.
www.nationaltrust.org.uk
Grant Recipient: The National Trust
Access Contact: The Property Manager
T: 01743 708162/708123   **F:** 01743 708155
E-mail: attingham@nationaltrust.org.uk
Open: House: 4 - 19 Mar, Sat and Sun 1 - 5pm. 25 Mar - 29 Oct daily except Wed & Thurs 1 - 5pm (last adm. 4.30pm). Guided tours 12 noon - 1pm only. Park: 1 Mar - 29 Oct 10am - 8pm, 4 Nov - 25 Feb 2007 weekends only, closed Christmas Day.
P Spaces: 150.
Wheelchair access: to lower ground and ground floors only (house), drives and paths (grounds), and shop. WC for the disabled. Guide Dogs allowed.
£ Adult: £6.50, £3.25 (house & grounds) £3.30, £1.65 (park & grounds). Family: £16.25. Booked Groups (15+) £5.50.

BENTHALL HALL
Broseley, Shropshire TF12 5RX
16th century stone house situated on a plateau above the gorge of the River Severn, with mullioned and transomed windows, carved oak staircase, decorated plaster ceilings and oak panelling. Also has a restored plantsman's garden, old kitchen garden and a Restoration church.
www.nationaltrust.org.uk
Grant Recipient: The National Trust
Access Contact: The Custodian
T: 01952 882159
E-mail: benthall@nationaltrust.org.uk
Open: 16 Apr - 28 June: Tues & Wed 2 - 5.30pm. 2 July - 27 Sept: Tues, Wed and Sun 2 - 5.30pm. Open BH Suns & Mons. Groups by arrangement with the custodian.
P Spaces: 50.
Wheelchair access to ground floor of Hall and part of garden only. No WC for the disabled. Guide Dogs allowed.
£ Adult: £4.40. Child: £2.20. Other: £2.75 & £1.35 (garden only).

BROSELEY PIPEWORKS
King Street, Broseley, Shropshire TF8 7AW
19th century clay pipe factory comprising a three storey factory range, bottle kiln, workers cottage and school room. Contents include pipe-making machinery and collection of smoking pipes. Main rooms contain the original equipment installed in the 1880s and used until the site was abandoned at the end of the 1950s.
www.ironbridge.org.uk
Grant Recipient: Ironbridge Gorge Museum Trust
Access Contact: Mr Glen Lawes
T: 01952 435 900   **F:** 01952 435 999
E-mail: information@ironbridge.org.uk
Open: Apr - Oct: 1 - 5pm.
P Overflow car park at adjacent site for 20.
Wheelchair access to ground floor and yard. WC for the disabled. Guide Dogs allowed.
£ Adult: £3.10. Child: £1.70. Senior: £2.30.

COMBERMERE ABBEY
Whitchurch, Shropshire SY13 4AJ
Originally founded in 1133 as a Cistercian Abbey, and it has now evolved into a complex medieval and 16th century building with extensive pasteboard Gothic enveloping dating from the early 19th century.
www.combermereabbey.co.uk
Grant Recipient: Mrs S Callender Beckett

Access Contact: Mrs Sarah Callender Beckett
T: 01948 662880
E-mail: estate@combermereabbey.co.uk
Open: 6 Apr - 28 Sept: Thurs afternoon, guided tours only 2pm & 4pm. Please tel in advance. Further access under review at time of publication, please check the English Heritage website or with the access contact. Heritage Open Days.
P Spaces: 50. Weather dependent.
& No wheelchair access or WC for the disabled. Guide Dogs allowed.
£ Adult: £5. Child: £3 (16 and under).

DUDMASTON

Quatt, Bridgnorth, Shropshire WV15 6QN
Queen Anne mansion of red brick with stone dressings, situated in parkland overlooking the Severn. Contains furniture, Dutch flower paintings, contemporary paintings and sculpture. Gardens, wooded valley and estate walks starting from Hampton Loade.
www.nationaltrust.org.uk
Grant Recipient: The National Trust
Access Contact: The Administrator
T: 01746 780866   **F:** 01746 780744
E-mail: dudmaston@nationaltrust.org.uk
Open: 2 Apr - 27 Sept: House: Tues, Wed & Sun 2 - 5.30pm. Garden: Mon, Tues, Wed & Sun 12 noon - 6pm. Shop: open as house 1 - 5.30pm. Tearoom: as garden 11.30am - 5.30pm.
P Spaces: 150.
& Wheelchair access to main and inner halls, Library, oak room, No 1 and Derby galleries, old kitchen, garden and grounds (some estate walks), shop and tea room. WC for the disabled. Guide Dogs allowed.
£ Adult: Child: £2.50. Family: £12.50. Garden only: £4. £4 (booked groups of 15+).

HOSPITAL OF THE HOLY AND UNDIVIDED TRINITY

Hospital Lane, Clun, Shropshire SY7 8LE
Founded in 1607 by Henry Howard, Earl of Northampton and built in 1618 with alterations of 1857. Dwellings and other rooms arranged around a square courtyard. A well preserved example of a courtyard-plan almshouses.
Grant Recipient: The Trustees of Trinity Hospital
Access Contact: Mrs JS Woodroffe
T: 01588 672303
Open: Gardens and chapel: daily (except Christmas Day). The Dining Hall and quadrangle: 23 - 25 June, 2 - 6pm. Other times by arrangement.
P Spaces: 70.
& Full wheelchair access. No WC for the disabled. Guide Dogs allowed.
£ No.

JACKFIELD TILE MUSEUM & FACTORY

Jackfield, Telford, Shropshire TF8 7LJ
Home to the Craven Dunnill factory, where decorative tiles were mass-produced from 1874 until just after the Second World War. Surviving example of a purpose-built Victorian tile factory and continues to manufacture products today.
www.ironbridge.org.uk
Grant Recipient: Ironbridge Gorge Museum Trust
Access Contact: Mr Glen Lawes
T: 01952 435 900   **F:** 01952 435 999
E-mail: information@ironbridge.org.uk
Open: Daily, 10am - 5pm. Closed 24 & 25 Dec & 1 Jan.
P Spaces: 30. Free.
& Full wheelchair access. WC for the disabled. Guide Dogs allowed.
£ Adult: £4.50. Child: £2.70. Other: £4.15.

JOHN ROSE BUILDING

High Street Coalport, Telford, Shropshire TF8 7HT
A range of china painting workshops, centre part dating from late 18th century, outer wings rebuilt early 20th century. Restored and converted to a Youth Hostel, craft workshops and shop. Main entrance is paved with mosaic celebrating the amalgamation of Coalport, Swansea and Nantgarw brands. Coalbrookdale cast iron windows of large dimension line both major elevations.
www.ironbridge.org.uk
Grant Recipient: Ironbridge Gorge Museum Trust
Access Contact: Mr Glen Lawes
T: 01952 435 900   **F:** 01952 435 999

E-mail: information@ironbridge.org.uk
Open: Access to exterior at all times. Shop: Mar - Oct, 11.30am - 5pm. Oct - Mar 11am - 4.30pm. Other times by arrangement.
P Spaces: 65. Museum car park.
& Youth Hostel: wheelchair access to ground and first floor (stair lift) with WC and shower facilities for the disabled. China Museum: majority accessible, visiting guide available on arrival. Guide Dogs allowed.
£ No.

LANGLEY GATEHOUSE

Acton Burnell, Shropshire SY5 7PE
This gatehouse has two quite different faces: one is of plain dressed stone; the other, which once looked inwards to long demolished Langley Hall, is timber-framed. It was probably used for the Steward or important guests. It was rescued from a point of near collapse and shows repair work of an exemplary quality.
www.landmarktrust.org.uk
Grant Recipient: The Landmark Trust
Access Contact: Mrs Victoria O'Keeffe
T: 01628 825920   **F:** 01628 825417
E-mail: vokeeffe@landmarktrust.org.uk
Open: The Landmark Trust is an independent charity, which rescues small buildings of historic or architectural importance from decay or unsympathetic improvement. Landmark's aim is to promote the enjoyment of these historic buildings by making them available to stay in for holidays. Langley Gatehouse can be rented by anyone, at all times of the year, for periods ranging from a weekend to three weeks. Bookings can be made by telephoning the Booking Office on 01628 825925. As the building is in full-time use for holiday accommodation, it is not normally open to the public. However the public can view the building by arrangement by telephoning the access contact (Vicky O'Keeffe on 01628 825920) to make an appointment. Potential visitors will be asked to write to confirm the details of their visit.
P Spaces: 2.
& No wheelchair access or WC for the disabled. Guide Dogs allowed.
£ No.

LOTON HALL

Alberbury, Shropshire SY5 9AJ
Country house, c1670, but extensively altered and enlarged in the early 18th and 19th centuries. Set in parkland which includes the ruins of the early 13th century Alberbury Castle. Home of the Leighton family since the 14th century.
Grant Recipient: Sir Michael Leighton
Access Contact: Mr Mark Williams
T: 01691 655334   **F:** 01691 657798
Open: House: 9 Jan - 13 Apr, Mons & Thurs by guided tour only at 10am or 12 noon. Garden and castle can also be viewed at the same times.
P Spaces: 30.
& Wheelchair access to ground floor only. 5 steps at front door – ramp can be put in place for wheelchair access. No WC for the disabled. Guide Dogs allowed.
£ Adult: £5. Child: Free. Senior: £3.

OLD MARKET HALL

The Square, Shrewsbury, Shropshire SY1 1HJ
Old market hall and court house, dated 1596 and listed Grade I. Recently repaired and refurbished to accommodate a Film and Digital Media Centre, including auditorium and cafe/bar.
www.oldmarkethall.co.uk
Grant Recipient: Shrewsbury & Atcham Borough Council
Access Contact: Mr David Jack
T: 01743 281250   **F:** 01743 281283
E-mail: davidjack@musichall.co.uk
Open: Daily, 10am -11pm. Auditorium closed to public when films are screened. Current screening times: Mon - Sun evening films. Matinee films most days.
P No.
& Full wheelchair access. WC for the disabled. Guide Dogs allowed.
£ Charges for performances only (Adult £4.80, child £3.30).

PRADOE

West Felton, Oswestry, Shropshire SY11 4ER
Georgian country house set in park and garden designed by John Webb. Grade II* listed house contains furniture dating

from 1803 - 1812 during initial occupation by the Kenyon family. Attached service ranges, walled kitchen garden and outbuildings including dairy, brewhouse and carpenter's shop, contain original early 19th century features, recently restored.
Grant Recipient: Colonel John F Kenyon
Access Contact: Col. John F Kenyon
T: 01691 610218   **F:** 01691 610913
Open: June - Sept: Mons & Tues 10am - 12pm or 1- 3pm, by arrangement.
P Spaces: 50.
& Wheelchair access to gardens and farm buildings only. No WC for the disabled. Guide Dogs allowed.
£ Adult: £5 (groups of not more than 30). Child: £2.

THE LYTH

Ellesmere, Shropshire SY12 0HR
Grade II* listed small country house, c1820, with minor later additions. Cast-iron verandah with trellised supports, one of the earliest and largest examples in the country. Birthplace of E & D Jebb, founders of Save the Children.
Grant Recipient: Mr L R Jebb
Access Contact: Mr L R Jebb
T: 01691 622339   **F:** 01691 624134
Open: To the exterior: 26 Mar, 21 May, 17 Sept, 8 Oct 2 - 6pm. Other times by arrangement with Mr Lionel Jebb.
P Spaces: 40.
& Full wheelchair access. No WC for the disabled. Guide Dogs allowed.
£ Adult: £2 (charity donation for visits to garden). Child: £1 (charity donation for visits to garden).

THE OLD MANSION

St Mary's Street, Shrewsbury, Shropshire SY1 1UQ
Early 17th century house with original staircase. The building was renovated in 1997 and now provides 4 bedroom suites for the Prince Rupert Hotel.
Grant Recipient: Mr A Humphreys
Access Contact: Mr J H L Humphreys
T: 01291 672 563
Open: By arrangement with the Prince Rupert Hotel (tel: 01743 499955).
P No. **&** No access. **£** No.

YEATON PEVEREY HALL

Yeaton Peverey, Shrewsbury, Shropshire SY4 3AT
Mock Jacobean country house, 1890-2 by Aston Webb. Previously a school, now reinstated as a family home. Principal rooms on the ground floor open to visitors.
Grant Recipient: Mr Martin Ebelis
Access Contact: Mr Martin Ebelis
T: 01743 851185   **F:** 01743 851186
E-mail: mae@earlstone.co.uk
Open: 20 & 21 Mar, 17 & 18 Apr, 8 & 9 May, 5 June: 12 noon - 5pm. When family is in residence by arrangement with written confirmation or introduction through known contact.
P Spaces: 6. Parking adjacent to the property for the disabled.
& Full wheelchair access. No WC for the disabled. Guide Dogs allowed.
£ Adult: £5, Child: £2.

SOMERSET

29 QUEEN SQUARE RAILINGS

Bristol BS1 4ND
Fronted by repaired, grant-aided railings, 29 Queen Square is an early Georgian town house, 1709-11, Grade II*. One of the few surviving original houses in Queen Square which was laid out in 1699 and has claim to be the largest square in England.
Grant Recipient: The Queen Square Partnership
Access Contact: Reception
T: 0117 975 0700
E-mail: southwest@english-heritage.org.uk
Open: Access to the exterior at all reasonable times to view the railings from the pavement.
P Paid parking in Queen Square and car park in The Grove (behind 29 Queen Square).
& Full wheelchair access. No WC for the disabled. Guide Dogs allowed.
£ No.

BATH ASSEMBLY ROOMS

Bennett Street, Bath, Somerset BA1 2QH
Built in 1771 by John Wood the Younger, now owned by the National Trust and administered by Bath and North East

Somerset District Council. Each of the rooms has a complete set of original chandeliers. The Museum of Costume is located on the lower ground floor.
www.museumofcostume.co.uk
Grant Recipient: Bath City Council/National Trust
Access Contact: Ms Rosemary Harden
T: 01225 477752   **F:** 01225 444793
E-mail: costume_enquiries@bathnes.gov.uk
Open: Daily: Jan, Feb, Nov & Dec 11am - 5pm; Mar - Oct 11am - 6pm when not in use for pre-booked functions. Last admission 1 hr before closing. Tel: 01225 477789 to check availability. No pre-booked functions during the day during Aug. Closed Christmas Day and Boxing Day.
Ⓟ On street car parking (pay and display).
♿ Full wheelchair access. WC for the disabled. Guide Dogs allowed
£ But charge for Museum of Costume.

BRITISH EMPIRE AND COMMONWEALTH MUSEUM
Clock Tower Yard, Temple Meads, Bristol BS1 6QH
Museum housed in world's earliest surviving railway terminus, which was completed in 1840 and was originally part of the Great Western Railway designed by I.K. Brunel. Over 220ft long with timber and iron roof spans of 72ft, this Grade 1 listed building has been nominated as a World Heritage Site. Contains the Passenger shed and the adjoining former Engine and Carriage shed.
www.empiremuseum.co.uk
Grant Recipient: Empire Museum Ltd
Access Contact: Mrs Anne Lineen
T: 0117 925 4980   **Fax:** 0117 925 4983
E-mail: anne.lineen@empiremuseum.co.uk
Open: From 1 Feb: daily 10am - 5pm, except 25/26 Dec. Access to exterior is unrestricted.
Ⓟ Spaces: 15 Additional parking in Station car park.
♿ Full wheelchair access. WC for the disabled. Guide Dogs allowed.
£ Adult: £6.50. Child: £3.95. Other: £5.50 (prices subject to change).

CHARD GUILDHALL
Fore Street, Chard, Somerset TA20 2YA
Grade II* listed building dating to 1834. Former Corn Exchange and Guildhall, now Town Hall.
Grant Recipient: Chard Town Council
Access Contact: Mr John Evans, Guildhall Manager
T: 01460 260 371   **F:** 01460 260 372
E-mail: john.evans@chard.gov.uk
Open: Accessible at all times.
Ⓟ No.
♿ Full wheelchair access. WC for the disabled. Guide Dogs allowed.
£ No.

CLEVEDON PIER
The Beach, Clevedon, Somerset BS21 7QU
Pier with attached toll house built c1860s to serve steamers bound for South Wales. Wrought and cast iron structure and shelters consisting of eight 100ft arched spans leading to a landing stage. The exceptionally slender spans are constructed from riveted broad-gauge railway track as designed by W H Barlow for the Great Western Railway. Scottish baronial style toll house contains shop and art gallery. Pier restored in 1999 after partial collapse 30 years earlier and is one of only two Grade 1 listed piers. This pier is of outstanding importance for its delicate engineering and the relationship of pier to landward buildings, which creates an exceptionally picturesque ensemble.
www.clevedonpier.com
Grant Recipient: The Clevedon Pier and Heritage Trust
Access Contact: Mrs Linda Strong
T: 01275 878846   **F:** 01275 790077
E-mail: clevedonpier@zoom.co.uk
Open: All year except 25 Dec: Mon - Wed, 10am - 5pm, Thurs - Sun 9am - 5pm. Please check opening times prior to visit.
Ⓟ Car parking on seafront.
♿ No wheelchair access to art gallery. No WC for the disabled. No Guide Dogs.
£ Adult: £1. Child: 50p. Conc: 75p.

ENGLISHCOMBE TITHE BARN
Rectory Farmhouse, Englishcombe, Bath BA2 9DU
Early 14th century cruck framed tithe barn. Recently restored with new crucks, masonry and straw lining to the roof, and filigree windows unblocked. There are masons and other markings on the walls.
Grant Recipient: Mrs Jennie Walker
Access Contact: Mrs Jennie Walker
T: 01225 425073
E-mail: jennie.walker@ukonline.co.uk
Open: BHs, 2 - 6pm; all other times by arrangement with Mrs Walker (tel: 01225 425073). Closed 18 Dec 2005 - 1 Mar 2006. Heritage Open Days.
Ⓟ Spaces: 34.
♿ Full wheelchair access. WC for the disabled. Guide Dogs allowed.
£ No.

FAIRFIELD
Stogursey, nr. Bridgwater, Somerset TA5 1PU
Elizabethan and medieval house and Grade II* listed. Undergoing repairs. Occupied by the same family for over 600 years. Woodland garden with views of the Quantocks.
Grant Recipient: Lady Gass
Access Contact: Mr D W Barke
T: 01722 555131 or 01278 732251   **F:** 01722 555140
Open: House: 26 Apr - 29 May & 7 June - 7 July: Weds, Thurs, Fris and BHs by guided tour at 2.30 & 3.30pm. Groups at other times by arrangement. Garden: open for NGS and other charities on dates advertised in Spring. No inside photography. No dogs except Guide Dogs.
Ⓟ Spaces: 30.
♿ Full wheelchair access. WC for the disabled.
£ Adult: £4. Child: £1. Other: Admission charges in aid of Stogursey Church.

FORDE ABBEY
Chard, Somerset TA20 4LU
Cistercian monastery founded in 1140 and dissolved in 1539 when the church was demolished. The monks' quarters were converted in 1640 into an Italian style "palazzo" by Sir Edmund Prideaux. Interior has plaster ceilings and Mortlake tapestries.
www.fordeabbey.co.uk
Grant Recipient: Trustees of the Roper Settlement
Access Contact: Mrs Clay
T: 01460 220231   **E-mail:** info@fordeabbey.co.uk
Open: Gardens: Daily, 10am - 4.30pm. House: Apr - Oct; Tues- Fri, Sun & BHs 12 noon - 4pm.
Ⓟ Spaces: 500.
♿ Wheelchair access to ground floor and garden. WC for the disabled. Guide Dogs allowed.
£ Adult: £7.50. Child: Free. Senior: £7. (Provisional).

GANTS MILL
Gants Mill Lane, Bruton, Somerset BA10 0DB
Working watermill with deeds dating back to owner John le Gaunt in 1290. Corn grinding and hydropower plant demonstrations and historical displays. Designer watergarden with sculptures, ponds, streams, rose pergolas. Collections of iris, delphiniums, penstemons, day lilies and dahlias. Riverside walk.
www.gantsmill.co.uk
Grant Recipient: Mr Brian Shingler
Access Contact: Brian & Alison Shingler
T: 01749 812393   **E-mail:** shingler@gantsmill.co.uk
Open: 15 May - end Sept: Suns, Thurs & BH, 2 - 5pm. Groups by arrangement. Refreshments available.
Ⓟ Spaces: 40. Parking close to site.
♿ Wheelchair access to gardens only. No WC for the disabled. Guide Dogs allowed.
£ Adult: £5. Child: £1. Other: Group reductions by arrangement.

GREAT HOUSE FARM
Theale, Wedmore, Somerset BS28 4SJ
17th century farmhouse with Welsh slate roof, oak doors and some original diamond paned windows. Inside is a carved well staircase with two murals on the walls. There are four servants rooms at the top, three of which are dark and occupied by Lesser Horseshoe bats.
Grant Recipient: Mr A R Millard
Access Contact: Mr A R Millard
T: 01934 713133
Open: Apr - Aug: Tues & Thurs 2 - 6pm by tel arrangement.
Ⓟ Spaces: 6.
♿ No wheelchair access or WC for the disabled. Guide Dogs allowed.
£ Adult: £2. Child: Free. Senior: £1.

HALL FARM HIGH BARN
Stogumber, Taunton, Somerset TA4 3TQ
17th century Grade II* listed building with seven bays of red local sandstone rubble with jointed cruck roof. South wall supported by four buttresses but there are none on the North wall. There are blocked windows on the South wall and two stub walls extend north. Lines of joist holes were provided for internal flooring and the two main entrances were to the north and south.
Grant Recipient: CM & R Hayes
Access Contact: CM & R Hayes
T: 01984 656321
Open: By arrangement with CM & R Hayes at Hall Farm.
Ⓟ Spaces: 4.
♿ Full wheelchair access. No WC for the disabled. Guide Dogs allowed.
£ No.

LANCIN FARMHOUSE
Wambrook, Chard, Somerset TA20 3EG
15th century farmhouse with old oak beams in places with the original smoking thatch, flagstone floors and breadoven.
Grant Recipient: Mr S J Smith
Access Contact: Mrs R A Smith
T: 01460 62290
Open: 18 Apr, 2 & 30 May, 20 & 27 June, 11 July, 5 & 19 Sept & 10 & 24 Oct 10am - 2.30pm. Also Tues - Thurs 10am - 5pm by arrangement.
Ⓟ Spaces: 5.   ♿ No access.   £ Adult: £2.

LORD MAYOR'S CHAPEL
College Green, Bristol BS1 5TB
13th century church with 16th century floor of Spanish tiles in the Poyntz Chapel. The only church in England that is owned, maintained and run by a City Council.
Grant Recipient: Bristol City Council
Access Contact: Mr Alan F Canterbury
T: 0117 922 2000/929 4350   **Fax:** 0117 929 4350
Open: Wed - Sat, 10am - 12pm & 1 - 4pm. Sunday service 11am. Heritage Open Days.
Ⓟ On street parking behind Council House and Trenchard St.
♿ No wheelchair access. No WC for the disabled. Guide Dogs allowed.
£ No.

PRIOR PARK COLLEGE OLD GYMNASIUM
Ralph Allen Drive, Bath, Somerset BA2 5AH
Built for Ralph Allen in the mid-18th century as an early and successful demonstration of the quality of Bath stone. The Chapel and Old Gymnasium are part of the mid-19th century additions to adapt the property as a Catholic seminary for Bishop Baines. Now a boarding and day school.
www.priorpark.co.uk
Grant Recipient: Governors of Prior Park College
Access Contact: C J Freeman
T: 01225 837491   **F:** 01225 835753
E-mail: bursar@priorpark.co.uk
Open: 21 - 25 Aug: daily 10.30am - 4pm. Group tours in school holidays or by arrangement. Please tel in advance.
Ⓟ Spaces: 50
♿ No wheelchair access. WC for the disabled. Guide Dogs allowed.
£ Please telephone for prices.

ROWES LEADWORKS
('Wildscreen at Bristol' and Firehouse restaurant), Harbourside, Bristol BS1 5DB
A former leadworks built in the 19th century. One of a few surviving structures associated with the industrial character of this area with a goods station and nearby warehouses. Now transformed into a restaurant/bar, The Firehouse Rotisseries. Attached to this is a modern canopied, large open structure, the entrance to 'Wildscreen at Bristol' which features imagery and interactive exhibits of the natural world. It includes an Imax cinema and living botanical house.
www.at-bristol.org.uk
Grant Recipient: Bristol City Council
Access Contact: Mr Mike Rippon, Operations Director
T: 0117915 7131   **Fax:** 0117 915 7200
E-mail: mike.rippon@at-bristol.org.uk
Open: All venues: daily 10am - 6pm. Public squares and spaces around the leadworks open all year round.
Ⓟ Spaces: 500. Pay parking operated by At-Bristol
♿ Full wheelchair access. WC for the disabled. Guide Dogs allowed.
£ Free to view building but charges for access to 'Wildscreen at Bristol' and the IMAX theatre.

ROWLANDS MILL

Rowlands, Ilminster, Somerset TA19 9LE

Grade II* stone and brick 3-storey millhouse and machinery, c1620, with a mill pond, mill race, overshooting wheel and waterfall. The millhouse is now a holiday let but the machinery has separate access and is in working condition.

Grant Recipient: Mr P G H Speke

Access Contact: Mr P G H Speke

T: 01460 52623   **F:** 01460 52623

Open: Millhouse Fridays & machinery Mon - Fri 10am - 4pm by written arrangement (at least 1 week's notice required). Heritage Open Days machinery only unless a Fri, then whole building.

🅿 Spaces: 7.

♿ Wheelchair access to ground floor only. No WC for the disabled. Guide Dogs allowed.

£ Adult £3. Child: Free.

ROYAL WEST OF ENGLAND ACADEMY

Queen's Road, Clifton, Bristol BS8 1PX

Bristol's first Art Gallery, founded in 1844, Grade II* listed and a registered museum. A fine interior housing five naturally lit art galleries, a new commercial gallery and a permanent fine art collection.

www.rwa.org.uk

Grant Recipient: Royal West of England Academy

Access Contact: Mrs Dee Smart

T: 0117 9735129   **Fax:** 0117 9237874

E-mail: info@rwa.org.uk

Open: Mon - Sat 10am - 5.30pm, Sun 2 - 5pm. BHs 11am - 4pm. Closed 25 Dec - 3 Jan & Easter Day. Heritage Open Days.

🅿 Parking for Disabled Badge Holders only (5 spaces).

♿ Wheelchair access to New Gallery on ground floor and Main Galleries accessible by lift (not Fedden Gallery) WCs fitted with handrails. Guide Dogs allowed.

£ Adult £3. Child: Free (under 16s). Senior/Student: £2.

ST GEORGE'S BRISTOL

Great George Street, Bristol, Somerset BS1 5RR

Grade II* listed Georgian former church, c1821-3, by Robert Smirke in Greek Revival style, now 550 seater concert hall. A Waterloo church, built as a chapel-of-ease to Cathedral of St Augine, and converted to a concert hall in 1987. The crypt now houses a café and art gallery.

www.stgeorgesbristol.co.uk

Grant Recipient: St George's Bristol

Access Contact: Mrs Jo Friend

T: 0117 929 4929   **F:** 0117 927 6537

E-mail: j.webb@stgeorgesbristol.co.uk

Open: For seasonal concert programmes - mainly evenings, some lunchtimes and Sun afternoons, contact Box Office on 0117 9230359 for brochure. Free access to crypt and art gallery from 1 hour before concerts. Tours can be arranged if dates comply with events schedule. Heritage Open Days.

🅿 Spaces: 3.

♿ Wheelchair access via Charlotte Street. The auditorium stalls, crypt/café/gallery and Box Office are accessible but preferable if you ring in advance as entry is not straightforward. WC for the disabled. Guide Dogs allowed.

£ But tickets required for concerts.

ST MARGARET'S ALMSHOUSES

Taunton, Somerset

Converted 16th century almshouses built on site of 12th century leper hospital. Listed Grade II*. 16th century conversion/repair undertaken through services of Abbot Bere of Glastonbury Abbey. Remained as almshouses until 1938 when it became HQ of the Rural Community Council and Somerset Guild of Craftsmen. Building stood unused from the late 1980s and became derelict. Purchased, repaired and converted into social housing by the Somerset Building Preservation Trust in 1999. Occupied by tenants of Falcon Rural Housing.

Grant Recipient: Somerset Building Preservation Trust

Access Contact: Mr Justin Roxburgh, Chief Executive

T: 01823 667 343

E-mail: justin@falconhousing.co.uk

Open: By arrangement only with Falcon Rural Housing.

🅿 Limited parking.

♿ Wheelchair access to ground floor. Guide dogs allowed, but with arrangement. WC for the disabled. No Guide Dogs.

£ No.

TEMPLE OF HARMONY

Halswell Park, Goathurst, Bridgwater TA5 2DH

18th century folly, a copy of the Temple of Verilis, forms part of the 18th century Pleasure Gardens at Halswell House. Restored in 1994.

www.somersite.co.uk/temple.htm

Grant Recipient: Somerset Buildings Preservation Trust

Access Contact: Mr Richard Mathews

T: 01278 786012   **F:** 01278 786012

E-mail: richard.p.mathews@totalise.co.uk

Open: June - Sept: Sat & Sun 2 - 5pm, Easter Weekend & May Day BH. Other times by arrangement with Mrs J Hirst, Honorary Treasurer, The Halswell Park Trust, 27 Durliegh Road, Bridgwater, Somerset TA6 7HX (tel: 01278 429342).

🅿 Spaces: 4.

♿ No wheelchair access or WC for the disabled. Guide Dogs allowed.

£ Adult: £1. Child: 50p. Senior: 50p.

SOUTH YORKSHIRE

HICKLETON HALL

Hickleton, South Yorkshire DN5 7BB

Georgian Mansion, Grade II* listed, built in the 1740s to a design by James Paine with later additions. The interior is noted for its plasterwork ceilings. Set in 15 acres of formal gardens laid out in the early 1900s, the Hall is now a residential care home.

Grant Recipient: Sue Ryder Care

Access Contact: Mr K Paynter

T: 01709 892070   **F:** 01709 890140

Open: By arrangement with Mr Paynter at Sue Ryder Care, Mon - Fri, 2 - 4pm.

🅿 Parking available.

♿ Wheelchair access to Hall only; no access to gardens. WC for the disabled. Guide Dogs allowed.

£ No.

MOATED SITE & CHAPEL

Thorpe Lane, Thorpe-in-Balne, nr. Doncaster DN6 0DY

Medieval chapel, moated site and fishponds. Built 12th century with 13th, 14th, 15th and 19th century alterations. Restored and re-roofed in 1994/5. In 1452 the chapel was the scene of the forcible abduction of Joan, wife of Charles Nowel, by Edward Lancaster of Skipton in Craven, which resulted in the passing of an Act of Parliament for the redress of grievance and the better protection of females.

Grant Recipient: Mr Attey

Access Contact: Mrs Attey

T: 01302 883160   **F:** 01302 883160

Open: By arrangement with Mrs Attey, the Manor House, Thorpe Lane, Thorpe-in-Balne, Doncaster, South Yorks DN6 0DY.

🅿 Spaces: 10.

♿ Partial access through the double doors at the front of the chapel facing Thorpe Lane – shallow wide step. No WC for the disabled. Guide Dogs allowed.

£ Donations for charity welcomed. St Mary's Church, Kirk Bramwith, near Doncaster.

THE LYCEUM THEATRE

Tudor Square, Sheffield, South Yorkshire S1 1DA

Grade II* listed theatre built 1897. The only surviving example of the work of WGR Sprague outside London. Special features include a domed corner tower, a lavish Rococo auditorium (1097 seats) and a proscenium arch with a rare open-work valance in gilded plasterwork. A notable example of a theatre of the period, with a largely unaltered interior.

www.sheffieldtheatres.co.uk

Grant Recipient: The Lyceum Theatre Trust

Access Contact: The Box Office

T: 0114 249 5999   **F:** 0114 249 6003

E-mail: info@sheffieldtheatres.co.uk

Open: Performances throughout the year. 21 scheduled backstage tours per year. Tours start at 10.30am. Group guided tours by arrangement. Contact the Box Office (tel: 0114 249 6000) or check the website for further information.

🅿 Spaces: 600. NCP adjacent to the theatre.

♿ Wheelchair access to all areas except two private entertaining rooms. WC for the disabled. Guide Dogs allowed.

£ Adult £3 (backstage tour). Other: Admission charge for performances.

STAFFORDSHIRE

10 THE CLOSE

Lichfield, Staffordshire WS13 7LD

Early 15th century timber-framed house, originally one-up one-down and part of a five-dwelling range in the Vicar's Close. Notable doors and solid tread staircase remains in attic.

Grant Recipient: Dean & Chapter of Lichfield Cathedral

Access Contact: Reverend Tony Whatmough

T: 01543 250 829

E-mail: tony@whatmough.org.uk

Open: By written arrangement.

🅿 Public car parks nearby.

♿ No wheelchair access or WC for the disabled. Guide Dogs allowed.

£ No.

BARLASTON HALL

Barlaston, nr. Stoke-on-Trent, Staffordshire ST12 9AT

Mid-18th century Palladian villa attributed to Sir Robert Taylor, with public rooms containing some fine examples of 18th century plasterwork. Extensively restored during the 1990s.

Grant Recipient: Mr James Hall

Access Contact: Mr James Hall

F: 01782 372391   **E-mail:** wadey54@mac.com

Open: 7 Mar - 12 Sept: Tues 2 - 5pm. No groups.

🅿 Spaces: 3.

♿ No wheelchair access.

£ Adult: £2.50. Child: £1.50. HHA members Free.

BIDDULPH GRANGE GARDEN

Biddulph, Staffordshire ST8 7SD

Garden with series of connected compartments designed to display specimens from James Bateman's extensive and wide ranging plant collection. Visitors are taken on a miniature tour of the world featuring the Egyptian court, China, a Scottish glen, as well as a pinetum and rock areas.

www.nationaltrust.org.uk

Grant Recipient: The National Trust

Access Contact: Property Manager

T: 01782 517999   **F:** 01782 510624

E-mail: biddulphgrange@nationaltrust.org.uk

Open: 25 Mar - 29 Oct: Wed - Fri 12 noon - 6pm & Sat & Sun 11am - 6pm (High Season). 4 Nov - 17 Dec: Sat & Sun 11am - 3pm (Low Season).

🅿 Spaces: 100.

♿ Wheelchair access to Lime Avenue, Lake, Pinetum, Cheshire Cottage, Egypt & East Terrace. Steps and undulating terrain in the garden. WC for the disabled. Guide Dogs allowed.

£ Adult: £5.30 (High Season), £2 (Low Season). Child: £2.60 (High Season), £1 (Low Season). Family: £13 (High Season), £5 (Low Season).

CHEDDLETON FLINT MILL

Cheddleton, Leek, Stoke-on-Trent, Staffs ST13 7HL

18th century complex for grinding flint comprising two working watermills. South Mill modified in 19th century and now contains displays relating to the pottery industry.

www.ex.ac.uk/~akoutram/cheddleton-mill

Grant Recipient: Cheddleton Flint Mill Industrial Heritage Trust

Access Contact: Mr E E Royle, MBE

T: 01782 502907

Open: Apr - Sept (incl. BHs), Sat - Sun 1pm - 5pm. Weekdays by arrangement.

🅿 Spaces: 18.

♿ Wheelchair access to ground floor only. No WC for the disabled. No Guide Dogs.

£ No.

CHILLINGTON HALL

Codsall Wood, nr. Wolverhampton, Staffs WV8 1RE

House by Sir John Soane with earlier wing by Francis Smith (1724). Home of the Giffard family for over 800 years. Extensive grounds with gardens landscaped by Capabilty Brown.

www.chillingtonhall.co.uk

Grant Recipient: Mr J W Giffard

Access Contact: Mr J W Giffard

T: 01902 850236   **F:** 01902 850 768

E-mail: mrsplod@chillingtonhall.co.uk

Open: Hall: Easter, May & Aug BH Sun & Mon. July: Suns. Aug: Thurs, Fri & Sun 2 - 5pm. Groups at other times by arrangement. Grounds: Easter - 1 June: Suns only.

🅿 Unlimited parking.

♿ Full wheelchair access. No WC for the disabled. Guide Dogs allowed.

£ Adult: £4 (£2 grounds only). Child: £2. HHA free.

CLAYMILLS PUMPING ENGINES

The Victorian Pumping Station, The Sewage Works, Meadow Lane, Stretton, Burton-on-Trent DE13 0DA

Large Victorian steam-operated sewage pumping station built in 1885. Four beam engines housed in two Italianate engine houses, two operational on steaming weekends. Boiler house with range of five Lancashire boilers, large Victorian steam-operated workshop with blacksmith's forge, steam hammer, and steam driven machinery. 1930s dynamo house with very early D.C. generating equipment, earliest dynamo 1889 (all operational). The site houses the largest number of steam engines in Britain still working in their original state (19).

www.claymills.org.uk

Grant Recipient: Severn Trent Water Ltd
Access Contact: Mr Roy Barratt
T: 01283 534960   F: 07092 275534
E-mail: webmaster@claymills.org.uk

Open: [illegible] - 5pm: Easter 16 & 17 Apr, Early May BH, 30 Apr & 1 May, End of May BH 28 & 29 May, 27 & 28 Aug, 16 & 17 Sept, 21 & 22 Oct, 30 & 31 Dec. Admission charged for steaming weekends, donations requested on other open days. Refreshments available. Heritage Open Days.

P Spaces: 100. Parking for the disabled adjacent to site. Parking for 1 coach.

Wheelchair access to ground floor only (boiler house, workshop, refreshment area, engine house). Interactive video link to Engine House. WC for the disabled. Guide Dogs allowed.

£ Adult: £4. Child: £2. Senior: £3. Family £10.

CLIFTON HALL

Clifton Campville, Staffordshire B79 0BE

Small country house built in 1705, perhaps by Francis Smith of Warwick for Sir Charles Pye. Two monumental wings flanking a courtyard, the intention being to link them with a central main building which was never constructed. This strange history explains why the Hall unusually developed out of what would have been the servants wing.

Grant Recipient: Mr Richard Blunt
Access Contact: Mr Richard Blunt
T: 01827 373681   F: 01827 373681
E-mail: richard@stauntonharoldhall.co.uk
Open: By arrangement only, any weekday 9am - 5pm all year.

P Spaces: 10.

Full wheelchair access. No WC for the disabled. Guide Dogs allowed.

£ Adult: £4.50. Child: £2. Other: £2.

HAMSTALL RIDWARE MANOR

Hamstall Ridware, Staffordshire WS15 3RS

Small scheduled ancient monument known as 'The Porch', with stone balcony, now restored and two stone fireplaces. Restored oak doors and windows. Some carvings on the stone balcony. Interior is made up of two rooms.

Grant Recipient: Mr and Mrs Shore
Access Contact: Mr and Mrs Shore
T: 0121 382 6540 office hrs only
Open: By arrangement with Mr and Mrs Shaw.

P No.

Partial wheelchair access. No WC for the disabled. Guide Dogs allowed.

£ No.

SHUGBOROUGH

Milford, Stafford, Staffordshire ST17 0XB

The present house was begun c1695. Between 1760 and 1770 it was enlarged and again partly remodelled by Samuel Wyatt at end of 18th century. The interior is particularly notable for its plaster work and other decorations. Ancestral home of the Earls of Lichfield. Houses the Staffordshire County Museum, Georgian working farm and Rare Livestock Breed project.

www.shugborough.org.uk

Grant Recipient: The National Trust
Access Contact: Property Manager
T: 01889 881388   F: 01889 881323
E-mail: shugborough.promotions@staffordshire.gov.uk
Open: House, servants' quarters, farm & gardens: 17 Mar - 27 Oct, daily 11am - 5pm (last adm. 4.30pm). Tours for booked groups daily, 10.30am. Evening tours also available.

P Spaces: 60.

Wheelchair access to ground floor of house and museum only. WC for the disabled. Guide Dogs allowed.

£ Adult: £10 (House & servants' quarters, farm & garden).

Child: £6 (House & servants' quarters, farm & garden). Other: £25 (family- all sites). NT members: free to house only, £6 all inclusive ticket.

SINAI HOUSE

Shobnall Road, Burton on Trent, Staffs DE14 2BB

Timber-framed E-shaped house, two-thirds derelict, on moated hill-top site, dating from the 13th century. House built variously during 15th, 16th and 17th centuries with later additions, including wall paintings and carpenters marks. 18th century bridge and plunge pool in the grounds.

Grant Recipient: Ms C A Newton
Access Contact: Ms C A Newton
T: 01283 544161/01283 840732
E-mail: knewton@brookesvernons.co.uk
Open: By arrangement only Min one week's notice required.

P Spaces: 10.

Temporary ramps to internal steps and no wheelchair WC for the disabled. Guide Dogs allowed.

£ Donations requested.

ST MARY'S (LICHFIELD HERITAGE CENTRE)

Market Square, Lichfield, Staffordshire WS13 6LG

Grade II* medieval guild church, rebuilt 1868-70 by James Fowler. Many original features are preserved and the building is a prominent landmark in the city. Now houses a Community Centre comprising a Heritage Centre, Social Centre for senior citizens, coffee and gift shops, as well as continuing to function as the parish church.

www.lichfieldheritage.org.uk

Grant Recipient: The Guild of St Mary's Centre
Access Contact: Mrs Bazeley
T: 01543 256611   F: 01543 414749
E-mail: info@lichfieldheritage.org.uk
Open: Lichfield Heritage Centre: open daily 10.30am - 5pm (last adm. 4pm), Suns 10.30am - 5pm (last adm. 4pm). Closed Christmas Day, Boxing Day and New Year's Day.

P Pay and display parking nearby.

Full wheelchair access. WC for the disabled. Guide Dogs allowed.

£ Adult: £3.50. Child: £1 (age 5-14, under 5s free). Conc: £2.50. Family: £8.

SUFFOLK

ABBEY FARM BARN

Snape, Saxmundham, Suffolk IP17 1RQ

Grade II* listed Aisled barn. Circa 1300. Built by resident monks living in adjacent Priory (no remains standing above ground). Refurbished and still used by farmer for storage.

Grant Recipient: Mr & Mrs Raynor
Access Contact: Mr and Mrs Raynor
T: 01728 688088   F: 01728 688989
E-mail: thecartshed@onetel.net.uk
Open: By arrangement.

P Spaces: 10.

Full wheelchair access. No WC for the disabled. Guide Dogs allowed.

£ No.

CHRISTCHURCH MANSION

Christchurch Park, Soane Street, Ipswich, Suffolk IP4 2BE

16th century red brick mansion with some blue brick diapering, set in fine parkland in the centre of town. The Mansion and its collections trace the lives of the three wealthy families who made it their home. Paintings, English domestic furniture, kitchen and servants' area.

www.ipswich.gov.uk/tourism/guide/mansion.htm

Grant Recipient: Ipswich Borough Council
Access Contact: Mr Phil Lown
T: 01473 433 574   F: 01473 433558
E-mail: museums.service@ipswich.gov.uk
Open: Nov - Mar: Tues - Sat 10am - 4pm, Sun 2.30pm - 4pm. Apr - Oct: Tues - Sat 10am - 4pm, Sun 12 - 4.30pm. For further information please contact Phil Lown, or the Mansion (tel: 01473 433554, fax: 01473 433564)

P Spaces: 1200. Public parking within 400 metres. Parking for the disabled adjacent to the Mansion.

Wheelchair access to most of ground floor and Wolsey Art Gallery. WC for the disabled. Guide Dogs allowed.

£ No.

CULFORD SCHOOL IRON BRIDGE

Culford, Bury St Edmunds, Suffolk IP28 6TX

Constructed for the second Marquis Cornwallis in the late 1790s by Samuel Wyatt, brother of James, to a design

patented by Wyatt. The bridge, in Culford Park, is one of the earliest surviving bridges with an unmodified cast-iron structure, being the earliest known example with hollow ribs.

Grant Recipient: Methodist Colleges and Schools
Access Contact: Michael Woolley
T: 01284 729318   F: 01284 729077
E-mail: bursar@culford.co.uk
Open: Access to the iron bridge and Culford Park is available at any time throughout the year.

P Spaces: 100.

Access for the disabled may be difficult as over grass and rough track. WC only available when Culford School is open and ramps in place. Guide Dogs allowed.

£ No.

FLATFORD MILL

Willy Lott's House and Flatford Bridge Cottage, Flatford, East Bergholt, Colchester, Suffolk CO7 6UL

Flatford watermill, 1733 datestone, incorporating possibly earlier but altered former granary range to rear and further 19th century range adjoining granary. The mill was in the possession of the Constable family from the mid 18th century. Willy Lott's farmhouse, late 16th century - 17th century. Grade 1 listing of both buildings reflects their significance in the life and work of John Constable. Both buildings are leased by the National Trust to the Field Studies Council. Flatford Bridge Cottage 16th century thatched cottage, upstream from Flatford Mill houses an exhibition on John Constable.

www.nationaltrust.org.uk

Grant Recipient: The National Trust
Access Contact: Property Manager
T: 01206 298260   F: 01206 299193
E-mail: flatfordbridgecottage@nationaltrust.org.uk
Open: Flatford Mill and Willy Lott's House are owned by the National Trust and leased to the Field Studies Council which runs arts-based courses for all age groups (for information on courses tel: 01206 298283). There is no general public access to these buildings, but the Field Studies Council will arrange tours for groups. Flatford Bridge Cottage is open Mar & Apr daily except Mon & Tues 11am - 5pm; May to end Sept daily 10.30am - 5.30pm; Oct daily 11am - 4pm; 1 Nov - 17 Dec daily except Mon & Tues 11am - 3.30pm. Closed Christmas and New Year. 6 Jan 2007 - 25 Feb Sat and Sun 11am - 3.30pm. For further information contact the Property Manager on 01206 298260.

P Spaces: 2000. Private pay car park 200 metres from Flatford Bridge Cottage. Parking near the Cottage for disabled visitors.

Wheelchair access to tea-garden and shop. Lavatory for the disabled available in car park owned by Babergh DC, 23 metres from the Cottage. Guide Dogs allowed.

£ £2.50 (adult). Guided walks (when available).

FRESTON TOWER

Freston, Babergh, Suffolk IP9 1AD

Elizabethan six-storey tower built in 1578 by Thomas Gooding, an Ipswich Merchant, to demonstrate his wealth and status and probably used as a look-out tower. Overlooks the estuary of the River Orwell.

www.landmarktrust.org.uk

Grant Recipient: The Landmark Trust
Access Contact: Mrs Victoria O'Keeffe
T: 01628 825920   F: 01628 825417
E-mail: vokeeffe@landmarktrust.org.uk
Open: The Landmark Trust is an independent charity, which rescues small buildings of historic or architectural importance from decay or unsympathetic improvement. Landmark's aim is to promote the enjoyment of these historic buildings by making them available to stay in for holidays. Freston Tower can be rented by anyone, at all times of the year, for periods ranging from a weekend to three weeks. Bookings can be made by telephoning the Booking Office on 01628 825925. The public can also view the building on eight Open Days throughout the year (dates to be set) or by arrangement; telephone the access contact Victoria O'Keeffe on 01628 825920 to make an appointment. Potential visitors will be asked to write to confirm the details of their visit. Heritage Open Days.

P Spaces: 2.

No wheelchair access or WC for the disabled. Guide Dogs allowed.

£ No.

HORSEMAN'S HOUSE

Boundary Farm, Framsden, Suffolk IP14 6LH

Mid 17th century brick stable. Gable ended with brick

pinnacles along upper edge with panels of diaper work in dark headers below round vents/owl holes. Original three bay, two storey structure housed horseman above his charges in unusually ornate accommodation for all.

Grant Recipient: Mr Bacon

Access Contact: Mr Bacon

T: 01728 860370   **F:** 01728 860370

E-mail: info@boundaryfarm.co.uk

Open: By arrangement with Mr Bacon.

P Spaces: 4.

Partial wheelchair access. WC for the disabled. Guide Dogs allowed.

£ No.

ICKWORTH HOUSE

Park & Garden, Horringer, Bury St Edmunds IP29 5QE

The Earl of Bristol created this eccentric house, with its central rotunda and curved corridors, in 1795 to display his collections. These include paintings by Titian, Gainsborough and Velazquez and a Georgian silver collection. The house is surrounded by an Italianate garden set in a 'Capability' Brown park with woodland walks, deer enclosure, vineyard, Georgian summerhouse, church, canal and lake.

www.nationaltrust.org.uk

Grant Recipient: The National Trust

Access Contact: Property Manager

T: 01284 735270   **F:** 01284 735175

E-mail: ickworth@nationaltrust.org.uk

Open: House: 20 Mar - 1 Oct: daily except Wed and Thurs 1 - 5pm (last adm. 4.30pm). 2 Oct - 5 Nov, 1 - 4.30pm. Garden: 20 Mar - 1 Oct, daily except Wed & Thurs 10am - 5pm (last adm. 4.30pm). 2 Oct - 18 Mar, 2007: daily except Wed and Thurs 11am - 4pm. Park open daily 8am - 8pm. Closed Christmas Day.

P Spaces: 2000.

Wheelchair access to House: ramped access (restricted access in House for large powered vehicles/chairs); lift to first floor; stairlift to basement (shop & restaurant) suitable for wheelchair users able to transfer; wheelchair on each floor. Garden largely accessible, some changes of level, gravel drive and paths. West Wing: all floors accessible. Separate parking in visitor car park (200 yds). WC for the disabled. Guide Dogs allowed.

£ Adult: £7, £3.40 (park & garden only). Child: £3.90 (park & garden only). Family: £17 (house, park & garden), £7.60 (park & garden).

MORETON HALL

Mount Road, Bury St Edmunds, Suffolk IP32 7BJ

White brick residence designed by Robert Adam in 1773 for Dr.Symonds, noted Cambridge professor and author. The design was inspired by the ruins of Emporor Diocletian's palace and many of the original Adam features remain on the ground and first floors. It is now the home of Moreton Hall Preparatory School.

www.moretonhall.net

Grant Recipient: Moreton Hall School Trust Ltc

Access Contact: Ms Doreen Young

T: 01284 753 532   **F:** 01284 769 197

E-mail: office@moretonhall.net

Open: By arrangement at any reasonable time, plus the Sat of Heritage Open Days weekend. Heritage Open Days.

P Spaces: 20. Free parking.

Wheelchair access to ground floor only. WC for the disabled. Guide Dogs allowed.

£ No.

RUINED CHURCH TOWER

Fornham St Genevieve, St Edmundsbury, Suffolk

Only the tower remains of the 15th century church. Church destroyed by fire in 1782.

Grant Recipient: Rossfleet Investments Ltd

Access Contact: Mr Steve Stuteley

T: 01953 717176   **F:** 01953 717173

Open: By arrangement with Steve Stuteley (Rossfleet Investments, Manor Farm, Bridgham, Norfolk). Heritage Open Days.

P No.

No wheelchair access or WC for the disabled. Guide Dogs allowed.

£ No.

SOMERLEYTON HALL & GARDENS

Somerleyton, Lowestoft, Suffolk NR32 5QQ

Early Victorian stately home, built in Anglo-Italian style for Sir Morton Peto by John Thomas upon former Jacobean mansion. Contains fine furnishings, paintings, ornate carved stonework and wood carving, and state rooms. Set in twelve acres of historic gardens including a yew hedge maze.

www.somerleyton.co.uk

Grant Recipient: The Rt Hon Lord Somerleyton GCVO

Access Contact: Mr Edward Knowles

T: 01502 730224   **F:** 01502 732143

E-mail: enquiries@somerleyton.co.uk

Open: 2 Apr - 29 Oct: Thurs, Sun & BH, plus Tues & Wed in July & Aug 10am - 5pm. Charges under review at time of publication, please check with the Hall for current information.

P Spaces: 200.

Full wheelchair access. WC for the disabled. Guide Dogs allowed.

£ Adult: £4.50 (Gardens only), £3 (Hall tour). Child: £2.50 (Gardens only), £1 (Hall tour). Senior: £3.50 (Gardens only) £3 (Hall tour).

ST LAWRENCE

Dial Lane, Ipswich, Suffolk IP1 1DL

15th century aisleless church with a 97 foot west tower, enlarged in the 19th century and recently restored. Declared redundant in 1975. Owned by Ipswich Borough Council.

Grant Recipient: Ipswich Historic Churches Trust

Access Contact: Mr J S Hall

T: 01473 232300/406270   **F:** 01473 406385

E-mail: james-hall@birketts.co.uk

Open: By arrangement with Mr Hall (tel: 01473 406270), office hours and weekdays only. At least 24 hours notice required. At other times and days subject to longer notice.

P Public parking in town centre car parks (10 minute walk).

No wheelchair access.   £ No.

ST PETER

College Street, Ipswich, Suffolk IP4 1DD

Large medieval church near the docks, owned by Ipswich Borough Council and redundant since the 1970s. Noted for a Tournai font and adjacent to Thomas Wolsey's gateway. Empty and unused.

Grant Recipient: Ipswich Historic Churches Trust

Access Contact: Mr J S Hall

T: 01473 232300/406270   **F:** 01473 406385

E-mail: james-hall@birketts.co.uk

Open: May - Sept: most Thurs 1.30 - 3.30pm (advisable to check in advance). Otherwise by arrangement with Mr Hall (tel: 01473 406270), office hours and weekdays only. 24 hours notice required. At other times and days subject to longer notice. Heritage Open Days.

P Car parks in town centre (½ mile).

Wheelchair access to all of church apart from the vestry and parts of the chancel. No WC for the disabled. Guide Dogs allowed.

£ No.

WALTON OLD HALL

Felixstowe, Suffolk

Remains of 13th century Manor House built by the Bigod family c-1292.

Grant Recipient: Suffolk Coastal District Council

Access Contact: Mrs Chris Robinson

T: 01394 444 518   **F:** 01394 385 100

E-mail: chris.robinson@suffolkcoastal.gov.uk

Open: Mon - Fri, 8am - 4pm, other times by arrangement.

P On street parking.

Wheelchair access to all areas but grass surfaces may limit access in poor weather conditions. No WC for the disabled. Guide Dogs allowed.

£ No.

SURREY

CAREW MANOR DOVECOTE

Beddington Park, Church Road, Beddington, Wallington, Surrey SM6 7NH

Early 18th century large octagonal brick dovecote with c1200 interior nesting boxes and original potence (circular ladder).

www.sutton.gov.uk

Grant Recipient: London Borough of Sutton

Access Contact: Ms Valary Murphy

T: 020 8770 4781   **F:** 020 8770 4777

E-mail: valary.murphy@sutton.gov.uk

Open: 26 Mar, 7 May, 2 July & 24 Sept 2 - 5pm. Guided tours of Carew Manor at 2pm & 3.30pm. Groups at other times by arrangement with Valary Murphy, The Heritage Service, Central Library, St Nicholas Way, Sutton, Surrey SM1 1EA (tel: 020 8770 4781). Heritage Open Days.

P Spaces: 30.

No wheelchair access or WC for the disabled. Guide Dogs allowed.

£ Adult: £3.50. Child: £2. Admission charges for guided tours of dovecote and Carew Manor, otherwise dovecote is free.

CLANDON PARK

West Clandon, Guildford, Surrey GU4 7RQ

Palladian mansion, built c1730 by Venetian architect Giacomo Leoni with a two-storeyed Marble Hall, collection of 18th century furniture, porcelain, textiles, carpets, the Ivo Forde Meissen collection of Italian comedy figures and a series of Mortlake tapestries. Grounds contain grotto, sunken Dutch garden, Maori Meeting House and Museum of the Queen's Royal Surrey Regiment.

www.nationaltrust.org.uk

Grant Recipient: The National Trust

Access Contact: Property Manager

T: 01483 222482   **F:** 01483 223479

E-mail: clandonpark@nationaltrust.org.uk

Open: House: 26 Mar - 29 Oct, daily except Mon, Fri &Sat (but open Good Fri, Easter Sat & BH Mons) 11am - 5pm (Last adm. 4.30pm). Museum: as house 12 noon - 5pm. Garden: as house 11am - 5pm.

P Spaces: 200.

Lift provides access to all areas of the house open to the public, some restrictions apply; please telephone for details. Grounds partially accessible, with some slopes and uneven terrain. WC for the disabled. Guide Dogs allowed.

£ Adult: £6.50, Child: £3.20. Other: £16.00 (family), £5 (group, Tues, Weds, Thurs & after 2pm Suns).

GREAT FOSTERS

Stroude Road, Egham, Surrey TW20 9UR

Grade II* registered garden. Laid out in 1918 by WH Romaine-Walker in partnership with GH Jenkins, incorporating earlier features. The site covers 50 acres and is associated with a late 16th century country house, converted to an hotel in 1927. The main formal garden is surrounded on three sides by a moat thought to be of medieval origin and is modelled on the pattern of a Persian carpet. Garden also includes a sunken rose garden, avenue of lime trees and a lake.

www.greatfosters.co.uk

Grant Recipient: Mr Richard Young

Access Contact: Mr Richard Young

T: 01784 433822   **F:** 01784 472455

E-mail: enquiries@greatfosters.co.uk

Open: At any time throughout the year.

P Spaces: 200.

Wheelchair access to ground floor of the house and most of the gardens. WC for the disabled. Guide Dogs allowed.

£ No.

GREAT HALL

Virginia Park, Christchurch Road, Virginia Water, Surrey GU25 4BH

By W H Crossland for Thomas Holloway and opened 1884. Built of red brick with Portland stone dressings and slate roofs in Franco-Flemish Gothic style. Formerly part of the Royal Holloway Sanatorium.

Grant Recipient: Virginia Park Management Co Ltd

Access Contact: Ms Liz Adams

T: 01344 845276   **F:** 01344 842428

E-mail: virginia.park@btinternet.com

Open: Entrance Hall, Staircase and Great Hall of former Sanatorium: Feb 15 & 25, Mar 22 & 26, Apr 12, 19 & 23, May 10, 24 & 28, June 14, 21 & 25, July 12, 19 & 23, Aug 9, 16 & 20, Sept 13, 21 & 24, Oct 11, 18 & 22, Nov 8, 22 & 26 10am - 4pm. Other times by tel arrangement with the Estate Office.

P Public car park nearby at Virginia Water Station.

Wheelchair access with assistance (steps into building to be negotiated). Downstairs entrance Hall but not the Great Hall (no lift). WC for the disabled. Guide Dogs allowed.

£ Adult £3.

PAINSHILL PARK

Portsmouth Road, Cobham, Surrey KT11 1JE

Restored Grade 1 Registered 18th century landscape garden of 150 acres, created by Charles Hamilton between 1738 and 1773. Contains a Gothic temple, Chinese bridge, ruined abbey, Turkish tent, grotto and 14 acre serpentine lake fed by

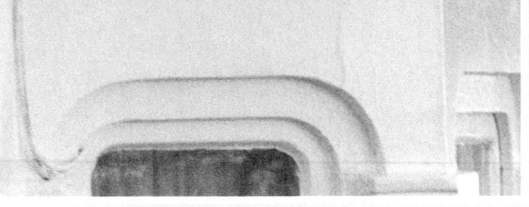

a large waterwheel. Europa Nostra medal winner for 'Exemplary Restoration'.
www.painshill.co.uk
Grant Recipient: Painshill Park Trust Ltd
Access Contact: Miss Sarah AM Hallett
T: 01932 868113   **F:** 01932 868001
E-mail: info@painshill.co.uk
Open: From 1 Mar daily: 10.30am - 6pm (last adm. 4.30pm) or dusk if earlier. Closed Christmas Day & Boxing Day. Guided tours by arrangement. Heritage Open Days.
P Spaces: 400. Parking for 8 coaches.
Wheelchair access to most of the site, apart from the Grotto and Alpine Valley. Wheelchairs and electric buggies available on request. Pre-book one week in advance. WC for the disabled. Guide Dogs allowed.
£ Adult: £6. Child: £3.50 (under 5s free). Other: £5.25; £18 (family - 2 adults and 2 children).

THE OLD MILL
Outwood Common, nr. Redhill, Surrey RH1 5PW
England's oldest working windmill, built in 1665.
www.outwoodwindmill.co.uk
Grant Recipient: Mrs Sheila Thomas
Access Contact: Mrs Sheila Thomas
T: 01342 843458   **F:** 01342 843458
E-mail: info@outwoodwindmill.co.uk
Open: Easter - Oct: Sun & BHs 2 - 6pm, plus groups by arrangement. Heritage Open Days.
P Spaces: 12.
Wheelchair access to ground floor of the mill only. WC for the disabled. Guide Dogs allowed.
£ Adult: £2. Child: £1.

SUSSEX

DE LA WARR PAVILION
The Marina, Bexhill-on-Sea, East Sussex TN40 1DP
Built in 1935 by architects Erich Mendholson and Serge Chermayeff was the first welded steel-framed building in this country. Its circular staircase and sweeping sea views make it unique as an iconic building of the Modernist movement.
www.dlwp.com
Grant Recipient: De La Warr Pavilion Trust
Access Contact: Ms Emma Morris
T: 01424 787900   **F:** 01424 787940
E-mail: info@dlwp.com
Open: Daily, 10am - 5pm. Closed Christmas Day. Heritage Open Days.
P Spaces: 100. Pay car park.
Full wheelchair access. WC for the disabled. Guide Dogs allowed.
£ No.

GLYNDE PLACE
Glynde, nr. Lewes, East Sussex BN8 6SX
Elizabethan manor house built in 1589 from local flint and stone from Normandy, then extensively added on to in the 18th century. Contains a collection of Old Masters, family portraits, furniture, embroidery and silver belonging to the family who have lived there for over 400 years.
Grant Recipient: Viscount Hampden
Access Contact: Viscount Hampden
T: 01273 858224   **F:** 01273 858224
E-mail: info@glyndeplace.co.uk
Open: May: Suns & BHs. June - Aug: Suns, Weds & BHss 2 - 5pm (last adm. 4.45pm). House open at other times by arrangement. Special prices for booked groups. Refreshments available.
P Spaces: 150.
Wheelchair access to tearoom and gardens. WC for the disabled. Guide Dogs allowed.
£ Adult: £5.50. Child: £2.75. Groups (25+): £4 on open days, £7.50 at other times.

LAMB HOUSE
(COROMANDEL LACQUER PANELS)
3 Chapel Hill, Lewes, East Sussex, BN7 2BB
The incised lacquer panels in the study of Lamb House are a unique surviving example of imported late 17th century Chinese lacquer work that remains as decorative wall panelling. Recently restored.
Grant Recipient: Professor Paul Benjamin
Access Contact: Professor Paul Benjamin

T: 01273 475657   **E-mail:** p.r.benjamin@sussex.ac.uk
Open: Weekends only by telephone or e-mail arrangement. Heritage Open Days.
P On-street parking.
Steps to front door. Wheelchair access to ground floor only. No WC for the disabled. No Guide Dogs.
£ No.

ROTUNDA TEMPLE
Brightling Park, Rother, East Sussex
Built c1812 as an eyecatcher by Sir Robert Smirke for John Fuller, wealthy philanthropist and eccentric. Small circular building with colonnade and dome: the centre-piece of Brightling Park.
Grant Recipient: Mr H C Grissell
Access Contact: Mr H C Grissell
T: 01424 838307   **F:** 01424 838467
E-mail: hchfarisscll@hotmail.co.uk
Open: By arrangement only. Temple can be viewed from public footpaths and other permitted access routes through Park.
P Parking in surrounding roads.
No wheelchair access or WC for the disabled. Guide Dogs allowed.
£ No.

ST MARY-IN-THE-CASTLE
Pelham Crescent, Hastings, East Sussex TN34 3AF
Built in 1828, architect Joseph Kay, forming an integral part of the design of Pelham Crescent. The Church has a horseshoe-shaped auditorium with gallery and is now used as an arts centre.
www.hastings.gov.uk
Grant Recipient: Friends of St Mary in the Castle
Access Contact: Ms Penny Precious
T: 01424 781154/01424 781122   **F:** 01424 781133
E-mail: pprecious@hastings.gov.uk
Open: Guided tours Tues - Sat by arrangement. Arts activities run throughout the year. Contact the Bookings Office (01424 781072 or 781154), the access contacts or check the website for further information. Heritage Open Days.
P Spaces: 400. Pay & Display parking opposite.
Full wheelchair access. WC for the disabled. Guide Dogs allowed.
£ Tours free but donations accepted. Events priced individually.

THE DOVECOTE
Alciston, East Sussex BN8 6NS
14th century dovecote of flint facings with green sand stone dressings on a chalk rubble core with chalk blocks and nesting boxes internally.
www.firleplace.co.uk
Grant Recipient: Trustees of the Firle Estate Settlement
Access Contact: Mr Jamie Evans-Freke
T: 01273 858567   **F:** 01273 858570
E-mail: jamie@firleplace.co.uk
Open: Access to the dovecote is by arrangement with the Estate Office.
P No.
Wheelchair access to the exterior. No WC for the disabled. Guide Dogs allowed.
£ No.

THE FLUSHING INN
4 Market Street, Rye, East Sussex TN31 7LA
15th century timber-framed building, now a restaurant, with large recently restored 16th century wallpainting.
www.theflushinginn.com
Grant Recipient: Mr Flynn
Access Contact: Mr Flynn
T: 01797 223292   **F:** 01797 229748
E-mail: j.e.flynn@talk21.com
Open: Restaurant open Wed - Sun for lunches & dinners, Mons lunch only & Tues closed. Closed first two weeks in Jan & June. Unless dining, visiting to view the Fresco is restricted to 10.30am - 12 noon.
P On-street parking, restricted to 1 hour, or public parking elsewhere in Rye.
Wheelchair access to Fresco with assistance (entrance steps to be negotiated). No WC for the disabled. Guide Dogs allowed.
£ No.

THE ROYAL PAVILION
Brighton, East Sussex BN1 1EE
Former seaside residence of George IV in Indian style with Chinese-inspired interiors. Originally a neo-classical villa by Henry Holland was built on the site in 1787, but this was subsequently replaced by the current John Nash building constructed between 1815-23.
www.royalpavilion.org.uk
Grant Recipient: Brighton & Hove City Council
Access Contact: Ms Cara Bowen
T: 01273 292810   **F:** 01273 292871
E-mail: cara.bowen@brighton-hove.gov.uk
Open: Apr - Sept: daily 9.30am - 5.45pm (Last adm. 5pm). Oct - Mar, daily 10am - 5.15pm (Last adm. 4.30pm). Closed 25/26 Dec. Charges are valid until 31 Mar 2006. Please check the English Heritage website or with the Royal Pavilion for current information.
P NCP car park on Church St. Parking for disabled available in the grounds of the Pavilion by arrangement.
Wheelchair access to ground floor only, reduced rate of admission is payable. WC for the disabled. Guide Dogs allowed.
£ Adult: £6.10, £2.35 (local residents, Oct - Feb only). Child: £3.60 under 16 (Oct - Feb, local residents free with paying adult). Conc: £4.30. Family: (2+4) £15.80, (1+4) £9.70. Prices valid until 31.3.06.

TITHE BARN
Court Farm, East Street, Brighton, West Sussex BN1 9PB
Grade II* listed medieval tithe barn. Mainly of timber construction with thatched roof.
Grant Recipient: Brighton and Hove County Council
Access Contact: Mr Richard Butler
T: 01273 291440   **F:** 01273 291467
E-mail: richard.butler@brighton-hove.gov.uk
Open: By arrangement with Richard Butler, Brighton and Hove County Council (or Thamar Stanley at Smiths Gore 01798 345983) and Eric Huxham - tenant at Court Farm (07802 453842).
P On-street parking within Falmer village.
Barn within working farm so access can be muddy. Guide dogs welcome but as a working farm care is requested. No WC for the disabled.
£ No.

WINDMILL HILL WINDMILL
Herstmonceux, Hailsham, East Sussex BN27 4RT
Grade II* listed, dating from 1815, the second tallest and largest post mill in body size. The mill last worked by wind in 1894 and has recently been authentically restored.
www.windmillhill.fsnet.co.uk
Grant Recipient: Windmill Hill Windmill Trust
Access Contact: Mrs B Frost
T: 01323 833033   **F:** 01323 833744
E-mail: admin@windmillhill.fsnet.co.uk
Open: Easter - Sept: Suns & BHs 2.30 - 5pm.
P Spaces: 4.
Wheelchair access to visitor centre. WC for the disabled. No Guide Dogs.
£ No.

TYNE & WEAR

FREEMASONS HALL
Queen Street East, Sunderland, Tyne & Wear SR1 2HT
Grade I listed oldest purpose-built Masonic meeting place in the world, c1785. Contains an ornate Lodge Room which remains virtually unaltered with elaborate thrones from 1735. Also has a cellar is in its original condition and the last remaining example of a Donaldson organ which was specially constructed for the building in 1785.
Grant Recipient: Queen Street Masonic Temple Ltd
Access Contact: Mr Colin Meddes
T: 0191 522 0115   **F:** 0191 522 0115
E-mail: colinmeddes@tiscali.co.uk
Open: Guided tours throughout the year by arrangement. Heritage Open Days Fri & Sat only 10am - 4pm.
P Spaces: 80.
Five external steps to main entrance: guides available to assist wheelchair users. Access ramp for the disabled due to be installed. WC for the disabled. Guide Dogs allowed.
£ No.

HIGH LEVEL BRIDGE
linking Newcastle & Gateshead, Tyne & Wear
Grade I listed railway and road bridge of ashlar and cast iron, 1849, designed by Robert Stephenson. One of the finest

pieces of architectural iron work in the world.

Grant Recipient: Network Rail

Access Contact: Mr Richard Bell

T: 01904389 876   F: 01904 389 819

E-mail: richard.bell@networkrail.co.uk

Open: Best viewed from adjacent riverbanks or via access road/footpath under bridge. Also may be viewed from the footways which cross the lower deck of the bridge. Access to the lower deck is normally available at all times, during 2006 access will be severely restricted to enable major refurbishment to take place. No access to the upper deck of the bridge.

ℙ On-street parking.

♿ Footways across lower deck of the bridge accessible for wheelchairs. No WC for the disabled. Guide Dogs allowed.

£ No.

THEATRE ROYAL

100 Grey Street, Newcastle-upon-Tyne NE1 6BR

Victorian theatre opened in 1837, rebuilt in 1899 by Frank Matcham in a richly-ornamented style. Classical façade with rare Hanoverian coat of arms. Traditional 4-tier 1,294 seat auditorium hosting annual programme of touring productions and international companies.

www.theatreroyal.co.uk

Grant Recipient: Newcastle Theatre Royal Trust Ltd

Access Contact: Mr Grahame Norris

T: 0191 232 0997   F: 0191 261 1906

E-mail: grahame.norris@newcastle.gov.uk

Open: Regular tours available depending on production schedule, contact theatre on 0870 905 5060 or 0191 232 0997 for details. Regular public programme except Suns. Café and Foyer: Mon - Sat from 10am. Possible refurbishment closure July - Sept 2006.

ℙ Public car parks in City centre.

♿ Wheelchair access to foyer, cafe and stalls. WC for the disabled. Guide Dogs allowed.

£ Adult: £3.50 (Tours). Child: £3.50 (Tours).

WASHINGTON OLD HALL

The Avenue, Washington Village, District 4, Washington, Tyne & Wear NE38 7LE

17th century manor house, incorporating the 12th century remains of the home of George Washington's ancestors. Recreated 17th century interiors and displays of 'Washingtonabilia' celebrating the close connection with the USA. Permanent exhibition on the recent tenement period of the property. Jacobean knot-garden and Nuttery.

www.nationaltrust.org.uk

Grant Recipient: The National Trust

Access Contact: Property Manager

T: 0191 4166879   F: 0191 4192065

E-mail: washington.oldhall@nationaltrust.org.uk

Open: 2 Apr - 29 Oct: Sun - Wed and Good Fri 11am - 5pm. Garden: as house 10am - 5pm. Tearoom: as house 11am - 4pm.

ℙ Spaces: 10.

♿ Wheelchair access to ground floor of house and upper garden. WC for the disabled. Guide Dogs allowed.

£ Adult: £4. Child: £2.50. Family: £10.50, £3.50 (£2 child, groups 10+).

WARWICKSHIRE

RAGLEY HALL

Alcester, Warwickshire B49 5NJ

Family home of the Marquess and Marioness of Hertford. Built in 1680 to a design by Robert Hooke in the Palladian style, with portico added by Wyatt in 1780. Contents include baroque plasterwork by James Gibb, family portraits by Sir Joshua Reynolds and a mural by Graham Rust completed in 1983. Surrounding park designed by 'Capability' Brown.

www.ragleyhall.com

Grant Recipient: Marquess of Hertford & Earl of Yarmouth

Access Contact: Mr Bryan McDonald

T: 01789 762090   F: 01789 764791

E-mail: bryanmcdonald@ragleyhall.com

Open: 25 Mar - 1 Oct: Thurs - Sun (plus BH Mons) 12 noon - 5.30pm (last adm. 4.30pm). Closing times may vary subject to events and functions. Park & gardens are open daily in school holidays. Group (20+) rates available: £6, adults & seniors, £3.50 child & school group.

ℙ Spaces: 4000.

♿ Wheelchair access via lift to first floor. WC for the disabled. Guide Dogs allowed.

£ Adult: £7.50. Child: £4.50 (age 5-16). Senior/Orange/Blue: £6.50. Family £25. Season: £75 (family), £25 (single).

STONELEIGH ABBEY

Kenilworth, Warwickshire CV8 2LF

16th century house built on site and incorporating remains of Cistercian Abbey founded in 1155. West wing designed by Francis Smith of Warwick between 1714-26 and northern wing reconstructed in 19th century by Charles S Smith of Warwick. South wing c1820. West wing contains a range of State Apartments. Also has restored Regency riding stables, 19th century conservatory and Humphrey Repton landscaped riverside gardens.

www.stoneleighabbey.org

Grant Recipient: Stoneleigh Abbey Preservation Trust (1996) Ltd

Access Contact: Estate Office

T: 01926 858535   F: 01926 850274

E-mail: enquire@stoneleighabbey.org

Open: Good Fri - end Oct: Tues - Thurs &Sun, plus BHs. Opening arrangements may change, please check with the Preservation Trust for current information.

ℙ Spaces: 400.

♿ Full wheelchair access. WC for the disabled. Guide Dogs allowed.

£ Adult: £6. Child: £2.50. Senior: £4. Grounds only: £2.50.

THE BATH HOUSE

Walton, Stratford-upon-Avon, Warwickshire LE17 5RG

Designed in 1748 by the architect Sanderson Miller. The upper room, where the bathers recovered, is decorated with dripping icicles and festoons of sea shells - the work of Mrs Delaney, better known for her flower pictures. Narrow steep staircases.

www.landmarktrust.org.uk

Grant Recipient: The Landmark Trust

Access Contact: Mrs Victoria O'Keeffe

T: 01628 825920   F: 01628 825417

E-mail: vokeeffe@.landmarktrust.org.uk

Open: The Landmark Trust is an independent charity, which rescues small buildings of historic or architectural importance from decay or unsympathetic improvement. Landmark's aim is to promote the enjoyment of these historic buildings by making them available to stay in for holidays. The Bath House can be rented by anyone, at all times of the year, for periods ranging from a weekend to three weeks. Bookings can be made by telephoning the Booking Office on 01628 825925. As the building is in full-time use for holiday accommodation, it is not normally open to the public. However the public can view the building by arrangement by telephoning the access contact (Victoria O'Keeffe on 01628 825920) to make an appointment. Potential visitors will be asked to write to confirm the details of their visit.

ℙ Spaces: 1.

♿ No wheelchair access or WC for the disabled. Guide Dogs allowed.

£ No.

CHARLECOTE PARK

Wellesbourne, Warwick, Warwickshire CV35 9ER

Owned by the Lucy family since 1247, Sir Thomas built the house in 1558. Now much altered, it is shown as it would have been a century ago. The balustraded formal garden gives onto a deer park landscaped by 'Capability' Brown.

www.nationaltrust.org.uk

Grant Recipient: The National Trust

Access Contact: Property Manager

T: 01789 470277   F: 01789 470544

E-mail: charlecote.park@nationaltrust.org.uk

Open: House: 4 Mar - 30 Sept, daily except Wed & Thurs 12 noon - 5pm; 1 Oct - 29 Oct, daily except Wed & Thurs 12 noon - 4.30pm. Park & gardens: 4 Mar - 29 Oct, daily except Wed & Thurs 10.30am - 6pm; 4 Nov - 14 Dec, Sat and Sun 11am - 4pm.

ℙ Spaces: 200. Overflow car park available.

♿ Wheelchair access to ground floor of house, restaurant and shop. WC for the disabled. Guide Dogs allowed.

£ Adult: £6.90. Child: £3.50. Family: £17. Group £5.90.

LORD LEYCESTER HOSPITAL

High Street, Warwick, Warwickshire CV34 4BH

14th century chantry chapel, Great Hall, galleried courtyard

and Guildhall. Acquired by Robert Dudley, Earl of Leicester in 1571 as a home for his old soldiers. Still operating as a home for ex-servicemen.

Grant Recipient: Patron & Governors of Lord Leycester Hospital

Access Contact: Lieut. Colonel G F Lesinski

T: 01926 491422   F: 01926 491422

E-mail: lordleycester@btinternet.com

Open: Tues - Sun 10am - 4pm (winter), 10am - 5pm (summer), plus BH Mons. Closed Good Fri and Christmas Day.

ℙ Spaces: 15.

♿ Wheelchair access to ground floor only. WC for the disabled. Guide Dogs allowed.

£ Adult: £4.90, £2 (garden only). Child: £3.90, free (garden only). Other: £4.40, £2 (garden only).

POLESWORTH NUNNERY GATEWAY

22-24 High Street, Polesworth, Tamworth B78 1DU

Abbey gatehouse, late 14th century with later alterations. Upper floors now in residential use.

Grant Recipient: Polesworth PCC

Access Contact: Mr R C Kind

T: 01827 896562   F: 01827 705450

E-mail: polesworthabbey@aol.com

Open: Exterior at all reasonable times, ground floor interior by arrangement with Mr R C Kind, 2 Whitehouse Road, Dordon, Tamworth B78 1QF. Heritage Open Days.

ℙ Spaces: 20. Parking in Abbey driveway, approx 20 vehicles.

♿ Wheelchair access to ground floor only. No WC for the disabled. Guide Dogs allowed.

£ No.

WEST MIDLANDS

RED HOUSE GLASSCONE

Wordsley, Stourbridge, West Midlands DY8 4AZ

Built around 1790, the Cone was used for the manufacture of glass until 1936 and is now one of only four left in the Country. Reaching 100ft into the sky, the Cone enclosed a furnace where glass was made for 140 years. In its 200 year history, the site has remained virtually unaltered and therefore provides an interesting insight into the history and tradition of glassmaking. Glassmaking and exhibitions tell the story of glassmaking in the area and the history of the glassworks.

www.dudley.gov.uk/redhousecone

Grant Recipient: Dudley Metropolitan Borough Council

Access Contact: Ms Sarah Hall

T: 01384 812752   F: 01384 812751

E-mail: sarah.hall@dudley.gov.uk

Open: Jan - 31 Mar: daily 10am - 4pm. 1 Apr - 31 Oct: Mon - Sat 10am - 5pm, Sun 10am - 4pm.

ℙ Spaces: 40.

♿ Full wheelchair access to the Cone, glassmaking area and all display areas. Lift to upper floor and galleries. Some studios are inaccessible. WC for the disabled. Guide Dogs allowed.

£ Audio guide: Adult £2.50 (adult). Conc £2. Child £1.50.

SOHO HOUSE MUSEUM

Soho Avenue, Handsworth, Birmingham B18 5LB

Soho House Museum is the former home of Matthew Boulton, Birmingham industrialist, entrepreneur and partner of James Watt. Designed by James and Samuel Wyatt, the house was once a meeting place of the Lunar Society and contains period rooms and displays on Boulton's manufacturing activities. The visitor centre houses a temporary exhibition gallery.

www.bmag.org.uk

Grant Recipient: Birmingham Museums & Art Gallery

Access Contact: Curator Manager

T: 0121 554 9122   F: 0121 554 5929

Open: 14 Apr (Good Fri) - 29 Oct: Tues - Sun 11.30am - 4pm, also open BH Mons. Heritage Open Days.

ℙ Spaces: 23.

♿ Full wheelchair access. WC for the disabled. Guide Dogs allowed.

£ No.

ST JAMES

Great Packington, Meriden, nr. Coventry CV7 7HF

Red brick building with four domes topped by finials in neo-classical style. Built to celebrate the return to sanity of King George III. The organ was designed by Handel for his librettist, Charles Jennens, who was the cousin of the 4th Earl

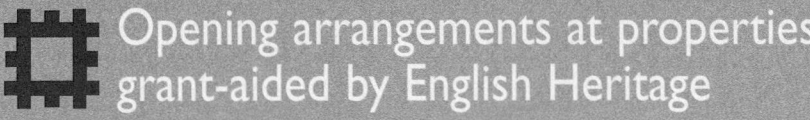

of Aylesford, who built the church.

Grant Recipient: St James Great Packington Trust
Access Contact: Packington Estate Office
T: 01676 522020   **F:** 01676 523399
E-mail: jameschurch@packingtonestate.co.uk
Open: Mon - Fri, 9am - 5pm: key can be obtained from the Estate Office at Packington Hall, preferably by phoning in advance (01676 522020). Other times by arrangement with Lord Guernsey (tel: 01676 522274).
P Spaces: 10.
Wheelchair access with assistance (entrance steps and heavy door to be negotiated). No WC for the disabled. Guide Dogs allowed.
£ Donations towards restoration welcomed.

THE BIG HOUSE
44 Church Street, Oldbury, West Midlands B69 3DE
Grade II* listed house dating from c1720. Originally with agricultural land and later the house and officers of a solicitor in 1857 when the land was sold. Restored and reopened in 2002 as Civic offices.
Grant Recipient: Sandwell Metropolitan Borough Council
Access Contact: Civic Affairs Officer
T: 0121 569 3041   **F:** 0121 569 3050
E-mail: ann_oneill@sandwell.gov.uk
Open: By arrangement with the Mayor's office via the Civic Affairs officer (tel: 0121 569 3041). The Mayor will also hold "Open House" at various times throughout the year.
P Market Street Public Car Park (30 spaces). Parking for the disabled (4 spaces) adjacent to property.
Full wheelchair access. WC for the disabled. Guide Dogs allowed.
£ No.

WIGHTWICK MANOR
Wightwick Bank, Wolverhampton WV6 8EE
Built 1887, the house is a notable surviving example of the Arts and Crafts Movement. Contains original William Morris wallpapers and fabrics, Pre-Raphaelite paintings, Kempe glass and de Morgan ware. Also has a 17 acre Victorian/Edwardian garden designed by Thomas Mawson.
www.nationaltrust.org.uk
Grant Recipient: The National Trust
Access Contact: Property Manager
T: 01902 761400/01902 760100   **F:** 01902 764663   **E-mail:** wightwickmanor@nationaltrust.org.uk
Open: By guided tour only 1 Mar - 23 Dec: Thurs, Fri & Sat (also BH Sun & Mon to ground floor only) 12.30 - 5pm. Family open days Weds in Aug 12.30 - 5pm. Admission by timed ticket issued from 11am at Visitor Reception. Other days by arrangement. Garden: Wed - Sat & BH Sun & Mon 11am - 6pm. First Thurs & Sat of each month: no guided tours, free flow only.
P Spaces: 50. For coach parking please tel 01902 760100.
Wheelchair access to ground floor only. WC for the disabled. Guide Dogs allowed.
£ Adult: £6.60, £3.20 (garden only). Child: £3.30, children free for garden only. Student: £3.30. Family: £16.50.

WEST YORKSHIRE

BOLLING HALL MUSEUM
Bowling Hall Road, Bradford BD4 7LP
Furnished house, mainly 17th and 18th centuries with some earlier parts. Large stained glass window with armorial glass, fine collection of 16th century oak furniture. Now a free public museum with temporary exhibition suite.
www.bradford.gov.uk
Grant Recipient: Bradford Metropolitan District Council
Access Contact: Miss Liz McIvor
T: 01274 431814   **F:** 01274 726220
E-mail: Liz.mcivor@bradford.gov.uk
Open: All year: Wed, Thurs and Fri 11am - 4pm; Sat 10am - 5pm; Sun 12 noon - 5pm. Closed on Mons (except Bank Holidays) and Christmas Day, Boxing Day and Good Fri.
P Spaces: 75. Free parking 100 metres from Museum.
Wheelchair access to ground floor only. WC for the disabled. Guide Dogs allowed.
£ No.

BRAMHAM PARK LEAD LADS TEMPLE
Wetherby, West Yorkshire LS23 6ND
Park folly, in the form of an open temple in the classical style, built in the 1750s by local craftsmen on the instructions of

Harriet Benson (about a mile from the house in woodland called Black Fen, close to a public footpath). The 'Lead Lads' were classical lead figures that stood on the three small blocks at the apex and base of the front pediment, and were lost to vandals many years ago.
www.bramhampark.co.uk
Grant Recipient: Trustees of the Bramham Settled Estate
Access Contact: The Estate Office
T: 01937 846000   **F:** 01937 846007
E-mail: enquiries@bramhampark.co.uk
Open: Close to a public footpath and accessible most of the year except closed 5 - 11 June & 14 Aug - 1 Sept.
P Car park for visitors to Bramham Park (1 mile).
WC for the disabled is not on site, but in visitors car park (1 mile). Guide Dogs allowed.
£ Adult: £4. Child: £2 (under 5s free). Senior: £2. No charge made for visitors via the footpath but charge made for visitors to the house and gardens

CROSSLEY PAVILION
The People's Park, King Cross Road, Halifax HX1 1EB
Grade II* listed building, designed by Sir Joseph Paxton and constructed in 1857. Contains seating and a statue of the park's benefactor, Sir Francis Crossley (1860), by Joseph Durham. Four gargoyle fountains supply pools flanking each side of the pavilion, set on formal terrace, balustrades and steps.
www.calderdale.gov.uk/tourism/parks/peoples.html
Grant Recipient: Calderdale Metropolitan Borough Council
Access Contact: People's Park Development Officer
T: 01422 323824   **F:** 01422 323824
Open: The Park: daily 8am - dusk. The Pavilion: visits by arrangement with Calderdale Metropolitan Borough Council Leisure Services, 25 Bedford Street North, Halifax, West Yorkshire HX1 5BH. Public toilets open during park hours. Information Centre open by arrangement as above. Heritage Open Days.
P On-street parking in Park Road (up to 10 spaces). Limited spaces in adjacent college.
There is one step into the pavilion, otherwise Full wheelchair access. WC for the disabled. Guide Dogs allowed.
£ No.

FRIENDS MEETING HOUSE
off Bolton Road, Addingham, Ilkley LS29
Land for burial ground purchased in 1666, followed by construction of Meeting House in 1669. A simple single cell building with rubblestone walls, mullioned windows, stone-slated roof and stone-flagged floor. Contains loose benches and an oak minister's stand of an unusual panelled design with turned balusters.
www.hct.org.uk
Grant Recipient: Historic Chapels Trust
Access Contact: Barry Cody
T: 01756 710587
Open: At all reasonable times by application to key holders Mr & Mrs Barry Cody, Riverview Cottage, Farfield, nr Addingham, West Yorks LS29 0RQ. Burial ground open for viewing and picnics. Heritage Open Days.
P Spaces: 2.
No wheelchair access or WC for the disabled. Guide Dogs allowed.
£ Donations box.

HAREWOOD HOUSE
Harewood, Leeds, West Yorkshire LS17 9LQ
Designed in neo-classical style by John Carr and completed in 1772. Contains Adam interiors, Chippendale furniture, an art collection and museum. Home of the Earl and Countess of Harewood.
www.harewood.org
Grant Recipient: The Trustees of Harewood House Trust Ltd
Access Contact: Mr Terence Suthers
T: 0113 218 1010   **F:** 0113 218 1002
E-mail: business@harewood.org
Open: Daily, 24 Mar - 29 Oct: Grounds and Bird Garden open 10am - 6pm (last adm. 4pm). House 11am - 4.30pm (last adm. 4pm). Grounds close at 6pm. Grounds and Bird Garden also open weekends between 4 Nov & 10 Dec. Guide dogs are not allowed in the Bird Garden but a free sound guide is available for the partially sighted visitor and a minder for the dog. Heritage Open Days.
P Spaces: 200. Unlimited overflow parking on grass.
Full wheelchair access. WC for the disabled. Guide Dogs allowed.
£ Adult: £11 (weekdays), £13 Sats, Suns & BHs. Child: £6.50

(Mon-Fri), £8 (Sat & Sun). Senior: £9. Family £35. Season tickets & concessions for disabled groups, 50% reduction for arrivals by public transport. Students free Wed.

HUDDERSFIELD STATION
St George's Square, Huddersfield HD1 1JF
Designed by J P Pritchett of York and built by local builder Joseph Kaye using local ashlar sandstone, the station is the oldest of the seven Grade I listed station buildings in use for railway passengers having opened on 3 Aug 1847. When the foundation stone was laid the year before a public holiday was declared and church bells were rung from dawn till dusk. The grandeur of the station is the result of it having been built at the joint expense of the Huddersfield & Manchester Rail & Canal Company and the Manchester & Leeds Railway Company.
Grant Recipient: Kirklees Metropolitan Council
Access Contact: Head of Design & Property Service
Open: Operational building open to the public every day except Christmas Day and Boxing Day. Please note that the building may also be closed on other days specified by Network Rail or other railway operators.
P Spaces: 20. One hour stay maximum in station car park.
Full wheelchair access to main buildings. Access with assistance to inner platforms. No WC for the disabled. Guide Dogs allowed.
£ No.

KIRKSTALL ABBEY
Leeds, West Yorkshire LS5 3EH
One of the best preserved examples of a ruined Medieval Cistercian Monastery in the country. Founded by monks from Fountains and the primary building work was completed in 1182. The Reredorter has been restored as a Visitor Centre.
www.leeds.gov.uk/kirkstallabbey
Grant Recipient: Leeds City Council
Access Contact: Ms Katherine Baxter
T: 0113 230 5492   **F:** 0113 230 5499
E-mail: katherine.baxter@leeds.gov.uk
Open: 1 Oct - 31 Mar: Tues, Wed, Sat, Sun 10am - 3pm. Tours (booked groups) Thurs. 1 Apr - 30 Sept: Tues - Sun (closed Mons) 11am - 4pm. Schools/tours can book for Tues - Fri all year. Heritage Open Days.
P Spaces: 70. Parking for 5 coaches and for the disabled.
Full wheelchair access. WC for the disabled. Guide Dogs allowed.
£ No.

NATIONAL COAL MINING MUSEUM FOR ENGLAND
Caphouse Colliery, New Road, Wakefield WF4 4RH
A colliery complex dating back to the 18th century with an underground tour into authentic coal workings. There are two major galleries of social history and technology and most of the historic buildings are open to the public. Facilities include a research library, restaurant, shop and education services.
www.ncm.org.uk
Grant Recipient: The National Coal Mining Museum for England Trust Ltd
Access Contact: Dr M Faull
T: 01924 848806   **F:** 01924 840694
E-mail: info@ncm.org.uk
Open: All year: daily 10am - 5pm except 24 - 26 Dec & 1 Jan.
P Spaces: 120.
Wheelchair access to all galleries and historic buildings and underground (limited tour) but not the screens. WC for the disabled. Guide Dogs allowed.
£ No.

NOSTELL PRIORY
Doncaster Road, Nostell, Wakefield WF4 1QE
Country house, c1736-1750, by James Paine for Sir Rowland Winn 4th baronet. Later Robert Adam was commissioned to complete the State Rooms. On display is a collection of Chippendale furniture, designed especially for the house, an art collection with works by Pieter Breughel the Younger and Angelica Kauffmann, an 18th century dolls house, complete with its original fittings and Chippendale furniture and an unrestored 18th century Muniments Room. Other attractions include lakeside walks, historic park, family croquet, giant chess set and open day for cabinets.
www.nationaltrust.org.uk
Grant Recipient: The National Trust

Access Contact: Property Manager

T: 01924 863892   F: 01924 866846

E-mail: nostellpriory@nationaltrust.org.uk

Open: House: 1 Apr - 5 Nov, daily except Mon & Tues (open Good Fri & BHs) 1 - 5pm. 9 Dec - 17 Dec: daily 12 noon - 4pm. Grounds, shop and tea room: 13 - 19 Feb: daily 11am - 4pm. 4 - 26 Mar: weekend only 11am - 6pm. 1 Apr - 5 Nov 11am - 6pm.

P Spaces: 120.

& Wheelchair access to ground floor of house with lift to first floor, tea room, children's playground and shop. No WC for the disabled. Guide Dogs allowed.

£ Adult: £6, £4 (grounds only). Child: £3.25, £1.75 (grounds only). Other: £16 (family, no family ticket for grounds only).

PONTEFRACT OLD TOWN HALL AND ASSEMBLY ROOMS

Bridge Street, Pontefract WF8 1PG

Grade II and II* Listed buildings. Old Town Hall built in 1785 and designed by Bernard Hartley. Assembly Rooms later added in 1882 and designed by Perkin & Bulmer. Currently used for productions, concerts and dance.

Grant Recipient: Wakefield Metropolitan District Council

Access Contact: Mrs Olive Rendell

T: 01924 305 573   F: 01924 306 963

E-mail: orendell@wakefield.gov.uk

Open: Mon - Thurs, 9 - 11.30am. Fri 9 - 10.30am. All other times by arrangement. Heritage Open Days.

P Car park nearby, disabled parking adjacent to property.

& Full wheelchair access. WC for the disabled. Guide Dogs allowed.

£ No.

TEMPLE NEWSAM HOUSE

Leeds Museums and Galleries, Leeds LS15 0AE

Tudor-Jacobean mansion in 1200 acre park. Birthplace of Henry Lord Darnley, husband of Mary Queen of Scots, and later the home of the Ingram family, Viscounts Irwin. Over 30 rooms open to the public with pre-eminent collections of paintings, furniture, metalwork, ceramics, textiles and wallpapers.

www.leeds.gov.co.uk/templenewsam

Grant Recipient: Leeds City Council

Access Contact: Mr Anthony Wells-Cole

T: 0113 264 7321   F: 0113 260 2285

E-mail: temple.newsam@leeds.gov.uk

Open: Jan - Dec: daily except Mon (open BH Mons) 10.30am - 5pm (4pm in winter). Last adm. 45 mins before closing. Heritage Open Days.

P Spaces: 200.

& Wheelchair access to all public areas except the first floor of the south wing. WC for the disabled. Guide Dogs allowed.

£ Adult: £3.50 (includes Audio Tour). Child: £2.50 (5-16), Free (under 5). Family: £8.

THE ROUNDHOUSE

Wellington Road, Leeds LS12 1DR

Grade II* railway roundhouse built in 1847 for the Leeds and Thirsk Railway by Thomas Granger. In full use by the North-Eastern Railway until 1904, now home to Leeds Commercial Van and Truck Hire.

Grant Recipient: Wellbridge Properties Ltd

Access Contact: Mr J D Miller

T: 0113 2435964   F: 0113 246 1142

E-mail: sales@leedscommercial.co.uk

Open: By written arrangement with the occupiers, Leeds Commercial, who manage the property as a working garage, or call in during office hours. Heritage Open Days.

P Spaces: 100. Free parking.

& Full wheelchair access. WC for the disabled. Guide Dogs allowed.

£ No.

THEATRE ROYAL & OPERA HOUSE

Drury Lane, Wakefield, West Yorkshire WF1 2TE

A 500 seat Victorian Theatre designed by Frank Matcham. Notable for the quality of decoration in the auditorium, it provides a year-round programme of events.

www.wakefieldtheatres.co.uk

Grant Recipient: Wakefield Theatre Royal & Opera House

Access Contact: Mr Murray Edwards/Executive Director

T: 01924 215531   F: 01924 215525

E-mail: murray.edwards@wakefieldtheatres.co.uk

Open: Programme of events published in Feb, July & Nov.

Guided tours once a month on Sat, groups on weekdays by arrangement, contact the Box Office 01924 211311 for further information.

P Spaces: 150.

& Wheelchair access to stalls area only. WC for the disabled. Guide Dogs allowed.

£ Adult £3. Child: Free. Admission charge for performances.

WILTSHIRE

AVONCLIFFE AQUEDUCT

Kennet & Avon Canal, Westwood, Wiltshire

19th century limestone aqueduct carrying the Kennet and Avon Canal over the River Avon and the railway line. The canal towpath crosses alongside the canal providing a foot link to Bradford-on-Avon or Bath.

www.britishwaterways.co.uk

Grant Recipient: British Waterways

Access Contact: Mr Kent Daniels

T: 01452 318000

E-mail: kentdaniels@britishwaterways.co.uk

Open: At all times.

P Spaces: 12.

& Wheelchair access to top of aqueduct from the small car park beside the canal. No WC for the disabled. Guide Dogs allowed.

£ No.

BARTON GRANGE FARM WEST BARN

Bradford on Avon, Wiltshire

Part of Barton Farm, once a grange of Shaftesbury Abbey (the richest nunnery in England), which includes the adjacent 14th century Tithe Barn. The West Barn was destroyed by fire in 1982 but has subsequently been rebuilt by the Preservation Trust and is now used as an 'Interpretation Centre'.

www.bradfordheritage.co.uk/PAGES/project.htm

Grant Recipient: Bradford on Avon Preservation Trust Ltd

Access Contact: Mr Chris Penny

T: 01225 866551   E-mail: chrispenny@lineone.net

Open: May - Sept: weekends & BHs 12 noon - 4pm. Also at other times throughout the year, please check with Mr Penny for further details. Heritage Open Days.

P Pay parking (15 spaces) near the site. Pay parking (200 spaces) at railway station.

& Wheelchair access to main building but not galleries. Entrance pathways are loose gravel. WC for the disabled. Guide Dogs allowed.

£ No.

HEMINGSBY

56 The Close, Salisbury, Wiltshire SP1 2EL

14th century canonical residence with spacious 18th century rooms and medieval Great Hall. Contains 15th century linenfold panelling. Large and interesting garden. Home of Canon William Fideon, a Greek scholar who escaped from Constantinople in 1453, and Canon Edward Powell, advocate of Catherine of Aragon and later hanged for denying the Act of Supremacy.

Grant Recipient: The Dean & Chapter of Salisbury Cathedral

Access Contact: Mr Peter Edds

T: 01722 555115   F: 01722 555140

E-mail: p.edds@salcath.co.uk

Open: By arrangement only. Exterior at all times.

P No.

& No wheelchair access or WC for the disabled. Guide Dogs allowed.

£ Donations for charity gratefully received.

LACOCK ABBEY

Lacock, nr. Chippenham, Wiltshire SN15 2LG

Founded in 1232 and converted into a country house c1540, the fine medieval cloisters, sacristy, chapter house and monastic rooms of the Abbey have survived largely intact. The handsome 16th century stable courtyard has half timbered gables, a clockhouse, brewery and bakehouse. Victorian woodland garden. Former residents include William Fox Talbot 'the father of modern photography'.

www.nationaltrust.org.uk

Grant Recipient: The National Trust

Access Contact: Property Manager

T: 01249 730459/730227   F: 01249 730501

E-mail: lacock.estate@nationaltrust.org.uk

Open: Abbey: 25 Mar - 29 Oct, daily 1 - 5.30pm (closed Tues & Good Fri). Museum, cloisters and garden: 25 Feb - 29 Oct, daily 11am - 5.30pm (closed Good Fri). Museum also open winter weekends, but closed 23 - 31 Dec.

P Spaces: 300.

& Wheelchair access to Abbey is difficult as four sets of stairs. Garden, cloisters and museum are accessible (non-wheelchair stairlift in museum). Limited parking in Abbey courtyard by arrangement. WC for the disabled at Red Lion car park, High Street, and abbey courtyard, RADAR lock. Guide Dogs allowed.

£ Adult: £7.80 (Abbey, museum, cloisters & garden), £6.30 (Abbey & garden), £4.80 (garden, cloisters & museum). Child: £3.90 (Abbey, museum, cloisters & garden), £3.20 (Abbey & garden), £2.40 (garden, cloisters & museum). Other: £20 (family: Abbey, museum, cloisters & garden), £16.10 (family: Abbey & garden), £12.20 (family: garden, cloisters & museum). Group rates.

LADY MARGARET HUNGERFORD ALMSHOUSES

Pound Pill, Corsham, Wiltshire SN13 9HT

Fine complex of Grade 1 listed 17th Almshouses, Schoolroom, Warden's House and Stables. Schoolroom with original 17th century furniture and Exhibition Room. Recently restored. Lady Margaret Hungerford founded the Almshouses for the care of six poor people and the schoolroom for educating poor children. Arms of the foundress are well displayed.

Grant Recipient: Trustees Of The Lady Margaret Hungerford Charity

Access Contact: Mr R L Tonge

T: 01225 742471   F: 01225 742471

E-mail: rtonge@northwilts.gov.uk

Open: 3 Apr - 2 Oct: Tues, Wed, Fri and Sat 1.30 - 4.00pm. Other dates: Sats 1.30pm - 4pm. Closed Dec & Jan. Groups welcome by appointment.

P Spaces: 100. Parking in the town within 100 yards.

& Wheelchair access to ground floor only. WC for the disabled. Guide Dogs allowed.

£ Adult: £2. Child: 50p. Senior/Conc: £1.75.

LARMER TREE GARDENS

nr Tollard Royal, Salisbury, Wiltshire SP5 5PY

Created by General Pitt Rivers in 1880 as a pleasure grounds for 'public enlightenment and entertainment', the Larmer Tree Gardens are set high on the Cranbourne Chase providing exceptional views of the surrounding countryside. One of the most unusual gardens in England containing an extraordinary collection of colonial and oriental buildings, a Roman Temple and an Open Air Theatre.

www.larmertreegardens.co.uk

Grant Recipient: Trustees of MALF Pitt-Rivers No. 1 Discretionary Settlement

Access Contact: Estate Secretary

T: 01725 516228/5   F: 01725 516321

E-mail: larmer.tree@rushmore-estate.co.uk

Open: Easter Sun - End of Oct: Sun - Thurs 11am - 5pm. Closed July, Fridays & Saturdays for private hire. Tea rooms: Suns & BHs.

P Spaces: 500.

& Wheelchair access to the sunken dell is difficult. WC for the disabled. Guide Dogs allowed.

£ Adult: £3.75. Child: £2.50 (over 5 yrs). Other: £3.

LYDIARD PARK

Lydiard Tregoze, Swindon, Wiltshire SN5 3PA

Ancestral home of the Bolingbrokes, the restored Palladian mansion contains family furnishings and portraits, plasterwork, rare 17th century painted window and room dedicated to 18th century society artist Lady Diana Spencer.

www.lydiardpark.org

Grant Recipient: Swindon Borough Council

Access Contact: Mrs Sarah Finch-Crisp

T: 01793 770401   F: 01793 770968

Open: House: Mon - Sat 10am - 5pm & Sun 2 - 5pm. Nov - Feb early closing at 4pm. Grounds: all day, closing at dusk. Heritage Open Days.

P Spaces: 400.

& Full wheelchair access. WC for the disabled. Guide Dogs allowed.

£ Adult: £2.20. Child: £1. Other: £1 (Swindon Card Holders).

MERCHANT'S HOUSE

132 High Street, Marlborough, Wiltshire SN8 1HN

17th century town house built by the Bayly family, mercers

between 1653 and c1700. Situated prominently in the High Street it contains a unique stripe-painted dining room c1665, painted balustrading to the oak staircase and a panelled chamber of the Commonwealth period.
www.themerchantshouse.co.uk
Grant Recipient: Merchant's House (Marlborough) Trust
Access Contact: Mr Michael Gray
T: 01672 511491 **F:** 01672 511491
E-mail: manager@themerchantshouse.co.uk
Open: Easter - end Sept: Fri & Sats 11am - 4pm. Other times by arrangement with the Secretary at Merchant's House.
P Parking for the disabled outside the building. Public parking in High Street.
No wheelchair access or WC for the disabled. Guide Dogs allowed.
£ Adult £3. Child 50p.

OLD BISHOP'S PALACE
Salisbury Cathedral School, 1 The Close, Salisbury, Wiltshire SP1 2EQ
13th century building, much altered over the centuries, with 13th century undercroft, Georgian drawing room and a chapel.
www.salisburycathedralschool.com
Grant Recipient: Salisbury Diocesan Board of Finance
Access Contact: Mr Neil Parsons
T: 01722 555302 **F:** 01722 410910
E-mail: bursar@salisburycathedralschool.com
Open: Guided tours on 10 days in July/Aug. Details can be obtained from the Visitors' Office at Salisbury Cathedral (tel: Jan Leniston: 01722 555124).
P No.
No wheelchair access. There is a WC for the disabled people in the cloister (100 yards). No Guide Dogs.
£ Adult: £2.50.

SALISBURY CATHEDRAL EDUCATION CENTRE (WREN HALL)
56c The Close, Salisbury, Wiltshire SP1 2EL
Originally north wing of adjacent Braybrook House, early 18th century. Former choristers' school (founded 13th century). Many of the original fixtures and fittings are still present. Items of particular interest are the teacher's and head teacher's desks, original wood panelling and various photographs and artefacts from the history of the schoolroom.
www.salisburycathedral.org.uk/education.php
Grant Recipient: The Dean & Chapter of Salisbury Cathedral
Access Contact: Mr Peter Edds
T: 01722 555115 **F:** 01722 555 140
E-mail: p.edds@salcath.co.uk
Open: By arrangement.
P As part of Close parking arrangements for members of the public.
No wheelchair access. WC for the disabled available within the Close. No Guide Dogs.
£ Donation to work of Centre invited.

THE CLOISTERS, IFORD MANOR
Bradford-on-Avon, Wiltshire BA15 2BA
Small stone-built cloister in gardens of Manor, completed 1914 by Harold Peto and based on 13th century Italian style. Interesting early contents. Used for concerts and opera evenings during the summer.
www.ifordmanor.co.uk
Grant Recipient: Mrs E Cartwright-Hignett
Access Contact: Mrs E Cartwright-Hignett
T: 01225 863146 **F:** 01225 862364
Open: Gardens only: Apr - Oct, Suns & Easter Mon 2 - 5pm; May - Sept, daily (except Mons & Fri), 2 - 5pm. Children under

10 not encouraged at weekends. Coaches and groups by arrangement only outside normal opening hours.
P Spaces: 100.
Wheelchair access by arrangement to Cloisters and part of the gardens. WC for the disabled. Guide Dogs allowed.
£ Adult: £4. Child: £3.50 (10-16, under 10 free). Conc: £3.50.

WILTON HOUSE
Wilton, Salisbury, Wiltshire SP2 0BJ
Ancestral home of the Earls of Pembroke for over 450 years, rebuilt by Inigo Jones and John Webb in the Palladian style with further alterations by James Wyatt c1801. Contains 17th century state rooms and an art collection including works by Van Dyck, Rubens, Joshua Reynolds and Brueghel. Surrounded by landscaped parkland.
www.wiltonhouse.com
Grant Recipient: Wilton House Charitable Trust
Access Contact: Mr Duncan Leslie
T: 01722 746720 **F:** 01722 744447
E-mail: tourism@wiltonhouse.com
Open: 13 Apr - 30 Sept: 10.30am - 5.30pm (last adm. 4.30pm). House closed on Sats but grounds open. House and gardens open on BHs.
P Spaces: 200.
Full wheelchair access. WC for the disabled. Guide Dogs allowed.
£ Adult: £9.75.   Child: £5.50. Senior: £8. Group rates on application.

WORCESTERSHIRE

ABBERLEY HALL CLOCK TOWER
Great Witley, Worcester, Worcestershire WR6 6DD
Victorian folly, built 1883-4, by J P St Aubyn in a fantastic mixture of 13th and 14th century Gothic styles. 161ft tall, it can be seen from six counties.
Grant Recipient: Abberley Hall Ltd
Access Contact: Mr John G W Walker
T: 01299 896275 **F:** 01299 896875
E-mail: johnwalker@abberleyhall.co.uk
Open: 20 & 21 July; other times by arrangement.
P Spaces: 20.
No wheelchair access or WC for the disabled.
£ Adult £3. Child: £1.50.

HANBURY HALL
Hanbury, Droitwich, Worcestershire WR9 7EA
Built in 1701, this William and Mary-style house contains painted ceilings and staircase. It has an orangery, ice house and Moorish gazebos. The re-created 18th century garden is surrounded by parkland and has a parterre, wilderness, fruit garden, open grove and bowling green pavilions.
www.nationaltrust.org.uk
Grant Recipient: The National Trust
Access Contact: Property Manager
T: 01527 821214 **F:** 01527 821251
E-mail: hanburyhall@nationaltrust.org.uk
Open: 4-12 Mar, Sat & Sun. 18 Mar - 1 Nov, Sat - Wed. House: 1 - 5pm. Garden: 11am - 5.30pm. 4 Grounds, tearoom and shop: 4 Nov - 10 Dec, 11am - 4pm.
P Spaces: 150. Car parking 200 metres from house. Buggy transfer available.
Wheelchair access to ground floor, gardens, tea room and shop. WC for the disabled. Guide Dogs allowed.
£ Adult: £6, £4 (garden only). Child: £3, £2 (garden only). Family: £15 (family). Group: £5.20.

HOPTON COURT CONSERVATORY
Cleobury Mortimer, Kidderminster DY14 0EF
Grade II* listed conservatory, c1830, of cast iron with a

rounded archway leading to a rear room roofed with curved glass. Two rooms either side, one housing the boiler beneath to supply heat by way of cast iron grilles running around the floor of the interior.
www.hoptoncourt.co.uk
Grant Recipient: Mr C R D Woodward
Access Contact: Mr Christopher Woodward
T: 01299 270734 **F:** 01299 271132
E-mail: chris@hoptoncourt.fsnet.co.uk
Open: Weekends of 13/14 May and 2/3 Sept 10am - 4.30pm. At other times by arrangement.
P Spaces: 150.
Full wheelchair access. WC for the disabled. Guide Dogs allowed.
£ Adult: £3.50.

LOWER BROCKHAMPTON
Brimsfield, Worcestershire WR6 5TB
A late 14th century moated manor house with a detached half-timbered 15th century gatehouse. Also, the ruins of a 12th century chapel. Woodland walks.
www.nationaltrust.org.uk
Grant Recipient: The National Trust
Access Contact: Property Manager
T: 01885 488099 **F:** 01885 482151
E-mail: brockhampton@nationaltrust.org.uk
Open: House: 4 Mar - 26 Mar, Sat & Sun (open BH Mons and Good Fri) 12 noon - 4pm. 1 Apr - 29 Oct: Wed - Sun 12 noon - 5pm (until 4pm in Oct) & BH 12 - 5pm. Woodland walks open all year, daily during daylight hours.
P Spaces: 60. Parking for the disabled near house. Car parking free when visiting house, £2 charge for non NT members at estate car park.
WC for the disabled in estate car park. Guide Dogs allowed.
£ Adult: £4. Child: £2. Family: £10 (family). Groups (15+) £3.50. £2 (car park).

ST MICHAEL'S RUINED NAVE & WEST TOWER
Abberley, Worcestershire
Ruins of tower, nave (both 12th century) and south aisle (c1260). Walls standing approximately 4ft high with many surviving features from Medieval church. 12th century chancel and south chapel, c1260, repaired in 1908 and still used for services.
Grant Recipient: Abberley Parochial Church Council
Access Contact: Mrs M A Nott
T: 01299 896392
Open: At all times.
P Spaces: 7. Also parking at Manor Arms Hotel.
Full wheelchair access to ruins but assistance required to visit interior of church. No WC for the disabled. Guide Dogs allowed.
£ Donations welcome (place in Green Box).

WALKER HALL
Market Square, Evesham, Worcestershire WR11 4RW
16th century timber-framed building adjoining Norman gateway, much altered. In the late 19th century the floor was removed and it became an open hall. In 1999 it was repaired and refitted to form offices (first floor) and a retail unit (ground floor).
Grant Recipient: Saggers & Rhodes
Access Contact: Messr Saggers & Rhodes
T: 01386 446623 **F:** 01386 48215
E-mail: wds@ricsonline.org
Open: Access to interior by arrangement.
P Spaces: 500. Parking in town centre car parks.
Wheelchair and guide dog access to ground floor only. WC for the disabled.
£ Charitable donation only.

English Civil War soldiers (Festival of History).
©English Heritage

indexes

plant sales pg 555

Properties and gardens offering collections of rare and unusual plants not generally available.

corporate hospitality pg 568

Properties able to accommodate corporate functions, wedding receptions and events.

education index pg 564

Properties providing facilities for schools/educational groups.

accommodation pg 567

Historic properties which offer accommodation - from basic comfort to ultimate luxury.

civil wedding venues pg 562

Places where the ceremony itself can take place and may also provide facilities for reception.

open all year pg 557

Properties and/or their grounds included in this list are open for all or most of the year.

special events pg 571

Historical re-enactments, festivals, country & craft fairs, concerts, fireworks, car & steam rallies.

Properties where plants are offered for sale

Floors Castle.　Floors Castle.　Wallington.

plants for sale

Properties included in this list are open to some extent for all or most of the year. See individual entries for details.

Turkey Mill

Lewes Castle

Anne of Cleves House

SOUTH WEST

EASTERN REGION

WALES

NORTH WALES

SOUTH WALES

NORTHERN IRELAND

Properties included in this list are open to some extent for all or most of the year. See individual entries for details.

open all year

Whitby Abbey. ©English Heritage.

Restoration House.

Borde Hill House & Gardens.

561

Places at which the marriage ceremony itself can take place – many will also be able to provide facilities for wedding receptions.

Full details about each property are available in the regional listings. There are numerous other properties included within *Hudson's* which do not have a Civil Wedding Licence but which can accommodate wedding receptions. In Scotland religious wedding ceremonies can take place anywhere, subject to the Minister being prepared to perform them.

ENGLAND

© Sarah Ward-Hendry
Loseley Park
Hall Place
Sarah Ward-Hendry

Cliveden.
© Sarah Ward-Hendry

Tower of London.
© Sarah Ward-Hendry

Adderbury Church.
© Sarah Ward-Hendry

The properties listed below provide special facilities for schools' groups. The range of these services varies, so it is vital that you contact the property directly when preparing to arrange a school trip. English Heritage offers free admission for pre-booked educational groups. For a free teacher's information pack: Tel: 020 7973 3385 or Email: education@english-heritage.org.uk or visit the website www.english-heritage.org.uk/education

ENGLAND

education

Hall Place.

Tower of London. ©HRP

Shugborough Hall ©NTPL

The historic properties listed below are not hotels. Their inclusion indicates that accommodation can be arranged, often for groups only. The type and standard of rooms offered vary widely – from the luxurious to the utilitarian. Full details can be obtained from each individual property.

Weston Park.

Tiverton.

Eastnor Castle

corporate hospitality venues

Properties which are able to accommodate corporate functions, wedding receptions and events. Some properties specialise in corporate hospitality and are open, only rarely, if ever, to day visitors. Others do both. See entry for details.

Belvoir Castle

Somerleyton House.

Tower of London.

©HRP

corporate hospitality venues

Beaulieu.

The Law Society.

Abbotsford.

Properties which are able to accommodate corporate functions, wedding receptions and events. Some properties specialise in corporate hospitality and are open only rarely, if ever, to day visitors. Others do both. See entry for details.

Doddington Hall & Gardens.

Raby Castle. Tower of London.

This is merely a selection of special events being staged in 2006 – more information can be obtained from individual property websites – for quick access to these sites visit: www.hudsonsguide.co.uk (this information is intended only as a guide, please check with individual properties before travelling).

JANUARY

29
Weston Park, Shropshire
Meynell & South Staffs Point-to-Point.

FEBRUARY

5
Kelmarsh Hall, Northamptonshire
Snowdrop Sunday.

11-12
Athelhampton House & Gardens, Dorset
Antique carpet exhibition.

11-19
Easton Walled Gardens, Lincolnshire
Snowdrop Spectacular, 11am-3pm.

12
Kelmarsh Hall, Northamptonshire
Snowdrop Sunday.

12
Weston Park, Shropshire
Albrighton Point-to-Point.

26
Wartnaby Gardens,
Leicestershire & Rutland
"Promise of Spring" – plants and bulbs for sale, 11am-3pm.

MARCH

3-5
Wilton House, Wiltshire
29th Annual Antiques Fair.

4-31
Fairfax House, Yorkshire
The John Butler Collection of Georgian Glass.

9
Boconnoc, Cornwall
History of Fabergé – evening lecture by Philip Birkenstein, Chairman of the St Petersburg Collection, and dinner.

10
Boconnoc, Cornwall
History of Fabergé – morning lecture by Philip Birkenstein, Chairman of the St Petersburg Collection, and lunch.

11-12
Exbury Gardens & Steam Railway, Hants
Early season steamer!   Engine Shed Open Day.

20-26
Hever Castle, Kent
Spring Garden Week.

26
Exbury Gardens & Steam Railway, Hampshire
Mothering Sunday Daffodils and Spring Train.

APRIL

1
Exbury Gardens & Steam Railway, Hants
New Forest Breakfast Walk.

1-2
Boconnoc, Cornwall
Cornwall Spring Flower Show.

1-30
Fairfax House, Yorkshire
The John Butler Collection of Georgian Glass.

7-9
Weston Park, Shropshire
Spring Horse Trials.

8-9
Catton Hall, Derbyshire
BASC Gamekeepers' Fair (enquiries 01889 565050).

8-9
Lamport Hall & Gardens, Northants.
Gardeners' Weekend.

8-9
Michelham Priory, Sussex
Spring Garden Festival.

10-30
Exbury Gardens & Steam Railway, Hampshire.
Art at Exbury.

14-17
Hever Castle, Kent
Easter Egg Trail.

15-16
Lamport Hall & Gardens, Northants.
Antique and Collectors Fair.

15-17
Exbury Gardens & Steam Railway, Hants
Easter Bunny Train.

16
Burton Constable Hall, Yorkshire
Easter Egg Hunt.

16
Floors Castle, Borders
Easter Eggstravaganza.

16
Michelham Priory, Sussex
Easter Egg Hunt.

16
Traquair, Borders
Easter Egg Eggstravaganza.

Raby Castle

© English Heritage.

Tower of London.

571

16-17

Eastnor Castle, Herefordshire
Easter Treasure Hunt.

16-17

Groombridge Place Gardens, Kent
Easter Eggstravaganza.

16-17

Kelmarsh Hall, Northamptonshire
Countryman Fair.

16-17

Rockingham Castle, Northamptonshire
Children's Easter Egg Hunt & family fun
quiz.

16-17

Weston Park, Shropshire
Midlands Festival of Transport.

18

Picton Castle, South Wales
RHS Lecture: Spring in the Woodland
Garden.

22-23

Rockingham Castle, Northamptonshire
Scarecrows at Rockingham.

23

Easton Walled Gardens, Lincolnshire
Annual Plant Fair, 11am-4pm.

27-30

Renishaw Hall Gardens, Derbyshire
Bluebell fortnight.

29-30

Catton Hall, Derbyshire
Mountain Bike Rally (enquiries 07956
276399).

29-30

Exbury Gardens & Steam Railway, Hants
Spring Fayre.

29-30

Hever Castle, Kent
Merrie is the Month of May – May Day
Revels with music, dance and The King's
Own Men foot soldiers.

29-30

Leonardslee Lakes & Gardens, Sussex
Bonsai Weekend.

29-30

Weston Park, Shropshire
Midlands Pets and People Show.

30

Bolsover Castle, Derbyshire
Knights' Tournament.

30

Catton Hall, Derbyshire
Classic Car Show, house and gardens
open (enquiries 01922 643385).

30

Eastnor Castle, Herefordshire
Arms and Armour.

30

Groombridge Place Gardens, Kent
Robin Hood.

30

Kelmarsh Hall, Northamptonshire
Hardy Plant Fair.

30

Lamport Hall & Gardens,
Northamptonshire
Spring Craft Festival.

30

Michelham Priory, Sussex
Celtic Weekend – Iron Age living history
day.

30

Wartnaby Gardens,
Leicestershire & Rutland
Plants for sale.

MAY

1

Bolsover Castle, Derbyshire
Knights' Tournament.

1

Catton Hall, Derbyshire
Classic Car Show, house and gardens
open (enquiries 01922 643385).

1

Eastnor Castle, Herefordshire
Arms and Armour.

1

Exbury Gardens & Steam Railway, Hants
Spring Fayre.

1

Groombridge Place Gardens, Kent
Robin Hood.

1

Hever Castle, Kent
Merrie is the Month of May – May Day
Revels with music, dance and The King's
Own Men foot soldiers.

1

Kelmarsh Hall, Northamptonshire
Hardy Plant Fair.

1

Lamport Hall & Gardens,
Northamptonshire
Spring Craft Festival.

1

Leonardslee Lakes & Gardens, Sussex
Bonsai Weekend.

1

Michelham Priory, Sussex
Celtic Weekend – Iron Age living
history day.

1

Weston Park, Shropshire
Midlands Pets and People Show.

1-4

Exbury Gardens & Steam Railway, Hants
Art at Exbury.

1-14

Renishaw Hall Gardens, Derbyshire
Bluebell fortnight.

1-31

Fairfax House, Yorkshire
The John Butler Collection of Georgian
Glass.

4-7

Hatfield House, Hertfordshire
Living Crafts.

7
Athelhampton House & Gardens, Dorset
NCCPG Plant Sale.

7
Boconnoc, Cornwall
Endurance Ride.

8-29
Exbury Gardens & Steam Railway, Hants
Exbury Award-Winning Blooms.

9
Floors Castle, Borders
Tapestry Trail Day.

13-14
Catton Hall, Derbyshire
South Derbyshire Steam & Country Show
(enquiries 0115 913 5823).

14
Kelmarsh Hall, Northamptonshire
Hot Air Balloons & Jazz.

14
Traquair, Borders
Traquair Garden Lovers Fair.

16-17
Boconnoc, Cornwall
House & Garden Fair.

20
Picton Castle, South Wales
Spring Plant Hunter's Fair.

20-21
1066 Battle of Hastings Abbey &
Battlefield, Sussex
Knights' Tournament.

20-22
Floors Castle, Borders
Horse Trials.

23
Picton Castle, South Wales
RHS Lecture: Gardening in harmony with
wildlife.

27-28
Arley Hall & Gardens, Cheshire
Arley Horse Trials & Country Fair.

27-28
Traquair, Borders
Medieval Fayre.

27-29
Harewood House, Yorkshire
Noddy's Here Again!

27-29
Hever Castle, Kent
Merrie England Weekend – Tudor weekend with archery, market stalls, music
and dance.

28-29
Eastnor Castle, Herefordshire
Steam & Woodland Country Fair.

28-29
Lamport Hall & Gardens,
Northamptonshire
19th Steam and Country Festival.

JUNE

1-30
Exbury Gardens & Steam Railway, Hants
Elizabeth Cameron Exhibition.

1-30
Fairfax House, Yorkshire
The John Butler Collection of Georgian
Glass.

3
Picton Castle, South Wales
Knights of Armis.

3-4
Cawdor Castle, Highlands & Skye
Special Gardens Weekend: guided tours
of gardens.

3-4
Exbury Gardens & Steam Railway, Hants
"We'll Meet Again", Exbury/HMS
Mastodon Wartime Memories Weekend.

4
Rockingham Castle, Northamptonshire
Medieval Jousting.

7-10
RHS Garden Wisley, Surrey
Wisley Music Festival.

8-11
Bramham Park, Yorkshire
Bramham International 3 Day Event.

10-11
Audley End House & Gardens, Essex
Knights' Tournament.

10-11
Exbury Gardens & Steam Railway, Hants
Petal Fall Weekend – children free.

10-11
Hatfield House, Hertfordshire
Flower Festival.

10-11
Weston Park, Shropshire
German Shepherd Dog Show.

11-15
Athelhampton House & Gardens, Dorset
Flower Festival.

16-22
Hever Castle, Kent
Rose Week.

17-18
Catton Hall, Derbyshire
Catton Park Horse Trials (enquiries
01283 716311).

17-18
Weston Park, Shropshire
International Model Air Show.

18
Harewood House, Yorkshire
Harewood Vintage & Classic Vehicle
Rally.

Raby Castle.
© English Heritage.

© English Heritage.

18
Saint Hill Manor, Sussex
Open Air Theatre: A Midsummer Night's Dream.

18
Wartnaby Gardens,
Leicestershire & Rutland
Plant Fair.

20
Picton Castle, South Wales
RHS Regional Lecture: The Garden at Highgrove by David Howard, Highgrove Head Gardener.

23-25
Kelmarsh Hall, Northamptonshire
Homes & Gardens Show.

24
Cawdor Castle, Highlands & Skye
RHS lecture on 'Plant Magic' by Sue Hoy, 11am in Cawdor Village Hall (booking required).

24
Exbury Gardens & Steam Railway, Hants
Hampshire Food Festival Breakfast Walk.

24
Lamport Hall & Gardens, Northants.
Theatre in the Garden: A Midsummer Night's Dream.

24-25
Arley Hall & Gardens, Cheshire
Arley Garden Festival.

24-25
Kirby Hall, Northamptonshire
Knights' Tournament.

25
Lamport Hall & Gardens, Northants.
Traditional Jazz in the Garden.

28
Easton Walled Gardens, Lincolnshire
Sweet Pea Day, 11am-4pm.

30
Easton Walled Gardens, Lincolnshire
Sweet Pea Day, 11am-4pm.

JULY

1
Arley Hall & Gardens, Cheshire
Blues on the Park.

1-2
Leonardslee Lakes & Gardens, Sussex
Vintage Engine Show.

1-31
Fairfax House, Yorkshire
The John Butler Collection of Georgian Glass.

2
Easton Walled Gardens, Lincolnshire
Sweet Pea Day, 11am-4pm.

8-9
Floors Castle, Borders
Gardeners' Festival.

8-9
Parham House & Gardens, Sussex
Annual Garden Weekend.

9
Picton Castle, South Wales
Open Air Theatre: Rain or Shine presents "A Midsummer Night's Dream".

10
Boughton Monchelsea Place, Kent
Open Air Shakespeare: "Macbeth".

11
Athelhampton House & Gardens, Dorset
Open Air Theatre: Queen Elizabeth the passion.

14-15
Catton Hall, Derbyshire
Bloodstock Music Festival (enquiries www.bloodstock.uk.com).

14-16
Kelmarsh Hall, Northamptonshire
Field Dog Fairs.

15
Wilton House, Wiltshire
Classical Firework Concert.

15-16
Old Sarum, Wiltshire
Knights' Tournament.

15-16
Leonardslee Lakes & Gardens, Sussex
Model Boat Regatta.

15-16
Michelham Priory, Sussex
Game & Country Fair.

15-16
Weston Park, Shropshire
Midlands Gardeners Weekend.

16
Burton Constable Hall, Yorkshire
Burton Constable Country Fair.

16
Chenies Manor House, Buckinghamshire
Plant & Garden Fair.

16
Groombridge Place Gardens, Kent
Wings, Wheels & Steam.

18
Picton Castle, South Wales
RHS Lecture: Ferns in your Garden.

21
Eastnor Castle, Herefordshire
A Midsummer Night's Dream performed by The Lord Chamberlain's Men.

21-23
Boconnoc, Cornwall
Steam Fair.

22
Catton Hall, Derbyshire
National Carriage Driving Trials (enquiries 01283 716311).

22
Hatfield House, Hertfordshire
Battle Proms Concert.

22
Hever Castle, Kent
Jousting Tournament.

22-23
Picton Castle, South Wales
Sealed Knot.

23
Hever Castle, Kent
Tudor Archery.

26
Easton Walled Gardens, Lincolnshire
Cut Flower Day, 11am-4pm.

28
Easton Walled Gardens, Lincolnshire
Cut Flower Day, 11am-4pm.

29
Exbury Gardens & Steam Railway, Hants
Chapterhouse Theatre – Twelfth Night.

29
Lamport Hall & Gardens, Northants.
Theatre in the Garden: "The Taming of
the Shrew".

29
Weston Park, Shropshire
Proms Spectacular.

29-30
Hever Castle, Kent
Jousting Tournament.

29-30
Scarborough Castle, Yorkshire
Knights' Tournament.

30
Easton Walled Gardens, Lincolnshire
Cut Flower Day, 11am-4pm.

30
Lamport Hall & Gardens,
Northamptonshire
Traditional Jazz in the garden.

31
Boughton Monchelsea Place, Kent
Open Air Theatre: "The Importance of
being Earnest".

AUGUST

1-31
Fairfax House, Yorkshire
The John Butler Collection of Georgian
Glass.

4-6
Hatfield House, Hertfordshire
National Pottery & Ceramics Festival.

5-6
Hever Castle, Kent
Jousting Tournament.

5-6
Traquair, Borders
Traquair Fair.

6
Athelhampton House & Gardens, Dorset
MG Day.

6
Groombridge Place Gardens, Kent
Hot Air Balloons & Ferraris.

6
Picton Castle, South Wales
Open Air Theatre: Chapter House
Theatre Company presents "Twelfth
Night".

10
Floors Castle, Borders
Shakespeare – The Merry Wives of
Windsor.

12
Hever Castle, Kent
Tudor Archery.

12-13
Catton Hall, Derbyshire
Sleepless in the Saddle Mountain Bike
Endurance Race (enquiries 07956
276399).

12-13
Kelmarsh Hall, Northamptonshire
"Festival of Living History".

13
Hever Castle, Kent
Jousting Tournament.

14-18
Eastnor Castle, Herefordshire
Children's Fun Week.

16
Athelhampton House & Gardens, Dorset
Open Air Theatre: Far From The
Madding Crowd.

18-20
Hatfield House, Hertfordshire
Hatfield House Country Show.

19-20
Hever Castle, Kent
Jousting Tournament.

19-20
Weston Park, Shropshire
V Festival.

22-24
RHS Garden Wisley, Surrey
Wisley August Flower Show.

24
Boconnoc, Cornwall
Open Air Theatre.

25-27
Bramham Park, Yorkshire
Leeds Festival.

26
Exbury Gardens & Steam Railway, Hants
Chapterhouse Theatre – Merry Wives of
Windsor.

26
Hever Castle, Kent
Jousting Tournament.

26-28
Exbury Gardens & Steam Railway, Hants
Exbury Scarecrow Festival.

26-28
Weston Park, Shropshire
The Noddy Tour.

27
Floors Castle, Borders
Massed Pipe Bands Family Day.

27-28
Eastnor Castle, Herefordshire
Knight's Treasure Hunt.

27-28
Harewood House, Yorkshire
Steam Rally.

27-28
Hever Castle, Kent
Tudor Archery.

27-28
Lamport Hall & Gardens, Northants.
Antique and Collectors' Fair.

27-28
Rockingham Castle, Northamptonshire
Vikings! of Middle England.

28
Athelhampton House & Gardens, Dorset
Village Fete.

28
Easton Walled Gardens, Lincolnshire
Garden Clinic, 11am-4pm – put your gardening questions to a panel of experts.

SEPTEMBER

1-30
Fairfax House, Yorkshire
The John Butler Collection of Georgian
Glass.

3
Boconnoc, Cornwall
Dog Show.

8-10
Hever Castle, Kent
Patchwork and Quilting.

9
Picton Castle, South Wales
Autumn Plant Hunters' Fair.

12
Picton Castle, South Wales
RHS Lecture: Simple Plant Propagation.

16-17
Weston Park, Shropshire
Midlands Game & Country Sports Fair.

23-24
Lamport Hall & Gardens, Northants.
Autumn Craft Festival.

25-28
Eastnor Castle, Herefordshire
Schools Programme: Victorian Eastnor.

OCTOBER

1
Eastnor Castle, Herefordshire
Victorian Eastnor.

1-31
Exbury Gardens & Steam Railway, Hants
Nerine "Jewel Lily" Exhibition.

1-31
Fairfax House, Yorkshire
The John Butler Collection of Georgian
Glass.

5-8
Weston Park, Shropshire
Autumn Horse Trials.

7-8
Parham House & Gardens, Sussex
Slow Food Fair.

9-15
Hever Castle, Kent
Autumn Colour Week.

14-15
Exbury Gardens & Steam Railway, Hants
Big Draw Weekend – children free.

14-15
Lamport Hall & Gardens,
Northamptonshire
Craft & Gift Fair.

14-31
Exbury Gardens & Steam Railway, Hants
Festival of Autumn Colour.

24-29
Exbury Gardens & Steam Railway, Hants
Exbury Ghost Train.

29
Michelham Priory, Sussex
Halloween Fun Day for Children.

29
Traquair, Borders
Halloween Experience.

31
Burton Constable Hall, Yorkshire
Halloween Ghost Tours.

NOVEMBER

1-5
Exbury Gardens & Steam Railway, Hants
Nerine "Jewel Lily" Exhibition.

1-5
Exbury Gardens & Steam Railway, Hants
Festival of Autumn Colour.

1-30
Fairfax House, Yorkshire
The John Butler Collection of Georgian
Glass.

4
Groombridge Place Gardens, Kent
Spectacular Fireworks.

5
Weston Park, Shropshire
Bonfire & Firework Extravaganza.

18-19
Michelham Priory, Sussex
Christmas Gift & Craft Fair.

29-30
Kelmarsh Hall, Northamptonshire
Christmas Fair.

DECEMBER

1-31
Fairfax House, Yorkshire
The John Butler Collection of Georgian
Glass.

1-31
Fairfax House, Yorkshire
Keeping of Christmas.

2-9
Arley Hall & Gardens, Cheshire
Christmas Floral Extravaganza.

3
Eastnor Castle, Herefordshire
Christmas at Eastnor.

9-10
Exbury Gardens & Steam Railway, Hants
Santa Steam Specials.

9-10
Floors Castle, Borders
Christmas Winter Wonderland.

16-17
Exbury Gardens & Steam Railway, Hants
Santa Steam Specials.

21-22
Exbury Gardens & Steam Railway, Hants
Santa Steam Specials.

Raby Castle.
© English Heritage

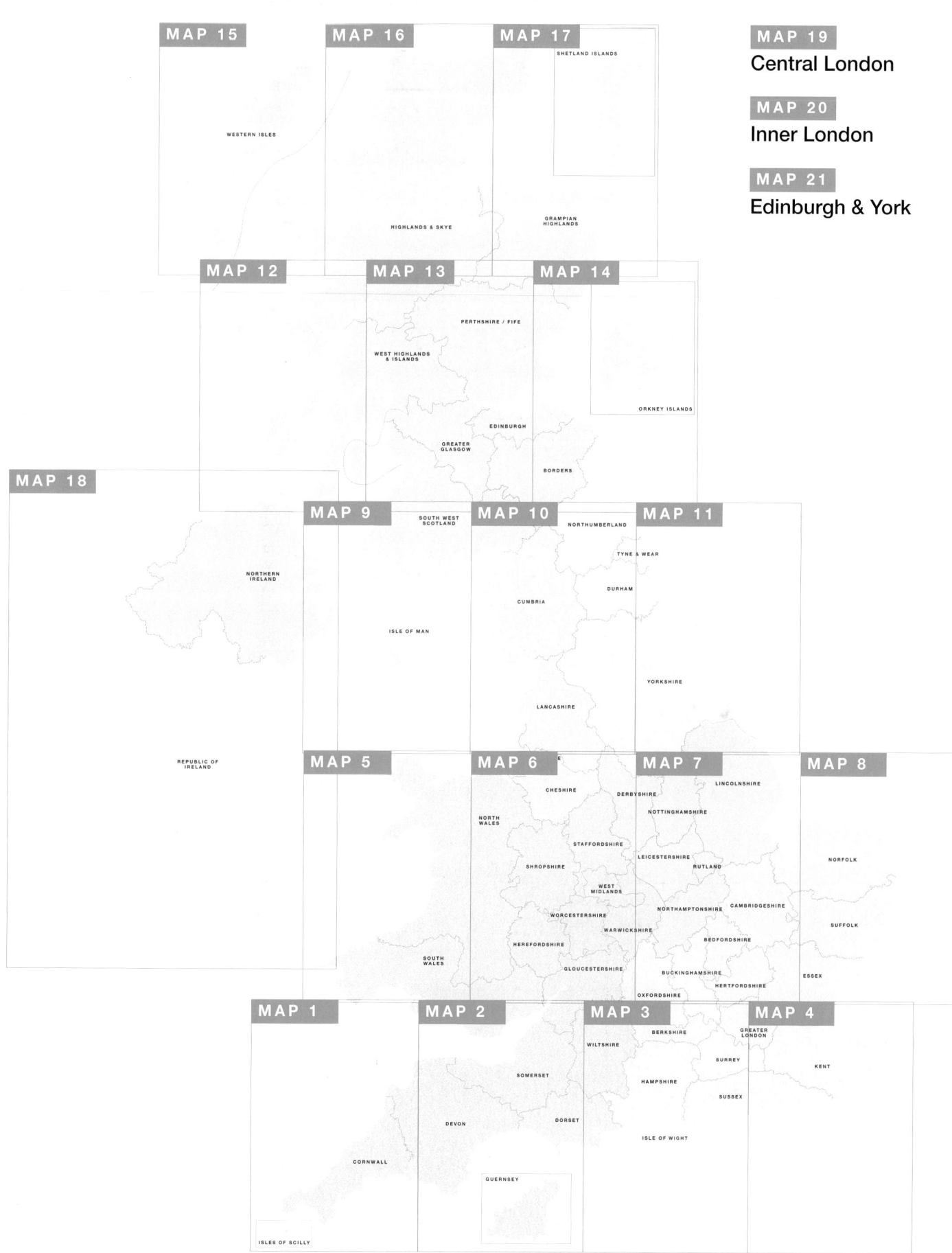

MAP 15

WESTERN ISLES

MAP 16

HIGHLANDS & SKYE

MAP 17

SHETLAND ISLANDS

GRAMPIAN
HIGHLANDS

MAP 19
Central London

MAP 20
Inner London

MAP 21
Edinburgh & York

MAP 12

MAP 13

PERTHSHIRE / FIFE

WEST HIGHLANDS
& ISLANDS

EDINBURGH

GREATER
GLASGOW

BORDERS

MAP 14

ORKNEY ISLANDS

MAP 18

NORTHERN
IRELAND

REPUBLIC OF
IRELAND

MAP 9

SOUTH WEST
SCOTLAND

ISLE OF MAN

MAP 10

NORTHUMBERLAND

CUMBRIA

TYNE & WEAR

DURHAM

LANCASHIRE

MAP 11

YORKSHIRE

MAP 5

NORTH
WALES

SOUTH
WALES

MAP 6

CHESHIRE

STAFFORDSHIRE

SHROPSHIRE

WEST
MIDLANDS

WORCESTERSHIRE

HEREFORDSHIRE

GLOUCESTERSHIRE

DERBYSHIRE

MAP 7

LINCOLNSHIRE

NOTTINGHAMSHIRE

LEICESTERSHIRE

RUTLAND

NORTHAMPTONSHIRE

WARWICKSHIRE

BEDFORDSHIRE

BUCKINGHAMSHIRE

OXFORDSHIRE

HERTFORDSHIRE

CAMBRIDGESHIRE

MAP 8

NORFOLK

SUFFOLK

ESSEX

MAP 1

CORNWALL

ISLES OF SCILLY

MAP 2

DEVON

SOMERSET

DORSET

GUERNSEY

MAP 3

WILTSHIRE

HAMPSHIRE

ISLE OF WIGHT

BERKSHIRE

SURREY

SUSSEX

MAP 4

GREATER
LONDON

KENT

577

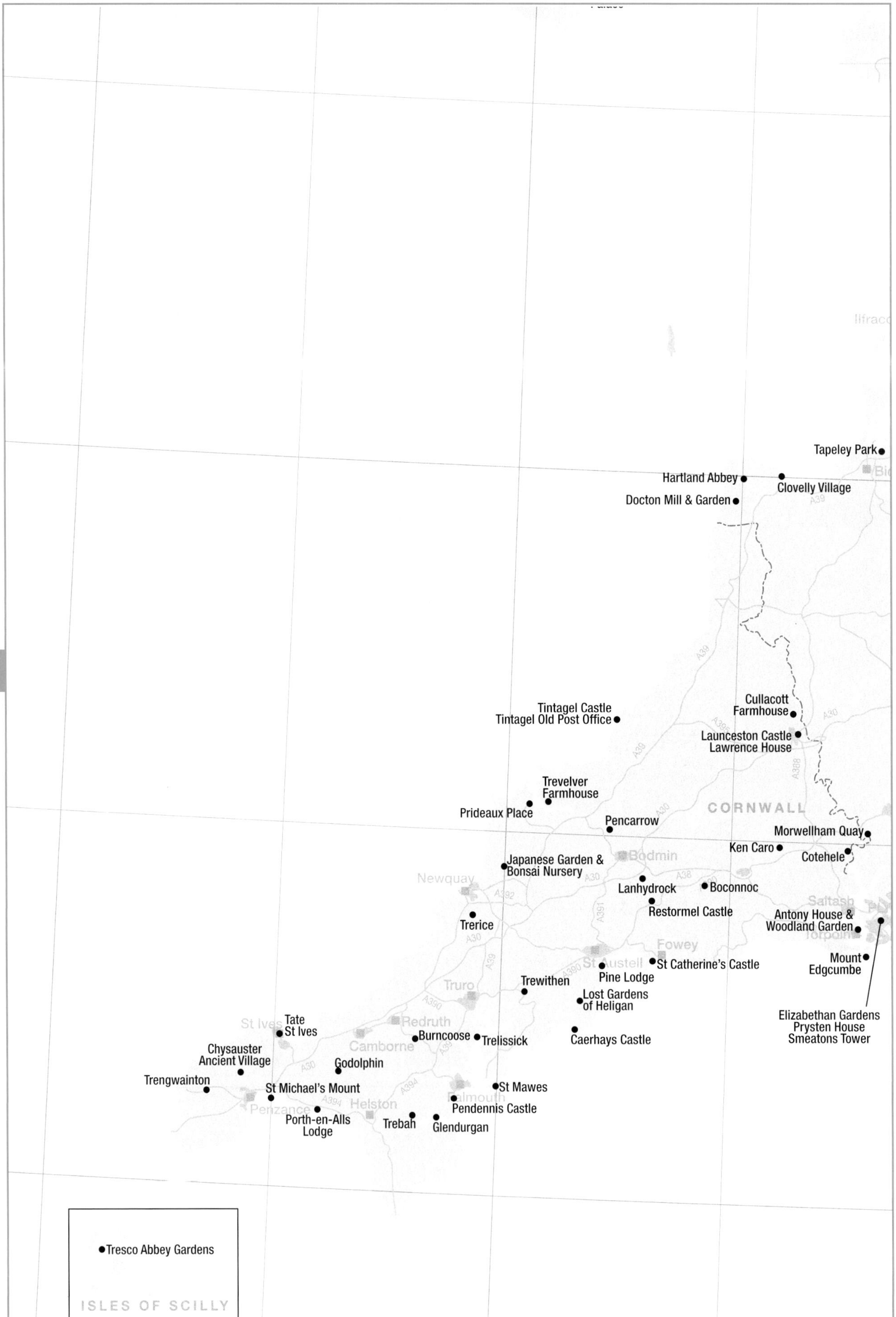

MAP 1

Tapeley Park ●

Hartland Abbey ●   ● Clovelly Village

Docton Mill & Garden ●

Cullacott
Farmhouse ●

Launceston Castle ●
Lawrence House

Tintagel Castle
Tintagel Old Post Office ●

Trevelver
Farmhouse ●

CORNWALL

Prideaux Place ●

Pencarrow ●

Morwellham Quay ●

Ken Caro ●   ● Cotehele

Bodmin

Japanese Garden & ●
Bonsai Nursery

Lanhydrock ●   ● Boconnoc

Restormel Castle ●

Newquay

Antony House & ●
Woodland Garden

Saltash

Trerice ●

Fowey

St Austell

Mount ●
Edgcumbe

Trewithen ●   Pine Lodge
● St Catherine's Castle

Truro

Lost Gardens ●
of Heligan

Elizabethan Gardens
Prysten House
Smeatons Tower

Tate ●
St Ives

Burncoose ●

Redruth

● Trelissick

Caerhays Castle ●

Chysauster ●
Ancient Village

Camborne

Godolphin ●

Trengwainton ●

St Michael's Mount ●

Helston

● St Mawes

Penzance

Porth-en-Alls ●
Lodge

Trebah ●   ● Glendurgan

Falmouth

Pendennis Castle ●

● Tresco Abbey Gardens

ISLES OF SCILLY

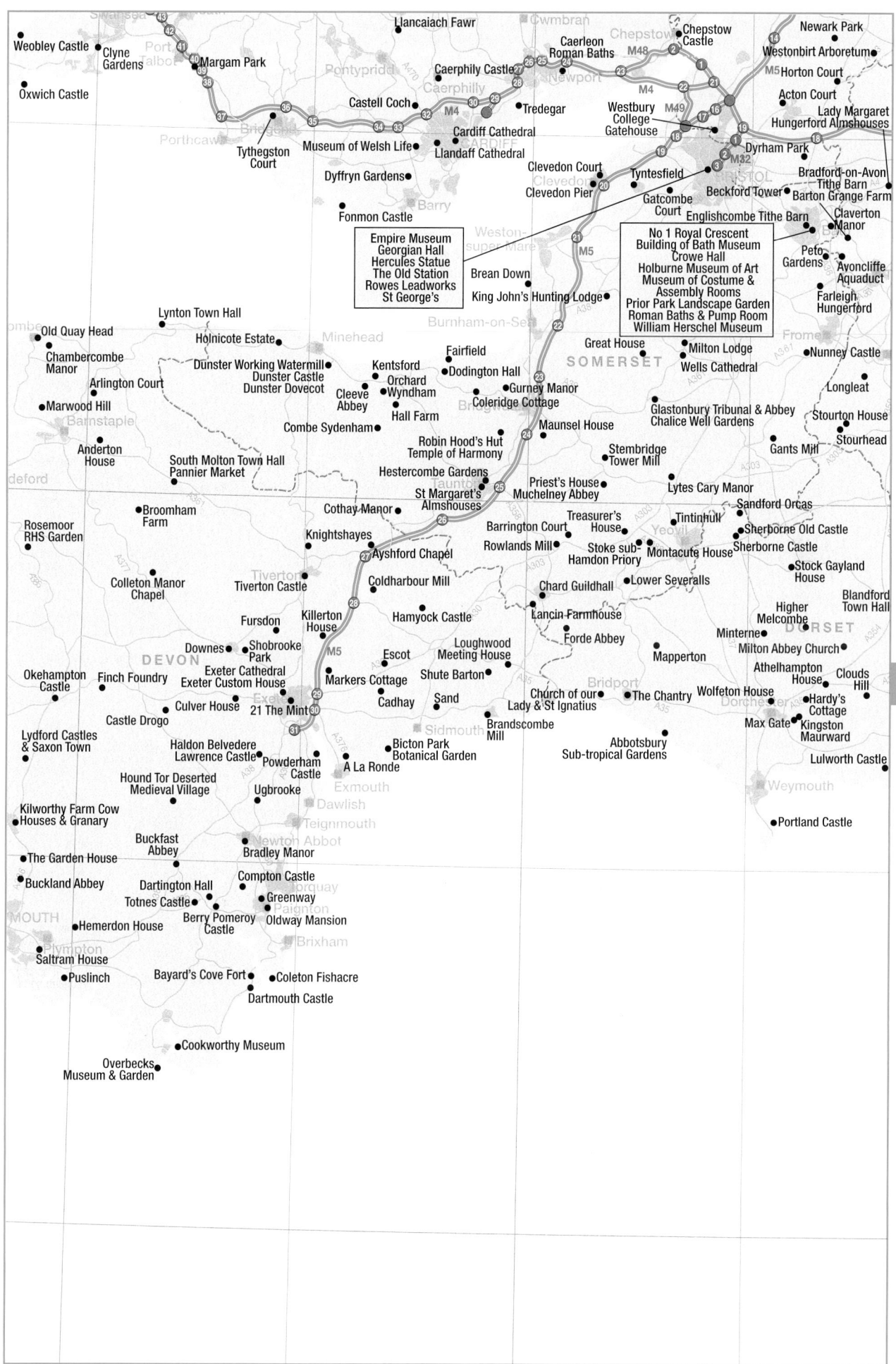

Weobley Castle
Clyne Gardens
Margam Park
Oxwich Castle
Tythegston Court
Museum of Welsh Life
Dyffryn Gardens
Fonmon Castle

Llancaiach Fawr
Caerphilly Castle
Castell Coch
Cardiff Cathedral
Llandaff Cathedral

Caerleon Roman Baths
Tredegar

Chepstow Castle
Chepstow

Newark Park
Westonbirt Arboretum
Horton Court
Acton Court
Lady Margaret Hungerford Almshouses

Westbury College Gatehouse
Dyrham Park

Clevedon Court
Clevedon Pier
Tyntesfield
Gatcombe Court
Englishcombe Tithe Barn
Beckford Tower

Bradford-on-Avon Tithe Barn
Barton Grange Farm
Claverton Manor
Peto Gardens
Avoncliffe Aquaduct
Farleigh Hungerford

Empire Museum
Georgian Hall
Hercules Statue
The Old Station
Rowes Leadworks
St George's

No 1 Royal Crescent
Building of Bath Museum
Crowe Hall
Holburne Museum of Art
Museum of Costume & Assembly Rooms
Prior Park Landscape Garden
Roman Baths & Pump Room
William Herschel Museum

Brean Down
King John's Hunting Lodge

Great House
Milton Lodge
Wells Cathedral
Nunney Castle
Longleat
Stourton House
Stourhead
Gants Mill

Lynton Town Hall
Old Quay Head
Chambercombe Manor
Arlington Court
Marwood Hill
Anderton House

Holnicote Estate
Dunster Working Watermill
Dunster Castle
Dunster Dovecot
Cleeve Abbey
Orchard Wyndham
Kentsford
Hall Farm
Combe Sydenham

Fairfield
Dodington Hall
Gurney Manor
Coleridge Cottage
Maunsel House

SOMERSET

Glastonbury Tribunal & Abbey
Chalice Well Gardens

South Molton Town Hall
Pannier Market

Robin Hood's Hut
Temple of Harmony
Hestercombe Gardens
St Margaret's Almshouses

Stembridge Tower Mill
Priest's House
Muchelney Abbey
Lytes Cary Manor

Rosemoor RHS Garden
Broomham Farm
Knightshayes
Cothay Manor
Barrington Court
Rowlands Mill
Treasurer's House
Stoke sub-Hamdon Priory
Tintinhull
Montacute House
Sandford Orcas
Sherborne Old Castle
Sherborne Castle

Colleton Manor Chapel
Tiverton Castle
Ayshford Chapel
Coldharbour Mill
Chard Guildhall
Lower Severalls
Stock Gayland House

Fursdon
Killerton House
Hamyock Castle
Lancin Farmhouse
Forde Abbey
Higher Melcombe
Minterne
Blandford Town Hall

DEVON
Downes
Shobrooke Park
Escot
Loughwood Meeting House
Mapperton
Milton Abbey Church
Athelhampton House
Clouds Hill

Okehampton Castle
Finch Foundry
Exeter Cathedral
Exeter Custom House
Culver House
21 The Mint
Markers Cottage
Cadhay
Shute Barton
Sand
Church of our Lady & St Ignatius
The Chantry
Wolfeton House
Milton Abbey
Hardy's Cottage
Max Gate
Kingston Maurward

Castle Drogo
Lydford Castles & Saxon Town
Haldon Belvedere
Lawrence Castle
Powderham Castle
A La Ronde
Bicton Park Botanical Garden
Brandscombe Mill
Abbotsbury Sub-tropical Gardens
Lulworth Castle

Hound Tor Deserted Medieval Village
Ugbrooke

Kilworthy Farm Cow Houses & Granary
Portland Castle

Buckfast Abbey
Bradley Manor

The Garden House
Buckland Abbey
Dartington Hall
Compton Castle
Greenway
Oldway Mansion
Totnes Castle
Berry Pomeroy Castle

Hemerdon House
Saltram House
Puslinch
Bayard's Cove Fort
Coleton Fishacre
Dartmouth Castle

Cookworthy Museum

Overbecks Museum & Garden

MAP 2

Chavenage

Buscot Old Parsonage
Buscot Park
Great Coxwell Barn
Culham Manor Dovecote
Milton Manor House
Aston Martin Club
Hughenden Manor
Clifton Open Air Museum
John Milton's Cottage
Church Farmhouse Museum

Priory Cottages
West Wycombe
Wildmere Farm Chapel
Wycombe Museum
Derby Almshouses
Boston Manor

Lydiard Park
Ardington House
Tudor House
Stonor
Freeman Mausoleum
Hall Barn
Clivedon
Pitzhanger Manor
Emery Walker's

Ashdown House
Tirrold House
Grey's Court
Taplow Court

BERKSHIRE
Mapledurham
Dorney Court
Eton College
Osterley Park

Corsham Court
Avebury Manor
Avebury Stone Circle
Welford Park
Basildon Park
St George's Chapel Castle
Windsor Castle
Frogmore House
Kew Garden

Lacock Abbey
WILTSHIRE
Donnington Castle
The Savill Garden
Great Fosters
The Octagon
Ham House
Strawberry Hill

Bowood House
Merchant House
Newbury
Royal Holloway Sanatorium
Garricks Temple
Hampton Cou

Great Chalfield
Sandham Memorial Chapel
Stratfield Saye House
Virginia Park
Great Hall
Claremont House
Whitehall

The Courts
Highclere
Camberl
Painshill

Broadleas Gardens
RHS Garden Wisley
Hatchlands Park
The Cobbe Collection

Stonehenge
The Vyne
Basing House
St Michael's Abbey
Clandon
Polesden Lacey
Box Hill

Heale Gardens
Whitchurch Silk Mill
Loseley Park
Guildford House
Goddards

Old Sarum
Hemingsby
The King's House
Mompesson House
Old Bishop's Palace
Salisbury Cathedral
Guildhall Gallery
Great Hall
Farnham Castle Keep
Winkworth Arboretum

Little Clarendon
Winchester Cathedral
Winchester City Mill
Wolvesey Castle
Uxenford Farm
Oakhurst Cottage
Ramster Gardens

Phillips House
Houghton Lodge
Northington Grange
Jane Austen's House

Wilton
HAMPSHIRE
Avington Park
Gilbert White's House
Leonardslee Gardens

Old Wardour Castle
Newhouse
Mottisfont Abbey
Hinton Ampner
Petworth House

Norrington Manor
King John's House
Manor Farmhouse
Weald & Downland Open Air Museum

Hamptoworth Lodge
Broadlands
Bishop's Waltham Palace
Uppark
Parham House

Lamer Tree Gardens
Breamore House
West Dean Gardens
Stansted Park
Bramber Castle
St Mary's

Chettle House
Furzey Gardens
Medieval Merchant's House
A3(M)
Bignor Roman Villa

Blandford Town Hall
Somerley
Netley Abbey
Boxgrove Priory
Arundel Castle
Arundel Cathedral

Edmonsham House
Eling Tide Mill
Titchfield Abbey
Fishbourne Roman Palace
Denmans
Marlipins Museum

Kingston Lacy
Beaulieu
Exbury
Portchester Castle
Calshot Castle
Fort Brockhurst
Boathouse No.6
Chichester Cathedral
Pallant House
Highdown Gardens

White Mill
Knoll Garden
Portsmouth Cathedral

Deans Court
Osborne House

MAP 3
Highcliffe Castle
Hurst Castle
Old Town Hall
Nunwell House
Bembridge Windmill

Brownsea Island
Yarmouth Castle
Carisbrooke Castle
Morton Manor

Lulworth Castle
Needles Old Battery
ISLE OF WIGHT

Corfe Castle
Mottistone Manor Gardens
Appuldurcombe House

Smedmore

L'Arcresse

Grandes Rocques
Bordeaux
St Sampson

Sausmarez Manor
Les Quartiers

King's Mill
St Peter Port

L'Erée
Caste
GUERNSEY

St Saviour

La Fosse

Torteval

580

Forty Hall
Salisbury House
Bruce Castle
Valentine's Mansion
William Morris Gallery
St Matthins
Lesnes Abbey
Royal Observatory
Queen's House
Ranger's House
Eltham Palace
Danson House
Red House
Hall Place
Morden Park
Carew Manor
Lullingstone Roman Villa
Little Holland House
Lullingstone Castle
Home of Charles Darwin
Quebec House
Titsey Place
Emmetts Garden
Riverhill
Knole
Great Comp Garden
Squerryes Court
Chartwell
Church House
Chiddingstone Castle
Outwood Old Mill
Hever Castle
Saint Hill Manor
Sackville College
Hammerwood Park
Groombridge Place
High Beeches Gardens
Standen
Wakehurst Place
The Priest's House
Bayham Old Abbey
Pashley Manor Gardens
Borde Hill
Clinton Lodge Garden
Merriments Gardens
Sheffield Park Garden
Rotunda Temple
1066 Battle of Hastings Abbey & Battlefield
Tithe Barn
Glynde Place
Michelham Priory
Windmill Hill Windmill
Herstmonceux Castle Garden
Firle Place
Preston Manor
Charleston
Pevensey Castle
Monk's House
The Royal Pavilion
The Dovecote, Alciston

Brendwood Cathedral
Tilbury Fort
Milton Chantry
Gad's Hill Place
Nurstead Court
Cobham Hall
Chatham Historic Dockyard
Temple Manor
Upnor Castle
Aylesford Priory
Maison Dieu
Archbishops' Palace
Old Soar
Turkey Mill
Stoneacre
Ightham Mote
Yalding Organic Gardens
Leeds Castle
Doddington Place
Boughton Monchelsea
Tonbridge Castle
Penshurst Place
Scotney Castle
Finchcocks
Sissinghurst Castle Garden
Bedgebury National Pinetum
Hole Park
Smallhythe Place
Great Dixter
Bateman's
Bodiam Castle
Flushing Inn
Lamb House
Camber Castle
St Mary-in-Castle
De La Warr Pavilion

Reculver Towers Roman Fort
Quex House
Herne Windmill
The Grange
Chart Gunpowder Mills
Richborough Roman Fort
Mount Ephraim Gardens
St Augustine's Abbey
Eastbridge Hospital of St Thomas
Belmont
Goodnestone Park
Deal Castle
Walmer Castle
St John's Commandery
Crabble Cornmill
South Foreland Lighthouse
White Cliffs of Dover
Roman Painted House
Dover Castle
Secret Wartime Tunnels
Dover Town Hall
Willesborough Windmill
Westenhanger Castle & Barns
Dymchurch Martello Tower

Restoration House
Rochester Castle
Rochester Cathedral

Lewes Castle
Barbican House
Anne of Cleves House

MAP 4

581

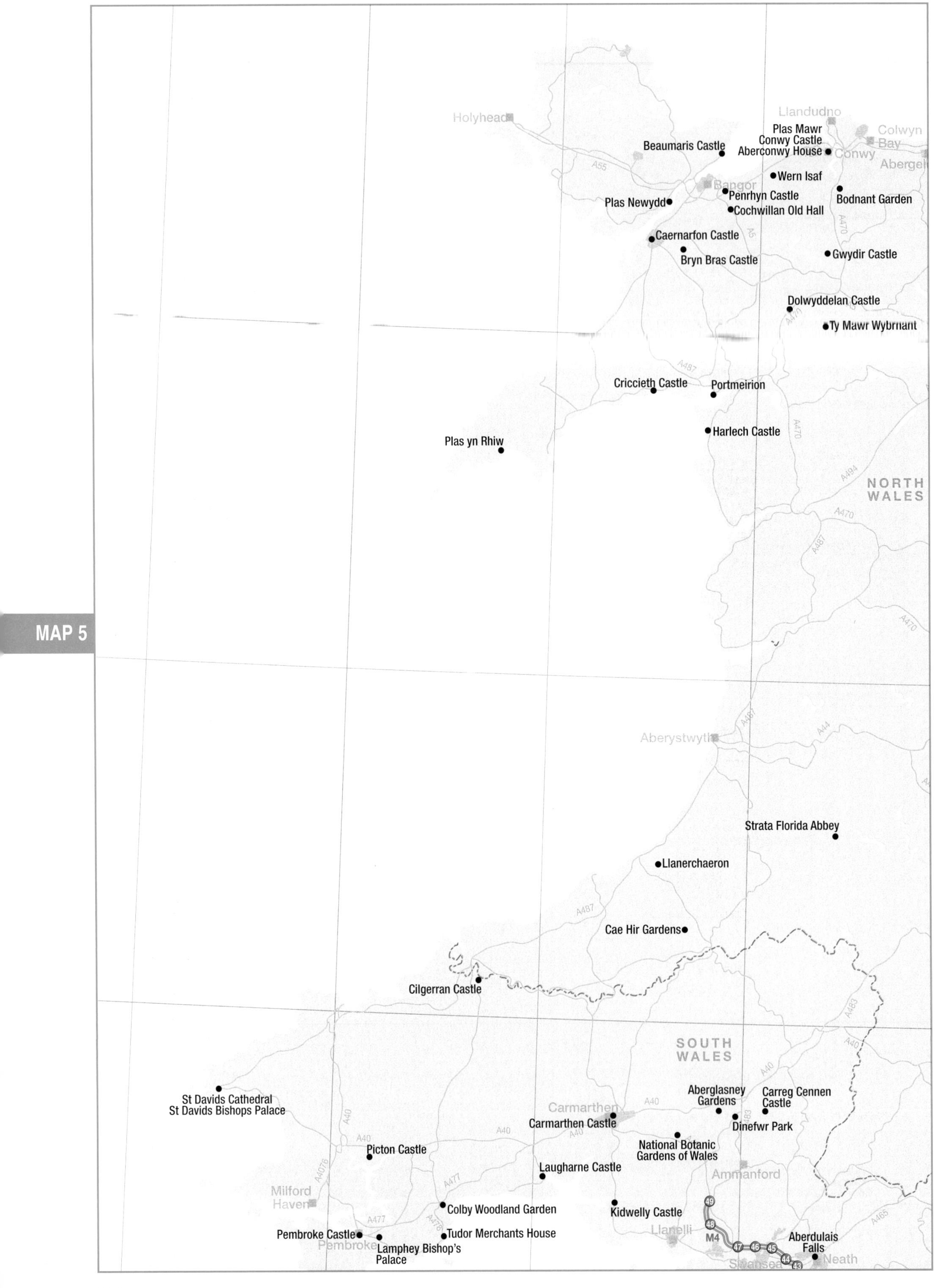

MAP 5
Holyhead
Llandudno
Plas Mawr
Conwy Castle
Aberconwy House
Conwy
Colwyn Bay
Abergele
Beaumaris Castle
A55
Wern Isaf
Bangor
Penrhyn Castle
Bodnant Garden
Plas Newydd
Cochwillan Old Hall
A470
A5
Caernarfon Castle
Bryn Bras Castle
Gwydir Castle
Dolwyddelan Castle
Ty Mawr Wybrnant
A487
Criccieth Castle
Portmeirion
Harlech Castle
A470
Plas yn Rhiw
A494
NORTH WALES
A470
A487
A470
A487
A44
Aberystwyth
Strata Florida Abbey
Llanerchaeron
A487
Cae Hir Gardens
Cilgerran Castle
A483
SOUTH WALES
A40
A40
St Davids Cathedral
St Davids Bishops Palace
A40
Aberglasney Gardens
Carreg Cennen Castle
Carmarthen
A40
A483
Dinefwr Park
Carmarthen Castle
A40
A40
A40
Picton Castle
National Botanic Gardens of Wales
Laugharne Castle
A4076
A477
Ammanford
Milford Haven
Colby Woodland Garden
Kidwelly Castle
49
48
A477
A478
Tudor Merchants House
Llanelli
M4
A465
Pembroke Castle
Pembroke
Lamphey Bishop's Palace
47
46
45
44
43
Aberdulais Falls
Swansea
Neath

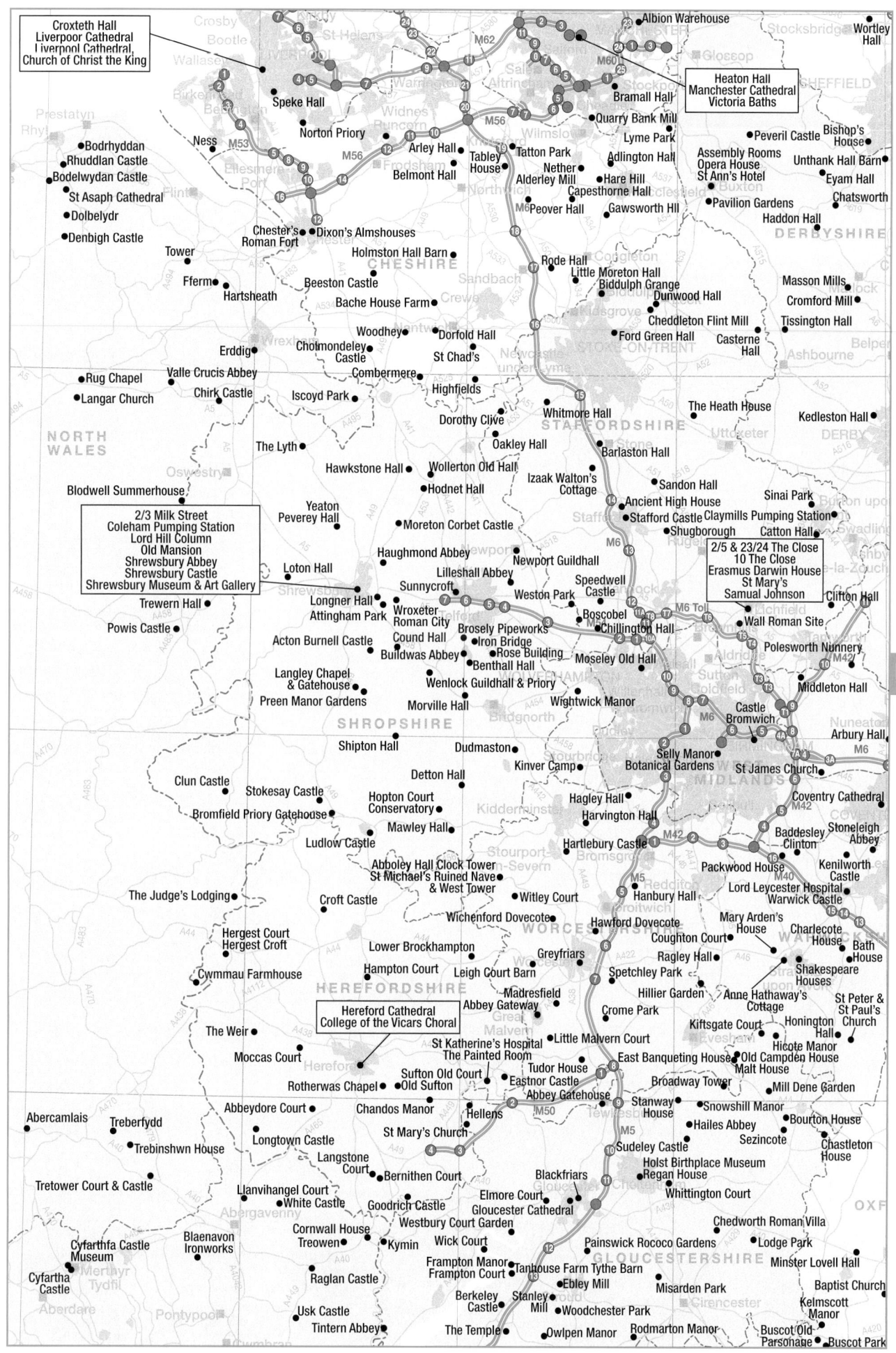

Croxteth Hall
Liverpool Cathedral
Liverpool Cathedral,
Church of Christ the King

Heaton Hall
Manchester Cathedral
Victoria Baths

2/3 Milk Street
Coleham Pumping Station
Lord Hill Column
Old Mansion
Shrewsbury Abbey
Shrewsbury Castle
Shrewsbury Museum & Art Gallery

2/5 & 23/24 The Close
10 The Close
Erasmus Darwin House
St Mary's
Samual Johnson

MAP 6

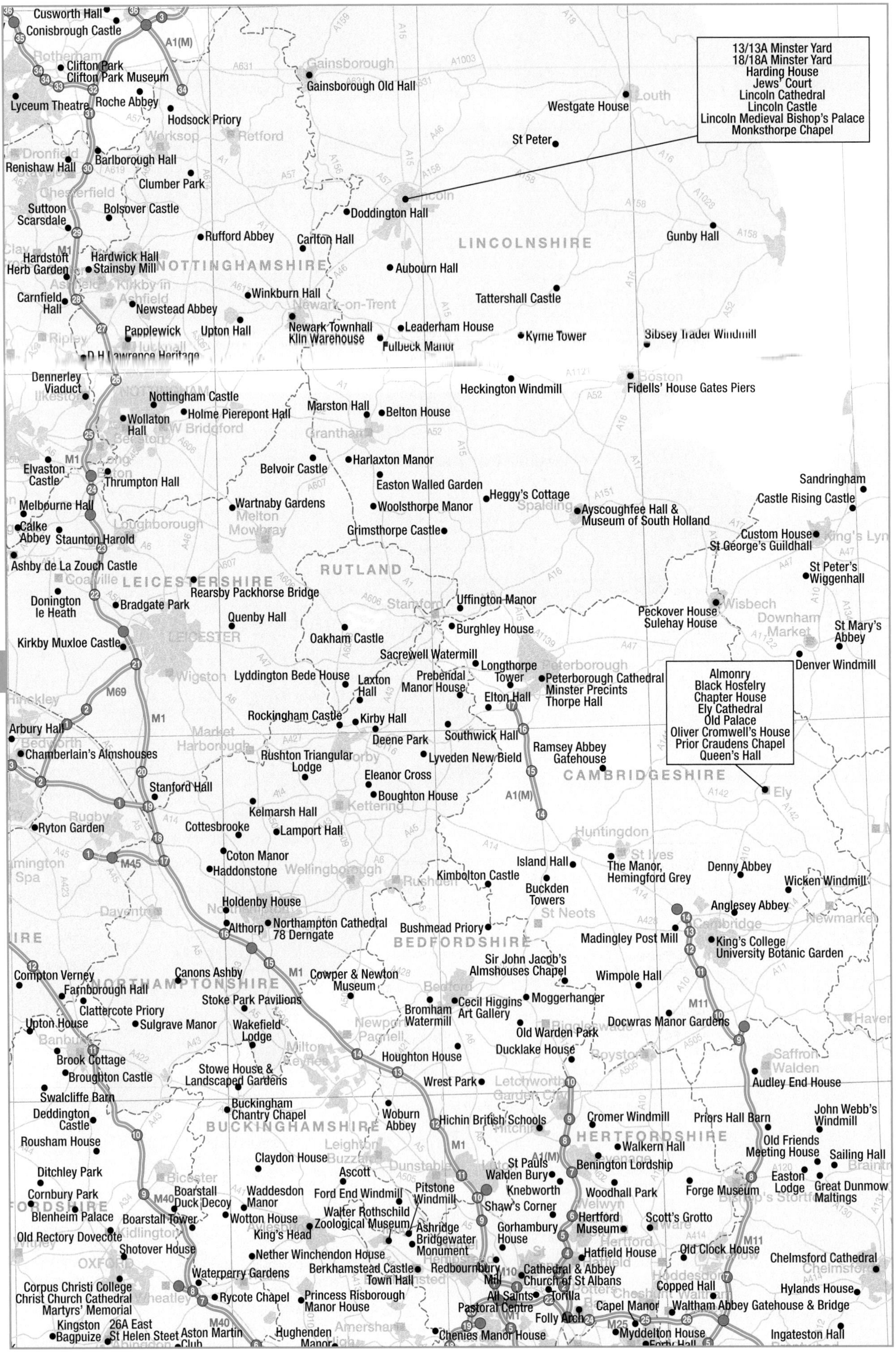

MAP 7

Cusworth Hall
Conisbrough Castle
A1(M)
Clifton Park
Clifton Park Museum
Lyceum Theatre
Roche Abbey
Hodsock Priory
Gainsborough Old Hall
Westgate House
St Peter

13/13A Minster Yard
18/18A Minster Yard
Harding House
Jews' Court
Lincoln Cathedral
Lincoln Castle
Lincoln Medieval Bishop's Palace
Monksthorpe Chapel

Barlborough Hall
Renishaw Hall
Clumber Park
Suttoon Scarsdale
Bolsover Castle
Hardstoft Herb Garden
Hardwick Hall
Stainsby Mill
Doddington Hall
Rufford Abbey
Carlton Hall
Gunby Hall

LINCOLNSHIRE

NOTTINGHAMSHIRE

Carnfield Hall
Newstead Abbey
Winkburn Hall
Aubourn Hall
Tattershall Castle
Papplewick
Upton Hall
Newark Townhall
Kiln Warehouse
Leaderham House
Kyme Tower
Sibsey Trader Windmill
D H Lawrence Heritage
Fulbeck Manor

Dennerley Viaduct
Heckington Windmill
Fidells' House Gates Piers

Nottingham Castle
Wollaton Hall
Holme Pierepont Hall
Marston Hall
Belton House

Elvaston Castle
Thrumpton Hall
Belvoir Castle
Harlaxton Manor
Sandringham
Castle Rising Castle
Melbourne Hall
Wartnaby Gardens
Easton Walled Garden
Heggy's Cottage
Custom House
St George's Guildhall
Calke Abbey
Staunton Harold
Woolsthorpe Manor
Grimsthorpe Castle
Ayscoughfee Hall & Museum of South Holland
St Peter's Wiggenhall
Ashby de La Zouch Castle

RUTLAND

LEICESTERSHIRE

Peckover House
Sulehay House
St Mary's Abbey

Donington le Heath
Bradgate Park
Rearsby Packhorse Bridge
Quenby Hall
Uffington Manor
Burghley House
Denver Windmill

Kirkby Muxloe Castle
Oakham Castle
Sacrewell Watermill
Longthorpe Tower
Peterborough Cathedral
Minster Precincts
Thorpe Hall

LEICESTER

Almonry
Black Hostelry
Chapter House
Ely Cathedral
Old Palace
Oliver Cromwell's House
Prior Craudens Chapel
Queen's Hall

Lyddington Bede House
Laxton Hall
Prebendal Manor House
Elton Hall

Arbury Hall
Rockingham Castle
Kirby Hall
Southwick Hall
Ramsey Abbey Gatehouse

CAMBRIDGESHIRE

Chamberlain's Almshouses
Deene Park
Lyveden New Bield
Ely

Stanford Hall
Rushton Triangular Lodge
Eleanor Cross
Boughton House
A1(M)

Ryton Garden
Kelmarsh Hall
Island Hall
The Manor, Hemingford Grey
Denny Abbey
Wicken Windmill

Cottesbrooke
Lamport Hall
Kimbolton Castle
Buckden Towers
Anglesey Abbey

Coton Manor
Haddonstone
King's College
University Botanic Garden

Holdenby House
Bushmead Priory
Madingley Post Mill

Compton Verney
Althorp
Northampton Cathedral
78 Derngate
Sir John Jacob's Almshouses Chapel
Wimpole Hall

NORTHAMPTONSHIRE

BEDFORDSHIRE

Farnborough Hall
Canons Ashby
Cowper & Newton Museum
Moggerhanger
Docwras Manor Gardens

Clattercote Priory
Stoke Park Pavilions
Cecil Higgins Art Gallery

Upton House
Sulgrave Manor
Wakefield Lodge
Bromham Watermill
Old Warden Park
Ducklake House
Audley End House

Brook Cottage
Broughton Castle
Stowe House & Landscaped Gardens
Houghton House
John Webb's Windmill

Swalcliffe Barn
Wrest Park
Cromer Windmill
Priors Hall Barn
Old Friends Meeting House

Deddington Castle
Buckingham Chantry Chapel
Woburn Abbey
Hichin British Schools
Walkern Hall
Sailing Hall

Rousham House
Claydon House
Ascott
Walden Bury
Benington Lordship
Woodhall Park
Forge Museum
Easton Lodge

BUCKINGHAMSHIRE

HERTFORDSHIRE

Ditchley Park
St Pauls
Knebworth
Great Dunmow Maltings

Cornbury Park
Boarstall Duck Decoy
Waddesdon Manor
Ford End Windmill
Pitstone Windmill
Shaw's Corner
Hertford Museum
Scott's Grotto

Blenheim Palace
Boarstall Tower
Walter Rothschild Zoological Museum
Gorhambury House
Old Clock House

Old Rectory Dovecote
Shotover House
Wotton House
King's Head
Ashridge Bridgewater Monument
Hatfield House
Chelmsford Cathedral

OXFORD

Nether Winchendon House
Berkhamsted Castle
Cathedral & Abbey Church of St Albans
Copped Hall
Hylands House

Corpus Christi College
Christ Church Cathedral
Martyrs' Memorial
Waterperry Gardens
Princess Risborough Manor House
Redbournbury
All Saints Pastoral Centre
Tortilla
Capel Manor
Waltham Abbey Gatehouse & Bridge

Kingston Bagpuize
26A East
St Helen Street
Rycote Chapel
Aston Martin Club
Hughenden Manor
Chenies Manor House
Folly Arch
Myddelton House
Forty Hall
Ingateston Hall

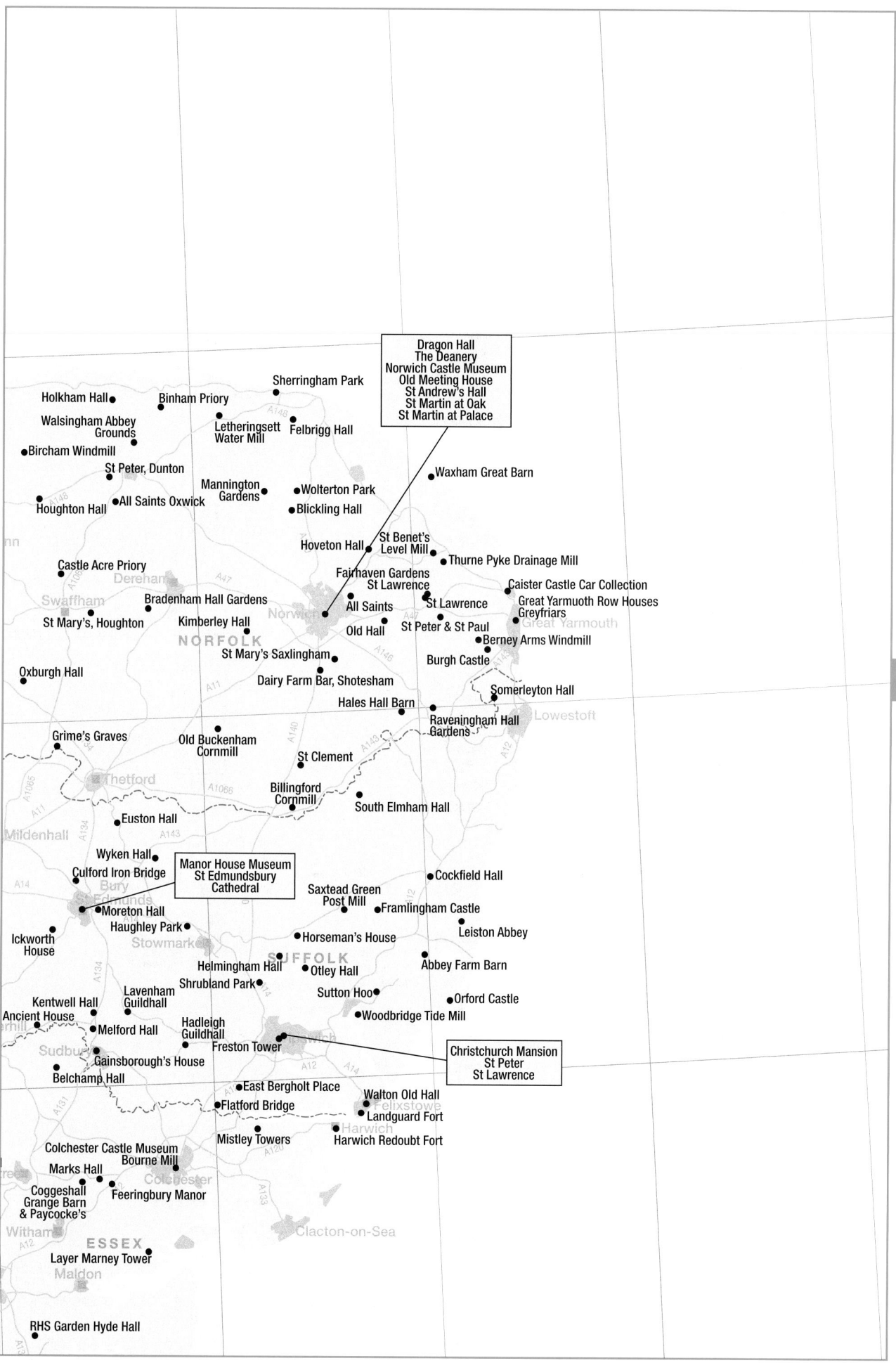

MAP 8

Dragon Hall
The Deanery
Norwich Castle Museum
Old Meeting House
St Andrew's Hall
St Martin at Oak
St Martin at Palace

Sherringham Park

Holkham Hall
Binham Priory
Walsingham Abbey
Grounds
Letheringsett
Water Mill
Felbrigg Hall
Bircham Windmill
St Peter, Dunton
Mannington
Gardens
Wolterton Park
Houghton Hall
All Saints Oxwick
Blickling Hall

Waxham Great Barn

Castle Acre Priory
Dereham
Hoveton Hall
St Benet's
Level Mill
Swaffham
Bradenham Hall Gardens
Thurne Pyke Drainage Mill
A47
Fairhaven Gardens
St Lawrence
St Mary's, Houghton
Kimberley Hall
Norwich
All Saints
St Lawrence
Caister Castle Car Collection
Great Yarmouth Row Houses
Greyfriars
Great Yarmouth
NORFOLK
Old Hall
St Peter & St Paul
St Mary's Saxlingham
Berney Arms Windmill
Oxburgh Hall
Dairy Farm Bar, Shotesham
Burgh Castle
Hales Hall Barn
Somerleyton Hall
Lowestoft
Grime's Graves
Old Buckenham
Cornmill
Raveningham Hall
Gardens
St Clement
Thetford
Billingford
Cornmill
South Elmham Hall
Mildenhall
Euston Hall
A143
Wyken Hall
Culford Iron Bridge
Manor House Museum
St Edmundsbury
Cathedral
Cockfield Hall
Saxtead Green
Post Mill
Bury
Edmunds
Moreton Hall
Framlingham Castle
Haughley Park
Leiston Abbey
Ickworth
House
Stowmarket
SUFFOLK
Horseman's House
Abbey Farm Barn
Helmingham Hall
Kentwell Hall
Lavenham
Guildhall
Otley Hall
Ancient House
Shrubland Park
Sutton Hoo
Orford Castle
Melford Hall
Hadleigh
Guildhall
Woodbridge Tide Mill
Sudbury
Freston Tower
Christchurch Mansion
St Peter
St Lawrence
Gainsborough's House
Belchamp Hall
East Bergholt Place
Walton Old Hall
Flatford Bridge
Felixstowe
Landguard Fort
Harwich
Mistley Towers
Harwich Redoubt Fort
Colchester Castle Museum
Bourne Mill
Marks Hall
Coggeshall
Grange Barn
& Paycocke's
Feeringbury Manor
Colchester
Witham
ESSEX
Clacton-on-Sea
Layer Marney Tower
Maldon
RHS Garden Hyde Hall

585

● Drumlanrig Castle

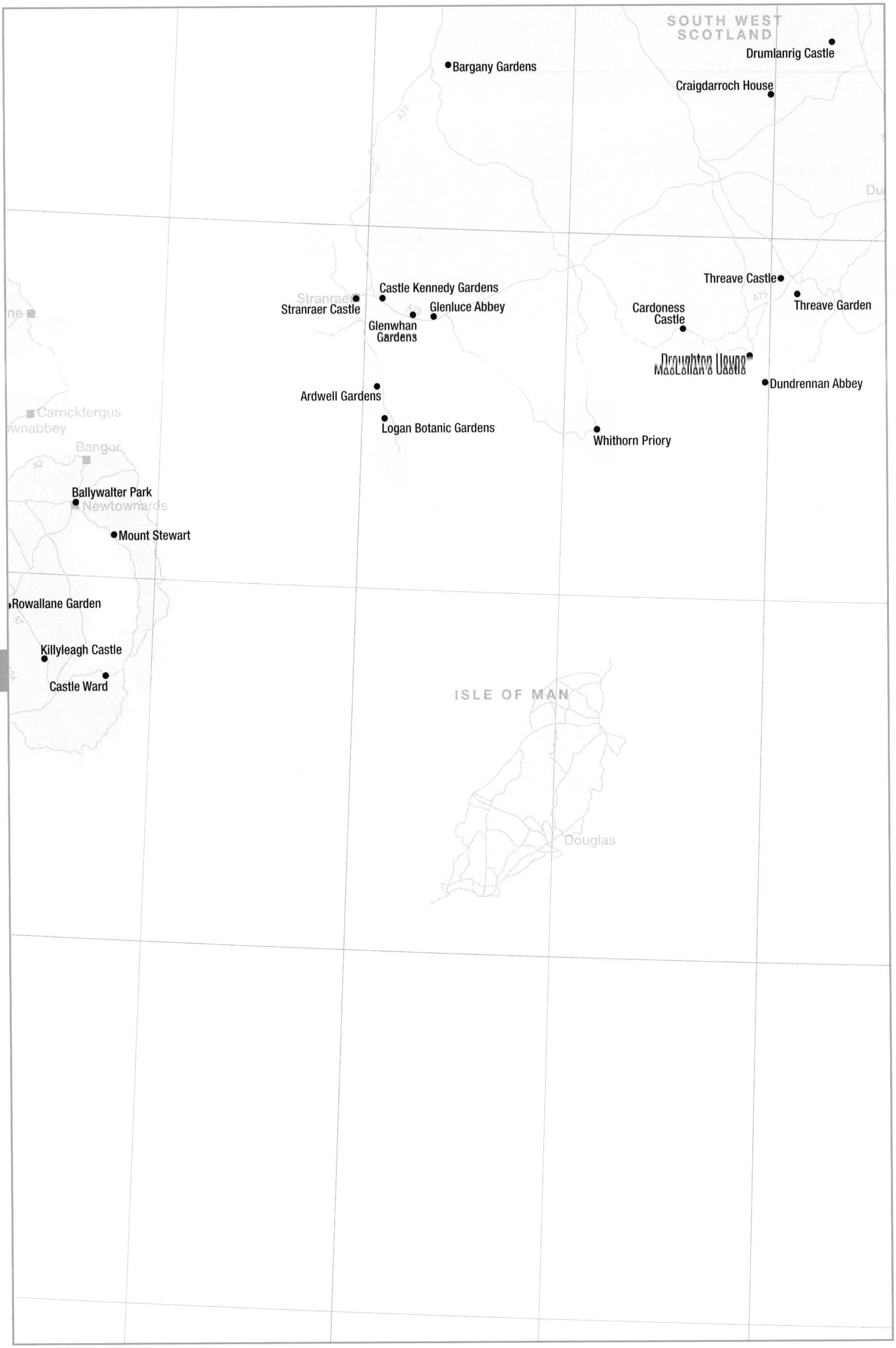

● Bargany Gardens

Craigdarroch House ●

Threave Castle ●

Castle Kennedy Gardens
Stranraer ●
Stranraer Castle ● Glenluce Abbey ●
Glenwhan
Gardens ●

Cardoness
Castle ●

Threave Garden ●

Broughton House ●
MacLellan's Castle ●

● Dundrennan Abbey

Ardwell Gardens ●

Logan Botanic Gardens ●

● Whithorn Priory

■ Carrickfergus
wnabbey

Bangor ■

Ballywalter Park ●
Newtownards

● Mount Stewart

● Rowallane Garden

Killyleagh Castle ●

MAP 9

Castle Ward ●

ISLE OF MAN

Douglas

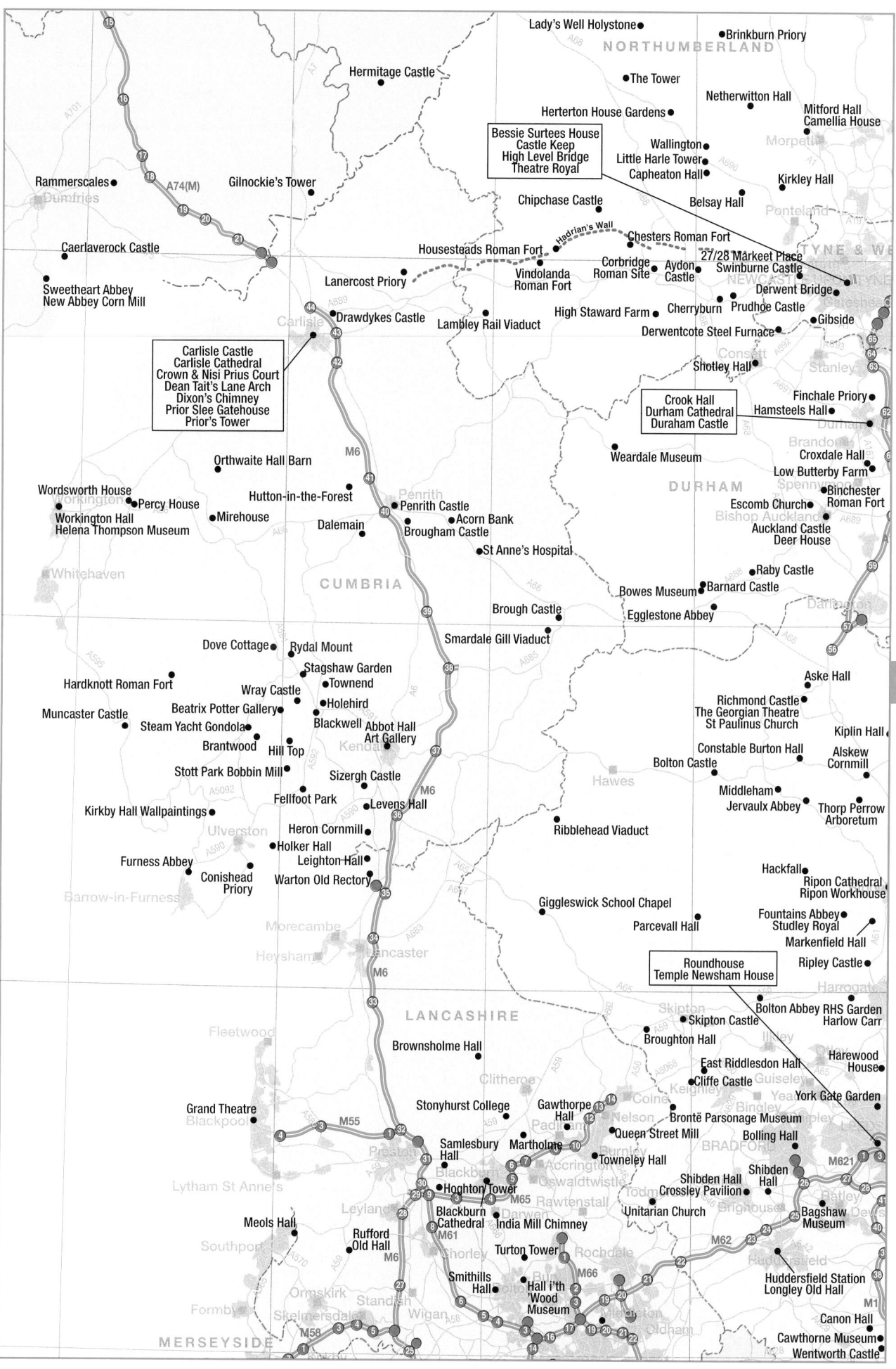

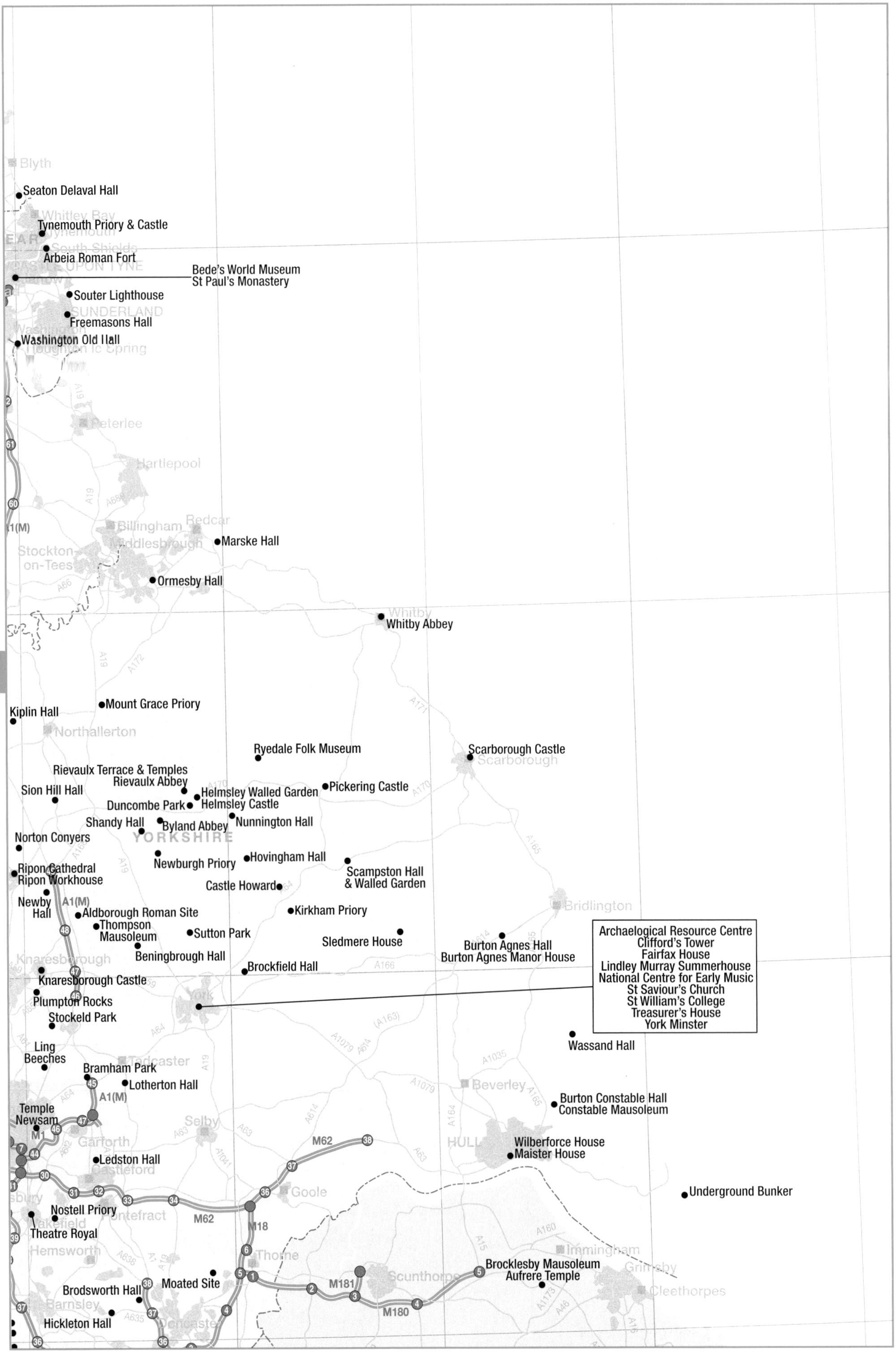

MAP 11

Blyth

Seaton Delaval Hall

Whitley Bay

Tynemouth Priory & Castle

Arbeia Roman Fort

Bede's World Museum
St Paul's Monastery

Souter Lighthouse

SUNDERLAND

Freemasons Hall

Washington Old Hall

Peterlee

Hartlepool

1(M)

Billingham
Middlesbrough
Redcar

Stockton-on-Tees

Marske Hall

Ormesby Hall

Whitby
Whitby Abbey

Kiplin Hall

Mount Grace Priory

Northallerton

Ryedale Folk Museum

Scarborough Castle
Scarborough

Rievaulx Terrace & Temples
Rievaulx Abbey

Sion Hill Hall

Helmsley Walled Garden
Pickering Castle

Duncombe Park
Helmsley Castle

Shandy Hall
Byland Abbey
Nunnington Hall

Norton Conyers

YORKSHIRE

Hovingham Hall

Newburgh Priory

Ripon Cathedral
Ripon Workhouse

Scampston Hall
& Walled Garden

Castle Howard

Newby Hall

A1(M)

Aldborough Roman Site

Kirkham Priory

Bridlington

Thompson Mausoleum

Sutton Park

Sledmere House

Beningbrough Hall

Burton Agnes Hall
Burton Agnes Manor House

Knaresborough
Brockfield Hall

Knaresborough Castle

Plumpton Rocks

Stockeld Park

Archaeological Resource Centre
Clifford's Tower
Fairfax House
Lindley Murray Summerhouse
National Centre for Early Music
St Saviour's Church
St William's College
Treasurer's House
York Minster

Ling Beeches

Wassand Hall

Bramham Park

Lotherton Hall

A1(M)

Tadcaster

Selby

Beverley

Temple Newsam

Garforth

HULL

Burton Constable Hall
Constable Mausoleum

M1

Ledston Hall

Castleford

M62

Wilberforce House
Maister House

Goole

Nostell Priory

Pontefract

M62

M18

Underground Bunker

Theatre Royal

Wakefield

Hemsworth

Thorne

Immingham
Grimsby

Brodsworth Hall

Moated Site

Scunthorpe

Brocklesby Mausoleum
Aufrere Temple

Barnsley

M181

Cleethorpes

Hickleton Hall

Doncaster

M180

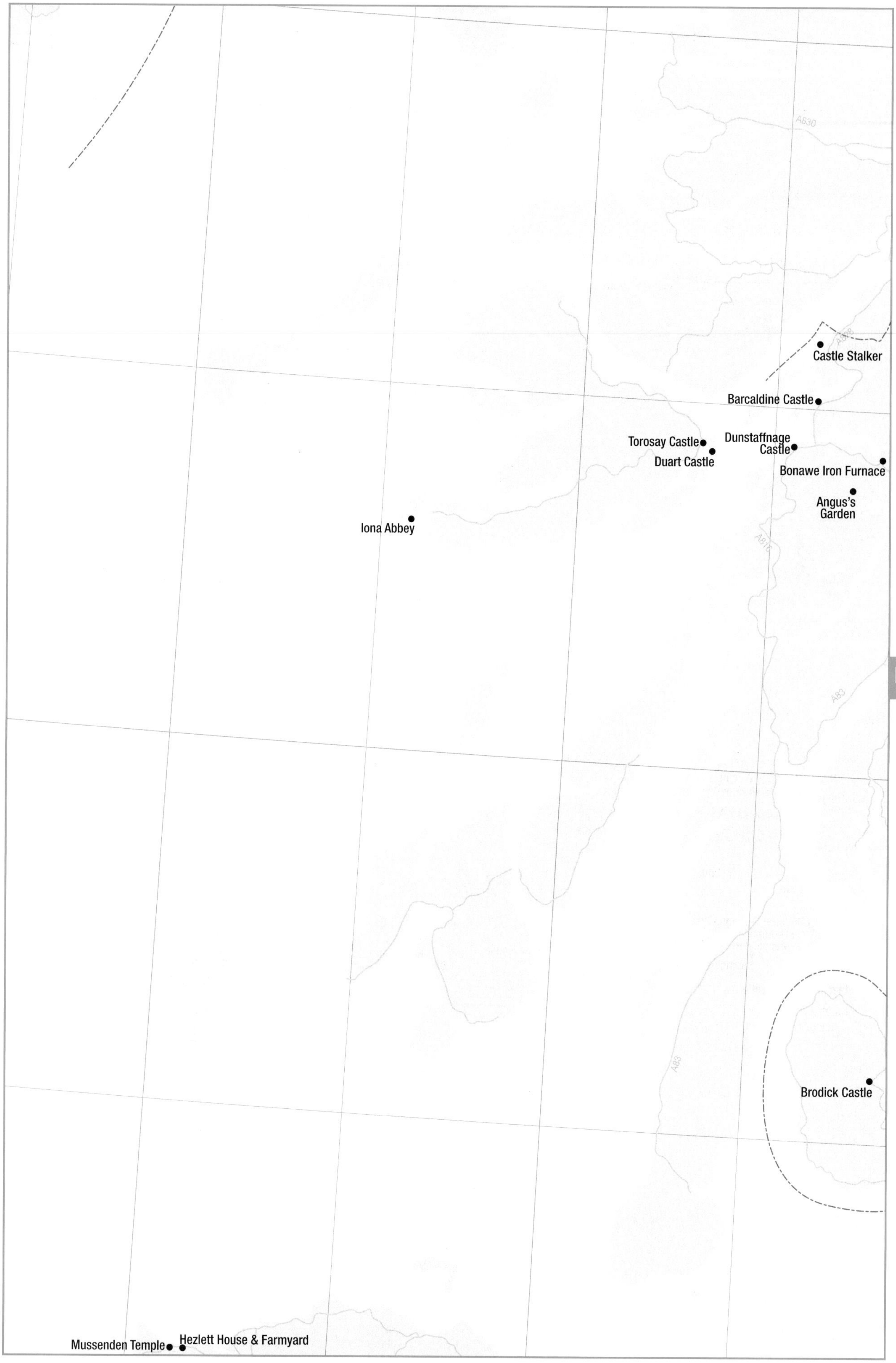
A830
A828
Castle Stalker
Barcaldine Castle
Torosay Castle
Duart Castle
Dunstaffnage Castle
Bonawe Iron Furnace
Angus's Garden
Iona Abbey
A816
A83
A83
Brodick Castle
Mussenden Temple
Hezlett House & Farmyard

MAP 12

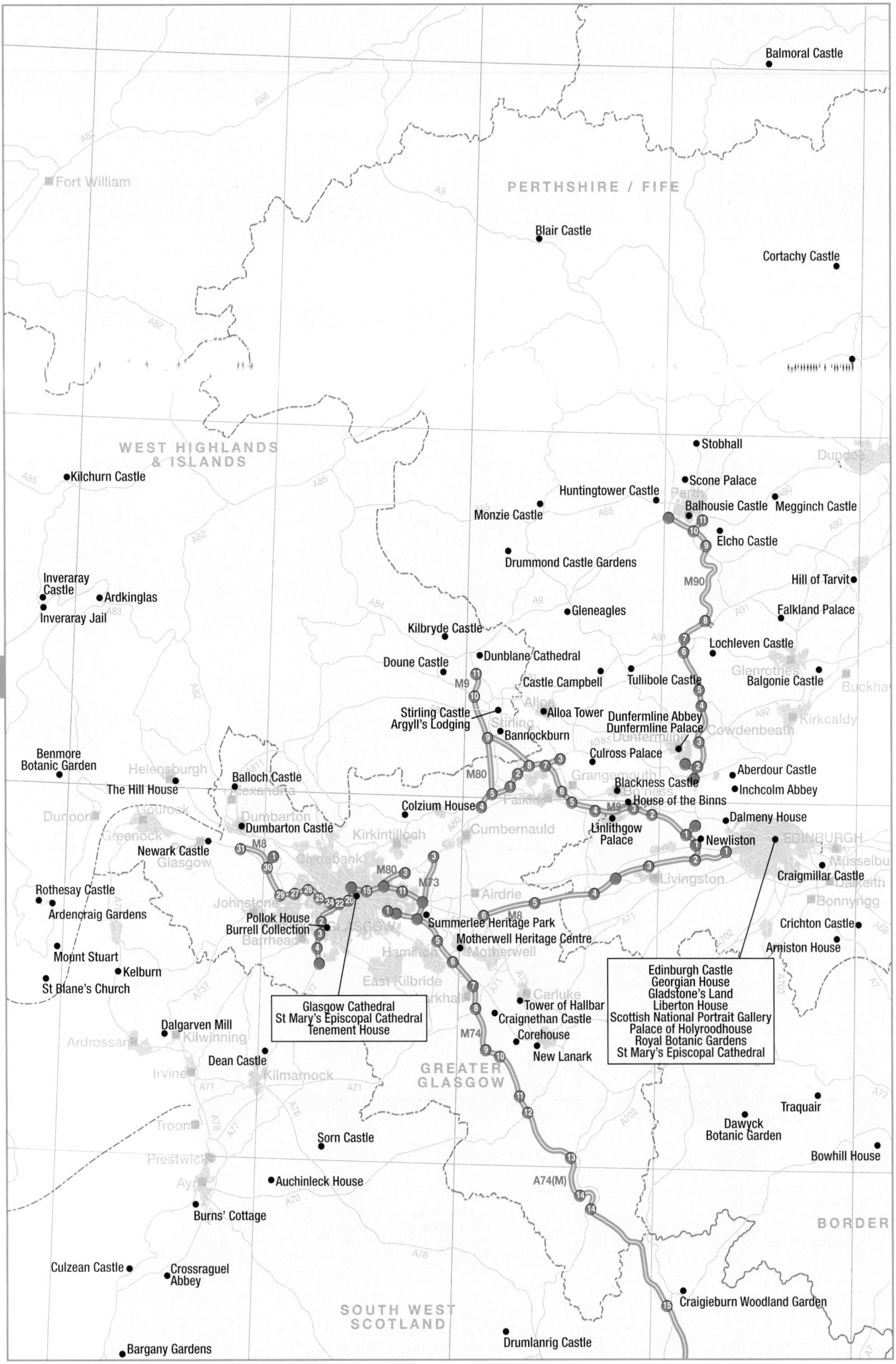

Balmoral Castle

PERTHSHIRE / FIFE

Fort William

Blair Castle

Cortachy Castle

Dundee

Stobhall

WEST HIGHLANDS
& ISLANDS

Scone Palace

Kilchurn Castle

Huntingtower Castle
Monzie Castle

Perth
Balhousie Castle   Megginch Castle

Elcho Castle

Drummond Castle Gardens

Hill of Tarvit

M90

Inveraray
Castle   Ardkinglas

Gleneagles

Inveraray Jail

Falkland Palace

Kilbryde Castle

Lochleven Castle

MAP 13

Doune Castle

Glenrothes

Dunblane Cathedral

Balgonie Castle

Buckhav

M9

Castle Campbell

Tullibole Castle

Stirling Castle
Argyll's Lodging

Alloa Tower

Alloa

Dunfermline Abbey
Dunfermline Palace

Cowdenbeath

Kirkcaldy

Stirling

Bannockburn

Culross Palace

Dunfermline

Benmore
Botanic Garden

Helensburgh

Balloch Castle

Colzium House

Blackness Castle

Aberdour Castle

Inchcolm Abbey

The Hill House

Alexandria

Dumbarton

House of the Binns

Dunoon

Gourock

Kirkintilloch

Cumbernauld

Grangemouth

Bo'ness

Linlithgow
Palace

Dalmeny House

EDINBURGH

Greenock

Dumbarton Castle

M80

Newliston

Musselbu

Newark Castle

M8

Clydebank

M80

Glasgow

Airdrie

Livingston

Craigmillar Castle

Dalkeith

Rothesay Castle

M73

Bonnyrigg

Ardencraig Gardens

Johnstone

Pollok House
Burrell Collection

Glasgow

Summerlee Heritage Park

Crichton Castle

Mount Stuart

Barrhead

Motherwell Heritage Centre

Arniston House

Kelburn

Hamilton

Motherwell

St Blane's Church

East Kilbride

Edinburgh Castle
Georgian House
Gladstone's Land
Liberton House
Scottish National Portrait Gallery
Palace of Holyroodhouse
Royal Botanic Gardens
St Mary's Episcopal Cathedral

Dalgarven Mill

Ardrossan

Kilwinning

Glasgow Cathedral
St Mary's Episcopal Cathedral
Tenement House

Tower of Hallbar
Craignethan Castle
Corehouse

Irvine

Dean Castle

Kilmarnock

M74

GREATER
GLASGOW

New Lanark

Traquair

Troon

Sorn Castle

Dawyck
Botanic Garden

Prestwick

Bowhill House

Ayr

Auchinleck House

A74(M)

Burns' Cottage

BORDER

Culzean Castle

Crossraguel
Abbey

SOUTH WEST
SCOTLAND

Craigieburn Woodland Garden

Bargany Gardens

Drumlanrig Castle

Crathes Castle●
●Drum Castle

●Dunnottar Castle

Arbuthnott House●

Edzell Castle & Garden●

House of Dun●
Brechin Castle●
●Dunninald

Arbroath Abbey●

ORKNEY ISLANDS
Carrick House●

Brock of Gurness●

Skaill House●
Skara Brae●
Ring of Brodgar Stone Circle & Henge●
Maeshowe●
Balfour Castle●

Tankerness House●
Bishop's Palace
Earl's Palace

Strathtyrum House●
St Andrews Castle
St Andrews Cathedral
●Cambo Gardens
Balcarres●
●Kellie Castle
●Charleton House
●Northfield

Red Row
Dirleton Castle●
Tantallon Castle●
Greywalls●
Gosford House●
Harelaw Farmhouse
Preston Mill●
Amisfield Mains●
Beanston
Hailes Castle●
Lennoxlove House●

EDINBURGH

Dunglass Collegiate Church●

Ayton Castle●

Duns Castle●
Paxton House●
Manderston●
Berwick Barracks
Berwick Ramparts
Berwick-upon-Tweed

Thirlestane Castle●

Norham Castle●

Harmony Garden
Melrose Abbey
Old Gala House●
Mellerstain House●
Hirsel Gardens●
Barmoor Castle●
Lindisfarne Priory
●Lindisfarne Castle

Etal Castle●
●Lady Waterford Hall
Smailholm Tower●
●Floors Castle
Belford Hall●
Bamburgh Castle●

Abbotsford●
Mertoun Gardens●
Dryburgh Abbey

Halliwells House Museum●
Monteviot House Gardens●
Chillingham Castle●
Preston Tower●

Jedburgh Abbey●
Ferniehurst Castle●
●Dunstanburgh Castle
Howick Hall Gardens●

Alnwick Castle●
Pottergate Tower

Drumlanrig's Tower●

Edingham Castle●

Lady's Well Holystone●
Cragside●
Warkworth Hermitage
Warkworth Castle●

BORDERS

NORTHUMBERLAND
●Brinkburn Priory

The Tower●

MAP 14

591

MAP 15

WESTERN ISLES

Black House

Dunvegan Castle

MAP 16

Dunrobin Castle

Castle Leod

Fort George

Brodie Castle
Dallas Dhu Distillery
Altyre Estate

Cawdor Castle

Inverness

Eilean Donan Castle

Urquhart Castle

HIGHLANDS & SKYE

Doune of
Rothiemurcus

MAP 17

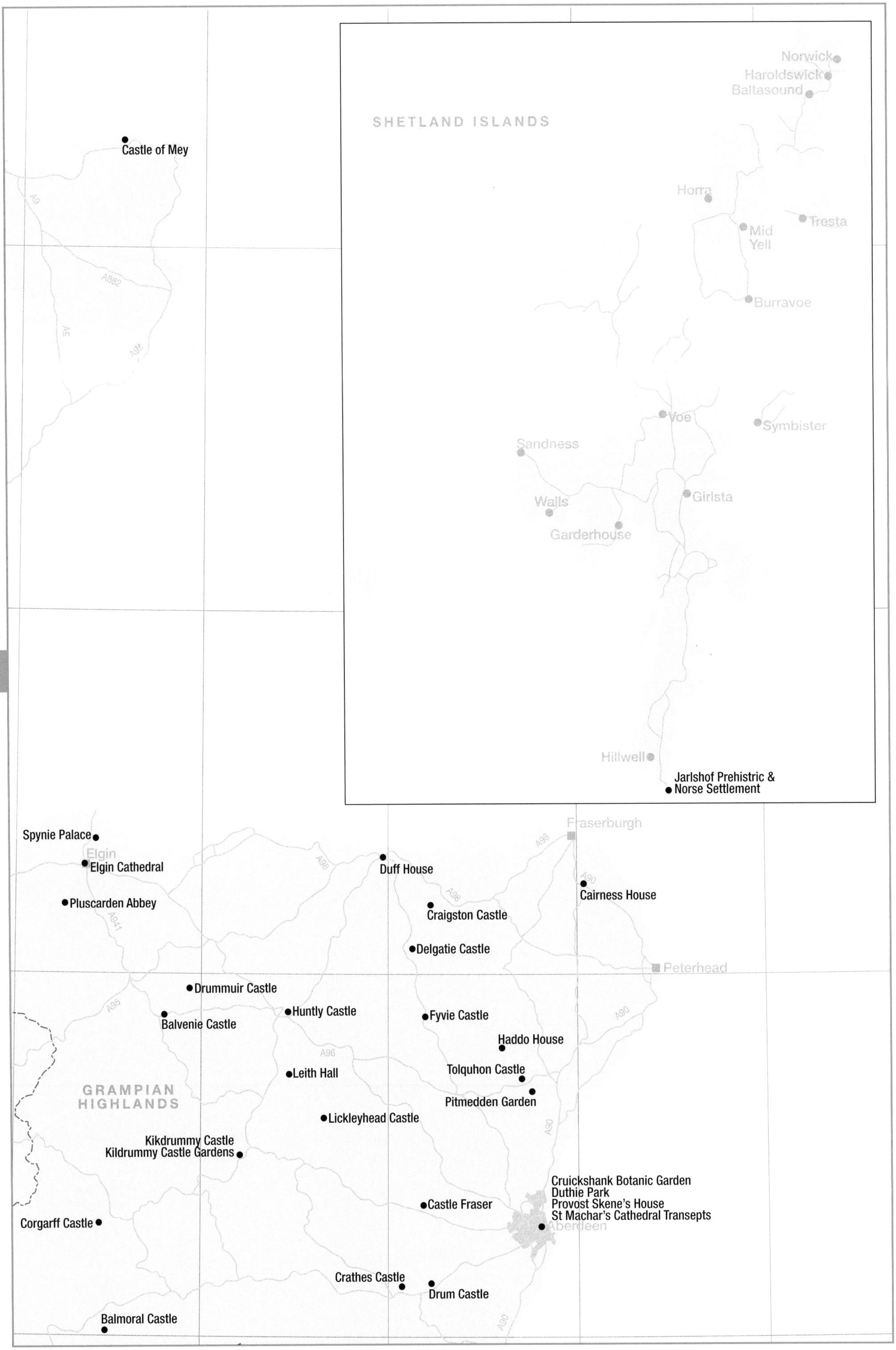

Castle of Mey
A9
A882
A9
A99
SHETLAND ISLANDS
Norwick
Haroldswick
Baltasound
Horra
Tresta
Mid
Yell
Burravoe
Voe
Symbister
Sandness
Girlsta
Walls
Garderhouse
Hillwell
Jarlshof Prehistric &
Norse Settlement
Fraserburgh
Spynie Palace
Elgin
Elgin Cathedral
Pluscarden Abbey
A941
A98
Duff House
A98
A98
A90
Cairness House
Craigston Castle
Delgatie Castle
Peterhead
Drummuir Castle
A95
Huntly Castle
Balvenie Castle
Fyvie Castle
A90
Haddo House
A96
Leith Hall
Tolquhon Castle
GRAMPIAN
HIGHLANDS
Pitmedden Garden
Lickleyhead Castle
A90
Kikdrummy Castle
Kildrummy Castle Gardens
Cruickshank Botanic Garden
Duthie Park
Provost Skene's House
St Machar's Cathedral Transepts
Castle Fraser
Corgarff Castle
Aberdeen
Crathes Castle
Drum Castle
A90
Balmoral Castle

Hezlett House & Farmyard

Mussenden Temple

Coleraine

LONDONDERRY

NORTHERN
IRELAND

Gray's Printing Press

Ballymena

Larne

Antrim Castle Garden

Carrickfergus

Barons Court

Springhill House &
Costume Collection

Cookstown

Newtownabbey
Bangor

Wellbrook Beetling Mill

BELFAST

Ballywalter Park

Newtownards

Mount Stewart

The Argory

Ardress

Craigavon

Portadown

Rowallane Garden

Castle Coole

Armagh

Killyleagh Castle

Florence Court

Castle Ward

Seaforde Gardens

Crom Estate

Derrymore House

Newry

Sligo

Cavan

Dundalk

Drogheda

Navan

Athlone

Galway

REPUBLIC OF
IRELAND

DUBLIN

Dun Laoghaire

Bray

Portlaoise

Carlow

LIMERICK

Kilkenny

Tipperary

Clonmel

WATERFORD

CORK

MAP 18

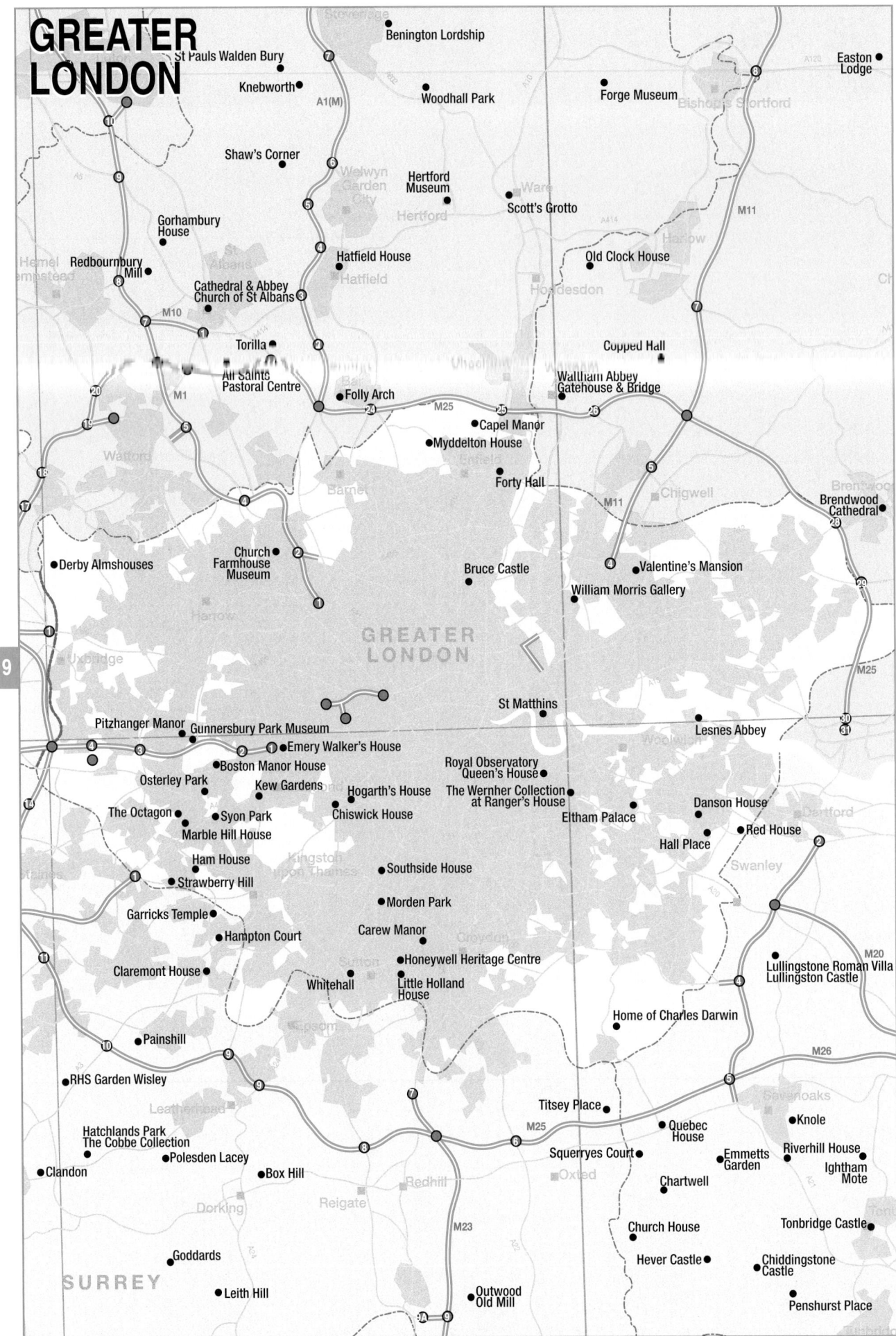

GREATER LONDON

MAP 19

Benington Lordship
St Pauls Walden Bury
Knebworth
Woodhall Park
Forge Museum
Easton Lodge

Shaw's Corner
Hertford Museum
Scott's Grotto
Old Clock House

Gorhambury House
Hatfield House
Redbournbury Mill
Cathedral & Abbey Church of St Albans
Copped Hall
Torilla
Waltham Abbey Gatehouse & Bridge
All Saints Pastoral Centre
Folly Arch
Capel Manor
Myddelton House
Derby Almshouses
Forty Hall
Brendwood Cathedral
Church Farmhouse Museum
Bruce Castle
Valentine's Mansion
William Morris Gallery

GREATER LONDON

Pitzhanger Manor
Gunnersbury Park Museum
St Matthins
Lesnes Abbey
Emery Walker's House
Boston Manor House
Royal Observatory Queen's House
Osterley Park
Kew Gardens
Hogarth's House
The Wernher Collection at Ranger's House
Danson House
The Octagon
Syon Park
Chiswick House
Eltham Palace
Red House
Marble Hill House
Hall Place
Ham House
Southside House
Strawberry Hill
Morden Park
Garricks Temple
Carew Manor
Hampton Court
Honeywell Heritage Centre
Lullingstone Roman Villa
Lullingston Castle
Claremont House
Whitehall
Little Holland House
Painshill
Home of Charles Darwin
RHS Garden Wisley
Titsey Place
Knole
Hatchlands Park The Cobbe Collection
Quebec House
Emmetts Garden
Riverhill House
Polesden Lacey
Squerryes Court
Clandon
Box Hill
Chartwell
Ightham Mote
Goddards
Church House
Tonbridge Castle
Leith Hill
Hever Castle
Chiddingstone Castle
Outwood Old Mill
Penshurst Place

SURREY

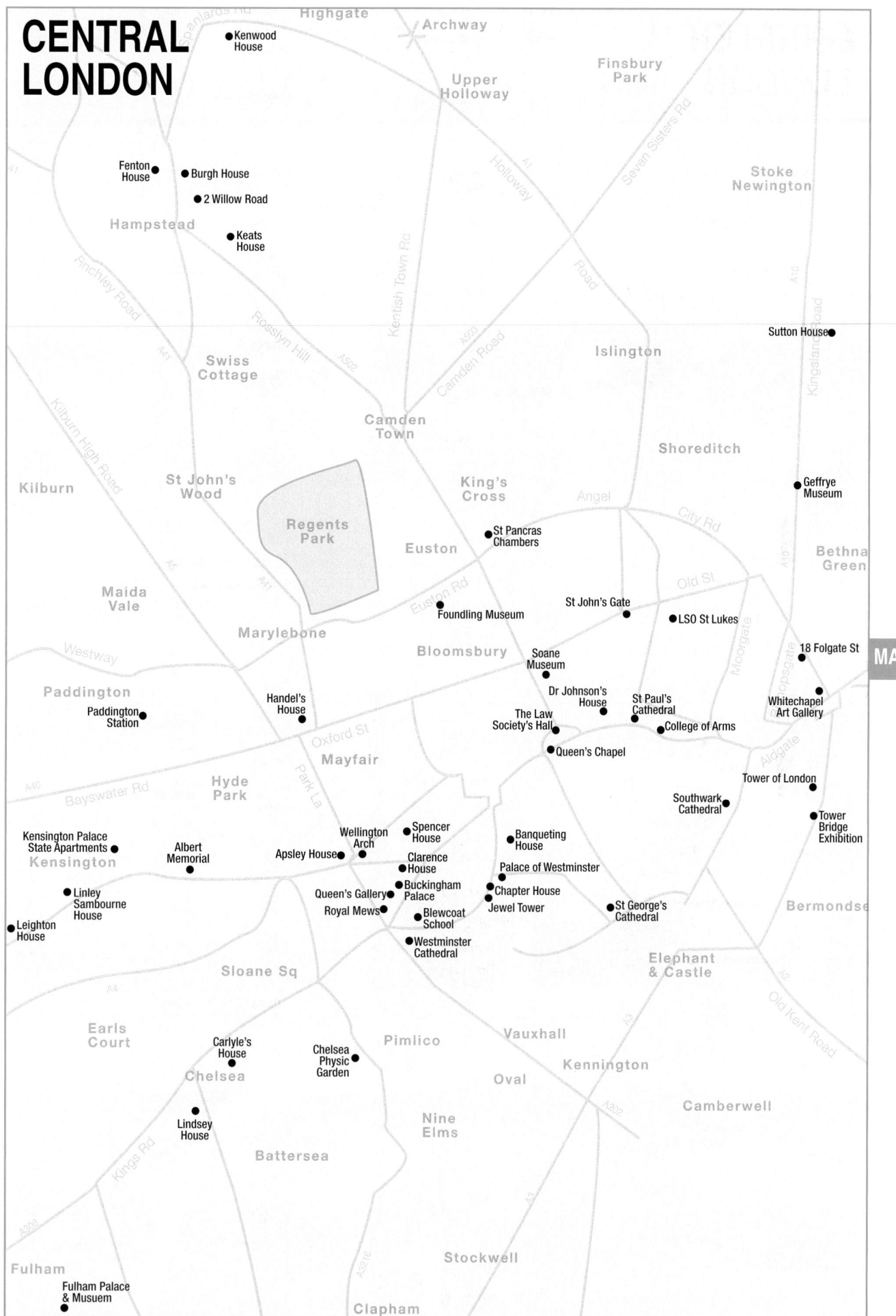

CENTRAL LONDON

Kenwood House

Highgate

Archway

Finsbury Park

Upper Holloway

Stoke Newington

Fenton House ● ● Burgh House

● 2 Willow Road

Hampstead

● Keats House

Swiss Cottage

Sutton House ●

Islington

Kilburn

St John's Wood

Camden Town

Shoreditch

Regents Park

King's Cross

Angel

Geffrye Museum ●

Maida Vale

Euston

St Pancras Chambers ●

Bethnal Green

Marylebone

Euston Rd

St John's Gate ●

Foundling Museum ●

LSO St Lukes ●

Bloomsbury

Soane Museum ●

18 Folgate St ●

MAP 20

Paddington

Handel's House ●

Dr Johnson's House ●

St Paul's Cathedral ●

Whitechapel Art Gallery ●

Paddington Station ●

Oxford St

The Law Society's Hall ●

College of Arms ●

Mayfair

Queen's Chapel ●

Hyde Park

Aldgate

Kensington Palace State Apartments ●

Albert Memorial ●

Spencer House ●

Wellington Arch

Apsley House ●

Banqueting House ●

Tower of London ●

Southwark Cathedral ●

Kensington

Clarence House ●

Palace of Westminster ●

Tower Bridge Exhibition ●

Linley Sambourne House ●

Queen's Gallery ●

Buckingham Palace ●

Chapter House ●

Bermondse

Leighton House ●

Royal Mews ●

Blewcoat School ●

Jewel Tower ●

St George's Cathedral ●

Westminster Cathedral ●

Sloane Sq

Elephant & Castle

Earls Court

Carlyle's House ●

Pimlico

Vauxhall

Chelsea Physic Garden ●

Kennington

Chelsea

Oval

Camberwell

Lindsey House ●

Nine Elms

Battersea

Fulham

Stockwell

Fulham Palace & Musuem ●

Clapham

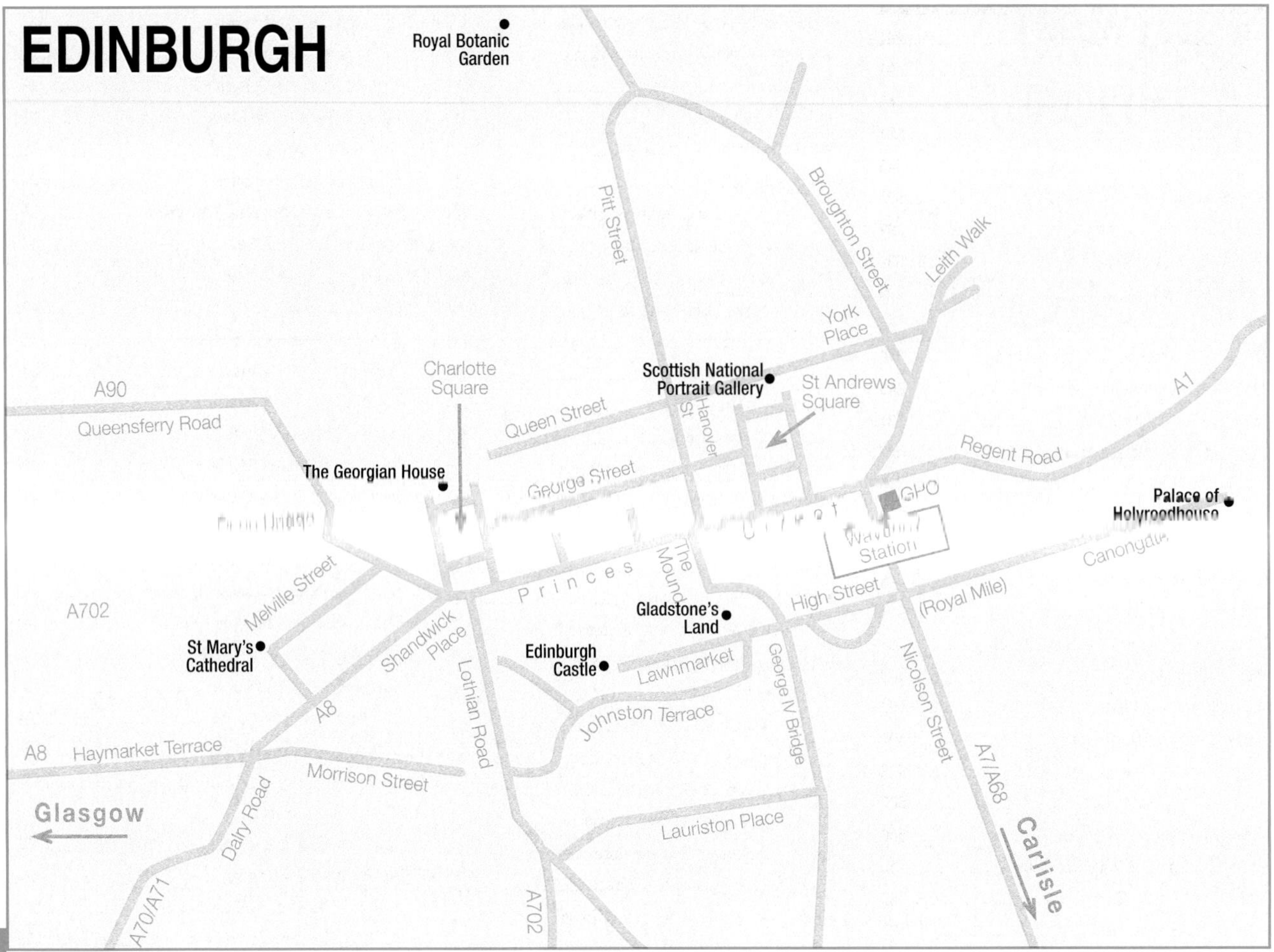

EDINBURGH

Royal Botanic
Garden

A90

Queensferry Road

Charlotte
Square

Scottish National
Portrait Gallery

St Andrews
Square

Pitt Street

Broughton Street

Leith Walk

York
Place

A1

Queen Street

Hanover St

Regent Road

The Georgian House

George Street

GPO

Waverley
Station

Palace of
Holyroodhouse

A702

Melville Street

Princes

The Mound

High Street

(Royal Mile)

Canongate

Nicolson Street

A7/A68

St Mary's
Cathedral

Shandwick
Place

Lothian Road

Gladstone's
Land

Edinburgh
Castle

Lawnmarket

George IV Bridge

Carlisle

A8   Haymarket Terrace

A8

Johnston Terrace

Morrison Street

Glasgow

Dalry Road

A70/A71

A702

Lauriston Place

MAP 21

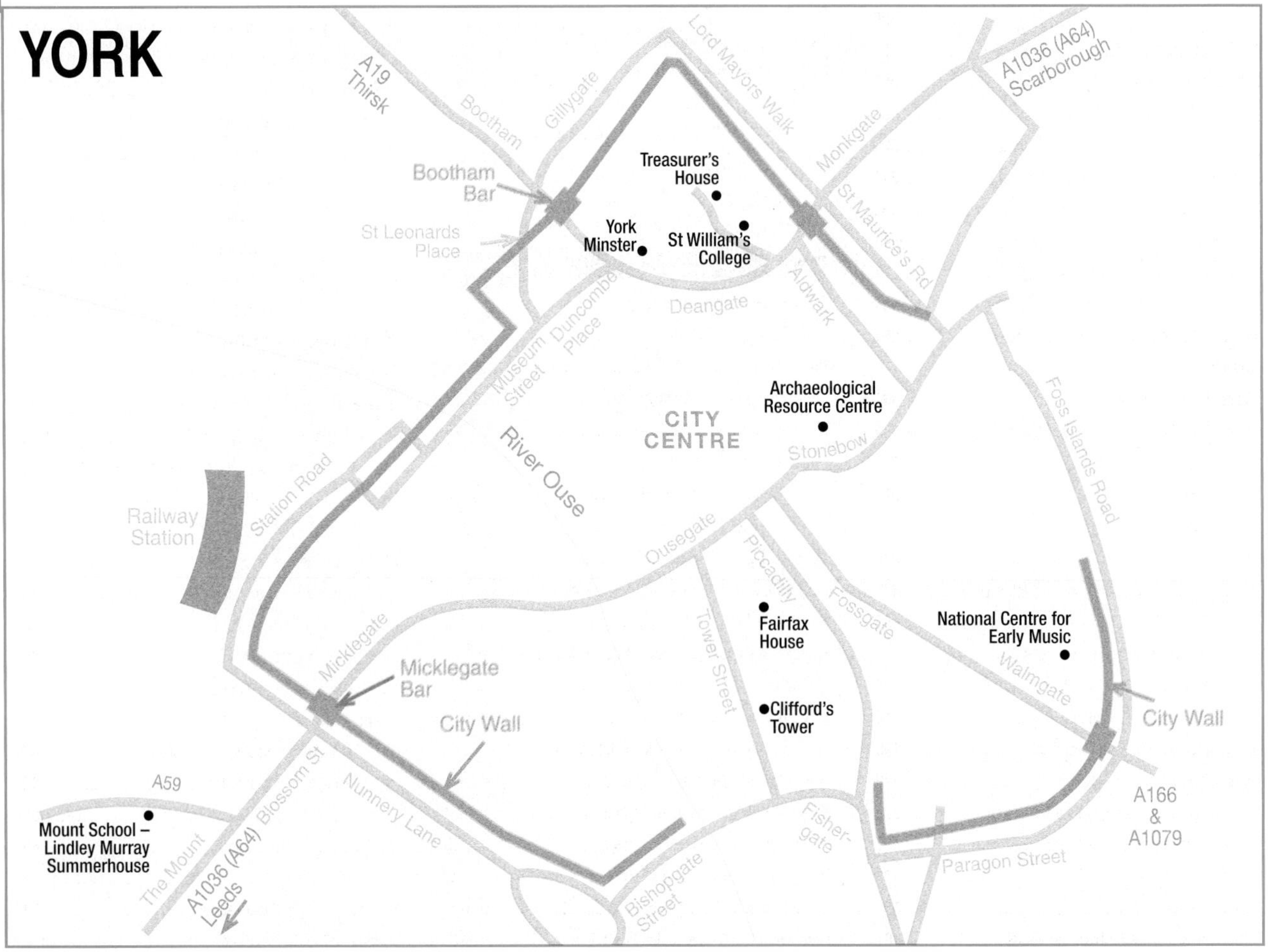

YORK

A19
Thirsk

Bootham

Gillygate

Lord Mayors Walk

Monkgate

A1036 (A64)
Scarborough

Bootham
Bar

Treasurer's
House

St Maurice's Rd

St Leonards
Place

York
Minster

St William's
College

Aldwark

Museum Duncombe
Street Place

Deangate

Foss Islands Road

Archaeological
Resource Centre

CITY
CENTRE

Stonebow

River Ouse

Ousegate

Railway
Station

Station Road

Piccadilly

Fossgate

Micklegate

Tower Street

Fairfax
House

National Centre for
Early Music

Micklegate
Bar

Walmgate

City Wall

City Wall

Clifford's
Tower

A166
&
A1079

A59

Mount School –
Lindley Murray
Summerhouse

The Mount

A1036 (A64) Blossom St
Leeds

Nunnery Lane

Fisher-
gate

Bishopgate
Street

Paragon Street

598

C

D

E

F

G

N

O

P